Imaging Technology

Imaging Technology

Edited by
Hua Lee

Assistant Professor of Electrical and
 Computer Engineering
University of Illinois at Urbana-Champaign

Glen Wade

Professor of Electrical Engineering
University of California at Santa Barbara

A volume in the IEEE PRESS Selected Reprint Series.

The Institute of Electrical and Electronics Engineers, Inc., New York

IEEE Order Number: PC01925

Library of Congress Cataloging in Publication Data
Main entry under title:

Imaging technology.

(IEEE Press selected reprint series)
Includes indexes.
1. Image processing—Addresses, essays, lectures.
I. Lee, Hua, 1952– . II. Wade, Glen.
TA1632.I495 1986   621.36'7   85-18221
ISBN 0-87942-199-1

Contents

Papers by Subject Category

THIS categorized list of papers is intended to help those readers who want to use this book on a category by category basis instead of reading it from cover to cover. Most of the papers appear in more than one category.

A. Holography

D. Gabor, ''Holography, 1948–1971,'' pp. 13–26.

J. W. Goodman, ''An Introduction to the Principles and Applications of Holography,'' pp. 27–39.

E. N. Leith, ''Quasi-Holographic Techniques in the Microwave Region,'' pp. 40–53.

T. S. Huang, ''Digital Holography,'' pp. 54–65.

H. Lee and G. Wade, ''Evaluating Quantization Error in Phase-Only Holograms,'' pp. 66–69.

R. K. Mueller, ''Acoustic Holography,'' pp. 83–99.

G. Wade, ''Acoustic Imaging with Holography and Lenses,'' pp. 100–109.

G. L. Fitzpatrick, ''Seismic Imaging by Holography,'' pp. 422–439.

B. Optical Processing

D. Gabor, ''Holography, 1948–1971,'' pp. 13–26.

J. W. Goodman, ''An Introduction to the Principles and Applications of Holography,'' pp. 27–39.

D. Casasent, ''Coherent Optical Pattern Recognition,'' pp. 70–82.

G. Wade, ''Acoustic Imaging with Holography and Lenses,'' pp. 100–109.

C. Acoustic-Ultrasonic Imaging

R. K. Mueller, ''Acoustic Holography,'' pp. 83–99.

G. Wade, ''Acoustic Imaging with Holography and Lenses,'' pp. 100–109.

P. N. Keating, T. Sawatari, and G. Zilinskas, ''Signal Processing Acoustic Imaging,'' pp. 110–124.

J. F. Havlice and J. C. Taenzer, ''Medical Ultrasonic Imaging: An Overview of Principles and Instrumentation,'' pp. 125–146.

G. S. Kino, ''Acoustic Imaging for Nondestructive Evaluation,'' pp. 147–162.

R. K. Mueller, M. Kaveh, and G. Wade, ''Reconstructive Tomography and Applications of Ultrasonics,'' pp. 229–249.

J. F. Greenleaf, ''Computerized Tomography with Ultrasound,'' pp. 250–257.

L. W. Kessler and D. E. Yuhas, ''Acoustic Microscopy—1979,'' pp. 471–481.

C. F. Quate, A. Atalar, and H. K. Wickramasinghe, ''Acoustic Microscopy with Mechanical Scanning—A Review,'' pp. 482–504.

D. Tomography/NMR Imaging

H. J. Scudder, ''Introduction to Computer Aided Tomography,'' pp. 163–172.

A. Macovski, ''Physical Problems of Computerized Tomography,'' pp. 173–178.

A. K. Louis and F. Natterer, ''Mathematical Problems of Computerized Tomography,'' pp. 179–189.

R. M. Lewitt, ''Reconstruction Algorithms: Transform Methods,'' pp. 190–208.

Y. Censor, ''Finite Series-Expansion Reconstruction Methods,'' pp. 209–219.

D. C. Munson, Jr., J. D. O'Brien, and W. K. Jenkins, ''A Tomographic Formulation of Spotlight-Mode Synthetic Aperture Radar,'' pp. 220–228.

R. K. Mueller, M. Kaveh, and G. Wade, ''Reconstructive Tomography and Applications to Ultrasonics,'' pp. 229–249.

J. F. Greenleaf, ''Computerized Tomography with Ultrasound,'' pp. 250–257

W. S. Hinshaw and A. H. Lent, ''An Introduction to NMR Imaging: From the Bloch Equation to the Imaging Equation,'' pp. 258–270.

Z. H. Cho, H. S. Kim, H. B. Song, and J. Cumming, ''Fourier Transform Nuclear Magnetic Resonance Tomographic Imaging,'' pp. 271–292.

K. A. Dines and R. J. Lytle, ''Computerized Geophysical Tomography,'' pp. 446–454.

E. Microwave Imaging

E. N. Leith, ''Quasi-Holographic Techniques in the Microwave Region,'' pp. 40–53.

D. C. Munson, Jr., J. D. O'Brien, and W. K. Jenkins, ''A Tomographic Formulation of Spotlight-Mode Synthetic Aperture Radar,'' pp. 220–228.

K. Tomiyasu, ''Tutorial Review of Synthetic-Aperture Radar (SAR) with Applications to Imaging of the Ocean Surface,'' pp. 293–313.

C. Elachi, T. Bicknell, R. L. Jordan, and C. Wu, ''Spaceborne Synthetic-Aperture Imaging Radars: Applications, Techniques, and Technology,'' pp. 314–349.

D. A. Ausherman, A. Kozma, J. L. Walker, H. M. Jones, and E. C. Poggio, ''Developments in Radar Imaging,'' pp. 350–385.

E. G. Njoku, ''Passive Microwave Remote Sensing of the Earth from Space—A Review,'' pp. 386–408.

F. Seismic Imaging

L. C. Wood and S. Treitel, ''Seismic Signal Processing,'' pp. 409–421.

G. L. Fitzpatrick, ''Seismic Imaging by Holography,'' pp. 422–439.

G. P. Gregori and L. J. Lanzerotti, ''Geomagnetic Depth Sounding by Means of Oceanographic and Aeromagnetic Surveys,'' pp. 440–445.

THE technology associated with imaging is rooted in concepts and inventions that go back many decades and even centuries. Much progress has been brought about by persons of great innovative talent. When we look at their accomplishments from the perspective of the modern era, we are logically impressed by what we see; their work exemplifies creativity in a fundamental way.

For hundreds of millenia, man's only effective instrument for producing an image was the unaided eye. Then, a few centuries ago, lenses, prisms, and related hardware were invented and have since served as important aids in forming and analyzing images. By now, the technological advances of the modern era have brought into being many different types of equipment, including high-speed digital computers, which enormously increase image processing and reconstruction capabilities.

The first great leap from naked-eye observation to instrument-aided vision was the invention of the eyeglass. We do not know the inventor or where he lived, but we do know his era. The first recorded use of eyeglasses took place about 700 years ago, Another 300 years passed before the telescope was invented.

Galileo's name is frequently associated with early telescopes. In 1609, when he heard about the instrument he decided to make one for himself and explore the heavens with it. Among other things, he discovered four moons circulating Jupiter. To him this was dramatic confirmation of Copernicus's idea of a moving earth and a heliocentric universe. What he saw seemed to prove that a body, like the earth with another body circulating around it, could itself circulate around a third body. So spectacular were Galileo's discoveries with his telescope that on the night of April 14, 1611, a banquet was given in his honor by a pioneer scientific society, the Academy of the Lynxes. It was on this occasion that Galileo's instrument was named the "telescope" by a Greek scholar who happened to be present. This was an early instance of what has developed into a custom of giving instruments of modern science names borrowed from ancient Greece.

Since the mid-1800's, humans have been able to record in permanent form a wide variety of the scenes their eyes perceive. This is done, of course, through photography, which was engendered by the discovery that exposure to sunlight changes the color of certain objects. Rugs fade, for example, and alchemists who splashed silver nitrate on their hands saw the effected areas turn black in the sunlight. Small experiments to control this phenomenon had been performed by the 18th century. However, it took years before the behavioral aspects of the silver compound could be determined and used to advantage. The chemistry associated with dissolving out unexposed silver on photographic plates was not confirmed until about 1839. Once this had happened, the remaining image could be "fixed," that is, made permanent.

Almost simultaneous with the discovery of these chemical steps, and even preceding it, was the development of greater understanding concerning the nature of light. It had long been known that light passing through a pinhole in a mask carries to an observation screen in an otherwise dark region behind the mask an image or reproduction of the view seen through the pinhole. The image is upside down and frequently soft and blurry. But it is recognizable. The simple apparatus to produce such an image is called a "camera obscura." During the 11th century, Arab experimenters had played with these cameras, and four centuries later, Leonardo da Vinci described in detail the "dark chambers" of his day. Afterwards it was learned that when a simple lens was substituted for the pinhole, the pictures became clearer and sharper. By the end of the 19th century, with the employment of photographic film in place of the observation screen, men began to achieve considerable success in the art and science of photography.

The fortunate combination of lens and photographic emulsion made possible the charting of stars, planets, and galaxies; the recording of optical spectra; the picturing of minute microscopic specimens; the storage of large amounts of data in the form of small recorded images; and a myriad of other uses. Because of the vast scope of its importance, the science of photography has been given much attention and has advanced steadily over the past century. Even today, new and important developments and uses are routinely being made.

One of the new uses has been in holography, a process similar to photography in some respects but fundamentally different in other respects. In photography, the light waves scattered from an object are processed by a lens in such a way that the waves converge onto the surface of photographic film and form a two-dimensional intensity pattern which constitutes the image recorded by the film. In holography, the film records an intensity pattern representing the scattered waves themselves rather than a converging or focused version of these waves. The process involves two steps. The first is to record the scattered waves on a photographic transparency. The second is to illuminate the transparency and reconstruct a replica of the original scattering waves. By looking into the hologram from which the scattered waves emerge, we can see a three-dimensional view of the object. Both the recording and the reconstructing are generally done with coherent light.

Photography and holography represent two important technological advances, but by now many others have come along which are also of importance and which enormously increase image processing and reconstruction capabilities. The tools presently in use range from the highly available and still widely employed human eyeball to the sophisticated and expensive microdensitometer-computer-image reproduction system.

Basically, imaging technology consists of manipulating image data by computers, either digital or analog. Very often, the fundamental job is simply to make a bad image into a good one. The term "imaging technology" is very broad. It can be regarded as a huge umbrella under which are found various aspects of optics, acoustics, electronics, microwave technology, mathematics, photography, holography, tomography, and, perhaps most important of all, computer science and technology. This large and exciting field is bringing into a number of areas of scientific, medical, and engineering endeavor, investigative instruments of great power. The technological developments in the field are having significant effects in remote sensing, diagnostic medicine, space exploration, nondestructive evaluation, oceanic search, microscopy, and a host of other applications.

Most of the modern imaging techniques were developed independently of each other. Nevertheless, striking similarities in the basic scientific principles behind many of them are apparent upon examination. This reprint volume is intended to serve as an introduction to the spectacular world of this modern technology. It is highly appropriate to assemble within a single set of covers a group of separate but related papers describing the techniques. In this fashion, various threads of commonality become exposed and emphasized.

Since the scope of what comprises imaging technology is broad, the coverage of this book can be divided into several parts by subject category. There are a total of 34 papers, all concerned with one or more of the fundamental aspects of imaging. It is possible to group these papers into such categories as holography, optical processing, acoustic imaging, tomography, microwave imaging, seismic imaging, microscopy, nondestructive evaluation, and the signal processsng techniques associated with imaging.

From the standpoint of simplicity in grouping the papers, it would have been nice to have been able to assign each paper to only one of the various categories. However, most of the papers clearly belong in more than one. For example, the paper by Munson, O'Brien, and Jenkins, "A Tomographic Formulation of the Spotlight Mode Synthetic Aperture Radar," fits three of the categories—tomography, microwave imaging, and signal processing.

Our categorization of the papers will help the reader. The majority of readers will not want to start with the first paper and proceed sequentially through the entire list. Rather, many will be interested in only one of the categories, or in a small group. The classification we have chosen should serve as an important aid for those who wish to be selective in reading the volume. It can be found on page vii, just after the table of contents.

Because of multiple listing, the 34 papers show up 57 times in the 8 categories. The fact that many papers appear in more than one category permits us to hope that the reading of a particular category will serve as a mechanism for intellectual cross-fertilization and thus enhance the educational and motivational value of the volume. The various imaging techniques associated with a given category are related not only to each other but to the techniques of a different category. A sequential reading of the papers in a particular group may 1) encourage the initiation of new applications, 2) help to overcome informational barriers between the various categories, and 3) upgrade the potential for future development.

We should point out that we have made free use of papers first published in the PROCEEDINGS OF THE IEEE. This journal requires of its authors a substantial amount of tutorial material and we wanted a marked tutorial component to characterize the articles in this volume. A large portion of the PROCEEDINGS' papers are from the following four special issues: "Special Issue on Holography," September 1971; "Special Issue on Remote Sensing," January 1975; "Special Issue on Acoustic Imaging," April 1979; "Special Issue on Computerized Tomography," March 1983.

We will now introduce each of the categories separately and we start with the first one, "Holography."

A. Holography

As previously stated, in holography we make a record of a beam of waves scattered from an object. This is done in such a way that a subsequent illumination of the record will reconstruct this object beam even in the absence of the object. Observation of the reconstructed beam will then yield a view of the object which, under idealized conditions, is indiscernible from the original object.

This method of imagery was invented almost four decades ago by Dennis Gabor, who in 1971 received a Nobel prize in physics for his work. Gabor's paper "Holography," from the June 1972 issue of the PROCEEDINGS OF THE IEEE, is the first reprint paper in this volume and the first to be listed under the category "Holography." The paper is the lecture Gabor gave in Stockholm when he received the Nobel prize and it tells the intriguing story of the early exciting years of this invention.

Holography was initiated as an interferometric technique for what Gabor called "wavefront reconstruction." He recognized that when a coherent reference wave is present simultaneously with coherent waves scattered by an object, information about both the amplitude and phase of the scattered waves can be recorded in the form of an interference pattern even when the recording medium responds only to intensity. He demonstrated that from such a record, a replica of the scattered wavefronts can be reconstructed and an image of the original object can be obtained. The record is called a hologram, a term coined by Gabor (from "holos" in Greek) to mean "whole recording."

The coherent waves involved in the recording process can be electromagnetic, acoustic, or even waves of matter such as those associated with an electron beam. In fact, the recording can be accomplished by one kind of wave and the reconstruction by another kind. Gabors' original interest was in electron microscopy. He devised holography as a lensless imaging process in which the hologram would be generated by a scattered electron beam but reconstruction would take place by means of an optical beam.

Gabor was influenced in his initial studies of wavefront reconstruction by W. L. Bragg's previous work on X-ray crystallography and by other work of a similar nature such as the work on interferometry. The concept of fringe patterns being generated by two intersecting coherent beams was well known, but Gabor went a step further. He realized that by illuminating such a pattern with a replica of one of the beams, he could generate a replica of the other beam. In short, he introduced the beam reconstruction process.

Although the work by Gabor was initiated in the 1940's and extended by himself and others throughout the 1950's, it was not until after the advent of the laser in the early 1960's, that the modern revolution in holography began. The pioneers in this effort were Leith and Upatnieks who suggested an important modification of Gabor's original technique that greatly generalized and improved the process. They also created a great popular interest in holography that extends to this day by vividly demonstrating its three-dimensional character. This success of optical holography prompted many researchers to investigate holography in other parts of electromagnetic spectrum and with other forms of radiation. Acoustic and microwave holography thus came into being.

The first experiments with acoustic and microwave holography were direct analogs of optical holography using square-law detectors of acoustic and electromagnetic radiation. But as these modalities were investigated, it was found that various aspects of holography could be exploited in the acoustical and microwave versions that were not possible in the optical versions. For example, in acoustical holography the reference wave can be added electronically, either in analog or digital fashion, or it can be left out altogether. Leaving it out is possible because the instantaneous amplitude and phase within a cycle of oscillation are known functions of time and hence time can be used as a reference.

Strong linkages exist between holography and numerous other pursuits of professional concern to IEEE members. The second paper in this category, Goodman's "An Introduction to the Principles and Applictions of Holography," reviews fundamental theory and describes applications such as three-dimensional imaging, interferometry, spatial filtering, and data storage. The third paper, by Leith entitled "Quasi-Holographic Techniques in the Microwave Region," relates range-Doppler radar, synthetic aperture radar, and chirp radar to holographic systems.

Computers have provided an additional dimension to holography in recent years. This point is brought out in Huang's paper, "Digital Holography." Computer techniques are described for simulating the holographic process, for calculating and recording holograms of artificial objects, for forming images from detected holographic data, and for generating binary holograms and kinoforms which are useful in spatial filtering and interferometry.

As previously stated, the word hologram means "whole recording" and reflects the fact that the object's beam amplitude and phase are both recorded. It is possible, however, to reconstruct a good image of an object even if only the phase is recorded. Under this circumstance, the recording is referred to by the somewhat contradictory term "phase-only hologram." This type of hologram is quite useful and has special characteristics which have been studied over the years. We include as the fifth paper in this category, a report of some of our own recent work, "Evaluating Quantization Error in Phase-Only Holograms."

Since holographic techniques are not limited to electromagnetic waves but can be useful for acoustic waves as well, we include a paper by Mueller, "Acoustic Holography," to describe various acoustic approaches such as those using scanning piezoelectric detectors of acoustic signals and laser-beam detectors of acoustically generated surface levitation. The applications presented include underwater viewing, biomedical diagnosis, acoustic microscopy, and seismic exploration.

Acoustic holography is also treated in Wade's paper entitled "Acoustic Imaging with Holography and Lenses." Several holographic systems using laser-beam readout such as Bragg-diffraction imaging, scanning laser acoustic microscopy, and liquid-surface holography are described.

A good example of computer-aided holography is in seismic exploration where computer algorithms are used to reconstruct maps of structural features of the earth at desired depths below the surface. The paper by Fitzgerald, entitled "Seismic Imaging by Holography," deals with this subject and describes holographic techniques for image enhancement. It discusses the application of these techniques to a variety of problems in the earth sciences.

Fitzgerald's paper concludes the group we have chosen to include in the "Holography" category. Many of these papers are quite old but because of their overall quality, their clarity of explanation, their historical significance and the innovative concepts they describe, we do not wish to replace them with newer papers. Nevertheless, the new work is important and should be cited. The International Society for Engineering (SPIE, from the original name, Society of Photo-Optical Instrumentation Engineers) has been particularly diligent in publishing in this area. *SPIE Proceedings* volume 532 (1985), "Holography: Critical Review of Technology," carries 15 papers describing the present state-of-the art, and *SPIE Proceedings* volume 523 (1985) contains 50 papers on applications of holography. For the layman, the March 1984 issue of the *National Geographic Magazine* features John Caufield's beautifully written tutorial description of holography and provides a hologram on its cover. The September/October 1980 issue of *Optical Engineering* (published by SPIE) is dedicated to Dennis Gabor and devotes 117 pages of largely tutorial material in treating many developments. The issue starts with E. N. Leith's article entitled "The Legacy of Dennis Gabor" and continues with broad coverage, including such topics as holographic interferometry and computer-generated holograms.

B. Optical Processing

Optical image processing involves manipulating information in images using light as the means of manipulation. In its most common form, an optical processor directs a beam of electromagnetic waves in the visible region onto a two-dimensional image field that spatially modulates the beam. This kind of processing is especially convenient when the image as well as the processing mechanism originates in optical form. The manipulation of images being processed results in their rearrangement in ways that are designed to bring out and enhance particular aspects of characteristics of the images.

Attractive features of optical processing include its capability for parallel processing and its speed. Once the input image has been recorded in the form of an input transparency, the remainder of the processing takes place at the velocity of light and proceeds in parallel fashion rather than sequentially. Optical processing has the additional advantage of great capacity.

Light as manipulated by lenses to produce magnification is an example of optical image processing and illustrates the capacity and the speed with which the processing takes place. In this sense, the word "lens" can be regarded as an apt acronym for large ensemble nanosecond system.

A simple optical processor, consisting of a fine-grained photographic transparency, a high-quality converging lens, and an observation screen, can be very quickly assembled in such a way as to perform complicated and useful processing of an image with enormous information content. For example, the input transparency may easily contain 10^9 resolvable data points in a two-dimensional array, each point possessing 8 bits of information. The system can perform a two-dimensional Fourier transformation on the data points in 2 or 3 ns. By adding a second lens and a second transparency with a desired pattern, the system can be made to multiply each of the transformed points by a predesignated quantity, take the inverse Fourier transform of the product set, and display the resulting pattern on the observation screen. The billion multiplications and the two transformations are accomplished almost simultaneously as the light propagates through the system at 3×10^8 m/s. In addition to the advantages of large capacity, high-speed, and parallelism, an optical image processor can be put together in a small, convenient package. A total volume of a fraction of cubic foot is easily feasible.

Optical image processing can be regarded as the manipulation of fields of photons. Such processing includes the acquisition and the treatment of the information contained in those fields. Acquiring and treating optical information is precisely what takes place whenever a living creature employs its ability to see. We are, therefore, led to the conclusion that optical image processing was developed naturally many millions of years ago when vision evolved in the animals inhabiting the earth.

The human eye, in particular, is a very sophisticated instrument for optical processing. The response of the eye to changes in intensity of illumination is nonlinear, appearing to be nearly logarithmic. This gives the eye an extremely large dynamic range. The retina, which contains the light sensitive elements (rods and cones) and the nerve connecting them to the brain's visual cortex, is responsible for some of the processing and can be regarded as an extension of the brain. When light activates one of the tiny receptors, a photo-chemical transition occurs, producing a nerve impulse which signals the visual cortex. The optical processing mechanisms of the brain permits edge-sharpening, intensity adaptation, and chromatic adaption. The perception of color, for example, is dependent on the spatial content of a scene being observed. It is not purely a local phenomenon, involving only the frequency of the light detected by the rods and cones in the eye.

For thousands of years this amazing instrument was man's only means of producing an image. But by now, the technological advances of the past and present have brought into being many types of equipment for image restoration, enhancement, manipulation, reconstruction, and processing in general. Holography, of course, is one of the most interesting and spectacular of these technological developments.

Whereas the converging lens is a critical component in the human eye for forming images, no lenses are needed in ordinary holography. And whereas the eye uses incoherent light, holography typically employs coherent light. The lens-and-retina combination of the eye is capable of producing a two-dimensional image; holograms can produce images in three-dimensions. Optical holography thus provides the basis for image-processing techniques not found in the eye or anywhere else in nature. Three of the four papers that we include in the section on optical processing were previously listed in Section A, "Holography." These papers have already been commented upon, but the remaining paper, "Coherent Optical Pattern Recognition" by D. Casasent has not been discussed. The paper treats pattern-recognition systems, techniques, and applications which involve the use of coherent light and whose objective is to determine the presence of a key object within a scene containing other objects and noise. The techniques described are excellent examples of a substantial repertoire of operations available in optical image processing and include both the modern holographic approaches and the more classical techniques utilizing lenses.

C. Acoustic-Ultrasonic Imaging

How to "see" with sound has intrigued engineers and scientists for decades. Bats, whales, and dolphins do it with ease but the human species has virtually no such natural ability. The history of engineering and science, however, is a vast demonstration that technological solution can compensate for deficiencies of nature. The technology associated with producing images with acoustic waves had its first great success with the development of sonar by the French in World War I. Since then, many other approaches to ultrasonic imaging have proven successful and the pace of the progress has steadily increased. That progress is what this section is all about.

Ultrasonic energy can give images of objects not obtainable with light, microwaves, X-rays, or any other form of radiation. Some examples are as follows: 1) a particular object may be surrounded by material completely opaque to light but relatively transparent to sound; 2) a given organ of the human body imbedded in soft tissue may be difficult to differentiate with X-rays but not with sound; 3) the submerged hulk of a sunken vessel in the murky waters of a shipping lane may be virtually impossible to find by means of light but easy to find by means of sound; and 4) the growth of a fetus in the mother's uterus cannot be safely monitored with invasive X-rays but can be observed without risk using benign ultrasound.

For these and many other reasons, modern embodiments of acoustical approaches to imaging are bringing to a number of areas of scientific, medical, and commercial endeavor well-engineered investigative instruments of great power. In hospitals, acoustical images are used for real-time diagnostics; in nuclear power plants, containment vessels are inspected with acoustical flaw-detection systems; and in biological laboratories, microspecimens are examined using acoustical microscopes that rival or surpass their optical counterparts in resolution, penetrability, and contrast. Many now-available commercial systems were in the research stage 15 years ago and less. The technological developments in the acoustic field are having significant effects in seismic exploration and oceanic search as well as in the above-mentioned areas of diagnostic medicine, nondestructive evaluation, and microscopy.

The papers in this section treat a number of the systems and instruments that carry out these tasks and introduce the concepts upon which they are based. The papers deal with these themes on levels ranging from purely tutorial exposition of principles and systems to basically technological description of the latest research progress. Many topics are covered from both analytical and experimental viewpoints and include general background, historical development, and fundamental categorization and detailed description of the modern systems, including their applications for acoustical imaging.

The first two papers of this section were previously listed in the holography classification and commented upon earlier. However, the remaining seven papers have yet to be described. The paper "Signal Processing in Acoustic Imaging," by Keating, Sawatari, and Zilinskas surveys processing methods for 1) extracting image data from noise, 2) improving resolution, 3) compensating for various kinds of errors, 4) recognizing patterns, 5) estimating bearings, 6) imaging passive sources, and 7) imaging objects in nonstationary environments by using adaptive methods. The authors observe that due to long wavelengths, acoustic imagery is inherently inferior to optical imagery. Signal processing therefore is extremely important. It can significantly improve acoustic imagery and becomes easier and easier to implement because of the ongoing revolution in digital electronics.

Havlice and Taenzer's paper, "Medical Ultrasonic Imaging: An Overview of Principles and Instrumentation," describes how ultrasonic acoustic imagery has become a substantial aid to the clinical radiologist, complementing imagery from X-ray and nuclear cameras. The authors present the basic principles of ultrasonic propagation in tissue and how these principles are used to design imaging systems.

In "Acoustic Imaging for Nondestructive Evaluation" G. Kino describes how ultrasonic imagery can be employed to search for various types of faults and to measure stress in manufactured parts and structures. Since acoustic images are maps of the mechanical properties of materials, the application of these images to nondestructive evaluation is very natural and constitutes a major advantage over other kinds of images. Kino shows that the acoustic techniques can locate the position of flaws quickly and accurately.

In "Reconstructive Tomography and Applications to Ultrasonics," Mueller, Kaveh, and Wade introduce the general subject of computer-assisted tomography and discuss several specific approaches to ultrasonic tomography including a Doppler-oriented approach. The major technical treatment in the paper describes how to take into account diffraction, whose effects are far more important for ultrasound than for X-rays because of the wavelength differences.

The theme of ultrasonic tomography is continued in

a more recent paper entitled "Computerized Tomography with Ultrasound," by J. Greenleaf. He discusses both theoretical and practical problems, beginning with a derivation of Eikonal (Greek for "image") reconstruction which assumes straight-line wave propagation and thus leaves out diffraction. He then derives the Born and Rytov approximations to the wave equation which include the effects of diffraction. He considers problems of implementation and discusses the strengths and weaknesses of the techniques of seismic backscatter reconstruction for use in tissue imaging.

Ultrasonic microscopes are discussed by Kessler and Yuhas in their paper "Acoustic Microscopy—1979." In contrast to the majority of the systems described by the previous papers of this classification in which low frequencies from 1 to 10 MHz are used, the microscopes use much higher frequencies, ranging from 100 MHz to the gigahertz region. The authors briefly relate the historical background for modern ultrasonic microscopes and then describe and compare in some detail the two most prominent systems: the scanning acoustic microscope (SAM) and the scanning laser acoustic microscope (SLAM). Resolution, imaging techniques, and applications for the two instruments are discussed. The authors conclude by predicting that SLAM and SAM will take their place alongside other types of microscopes as standard analytical instruments.

The classification concludes with a second paper on ultrasonic microscopy, this one by Quate, Atalar, and Wickramasinghe entitled "Acoustic Microscopy with Mechanical Scanning—A Review." The authors provide a captivating tutorial examination of the scanning acoustic microscope, along with a number of impressive images of biological cells, integrated circuits, and minute structure in solid-state material. The results they present constitute convincing evidence of a promising future for SAM.

D. Tomography/NMR Imaging

The word "tomography" has historically referred to a technique of X-ray photography in which only one plane of internal structure within the object is photographed in sharp focus. The structure in the other planes shows up blurred in the photograph. The tomogram thus produced appears to be an X-ray image of the slice of the object in the focused plane. This kind of tomography has been performed in our hospitals for many years by a system using a moving X-ray source and moving photographic film.

Now, however, a new kind of tomography is available. Far more accurate and useful than the tomograms described above are tomograms reconstructed by digital computation. Because of its accuracy and clarity, computer-aided tomography (CAT) has brought about a revolution in radiography giving the practicing physician a new degree of access to what is going on inside a patient's body. In recognition of this fact, the 1979 Nobel prize in Physiology and Medicine went to two leading workers in this field, G. N. Hounsfield, an English electrical engineer, and A. M. Cormack, a U.S. physicist.

X-rays are not the only kinds of radiation for which computer tomography is feasible. Microwaves, electron beams, ultrasound, fast sub-atomic particles from accelerators, gamma-ray emission from such sources as positron annihilation, and even magnetic fields can be used.

By comparing an ordinary X-ray image to an X-ray tomogram we can quickly see the advantages of tomography. In a conventional X-ray system, the rays diverge from a single source to project an image onto a piece of film. The image is a shadowgraph of the structure along the paths of the rays. But structural elements, cleanly separated in the three-dimensional object, often overlap in the final two-dimensional image in such a way as to make them hard to distinguish. In CAT there is no overlap. A tomogram is computed from a large number of projections and has the form of a two-dimensional mapping of the discrete non-overlapping structural elements in a single plane of the body. The irradiating rays are confined solely to that plane, not being permitted to penetrate into other regions of the body. Thus, there is no blurred structure in these tomograms. Ordinary X-ray technology is combined with sophisticated digital processing to make this kind of tomography possible.

The X-ray source and detector are moved around the body and, typically, hundreds of projections are made. They each correspond to a different orientation of the rays passing through the body. Instead of being recorded on film, the information is sent to a computer for calculating the tomogram. With this approach, generically referred to as synthetic imaging, it is possible in principle to obtain the image of any cross-section within the body. The technique has proven invaluable for the diagnosis of brain tumors and for many other pathologies.

Transmission modes of operation are the only modes possible with X-rays. But microwaves and acoustic waves can be reflected and reflection modes are therefore possible with such radiation. It is also possible to make use of coherence and record complex amplitudes (including phase) rather than only intensity as in the case of X-rays. One system that appears to have a particularly attractive potential employs CW coherent waves and uses complex amplitude data from Doppler-shifted reflections to produce the tomograms.

This latter technique is sometimes called "coherent Doppler reflection tomography" (CDRT). When an object is in motion with respect to a stationary transmitter-receiver unit, points of reflection within the object return echoes that are Doppler-shifted in frequency by an amount depending on the velocity of the individual points. In a conceptually simple version of CDRT, the output from the transmitter is a sheet beam of CW sinusoidal waves. The object irradiated by the sheet beam rotates at uniform angular velocity about an axis perpendicular to the plane of the beam. All the points of reflection lying on a line of constant cross range have the same component of velocity in the direction pointing towards the receiver. All the echoes produced by this line of point reflectors will have the same Doppler-shifted frequency in traveling toward the receiver. By measuring the receiver output at any particular frequency, we obtain the value of the line integral of the scattered radiation for the cross range corresponding to that frequency. The output at other frequencies gives the line integral for scattered radiation at other cross ranges. An instantaneous plot of receiver output as a function of frequency can be interpreted as a projection. With the passage of time, the object will rotate continuously to new positions and new projections will be produced. In this fashion a continuum of projections, one coming rapidly after another, is generated. Many projections can be recorded as the body is rotated through 360°. A computer can be programmed to use the data from these projections to produce the distribution of point reflections in the irradiated object slice. A plot of this distribution constitutes the tomogram.

As previously mentioned, we can also produce tomograms by using magnetic fields. That is what is done in nuclear-magnetic resonance (NMR) tomography, a type of imaging showing signs of becoming the basis for another important revolution in clinical medicine. NMR refers to resonance that occurs in the nuclei of the atoms of certain chemical elements. When these elements are placed in strong magnetic fields and excited by electric fields of the right frequency, certain nuclei will resonate, expelling electromagnetic energy at the resonant frequency. A technique based on detecting this radiated energy has long been used to identify various types of nuclei in chemical compounds.

Not all atoms exhibit NMR. Hydrogen, present throughout the human body, is one that does. The frequency of its radiated energy depends on the strength of the applied magnetic field; the magnitude, on the concentration of the resonating atoms. We therefore apply a magnetic field that varies in known fashion across the slice to be imaged. By measuring the frequency of the radiation that emerges we know where within the slice the radiation came from. By measuring its magnitude we know the density of the hydrogen radiators. This information is all that is needed to produce a two-dimensional image. Instead of showing only what types of nuclei are contained in a test sample (as is the case with ordinary NMR testing), the measurements described above show the location and density of the concentrations of hydrogen throughout the object. Location and density, of course, constitute the essence of any tomogram.

NMR tomography is quickly becoming a mature technique. It is both safer and superior to X-ray tomography. Rapid advances are presently taking place with no slowing of the rate of improvement yet in sight.

NMR tomography is safer than X-ray tomography because it involves no ionizing radiation. It is superior because it works by source, not by attenuation. What X-rays do is exploit the varying degrees of transparency of different parts of the body. Bones are less transparent to X-rays than flesh, so they attenuate more severely the flow of the rays. Using X-rays is as though one were shining light through a setting of crystal bowls or goblets. A silhouette of these items can be projected onto a wall behind the setting to provide an image or shadowgraph. But NMR makes the object points visible as individual sources, not as obstacles. With NMR it's as though one were shining the light into the setting and observing the details as the various items reflect the light.

Images produced by NMR tomography are already much better than those produced by X-ray tomography. Nevertheless, NMR tomography can be expected to show much improvement in the future, whereas X-ray tomography has reached the point of saturation as far as further improvement is concerned.

The type of computed tomography based on gamma-ray emission from positron annihilation is particularly attractive from a functional point of view. In this tomography, frequently called PET as an acronym for positron-emission tomography, the computed image yields the location and concentration of positron-emitting radioisotopes. The clinical value of PET lies in the fact that the distribution of such an isotope, administered to the patient either by inhalation or by injection, gives physicians information about the functional state of various organs. Dynamic studies can be easily made which show the time dependence of the distribution, and this is of great importance in nuclear medicine.

The mathematical approach to positron-emission tomography (PET) is quite similar to that of X-ray computed tomography. An understanding of either aids in understanding the other. Common to both are the computer algorithms for reconstructing tomograms from the projections. All such algorithms are based on the assumption that the projections are line integrals of the quantity of interest. In PET the line integral is of the distribution of the positron-emitting radioisotopes. In CAT, the line integral is of the attenuation experienced by the rays as they propagate through the body.

The first paper of this classification is by H. J. Scudder and is entitled ''Introduction to Computer Aided Tomography.'' This paper provides the reader with basic understanding of both the physics and the mathematics that underlie the techniques of tomography. The physics of X-ray photon interaction with matter is treated and the question of beam hardening is discussed. Beam hardening gives rise to nonlinearity, triggered by the fact that an X-ray beam consists of photons of different energies. The reconstructed tomogram is a map of the attenuation coefficients at all the points in the imaged cross-section. Because the attenuation at a given point is generally greater for photons of lower energy, the lower energy photons are more rapidly eliminated. This causes the spectrum of energy distribution of the X-ray beam to change, or harden, as the beam passes through the object. X-ray beams reaching a particular point inside the body from different directions are likely to have different spectra, having passed through different materials before reaching the point. These beams will therefore be attenuated differently at that point and this makes it difficult to assign a single value for the attenuation coefficient there.

Scudder presents a mathematical derivation of the equations associated with convolution-back projection. He first treats the mathematics on a continuous basis and then shows how to perform the calculations on a quantized-discrete basis suitable for use by a digital computer.

The second paper in this classification, by A. Macovski, is entitled "Physical Problems of Computerized Tomography." The author points out that accurate tomograms can be reconstructed if the projections are accurately known at all angles. Under these circumstances, the tomographic reconstruction will provide an artifact-free image. In many physical systems, however, the measurements fail to accurately represent a complete set of projections. The inadequacy of the measurements can include nonlinearities, noise, and insufficient data. Macovski explores various inadequacies of this kind and discusses their effect on the reconstructions.

Louis and Natterer shift back to concerns about mathematics in their paper "Mathematical Problems of Computerized Tomography." They discuss the extent to which it is possible to reconstruct an image of an object from acquired data and the extent to which the reconstruction process is stable with respect to data errors. Finally, they present algorithms to accomplish the reconstruction.

The paper by E. M. Lewitt entitled "Reconstruction Algorithms: Transform Methods," is a tutorial presentation which introduces the principles and implementation of a group of reconstruction algorithms classified as "transform" methods as opposed to "series-expansion" methods. Transform methods are essentially numerical means for solving a closed-form inversion formula. A number of the methods are discussed in detail by the author. The mathematical model associated with these methods involves known and unknown functions whose arguments come from a continuum of real numbers. Unknown functions can be solved by producing inversion formulas, which are then discretized for digital computation.

In the series-expansion method, the mathemical model starts with discretization in the image domain. The discrete formulation leads immediately to a system of equations whose solution is found numerically. Y. Censor, in his paper "Finite Series-Expansion Reconstruction Methods," treats this approach. He shows that the fundamental difference between the series-expansion approach and the transform approach is that discretization takes place at the outset in the former but only at the end in the latter.

Synthetic aperture radar (SAR) is a well-developed technique for producing high-resolution images of the terrain below and off to one side of a traveling airplane or space vehicle. The data to be processed are collected by airborne or spaceborne microwave radar which illuminates the target area from different perspectives. One form of SAR utilizes a "spotlight" mode of operation in which the antenna is steared so that the same terrain area remains illuminated during a long data-collection interval. Although computer-aided tomography and spotlight-mode synthetic aperture radar were developed independently, the operation of the two have a striking similarity of principles. Munson, O'Brien, and Jenkens, in their paper "A Tomographic Formulation of Spotlight-Mode Synthetic Aperture Radar," show that spotlight-mode SAR is indeed a tomographic imaging system and can profitably be analyzed from this point of view. The authors point out important differences as well as remarkable similarities between the two types of systems.

The next two papers in this classification, one by Mueller, Kaveh, and Wade and one by J. F. Greenleaf, both concern ultrasonic tomography and were reviewed in the last section. The following paper by Hinshaw and Lent, "An Introduction to NMR Imaging: From the Bloch Equation to the Imaging Equation," treats NMR tomography which, as we have discussed, is the latest and in many ways the most potentially effective addition to the tools of diagnostic radiologists. The authors assume that the reader is familiar with X-ray computerized tomography but not with NMR tomography. The Bloch equation referred to in the title was first given by Felix Bloch in 1946. He and Edward Purcell shared the 1952 Physics Nobel Prize for their work in nuclear magnetic resonance. Hinshaw and Lent describe the appropriate physical system capable of exploiting the Bloch equation to produce clinically useful tomograms.

The NMR approach to tomography is treated also by Cho, Kim, Song, and Cumming in their paper "Fourier Transform Nuclear Magnetic Resonance Tomographic Imaging." The authors review the principles of NMR tomography from an engineering and physics point of view and present computer simulations to clarify the concepts. They describe in detail four major types of such imaging and discuss ways to improve performance.

The last paper of this classification is "Computerized Geophysical Tomography" by Dines and Lytle. The paper deals with the data processing of electromagnetic or seismic signals that propagate through regions of geophysical interest between borehole arrays. This approach to tomographic imaging involves spatially truncated projections that are limited in view angle. Possible applications include detecting hazardous regions in mining and underground construction, assessing sites for nuclear reactors and waste storage, and determining the location and volume of commercially important mineralogical deposits. Dines and Lytle show that an iterative-solution algorithm is suitable for the kinds of problems involved. They demonstrate the performance of their algorithm using computer-generated data. They then apply the algorithm to experimental data collected by continuous-wave electromagnetic transmission probing.

E. Microwave Imaging

The tomographic and holographic systems described in previous sections are related to certain microwave imaging systems and particularly, as we have discussed, to synthetic aperture radar (SAR). However, in SAR, Doppler processing is employed and the energy is usually emitted in short pulses. One version of SAR is born aloft by a plane or spacecraft following a straightline path at uniform velocity. Imagine an aircraft carrying a small broad-beam antenna which points in a fixed direction off to one side and down. Radar pulses are transmitted from a sequence of positions along the flight path and the complex amplitude of the echoes are holographically recorded on film. There is often tomographic character to the operation of such systems also by properly combining the received waveforms, it is possible to synthesize an effective aperture thousands of meters long and achieve resolution in the along-track direction commensurate with such a length.

The data gathered by an SAR is ordinarily processed by optical rather than digital means. Film transparency, coherent light, and special lenses are used. The technology has been under intensive development for almost 30 years and has reached a high level of sophistication. Excellent and even spectacular results have been achieved for a couple of decades. Resolution thousands of times finer than the diffraction limit of the actual receiving antenna is available. Optical processing can be accredited with having made this enormous success possible. Nevertheless, the reason for the dominance of optical processing over digital processing is largely historical. When SAR was first developed, powerful optical techniques were available but not powerful digital techniques. Since those early days, the digital computer has experienced phenomenonal development and has become an extremely powerful and versatile tool. It is by now an instrument of ever-more pervasive influence and its use is extending into the synthetic aperture domain. From an examination of the research literature, it is apparent that much significant recent progress in this field has been associated with the increasing use of the digital computer. Various image processing operations routinely carried out by digital computers, such as edge sharpening, contrast enhancement, the use of pseudo-color, and pattern recognition, are increasingly being investigated and employed. Some advantages of the digital approach now coming to light are that 1) the results are more accurate and hence more reproducible, 2) the processing is more convenient to perform, 3) under many circumstances it can be done more rapidly, and 4) it is more versatile and can be more readily extended to take care of such difficult tasks as aircraft-motion compensation, etc.

One can predict substantial future progress with both optical and digital technology and its increasing effectiveness in terms of cost, we can confidently expect digital approaches to play an ever-expanding role in synthetic aperture technology and other microwave imaging approaches, perhaps at the expense of optical approaches.

The first two papers listed in this section (Leith's paper, "Quasi-holographic Techniques in the Microwave Region," and Munson, O'Brien, and Jenkins' paper "A Tomographic Formulation of Spotlight-Mode Synthetic Aperture Radar") have previously been reviewed in other sections.

The next paper, by K. Tomiyasu, entitled "Tutorial Review of Synthetic-Aperture Radar (SAR) with Applications to Imaging of the Oceans Surface," is understandable to readers with no previous knowledge of the subject. The fundamentals of SAR operations are explained as well as the physical significance of synthetic aperture. The question of azimuth ambiguity is clearly presented. The author corrects some incomplete and misleading concepts that are widely held concerning SAR. The imaging of ocean waves is discussed as an important and challenging application of synthetic aperture radar.

The paper entitled "Spaceborne Synthetic-Aperture Imaging Radars: Applications, Techniques and Technology" by Elachi, Bicknell, Jordan, and Wu, reviews many aspects of the development and applications of SAR technology. The paper particularly addresses in detail all the features of spaceborne SAR's, with particular emphasis on those features that are unique to spaceborne systems. For example, the treatment takes into account the effects of the earth's rotation. The authors summarize the characteristics of specific systems such as the Seasat SAR and SIR-A. They discuss possible future developments and point out that one of the most challenging aspects of past and present SAR development has been digital processing of the data. The authors review various fields of application of SAR imaging with specific examples given in the areas of geology, oceanography, and studies of polar ice and renewable resources.

The next paper in this section, by Ausherman, Kozma, Walker, Jones, and Poggio entitled "Developments in Radar Imaging," presents an introduction to range-Doppler imaging and describes some common forms. The authors develop in detail the fundamentals of this type of imaging and discuss various processing approaches involving motion of object components through resolution cells. They describe such techniques of SAR as the strip-map mode, the spotlight mode, and the delay-Doppler mode. They enunciate the general properties of radar images and the necessary requirements for them to be useful. They point out that, however different the techniques may appear on the surface, they are basically equivalent and can be developed from a common theoretical background.

The last paper of this section is by E. G. Njoku and is entitled "Passive Microwave Remote Sensing of the Earth from Space—A Review." The paper surveys progress achieved with space-based microwave radiometry. The author focuses on sensor characteristics and decribes specific results. He starts with a brief examination of historical developments and then discusses the basic concepts for spacecraft radiometry. He summarizes the significant accomplishments obtained with these systems and includes several excellent maps. By treating each sensor sequentially, the author traces with great clarity the development of passive microwave sensing from space and spells out the options and possibilities for the future.

F. Seismic Imaging

The major impetus in developing seismic imaging has been commercial interest in searching for oil. It is obviously very difficult to tell from above ground exactly where oil has collected beneath its surface. A typical approach is to use explosive charges and sensitive sensors to measure the intensity and travel-time of acoustic shockwaves moving through the earth. In one simplified approach, a geophysicist bores a shallow hole into the ground, lowers in a charge and sets it off. Shockwaves are created which reflect sharply from hard rock but not from soft dirt. The length of time it takes the waves to reach an underground layer of rock and return to a sensor at the surface shows how deep the layer is. Sensors are generally called geophones. The impulses received by them are recorded and processed. Seismic imaging includes acquiring and recording the data and then interpreting the recording. Systems to do this were first developed about 60 years ago and have been in use ever since.

This type of imaging is based on echo-ranging and is fundamentally similar to radar and sonar. It starts with an explosion which generates an intense signal approximating an impulse. The signal travels to the inaccessible structure to be imaged and returns by reflection. The data acquisition consists of detecting the reflected signal. Processing is required to help unravel the physical characteristics of the structure producing the echoes. This structure is necessarily confined to a limited underground region of the earth near where the charge was set off. In this fashion we image a portion of the interior of the earth from a finite aperture on its surface. The measurements are made at relatively few points within this limited aperture. The earth acts as an elastic medium for propagating the acoustic shockwaves. Typically, a number of shots are laid out at equally spaced intervals along a surveyed line. The geophones are usually located at similarly spaced intervals on one or both sides of the shots. The geophone outputs are thus due to signals reflected, diffracted, or refracted back to the earth's surface from the reflective elements being explored.

Seismic data acquisition, as practiced at present, is inherently multi-dimensional in character. The acoustic wavefields which propagate beneath the earth's surface have both temporal and spatial variations. Seismic signal processing is concerned with utilizing the full multi-dimensional character of the recorded wavefields. Concepts of both holography and tomography are applicable.

The first paper in this section, by Wood and Treitel, is "Seismic Signal Processing," and it reviews a number of distinctly different processing techniques. The authors point out that seismic prospecting for oil and gas has undergone a "digital revolution" during the last few years. This progress has affected all three of the categories that seismic signal processing is generally divided into data acquisition, data processing, and data interpretation. The paper, however, deals mainly with data processing; acquisition and interpretation being covered only where necessary. The paper emphasizes techniques associated with exploration in offshore areas where reverberations in the water interfere with reflections from the regions below. The authors describe a method called predictive deconvolution that has been successful in attenuating these reverberations, making it possible to detect and process reflections from structures in the earth below the water. The authors point out that seismic signal processing is neither pure science nor pure art and that the optimum processing sequences depend upon geological conditions and vary from area to area.

The paper by G. L. Fitzpatrick treats holographic techniques in seismic imaging and has already been reviewed in the first section "Holography."

The next paper, entitled "Geomagnetic Depth Sounding by Means of Oceanographic and Aeromagnetic Surveys," by Gregori and Lanzerotti, deals with a passive approach to seismic imaging. Geomagnetic surveys by means of airborne or shipborne magnetometers have been conducted for a long time and now cover a large fraction of the earth's surface. There is a time-varying part of the geomagnetic field that is normally associated with induction and local conductivity anomalies involving induced telluric currents. This time-varying component normally is subtracted from the data as an unwanted nuisance, but in this paper the authors show how to make use of it. They discuss techniques for analyzing the data to provide important information in locating ocean ridges, volcanic islands, island arcs, and geothermal fluxes. They believe that these analyses can be carried out with the data already available. The authors focus on a convenient filtering method for the geomagnetic field referred to as Parkinson filtering.

The paper by Dines and Lytle deals with geophysical tomography and has been reviewed in Section D.

The final paper in this section is by E. A. Robinson and is entitled "Spectral Approach to Geophysical Inversion by Lorentz, Fourier, and Radon Transforms." The geophysical inversion referred to in the title refers to an attempt to determine the structure of the interior of the earth from data recorded at the surface. The paper gives a survey of production-type data-processing methods in everyday use in geophysical exploration. Specifically, the author describes a number of spectral approaches involving lattice methods, the Fourier transform, and the Radon transform.

G. Microscopy/Nondestructive Evaluation

As the title indicates, this section includes papers dealing with both microscopy and nondestructive evaluation (NDE). It is justifiable to put the two fields together in this reprint volume because microscopes play a prominent part in many kinds of NDE. An important application for microscopy has long veen in evaluating the integrity of the microstructure of various manufactured parts without damaging the parts. For example, silicon nitride turbine blades can be examined by a scanning laser acoustic microscope not only to detect flaws but to define the elestic microstructure of the blades. The profiles of metal and semiconductor films on silicon can be measured with a scanning acoustic microscope to an accuracy of tens of angstroms. A new fiber-optic microscope can be used to measure acoustic waves near cracks and thermal conduction changes near other defects by photoacoustic methods.

The importance of nondestructive evaluation is unquestioned. The nuclear-reactor accident at Three-Mile Island was due in part to undetected mechanical faults. The existence, growth and spread of such faults in a manufactured item becomes more unpredictable as the item becomes more complex. In the case of nuclear and other modern systems, the materials problems are not completely understood. Flaws can develop in startling ways. Many new military and commercial aircraft are built with composite materials consisting of epoxy reinforced with carbon and other fibers. These composites are light, strong, and economical and can be molded into complicated shapes. They are hard to test for faults without destroying them, either during their manufacture or their use.

Many manufactured items do not require microscopy, but an integrated circuit (IC) is quite a different matter. The scale is small and the structure, complex. Mechanical faults in IC's are extremely important: thin films may adhere improperly to substrates, connecting leads may break, cracks may develop, and semiconductor substrates, may not be bonded properly to ceramic bases. Techniques are needed to evaluate the properties of mechanical structures both during their manufacture and during their operation. The evaluation of these properties without destroying the unit being evaluated is of tremendous importance and constitues the essence of NDE.

The first three papers listed in this section by Kino, Kessler and Yuhas, and Quate, Atalar, and Wickramasinghe have appeared in other sections and have already been reviewed. The first new paper is "Laser Scanning Microscopy" by Alford, Vanderneut, and Zaleckas. The authors describe a type of optical microscopy in which the surface of the object is scanned, point by point, by a focused laser beam which in its simplest form moves over a predetermined raster pattern. The image of the object is then generated by an electronic system just as with a scanning electron microscope. As the object is scanned, the reflected and scattered radiation is detected. This approach to optical microscopy provides a whole series of possible controls and variable to optimize. The authors review optimization involving detection, illumination, and scanning. They then describe a number of applications in biomedical research, in semiconductor microelectronics, and in a variety of other industrial areas. They show that laser scanning microscopy offers a number of unique advantages over more conventional microscopy.

The next paper is by J. R. Wait, entitled "Review of Electomagnetic Methods in Nondestructive Testing of Wire Ropes." The failure of a wire rope on an aerial tramway can result in injury or death. Elevators, mine hoists, ski lifts, helicopters, and a number of suspension structures all make extensive use of wire ropes in life-sustaining situations. The condition of these ropes is of great importance and needs to be carefully monitored by nondestructive methods. There are several methods available starting with careful visual inspection. Other methods imply electromagnetic fields, X-rays or mechanical waves. In this tutorial paper, Wait reviews the progress involving the electromagnetic methods.

One common approach is to induce currents into the wire ropes by means of a solenoid which encircles the rope. The impedance of the solenoid is related to the cross-sectional area and the electrical properties of the rope. The scattered magnetic field external to the rope is measurable with coils. It is this field that is of most interest in this approach.

The most useful work to date has been empirical in nature. No attempt has yet been made to deduce the magnitude of the secondary fields due to internal flaws. Instead, a large number of ropes have been experimentally tested and the results published.

Analytical approaches thus far have considered only highly idealized situations. The anisotropic nature of wire ropes has not yet been addressed. The author concludes "that much research remains to be done."

Nevertheless, some important analytical work has been done. The work has proceeded by making use of closely related investigations in other fields such as geophysical prospecting. A unique aspect of the work is that it deals with the concept of probing the entire vector nature of the secondary fields rather than just one or two scaler components.

The results are of interest to anyone needing to test the internal structure of conductive and magnetic materials by nondestructive means. Some of the concepts are therefore relevant to the exploration of natural resources by remote sensing.

H. Signal Processing

This last section consists entirely of papers that have already appeared at least once in the previous sections. The papers are related to each other in that a substantial content of each is concerned with the general question of signal processing. The fundamental task of signal processing for images is to change an image which would otherwise be deficient in some way into one which is more suitable. A substantial number of important techniques have been developed for processing signals carried by energy which reflects from or passes through an object or piece of terrain. These papers deal with these techniques.

The general imaging process can be broken down into the categories of data acquisition, signal processing of the data, and image interpretation. This section deals with the second of these categories.

The signal processing procedures often have a single goal: to solve the inverse problem in which propagating energy is first modulated by an object and then received by sensors. The received signal serves as data and the signal processing is designed to use that data to find out what it was that modulated the energy in the first place.

Great progress has been made in signal processing recently. Because of advances in the hardware associated with integrated-circuit technology, the digital approach to signal processing has grown at a tremendous rate during the past two decades. The software has advanced also. Fast-processing algorithms are now available in such diverse areas as biomedical engineering, acoustics, sonar, radar, seismology, speech communication, data communication, nuclear science, and in many other areas. To process at high-speed we can utilize both LSI chips and special-purpose computers oriented specifically toward the task at hand. The progress continues to be of such a scale that it suggests that the revolution in digital image processing will continue for quite some time. The signal processing techniques can confidently be expected to constitute an important part of the work in imaging for a long time to come.

Holography, 1948–1971

DENNIS GABOR

I HAVE THE ADVANTAGE in this lecture, over many of my predecessors, that I need not write down a single equation or show an abstract graph. One can of course introduce almost any amount of mathematics into holography, but the essentials can be explained and understood from physical arguments.

Holography is based on the wave nature of light, and this was demonstrated convincingly for the first time in 1801 by Thomas Young, by a wonderfully simple experiment (see Fig. 1). He let a ray of sunlight into a dark room, placed a dark screen in front of it, pierced with two small pinholes, and beyond this, at some distance, a white screen. He then saw two darkish lines at both sides of a bright line, which gave him sufficient encouragement to repeat the experiment, this time with a spirit flame as light source, with a little salt in it, to produce the bright yellow sodium light. This time he saw a number of dark lines, regularly spaced; the first clear proof that light added to light can produce darkness. This phenomenon is called interference. Thomas Young had expected it because he believed in the wave theory of light. His great contribution to Christian Huygens's original idea was the intuition that monochromatic light represents regular sinusoidal oscillations, in a medium which at that time was called "the ether." If this is so, it must be possible to produce more light by adding wavecrest to wavecrest, and darkness by adding wavecrest to wavetrough.

Light which is capable of interferences is called "coherent," and it is evident that in order to yield many interference fringes, it must be *very* monochromatic. Coherence is conveniently measured by the path difference between two rays of the same source, by which they can differ while still giving observable interference contrast. This is called the coherence length, an important quantity in the theory and practice of holography. Lord Rayleigh and Albert Michelson were the first to understand that it is a reciprocal measure of the spectroscopic line width. Michelson used it for ingenious methods of spectral analysis and for the measurement of the diameter of stars.

Let us now jump a century and a half, to 1947. At that time I was very interested in electron microscopy. This wonderful instrument had at that time produced a hundredfold improvement on the resolving power of the best light microscopes, and yet it was disappointing, because it had stopped short of resolving atomic lattices. The de Broglie wavelength of fast electrons, about 1/20 angstrom, was short enough, but the optics was imperfect. The best electron objective which one can make can be compared in optical perfection to a raindrop rather than to a microscope objective, and through the theoretical work of O. Scherzer it was known that it could never be perfected. The theoretical limit at that

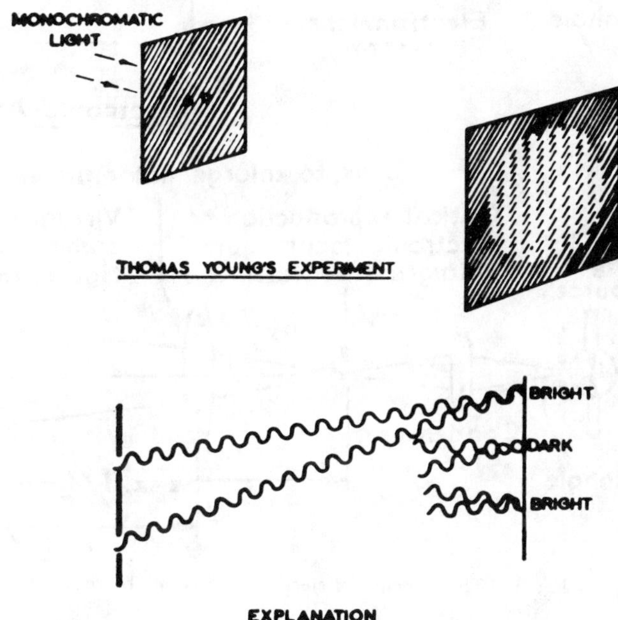

Fig. 1.   Thomas Young's interference experiments, 1801.

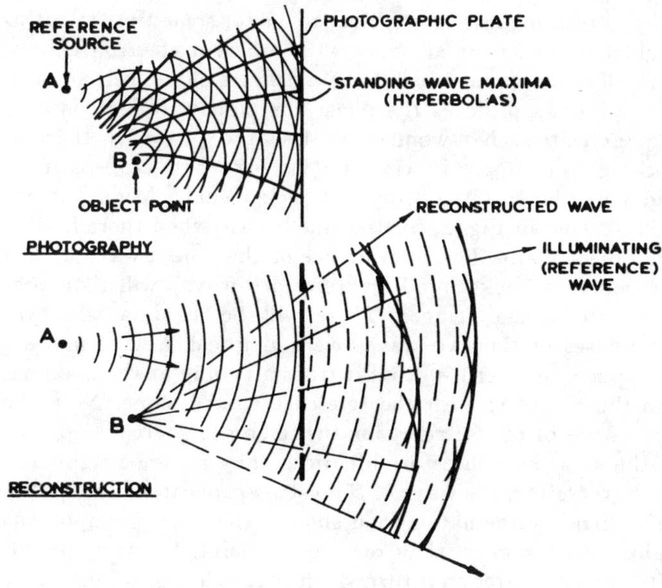

Fig. 2.   The basic idea of holography, 1947.

time was estimated at 4 Å, just about twice what was needed to resolve atomic lattices, while the practical limit stood at about 12 Å. These limits were given by the necessity of restricting the aperture of the electron lenses to a few 1/1000 radian, at which angle the spherical aberration error is about equal to the diffraction error. If one doubles this aperture so that the diffraction error is halved, the spherical aberration error is increased 8 times, and the image is hopelessly blurred.

After pondering this problem for a long time, a solution suddenly dawned on me, one fine day at Easter 1947, more or

Manuscript received February 21, 1972. Lecture delivered by D. Gabor on the occasion of his receiving the 1971 Nobel Prize for Physics, Stockholm, Sweden, December 13. Copyright © The Nobel Foundation 1972.

The author is Professor Emeritus and Senior Research Fellow, Imperial College of Science and Technology, University of London; and Staff Scientist, CBS Laboratories, Stamford, Conn.

Reprinted from *Proc. IEEE*, vol. 60, pp. 655–668, June 1972.

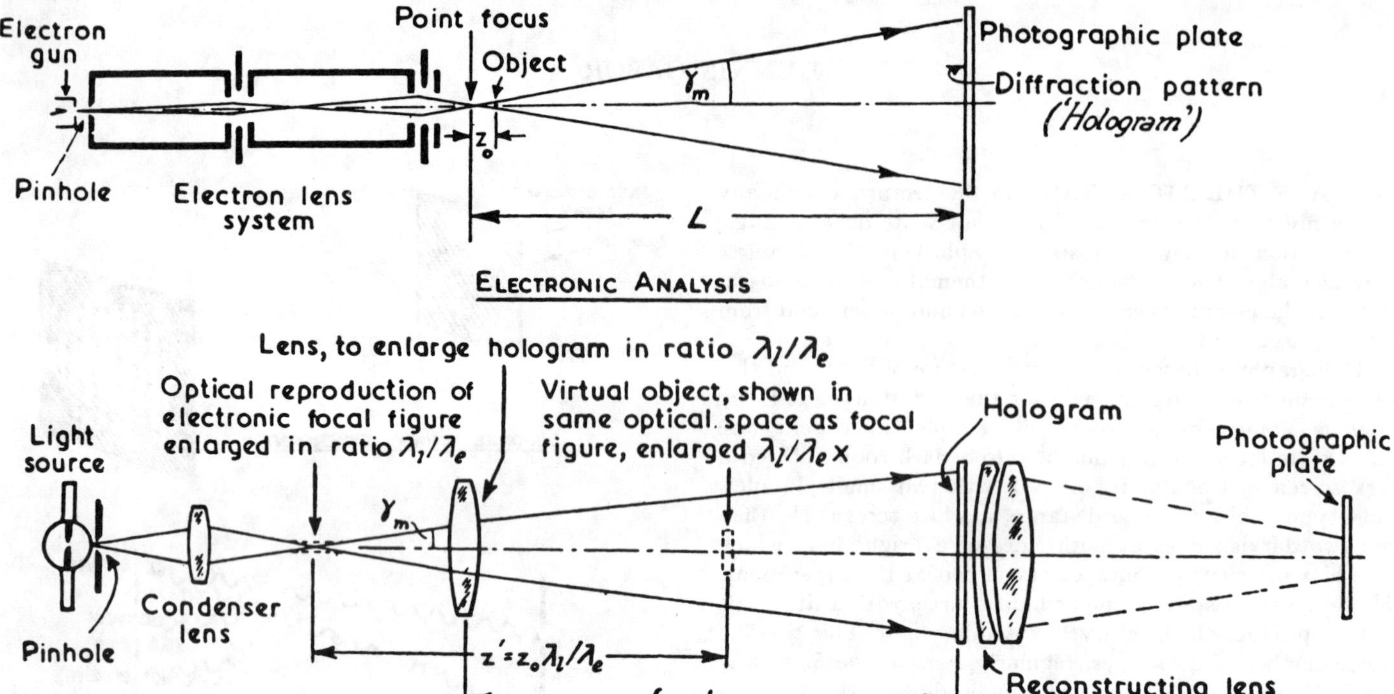

Fig. 3. The principle of electron microscopy by reconstructed wavefronts (Gabor, *Proc. Roy. Soc.*, vol. A197, p. 454, 1949 [1]).

less as shown in Fig. 2. Why not take a bad electron picture, but one which contains the *whole* information, and correct it by optical means? It was clear to me for some time that this could be done, if at all, only with coherent electron beams, with electron waves which have a definite phase. But an ordinary photograph loses the phase completely, it records only the intensities. No wonder we lose the phase, if there is nothing to compare it with! Let us see what happens if we add a standard to it, a "coherent background." My argument is illustrated in Fig. 2, for the simple case when there is only one object point. The interference of the object wave and of the coherent background or "reference wave" will then produce interference fringes. There will be maxima wherever the phases of the two waves were identical. Let us make a hard positive record, so that it transmits only at the maxima, and illuminate it with the reference source alone. Now the phases are of course right for the reference source A, but as at the slits the phases are identical, they must be right also for B; therefore, the wave of B must also appear, *reconstructed*.

A little mathematics soon showed that the principle was right, also for more than one object point, for any complicated object. Later on it turned out that in holography Nature is on the inventor's side; there is no need to take a hard positive record; one can take almost any negative. This encouraged me to complete my scheme of electron microscopy by reconstructed wavefronts, as I then called it and to propose the two-stage process shown in Fig. 3. The electron microscope was to produce the interference figure between the object beam and the coherent background, that is to say the non-diffracted part of the illuminating beam. This interference pattern I called a "hologram," from a Greek word "holos"—the whole, because it contained the whole information. The hologram was then reconstructed with light, in an optical system which corrected the aberrations of the electron optics [1].

In doing this, I stood on the shoulders of two great physi-

cists, W. L. Bragg and Fritz Zernike. Bragg had shown me, a few years earlier, his "X-ray microscope," an optical Fourier-transformer device. One puts into it a small photograph of the reciprocal lattice, and obtains a projection of the electron densities, but only in certain exceptional cases, when the phases are all real, and have the same sign. I did not know at that time, and neither did Bragg, that Mieczislav Wolfke had proposed this method in 1921, but without realising it experimentally. So the idea of a two-stage method was inspired by Bragg. The coherent background, on the other hand, was used with great success by Fritz Zernike in his beautiful investigations on lens aberrations, showing up their phase, and not just their intensity. It was only the reconstruction principle which had escaped them.

In 1947 I was working in the Research Laboratory of the British Thomson-Houston Company in Rugby, England. It was a lucky thing that the idea of holography came to me *via* electron microscopy, because if I had thought of optical holography only, the Director of Research, L. J. Davies, could have objected that the BTH company was an electrical engineering firm, and not in the optical field. But as our sister company, Metropolitan Vickers were makers of electron microscopes, I obtained the permission to carry out some optical experiments. Fig. 4 shows one of our first holographic reconstructions. The experiments were not easy. The best compromise between coherence and intensity was offered by the high pressure mercury lamp, which had a coherence length of only 0.1 mm, enough for about 200 fringes. But in order to achieve spatial coherence, we (my assistant Ivor Williams and I) had to illuminate, with one mercury line, a pinhole of 3 microns diameter. This left us with enough light to make holograms of about 1 cm diameter of objects, which were microphotographs of about 1 mm diameter, with exposures of a few minutes, on the most sensitive emulsions then available. The small coherence length forced us to arrange everything in one axis. This is now called "in line"

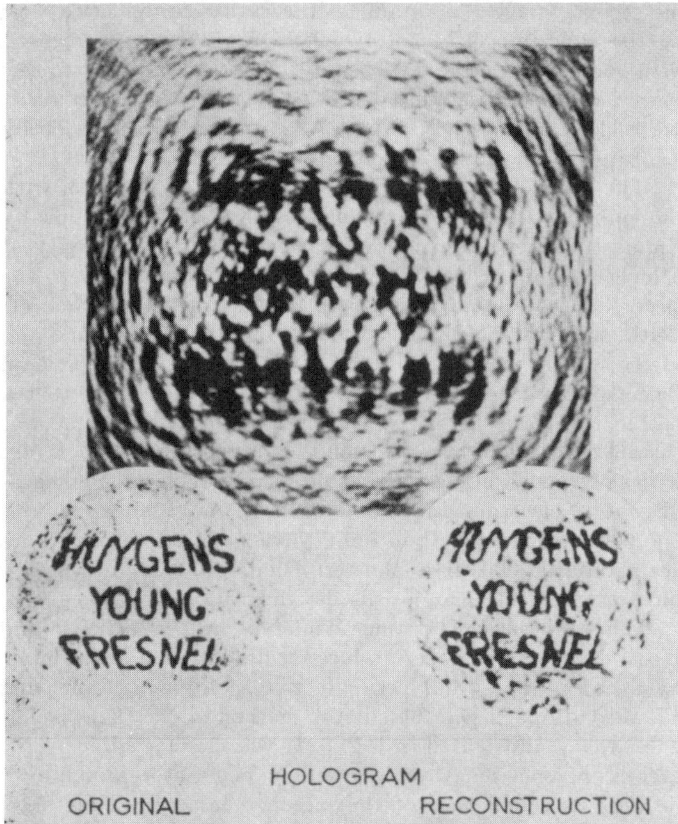

Fig. 4.   First holographic reconstruction, 1948.

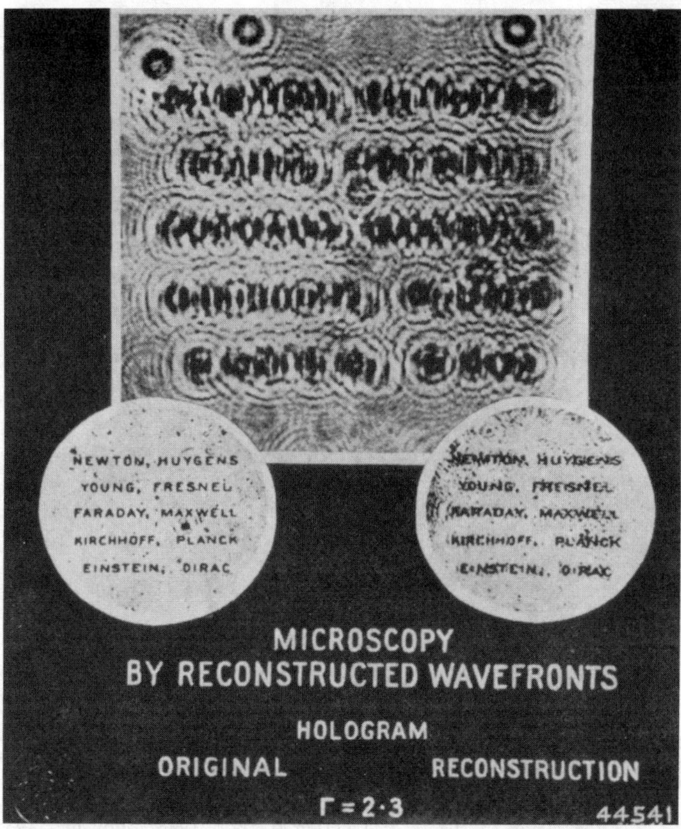

Fig. 5.   Another example of early holography, 1948 (Gabor, *Proc. Roy. Soc.*, vol. A197, p. 454, 1949 [1]).

holography, and it was the only one possible at that time. Fig. 5 shows a somewhat improved experiment, the best of our series. It was far from perfect. Apart from the *schlieren*, which cause random disturbances, there was a systematic defect in the pictures, as may be seen by the distortion of the letters. The explanation is given in Fig. 6. The disturbance arises from the fact that there is not one image but *two*. Each point of the object emits a spherical secondary wave, which interferes with the background and produces a system of circular Fresnel zones. Such a system is known after the optician who first produced it, a Soret lens. This is, at the same time, a positive and a negative lens. One of its foci is in the original position of the object point, the other in a position conjugate to it, with respect to the illuminating wavefront. If one uses "in-line holography" both images are in line, and can be separated only by focusing. But the separation is never quite perfect, because in regular coherent illumination every point leaves a "wake" behind it, which reaches to long distances.

I will tell later with what ease modern laser holography has got rid of this disturbance, by making use of the superior coherence of laser light which was not at my disposal in 1948. However, I was confident that I could eliminate the second image in the application which alone interested me at that time: seeing atoms with the electron microscope. This method, illustrated in Fig. 7, utilized the very defect of electron lenses, the spherical aberration, in order to defeat the second image. If an electron hologram is taken with a lens with spherical aberration, one can afterwards correct *one* of the two images by suitable optics, and the other has then twice the aberration, which washes it out almost completely. Fig. 7 shows that a perfectly sharp reconstruction, in which as good as nothing remains of the disturbance caused by the second image, can be obtained with a lens so bad that its definition

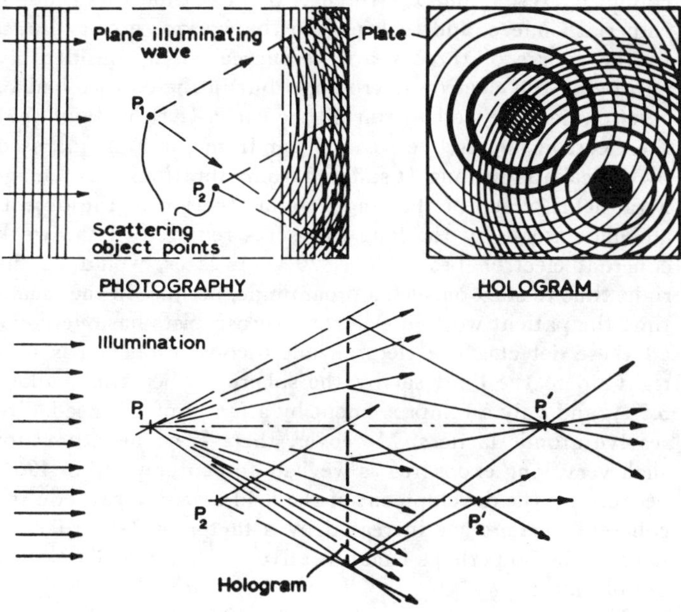

Fig. 6.   The second image. Explanation in terms of Soret lenses as holograms of single object points.

is at least 10 times worse than the resolution which one wants to obtain. Such a very bad lens was obtained using a microscope objective the wrong way round, and using it again in the reconstruction.

So it was with some confidence that two years later, in 1950, we started a programme of holographic electron microscopy in the Research Laboratory of the Associated Electrical Industries, in Aldermaston, under the direction of Dr.

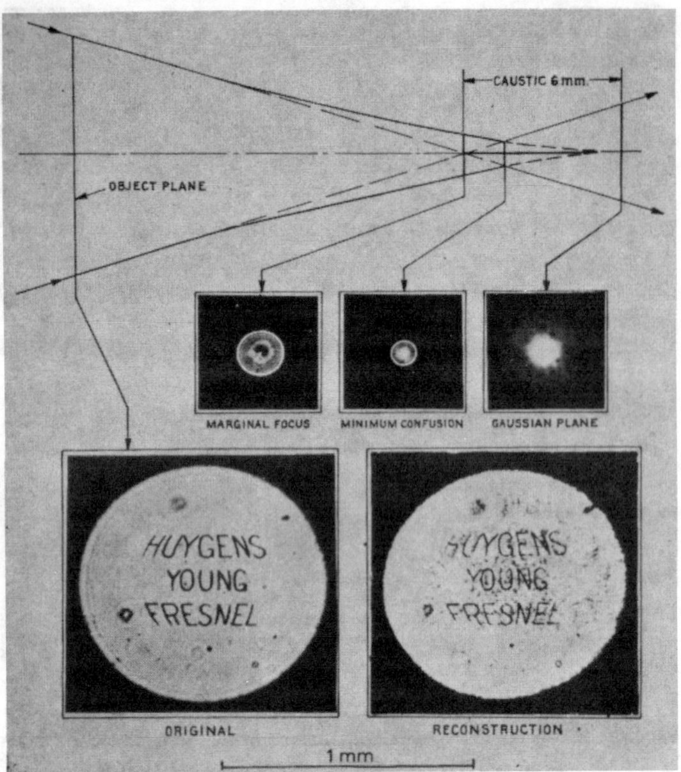

Fig. 7. Elimination of the second image by compensation of the spherical aberration in the reconstruction (Gabor, 1948; published 1951 [1]).

T. E. Allibone, with my friends and collaborators M. W. Haine, J. Dyson, and T. Mulvey,[1] By that time I had joined Imperial College, and took part in the work as a consultant. In the course of three years we succeeded in considerably improving the electron microscope, but in the end we had to give up, because we had started too early. It turned out that the electron microscope was still far from the limit imposed by optical aberrations. It suffered from vibrations, stray magnetic fields, creep of the stage, contamination of the object, all made worse by the long exposures required in the weak coherent electron beam. *Now*, 20 years later, would be the right time to start on such a programme, because in the meantime the patient work of electron microscopists has overcome all these defects. The electron microscope resolution is now right up to the limit set by the spherical aberration, about 3.5 Å, and only an improvement by a factor of 2 is needed to resolve atomic lattices. Moreover, there is no need now for such very long exposures as we had to contemplate in 1951, because by the development of the field emission cathode the coherent current has increased by a factor of 3–4 orders of magnitude. So perhaps I may yet live to see the realisation of my old ideas.

My first papers on wavefront reconstruction evoked some immediate responses. G. L. Rogers [2] in Britain made important contributions to the technique, by producing among other things the first phase holograms, and also by elucidating the theory. In California, Alberto Baez [3], Hussein El-Sum, and P. Kirkpatrick [4] made interesting forays into X-ray holography. For my part, with my collaborator W. P. Goss, I constructed a holographic interference microscope, in which

the second image was annulled in a rather complicated way by the superimposition of two holograms, "in quadrature" with one another. The response of the optical industry to this was so disappointing that we did not publish a paper on it until 11 years later, in 1966 [5]. Around 1955 holography went into a long hybernation.

The revival came suddenly and explosively in 1963, with the publication of the first successful laser[2] holograms by Emmett N. Leith and Juris Upatnieks of the University of Michigan, Ann Arbor. Their success was due not only to the laser, but to the long theoretical preparation of Emmett Leith, which started in 1955. This was unknown to me and to the world, because Leith, with his collaborators Cutrona, Palermo, Porcello, and Vivian applied his ideas first to the problem of the "side-looking radar" which at that time was classified [6]. This was in fact two-dimensional holography with electromagnetic waves, a counterpart of electron holography. The electromagnetic waves used in radar are about 100 000 times longer than light waves, while electron waves are about 100 000 times shorter. Their results were brilliant, but to my regret I cannot discuss them for lack of time.

When the laser became available, in 1962, Leith and Upatnieks could at once produce results far superior to mine, by a new, simple, and very effective method of eliminating the second image [7]. This is the method of the "skew reference wave," illustrated in Fig. 8. It was made possible by the great coherence length of the helium–neon laser, which even in 1962 exceeded that of the mercury lamp by a factor of about 3000. This made it possible to separate the reference beam from the illuminating beam; instead of going through the object, it could now go around it. The result was that the two reconstructed images were now separated not only in depth, but also angularly, by twice the incidence angle of the reference beam. Moreover, the intensity of the coherent laser light exceeded that of mercury many millionfold. This made it possible to use very fine-grain low-speed photographic emulsions and to produce large holograms, with reasonable exposure times.

Fig. 9 shows two of the earliest reconstructions made by Leith and Upatnieks, in 1963, which were already greatly superior to anything that I could produce in 1948. The special interest of these two images is, that they are reconstructions from *one* hologram, taken with different positions of the reference beam. This was the first proof of the superior storage capacity of holograms. Leith and Upatnieks could soon store 12 different pictures in one emulsion. Nowadays one can store 100 or even 300 pages of printed matter in an area which by ordinary photography would be sufficient for one.

From then on progress became very rapid. The most spectacular result of the first year was the holography of three-dimensional objects, which could be seen with the two eyes. Holography was of course three dimensional from the start, but in my early small holograms one could see this only by focusing through the field with a microscope or short-

[1] Supported by a grant of the DSIR (Direction of Scientific and Industrial Research), the first research grant ever given by that body to an industrial laboratory.

[2] I have been asked more than once why I did not invent the laser. In fact, I have thought of it. In 1950, thinking of the desirability of a strong source of coherent light, I remembered that in 1921, as a young student, in Berlin, I had heard from Einstein's own lips his wonderful derivation of Planck's law which postulated the existence of stimulated emission. I then had the idea of the pulsed laser: Take a suitable crystal, make a resonator of it by a highly reflecting coating, fill up the upper level by illuminating it through a small hole, and discharge it explosively by a ray of its own light. I offered the idea as a Ph.D. problem to my best student, but he declined it, as too risky, and I could not gainsay it, as I could not be sure that we would find a suitable crystal.

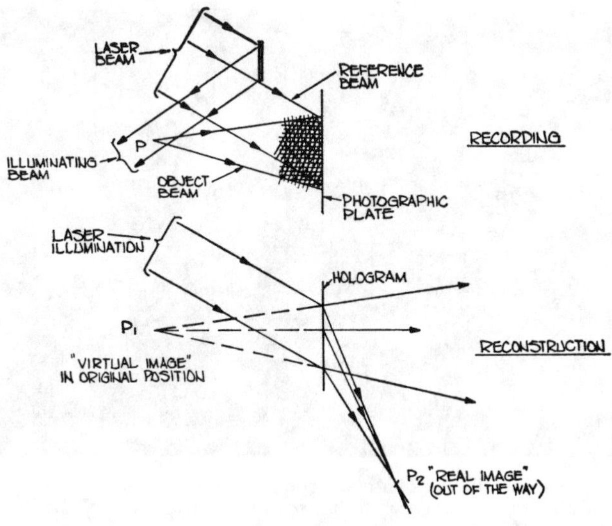

Fig. 8.   Holography with skew references beam.
(E. N. Leith and J. Upatnieks, 1963.)

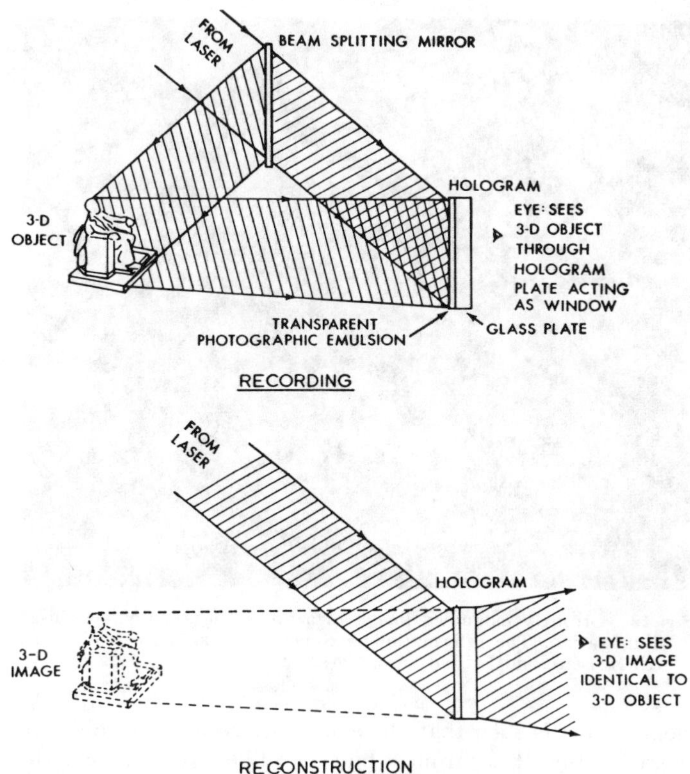

Fig. 10.   Three-dimensional holography of a
diffusing object with later light.

Fig. 9.   First example of multiple image storage in one hologram
(E. N. Leith and J. Upatnieks, *J. Opt. Soc. Amer.*, Nov. 1964).

Fig. 11.   Three-dimensional reconstruction of a small statue of Abraham Lincoln. (Courtesy of Prof. G. W. Stroke, State University of New York, Stony Brook.)

focus eyepiece. But it was not enough to make the hologram large, it was also necessary that every point of the photographic plate should see every point of the object. In the early holograms, taken with regular illumination, the information was contained in a small area, in the diffraction pattern.

In the case of rough diffusing objects no special precautions are necessary. The small dimples and projections of the surface diffuse the light over a large cone. Fig. 10 shows an example of the setup in the case of a rough object, such as a statuette of Abraham Lincoln. The reconstruction is shown in Fig. 11. With a bleached hologram ("phase hologram") one has the impression of looking through a clear window at the statuette itself. (Courtesy of Professor George W. Stroke [8].)

If the object is non-diffusing, for instance if it is a transparency, the information is spread over the whole hologram area by illuminating the object through a diffuser, such as a frosted glass plate. The appearance of such a "diffused" hologram is extraordinary; it looks like noise (Fig. 12). One can call it "ideal Shannon coding," because Claude E. Shannon has shown in his Communication Theory that the most effi-

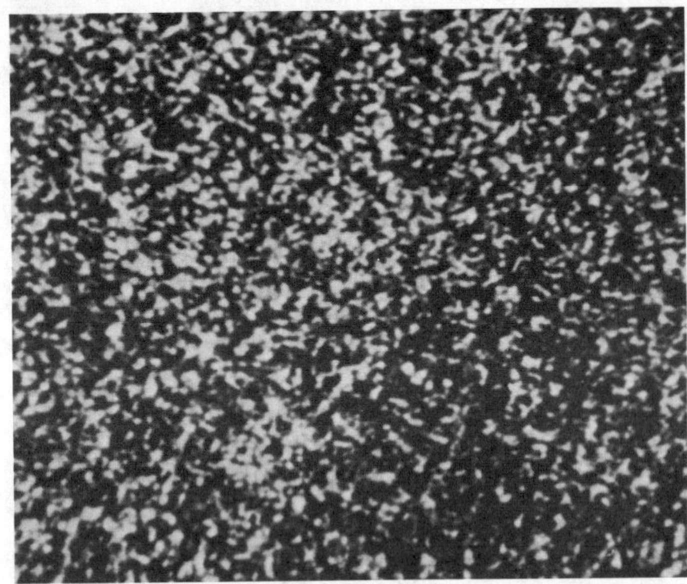

Fig. 12. Strongly magnified image of a hologram taken with diffused illumination. The information is conveyed in a "noise-like" code. (E. N. Leith and J. Upatnieks, 1964.)

Fig. 13. Reconstruction of a plane transparency, showing a restaurant, from a hologram taken with diffused illumination. (E. N. Leith and J. Upatnieks, 1964.)

Fig. 14. Equipment of a modern holographic laboratory. (Courtesy of Prof. G. W. Stroke, State University of New York, Stony Brook.)

cient coding is such that all regularities seem to have disappeared in the signal; it must be "noise-like." But where is the information in this chaos? It can be shown that it is not as irregular as it appears. It is not as if grains of sand had been scattered over the plate at random. It is rather a complicated figure, the diffraction pattern of the object, which is repeated at random intervals, but always in the same size and the same orientation.

A very interesting and important property of such diffused holograms is that any small part of it, large enough to contain the diffraction pattern, contains information on the whole object, and this can be reconstructed from the fragment, only with more noise. A diffuse hologram is therefore a *distributed memory*, and this has evoked much speculation whether human memory is not perhaps, as it were, holographic, because it is well known that a good part of the brain can be destroyed without wiping out every trace of a memory. There is no time here to discuss this very exciting question. I want only to say that in my opinion the similarity with the human memory is functional only, but certainly not structural.

It is seen that in the development of holography the hologram has become always more unlike the object, but the reconstruction always more perfect. Fig. 13 shows an excellent reconstruction by Leith and Upatnieks of a photograph, from a diffuse hologram like the one in the previous figure.

The pioneer work carried out in the University of Michigan, Ann Arbor, led also to the stabilization of holographic techniques. Today hundreds if not thousands of laboratories possess the equipment of which an example is shown in Fig. 14; the very stable granite slab or steel table, and the various optical devices for dealing with coherent light, which are now manufactured by the optical industry. The great stability is absolutely essential in all work carried out with steady-state lasers, because a movement of the order of a quarter wavelength during the exposure can completely spoil a hologram.

However, from 1965 onwards there has developed an important branch of holography where high stability is not required, because the holograms are taken in a small fraction of a microsecond, with a pulsed laser.

Imagine that you had given a physicist the problem: "Determine the size of the droplets which issue from a jet nozzle, with a velocity of 2 Mach. The sizes are probably from a few microns upwards." Certainly he would have thrown up his hands in despair! But all it takes now, is to record a simple in-line hologram of the jet, with the plate at a safe distance, with a ruby laser pulse of 20–30 nanoseconds. One then looks at the "real" image (or one reverses the illuminating beam and makes a real image of the virtual one), one dives with a microscope into the three-dimensional image of the jet and focuses the particles, one after the other. Because of the large distance, the disturbance by the second image is entirely negligible. Fig. 15 shows a fine example.

As the research workers of the TRW laboratories have shown, it is possible to record in one hologram the infusoriae in several feet of dirty water, or insects in a meter of air space. Fig. 16 shows two reconstructions of insects from one hologram, focusing on one after the other. The authors, C. Knox and R. E. Brooks have also made a cinematographic record of a holographic film, in which the flight of one mosquito is followed through a considerable depth, by refocusing in every frame [9].

Another achievement of the TRW group, Ralph Wuerker

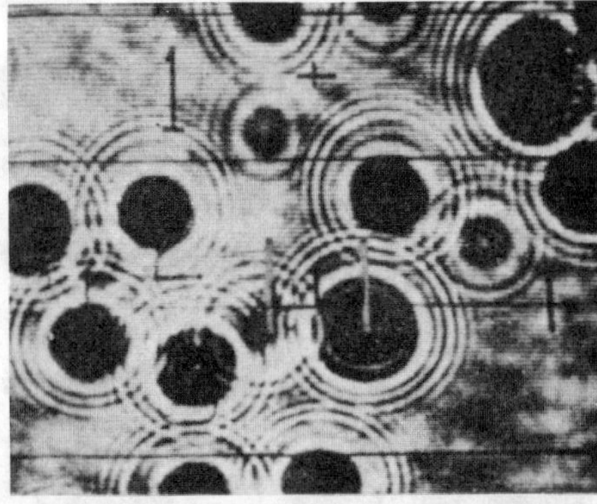

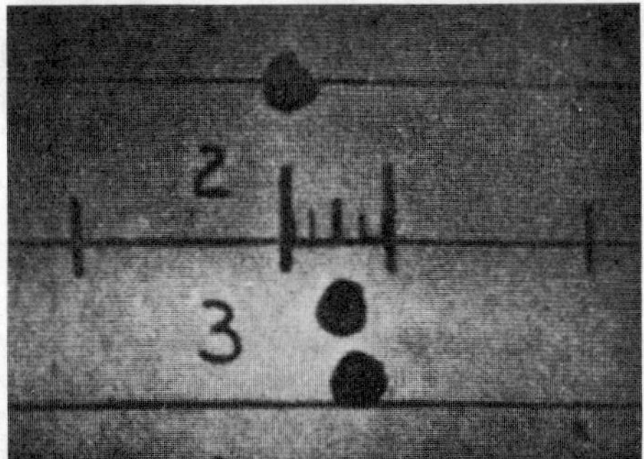

Fig. 15. Holography of jets. (Courtesy of Laser Holography, Inc., Santa Barbara, Calif.)

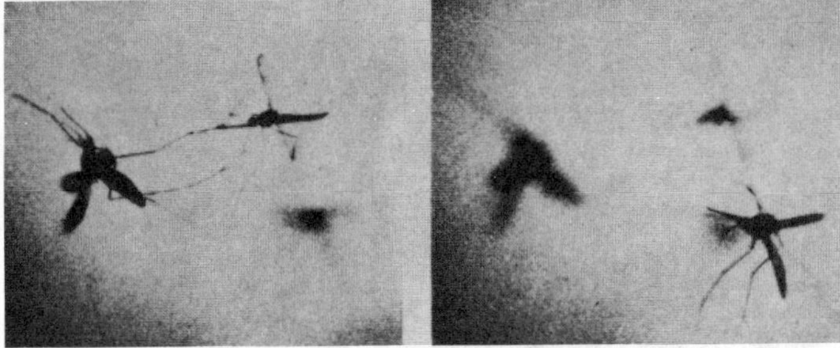

Fig. 16. Observation of mosquitos in flight. Both pictures are extracted from one hologram. (Courtesy of C. Knox and R. E. Brooks, TRW, Redondo Beach, Calif.)

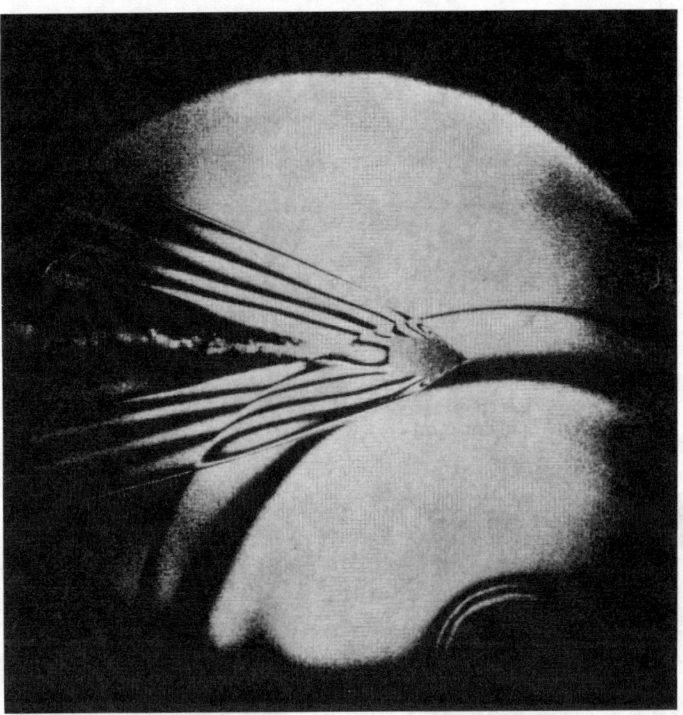

Fig. 17. Dynamic holographic interferometry. This reconstruction of a holographic interferogram shows the interaction of two air shock fronts and their associated flows. (Courtesy of Dr. R. F. Wuerker and his associates, TRW Physical Electronics Lab., Redondo Beach, Calif.)

Fig. 18. Holographic portrait. (L. Siebert, Conductron Corp., now merged into McDonnell–Douglas Electronics Co., St. Charles, Mo.)

and his colleagues, leads us into another branch of holography, to holographic interferometry. Fig. 17 shows a reconstruction of a bullet, with its train of shockwaves, as it meets another shockwave. But it is not just an image, it is an interferometric image. The fringes show the *loci* at which the retardation of light is by integer wavelengths, relative to the quiet air, before the event. This comparison standard is obtained by a previous exposure. This is therefore a double-exposure hologram, such as will be discussed in more detail later [10].

Fig. 18 shows another high achievement of pulse holography: a holographic three-dimensional portrait, obtained by L. Siebert in the Conductron Corporation (now merged into McDonnel-Douglas Electronics Company, St. Charles, Mo.). It is the result of outstanding work in the development of lasers. The ruby laser, as first realised by T. H. Maiman, was capable of short pulses, but its coherence length was of the order of a few centimeters only. This is no obstacle in the case of in-line holography, where the reference wave proceeds almost in step with the diffracted wavelets, but in order to take a scene of, say, one meter depth with reflecting objects one

must have a coherence length of at least one meter. Nowadays single-mode pulses of 30 nanosecond duration with 10 joule in the beam and coherence lengths of 5–8 meters are available, and have been used recently for taking my holographic portrait shown in the exhibition attached to the lecture.

In 1965, R. L. Powell and K. A. Stetson in the University of Michigan, Ann Arbor, made an interesting discovery. Holographic images taken of moving objects are washed out. But if double exposure is used, first with the object at rest, then in vibration, fringes will appear, indicating the lines where the displacement amounted to multiples of a half wavelength. Fig. 19 shows vibrational modes of a loudspeaker membrane,

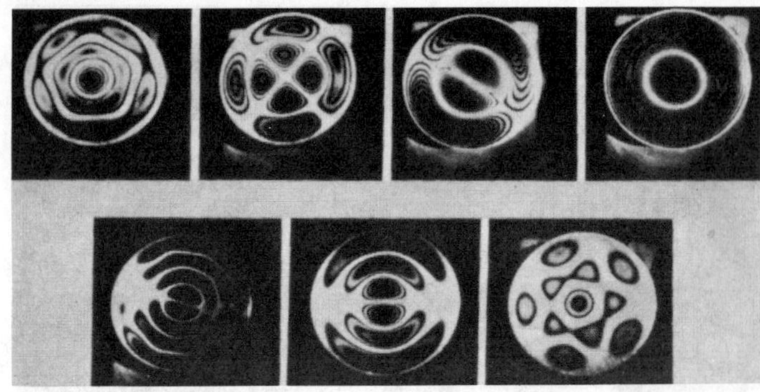

Fig. 19. Vibrational modes of a loudspeaker membrane, obtained by holographic interferometry. (R. L. Powell and K. A. Stetson, University of Michigan, Ann Arbor, 1965.)

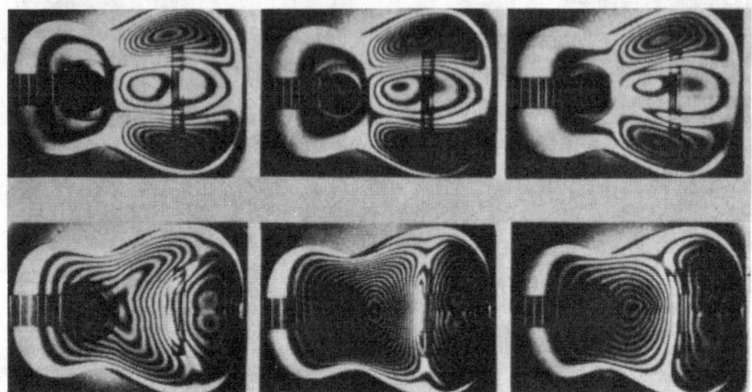

Fig. 20. Vibrational modes of a guitar, recorded by holographic interferometry. (Courtesy of Dr. K. A. Stetson and Prof. E. Ingelstam.)

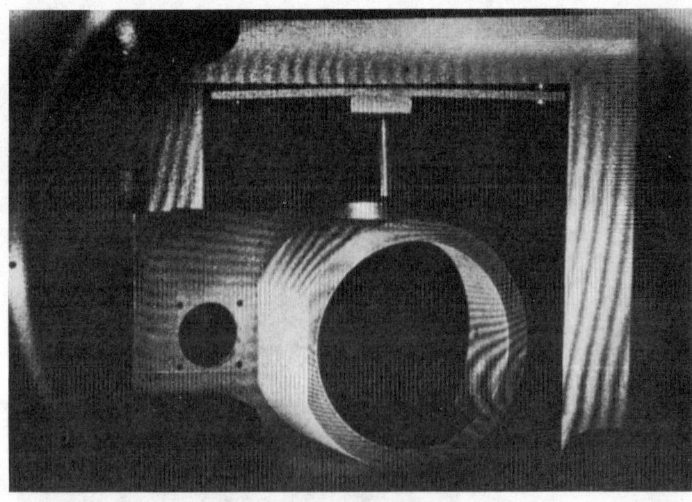

Fig. 21. An early example of holographic interferometry by double exposure. (K. Haines and B. P. Hildebrand, University of Michigan, Ann Arbor, 1965.)

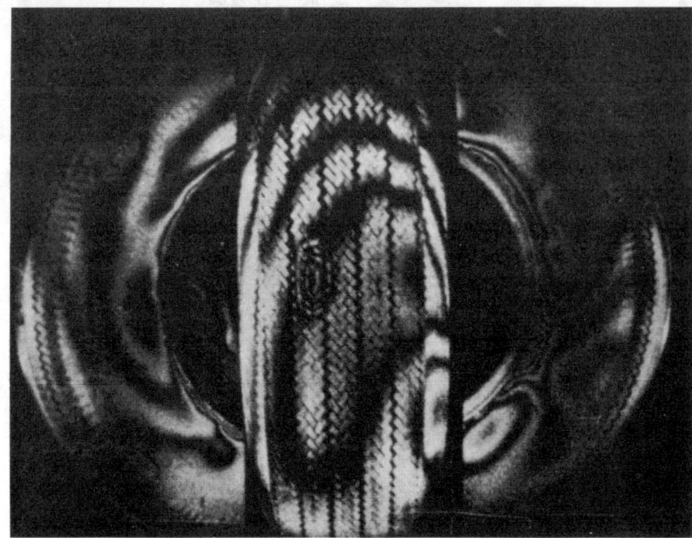

Fig. 22. Non-destructive testing by holography. Double-exposure hologram, revealing two flaws in a tyre. (Courtesy of Dr. R. Grant and GCO, Ann Arbor, Mich.)

recorded in 1965 by Powell and Stetson [11], Fig. 20 the same for a guitar, taken by K. A. Stetson in the laboratory of Professor Erik Ingelstam [12].

Curiously, both the interferograms of the TRW group and the vibrational records of Powell and Stetson preceded what is really a simpler application of the interferometrical principle, and which historically ought to have come first—if the course of science would always follow the shortest line. This is the observation of small deformations of solid bodies by double exposure holograms. A simple explanation is as follows: We take a hologram of a body in state A. This means that we freeze in the wave A by means of a reference beam. Now let us deform the body so that it assumes the state B, and take a second hologram in the same emulsion with the same reference beam. We develop the hologram, and illuminate it with the reference beam. Now the two waves A and B, frozen in at different times, and which have never seen one another, will be revived simultaneously, and they interfere with one another. The result is that Newton fringes will appear on the object, each fringe corresponding to a deformation of a half wavelength. Fig. 21 shows a fine example of such a holographic interferogram, made in 1965 by K. Haines and B. P. Hildebrand. The principle was discovered simultaneously and independently also by J. M. Burch in England.

Non-destructive testing by holographic interferometry is now by far the most important industrial application of holography. It gave rise to the first industrial firm based on holography, GCO (formerly G. C. Optronics), in Ann Arbor, Mich., and the following examples are reproduced by courtesy of GCO. Fig. 22 shows the testing of a motor car tyre. The

front of the tyre is holographed directly, the sides are seen in two mirrors, right and left. First a little time is needed for the tyre to settle down and a first hologram is taken. Then a little hot air is blown against it, and a second exposure is made, on the same plate. If the tyre is perfect, only a few, widely spaced fringes will appear, indicating almost uniform expansion. But where the cementing of the rubber sheets was imperfect, a little blister appears, as seen near the centre and near the top left corner, only a few thousandths of a millimeter high, but indicating a defect which could become serious. Alternately, the first hologram is developed, replaced exactly in the original position, and the expansion of the tyre is observed "live."

Other examples of non-destructive testing are shown in Fig. 23; all defects which are impossible or almost impossible to detect by other means, but which reveal themselves unmistakeably to the eye. A particularly impressive piece of equipment manufactured by GCO is shown in Fig. 24. It is a holographic analyser for honeycomb sandwich structures (such as shown in the middle of Fig. 23) which are used in

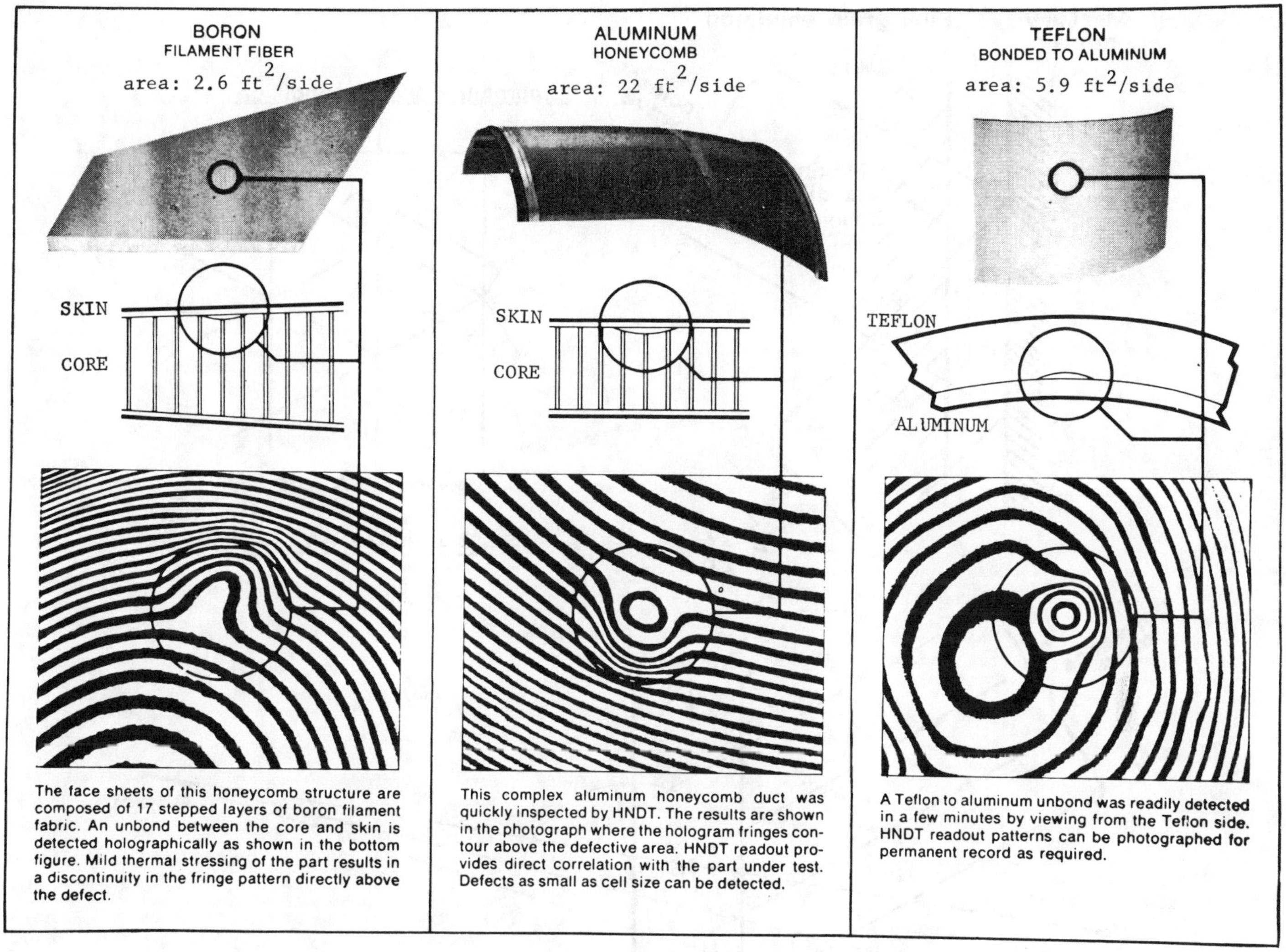

<table>
<tr>
<td>

BORON
FILAMENT FIBER
area: 2.6 ft^2/side

The face sheets of this honeycomb structure are composed of 17 stepped layers of boron filament fabric. An unbond between the core and skin is detected holographically as shown in the bottom figure. Mild thermal stressing of the part results in a discontinuity in the fringe pattern directly above the defect.

</td>
<td>

ALUMINUM
HONEYCOMB
area: 22 ft^2/side

This complex aluminum honeycomb duct was quickly inspected by HNDT. The results are shown in the photograph where the hologram fringes contour above the defective area. HNDT readout provides direct correlation with the part under test. Defects as small as cell size can be detected.

</td>
<td>

TEFLON
BONDED TO ALUMINUM
area: 5.9 ft^2/side

A Teflon to aluminum unbond was readily detected in a few minutes by viewing from the Teflon side. HNDT readout patterns can be photographed for permanent record as required.

</td>
</tr>
</table>

Fig. 23. Examples of holographic non-destructive testing. (Courtesy of GCO, Ann Arbor, Mich.)

Fig. 24. Holographic analyzer Mark II for sandwich structures. (GCO, Ann Arbor, Mich.)

Fig. 25. Holographically produced contour map of a medal, made by a method initiated by B. P. Hildebrand and K. A. Haines (*J. Opt. Soc. Amer.*, vol. 57, p. 155, 1967). Improved by J. Varner, University of Michigan, Ann Arbor, 1969.

aeroplane wings. The smallest welding defect between the aluminum sheets and the honeycomb is safely detected at one glance.

While holographic interferometry is perfectly suited for

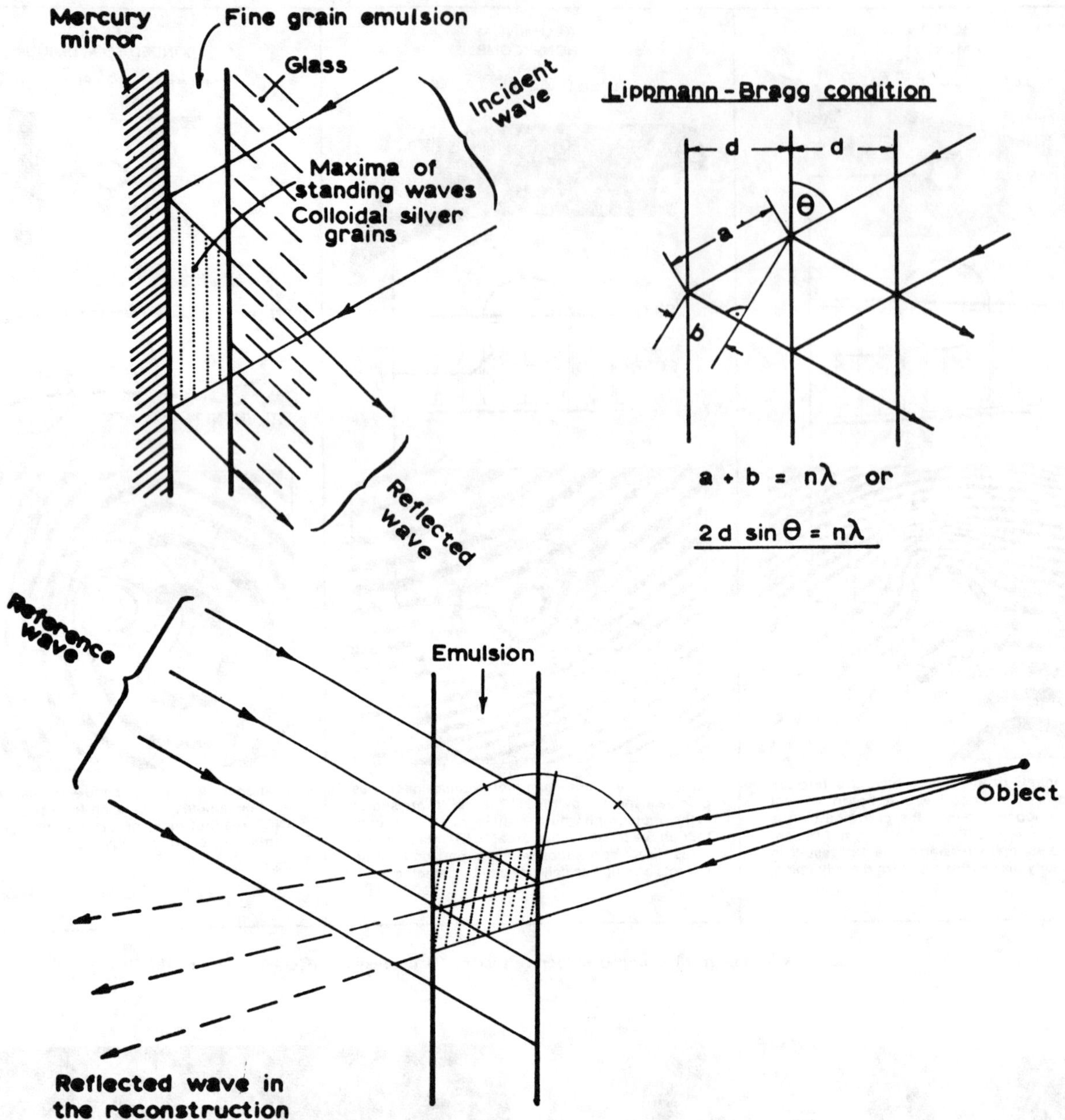

Fig. 26.   Lippmann–Denisyuk reflection holography in natural colours.

the detection of very small deformations, with its fringe unit of 1/4000 mm, it is a little too fine for the checking of the accuracy of workpieces. Here another holographic technique called "contouring" is appropriate. It was first introduced by Haines and Hildebrand [13], in 1965, and has been recently much improved by J. Varner, also in Ann Arbor, Mich. Two holograms are taken of the same object, but with two wavelengths which differ by, e.g., one percent. This produces *beats* between the two-fringe system, with fringe spacings corresponding to about 1/40 mm, which is just what the workshop requires (Fig. 25).

From industrial applications I am now turning to another important development in holography. In 1962, just before the "holography explosion" the Soviet physicist Yu. N. Denisyuk [13] published an important paper in which he combined holography with the ingenious method of photography in natural colours, for which Gabriel Lippmann received the Nobel Prize in 1908. Fig. 26 illustrates Lippmann's method and Denisyuk's idea. Lippmann produced a very fine-grain

emulsion, with colloidal silver bromide, and backed the emulsion with mercury, serving as a mirror. Light falling on the emulsion was reflected at the mirror, and produced a set of standing waves. Colloidal silver grains were precipitated in the maxima of the electric vector, in layers spaced by very nearly half a wavelength. After development, the complex of layers, illuminated with white light, reflected only a narrow waveband around the original colour, because only for this colour did the wavelets scattered at the Lippmann layers add up in phase.

Denisyuk's suggestion is shown in the second diagram. The object wave and the reference wave fall in from opposite sides of the emulsion. Again standing waves are produced, and Lippmann layers, but these are no longer parallel to the emulsion surface, they bisect the angle between the two wavefronts. If now, and this is Denisyuk's principle, the developed emulsion is illuminated by the reference wave, the object will appear, in the original position and (unless the emulsion has shrunk) in the original colour.

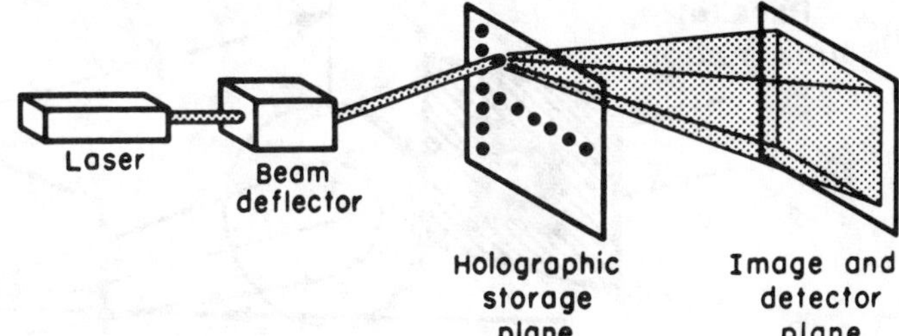

Fig. 28. Holographic flying spot store. (L. K. Anderson and R. J. Collier, Bell Telephone Labs., 1968.)

Fig. 27. First two-colour reflecting hologram, reconstructed in white light (L. H. Lin, K. S. Pennington, G. W. Stroke, and A. E. Labeyrie [14].)

Note: This photograph appeared in color in the original publication.

Though Denisyuk showed considerable experimental skill, lacking a laser in 1962 he could produce only an "existence proof." A colour reflecting hologram which could be illuminated with white light was first produced in 1965 by G. W. Stroke and A. Labeyrie [14a] and a two-colour version of it subsequently by L. H. Lin, K. S. Pennington, G. W. Stroke, and A. Labeyrie [14b] is shown in Fig. 27.

Since that time single-colour reflecting holograms have been developed to high perfection by new photographic processes, by K. S. Pennington [15] and others, with reflectances approaching 100 percent, but two, and even more, three-colour holograms are still far from being satisfactory. It is one of my chief preoccupations at the present to improve this situation, but it would take too long, and it would be also rather early to enlarge on this.

An application of holography which is certain to gain high importance in the next years is information storage. I have mentioned before that holography allows storing 100–300 times more printed pages in a given emulsion than ordinary microphotography. Even without utilizing the depth dimension, the factor is better than 50. The reason is that a diffused hologram represents almost ideal coding, with full utilization of the area and of the gradation of the emulsion, while printed matter uses only about 5–10% of the area, and the gradation not at all. A further factor arises from the utilization of the third dimension, the depth of the emulsion. This possibility was first pointed out in an ingenious paper by P. J. van Heerden [16], in 1963. Theoretically it appears possible to store one bit of information in about one wavelength cube. This is far from being practical, but the figure of 300, previously mentioned, is entirely realistic.

However, even without this enormous factor, holographic storage offers important advantages. A binary store, in the form of a checkerboard pattern on microfilm can be spoiled by a single grain of dust, by a hair or by a scratch, while a diffused hologram is almost insensitive to such defects. The holographic store, illustrated in Fig. 28, is according to its author L. K. Anderson [17] (1968) only a modest beginning, yet it is capable of accessing for instance any one of 64×64 printed pages in about a microsecond. Each hologram, with a diameter of 1.2 mm can contain about 10^4 bits. Reading out this information sequentially in a microsecond would of course require an impossible waveband, but powerful parallel reading means can be provided. One can confidently expect enormous extensions of these "modest beginnings" once the project of data banks will be tackled seriously.

Another application of holography which is probably only in an early stage is pattern and character recognition. I can only briefly refer to the basic work which A. Vander Lugt [18] has done in the field of pattern recognition. I will be sufficient to explain the basic principle of character recognition with the aid of Fig. 29.

Let us generalize a little the basic principle of holography. In all previous examples a complicated object beam was brought to interference with a simple plane or spherical reference beam, and the object beam was reconstructed by illuminating the hologram with the reference beam. But a little mathematics shows that this can be extended to any reference beam *which correlates sharply with itself*. The autocorrelation function is an invariant of a beam; it can be computed in any cross section. One can see at once that a spherical wave correlates sharply with itself, because it issues from a "point." But there are other beams which correlate sharply with themselves, for instance those which issue from a fingerprint, or from a Chinese ideogram, in an extreme case also those which issue from a piece of frosted glass. Hence it is quite possible for instance to translate, by means of a hologram, a Chinese ideogram into its corresponding English sentence and *vice versa*. Dr. Butters and M. Wall of Loughborough University have recently created holograms which from a portrait produce the signature of the owner, and *vice versa*.[3] In other words,

[3] Quoted from Basil de Ferranti, "The computer, a challenge to the human brain," *Proc. Roy. Inst. of Great Britain*, p. 165, Aug. 1971.

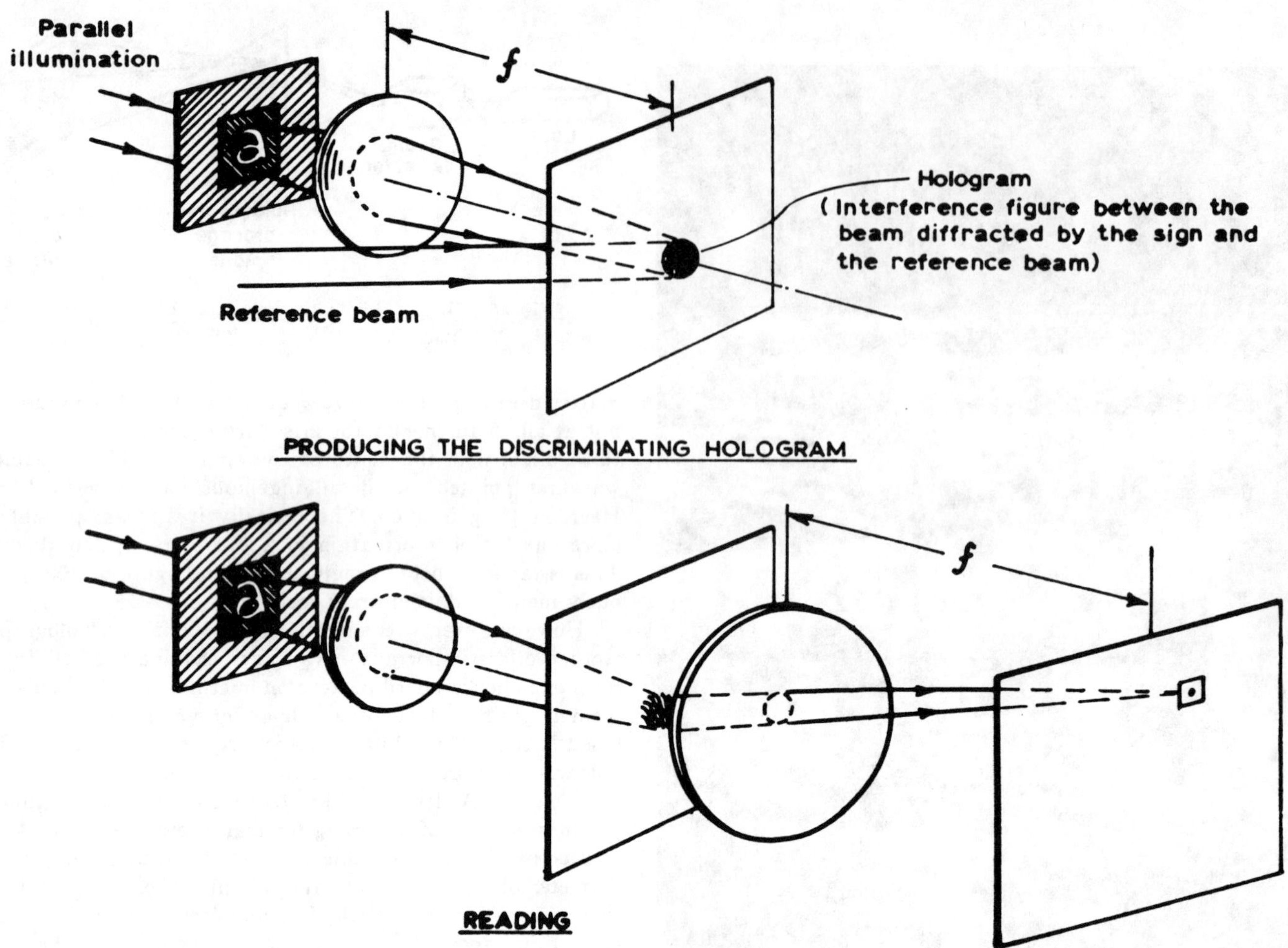

Fig. 29.   The principle of character recognition by holography.

a hologram can be a fairly universal translator. It can for instance translate a sign which we can read to another which a machine can read.

Fig. 29 shows a fairly modest realisation of this principle. A hologram is made of a letter "a" by means of a plane reference beam. When this hologram is illuminated with the letter "a" the reference beam is reconstructed, and can activate for instance a small photocell in a certain position. This, I believe, gives an idea of the basic principle. There is of course much more needed to make a practical system of it, because there are so many ways of printing letters, but it would take me too long to explain how to deal with this and other difficulties.

With character recognition devices we have already taken half a step into the future, because these are likely to become important only in the next generation of computers or robots, to whom we must transfer a little more of human intelligence. I now want to mention briefly some other problems which are half or more than half in the future.

One, which is already very actual, is the overcoming of laser speckle. Everybody who sees laser light for the first time is surprised by the rough appearance of objects which we consider as smooth. A white sheet of paper appears as if it were crawling with ants. The crawling is put into it by the restless eye, but the roughness is real. It is called "laser speckle" and Fig. 30 shows a characteristic example of it. This is the appearance of a white sheet of paper in laser light, when viewed with a low-power optical system. It is not really noise; it is information which we do not want, information on the microscopic

unevenness of the paper in which we are not interested. What can we do against it?

In the case of rough objects the answer is, regrettably, that all we can do is to average over larger areas, thus smoothing the deviations. This means that we must throw a great part of the information away, the wanted with the unwanted. This is regrettable but we can do nothing else, and in many cases we have enough information to throw away, as can be seen by the fully satisfactory appearance of some of the reconstructions from diffuse holograms which I have shown. However, there are important areas in which we can do much more, and where an improvement is badly needed. This is the area of microholograms, for storing and for display. They are made as diffused holograms, in order to ensure freedom from dust and scratches, but by making them diffused, we introduce speckle, and to avoid this such holograms are made nowadays much larger than would be ideally necessary. I have shown recently [19], that the advantages of diffuse holograms can be almost completely retained, while the speckle can be completely eliminated by using, instead of a frosted glass, a special illuminating system. This, I hope, will produce a further improvement in the information density of holographic stores.

Now let us take a more radical step into the future. I want to mention briefly two of my favourite holographic brain-children. The first of these is Panoramic Holography, or one could also call it Holographic Art.

All the three-dimensional holograms made so far extend to a depth of a few meters only. Would it not be possible to

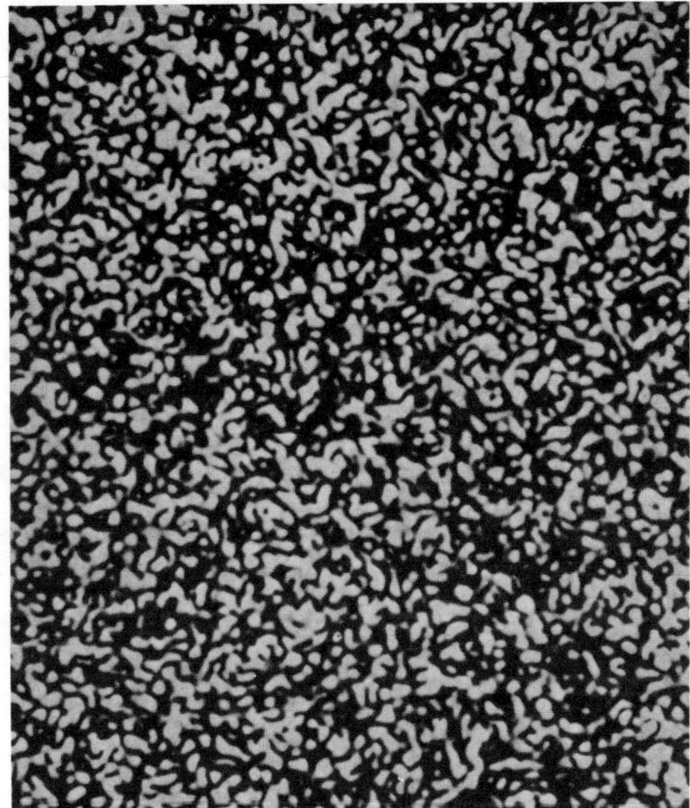

Fig. 30.   Laser speckle. The appearance of, for example, a white sheet of paper, uniformly illuminated by laser light.

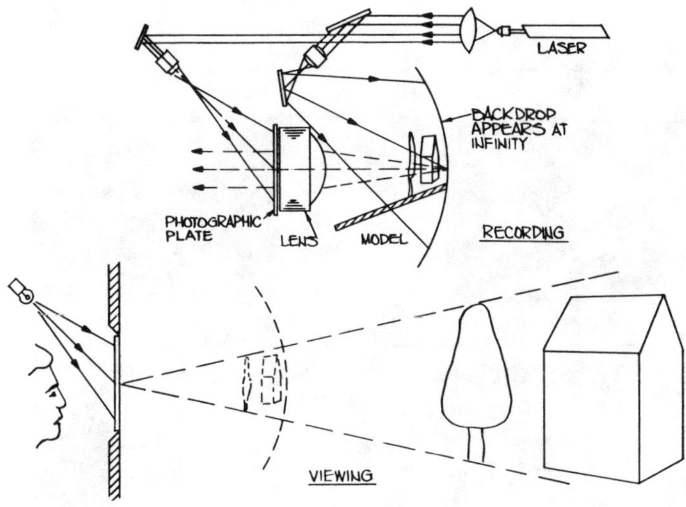

Fig. 31.   Panoramic holography.

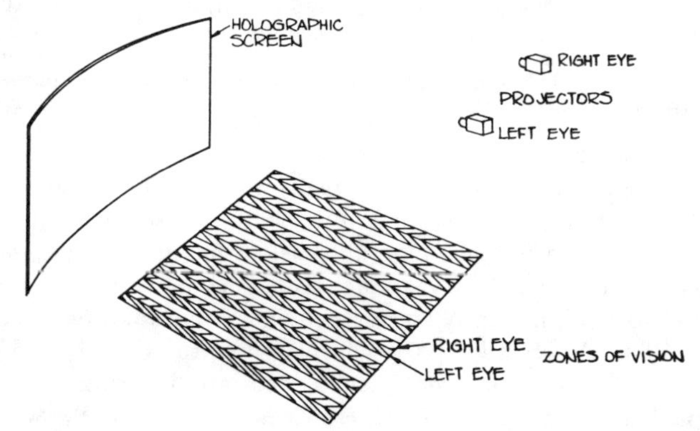

Fig. 32.   Three-dimensional cinematography with holographic screen.

extend them to infinity? Could one not put a hologram on the wall, which is like a window through which one looks at a landscape, real or imaginary? I think it can be done, only it will not be a photograph but a work of art. Fig. 31 illustrates the process. The artist makes a model, distorted in such a way that it appears perspectivic, and extending to any distance when viewed through a large lens, as large as the hologram. The artist can use a smaller lens, just large enough to cover both his eyes when making the model. A reflecting hologram is made of it, and illuminated with a strong small light source. The viewer will see what the plate has seen through the lens; that is to say a scene extending to any distance, in natural colours. This scheme is under development, but considerable work will be needed to make it satisfactory, because we must first greatly improve the reflectance of three-colour holograms.

An even more ambitious scheme, probably even farther in the future, is three-dimensional cinematography, without viewing aids such as Polaroids. The problem is sketched out in Fig. 32. The audience (in one plane or two) is covered by zones of vision, with the width of the normal eye spacing, one for the right eye, one for the left, with a blank space between two pairs. The two eyes must see two different pictures; a stereoscopic pair. The viewer can move his head somewhat to the right or left. Even when he moves one eye into the blank zone, the picture will appear dimmer but not flat, because one eye gives the impression of "stereoscopy by default."

I have spent some years of work on this problem, just before holography, until I had to realise that it is strictly insolvable with the orthodox means of optics, lenticules, mirrors, prisms. One can make satisfactorily small screens for small theatres, but with large screens and large theatres one falls into a dilemma. If the lenticules or the like are large, they will

be seen from the front seats; if they are small, they will not have enough definition for the back seats.

Some years ago I realised to my surprise, that holography can solve this problem too. Use a projector as the reference source, and for instance the system of left viewing zones as the object. The screen, covered with a Lippmann emulsion, will then make itself automatically into a very complicated optical system such that when a picture is projected from the projector, it will be seen only from the left viewing zones. One then repeats the process with the right projector, and the right viewing zones. In the case of volume, (Lippmann–Denisyuk) holograms display the phenomenon of directional selectivity. If one displaces the illuminator from the original position by a certain angle, there will be no reflection. We put the two projectors at this angle (or a little more) from one another, and the effect is that the right picture will not be seen by the left eye and *vice versa*.

There remains of course one difficulty, and this is that one cannot practice holography on the scale of a theatre, and with a plate as large as a screen. But this too can be solved, by making up the screen from small pieces, not with the threatre but with a *model* of the theatre, seem through a lens, quite similar to the one used in panoramic holography.

I hope I have conveyed the feasibility of the scheme, but I feel sure that I have conveyed also its difficulties. I am not sure whether they will be overcome in this century, or in the next.

Ambitious schemes, for which I have a congenital inclina-

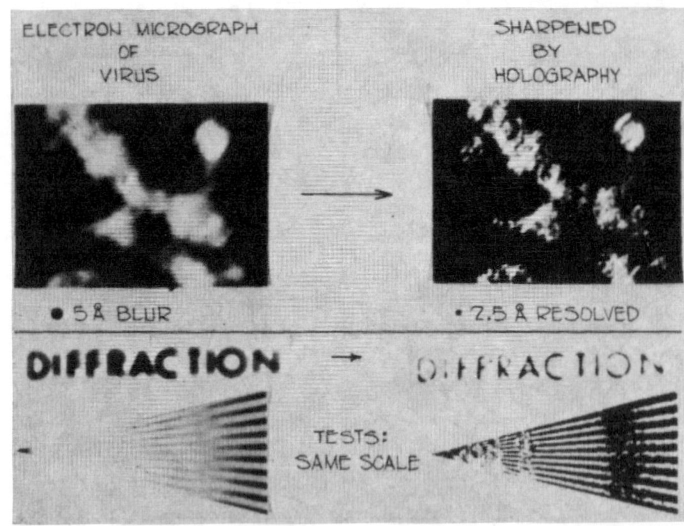

Fig. 33. Scanning transmission electron micrograph (Prof. A. Crewe, University of Chicago), holographically deblurred (by Prof. G. W. Stroke, 1971). The bottom photographs prove that the effect could not be obtained by hard printing, because some spatial frequencies which appear in the original with reversed phase had to be phase-corrected.

tion, take a long time for their realisation. As I said at the beginning, I shall be lucky if I shall be able to see in my lifetime the realisation of holographic electron microscopy, on which I have started 24 years ago. But I have good hope, because I have been greatly encouraged by a remarkable achievement of G. W. Stroke [20], which is illustrated in Fig. 33. Professor Stroke has recently succeeded in deblurring micrographs taken by Professor Albert Crewe, Chicago, Ill., with his scanning transmission electron microscope, by a holographic filtering process, improving the resolution from 5 angstrom to an estimated 2.5 angstrom. This is not exactly holographic electron microscopy, because the original was not taken with coherent electrons, but the techniques used by both sides, by A. Crewe and by G. W. Stroke are so powerful, that I trust them to succeed also in the next, much greater and more important step.

Summing up, I am one of the few lucky physicists who could see an idea of theirs grow into a sizeable chapter of physics. I am deeply aware that this has been achieved by an army of young, talented, and enthusiastic researchers, of whom I could mention only a few by name. I want to express my heartfelt thanks to them, for having helped me by their work to this greatest of scientific honours.

BIBLIOGRAPHY AND REFERENCES

It is impossible to do justice to the hundreds of authors who have significantly contributed to the development of holography. The number of articles exceeds 2000, and there are more than a dozen books in several languages.

An extensive bibliography may be found for instance in, T. Kallard, Ed., *Holography*. New York: Optosonic Press, 1969 and 1970.

Books

E. S. Barrekette, W. E. Kock, T. Ose, J. Tsujiuchi, and G. W. Stroke, Eds., *Applications of Holography*. New York: Plenum, 1971.

H. J. Caulfield and S. Lu, *The Applications of Holography*. New York: Wiley–Interscience, 1970.

R. J. Collier, C. B. Burckhardt, and L. H. Lin, *Optical Holography*. New York: Academic Press, 1971.

J. B. DeVelis and G. O. Reynolds, *Theory and Applications of Holography*. Reading, Mass.: Addison Wesley, 1967.

M. Françon, *Holographie*. Paris, France: Masson et Cie, 1969.

H. Kiemle und D. Röss, *Einführung in die Technik der Holographie*. Frankfurt am Main, Germany: Akademische Verlagsgesellschaft, 1969. English translation: *Introduction to Holographic Techniques*. New York: Plenum, 1972, in print.

W. E. Kock, *Lasers and Holography (An Introduction to Coherent Optics)*. Garden City, N. Y.: Doubleday, 1969 (Russian translation, Moscow, USSR: Mir, 1967).

Yu. I. Ostrovsky, *Holography* (in Russian). Leningrad, USSR: Nauka, 1970.

E. R. Robertson and J. M. Harvey, Eds., *The Engineering Uses of Holography*. Cambridge, England: Cambridge Univ. Press, 1970.

G. W. Stroke, *An Introduction to Coherent Optics and Holography*. New York: Academic Press, 1st ed. 1966; 2nd ed. 1969.

J. C. Vienot, P. Smigielski, and H. Royer, *Holographie Optique (Developpements. Applications)*. Paris, France: Dunod, 1971.

Papers

[1] D. Gabor, "A new microscopic principle," *Nature*, vol. 161, pp. 777–778, 1948.
——, "Microscopy by reconstructed wavefronts," *Proc. Roy. Soc.*, vol. A197, pp. 454–487, 1949.
——, "Microscopy by reconstructed wavefronts: II," *Proc. Roy. Soc.* (London), vol. 64, pt. 6, pp. 449–469, 1951.

[2] G. L. Rogers, "Experiments in diffraction microscopy," *Proc. Roy. Soc.* (Edinburgh), vol. 63A, p. 193, 1952.

[3] A. Baez, "Resolving power in diffraction microscopy," *Nature*, vol. 169, pp. 963–964, 1952.

[4] H. M. A. El-Sum and P. Kirkpatrick, "Microscopy by reconstructed wavefronts," *Phys. Rev.*, vol. 85, p. 763, 1952.

[5] D. Gabor and W. P. Goss, "Interference microscope with total wavefront reconstruction," *J. Opt. Soc. Amer.*, vol. 56, pp. 849–858, 1966.

[6] L. J. Cutrona, E. N. Leith, L. J. Porcello, and W. E. Vivian, "On the application of coherent optical processing techniques to synthetic-aperture radar," *Proc. IEEE*, vol. 54, pp. 1026–1032, Aug. 1966.

[7] E. N. Leith and J. Upatnieks, "Wavefront reconstruction with continuous tone transparencies," *J. Opt. Soc. Amer.*, vol. 53, p. 522, 1963.
——, "Wavefront reconstruction with continuous-tone objects," *J. Opt. Soc. Amer.*, vol. 53, pp. 1377–1381, 1963.

[8] From D. Gabor, W. E. Kock, and G. W. Stroke, "Holography," *Science*, vol. 173, pp. 11–23, 1971. This is one of the first 3-D diffused light holograms recorded by G. W. Stroke at the University of Michigan, where he originated this work. An early reference is G. W. Stroke, "Theoretical and experimental foundations of high-resolution optical holography," presented in Rome, Italy, on Sept. 14, 1964; also in *Pubbliciazioni IV Centenario della Nascita di Galileo Galilei*. Firenze, Italy: G. Barbera, 1966, pp. 53–63.

[9] C. Knox and R. E. Brooks, "Holographic motion picture microscopy," *Proc. Roy. Soc.* (London), vol. B174, pp. 115–121, 1969.

[10] G. W. Stroke and A. E. Labeyrie, "Two-beam interferometry by successive recording of intensities in a single hologram," *Appl. Phys. Lett.*, vol. 8, pp. 42–44, Jan. 15, 1966.
L. O. Heflinger, R. F. Wuerker, and R. E. Brooks, *J. Appl. Phys.*, vol. 37, pp. 642–649, Feb. 1966.

[11] J. M. Burch, "The application of lasers in production engineering," *Production Eng.*, vol. 44, pp. 431–442, 1965.
R. L. Powell and K. A. Stetson, "Interferometric vibration analysis by wavefront reconstruction," *J. Opt. Soc. Amer.*, vol. 55, pp. 1593–1598, 1965.

[12] K. A. Stetson, thesis (under direction of E. Ingelstam), Royal Institute of Technology, Stockholm, Sweden, 1969.

[13] Yu. N. Denisyuk, "Photographic reconstruction of the optical properties of an object in its own scattered radiation," *Dokl. Akad. Nauk SSR*, vol. 144, pp. 1275–1278, 1962.

[14a] G. W. Stroke and A. E. Labeyrie, *Phys. Lett.*, vol. 20, no. 4, pp. 368–370, Mar. 1, 1966.

[14b] L. H. Lin, K. S. Pennington, G. W. Stroke, and A. E. Labeyrie, *Bell Syst. Tech. J.*, vol. 45, p. 659, 1966.

[15] K. S. Pennington and J. S. Harper, "Techniques for producing low-noise, improved-efficiency holograms," *Appl. Opt.*, vol. 9, pp. 1643–1650, 1970.

[16] P. J. Van Heerden, "A new method of storing and retrieving information," *Appl. Opt.*, vol. 2, pp. 387–392, 1963.

[17] L. K. Anderson, "Holographic optical memory for bulk data storage," *Bell Lab. Rec.*, vol. 46, p. 318, 1968.

[18] A. Vander Lugt, "Signal detection by complex spatial filtering," *IEEE Trans. Inform. Theory*, vol. IT-10, pp. 139–145, Apr. 1964.

[19] D. Gabor, "Laser speckle and its elimination," *IBM J. Res. Develop.*, vol. 14, pp. 509–514, Sept. 1970.

[20] G. W. Stroke, "Image deblurring and aperture synthesis using 'a posteriori' processing by Fourier-transform holography," *Opt. Acta*, vol. 16, pp. 401–422, 1971.
——, "Sharpening images by holography," *New Scientist*, vol. 51, pp. 671–674, 1971.
G. W. Stroke and M. Halioua, "Attainment of diffraction-limited imaging in high-resolution electron microscopy by 'a posteriori' holographic image sharpening," *Optik*, 1972, in print.

An Introduction to the Principles and Applications of Holography

JOSEPH W. GOODMAN, MEMBER, IEEE

Invited Paper

Abstract—Holography has strong historical ties with electrical engineering and potential application to many electrical engineering problems. The basic problem addressed by holography is introduced in both physical and mathematical terms. The analogy between the hologram of a point-source object and the linear FM signals of chirp radar is stressed, and the first-order imaging properties of holograms recorded in arbitrary geometries are derived.

Various types of holograms are described, including thin, thick, transmission, reflection, amplitude, and phase holograms. The important properties of each type of hologram are introduced.

A survey of various applications of holography is presented, with introductions to the use of holography in interferometry, microscopy, imaging through distorting media, optical data processing, and optical data storage. The use of simple holograms as optical elements is also described.

I. INTRODUCTION

DURING the past decade the field known as holography has undergone dramatic changes with regard to both theoretical understanding and practical application. The ideas that ten years ago were regarded primarily as an optical curiosity have developed into a branch of technology with a diversity of demonstrated applications. Why should this field, so closely tied to physical optics and seemingly so far from the more traditional areas of electrical and electronic phenomena, be of particular interest to electrical engineers? There are a variety of answers to this question.

First, there is a strong historical tie between holography and electrical engineering, for many of the most important innovative advances in the field have been made by individuals who, at the time of their contributions, were concerned with areas closely associated with the electronic sciences. Most important, of course, was the original conception of the idea behind holography by Dennis Gabor in 1948 [1] (see also [2]–[4]). Holography was envisioned by Gabor as a potential means for overcoming the spherical aberration of electron lenses in the electron microscope. A second example is the pioneering work of Leith and Upatnieks [5], who applied techniques developed in connection with synthetic aperture radars [6]–[10] to holography, thereby removing many of the practical difficulties previously encountered by Gabor. (For a discussion of the close connection between holography and synthetic aperture radars, see the paper by Leith in this issue.[1])

Above and beyond the purely historical connections, the language, concepts, and mathematical tools of electrical engineering have proved extremely useful in holography and have played an important role in its development. Notable examples are the work of Lohmann [11], based on analogies with single-sideband modulation techniques, and again the work of Leith and Upatnieks, whose

papers (e.g., [5], [12]–[15]) make liberal use of concepts from communication and information theory.

Finally, holography is of growing importance to electrical engineers because of the significant roles it can now play and will undoubtedly play in the future in the design of electronic, acoustical, and electrooptical systems of various kinds. Some of the present and future capabilities of holography in this regard are discussed in Section IV of this paper, as well as in related papers in this issue.

The goal of this paper is to present a tutorial review of the principles of holography and an introduction to a variety of its applications. An effort has been made, wherever possible, to present the discussion in terms familiar to most electrical engineers. Primary attention is devoted to optical holography, but the reader is reminded, with the help of the accompanying papers, that holographic principles can also be applied in other regions of the electromagnetic spectrum and indeed with nonelectromagnetic waves. The reader interested in pursuing the subject of holography in greater depth may wish to consult any of the several books on the subject that now exist [16]–[20]. In addition, several excellent review articles have been published [21]–[23].

II. FUNDAMENTALS

A. The Central Problem of Holography

The central problem addressed by holography is that of "wavefront reconstruction," by which we mean recording, and later reconstituting, the amplitude and phase distributions of a monochromatic (or nearly monochromatic) wave disturbance incident on a prescribed surface. The difficulties associated with this task in the optical region of the spectrum arise first in connection with the measurement of phase, for detector response is governed by the intensity (i.e., squared amplitude) of the wave and is quite independent of phase. To overcome this difficulty it is necessary to resort to an interferometric recording process, which effectively encodes the phase distribution of the incident wave as a measurable modulation (generally spatial, but in some cases temporal) of the intensity distribution. Thus the wave of interest is allowed to interfere with a mutually coherent "reference" wave, such that fringes of interference are formed and recorded. Gabor referred to such a recording as a "hologram," a term derived from the Greek word "holos" and meaning a "complete record."

Seldom is the hologram itself the desired end product. Rather the recording process is only the first step in what normally is a two-step process, the second step consisting of the construction of a new wave from the detected data. Generally the amplitude and phase distributions of the new wave are desired to be identical (up to a possible scaling of the spatial coordinates) with those of the original wavefront. In some cases, however, the reconstructed wave is intentionally made to differ from the original wave in some desired fashion.

The reader may well wonder just what is accomplished by this rather laborious two-step process, which produces in the end little

Manuscript received March 10, 1971; revised June 16, 1971. This work was supported by the Office of Naval Research. *This invited paper is one of a series planned on topics of general interest—The Editor.*

The author is with the Department of Electrical Engineering, Stanford University, Stanford, Calif. 94305.

[1] E. N. Leith, "Quasi-holographic techniques in the microwave region," this issue, pp. 1305–1318.

Reprinted from *Proc. IEEE*, vol. 59, pp. 1292–1304, Sept. 1971.

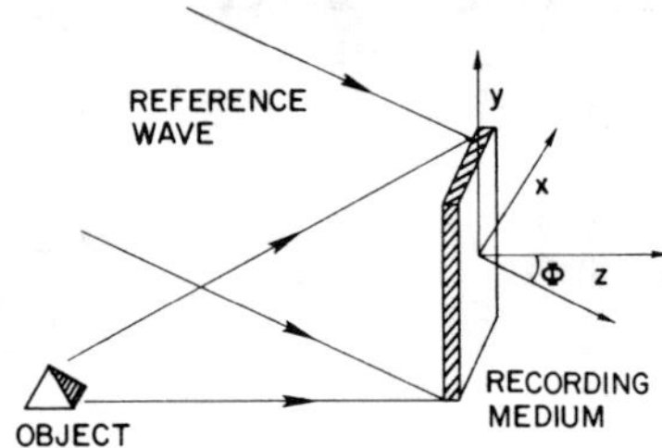

Fig. 1.   Recording a hologram.

more than a duplicate of the wavefront that was already available at the start. The answers to this question will become apparent in detail only when the various applications of holography are considered. In most cases it is not the wavefront itself that is of ultimate interest, but rather some object (possibly three-dimensional) through which the wave has passed, or from which it has been reflected during propagation to the recording plane. The ability to record information about that object in the form of a hologram, rather than as a directly formed image, introduces a variety of advantages, particularly with respect to the kind and quality of information that can ultimately be recovered. For example, the image generated when the hologram is illuminated may be three-dimensional. A more detailed discussion of these advantages is best presented after the holographic process has been described in greater depth, and is therefore postponed until Section IV.

B. The Basic Mathematics of Holography

The physical quantities dealt with in this analysis are complex-valued functions defined on three-dimensional space and representing the scalar amplitude and phase distributions of a monochromatic wave. If the wave of concern is electromagnetic, the scalar amplitude may be regarded as that of a single polarization component, it being tacitly assumed that all waves are identically polarized and that their polarizations are unaffected by the various operations involved. Such an assumption must be used with some caution, for polarization effects can be important in practice [24]–[26]. As a first approximation, a more complete theory can be developed by treating the two polarization components independently.

With reference to Fig. 1, let there exist in the plane $z=0$ a detection medium, for example a photographic emulsion if the waves are optical. For the present, the physical thickness of the medium will be ignored. Let there impinge upon this medium from the left two monochromatic waves, each with wavelength λ. One wave, which we refer to here as the "object" wave, has been reflected from or transmitted by some object of interest; the complex amplitude of this incident wave is represented by $U_0(x, y)$. The second wave, which we refer to as the "reference" wave, has complex amplitude $U_r(x, y)$ at the recording medium. The physically measurable quantity at the detector is the intensity distribution of the incident wave, which can be written

$$I(x, y) = |U_r + U_0|^2 = |U_r|^2 + |U_0|^2 + U_r^*U_0 + U_rU_0^*. \quad (1)$$

Note in particular that the third term of (1) contains U_0, so there is some hope that perhaps both amplitude and phase information can be recovered.

If optical reconstruction of the wavefront U_0 is desired, the detected intensity pattern must somehow be transferred to a spatial modulator which will impress upon an incident optical wave the desired pattern of amplitude and phase. A photographic transparency provides the simplest modulator of this kind, although many other materials can and have been used, including embossed vinyl tape [27], thermoplastics [28], [29], electrooptic crystals [30],

ferromagnetic films [31], photopolymers [32], and photochromics [33].

To attempt by direct means to impress upon an incident optical wave a prescribed distribution of both amplitude and phase is an enormously difficult task, requiring simultaneous and independent control of both attenuation and phase shift through the modulator. In practice it is possible to control either attenuation or phase shift, but not both independently. Suppose, however, that it is possible to achieve an amplitude transmittance $t_A(x, y)$ (i.e., the ratio of transmitted complex field to incident complex field at each point) that is simply proportional to the intensity $I(x, y)$ of the holographic interference pattern. For example, over a limited dynamic range the amplitude transmittance of a developed photographic transparency can be approximated by

$$t_A(x, y) \cong t_b + \beta\Delta I(x, y) \quad (2)$$

where t_b and β are constants while ΔI represents the variations of intensity about its mean level. A similar proportionality can be achieved for a purely phase-shifting medium, such as a bleached photographic transparency, through the linearization

$$t_A(x, y) = \exp\{j\mu\Delta I(x, y)\} \cong 1 + j\mu\Delta I(x, y) \quad (3)$$

($\mu=$constant) valid for small modulation depths. In practice neither a pure attenuation nor a pure phase shift can be realized, but (2) and (3) provide adequate models for thin modulation media that operate primarily through attenuation or primarily through phase shift.

To proceed with our discussion of the reconstruction process, suppose that proportionality between t_A and I is achieved. Let the modulator be illuminated by a replication of the original reference wave $U_r(x, y)$. Neglecting unimportant constants, the field $U_c(x, y)$ appearing immediately behind the modulator is

$$U_c(x, y) = U_r(x, y)I(x, y)$$
$$= U_r|U_r|^2 + U_r|U_0|^2 + |U_r|^2U_0 + U_r^2U_0^*. \quad (4)$$

Now if the reference wave has been chosen to have approximately constant intensity $|U_r|^2$, the third term above is clearly a duplication of the original object wavefront, and if it can be separated from the other components the wavefront reconstruction process will have succeeded.

Separation of the various reconstructed wave components represented in (4) posed the most serious obstacle to useful application of Gabor's invention until the early 1960s, when Leith and Upatnieks introduced the concept of an "offset reference" hologram [5]. The basic idea behind this innovation is best illustrated by considering a very specific reference wave, namely a plane wave with wave vector in the y-z plane inclined at an angle Φ with respect to the z axis (cf. Fig. 1). The field distribution at the detector due to this wave is of the form

$$U_r(x, y) = A \exp\{-j2\pi\alpha y\} \quad (5)$$

where A is a constant and $\alpha=\sin \Phi/\lambda$. In addition let the object wave U_0 be expressed in terms of its amplitude and phase distributions

$$U_0(x, y) = a(x, y) \exp[j\theta(x, y)]. \quad (6)$$

The pattern of interference now becomes

$$I(x, y) = A^2 + a^2(x, y) + Aa(x, y) \exp\{j[2\pi\alpha y + \theta(x, y)]\}$$
$$+ Aa(x, y) \exp\{-j[2\pi\alpha y + \theta(x, y)]\}$$
$$= A^2 + a^2(x, y) + 2Aa(x, y) \cos[2\pi\alpha y + \theta(x, y)]. \quad (7)$$

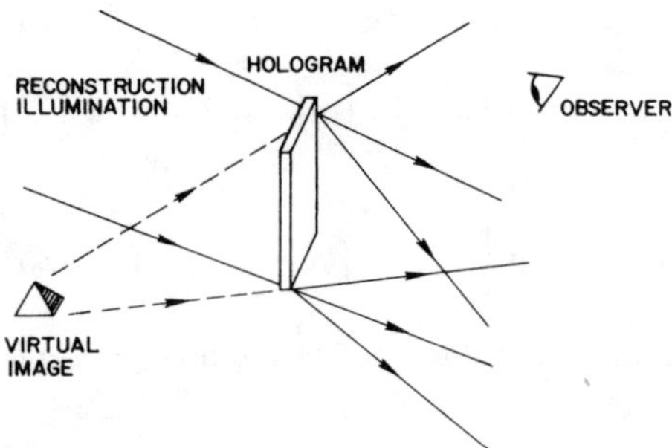

Fig. 2.   Reconstructing a virtual image.

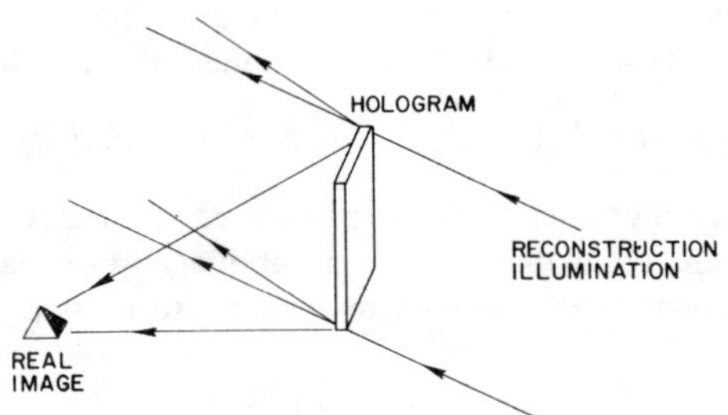

Fig. 3.   Reconstructing a real image.

Clearly, the amplitude and phase distributions of the object wave have been encoded, respectively, as amplitude and phase modulations of a spatial carrier of frequency α.

Let the recorded hologram now be illuminated by a duplication of the reference wave. The transmitted field has the following components:

$$U_c(x, y) = A^3 \exp\{-j2\pi\alpha y\} + Aa^2(x, y)\exp\{-j2\pi\alpha y\} + A^2 a(x, y)$$
$$\cdot \exp\{j\theta(x, y)\} + A^2 a(x, y)\exp\{-j[4\pi\alpha y + \theta(x, y)]\}. \quad (8)$$

Up to an unimportant constant, the third term of this equation is a duplication of the original wavefront. The first two terms are multiplied by $\exp(-j2\pi\alpha y)$, which indicates they will propagate away from the modulator in the general direction of travel of the reference wave. The fourth term contains a factor $\exp\{-j4\pi\alpha y\}$, which indicates that it will propagate away at an even steeper angle. Thus a properly situated observer will intercept the reconstructed wavefront without interference, and will accordingly see behind the hologram a virtual image of the object that gave rise to U_0 (see Fig. 2).

If the hologram is illuminated not by the original reference wave but rather by its complex conjugate U_r^*, the fourth term of (7) yields a wave proportional to U_0^*. As consideration of the simple case of a point-source object shows, U_0^* corresponds to a wave converging towards a real image of the original object. One way to generate the required illumination U_r^* is to illuminate the hologram by a plane wave with direction of propagation opposite to that used during recording. Thus referring to Fig. 3, the hologram is illuminated from the right, and the wavefront U_0^* is created to the left of the transparency. The result is the formation of a real image of the object, with each image point coming to focus at the location of the object point that gave rise to it. Again the various extraneous reconstructed waves will propagate away from the image, provided the carrier frequency is chosen sufficiently high.

C. The Elementary Signals of Holography

A hologram of a complex object may be viewed as being built up as a superposition of "elementary signals" which are the holograms of individual point-source components of the object. Strictly speak-

ing, this view is not quite correct, for it neglects the signals generated by interference of each object point with all other object points, i.e., the $|U_0|^2$ term of (1). Nonetheless, under most conditions these object-object intermodulation terms do not diffract light in the direction of the desired images, and therefore there is some justification in neglecting them. As we shall see, there is a marked similarity between the hologram of a point-source object and the more familiar "chirp" signals of radar and communication theory.

For simplicity, let the reference wave again be the plane wave described by (5), and let the object wave be a simple spherical wave expanding about the source point (x_0, y_0, z_0), where z_0 is a negative number. At the recording plane, the object wave is of the form

$$U_0(x, y) = a \exp\left\{j\frac{2\pi}{\lambda}[z_0^2 + (x - x_0)^2 + (y - y_0)^2]^{1/2}\right\}. \quad (9)$$

To concentrate on the first-order properties of the imaging process, it is necessary to make a small angle or paraxial approximation, representing the square root in (9) by the first two terms of its binomial expansion. Thus the spherical wavefront is approximated by a paraboloid,

$$\exp\left\{j\frac{2\pi}{\lambda}[z_0^2 + (x - x_0)^2 + (y - y_0)^2]^{1/2}\right\}$$
$$\approx \exp\left\{-j\frac{2\pi z_0}{\lambda} - j\frac{\pi}{\lambda z_0}[(x - x_0)^2 + (y - y_0)^2]\right\} \quad (10)$$

where we have used the fact that z_0 is negative. Inclusion of higher order terms in the binomial expansion is necessary if predictions of the aberrations associated with the holographic process are to be made [34]–[37], but this rather specialized subject will not be treated here. Introducing (10) and (5) in (1), the intensity distribution at the detector is found to be

$$I(x, y) = I_r + I_0 + 2\sqrt{I_r I_0}$$
$$\cdot \cos\left\{2\pi\alpha y - \frac{\pi}{\lambda z_0}[(x - x_0)^2 + (y - y_0)^2] + \phi\right\} \quad (11)$$

where $I_r = A^2$, $I_0 = a^2$, and $\phi = 2\pi z_0/\lambda$ is a constant phase angle. Equation (11) represents what we call an "elementary signal."

Neglecting the constants I_r and I_0, the elementary signal bears a strong resemblance to the "chirp" (i.e., linear FM) signals so widely encountered in the theory of modern radar [38], [39]; it is in fact the two-dimensional analog of such signals. Let $\psi(x, y)$ represent the argument of the consinusoidal term in (11), i.e.,

$$\psi(x, y) = 2\pi\alpha y - \frac{\pi}{\lambda z_0}[(x - x_0)^2 + (y - y_0)^2] + \phi. \quad (12)$$

The "local frequency" (analogous to instantaneous frequency) of the fringe pattern is a vector quantity $\mathbf{v}(x, y)$ defined by

$$\mathbf{v}(x, y) \triangleq \frac{1}{2\pi}\nabla\psi(x, y) = \frac{1}{2\pi}\frac{\partial\psi}{\partial x}\hat{x} + \frac{1}{2\pi}\frac{\partial\psi}{\partial y}\hat{y} \quad (13)$$

where $\hat{x}$ and $\hat{y}$ are unit vectors. Performing the required differentiations, the vector components are found to be

$$v_X = \frac{1}{2\pi}\frac{\partial\psi}{\partial x} = -\frac{(x - x_0)}{\lambda z_0}$$

$$v_Y = \frac{1}{2\pi}\frac{\partial\psi}{\partial y} = \alpha - \frac{(y - y_0)}{\lambda z_0}. \quad (14)$$

Thus each vector component of spatial frequency sweeps linearly

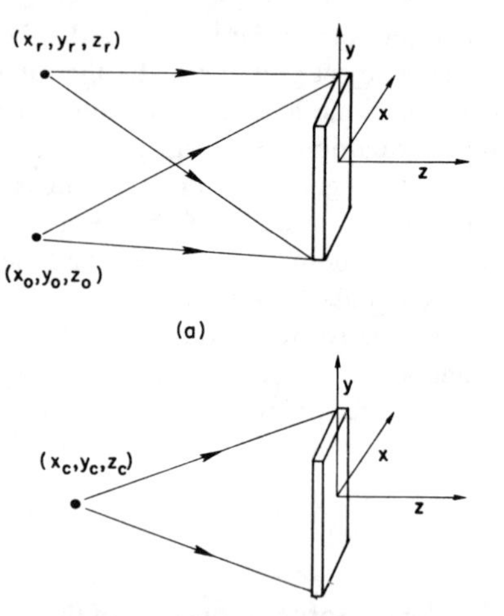

(a)

(b)

Fig. 4.　Generalized geometries. (a) Recording a hologram.
(b) Reconstructing images.

with its corresponding space coordinate. The length v of the local frequency vector is

$$v = \left\{\left[\alpha - \frac{(y - y_0)}{\lambda z_0}\right]^2 + \left[\frac{x - x_0}{\lambda z}\right]^2\right\}^{1/2}. \tag{15}$$

The encoding of a point-source object into the extended fringe pattern of (11) is significant in several respects. Most important, the highly localized point-source object has been dispersed by the propagation phenomenon to yield a detected signal occupying an extended region of the space domain. When the object wave arises from a complex source which has a large dynamic range of brightness, the redistribution of signal energy often results in a considerable relaxation of the dynamic range requirements at the detector. In addition, a spatial redundancy is introduced such that localized imperfections of the recording medium are often of little consequence.

The importance of the elementary signals represented by (11) was recognized at an early time in the history of holography by Rogers [40], who pointed out their similarity to Fresnel zone plates. The zone plate interpretation of holography provides a very physical way of explaining the holographic process [41]. The "chirp" signal interpretation likewise has many advantages, for many of the known properties of pulse compression systems can be drawn upon in discussing the properties of the reconstructed images.

D. Generalized Hologram Geometries

The assumption of a plane reference wave in the previous sections was made for analytical simplicity, but is by no means a necessary restriction in practice. Similarly, the assumption of a reconstruction wave which duplicates the original reference wave (or its conjugate) is not necessary unless the hologram thickness becomes comparable with, or greater than, the finest recorded fringe, in which case Bragg diffraction effects are important (see Section III). Several important properties of holograms as image-forming devices are discovered when a more general geometry is considered.

Let the object wave be generated by a point source at coordinates (x_0, y_0, z_0) and the reference wave be generated by a point source at coordinates (x_r, y_r, z_r), as shown in Fig. 4a. The wavelength used during the recording process is represented by λ_1. Let the resulting hologram transparency be illuminated by a spherical wave of wavelength λ_2 arising from a point source at coordinates (x_c, y_c, z_c), as shown in Fig. 4(b).

If the spherical wavefronts are again approximated by paraboloids and constant phase factors are dropped, the incident wavefronts are

$$U_r(x, y) \cong A \exp\left\{-j\frac{\pi}{\lambda_1 z_r}[(x - x_r)^2 + (y - y_r)^2]\right\} \tag{16}$$

$$U_0(x, y) \cong a \exp\left\{-j\frac{\pi}{\lambda_1 z_0}[(x - x_0)^2 + (y - y_0)^2]\right\}. \tag{17}$$

Similarly, the wavefront illuminating the hologram during reconstruction is

$$U_c(x, y) \cong B \exp\left\{-j\frac{\pi}{\lambda_2 z_c}[(x - x_c)^2 + (y - y_c)^2]\right\}. \tag{18}$$

Assuming the ideal detector characteristic described by (2), the two important terms of amplitude transmittance of the hologram are

$$t_1(x, y) \propto U_c(U_r^* U_0), \qquad t_2(x, y) \propto U_c(U_r U_0^*). \tag{19}$$

If the required multiplications are performed and the two resulting wavefronts are compared with a parabolic approximation to a spherical reconstructed wave corresponding to an image point at (x_i, y_i, z_i)

$$U_i(x, y) \cong D \exp\left\{-j\frac{\pi}{\lambda_2 z_i}[(x - x_i)^2 + (y - y_i)^2]\right\} \tag{20}$$

the following identifications can be made, where the upper set of signs applies to one wave and the lower set to the other:

$$x_i = \pm\frac{\lambda_2 z_i}{\lambda_1 z_0}x_0 \mp \frac{\lambda_2 z_i}{\lambda_1 z_r}x_r - \frac{z_i}{z_c}x_c$$

$$y_i = \pm\frac{\lambda_2 z_i}{\lambda_1 z_0}y_0 \mp \frac{\lambda_2 z_i}{\lambda_1 z_r}y_r - \frac{z_i}{z_c}y_c$$

$$z_i = \left(\frac{1}{z_c} \pm \frac{\lambda_2}{\lambda_1 z_r} \mp \frac{\lambda_2}{\lambda_1 z_0}\right)^{-1}. \tag{21}$$

When z_i is a negative number, the image is virtual, for the wave appears to be diverging from a point lying to the left of the hologram in Fig. 4(b). When z_i is positive, the image is real, for the light comes to a focus to the right of the hologram. Note that in general it is not necessary that one image be real and the other virtual. For example, when $\lambda_1 = \lambda_2$, $z_r = z_0$, and $z_c > 0$, both images are real, while when $\lambda_1 = \lambda_2$, $z_r = z_0$, and $z_c < 0$ both images are virtual.

From the results presented in (21) it is a simple matter to show that, for objects more complex than a single point source, the images produced by the holographic process may be magnified or demagnified with respect to the object that gives rise to them. The transverse magnification M_t is found from (21) to be

$$M_t = \left|\frac{\partial x_i}{\partial x_0}\right| = \left|\frac{\partial y_i}{\partial y_0}\right| = \left|\frac{\lambda_2 z_i}{\lambda_1 z_0}\right| = \left|1 - \frac{z_0}{z_r} \mp \frac{\lambda_1 z_0}{\lambda_2 z_c}\right|^{-1} \tag{22}$$

while the longitudinal magnification M_l is

$$M_l = \left|\frac{\partial z_i}{\partial z_0}\right| = \frac{\lambda_1}{\lambda_2} M_t^2. \tag{23}$$

The possible use of these magnifications in microscopy, particularly X-ray microscopy, were studied by El-Sum in the 1950s [42].

An important conclusion to be drawn from the preceding equations is that, if the images are ultimately formed with radiation of different wavelength than used for recording, the longitudinal and transverse magnifications will not be the same. For a three-dimensional object, the result is an apparent distortion of the image. To emphasize this point, consider a microwave hologram recorded with

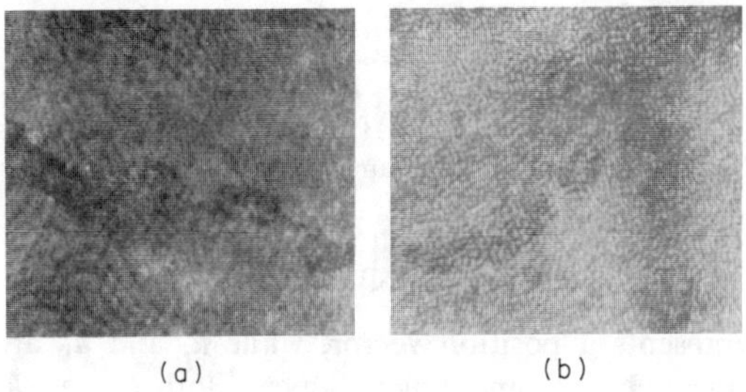

Fig. 5. Holograms of diffuse objects. (a) View with the naked eye. (b) High magnification.

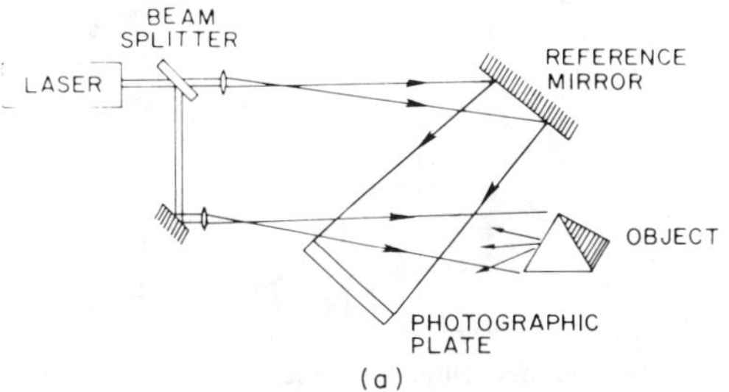

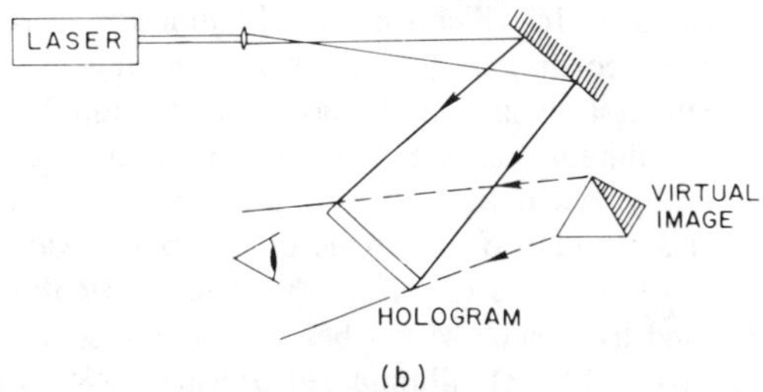

Fig. 6. Hologram of a three-dimensional object. (a) Recording. (b) Viewing the virtual image.

Fig. 7. Photographs of the virtual image of a three-dimensional object, illustrating a change of both focus and perspective.

wavelength $\lambda_1 = 10$ cm. For the sake of argument, suppose that a photographic hologram of the same size as the original detecting array is produced (such a large transparency would, of course, hardly be desirable in practice). Let this transparency be illuminated by red light from an He–Ne laser ($\lambda = 632.8$ nm). The longitudinal magnification is then about 1.6×10^5 times greater than the transverse magnification.

A partial solution to this problem is afforded by scaling the linear size of the hologram by a factor m between recording and reconstruction, a step that would generally be necessary in any case to achieve a transparency of reasonable size. If $m < 1$, the size of the hologram has been reduced, while if $m > 1$ it has been increased. In this case the transverse and longitudinal magnifications become [34]

$$
M_t = m\left[1 - \frac{z_0}{z_r} \mp m^2 \frac{\lambda_1}{\lambda_2} \frac{z_0}{z_c}\right]^{-1}
$$

$$
M_l = \frac{\lambda_1}{\lambda_2} M_t^2. \tag{24}
$$

The transverse and longitudinal magnifications can be made equal, independent of position, by making M_t equal to λ_2/λ_1 and scaling the linear size of the hologram by a factor $m = \lambda_2/\lambda_1$ [35]. For the particular example outlined above, the hologram must be reduced in size by a factor 0.6×10^{-5}. If the original microwave array is 10 m long, the detected data must be transferred to a hologram of length 60 μm to achieve equal transverse and longitudinal magnifications. Unfortunately, the resulting hologram is so small that the virtual image cannot be viewed with any useful parallax. In addition, the resulting transverse demagnification may be so great as to require the use of a microscope to view the image.

E. Holograms with Diffused Illumination and Holograms of Three-Dimensional Objects

When the object of interest is a simple transparency, it is generally advantageous to illuminate that transparency with highly diffused laser light during the recording process [13]. Thus rather than simply expanding the output of a laser to fully illuminate the transparency of interest, a diffusing medium, such as opal glass, is inserted between the laser and the transparency, generally in close proximity to the transparency. The effect of the diffuser is to introduce an extremely complex phase distribution across the illuminating wave, or equivalently to randomize (in an ensemble sense) the phase of the light transmitted by each point on the object transparency. As a consequence, the elementary signals described by (11) add at the recording plane with unrelated spatial phases, producing a hologram that appears to the eye to be uniformly gray. Fig. 5(a) shows a hologram formed with diffuse object illumination, while Fig. 5(b) shows a highly magnified portion of that same hologram. The extremely complex patterns observed on a microscopic scale represent the information-bearing structure of the hologram.

Two advantages are gained by the use of diffused illumination.

First, the energy distribution across the hologram is spread out more evenly than would otherwise be the case, resulting in a reduction of the dynamic range required of the recording medium. Second, because the original phase relations between elementary signals on the hologram are randomized by the diffuser, large regions where the elementary signals would have added with destructive interference are eliminated, and the entire virtual image of the transparency can be viewed through any portion of the hologram. Thus the use of diffused illumination increases the degree of spatial redundancy present in the holographic recording. These advantages are gained only at a price, however, for the images formed from such holograms have a mottled appearance or granularity that is generally referred to as "speckle" [43], [44] and which arises because of the diffused nature of the illumination. Speckle not only reduces the esthetic qualities of the images, but in addition leads to a loss of effective resolution. Several methods for eliminating or minimizing speckle have been proposed and demonstrated [45]–[47], often through the use of specially constructed diffusing plates.

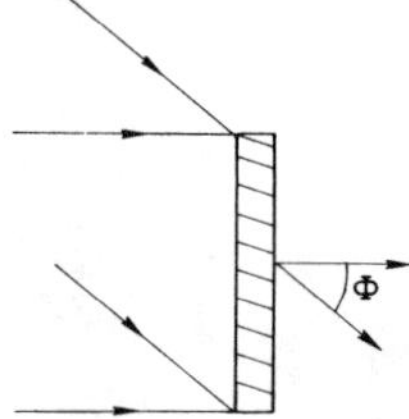

Fig. 8.   Interference fringes in a thick recording medium.

A second situation in which diffused illumination arises quite naturally is in the recording of holograms of three-dimensional objects, as first successfully accomplished by Leith and Upatnieks [13]. Most three-dimensional scenes containing figurines, models, or more naturally occurring objects are composed primarily of surfaces that are rough on the scale of an optical wavelength. Thus the object itself serves to diffuse the reflected light, and the holograms formed from such scenes bear a strong resemblance to those recorded from diffusely illuminated transparencies. Fig. 6(a) illustrates a typical geometry used for recording holograms of three-dimensional objects, while Fig. 6(b) illustrates the means by which the virtual image would be viewed. Fig. 7(a) and (b) shows two photographs of the virtual image produced by such a hologram, illustrating the different views of the object obtained through different parts of the hologram. The dramatic nature of the three-dimensional images obtained from such holograms is largely responsible for the great popular interest in holography. However, as we shall see in Section IV, many of the important applications of holography are quite independent of this three-dimensional imaging capability.

III. Various Types of Holograms

In recent years, a wide variety of different types of holograms have been discussed in the literature, many of which have proved to be very useful and important from a practical point of view. Here we briefly review the properties of several different types of holograms; more detailed discussions of this material are available in the literature [15], [23], [48], [49].

A. Thin versus Thick Holograms

The importance of the third dimension, i.e., depth, of a holographic recording was recognized at an early date by Denisyuk [50] and by van Heerden [51]. Strictly speaking, a hologram may be considered a thin diffracting structure only if its optical thickness is less than a wavelength. In practice, however, it is not the relation of thickness to wavelength that influences the characteristics of the hologram, but rather the relationship between the thickness and the period of the finest fringe recorded on the hologram. If the finest fringe period is larger than the thickness, the hologram behaves essentially as a two-dimensional diffracting structure. If the fringe period is smaller than the thickness, then that fringe behaves as a three-dimensional diffracting structure. In practice, a given hologram contains many different fringe structures, some of which may be fine and some coarse, so the hologram may exhibit properties of both thin and thick structures.

Fig. 8 illustrates the formation of fringes in the volume of an emulsion for the particular case of plane object and reference waves. Regions of constructive and destructive interference move through the emulsion at an angle that bisects the angle Φ between the two interfering waves. The result is a grating structure that exists through the volume of the emulsion.

To discuss this phenomenon in greater depth, let the complex amplitudes of the object and reference waves in the emulsion be represented by

$$U_r(p) = A \exp\{jk_r \cdot p\}$$

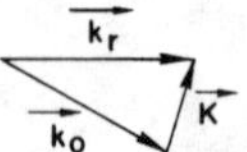

Fig. 9.   Wave-vector diagram, hologram recording.

$$U_0(p) = a \exp\{jk_0 \cdot p\} \tag{25}$$

where p represents a position vector, while k_r and k_0 are wave vectors of the reference and object waves. Both k_r and k_0 have lengths $2\pi/\lambda$, where λ is again the wavelength of the light (in the emulsion). The intensity $I(p)$ of the light at each point p in the emulsion is given by

$$I(p) = |U_r + U_0|^2 = A^2 + a^2 + 2Aa \cos\left[(k_r - k_0) \cdot p\right]. \tag{26}$$

Thus we may specify an effective K vector for the fringes in the emulsion by the definition

$$K \triangleq k_r - k_0. \tag{27}$$

The direction of K indicates the normal to the fringes in the emulsion, while the length of K is related to the fringe period Λ (measured normally between two fringes) by

$$|K| = \frac{2\pi}{\Lambda}. \tag{28}$$

As shown in Fig. 9, which pictorially represents (27), the fact that $|k_r| = |k_0|$ implies that the direction of K is indeed such that the fringes run at an angle which bisects the angle Φ between the incident wave vectors. Simple trigonometry also shows that the fringe period Λ is given by

$$\Lambda = \frac{\lambda}{2 \sin \dfrac{\Phi}{2}}. \tag{29}$$

A grating of thickness T may be regarded as "thin" if $\Lambda \gg T$, while it must be regarded as "thick" when $\Lambda \ll T$. For Kodak 649F plate, which is widely used in holography, the thickness ($\sim 16\,\mu$) and refractive index (~ 1.5) are such that a hologram behaves as a thin structure only for external reference-object angles of 10° or less.

For a thick hologram, the brightness of the reconstructed image is governed by Bragg diffraction, and is in general sensitive both to the angle at which the hologram is illuminated and to the wavelength of the illumination. A qualitative understanding of these dependences can be obtained from the following reasoning. A plane optical wave will be strongly reflected from a grating of *infinite* thickness only if the wave vector k_c of the illumination, the grating vector K, and the wave vector k_i of the reflected light satisfy

$$k_c - k_i = \pm K \tag{30}$$

for only then will the scattered contributions from all depths of the grating add constructively. Neglecting the effects of emulsion shrinkage, the two most important ways this condition can be satisfied are those illustrated in Fig. 10(a) and (b). First, referring to Fig. 10(a), if the hologram is illuminated by a wave with wave vector k_c identically equal to the wave vector k_r of the original reference wave, then an image wave with wave vector $k_i = k_0$ will be generated. For a more general situation in which the object wave contains an entire family of wave-vector components, this illumination yields a virtual image of the object. On the other hand, as illustrated in Fig. 10(b), if the hologram is illuminated by a wave with wave vector $k_c = -k_r$, then an image wave with wave vector $k_i = -k_0$ will be generated. When the object wave contains a family of wave-vector components, this illumination yields a real image of the object.

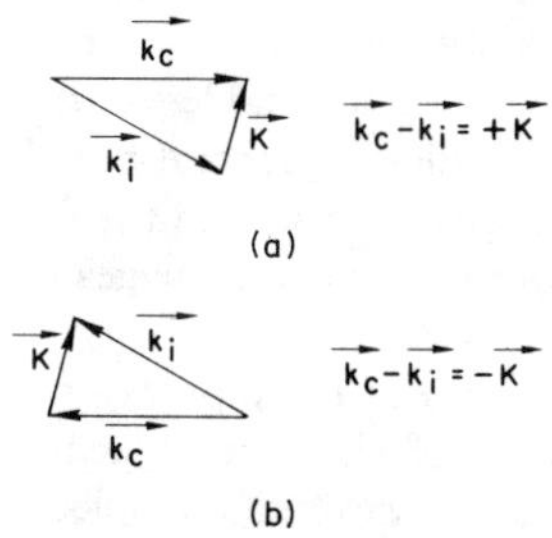

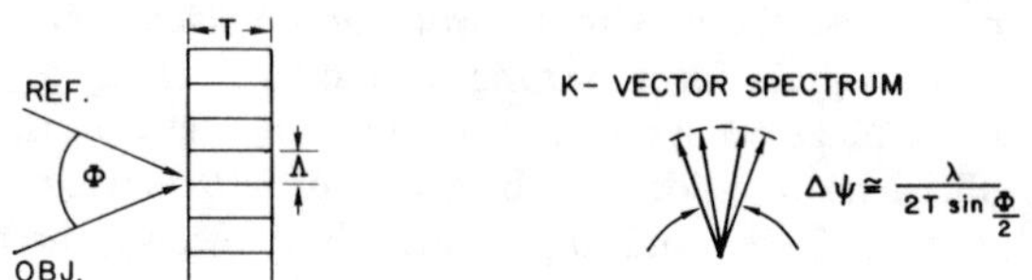

Fig. 10.   Wave-vector diagrams for forming a virtual and a real image.
(a) Virtual image. (b) Real image.

Fig. 11.   Grating vector components for a hologram of finite thickness.

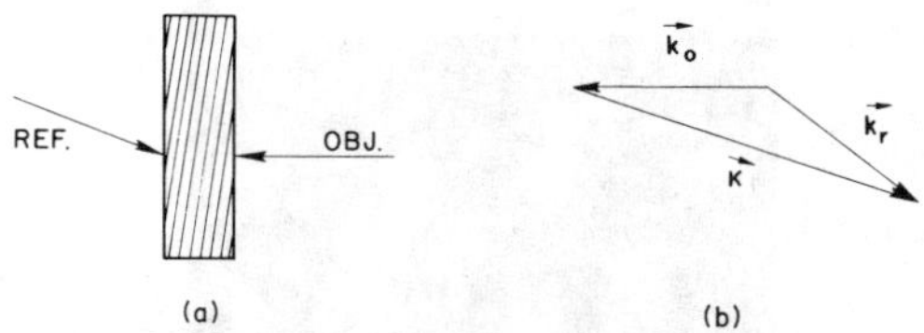

Fig. 12.   A thick reflection hologram. (a) Recording geometry.
(b) Wave-vector diagram.

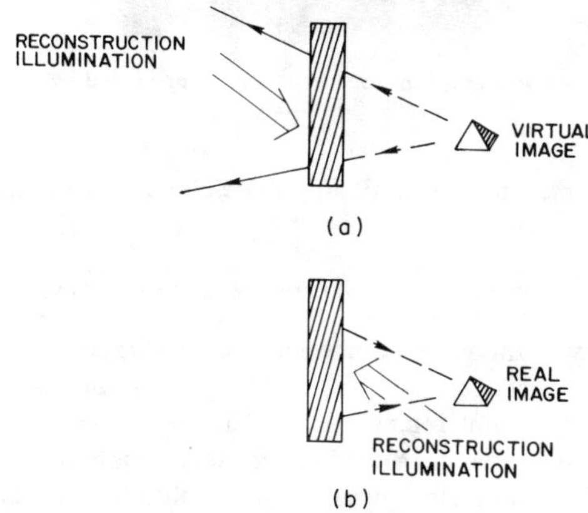

Fig. 13.   Obtaining images from a thick reflection hologram.
(a) Virtual image. (b) Real image.

In practice the grating is not infinitely thick, but rather has some finite thickness T. In this case we may regard the grating as containing an angular spectrum of grating-vector components, all with the same length $2\pi/\Lambda$, but distributed in direction over an approximate angle $\Delta\psi$, as shown in Fig. 11. When the bisector of the reference-object angle Φ is normal to the emulsion, we have that $\Delta\psi \cong \Lambda/T$, and using (29)

$$\Delta\psi \cong \frac{\lambda}{2T \sin \dfrac{\Phi}{2}}. \tag{31}$$

Thus the angular spread of the grating vectors is smallest when Φ is near 180°.

As a consequence of the spread of the angular directions of grating vectors, exact Bragg alignment of the readout wave is not required. Rather it is only necessary that the wave vector k_c of the illumination be properly aligned with any one of the grating vector components. Rotational alignment of the hologram is found to be most critical when $\Phi \approx 90°$, while the wavelength selectivity is greatest when $\Phi \approx 180°$ and the reference and object waves enter from opposite sides of the plate, a condition we examine in Section III-B.

Because of the Bragg effect it is possible to utilize all three dimensions of the recording medium for information storage. Thus both angular and wavelength multiplexing of stored images are possible [33], [52], and very high information densities can be achieved. A general discussion of the information storage capabilities of thick holograms has been given by Gabor and Stroke [53].

B. Transmission versus Reflection Holograms

For the most common types of holograms, the images of interest are formed with transmitted light. It is also possible, however, to construct holograms that form images by means of reflected light. For example, if a hologram recorded on a silver halide material develops a relief pattern that is directly related to the original exposure (as often happens in practice [54]), then deposition of a metallized layer on the emulsion surface can create a highly reflective hologram from which images can be obtained [55]. Similar techniques can be applied for holograms recorded on thermoplastic materials [56].

A more complex type of reflection hologram can be produced if the recording medium is thick [57]. With reference to Fig. 12(a), let the object and reference waves be incident from opposite sides of the emulsion, with an angular separation Φ approaching 180°. In this case the recorded fringes run nearly parallel to the emulsion surface, and from (29) we see that the fringe period Λ is approximately $\lambda/2$. The k-vector diagram appropriate for this case is illustrated in Fig. 12(b). For reconstruction of a virtual image, the Bragg condition requires that the hologram be illuminated by a duplication of the original reference wave, in which case the image appears in reflected light, as shown in Fig. 13(a). The geometry for reconstructing a real image is shown in Fig. 13(b), where it is clear that again the image is formed in reflected light.

The wavelength selectivity of a thick grating structure is highest when $\Phi \approx 180°$ [15], and as a consequence, the images formed by thick reflection holograms may be viewed with white light sources. In practice, the color of the reconstructed image is not the same as the color of the light used during recording, but rather is shifted towards shorter wavelengths by emulsion shrinkage that occurs during the fixing of the emulsion. This problem can be overcome by omitting the fixing step, or by reswelling the emulsion. Fig. 14 shows a photograph of the virtual image produced by a thick reflection hologram.

C. Amplitude Holograms

A hologram may be classified as an amplitude hologram if absorption is the primary mechanism by means of which stored information is transferred to the reconstructed optical field. The properties of such a hologram depend on whether it is thin or thick in the sense described in Section III-A.

A thin amplitude hologram is best described in terms of its amplitude transmittance, as was done in (2). Since holograms are really modulated diffraction gratings, we concentrate attention on the simple case of a sinusoidal amplitude grating, as described by

$$t_A(x, y) = \tfrac{1}{2}[1 + \cos 2\pi\alpha y]. \tag{32}$$

Such an amplitude transmittance could in principle be obtained from a perfectly linear holographic material exposed to two equal-intensity plane waves. The field transmitted by such a hologram

Fig. 14.   Photograph of the virtual image produced by a thick reflection hologram.

when it is illuminated by a unit amplitude plane wave contains three wave components,

$$U_c(x, y) = \tfrac{1}{2} + \tfrac{1}{4} \exp(j2\pi\alpha y) + \tfrac{1}{4} \exp(-j2\pi\alpha y). \tag{33}$$

The intensity of the wave component $\tfrac{1}{4} \exp(j2\pi\alpha y)$, which leads to one of the two reconstructed images, is $\tfrac{1}{16}$. Since the hologram was illuminated by a unit intensity wave, only $\tfrac{1}{16}$ of the incident light contributes to the reconstructed image. Accordingly we say that the maximum diffraction efficiency of a thin amplitude hologram is $\tfrac{1}{16}$ or 6.25 percent. In practice, the perfect recording linearity implied by (32) cannot be achieved, and the contrast of the sinusoidal grating must be reduced to maintain linearity. Diffraction efficiencies somewhat less than 6.25 percent are therefore achieved in practice, typical numbers being in the range 1 to 2 percent.

A thick amplitude hologram formed by interference of two plane waves is described by an absorption coefficient β that varies sinusoidally with distance, i.e.,

$$\beta(x, y) = \beta_0 + \beta_1 \cos(2\pi\alpha y). \tag{34}$$

An analysis by Kogelnik, using coupled mode theory [48], [49], has shown that the diffraction efficiency of this type of hologram depends on whether the hologram is made to be viewed with transmitted light or with reflected light. The maximum theoretical diffraction efficiency for a transmission hologram was found to be 3.7 percent, while that for a reflection hologram is 7.2 percent.

D. Phase Holograms

When the primary mechanism by which a hologram modulates an incident wave is either a change of dielectric constant or a change of physical thickness, the hologram is called a phase hologram. Because phase holograms can in principle be lossless diffracting structures, their diffraction efficiencies can be much higher than those of amplitude holograms. However, modulation of phase is intrinsically a nonlinear operation, and some care must be taken to avoid image degradations caused by nonlinearities.

For a thin phase hologram [58], [59], the most suitable description is again in terms of amplitude transmittance, as indicated previously in (3). Again treating the case of a simple sinusoidal grating, the amplitude transmittance is of the form

$$t_A(x, y) = \exp\{j\mu \sin 2\pi\alpha y\} \tag{35}$$

where μ is the peak phase modulation amplitude. Expanding the exponential in a Fourier series, we find

$$t_A(x, y) = \sum_{q=-\infty}^{\infty} J_q(\mu) \exp(j2\pi q\alpha y) \tag{36}$$

where J_q is a Bessel function of the first kind, order q. The $q=0$ component leads to an undiffracted component of transmitted light,

while the $q = \pm 1$ components correspond to the usual first-order images. Values of q greater than 1 and less than -1 lead to so-called "higher order images," which in general bear little resemblance to the original object, and therefore are of little interest, provided their angular separation from the primary images is sufficiently great to prevent overlap.

The diffraction efficiency of a thin phase grating is equal to $J_1^2(\mu)$, and has a maximum value of 33.9 percent, achieved when the modulation depth μ equals 1.8. However, if the object is more complicated than the simple plane wave implicitly assumed in writing (34), the choice of an rms modulation depth as large as 1.8 leads to an unacceptable degree of intermodulation distortion in the primary images. In practice, the maximum diffraction efficiency consistent with good image quality is in the range of 5 to 10 percent.

If a surface blaze occurs on a thin sinusoidal phase grating, diffraction efficiencies considerably in excess of 33.9 percent can be achieved, both in theory and in practice [60]. However, the blazed phase hologram is again intrinsically nonlinear [61], and for objects more complex than a single plane wave the achievable diffraction efficiency is severely limited by image distortions.

A thick phase hologram formed by interference of two plane waves is characterized by a refractive index ε that varies sinusoidally with space

$$\varepsilon = \varepsilon_0 + \varepsilon_1 \cos 2\pi\alpha y. \tag{37}$$

Under the condition of Bragg alignment it is theoretically possible to achieve a diffraction efficiency of 100 percent from thick sinusoidal phase gratings of both the transmission and reflection types [48], [49]. In practice, diffraction efficiencies in the 60 to 70-percent range can typically be achieved with Kodak 649F plate. For the special case of a dichromated gelatin recording medium, diffraction efficiencies as high as 90 percent have been achieved [62], [63], but the storage mechanism is believed to involve surface cracking rather than the internal refractive index modulation of (37) [64].

When the object of interest is a complex diffuse subject rather than a simple plane wave, the theoretical results must be modified. Upatnieks and Leonard [65] have shown that, for a diffuse object with angular subtense smaller than the angle $\Delta\psi$ of (31), the speckle effect (i.e., the granularity of the diffusely reflected or diffusely transmitted coherent light) limits the theoretically achievable diffraction efficiency to 64 percent. However, if the angular subtense of the object is greater than $\Delta\psi$, this conclusion is no longer valid, and higher diffraction efficiencies are theoretically possible. In practice, diffraction efficiencies higher than 50 percent are seldom achieved with diffuse objects.

IV. Applications of Optical Holography

In this section, various applications of holography are discussed. Attention is restricted to optical holography, since microwave and acoustic holography are covered elsewhere in this issue.

A. Interferometry

In 1965 several groups of workers discovered more or less simultaneously that holography offers important new methods for testing and measurement through interferometry [66]–[72]. While a considerable variety of techniques for holographic interferometry exists, all rest on the ability of a hologram to store and regenerate both the amplitude and phase distributions of a complex optical disturbance.

Perhaps the simplest and most fundamental technique is that called "double-exposure" holographic interferometry [73]. Let a hologram be recorded with reference wave U_r, but let the exposure take place in two steps, first with an object wave U_{01} and second

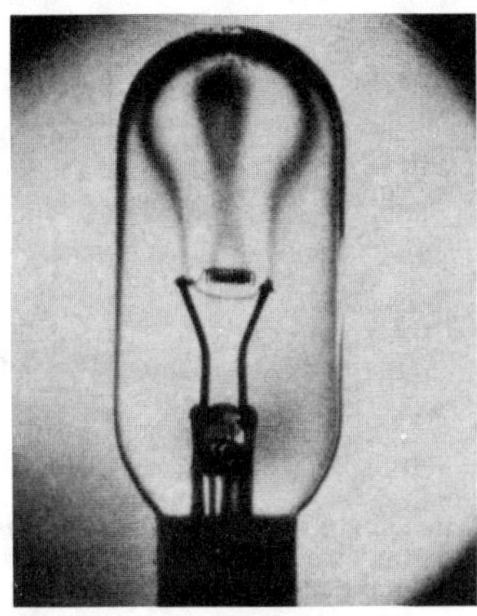

Fig. 15. Image obtained from a double-exposure hologram of a light bulb (courtesy of R. E. Brooks, L. O. Heflinger, and R. F. Wuerker).

with an object wave U_{02}. Since the exposures take place sequentially, the two interference patterns are superimposed independently on the emulsion, the effective intensity pattern being

$$I(x, y) = |U_r + U_{01}|^2\tau_1 + |U_r + U_{02}|^2\tau_2 \qquad (38)$$

where τ_1 and τ_2 are weighting factors representing the fractions of time devoted to each individual exposure. If the developed hologram is illuminated by a duplication of U_r, and if the usual conditions of linearity are satisfied, one component of the reconstructed field has the form

$$U_c' \propto |U_r|^2(U_{01}\tau_1 + U_{02}\tau_2). \qquad (39)$$

Thus a linear superposition of the two object waves is generated, and these two waves will interfere.

There are several fundamental aspects of this type of interferometry that should be noted. Most important, it is a method of *differential* interferometry, for only changes of the object wave between exposures create interference fringes. If the object under study is completely stationary, and if all conditions of object illumination are the same for the two exposures, no interference fringes are seen in the reconstructed image, for U_{01} and U_{02} are identical. If, however, the object or the medium within which it is situated are perturbed between exposures, fringes are observed in the three-dimensional space of the holographic image. From this fringe structure, much information about the perturbations can be derived. The differential nature of this process allows interferometry to be performed with low quality optical elements, and even through highly inhomogeneous structures that would otherwise preclude the use of interferometric techniques. Fig. 15 shows the interference fringes generated by a hologram exposed before and after a common light bulb has been turned on. The fringes are generated by changes of the index of refraction caused by patterns of gas flow within the glass envelope.

Two additional important properties of double-exposure holographic interfereometry are that it allows interference between two wave fields that existed at entirely different times, and even between two wave fields that have entirely different wavelengths.

The concept of double-exposure holographic interferometry is readily extended to multiple-exposure holographic interferometry, in which case three or more wave fields can be simultaneously reconstructed and caused to interfere. Generalization from multiple exposure to continuous exposure is also possible; continuous-exposure holography has found application particularly in the study of vibrating structures [66], [74].

Another variety of holographic interferometry is two-frequency holography, for which the object is illuminated by a source with two

separate frequencies and the image reconstructed with a single-frequency source. Each illumination frequency creates a separate and independent hologram; when the recording is properly illuminated, two separate wave fields are generated and interfere. Such techniques have been used for the generation of depth contours for profile measurement [68].

Finally, it is possible to perform "real-time" holographic interferometry by causing a holographic image to directly interfere with the object from which the hologram was made [70]. Deformations of the object can then be monitored in real time. Alternatively, real objects can be tested against an "ideal" object represented, for example, by a computer-generated hologram.

The reader interested in pursuing the topic of holographic interferometry will find a wealth of material in the recent optics literature (see, for example, [75], [76]).

B. High-Resolution Volume Imagery (Holographic Microscopy)

With a conventional imaging system, i.e., a system that uses lenses and/or mirrors as the image-forming elements, high transverse resolution is achieved only at the price of a limited depth of focus. Thus only a limited volume of object space can be recorded in a sharply focused image with a single photograph. On the other hand, with holography a single photographic recording can yield high-resolution images of a very large volume of object space. For example, if a hologram of a large object volume is properly illuminated, a real image of that entire object volume is formed behind the hologram. By sequentially examining the image at various distances from the hologram, the entire object volume can be searched with high transverse resolution.

The previously described property of holography has been usefully exploited in a number of applications, including the measurement of particle sizes in aerosols [77], the study of large volumes of living biological specimens [78], and in more general microscopy [79], [80]. This property is probably most important for the study of three-dimensional dynamic or transient phenomena with high resolution.

C. Imaging through Distorting Media

Because a hologram records information about the phase of an optical wave, several holographic methods for forming high-resolution images in the presence of wavefront distortions have proven possible. The first method of interest [81], [82] may be applied when the distorting medium is constant in time and movable in space. With reference to Fig. 16, suppose that a thin distorting medium with amplitude transmittance

$$t_A(\xi, \eta) = \exp\{jW(\xi, \eta)\} \qquad (40)$$

lies between the object and the recording plane. The wavefront immediately to the right of the distorting medium may be represented by $U_0(\xi, \eta) \exp\{jW(\xi, \eta)\}$, where $U_0(\xi, \eta)$ is the wavefront that would be present in the absence of the distorting medium. The distorted wavefront propagates to the recording plane, where a hologram is recorded. Let the hologram be illuminated by a wave traveling in a direction opposite to that of the reference wave, such that a real image is formed. Since the phase distribution in the real image is conjugate to that of a corresponding wave in the original object space, at the real image of the distorting medium there is a field distribution $U_0^*(\xi, \eta) \exp\{-jW(x, y)\}$. If the original distorting medium is now inserted to coincide with its real image, the field transmitted is

$$U_0^*(\xi, \eta) \exp\{-jW(\xi, \eta)\} \exp\{jW(\xi, \eta)\} = U_0^*(\xi, \eta). \qquad (41)$$

Thus the effect of the distorting medium has been cancelled, and an undistorted real image is recovered.

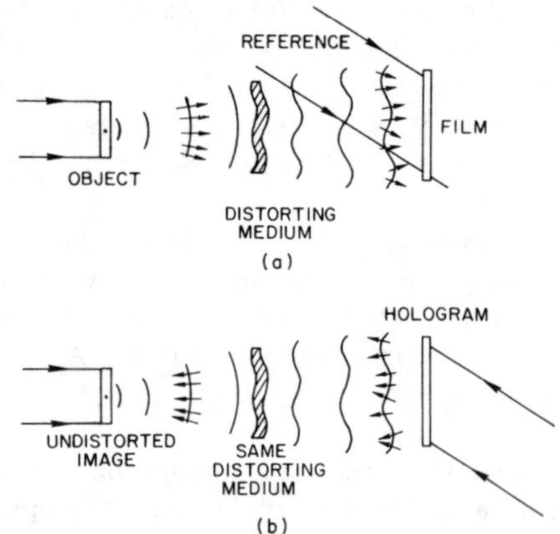

Fig. 16. Holographic imaging through a distorting medium. (a) Recording the hologram. (b) Recovering the image.

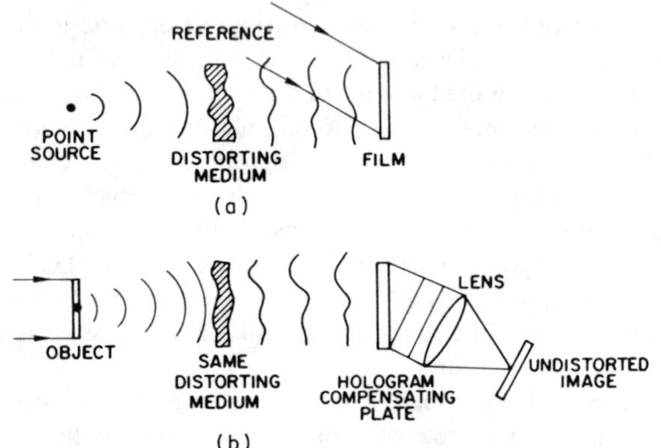

Fig. 17. Recording (a) and using (b) a hologram compensating plate.

This method clearly has potential application to the problem of storing information in a secure fashion, such that only authorized individuals (i.e., those with the correct "decoding plate") can have access to it. However, the very stringent requirements regarding precise positioning of the decoding plate pose serious practical difficulties. A somewhat simpler problem to which the idea has been successfully applied by Loth and Collins [83] is the removal of aberrations in low quality microscope objectives, the same objective being used both in recording and in reconstruction.

A second method of interest is illustrated in Fig. 17. In this case the distorting medium may be immovable, but it must be essentially unchanging in time. A hologram of a point-source object is first recorded through the distorting medium. If the wavefront incident on this hologram is exp $\{jW(x, y)\}$, then the portion of the hologram transmittance that normally contributes to a real image is exp $\{-jW(x, y)\}$. If a more general object is now to be viewed through the distorting medium, each object point generates a wavefront with distortions of the form exp $\{jW(x, y)\}$. If the object wave passes through the hologram, and if the light diffracted by the "real-image" term of the hologram transmittance is viewed, the wavefront distortions are cancelled, allowing an undistorted image to be formed by a conventional imaging system. Thus the hologram has served as a "compensating plate." This technique has been applied to the compensation of lens aberrations with some success [84].

A third and final technique, which may be applied to movable or immovable and time-invariant or time-varying distortions is illustrated in Fig. 18. In this case both the reference and object waves pass through the distorting medium [85]. If the reference and object are not too widely separated, the distortions of both the object and reference wavefronts are identical. Interference of the two identically distorted wavefronts yields a hologram that is free from distortions

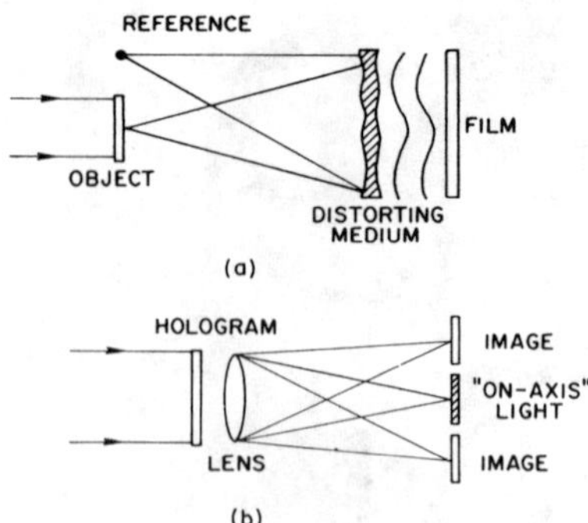

Fig. 18. Holographic imaging through a distorting medium, reference, and object waves both passing through the distorting medium. (a) Recording the hologram. (b) Obtaining images.

and from which a high quality image can be obtained. Application of this method to the problem of imaging through atmospheric inhomogeneities has been investigated [86], [87], and some improvement of image quality has been observed with holography over long paths through the atmosphere [88].

D. Holograms as Optical Elements

Holograms have been found useful in a number of specialized applications as optical elements, playing the role of specialized lenses or gratings. A hologram of a point-source object is basically a focusing element which in many respects behaves like a lens. The obvious advantages of a hologram in this respect are that it can be more lightweight and compact than a lens. A less obvious advantage in some applications follows from the fact that holograms can be physically overlapped in the emulsion, whereas two lenses cannot physically overlap. Thus a holographic "fly's-eye" lens can have elements that are larger than the element-to-element spacing, and therefore can achieve higher resolution than might otherwise be possible. A chief disadvantage of holographic elements of this kind is their very large chromatic aberration.

Holographic lenses have found application as focusing elements in the page composer of a holographic memory [89]. Holographic gratings have been used both for spectral analysis [90] and for coupling light waves into thin films [91]. In addition, a holographic element has been used to produce line scanning in a unique scanner [92].

E. Holograms in Coherent Optical Data Processing Systems

While a complete and detailed review of the broad field of coherent optical data processing is beyond the scope of this paper, some attention will be devoted to the important role holographic techniques can play in such systems. More detailed reviews of this field can be found in the literature [6], [93]–[96].

Coherent optical data processing systems depend on the ability of simple positive (i.e., converging) lens to perform a two-dimensional Fourier transformation of a coherent field distribution impressed across its front focal plane. More specifically, if a complex amplitude distribution $U_0(x_0, y_0)$ is impressed across the front focal plane (coordinates x_0, y_0) of a positive lens of focal length f, then across the rear focal plane (coordinates x_f, y_f) there will appear a field distribution

$$U_f(x_f, y_f) = \frac{1}{\lambda f} \int\int_{-\infty}^{\infty} U_0(x_0, y_0)$$

$$\cdot \exp\left\{-j\frac{2\pi}{\lambda f}(x_0 x_f + y_0 y_f)\right\}dx_0\, dy_0. \quad (42)$$

If two such lenses are separated by a distance $2f$, as shown in Fig. 19, then the lens L_1 displays the Fourier spectrum of the input

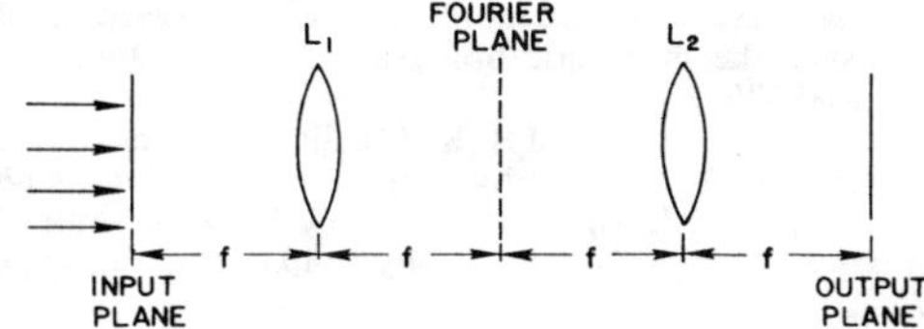

Fig. 19.   A simple coherent optical data processing system.

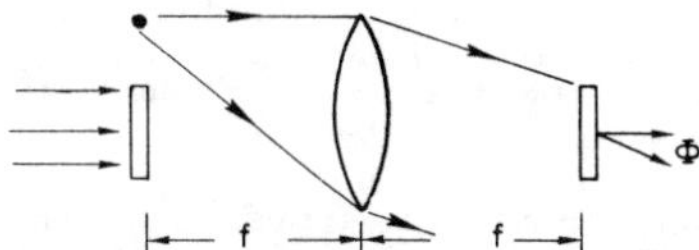

Fig. 20.   Recording an interferometrically generated spatial filter.

transparency in the Fourier plane, where the spectral components can be modified in amplitude and/or phase, and the lens L_2 performs a second transformation to yield a linearly filtered image of the original input. If a linear filtering operation with two-dimensional transfer function $H(f_X, f_Y)$ is desired, this operation can be realized by placing in the Fourier plane a transparency with amplitude transmittance proportional to H, i.e.,

$$t_A(x_f, y_f) \propto H\left(\frac{x_f}{\lambda f}, \frac{y_f}{\lambda f}\right). \tag{43}$$

A major practical problem encountered in the realization of such filtering systems arises from the necessity to control *both* the amplitude and the phase transmission through the focal plane with complicated but related distributions. Major advances in this regard were made by Kozma and Kelly [97] by introducing the use of carrier frequency transparencies and by Vander Lugt [98] by introducing the interferometrically generated (or holographic) frequency-plane filter. If it is desired to synthesize an optical filtering system with a particular impulse response h, the required frequency plane filter may be generated with the recording system illustrated in Fig. 20. A transparency with amplitude transmittance proportional to h (which is often of simple form in practice) is introduced in the front focal plane of the transforming lens. Incident on the photographic emulsion in the rear focal plane of the lens is the sum of a plane wave inclined at angle Φ to the normal (analogous to the reference wave of holography) and a wave with amplitude distribution proportional to $H(x_f/\lambda f, y_f/\lambda f)$, where H is the desired transfer function. Assuming that the amplitude transmittance of the developed transparency can be made proportional to the intensity of the exposing light, we have

$$t_A(x_f, y_f) \propto \left| \exp\left(-j2\pi\alpha y_f\right) + H\left(\frac{x_f}{\lambda f}, \frac{y_f}{\lambda f}\right) \right|^2$$

$$= 1 + |H|^2 + H \exp\left(j2\pi\alpha y_f\right) + H^* \exp\left(-j2\pi\alpha y_f\right) \tag{44}$$

where $\alpha = \sin \Phi/\lambda$. If this transparency is inserted in the frequency plane of the coherent processing system of Fig. 19, at the output several different distributions of light appear. About the optical axis there appears an image of the input transparency which has been filtered by a transfer function $1 + |H|^2$. This output term is generally not of interest. Deflected to opposite sides of the output plane are two additional images, one filtered by transfer function H and the second by transfer function H^*. If the spatial frequency α is chosen sufficiently high, the three distributions are physically separated in space, and by choosing the proper region of the output plane the experimenter can realize a transfer function H or H^*, as he may desire.

The significance of the holographic frequency-plane filter is that, due to the spatial carrier frequency introduced, it allows effective control over both the amplitude and the phase of the transfer function by means of a purely absorbing frequency-plane transparency. True simultaneous control of amplitude and phase transmission through the frequency plane is therefore not required when this type of filter is used. This property has led to a considerable extension of the types of problems to which coherent optical data processing systems can be applied.

An important byproduct of the interferometric approach to filter generation is the presence of the term H^* in (44). Since this is precisely the transfer function of a filter "matched" to the signal h [99], matched filter detection and recognition systems can readily be synthesized optically [98], [100]. In addition, by sandwiching an interferometrically generated filter transparency with a second transparency with amplitude transmittance proportional to $|H|^{-2}$, a new filter can readily be generated [101] such that its transfer function G is given by

$$G = \frac{H^*}{|H|^2} = \frac{1}{H}. \tag{45}$$

Thus G is an inverse filter and may be used, for example, for image deblurring [102].

F. Holographic Data Storage and Retrieval Systems

Of the various applications of holography that have been proposed, those with the greatest potential for wide-spread commercial use are undoubtedly in the data storage field. Examples include the use of holography for the storage of TV program material in vinyl tape cassettes [27], holographic read-only memories for storage of digital data [103]–[105], holographic storage of consumer credit status for credit verification purposes [106], and the use of holography in a microfiche system [107].

There are a multitude of reasons for considering holography as a means for data storage, particularly for high-density storage. Most widely mentioned, perhaps, is the highly redundant nature of a holographic recording. If a portion of the hologram is obliterated by a dust speck or a scratch, there need be no localized loss of information, for the entire image can still be recovered, albeit with some small loss of resolution. For applications requiring the storage and recovery of visual data, this type of protection can be extremely valuable. For applications involving the storage of digital data, similar protection can be provided by direct image storage using error correcting codes [108], probably with more efficient use of the resolvable spots available on the recording medium. However, the advantage of holography in this case lies with the extreme simplicity of the "decoding" operations: the stored data are recovered at the speed of light with no decoding computations required.

A second important advantage of holography, particularly in a high-density storage system, comes from the ability to obtain high magnification of the image data without a corresponding magnification of the registration errors. This property is most pronounced when the hologram is recorded using a reference point source that lies coplanar with the object data to be stored. For this so-called "lensless Fourier transform" recording geometry, the image obtained from the hologram suffers absolutely no motion as the hologram is translated in the reading beam, yet the magnification can be high in the sense that a large image can be obtained from a tiny hologram. Closely related to this insensitivity to translational movement is an insensitivity to the movement of the hologram along the optical axis, a property not shared by conventional imaging systems operating with similar magnifications.

With respect to the storage of digital data in a read-only holographic memory, a page-organized memory storing 10^8 bits with an access time of 1 μs to a single page of 10^4 bits appears feasible [105]. Efforts are underway to attempt to find suitable materials for a read-write memory [29], [31], but at this early stage it is difficult to judge the likelihood of success in this regard. Mention should also be made of a recent proposal for an associative memory based on holographic techniques [109].

Ultimately, of course, the success of holographic data storage systems will rest on economic questions. Can the data be stored holographically with less cost than offered by an alternative approach with similar performance? At present there are considerable grounds for optimism in this regard. However, the future will depend not only on advances in holography but also on advances in other competitive areas of technology.

REFERENCES

[1] D. Gabor, "A new microscope principle," *Nature*, vol. 161, May 1948, pp. 777–778.

[2] ——, "Microscopy by reconstructed wavefronts," *Proc. Roy. Soc., Ser. A*, vol. 197, July 1949, pp. 454–487.

[3] ——, "Microscopy by reconstructed wavefronts: II," *Proc. Phys. Soc. London* (Gen.), vol. 64, June 1951, pp. 449–469.

[4] D. Gabor and W. P. Goss, "Interference microscope with total wavefront reconstruction," *J. Opt. Soc. Am.*, vol. 56, July 1966, pp. 849–858.

[5] E. N. Leith and J. Upatnieks, "Reconstructed wavefronts and communication theory," *J. Opt. Soc. Am.*, vol. 52, Oct. 1962, pp. 1123–1130.

[6] L. J. Cutrona, E. N. Leith, C. J. Palermo, and L. J. Porcello, "Optical data processing and filtering systems," *IRE Trans. Inform. Theory*, vol. IT-6, June 1960, pp. 386–400.

[7] L. J. Cutrona, E. N. Leith, L. J. Porcello, and W. E. Vivian, "On the application of coherent optical processing techniques to synthetic-aperture radar," *Proc. IEEE*, vol. 54, Aug. 1966, pp. 1026–1032.

[8] E. N. Leith, "Optical processing techniques for simultaneous pulse compression and beam sharpening," *IEEE Trans. Aerosp. Electron. Syst.*, vol. AES-4, Nov. 1968, pp. 879–885.

[9] E. N. Leith and A. L. Ingalls, "Synthetic antenna data processing by wavefront reconstruction," *Appl. Opt.*, vol. 7, Mar. 1968, pp. 539–544.

[10] R. O. Harger, *Synthetic Aperture Radar Systems: Theory and Design.* New York: Academic Press, 1970.

[11] A. Lohmann, "Optical single-sideband transmission applied to the Gabor microscope," *Opt. Acta*, vol. 3, June 1956, pp. 97–99.

[12] E. N. Leith and J. Upatnieks, "Wavefront reconstruction with continuous-tone objects," *J. Opt. Soc. Am.*, vol. 53, Dec. 1963, pp. 1377–1381.

[13] ——, "Wavefront reconstruction with diffused illumination and three-dimensional objects," *J. Opt. Soc. Am.*, vol. 54, Nov. 1964, pp. 1295–1301.

[14] ——, "Photography by laser," *Sci. Amer.*, vol. 212, June 1965, pp. 24–35.

[15] E. N. Leith, A. Kozma, J. Upatnieks, J. Marks, and N. Massey, "Holographic data storage in three-dimensional media," *Appl. Opt.*, vol. 5, Aug. 1966, pp. 1303–1311.

[16] G. W. Stroke, *An Introduction to Coherent Optics and Holography.* New York: Academic Press, 1966.

[17] J. B. De Velis and G. O. Reynolds, *Theory and Applications of Holography.* Reading, Mass.: Addison-Wesley, 1967.

[18] H. M. Smith, *Principles of Holography.* New York: Wiley, 1969.

[19] H. J. Caulfield and S. Lu, *The Applications of Holography.* New York: Wiley, 1970.

[20] R. J. Collier, L. Lin, and C. Burckhardt, *Optical Holography.* New York: Academic Press, 1971.

[21] R. J. Collier, "Some current views on holography," *IEEE Spectrum*, vol. 3, July 1966, pp. 67–74.

[22] E. N. Leith and J. Upatnieks, "Recent advances in holography," in *Progress in Optics*, vol. 11, E. Wolf, Ed. Amsterdam: North-Holland, 1967.

[23] J. C. Urbach and R. W. Meir, "Properties and limitations of hologram recording materials," *Appl. Opt.*, vol. 8, Nov. 1969, pp. 2269–2281.

[24] A. W. Lohmann, "Reconstruction of vectorial wavefronts," *Appl. Opt.*, vol. 4, Dec. 1965, pp. 1667–1668.

[25] H. W. Rose, T. L. Williamson, and S. A. Collins, Jr., "Polarization effects in holography," *Appl. Opt.*, vol. 9, Oct. 1970, pp. 2394–2396.

[26] C. B. Burckhardt, "Diffraction of a plane wave at a sinusoidally stratified dielectric grating," *J. Opt. Soc. Am.*, vol. 56, Nov. 1966, pp. 1502–1509.

[27] R. Bartoline, W. Hannan, D. Karlsons, and M. Lurie, "Embossed hologram motion pictures for television playback," *Appl. Opt.*, vol. 9, Oct. 1970, pp. 2283–2290.

[28] J. C. Urbach and R. W. Meier, "Thermoplastic xerographic holography," *Appl. Opt.*, vol. 5, Apr. 1966, p. 666–667.

[29] L. H. Lin and H. L. Beauchamp, "Write-read-erase in situ optical memory using thermoplastic holograms," *Appl. Opt.*, vol. 9, Sept. 1970, pp. 2088–2092.

[30] H. R. Farrah, E. Marom, and R. K. Mueller, "An underwater viewing system using sound holography," in *Acoustical Holography*, vol. 2, A. Metherell and L. Larmore, Eds. New York: Plenum, 1970.

[31] R. S. Mezrich, "Magnetic holography," *Appl. Opt.*, vol. 9, Oct. 1970, pp. 2275–2279.

[32] J. A. Jenny, "Holographic recording with photopolymers," *J. Opt. Soc. Am.*, vol. 60, Sept. 1970, pp. 1155–1161.

[33] A. A. Friesem and J. L. Walker, "Thick absorption recording media in holography," *Appl. Opt.*, vol. 9, Jan. 1970, pp. 201–214.

[34] R. W. Meier, "Magnification and third-order aberrations in holography," *J. Opt. Soc. Am.*, vol. 55, Aug. 1965, pp. 987–992.

[35] E. N. Leith, J. Upatnieks, and K. A. Haines, "Microscopy by wavefront reconstruction," *J. Opt. Soc. Am.*, vol. 55, Aug. 1965, pp. 981–986.

[36] J. A. Armstrong, "Fresnel holograms: Their imaging properties and aberrations," *IBM J. Res. Develop.*, vol. 9, May 1965, pp. 171–178.

[37] E. B. Champagne, "Nonparaxial imaging magnification and aberration properties in holography," *J. Opt. Soc. Am.*, vol. 57, Jan. 1967, pp. 51–55.

[38] J. R. Klauder, A. C. Price, S. Darlington, and W. J. Alberscheim, "The theory and design of chirp radars," *Bell Syst. Tech. J.*, vol. 39, July 1960, pp. 745–808.

[39] A. W. Rihaczek, *Principles of High-Resolution Radar.* New York: McGraw-Hill, 1969.

[40] G. L. Rogers, "Gabor diffraction microscopy: The hologram as a generalized zone-plate," *Nature*, vol. 166, Aug. 1950, p. 237.

[41] W. Kock, *Lasers and Holography.* Garden City, N. Y.: Doubleday, 1968.

[42] H. M. A. El-Sum, "Reconstructed wavefront microscopy," Ph.D. dissertation, Dept. of Physics, Stanford University, Stanford, Calif., 1952 (available from University Microfilm, Inc., Ann Arbor, Mich.).

[43] J. D. Rigden and E. I. Gordon, "The granularity of scattered optical maser light," *Proc. IRE* (Corresp.), vol. 50, Nov. 1962, pp. 2367–2368.

[44] P. S. Considine, "Effects of coherence on imaging systems," *J. Opt. Soc. Am.*, vol. 56, Aug. 1966, pp. 1001–1009.

[45] E. N. Leith and J. Upatnieks, "Imagery with pseudo-randomly diffused coherent illumination," *Appl. Opt.*, vol. 7, Oct. 1968, pp. 2085–2089.

[46] H. J. Gerritsen, W. J. Hannan, and E. G. Ramberg, "Elimination of speckle noise in holograms with redundancy," *Appl. Opt.*, vol. 7, Nov. 1968, pp. 2301–2311.

[47] C. B. Burckhardt, "Use of a random phase mask for the recording of Fourier transform holograms of data masks," *Appl. Opt.*, vol. 9, Mar. 1970, pp. 695–700.

[48] H. Kogelnik, "Response and efficiency of five hologram types," in *Modern Optics*, J. Fox, Ed. Brooklyn, N. Y.: Polytechnic Press, 1967.

[49] ——, "Coupled wave theory for thick hologram gratings," *Bell Syst. Tech. J.*, vol. 48, Nov. 1969, pp. 2909–2947.

[50] Y. N. Denisyuk, "Photographic reconstruction of the optical properties of an object in its own scattered radiation field," *Sov. Phys.—Dokl.*, vol. 7, Dec. 1962, pp. 543–545.

[51] P. J. van Heerden, "A new optical method of storing and retrieving information," *Appl. Opt.*, vol. 2, Apr. 1963, pp. 387–392.

[52] L. H. Lin, K. S. Pennington, G. W. Stroke, and A. E. Labeyrie, "Multicolor holographic image reconstruction with white-light illumination," *Bell Syst. Tech. J.*, vol. 45, Apr. 1966, pp. 659–660.

[53] D. Gabor and G. W. Stroke, "The theory of deep holograms," *Proc. Roy. Soc., Ser. A*, vol. 304, Apr. 1968, pp. 275–289.

[54] H. M. Smith, "Photographic relief images," *J. Opt. Soc. Am.*, vol. 58, Apr. 1968, pp. 533–539.

[55] A. K. Rigler, "Wavefront reconstruction by reflection," *J. Opt. Soc. Am.*, vol. 55, Dec. 1965, p. 1693.

[56] J. C. Urbach, private communication.

[57] G. W. Stroke and A. Labeyrie, "White-light reconstruction of holographic images using the Lippmann-Bragg diffraction effect," *Phys. Lett.*, vol. 20, Mar. 1966, pp. 368–370.

[58] W. T. Cathey, Jr., "Three-dimensional wavefront reconstruction using a phase hologram," *J. Opt. Soc. Am.*, vol. 55, Apr. 1965, p. 457.

[59] G. L. Rogers, "Experiments in diffraction microscopy," *Proc. Roy. Soc., Ser. A* (Edinburgh), vol. 63, Feb. 1952, pp. 193–221.

[60] N. K. Sheridon, "Production of blazed hologram," *Appl. Phys. Lett.*, vol. 12, May 1968, pp. 316–320.

[61] D. Kermisch, "Wavefront-reconstruction mechanism in blazed holograms," *J. Opt. Soc. Am.*, vol. 60, June 1970, pp. 782–786.

[62] T. A. Shankoff, "Phase holograms in dichromated gelatin," *Appl. Opt.*, vol. 7, Oct. 1968, pp. 2101–2105.

[63] L. H. Lin, "Hologram formation in hardened dichromated gelatin films," *Appl. Opt.*, vol. 8, May 1969, pp. 963–966.

[64] R. K. Curran and T. A. Shankoff, "The mechanism of hologram formation in dichromated gelatin," *Appl. Opt.*, vol. 9, July 1970, pp. 1651–1657.

[65] J. Upatnieks and C. Leonard, "Efficiency and image contrast of dielectric holograms," *J. Opt. Soc. Am.*, vol. 60, Mar. 1970, pp. 297–305.

[66] R. L. Powell and K. A. Stetson, "Interferometric vibration analysis by wavefront reconstruction," *J. Opt. Soc. Am.*, vol. 55, Dec. 1965, pp. 1593–1598.

[67] R. E. Brooks, L. O. Heflinger, and R. F. Wuerker, "Interferometry with a holographically reconstructed comparison beam," *Appl. Phys. Lett.*, vol. 7, Nov. 1965, pp. 248–249.

[68] B. P. Hildebrand and K. A. Haines, "Multiple-wavelength and multiple-source holography applied to contour generation," *J. Opt. Soc. Am.*, vol. 57, Feb. 1967, pp. 155–162.

[69] J. M. Burch, "The application of lasers in production engineering," *Prod. Eng.*, vol. 44, Sept. 1965, pp. 431–442.

[70] R. J. Collier, E. T. Doherty, and K. S. Pennington, "Application of moire techniques to holography," *Appl. Phys. Lett.*, vol. 7, Oct. 1965, pp. 223–225.

[71] M. H. Horman, "Application of wavefront reconstruction to interferometry," *J. Opt. Soc. Am.*, vol. 55, May 1965, p. 615.

[72] D. Gabor, G. W. Stroke, R. Restrick, A. Funkhouser, and D. Brumm, "Optical image synthesis (complex amplitude addition and subtraction) by holographic Fourier transformation," *Phys. Lett.*, vol. 18, Aug. 1965, pp. 116–118.

[73] L. O. Heflinger, R. F. Wuerker, and R. E. Brooks, "Holographic interferometry," *J. Appl. Phys.*, vol. 37, Feb. 1966, pp. 642–649.

[74] C. C. Aleksoff, "Temporally modulated holography," *Appl. Opt.*, vol. 10, June 1971, pp. 1329–1341.

[75] E. R. Robertson and J. M. Harvey, Eds., *The Engineering Uses of Holography.* Cambridge: Cambridge University Press, 1970.

[76] B. Ragent and R. M. Brown, Eds., "Holographic instrumentation applications," NASA Rep. SP-248, 1970.

[77] B. J. Thompson, J. H. Ward, and W. R. Zinky, "Application of hologram techniques for particle size analysis," *Appl. Opt.*, vol. 6, Mar. 1967, pp. 519–526.

[78] C. Knox, "Holographic microscopy as a technique for recording dynamic microscopic subjects," *Science*, vol. 153, Aug. 1966, pp. 989–990.

[79] R. F. van Ligten, "Holographic microscopy," in *Holography Seminar Proc.* Redondo Beach, Calif.: Soc. Photo-Optical Instrum. Engineers, 1968.

[80] M. E. Cox, R. G. Buckles, and D. Whitlow, "Cineholomicroscopy of small animal microcirculation," *Appl. Opt.*, vol. 10, Jan. 1971, pp. 128–131.

[81] E. N. Leith and J. Upatnieks, "Holographic imagery through diffusing media," *J. Opt. Soc. Am.*, vol. 56, Apr. 1966, p. 523.

[82] H. Kogelnik, "Holographic image projection through inhomogeneous media," *Bell Syst. Tech. J.*, vol. 44, Oct. 1965, pp. 2451–2455.

[83] L. Toth and S. A. Collins, "Reconstruction of a three-dimensional microscopic sample using holographic techniques," *Appl. Phys. Lett.*, vol. 13, July 1968, pp. 7–9.

[84] J. Upatnieks, A. Vander Lugt, and E. Leith, "Correction of lens aberrations by means of holograms," *Appl. Opt.*, vol. 5, Apr. 1966, pp. 589–593.

[85] J. W. Goodman, W. H. Huntley, Jr., D. W. Jackson, and M. Lehmann, "Wavefront-reconstruction imaging through random media," *Appl. Phys. Lett.*, vol. 8, June 1966, pp. 311–313.

[86] J. D. Gaskill, "Imaging through a randomly inhomogeneous medium by wavefront reconstruction," *J. Opt. Soc. Am.*, vol. 58, May 1968, pp. 600–608.

[87] ——, "Atmospheric degradation of holographic images," *J. Opt. Soc. Am.*, vol. 59, Mar. 1969, pp. 308–318.

[88] J. W. Goodman, D. W. Jackson, M. Lehmann, and J. Knotts, "Experiments in long-distance holographic imagery," *Appl. Opt.*, vol. 8, Aug. 1969, pp. 1581–1586.

[89] W. C. Stewart and L. S. Cosentino, "Optics for a read-write holographic memory," *Appl. Opt.*, vol. 9, Oct. 1970, pp. 2271–2275.

[90] J. Cordelle, J. Flammand, G. Pieuchard, and A. Labeyrie, "Aberration-corrected concave gratings made holographically," in *Optical Instruments and Techniques*, J. H. Dickson, Ed. Newcastle-on-Tyne, England: Oriel Press, 1970.

[91] H. Kogelnik and T. P. Sosnowski, "Thin-film coupling with holographic Bragg gratings," *J. Opt. Soc. Am.*, vol. 60, Nov. 1970, p. 1543.

[92] D. H. McMahon, A. R. Franklin, and J. B. Thaxter, "Light beam deflection using holographic scanning techniques," *Appl. Opt.*, vol. 8, Feb. 1969, pp. 399–402.

[93] E. L. O'Neill, "Spatial filtering in optics," *IRE Trans. Inform. Theory*, vol. IT-2, June 1956, pp. 56–65.

[94] A. B. Vander Lugt, "A review of optical data-processing techniques," *Opt. Acta*, vol. 15, Jan.–Feb. 1968, pp. 1–34.

[95] A. R. Shulman, *Optical Data Processing.* New York: Wiley, 1970.

[96] J. W. Goodman, *Introduction to Fourier Optics.* New York: McGraw-Hill, 1968, ch. 7.

[97] A. Kozma and D. L. Kelly, "Spatial filtering for detection of signals submerged in noise," *Appl. Opt.*, vol. 4, Apr. 1965, pp. 387–392.

[98] A. Vander Lugt, "Signal detection by complex spatial filtering," *IEEE Trans. Inform. Theory*, vol. IT-10, Apr. 1964, pp. 139–145.

[99] G. L. Turin, "An introduction to matched filters," *IRE Trans. Inform. Theory*, vol. IT-6, June 1960, pp. 311–329.

[100] A. B. Vander Lugt, F. B. Rotz, and A. Klooster, Jr., "Character reading by optical spatial filtering," in *Optical and Electro-Optical Information Processing*, J. T. Tippett, D. A. Berkowitz, L. C. Clapp, C. J. Koester, and A. Vanderburg, Jr., Eds. Cambridge, Mass.: M.I.T. Press, 1965, ch. 7.

[101] G. W. Stroke, "A new holographic method for a posteriori image-deblurring restoration of ordinary photographs using 'extended-source' lensless Fourier-transform holography compensation," *Phys. Lett.*, vol. 27a, Aug. 1968, pp. 405–406.

[102] ——, "Image deblurring and aperture synthesis using a posteriori processing by Fourier transform holography," *Opt. Acta*, vol. 16, July–Aug. 1969, pp. 401–422.

[103] J. A. Rajchman, "Promise of optical memories," *J. Appl. Phys.*, vol. 41, Mar. 1970, pp. 1376–1383.

[104] ——, "An optical read-write mass memory," *Appl. Opt.*, vol. 9, Oct. 1970, pp. 2269–2271.

[105] L. K. Anderson, "High capacity holographic optical memory," *Microwaves*, vol. 9, Mar. 1970, pp. 62–66.

[106] E. H. Chrysty and K. K. Sutherlin, "Validating credit cards using holography," *1970 IEEE Int. Conv. Dig.* (New York, March 23–26), pp. 338–339.

[107] A. A. Friesem, E. N. Tompkins, and G. E. Hoffmann, "Holographic application in high density document storage and retrieval," presented at 15th Ann. Technical Symp. Society of Photo-Optical Instrum. Engineers, Los Angeles, Calif., Sept. 1970.

[108] I. B. Oldham, R. T. Chien, and D. T. Tang, "Error detection and correction in a photo-digital memory system," *IBM J. Res. Develop.*, vol. 12, Nov. 1968, pp. 422–430.

[109] M. Sakaguchi, N. Nishida, and T. Nemoto, "A new associative memory system utilizing holography," *IEEE Trans. Comput.*, vol. C-19, Dec. 1970, pp. 1174–1181.

Quasi-Holographic Techniques in the Microwave Region

EMMETT N. LEITH, FELLOW, IEEE

Invited Paper

Abstract—Various microwave processes, including synthetic-aperture radar and linearly frequency-modulated pulse compression, are described as analogs of holography. The holographic viewpoint often leads to a new understanding and to new methods of signal processing.

I. Introduction

FOLLOWING the intensification of holographic activity in the 1960s, various researchers reported experiments that were direct microwave counterparts of the optical holography which preceded them [1]–[3]. This work, which has by no means been extensive, may be termed true microwave holography. As the title of our paper implies, we deal not with this rather restrictive field, but with a much broader one which embodies holographic-like techniques. With the broader license we gain access to a rather large body of material, of which we must discard all but a select portion.

There exists in the field of communication science a variety of techniques that resemble holography to various degrees, both in concept and in their mathematical formulation. Further, when these processes are carried out with the aid of coherent optical systems, the resemblance to holography becomes striking indeed. Yet these processes have developed quite independently of holography and in no way depend upon principles originating in holography.

We select four such techniques for our discussion: the synthetic aperture, the chirp radar, the rotating-target-imaging system, and the beam-forming technique. Each in its own way resembles holography, and viewing them as holographic processes offers, in some cases, new insights that lead to new implementations. The first three constitute special cases of the range-Doppler radar system, so we begin by introducing this rather basic system concept.

II. The Range-Doppler Principle

In the range-Doppler radar system, shown in Fig. 1, the task is to measure the range, radial velocity, and relative reflectivity of a distribution of scatterers. A wave

$$f(t) = a(t) \exp j[\omega_0 t + \phi(t)] \tag{1}$$

is radiated: $f_0 = \omega_0/2\pi$ is the RF carrier frequency and a and ϕ are, respectively, the amplitude and phase modulations impressed on the wave. A point object at range r returns to the radar a signal,

$$g(t) = \sigma f\left(t - \frac{2r}{c}\right) = \sigma a\left(t - \frac{2r}{c}\right) \exp j\left[\omega_0\left(t - \frac{2r}{c}\right) + \phi\left(t - \frac{2r}{c}\right)\right] \tag{2}$$

which is just the radiated signal time delayed and Doppler shifted; σ is a complex constant containing such factors as the complex reflectivity of the object and the attenuation with distance which, in the radar case, because of the round trip factor, becomes the inverse fourth-power factor. The Doppler shift is implicit in the variable r,

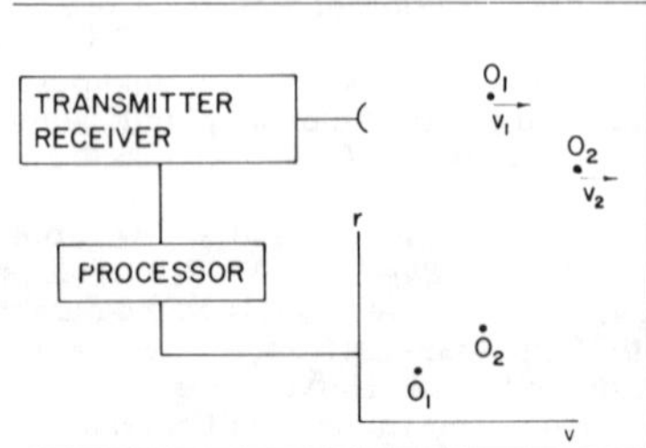

Fig. 1. Pulse-Doppler radar, showing two point objects imaged in a range-velocity display. Ranges are r_1 and r_2, radial velocities are v_1 and v_2.

which is a time-varying function. Let the radial velocity be v_1, which for simplicity we suppose to be constant; thus

$$r = r_1 + v_1 t \tag{3}$$

where r_1 is the range at time $t=0$. We insert (3) into (2) and make the customary narrow-band approximations[1]

$$a\left[t - \frac{2(r_1 + v_1 t)}{c}\right] \cong a\left(t - \frac{2r_1}{c}\right) \tag{4a}$$

$$\phi\left[t - \frac{2(r_1 + v_1 t)}{c}\right] \cong \phi\left(t - \frac{2r_1}{c}\right). \tag{4b}$$

The return signal $g(t)$ is then

$$
\begin{aligned}
g(t) &= \sigma a\left(t - \frac{2r_1}{c}\right) \exp j\left[\omega_0\left(t - \frac{2r_1}{c} - \frac{2v_1 t}{c}\right) + \phi(t) - \frac{2r_1}{c}\right] \\
&= \sigma a\left(t - \frac{2r_1}{c}\right) \exp j\left[\left(\omega_0 - \frac{4\pi v_1}{\lambda_0}\right)t + \phi\left(t - \frac{2r_1}{c}\right) - \frac{4\pi}{\lambda_0} r_1\right] \\
&= \sigma f\left(t - \frac{2r_1}{c}\right) \exp\left(-j \frac{4\pi v_1}{\lambda_0} t\right)
\end{aligned} \tag{5}
$$

where the bulk phase delay $\exp -j(4\pi r_1/\lambda_0)$ has been incorporated into σ. The round trip delay time $2r_1/c$ can be written as t_1, while the term $4\pi v_1/\lambda_0$ is a Doppler shift which we represent as ω_{d1}. Measurements are made of both the time delay and the Doppler shift, from which the range and the radial velocity are readily determined. One of the fundamental problems, then, is to determine optimum forms for $f(t)$ since our ability to make these measurements is strongly dependent on the form of this signal.

The range-Doppler measurement is performed by cross correlating the return signal with a reference function

$$r_c(t) = f(t) \exp(-j\omega_r t) \tag{6}$$

which is a frequency-shifted replica of the radiated pulse, yielding

---

Manuscript received March 4, 1971; revised May 28, 1971. *This invited paper is one of a series planned on topics of general interest—The Editor.* The author is with the University of Michigan, Ann Arbor, Mich. 48104.

[1] If a and ϕ are narrow-band functions, centered about zero frequency, then in a short time interval $(2v_1/c)^t$, these functions will have changed negligibly even though the RF carrier term $\exp (j\omega_0 t)$ may have changed considerably.

Reprinted from *Proc. IEEE*, vol. 59, pp. 1305–1318, Sept. 1971.

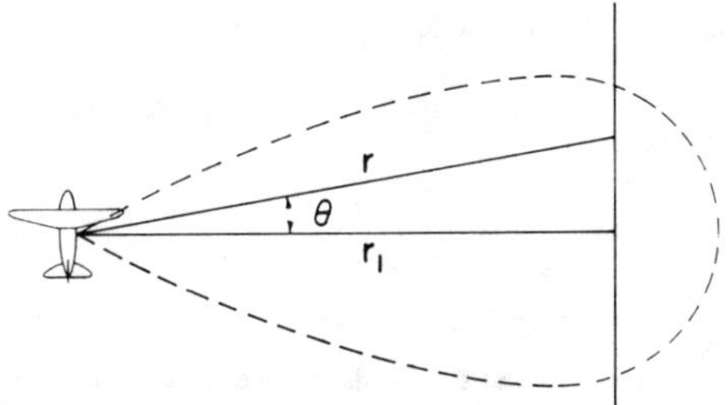

Fig. 2.   Synthetic-aperture geometry.

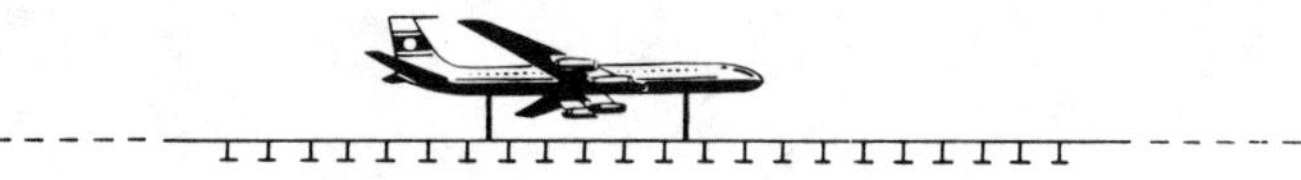

Fig. 3.   An aircraft utilizing a real antenna which achieves the resolution of a synthetic antenna.

$$u(t_r, \omega_r) = r_c \circledast g$$

$$= \sigma \exp(j\omega_r t_r) \int f(t - t_r) f^*(t - t_1)$$

$$\cdot \exp\left[-j(\omega_r - \omega_{d1})t\right] dt \qquad (7)$$

where $\circledast$ represents the cross-correlation operation. This equation is readily placed in the standard form

$$|u(\tau', w')|^2 = |\sigma|^2 \left| \int f(t' + \tau') f^*(t') \exp(-j\omega' t') \, dt' \right|^2 \qquad (8)$$

by the substitutions $t' = t - t_1$, $\tau' = t_1 - t_r$, and $\omega' = \omega_r - \omega_{d1}$. Equation (8) is known as the ambiguity function of f. The ambiguity function, somewhat analogous to an impulse response or a point-spread function, describes how the system images the object field into a two-dimensional range-Doppler space. The waveform $f(t)$ is designed to give an ambiguity function with a sharp peak at $\tau' = \omega' = 0$ with low secondary responses. There are limitations to how well this can be achieved. Note that when there are no Doppler shifts, the ambiguity function becomes just the magnitude squared of the autocorrelation function.

The similarity to holography is evident: simultaneously within the radar wave detected at the receiver may be many superimposed signals, originating from a range-velocity object space, and the requirement is to unscramble the signals and thereby reconstruct the original object space. The correlation operation accomplishes this, displaying each object point as a response in a τ_r, ω_r space, centered about the original location t_1, ω_{d1}. When the data are stored in a manner such that they can be interrogated with light, and when the range-Doppler analysis is carried out by coherent optical-processing techniques, the resemblance to holography becomes strong. In some of the specific instances to be discussed the holographic analogy is stronger yet.

III. The Synthetic Antenna

In the synthetic-aperture technique, a special case of range-Doppler radar, the Doppler shifts are generated primarily by the motion of the radar platform. The system can be described in a variety of ways, with each offering its own special insight into the process. Here we view the process in three rather different ways: as a somewhat modified range-Doppler system; as a synthetic antenna; and finally, as holography.

The radar may be carried by an airplane or, equally well, by any other relatively fast-moving vehicle. In the usual embodiment, shown in Fig. 2, the antenna is mounted in a sidelooking configuration, although this is by no means always the case. The radial velocity between an object point and the radar is proportional to the sine of the bearing angle θ of the point. Thus at any instant there is a one-to-one correspondence between Doppler shift and position in the beam. The Doppler analysis thus yields resolution in the along-track dimension, and a range-Doppler display becomes an image of the object field over which the beam passes.

In general, the Doppler analysis provides azimuth resolution

considerably better than that produced by the angular extent of the beam so that, at any range r_1 a large number of object positions simultaneously in the beam can be resolved. If we compare this situation with conventional radar, wherein azimuth resolution is just the beamwidth, the resulting image seems to have been produced by a radar system having a narrower beam, hence a longer antenna, than is actually the case. This observation leads to the synthetic-antenna concept.

A long receiving antenna yielding resolution comparable to the Doppler processing technique could, indeed, be a very long antenna. It would have a length equal to the distance that our platform moves during the time that a signal is received from a scattering point. This distance would be the linear width of the radiated beam at the range of interest, or possibly less if we choose not to utilize all the available data. In general, such an antenna would have an unmanageable length, as Fig. 3 suggests.

The long antenna achieves a narrow receiving beam through the coherent summation of the signals received on the individual elements. However, there is no fundamental requirement that the many elements exist simultaneously; a single element carried on the aircraft could serve in sequence the function of each element. This single element, through the forward motion of the aircraft, would in turn occupy the position of each array element of the long antenna. The signal received at that position could be stored and, when all the signals have been collected, they could be combined just as the large array would have done. The result, in either case, would be indistinguishable. The small antenna has then functioned as a large array, or equivalently, has formed a synthetic antenna.

A. Analysis

The analysis can proceed either from the Doppler analysis or from the synthetic-aperture viewpoint. We choose the former, thus utilizing the results already presented.

As previously, $f(t)$ is the radiated wave and

$$g(t) = \sigma a\left(t - \frac{2r}{c}\right) \exp\left\{j\left[\omega_0\left(t - \frac{2r}{c}\right) + \phi\left(t - \frac{2r}{c}\right)\right]\right\} \qquad (9)$$

is the signal received from a point object at range r, as in Fig. 2. Let the wave be unmodulated; thus, $a = a_0$ (a constant), and $\phi = 0$. Resolution in range is, of course, not available with this waveform, but for the moment we consider only a single range. Later we introduce pulsing for ranging purposes, and finally, we consider an arbitrary waveform. The returned signal is thus

$$g(t) = \sigma a_0 \exp\left[j\omega_0\left(t - \frac{2r}{c}\right)\right] = \sigma a_0 \exp\left(j\omega_0 t - \frac{4\pi}{\lambda_0} r\right). \qquad (10)$$

The Doppler shift is the time derivative of the phase delay,

$$\omega_d = -\frac{4\pi}{\lambda_0} \frac{dr}{dt} \qquad (11)$$

which is readily found to be

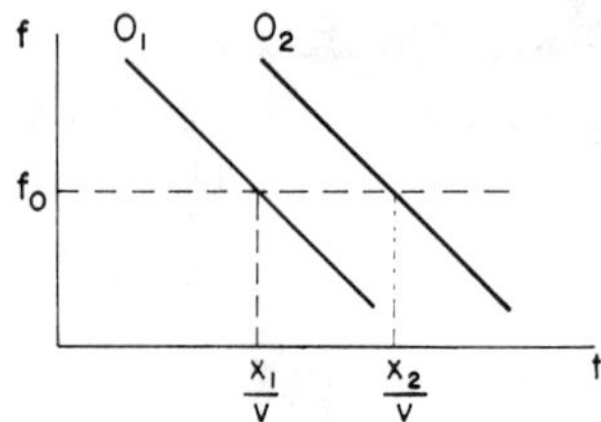

Fig. 4.   Doppler frequency as function of time, for two point objects
O_1 and O_2, located at positions x_1 and x_2.

$$\omega_d = -\frac{4\pi}{\lambda} v \sin\theta \tag{12}$$

where v is the aircraft velocity. If the observation time is sufficiently short that the object bearing, and hence the Doppler frequency remain constant, then the previously noted one-to-one correspondence between Doppler frequency and target-bearing angle applies, and a Doppler analysis yields the azimuthal resolution we seek.

In practice the integration times are much longer, perhaps over the entire duration that the point object is in the beam; consequently, the Doppler shift is not constant and this quite simple approach does not suffice. Instead, we make the small angle approximation,

$$r = \sqrt{r_1^2 + (x - x_1)^2} \cong r_1 + \frac{1}{2}\frac{(x - x_1)^2}{r_1} \tag{13}$$

(satisfactory for the usual case of a beamwidth less than $10°$) which yields

$$g(t) = \sigma a_0 \exp j\left[\omega_0 t - \frac{2\pi}{\lambda_0 r_1}(x - x_1)^2\right] \tag{14}$$

where an inconsequential constant phase term, $-(4\pi/\lambda_0)r_1$ has been, as before, incorporated into σ.

Taking the aircraft position to be $x = vt$, it is apparent that the received signal can be expressed purely as a function of either position x or of time:

$$g(t) = \sigma a_0 \exp j\left[\omega_0 t - \frac{2\pi}{\lambda_0 r_1}(vt - x_1)^2\right] \tag{15a}$$

$$g\left(\frac{x}{v}\right) = \sigma a_0 \exp j\left[\omega_0 \frac{x}{v} - \frac{2\pi}{\lambda_0 r}(x - x_1)^2\right]. \tag{15b}$$

We have use for both forms.

The Doppler-shifted signal has frequency

$$f = \frac{1}{2\pi}\frac{d}{dt}\left[\omega_0 t - \frac{2\pi}{\lambda_0 r_1}(vt - x_1)^2\right] \tag{16}$$

$$= f_0 - f_d$$

where

$$f_d = \frac{2v}{\lambda_0 r_1}(vt - x_1) \tag{17}$$

is the Doppler shift. Hence as depicted in Fig. 4, the signal reflected from object point O_1 undergoes a linear frequency shift as the beam sweeps past. The Doppler shift is maximum as the object enters the beam, since then the radial velocity is maximum. Abeam of the aircraft the radial velocity component, and hence also the Doppler shift, is zero. In the trailing portion of the beam, the object is receding and the Doppler shift is thus negative. A second object O_2 which enters the beam later, produces a similar Doppler history, except that each frequency occurs at a later time.

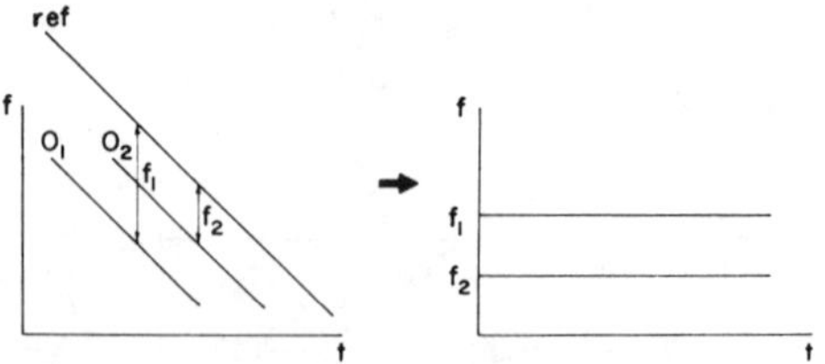

Fig. 5.   Conversion of the signal histories to constant frequencies.

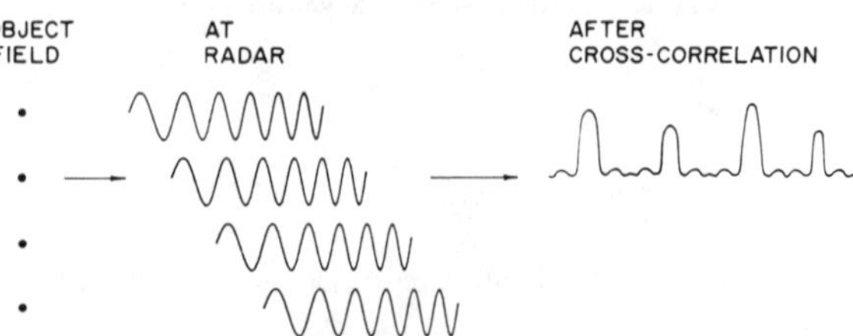

Fig. 6.   The imaging process, showing an object field, the signal received at the radar, and the signal after cross-correlation processing.

Since all object points generate the same Doppler spectrum as they proceed across the beam, a Doppler analysis is no longer appropriate and the earlier analyses must be modified. One possible solution is to mix the incoming signal with an internally generated signal swept in frequency at the same rate as each Doppler history, as illustrated in Fig. 5. Each signal history is converted into a constant-frequency signal, resulting in a one-to-one correspondence between object position and frequency. The Doppler analysis now provides the desired resolution.

Rather than such mixing, let the received signal be cross correlated with an internally generated signal r_c having the same form as the signal from a point object:

$$u = \int_{-L/2}^{L/2} \sigma a_0 \exp j\left[\frac{\omega_0}{v}x - \frac{2\pi}{\lambda_0 r_1}(x - x_1)^2\right]$$

$$\cdot \exp -j\left[\frac{\omega_0}{v}(x - x') - \frac{2\pi}{\lambda_0 r_1}(x - x')^2\right]dx$$

$$= g \circledast r_c \tag{18}$$

where L is the length of the data we process—perhaps one beamwidth, perhaps less. Note that the terms in x^2 cancel; thus the correlation process in fact accomplishes the FM removal suggested previously. Indeed, such an FM removal followed by the appropriate Doppler filtering would constitute exactly the cross-correlation operation of (18). Integration of (18) yields

$$u = K\sigma \operatorname{sinc}\frac{2(x' - x_1)L}{\lambda_0 r_1} \tag{19}$$

where K is a constant and sinc $\gamma = \sin(\pi\gamma)/\pi\gamma$.

The above cross correlation (which, of course, could alternatively be described as a matched filtering) completes the imaging process. The signal at the receiver is a superposition of linearly frequency modulated signals with relative displacements in accordance with the positions of the point objects producing them, as seen in Fig. 6. The correlation process compresses each elemental signal into a narrow spike; the signals, now resolved, constitute a fine-resolution image of the object field. The process, both in the broad concept and in the mathematical formulation, strongly resembles a conventional imaging process at optical wavelengths; the implementation, however, is remarkably different, although we note with anticipation that it need not be.

Having described the synthetic-aperture process as it occurs at a single range, we introduce pulse modulation to provide range resolution. The analysis previously given is not essentially altered. The pulse modulation constitutes a sampling process on the Doppler frequency histories, and if the sampling rate, or pulse-repetition frequency, is adequate, the complete signals can readily be reconstituted from the samples. And, of course, range resolution is achieved in the usual manner, being determined by the pulse duration. The cross-correlation process is performed independently for each range element; the result is a two-dimensional radar image, in range and along-track coordinates, of the original object field.

B. Implementation: Optical Processing

In the early period of synthetic-aperture radar (1951–1955), many methods were devised for processing the stored data; processing techniques were developed around such devices as storage tubes, recirculating delay lines, and filter banks. Because the quantity of data produced by a synthetic antenna system is enormous, utilization of even a moderate fraction of the data results in difficult storage and processing problems. If integration times were to be sufficiently long as to require the linear FM approximation (14), instead of the constant-frequency approximation, and thereby produce a synthetic antenna focused at all ranges, then each range would have to be processed in a separate channel, since this FM rate is range dependent. Thus both the storage and the processing requirements are severe.

Photographic film, because of its high-density storage capabilities, was found to be an attractive storage medium; optical correlators, because of their multichannel capability stemming from their ability to image in two dimensions, appeared as attractive candidates for the processor. Additionally, these two solutions are quite compatible; photographically stored data are in an ideal form for the optical processor input.

The typical transducer for storing the electrical signal photographically consists of a cathode-ray tube and a camera, as illustrated in Fig. 7. Each range sweep is displayed as an intensity-modulated line and photographed. Successive line traces are recorded side-by-side, resulting in a two-dimensional raw data record, with range being distance across the film. Fig. 8 shows the object-space geometry, a range swath, a point object, and the resulting data record.

The stored data are a scaled record of the data collected along the flight path, where $x \rightarrow px$ and p is the scaling factor. The signal, recorded as photographic transmittance, is thus

$$g_0(x) = \sigma a_0 \cos\left[\alpha x - \frac{2\pi p^2}{\lambda_0 r_1}\left(x - \frac{x_1}{p}\right)^2\right] \qquad (20)$$

where $\alpha/2\pi$ is a spatial frequency related to the video-carrier frequency of the electrical signal at the recorder. Similarly, the reference function is

$$r_0(x) = \cos\left(\alpha x - \frac{2\pi p^2}{\lambda_0 r_1} x^2\right). \qquad (21)$$

Although we neglect it in the equations, an amplitude scaling factor is needed since photographic transmittance cannot exceed unity. The cross-correlation process yields

$$g_0 \circledast r_0 = K\sigma \operatorname{sinc} \frac{2p\left(x' - \frac{x_1}{p}\right)L}{\lambda_0 r_1} \qquad (22)$$

which is analogous to (19), except that, because of the scaling, distances are measured in a miniaturized image space.

The optical processing method is shown in Fig. 9. Observation of

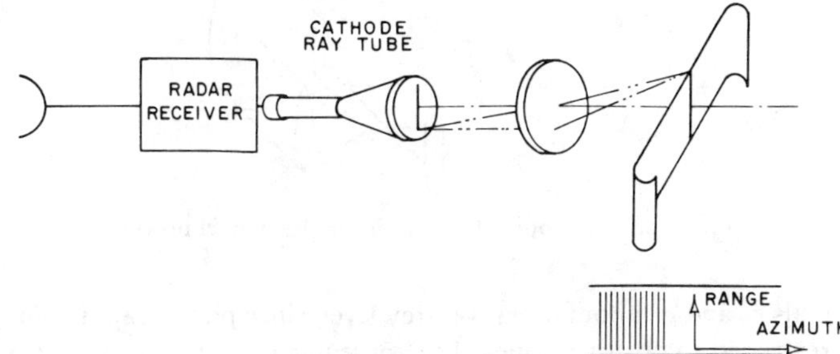

Fig. 7.   Producing the data record.

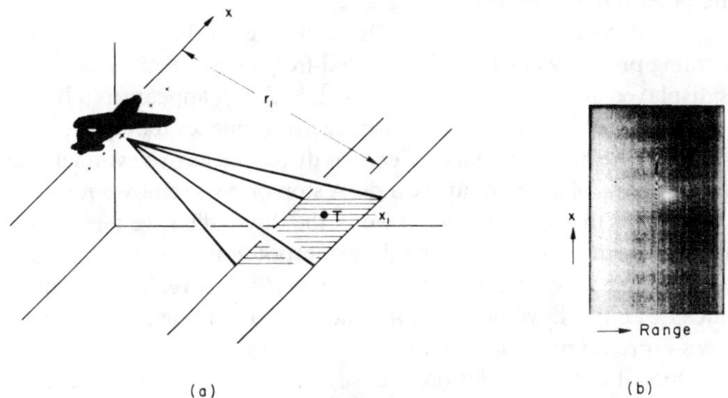

Fig. 8.   The radar system geometry. (a) A point object.
(b) The resulting data record.

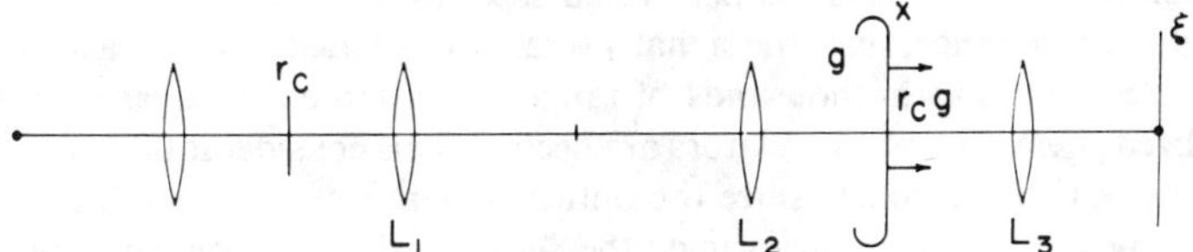

Fig. 9.   A coherent optical system for cross correlation.

(18) shows the cross-correlation process to consist of three elementary suboperations: a multiplication; an integration; and a displacement of one function relative to the other. Each is readily performed optically.

Imaging of the transparency r_0 onto g_0 produces the multiplication. To produce the integration, we utilize the well-known Fourier transforming properties of lenses. The signal g_0 is placed in the front focal plane of L_3, and in the back focal plane the light distribution [4]

$$q(x) = \int r_0 g_0 \exp\left(j\frac{\pi}{\lambda_l F} x\xi\right) dx \qquad (23)$$

is formed, where λ_l is the wavelength of the light and F the focal length of the lens. If our observation is confined to the axial point $\xi = 0$, (23) becomes a simple integration. Thus a pinhole is placed on axis and the illumination in the pinhole is continuously photographed as the signal record moves through the aperture. In this manner, the cross-correlation operation of (22) is formed. As the signal record moves, each elemental signal is brought into alignment with the reference function, and the output at that instant is a measure of the reflectivity σ of the image point that produced the signal. Thus the overlapping signals are unscrambled, producing a fine-resolution image from the raw data record.

But the optical implementation had its problems, which in hindsight may seem trivial, yet appeared quite challenging when they first arose. The first such difficulty now appears; we must write the

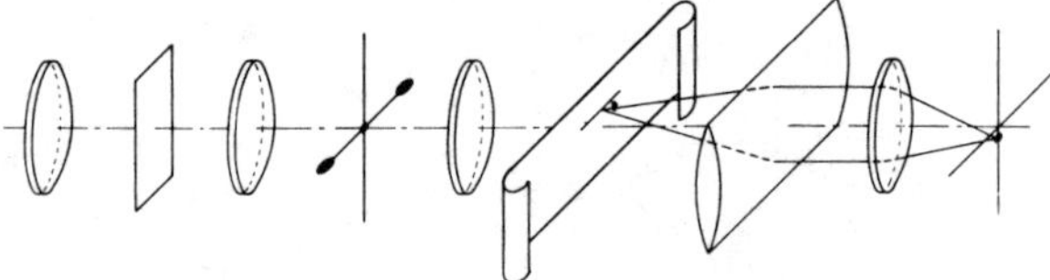

Fig. 10. A coherent optical system for multichannel processing.

signals r_0 and g_0 about a bias or grey level, since photographic film is restricted to positive values. The consequence is that we produce $(r_b + r_0) \circledast (g_b + g_0)$ instead of $r_0 \circledast g_0$, where r_b and g_b are the required bias terms. Four terms result, three of which are extraneous and have the potential for ruining our results.

We dispose of this threat by invoking again the Fourier transforming property of lenses. The spatial-frequency spectrum of $r_b + r_0$ is displayed at the back focal plane of lens L_1; r_b appears as a bright spot on axis, while r_0, having no zero-frequency component (a consequence of the spatial carrier α), is displayed as two symmetrical distributions of light about the axis. A stop on axis removes r_b, while r_0 passes to the signal record. Two of the three offensive terms have at once been eliminated, including the potentially disastrous one $r_b \circledast g_b$. The surviving extraneous term $r_0 \circledast g_b$ is really innocuous since r_0 and g_b have nonoverlapping spectra, and hence produce a cross-correlation value of zero.

Optical cross correlation is easily implemented, but so is electronic cross correlation. What then is the motivation for performing the awkward and time-consuming recording procedure required for the optical method? The answer, already indicated, is that this correlation process must be performed separately for each resolution element in range, since the signal g is range dependent. For a reasonable range swath, thousands of range-resolution elements are utilized; hence, many correlators are needed. This consideration led to the optical approach, since the optical system can accommodate a two-dimensional input format; the yet unused dimension can thus create a multichannel processing capability. We may handle as many channels and perform as many independent correlations as there are resolvable elements across the input aperture. Fig. 10 shows a pictorial view of the same optical system shown first in Fig. 9. The reference-transparency function now appears as a two-dimensional function $r_0(x, r)$ and when imaged onto the signal record, supplies the proper reference function for each range.

The optical system, in a sense, performs too much. The integrating lens L_3 performs an integration in two dimensions—and the integration in range would superimpose all range elements, thus destroying all resolution in range. The cylindrical lens corrects this difficulty. The cylindrical lens and spherical lens together image, in the range dimension, the raw data film onto the output plane. As before, the spherical lens L_3 integrates in the x dimension, displaying the result along a vertical line through the axis. A recording film behind the slit records the image.

C. Further Evolution of the Optical Technique

At this stage, the processor is certainly a successful and useful device. The inventive process, however, did not stop here; improvements were indeed possible and were soon forthcoming. A shortcoming of the previously mentioned system is the large light attenuation loss; the reference-function transparency absorbs about half of the incident light; worse yet, most of the transmitted light remains in the zero order, only to be removed further downstream by the axial stop. Perhaps only 0.001 percent of the light incident on r_0 reaches the output slit.

To correct this shortcoming, we start with the observation that the transparency r_0, being a real function, has redundancy in its

spectrum in the form of conjugate sidebands. Thus we need not pass both sidebands and the axial stop in the focal plane of L_1 can be replaced with a half-plane stop which, in addition, removes one sideband. The resulting image is unaffected.

Except, of course, for the additional 50-percent light loss. Yet, pursuing this train of thought further eventually leads to considerable improvement of light utilization efficiency and to developments of even greater significance. Writing the reference function in its exponential form

$$K[r_b + \cos(\alpha x - \phi)] = K[r_b + \tfrac{1}{2} \exp[j(\alpha x - \phi)]$$
$$+ \tfrac{1}{2} \exp[-j(\alpha x - \phi)]] \quad (24)$$

where

$$\phi = \frac{2\pi p^2}{\lambda_0 r} x^2$$

we can readily demonstrate that each sideband represents one of the two exponential terms; thus the single sideband mode is equivalent to operating with a complex reference function $\exp[\pm j(\alpha x - \phi)]$. If the complex reference function could be generated directly instead of being derived from the cosine function, an enormous reduction of light attenuation would result, for the SSB-reference function considered as a transparency is a pure-phase function and transmits in principle all the light in its path. To produce the phase transparency is easy in principle; we have only to properly figure a glass blank, cutting its thickness in accordance with the argument of r_0.

But in practice the problem is formidable, for in general only a few simple shapes, such as spheres, cylinders, and some aspherics can be accurately produced; arbitrary thickness functions are beyond present-day art.

However, further inspection of the argument $\alpha x - \phi$ reveals some interesting possibilities. The term αx represents a linearly increasing phase shift and is supplied by a simple prism. Further, since prisms do nothing more than bend light rays, the prism term is clearly unneeded. This term is required in the cosine transparency for various reasons: for example, it makes possible the separation and subsequent removal of the bias term. In the complex transparency, it serves no purpose.

The second term of the argument, $\phi = 2\pi p^2 x^2/(\lambda_0 r)$, being quadratic in x, is realized as a cylindrical lens [4]. Such lenses can be readily obtained; hence, the complex transparency can be synthesized. So it appears, until we note the term r in the denominator. The focal length is determined by the coefficient of x^2, and from basic principles [4] is found to be

$$F_x = \frac{1}{2p^2} \frac{\lambda_0}{\lambda_l} r \quad (25)$$

where λ_l is the wavelength of the light used. The "cylindrical" lens thus has a focal length which varies linearly along its length, and thus could better be described as a conical lens. One could plausibly expect that its fabrication is not feasible.

However, not only is this supposition incorrect, but indeed such lenses had already been produced for quite unrelated purposes. The conical lens can be derived from the axicon [5], a lens in the form of a rather flat cone (Fig. 11). A sector, or "pie" slice from an axicon of proper specification is an exceedingly accurate approximation to the conical lens. Obtaining the conical lens was then merely a matter of selecting the proper axicon from the dealer's stock. The feasibility and availability of the conical lens was a most fortuitous circumstance.

The resulting optical correlator, shown in Fig. 12, is improved

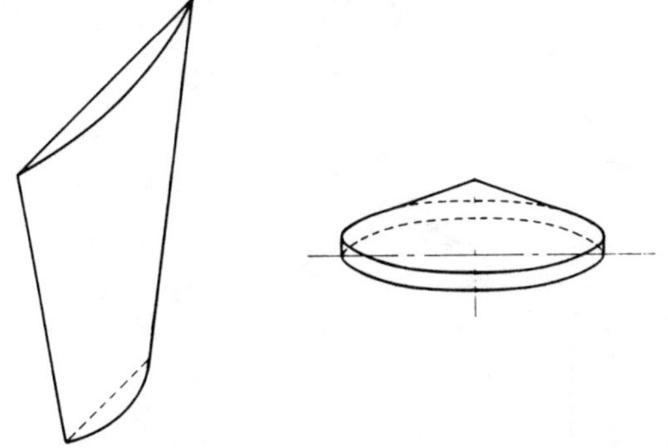

Fig. 11.   The conical lens and the axicon lens from which the former was derived.

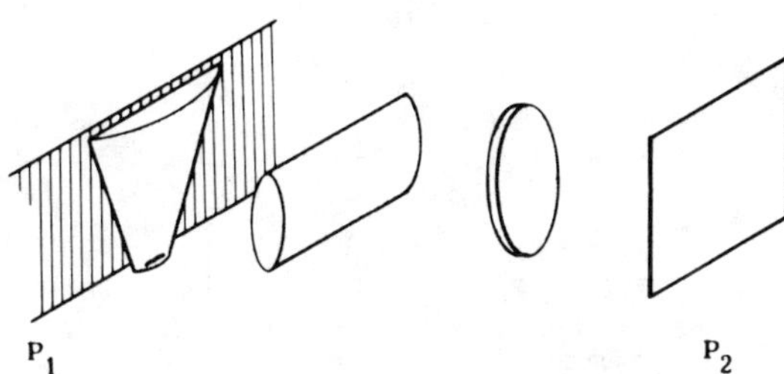

Fig. 12.   The optical cross correlator with conical lens.

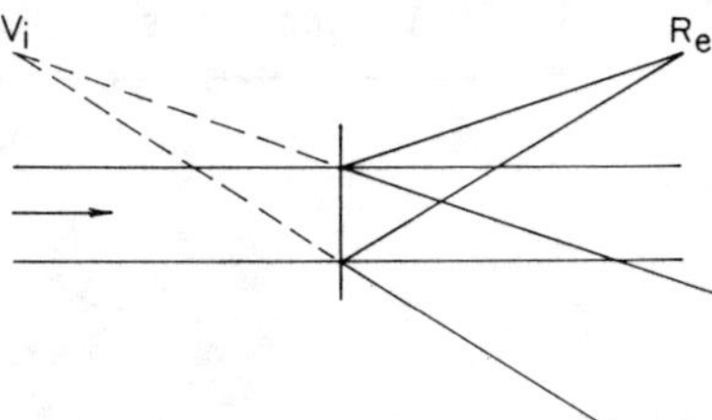

Fig. 13.   The focusing properties of a Fresnel zone plate. Collimated light impinges on the structure. Part of the emergent light forms a real image R_e, part forms a virtual image V_i. A portion emerges unchanged and continues as a collimated beam.

by a factor 20 in its light utilization efficiency. Additionally, the optical system is considerably simplified. Since there is no bias term to remove, the conical lens may be placed in direct contact with the signal record, thereby eliminating two lenses and a spatial filter. The system comprises a most unlikely combination of lenses, but accomplishes a task that would otherwise be difficult indeed.

These developments were gratifying from an instrumentation viewpoint, but they appeared to undermine the theory that had produced them. The correlator elements, including also now the reference function, are lenses. Lenses form images only from other images or from original objects. The image we produce at the output slit must indeed exist quite independently of the lenses to which theory had led.

Further considerations indicate that this supposition is true. For if the reference function is a lens, so must the signal from each object point also be a lens, since the reference function has the same functional form as such a signal. Each object-point signal is, of course, a Fresnel zone-plate lens, and illumination of such a structure with a collimated beam produces two primary foci—one real and one virtual (Fig. 13). The images formed by the Fresnel zone-plate signal can be shown to possess precisely the structure of the image produced by the correlation process previously described. Thus by reducing the optical system to only three lenses, we are, it appears, led to abolishing even these, as well as the correlation theory upon which all had been based.

At this stage a new viewpoint emerged which restored the rational basis of the process. In the ensuing months, beginning in late 1955, the theory of synthetic-aperture radar (in combination with optical processing) was recast in terms of holography. The various elements and functions of the system were now viewed in an altogether different way. The communication theory tools were laid aside, to be replaced with those of geometrical and physical optics. Terms such as linear filter, spectrum, and sideband gave way to optical ones like diffraction lens, focal length, and f number. Ray diagrams became the basic tool of analysis. As a result, the process became understood in a more pictorial way than before; problems that previously were solved using mathematical formulas could now be solved by optical diagrams and elementary ray tracing.

The signal record was no longer to be regarded as merely stored data, but as a scaled-down hologram of the wavefield impinging on the aircraft flight path. Illumination with coherent light produces, in miniature, an optical replica of this wavefield. Images are produced, as in conventional holography, but these images have resolution corresponding to the data-collecting aperture rather than to the aperture of the real antenna. Hence the synthetic aperture is realized through conversion into an equivalent real aperture of a holographic optical system.

The image thus formed is defective in various respects. For example, the signals have focal lengths proportional to the range of their origin; thus the locus of focal positions is a tilted plane, as shown in Fig. 14. A similar tilted plane, corresponding to the real image foci, forms on the other side of the signal record. Since the signals are cylindrical zone-plate lenses, having focal power in the x dimension only, the images are defocused in range. Range resolution, formed by the pulse modulation, is present on the raw data record, which is therefore the plane of range focus. The radar system is thus anamorphic, and a compensating anamorphic property must be introduced into the optical system. The tilted plane must be untilted and then brought into coincidence with the plane of range focus.

As before, a conical lens, having a focal length equal but opposite to the negative focus of the signal record, is placed against the signal record, thus reimaging the tilted plane at infinity and erecting it in the process (Fig. 15). Next, a cylindrical lens placed one focal length from the signal record images the signal record at infinity, thereby bringing the two planes into coincidence. A conventional spherical lens then forms a real image, free from the original defects.

The optical system is identical to the previous one, but the function of each element is described in a different way; the cross correlator has become an anamorphic imaging system. Thus we find that diverse theories from the two traditionally unrelated disciplines of communication theory and physical optics have produced an identical equipment synthesis!

The optical analysis can be carried much further [6]. We may consider, for example, the character of the image (or image data) at various steps of the process. A square in object space, formed by four point objects, is mapped onto the data record via the transformation $x \to px$ and $r \to qr$, and since in general $p \neq q$, the data record is elongated in one dimension. Similarly, the image formed from the hologram, under collimated illumination, will be elongated.

The lens system produces yet a further transformation, which we can best explain by considering the anamorphic system as two distinct imaging systems, one for each dimension, x and r (Fig. 16). In the r dimension, the cylindrical and spherical lenses (with focal length F_{cy} and F, respectively) form a simple telescope with magnification

$$M_r = \frac{F}{F_{cy}} \tag{26}$$

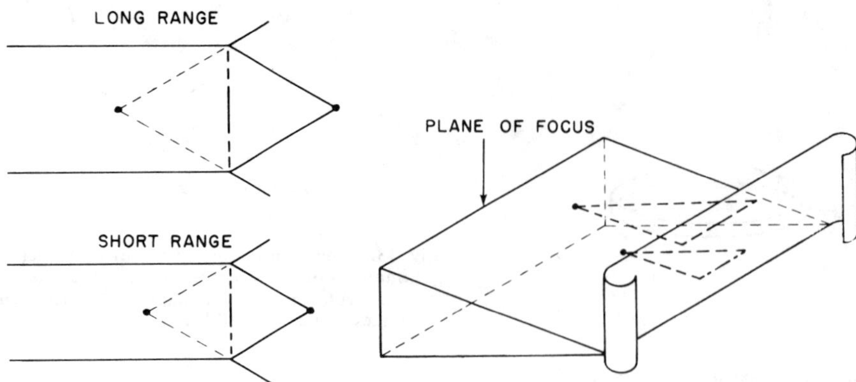

Fig. 14. Focal properties of the signal record.

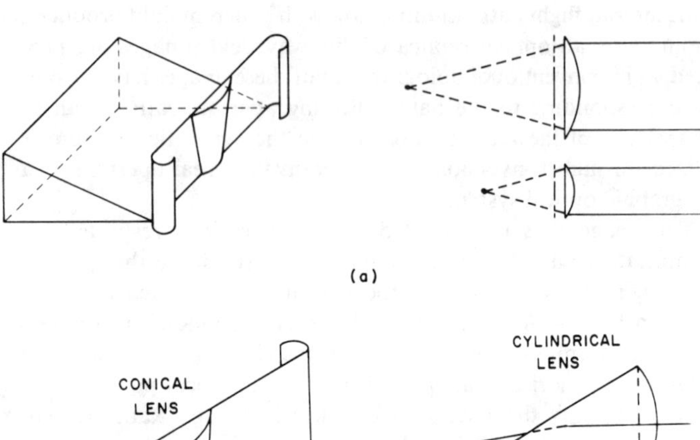

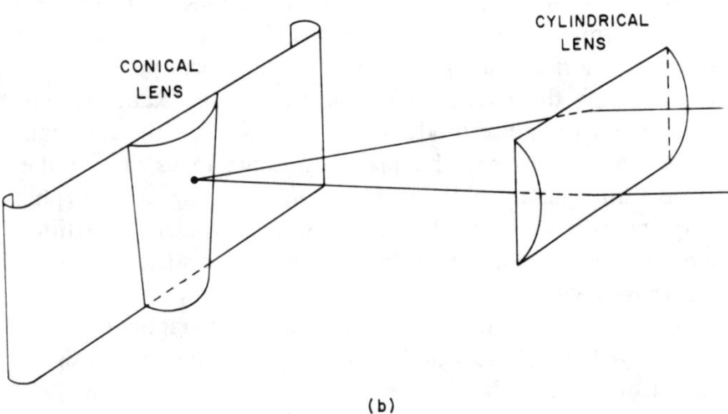

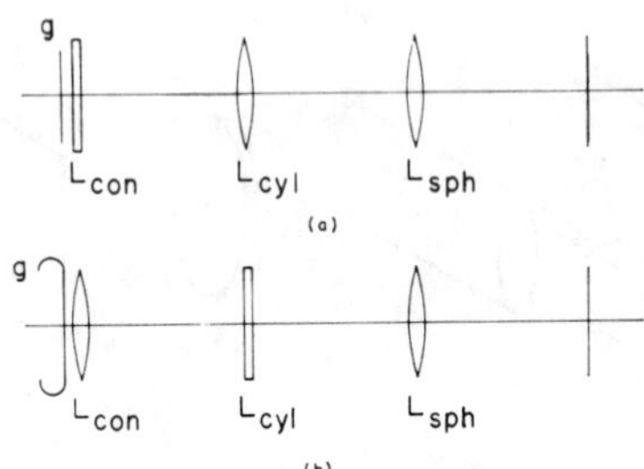

Fig. 16. The anamorphic lens system as viewed in r and x meridians. (a) The r meridian. (b) The x meridian.

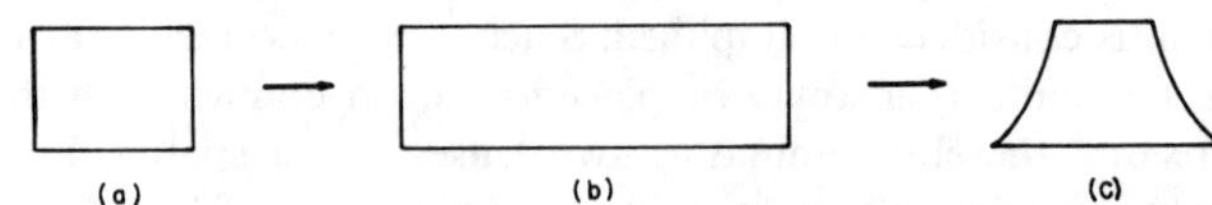

Fig. 17. Transformations on the image. (a) The object. (b) The image formed by the data record. (c) The image formed by the anamorphic lens system.

$$\frac{M_x}{M_r} = \frac{F_{cy}}{F_x} = \frac{p}{q}.\tag{28}$$

But since F_x is range dependent, the proper aspect ratio can be attained at one range only. At other ranges, the image will be distorted and the object-space square is ultimately mapped into the peculiar shape shown in Fig. 17. The variable magnification is produced by the conical lens, and is the price paid for removing the anamorphism.

The variable scale factor can be removed, however, using the scanning slit introduced previously. As the signal record moves through the aperture, the image moves past the slit, with the magnified parts moving proportionately faster. The image recorded on the moving film behind the slit will have a proper aspect ratio provided the velocity ratio of the two films is made equal to the ratio p/q quite independently of the various lens focal lengths.

Alternatively, an equivalent conical lens, placed in a plane where the Fourier transform of the signal is formed, acts as a spatial-matched filter and removes the anamorphism without introducing the variable magnification distortion. This assertion can be demonstrated either with geometrical optics, which is a rather tedious procedure, or with linear-filter theory, which yields the same result by a short verbal statement. For, contrary to the impression that may now have been created, the optical approach is not always the more succinct.[2]

The holographic viewpoint and the physical and geometrical optics analyses that thereby become available not only offer new

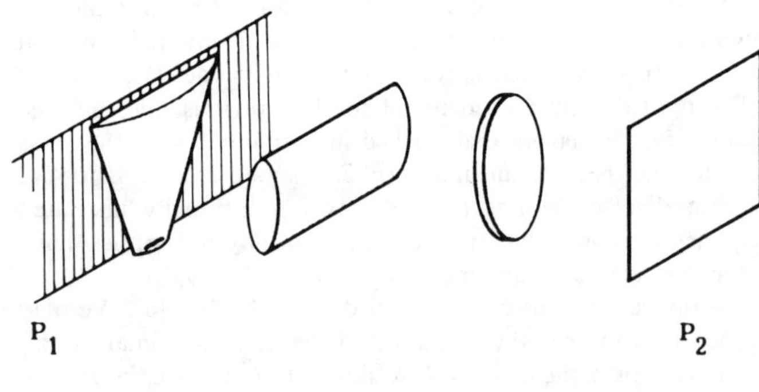

Fig. 15. Development of an anamorphic lens system for compensation of the radar image.

whereas, in the x dimension, the conical and spherical lenses form a simple telescope with magnification

$$M_x = \frac{F}{F_x} = \frac{F}{\left(\frac{1}{2p^2}\frac{\lambda_0}{\lambda_l}r\right)}\tag{27}$$

where F_x is the focal length of the conical lens. The proper aspect ratio can be restored by choosing the magnification ratio so as to compensate for the nonequality of p and q:

---

[2] These demonstrations are left to the reader.

(a)

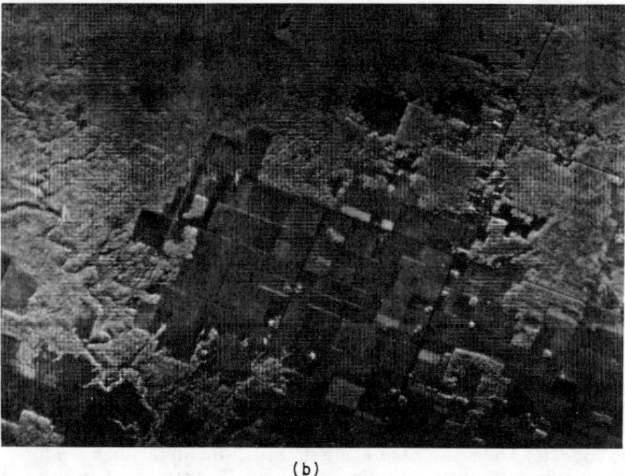

(b)

Fig. 18.   An example of synthetic-aperture radar imagery.
(a) A raw data record. (b) A processed image.

insights into the synthetic-aperture process, they also give rise to implementations that are not readily suggested by other approaches. The holographic viewpoint has, therefore, been quite valuable.[3]

A radar image formed by optically processing data gathered by a synthetic-antenna radar is shown in Fig. 18. The radar picture, which is of a rural area in Northern Michigan, shows a variety of scenery, including rivers, wooded areas, and farmland. Highways and rural buildings are clearly visible, as well as shadows cast by wooded tracts. From the shadowing, it is obvious that the radar-carrying aircraft was to the north of the illuminated area, yet the picture appears to have been taken from directly above. This rendition of perspective is characteristic of the synthetic-antenna radar system.

D. History of the Synthetic Antenna

The synthetic-aperture technique, developed under military sponsorship, has a history stemming from 1951. Many hundreds of persons contributed to its development. The most comprehensive account of the early history is given in a paper by Sherwin, Ruina, and Rawcliffe [5]. The synthetic-antenna concept is generally credited to Wiley, who noted in 1951 that stationary objects within the beam of a moving radar could be resolved by Doppler filtering. Similar conclusions were reached by Sherwin, Kovaly, Prothe,

---

[3] The development related here obviously has a logic: each step seems to point to the next, as though the historical development may really have proceeded in this manner. In general it did, except that the conical lens was, in fact, suggested by the holographic viewpoint, and was the first of many innovations arising from this concept. Some of these, unlike the conical lens, are almost inexplicable except by holographic concepts.

Newell, Ruina, and Rawcliffe at the University of Illinois [5]. The resolution improvement was explained by introducing the synthetic-antenna concept. In an extensive flight program, the group successfully demonstrated their ideas. Other significant contributions include the "zero-beat" processing concept by Hausz, and the Redap, or reëntrant recirculating delay-line processor developed by Steinberg and Sunstein [5].

In 1954 an extensive report describing many new and sophisticated ideas, including optical processing, was produced at the University of Michigan, the primary contributors being Vivian and Cutrona. The optical method, as originally described, utilized incoherent illumination. Although cumbersome and never implemented, it was the forerunner of the elegant version we have thus described.

Coherent optical configurations were examined in 1955 by Porcello and myself after annoying diffraction effects produced problems with the incoherent methods. The single sideband approach, the interpretation of the reference function and signals as lenses, and the subsequent fusion of holography and synthetic-aperture radar, are the author's work, performed during the period 1955–1956. The Michigan system was first flown in 1957 and, after a few flights, produced excellent results [6], [7].

The holographic viewpoint today has gained wide acceptance and is the usual method of explaining the processing system [8]. Yet, when first introduced and for several years afterward, it found little acceptance. This situation gradually changed when theory was reduced to practice and experimental results became available. By 1960 the holographic view became dominant, and has so remained. This situation is not entirely satisfactory, for the holographic viewpoint puts undue emphasis on the optical-processing aspect, which is always a minute part of the entire system. Furthermore, the optical-processing method must be regarded as a complement rather than a replacement for the electronic-processing methods, for the latter have continued to flourish.

IV. Pulse Compression

Radar systems employing conventional pulsing are beset with two conflicting requirements: to achieve fine resolution, the pulse should be narrow; to achieve a long-range capability, the average radiated power should be high. High power can be obtained by a) increasing the pulse duration, which causes loss of resolution; by b) increasing the pulse-repetition frequency, which results in the ambiguity problem of pulses returning to the receiver simultaneously for two or more ranges; or by c) increasing the pulse intensity, or peak power, a process limited by insulation problems in the transmitter.

The pulse-compression technique is a fourth possibility which avoids all of the previously mentioned difficulties. A coded pulse is radiated and, upon reception, is compressed by correlation techniques to a fraction of its original duration. Thus high-average power is attained without the need for high-peak power and without reduction of range resolution.

The pulse-compression radar fits into the category of pulse-Doppler radar. Thus the holographic analogy noted earlier applies and indeed becomes quite striking when the coded waveform is of the linearly frequency modulated or "chirp" variety.

A. Analysis and Instrumentation

Let the radiated pulse be

$$f(t) = a \exp\left(j\left[\omega_0 t + \phi(t)\right]\right), \qquad \text{for } \frac{T}{2} \le t \le \frac{T}{2}$$

$$= 0, \qquad\qquad \text{for } |t| > \frac{T}{2}. \tag{29}$$

The return signal $g(t) = \sigma f(t - t_1)$ is cross correlated with the reference

Fig. 19.　Two forms of pulse coding. (a) A multiphase pulse train, with phases $\phi_1, \cdots, \phi_n$. (b) A chirp pulse.

function $r_c(t)$, which, since we consider only stationary object points, is not frequency shifted and is, therefore, just a replica of the radiated pulse $f(t)$:

$$u = \sigma \int f(t - t_r) f^*(t - t_1)\, dt. \tag{30}$$

This operation is usually performed passively using a matched filter. The result is the autocorrelation function of the transmitted pulse, centered about the time-delay value t_1. Evidently, we should choose a code $a \exp\left[j\phi(t)\right]$ having an autocorrelation function with a narrow main lobe and low sidelobes.

The width of the compressed pulse is approximately the reciprocal of the bandwidth W. The compression ratio is thus the time-bandwidth product TW of the pulse. A narrow uncoded pulse thus has a TW product of unity. The coding, then, has the purpose of increasing the TW product of the pulse, or equivalently, of increasing the bandwidth over that of an uncoded pulse of the same duration.

Two types of encoding have commonly been used: the multiphase pulse train and the chirp pulse. In the former type, the radiated pulse consists of a sequence of abutting subpulses, all of constant amplitude, but of varying phase [Fig. 19(a)]. The phases, $\phi_1, \cdots, \phi_n$, are chosen so as to yield a desirable autocorrelation function. Sophisticated techniques exist for finding such codes.

The well-known shift register codes are often used. Here the ϕ's assume two values, 0 and π: the code then consists, to within a multiplicative constant, of a sequence of $+1$'s and -1's arranged in what can be described as a pseudorandom ordering. The autocorrelation function (actually the sequence correlated with its periodic extension) is n when the sequences match and -1 otherwise, where n is the number of pulses in the sequence.

The chirp or linearly frequency-modulated pulse [Fig. 19(b)] is the more commonly used waveform for pulse compression. Ease of generation and ease of processing make it attractive. Furthermore, the autocorrelation function of a linearly FM pulse is, in general, just as satisfactory as that of the more complex codes. Either type of pulse may, of course, be compressed by optical means.

Optical correlators of various types are available to compress the pulse. A basic system, shown in Fig. 20(a), is applicable to any type of waveform. The signal from the radar receiver is converted into an ultrasonic wave, which passes through an ultrasonic delay line and is absorbed at the other end. Illumination of the delay line with a coherent light beam results in spatial modulation of the light beam in a manner analogous to the behavior of the photographic signal record previously described. The signal may then be correlated with a reference mask exactly as was done with the synthetic-aperture data. An alternative technique, the frequency-domain synthesis, is shown in Fig. 20(b). The Fourier transform $F(\omega)$ of the waveform is displayed as a spatial-frequency distribution at P_2. A transparency bearing $F^*(\omega)$ is introduced at P_2, and the compressed pulse appears at the output plane P_3.

A major problem, that of implementing the complex filter $F^*(\omega)$ made the frequency-domain synthesis only a conceptual solution until 1961 when Kozma and Kelly, using a technique which today is known as computer-generated holography, synthesized on photographic film a transparency bearing the spectrum of a shift register code [9]. Results are shown in Fig. 21.

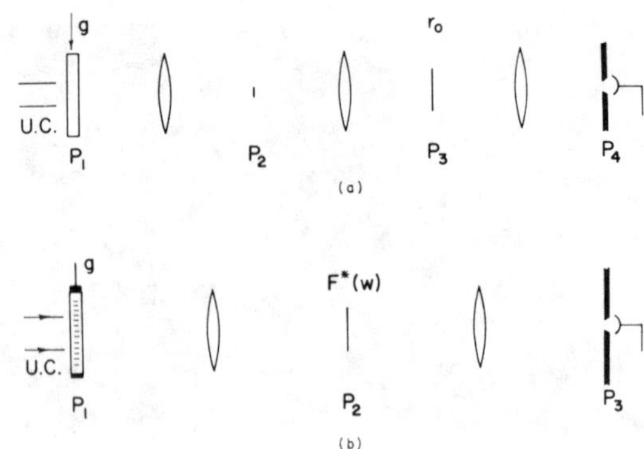

Fig. 20.　Two forms of optical processor. (a) The spatial-domain synthesis. (b) The spatial-domain synthesis. In (a), g (in an ultrasonic cell U.C.) is imaged, after spatial filtering at P_2 onto r_0. The correlated output is sensed by a photo detector at P_4. In (b), the signal g is imaged through a spatial-matched filter at P_2 and the filtered signal is detected at P_3.

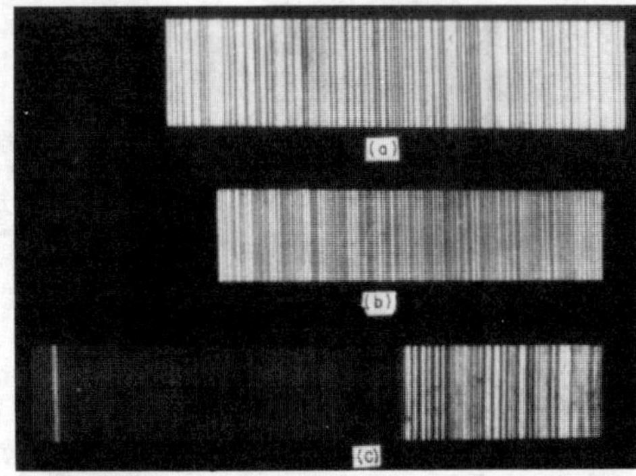

Fig. 21.　Spatial-matched filtering for a shift register code. (a) A shift register sequence, written on a spatial carrier. (b) The spatial-matched filter for the code. (c) The result of imaging the structure (a) through the filter (b). The compressed pulse is shown on the left. The structure on the right is the zero-order term produced by the filter and is of no significance. (Courtesy of A. Kozma and D. Kelly.)

The systems of Fig. 20 are general, applying to any pulse form. However, we stress here the chirp pulse because then the resemblance to holography is strongest. The return from an object field is then a superposition of superimposed but displaced chirp signals that, on recording, become the familiar zone plates of holography.

For the chirp pulse, the autocorrelation function may be readily calculated. Indeed we did exactly this in spatial coordinates (18) when discussing the synthetic antenna, since that process also gives rise to linearly frequency modulated signals.

The optical system is considerably simplified for the chirp pulse, as then we may advantageously use the zone-plate or self-compressing properties of the signals. These properties arise whether the signal is stored in a delay line, on photographic film, or on any medium that can be interrogated with coherent light. The recorded signal from an object field is then indistinguishable from a hologram (a one-dimensional one, of course), and when coherently illuminated forms the usual true and conjugate images of the holographic process corresponding to the two primary foci of the Fresnel zone plate. As with the synthetic-aperture case, these images are identical to the result obtained using cross correlation or matched filtering. This conclusion, while intuitively expected, can be readily demonstrated by regarding free space as a matched filter for the chirp pulse.

The chirp signal from a point object,

$$g(t) = \sigma a_0 \exp j\left[\omega_0\left(t - \frac{2r_1}{c}\right) + \frac{1}{2}k\left(t - \frac{2r_1}{c}\right)^2\right]$$

$$= \sigma a_0 \exp j\left[\frac{4\pi}{\lambda_0}\left(\frac{c}{2}t - r_1\right) + \frac{2k}{c^2}\left(\frac{c}{2}t - r_1\right)^2\right] \tag{31}$$

which may be expressed in spatial coordinates by using the relation $r=(c/2)t$, can be recorded using a scaling process $r \rightarrow qr$, producing

$$\sigma a_0 \cos\left[\alpha\left(r - \frac{r_1}{q}\right) + \frac{2kq^2}{c^2}\left(r - \frac{r_1}{q}\right)^2\right]. \tag{32}$$

Using the Fourier transform relation

$$\mathscr{F}\{\exp(j\gamma x^2)\} = \frac{\pi}{\gamma}\exp\left(j\frac{\omega^2}{4\gamma}\right)$$

the Fourier transform of the signal is readily shown to be

$$K\left[\exp j\beta(\omega_r - \alpha)^2 \exp -j\omega_r\frac{r_1}{q} + \text{complex conjugate}\right] \tag{33}$$

where K is a constant and $\beta = c^2/(8q^2k)$.

Free space can be regarded as a spatial filter, dispersive in nature and having the transfer function [4],

$$H(\omega_x, \omega_y) = \exp(jkz)\exp\left[-j\frac{\lambda z}{4\pi}(\omega_x^2 + \omega_y^2)\right] \tag{34}$$

a result readily obtained by Fourier transforming the usual Kirchhoff expression for Fresnel diffraction [4]. Let the pulse be recorded along the x dimension; then $\omega_r \sim \omega_x$. At a position in the diffraction field a distance z from the signal transparency, the spectrum (33) is multiplied by the transfer function of the intervening space. The first term of (33) has its quadratic phase factor perfectly compensated when

$$z = \frac{\pi c^2}{2kq^2\lambda_0}. \tag{35}$$

We expect this value of z to be just the focal length of the Fresnel zone plate, a hypothesis readily confirmed by inspection of (32), and by noting that a lens of focal length F introduces a quadratic phase factor $\exp j[(\pi/\lambda F)(x^2+y^2)]$.

The demonstration may be completed by Fourier transforming the product of signal spectrum and transfer function, and converting back to time coordinates, whereupon the result is identical to that obtained by direct matched filtering of the temporal signal $g(t)$.

There are several significant differences between the free-space filter and some of the electronic chirp filters. The chirp filters (at least in the 1950s) were expensive, bulky, heavy, highly attenuating, and not always linear; sometimes they became somewhat detuned. Free space, on the other hand, has none of these shortcomings.

In converse to the present discussion, the holographic process may be modeled as a pulse-compression process, an approach used by Upatnieks and me in our earliest holography paper [11].

B. Combined Beam Sharpening and Pulse Compression

Obviously, pulse-compression and synthetic-antenna techniques can be combined. A chirp or other coded waveform can be radiated and then compressed upon reception, whereupon the beam-sharpening operation can be carried out just as if the radiated pulse had not been coded.

More interesting, however, is the case where the coded pulse is stored and later processed by optical means. Under this circumstance the beam-sharpening and pulse-compression operations can be treated as orthogonal aspects of a single two-dimensional operation. An optical system, because of its inherent capability for treating two-dimensional signals, can readily perform the combined operation [12].

As previously, we stress the chirp method. The recorded signal from a point object has the form

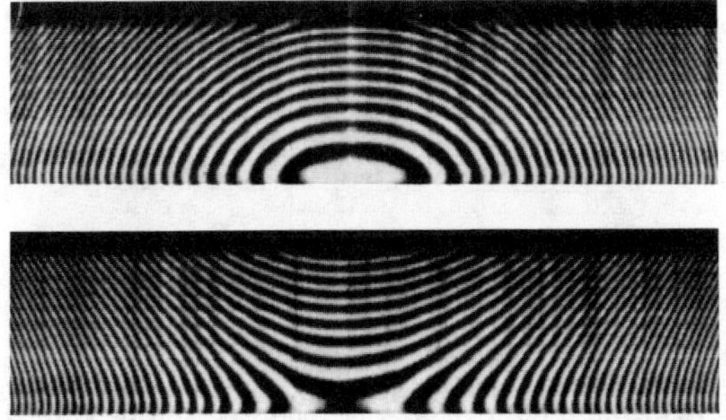

Fig. 22.   Elliptical and hyperbolic zone plates produced by a pulse-Doppler radar system.

$$\sigma a \cos\left[\alpha x - \frac{2\pi p^2}{\lambda_0 r_1}\left(x - \frac{x_1}{p}\right)^2 + \frac{2kq^2}{c^2}\left(r - \frac{r_1}{q}\right)^2\right] \tag{36}$$

where the first quadratic phase factor is due to the Doppler shift and the second arises from the chirp waveform. The signal is a two-dimensional zone plate with a different focal length in each dimension [12]. Inspection shows the focal length to be

$$F_x = \pm \frac{1}{2p^2}\frac{\lambda_0}{\lambda_l}r_1 \tag{37}$$

$$F_r = \pm \frac{\pi c^2}{2kq^2\lambda_l} \tag{38}$$

for the x and r dimensions, respectively.

The zone plate is generally anamorphic since the factors determining the focal length are different for each dimension. Proper selection of the FM rate and other parameters can make the focal lengths equal, but for one range element only.

For an extended target field, the plane of azimuth focus is the tilted plane described previously. The plane of range focus, however, is no longer the signal record itself, but is a plane parallel to the signal record and located one focal length F_r in front of or behind the record, depending on whether we utilize the real or virtual image term.

The one-dimensional multichannel optical processor of Fig. 12 is converted into a two-dimensional multichannel processor merely by moving the cylindrical lens a distance F_r along the optic axis so that the range focal plane lies in the front focal plane of the cylindrical lens. This quite simple expedient has, at once, given us a two-dimensional processor. The pulse-compression operation has indeed been obtained without cost.

The quadratic coefficients of $(x - x_1/p)^2$ and $(r - r_1/q)^2$ may have like or unlike signs, depending on whether the frequency sweep rate k is positive or negative. If the coefficients have like signs, the constant-phase contours are ellipses; if the signs are unlike, the contours are hyperbolas. Signals of each type are shown in Fig. 22. The elliptical type is conceptually simpler. One order has a positive focal length in each meridian; that is, F_x and F_r, although not equal, are each positive for that order. The other order has a negative focal length in each meridian.

The hyperbolic type has F_x and F_r with unlike signs. One order has a focal length that is positive in one meridian and negative in the other, while the other order has the signs reversed.

Either type of zone plate can be handled, but the elliptical type is preferable since the anamorphic properties of the correcting-optical system can be less severe.

C. Terminologies: Electrical and Optical

There is a well-established mathematical formalism derived from linear-filter theory for describing the action of the chirp filter. Like-

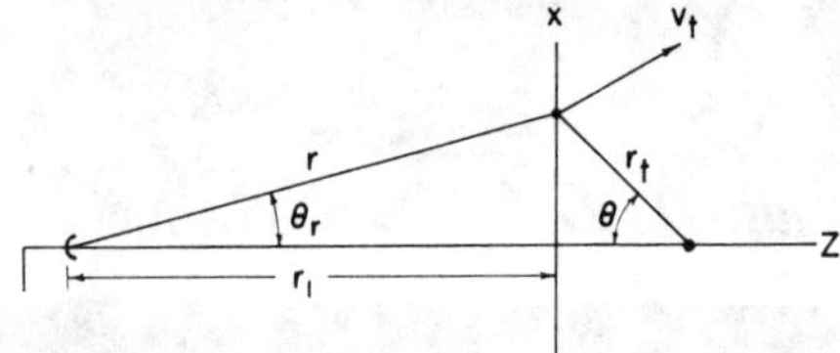

Fig. 23.   Geometry of the rotating body range-Doppler radar system.

wise, the focusing action of a zone plate is well described by the concepts of physical optics. Since the two phenomena are essentially identical, we can compare them and draw some analogies between the two sets of terminologies. We might, for example, describe the pulse compression in the usual way and then apply the concepts of physical optics to a zone plate formed by recording the pulse.

Comparison of the two terminologies reveals interesting relations. The focal-length expression F_r (38) shows focal length to correspond in a proportional way to the reciprocal of the FM rate k. Similarly, bandwidth and f number are inversely related. The electrical signal has bandwidth $W_t = kT$, where T is the pulse duration. For the optical case, the resolution can be found by the usual expression resolution $= \lambda \cdot f$-number, or from calculation of the bandwidth. The results, as to be expected, will agree.

The time-bandwidth product (TW), important in communication theory, has no established counterpart in optics, although the term space-bandwidth production is gaining acceptance. The TW product is an important characteristic of a signal, partly because it defines the number of degrees of freedom of a signal, and partly because of its invariance to many transformations. The reader can verify from a few simple calculations that the TW product has remained invariant under the recording transformation.

D. Historical Summary

The pulse-compression method was invented independently by several researchers during the 1940s [13]. This work continued into the 1950s at a number of establishments, including Sperry and Bell Laboratories. The earliest detailed description in the published literature is by Klauder, Price, Darlington, and Albersheim [10]. Investigation of optical methods for compression of the pulse was initiated by the author in 1957, the salient facets of the effort being the utilization of the zone-plate properties of the chirp pulse, and the combining of pulse compression and synthetic aperture into a single two-dimensional operation, performed by coherent optical methods [14], [15], [10]. This two-dimensional optical-processing method was independently suggested by Curtis and Smith at RCA [16]. Optical-processing methods, along different lines, were carried out by Lambert and his group at Columbia University [17], using ultrasonic delay lines to provide, in real time, a range-Doppler analysis of the incoming signal. Dickey of General Electric reported on optical techniques for pulse compression at a symposium in 1959 [18].

V. RANGE-DOPPLER RADAR FOR ROTATING BODIES

The range-Doppler principle, when applied to rotating bodies, can yield excellent resolution, as evidenced by the dramatic radar imagery of planets that has been thus obtained. The technique is akin to the synthetic-aperture principle, but with some additional aspects of considerable significance.

A system of particles, shown in Fig. 23, rotates with constant angular velocity about a common axis. The particles could represent point scatterers on a single rigid body. A pulse-Doppler radar a distance r from the object point O_1 radiates a signal

$$f(t) = a \exp\left[j(\omega_0 t + \phi)\right] \quad (39)$$

and receives from O_1 a signal

$$g(t) = \sigma a\left(t - \frac{2r}{c}\right) \exp j\left[\omega_0\left(t - \frac{2r}{c}\right) + \phi\left(t - \frac{2r}{c}\right)\right]. \quad (40)$$

If $r \gg r_t$, the approximations

$$a\left(t - \frac{2r}{c}\right) = a\left(t - \frac{2r_1}{c}\right)$$

$$\phi\left(t - \frac{2r}{c}\right) = \phi\left(t - \frac{2r_1}{c}\right) \quad (41)$$

are valid. If the observation time is sufficiently short, then r_1 and the radial velocity v_r (which we take as being approximately v_z) can be considered constant, and the range $r(t)$ can be written

$$r(t) = r(t = 0) + v_z t \quad (42)$$

where $v_z = \omega_t r_t \sin \theta_0$, and ω_t is the angular velocity. The signal $g(t)$ may then be written

$$g(t) = \sigma f\left(t - \frac{2r_1}{c}\right) \exp -j\left[\frac{4\pi}{\lambda_0} r(t = 0) + \omega_d t\right] \quad (43)$$

where

$$f_d = \frac{\omega_d}{2\pi} = \frac{2}{\lambda_0} \omega_t r_t \sin \theta_0 \quad (44)$$

is the Doppler frequency shift. Contours of constant Doppler shift are found by setting

$$\omega_d = \frac{4\pi}{\lambda_0} \omega_t x_t = C \quad (45)$$

where C is a constant and $x_t = r_t \sin \theta_0$. The Doppler contours, given by

$$x_t = \frac{C\lambda_0}{4\pi\omega_t} \quad (46)$$

are thus planes parallel to the plane defined by the axis of rotation and the line between radar and the rotating system axis. Iso-range contours are planes normal to this line and thus normal to the iso-Doppler planes, provided the radar is sufficiently distant. Thus a range-Doppler analysis produces an x, r image of the rotating-particle system.

Implicit in the foregoing analysis is an axis of rotation normal to the radius vector r_0. A minor extension of the preceding analysis shows an essentially similar result when this condition is not met.

The Doppler resolution $\Delta\omega_d$ is determined by the time of observation

$$\Delta\omega_d = \frac{2\pi}{T} \quad (47)$$

from which the x resolution is found to be

$$\Delta x = \frac{\lambda_0}{2\omega_t T}. \quad (48)$$

The resolution in range is, as usual, roughly the reciprocal of the bandwidth of $f(t)$

$$\Delta r \cong \frac{1}{\Delta W}. \quad (49)$$

Both range and cross-range resolution are independent of distance;

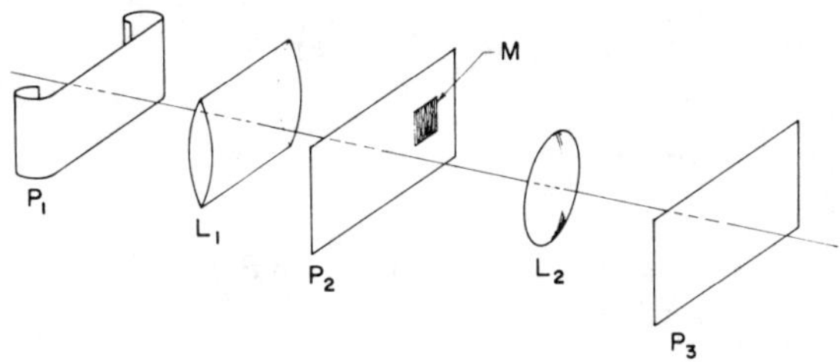

Fig. 24.   Optical processing system for range-Doppler analyses of rotating body data. *M* is a spatial-matched filter, which operates on one sideband of the signal.

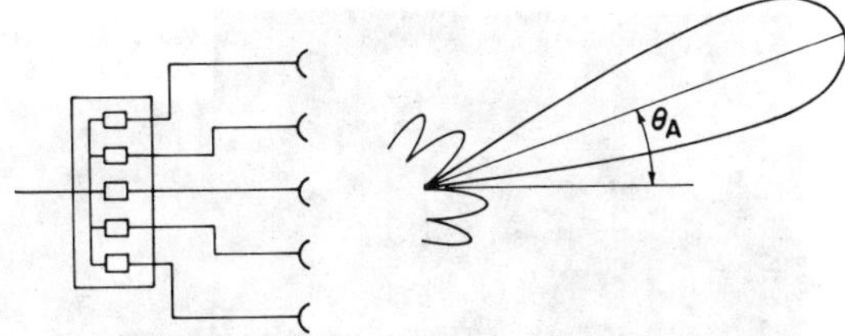

Fig. 25.   Image of a portion of the planet Venus obtained from a pulse-Doppler radar system at the Jet Propulsion Laboratory of the California Institute of Technology, with optical processing at the University of Michigan. (Courtesy of L. Porcello, C. Heerema, and N. Massey.)

therefore, the system has potential for excellent resolution at large distances.

Rotating-target returns have been range-Doppler processed by various methods, including digital, electronic analog, and optical. The optical-processing procedure is similar to that for combined pulse compression and synthetic-antenna beam sharpening. A pulsed waveform $f(t)$ is radiated repetitively and successive pulse returns are recorded adjacently, thus forming a two-dimensional signal record. The optical-processing system is shown in Fig. 24. A cylindrical lens produces a Fourier transformation on the range variable, thus forming the pulse spectrum at P_2. The pulse is compressed by means of a spatial-matched filter at P_2 and the processed image is displayed at P_3 after a transformation by lens L_2. The same lens forms at P_3, through its Fourier transforming properties, a Doppler analysis along the x direction.

For the x dimension, the data record is indistinguishable from a Fourier transform hologram. Under coherent illumination, the record forms, at infinity, an image which is displayed as a real image in the back focal plane of a lens.

The velocity tangential to the line between radar and object is

$$v_x = v_t \cos \theta_0 = \omega_t r_t \cos \theta_0 \tag{50}$$

but since $r_t \sin \theta_0 = z_t$,

$$v_x = \omega_t x_t \tag{51}$$

showing that all particles at constant range r from the radar have the same cross-range velocity (although, for different ranges, v_x will be different). If we view the particles in a coordinate system that moves with the same tangential velocity v_x, the radar resembles a synthetic-aperture system, and the signal received at the antenna can be regarded as a sampling of wavefronts impinging on the antenna flight path. The holographic viewpoint thus applies equally well to both types of systems.

The resolution, however, is considerably better than with the conventional synthetic antenna. The latter has resolution

$$\Delta x = \frac{\lambda_0 r}{2A} \tag{52}$$

where A is the aperture generated. The rotating-body system has resolution given by (48) and since the travel distance, or synthetic-antenna length, is $A' = r_t \omega_t T$, the resolution can be expressed as

$$\Delta x = \frac{\lambda_0 r_t}{2A'}. \tag{53}$$

Combining (52) and (53) yields

$$A = A' \frac{r}{r_t}. \tag{54}$$

The resolution is better than for an equal synthetic aperture by the

ratio of the object distance to the length of the rotation axis. For distant objects, such as a planet, this resolution-improvement factor can be several thousand. The resolution is essentially as good as if the synthetic aperture were at the axis of rotation.

An object point at angular position θ_r, with respect to the antenna, has a Doppler shift

$$\omega_d = \frac{4\pi}{\lambda_0} v \sin \theta_0 \tag{55}$$

thus appearing to arrive at an angle θ_0. Hence the reconstruction process converts an object field angle θ_r into an image field angle θ_0, a viewpoint consistent with regarding the synthetic antenna as being effectively at the axis of rotation.

One of the most fascinating examples of rotating-target imagery is that carried out on the planet Venus at the Jet Propulsion Laboratory (JPL) of the California Institute of Technology [19]. The JPL radar transmitted, at a wavelength of 12.5 cm, a binary-coded pulse of duration 51 100 μs; the pulse was divided into 511 subpulses of phase 0 or π. The code was repeated without interruption for 5 min corresponding to the round trip transit time between Earth and Venus. At the end of this time, the transmission ceased and the reflected signal from Venus was picked up by the receiver and the results stored on magnetic tape. The Doppler bandwidth of the received signal was approximately ± 15 Hz.

The stored data were range-Doppler analyzed by means of a digital computer which compressed the pulse and performed the Doppler analysis.

The data were also processed by optical means, which relates the process more to holography [20]. The data, stored on tape, were recorded photographically through the display of a line trace on a cathode-ray tube, in the manner described in connection with the synthetic-aperture technique. The photographic record was then processed optically, yielding an image, shown in Fig. 25, with resolution of about 15 km in range and about 180 km in the cross-range direction.

Note that the surface of a sphere has two points with the same range and velocity, one in the upper hemisphere and the other in the lower. Unless special means are used to suppress one set of images, the two hemispheres will not be imaged separately, a deficiency present in the image of Fig. 25.

The signal-to-noise ratio of the resulting image, always a problem because of the large signal attenuation resulting from the enormous distances involved, can be significantly increased by the use of post-detection integration. This is accomplished simply by continuing the exposure while moving the data film through the aperture until all of the data have been utilized. All of the data in the aperture at one time are coherently integrated, thus producing an image in accordance with the theory previously given. The length of data that can be usefully integrated coherently is limited by various phase errors to about 2 s; beyond this, there is no improvement in Doppler resolution. A continuum of 2-s sections of data were summed incoherently (i.e., on an intensity basis). Thus each 5-min radiation

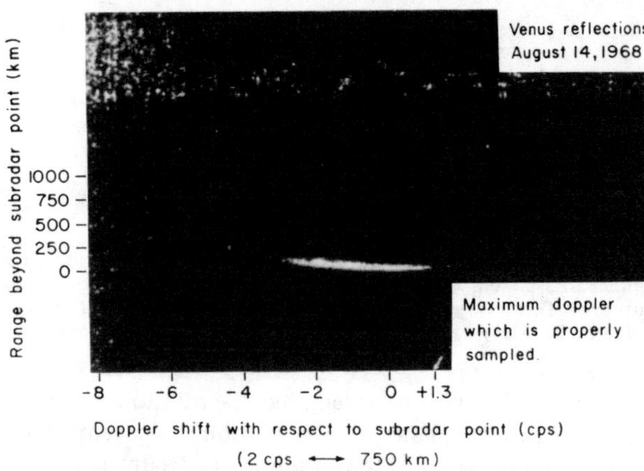

Fig. 26.   Beamforming and steering on a phase-array system.
The beam is aimed in the direction of θ_A.

period results in the incoherent summation of 150 images, thus producing considerable S/N improvement over a single exposure.

VI. Phased-Array Beamforming

Another significant holographic-like technique, beam formation on phase-array systems, unlike the other previously described, does not fall into the category of range-Doppler radar; indeed, phased-array systems need not be radar devices, and they may be passive as well as active.

The phased-array antenna system we describe here is an array of receiving elements in which the received signals, instead of being summed at the antenna, are separately fed into a processing system, either analog or digital, which can process the signals in a variety of different ways. In particular, the signals may be summed with progressive linear-phase delays; e.g., the signal on each array element may be delayed 10° with respect to that on the adjacent element on the left. Such a pattern of summation gives the array a somewhat skewed receiving pattern (Fig. 26). Summing with no phase delay produces a beam pattern centered about the normal to the array.

Generation of a beam pattern in this manner is called beamforming. By controlling the delay pattern, the beam pattern can be steered in any desired direction—a process called beam steering. The signals can each be divided into many portions, each sent into a separate beamforming device which forms a beam in a different direction. Thus unlike the conventional array, the phased-array system can form a narrow beam simultaneously in many directions.

Let $g(x_k, t)$ be the signal received in the kth element. The beamforming process then produces

$$u = \sum_k w(x_k)g(x_k, t) \qquad (56)$$

where $w(x_k)$ is a complex weighting function whose phase component represents the phase delay and whose modulus represents an apodization factor. If the number of elements is large, the summation may be approximated by the integral

$$\int_{-\infty}^{\infty} w(x)g(x, t)\, dx. \qquad (57)$$

For a uniform weighting function and a linear-phase delay,

$$w = \exp\ (j\alpha x), \qquad \frac{-L}{2} \leq x \leq \frac{L}{2}$$

$$= 0, \qquad\qquad |x| > \frac{L}{2} \qquad (58)$$

and for a plane wave incident at angle θ

$$g = \exp j\left(\frac{2\pi}{\lambda_0}\sin\theta\right). \qquad (59)$$

Equation (57) becomes

$$u = \int_{-L/2}^{L/2} \exp j\left(\alpha + \frac{2\pi}{\lambda_0}\sin\theta\right)x$$

$$= K\ \text{sinc}\left(\frac{\alpha}{\pi} + \frac{2}{\lambda_0}\sin\theta\right)\frac{L}{2}. \qquad (60)$$

The array thus has a receiving pattern with a maximum in the direction θ_A such that

$$\alpha + \frac{2\pi}{\lambda_0}\sin\theta_A = 0. \qquad (61)$$

It is evident that quadratic-phase factors may be introduced so as to cause the array to be focused at a point short of infinity.

The beamforming process, as given in (57) with weighting function $\exp\ (j\alpha x)$, is a Fourier transformation. This result is expected in view of the well-known Fourier transform relationship between the antenna illumination function and the far-field antenna receiving pattern. Each point of the Fourier transform represents one of the beams; hence, a device, analog or digital, that Fourier transforms the incident signal $g(x)$ thus forms all the beams.

The beamforming process is obviously akin to the holographic process; the wave-field incident on the array is recreated as an electrical signal, and the second (the electrical) step of the process inverts the process, thereby forming an image of the source distribution.

This simularity suggests carrying out the second step by recording the wave field as a hologram, with subsequent reconstruction at optical frequencies. Alternatively, from the viewpoint of optical data processing, the Fourier-transform relation of (57) also suggests the optical approach, since lenses readily produce Fourier transformations.

The data received on each array element are recorded on photographic film or other device that can serve as the input to an optical system. The recording process, in general, should preserve the geometry so that the reconstruction process duplicates the propagation process that formed the data. The signal thus recorded is coherently illuminated and Fourier transformed by means of a lens. In the Fourier-transform plane, each point represents a beam; or stated equivalently, the Fourier-transform plane is an image of the far-field source distribution sensed by the array. The latter view implies that the entire space sensed by the array is mapped into an optical space, with mapping equations similar to those governing synthetic-aperture systems, or in general, holographic systems.

The process of transferring the data to film may be performed in many ways. For example, the signal on each element may be sampled, the sampled function displayed as an intensity-modulated trace on a cathode-ray tube, and the data transferred to film in the manner described for the synthetic aperture.

Numerous variants of the optical method are possible. The two-dimensional processing capability of the optical system permits two-dimensional arrays to be handled. The signal recorded on each spot on the data film can represent the signal at a single instant, or, in the case of a highly monochromatic signal, the point can represent an integration over time, as in the case of optical holography. In the case where the array is one-dimensional, and we desire to display, as a function of time, the signal $g(x, t)$ on each array element, we may let one dimension of the recording film, say the width dimension, represent the dimension x, while letting distance along the length of the film represent time. This leads to the multichannel system wherein the beamforming process is performed in one dimension, while each signal (a time function) can be filtered, cross correlated with another signal, or otherwise processed. Cylindrical optics can be useful in such situations. An example of the flexibility of the optical approach is given by Beste and Leith [21], wherein a single optical system performs simultaneously on two separate arrays and correlates the signal on one array with that on the other.

Arrays other than linear or planar may be treated. Circular arrays provide an interesting example. The recording process, through its considerable flexibility, permits transformations of the geometry; thus a circular array may be transformed upon recording into a linear array.

The phased-array system may be either active or passive. Coherence between the source and the equivalent "reference function" in the receiver is not necesssary, nor need there be coherence between any of the radiators in the object field. Thus a flexibility exists that is generally absent from optical holography.

VII. Other Holographic-like Systems

The quasi-holography systems already discussed are probably the major ones, but the list is by no means exhausted.

The so-called "hologram radar," suggested by Brown in 1964 as a direct microwave counterpart of optical holography, is, as Brown later noted, better regarded as a union of the synthetic-aperture and the phased-array techniques [22]. An airborne antenna aimed directly below is used in the synthetic-aperture mode. This antenna is an array of dipole elements oriented normal to the flight path, and resolution in the cross-track dimension is produced by the beamforming techniques of Section VI. The radar either is not pulsed or is pulsed only so that the transmitter will be off during the receiving time. Resolution in range is achieved by the three-dimensional imaging effects well known in holography.

A modification of this technique, using the phased-array method in combination with the rotating-target method, was reported by Larson, Johansen, and Zelenka [23].

Kock has recently reported on a variety of microwave processes that fall into the category of quasi-holography, including end-fire synthetic arrays and moving-target-indication radars [24]–[31].

Some early work by Rogers [28] is worth noting, although it was not done at microwave frequencies and was proposed as a direct extension of Gabor's original work and, therefore, qualifies as true rather than quasi-holography. Rogers described the formation of holograms from radio waves reflected from inhomogeneities in the ionosphere. As the inhomogeneity moves, its diffraction pattern on the ground moves across a receiver. The detected signal is then recorded on film as a hologram, from which an image of the inhomogeneity can be formed. Images of both atmospheric inhomogeneities and an aircraft in flight were thus obtained.

VIII. Concluding Comments

Viewing these various processes as holographic often is helpful in increasing one's understanding of them, particularly through being able to visualize them in a very physical and pictorial way. In general, the techniques of geometrical and physical optics are at once brought to bear. Occasionally, techniques are suggested that would have had little likelihood of arising from a communication theory view.

Acknowledgment

The author wishes to thank L. J. Cutrona, who perhaps more than any other individual contributed to the success of synthetic-aperture radar; A. Ingalls, who in the years 1956–1959 helped enlarge on the holographic viewpoint; A. Kozma, who most successfully used the holographic viewpoint to develop new optical-processing concepts for synthetic-aperture radar; and C. J. Palermo, whose contributions to coherent optics include, among many others, the suggestion of optical beamforming.

References

[1] R. P. Dooley, "*X*-band holography," *Proc. IEEE* (Corresp.), vol. 53, Nov. 1965, pp. 1733–1735.
[2] D. E. Duffy, *J. Opt. Soc. Amer.*, vol. 56, 1966, p. 832.
[3] G. Tricoles and E. L. Rope, *J. Opt. Soc. Amer.*, vol. 56, 1966, p. 542; also vol. 57, 1967, p. 97.
[4] J. W. Goodman, *Introduction to Fourier Optics.* New York: McGraw-Hill, 1968, see for example p. 60.
[5] C. W. Sherwin, J. P. Ruina, and R. D. Rawcliffe, "Some early developments in synthetic aperture radar systems," *IRE Trans. Mil. Electron.*, vol. MIL-6, Apr. 1962, pp. 111–115.
[6] L. J. Cutrona, W. E. Vivian, E. N. Leith, and G. O. Hall, "A high-resolution radar combat-surveillance system," *IRE Trans. Mil. Electron.*, vol. MIL-5, Apr. 1961, pp. 127–131.
[7] L. J. Cutrona, E. N. Leith, L. J. Porcello, and W. E. Vivian, "On the application of coherent optical processing techniques to synthetic-aperture radar," *Proc. IEEE*, vol. 54, Aug. 1966, pp. 1026–1032.
[8] E. N. Leith and A. L. Ingalls, *Appl. Opt.*, vol. 7, 1968, p. 539.
[9] A. Kozma and D. L. Kelly, *Appl. Opt.*, vol. 5, 1965, p. 387.
[10] J. R. Klauder, A. L. Price, S. Darlington, and W. J. Albersheim, *Bell Syst. Tech. J.*, vol. 34, 1960, p. 745.
[11] E. N. Leith and J. Upatnieks, *J. Opt. Soc. Amer.*, vol. 52, 1962, p. 1123.
[12] E. N. Leith, "Optical processing techniques for simultaneous pulse compression and beam sharpening," *IEEE Trans. Aerosp. Electron. Syst.*, vol. AES-4, Nov. 1968, pp. 879–885.
[13] *Modern Radar*, R. Berkowitz, Ed. New York: Wiley, 1965, p. 212.
[14] E. N. Leith, in *Proc. 5th Annu. Radar Symp.* Ann Arbor, Mich.: University of Michigan, Feb. 1959.
[15] ——, in *Proc. 2nd Conf. Pulse Compression.* Rome, N. Y.: Rome Air Development Center, Aug. 1959.
[16] W. C. Curtis, private communication, 1959.
[17] L. Lambert, "Optical correlation," see for example, ch. 3 of [13].
[18] F. Dickey, in *Proc. 2nd Conf. Pulse Compression.* Rome, N. Y.: Rome Air Development Center, Aug. 1959.
[19] R. M. Goldstein and R. L. Carpenter, *Science*, vol. 139, 1963, p. 910.
[20] L. J. Porcello, C. E. Heerema, and N. G. Massey, *J. Geophys. Res.*, vol. 74, 1969, p. 27.
[21] D. C. Beste and E. N. Leith, "An optical technique for simultaneous beamforming and cross-correlation," *IEEE Trans. Aerosp. Electron. Syst.*, vol. AES-2, July 1966, pp. 376–384.
[22] W. M. Brown, private communication, 1964.
[23] R. W. Larson, E. L. Johansen, and S. J. Zelenka, "Microwave holography," *Proc. IEEE* (Lett.), vol. 57, Dec. 1969, pp. 2162–2164.
[24] W. E. Kock, "Stationary coherent (hologram) radar and sonar," *Proc. IEEE* (Lett.), vol. 56, Dec. 1968, pp. 2180–2181.
[25] ——, "A hologram form of bistatic radar or sonar," *Proc. IEEE* (Lett.), vol. 57, Jan. 1969, p. 100.
[26] F. Tuttle and W. E. Kock, "A holographic pulse compression technique employing amplitude modulation," *Proc. IEEE* (*Special Issue on Computers in Industrial Process Control*) (Lett.), vol. 58, Jan. 1970, pp. 153–154.
[27] W. E. Kock, "Passive (cooperative) hologram radar," *Proc. IEEE* (Lett.), vol. 58, Aug. 1970, p. 1297.
[28] ——, "Pulse compression with periodic gratings and zone plate gratings," *Proc. IEEE* (Lett.), vol. 58, Sept. 1970, pp. 1395–1396.
[29] ——, "Holographic amplitude pulse compression for synthetic aperture radar," *Proc. IEEE* (*Special Issue on Optical Communication*) (Lett.), vol. 58, Oct. 1970, pp. 1773–1774.
[30] ——, "Synthetic end-fire hologram radar," *Proc. IEEE* (Lett.), vol. 58, Nov. 1970, pp. 1858–1859.
[31] ——, "Holographic techniques in continuous wave bistatic radars," *Proc. IEEE* (Lett.), vol. 58, Nov. 1970, pp. 1863–1864.

Digital Holography

THOMAS S. HUANG, MEMBER, IEEE

Invited Paper

Abstract—The basic techniques in generating and reconstructing holograms on a digital computer are described. Some applications of computer holography, including optical spatial filtering and the testing of optical surfaces, are discussed. Finally, the results on the effects of sampling and quantizing holograms are reviewed.

I. INTRODUCTION

THERE HAS BEEN considerable interest recently in the field of digital holography, i.e., the computer generation and reconstruction of holograms [42], [16], [19]. Computer-generated holograms find applications in optical spatial filtering (for image enhancement, matched-filter pattern detection, code translation, etc.), testing optical surfaces, three-dimensional computer display, automobile design, and the optimum packaging of spacecraft payload. The computer reconstruction of holograms is invaluable in acoustical and microwave holography. And both the generation and the reconstruction of holograms by computer are useful in computer-simulation studies of holographic processes, and in image transmission. Finally, it might be mentioned that for many researchers in optics, the most fruitful aspect of digital holography is perhaps the extensions of the physical process which are permitted by the use of the computer as an imaging element.

The computer generation of holograms involves two major steps. First, we make a mathematical model of the object and calculate the light wave produced by it in a plane in space (the hologram plane). Second, we find a way of displaying the results of our calculation (which are usually complex-valued) and record the display on film or similar material in such a way that the original light wave can be optically reconstructed from this recording (which is called the hologram). These two steps in generating computer holograms are discussed in Sections II and III. In Section IV, we mention some applications of computer-generated holograms.

In the computer reconstruction of holograms (optical, acoustical, or microwave), we scan the hologram plane with a detector and feed the information into a computer. The computer then does the necessary calculations to reconstruct the original object. The reconstruction may be displayed for example on a CRT. We shall describe the computer reconstruction of holograms briefly in Section V.

In both computer generation and computer reconstruction, the hologram data have to be digitized (i.e., sampled in space and quantized in amplitude). The effects of digitization on the quality of the reconstructed image are discussed in Sections VI and VII.

Finally, some alternative approaches to digital holography are mentioned in Section VIII.

II. RECORDING THE LIGHT-WAVE PATTERN

A. Direct Recording of Amplitude and Phase

Let the computer-calculated light-wave distribution in the hologram plane be

$$g(x, y) = A(x, y) \exp (i\phi(x, y)) \tag{1}$$

Manuscript received June 7, 1971; revised July 8, 1971. This work was supported by the NIGMS under Grant 5 PO1 GM14940-05, and by the Associated Press. *This paper is one of a series planned on topics of general interest—The Editor.*

The author is with the Department of Electrical Engineering and Research Laboratory of Electronics, Massachusetts Institute of Technology, Cambridge, Mass. 02139.

where (x, y) are the spatial coordinates in the hologram plane, and A and ϕ are, respectively, the magnitude and the phase angle of g.

A direct way of recording $g(x, y)$ is to make two transparencies. The first one has density variations only but no thickness variation, its amplitude transmittance being proportional to $A(x, y)$. The second one has thickness variations only but no density variations, its amplitude transmittance being proportional to $\exp(i\phi(x, y))$.

The first transparency is relatively easy to make. It requires only a display-recording device with gray-scale capabilities (such as a CRT scanner) and careful control of the exposure and development of the film. To eliminate film thickness variation, a liquid gate may be needed. The second transparency is much harder to produce. One possibility is to expose a film with an intensity distribution proportional to $\phi(x, y)$ and then bleach the film. The resulting transparency will be completely transparent but with a relief image on it. The thickness of the transparency is approximately $a + k\phi(x, y)$, where a and k are real constants. The two transparencies superimposed on each other constitute the hologram. A uniform plane wave incident on this hologram will produce a light wave proportional to the original $g(x, y)$.

If the object we are making a hologram of is diffusely illuminated, then the magnitude $A(x, y)$ of $g(x, y)$ turns out to be relatively unimportant for reconstruction, i.e., we can optically reconstruct the original object from the second transparency (which contains only the phase $\phi(x, y)$) alone. In fact, Kermisch [44] showed that in such reconstruction, 78 percent of the energy of the incident plane wave goes to the reconstructed object, while 22 percent creates noise which consists of essentially convolutions of the original object with itself. This type of phase recording has recently been studied extensively by Lesem *et al.* [58], [59] at IBM. They call it the kinoform. It is to be emphasized that the kinoform is completely different from the conventional phase hologram which is made by bleaching an optical hologram [13]. We would also like to mention here an interesting extension of kinoform by Kirk and Jones [46].

B. Using a Reference Wave

To avoid the necessity of making a relief image, we can use a reference wave as in the case of optical holograms [53]. After we have calculated the light wave $g(x, y)$ due to the object, we add a reference wave $r(x, y)$ to it, and square the absolute value of the sum to get

$$h(x, y) = |g(x, y) + r(x, y)|^2. \tag{2}$$

The reference wave can be a plane wave, in which case

$$h(x, y) = |g(x, y) + B \exp(ibx)|^2 \tag{3}$$

or

$$h(x, y) = A^2(x, y) + B^2 + 2B\,A(x, y)\cos(bx - \phi(x, y)) \tag{4}$$

where B and b are real constants, and A and ϕ are as defined in (1). We then produce a film transparency with an amplitude transmittance proportional to $h(x, y)$, which is real and positive.

To reconstruct optically, we have a plane wave $B \exp(ibx)$ incident upon the hologram, producing a light wave that contains four components. Two of the components are, respectively, proportional to $g(x, y)$, the original wave, and $g^*(x, y) \exp(i2bx)$, where * denotes complex conjugation. The other two components constitute noise; i.e., they are undesired. We note that the two desired components are due to the last term at the right-hand side of (4). As far as we are concerned, the first two terms at the right-hand side of (4) are there for the sole purpose of biasing, i.e., making $h(x, y)$ positive for all (x, y) so that we can record it on film as a density variation. In making holograms optically, the use of $(A^2(x, y) + B^2)$ as the bias is con-

venient, since (3) is easy to perform by photooptical means. However, when we make holograms on the computer, we are much more flexible. We can use other forms of biases.

Burch [6] suggested the use of a constant bias, yielding the hologram

$$h_1(x, y) = K + 2BA(x, y)\cos(bx - \phi(x, y)) \tag{5}$$

where K is a constant which is just large enough to make $h_1(x, y)$ positive for all (x, y). Huang and Prasada [39] proposed the hologram

$$h_2(x, y) = 2BA(x, y) + 2BA(x, y)\cos(bx - \phi(x, y)). \tag{6}$$

The advantage of Burch's hologram is that the noise component in the reconstruction is just a plane wave. The advantage of the Huang-Prasada hologram is that its fringe contrast is higher than that of either (4) or (5), making the accuracy requirements on the display-recording device and on film exposure and development less stringent.

C. Fourier-Transform Holograms—Lohmann's Method

The flexibility of computer calculation makes it possible for us to do things which have no analogy in optical holography. In this and the following sections we shall describe two ingeneous methods of recording Fourier-transform holograms.

For Fourier-transform holograms, the light distribution at the hologram plane due to the object is

$$g(x, y) = \iint_{-\infty}^{\infty} p(u, v) \exp(-i(2\pi/\lambda f)(ux + vy))\,du\,dv \tag{7}$$

where $p(u, v)$ is the light amplitude distribution at the two-dimensional object, (u, v) the spatial coordinates in the object plane, λ the wavelength of the light, and f the focal length of the lens used to produce the Fourier transform.

In computer calculation, $g(x, y)$ will be sampled in space. Each sample has a generally complex value. Assume that we calculate $g(x, y)$ at $x, y = md$; $m = 0, 1, 2, \cdots$, and $d = $ constant. The sampled hologram is then

$$\hat{g}(x, y) = \sum_m \sum_n g(md, nd)\delta(x - md, y - nd) \tag{8}$$

where $\delta(x, y)$ is the two-dimensional unit impulse function. Equation (8) cannot be directly recorded on a film with density variations only, since $g(md, nd)$ is complex-valued. The gist of Lohmann's method [3]–[5], [64]–[66], is to display only the magnitude $|g(md, nd)|$ of each sample, but to shift the position of each sample (in the x-direction, say) by an amount Δ_{mn} proportional to the phase angle $\phi(md, nd)$ of $g(md, nd)$. That is, the mathematical expression of Lohmann's hologram is

$$g_l(x, y) = \sum_m \sum_n |g(md, nd)|\delta(x - md - \Delta_{mn}, y - nd). \tag{9}$$

In Lohmann's original work, the magnitude of each sample was not recorded as a transmittance variation of the sample point. Rather, a completely transparent slit was used to represent each sample, the area of the slit being proportional to $|g(md, nd)|$. Lohmann's original holograms are therefore similar to newspaper halftone pictures and are binary; i.e., each point on the hologram has a transmittance of either 0 or 1.

In optical reconstruction, a uniform plane wave passes through Lohmann's hologram, and then a lens is used to perform the Fourier transformation of $g_l(x, y)$. The first-order diffraction pattern at the back focal plane of the lens turns out to be $p(u, v)$, the reconstructed original image.

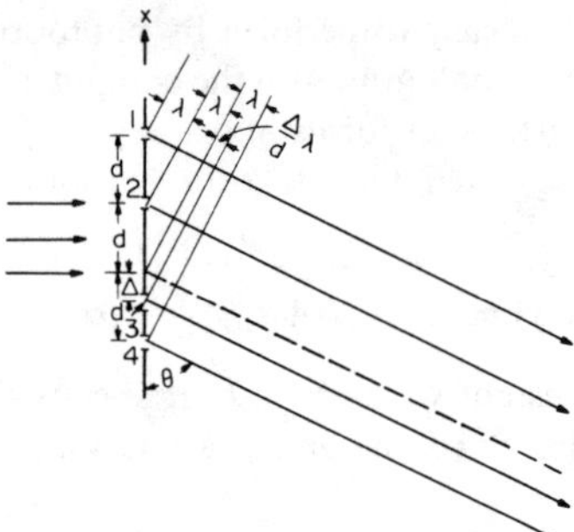

Fig. 1.   Lohmann's method.

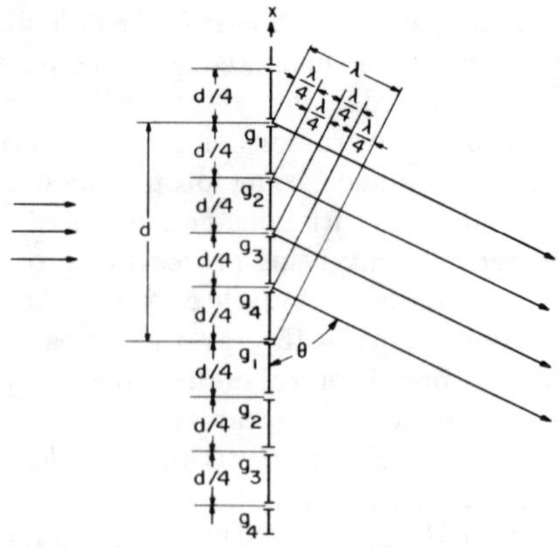

Fig. 2.   Lee's method.

A detailed mathematical analysis of the reconstruction was given by Lohmann and Paris [64]. Here we give a heuristic argument [3] to indicate why the process works. In Fig. 1 we show a sideview of a part of a Lohmann hologram. Three of the sample points (1, 2, and 4) have zero phase, so they are located at their regular grid positions. However, sample point 3 has a nonzero phase angle (ϕ_3, say), so it is shifted a distance Δ from its regular grid position. When a uniform plane wave coming from the left impinges on the pinholes representing the sample points, light is scattered in all directions to the right of the hologram. The far-field diffraction pattern will be essentially the Fourier transform of the hologram. If we look at the far field at an angle $\theta = \cos^{-1}(\lambda/d)$ with respect to the x axis, we observe that the phase differences between the light from sample points 1, 2, and 4 are multiples of 2π, while the phase differences between the light from sample point 3 and that from the other three sample points are multiples of 2π plus $(2\pi/d)\Delta$. Therefore, by choosing Δ to make $(2\pi/d)\Delta = \phi_3$ we can create the proper phase relationships between the sample points on the hologram. When a lens is used, the far field is brought to the back focal plane of the lens, and the far-field pattern in the θ-direction becomes the first-order diffraction pattern.

D. Fourier-Transform Hologram—Lee's Method

An alternative method of recording sampled Fourier-transform holograms was developed by Lee [50]–[52]. In Lee's method, each complex-valued sample $g(md, nd)$ is represented by four positive real samples on the hologram. Let g_r and g_i be, respectively, the real and the imaginary parts of g, and let

$$g_1 = \begin{cases} g_r, & \text{if } g_r \geq 0 \\ 0, & \text{if } g_r < 0 \end{cases} \tag{10}$$

$$g_3 = \begin{cases} -g_r, & \text{if } g_r < 0 \\ 0, & \text{if } g_r \geq 0 \end{cases} \tag{11}$$

$$g_2 = \begin{cases} g_i, & \text{if } g_i \geq 0 \\ 0, & \text{if } g_i < 0 \end{cases} \tag{12}$$

$$g_4 = \begin{cases} -g_i, & \text{if } g_i < 0 \\ 0, & \text{if } g_i \geq 0. \end{cases} \tag{13}$$

Then

$$g = g_1 - g_3 + ig_2 - ig_4 \tag{14}$$

where g_1, g_2, g_3, and g_4 are all real and positive.

In Fig. 2 we show a sideview of a part of a Lee hologram. Each complex-valued sample g is represented by four equally spaced positive real samples g_1, g_2, g_3, and g_4. The optical reconstruction procedure is identical to that of a Lohmann hologram. Again we explain heuristically why it works. With a uniform plane wave impinging from the left, we again look at the far-field diffraction pattern of the

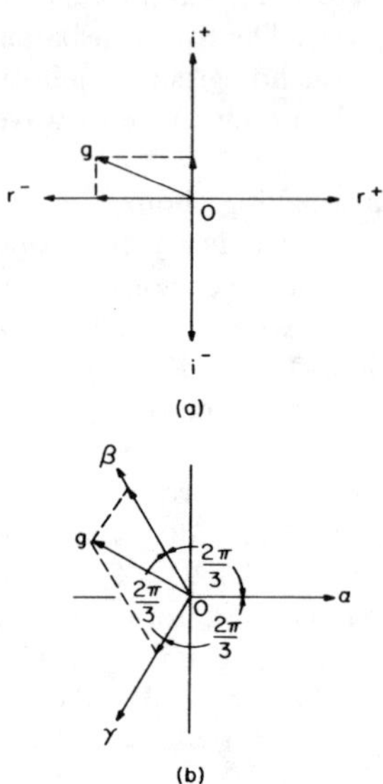

Fig. 3.   Interpreting Lee's method. (a) Resolving a complex number into four positive real components. (b) Burckhardt's simplification (reducing the number of components to three).

hologram in the $\theta = \cos^{-1}(\lambda/d)$ direction. We observe that the path differences between the light from g_2, g_3, and g_4, respectively, and that from g_1 are $(\lambda/4)$, $(\lambda/2)$, and $(3\lambda/4)$, respectively. But these path differences correspond to $\pi/2$, π, and $3\pi/2$, and $\exp(i)(\pi/2)=i$, $\exp(i\pi)=-1$, and $\exp(i)(3/2)\pi=-i$. Therefore, as far as the first-order far-field pattern is concerned, the four samples g_1, g_2, g_3, and g_4 taken together are equivalent to a single complex-valued sample g, as given by (14).

Equation (14) can be interpreted as a vector resolution in the complex-number plane as depicted in Fig. 3(a). We have a set of four base vectors: $r^+ = (1, 0)$, $r^-(-1, 0)$, $i^+ = (0, 1)$, and $i^- = (0, -1)$. It should be obvious that any vector g can be expressed as

$$g = g_1 r^+ + g_2 i^+ + g_3 r^- + g_4 i^- \tag{15}$$

where g_1, g_2, g_3, and g_4 are all positive. In fact, at most two of the four components can be nonzero. From this interpretation, Burckhardt [8] suggested that it is possible to reduce the number of base vectors to three by using the set $\{\alpha, \beta, \gamma\}$ shown in Fig. 3(b). Any vector g can be expressed as

$$g = a\alpha + b\beta + c\gamma \tag{16}$$

where a, b, and c are all positive, and at most two of them are nonzero. By employing Burckhardt's solution, we need to use only three positive real samples to represent one complex-valued sample.

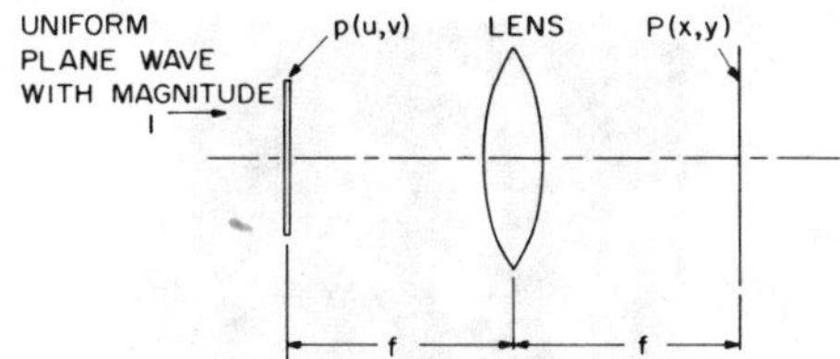

Fig. 4. Basic optical setup for Fourier transformation.

We mention in passing that, just as in the case of Lohmann holograms, the halftone technique can be applied to Lee holograms to make them binary.

E. Recording any Wavefront with Lohmann's and Lee's Methods

The methods of Lohmann and Lee can be used to record not only Fourier transforms but also any light wave distribution $f(u, v)$. What we do is to first calculate the Fourier transform $F(x, y)$ of $f(u, v)$ and then record this $F(x, y)$ by either Lohmann's or Lee's method. To optically recreate $f(u, v)$, we pass a uniform plane wave through our hologram and use a lens to take the Fourier transform. Then the first-order pattern at the back focal plane of the lens will be the desired $f(u, v)$.

III. CALCULATING THE LIGHT-WAVE PATTERN

A. Two-Dimensional Fourier-Transform Hologram

The basic setup for taking a Fourier transform optically is shown in Fig. 4. A transparency with amplitude transmittance $p(u, v)$ is located in the front focal plane of the lens, where (u, v) are the spatial coordinates in that plane. When a uniform plane wave with unit magnitude impinges on the transparency from the left, the light distribution at the back focal plane of the lens becomes the Fourier transform of $p(u, v)$:

$$P(x, y) = \iint_{-\infty}^{\infty} p(u, v) \exp\left(-i(2\pi/\lambda f)(ux + vy)\right) du dv \quad (17)$$

where (x, y) are the spatial coordinates in the back focal plane, λ is the wavelength of the light, and f the focal length of the lens.

To perform the Fourier transformation on the computer, we use a sampled version of $p(u, v)$ and calculate its discreet Fourier transform (DFT), which gives us approximately a sampled version of $P(x, y)$. The more samples we take of p, the better the approximation. If we use N samples of $p(u, v)$, then we will get N samples for $P(x, y)$. If we use the fast Fourier transform (FFT) algorithm [30], the computation time required is

$$T = (2N \log_2 N)t \quad (18)$$

where t is the time for the computer to do one complex multiplication and one complex addition. For a typical computer, such as the IBM 7094, $t \approx 30$ μs. Using $N = 256 \times 256$, we get $T \approx$ min. After having calculated $P(x, y)$, we can record it using any of the methods described in Section II. An example of a two-dimensional Fourier-transform hologram of the Lee type is shown in Fig. 5.

We note that for most images we are interested in, their Fourier transforms have very large dynamic ranges—the magnitudes of the dc and low-frequency components being much larger than those of higher frequencies. This poses a severe problem in recording the Fourier transform on film. To alleviate this problem, we can multiply the original image $p(u, v)$ by a random phase factor $\exp(i\theta(u, v))$ before we calculate the Fourier transform. Then the magnitudes of the Fourier coefficients will be much more uniform. The optical analogy of adding the random phase factor is to place a diffuser (e.g., ground glass) right in front of the transparency in Fig. 4. Examples of computer-generated Lee holograms of images multi-

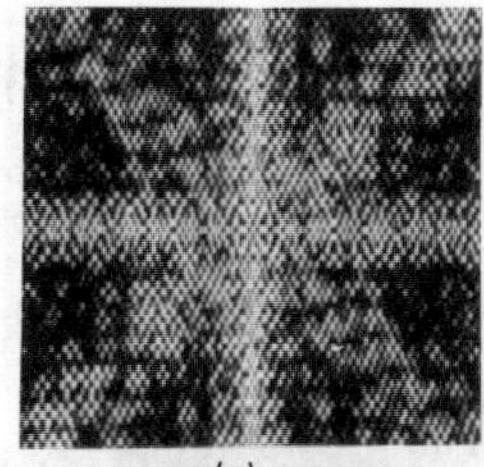

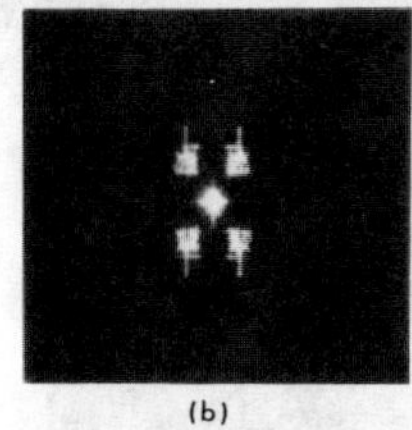

Fig. 5. A two-dimensional Fourier-transform Lee hologram.
(a) The hologram. (b) Optical reconstruction.

plied by random phase factors are shown in Figs. 6 and 7. Note that the hologram in Fig. 6(a) is binary.

B. Three-Dimensional Fourier-Transform Hologram

Although a lens cannot take the exact Fourier transform of a three-dimensional object, the concept of Fourier-transform holography can be generalized to three-dimensional objects [85], [86], [4], [50]. Consider the setup in Fig. 8, where a three-dimensional object is located near the front focal plane of the lens. If we model the three-dimensional object as a source amplitude distribution $p(u, v, z)$, then the light amplitude distribution at the back focal plane of the lens is (except for a multiplicative constant)

$$P(x, y) = \iiint_{-\infty}^{\infty} p(u, v, z) \exp\left(-i\right)(\pi/\lambda f^2)z(x^2 + y^2)$$
$$\cdot \exp\left(-i\right)(2\pi/\lambda f)(ux + vy) du dv dz. \quad (19)$$

This integral can be evaluated for simple objects such as finite segments of straight lines, planes, and simple curves at various orientations in the three-dimensional object space. For more complicated objects, we can approximate the integral by

$$P(x, y) \approx \sum_{k=0,1,2,\cdots} \left\{ \exp\left(-i\right)(\pi/\lambda f^2)k\Delta z(x^2 + y^2) \iint_{-\infty}^{\infty} p(u, v, k\Delta z) \right.$$
$$\left. \cdot \exp\left(-i\right)(2\pi/\lambda f)(ux + vy) du dv \right\} \quad (20)$$

where Δz is a constant. What we have done was to approximate the three-dimensional object by a sum of its equally spaced cross sections perpendicular to the z axis. In computer calculation, the integral in each term of the summation in (20) can be computed by an FFT algorithm.

After having computed $P(x, y)$ of (20), we can again record it using any of the methods described in Section II. In optical reconstruction using a lens, cross sections of the object will be reconstructed in the appropriate planes around the back focal plane of the lens. A three-dimensional Fourier-transform hologram of the Lee type is shown in Fig. 9(a). In this case, the object consists of two cross sections. On one of the cross sections we have the letter "E," while on the other the symbol "$+$." The reconstructions are shown in Fig. 9(b) and (c).

C. Two-Dimensional Fresnel Holograms

For Fresnel holograms, the light distribution in the hologram plane due to the object is the Fresnel diffraction pattern of the ob-

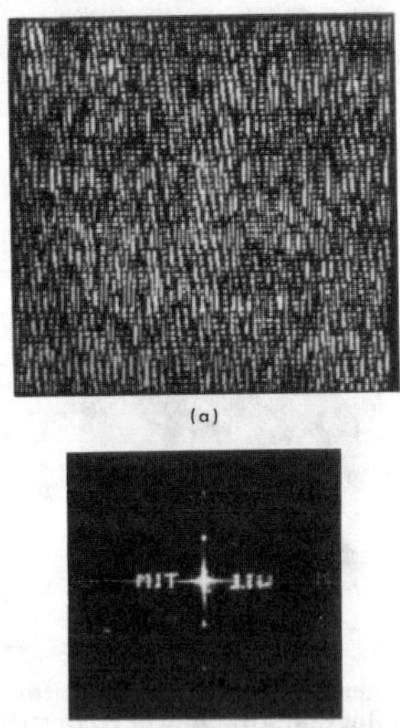

Fig. 6.   A two-dimensional Fourier-transform binary Lee hologram using random phase factor. (a) The hologram. (b) Optical reconstruction.

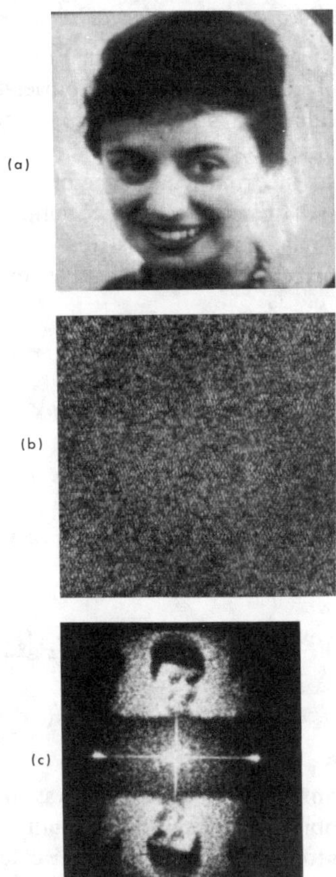

Fig. 7.   A two-dimensional Fourier-transform Lee hologram of a continuous-tone image using random phase factor. (a) The original. (b) The hologram. (c) Optical reconstruction.

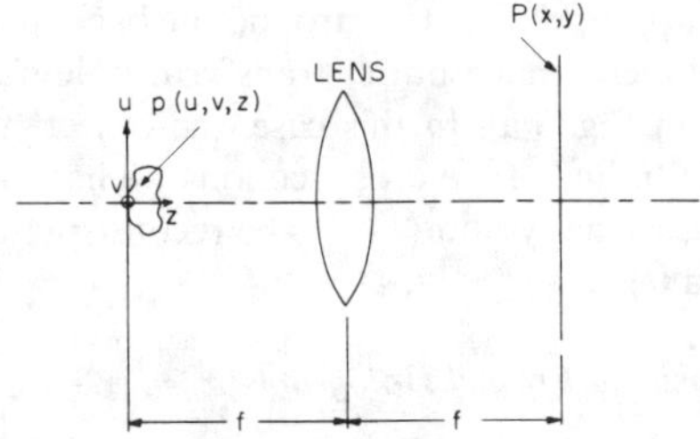

Fig. 8.   Optical Fourier transformation generalized to three-dimensional object.

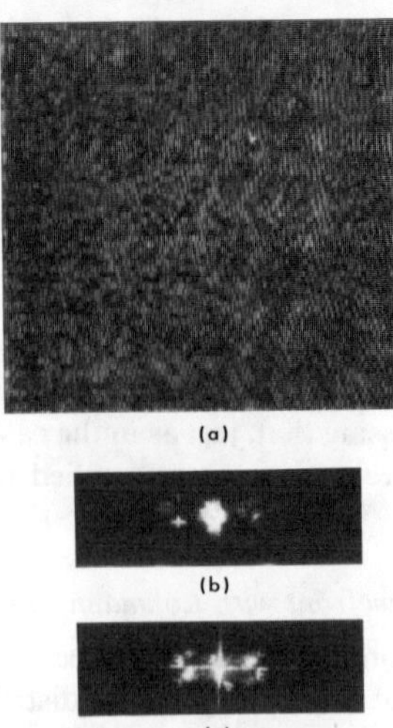

Fig. 9.   A three-dimensional Fourier-transform Lee hologram. (a) The hologram. (b) Optically reconstructed image at the back focal plane of the lens. (c) Reconstructed image at a plane shifted from the back focal plane.

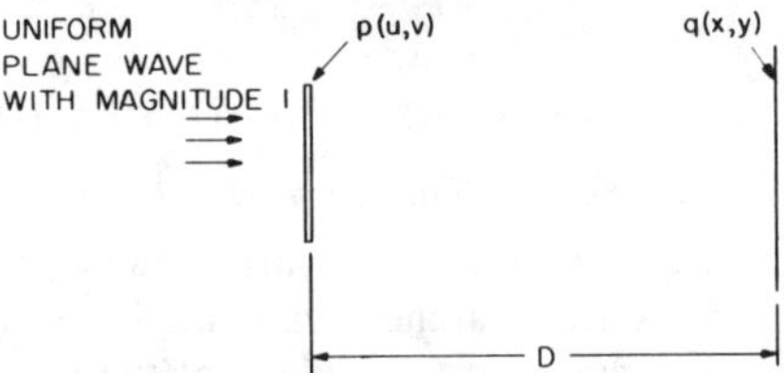

Fig. 10.   Optical setup for the generation of Fresnel diffraction pattern of a two-dimensional image.

ject. Fig. 10 shows an optical setup for the generation of the Fresnel diffraction pattern of a two-dimensional object in the form of a transparency with a transmittance $p(u, v)$, where (u, v) are the spatial coordinates in the transparency plane. When a uniform plane wave with unity magnitude impinges on the transparency from the left, the light distribution in the hologram plane, which is located a distance D to the right of the object transparency, is

$$q(x, y) = p(x, y) \otimes h_D(x, y) \tag{21}$$

where

$$h_D(x, y) = K \exp(i)(\pi/\lambda D)(x^2 + y^2). \tag{22}$$

K is a constant, and $\otimes$ denotes convolution. Equation (21) can be rewritten as

$$q(x, y) = \exp(i)(\pi/\lambda D)(x^2 + y^2) \iint_{-\infty}^{\infty} p(u, v) \exp(i)(\pi/\lambda D)(u^2 + v^2)$$
$$\exp(-i)(2\pi/\lambda D)(ux + vy) \, du dv. \tag{23}$$

To calculate $q(x, y)$ on the computer [55], [57], we can follow (23). We first multiply $p(u, v)$ by a quadratic phase factor, then take the Fourier transform using the FFT algorithm, and finally multiply the transform by another quadratic phase factor.

Alternatively, we note that from (21),

$$Q(\alpha, \beta) = P(\alpha, \beta)H_D(\alpha, \beta) \tag{24}$$

where Q, P, and H_D are the Fourier transforms of q, p, and h_D, respectively. Therefore, to calculate $q(x, y)$, we can first calculate the Fourier transform of p, then multiply it by H_D, and finally take the inverse Fourier transform of the product to get q. After having calculated $q(x, y)$, we can record it using any of the methods described in Section II.

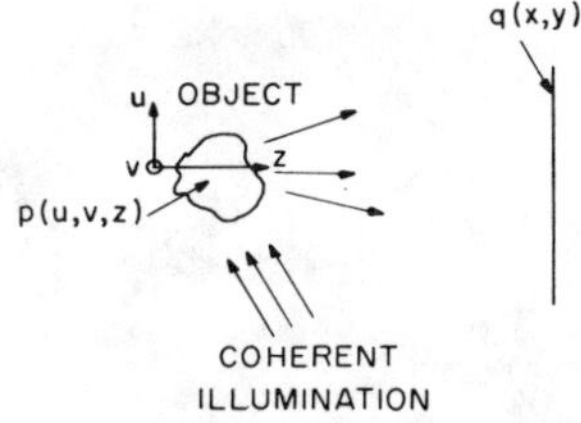

Fig. 11. Optical setup for the generation of Fresnel diffraction pattern of a three-dimensional object.

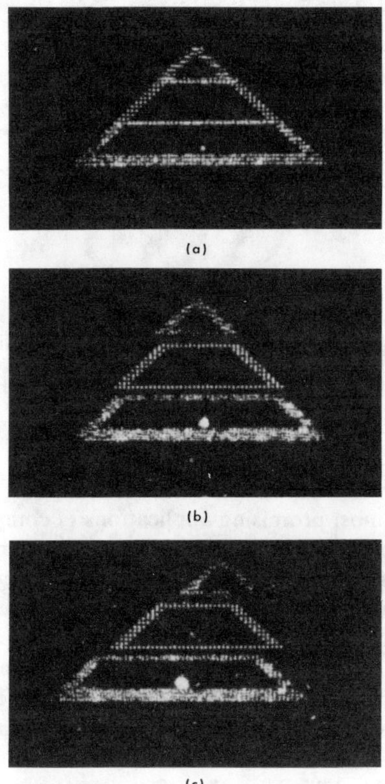

Fig. 12. Photographs of three-dimensional kinoform-generated images; each of the three geometrical figures is located in a different plane. (a) On-axis view. (b), (c) Off-axis views showing separation and parallax. (Courtesy of *IBM J. Res. Develop.*)

We mention in passing that diffuse illumination can again be simulated on the computer by multiplying $p(u, v)$ by a random phase factor.

D. Three-Dimensional Fresnel Holograms

In Fig. 11 we show an optical setup for the generation of Fresnel diffraction pattern of a three-dimensional object. To calculate the Fresnel diffraction pattern $q(x, y)$ on a computer, we can do again what we did in the case of three dimensional Fourier-transform holograms. We model the object by a source distribution $p(u, v, z)$ and then approximate it by its cross sections $p(u, v, k\Delta z)$; $k = 0, 1, 2 \cdots$. We then calculate $q(x, y)$ by summing up the contributions due to these cross sections. The contribution due to each cross section can be calculated by the methods discussed in Section III-C. An example of the optical reconstruction from a three-dimensional Fresnel hologram in the form of a kinoform [58] is shown in Fig. 12. The original object consists of three cross sections, each of which contains a geometrical figure.

In the computer calculation of $q(x, y)$ we are dealing with samples of $p(u, v, k\Delta z)$. Therefore, we are actually modeling the object as a collection of point sources. Waters [84] developed a technique of making holograms where he recorded on the hologram the Fresnel zone plate patterns [77] corresponding to the point sources.

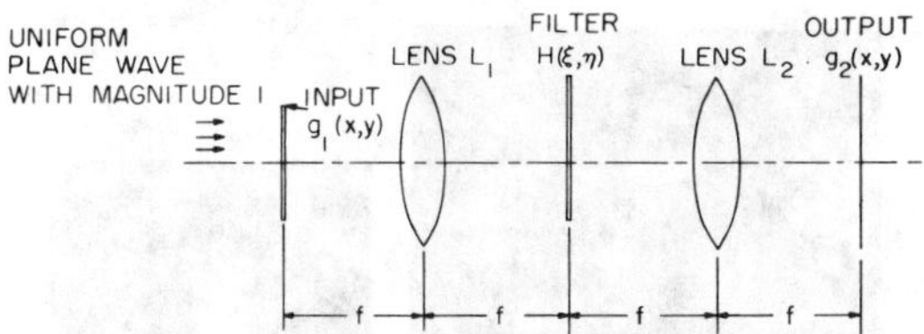

Fig. 13. The basic setup for doing coherent optical spatial filtering.

Finally, we mention that for simple objects it is sometimes possible to derive closed-form solutions for the diffraction patterns in the hologram plane [72], [37]. The computer can then be used to calculate numerical values from these solutions.

E. The Hidden-Line Problem

In our discussions of three-dimensional holograms in Section III-B and D, we have ignored the hidden-line problem. In optical reconstructions from holograms made by the methods described there, we can see through the objects. This is undesirable if the original object is opaque. In the reconstruction, we do not want to see the back side of the object which is supposed to be obstructed by the front surface of the object.

One way to solve the hidden-line problem is as follows. In calculating the light value due to the object in any particular point in the hologram plane, we sum up the contributions due to only those object points that can be seen from the particular hologram point in question.

An alternative way of solving the hidden-line problem, which is computationally more efficient, was suggested by Ichioka *et al.* [41]. The three-dimensional object $p(u, v, z)$ is approximated by its cross sections $p(u, v, k\Delta z)$; $k = 0, 1, 2, \cdots$. Assume light is propagating in the positive z-direction. We first calculate the Fresnel diffraction pattern of $p(u, v, 0)$ at the plane $z = \Delta z$. Call the result $p_0(u, v, \Delta z)$. Then we calculate the Fresnel diffraction pattern of $p_0(u, v, \Delta z) \cdot p(u, v, \Delta z)$ at the plane $z = 2\Delta z$. Call the result $p_1(u, v, 2\Delta z)$. Then we calculate the Fresnel diffraction pattern of $p_1(u, v, 2\Delta z)p(u, v, 2\Delta z)$ at the plane $z = 3\Delta z$. And so on until we get to the hologram plane. A three-dimensional Fourier-transform hologram was successfully made by Ichioka *et al.* using this method.

IV. Applications of Computer-Generated Holograms

A. Coherent Optical Spatial Filtering

The computer generation of two-dimensional Fourier-transform holograms provides a convenient and sometimes the only way of synthesizing complex optical spatial filters. Fig. 13 shows the basic setup for doing coherent optical spatial filtering [83]. The input image $g_1(x, y)$ is represented by the amplitude transmittance variation in the transparency at the front focal plane of lens L_1. The filter transparency has an amplitude transmittance equal to $H(\xi, \eta)$, the frequency response of the desired filter. The spatial frequency variables ξ and η are related to the spatial variables x and y by

$$\begin{cases} \xi = \dfrac{x}{\lambda f} \\ \eta = \dfrac{y}{\lambda f} \end{cases} \qquad (25)$$

where λ is the light wavelength, and f the focal length of the lenses. The light distribution at the back focal plane of lens L_2 is the desired output

$$g_2(x, y) = g_1(x, y) \otimes h(x, y) \qquad (26)$$

where $h(x, y)$ is the Fourier transform of $H(\xi, \eta)$, and therefore the impulse response of the filter.

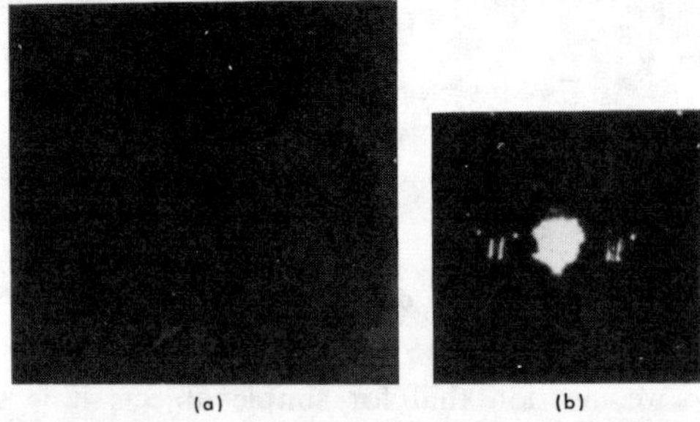

Fig. 14.   (a) A differentiation filter. (b) Output pattern obtained by using the letter T as the input.

Fig. 15.   (a) A code-translation filter. (b) The input triangle is shown in the middle, the output triangle on the side.

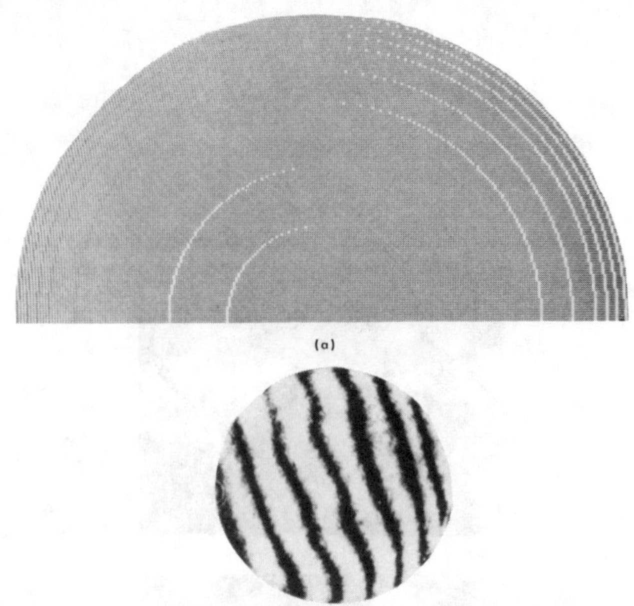

Fig. 16.   (a) Lohmann hologram of defocused parabolic wavefront. (b) Interferogram resulting from interfering parabolic wavefront produced by hologram with wavefront produced by parabolic mirror. (Courtesy of *Applied Optics*.)

The desired filter frequency response $H(\xi, \eta)$ is generally complex-valued. The methods discussed in Section II can be used to record it. In fact, what we do is to make a Fourier-transform hologram of $h(x, y)$ and use it as the filter. If the direct recording method (Section II-A) is used, the output will be obtained on axis; while if the reference-beam (Section II-B), Lohmann's (Section II-C), or Lee's (Section II-D) method is used, the desired output will be obtained off axis.

Coherent optical spatial filtering finds applications in many areas, such as image enhancement, matched filtering, and code translation. Two examples where Lee's method was used to synthesize the filters are shown in Figs. 14 and 15. Fig. 14 illustrates a differentiator. The frequency response of the filter is $i2\pi\xi$. Fig. 15 illustrates a code translator whose response to an input triangle is a different triangle (which is the input triangle rotated by 180°). The frequency response of the filter is simply equal to the ratio of the Fourier transform of the output triangle to that of the input triangle.

We mention in passing that computer-generated holograms can also be used to do noncoherent optical spatial filtering [74], [63], [67]. However, in noncoherent filtering the form of the impulse response of the filter is restricted.

B. Testing of Optical Surfaces

One of the most promising applications of computer-generated holograms is the testing of optical surfaces. A hologram is made of a standard wavefront calculated in the computer. Then the optically reconstructed wavefront from the hologram is interfered with the wavefront from the surface under test. MacGovern and Wyant [69] at Itek used a Lohmann hologram to test an $f/5$ parabola. Fig. 16(a) shows the Lohmann hologram. Fig. 16(b) shows the fringes resulting from the test—a modified Twyman–Green interferometer was used with some tilt introduced between the two wavefronts. The hologram was tested to 1/15 wave. Therefore, most of the departure from straightness of the fringes may be directly attributed to errors in the parabola.

C. Simulation of Holographic Processes

The computer generation and reconstruction of holograms can be used to study various holographic effects such as the effects of film nonlinearity and noise on the quality of the reconstructed image. The advantages of using a computer are that the parameters in the holographic processes can be controlled precisely and that dust and defects of optical elements are totally absent.

Carter and Dougal [11] used computer simulation to verify some theoretical results concerning the effect of finite hologram resolution on the range of field recorded in hologram and the resolution of the reconstructed image. Milder and Wells [73] demonstrated by computer simulation ways of solving two practical problems in acoustical holography: how to constrain the spatial extent of the hologram plane, and how to retain the range-gating features so valuable in sonar and radar.

D. Three-Dimensional Computer Display

One of the most exciting potential applications of computer-generated holograms is three-dimensional computer display. In many important problems the results we calculate on the computer are three-dimensional in nature. For example, we may feed into a computer the two-dimensional X-ray shadowgrams of a biological specimen and then calculate the three-dimensional internal structure of the specimen [82]. One truly three-dimensional way of displaying such results is to calculate on the computer a hologram of

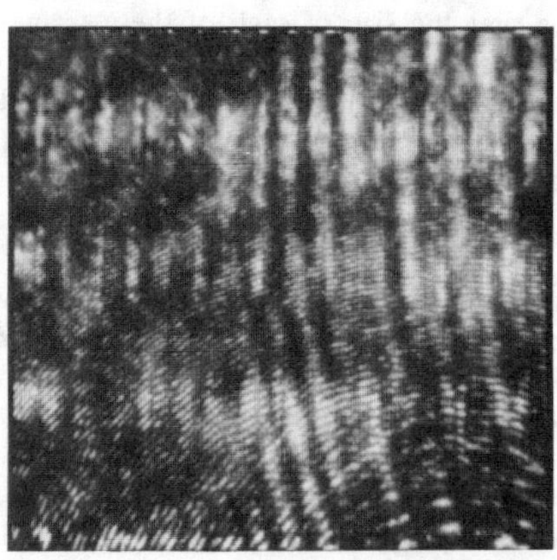
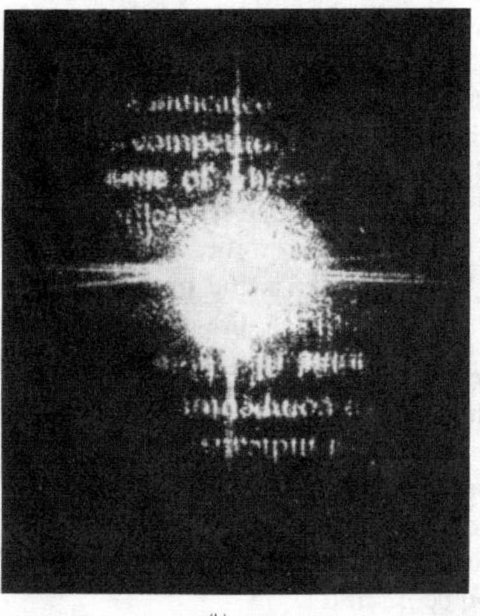
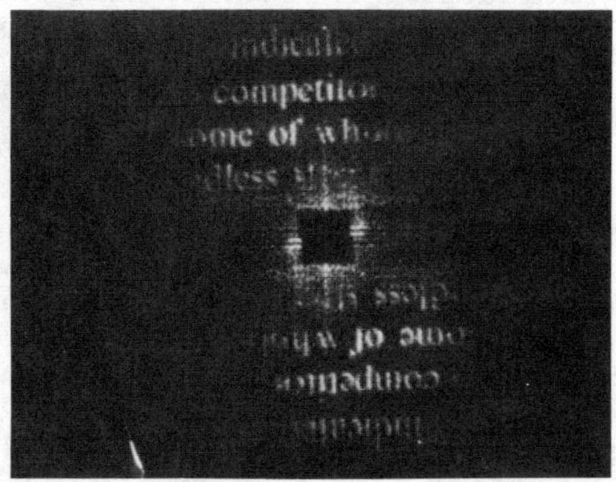

(a)   (b)   (c)

Fig. 17. Optical versus computer reconstruction of a Fourier-transform hologram. (a) Scanned hologram. (b) Optical reconstruction from a reduced version of (a). (c) Computer reconstruction.

the three-dimensional object, record it on some suitable medium (e.g., photochromic film or dark-trace-phosphor CRT surface) and reconstruct the object by passing laser light through the medium.

One major difficulty in carrying out this procedure is the high resolution requirement of the hologram of most three-dimensional objects of practical interest [54], [7], [60], [36], [28], [38], [35]. A practical three-dimensional holographic computer display system is yet to be developed.

V. Computer Reconstruction of Holograms

A. Fourier-Transform Holograms

In making acoustical and microwave holograms (and in some cases optical holograms), the hologram plane is scanned point by point by a detector [31], [33], [71], [70], [2]. Instead of trying to create a film transparency of appropriate size from the data thus gathered and then get an optical reconstruction, it is often much more convenient to feed the data directly into a computer and reconstruct the original object by computer calculation. Because this latter approach eliminates several intermediate steps, it usually gives a reconstruction of better quality.

We shall restrict our attention to two-dimensional holograms. Holograms of three-dimensional objects can be reconstructed section by section. An acoustical, microwave, or optical Fourier-transform hologram $h(x, y)$ has the form of (2) or (3) in Section II-B, where $g(x, y)$ is the Fourier transform of the original two-dimensional object $p(u, v)$. On a computer we can reconstruct $p(u, v)$ by simply taking the Fourier transform of the hologram $h(x, y)$. The Fourier transform of the last term at the right-hand side of (4) gives us two reconstructed images shifted away from the origin. The Fourier transform of the first two terms gives us a function centered around the origin. If the constant b is large enough, the desired reconstructed images will not overlap the undesired component near the origin.

An example of optical versus computer reconstruction of a Fourier-transform hologram is shown in Fig. 17. An optically made hologram was scanned and fed into a computer. Fig. 17(c) shows a display of the computer reconstruction. Then the scanned hologram was displayed on a CRT [Fig. 17(a)]. A picture was taken of the display and photoreduced to a size suitable for optical reconstruction. Fig. 17(b) shows the optical reconstruction. As we mentioned earlier, since the computer reconstruction eliminated several intermediate steps, it gave a better reconstruction.

B. Fresnel Holograms

An acoustical, microwave, or optical Fresnel hologram with a plane-wave reference beam has the form

$$h(x, y) = |q(x, y) + B \exp(ibx)|^2 \tag{27}$$

or

$$h(x, y) = |q(x, y)|^2 + B^2 + Bq(x, y) \exp(-ibx)$$
$$+ Bq^*(x, y) \exp(ibx) \tag{28}$$

where B and b are constants, and $q(x, y)$ is given by (21) or (23) of Section III-C, where $p(u, v)$ is the original object. To reconstruct $p(u, v)$, we first take the Fourier transform of $h(x, y)$ to get

$$H(\xi, \eta) = K(\xi, \eta) + BQ\left(\xi - \frac{b}{2\pi}, \eta\right) + BQ\left(-\xi - \frac{b}{2\pi}, \eta\right) \tag{29}$$

where ξ and η are frequency variables, $Q(\xi, \eta)$ is the Fourier transform of $q(x, y)$, and $K(\xi, \eta)$ that of $|q(x, y)|^2 + B^2$. For a large enough b, the three terms at the right-hand side of (29) will not overlap each other. Therefore, we can extract $Q(\xi, \eta)$ from $H(\xi, \eta)$. From (24) we can get the Fourier transform $P(\xi, \eta)$ of $p(u, v)$ by dividing $Q(\xi, \eta)$ by $H_D(\xi, \eta)$. Finally, taking the inverse Fourier transform of $P(\xi, \eta)$, we obtain $p(u, v)$, our reconstructed object [55].

Sondhi [79] did an experiment in which he measured the sound Fresnel diffraction pattern $q(x, y)$ (without any reference beam) of an object $p(u, v)$ and then reconstructed p from q on a digital computer. The method he used in obtaining p from q was essentially the one we described in the preceding paragraph.

Wolf [88], [89] has recently developed an inverse scattering theory by which the three-dimensional structure of a weakly scattering, semitransparent object can be computationally determined from holographic measurements. Applying Wolf's theory, Carter [10] successfully reconstructed a two-dimensional rectangular scatterer from its Fresnel diffraction pattern.

VI. Digitization Effects—Fourier-Transform Holograms

A. Sampling

In both the computer generation and reconstruction of holograms, we have to sample the hologram in space and quantize the amplitude of each sample to a finite number of levels. In Sections VI and VII, we shall discuss the effects of sampling and quantization on the quality of the reconstructed image from the hologram. We first consider the sampling of Fourier-transform holograms.

1) Direct Recording: In the direct-recording (Section II-A) type of Fourier-transform holograms, the amplitude transmission of the hologram is

$$P(\xi, \eta) = \iint_{-\infty}^{\infty} p(u, v) \exp(-i2\pi)(\xi u + \eta v)\, du\, dv \qquad (30)$$

where $p(u, v)$ is the original object, u and v are spatial coordinates (measured, for example, in millimeters), and ξ and η are spatial frequencies (measured, for example, in cycles per millimeter). The variables ξ and η are related to the actual spatial coordinates of the hologram by a constant scale factor which we can choose at will (in making computer holograms) to make the size of the hologram appropriate for optical reconstruction. Let the size of the image $p(u, v)$ be $L \times L$, and let the sampling periods we use for $P(\xi, \eta)$ be $\Delta\xi$ and $\Delta\eta$. Then by the Whittaker-Shannon sampling theorem [87], [76], the optical reconstruction from our sampled hologram will be

$$\bar{p}(u, v) = \sum_{m=-\infty}^{\infty} \sum_{n=-\infty}^{\infty} p\left(u - \frac{1}{\Delta\xi}, v - \frac{1}{\Delta\eta}\right) \qquad (31)$$

assuming that each sample of the hologram is an infinitely small point. The reconstruction then is a sum of periodically shifted versions of the original object. In order to make these versions nonoverlapping, we require

$$\begin{cases} \Delta\xi \le \dfrac{1}{L} \\[2mm] \Delta\eta \le \dfrac{1}{L}. \end{cases} \qquad (32)$$

In practice, the samples cannot be ideal points. The nonzero size of the hologram samples has the effect of attenuating the higher order terms in the reconstruction [the right-hand side of (31)]. This effect is, in fact, often desirable since we usually want only the 0th-order ($m = 0 = n$) term. Suppose the function $P(\xi, \eta)$ is essentially zero for $|\xi| > W$ or $|\eta| > W$. Then the size of the hologram will be $W \times W$. To avoid the overlapping of the various terms in the reconstruction, we can sample the hologram at a period $\Delta\xi = (1/L)$, $\Delta\eta = (1/L)$. The total number of samples required for the entire hologram is then $N = (WL)^2$. To reduce the computation time and the resolution requirement of the display-recording device, we wish to use as few samples as possible. If we only use $M(<N)$ samples, what would be the effect on the reconstruction? It depends on how we take the samples.

If we sample the entire hologram uniformly at a period $\Delta\xi = (W/\sqrt{M}) > (1/L)$, $\Delta\eta = (W/\sqrt{M}) > (1/L)$, then in the reconstruction the terms at the right-hand side of (31) will overlap each other. This effect is called aliasing. If we use only the center part of the hologram with a size $(\sqrt{M}/L)/(\sqrt{M}/L)$ and sample that part with $\Delta\xi = (1/L)$, $\Delta\eta = (1/L)$, then in the reconstruction there is no aliasing but the resolution of the image is degraded. Finally, if we use the entire hologram and distribute our M samples randomly over the hologram, then the reconstruction will be degraded by noise but no aliasing will occur [14], [15], [61], [62].

2) Lohmann and Lee Methods: When the Fourier transform $P(\xi, \eta)$ is recorded by Lohmann's (Section II-C) or Lee's (Section II-D) method, it can be shown that the reconstruction (which is the inverse Fourier transform of the hologram) again consists of a sum of periodically shifted terms. However, these terms are no longer simply shifted versions of each other. The ($m = \pm 1$, $n = 0$) terms are

equal to the original object, but the other terms are generally related to the original object in a complicated manner. However, experimental evidence indicates that the size of each of these terms is approximately the same as the original object ($L \times L$). Therefore, to avoid aliasing (32) can be used as a guideline. That is, we can make the spacing in the basic grid for the complex samples equal to $(1/L)$.

In a Lohmann hologram, the actual sample we display and record is the magnitude of the complex sample and it is shifted (in the ξ direction, say) from its basic grid position by a distance proportional to the phase angle of the complex sample. Therefore, if we use WL samples over the width of the hologram, the resolution requirement is actually WLS cells per width of hologram in the ξ direction, where S is the number of quantization levels we use for the phase angle of the Fourier transform. The resolution required in the η direction is just WL cells.

In a Lee hologram we actually display four positive real samples (spread out in the ξ direction, say) instead of one complex sample. Therefore, the resolution requirement in the ξ direction and η direction are, respectively, $4WL$ and WL cells per width of hologram.

If we decide to make binary holograms, then the resolution requirement will be increased by a factor m in the ξ direction and n in the η direction, where m and n are any positive integers such that mn is equal to the number of quantization levels we use for the magnitude and the real and imaginary parts of the Fourier transform.

3) Reference-Beam Recording: When a reference beam is used, the transmittance of the Fourier-transform hologram is

$$H(\xi, \eta) = \left| P(\xi, \eta) + B \exp(i2\pi b\xi) \right|^2 \qquad (33)$$

where $P(\xi, \eta)$ is the Fourier transform of the original object $p(u, v)$ as defined in (30), and B and b are real constants. The inverse Fourier transform of $H(\xi, \eta)$ is

$$h(u, v) = B^2 \delta(u, v) + R_{pp}(u, v) + Bp(u - b, v) + Bp(-u - b, -v) \qquad (34)$$

where $\delta(u, v)$ is the two-dimensional unit impulse function, and $R_{pp}(u, v)$ is the autocorrelation function of $p(u, v)$. If the size of $p(u, v)$ is $L \times L$, then the size of $R_{pp}(u, v)$ will be $2L \times 2L$. To avoid overlapping of terms at the right-hand side of (34), we require

$$b \ge \tfrac{3}{2}L. \qquad (35)$$

If we use a value for B which is much greater than the value of $p(u, v)$, then $R_{pp}(u, v)$ is small compared to the other terms at the right-hand side of (34) and can be neglected. Then we only require

$$b \ge \frac{L}{2} \qquad (36)$$

the size of $h(u, v)$ is $(2b + L) \times L$, assuming $b \ge (L/2)$.

When $H(\xi, \eta)$ is sampled, the optical reconstruction will consist of a sum of periodically shifted versions of $h(\xi, \eta)$. To avoid aliasing, we require

$$\begin{cases} \Delta\xi \le \dfrac{1}{2b + L} \\[2mm] \Delta\eta \le \dfrac{1}{L}. \end{cases} \qquad (37)$$

B. Quantization

1) Fine Quantization: When the number of quantization levels used is relatively large, we can model the quantization noise as additive white noise independent of the signal being quantized. Using this model, Anderson and Huang [1] analyzed the effects of quantization in various types of Fourier-transform holograms.

In the direct-recording and the Lohmann holograms, the noise is added to the magnitude and the phase of the Fourier transform, while in the reference-beam and the Lee holograms, the noise is added to the real and imaginary parts.

It can be shown that the effect of uniform quantization of the magnitude or the real and imaginary parts is to introduce independent white noise in the amplitude of the reconstructed image (the noise power being equal to that of the quantization noise). When we observe the intensity of the image, this noise becomes multiplicative. The effect of either logarithmic magnitude quantization or uniform phase quantization is to introduce an additive noise in the amplitude of the reconstructed image whose power density spectrum is proportional to the square of the Fourier transform of the original image. Since most images contain largely low spatial frequencies so does the noise. When we observe the intensity of the image, the noise again becomes multiplicative.

2) Phase Quantization: When the number of quantization levels is small, a more exact analysis becomes necessary. Goodman and Silvestri [34], [21], [22] studied the effect of phase quantization. For the one-dimensional case, the result is as follows. Let

$$P(\xi) = |P(\xi)| \exp j\phi(\xi) = \int_{-\infty}^{\infty} p(u) \exp(-i2\pi\xi u)\, du. \quad (38)$$

If we quantize $\phi(\xi)$ uniformly but leave $|P(\xi)|$ alone, the inverse transform becomes

$$g(u) = \sum_{m=-\infty}^{\infty} \mathrm{sinc}\left[m + \frac{1}{N}\right] g_m(u) \quad (39)$$

where

$$g_m(u) = \int_{-\infty}^{\infty} |P(\xi)| \exp(i)(Nm + 1)\phi(\xi) \exp(i2\pi\xi u)\, d\xi \quad (40)$$

and

$$\mathrm{sinc}\, x = \frac{\sin \pi x}{\pi x} \quad (41)$$

and N is the number of quantization levels used for $\phi(\xi)$. Note that $g_0(u) = p(u)$.

If $p(u)$ consists of a small object in a large empty field, then $g_m(u)$, for $m \neq 0$, are shifted versions of $g_0(u)$. If $p(u)$ is diffuse (i.e., has a random phase), then $g_m(u)$ is approximately the $(Nm+1)$th-order self-convolution of $g_0(x)$.

The reader may also be interested in some results on phase holograms derived by Dammann [23]–[25].

3) Reference-Beam Holograms: The results we shall describe below on the quantization effects of reference-beam holograms apply to both Fourier-transform and Fresnel holograms.

The transmittance of a reference-beam hologram is, as we recall,

$$h(x, y) = |g(x, y) + B \exp(ibx)|^2 \quad (42)$$

where $g(x, y)$ is the light distribution in the hologram plane due to the object, x and y are spatial coordinates in the hologram plane, and B and b are constants. Kozma and Kelly [49] analyzed the effect of hard clipping (i.e., two-level quantization) on a modified version of this type of hologram. Specifically, they considered the one-dimensional hologram

$$t(x) = \frac{1}{2} + \frac{1}{2} \frac{A(x) \cos(bx - \phi(x))}{|A(x) \cos(bx - \phi(x))|} \quad (43)$$

where $A(x) \exp j\phi(x) = h(x)$ is the original object. They showed that $t(x)$ can be expanded into an infinite series

$$t(x) = \frac{1}{2} + \sum_{m=1,3,5\cdots}^{\infty} \frac{2(-1)^{(m-1)/2}}{m\pi} \cos\left[mbx + m\phi(x)\right] \quad (44)$$

from which we observe that the first-order ($m=1$) term will give the phase-only reconstruction of the original object. By using a large enough b, we can make the reconstruction due to the $m \neq 1$ terms not to overlap the first-order reconstruction.

A similar analysis can be performed for the general case of quantizing $h(x, y)$ of (42) to an arbitrary number of levels. In fact, Tokarski [81] suggested that we may expand the quantized $h(x, y)$ into a Fourier series in ϕ:

$$t(x, y) = \sum_{m=0}^{\infty} t_m(A(x, y)) \cos\{m[\phi(x, y) - bx]\} \quad (45)$$

where

$$A(x, y) \exp j\phi(x, y) = h(x, y).$$

The first-order ($m=1$) term in (45) gives a correct-phase distorted magnitude reconstruction of the original object. Again by using a large enough b, we can make the other terms not to overlap the first-order reconstruction.

The reader may want to refer to some of the more elaborate studies [47], [27], [32], [48]. The recent theoretical and experimental studies of Sass [75] on hard-clipped reference-beam Fourier-transform holograms may also be mentioned here.

C. Optimum Digitization

The total number of bits (in the case of binary holograms, the total number of resolution cells) used for a digitized hologram is equal to the product of the total number of samples and the number of quantization bits per sample. Given a fixed number of bits per hologram, what is the optimum way of distributing this number between sampling and quantization? This question is very difficult to answer in general. However, Gabel and Liu [29] succeeded in solving this optimization problem for Lohmann filters under the least mean-square error criterion.

VII. Digitization Effects—Fresnel Holograms

A. Sampling

Using the angular spectrum of plane waves, Cathey [12] showed that to avoid aliasing in the reconstruction of a Fresnel hologram, the sampling rate must be at least twice the highest spatial frequency of the hologram. Let θ be the maximum angular separation between the reference beam and the object or between points on the object in case no reference beam is used. Then the highest spatial frequency on the hologram is [31]

$$f_{\max} = \frac{\sin \theta}{\lambda} \quad (46)$$

where λ is the light wavelength. The sampling interval should, therefore, be smaller than $\lambda/2 \sin \theta$.

The aliasing phenomenon in the reconstruction of sampled Fresnel holograms was also analyzed by Carter [9] using the concept of Fresnel zone plates.

The effects of the nonzero size of the samples were studied by Cathey [12]. He showed the nondistorted images can be reconstructed only if the samples are ideal points. In the case of nonzero size samples, spatial frequency distortion will occur.

Finally, we mention the interesting experiment of Enloe *et al.* [26] of BTL on the transmission and reconstruction of a scanned hologram.

B. Quantization

The effects of quantizing a reference-beam type Fresnel hologram have been discussed in Section VI-B3. The effects of quantizing Fresnel holograms of the direct-recording type have not yet been studied.

The reader may be interested in some experimental results of Keeton [43] on sampled and quantized Fresnel holograms.

VIII. CONCLUDING REMARKS

We have discussed in this paper some of the basic techniques of generating and reconstructing holograms on a digital computer. The computer reconstruction of holograms finds applications mainly in acoustical and microwave holography. The computer generation of holograms have proven useful in optical spatial filtering and the testing of optical surface. However, the most exciting potential application of computer hologram, viz., three-dimensional computer display is yet to become a practical reality.

We have restricted our discussions in this paper to those techniques of generating holograms where the diffraction pattern in the hologram plane due to the object is calculated on the computer and then recorded as the hologram. Other alternative approaches to digital holography have been proposed and developed [68], [18], [80], [17], [20], [78], [45]. Some of these approaches may very well be more useful in the development of a successful three-dimensional computer display system.

In conclusion, let us emphasize again what we have mentioned at the beginning of our paper: the most exciting aspect of digital holography is that it has served as prologue for the use of the computer as an optical element in a generalized sense. The past few years have given us advances such as the kinoform, advances which use the digital computer's unique properties and which have no strict analogs in the physical world.

ACKNOWLEDGMENT

The author wishes to thank Prof. J. W. Goodman, who kindly invited him to write this review paper, and an anonymous reviewer, who pointed out a number of important references and made some very helpful comments.

REFERENCES

[1] G. B. Anderson and T. S. Huang, "Errors in frequency-domain processing of images," in *1969 Spring Joint Computer Conf., AFIPS Conf. Proc.*, vol. 34, pp. 173–185.

[2] Y. Aoki, "Microwave holograms and optical reconstruction," *Appl. Opt.*, vol. 6, no. 11, Nov. 1967, pp. 1943–1946.

[3] B. R. Brown and A. W. Lohmann, "Complex spatial filtering with binary masks," *Appl. Opt.*, vol. 5, no. 6, June 1966, pp. 967–969.

[4] ——, "Computer-generated binary holograms," *IBM J. Res. Develop.*, vol. 13, no. 2, Mar. 1969, pp. 160–168.

[5] B. R. Brown, A. W. Lohmann, and D. P. Paris, "Computer generated optical-matched filtering," *Opt. Acta.*, vol. 13, 1966, p. 377.

[6] J. J. Burch, "A computer algorithm for the synthesis of spatial frequency filters," *Proc. IEEE* (Lett.), vol. 55, Apr. 1967, pp. 599–601.

[7] C. B. Burckhardt, "Information reduction in holograms for visual display," *J. Opt. Soc. Amer.*, vol. 58, no. 2, Feb. 1968, pp. 241–246.

[8] ——, "A simplification of Lee's method of generating holograms by computer," *Appl. Opt.*, vol. 9, no. 8, Aug. 1970, p. 1949.

[9] W. H. Carter, "Aliasing in sampled holograms," *Proc. IEEE* (Lett.), vol. 56, Jan. 1968, pp. 96–98.

[10] ——, "Computational reconstruction of scattering objects from holograms," *J. Opt. Soc. Amer.*, vol. 60, no. 3, Mar. 1970, pp. 306–314.

[11] W. H. Carter, and A. A. Dougal, "Field range and resolution in holography," *J. Opt. Soc. Amer.*, vol. 56, no. 12, Dec. 1966, pp. 1754–1759.

[12] W. T. Cathey, Jr., "The effect of finite sampling in holography," *Optik*, vol. 27, 1968, pp. 317–326.

[13] ——, "Phase holograms, phase-only holograms, and kinoforms," *Appl. Opt.*, vol. 9, no. 6, June 1970, pp. 1478–1479.

[14] H. J. Caulfield, "Wavefront sampling in holography," *Proc. IEEE* (Lett.), vol. 57, Nov. 1969, pp. 2082–2083.

[15] ——, "Image degraded in undersampled holograms," *Phys. Lett.*, vol. 28A, no. 9, Feb. 10, 1969, pp. 600–601.

[16] H. J. Caulfield and S. Lu, "Applications of computer generated holograms," in *The Applications of Holography*. New York: Wiley–Interscience, 1970, ch. 10.

[17] H. J. Caulfield, S. Lu, and J. L. Harris, "Biasing for single-exposure and multiple-exposure holography," *J. Opt. Amer.*, vol. 58, no. 7, July 1968, pp. 1003–1004.

[18] A. Chutjian and R. J. Collier, "Recording and reconstructing three-dimensional images of computer-generated subjects by Lippmann integral photography," *J. Opt. Soc. Amer.*, vol. 57, 1967, p. 1405.

[19] R. J. Collier, C. B. Burckhardt, and L. H. Lin, *Optical Holography*. New York: Academic Press, 1971.

[20] R. L. Conger, L. T. Long, and J. A. Parks, "Synthesis of Fresnel diffraction patterns by overlapping zone plates," *Appl. Opt.*, vol. 7, no. 4, Mar. 1968, pp. 623–624.

[21] W. J. Dallas, "Phase quantization—A compact derivation," *Appl. Opt.*, vol. 10, no. 3, Mar. 1971, pp. 673–674.

[22] ——, "Phase quantization in holograms—a few illustrations," *Appl. Opt.*, vol. 10, no. 3, Mar. 1971, pp. 674–676.

[23] H. Dammann, "Computer generated quaternary phase-only holograms," *Phys. Lett.*, vol. 29A, 1969, pp. 301–302.

[24] ——, "Blazed synthetic phase-only holograms," *Optik*, vol. 31, 1970, pp. 95–104.

[25] ——, "Phase holograms of diffuse objects," *J. Opt. Soc. Amer.*, vol. 60, no. 12, Dec. 19, 1970, pp. 1635–1639.

[26] L. H., Enloe, J. A. Murphy, and C. B. Rubinstein, "Hologram transmission via television," *Bell Syst. Tech. J.*, vol. 45, Feb. 1966, pp. 335–339.

[27] A. A. Friesem and J. S. Zelenka, "Effects of film nonlinearities in holography," *Appl. Opt.*, vol. 6, 1967, pp. 1755–1759.

[28] D. Fritzler and E. Marom, "Reduction of bandwidth required for high resolution hologram transmission," *Appl. Opt.*, vol. 8, June 1969, pp. 1241–1243.

[29] R. A. Gabel and B. Liu, "Minimization of reconstruction errors with computer generated binary holograms," *Appl. Opt.*, vol. 9, May 1970, pp. 1180–1191.

[30] B. Gold and C. Rader, *Digital Processing of Signals*. New York: McGraw-Hill, 1969.

[31] J. W. Goodman, "Digital image formation from detected holographic data," in *Acoustical Holography*, vol. 1, A. F. Metherell, H.M.A. El-Sum, and L. Larmore, Eds. New York: Plenum, 1969.

[32] J. W. Goodman and G. R. Knight, "Effects of film nonlinearities on wavefront-reconstruction images of diffuse objects," *J. Opt. Soc. Amer.*, vol. 58, Sept. 1968, pp. 1276–1283.

[33] J. W. Goodman and R. W. Lawrence, "Digital image formation from electronically detected holograms," *Appl. Phys. Lett.*, vol. 11, Aug. 1, 1967, pp. 77–79.

[34] J. W. Goodman and A. M. Silvestri, "Some effects of Fourier domain phase quantization," *IBM J. Res. Develop.*, vol. 14, Sept. 1970, pp. 478–484.

[35] K. A. Haines, "Bandwidth reduction in holography, using periodic dispersion structures," *Appl. Opt.*, vol. 9, pp. 1946–1949.

[36] K. A. Haines and D. B. Brumm, "Holographic data reduction," *Appl. Opt.*, vol. 7, June 1968, pp. 1185–1189.

[37] R. Hickling, "Scattering of light by spherical liquid droplets using computer-generated holograms," *J. Opt. Soc. Amer.*, vol. 58, Apr. 1968, pp. 455–460.

[38] B. P. Hildebrand, "Hologram bandwidth reduction by space-time multiplexing," *J. Opt. Soc. Amer.*, vol. 60, Feb. 1970, pp. 259–264.

[39] T. S. Huang and B. Prasada, "Considerations on the generation and processing of holograms by digital computers," MIT/RLE Quar. Prog. Rep. 81, Apr. 15, 1966, pp. 199–205.

[40] Y. Ichioka, M. Izumi, and T. Suzuki, "Halftone plotter and its applications to digital optical information processing," *Appl. Opt.*, vol. 8, 1969, pp. 2461–2471.

[41] ——, "Scanning halftone plotter and computer-generated continuous-tone hologram," *Appl. Opt.*, vol. 10, Feb. 1971, pp. 403–411.

[42] J. A. Jordan, Jr., "The conference on holography and the computer," *IBM J. Res. Develop.*, vol. 14, Sept. 1970, pp. 476–477.

[43] S. C. Keeton, "A sampled computer-generated binary hologram," *Proc. IEEE* (Lett.), vol. 56, Mar. 1968, pp. 325–327.

[44] D. Kermisch, "Image reconstruction from phase information only," *J. Opt. Soc. Amer.*, vol. 60, Jan. 1970, pp. 15–17.

[45] M. C. King, A. M. Noll, and D. H. Berry, "A new approach to computer-generaged holography," *Appl. Opt.*, vol. 9, Feb. 1970, pp. 471–475.

[46] J. P. Kirk and A. L. Jones, "Analysis of a phase-only complex-valued spatial filter," presented at the 1970 Spring Meet. Opt. Soc. of Amer.; a

written version to appear in *J. Opt. Soc. Amer.*, July 1971.

[47] A. Kozma, "Photographic recording of spatially modulated coherent light," *J. Opt. Soc. Amer.*, vol. 56, Apr. 1966, pp. 428–432.

[48] A. Kozma, G. W. Jull, and K. O. Hill, "An analytical and experimental study of nonlinearities in hologram recording," *Appl. Opt.*, vol. 9, Mar. 1970, pp. 721–731.

[49] A. Kozma and D. L. Kelly, "Spatial filtering for detection of signals submerged in noise," *Appl. Opt.*, vol. 4, Apr. 1965, pp. 387–392.

[50] W. H. Lee, "Computer generation of holograms and spatial filters," Sc.D. dissertation, M.I.T., Department of Electrical Engineering, Sept. 1969.

[51] ——, "Sampled Fourier-transform hologram generated by computer," *Appl. Opt.*, vol. 9, Mar. 1970, pp. 639–643.

[52] ——, "Filter design for optical data processors," *Pattern Recog.*, vol. 2, May 1970, pp. 127–137.

[53] E. N. Leith and J. Upatnieks, "Reconstructed wavefronts and communication theory," *J. Opt. Soc. Amer.*, vol. 52, 1962, p. 1123.

[54] E. N. Leith, J. Upatnieks, B. P. Hildebrand, and K. A. Haines, "Requirements for a wavefront reconstruction television facsimile system," presented at SMPTE Tech. Conf., Los Angeles, Calif., 1965.

[55] L. B. Lesem, P. Hirsch, and J. A. Jordan, Jr., "Computer generation and reconstruction of holograms," *Proc. Symp. Modern Optics.* New York: Polytechnic Institute of Brooklyn, 1967.

[56] ——, "Holographic display of digital images," *Proc. 1967 Fall Joint Comp. Conf.*, vol. 31. Washington, D. C.: Thompson Books, pp. 41–47.

[57] ——, "Computer synthesis of holograms for 3-d display," *Commun. ACM*, vol. 11, Oct. 1968, pp. 661–674.

[58] ——, "The kinoform: a new wavefront reconstruction device," *IBM J. Res. Develop.*, vol. 13, Mar. 1969, pp. 150–155.

[59] ——, "The promise of kinoform," *Opt. Spectra*, vol. 4, Dec. 1970, pp. 18–21.

[60] L. H. Lin, "A method of hologram information reduction by spatial frequency sampling," *Appl. Opt.*, vol. 7, Mar. 1968, pp. 545–548.

[61] Y. T. Lo, "A mathematical theory of antenna arrays with randomly spaced elements," *IEEE Trans. Antennas Propagat.*, vol. AP-12, May 1964, pp. 257–268.

[62] Y. T. Lo and R. J. Simcoe, "An experiment on antenna arrays with randomly spaced elements," *IEEE Trans. Antennas Propagat.*, vol. AP-15, Mar. 1967, pp. 231–235.

[63] A. W. Lohmann, "Matched filtering with self-luminous objects," *Appl. Opt.*, vol. 7, Mar. 1968, pp. 501–563.

[64] A. W. Lohman and D. F. Paris, "Binary Fraunhofer holograms generated by computer," *Appl. Opt.*, vol. 6, Oct. 1967, pp. 1739–1748.

[65] ——, "Computer generated spatial filters for coherent data processing," *Appl. Opt.*, vol. 7, Apr. 1968, pp. 651–655.

[66] A. W. Lohmann, D. P. Paris, and H. W. Werlich, "A computer-generated spatial filter applied to code translation," *Appl. Opt.*, vol. 6, June 1967, pp. 1139–1140.

[67] A. W. Lohmann and H. W. Werlich, "Incoherent matched filtering with Fourier holograms," *Appl. Opt.*, vol. 10, Mar. 1971, pp. 670–672.

[68] S. Lu, H. W. Hemstreet, Jr., and H. T. Caulfield, "Holography of moving objects," *Phys. Lett.*, vol. 25A, Aug. 28, 1967, pp. 294–295.

[69] A. J. MacGovern and J. C. Wyant, "Computer-generated holograms for testing optical elements," *Appl. Opt.*, vol. 10, Mar. 1971, pp. 619–624.

[70] A. F. Metherell and H. N. A. El-Sum, "Simulated reference in a coarsely sampled acoustical hologram," *App. Phys. Lett.*, vol. 11, July 1, 1967, pp. 20–22.

[71] A. F. Metherell, "The relative importance of phase and amplitude in acoustical holography," in *Acoustical Holography*, vol. 1, A. F. Metherell *et al.*, Eds. New York: Plenum, 1969.

[72] A. J. Meyer and R. Hickling, "Holograms synthesized on a computer-operated cathode-ray tube," *J. Opt. Soc. Amer.*, vol. 57, Nov. 1967, pp. 1388–1389.

[73] D. M. Milder and W. H. Wells, "Acoustic holography with crossed linear arrays," *IBM J. Res. Develop.*, vol. 14, Sept. 1970, pp. 492–500.

[74] J. C. Patau, L. B. Lesem, P. M. Hirsch, and J. A. Jordan, Jr., "Incoherent filtering using kinoforms," *IBM J. Res. Develop.*, vol. 14, Sept. 1970, pp. 485–491.

[75] A. R. Sass, "Binary-intensity holograms," *J. Opt. Soc. Amer.*, vol. 61, July 1971, pp. 910–915.

[76] C. E. Shannon, "Communication in the presence of noise," *Proc. IRE*, vol. 37, Jan. 1949, pp. 10–21.

[77] A. R. Shulman, "Zone plates," in *Optical Data Processing.* New York: Wiley, 1970, ch. 9.

[78] W. J. Siemeno-Wapniarski and M. P. Givens, "The experimental production of synthetic holograms," *Appl. Opt.*, vol. 7, Mar. 1968, pp. 535–538.

[79] M. M. Sondhi, "Reconstruction of objects from their sound-diffraction patterns," *J. Acoust. Soc. Amer.*, vol. 46, pt. 2, Apr. 1969, pp. 1158–1164.

[80] G. W. Stroke, F. H. Westervelt, and R. G. Zech, "Holographic synthesis of computer-generated holograms," *Proc. IEEE* (Lett.), vol. 55, Jan. 1967, pp. 109–111.

[81] J. M. J. Tokarski, "The effect of the hologram record of a nonlinear relationship between amplitude transmission and exposure," *Appl. Opt.*, vol. 7, May 1968, pp. 989–990.

[82] O. J. Tretiak, M. Eden, and W. Simon, "Internal structure from X-ray images," in *Proc. 8th ICMBE* (Chicago, July 20–25), 1969.

[83] A. B. Vander Lugt, "Signal detection by complex spatial filtering," *IEEE Trans. Inform. Theory*, vol. IT-10, Apr. 1964, pp. 139–145.

[84] J. P. Waters, "Holographic image synthesis utilizing theoretical methods," *Appl. Phys. Lett.*, vol. 9, Dec. 1, 1966, pp. 405–407.

[85] ——, "Three-dimensional Fourier-transform method for synthesizing binary holograms," *J. Opt. Soc. Amer.*, vol. 58, Sept. 1968, pp. 1284–1288.

[86] J. P. Waters and F. Michael, "High resolution images from CRT-generated synthetic holograms," *Appl. Opt.*, vol. 8, Mar. 1969, pp. 714–715.

[87] E. T. Whittaker, "On the functions which are represented by the expansion of the interpolation theory," *Proc. Roy. Soc. Edinburgh, Sect. A*, vol. 35, 1915, p. 181.

[88] E. Wolf, "Three dimensional structure determination of semi-transparent objects from holographic data," *Optics Commun.*, vol. 1, Sept./Oct. 1969, pp. 153–156.

[89] ——, "Determination of the amplitude and the phase of scattered fields of holography," *J. Opt. Soc. Amer.*, vol. 60, 1970, pp. 18–20.

Evaluating Quantization Error in Phase-Only Holograms

HUA LEE, MEMBER, IEEE, AND GLEN WADE, FELLOW, IEEE

Abstract—Backward projection is useful in assessing the quality of images that can be reconstructed from holograms. Backward projection is employed to determine image degradation caused by using phase information only in making a hologram rather than both phase and amplitude information. It is shown that the phase-only technique can produce high-quality images at low bit rates. An image deterioration factor is defined to serve as a reference in evaluating the performance of this type of hologram.

INTRODUCTION

AN ORDINARY hologram is made by recording both phase and amplitude information. It is possible, however, to produce a hologram using only the phase information and hence ignoring the amplitude information. In an analysis to assess the quality of a reconstructed image from such a hologram and to physically interpret the reconstruction technique, we have employed the derivation and the image-forming concepts associated with generalized backward projection [1]. Our analysis shows that the phase contains the most important part of the information required for good resolution and highly resolved images can be produced without taking into account the amplitude variations. This conclusion has already been suggested and supported by other research [2], [3], [4].

If the hologram is to be processed by digital means, quantization is necessary and has a significant bearing on the resolving power of the system. In our analysis of phase-only holograms, we ignore the amplitude distribution of the detected wave fields, of course, and assume that the phase variation is uniformly quantized. We examine the consequent reconstruction and quantify the image degradation. Our definition of degradation error is composed in such a way as to permit measuring the resolving power of the hologram. Our analysis thus gives a numerical evaluation of the degradation. It readily demonstrates the convergence to the Rayleigh diffraction limit lower bound as we increase the number of quantization levels to infinity. By examining cumulative effects during image formation, we establish an analytical deterioration factor which aids in quantifying the quantization performance.

BACKWARD PROJECTION METHOD

Consider a linear data acquisition system in which the received wavefield $g(x)$ is related to the unknown object function $f(x)$ by the integral

$$g(x) = \int_A h(x, \alpha) f(\alpha) \, d\alpha, \tag{1}$$

where $h(x)$ is the impulse response and A denotes the object region. The space variable x can be a vector for multidimensional cases.

The backward projection method consists of two major steps in image reconstruction, namely, the normalization process and the adjoint operation. The resultant image $\hat{f}(x)$ can be found by applying the adjoint operator to the normalized wavefield $n(x) g(x)$

$$\hat{f}(x) = \int_B h^*(\alpha, x) \, [n(\alpha) g(\alpha)] \, d\alpha, \tag{2}$$

where the asterisk denotes complex conjugation and B represents the receiving aperture [5]. The normalization factor $n(x)$ provides an amplitude correction to compensate for the attenuation due to wave propagation from the object region to the receiving aperture. The real and positive normalization factor is a function of the receiving position and can be obtained by

$$n(x) = \left[\int_A |h(\alpha, x)|^2 \, d\alpha \right]^{-1}. \tag{3}$$

For linear and space invariant systems, (1) becomes a convolution integral of $h(x)$ and $f(x)$, and (2) is a correlation between $h^*(x)$ and $[n(x) g(x)]$.

The estimation error of the backward projected image is defined as

$$E_1 \triangleq \int_A |f(x) - \hat{f}(x)|^2 \, dx. \tag{4}$$

Fig. 1 shows the backward projected image of a point object located at the center of the object region, using both amplitude and phase of the received wavefield. The distance between the object region and the receiving aperture is 100λ where λ is the wavelength. The object region and the receiving aperture are each 200λ in length. The sample spacing is $\lambda/2$. This is to satisfy the Nyquist rate because the cutoff of the lowpass transfer function of the data acquisition system is $1/\lambda$ [6]. A total of 400 data samples are processed to perform the image reconstruction. For comparison purposes, the same detection system and data samples are used throughout this paper.

Equation (1) can be written in the form of an approximate Rayleigh–Sommerfeld integral for acoustical data acquisition systems

$$g(x) = \int_A \frac{f(\alpha)}{j\lambda r} \exp \{j2\pi r/\lambda\} \, d\alpha, \tag{5}$$

Manuscript received September 8, 1981; revised May 7, 1982.
The authors are with the Department of Electrical and Computer Engineering, University of California, Santa Barbara, CA 93106.

Reprinted from *IEEE Trans. Sonics Ultrason.*, vol. SU-29, pp. 251–254, Sept. 1982

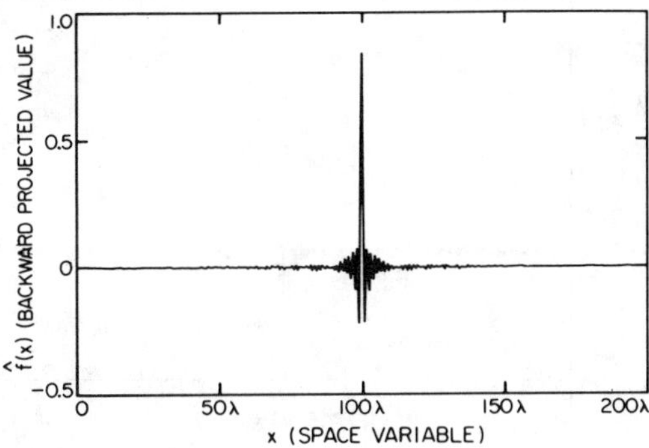

Fig. 1. Image reconstruction of a point object from backward projection using both phase and amplitude of detected signals.

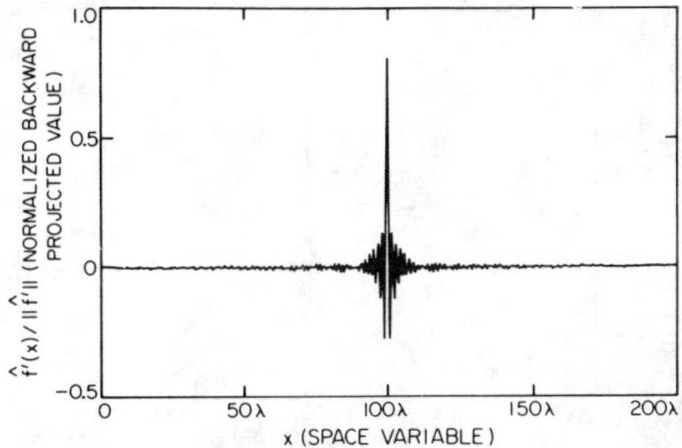

Fig. 2. Normalized image reconstruction of a point object from backward projection using only the phase variation of detected signals.

where r is the distance between the point x and the point α [5]. To examine the point-spread-function of the imaging system, we use a unit impulse to represent a point object source. The wavefield generated by the point source is then

$$g(x) = \frac{1}{j\lambda r_0} \exp\{j2\pi r_0/\lambda\}, \tag{6}$$

where r_0 is the distance between the position x and the point object. Therefore, the resultant image of the point object can be formed by backward projecting the normalized wavefield

$$\hat{f}(x) = \int_B \frac{n(\alpha)\,g(\alpha)}{-j\lambda r'} \exp\{-j2\pi r'/\lambda\}\,d\alpha$$

$$= \int_B \frac{n(\alpha)}{\lambda^2 r_0 r'} \exp\{j2\pi(r_0 - r')/\lambda\}\,d\alpha, \tag{7}$$

where r' is the distance between x and α.

Because $n(\alpha)$, λ^2, r_0, and r' are all real and positive quantities, (7) can be regarded as an integral over vectors having amplitudes $n(\alpha)/\lambda^2 r_0 r'$ and phases $2\pi(r_0 - r')/\lambda$. The phases will be zero and (7) will become an integral of real and positive scalar only when $r_0 = r'$. Hence, (7) accumulates real and positive scalars to generate a greater value when the reconstruction reaches the point object's position. With the appearance of the phase terms, the integral begins to introduce vector cancellation instead of solely scalar accumulation and the integral diminishes in value. This behavior implies that the image formation depends upon the amplitude accumulation as well as the vector cancellation. This behavior is governed by the phase variation of the detected wavefield.

Phase-Only Holographic Imaging

The complex received wavefield can be expressed in polar form by

$$g(x) = G(x) \exp\{j\theta(x)\}. \tag{8}$$

It should be kept in mind that both the amplitude $G(x)$ and the phase $\theta(x)$ are functions of the space variable. The phase-only holographic technique removes the amplitude distribution of the detected signal and simplifies the reconstruction $\hat{f}'(x)$ to an integral over unit vectors

$$\hat{f}'(x) = \int_B \exp\{j\theta(\alpha)\} \exp\{-j2\pi r'/\lambda\}\,d\alpha, \tag{9}$$

where r' is the distance between the point α at the receiving aperture and the point x in the object region. Because the amplitude variation of the received wavefield and the amplitude weighting during the reconstruction are all ignored by the phase-only approach, the reconstruction introduces ambiguous scaling. Therefore, the resultant images are usually normalized to indicate the relative object distributions. Accordingly we modify the definition of the estimation error for phase-only reconstruction to

$$E_2 \triangleq \int_A \left| \frac{f(x)}{\|f\|} - \frac{\hat{f}'(x)}{\|\hat{f}'\|} \right|^2 dx, \tag{10}$$

where $\|f\|$ and $\|\hat{f}'\|$ are the norms of $f(x)$ and $\hat{f}'(x)$, respectively.

$$\|f\| \triangleq \left[\int_A |f(x)|^2\,dx \right]^{1/2} \tag{11a}$$

$$\|\hat{f}'\| \triangleq \left[\int_A |\hat{f}'(x)|^2\,dx \right]^{1/2} \tag{11b}$$

The resolving ability of the phase-only technique can be evaluated by examining the image formation process of the point object. The phase variation of the received wavefield of a distant point object is $2\pi r_0/\lambda$. Then the resultant image becomes

$$\hat{f}'(x) = \int_B \exp\{j2\pi(r_0 - r')/\lambda\}\,d\alpha. \tag{12}$$

It integrates over unity only when $r_0 = r'$, and over unit vectors with various phases otherwise. Hence, the phase-only approach performs scalar accumulation and vector cancellation very similar to (7) and results in compatible resolving ability.

Fig. (2) shows the normalized phase-only reconstruction of a point object referring to the same set of detected data samples and the same imaging arrangement. The estimation error is about 0.3832% which is calculated in accordance with the definition indicated by (10).

Quantization Performance Evaluation

Due to the utilization of the phase-only holographic technique, the detection objective is reduced from a two-dimensional complex wavefield distribution to a scalar phase varia-

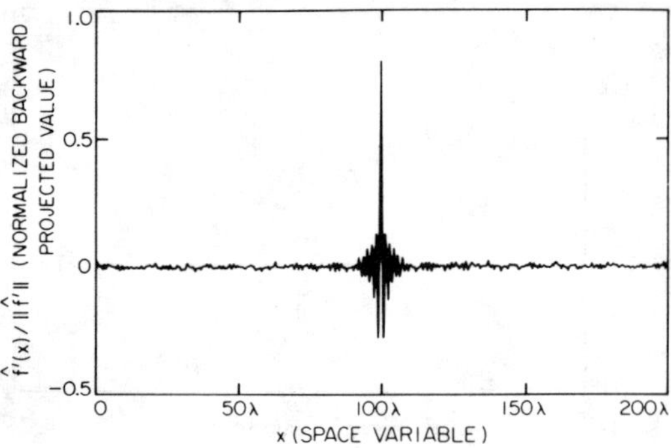

Fig. 3. Normalized phase-only reconstruction of a point object with 3 bits/sample quantization.

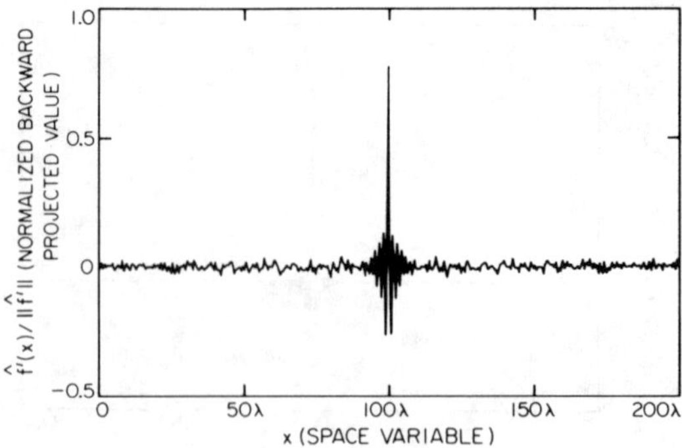

Fig. 4. Normalized phase-only reconstruction of a point object with 2 bits/sample quantization.

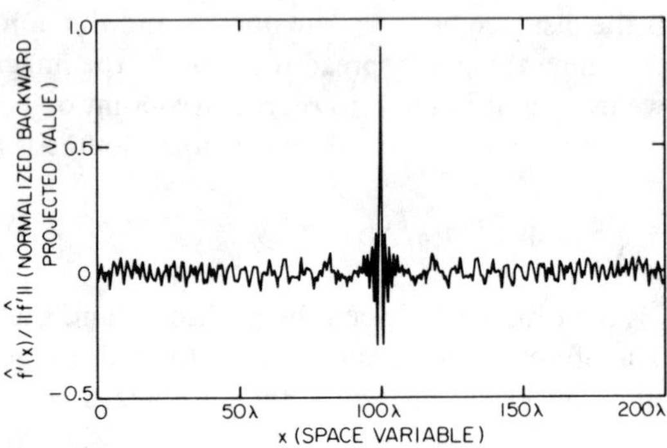

Fig. 5. Normalized phase-only reconstruction of a point object with 1 bit/sample quantization.

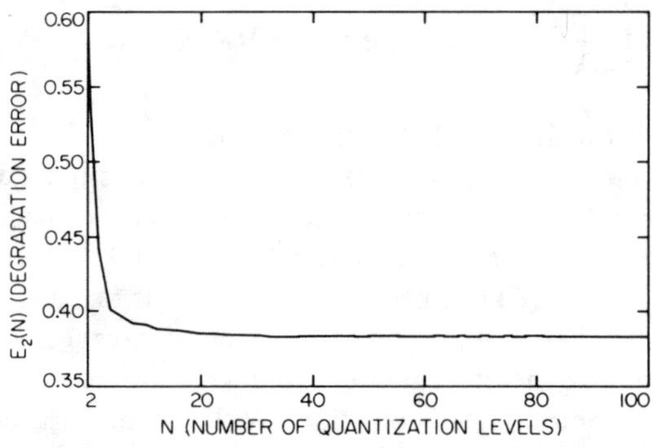

Fig. 6. Degradation error of phase-only reconstructions corresponding to the number of quantization levels.

tion. Therefore, it considerably decreases the amount of variables to be processed. Because the values of the scalar phase variation are bounded between 0 and 2π, uniform quantization can be applied to further simplify the operation.

As a number of quantization levels are assigned to the received wavefield, the phase $\theta(x)$ is quantized uniformly and we define the quantization phase error $\phi(x)$ as

$$\phi(x) = \theta(x) - \hat{\theta}(x), \tag{13}$$

where $\hat{\theta}(x)$ is the quantized phase value. The phase error is bounded between $-\pi/N$ and π/N for N quantization levels. Consider the case that the object function is a point source. Phase error is introduced to the unit vector $\exp\{j2\pi(r_0 - r')/\lambda\}$ in (12), and the resultant image becomes a function of N as well as a function of the space variable x since $\phi(x)$ depends on N:

$$\hat{f}'(x, N) = \int_B \exp\{j[2\pi(r_0 - r')/\lambda - \phi(\alpha)]\}\, d\alpha. \tag{14}$$

If $r_0 = r'$, the phase error $\phi(x)$ moves the unit vectors $\exp\{j2\pi(r_0 - r')/\lambda\}$ away from the real axis and decreases the effectiveness of the scalar accumulation to resolve the point object. Due to the phase error, (14) becomes an integral over the phase error vectors instead of unity for $r_0 = r'$:

$$\int_B \exp\{j[2\pi(r_0 - r')/\lambda - \phi(\alpha)]\}\, d\alpha \bigg|_{r_0 = r'}$$

$$= \int_B \exp\{-j\phi(\alpha)\}\, d\alpha. \tag{15}$$

Fewer quantization levels increase the range of the phase error, move the phase error vectors $\exp\{-j\phi\}$ farther away from the real axis and cause predictable degradation to the quality of the resultant images. Figs. (3), (4), and (5) show the normalized reconstructions of a point object using 3 bits, 2 bits, and 1 bit per sample quantizations, respectively.

Here, we use a unit amplitude point object as a reference and evaluate the quantization performance with respect to various numbers of quantization levels assigned to the process by calculating the degradation error defined by (10).

Fig. (6) shows the degradation based on (10) drops as the number of quantization levels increases. However, the lower bound of the curve cannot reach zero due to the Rayleigh resolution limit and the finite aperture size. The error is 0.572% for 1 bit per sample quantization and 0.387% for 4 bits. Some of the numerical results are shown in Table I.

TABLE I

Number of Quantization Levels per Data Sample	Degradation Error of the Normalized Point-Spread-Function (percent)
2 (1 bit)	0.572
4 (2 bits)	0.442
6	0.401
8 (3 bits)	0.396
10	0.392
12	0.391
14	0.387
16 (4 bits)	0.387

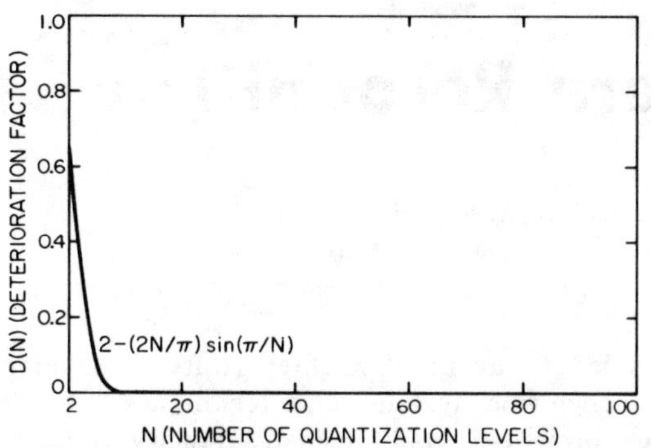

Fig. 7. Deterioration effect as a function of the number of quantization levels.

In this case, the lower bound of the curve is 0.383% and the resolution improvement is insignificant for quantization bit-rates greater than 4 bits/sample. Similar evaluations are also performed by changing the wavelength, the size of the aperture, the sampling rate, and the distance between the object and aperture planes. The numerical results show the same trajectory except for the different upper and lower bounds.

Here, we observe the deterioration of the accumulation effect in (15) to establish an overall and analytical quantization performance evaluation. During the backward projection, each detected phase-only data sample contributes a unit vector exp $\{-j\phi\}$ to the reconstruction of the point object, where ϕ denotes the phase error due to quantization. The quantization error of this projection is then $|1 - \exp \{-j\phi\}|^2$. Assuming the probability density function of the quantization phase error is constant, then

$$p(\phi) = N/2\pi \quad -\pi/N < \phi \leqslant \pi/N. \tag{16}$$

We define the deterioration factor $D(N)$ as the mean error cause by quantization of N levels:

$$D(N) \triangleq \int_{-\pi/N}^{\pi/N} |1 - \exp \{-j\phi\}|^2 \, p(\phi) \, d\phi$$

$$= \int_{-\pi/N}^{\pi/N} (2 - 2\cos\phi) \, p(\phi) \, d\phi$$

$$= 2 - \frac{2N}{\pi} \sin \frac{\pi}{N} \quad N = 2, 3, \cdots. \tag{17}$$

Shown as Fig. (7), $D(N)$ is a monotonically decreasing function with upper and lower bounds $(2 - (4/\pi))$ and zero, respectively. The trajectory matches that of $E_2(N)$ for various types of receiving apertures. Therefore, we may have a linear relation between the quantization performance and the deterioration factor:

$$E_2(N) \approx a_1 D(N) + a_2. \tag{18}$$

The linear relation holds when the aperture size and the sampling rate are sufficiently large to make the assumption of constant probability density function valid. The positive values a_1 and a_2 will be different for different data acquisition systems. They are governed by Rayleigh resolution limit, aperture size, sampling rate, and wavelength employed. Both of them can be decreased by having larger aperture, higher sampling frequency, and shorter wavelength.

Conclusion

To achieve rapid, high quality imaging, the data acquisition in acoustical imaging systems demands high bit-rates. But high bit-rates bring technical difficulties to data storage and transmission. Therefore, bit-rate reduction becomes an important topic in acoustical signal coding and reconstruction.

The phase-only holographic technique simplifies the coding and the implementation of the data acquisition due to the removal of the amplitude distribution of the received wavefield. The analysis of the deterioration and the numerical results illustrate the possibility of low bit-rate, high-quality imaging. The derivation of the deterioration factor provides a guideline for how high the bit-rate should be in order to achieve tolerable degradation.

Vector quantization has been successfully applied to speech coding [7]. The bit-rate in image processing can be furthermore reduced by performing vector quantization on the phase-only data samples. The reduction in the bit-rate will be significant when the phase variation over the receiving aperture is well-correlated statistically.

References

[1] H. Lee, C. Schueler, G. Wade, and J. Fontana, "Digital reconstruction of acoustical holograms in the space domain with a vector space approximation," in *Acoustical Imaging*, vol. 9, K. Wang, Ed. New York: Plenum Press, 1979, pp. 631–642.

[2] A. F. Metherell, "The relative importance of phase and amplitude in acoustical holography," in *Acoustical Holography*, vol. 1, Metherell Ed. New York: Plenum Press, 1969, Ch. 14.

[3] J. Power, J. Landry, and G. Wade, "Computed reconstructions from phase-only and amplitude-only holograms," *Acoustical Holography*, vol. 2, Metherell Ed. New York: Plenum Press, 1969, ch. 13.

[4] A. V. Oppenheim and J. S. Lim, "The importance of phase in signals," *IEEE Proc.*, vol. 69, no. 5, pp. 529–541, May 1981.

[5] H. Lee, "Development and analysis of the backward projection method for acoustical imaging," Ph.D. dissertation, University of California, Santa Barbara, 1980, p. 12.

[6] J. W. Goodman, *Introduction to Fourier Optics*. New York, McGraw-Hill, 1968, pp. 42–54.

[7] A. Buzo, A. H. Gray, Jr., R. M. Gray, and J. D. Markel, "Speech coding based upon vector quantization," *IEEE Trans. Acous., Speech, Signal Processing*, vol. 28, no. 5, pp. 562–574, Oct. 1980.

Coherent Optical Pattern Recognition

DAVID CASASENT, FELLOW, IEEE

Abstract—Pattern-recognition systems, techniques, and applications using coherent optical systems are reviewed. Many optical pattern-recognition system architectures exist that include time-domain optical correlators and the optical joint transform correlator and refinements in the original optical matched spatial filter synthesis processor. Advanced optical pattern-recognition systems are also described such as hybrid optical/digital processors and diffraction-pattern sampling systems using specially shaped Fourier plane detector arrays. The optical space-variant pattern-recognition systems described are examples of the growing repertoire of operations now achievable in optical computers.

I. INTRODUCTION

THE BASIS of coherent optical Fourier transform (FT) theory began with the microscopy image resolution work of Abbe [1], the spatial-filtering experiments of Porter [2], and the phase-contrast microscope of Zernike [3]. However, it was Marechal and Croce [4] in 1953 who provided the basic analysis of coherent optical systems in terms of spatial-frequency response and thus gave new meaning to the work of Abbe. Significant developments in optical spatial filtering began with the marriage of communications theory and optics in the classic work of O'Neill [5] who unified much of the earlier research.

The objective of the types of pattern-recognition systems to be discussed is to determine the presence (and usually the location) of a key object or signal within an input containing other data (referred to as noise). Depending on the specific application, the pattern-recognition problem can be classified as the extraction of a signal buried in noise, character recognition in which one or several members of a given set are searched for, or the location of one key object in diverse backgrounds. Turin [6] provides an excellent description of matched filters for such diverse scenarios.

Optical pattern recognition, as one generally views it today, began with the optical realization of a complex matched spatial filter by vander Lugt [7]. This work was based upon sidelooking radar-processing concepts developed by Cutrona *et al.* [8] and the holography work of Leith and Upatnieks [9]. These early successes and developments, plus the commercial availability of continuous-wave lasers caused a rapid maturing in the field of optical data processing.

Many developments have occurred in the fifteen years since the first optical matched filtering paper. The intrigue of processing data in parallel and in real-time has captured the imagination and tapped the inventiveness of many researchers.

Manuscript received May 16, 1978; revised October 4, 1978. This work was supported by the Air Force Office of Scientific Research under Contract AFOSR75-2851, administered by the Air Force Systems Commands; the Office of Naval Research under Contract NR-366-005; and the National Science Foundation under Contract ENG77-20038; and other agencies for much of the author's work included in this survey.

The author is with the Department of Electrical Engineering, Carnegie-Mellon University, Pittsburgh, PA 15213.

This has led to an increasing repertoire of coherent optical pattern-recognition systems and techniques. In this survey paper, we provide a vitally needed summary of optical pattern recognition over these recent fifteen years, and a consolidated summary of the system architectures [10], operations achievable [11], and applications [12]–[15] of this aspect of the more general field known as optical computing [14].

Cutrona *et al.* [16] describe a wealth of optical pattern-recognition system architectures and their use in signal processing. When coded signal waveforms are used, signal-processing systems become multichannel 1-D versions of the more conventional 2-D pattern-recognition topologies, and we thus include advancements in such work in this survey.

Optical pattern recognition is but one aspect of the larger field of optical computing [14]. Space does not permit detailed discussions of all optical techniques related and associated with pattern recognition. Recent advances in non-coherent optical pattern recognition are discussed elsewhere [17]. Similarly, image enhancement and restoration techniques [18] and image deblurring methods [19], [20] in which the output is a corrected image are not discussed. Rather, preference is given to systems whose output contains the final desired pattern-recognition decision and data. We will concentrate on coherent optical-processing systems in which the optical system itself performs the actual processing and the pattern recognition of the data, rather than serving only as the data collection vehicle or as an image enhancement preprocessor.

In the type of coherent optical processor considered in this paper, the data to be processed is assumed to be an image or some similar two-dimensional pattern. This input data is entered into the optical processor as a transparency, e.g., a 35-35-mm slide of the input scene. Such a transparent pattern is then illuminated with parallel coherent (laser) light of uniform amplitude (spatially). This spatially uniform light passes through the transparent input medium and emerges spatially modulated in amplitude proportional to the two-dimensional amplitude transmittance pattern recorded on the input medium. This process is thus quite analogous to the operation of a simple slide-projector, but yet demonstrates the two-dimensional feature of such processors.

However, because the input illumination used is coherent laser light, a multitude of operations quite useful in pattern recognition are obtainable. The fundamental operation performed in such coherent optical processors is the Fourier transform (FT) (Section II). As the input data is a spatial pattern rather than temporal, we represent it in 1-D by $f(x)$ and in 2-D by $f(x_1, y_1)$. Thus in optics, we speak of a spatial FT, in which distance in the input data plane is directly analogous to time in the more conventional temporal FT. As we describe in subsequent sections, the normal linear-systems operations of correlation and convolution (often used in pattern recognition) can be realized in such optical processors. For now

Reprinted from *Proc. IEEE*, vol. 67, pp. 813–825, May 1979.

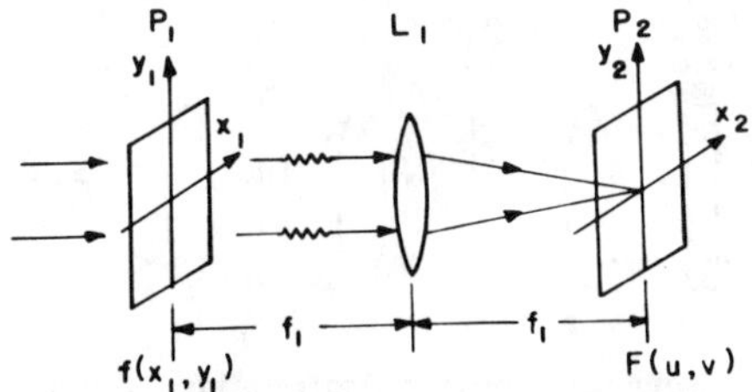

Fig. 1. Schematic of the conventional optical FT system.

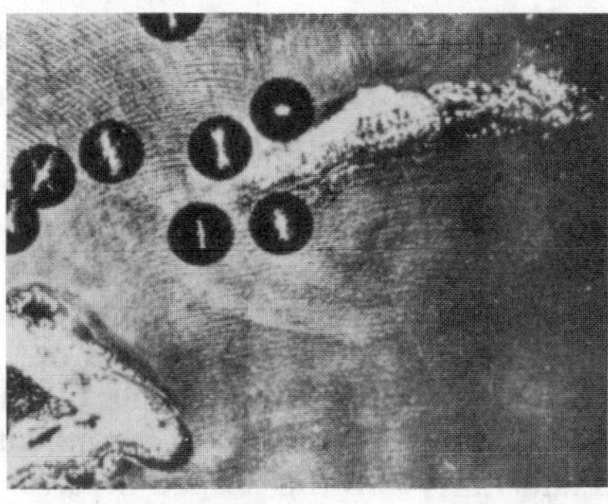

Fig. 2. Example of the optical FT. The inserts show the FT of the corresponding regions of the input plane P_1 pattern [13]. The direction, velocity, and amplitude of the ocean waves can be found from these FT data.

we only note that these operations are realizable on two-dimensional input data and in parallel (i.e., the input light operates in parallel on all pixels of data present in the input plane).

The ability of an optical processor to operate in parallel on 2-D input data and to perform operations such as the FT, correlation and convolution, is why such systems have been considered for pattern recognition and other applications. The final feature of such systems that makes them attractive alternatives to digital processors is the speed with which these parallel operations can be performed. The coherent laser light is used only as the optimum carrier upon which to modulate or impress the input data and as the information bearing carrier that flows through the system. The speed with which this light carrier moves is roughly 1 ns/ft (1 ns = 10^{-9} s). Thus for a three-foot optical system, the required processing time for parallel 2-D pattern-recognition operations would be 3 ns (excluding input data recording and output data detection times). It is too premature and early in the development of optical processors and not the purpose of this paper to expand upon the size, weight, and cost effectiveness of such systems compared to digital or other alternative analog methods. It is also not the purpose of this paper to compare optical and digital pattern-recognition systems. Rather, our emphasis is to convey the operations achievable and to summarize recent progress made in optical pattern-recognition research.

II. OPTICAL FOURIER TRANSFORM

The basic operation in nearly all coherent optical systems is the FT. It is well known [21] that if an input transparency with amplitude transmittance $f(x_1, y_1)$, placed in the front-focal plane P_1 of a spherical lens L_1 (of focal length f_L), is illuminated with collimated coherent laser light (of wavelength λ), then the light amplitude distribution in the back-focal plane P_2 of L_1 is the complex 2-D FT of $f(x_1, y_1)$. We represent the 2-D optical spatial-FT of $f(x_1, y_1)$ by $F(u, v)$, where

$$F(u, v) = \frac{1}{\lambda f_L} \iint_{-\infty}^{+\infty} f(x_1, y_1) \exp\left[j2\pi(ux_1 + vy_1)\right] dx_1 \, dy_1.$$

$$(1)$$

The schematic of this simple optical-FT system is shown in Fig. 1. We denote space functions by lower case variables (e.g., f, g, h) and their FT's by the corresponding upper case variables (e.g. F, G, H). Distances in the input plane P_1 are denoted by (x_1, y_1). The spatial distances (x_2, y_2) in the FT plane P_2 are related to the spatial frequencies (u, v) present in the input plane P_1 data by

$$u = x_2/\lambda f_L \qquad v = y_2/\lambda f_L \qquad (2)$$

where the units of x and y are typically millimeter and the units of u and v are cycles per millimeter (analogous to cycles/time or Hertz in the conventional temporal FT).

An understanding of the anatomy of an optical FT is vital to obtain the insight necessary to follow the future operations and applications to be discussed. In general, the transmittance of P_1 must be real and positive and thus input data must be recorded on a bias (the acoustooptical transducers discussed in Section III and film-thickness variations, which we ignore, are exceptions). Thus if the input is a sinewave, its optical FT at P_2 appears as a dc spot on-axis plus two symmetrically located spots of light on each side of dc. The locations $\pm x_2'$ of these two spots correspond to the input spatial frequency u' of the sinewave as in (2). If the input sinewave is recorded horizontally (vertically), the FT-plane spots appear along the horizontal u or x_2 axis (vertical v or y_2 axis) at P_2. If the frequency u' of the input sinewave is increased (decreased), the separation of the two off-axis FT-plane spots from the origin of P_2 increases (decreases). If the input sinewave is recorded at $+45°$ to the input x_1 axis, the spots of light comprising the FT-pattern occur on a line inclined at $-45°$ to the x_2 axis of the FT plane.

Thus the location of a spot of light in the optical FT-plane P_2 indicates the presence of a given spatial frequency in the input data, as well as the orientation of this data in the input plane. The amplitude of each spot of light in P_2 indicates the amount of that spatial frequency component present in the input data. Low spatial frequencies lie closer to the origin of P_2.

A simple example of the information content available in the optical FT plane pattern is shown in Fig. 2. This figure shows an aerial photograph of a portion of the Caribbean with the optical FT-pattern of various regions of the input shown in the inserts [13]. Close examination of each FT-pattern will show a series of spots of light at different orientations. The direction of the FT-light pattern indicates the direction of the ocean currents and the spacing of the spots indicates the velocity of the ocean currents in the corresponding region of the input scene.

Although the classic optical pattern-recognition system one envisions is a correlator topology, pattern recognition can often be achieved by analysis of the contents of the FT plane alone. When such a simplified optical system is usable, it is clearly preferable to the more sophisticated optical correlators to be described later. The optical FT pattern is usually referred to as the diffraction pattern. We now consider a diffraction-pattern system for pattern recognition that uses a unique frequency plane detector at P_2 of Fig. 1.

A. Pattern Recognition by Diffraction Pattern Sampling

Advances in integrated circuit and detector technology as well as statistical and nonparametric digital pattern-recognition algorithms have benefitted optical pattern recognition just as they have advanced the sophistication of digital pattern recognition. The diffraction-pattern sampling system to be discussed is the simplest and most hardened hybrid optical/ digital system. It is commercially available from Recognition Systems, Inc. The key opto-electronic element in this system is a special Fourier plane detector consisting of thirty-two wedge-shaped and thirty-two ring-shaped detector elements in the two semicircular halves of a one-inch diameter silicon detector [22]. (Many other Fourier plane detectors exist, and digital-computer systems to model this wedge/ring detector (WRD) have been described [23]. We restrict discussion to this FT plane sampling system as representative of such pattern-recognition processors.) The outputs from all sixty-four elements in this WRD are available in parallel and can be multiplexed, electronically preprocessed, and fed to a digital computer for final analysis.

The detector is placed in the FT plane P_2 of the optical system of Fig. 1. The outputs of the ring-shaped detector elements provide the analyst with information on the spatial frequencies present in the input data, on the amount of each spatial frequency present, and thus a measure of the information content of the input data. The outputs of the wedge detector elements provide data on the orientation of the information in the input plane.

When the WRD is used in a pattern-recognition application, the outputs of only selected wedge or ring detector elements are used, thus resulting in a large reduction in data analysis. However, to determine which WRD outputs are to be used and how sums or differences of selected detector outputs are to be weighted, a test set of inputs is used. All WRD outputs are collected for all of these test inputs. Statistical tests are then applied to determine if these data are separable and if recognition algorithms can be developed. Nonparametric pattern-recognition methods are then developed for these data. Once the recognition routine has been determined analysis of future inputs is automatic and rapid.

This type of optical pattern recognition is useful in applications requiring coarse sorting and the analysis of large amounts of data. When such a method is appropriate, a system using WRD data is faster and cheaper than an optical correlator because it requires the analysis of far less data than that contained in the entire input (usually only five or fewer ring measurements are needed in the final system). If all points in the input plane pattern are needed to sort the data, matched spatial filtering or other correlation pattern-recognition methods are required. However, if the resolution of the input data is finer than what is needed and if the input pattern is large and generally uninteresting except for certain smaller key regions, then diffraction pattern sampling using the WRD at P_2 of Fig. 1 is an appropriate pattern-recognition technique.

Many uses of the WRD diffraction pattern-sampling system have been demonstrated [22]. These include: distinguishing urban from nonurban imagery [24] (by the higher spatial frequency data present in urban imagery at higher rings); distinguishing various physiographic regions of an image [25]; and analysis of X-ray images to determine the presence of black lung disease [26]. In this last case, textural image data is used. Sixty-two features of each of six lung zones are

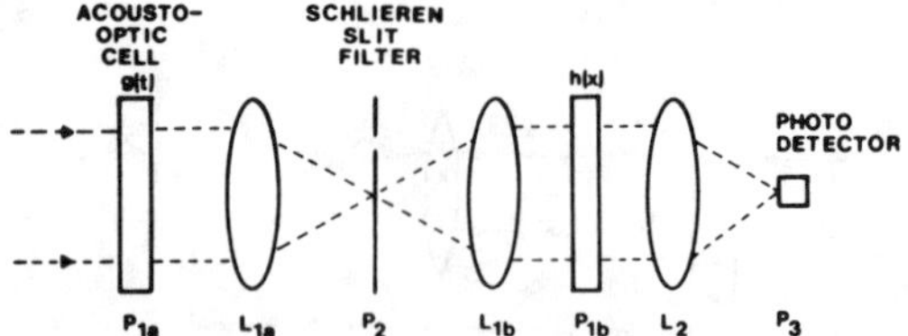

Fig. 3. Schematic of a real-time spatial integrating 1-D optical correlator.

measured, feature extraction is achieved by a step-wise discriminant analysis, and a correct classification of over 86 percent of the X-rays examined was achieved using the data from only two to five ring detectors. Detection of muscular dystrophy, the screening of cervical cytologic samples for malignancy, a flow cell analysis system, measurement of line-widths in photomasks, the inspection of griege goods, the determination of the printability of paper and the analysis of handwriting are among other more well-known laboratory and factory applications of this WRD-system [22].

The WRD-system is best suited for more general pattern-analysis applications. The recognition of specific image features generally requires the use of more sophisticated pattern-recognition methods. This is due to the loss of resolution and the phase portion of the FT that occurs when only the diffraction pattern is sampled. Hereafter, we discuss only optical pattern-recognition systems that achieve correlation and matched spatial filtering. These systems are more powerful, but are more complex and less extensively available commercially.

III. Time-Domain Optical Pattern Recognition

Correlation is still the basic optical pattern-recognition operation. In 1-D, we describe the correlation of two time functions or signals by

$$p(\tau) = \int_{-\infty}^{\infty} g(t)\, h(t + \tau)\, dt = g \circledast h \qquad (3)$$

where g is the input function, h is the reference function, and τ is the shift parameter. To realize the parallel processing advantages of an optical processor in real time, transducers capable of introducing the input data into the system in real time are needed. The most available and proven real-time optical transducers are acoustooptic cells [27]. In these devices, the input signal is fed to a transducer on the acoustooptic cell and a sound wave proportional to the input signal travels along the cell. Korpel, Minkoff, King, and Lambert *et al.* pioneered much of the research and applications of these devices, especially in radar processing [28]–[31]. These systems usually realize the correlation operation in the time domain and thus we discuss them separately here. These acoustooptic cells are 1-D transducers and thus the resultant correlators are only 1-D and hence are generally restricted to signal pattern-recognition applications. Because of the large center frequencies (up to 1 GHz) and bandwidths (up to 500 MHz) of available acoustooptic cells, such systems are of direct use in radar signal pattern recognition. Many of these concepts originated elsewhere and are reviewed in [32].

The schematic of a spatial integrating 1-D correlator is shown in Fig. 3. The operation of these systems is straightforward. The coded reference signal $h(t)$ is stored at P_{1b} as $1 + h(x_1)$. The real-time received input signal $g(t)$ is applied to

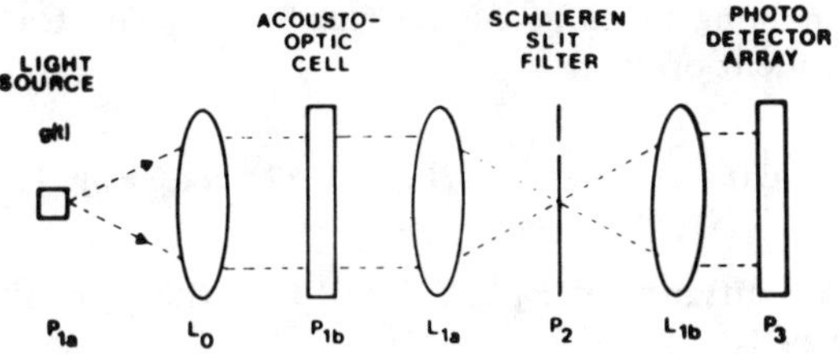

Fig. 4. Schematic of a time integrating real-time 1-D optical correlator.

the transducer at P_{1a}. As this signal moves through the input P_{1a} aperture, it causes a spatial variation in the index of refraction of the cell. This results in a signal in P_{1a} that varies in space (distance x_1 along the cell) and time t. We thus represent this signal as $g(x_1 + v_s t)$, where v_s is the velocity of the sound wave which moves vertically in the x_1 direction in Fig. 3. The wavefront leaving P_{1a} is phase-modulated by $g(x_1 + v_s t)$ and is described by

$$t_1(x_1, t) = a_0 \exp(j\omega t) \exp[jbg(x_1 + v_s t)] \qquad (4)$$

where b is a constant and $a_0 \exp(j\omega t)$ describes the plane-wave input of uniform amplitude a_0 traveling in time. The L_{1a} and L_{1b} imaging system and slit filter convert the phase modulation in (4) to amplitude modulation by passing only the first-order term in the transform of (4). The filtered image of t_1 incident on P_{1b} is then

$$t_1'(x_1, t) = jba_0 g(x_1 + v_s t) \exp(j\omega t) \qquad (5)$$

and the light distribution transmitted through P_{1b} is $t_1'[1 + h(x_1)]$.

Lens L_2 produces the FT of this product of two filtered signals at P_3, where the FT is evaluated only on-axis by a single photodetector at $u = 0$. L_2 thus effectively integrates $t_1'[1 + h(x_1)]$ over a spatial distance $v_s T$ where T is the time aperture or time window of the input acoustooptic cell. The time history of the output of the photodiode at P_3 is thus (omitting terms with signal functions with no Fourier components with periods of the order of $v_s T$ or larger).

$$u_3(t) = \left| \int_0^{v_s T} g(x + v_s t) h(x) \, dx \right|^2$$

or the magnitude squared of the desired correlation of the input and reference signals. Since this correlation is performed in space and displayed in time, the name spatial-integrating correlator is used. With the correlation shift τ between the two functions obtained by the movement of $g(t)$ through the acoustooptic cell, this and similar systems using moving-window transducers are time-domain correlators.

A time-integrating version of this correlator [33] is shown in Fig. 4. This topology is similar to a noncoherent processor described earlier by Bromley [17] and later extended by Goodman [34] for use with a linear input LED array for matrix-vector multiplication applications. In this system, the time-output intensity from an LED is modulated by the input signal $g(t)$ and the input light is now

$$I_1(t) = B_1 + g(t) \qquad (7)$$

where B_1 is the input bias level. The reference signal is added to a bias B_2 and used to amplitude modulate the center carrier frequency of an acoustooptic cell. The light distribution

incident on the output detector array is now

$$u_3(x, t) = [B_1 + g(t)] [B_2 + h(x + v_s t)]. \qquad (8)$$

In this topology, integration of the product in (8) is performed on the output detector array and the dc bias terms are removed by ac coupling. Once again the desired correlation of g and h results. In this system, the correlation is performed in time and displayed in space. We thus refer to this as a time-integrating correlator.

Extensions of these 1-D systems to multichannel correlators and the use of heterodyne detection to yield complex correlations are among the many extensions possible in these time-domain pattern-recognition systems [32]. The interaction of bulk laser light and surface acoustic waves represents another viable 1-D optical signal processing approach that promises small size systems of high bandwidth [35].

IV. FREQUENCY-DOMAIN OPTICAL PATTERN RECOGNITION

The architecture of the correlators described in Section III was determined by the real-time acoustooptic input transducer used in which the signal moved through the input plane. Although permitting processing of high-bandwidth input data, the space or time bandwidth product of acoustooptic cells is limited to 2000 and the time apertures are typically limited to 10 μs. In addition, these systems are basically 1-D correlators and more conducive for signal rather than image pattern recognition. Optical systems with a fixed rather than moving input data frame and systems that achieve correlation by multiplication in the frequency domain rather than the time domain or space domain are more customarily used in image and 2-D pattern recognition.

The basic equations from linear-system theory that describe such correlators are:

$$p(x, y) = g(\xi, \eta) \circledast h(\xi, \eta) = \text{correlation}$$

$$= \iint_{-\infty}^{\infty} g(\xi, \eta) h^*(x + \xi, y + \eta) \, d\xi \, d\eta$$

$$= \mathcal{F}^{-1}[G(u, v) H^*(u, v)] \qquad (9)$$

$$r(x, y) = g(\xi, \eta) * h(\xi, \eta) = \text{convolution}$$

$$= \iint_{-\infty}^{\infty} g(\xi, \eta) h(x - \xi, y - \eta) \, d\xi \, d\eta$$

$$= \mathcal{F}^{-1}[G(u, v) H(u, v)]. \qquad (10)$$

We represent the inverse FT by $\mathcal{F}^{-1}$ and the forward FT by $\mathcal{F}$. Optically these two operations are essentially equivalent if the output coordinate axes are properly defined. From the last formulations in (9) and (10), we see that the convolution of two functions can be produced by forming the FT of the product of the FT's of the two functions. When the conjugate transform of the reference function is used (a superscript * denotes complex conjugate), the correlation results. Several 2-D optical correlator architectures are now described and examples of the outputs of such systems are presented.

A. Frequency Plane Correlator

The optical system of Fig. 5 directly implements (9). With $g(x_1, y_1)$ placed at P_1, the light distribution incident on P_2 is $G(u, v)$. With the transmittance of P_2 described by $H^*(u, v)$,

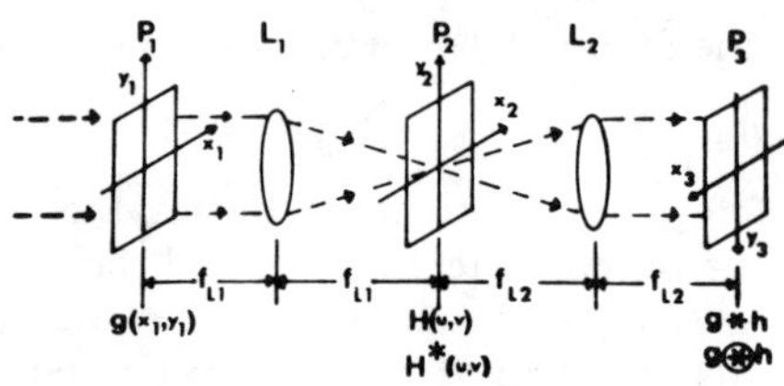

Fig. 5. Schematic of a frequency plane correlator (FPC) with a matched spatial filter (MSF) of the reference function recorded at P_2.

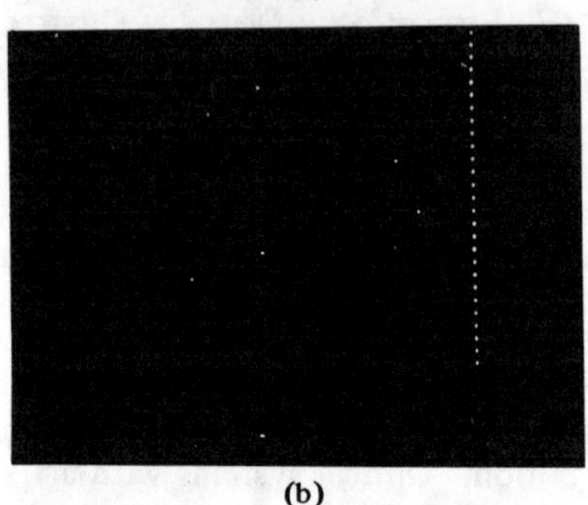

(a)

(b)

Fig. 6. Representative example of optical pattern recognition using the system of Fig. 5. (a) Input plane P_1 pattern. (b) Output correlation plane P_3 pattern with a matched spatial filter of the word "RADAR" recorded at P_2 of Fig. 5. The location of the correlation peaks correspond to the locations of the word "RADAR" in the input paragraph of text [36].

the light distribution leaving P_2 is $G(u, v) H^*(u, v)$. Lens L_2 forms the FT of this product $G(u, v) H^*(u, v)$ of two transforms as described by (9). Thus the desired correlation of g and h results at P_3 of Fig. 5. The display of an optical-correlation plane differs significantly from a digital correlation with the coordinates of P_3 being the (x, y) shift parameters of the correlation. The optical-correlation pattern in P_3 consists of peaks of light. The presence of a peak of light in P_3 indicates the presence of h in g, the location of the peak of light denotes the location of h in g, and the amplitude of the peak denotes the degree to which h and the associated region of the input g agree. This coding of the locations and amplitudes of the peaks of light at P_3 in an optical-output correlation plane are best shown by example. In Fig. 6 we show the input plane pattern (a paragraph of text = g) and the resultant output correlation plane pattern (with H^* being the conjugate transform of the word "RADAR"). The reader can convince himself that the locations of the peaks of light in Fig. 6(b) correspond to the locations of the word "RADAR" in the input paragraph of text.

We can describe the example of Fig. 6 mathematically with increased insight into the process that occurs. To achieve such a formulation, we describe the input by

$$g(x, y) = f(x, y) + \sum_{n=1}^{6} h(x - x_n, y - y_n) \qquad (11)$$

where h represents the word "RADAR," (x_n, y_n) denote the six locations of this word in the full input g, and f describes

the remaining portions of the full input. The transform of (11) incident on P_2 is

$$G(u, v) = F + \sum_{n=1}^{6} H \exp\left[-j2\pi(ux_n + vy_n)\right]. \qquad (12)$$

The transmittance of P_2 is H^* and thus the light distribution leaving P_2 is

$$U_2(u, v) = GH^* = FH^* + \sum_{n=1}^{6} HH^* \exp\left[-j2\pi(ux_n + vy_n)\right]. \qquad (13)$$

Lens L_2 forms the FT of U_2 and at P_3 we obtain

$$u_3(x, y) = \mathcal{F}[U_2] = \mathcal{F}[GH^*]$$

$$= f \circledast h + \sum_{n=1}^{6} h \circledast h * \delta(x - x_n, y - y_n)$$

$$= \sum_{n=1}^{6} \delta(x - x_n, y - y_n). \qquad (14)$$

In the last expression in (14), the autocorrelation $h \circledast h$ of h was assumed to be a delta function of normalized unit amplitude (i.e. $h \circledast h = 1$) and the key object and the other regions of the input are assumed to be uncorrelated (i.e., $f \circledast h = 0$). The resultant correlation of g and h thus reduces to six delta functions at locations (x_n, y_n) corresponding to the six locations of h in g.

The correlator of Fig. 5 is the classic matched spatial filter (MSF) system devised by Vander Lugt [7] in 1964. The H^* pattern recorded at P_2 is an MSF. We refer to this as a frequency plane correlator (FPC) since the desired correlation is achieved by multiplying the FT's of g and h. One of Vander Lugt's major contributions was the description of how a filter function with complex transmittance H^* could be recorded on an intensity-sensitive medium at P_2. The scheme used is similar to the holographic-synthesis procedure originated by Gabor [37], and developed by Leith and Upatnieks [9] for 3-D imaging applications.

B. Matched Spatial Filter

The MSF synthesis procedure as described by Vander Lugt assumed g to be the signal-plus-noise and the application directly envisioned was the recovery of a signal h buried in noise. In our pattern-recognition application, those portions of the input that do not agree with the signal or reference function h are effectively the noise or the function f in (11). To record H^* at P_2, the function h is placed at P_1 and the interference of its transform H (formed by L_1 at P_2) and a plane wave reference beam $U_R = \exp(j2\pi\alpha x_2)$ of unit amplitude is recorded at P_2, where $\alpha = (\sin\theta)/\lambda$ is the spatial frequency due to the off-axis angle θ between the reference and signal beams. The pattern recorded at P_2 and the subsequent transmittance of P_2 is

$$t_2(x_2, y_2) = |H + U_R|^2 = 1 + |H|^2$$

$$+ H \exp(j2\pi\alpha x_2) + H^* \exp(-j2\pi\alpha x_2). \qquad (15)$$

The last term in (15) is proportional to the desired transmittance H^* of P_2. To see how the effects of this term are separated from the other three terms in (15), we consider the correlation process itself in detail.

During correlation, g is placed at P_1 and the full transmittance of P_2 is t_2 given by (15). The light distribution leaving P_2 is Gt_2 and L_2 of focal length f_{L2} forms the FT of this product at P_3, where we find

$$u_3(x_3, y_3) = \mathcal{F}[Gt_2] = g \text{ at } x_3 = y_3 = 0$$
$$+ h \circledast h * g \text{ at } x_3 = y_3 = 0$$
$$+ g * h \text{ at } x_3 = \alpha\lambda f_{L2}, y_3 = 0$$
$$+ g \circledast h \text{ at } x_3 = -\alpha\lambda f_{L2}, y_3 = 0. \quad (16)$$

From (16), we see that the desired correlation $g \circledast h$ can be separated from the other three terms in the output plane pattern by proper choice of the reference to signal-beam angle θ. The region of the correlation plane shown in Fig. 6 is the portion centered at $x_3 = -\alpha\lambda f_{L2}, y_3 = 0$.

The FPC optical pattern-recognition system of Fig. 5 is useful when a single fixed reference function is to be located. In many applications (i.e., character recognition), multiple and composite MSF's are useful to allow a parallel pattern-recognition search to be performed. Several multiple MSF approaches are summarized in [38]. Much of the work in this area relates to optical data storage [39]. Optical pattern-recognition techniques have been applied to a multitude of applications including diatom (water pollution particle) [40], text [41], aerial imagery [42], and key-object [43] recognition. Single, multiple, and averaged MSF's have been used in [40] and [43] to reduce the number of required filters and to enchance the capacity of the recognition system.

C. Joint Transform Correlator

An alternate optical pattern-recognition topology [44] is shown in Fig. 7. In this architecture, the two functions to be correlated (g and h, assumed to be of spatial extent b) are placed side by side at P_1 with a center-to-center separation $2b$. The transmittance of P_1 (in 1-D, for simplicity only) is

$$u(x_1) = g(x_1 - b) + h(x_1 + b). \quad (17)$$

Lens L_1 forms the FT of (17) or a joint transform pattern that is recorded at P_2. The subsequent transmittance of P_2 is

$$t_2(u) = |G \exp(-j2\pi ub) + H \exp(+j2\pi ub)|^2$$
$$= |G|^2 + |H|^2 + GH^* \exp(-j4\pi ub) + G^*H \exp(+j4\pi ub). \quad (18)$$

P_2 is now illuminated with a plane wave of read-light (shown incident on P_2 in reflection in Fig. 7).

With P_2 in the front focal plane of L_2, the pattern at P_3 is the FT of (18) or

$$u_3(x_3) = g \circledast g \text{ at } x_3 = 0$$
$$+ h \circledast h \text{ at } x_3 = 0$$
$$+ g \circledast h \text{ at } x_3 = +2b$$
$$+ h \circledast g \text{ at } x_3 = -2b. \quad (19)$$

Proper choice of the separation $2b$ between the inputs in Fig. 7 enables the desired $g \circledast h$ term in the output pattern of (19) to be separated from the other terms. This is similar to how the choice of θ in the FPC system of Fig. 5 enabled the desired correlation term to be separated from other terms in that output plane. This is referred to as a joint transform correlator (JTC) [44].

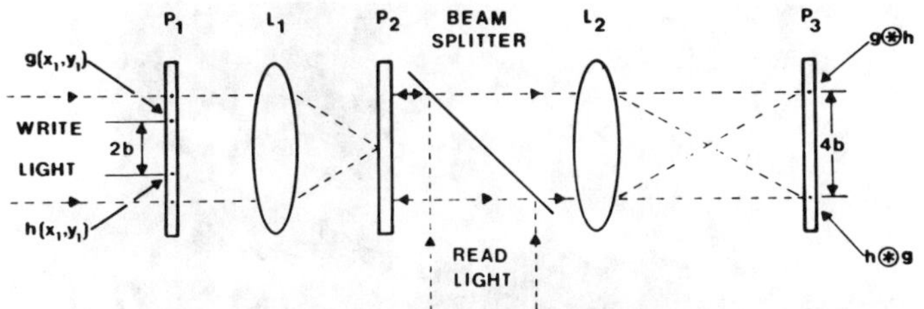

Fig. 7. Schematic of a joint transform correlator (JTC) for optical pattern recognition.

D. Real-Time Optical Pattern Recognition

Since the advantages of optical pattern recognition include real-time and parallel processing, reusable and real-time 2-D electrooptical transducers are necessary at the input plane P_1, and often at the transform plane P_2 in the systems of Figs. 5 and 7, if real-time operation is to be realized. The devices used for these purposes are known as spatial light modulators (SLM) [45], [46]. The architecture of the optical pattern-recognition system of Fig. 7 assumed an optically addressed and reflex-mode readout SLM at P_2 with different write and read wavelengths. Most optically sensitive SLM's operate in this manner.

The example shown in Fig. 6 was performed in real-time on the FPC system of Fig. 5 using an electron-beam addressed electrooptic crystal input plane P_1 transducer. The input paragraph of text was scanned onto a special target crystal by a current-modulated electron gun, quite similar to the operation of a television. A collimated laser beam was then passed through this crystal and emerged spatially modulated with the input data. The electrooptic effect [47] is used in this and similar devices to modulate an input light wave proportional to the spatially varying voltage or charge pattern across the crystalline material [45], [46].

Another real-time optical pattern-recognition application nearing completion at General Motors [48] is shown in Fig. 8. The application involved the recognition and location of the position of a 3-D object (a relay for the example shown in Fig. 8) on an assembly line. The output of this optical pattern-recognition system is to be interfaced to a robot as part of an automated assembly line. In operation, a diffusely illuminated image of the assembly line is continuously focused onto the photoconductor side of an SLM at P_1 of Fig. 5. The image on the liquid-crystal input transducer used is read out continuously in reflection in coherent laser light. Since the decay time of the liquid-crystal SLM is only 20 ms, the liquid-crystal input transducer serves as a noncoherent-to-coherent input P_1 image converter for the FPC system of Fig. 5. Several images of the input object (a relay) on the assembly line are shown in Fig. 8(b). An MSF of the key object to be searched for (the relay) is stored on film at P_2 of Fig. 5. The peak in the output correlation plane P_3 pattern and its cross sectional scan are shown in Fig. 8(a) for several locations of the input relay on the moving assembly line in real time.

To change the key object to be searched for, only the film at P_2 need be changed. A modified scan and prism system is presently under consideration at General Motors to enable recognition of a key object to be maintained in the presence of expected rotational and scale differences between the input and reference (or MSF) imagery. In Sections V and VI, we consider alternate methods by which such distortion invariance and increased optical pattern-recognition flexibility can be realized.

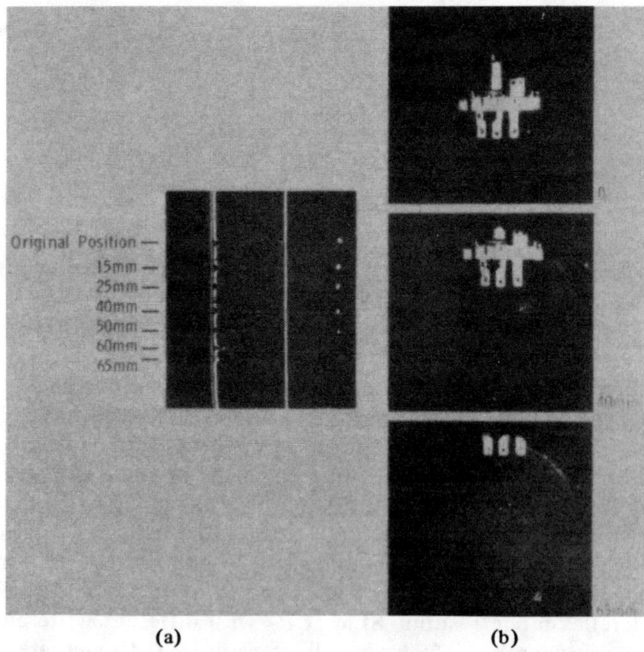

(a)　　　　　　　(b)

Fig. 8. (a) Example of a real-time optical pattern recognition [48]. (b) Output correlation peak and its cross sectional scan for various locations of the input object (a relay) in the input field of view.

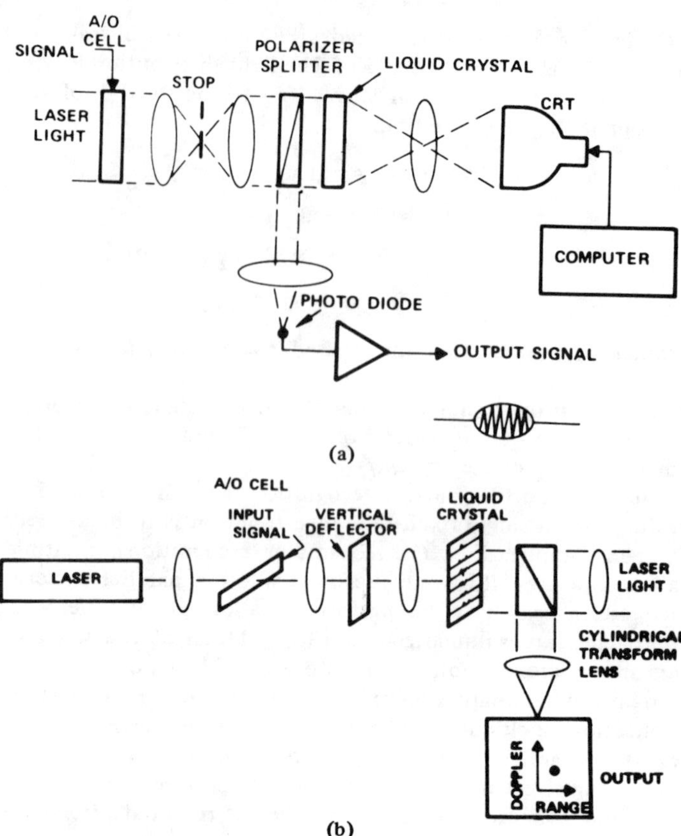

Fig. 9. Schematic of a 2-D real-time optical signal processor. (a) Pulse compression section. (b) Doppler processing section [49].

An alternate real-time 2-D optical pattern-recognition system [49] intended for signal-processing applications, specifically the generation of the ambiguity function (range versus Doppler) for any coded input waveform, is shown in block diagram form in Fig. 9. This topology combines the high bandwidth features of the acoustooptic correlators described in Section III with the 2-D nature of an optical processor. In signal correlations, coded waveforms are generally employed and the target's range and Doppler vary. The desired target data (its range and Doppler) is best conveyed by an ambiguity surface [50] with range τ and Doppler v axes. This output can be realized in a multichannel correlator in which different Doppler shifted versions of the reference signal are recorded on different lines. Each of these signals is then correlated with the received signal in 1-D. The resultant 2-D plot (correlation or range τ horizontal and Doppler vertical) is an ambiguity function, widely used in radar. This basic signal pattern-recognition problem thus deserves note in this paper. Many methods exist by which this operation can be realized. One of the more promising and developed ones is shown schematically in Fig. 9 and is described below.

In the pulse compression section (Fig. 9(a)), the coded radar waveform to be used is generated by computer or other methods and displayed on a CRT from which it is continuously imaged onto a liquid crystal. The received input radar signal is fed to an acoustooptic input transducer. This received input signal is continuously imaged onto the reference signal (on the liquid crystal) in reflection, the product integrated and heterodyne detected by a photodiode, whose time-history output is the correlation of the transmitted coded radar signal and the reflected signal received from various targets for various transmitted pulses in the pulse burst. If this process is continued for N pulses in a pulse burst waveform, N output correlations appear in time from the photodiode. These outputs are separated in time by one pulse period and correspond to the returns from targets at a specific range, with each of the N-returns modulated by the target's Doppler. If these

correlations, corresponding to the returns due to sequential transmitted pulses, are recorded on separate horizontal lines, they will align vertically for a target at a given range.

To obtain Doppler data on the target, one must integrate across these N correlations. To achieve this, the output from the photodetector is fed to a second acoustooptic cell (Fig. 9(b)). A laser is pulsed on in synchronization with the PRF of the code and passed through a 1-D deflector. In the resultant pattern recorded on the second liquid crystal, each of the N correlations from the pulse compression section are recorded on N separate lines. The vertical scanning system for this 2-D pattern is synchronized to the PRF of the transmitted waveform. This second liquid crystal is then read from the right side and the 1-D vertical FT of the pattern on this liquid crystal yields the desired range/Doppler ambiguity function. This system is scheduled for completion and delivery in late 1978.

V. Weighted MSF Synthesis

As implied in Section IV, practical pattern-recognition systems of any kind must be able to operate even with various distortions (scale, rotation, aspect, etc.) present between the input and reference functions. Such flexibility is achieved in digital pattern recognition by sophisticated software algorithms. Recent programs intended to increase the flexibility of optical pattern-recognition systems are addressing such practical problems with encouraging results. One approach toward this goal involves control of the MSF synthesis process [42]. To describe this method, we rewrite (15) as

$$t_2(x_2, y_2) = 1 + 1/K + (2/\sqrt{K}) \cos \psi \qquad (20)$$

where $K = A^2/|H|^2$ is the ratio of the intensities of the reference and signal beams and where $\psi = 2\pi\alpha x_2 + \text{Arg }(H)$ describes the recorded MSF as a fringe pattern at spatial frequency α with the phase of H encoded as a phase modulation on this carrier frequency α.

At this point, it is necessary to discuss one feature of all MSF optical pattern-recognition systems. We refer to the limited dynamic range of the P_2 recording material. The optical FT of an image contains a large dc term (that contains no information useful in distinguishing objects) and higher frequency components of far lower intensity (that contain the data needed to distinguish or discriminate one object from another similar one). The bias on the MSF material is properly adjusted so that this dc term saturates the MSF material, whereas high modulation is given to the lower intensity and higher spatial frequency data. Thus in practice, an optical FPC system correlates the ac rather than the dc portions of imagery.

Referring to (20), we see that since H varies spatially (with x_2 and u) so does K and hence, so does the modulation of the fringe pattern. Recently [42] use has been made of this fact to choose the spatial frequency f^* at which $K = 1$ (corresponding to full modulation). This effectively weights specific spatial frequencies in the MSF. The use of this adjunct to optical pattern recognition is best shown by example. The image of Fig. 10(a), characterized by regions A, B, and C that are respectively predominantly rural, urban and structured was used as the test image. An MSF of the full image was made with $K = 2$ at various spatial frequencies f^* and correlated with the three indicated isolated regions of Fig. 10(a). In Fig. 10(b) we show the variation of the peak intensity I_p of these correlations with the f^* band in which $K = 1$ during MSF synthesis. The correlation for the urban input (curve B) clearly peaks at a larger f^* setting than for the rural input (curve A), with the correlation for the structured image region (curve C) peaking at an intermediate f^* setting. From this example, we clearly see that control of K and f^* can greatly effect the resultant correlation. The WRD detector (Section II-A) was used to facilitate rapid evaluation of the effects of f^* and K settings on the output correlation [42].

This same technique, which we refer to as weighted MSF synthesis, is also useful in controlling the effect of various expected image-degradations on I_p and signal-to-noise ratio (SNR) of the output correlation [42]. Many different expected degradations can occur between the input and reference image. In Fig. 10(c) we consider rotational misalignments between the key object as it appears in the input and reference scenes and the effect that selection of the proper f^* band can have on the SNR of the output correlation. As shown, setting $K = 1$ at a large f^* (band H) results in a larger SNR than lower f^* choices. However, as the angle θ of rotational misalignment between the input and reference image increases, the SNR of the correlation with the MSF formed with $K = 2$ in band H rapidly decreases. Conversely, a lower f^* choice (band B) results in a lower initial SNR, but a far lower SNR loss with θ variations.

Thus when image degradations are present, lower f^* settings are preferable. The reason is simply that when emphasizing high-input spatial frequencies (by high f^* settings), these are the first components lost when degradations occur between the input and reference imagery. By emphasizing lower input spatial frequency components (by lower f^* settings) and sacrificing some initial SNR and I_p (Fig. 10(c)), we find the resultant correlation preferable when differences or degradations are expected between the input and reference images.

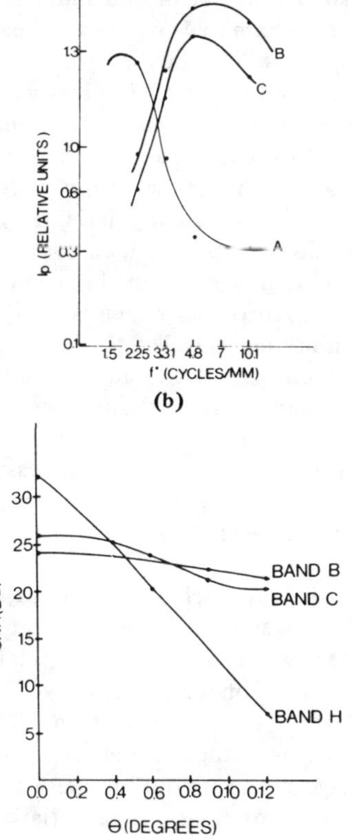

Fig. 10. Optical pattern recognition by weighted MSF control [42]. (a) Input scene. (b) I_p versus f^* for input regions A, B, C. (c) SNR versus θ for various f^* bands.

Many types of image differences have been examined [51] such as scenes of the same area taken years apart, in different seasons, from different aspect angles, and radar images taken from different headings or from different sensors, etc. The magnitude of the I_p and SNR correlation loss for each of these degradation sources were found. For the imagery analyzed, textural-image differences (snow cover in winter scenes and new structure in imagery taken years apart) were found to have less of a degrading effect on the correlation than geometrical image distortions (due to heading or aspect differences). Weighted MSF synthesis control was found to be helpful in reducing the correlation loss due to geometrical-image differences if the spectrum of the imagery was broad

Fig. 11. Multisensor imagery exhibiting intensity disparity [55].

and if the image degradation could be classified by a narrow-band distortion function. Aspect differences satisfy these criteria, whereas slant range error and radar shadow effects in the SLAR imagery examined (opposite headings and low depression angles) were of such a broad-band nature that extensive compensation for correlation loss was not possible.

Another expected source of image differences arises when images taken from different sensors are correlated [52]. In a missile guidance application, the stored reference image is usually assumed to be a high-quality aerial image and the input image a real-time radar map. In such cases, intensity differences occur in various image regions between the two scenes. The intensity of a given object depends on the nature of the object, the illuminating wavelength, and so many other factors that one cannot predict in advance how a given scene will appear in a radar image without *a priori* knowledge of the content of the various regions of the scene. We refer to this aspect of multisensor image processing as intensity disparity image pattern recognition. Similar intensity differences arise between imagery taken from the same sensor at different times.

One of the classic approaches to intensity disparity is to differentiate both images [53]. The premise here is that only the edges of the regions in such scenes are the features that are common between such imagery. However, this is a purely statistical contribution to the correlation. This contribution decreases as we increase the number N of uniquely shaped regions in the image with random intensity variations. There are also various types of image differentiation [54]. If we consider an MSF in which K is set to 1 (optimum modulation) at a high spatial frequency f^* (thus emphasizing the high spatial frequency portion of the input image), we are effectively performing one type of image differentiation. A plot of the transmittance of such an MSF shows that it represents a high-pass filtered transfer function with a 6-dB cutoff at the f^* spatial frequency at which K was set to unity during MSF synthesis.

Thus, in performing the correlation $g \circledast h$ using an MSF, the reference scene h can be modified to be a high-pass filtered version h' by the action of the MSF (and so is g). The correlation $g' \circledast h'$ of the input and a high-pass filtered reference function is thus performed. By varying f^*, we can control the degree of image differentiation used and arrive at the optimum combination of statistical and deterministic (edge-enhanced) pattern recognition. An example of one set of multisensor imagery is shown in Fig. 11. The left portion of the image exhibits several fields of various degrees of random

intensity variations and of somewhat unique shapes. This portion of the image can be viewed as a set of N key objects (where N is somewhat small), whereas the remaining portion of the image contains little information content. By the proper choice of the spatial frequency f^*, we have successfully correlated all four images in this and similar image sets using only one MSF formed from one of the images. Similar multispectral correlations on various other image sets (including a completely contrast-reversed image pair) have been achieved by this method [55].

VI. SPACE-VARIANT PATTERN RECOGNITION

As noted in Sections IV and V, geometrical differences between the input and reference imagery severely degrade correlations. Scale and rotation are the most common geometrical differences. These can be accommodated by use of multiple MSF's at P_2 of Fig. 5. However, this approach requires that multiple output correlation planes be scanned and always results in a considerably reduced output light intensity. In another approach to producing a scale-invariant optical correlator, the input plane P_1 in Fig. 5 is placed behind L_1. A scaling correlator results in which a scale search of the input function can be performed by varying the distance from P_1 to P_2. Rotational differences in the orientation of the MSF can also be accommodated by rotating P_1 or P_2. In both of these latter schemes, the time required to manually search scale and rotational differences is not compatible with the real-time processing advantages of an optical pattern-recognition system. In this section, we consider a real-time optical processing approach to the problem of geometrical differences in pattern recognition. The resultant optical processor will be a space variant rather than a space-invariant system.

One of the major limitations in the realization of a practical recognition system has been the space invariance of an optical processor. This feature allows these systems to be described by the convolution integral in (10). With reference to Fig. 5, the input function is g, the system's impulse response is h (the transform of the system's transfer function H recorded at P_2), and the content of the output plane P_3 pattern is the convolution of g and h. Considerable research, presently in progress, is concerned with producing various types of space-variant optical systems (whose impulse response varies spatially with input position). One program in this area directly related to pattern recognition involves the use of coordinate transformation preprocessing [56] as initially described by Huang [57] and Sawchuck [58]. We describe two examples of such optical systems in detail below.

We consider first a space-variant optical pattern-recognition system whose output correlation is invariant to scale differences between the input and reference functions. By applying a logarithmic transformation to the input and reference functions, we obtain (in 1-D for simplicity) $g' = g(\exp x)$ and $h' = h(\exp x)$. The FT of these functions yields G' and H' (or H'^*). It has been shown [56] that the FT of g' is the Mellin transform [59] of g. Of particular interest is the case when $h(x) = g(ax)$ (i.e., g and h differ by a scale factor a). In this case the Mellin transforms M_g and M_h of g and h are related by

$$M_g(u) = M_h(u) \exp(-j2\pi u \ln a) \exp(-j2\pi \alpha x_2). \quad (21)$$

This follows from the definitions of M_g and M_h as the FT's of g' and h'. The final exponential factor in (21) is due to the spatial carrier α on which M_h is recorded (as in the MSF synthesis and correlation operation described in Section IV).

When realized using the FPC system of Fig. 5, g' is placed at P_1 and M_h^* is recorded at P_2 of Fig. 5. The light incident on P_2 is M_g (the FT of g') and the light distribution leaving P_2 is $M_g M_h^*$. Lens L_2 in Fig. 5 forms the FT of $M_g M_h^*$ at P_3 where we find

$$u_3 = \mathcal{F}[M_g M_h^*] = \mathcal{F}[M_h M_h \exp[-j2\pi(u \ln a + \alpha x_2)]]$$

$$= h \circledast h * \delta(x_3 - \ln a\, \alpha\lambda f_L). \tag{22}$$

From (22), we see that the resultant correlation is displaced from its normal location $x_3 = \alpha\lambda f_L$ by an amount proportional to the natural logarithm of the unknown scale factor "a" between the two functions. Thus from the location of the correlation peak we can determine "a." Of more importance is the fact that the output correlation is identical to the autocorrelation $h \circledast h$, just as if $g \equiv h$ with no scale difference present.

We now consider a space-variant optical pattern-recognition system that is invariant to rotational differences between the input and reference images. The same coordinate preprocessing approach is again used. The two functions are h and g (a rotated version of h with rotational angle θ_0). We first convert both $h(x, y)$ and $g(x, y)$ to new functions $h'(\xi, \eta)$ and $g'(\xi, \eta)$ by the coordinate transformations $\xi = \tan^{-1}(y/x)$ and $\eta = \sqrt{x^2 + y^2}$ (i.e., a polar transform). This transformation now converts a rotation by θ_0 into a shift. The 1-D conjugate transform H'^* of the coordinate transformed undistorted function h' is formed and stored at P_2 of Fig. 5.

With g' recorded at P_1 of Fig. 5, the light distribution leaving P_2 is $G'H'^*$. To best understand how the rotational invariance is achieved, we separate the original function g into two parts g_1 and g_2 (where in polar-coordinates, g' occupies the 0 to $-\theta_0$ portion of θ space and g_2' occupies the remaining 0 to $2\pi - \theta_0$ region). The portions G_1' and G_2' of the FT's of the coordinate-transformed polar functions $g'(\xi, \eta) = g'(\theta, r)$ are related to the FT's G_1 and G_2 of the corresponding portions g_1 and g_2 of the original $g(x, y)$ image by

$$G' = G_1' + G_2' = G_1 \exp(-j\omega_\theta \theta_0) + G_2 \exp[-j\omega_\theta(2\pi - \theta_0)] \tag{23}$$

where ω_θ denotes the Fourier plane spatial frequency variable associated with the polar-angle variable $\theta = \xi$.

The light leaving P_2 is now $G'H'^*$ and its FT formed at P_3 of Fig. 5 by L_2 is

$$u_3 = \mathcal{F}[G'H'^*] = g_1' \circledast h + g_2' \circledast h$$

$$= h_1 \circledast h * \delta(\theta - \theta_0) + h_2 \circledast h$$

$$* \delta(\theta + 2\pi - \theta_0). \tag{24}$$

From (24), we see that the output correlation is now divided into two correlation peaks separated in distance by 2π in P_3 space. The sum of these two correlation peaks is

$$u_3 = h_1 \circledast h + h_2 \circledast h = h \circledast h \tag{25}$$

or the output correlation of two rotated functions equals the autocorrelation of the original unrotated functions. There is thus no correlation loss even if the input and reference functions are rotated versions of one another with an unknown rotational angle θ_0. From (24) we see that the location of the output correlation peak is proportional to the unknown rotational angle θ_0 and thus θ_0 can also be found from the output correlation.

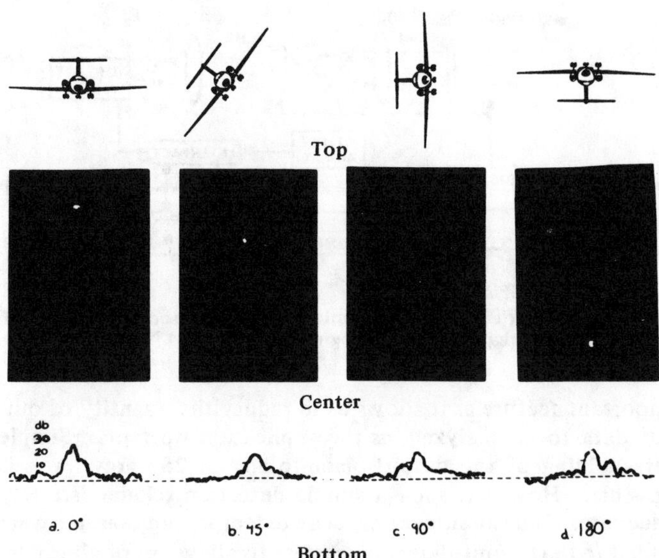

Fig. 12. Rotation-invariant optical pattern recognition. (Top) input. (Center) output correlation plane. (Bottom) cross-sectional scan of the correlation peak.

An example of this rotation invariance is shown in Fig. 12. The reference image chosen was an airplane, an MSF of the polar transformed version of the airplane was recorded at P_2 of Fig. 5. As the input was rotated (Fig. 12, top), its polar transform was formed and recorded at P_1. The resultant output correlation plane pattern (Fig. 12, center) and its cross sectional scan (Fig. 12, bottom) show the predicted results. The location of the output correlation peak changes proportional to the rotational misorientation between the input and reference and the output correlation peak remains essentially invariant to the input rotational differences.

The log coordinate transformation required in the Mellin transform correlator can easily be realized by use of log modules in the deflection system of the input plane SLM. The polar transforms in Fig. 12 were realized in real time using a specially modified camera. Extensions of these optical space-variant pattern-recognition methods and the formulation of a system invariant to multiple distortions are described in detail elsewhere [60].

VII. Hybrid Optical/Digital Correlators

The final embodiment of any optical processor will be a hybrid system [36] in which the best features of optical and digital processing are properly married. The architecture of one such hybrid system that has been assembled [61] is shown in Fig. 13. The upper portion of this schematic shows the FPC system of Fig. 5 with real-time SLM's at the input and filter planes. Digital control of the content of these SLM's and control of the system's WRITE, READ, and ERASE cycle are implied in the flowlines shown. The digital preprocessor in Fig. 13 is used for format control and as a scan converter. As shown, the outputs at the FT and correlation planes are detected by a 2-D array and analyzed by a microprocessor array (250-ns cycle time, Intel 3000 series) to extract the desired information (usually the location of the correlation peak). A buffer memory within the interface allows interframe operations to be performed such as change detection and output time history of correlation peaks to be found.

The microprocessor-interface system allows us to digitize the output correlation plane to a variable resolution. This is an

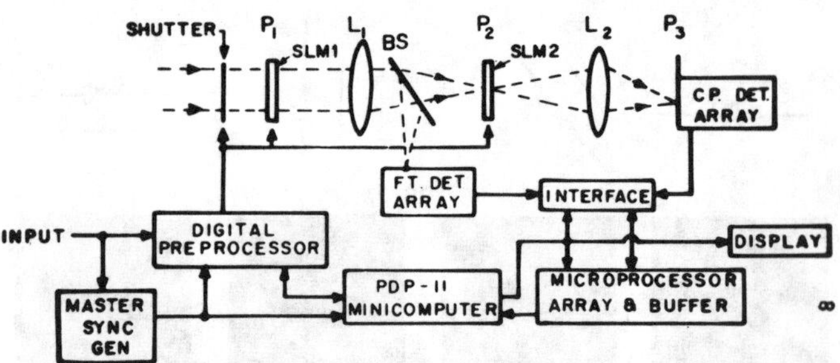

Fig. 13. Schematic diagram of a microprocessor-based hybrid optical/
digital pattern-recognition system [61].

important feature as it allows us to reduce the quantity of output data to be analyzed, as the application warrants. Simple thresholding of the output plane to any of 256 gray levels is possible. However, such a simple detection scheme is rarely adequate. Thus an integrator, peak detector, and counter were added to the output-detection system to allow use of alternate-detection criteria such as the area under the correlation peak or whether the output signal exceeds a given threshold level for a given amount of time. We have shown earlier [42] that the area of the correlation peak decreases less rapidly than I_p with rotation, scale, or other distortion parameters. Thus use of such alternate detection methods is another way by which the pattern-recognition system's sensitivity to differences between the input and reference imagery can be reduced.

An alternate version of a hybrid-correlator can be realized by placing a TV or linear CCD/photodiode detector in the frequency plane P_2 of the JTC system of Fig. 7. Lens L_2 and plane P_3 in Fig. 7 are not used now, rather the transform of the data at P_2 previously performed by L_2 is now realized by a digital fast Fourier transform (FFT) or spectrum-analyzer system [62]–[64].

To accomplish the processing previously performed by L_2 in Fig. 7 on the joint-transform pattern of (17), the pattern in (18) is detected and scanned as a time or video signal $v(t)$. An FT operation on $v(t)$ is realized by multiplying $v(t)$ by quadrature sinusoids ($\sin \omega_0 t$ and $\cos \omega_0 t$); the two separate products are then integrated over one line scan time of the output detector, squared, and summed. From (18), we see that the $|G|^2 + |H|^2$ envelope is the slowly varying part of the output video signal, whereas the important part of $v(t)$ is the cosine function.

If the input and reference patterns are equal, $g = h$ and (18) becomes

$$v(t) = 2|H|^2(1 + \cos 4\pi bu). \qquad (26)$$

For this case the frequency of the cosine depends upon the separation between the input and reference in P_1 or, therefore, the location of h in g. If g is displaced from h by $2.5b$ rather than $2b$, then (26) becomes

$$v(t) = 2|H|^2[1 + \cos(4\pi bu + \pi bu)] \qquad (27)$$

from which we see that the location of h in g can be found from the frequency of the cosine pattern.

To demonstrate this principle, a landing field was chosen as the key reference object h to be located (Fig. 14(a), left) in a larger input scene (Fig. 14(a), right). Several of the input image pairs at P_1 of the JTC system are shown in Fig. 14(a), with the separation between h and g in the two images increasing. The joint transform of each input image pair was de-

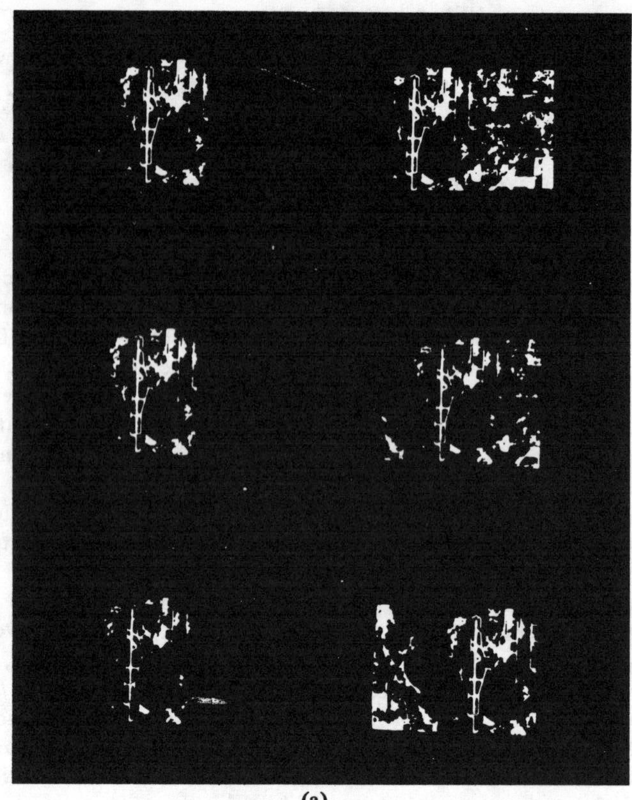

(a)

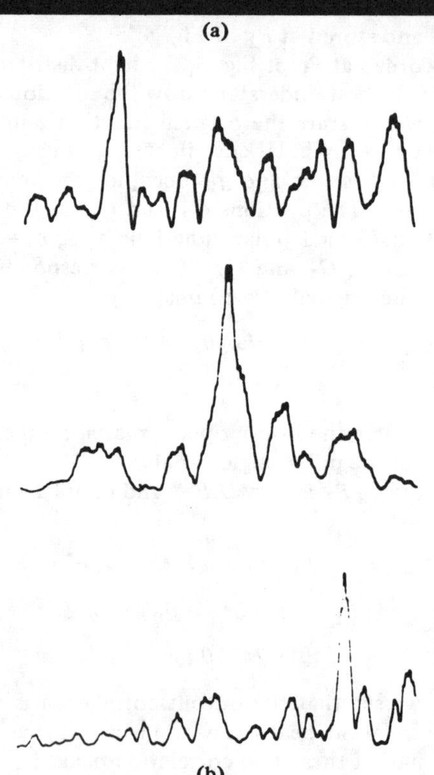

(b)

Fig. 14. Experimental demonstration of a hybrid optical coherence measure pattern-recognition system [64]. (a) Inputs. (b) Cross-sectional scan of the output correlation.

tected, scanned, and quadrature modulated as noted earlier. As the frequency of the local oscillator was swept with time, the output was displayed (Fig. 14(b)). The horizontal axis in Fig. 14(b) thus corresponds to different mixing oscillator frequencies or equivalently to testing different displacements or shifts of the input function. As shown, the location of the peak output from the electronically processed joint-transform pattern shifts right as the location of h in g shifts right. The presence of a peak indicates the presence of h in g and the location of the peak indicates the location of h in g.

Returning to (26) and (27), we see that the amplitude of the recorded cosine pattern depends on the product of the magnitudes of the FT's of the two input functions. If g and h are identical except for their strength, i.e., $g(x) = ah(x)$ in 1-D, the detected pattern is

$$t_2 = |H|^2(1 + a + 2a \cos 4\pi bu). \tag{28}$$

From (28), we find that the modulation is reduced proportional to the reduced signal strength of g. Since the amplitude $2a$ of the cosine term can easily be found from the electronically processed output, the vertical scale in the output pattern (Fig. 14(b)) can appropriately be adjusted and thus a normalized correlation produced.

Another feature of electronic postprocessing and further insight into the operation of the original JTC-system can be seen by considering the case when $h \neq g$. The fringe pattern at P_2 is now no longer a pure cosine but is phase modulated (spatially) by the difference between the phases of the transforms G and H. The power spectral density at the carrier frequency $2b$ is now decreased proportional to the degree of mismatch of g and h. Thus from the magnitude of the output-spectral density, we have a measure of the spectral purity of the video signal and equivalently the coherence or similarity of the two inputs. The carrier period variance and carrier phase variance can easily be found (e.g., from a phase-locked loop on the output) and hence a "coherence measure correlator" results.

However, electronic postprocessing also allows increased flexibility since the signals can be modified prior to quadrature modulating and processing them. This luxury and flexibility is not present in the full optical system of Fig. 7, since L_2 must take the FT of the P_2 pattern (the joint transform of G and H) and once detected P_2 cannot easily be modified. In practice g and h will differ as noted in Sections IV and V. For the case when the distortion present in g can be described by the action of a linear-space invariant system with impulse response f, we can describe g by $g = h * f$. In many instances the distortion f is known or reasonable distortion functions can be assumed *a priori*. In such cases, the electronic postprocessor of the P_2 data can be modified (for example, by phase-modulating the local oscillator in the detection system with the transfer function F of the assumed distortion function f). An "equalizing correlator" (a term borrowed from communications) then results in which various distortions present in g that are not in h can be removed (or their effects equalized). Experimental confirmation of the "equalizing optical correlator" has also been reported [64].

An alternate technique by which improved discrimination can be achieved in optical pattern recognition was suggested by Caulfield and Maloney [65]. In this approach, linear combinations of the system's responses to various input characters are formed in a second processing stage.

Electronic preprocessing and postprocessing techniques have recently been used to enable bipolar correlations to be performed on incoherent processors [66]-[69]. The use of computer-generated holograms to synthesize spatial filters [70], [71] of functions not easily physically realizable represents yet another use of digital techniques in optical pattern recognition.

VII. Summary

Although many survey articles, special issues, and books exist on optical computing, this article is the first to address only the issue of optical pattern recognition—thus allowing a unified treatment in some depth. When we think of optical pattern recognition, we usually consider only the optically matched spatial-filtering system of 1964. However as shown, many advances have occurred since 1964. A wealth of new architectures for optical pattern-recognition systems exist and have been demonstrated and many refinements have occurred in the original Vander Lugt correlator.

Research in optical pattern recognition is now addressing more practical and real pattern-recognition problems. These directed research efforts and major advances in optoelectronic and solid state components, plus advances in digital electronics and digital pattern-recognition algorithms have affected optical pattern-recognition systems. A rapidly increasing repertoire of new operations (such as space-variant ones) are now possible in optical processors. Many of these have already been applied to pattern-recognition applications.

Many other optical processing operations not discussed in this survey exist that do not use the classic FT property of a lens. These include an optical system to realize the discrete FFT [72], optical systems operating in residue arithmetic [73]-[75] and many others [11]. In time, these and other optical processing methods will be applied to pattern-recognition applications. This will further increase the capability of optical pattern-recognition systems, while retaining the high-speed parallel processing, and large-space-bandwidth product features of optical processors that have made them attractive for the past twenty years.

Acknowledgment

The author thanks his present and past Ph.D. students who performed most of the experiments whose results are included, especially Dr. Warren Sterling, Dr. Demetri Psaltis, and Dr. Alan Furman.

References

[1] E. Abbe, "Beitrage zur theorie des mikroskops und der mikroskopischen Wahrnehmung," *Arch. Mikroskop. Anat.*, vol. 9, pp. 413–468, 1873.

[2] A. B. Porter, "On the diffraction theory of microscope vision," *Phil. Mag.*, vol. 11, p. 154, 1906.

[3] F. Zernike, "Das Phasenkontrastverfahren bei der mikroskopischen beobachtung," *Z. Tech. Phys.*, vol. 16, p. 454, 1935.

[4] A. Marechal and P. Croce, "Un filtre de frequences spatiales pour l'amelioration du contrast des images optiques," *C. R. Acad. Sci.*, vol. 127, p. 607, 1953.

[5] E. L. O'Neill, "Spatial filtering in optics," *IRE Trans. Inform. Theory*, vol. IT-2, pp. 56–65, June 1956.

[6] G. L. Turin, "An introduction to matched filters," *IRE Trans. Inform. Theory*, vol. IT-6, pp. 311–329, June 1960.

[7] A. Vander Lugt, "Signal detection by complex spatial filtering," *IEEE Trans. Inform. Theory*, vol. IT-10, pp. 139–145, Apr. 1964.

[8] L. J. Cutrona *et al.*, "On the application of coherent optical processing techniques to synthetic aperture radar," *Proc. IEEE*, vol. 54, pp. 1026–1032, Aug. 1966.

[9] E. N. Leith and J. Upatnieks, "Reconstructed wavefronts and communication theory," *J. Opt. Soc. Amer.*, vol. 52, pp. 1123–1130, Oct. 1962.

[10] D. Casasent, "Optical pattern and character recognition," in *Handbook of Holography*, H. J. Caulfield, Ed. New York: Academic Press, 1979.

[11] J. W. Goodman, "Operations achievable with coherent optical information processing systems," *Proc. IEEE*, vol. 65, pp. 29–38, 1977.

[12] J. T. Tippett *et al.*, Eds., *Optical and Electro-Optical Information Processing*. Cambridge, MA: M.I.T. Press, 1965.

[13] A. Vander Lugt, "Coherent optical processing," *Proc. IEEE*, vol.

62, pp. 1300–1319, 1974.

[14] *Proc. IEEE, Special issue on Optical Computing*, vol. 65, Jan. 1977.

[15] D. Casasent, Ed., *Optical Data Processing: Applications, Vol. 23, Topics in Applied Physics.* Heidelberg, Germany: Springer-Verlag, 1978.

[16] L. J. Cutrona, E. N. Leith, C. J. Palermo, and L. J. Porcello, "Optical data processing and filtering systems," *IRE Trans. Inform. Theory*, vol. IT-6, pp. 386–400, June 1960.

[17] M. Monahan, K. Bromley, and R. P. Bocker, "Incoherent optical correlators," *Proc. IEEE*, vol. 65, pp. 121–129, Jan. 1977.

[18] P. S. Consodine and R. A. Gonsalves, "Optical image enhancement and image restoration," in *Optical Data Processing: Applications, Vol. 23, Topics in Applied Physics.* Heidelberg, Germany: Springer-Verlag, 1978.

[19] G. W. Stroke, *et al.*, "Image improvement and three-dimensional reconstruction using holographic image processing," *Proc. IEEE*, vol. 65, pp. 39–62, Jan. 1977.

[20] S. H. Lee, "Recent developments in optical information processing using non-linearity and feedback," in *Optical Information Processing*, vol. 2, E. S. Barrekette *et al.*, Ed., New York: Plenum, 1978, pp. 171–191.

[21] J. W. Goodman, *Introduction to Fourier Optics.* New York: McGraw-Hill, 1968.

[22] H. Kasdan and D. Mead, "Out of the laboratory and into the factory: optical computing comes of age," in *Proc. Electronic Optic System Design Conf.* (Anaheim, CA) Oct. 1975.

[23] H. Stark, "An optical-digital computer for parallel processing of images," *IEEE Trans. Comput.*, vol. C-24, pp. 340–347, Apr. 1975.

[24] G. Lendaris and G. Stanley, "Diffraction pattern sampling for automatic pattern recognition," *Proc. IEEE*, vol. 58, pp. 198–216, Feb. 1970.

[25] G. Stanley and G. Lendaris, "Diffraction pattern sampling for automatic pattern recognition," *Soc. Photo-Opt. Instrum. Eng.*, vol. 18, pp. 127–153, June 1969.

[26] R. Kruger, W. Thompson and A. Turner, "Computer diagnosis of pneumoconiosis," *IEEE Trans. Syst. Man Cybern.*, vol. SMC-4, pp. 40–49, Jan. 1974.

[27] *Optical Eng., Special Issue on Acoustooptics*, vol. 16, Sept. 1977.

[28] L. Lambert, M. Arm and A. Aimette, chapter 38 in *Optical and Electro-Optical Information Processing*, J. T. Tippet *et al.*, Eds., Cambridge, MA: M.I.T. Press, 1965, pp. 715–748.

[29] L. Lambert, "Electro-Optical Correlation Techniques," in *Textbook of Modern Radar Techniques.* New York: Wiley, 1966.

[30] W. T. Maloney, "Acousto-optical approaches to radar processing," *IEEE Spectrum.*, vol. 6, pp. 40–49, Oct. 1969.

[31] E. B. Felstead, "A simple real-time incoherent optical correlator," *IEEE Trans. Aerosp. Electron. Syst.*, vol. AES-3, pp. 907–914, Nov. 1967.

[32] L. Flores and D. Hecht, "Acousto optic signal processors," *Proc. Soc. Photo-Opt. Instrum. Eng.*, vol. 118, pp. 182–192, Aug. 1977 (IEEE Cat. No. 77CH1265-8C).

[33] R. Sprague and C. Koliopolous, "Time integrating acoustooptic correlator," *Appl. Opt.*, vol. 15, pp. 89–92, Jan. 1976.

[34] J. W. Goodman, A. R. Dias and L. M. Woody, "Fully parallel, high-speed incoherent optical method for performing discrete Fourier transforms," *Opt. Letts.*, vol. 1, pp. 1–3, Jan. 1978.

[35] J. Lee, B. Udelson, and N. Berg, "Acousto-optic signal processing for radar applications," *Proc. Soc. Photo-Opt. Instrum. Eng.*, vol. 128, pp. 192–201, Sept. 1977.

[36] D. Casasent and W. Sterling, "A hybrid optical/digital processor: hardware and applications," *IEEE Trans. Comput.*, vol. C-24, pp. 348–357, Apr. 1975.

[37] D. Gabor, "Microscopy by reconstructed wavefronts. I and II," *Proc. Roy. Soc.* (Ser. A), vol. 197, p. 454, 1959 and (Gen.) vol. 64, p. 449, 1951.

[38] C. L. Burckhardt, "Storage capacity of an optically formed spatial filter for character recognition," *Appl. Opt.*, vol. 6, pp. 1359–1366, Aug. 1967.

[39] Di Chen and J. D. Zook, "An overview of optical data storage technology," *Proc. IEEE*, vol. 63, pp. 1207–1230, Aug. 1975.

[40] S. Almeida and J. K-T Eu, "Water pollution monitoring using matched spatial filters," *Appl. Opt.*, vol. 15, pp. 510–515, Feb. 1976.

[41] A. Vander Lugt, F. B. Rotz and A. Klooster, "Character reading by optical spatial filtering," in *Optical and Electro-Optical Information Processing*, J. T. Tippet *et al.*, Eds., Cambridge, MA: M.I.T. Press, 1965, pp. 125–141.

[42] D. Casasent and A. Furman, "Optimization of parameters in matched spatial filter synthesis," *Appl. Opt.*, vol. 16, pp. 1662–1669, June 1977. See also D. Casasent and A. Furman, "Sources of correlation degradation," *Appl. Opt.*, vol. 16, pp. 1552–1661, June 1977.

[43] K. Leib *et al.* "Aerial reconnaissance film screening using optical matched-filter image-correlator technology," *Appl. Opt.*, vol. 17, pp. 2892–2899, Aug. 1978.

[44] J. Rau, "Detection of difference in real distributions," *J. Opt. Soc. Amer.*, vol. 56, pp. 1490–1494, Nov. 1966.

[45] D. Casasent, "Spatial light modulators," *Proc. IEEE*, vol. 65, pp. 143–157, Jan. 1977.

[46] *Opt. Eng., Special Issue on Real Time Spatial Light Modulators*, vol. 17, July 1978.

[47] B. H. Billings, "The electro-optic effect in uniaxial crystals of the dihydrogen phosphate type, I. Theoretical," *J. Opt. Soc. Amer.*, vol. 39, p. 797, Oct. 1949.

[48] A. Gara, "Real-time optical correlation of 3-D scenes," *Appl. Opt.*, vol. 16, No. 1, pp. 149–153, Jan. 1977.

[49] H. Brown and B. Markevitch, "Radar signal optical processor," *Proc. Soc. Photo-Opt. Instrum. Eng.*, vol. 128, pp. 204–209, Sept. 1977.

[50] P. M. Woodward, *Probability and Information Theory with Applications to Radar.* New York: Pergamon, 1955.

[51] D. Casasent and M. Saverino, "Optical image processing for missile guidance," *Proc. Photo-Opt. Instrum. Eng.*, vol. 118, pp. 11–20, Aug. 1977.

[52] R. Y. Wong, "Sensor transformations," *IEEE Trans. Syst. Man Cybern.*, vol. SMC-7, pp. 836–841, Dec. 1977.

[53] R. Y. Wong, "Sequential scene matching using edge features," *IEEE Trans. Aerosp. Electron. Syst.*, vol. AES-14, pp. 128–140, Jan. 1978.

[54] G. S. Robinson, "Detection and coding of edges using directional masks," *Opt. Eng.*, vol. 16, pp. 580–585, Nov. 1977.

[55] D. Casasent and Y. Barniv, "Coherent optical processing for multi-sensor image processing," *Proc. Photo-Opt. Instrum. Eng.*, vol. 137, Mar. 1978.

[56] D. Casasent and D. Psaltis, "New optical transforms for pattern recognition," *Proc. IEEE*, vol. 65, pp. 77–84, 1977.

[57] G. Robbins and T. S. Huang, "Inverse filtering for linear shift invariant image systems," *Proc. IEEE*, vol. 60, pp. 862–872, July 1972.

[58] A. A. Sawchuk, "Space variant motion degradation and restoration," *Proc. IEEE*, vol. 60, pp. 854–861, July 1972.

[59] R. Bracewell, *The Fourier Transform and Its Applications*, New York: McGraw-Hill, 1965.

[60] D. Casasent and D. Psaltis, "Deformation-invariant, space-variant optical pattern recognition," in *Progress in Optics, vol. XVI*, E. Wolf, Ed. New York: North Holland Publ., 1978.

[61] D. Casasent, J. Hackwelder, and P. DiLeonardo, "A microprocessor-based optical/digital processor," *Proc. Soc. Photo-Opt. Instrum. Eng.*, vol. 117, pp. 26–32, Aug. 1977.

[62] E. Rau, "Real-time complex spatial modulation," *J. Opt. Soc. Amer.*, vol. 57, pp. 798–802, June 1967.

[63] C. W. Weaver *et al.*, "The optical convolution of time functions," *Appl. Opt.*, vol. 9, pp. 1672–1682, July 1970.

[64] D. Casasent and A. Furman, "Equalizing and coherence measure correlators," *Appl. Opt.*, vol. 17, 1978.

[65] H. J. Caulfield and W. T. Maloney, "Improved discrimination in optical character recognition," *Appl. Opt.*, vol. 8, pp. 2354–6, Nov. 1969.

[66] A. W. Lohmann, "Incoherent processing of complex data," *Appl. Opt.*, vol. 16, pp. 261–263, Feb. 1977.

[67] A. W Lohmann and W. T. Rhodes, "Two pupil synthesis of optical transfer functions," *Appl. Opt.*, vol. 17, pp. 1141–1151, Apr. 1978.

[68] W. Stoner, "Incoherent optical processing via spatially offset pupil masks," *Appl. Opt.*, vol. 17, pp. 2454–2467, Aug. 1978.

[69] A. Furman and D. Casasent, "Bipolar incoherent optical pattern recognition by carrier encoding," *Appl. Opt.*, submitted for publication.

[70] A. W. Lohmann and D. P. Paris, "Computer generated spatial filters for coherent optical data processing," *Appl. Opt.*, vol. 7, p. 651, 1968.

[71] W. H. Lee, "Sampled Fourier transform hologram generated by computer," *Appl. Opt.*, vol. 9, p. 639 1970.

[72] J. W. Goodman, A. R. Dias, and L. M. Woody, "Fully parallel, high-speed, incoherent optical method for performing discrete Fourier transforms," *Opt. Lett.*, vol. 2, pp. 1–3, Jan. 1978.

[73] Y. Tsunoda, A. Huang, and J. W. Goodman, "Proposed optoelectronic residue matrix vector multiplier," *Appl. Opt.*, 1979.

[74] S. A. Collins, Jr., "Numerical optical data processor," *Proc. Soc. Photo-Opt. Instrum. Eng.*, vol. 128, pp. 313–319, Sept. 1977.

[75] D. Psaltis and D. Casasent, "A correlation-based approach to optical residue arithmetic," *Appl. Opt.*, 1979.

Acoustic Holography

ROLF K. MUELLER, SENIOR MEMBER, IEEE

Invited Paper

Abstract—In the middle and late 1960s, holography, applied to acoustics, generated a considerable upsurge of activity in the already mature acoustic imaging technology. It brought both coherent optics and digital data processing to bear upon the problems of acoustic imaging and introduced fresh approaches to the visualization of sound fields. These developments are reviewed and the wide range of potential applications for acoustic holography is discussed. In most cases, the status is that of proved feasibility awaiting broader application.

I. Introduction

ACOUSTIC imaging was in the early 1960s, before holography entered the field, an already mature technology. Most of its basic ideas had been generated in the 1930s in Europe and USSR [1]. The field developed in two clearly distinct directions: ultrasonic cameras and sonar-related devices.

Ultrasonic cameras are imaging devices which use lenses or shadow projection (proximity focusing) to produce an ultrasonic image on an area detector which transposes the ultrasound into a visual image. The frequency is typically in the megahertz range. These devices are generally used in nondestructive testing and medical diagnostics.

Sonar-related imaging devices are based on pulse echo ranging and direction scanning, using mechanical or electronic scanning of single elements or arrays which might function as transmitters, receivers, or both. These systems derive their technological base from the radar field and are developed to high sophistication in naval underwater search and surveillance. Stationary and mobile imaging systems, ranging in frequency from 10 Hz to several megahertz, have been described. Their use is not limited to navy-related applications: sonar-type systems, especially in the higher frequency domain, are used in diagnostics and nondestructive testing.

With holography, a novel and fertile concept was introduced into acoustic imaging, which spurred new and extensive developments in both the camera and sonar fields. We shall briefly recapitulate the basic concepts of holography as a background for understanding its impact on acoustic imaging and as a basis for the subsequent discussions.

It is well known in optics that light which passes through an aperture is fully described by the phase and amplitude distribution in the aperture. According to Huygens' principle, this is sufficient to reconstruct the light wave at any point behind the aperture. If we describe phase and amplitude in the aperture plane $z=0$ by the complex function $F(x, y)$, we obtain for the wave $f(x, y, z)$ which develops behind the aperture, according to Huygens' principle [2]

$$f(x, y, z) = F(x, y) * G(x, y, z) \qquad (1)$$

where the symbol $*$ denotes convolution and G is a spherical wave

originating in the aperture plane. Thus $G = e^{i2\pi r/\lambda}/r$ with $r=\sqrt{x^2+y^2+z^2}$, which becomes in Fresnel's approximation $r=z + [(x^2+y^2)/2z]$. Hence the wave behind the aperture $f(x, y, z)$ is fully described if phase and amplitude distribution $F(x, y)$ of the impinging wave is given in the aperture plane.

In acoustics, where linear detectors such as microphones or hydrophones are available, it is trivial to obtain phase and amplitude. In optics, where one has only intensity-sensitive detectors, one has to resort to interferograms; that is, a recording of the interference pattern of the wavefront of interest with a known and simple reference wave as, for example, a plane wave $e^{i\mathbf{k}\cdot\mathbf{r}}$. The intensity distribution which constitutes the interference pattern is

$$I(x, y) = |F(x, y) + e^{i(k_1 x + k_2 y)}|^2$$
$$= 1 + |F|^2 + Fe^{-i(k_1 x + k_2 y)} + F^* e^{i(k_1 x + k_2 y)} \qquad (2)$$

provided that the object wave and the reference wave are mutually coherent over the aperture plane. To obtain large area coherence with prelaser light sources was quite an experimental feat; however, it became easy with highly coherent laser sources. A photographic plate, suitably exposed, records a density pattern which is proportional to the intensity distribution of (2). In principle, therefore, one can determine the amplitude and phase of an optical wave over an aperture as large as the coherence of the light permits. Amplitude and phase, however, are not in themselves of interest since we are concerned with recording or displaying imagery.

It was Gabor [3] who showed how information encoded in an interferogram can be extracted in an eminently useful form. Consider an optical transparency with an amplitude transmission proportional to the intensity of the two interfering beams, the reference and object beams of (2). If such a transparency (which Gabor called a hologram) is illuminated by the reference beam, one obtains in the plane immediately behind it an amplitude and phase distribution $H(x, y)$ which contains, besides some other additive terms, a term equal to the phase and amplitude distribution of the object wave $F(x, y)$.

$$H(x, y) = (1 + |F|^2)e^{i(k_1 x + k_2 y)} + F(x, y) + F^*(x, y)e^{i2(k_1 x + k_2 y)}. \qquad (3)$$

According to Huygens' principle, therefore, a wave develops behind the hologram which contains, due to the second term on the right-hand side of (3), an exact replica of the object wave, giving the viewer the feeling that he is looking at an object through a window rather than at an illuminated hologram. This effect is quite striking, and a wide literature [4] now exists on the subject.

For our present purpose, however, the importance of this reconstruction process lies in the fact that it is not limited to optical interferograms. This again was recognized by Gabor [3], who introduced holography in 1948, motivated by the desire to improve electron microscopy by optically reconstructing holograms which had been produced by interfering electron beams. Gabor's idea, which is as applicable to sound as to electron waves, is to transfer spatial

Manuscript received April 30, 1971; revised July 2, 1971. *This invited paper is one of a series planned on topics of general interest—The Editor.*

The author is with Bendix Research Laboratories, Southfield, Mich. 48076.

Reprinted from *Proc. IEEE*, vol. 59, pp. 1319–1335, Sept. 1971.

modulation from invisible image-carrying wave fields onto a light beam. Once this is done, one can use the highly developed optical imaging technology to generate images better than those possible in the original medium.

This modulation transfer brings with it an unavoidable image distortion [5]. If, for example, an acoustic plane wave reference hologram was made with sound of wavelength λ_s and played back without scale change with a collimated light beam of wavelength λ_L, the reconstructed wave would appear to come from an object field with unchanged lateral (x, y) dimensions but with a depth distortion proportional to the wavelength ratio λ_s/λ_L.

If one changes the linear scale of the hologram by a factor m, both lateral dimensions will change by the same factor, that is

$$x' = mx \tag{4}$$

$$y' = my \tag{5}$$

and the depth dimension, following the well-known optical imaging relation [2], will change to

$$z' = m^2 \frac{\lambda_s}{\lambda_L} z. \tag{6}$$

Thus to obtain undistorted imagery, one would have to choose $m = \lambda_L/\lambda_s$. In the most common domain of ultrasound, m is of the order of 10^{-3}. The undistorted imagery is therefore so small that one has to use optical magnification to obtain useful images, thereby regenerating the depth distortion. This situation rules out obtaining anything approaching the realistic three-dimensional reconstruction of optical holography in the acoustic domain. Thus we have to find other reasons to explain the strong upsurge of interest in acoustic imaging with the advent of holography.

One of the more obvious reasons for the fast growth of interest in acoustic holography was the availability of coherent sources. Optical holography was held back for more than a decade because coherent sources were not available. Almost all acoustic sources used for imaging are already coherent and, therefore, conventional imaging devices can be readily turned into holographic equipment. Furthermore, not only intensity-sensitive detectors are available in acoustics, but also linear detectors, which opens new possibilities for holographic recording. The processes for recording amplitude and phase and for generating the holograms for optical reconstruction then became separable tasks and could be independently studied and optimized. Concepts like phase-only holograms [6], [7], for example, were easily realized by separating phase and amplitude information before assembling a hologram. Schemes for generating synthetic reference beams [8]–[10] were invented, thereby bringing new electronic approaches into acoustic imaging.

The relatively large wavelength available in acoustics permitted such sampling techniques [11]–[13] as scanning the aperture or employing receiving or transmitting arrays. This latter development was, at least as far as equipment is concerned, a takeoff from sonar techniques where digital data handling is widely practiced. Therefore, as this technology matured, the assembly of a hologram from observed phase and amplitude data and the subsequent optical reconstruction and imaging process was understood as analog optical data processing. The rediscovery of the fast Fourier transform algorithm [14] (which occurred around the time of peak activity in acoustic holography), the availability of fast computers and array processors [15], and the relatively small amount of data to be processed in acoustic (as compared to optical) holograms made digital processing a distinct and widely discussed possibility for image reconstruction, thus adding a new dimension to acoustic imaging.

The renewed interest in acoustic imaging brought many additional workers to the field who developed new methods for detecting sound. One method which deserves special interest uses laser scanning [16] and coherent phase contrast methods [17], [18] to pick up acoustic phase and amplitude information from sonically excited surfaces. Another new imaging method of special interest utilizes volume interaction between sound and light to transfer spatial modulation from one wave field to the other. This method, Korpel's Bragg imaging concept [19], is related to Lippman-type holography [2] and will therefore be included in this review.

II. Methods and Techniques

In the following subsections we shall discuss various holographic imaging devices based on a wide range of techniques. In some instances, the image reconstruction will appear as an integral part of the holographic imaging system; in others, the final output of the apparatus will be an acoustic hologram presented either on a TV monitor or some other graphic output device. In the latter case, image reconstruction can proceed by generating a photographic transparency from the hologram display and reconstructing an optical image in the usual fashion. This procedure, however, introduces long time delays which might be objectionable even for still pictures and completely rules out real-time operation. The real-time capability, however, which some of the fast scanning hologram recording devices possess, can be preserved by electrooptical hologram processors, which are discussed in one of the following subsections, together with digital reconstruction of images from electronically recorded holographic data. Another subsection is devoted to a novel acoustic imaging technique introduced by Korpel in 1966, the so-called Bragg diffraction imaging [20]. This technique, if not classified as holography, is at least very closely related to it and has its purely optical analogs in thick emulsion and volume-recorded holography [21]. A final subsection will contain some comments on image quality. Acoustic images—at least those of the long wavelength variety—are plagued by a number of problems such as relatively low resolution, high specular reflection, extensive speckle, and others which are not specific to any particular method.

Section II has been written in such a manner that the reader does not have to follow the equations in order to understand the concepts; he may feel free to disregard them entirely.

A. Intensity-Sensitive Area Detectors

Acoustic holograms made on intensity-sensitive area detectors were the first to be reported in the literature [22]. They are generated analogously to optical holograms by a sound wave (which is reflected from or transmitted through an object) and a reference wave impinging together on an intensity-sensitive area detector. The intensity pattern of the two interfering beams is then recorded as the acoustic hologram. In some cases, for the purpose of reconstruction, an optical transparency has to be prepared. In others, the acoustic hologram itself can be used as the light modulator. All intensity-sensitive area detectors suitable for conventional acoustic imaging are potential holographic material. These detectors, together with their sensitivity and response time, are listed in Table I. To compare these detectors with amplitude-sensitive which will be discussed later, see [24]–[29] and Table II in Section II-B.

Of all the detectors listed, the liquid-gas interface received the most attention [30]–[33] because it can be directly used as the light modulator, thereby avoiding intermediate processing. We shall discuss three versions of this system in some detail, since its evolution gives an interesting example of how holography induced an interesting new approach in an old, direct imaging technique. These three versions are the following:

lensless holography

TABLE I

Typical Intensity-Sensitive Area Detectors

Method	Sensitivity (W/cm²) (Experimental Value)	Time Constant (s)	Experimental Frequency Used	Reference
Photographic plate in developer bath	1	10^{-4}		[1]
Thermosensitive dyes	1	1		[1]
Cholesteric liquid crystals	10^{-3}	10^{-1}		[23]
Liquid surface deformation	10^{-3}	10^{-3}	(7 MHz)	[1]

focused image holography

time-independent spatial carrier imaging.

Sound reflected from a surface exerts a pressure—the so-called radiation pressure—on the surface. This pressure is proportional to the impinging intensity. The surface reacts to this pressure and deforms until gravity and surface tension restore a new balance. The deformation h of the surface measured normal to the undisturbed (planar) surface is related to the impinging intensity by

$$h \propto I_s * K. \tag{7}$$

The symbol $*$ indicates convolution, I_s is the sound intensity, and K the impulse response of the liquid surface. Under Fourier transform, (7) simplifies to:

$$\tilde{h} \propto \tilde{I}_s \cdot \tilde{K} = \tilde{I}_s/(1 + \gamma^2 v^2) \tag{8}$$

where $\tilde{h}$, $\tilde{I}$, and $\tilde{K}$ are the Fourier transforms of h, I, and K. The Fourier transform $\tilde{K}$ of the impulse response K is the modulation transfer function of the liquid surface

$$\tilde{K} = \frac{1}{1 + \gamma^2 v^2} \tag{9}$$

where $v = \sqrt{v_x^2 + v_y^2}$ is the spatial frequency and γ a characteristic length which depends on surface tension σ and the density ρ of the liquid

$$\gamma = 3.2 \times 10^{-2} \sqrt{\sigma/\rho} \ [\text{cm}]. \tag{10}$$

For the water-air interface, γ is around 2 mm.

Equation (8), the most important for the following discussion, states that the water surface records the sound intensity, via a modulation transfer function $\tilde{K} = 1/(1 + \gamma^2 v^2)$ that transforms intensity into a surface deformation h. If the intensity distribution varies slowly relative to the characteristic length γ, the surface deformation h is, for all practical purposes, proportional to the sound intensity. The amplitude of h ranges typically between 100 Å and 1000 Å.

In liquid surface imaging and holographic systems, light is reflected from the deformed surface, picking up in this manner the information contained in the deformed surface as phase modulation. In order to generate optical images, this phase modulation is transformed into intensity modulation by optical Schlieren [2] or phase-contrast methods. For direct imaging this poses a problem, because most optical Schlieren methods give poor imaging for the coarse detail normally available in acoustic images. The method is, however, at least conceptually very well suited for the holographic approach, since the information is modulated onto a rapidly varying high-spatial-frequency carrier.

1) Lensless Holography: Fig. 1 shows a schematic of a lensless water surface holography system. The object is an acoustic trans-

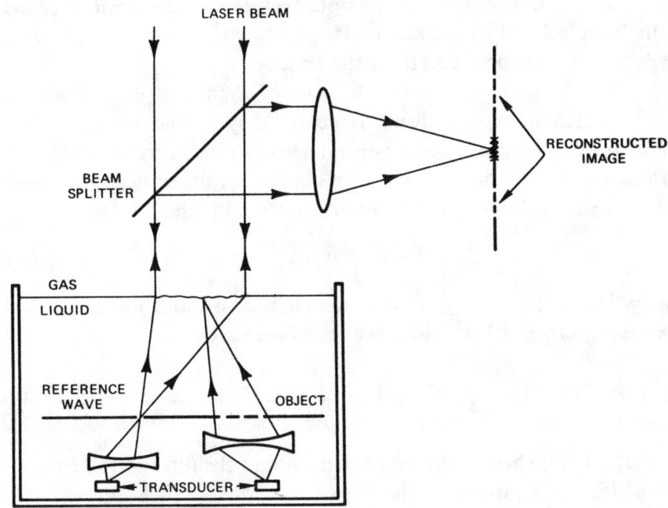

Fig. 1. Liquid surface holography system, generating a Fourier transform hologram at the liquid surface (after Mueller and Sheridon [22]).

parency, which is configured so that the interference pattern at the water surface is essentially the Fourier transform of the object transmission function $f_s(x, y)$. The intensity at the water surface in Fresnel's approximation is

$$I_s(x, y) = R^2 + |\tilde{f}_s|^2 + R(\tilde{f}_s \cdot e^{-i(2\pi lx/\lambda_s z_s)} + \tilde{f}_s^* \cdot e^{i(2\pi lx/\lambda_s z_s)}) \tag{11}$$

where R is the amplitude of the reference beam, l is the separation between the optical axis of reference and illumination beams, z_s the distance of the object from the hologram plane, and $\tilde{f}_s$ the Fourier transform of the object transmission function:

$$\tilde{f}_s = \iint f_s(x', y') e^{i(2\pi/\lambda_s z_s)(xx' + yy')} \, dx' \, dy'. \tag{12}$$

Note that the interference terms in (11) are fast varying functions, due to the fact that the relatively slow varying functions $\tilde{f}_s$ and $\tilde{f}_s^*$ are modulated onto a high-spatial-frequency carrier $e^{i(2\pi lx/\lambda_s z_s)}$. The spatial frequency $2\pi l/\lambda_s z_s$ is, for ultrasound of 10 MHz in water, one order of magnitude larger than $1/\gamma$; the modulation transfer function $\tilde{K}$ around this spatial frequency is therefore, in good approximation, $\tilde{K} \propto 1/v^2$.

If we disregard the inconsequential constant term R^2 and the small second order term $|\tilde{f}_s|^2$, the surface deformation due to the intensity distribution (11) is

$$h \propto (\tilde{f}_s \cdot e^{-i(2\pi lx/\lambda_s z_s)} + \tilde{f}_s^* e^{i(2\pi lx/\lambda_s z_s)}) * K. \tag{13}$$

If a plane optical wave u_0 is reflected from the deformed surface, one obtains a reflected wave at the water surface of the form

$$u = u_0 \cdot e^{i(4\pi h/\lambda_L)} \approx u_0 \left(1 + i \frac{4\pi}{\lambda_L} h\right). \tag{14}$$

The last part of (14) follows from the fact that the surface deformation is, as mentioned previously, small compared to the wavelength of the light λ_L. In order to obtain an optical reconstruction of the object function f_s, we have to generate a Fourier transform of the reflected wavefront. With coherent illumination of the deformed surface, this can be done easily by a transfer lens. We then obtain for the optical amplitude in its Fourier plane $\tilde{u}$ (neglecting the effects of the finite aperture of the optical system):

$$\tilde{u} \propto \left\{ \delta(v_x - 0, v_y - 0) + i \frac{4\pi}{\lambda_L} \tilde{h} \right\} \tag{15}$$

v_x, v_y are the coordinates of the optical system in the Fourier plane, which are related to the spatial frequency v of (9) by $v = (2\pi/\lambda_L z_L)v$, where z_L is the focal length of the lens.

The δ function represents the center bright spot into which the undiffracted light is focused. A center stop in the Fourier plane removes this light as does a neutral density filter with an amplitude transmission function v^2/v^2_{max}. One obtains for the optical amplitude behind such a filter in the Fourier transform plane

$$\tilde{u}' \propto \tilde{h} \cdot v^2. \tag{16}$$

Equation (16) gives, after some simple algebra and use of the approximation, $\tilde{K} = 1/v^2$ which we discussed earlier;

$$\bar{u}' \propto \left\{ f_s\left(\frac{\lambda_s z_s}{\lambda_L z_L} v_x + l, \frac{\lambda_s z_s}{\lambda_L z_L} v_y\right) + f_s\left(l - \frac{\lambda_s z_s}{\lambda_L z_L} v_x, -\frac{\lambda_s z_s}{\lambda_L z_L} v_y\right) \right\}. \tag{17}$$

Equation (17) shows that we obtain, behind the filter in the Fourier plane (u_x, v_y), an image of the object function $f_s(x', y')$ centered at

$$v_x = -\frac{\lambda_L z_L}{\lambda_s z_s} l$$

and its inverse centered at

$$v_x = \frac{\lambda_L z_L}{\lambda_s z_s} l$$

both changed in scale by $\lambda_L z_L/\lambda_s z_s$ but undistorted within our approximation. In general, the ratio λ_L/λ_s is very small compared to unity so that the images have to be viewed through a microscope.

Unfortunately, the experimental results do not verify these analytical predictions. Image reconstructions obtained with this method are plagued with severe aberrations because the reference beam unavoidably deforms the water surface. Only if the reference beam causes a constant or a spherical deformation of the water surface in the hologram area is the foregoing analysis valid. In practice, however, departures from sphericity are unavoidable. These aberrations are of low spatial frequency but their amplitude is of the same order as the surface levitation due to the reference beam, which is, for practical power levels, large compared to the optical wavelength. If we introduce an aberration function $W(x, y)$ which measures the deviation from sphericity of the reference-induced levitation, we obtain an additional phase term $e^{i4\pi W/\lambda_L}$ in the reflected light. Because of the condition $W \gg \lambda_L$, the Fourier transform of this term has extensive higher frequency components, even if W itself varies slowly over the hologram aperture. We obtain, therefore, a severely blurred image of the form

$$f'_s = f_s * e^{i4\pi \tilde{W}/\lambda_L} \tag{18}$$

in the image plane (v_x, v_y), instead of the perfect image of (17). The blurred image renders this method rather useless.

2) Focused Image Holography: However, a method introduced by Smith and Brenden [32] gets around the blurred image difficulty. Instead of generating a Fourier transform of the object function, Brendon uses an acoustic projection system to image the object into the water surface. This image, together with a reference wave, generates a focused image hologram at the water surface (see Fig. 2). Using the same notation as in the preceding section, we obtain for the surface deformation

$$h \propto W(x, y) + R(f_s \cdot e^{-i(2\pi \cos \alpha/\lambda_s)x} + f_s^* \cdot e^{i(2\pi \cos \alpha/\lambda_s)x}) * K \tag{19}$$

where W is again the nonspherical surface deformation due to the reference beam. It is now the acoustic image f_s, and not its Fourier transform $\tilde{f}_s$ modulated onto the high frequency carrier

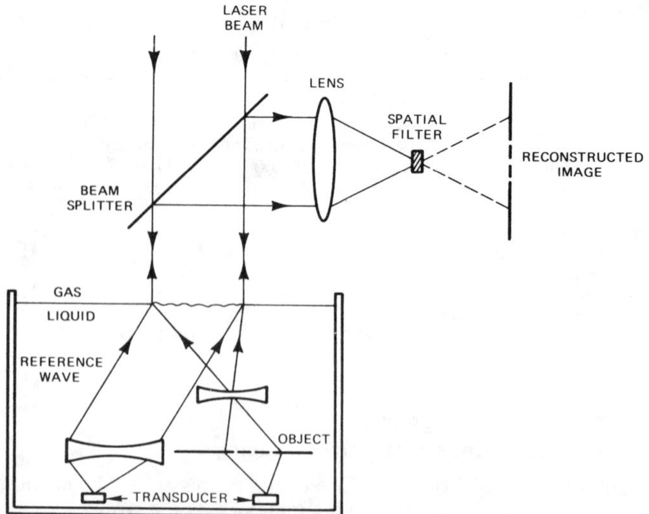

Fig. 2.   Holographic system, generating a focused image hologram at the liquid surface (after Brenden [32]).

$\exp [i2\pi \cos \alpha(x/\lambda_s)]$, which appears at the surface and is picked up as phase modulation in a light beam reflected from the water surface

$$u = u_0 \cdot e^{i(4\pi h/\lambda_L)}. \tag{20}$$

A phase-contrast imaging system, using a center stop method [2] (such as the v^2/v^2_{max} filter in the pupil plane discussed earlier), generates in the image plane a light distribution which is essentially the second derivative of the light distribution obtained at the water surface [34]:

$$u' \propto \nabla^2 e^{i(4\pi h/\lambda_L)} \propto \left\{ \nabla^2\left(\frac{h}{\lambda_L}\right) + 4\pi i\left[\nabla\left(\frac{h}{\lambda_L}\right)\right]^2 \right\} e^{i(4\pi h/\lambda_L)}. \tag{21}$$

The light now carries an amplitude modulation in addition to an inconsequential phase modulation. The amplitude modulation,

$$\{[\nabla^2(h/\lambda_L)]^2 + 16\pi^2[\nabla(h/\lambda_L)]^4\}^{1/2}$$

which becomes rather involved if h is introduced from (19), can be drastically simplified. The slow-varying (reference-beam induced) surface deformation term W in (19), which caused the severe aberrations in the previously considered case, is strongly suppressed because its derivatives are small compared to the derivatives of the rapidly oscillating spatial carrier $\exp [i2\pi \cos \alpha(x/\lambda_s)]$ onto which the acoustic image is modulated. Neglecting the term W, we are left with only the rapidly varying part of the surface disturbance h which we shall designate by h' in the following.

As discussed earlier, h'/λ_L is small compared to unity. We obtain, therefore, in good approximation

$$\{[\nabla^2(h/\lambda_L)]^2 + 16\pi^2[\nabla(h/\lambda_L)]^4\}^{1/2} \approx |\nabla^2(h/\lambda_L)|. \tag{22}$$

If we further consider that, for sufficiently high spatial frequencies, $\nabla^2 h'$ is proportional to the high frequency portion of the acoustic intensity at the water surface [30], we obtain finally for the light distribution in the image plane

$$u' \propto \nabla^2\left(\frac{h}{\lambda_L}\right) e^{i(4\pi h/\lambda_L)}$$

$$\approx (f_s \cdot e^{-i(2\pi \cos \alpha/\lambda_s)x} + f_s^* e^{i(2\pi \cos \alpha/\lambda_s)x}) e^{i(4\pi h/\lambda_L)} \tag{23}$$

and, therefore, for the light intensity:

$$I_L \propto 2|f_s|^2 + \text{Real} \{f_s^2 \cdot e^{i(4\pi \cos \alpha/\lambda_s)x}\}. \tag{24}$$

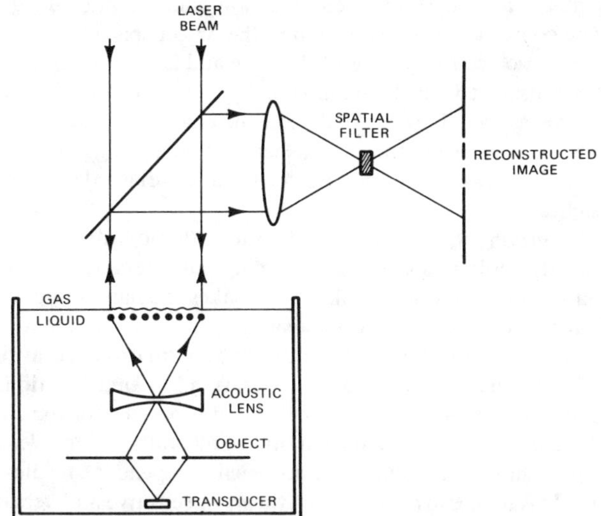

Fig. 3. Acoustic imaging system, generating a direct image on the water surface modulated by a subsurface wire grating (after Green [33]).

TABLE II

TYPICAL AMPLITUDE-SENSITIVE AREA DETECTORS

Mode	Minimal Intensity for 30 Frame/s Operation (Experimental Value) (W/cm^2)	Experimental Frequency Used (MHz)	Reference
Piezoelectric array	10^{-11}		[1][a]
Piezoelectric area detector with electron beam scanning	10^{-8}	3.58	[27]
Piezoresistive area detector with electron beam scanning	10^{-7}	4	[2][b]
Solid surface deformation laser scan readout	10^{-7}	8.5	[24]

[a] Bendix Research Laboratories experiment unpublished (limitation caused from electronics).
[b] J. E. Jacobs (Northwestern Univ.), private communication.

If the reference beam inclination angle α is chosen so that $\lambda_s/\cos \alpha$ is smaller than any significant detail in the acoustic image, one can suppress the second term in (24) without loss of image detail. One then obtains, within the approximation used, an undistorted image $|f_s|$ of the insonified object.

Smith and Brenden's method, therefore, achieves a very effective rejection of the aberrations which severely limited the lensless holographic method. The quality of the experimentally obtained imagery is very good (see later Figs. 12–14).

In spite of its success, the new process has lost one of the main features which recommend holography as an approach to acoustic imaging, that is, the relegation of the imaging from the acoustic to the optical domain. If this is not realized, the question arises: Why the holographic embodiment, which we shall discuss in the next section.

3) *Time-Independent Spatial Carrier Imaging:* Green [33] has shown recently that one of the important functions of the reference beam in the focused image approach is, rather than supplying a phase reference, to supply the spatial carrier onto which the image is modulated. According to Green, this can be done in a much simpler manner by putting a wire grating close to the surface and projecting the image through this grating, as shown in Fig. 3. This results in a surface deformation of

$$h \propto |f_s|^2(1 + \Sigma a_n \cos nv_0 x) * K \approx |f_s|^2 + \frac{a_1}{v_0^2} |f_s|^2 \cos v_0 x \quad (25)$$

where v_0 is the basic frequency of the grating. Equation (25) shows an important difference between the surface deformation in Green's and Smith and Brenden's methods. In Green's case, the amplitude of the high-frequency surface ripple h' is proportional to the acoustic intensity $|f_s|^2$ which passes through the insonified object. In Smith and Brenden's holographic approach, however, it is proportional to both the amplitude of the reference beam R and the amplitude f_s of the beam transmitted through the object. Using the holographic method therefore one can obtain a given depth in surface modulation with a smaller sound intensity at the object by appropriately increasing the reference beam intensity. This can become an important consideration in medical applications. The image quality, however, is comparable in both methods. The fact that, in Green's method, the optical intensity at the image plane is proportional to the square of the acoustic intensity transmitted through the object

is of minor importance since this can be compensated, if desired, by an appropriately chosen response characteristic of the optical detector.

B. Amplitude-Sensitive Area Detectors

In acoustics, linear receivers (see Table II) can be used to detect the space and time dependence of an acoustic field impinging on a given area. These data, according to Huygens' principle, can be used to analytically reconstruct the sound field and obtain imagery through computer reconstruction; thus the generation of a hologram, in the sense of an actual or simulated interference pattern, is bypassed. The increasing speed of digital computers and advances in array processors promise to make this a practical approach to acoustic imaging. We shall discuss the state of the art of that technology, however, in one of the following sections. In the present section, we will be concerned with holography systems in the restricted sense that the information obtained from the amplitude-sensitive detectors is processed into a form suitable for optical image reconstruction, that is, into an optical hologram, or into a reconstructed image from such a hologram.

The acoustic data can be acquired in a variety of ways. If the acoustic field is stationary, it can be sampled over a given aperture area with a mechanically scanned small microphone or hydrophone [35], [36]. This technique, though rather time-consuming, is useful for applications which require large apertures but not rapid operation [37]. Much faster sampling operations are possible with simultaneously sampling detector arrays [15] or with electron-beam-scanned piezoelectric area detectors [38], such as the Sokoloff tube. A third approach is to use the *dynamic* (linear) response [16], [17], [39] of optically reflecting surfaces to phase-modulate impinging light with the acoustic excitation. This technique can be used in a scanning or imaging mode, and is the most versatile and successful of the three. Before we describe some of the amplitude-sensitive detection systems reported in the literature, we shall outline the general method for generating holograms.

An ideal linear area detector generates a signal $S(x, y, t)$ which is, for each position x, y in the detection area, proportional to the local acoustic excitation $A(x, y) \cos [\phi(x, y) - \omega_s t]$. That is

$$S \propto A(x, y) \cos [\phi(x, y) - \omega_s t] = \text{Real } F_s e^{-i\omega_s t} \quad (26)$$

with the complex amplitude F_s defined as

$$F_s = A(x, y)e^{i\phi(x,y)}. \quad (27)$$

In the case of slow sampling systems or fixed arrays, a straightforward way to generate the necessary data to construct a hologram is to add electronically to the signal $S(x, y, t)$ at every sampling position (x, y) a signal simulating the local amplitude and phase of an appropriately chosen reference wave $R \cos(kx - \omega_s t)$. After rectification, the resulting dc output for each sampling position is

$$|F_s|^2 + |R|^2 + F_s R^* + F_s^* R \tag{28}$$

which exactly corresponds to the required local amplitude transmission for an off-axis hologram.

For fast scanning systems, a better way to obtain such data is as follows. The detected signal $S(x, y, t)$ is mixed with a reference signal $R \cos \omega_r t$ which oscillates at a frequency ω_r rather than at the acoustic frequency ω_s. The mixing process yields, among others, a component $AR \cos(\phi - \omega' t)$ which oscillates with a carrier frequency $\omega' = (\omega_s - \omega_r)$. This component can be isolated with a suitable bandpass filter and used directly to generate an off-axis hologram on a CR tube or TV monitor, if we add a bias term B and interpret the carrier frequency ω' as spatial-carrier-frequency β readout by scanning the coordinate x with the scanning velocity v, yielding

$$B + AR \cos[\phi(x, y) - \beta x]. \tag{29}$$

The synthetic reference hologram [8]–[10], (29), does not contain the undesirable noise-generating term $|F_s(x, y)|^2$ of (28). It has, instead of $|R|^2$, an adjustable bias term B which can be optimized for highest contrast. Using this method, one can generate any spatial carrier $\beta = \omega'/v$ by appropriate choice of the frequency offset. It is of interest to note that, in these synthetic reference holograms, the spatial carrier frequency β is not limited by the acoustic wavelength as is the case in interference holograms. Rather, its upper limit is determined only by the wavelength of the reconstruction wave. This means that the full range of acoustic resolution is available in linear systems for image information.

The sampling process introduces some unavoidable data degradation. In the case of continuous scanning, the degraded signal is simply the actual acoustic excitation smeared out over the sampling aperture (the transducer area in the slow scanning and array case, or the electron or laser beam cross section in the fast scanning schemes). This results in the suppression of spatial frequencies higher than the reciprocal of the scanning aperture diameter. This effect does not really represent a limitation for electron- and laser-beam scanning since both beams can be easily focused to sufficiently small diameter, thus narrowing the scanning aperture. The issue then becomes a resolution-versus-sensitivity compromise.

The situation is different in fixed arrays. Here each sampling position has not only an individual detector but, in general, also data processing circuitry. At a minimum, this circuitry contains a mixer for introducing the reference, an integrator, and possibly gating circuitry and readout provisions. The system complexity increases sharply with the number of elements and is inversely proportional to the square of the sampling interval d. This provides a strong incentive to make d as large as the system requirements permit, that is, one-half the reciprocal of the highest spatial frequency v_{max} which has to be resolved in the acoustic excitation. In systems with reasonable numerical apertures, the maximum spatial frequency which has to be accommodated is simply related to the field of view Ω for which the system is designed. The relation is

$$v_{max} = \frac{\sin \Omega}{\lambda_s} \tag{30}$$

and, therefore, if Ω is specified, the sampling distance has to be $d \leq \lambda_s/\sin \Omega$. If this condition is not satisfied, aliasing occurs; that is,

ghost images appear in the reconstruction which cannot unequivocally be coordinated with position in the object space.

Since piezoelectric systems of the slow and fast scanning variety have been discussed widely in individual papers [35], [36], [38] and review articles [40]–[42], we shall refer the reader to these and limit our present discussion to some aspects of integrating array detection and to less widely discussed dynamic surface deformation approaches.

1) Integrating Arrays: In array detectors, the acoustic excitation is observed simultaneously at all sampling points and the obtained information processed in parallel. This makes the handling of nonstationary fields possible, as, for example, in range gating where objects insonified by short bursts of radiation are observed at time intervals of specified position and duration. In quasi-stationary situations, information can be collected and processed for the duration of the image upgrading or repetition time, rather than over the very much shorter sampling time for each independent resolution element. This makes array detectors the most sensitive and versatile receivers available.

In order to utilize arrays optimally for holographic purposes, it is necessary to assure that the entire array is used for image information. The simple mixing with a reference beam mentioned earlier does not give this optimal utilization because either half of the spatial bandwidth is used to accommodate the conjugate image as an off-axis hologram, or the two images each cover the whole spatial bandwidth but are inextricably mixed as in an on-axis hologram.

The acoustic excitation at a sampling site x_i, y_j is $A(x_i, y_j) \cos[\phi(x_i, y_j) - \omega_s t]$. It can be fully represented by two numbers, e.g., $A \cos \phi$ and $A \sin \phi$, which may be obtained from $A \cos(\phi - \omega_s t)$ by mixing with $\cos \omega_s t$ and $\sin \omega_s t$ and integrating. If these two values are available at each sampling site, an offset hologram can be generated which fully utilizes the array resolution.

One way of generating such a hologram is to display the sum $A \cos \phi \cdot \cos \beta x + A \sin \phi \cdot \sin \beta x = A \cos(\phi - \beta x)$ against a constant bias term. This gives an off-axis hologram with complete image separation if we choose $\beta = \pi/d$. Such a hologram display requires, in the x direction, twice the number of resolution elements x_n as the array itself, that is, $x_n = n(d/2)$ where n ranges from 0 to $2N$. The multipliers, $\cos \beta x_n$ and $\sin \beta x_n$, assume the values

n	0	1	2	3	4	5	$\cdots$
$\cos \beta x_n$	1	0	-1	0	1	0	$\cdots$
$\sin \beta x_n$	0	1	0	-1	0	1	$\cdots$

at the sampling points x_n. Since sample values at the intermediate (odd) points are not directly available, they have to be obtained from the neighboring samples by averaging.

2) Dynamic Surface Deformation for Linear Area Detection: The dynamic surface deformation is different in nature from the radiation-pressure-induced liquid surface deformation discussed in a previous section. Consider a thin film, completely transparent to sound, immersed in an acoustic medium. If sound passes through such a film, no radiation pressure develops but the film, nevertheless, moves with the sound, following the motion of the acoustic medium. This excursion is proportional to the square root of the intensity and inversely proportional to the frequency. For a normally impinging plane wave in water, the excursion Δ is

$$\Delta = \frac{3.5}{\omega_s} I_s^{1/2} \text{ [cm]} \tag{31}$$

where ω_s is the frequency and I_s the sound intensity in watts per square centimeter.

If such a film is made reflective to light, as suggested by Gabor [17], the acoustic excitation passing through the film can be picked up as phase modulation on a coherent light beam. This linear deformation also occurs on liquid-air interfaces, but it is generally masked by the strong radiation-pressure effect. However, this linear term is the dominant one on a solid-gas interface which does not yield to radiation pressure, and systems to detect it by phase-modulation schemes were proposed by several authors [16]–[18], [39].

A system proposed by Korpel and Desmares [16] is shown schematically in Fig. 4. A laser beam scanned over the reflecting interaction surface picks up the local acoustic excitation as phase modulation. The lens L images the exit pupil of the beam deflector onto the entrance pupil of the detector. The detector, a knife edge in front of a photodiode, transforms a phase modulation into amplitude modulation and generates a signal proportional to the acoustic excitation. This signal is then processed, as previously discussed, to give an offset hologram displayed on the CR tube from which a photographic record can be made for optical reconstruction. This method is, in its electronic processing concepts, very similar to holographic systems that use a piezoelectric area detector scanned by an electron beam [38]. However, it is less limited in resolution and aperture and is especially suitable for high frequency imaging. It is, for this reason, one of the most promising candidates for an ultrasonic microscope [43], [44].

Instead of scanning the acoustically excited reflecting surface with a laser beam, several authors [17], [18] have described schemes in which the surface is homogeneously illuminated and imaged with a phase contrast system onto the photocathode of an image dissector tube. The resulting electron image is then scanned electronically. This scheme is less sensitive than the laser scanning technique but has the advantage that it is capable of displaying either a hologram, or its optical reconstruction, depending on where the photocathode of the image tube is located in the optical system. Fig. 5 shows a schematic of such a system. It essentially follows Green's approach [18].

We will first consider the holographic display mode of the previously described system. The properly illuminated interaction surface is imaged on the photocathode of the image dissector. An optical (planar) reference wave, frequency-modulated with a frequency ω_r, which is different from the acoustic frequency, also impinges on the photocathode. The intensity at the photocathode is then

$$I_1 = \left| 1 + i\frac{4\pi}{\lambda_L} A \cos(\phi - \omega_s t) + R e^{-i\omega_r t} \right|^2. \tag{32}$$

The intensity contains a term oscillating with the difference frequency, $\Delta\omega = \omega_s - \omega_r$, which can be picked out of the image dissector signal by proper filtering. This term is proportional to $RA \cos(\phi - \Delta\omega t)$ which can be displayed in the usual way as an offset hologram on the TV monitor.

In order to operate in a reconstruction mode, the system has to be focused to a plane $z_s \cdot \lambda_s/\lambda_L$ behind the acoustooptical interaction surface, if z_s is the distance of the insonified object behind this surface. The image of this hypothetical plane on the photocathode is again mixed with the frequency-modulated optical reference $R e^{-i\omega_r t}$. In this case, it can be easily shown that the difference-frequency term corresponds to the image of the insonified object; it can be filtered out, rectified, and displayed directly on the monitor. The conjugate image in this reconstruction process is tagged with the sum fre-

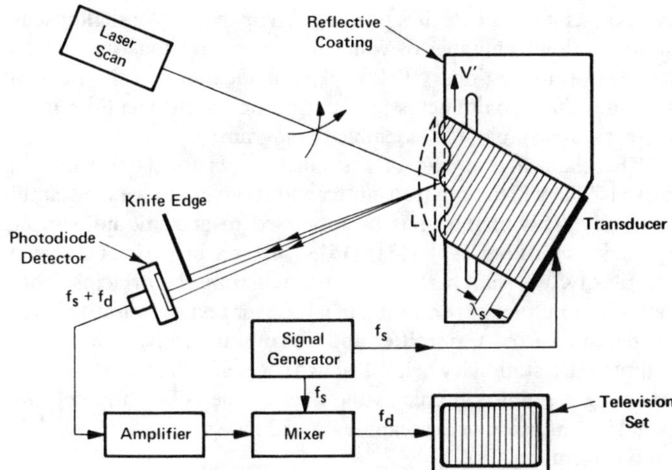

Fig. 4. Rapid sampling of acoustic surface excitation by laser scanning (from Korpel [16]).

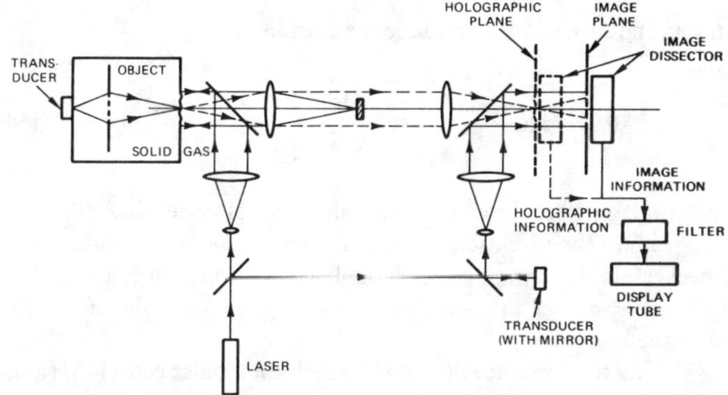

Fig. 5. Rapid electronic sampling of phase-contrast image of acoustic surface excitation with image dissector tube. (With the photocathode at plane H [18], holographic information is recorded. With the photocathode at plane I the same setup produces an optical reconstruction of the acoustic image.)

quency $(\omega_s + \omega_r)$, and the nonimage-forming components are the dc terms. This shows how powerful a tool optical heterodyning and temporal filtering can be in cases where linear detection is possible. Furthermore, in the case of high-frequency sound imaging, the requirements for frequency response of the data handling system are determined only by the difference in frequency $(\omega_s - \omega_r)$, which can be adjusted to suit.

A method to obtain an acoustic hologram from a dynamically deformed surface, which is quite different from the scanning schemes discussed earlier, was proposed by Metherell [10]. His approach is based on the fact that a record of the instantaneous value $S(x, y, t_0)$ of the surface excitation $S(x, y, t) = A(xy) \cos(\phi - \omega_s t)$ is equivalent to the information-carrying part of an on-axis hologram. In order to get $S(x, y, t_0)$, Metherell records consecutively on the same photographic plate two pulsed optical holograms spaced in time by an odd number of acoustic half-periods and having their optical reference waves in quadrature.

The reconstruction of such a hologram gives a phase-contrast image of $S(x, y, t_0)$ over the excited surface, which, in turn, can be used as an acoustic hologram.

C. Synthetic Apertures

In the methods discussed in previous sections, holograms were constructed essentially by mapping a stationary acoustic field point by point as it actually exists over a given aperture. We shall discuss in this section techniques by which holograms are constructed from samples of nonstationary fields taken at locations in the physical aperture which do not necessarily correspond to the locations in the synthetic aperture of the assembled hologram.

The classical example of a synthetic aperture is side-looking radar [45] in which both transmitter and receiver are scanned simultaneously. This method has been applied to acoustic holography by various authors [11]–[13], [15], [46] and in various stages of complexity. We shall here, in order to illustrate the principle, compare the simultaneous scanning of a receiver and a transmitter with the case of a fixed transmitter and a scanning receiver (that is, the mapping of a stationary field). The two cases are illustrated in Fig. 6, assuming a point scatterer as the object. The coherently detected signal as a function of the scanning coordinate x is, in the case of the fixed transmitter

$$F(x) = \cos\left(\frac{2\pi r_0}{\lambda_s} + \frac{2\pi r(x)}{\lambda_s}\right) = \cos\left(\beta_0 + \frac{2\pi z_0}{\lambda_s}\left(1 + \frac{(x - x_0)^2}{z_0^2}\right)\right) \quad (33)$$

and, in the case of the simultaneous scanning,

$$F(x) = \cos\frac{4\pi r(x)}{\lambda_s} = \cos\left(\frac{4\pi z_0}{\lambda_s}\left(1 + \frac{(x - x_0)^2}{2z_0^2}\right)\right). \quad (34)$$

The result in both cases is a one-dimensional zone plate that is a hologram of the point scatterer. In the simultaneous scanning case, however, the hologram appears as if it were taken with a field half the wavelength of the actual ultrasound used and, therefore, has twice the resolution.

This method can be expanded by including pulse echo [45] ranging for determining the coordinate y perpendicular to the scanning coordinate x. This technique, which is the actual practice in side-looking radar, has been applied to acoustics by Walker [46].

Another extension of this approach (discussed in detail by Hildebrend and Haines [11]) is to move the receiver and the transmitter independently. The hologram construction then becomes rather complex, but the additional degree of freedom opens new and interesting possibilities.

A different approach to synthetic apertures, combining parallel processing of a receiver array with sequential operation of a transmitter array, was originally proposed by Wells [47]. He showed that, with a crossed array of N receivers and N transmitters, as shown in Fig. 7, one can obtain approximately the same result as with a square array of N^2 receivers in stationary operation. The basic idea is that, in the usual second-order approximation, the phase of a wave emitted by a point scatterer which is illuminated by transmitter j and observed at receiver k is the same as the phase which would be observed at location (j, k) of a full array under stationary illumination with a transmitter located at the origin.

There are only $2N$ nonmoving elements required to obtain the N^2 data points necessary to construct a hologram from the aperture spanned by the crossed array. The tradeoff here is complexity against time required to obtain the N^2 data points with a desired signal-to-noise ratio.

The crossed array proposed by Wells is the only way in which N receivers and M transmitters can be arranged to give an $N \times M$ array simulation without first-order aberrations. This is convenient but not necessary, because known aberrations can be corrected by electronic processing of the data in the course of assembling the hologram. More general schemes, proposed by Marom *et al.* [15] and Kreutzer [12], have more degrees of freedom and, therefore,

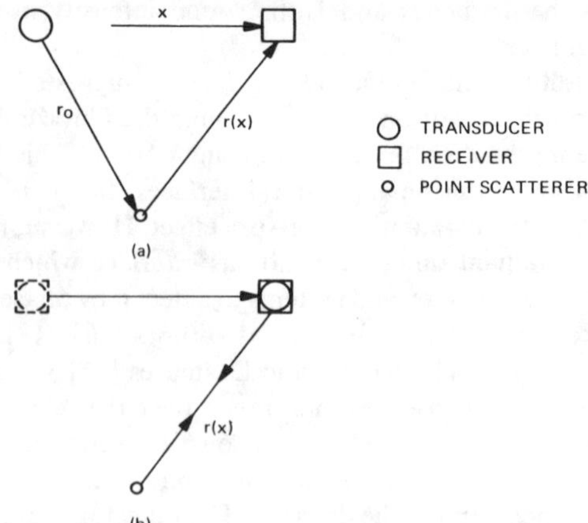

Fig. 6. Scanning modes. (a) Transmitter and receiver scanning simultaneously. (b) Transmitter fixed receiver scanning.

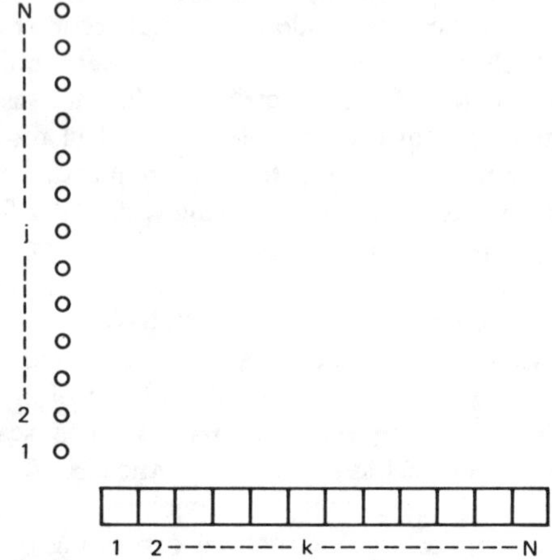

Fig. 7. Crossed linear array of N receivers and N sequentially fired transmitters synthesizes a full array of N^2 sampling points (from Wells [44]).

permit compromises between added complexity and adaptation to existing requirements.

D. Reconstruction Devices

We have, in the foregoing sections, discussed a number of methods to obtain the data necessary to construct acoustic holograms. In some cases, the information was already in a form which permitted further optical processing to reconstruct the image of the insonified object. In other cases, the final product was a hologram displayed on a TV monitor or in some other display device. In order to reconstruct an image from such a hologram, two routes are open to us—one is to use the information to make an area light modulator which is useful for coherent processing, or to use the information which already exists in electronic form to reconstruct images by means of a computer. We shall, in this section, discuss these two possibilities.

1) Optical Reconstruction: A simple and straightforward approach to optical reconstruction is to photograph the acoustic hologram displayed either on TV monitors or on image recorders and use the photographic transparency as an optical hologram for reconstruction. This approach is widely used because it is easily available. It has, however, the severe disadvantage that it introduces a considerable time lag between hologram generation and image reconstruction. This is particularly objectionable where real-time viewing is desirable and where the hologram-generating part of the

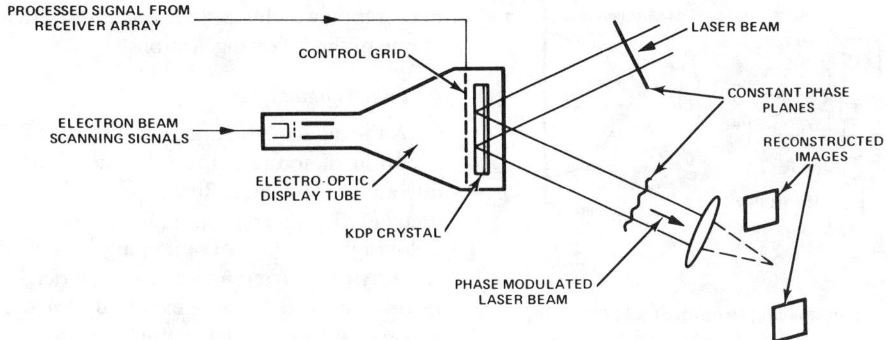

Fig. 8.   Schematic of electrooptical light modulator tube (from Goetz [48]).

system is capable of real-time operation, that is, capable of producing a new or upgraded hologram at TV frame rates.

A number of different electrooptical area modulators which are compatible with this requirement have been described in the literature [48]–[51]; some, as for example, the eidophor [52], are commercially available.

However, only one scheme—the electrooptical KDP modulator [48], [49]—has been demonstrated to be useful for coherent optical data processing, including the reconstruction of holograms.

The reason why it is so much easier to generate good direct imagery, rather than good holographic reconstruction within the same resolution requirement, has been discussed in great detail in Section II-A, in which the water surface deformation method was considered as a real-time holographic playback system. We have seen that any deviation from flatness (or homogeneity) in the processor, though harmless for direct imaging, severely limits holographic reconstruction. The reason is that the reconstructed image in holography appears not in the plane which images the processor surface, but in the Fourier transform plane, where the image is convolved with a rapidly varying function introduced by the deviations from flatness in the processor (see (18)).

The electrooptical modulator mentioned earlier is still in a developmental stage. A system described by Goetz [48] (schematically shown in Fig. 8) can handle, depending on the operating temperature, up to 400 resolved points per line, which is well within the requirements of ultrasonic holography in the 100-kHz to 1-MHz range. Its application is seen as the image reconstructor in an underwater viewing system [15], [53] which processes the information obtained from a piezoelectric array. The system will be discussed in the application section in more detail.

2) Computer Reconstruction: One can consider an optical hologram reconstruction system as an analog computer with very extensive parallel processing capability. The same task on a digital computer, which performs all operations sequentially, would seem to pose a very difficult problem. However, in all the scanning systems and arrays discussed earlier, the information is acquired sequentially and available in electronic form before it is reassembled into a hologram (on the face of a CR tube or other display device) for optical processing. Furthermore, the number of data to be processed in an acoustic hologram is small enough in magnitude to be manageable in terms of present-day medium-sized computers, especially since the rediscovery of the fast Fourier transform algorithm [54] by Cooley and Tukey in 1965. Considerable advances have since been made in hard-wired array processors, specially designed to handle two-dimensional Fourier transforms [14].

Table III lists the processing times required by commercially available systems to reconstruct one image plane from holograms

TABLE III

EXECUTION TIME FOR TYPICAL FAST-FOURIER-TRANSFORM PROCESSORS

	Maximum Value of N Processed ($K = 1024$)	Execution Time for N_{max} (s)	Execution Time for $N = 100 \times 100$ (s)
Computer signal processors CSS-3	32 K	22.6	6.3
Computer signal processors CSP-30	65 K	3.2	0.4
IBM array processor 2938-1	32 K	2.20	0.52
IBM array processor 2938-2	32 K	1.50	0.32
Sylvania ASP	65 K	13.6	$\dfrac{8^a}{\text{no. AU}}$
Time/date 1923 real-time analyzer FFT	8 K	0.12	0.13

[a] Where no. AU refers to the number of arithmetic units used.

with typical numbers of resolved points. It can be seen from this table that digital reconstruction has not quite reached real-time operation but is approaching it for small arrays. In applications with large numbers of data points, such as seismic exploration, the time lapse between data acquisition and image reconstruction is not essential and, therefore, processing time does not pose any limitations.

Computer reconstruction has, where applicable, considerable advantages. All nonrandom image degradation can be corrected more easily with a digital computer than in the analog optical case. Moreover, complex image processing can be achieved when desired in the course of the reconstruction process; for example, a digital computer directly handles the complex amplitude distribution over the hologram aperture which linear receivers can furnish. Thus one does not have to carry a conjugate image through the reconstruction process, thereby avoiding added complexity and noise at the image plane.

In summary, computer reconstruction has to be considered as a very real possibility for acoustic holography.

E. Bragg Diffraction Imaging

The availability of lasers in the middle 1960s not only made the rapid development of acoustic holography possible but also revived and stimulated the study of other acoustooptic interactions. One very interesting result of such studies was a novel acoustic imaging

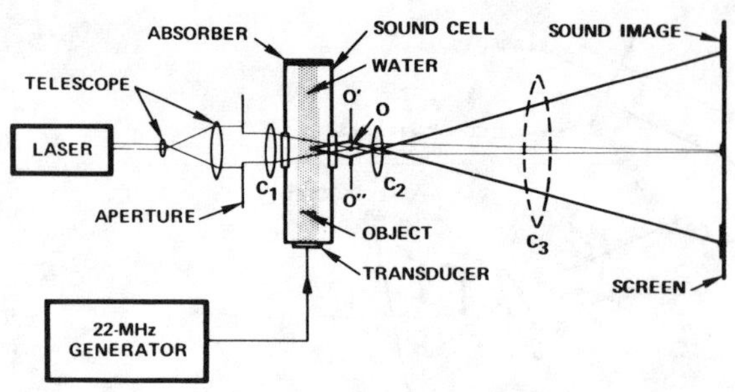

Fig. 9. Bragg diffraction imaging (from Korpel [19]).

method reported by Korpel [20] in 1966. He showed that both phase and amplitude distribution of a sound beam is modulated onto a light beam if it travels through some common space with the sound. It is, therefore, possible to obtain an optical image of the sound source distribution which can be, for example, a properly insonified object. The mechanism which is active in the transfer of phase and amplitude information from the sound wave to the light wave is Bragg diffraction of the light off the (three-dimensional) phase grating which the sound generates.

This method is related to Lippman-Denisyuk [55] volume holography in which the image information is also modulated onto the light by Bragg diffraction.

Korpel demonstrated his new method originally with ultrasound of 22 MHz. For this frequency, the ratio λ_L/λ_s of light to sound wavelength is very small, leading to a Bragg condition for the angle θ between the sound and light wave propagation vectors

$$\cos \theta = \frac{\lambda L}{2\lambda_s} \ll 1 \quad \text{or} \quad \theta = \pm \frac{\pi}{2} - \frac{\lambda_L}{2\lambda_s}. \tag{35}$$

This shows that the two interacting beams have to travel almost perpendicular to each other. In Fig. 9, Korpel's original experimental setup is schematically shown. He uses Bragg diffraction holography in two dimensions, relying on shadow projection for imaging in the remaining third dimension. In a later publication [19], he reports fully holographic imaging using this method. The imaging conditions are the same as in other holographic methods discussed earlier. For unchanged lateral dimensions, the depth dimension is enlarged by a factor λ_s/λ_L, a situation which can only be corrected optically by lateral demagnification of $m = \lambda_L/\lambda_s$ which gives rise to unacceptably small imagery.

An interesting version of Bragg imaging, which uses collinear interaction between sound and light, has been reported by Quate et al. [44] in several publications. The method makes use of the fact that, in birefringent crystals, Bragg's condition (index matching) can be achieved between the ordinary and extraordinary rays traveling in the same direction collinearly with sound of a characteristic frequency ω_s

$$\left|\frac{\omega_s}{V}\right| = |k_o| - |k_{eo}| \tag{36}$$

where V is the velocity of longitudinal sound waves, and k_o and k_{eo} the propagation vectors of the ordinary and extraordinary rays. This collinear interaction has two very desirable characteristics. First, a high efficiency in modulation transfer can be achieved since the interaction path can be made long, which, in a parametric process (such as Bragg diffraction), increases the modulation transfer proportionally. Second, since ordinary and extraordinary rays have orthogonal polarization, the information-carrying beam can be easily separated from the undiffracted beam by a polarization filter. This method is applied in a very promising approach to ultrasonic

microscopy which we shall discuss together with other approaches in one of the following sections.

F. Image Quality

An ideal acoustic imaging system maps point by point the distribution of sound sources (sound emitting or insonified objects) into an optical image. Real systems do this only approximately with unavoidable aberrations and loss of information. In an acoustic holography system, the mapping is achieved by optical wavefront reconstruction from an acoustic interferogram and subsequent optical imaging. It is to be expected that the acoustic portion of the process introduces limitations to the quality of the obtainable imagery, against which aberrations [5] in the optical part of the system are negligible.

The most important limitation pertinent to all acoustic imaging, not only to the holographic approach, arises from the relatively large wave length λ_s of ultrasound as compared to the wavelength λ_L of the light with which the acoustic image is viewed. For ultrasound in water of 1 MHz the wavelength ratio λ_s/λ_L is about 250.

One effect caused by a large wavelength ratio [56], which we shall consider first, is that the surface texture of insonified objects is smoother to sound waves by a factor λ_s/λ_L than their visual appearance indicates. Most objects are, therefore, specularly reflecting for ultrasound which gives rise to imagery that is hard to interpret. Diffuse illumination remedies this problem but is not always applicable (e.g., underwater viewing).

In holographic systems, however, diffuse insonification of the object field or diffuse reflection from unidirectionally insonified objects present another problem, speckle [56]–[58] which gives rise to a coarse grainy appearance. The grain size of the speckle pattern increases linearly with decreasing aperture. Fig. 10 shows the effect of specular reflection under unidirectional illumination and the speckle resulting from diffuse illumination of simple objects imaged with various aperture sizes in an optical simulation experiment.

Another limitation related to the long wavelength is the relatively low resolution of acoustic imaging systems as compared with that of optical systems having the same geometry [59]. The reduction factor is again the wavelength ratio λ_s/λ_L which follows directly from (37) that relates the resolution r to aperture diameter A, object distance z_s, and wavelength λ_s

$$r \approx A/\lambda_s z_s \text{ line pairs/cm} \tag{37}$$

if all distances are measured in centimeters. For a 30-cm aperture and an object distance of 1 m, one obtains with ultrasound of 1 MHz a resolution of two line pairs per centimeter.

A very significant first-order aberration also related to the wavelength ratio λ_s/λ_L occurs in the reconstruction of acoustic holograms. One can, through suitable choice of the optical system, select any given lateral magnification M_{lat} in the reconstructed image; the longitudinal magnification M_{long}, however, is then fixed and is related to the lateral magnification by

$$M_{long} = \lambda_s/\lambda_L (M_{lat})^2 \tag{38}$$

which, as discussed earlier, excludes a true three-dimensional display of the acoustically imaged object for large values of the wavelength ratio λ_s/λ_L. This is not a great loss, however, since the resolution limitation discussed earlier requires all available aperture for the generation of acceptable image quality. Therefore, a three-dimensional display, in the sense of optical holograms (where the parallax effect is experienced by sequentially utilizing different portions of the aperture), is not possible.

Another source of image degradation, which is typically holographic in origin, comes from the fact that the optically recon-

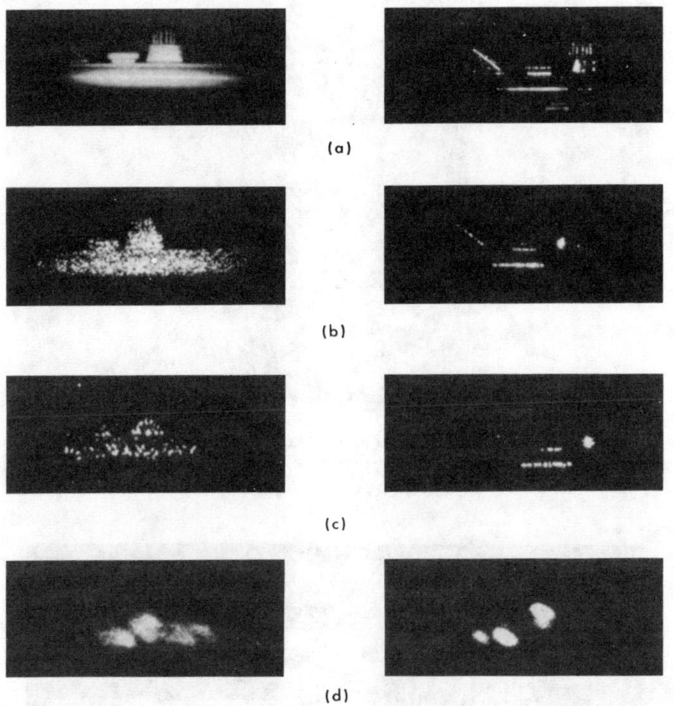

Fig. 10. Optically simulated acoustic pictures of submarine model. Diffuse reflection causing speckle—left. Specular reflection causing highlights— right. (From W. A. Penn and J. L. Chovan [56].) (a) Ordinary optical image. (b) 2000 λ (equivalent to 400 $\lambda/\theta_{\text{subtended}}$). (c) 800 λ (equivalent to 160 $\lambda/\theta_{\text{subtended}}$). (d) 200 λ (equivalent to 40 $\lambda/\theta_{\text{subtended}}$).

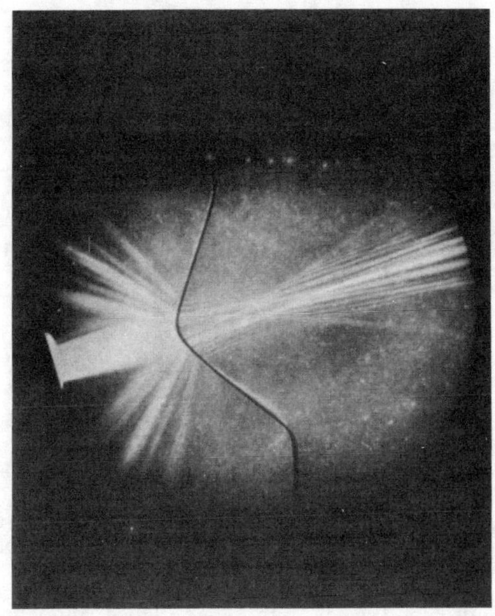

Fig. 11. Schlieren photograph of an ultrasound beam of 5 MHz striking a thin sheet of aluminum (from Berger [1] courtesy of Automation Industries, Boulder, Colo.).

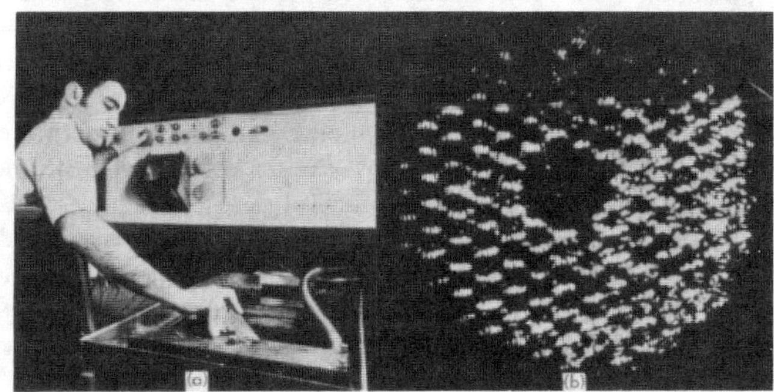

Fig. 12. (a) Holosonics holographic ultrasound imaging system. (b) Honeycomb structure (1/2-in period) with intentionally introduced nonbonding area as imaged by the Holosonic system at 5 MHz (courtesy of Holosonics, Inc.).

structed wave is not a true replica of the acoustic wave but is modified by the modulation transfer functions of both the acoustic recording and the optical reconstruction processes. We have earlier discussed the water surface-relief method as an example for this kind of image degradation.

Finally, a problem arises in acoustic imaging, if one wants to image flaws or discontinuities inside an optically opaque solid. Multiple internal reflections [60], the occurrence of surface waves, and the transformation of pressure into shear waves complicate severely the task of interpreting the obtained imagery, even if the solid is of simple shape. Problems of this nature arise in NDT and seismic applications. In Fig. 11, the sound waves emanating in various directions from a simple metal strip, insonified by a beam of 1-MHz sound, illustrates the point in case.

III. APPLICATIONS

A. Nondestructive Testing

Effective acoustic imaging devices as tools for nondestructive testing have been sought ever since acoustic imaging became a technical reality. It is, therefore, not surprising that many laboratories directed their acoustic holography work toward that goal [12], [32], [61], [62]. Very substantial advances have been made through these efforts and we shall discuss some of the results obtained by different groups. However, a note of caution seems in order. Due to the complexity of realistic test pieces and due to the intricacies of sound propagation in solid material, one obtains, in many cases, information which is difficult to interpret and which might not yield the desired clues as easily as simpler approaches. There is, however, no doubt in this reviewer's mind that acoustic holographic methods will occupy a place in the rapidly expanding NDT field.

A real-time holographic imaging system, based on Brenden's "focused image" holography [32] using the liquid surface pressure relief method (discussed in an earlier section), is the first holographic imaging system offered commercially for NDT and medical applica-

tions. The system is shown in Fig. 12(a) and an acoustic image of a honeycomb structure with an intentionally introduced bonding defect obtained with this system in Fig. 12(b). Mechanical scanning systems which do not have real-time capability have been studied for their potential applications in NDT. Images of high quality have been obtained with this method. Fig. 13, for example, shows an acoustic image of a British penny taken with a scanning transmitter/receiver combination (see Section II-C) by Aldridge et al. [62]. Such transmitter/receiver combinations can be used in either transmission or reflection mode. They also permit scanning over large areas with the possibility of coupling directly into the test material.

The holographic approach is not limited to simple imaging. Pulse-echo methods [45], in conjunction with holographic imaging, can be used to reject multiply reflected signals and thus simplify the interpretation. Finally, through holographic matched filtering [63], mass produced parts can be compared acoustically with a master via a holographic matched filter in a manner analogous to optical matched filter techniques.

B. Medical Diagnostics

Medical diagnostics is, as NDT, a field of potential application for acoustic imaging and holography. The visualization of soft tissue

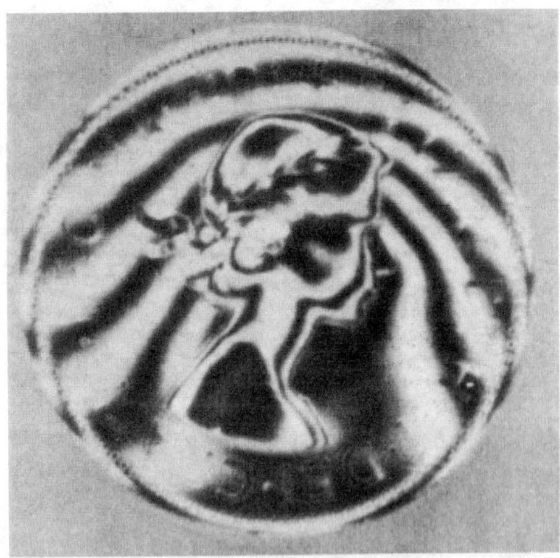

Fig. 13. Acoustic image of British penny obtained with scanning transmitter and receiver combination at 10 MHz (from Aldridge *et al.* [62]).

Fig. 14. Acoustic image of lower arm obtained with holosonics holographic imaging system (courtesy of Holosonics, Inc.).

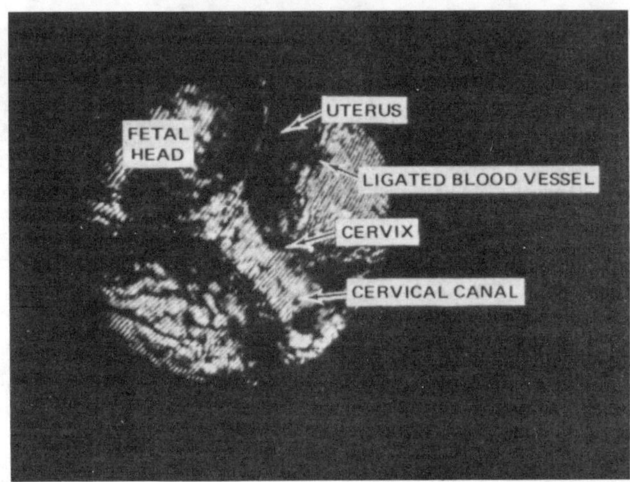

Fig. 15. Acoustic hologram of human uterus showing the fetal head—one-half size (courtesy of Dr. M. R. Sikov, Battelle Pacific Northwest Labs., Richland, Wash.).

such as glands, blood vessels, tumors, etc. (which cannot be seen with X rays) is a definite possibility, and as Figs. 14 and 15 show, an experimentally verified capability of acoustic imaging systems. Their acceptance and use is, however, very limited, in spite of this intriguing potential. With very few exceptions, it is confined to research applications rather than diagnostic use.

The reasons are that fast and highly sensitive systems which can accommodate larger apertures than presently available are required in order to be useful for general diagnostic purposes. Furthermore, the need for a coupling agent such as water between patient and transducers makes the design of a general purpose diagnostic system difficult and rather cumbersome. However, the promise which lies in acoustic and especially holographic imaging systems is so great that it appears to be only a question of time before these systems will find their use in medical diagnostics. Several laboratories are working toward this goal, with Battelle Northwest leading with the liquid surface relief method. Recently a very significant effort has been initiated as a joint CBS Laboratories–Stoneybrook SUNY program[1] aimed toward implementing Gabor's reflecting membrane approach (Section II-B) for diagnostic application.

C. Ultrasonic Microscopy

Acoustic waves in the frequency range of 0.1 to 3 GHz have wavelengths in water ranging from 15 to 0.5 μm, comparable to the wavelengths of infrared to visible light. It is, therefore, quite conceivable that sound waves can provide a means for viewing microscopic objects with a resolution approaching that of optical microscopes. This is particularly so because the technology of generating and processing sound at microwave frequencies [64] is a well developed art. Such ultrasonic microscopes would be of great interest for biological application since they can utilize differences in mechanical properties of biological specimens, rather than differences in optical properties, for the generation of high-contrast imagery. A serious difficulty is the very high attenuation of sound in this frequency domain, which will ultimately limit the resolution obtainable with ultrasonic microscopes. The two approaches reported in the literature and discussed in the following, however, are not approaching this limit yet.

One method pursued by Korpel and co-workers is based on Korpel's laser scanning method [16] discussed in Section II-B to detect and read acoustic excitation of a solid surface. The other method pursued by Quate *et al.* [44], [65], [66] is based on Bragg diffraction imaging discussed in Section II-E.

In Quate's method, which used collinear sound-light interaction in $LiNO_4$ (see Fig. 16), the sound frequency of 860 MHz is determined by the elastic and optical constants of $LiNO_4$ and the frequency of the laser light used. Index matching in the collinear interaction further requires collimation of the sound beam, which is accomplished with an acoustic condenser lens (see Fig. 16). The image quality obtainable is, therefore, limited by the quality of this acoustic lens. In Korpel's approach [19], the image data acquisition imposes no constraints on the sound frequency and does not require any beam shaping or acoustic preimaging. All image data processing is done optically after holographic wavefront reconstruction. This makes Korpel's method acoustically simpler and less restricted in the choice of frequencies. The performance of the two systems, however, was at the time of this review comparable, and both were very promising.

Fig. 17 shows an image, obtained with Quate's system, of a test specimen consisting of a 50-μ periodic mesh (30-μ open space 20-μ wire). The acoustic wavelength in the water, in which the specimen

---

[1] G. W. Stroke, private communication. Some further discussion of this work is given in *Science*, vol. 173, 1971, p. 11.

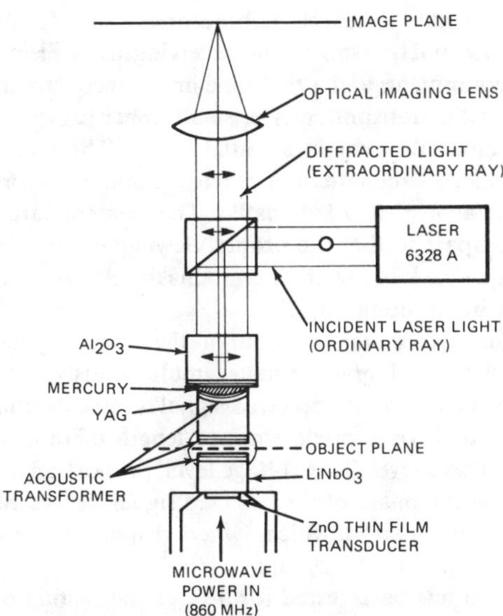

Fig. 16.   Ultrasonic microscope using Bragg diffraction method (from Havlice *et al.* [65]).

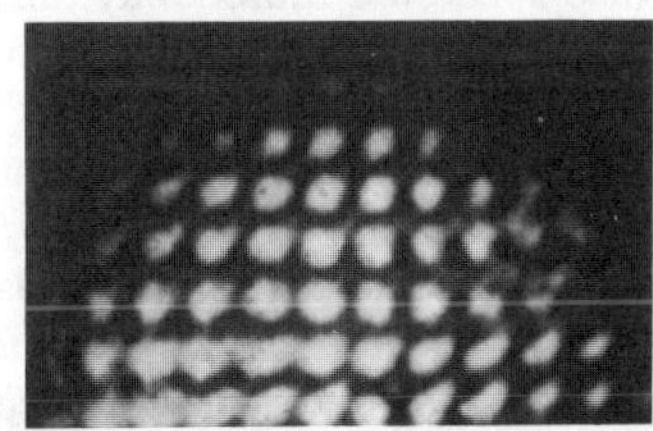

Fig. 17.   Acoustic image of a 50-μ periodic mesh (20-μ wire) obtained with Bragg diffraction microscope shown schematically in Fig. 19 (from Havlice *et al.* [65]).

Fig. 18.   Acoustic image of a 100-μ periodic mesh (25-μ wire) obtained by laser scan microscope (from Korpel).

Fig. 19.   Vehicle-mounted hydraulic vibrator. A typical acoustic source for seismic work (courtesy of Bendix United Geophysical Corp.).

was suspended, was 2 μ. The resolution of the system, however, is determined by the wavelength in the YAG crystal and the numerical aperture of the acoustic lens system. It came out to be 22 μ, which is borne out by the imagery.

In Fig. 18 a test specimen consisting of a 100-μ periodic mesh (75-μ open space 25-μ wire) imaged with Korpel's system is shown. Here the frequency is 100 MHz and the wavelength in water is 15 μ. The expected resolution lies between one and two wavelengths, which is again borne out by the imagery.

D. Seismic Holography

Seismic holography is an extension of acoustic holography to very long (10- to 300-m) wavelength radiation. The application of long wavelength (seismic) holography to large-scale underground exploration is still in its initial development stages, but it holds promise to aid in the accumulation of geological information for scientific purposes, for preexcavation surveys, and for seismic exploration in the mining and oil industries [67]–[72].

In seismic holography, object distances are measured in hundreds of meters and for many applications, resolutions of several decameters are sufficient. Because distances are large and the range decreases with frequency, low frequencies (10–1000 Hz) are required for this type of work. The low frequencies and consequently long wavelengths require apertures measured in kilometers, which make synthetic aperture approaches (discussed in Section II-B) the method of choice.

The major components of a seismic system are the same as for other acoustic holography applications, i.e., a transmitter, receiv-

ing array, electronic signal processing, and a reconstruction display device. The physical size of the equipment is much larger, however. The seismic energy source must be capable of radiating kilowatts of energy into the earth. A typical vehicle-mounted servo-hydraulic vibrator is shown in Fig. 19.

The interpretation of holographic data from a complex medium such as the earth involves many more difficulties than are encountered in a homogeneous medium, such as water. Inhomogeneities in the earth ranging from formation changes to macroscopic variations in physical properties within formations cause complexities in elastic wave propagation. Velocity varies with lithology, and refraction occurs as the energy passes from one type of rock into another. These events serve to degrade the coherence of the seismic waves and generate noise.

Several of the problems previously mentioned are similar to those encountered using conventional seismic profiling (pulse-echo methods) to map the earth's structure. The development of sophisticated signal processing and filtering techniques, however, has made it possible to interpret the seemingly meaningless seismograms into realistic vertical cross sections of the earth [72]. Similarly, it is expected that the development of sophisticated holographic processing techniques will eventually allow reasonable underground viewing of rather large areas.

The first earth holography field experiment was reported by Lerwill [68] (England) in 1969. He used mechanical vibrators operating at 90 Hz for his source, and rather than recording over a large area, he used a single 4350-ft line with geophone detectors spaced at 25-ft sampling intervals. Using a wavefront recognition technique for reconstruction, he was able to resolve a known reflecting layer at a depth of about 2500 ft (Fig. 20).

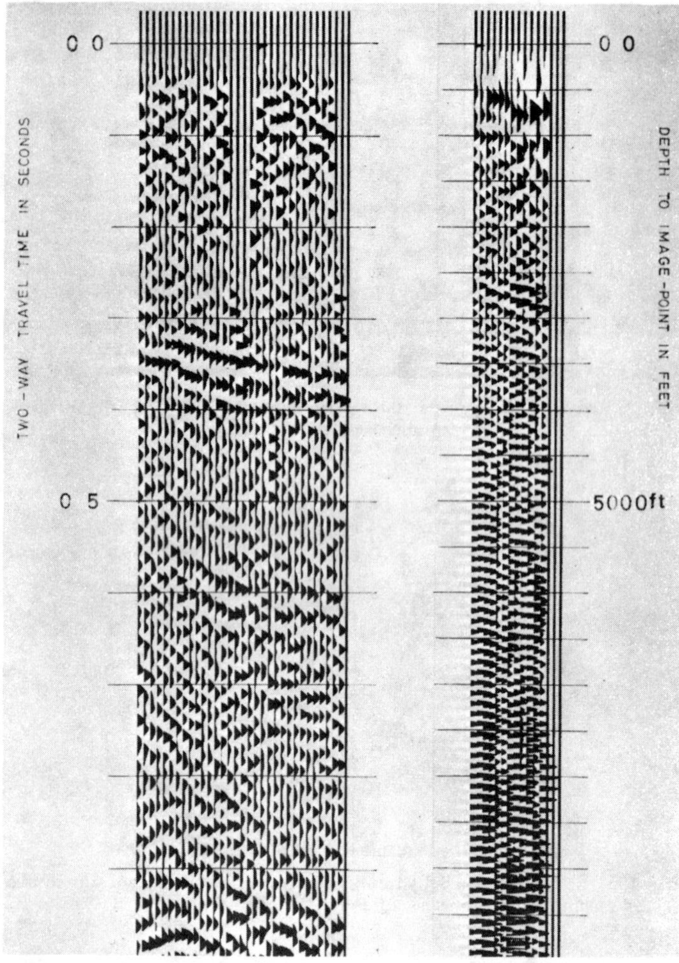

Fig. 20. Conventional seismic data compared with a holographic reconstruction (from Lerwill [68]). Left—Conventional seismic data; right—holographic reconstruction.

Fitzpatrick [73] (U.S. Bureau of Mines) has recently completed a holographic field experiment in which he successfully imaged a void in the ground of about 2 wavelengths diameter. The void was located about 80 ft below the surface of the ground. Instead of a monofrequency source, he used an explosive charge, detonated at 200 ft below the surface, as his source energy. The frequency component of the radiated spectrum corresponding to a wavelength of 50 ft was used to generate the hologram. These results are to be published in the near future.

Several methods using broad-band sources to maintain the high depth resolution of pulse sources combined with holographic methods for lateral resolution have been proposed by different authors [69], [71], but no experimental results were available at the time of this review.

E. Underwater Viewing System

The idea of combining holography with acoustics as a technique for underwater viewing [15], [56], [74]–[76] has been under study in recent years since such a combination offers certain advantages over conventional search and surveillance techniques, such as direct optical viewing and sonar. Direct optical viewing is limited to ranges of several feet under turbid water conditions, and conventional sonar cannot provide a recognizable image for accurate identification and classification of the target. On the other hand, acoustic holography is capable of producing good images, which are relatively unaffected by water turbulence and turbidity, of underwater objects over a comparatively large field of view.

An acoustic underwater viewing system (Fig. 21) has been de-veloped by Bendix Research Laboratories [15]. Its major components are a sound transmitter, the receiving array, electronic signal processing equipment, and a real-time image reconstruction device.

The acoustic transmitter is a small spherical shell of piezoelectric ceramic vibrating in a radial mode. The receive array is composed of lead zirconate titanate slugs mounted to form a planar matrix in an acoustically soft baffle. The elements are placed 4.5 wavelengths apart so that the proper viewing aperture is achieved. The housing in back of the array contains the electronic boards that generate the holographic signal.

The signal processing portion of the system generates electronically all the holographic data simultaneously. At each individual receiver element, the received signal is mixed with a reference signal, integrated for a predetermined length of time, and finally stored as a voltage level. This voltage level, proportional to both the amplitude and the phase of the detected signal, represents the local holographic information which, when displayed for all points, makes up the complete hologram.

The system has been tested for a target consisting of pressure-release disks (7.5-in diameter) irradiated in reflection (Fig. 22). A transmitter was placed next to the hydrophone array, while the target was at a distance of 2 m from the receive array.

The hologram displayed on a cathode-ray tube for the target is shown in Fig. 23(a) and its optical reconstruction in Fig. 23(b). In the reconstruction, the focused real image (upper left) and the unfocused virtual image (bottom right) are seen around the zero-order central spot.

The hologram can be reconstructed and displayed in real time [47], if a coherent light area modulator [15] is used (see Section II-D). In this device, the linear electrooptical effect of an optically active crystal is used to phase-modulate light via a scanning electron beam that records information as a charge pattern on the crystal. The information will be supplied directly from the acoustic array. The hologram is thus written on the crystal, and reconstruction is obtained by passing a laser beam through the actuated crystal in real time. The image is magnified by associated optics and then displayed.

An example of an image reconstructed by the display tube is shown in Fig. 24, together with the hologram from which it was made.

IV. Conclusion

Acoustic holography is the newest branch in acoustic imaging technology. It underwent very rapid development during the last few years and stimulated the general field of acoustic imaging through the introduction of novel techniques for visualizing acoustic excitation. The fact that linear area detectors are available in acoustics gave rise to holographic techniques which have no analog in optical holography, such as the electronic simulation of a reference wave, or the unique combinations of spatial and temporal processing of image information. The total amount of image data to be handled is far less here than in the optical case, so that computer reconstruction of actual acoustic holograms is practical and real-time operation is feasible in some applications.

Applications of this technology are now appearing more slowly perhaps than many of us hoped to see. Holosonics, Inc., offered the first commercially available holographic imaging system for NDT and medical diagnostics. Ultrasonic microscopy has been shown to be possible and offers very great promise for biomedical applications. Seismic holography, as a means of resource exploration in marine and terrestrial environment, is widely discussed, and several large-scale experiments have been carried out, which now await evaluation. Finally, the underwater viewing application is under consideration and evaluation by the U.S. Navy.

To summarize the status, the technological innovations have

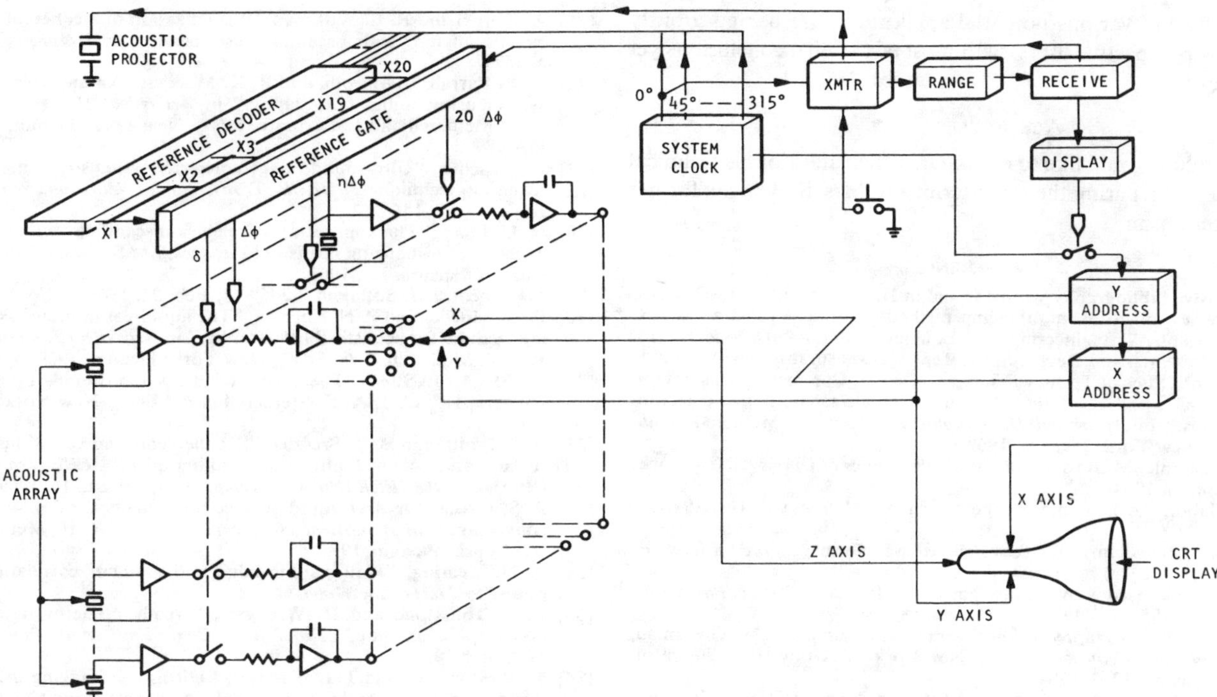

Fig. 21.   Block diagram of holographic underwater viewing system (from Marom *et al.* [15]).

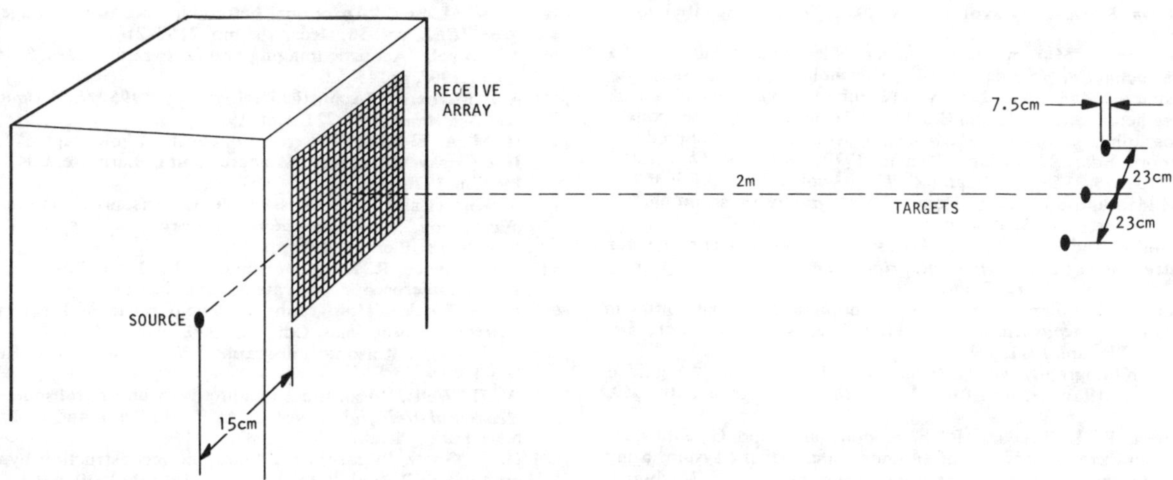

Fig. 22.   Acoustic array test configuration (targets are scattering points).

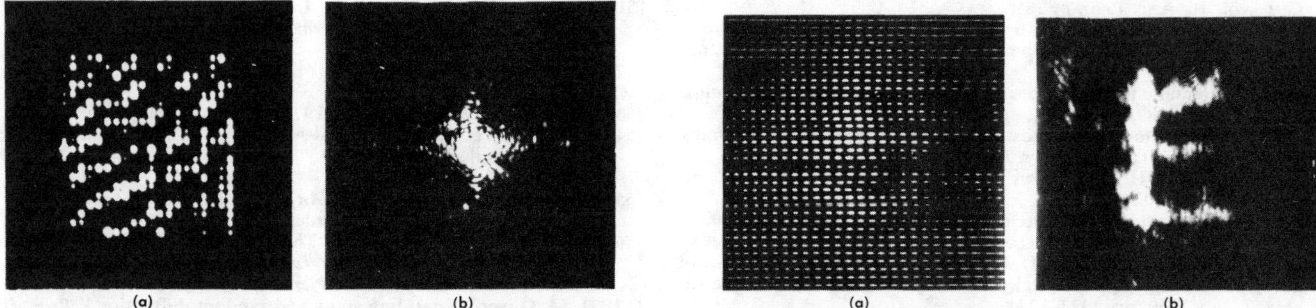

Fig. 23.   Acoustic hologram of 3 disks and its optical reconstruction. (a) Underwater acoustic hologram of 3 disks taken by 20 × 20 transducer array. (b) Optical reconstruction.

Fig. 24.   Acoustic hologram and reconstruction of letter *E*. (a) Acoustic hologram of letter *E*, taken by scanning transducer. (b) Real-time reconstruction with DKDP light modulator.

been made, and various potential applications are being seriously studied by prospective users, with most of the final conclusions yet to be drawn.

ACKNOWLEDGMENT

The author would like to thank Dr. T. Sawatari for his technical assistance in preparing the manuscript and Mrs. S. Benigna for her editorial criticism.

REFERENCES

[1] Extensive bibliography will be found in H. Berger and R. E. Dickens, "A review of ultrasonic imaging methods, with a selected annotated bibliography," Engineering and Equipment (TID-4500, second ed.), AFC Research and Development Rep. ANL-6680, July 1963 (available from the Office of Technical Services, Dep. of Commerce, Washington 25, D. C.), and H. Berger, "A survey of ultrasonic image detection methods," in *Acoustical Holography*, vol. 1, A. F. Metherell *et al.*, Eds. New York: Plenum, 1969.

[2] For example, M. Born and E. Wolf, *Principles of Optics*. New York: Pergamon, 1964.

[3] D. Gabor, "A new microscope principle," *Nature*, vol. 161, 1948, p. 777.
—, "Microscopy by reconstructed waveforms," *Proc. Roy. Soc.*, *Ser. A*, vol. 197, 1949, p. 454.
—, "Microscopy by reconstructed wavefronts: II," *Proc. Phys. Soc.*, vol. B64, 1951, p. 449.

[4] Extensive bibliography will be found in, for example, J. W. Goodman, *Introduction to Fourier Optics*. New York: McGraw-Hill, 1968; also, this issue, pp. 1292–1304.

[5] R. W. Meier, "Magnification and third-order aberration in holography," *J. Opt. Soc. Amer.*, vol. 55, 1965, p. 987.

[6] L. Larmore, H. M. A. El-Sum, and A. F. Metherell, "Acoustical holograms using phase information only," *Appl. Opt.*, vol. 8, 1969, p. 1533.

[7] A. Lohmann, "Comments about phase-only holograms," in *Acoustical Holography*, vol. 2, A. F. Metherell and L. Larmore, Eds. New York: Plenum, 1970, p. 203.

[8] F. L. Thurstone, "Ultrasound holography and visual reconstruction," *Proc. Symp. Biomed. Eng.*, vol. 1 (Milwaukee, Wis., Marquette Univ.), 1966, p. 12.

[9] R. K. Mueller, E. Marom, and D. Fritzler, "Electronic stimulation of a variable inclination reference for acoustic holography via the ultrasonic camera," *Appl. Phys. Lett.*, vol. 12, June 1, 1968, p. 394.

[10] A. F. Metherell, S. Spinak, and E. J. Pisa, "Temporal reference acoustical holography," in *Acoustical Holography*, vol. 2, A. F. Metherell and L. Larmore, Eds. New York: Plenum, 1970; also *Appl. Phys. Lett.*, vol. 13, Nov. 15, 1968, p. 340; and *Appl. Opt.*, vol. 8, 1969, p. 1543.

[11] B. P. Hildebrand and K. A. Haines, "Holography by scanning," *J. Opt. Soc. Amer.*, vol. 59, 1969, p. 1.

[12] J. L. Kreuzer and P. E. Vogel; "Acoustic holographic techniques for nondestructive testing," in *Acoustical Holography*, vol. 1, A. F. Metherell *et al.*, Eds. New York: Plenum, 1970, p. 73.

[13] G. Wade, M. Wollman, and K. Wang, "A holographic system for use in the ocean," in *Acoustical Holography*, vol. 3, A. F. Metherell, Ed. New York: Plenum, 1971, p. 211.

[14] Extensive bibliography will be found in G. D. Bergland, "A guided tour of the fast Fourier transform," *IEEE Spectrum*, vol. 6, July 1969, pp. 41–52.

[15] E. Marom, R. K. Mueller, R. F. Koppelmann, and G. Zilinskas, "Design and preliminary test of an underwater viewing system using sound holography," in *Acoustical Holography*, vol. 3, A. F. Metherell, Ed. New York: Plenum, 1971, p. 191.

[16] A. Korpel and P. Desmares, "Rapid sampling of acoustic holograms by laser-scanning techniques," *J. Acoust. Soc. Amer.*, vol. 45, 1969, p. 881.

[17] D. Gabor, "Tilted phase contrast method," U. S. Patent 548 939.

[18] P. S. Green, A. Macovski, and S. D. Ramsey, "Coherent optical detection of ultrasonic images using electronic scanning," *Appl. Phys. Lett.*, vol. 16, Apr. 1970, p. 265.

[19] A. Korpel, "Acoustic imaging by diffracted light, I. Two-dimensional interaction," *IEEE Trans. Sonics Ultrason.*, vol. SU-15, July 1968, pp. 153–157.
—, "Astigmatic imaging properties of Bragg diffraction," *J. Acoust. Soc. Amer.*, vol. 49, Mar. 1971, pp. 1059–1061.

[20] —, "Visualization of the cross-section of a sound beam by Bragg diffraction of light," *Appl. Phys. Lett.*, vol. 9, Dec. 1966, p. 425.

[21] A. A. Friesem, "Holograms on thick emulsions," *Appl. Phys. Lett.*, vol. 7, 1965, pp. 102–103.

[22] R. K. Mueller and N. K. Sheridon, "Sound holograms and optical reconstruction," *Appl. Phys. Lett.*, vol. 9, Nov. 1, 1966, p. 328.

[23] C. F. Augustine, C. Deutsch, D. Fritzler, and E. Marom, "Microwave holography using liquid crystal area detectors," *Proc. IEEE* (Lett.), vol. 57, July 1969, pp. 1333–1334.

[24] A. Korpel, "Methods of acoustic microscopy," in *Acoustical Holography*, vol. 3, A. F. Metherell, Ed. New York: Plenum, 1971, p. 23.

[25] A. Korpel and R. L. Withman, "Visualization of a coherent light field by heterodyning with a scanning laser beam," *Appl. Opt.*, vol. 8, 1969, p. 1577.

[26] H. R. Farrah, E. Marom, and R. K. Mueller, "An underwater viewing system using sound holography," in *Acoustical Holography*, vol. 2, A. F. Metherell and L. Larmore, Eds. New York: Plenum, 1970, pp. 173–184.

[27] J. E. Jacobs, "Ultrasound image converter systems utilizing electron-scanning techniques," *IEEE Trans. Sonics Ultrason.*, vol. SU-15, July 1968, pp. 146–152.

[28] N. U. Phan, "The application of television scanning techniques to the problem of visualizing ultrasound images," M.S. thesis, Northwestern Univ., Evanston, Ill., 1961.

[29] J. E. Jacobs, U. S. Patent 3 236 944, Feb. 22, 1966.

[30] R. K. Mueller and P. N. Keating, "The liquid-gas interface as a recording medium for acoustical holography," in *Acoustical Holography*, vol. 1, A. F. Metherell *et al.*, Eds. New York: Plenum, 1969, p. 49.

[31] H. M. A. El-Sum, "The scope of the symposium," in *Acoustical Holography*, vol. 1, A. F. Metherell *et al.*, Eds. New York: Plenum, 1969.

[32] R. B. Smith and B. B. Brenden, "Refinements and variations in liquid surface and scanned ultrasound holography," *IEEE Trans. Sonics Ultrason.* (1968 IEEE Ultrason. Symp. Dig.), vol. SU-16, 1969, p. 29.

[33] P. S. Green, "A new liquid surface-relief method of acoustic image conversion," in *Acoustical Holography*, vol. 3, A. F. Metherell, Ed. New York: Plenum, 1971, p. 173.

[34] P. N. Keating, "Holographic edge and gradient correlation," submitted to *J. Opt. Soc. Amer.*

[35] F. L. Thurstone and H. W. Tyrer, "Acoustic energy detection for holographic imaging," *Proc. Ann. Conf. Eng. Med. Biol.*, vol. 10, 1968, p. 8.10.

[36] K. Preston, Jr., and J. L. Kreuzer, "Ultrasonic imaging using a synthetic holographic technique," *Appl. Phys. Lett.*, vol. 10, Mar. 1967, p. 150.

[37] J. B. Farr, "Acoustical holography experiments using digital processing," in *Acoustical Holography*, vol. 2, A. F. Metherell and L. Larmore, Eds. New York: Plenum, 1970, p. 225.

[38] E. Marom, D. Fritzler, and R. K. Mueller, "Ultrasonic holography by electronic scanning of a piezoelectric crystal," *Appl. Phys. Lett.*, vol. 12, Jan. 1968, p. 26.

[39] G. A. Massey, "An optical heterodyne ultrasonic image converter," *Proc. IEEE*, vol. 56, Dec. 1968, pp. 2157–2161.

[40] A. Korpel, "Acoustic imaging and holography," *IEEE Spectrum*, vol. 5, Oct. 1968, pp. 45–52.

[41] A. F. Metherell, "Acoustical holography," *1969 IEEE Conv. Dig.*, p. 66; also *Sci. Amer.*, vol. 221, Oct. 1969, p. 36.

[42] H. M. A. El-Sum, "Progress in acoustical holography," in *Acoustical Holography*, vol. 2, A. F. Metherell and L. Larmore, Eds. New York: Plenum, 1970, p. 7.

[43] A. Korpel and L. W. Kessler, "Comparison of methods of acoustic microscopy," in *Acoustical Holography*, vol. 3, A. F. Metherell, Ed. New York: Plenum, 1971, p. 23.

[44] J. F. Havlice, R. Kompfner, and C. F. Quate, "Progress towards an acoustic microscope," private communication.

[45] W. E. Kock, "Holography can help radar find new performance horizons," *Electronics*, Oct. 12, 1970.

[46] J. Walker, "Ultrasonic holography," Willow Run Labs. Rep. 2420-5-P, July 1969.

[47] W. H. Wells, "Acoustical imaging with linear transducer arrays," in *Acoustical Holography*, vol. 2, A. F. Metherell and L. Larmore, Eds. New York: Plenum, 1970, p. 87.

[48] G. G. Goetz, "Real-time holographic reconstruction by electro-optic modulation," *Appl. Phys. Lett.*, vol. 17, July 1970, p. 63.

[49] G. Groh and G. Marie, "Information input in an optical pattern recognition system using a relay tube based on the Pockels effect," presented at Holographie-Applications Symposium International, Besancon, France, July 6–11, 1970.

[50] K. P. Preston, Jr., "An array optical spatial phase modulator," presented at IEEE Int. Solid-State Circuits Conf., Philadelphia, Pa., Feb. 1969.

[51] W. E. Glenn and R. J. Doyle, "Lumatron, a high resolution storage *A* and *P* projection display device," presented at 1970 IEEE Conf. Display Devices, Dec.

[52] E. Baumann, "Eidophor colour projection system," *Television Soc. J.*, vol. 9, Oct.–Dec. 1959, p. 127.

[53] *Naval Research Reviews*, Feb. 1971.

[54] J. W. Cooly and J. W. Tukey, "An algorithm for the machine calculation of complex Fourier series," *Math. Comput.*, vol. 19, Sept. 1965, p. 297.

[55] For example, G. W. Stroke, *An Introduction to Coherent Optics and Holography*. New York: Academic Press, 1969.

[56] W. A. Penn and J. L. Chovan, "The application of holographic concepts to sonar," in *Acoustical Holography*, vol. 2, A. F. Metherell and L. Larmore, Eds. New York: Plenum, 1970, p. 133.

[57] B. M. Oliver, "Sparkling spots and random diffraction," *Proc. IEEE*, vol. 51, Jan. 1963, pp. 220–221.

[58] R. K. Mueller, H. R. Farrah, and E. Marom, "Acoustic holography,"

Bendix Tech. J., vol. 2, Summer 1969, p. 15.

[59] R. K. Mueller, E. Marom, and D. Fritzler, "Some problems associated with optical image formation from acoustic holograms," *Appl. Opt.*, vol. 8, 1969, p. 1537.

[60] H. Berger, "A survey of ultrasonic image detection methods," in *Acoustical Holography*, vol. 1, A. F. Metherell *et al.*, Eds.   New York: Plenum, 1969, p. 27.

[61] H. Beiger, "Ultrasonic imaging system for nondestructive testing," *J. Acoust. Soc Amer.*, vol. 45, 1969, p. 859.

[62] E. E. Aldridge, A. B. Clare, and D. A. Shepherd, "Ultrasonic holography in nondestructive testing," in *Acoustical Holography*, vol. 3, A. F. Metherell, Ed.   New York: Plenum, 1971, p. 129.

[63] A. Vander Lugt, "Signal detection by complex spatial filtering," *IEEE Trans. Inform. Theory*, vol. IT-10, Apr. 1964. pp. 139–145.

[64] *IEEE Proc. (Special Issue on Ultrasonics)*, Oct. 1965.

[65] J. F. Havlice, C. F. Quate, and J. W. Goodman, "Acoustic microscope-visualization of acoustic beams," *Electron. Res. Rev.*, Stanford Univ., vol. 11, Aug. 1969.

[66] J. F. Havlice, C. F. Quate, and B. Richardson, "Visualization of sound beams in quartz and sapphire near 1 GHz," presented at IEEE Symp. Sonics Ultrason., Vancouver, Canada, 1967.

[67] J. B. Farr, "Earth holography: A potential new seismic method," presented at the 38th Ann. Meet. of the Soc. of Exploration Geophysicists, Colorado, Oct. 1968, Paper R-17.

[68] W. E. Lerwill, "Holography at seismic frequency," presented at European Association Exploration Geophysicist (EAEL) Conf., Venice, Italy, 1969.

[69] A. Fontanel and G. Grau, "Application of impulse seismic holography," presented at the 39th Annual Int. Meet. of the Soc. of Exploration Geophysicists, Institut Francais du Petrolo reprint, reference 17353, Sept. 1969.

[70] D. Silverman, "Mapping the earth with elastic wave holography," *IEEE Trans. Geosci. Electron.*, vol. GE-7, Oct. 1969, pp. 190–199.

[71] R. A. Peterson, "Seismography 1970. The writing of the earth waves," presented at the Symp. of the Pacific Coast Section of the Soc. of Exploration Geophysicists on Seismic Waves from Vibrational Sources, Los Angeles, Calif., Nov. 1969.

[72] F. Levin, "Oil exploration technology," *Sci. Technol.*, Feb. 1969.

[73] G. L. Fitzpatrick, Denver Mining Research Center, U. S. Bureau of Mines, Denver, Colo., private communication.

[74] H. R. Farrah, E. Marom, and R. K. Mueller, "An underwater viewing system using sound holography," in *Acoustical Holography*, vol. 2, A. F. Metherell and L. Larmore, Eds.   New York: Plenum, 1970, p. 173.

[75] S. C. Daubin, "System requirements for underwater acoustic holographic mapping," *IEEE Trans. Geosci. Electron.*, vol. GE-8, Oct. 1970, pp. 313–320.

[76] G. Wade and M. Wollman, "Acoustic holographic system for underwater search," in *Acoustical Holography*, vol. 3, A. F. Metherell, Ed.   New York: Plenum, 1971, p. 225.

Acoustic Imaging with Holography and Lenses

GLEN WADE, FELLOW IEEE

I see . . . (an) important application of vision by ultrasound in medical diagnostics, where it could not only replace X rays, but score above them by making visible fetuses, clogged veins and arteries, and incipient tumors.—Dennis Gabor, 1970 [1].

Abstract—Acoustic energy can often give a view of an object not available with light or even with X rays. A number of basically different acoustic systems have been made to give excellent orthoscopic images in real time. These systems range from the purely holographic to the purely lens types. They read out image information contained on waves of scattered sound either by using a laser beam or by employing piezoelectric elements.

In all of the laser systems, phase information is preserved, whereas in the piezoelectric systems it is not. Retaining the phase makes it difficult to eliminate from the image such detrimental interference products as speckle and ringing. Also, the high-energy laser photons are extremely noisy and may cause problems in sensitivity for the laser-beam systems.

In spite of the problems, much progress has been made, and we can resonably expect that the new systems will eventually find employment in such applications as medical diagnosis, acoustic microscopy, nondestructive testing, oceanic search, and perhaps seismic sensing.

INTRODUCTION

THE IDEA of being able to "see" with sound has long been intriguing to humans. Sound waves which are scattered from objects carry much the same image information as do light waves. By nature, man is not equiped to efficiently utilize this information and from it obtain mental images. However, many animals such as bats can data-process scattered sound very rapidly. Only recently has this fact been fully appreciated. In 1793, the Italian scientist Spallanzani concluded that bats must have some "new organ or sense" that humans do not have and are not aware of. It was not until 1920 that the principle of operation of the "new sense" was found to be similar to that used by the sonar systems of World War I. By now it is well known that several cetaceans, such as the dolphin, also have excellent capability for visualizing objects by means of sonic energy.

One important application for acoustic imaging is in medical diagnosis as was pointed out in detail by the excellent expository article of Erickson, Fry, and Jones which appeared in this TRANSACTIONS last year [2]. The human body is opaque to visible light, but, as in the case of X rays, it is relatively transparent to ultrasound. Soft bodily tissues frequently provide little contrast in opacity to X rays. Therefore, in diagnostic radiology, artificial contrast agents are sometimes introduced into the body by invasive techniques involving a hazard to the patient which may range from discomfort to death. In addition, the cumulative effect of the X rays by themselves may impose severe damage to the tissue. These types of drawbacks are not prevalent in acoustic imaging. Biological objects which fail to exhibit good contrast for X rays may well show striking contrast for sound. Different soft tissues can often be seen with excellent clarity in an ultrasonic image. Cancerous or diseased tissue can frequently be distinguished without difficulty from normal tissue. In addition, there is a threshold level of acoustic intensity below which there will be no damage to irradiated biological tissue, either immediately or on a cumulative basis.

Another application of acoustic imaging is in nondestructive testing. With the development of nuclear reactors, deep-ocean vehicles, jet-powered aircraft, manned spacecraft and other technological innovations of the last 30 years, the need for nondestructive methods to detect flaws and inclusions in various components and structures has greatly increased. Radiographic processes involving X rays, gamma rays, and neutrons have been used with reasonable success but are relatively costly, particularly for thick objects where high penetrating power is needed. The search for other approaches has inevitably led to ultrasound, well known for its ability to pierce many important materials. In fact, for a number of years, ultrasonic systems of the pulse-echo type have been successfully employed in nondestructive testing. Like radar, these systems provide a map of the regions under investigation producing, by means of the so-called *B*-scan, cross-sectional "images" of the internal structure of the object. These images are sometimes referred to as artificial images. They are not of the true-focused or holographic type with which this article is concerned. They are also not orthographic in character but rather are like the sector scans obtained with radar and sonar systems. In medical science, they are frequently called tomograms. They have proven to be very useful, not only in nondestructive testing but, as described in [2], also in medical diagnosis. The pulse-echo approach works particularly well for objects

Manuscript received May 27, 1975.

The author is with the Department of Electrical Engineering and Computer Science, University of California, Santa Barbara, Calif. 93106.

Reprinted from *IEEE Trans. Sonics Ultrason.*, vol. SU-22, pp. 385–394, Nov. 1975.

of small area. Large-area coverage by such a system requires complex mechanical scanning or the use of numerous transducers in an array. Real-time operation is also a problem. Therefore, other methods of acoustic imaging, especially where the performance is in real time, offer alternative approaches.

Microscopy is another important area for applying acoustic imaging. An acoustic microscope, as opposed to its optical counterpart, is capable of differentiating microstructure on the basis of mechanical and elastic properties rather than optical properties. In optics, dielectric variations produce the wave scattering. In acoustics, waves are scattered by variations in elastic qualities. Many biological specimens show little intrinsic optical contrast but large intrinsic acoustic contrast. Thus not only is optical opacity circumvented by employing ultrasound, but also optical transparency in which lack of contrast is a problem.

One of the first persons to systematically explore the usefulness of ultrasound for "imaging" was S. J. Sokolov at the University of Leningrad over a twenty-year period starting in the 1920's. He devised several techniques for producing optical patterns corresponding to various objects, usually metallic, that were irradiated with sonic beams in the megahertz region and above. Most of his schemes were proposed in order to detect inhomogeneities within the objects such as flaws and voids, the classical problem of nondestructive testing. However, one of his ideas involved using sound at 3 GHz where the wavelength would be extremely small (half a micrometer in water) and capable of resolving truly minute objects. The name he gave to the corresponding device was the "ultrasonic microscope" [3]. Technological impracticalities prevented Sokolov from operating at such a high frequency, and the principle he put forth (that of reading out localized electronic charge developed on a piezoelectric crystal in response to an acoustic input) has since become embodied in a well-known device, called the Sokolov tube, for low-frequency acoustic imaging [4].

In another of his schemes, inhomogeneities in metal objects were made "visible" by reflecting collimated light from the surface of an oil film contacting the metal [5] in a fashion reminiscent of modern liquid-surface acoustic holography. Lasers, of course, were not available to Sokolov and his light source (a mercury arc) was not as coherent as he might have wished. It has been pointed out [6] that the static ripples formed on the oil surface did, by themselves, constitute a type of embossed hologram. Sokolov can therefore be regarded as having produced holograms a number of years before Gabor invented holography. Of course, Sokolov had no way of understanding holography as we understand it today, and his reconstructed "images" were not of high quality.

In still another of Sokolov's schemes, light was diffracted after being passed through a glass container filled with turpentine [7] in a manner somewhat similar to that of modern Bragg-diffraction imaging [8]–[10]. The sound was first directed through a metal test piece and then into the turpentine. Sokolov's system utilized the arrangements of Debye and Sears and of Lucas and Biquard to display the diffraction spectra of the light as produced by interaction with the sound. Thus, strictly speaking, Debye–Sears diffraction rather than Bragg diffraction was involved. Also no actual images were formed. The intensity and number of orders of the diffraction spectra displayed depended upon the strength and the wavefront configuration of the sound in the liquid. For a homogeneous mass of metal, the sound power reaching the acoustic cell would be relatively strong and the wave-fronts planar. The intensity and the number of orders would then be high. However, if there were flaws in the metal, the sound passing through it would be scattered and damped, and the intensity and number of orders would be reduced.

Since the days of Sokolov, a multiplicity of other methods have been proposed for acoustic imaging. The invention of holography and the advent of the laser have been particularly influential in stimulating new thought and effort in this area. A number of exciting experimental results accompanied by relevent analytical advances have recently taken place. By now a wide variety of system concepts exists, and several of them have demonstrated astonishing capability. The systems range from purely holographic to purely lens types. The applications being considered include seismic sensing and oceanic underwater imaging as well as microscopy, medical diagnosis, and nondestructive testing. Obviously, in a paper of limited size it is not possible to treat all of the systems now being explored. The ones chosen for coverage are, in each case, systems which operate in real time (or can easily be made to operate in that fashion), give orthographic images in true perspective, and for which there has been important recent progress. Therefore, a number of excellent systems, such as those employing conventional pulse-echo techniques or the Sokolov tube, will not be discussed. The systems treated here either use a laser beam to read out the image information, or the read-out is accomplished by means of piezoelectric acoustic transducers.

TYPES OF ACOUSTIC IMAGING SYSTEMS

All of the systems treated in this paper which employ laser beams are either holographic or can be thought of in terms of holography. However, some of these systems are of a distinctly hybrid nature when it comes to how they can be made to operate. They can function either in a holographic mode or a mode that is completely nonholographic. The holographic nature of these systems may be quite unimportant from a practical standpoint and not at all critical to the production of good images. However, even in these cases, the holographic character of the system can be useful for the purpose of categorization, especially if we wish to relate one system to another [6]. Historically, the advent of acoustic holography has served to stimulate great breadth of thought in the whole area of acoustic imaging and has had a particularly important bearing on the conception and development of the systems using lasers.

The other systems which will be treated do not employ laser-beam readout and are not basically holographic, although they also can readily be modified to function in a holographic mode if this is wanted. However, in their present operation, the necessary focusing is accomplished through the use of acoustic lenses, and the image information is read out by means of piezoelectric transducers. In terms of sensitivity and freedom from certain spurious image elements (speckle and ringing), this latter category of systems is inherently superior to the former category. That this is so can be seen from the simple arguments presented below.

Any system that is fundamentally holographic in nature uses coherent waves and operates in such a way as to retain the phase information associated with these waves. In most nonholographic systems, this information is not preserved. In all the laser systems treated in this paper, the phase is preserved, whereas in the piezoelectric systems it is not. Retaining the phase makes a fundamental difference as far as the presence of such interference products as speckle and ringing are concerned. Speckle refers to randomly positioned variations in image intensity due to phase cancellation and phase reinforcement among all of the coherent spatial wave components impinging upon the image plane. Ringing refers to the systematic variations, also due to phase cancellation and phase reinforcement, which show up in the image as fringes. Ringing can be thought of as a more orderly manifestation than speckle of the interference phenomenon. The fringes are particularly prominent in the vicinity of the images of sharp edges. Thus the coherent spatial wave components used in forming an image can and do interfere with each other to produce interference products that would not be present if the components were incoherent.

In ordinary sight we use incoherent light and do not have to cope with speckle or ringing. We are therefore not used to seeing interference fringes and spots in the images formed on the retinas of our eyes. When we observe speckle and ringing in images produced by coherent systems, it is difficult to interpret what we are seeing. These spurious elements are not the same as noise. They actually represent information, but a type of information we normally do not use. If we were clever enough, perhaps we could garner meaning from them. However, because of our lack of ability to interpret what we are seeing, they ordinarily detract from, rather than add to, our understanding of the object.

Speckle and ringing are particularly annoying in still-life pictures. They seem to go away if the image is moving. The reason for this is physiological. When the eye looks at a moving image produced by a real-time holographic system, the spurious elements change shape and shift position rapidly. A visual averaging or integrating effect

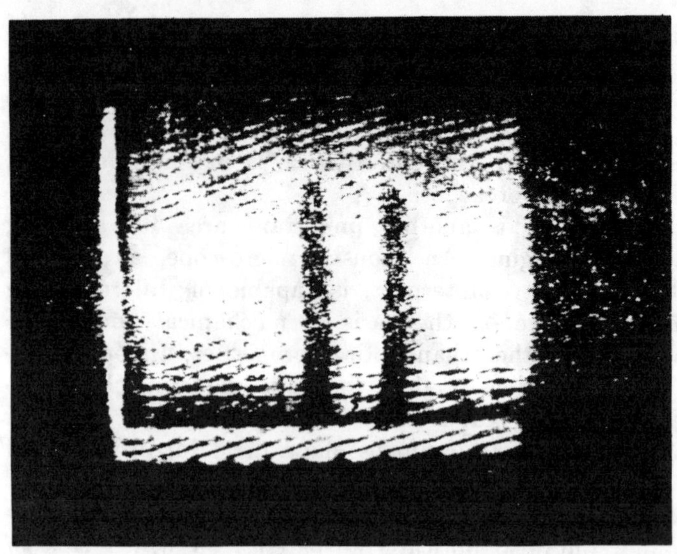

Fig. 1. Ringing and speckle in a stationary image from a Bragg-diffraction system. The object is a 7-mm-thick aluminum plate with two 1.5-mm-diameter internal holes drilled into one of its edges [10]. The ringing is particularly noticeable appearing in the form of several different sets of parallel fringes.

takes place that, from the viewpoint of the observer, seems to smooth out the deviations. Thus in a moving image, an observer will often not find the speckle and the ringing to be particularly disturbing and may actually be quite unaware that the spurious elements are even present. However, if a photograph is taken of the image at some instant of time, the motion, and hence the averaging, are eliminated and the interference products show up.

The problem of ringing and speckle in such a photograph is illustrated in Fig. 1. The system in this case is one which employs Bragg diffraction of laser light from coherent sound in order to produce an optical replica of an acoustic beam which has been scattered from the object. By processing this laser light with a conventional lens system, the image is obtained. When light is Bragg-diffracted from sound, the phase information associated with the sound is retained in the diffracted light. The images from a Bragg system, therefore, usually contain much ringing and speckle. The ringing is especially prominent in the figure and shows up mainly as sets of parallel fringes associated with various edges in the object or in the system itself.

As previously mentioned, sensitivity is another characteristic for which piezoelectric readout is inherently superior to laser-beam readout. This is due to the fact that the high-energy laser photons are extremely noisy and by themselves constitute the major source of unremovable noise in all the laser systems. This makes it difficult for such a system to detect small differences in the intensity of sound components which are scattered by an object even if the laser power level is relatively high [11]. The equivalent noise temperature of the readout process alone is directly proportional to the frequency of the light and amounts to about 10 000° K. Therefore, if two adjacent object elements scatter the sound with only

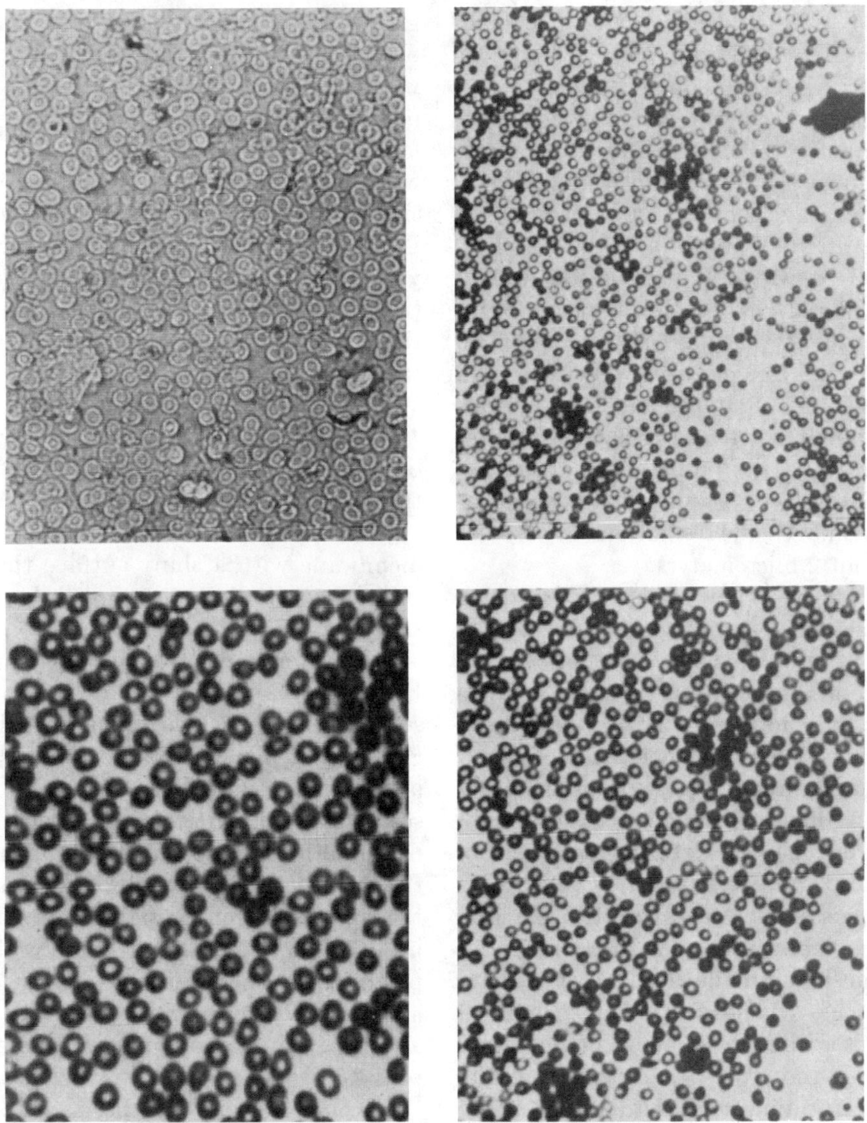

Fig. 2. Comparison of an optical image (upper left) with three acoustical images from Stanford's scanning acoustic-beam microscope. The images are of unstained human red blood cells.

slight dissimilarities, the two elements will not be distinguishable from each other in the final image. The chief source of unremovable noise in the piezoelectric systems is thermal noise. Under ordinary operating conditions this type of noise would have an equivalent temperature of only about 300° K. Thus the ultimate sensitivity of the laser systems can be expected to be almost two orders of magnitude worse than that for the piezoelectric systems. Recent analytical study has confirmed this expectation [11]. At the present stage of development of these systems, the ideal performance hypothesized in the above study has not yet been approached in any of the systems, and the difference in the sensitivity actually achieved is even greater than two orders of magnitude.

For medical use, high sensitivity is very important. The object being imaged must, of course, be insonified. If the object is a living human organ, the power level of insonification must be low enough to prevent damage to the organ. Since the piezoelectric systems offer the possibility of producing effective images with the least tissue exposure to ultrasound, these systems have a substantial advantage over the laser systems. However, in applications other than medical diagnosis, where operation at higher power is permissible, the laser systems may well be quite competitive, particularly if phase retension is important.

REAL-TIME ORTHOGRAPHIC IMAGES

Perhaps the most spectacular of the real-time acoustic images are those from acoustic microscopes. When first we consider ordinary sound, it is difficult to imagine that sonic waves could possibly be useful in obtaining highly resolved images of minute objects. It is easy to conceive of this being done with ordinary light whose wavelengths we all know to be very short or with electrons whose size we recognize to be negligibly small. Yet sound might at first glance appear to be entirely too cumbersome. Certainly this would be true if we were talking about sound in air where the frequency spectrum is severely limited. However, consider sound in water where the spectrum is much larger. Because sound velocity is extremely slow compared to that of light, sound wavelengths are extremely short compared to those of electromagnetic waves at the same frequencies. For example, at 1.5 MHz where the EM vacuum wavelength is 200 meters, the sound wavelength in water is only 1 mm. At 1.5 GHz the sound wavelength is down to 1 micrometer, and at double that frequency, it reduces to that of visible light.

Fig. 2 illustrates the quality of image obtainable when the frequency is 600 MHz. The pictures were furnished by Professor Calvin F. Quate of Stanford and show various images of unstained human red blood cells. The photograph on the left is of an optical image and the other three are of acoustical images with different magnifications. For the acoustical images, the resolution of Professor Quate's system was about 2 micrometers.

The system is of the lens type and reads out the image information with a piezoelectric transducer. It can be thought of as an acoustic equivalent of the scanning electron-beam microscope. Actually, Professor Quate's system, at this writing, has not been made to operate in real time, the period for one frame being one second. However, an order of magnitude speed-up could be accomplished without difficulty and we do not hesitate to place this system in the real-time category in terms of potentiality.

In the Quate system, a sound beam from a transmitting transducer is focused by an acoustic lens to a small spot in the object plane. The spot is made to scan out a raster pattern over the object by rapidly moving the object through such a pattern within its plane. The scattered sound is then gathered by another lens and projected onto a receiving transducer. The time variation in the output from this transducer, after suitable processing, is converted into a corresponding spatial variation of intensity on the screen of a cathode ray tube by means of synchronous scanning. The details of the system have recently appeared in the literature [12].

The acoustic images of the blood cells in Fig. 2 compare favorably with the optical ones. Each blood cell averages about 7 micrometers in diameter. Obviously, for objects of this size the resolution is adequate in both systems. However, for contrast, the story is different. The contrast is much better acoustically than optically, and this fact illustrates a chief advantage and utility of acoustic microscopy.

The capability of a very different kind of microscope is impressively shown by the three images of Fig. 3, which were furnished by Lawrence W. Kessler of Sonoscan. The microscope was developed by Dr. Kessler and collegues while Dr. Kessler was still with Zenith [13]. It has recently been packaged by Sonoscan and is the only acoustic microscope now commercially available.

This microscope has the unique feature that it can be adjusted to give simultaneously both an acoustic and an optical image of the same object. In fact, the photographs in the figure show three simultaneous images. The object in this case was a fruit-fly larva, and the images were displayed on the screens of three color television monitors. Fig. 3(a) presents the optical image of the larva, 3(b) the acoustic image, and 3(c) a superposition of the preceding two images. Thus 3(c) displays the simultaneous sum of the optical and acoustic information. It is color coded. Since the optical image is shown in yellow and the acoustic in blue, the bicolored representation maintains the identity of the source of the information. It is thus more useful, as well as more spectacular, than such a superposition would be if displayed in black and white.

The Sonoscan system is of the type that employs laser-beam readout. The sound waves are first scattered from the object to be viewed into the water bath in which the object is placed. The waves then impinge upon a solid membrane with a shiny surface that serves as one of the sides of the tank containing the bath. As they strike the solid surface, the waves generate a moving ripple pattern on the interface between the membrane and the water. Even though no reference beam is used in the system, the surface records what might be called a "dynamic hologram." The image is read out by using a scanning focused laser beam to produce a spot on the surface. The spot scans through a raster pattern on the "holographic" plane and is reflected from the shiny surface. In striking the surface, the beam becomes angularly modulated by the dynamic ripple contained on the surface. The image information is converted into weak electrical signals by passing the reflected laser beam through a knife-edge and photodiode combination. The signals are amplified and decoded resulting in an acoustic micrograph displayed on a synchronously-scanned television screen [13].

The larva shown in the displays of Fig. 3 was about 1 mm in diameter and 4 mm long. This latter dimension is considerably greater than the uniform region of the sound field, therefore, only a portion of the specimen could be imaged at any one time. In each of the images, the larva head is located beyond the display to the right. Obviously more fine detail is visible in the acoustic image (Fig. 3(b)) than in the optical one (Fig. 3(a)). Extending back from the head is a system of tubes through which oxygen is delivered to the cells, and many small bubbles are present. There are two main branches of the system, and these show up more clearly acoustically than optically. One would expect this to be the case because the impedance mismatch for sound waves in passing through a region containing bubbles is much greater than for light waves. Also, in general, the optical opacity of the specimen is greater than the acoustic opacity. Much of the internal detail is masked from view in the optical image but not in the acoustic image. Certain inner structure of the larva would be entirely unobservable optically without sacrificing the specimen by slicing it up or dissecting out its organs. Even with X rays, where opacity is not a problem and where differentiation between hard, calcified tissue and soft tissue is easy to produce, it is still difficult

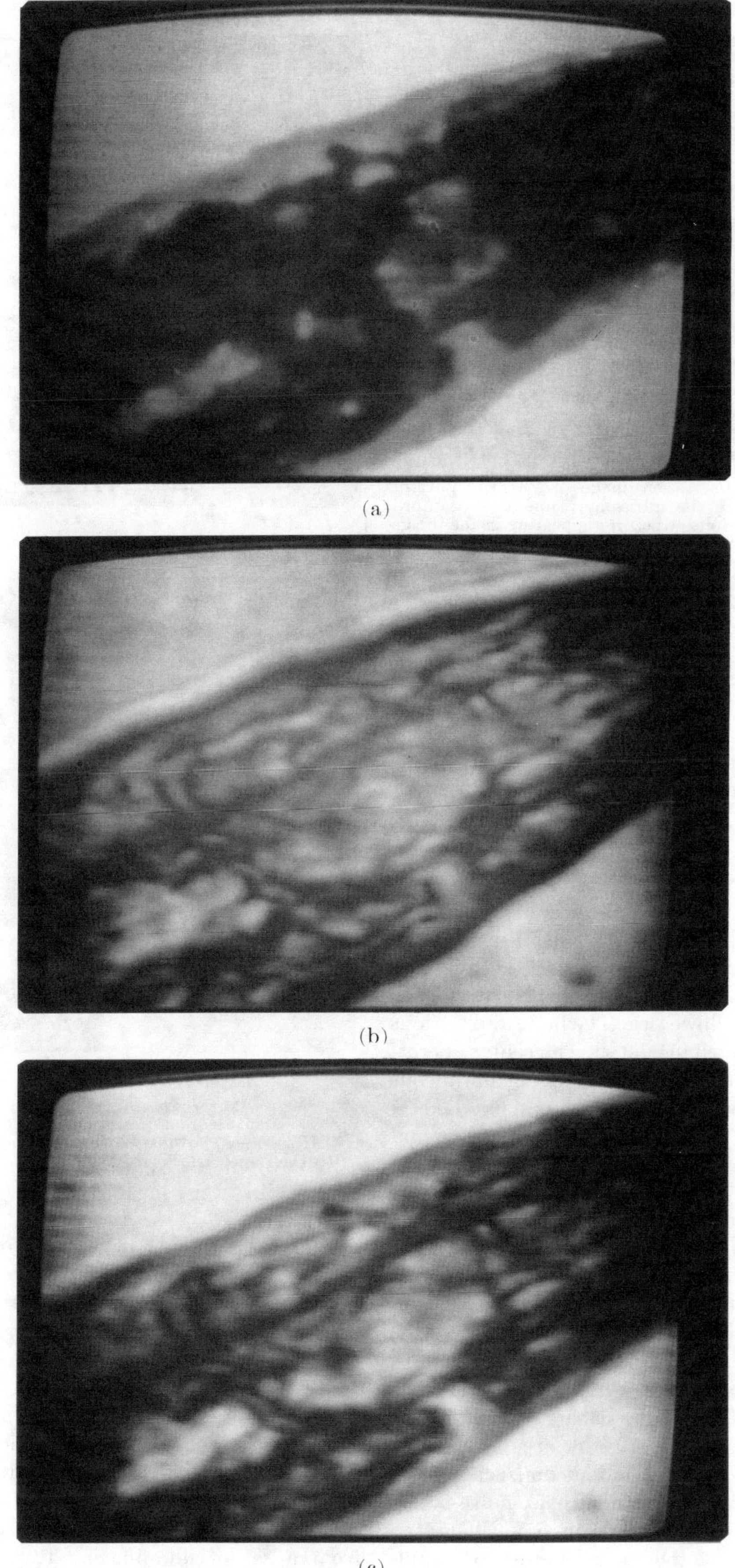

Fig. 3. Optical and acoustic images of a section of a fruit-fly larva obtained by a microscope developed at Zenith. (a) Optical image. (b) Acoustic image. (c) Superposition of (a) and (b).

Note: These photographs appeared in color in the original publication.

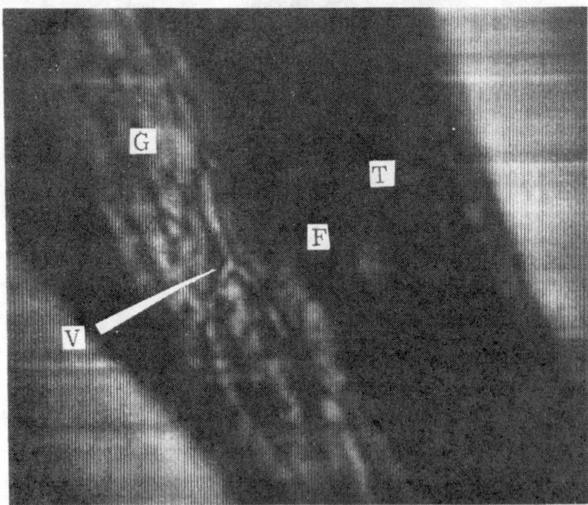

Fig. 4. Acoustic through-transmission image (2 MHz) of part of the lower leg as viewed by the ultrasonic camera of Stanford Research Institute. The various structures appearing in the image include the tibia (T), fibula (F), gastrocnemius muscle (G), and bifurcation of superficial vein (V).

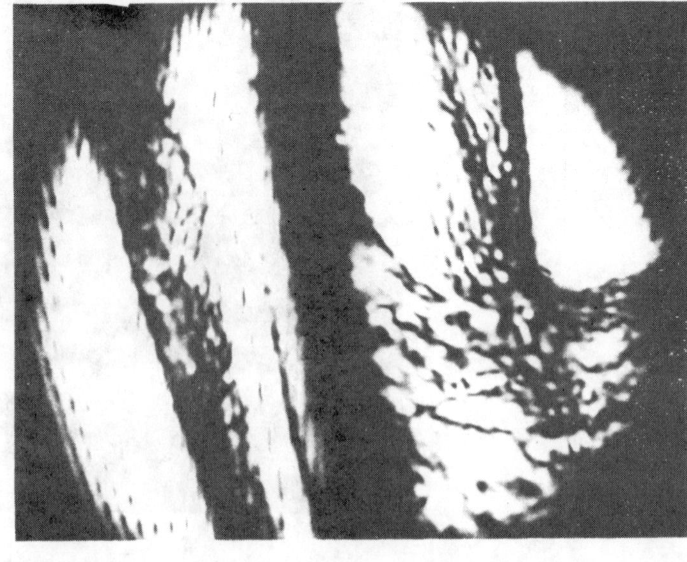

(a)

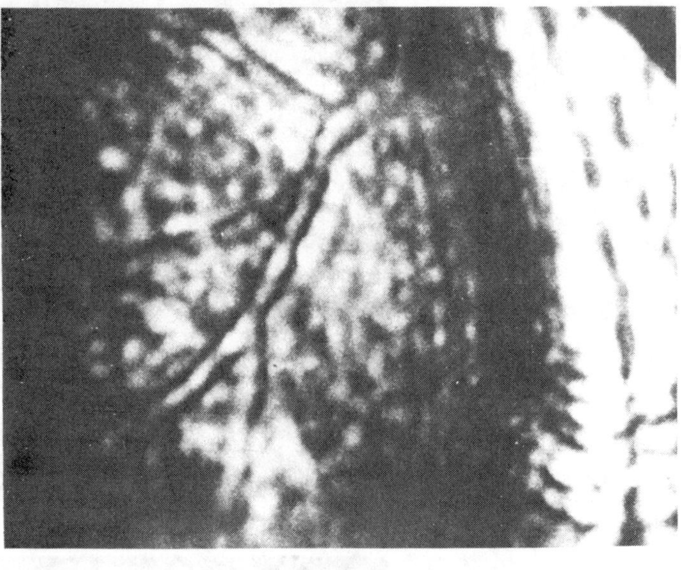

(b)

Fig. 5. Acoustic images from the liquid-surface holographic system of Holosonics showing (a) the upper arm just above the elbow, and (b) the upper arm in the region of the biceps.

to distinguish between various soft tissues. Soft tissue differentiation is readily apparent, however, in acoustic micrographs without the need for chemical staining. For some experimental situations, considerable optical detail as well as acoustic detail is present, and one image tends to complement the other. Under these circumstances, the simultaneous superposition of both the optical and the acoustic signals may be greatly advantageous and can be accomplished with striking effectiveness as demonstrated in Fig. 3(c).

A number of remarkable images of various parts of the human body have been obtained with an ultrasonic camera developed by Philip Green and colleagues at Stanford Research Institute (SRI) [14]. Fig. 4 displays one such image showing part of the lower leg. The bone and various blood vessels are seen in striking detail. The center operating frequency for this image was 2 MHz, the instantaneous frequency being swept over a total range of about 1 MHz (that is, from 1.5 to 2.5 MHz) to insure incoherence and thereby eliminate speckle and ringing.

The system is capable of imaging many internal organs of the body trunk, including the colon, the kidneys, the stomach, and the heart. In the abdominal region, for example, the spine, the lower ribs, and the costal cartilage can be viewed without difficulty. Muscles, tendons, and vascular structure are easy to identify. The fact that the viewing is in real time and in true perspective (that is, orthographic rather than cross-sectional) means that spatial relationships between various anatomical structures are readily determined.

This system uses piezoelectric readout and is astonishingly sensitive. Employing a maximum peak-pulse-power density of only 18 mW/cm², the instrument will give a good transmission image of the *in vivo* kidney of a full-grown man. The highest insonification intensity obviously occurs at the surface of the skin facing the insonifying transducers. As the waves penetrate the body, they are attenuated at a rate of about 3 dB per cm. Because the system is pulsed with a duty cycle of 1:60, the average power density even at the entering skin surface is only 0.3 mW/cm². The receiver, an array of piezoelectric transducers, has a threshold sensitivity of the order of 10^{-11} W/cm². This means that the viewing of bodily organs can take place through a considerable depth of tissue, even though the insonification intensity is well below that employed in current diagnostic practice.

The operation is as follows. The object to be imaged is flooded with pulses of ultrasonic energy emanating from a set of illuminating transducers. The impinging acoustic waves scatter from the object and are collected and focused into an acoustic image by means of two plastic ultrasonic lenses. The image is then detected by a linear horizontal array of 192 tiny receiving transducers in a most ingenious fashion. At any time instant, the receiving array can, of course, detect only 192 resolution elements. These elements extend in a straight line horizontally from one side of the focused image to the other. The complete picture contains about 400 interlaced horizontal lines and is obtained by repeatedly sweeping the focused image up and down across the stationary line of receiving transducers. The sweeping is accomplished by using two counterrotating plastic ultrasonic prisms located between the two image-forming lenses.

As is apparent from Fig. 5, high-quality orthographic images of potential value in medical diagnosis can be obtained from yet another type of ultrasonic system. The figure shows two transmission images of a boy's upper arm just above the elbow as viewed with the liquid-surface holographic instrument developed by Brenden and colleagues at Holosonics [15], [16]. Note the considerable differentiation between the several types of soft tissue displayed. In Fig. 5(a), one can plainly distinguish various muscles and muscle attachments such as the triceps, the biceps, the attachments of the biceps to the radius in the forearm, and the attachments of some of the muscles of the forearm to the humerus in the upper arm. In the case of the humerus, the true bone edge is not as sharply displayed as it would be with X rays because of the superimposed imaging of the tendons from the forearm muscles. In fact, the attachment pads literally glow with ultrasound and are easy to identify.

The image in Fig. 5(b) shows a portion of the region of the biceps just above the part viewed in Fig. 5(a). A blood vessel is strikingly displayed along with three of its branches.

These two images demonstrate very well the impressive power of acoustic waves to delineate the structure of soft tissue. However, they also demonstrate one of the problems with imagers which employ coherent waves. As was described previously, ringing and speckle are a by-product of coherency. Consider in particular Fig. 5(b) where ringing is especially noticeable. There are several prominent spuriously-generated lines or line segments to the right of the region where the bicep structure actually terminates. Of course, what appears here is a stationary, still-life photograph of an image originally in motion and produced in real time. As previously stated, the severity of the ringing and speckle problem is diminished when moving images are being viewed.

A comparison of sensitivity in the two types of systems can be made by examining the operation of this laser-beam system in the same fashion we have already examined that of the previously-discussed piezoelectric system. For biological imaging of the kind illustrated in Fig. 5, the Holosonics system ordinarily operates with an average sound intensity of about 20 mW/cm² and a peak of almost 1 W/cm². Although these levels are frequently accepted as being safe for human insonification, there is still a question as to whether somewhat lower figures would

not be better. In our work at the University of California at Santa Barbara (UCSB), the campus safety committee has restricted us to a figure of 0.1 W/cm² peak. In fact, the committee would prefer that in actual experiments we stay well below that level. If the Holosonics system were to employ a peak figure less than 0.1 W/cm², the quality of the images would of course decrease. Let us assume, as before, that biological tissue has an absorption coefficient of about 3 dB/cm. Suppose we wish to obtain a transmission image of a human kidney through the midsection of the body with the Holosonics system. The total object thickness (the thickness of the midsection) will be taken to be 30 cm. If we start with an intensity of 0.1 W/cm² peak and 2 mW/cm² average at the surface of the skin facing the insonifying transducer, we will have only 10^{-10} W/cm² peak and 2×10^{-12} W/cm² average at the skin surface on the other side. These values are too low for effective imaging in the present Holosonics system. Thus by invoking the safety standards currently employed in laboratory experiments at UCSB, the use of this laser-beam equipment would be limited to biological objects somewhat thinner than the hypothetical midsection of the preceding example. On the other hand, as previously noted, the SRI piezoelectric system can meet these standards without difficulty, having already given a good transmission image of the *in vivo* kidney of a full-grown man with a peak intensity of only 18 mW/cm².

The acoustical method employed in the Holosonics system is generally referred to as focused liquid-surface holography. A single acoustic transducer produces a beam of sound which insonifies the object to be imaged. The sound waves scattered from the object then pass through a double lens and mirror combination to produce an acoustic image on the surface of the liquid in which the object is located. These focused sound waves are then mixed with those from a second undisturbed acoustic beam at the same frequency. This latter beam is called the reference beam and serves the traditional purpose of all other reference beams in holography, that of producing an interference pattern in the hologram plane. In this case, the hologram plane is the surface of the liquid. The interference pattern takes the form of ripples on the surface. There are dc components associated with the ripples which can be regarded as constituting an embossed hologram. As such, the hologram can be used directly and in real time to spatially modulate a coherent beam of laser light and thus produce the image. A low-power laser is, therefore, employed to illuminate the liquid surface. The laser light is reflected from the surface and diffracted by the ripples and is then spatially filtered and focused onto a television camera tube. An image of the object may then be displayed on a TV monitor, and if desired, a video tape can be made at the same time.

The Holosonics system was the first of the medical instruments to achieve sufficient development to warrant a program of clinical evaluation. Such a program has existed from early in 1972 and extends to the present time in a continuing effort to determine the instrument's diagnostic potential. Another holographic instrument has also undergone evaluation in a clinical setting [17]. The work on this instrument was carried out at Actron and involves a technique of substantially different character from any of the techniques previously mentioned. The method employed is referred to as "linearized subfringe holographic interferometry" [18]. Although the instrument does not operate in real time and therefore, strictly speaking, falls outside the purview of this review, it can nevertheless show an object in motion. It possesses a number of unique and interesting features which merit at least brief mention here.

The technique employs a clever extension of conventional time-averaged holography in which a laser is used to make an optical hologram. In this system the hologram records the fringe pattern associated with the tiny acoustical vibrations that are registered on a solid surface by an impinging acoustic beam which has been scattered from the object to be imaged. Actually, not just one such hologram is made of the object, but a large number, each in rapid sequence. These holograms then constitute the various frames of a holographic movie. When the frames are put together the movie can be made to reconstruct the object in its precise original motion. A radiologist, using the holographic viewer developed for the system, can either run the movie with the focus at a selected plane, or he can stop the action to focus on different depths within the object in any one frame.

The single most unique characteristic of this system is that the entire volume of the object is recorded in each hologram. Thus, as indicated above, the viewer has the advantage of being able to focus throughout the entire volume using only a single hologram if he wishes to do so. However, at least three disadvantages may be associated with the system. First, it will not image in real time. Second, because coherent waves are used in the system, the images are plagued with the diffraction artifacts which we have been calling ringing and speckle. Finally, the readout is not piezoelectric, and the peak and average intensity levels required for imaging are substantially higher than in the SRI system.

Although a handicap in medical diagnosis, the relative insensitivity of the laser-beam systems may not be a critical factor in nondestructive testing of manufactured parts where high acoustic power can be used without damaging the parts. Thus the Holosonics liquid-surface system may well turn out to be more attractive for industrial examination than it is for medical examination [15]. This same conclusion may also be valid for the Bragg-diffraction imagers [19]. Recent work, with nondestructive testing in mind, has been done at both TRW and UCSB where Bragg-diffraction systems were pulsed and range-gated to provide depth discrimination in a reflection mode of operation. Bragg-diffraction is perhaps the simplest of the real-time orthoscopic imaging methods and, by and large, uses less costly components. Besides

a laser and a sound cell, the only other components needed are two spherical lenses for collimating the laser beam, three cylindrical lenses for focusing it, and an observation screen for viewing the image. In principle, such a system can instantaneously construct optical replicas of any sound field whatsoever, retaining phase information as well as amplitude information.

SUMMARY AND CONCLUSIONS

Orthographic ultrasonic imaging in real time is currently a subject of great interest to many research groups. In the last decade, a number of new systems have been devised, and some have shown sufficient promise to warrent substantial effort in their development. It has long been recognized that acoustic energy can often give a view of an object not available with light. For example, many objects are opaque to light but relatively transparent to sound. In addition, inconsistent biological tissue frequently provides little contrast for optical radiation and even X ray radiation but, as we have seen, excellent contrast for sonic radiation.

The attempt to use sound for imaging has a lengthy history. However, over the last ten years there has been a spurt of research activity in this field, stemming from the advent of the laser and optical holography, and concentrating particularly on orthographic imagers. The work in real-time true-perspective imaging with sound has matured to the extent that several systems are presently being examined in clinical or industrial settings to assess their value in various practical ways. The period of rapid experimental achievement and solid theoretical development seems to have already peaked and is perhaps now on the decline to some extent, but a new period of careful and detailed examination of practical applications and potentialities is in the offing.

Nevertheless, there are still a number of interesting and important problems to be solved. The sensitivity of various systems needs to be improved, especially of those systems being considered for use in medical diagnostics. However, it appears that the solution to this problem is in sight, particularly in view of the demonstrated quality of the images obtainable from systems employing piezo-electric readout. The presence of spurious image elements caused by interference between coherent wave components (ringing and speckle) is a drawback for several of the systems. However, even in this case, a valid solution appears to have been strongly suggested by the success of the systems using noncoherent sound. Other problems, of course, could also be cited, such as those concerning less glamorous aspects of the systems like cost, reliability, complexity, and ease of operation.

The solutions to these problems must be provided, and improvements must be brought about before the full potential of orthographic acoustic imaging will be realized in practical applications. There are many unanswered questions and unexplored techniques to be checked out. Obviously, much work remains to be done. Nevertheless, this work is being done, and it now appears more and more likely that someday we will be able to look back at the present activity and say that it was worthwhile. From what has already been accomplished we can reasonably expect that the new systems will find employment not only in medical diagnosis, acoustic microscopy, and non-destructive testing, the areas emphasized in this paper, but also in such applications as seismic sensing and oceanic search, which have not been covered here.

REFERENCES

It had originally been intended to provide a bibliography of important texts and research papers not specifically included in the 19 citations of this section. However, after assembling the bibliography, it was discovered that all the items listed were members of a much more complete compilation of 376 references contained in [2] and published last year in this TRANSACTIONS. Therefore, rather than providing the new bibliography, it is recommended to those interested in further reading that they consult the very excellent list previously furnished in [2].

[1] Editorial Staff, "An interview with the father of holography," *Optical Spectra*, Vol. 4, No. 9, pp. 32–33, October 1970.

[2] K. R. Erikson, F. J. Fry, and L. P. Jones, "Ultrasound in medicine—A review," *IEEE Trans. Sonics and Ultrasonics*, Vol. SU-21, No. 3, pp. 144–170, July 1974.

[3] S. J. Sokolov, "Ultrasonic microscope," *Akademia Nauk SSSR; Doklady (Tekhnicheskaya Fizika)*, Vol. 64, pp. 333–335, 1949.

[4] J. E. Jacobs and D. A. Peterson, "Advances in the Sokoloff tube," in *Acoustical Holography*, Vol. 5, P. S. Green, Ed. New York: Plenum, 1974, pp. 633–645.

[5] S. J. Sokolov, "Ultrasonic oscillations and their applications," *Techn. Physics USSR*, Vol. 2, p. 522, 1935.

[6] G. Wade, "Recent developments in acoustic holography and imaging," *CRC Critical Reviews in Solid State Sciences*, Vol. 3, Issue 3, pp. 335–372, 1973.

[7] S. J. Sokolov, "Uber die praktische ausnutzung der beugung des lichtes an ultraschallwellen," *Phys. Z.*, Vol. 36, p. 142, 1935.

[8] A. Korpel, "Visualization of the cross-section of a sound beam by Bragg-diffraction of light," *Appl. Phys. Lett.*, Vol. 9, pp. 425–427, Dec. 1966.

[9] H. V. Hance, J. K. Parks and C. S. Tsai, "Optical imaging of a complex ultrasonic-field by diffraction of a laser beam," *J. Appl. Phys.*, Vol. 38, No. 4, pp. 1981–1983, March 1967.

[10] J. Landry, J. Powers, and G. Wade, "Ultrasonic imaging of internal structure by Bragg-diffraction," *Appl. Phys. Lett.*, Vol. 15, pp. 186–188, Sept. 1969.

[11] K. Wang and G. Wade, "Threshold contrast for three real-time acoustic imaging systems," in *Acoustical Holography*, Vol. 5, P. S. Green, Ed. New York: Plenum, 1974, pp. 239–247.

[12] R. A. Lenoms and C. F. Quate, "Acoustic microscope—Scanning version," *Appl. Phys. Lett.*, Vol. 24, No. 4, pp. 163–165, Feb. 1974.

[13] L. W. Kessler, P. R. Palermo, and A. Korpel, "Practical high-resolution acoustic microscopy," in *Acoustical Holography*, Vol. 4, G. Wade, Ed. New York: Plenum, 1972, pp. 51–71.

[14] P. S. Green, L. F. Schaefer, E. D. Jones, and J. R. Suarez, "A new, high-performance ultrasonic camera," in *Acoustical Holography*, Vol. 5, P. S. Green, Ed. New York: Plenum, 1974, pp. 493–503.

[15] B. B. Brenden, "Real-time acoustical imaging by means of liquid-surface holography," in *Acoustical Holography*, Vol. 4, G. Wade, Ed. New York: Plenum, 1972, pp. 1–9.

[16] G. W. Stroke, W. E. Kock, Y. Kikuchi, and J. Tsujiuchi, Eds., *Ultrasonic Imaging and Holography*, New York: Plenum, 1974.

[17] K. R. Erikson, B. J. O'Loughlin, J. J. Flynn, E. J. Pisa, J. E. Wreede, R. E. Greer, B. Stauffer, and A. F. Metherell, "Through-transmission acoustical holography for medical imaging—A status report," presented at the Sixth International Symposium on Acoustical Holography and Imaging, San Diego, California, February 1975. (To be published in *Acoustical Holography*, Vol. 6, N. O. Booth, Ed. New York: Plenum.)

[18] A. F. Metherell, "Linearized subfringe interferometric holography," in *Acoustical Holography*, Vol. 5, P. S. Green, Ed. New York: Plenum, 1974, pp. 41–58.

[19] G. Wade, H. Keyani, and S. C. Pei, "New experiments and analysis in Bragg-diffraction imaging," *IEEE Trans. on Computers*, Vol. c-24, No. 4, pp. 395–401, April 1975.

Signal Processing in Acoustic Imaging

PATRICK N. KEATING, TAKEO SAWATARI, AND GENE ZILINSKAS

Abstract—A review of signal processing methods which can be used to improve the effectiveness of systems designed for acoustic imaging and bearing estimation is presented. Topics covered include a) signal processing for increased resolution, b) the processing of stochastic acoustic signals, c) image processing, enhancement, and pattern recognition. The discussion of resolution processing includes lateral resolution improvement by both superresolution techniques and aperture synthesis, and improvement of both range and Doppler resolution. The stochastic signal-processing section addresses adaptive processing, as well as methods of imaging in the case of incoherent, noisy signals.

I. INTRODUCTION

ACOUSTIC imaging is a field which has grown considerably over the past ten years, and which has important applications in medicine, nondestructive testing, and in underwater and undersea applications. Acoustic imaging can be conveniently divided into a) active imaging (where a transmitter produces acoustic energy which is either reflected from, or transmitted through, the object of interest) and b) passive imaging, where the object itself is the source of the acoustic energy. Its use ranges from the submillimeter distances of acoustic microscopy to hundreds of miles in some passive sonar applications. Correspondingly, the frequencies employed vary from the gigahertz range down to a few hertz, and the wavelengths from a few micrometers to thousands of meters.

In almost all cases, the imagery obtained by acoustic radiation is clearly inferior to the imagery we are all familiar with via optical radiation. The primary reason for this is the longer wavelengths of acoustic radiation, which means that available apertures are normally considerably smaller than optical apertures in terms of wavelengths. As a result, signal-processing techniques to obtain improved resolution have long been of considerable interest.

Again, the noise environment in acoustical imaging is often severe, and significant effort has gone into signal processing for the extraction of imaging data from noise. On the other hand, because of the low-propagation velocities, acoustic signals can be gated to provide range discrimination, and signal-processing techniques have frequently been used to improve performance in this area.

Not only are signal-processing methods necessary and desirable in acoustic imaging, but they are also more readily implemented. The linear detectors available for acoustic radiation allow more signal-processing possibilities to be implemented than in the optical case, where square-law detection, without phase information, is the general rule. For example, in the acoustic case, the frequency of the acoustic return can readily be determined, and, hence, Doppler shifts and information about the velocity of a given object. Again, signal-processing techniques can be used to enhance this process, or to make it compatible with other requirements. Furthermore, the linear detection feature makes approaches which use cross correlation between the signals obtained from the different detectors particularly useful for stochastic signals, especially in processing for passive systems. This same feature also allows sophisticated adaptive processing (i.e., processing which adapts to different noise environments) to be implemented. Finally, image processing and pattern-recognition techniques which are common to optical imaging have also been used in the acoustic case.

The scope of this paper is such that acoustic imaging is taken to include one-dimensional imaging (such as bearing estimation in Navy applications) and three- and four-dimensional imaging, as well as the more familiar two-dimensional images analogous to visual imagery. We include sonar bearing estimation techniques along with more conventional imaging methods because we believe that each of these fields can learn from the other in many important ways, especially in the area of signal processing. The companion papers in this issue treat the different subclasses of acoustic imaging in some detail, and, therefore, this paper will ignore applications and will spend very little time on the image formation process, only discussing it briefly in order to show its impact on the signal-processing options available. Because it is the subject of a companion article in this issue, the processing techniques used with acoustic tomography will not be included in this paper, except when they are of more general significance. The extensive signal processing associated with certain seismic applications will also not be included in the scope of this paper. The emphasis here will be on advanced signal-processing methods which can be used to improve the effectiveness of systems for acoustic imaging and bearing estimation.

We believe that the main point to be made regarding the future of signal processing in acoustic imaging is as follows. On the one hand, signal processing can significantly improve the imagery obtained by means of acoustic radiation; and, on the other hand, it is becoming easier to implement because of the revolution in digital electronics. We believe that the microprocessor revolution will have an enormous impact on the field, especially on imaging systems in which the image is formed digitally, and cite the example of X-ray computerized axial-tomography as an indication of the substantial improvements which may be possible.

II. IMAGE-FORMATION

The propagation of acoustic radiation between the object and the detector, or array of detectors, produces a transformation of the spatial information. All imaging systems with lateral resolution (except for the trivial case of proximity

Manuscript received May 4, 1978; revised August 21, 1978.
P. N. Keating and T. Sawatari are with Bendix Research Laboratories, Southfield, MI 48076.
G. Zilinskas is with Bendix Electrodynamics Division, Sylmar, CA 91342.

Reprinted from *Proc. IEEE*, vol. 67, pp. 496–510, Apr. 1979.

imaging) require some means for inverting this transformation produced by propagation. In the near field, this is a complicated convolution transformation. However, in the Fresnel region and in the far field, this transformation simplifies to essentially a Fourier transform (with additional quadratic phase terms in the Fresnel-zone case). In other words, except in the very near field, the image distribution is

$$I(x) = C \exp\left(\frac{ik}{2R}\, x^2\right) \int d^2 y\, H(y) \exp\left(\frac{ik}{2R}\, y^2\right)$$
$$\cdot \exp\left(\frac{-ik}{R}\, x \cdot y\right) \quad (1)$$

where x is a two-dimensional vector in the image plane, y is a two-dimensional vector in the system input plane, $H(y)$ is the field distribution on this input plane, R is the distance between object and input plane, $k = 2\pi/\lambda$ is the wave vector for the radiation used, and C is a constant. The input plane of a system is a plane in the acoustic medium immediately prior to any processing (e.g., the hologram plane in a holographic system, the array-plane in a phased array system or a plane prior to the lens in a lens-imaging system). Means for inverting the transformation include shaped transducers and lenses (which carry out an inverse transform in the acoustic domain), optical holographic reconstruction (an inverse transform in the optical domain), and computer reconstruction, time-delay beamforming, etc., which involve inverse transforms in the electrical domain. As in all imaging systems, the basic lateral resolution available is determined by the dimensions of the aperture in wavelengths; i.e., the minimum geometrical separation of two point-images in quadrature phase relation is given by

$$\delta = \frac{\lambda R}{D} \quad (2)$$

where D is the diameter of the aperture. However, we can often reduce sidelobe effects on image quality by sacrificing the resolution mentioned above. This can be done by shading or apodizing the aperture of the system [1]. The opposite process, sacrificing sidelobe reduction to increase resolution, is that of superresolution, discussed in Section III-A. Other methods of increasing lateral resolution are also described in Section III-A.

Many acoustic-imaging systems not only employ the lateral discrimination common in optical systems, but, because of the low acoustic velocity, also utilize range discrimination by means of time-gated ranging. A-scan systems use nothing but ranging (and are not really imaging systems), while B-scan and C-scan systems utilize both range discrimination and one dimension of lateral discrimination [2]. More complex systems may use more dimensions of discrimination, or resolution, sometimes including frequency discrimination, i.e., Doppler resolution. Signal-processing techniques for improving range and Doppler resolution are described in Section III-B.

It is not the purpose of this paper to discuss the image-formation process in any detail. However, it is necessary to take it into account when discussing signal processing, since the image-formation process impacts the type of signal processing which can be done. For example, if the image formation is carried out in the acoustic [3], [4] or optical domain [5]–[8], a great deal of sophisticated signal-processing is inappropriate. In general, it is only when the image

is formed in the electrical domain (and preferably digitally) that significant signal processing can conveniently be carried out.

The most flexible approach to the formation of images and use of signal-processing methods is to digitize the data from the acoustic array and to use a digital computer to reconstruct the image. It was recognized quite early that only one Fourier transform is necessary in the Fresnel and far-field regions [9], [10], although several workers have used more complicated convolution methods using two transforms [11], [12]. One recent development which may impact this area is the development of new Fourier transform algorithms which require fewer multiplications than the FFT, such as the work of Winograd [13]. However, we believe that these may not have significant impact because there is a corresponding increase in program complexity and number-shifting overhead which makes their advantages marginal.

Other image-formation methods used in the electrical domain include analog processing [14], the use of surface-acoustic-wave devices [15], and charge-transfer devices [16]. However, digital processing is by far the most flexible approach and the most suitable for implementing performance improvements via signal processing. Moreover, the rapid advances made in microcomputer technology tend to indicate that digital signal processing will be an extremely important part of the future in acoustic imaging.

The image-formation methods described above are appropriate when the medium between the detector and the object is homogeneous. If, however, the medium is inhomogeneous, or if the inhomogeneity of the medium is itself the property to be measured, acoustic tomography is now available. This method (also called "algebraic reconstruction") [17]–[19] is a technique to calculate the spatial distribution of refractive-index or acoustic-velocity from time-of-flight and amplitude-profile data by dividing the space into small cells. Computer-aided tomography has had considerable success in radiography and it is expected that this technique will soon be important in acoustics. However, we shall not discuss it in this review because it is the subject of a companion paper.

III. Signal Processing for Resolution

This section consists of a discussion of improvements in system resolution which can be obtained by signal processing. While the term "resolution" often tends to carry with it the meaning lateral resolution, we intend it to also include range resolution and Doppler (i.e., velocity) resolution, and these will be discussed in a subsection below. It is also convenient to have separate subsections on synthetic aperture methods and superresolution techniques, although both are directed towards increased lateral resolution. Signal processing which increases lateral resolution is particularly important in acoustic imaging because apertures (in terms of wavelengths) are normally very much smaller than those available in optical imaging.

A. Lateral Resolution Processing

Before any extended discussion of aperture synthesis or superresolution, it is important to address the need to make proper use of the full resolution obtainable from the acoustic aperture. While this might appear to be a minor point, there are some subtleties involved which are not well known.

If a one-dimensional aperture contains N equally spaced linear detectors or N equally spaced sampling points, then

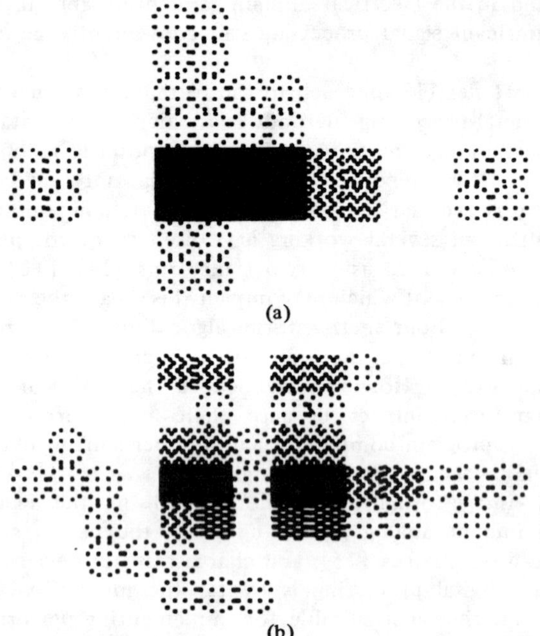

(a)

(b)

Fig. 1. Experimental imagery obtained for two coherent point sources in antiphase via (a) 20 × 20 intensity display and (b) 40 × 40 interpolated intensity display. The two points which are not resolved in (a) are clearly resolved in (b) (after Keating *et al.* [20]).

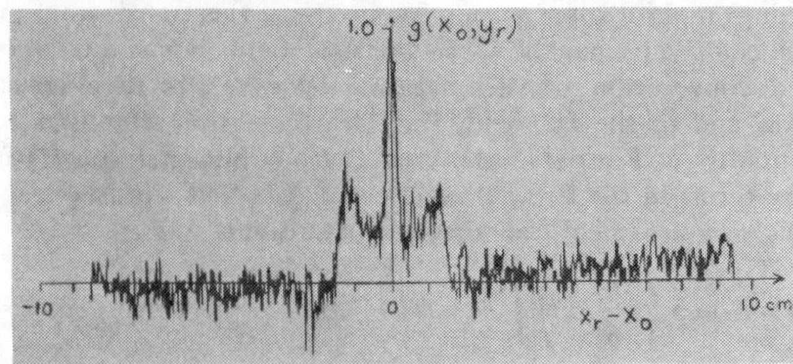

Fig. 2. A reconstructed image of a point reflector obtained by a medical imaging system equivalent to side-looking radar (courtesy of M. L. Dick *et al.* [26]).

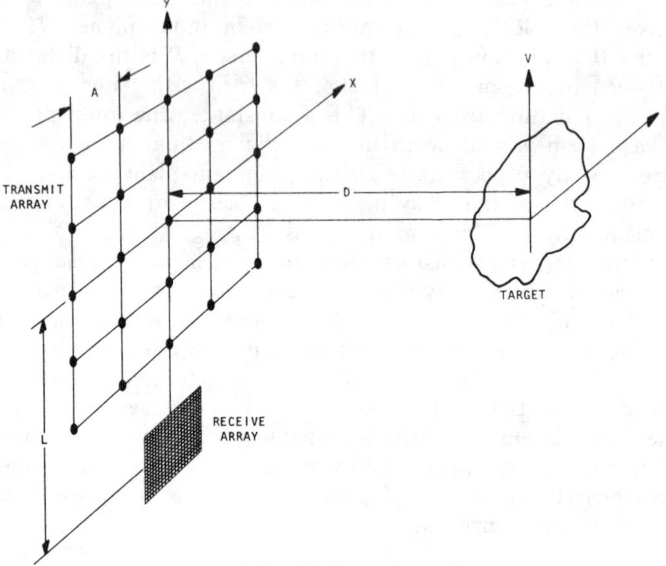

Fig. 3. Synthetic aperture geometry using square receiver and square transmitter arrays.

there are $2N$ words of input information (phase and amplitude) for each frequency band.[1] If this is processed to form an image by straightforward methods (e.g., an FFT), one normally ends up with $2N$ output words of information (again phase and amplitude). No information has been lost. However, most imaging systems display only intensity and thus N words of information are the final output. Half of the information has been lost. By examining the Rayleigh criterion, one may readily show [20], [21] that there should be twice as many points in the intensity display, spaced half as far apart as in a phase/amplitude display. One then ends up with the required $2N$ output words and the full resolution capability of the acoustic aperture which is being used.

The experimental results shown in Fig. 1 demonstrate this point. In Fig. 1(a), it can be noted that the two sources cannot be resolved in the 20 × 20 intensity display, even though their separation is slightly greater than the Rayleigh distance and they are in antiphase. The limitation lies in the display, as Fig. 1(b) shows, and not in the system aperture. The image display shown in Fig. 1(b) was obtained from exactly the same array data as that in Fig. 1(a) and the only difference in processing was interpolation to obtain the 40 × 40 display. The two sources are clearly resolved in the interpolated image display. A more detailed exposition of this point is given in [20].

1) Synthetic-Aperture Processing: One way to improve lateral resolution without a full increase in the number of receiver elements is to synthesize a receiver aperture which is larger than the actual aperture. Two different approaches can be noted: a) the receiver aperture is synthesized by motion of either the object, or the receiver, or the transmitter, or any

two of these [16]–[20], b) the receiver aperture is synthesized by multiplexing transmitters, so that no motion is involved [21]–[24].

The most common version of the first approach is, of course, the direct acoustic equivalent [22]–[26] of side-looking radar. In other words, a transmitter and detector, or detector array, are mounted on a vehicle which moves at constant velocity at a fixed distance from an object plane. Fig. 2 shows an image formed by this technique by Dick *et al.* [26]— a point target which was generated by the acoustic equivalent of side-looking radar. The point target was placed at 5.0 cm from the detector plane in which a single detector was scanned linearly. The length of the original pulse was 0.28 cm and the dimension of the detection aperture was 1.0 cm. The width of the point image is 0.3 cm and the sidelobes fall off to zero at ±2.0 cm. These results match the theoretically predicted results. Other versions have been analyzed [27] but have not been significantly used. However, because of the relatively slow propagation velocity, synthetic-aperture sonar encounters ambiguity problems not present in synthetic-aperture radar, and these severely limit the area search-rate unless steps are taken to remove them [25]. Possible steps include a) the use of arrays of detectors to increase the coverage and b) the use of different codes on successive pings, so that the pulse-repetition rate and vehicle velocity can be increased without ambiguities. Another potential problem is the fact that acoustic media (the ocean, in particular) are

---

[1] In the case of square-law detection, only N words are obtained. However, half of the image space is then occupied by the conjugate image, and thus only $N/2$ nonredundant words are output in an intensity display, and the need for doubling of the display sampling is still present.

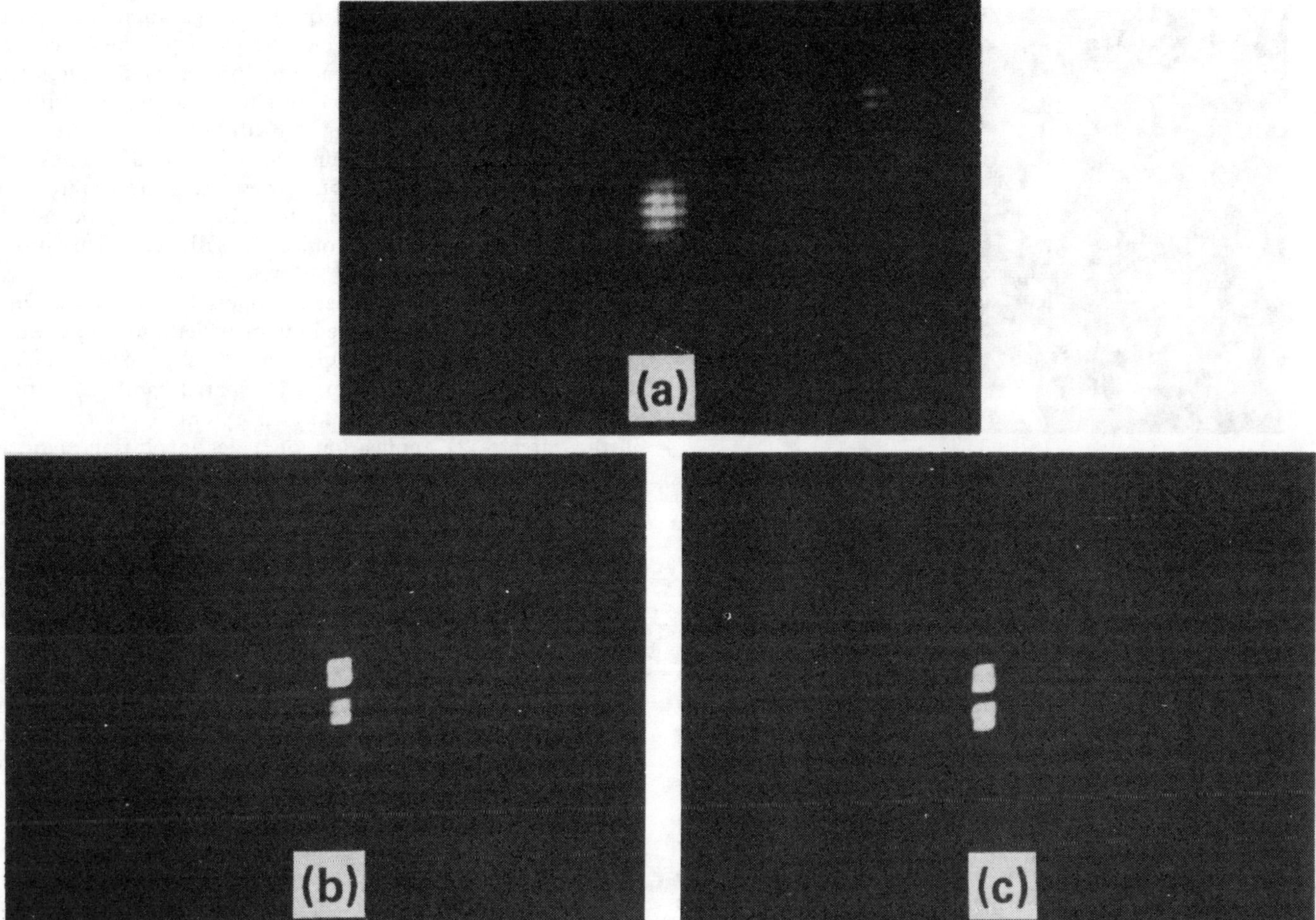

Fig. 4. Reconstructed images by 10 × 10 receiver array hologram (top), by synthetic aperture (20 × 20) hologram (left) and by 20 × 20 receiver array hologram (right) with a single transmitter (after Keating *et al.* [30]).

generally less ideal than air is as a microwave medium. However, tests have shown that the ocean appears to be sufficiently stable to allow substantial apertures to be synthesized [32].

The simplest version of transmitter-multiplexed aperture synthesis is the Wells cross [28], which uses a vertical array of receivers and a horizontal transmitter array. Another geometry (Fig. 3) which has been used several times [27]–[31], primarily for cost-reduction, is that of a square-receiver array and a large-transmitter array with few elements. For example, if receiver channels are $50 each and transmitter channels are $200 each, a real 96 × 96 receive aperture is $461 000, whereas a 24 × 24 receive array and a 4 × 4 transmitter array synthesizes the same aperture for $32 000. A Well's cross of 96 receivers and 96 transmitters is $24 000. However, it must be noted that, unless the target is stationary (or perhaps moving at known velocity), it is necessary to pulse all transmitters simultaneously and, therefore, each transmitter pulse must be coded so that its contribution at each detector can be separated from the others. It is, therefore, impractical to have too many transmitters, and 32 × 32 receivers and 3 × 3 transmitters (at $53 000) are probably more practical for synthesis of the 96 × 96 aperture. An early experiment sin this area [29] was unsuccessful because there are phase shifts which must be compensated for, but cannot practically be removed using optical reconstruction. With digital processing, however, this phase compensation can be carried out easily [30]. A typical example of the

reconstructed imagery obtained with phase-compensated aperture-synthesis is shown in Fig. 4. The target was two small glass-shell spheres (3 cm in diameter) with a separation of 4 cm. Fig. 4(a) shows the reconstructed image obtained from a small hologram (10 × 10 array). The lateral resolution expected with this aperture is 8 cm in terms of the Rayleigh criterion. With this resolution, the two points are unresolved by this limited aperture. Fig. 4(b) shows the synthesized image formed by the coherent superposition of four images obtained by 10 × 10 receiver array with each of four transmitters; one of them is Fig. 4(a). A successfully synthesized image should be equivalent to the image obtained by a single 20 × 20 array hologram. Fig. 4(c) shows the reconstructed images of the same target using a real 20 × 20 array hologram, which gives a resolution of 4 cm.

An interesting variation using this geometry is that of Nitadori [31], [33] where a large unfilled transmitter array is used as a phased array to produce a set of high-resolution beams which may be regarded as grating lobes. The smaller filled receiver aperture receives the return signal from the several highly localized regions illuminated by the grating lobes, and can, via reconstruction, discriminate among the contributions from the different localized regions because of the small detector spacing. The set of grating lobe beams is then scanned over a range equal to the distance between adjacent lobes by electrical phasing of the transmitter array. This approach has several advantages, including reduced

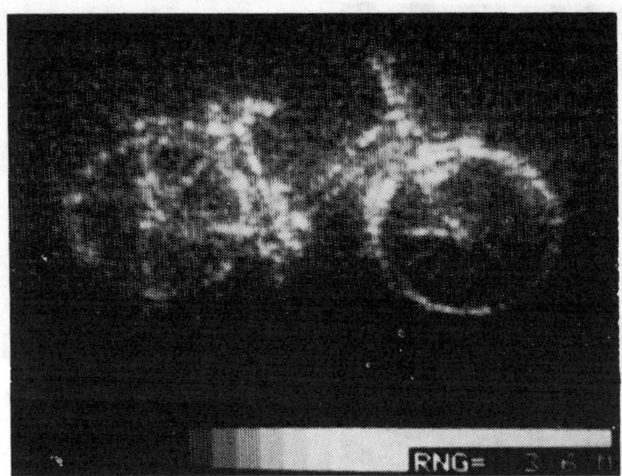

Fig. 5. Underwater image of a bicycle using Nitadori's synthetic aperture system (courtesy of K. Mano and K. Nitadori [33]).

dependence on mechanical stability of the transmitter/receiver platform and reduced sensitivity to phase shifts due to the medium and to motion of the object. Imagery obtained in this manner is shown in Fig. 5. The picture consists of 256×256 picture elements and the Rayleigh resolution is 3 cm (measured) at a range of 4.3 m. The main disadvantage of this approach is that phasing of the transmitter array is somewhat tricky; however, this may not be a serious problem.

2) Superresolution Processing: When more than two discrete objects or targets are within the classical limit of the resolution of the system, conventional image formation techniques are usually not able to separate the targets nor to determine their locations to an accuracy within the resolution. Because of the limited apertures available in acoustic imaging, approaches to increase the resolution via signal processing (i.e., superresolution techniques) are of significant interest. Three different classes of method can be noted: a) analytic continuation methods, b) multiplicative (cross-sensor) methods, and c) entropy-maximization methods.

Di Francia [34] first suggested the possibility of super-resolution in optics. Since then, several investigators have proposed various superresolution techniques. Harris [35], for example, has established an analytic continuation method based on sampling theory. A similar approach has been proposed by Barnes [36] and Frieden [37]. They have developed a technique based on expanding the aperture function in terms of prolate spheroidal wave functions, which are a set of band-limited functions whose finite Fourier transform is proportional to the same function. However, all of these approaches are known to be more or less equally noise sensitive; e.g., if we want to increase the resolution 3 times more than the classic resolution while maintaining the field of view to one resolution element of the original array, Harris' approach requires at least a 30-dB signal-to-noise ratio in the original signal. Yet we can only expect the signal-to-noise amplitude ratio in the restored data to be around 0.7.

Because of the high noise sensitivity, the above techniques have not been used to gain lateral resolution in acoustic-imaging systems. However, a method recently proposed by Gerchberg [38] is designed to be more robust against noisy environments. This approach, called the error-energy reduction method, is an extension of Harris' method. With this method, the input (far-field holographic) data are first Fourier transformed to yield the conventional image. The image is

then modified by setting all of the image points outside the known extent of the true object to zero.[2] The image thus modified is Fourier transformed to form a far-field hologram over a larger aperture than originally available, with the original hologram data being substituted only where it was available (i.e., over the original aperture) and the new data being used outside this region. These steps are iterated until a criterion based on the estimated object energy outside the known extent of the true object is satisfied. This process has been shown to converge [39].

A similar approach has been proposed to obtain accurate bearing estimation of localized targets when they are clustered [40]. This method, developed specifically for sonar applications, involves three steps: 1) spatial-bandpass filtering to reject noise outside the known extent (clustered region) of the targets, 2) application of a deconvolution algorithm which is identical to Harris' analytic continuation method, and 3) application of a Bendix adaptive null-processing technique (see Section IV). This method was designed to be rapid and relatively robust against noise. This method and Gerchberg's improve the noise tolerance over Harris' by as much as the array gain if the object region of interest is one resolution element (one beamwidth).

The cross-sensor (multiplicative) approach has been used in the acoustics field by several workers [41]-[43] and does increase the resolution in a certain sense. However, because convolution in the holographic plane is equivalent to multiplication in the image plane, this process is almost identical to the trivial process of multiplying the image by itself, and thus analogous to the use of high-gamma film in photography to increase contrast. In other words, we do not believe that cross-sensor multiplicative approaches to superresolution are of significant value since the same effect can be obtained more rapidly by multiplication in the image domain.

The most interesting recent development in the field of superresolution is the application of maximum-entropy techniques, used earlier in power-spectrum estimation, to the imaging problem. This approach is an almost entirely statistical approach and may be regarded as an extension of maximum-likelihood estimation (MLE) discussed later in Section IV-A. In fact, the original reason for the maximum-entropy approach to imaging problems was as an estimation technique based on relatively fundamental work by Jaynes [44]. It is included in this section rather than in Section IV only because it produces important superresolution effects. One of the best descriptions of this approach in the field of optical imaging is that by Frieden [45]. Frieden has shown that Jaynes' work leads to the conclusion that the maximum-likelihood image distribution based on specific known data is the image distribution with maximum entropy, i.e., the image distribution which can be obtained in the largest number of ways. Furthermore, he shows that this image distribution estimated via maximum entropy is not intrinsically band limited and can therefore, in principle, provide superresolution.

Solution of the problem involves maximizing the sum of the object entropy and the noise entropy, subject to the constraints that the result is consistent with the measured data. The object entropy, for example, is defined by $-\Sigma_j O_j \ln O_j$, where O_j is the object intensity in the jth pixel and is always

---

[2] It should be noted that the necessary condition for application of this technique, as well as the others mentioned above, is that the object is significantly smaller than the field-of-view of the system.

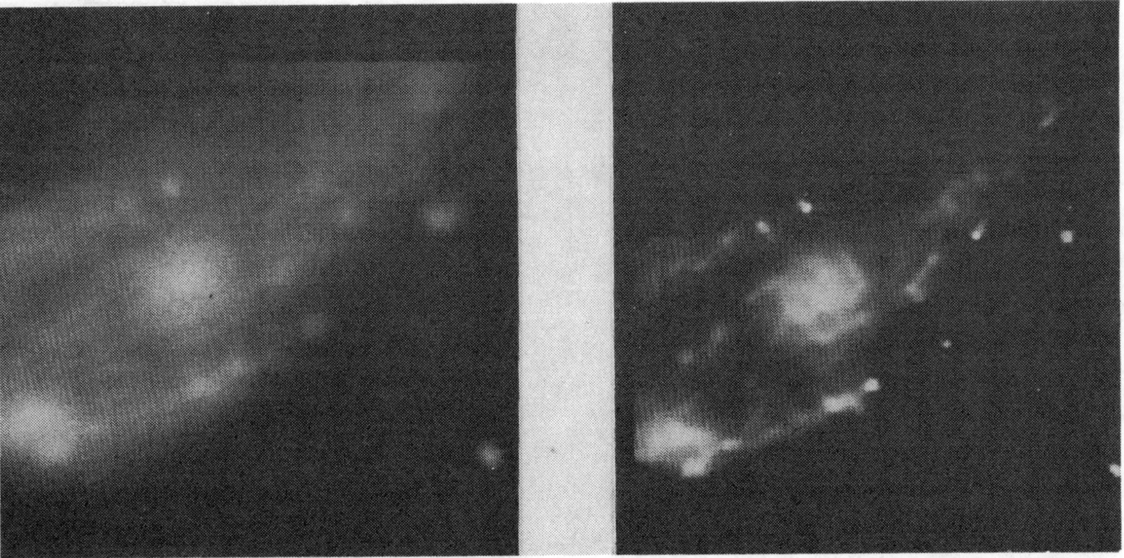

Fig. 6. Superresolution processing improvements in optical imagery. Left, the "Bird" nebula, Kitt Peak National Observatory data, blurred by atmospheric turbulence. Right, maximum entropy restoration of "Bird." The spread function was estimated from the lower-right star-image data (courtesy of B. R. Frieden).

positive or zero. The formal solution for M-image pixels and J pixels in the "restored" object ($J > M$) is [45]

$$\hat{O}_j = \exp\left[-1 - \mu - \sum_{m=1}^{M} \lambda_m S(y_m, x_j)\right], \quad j = 1, 2, \cdots, J \tag{3}$$

for the restored object intensity value in the jth pixel, and

$$\hat{N}_m = \exp\left[-1 - \lambda_m/\rho\right], \quad m = 1, 2, \cdots, M \tag{4}$$

for the mth noise value (biased so that $N_m > 0$ always). Here, μ and the λ_m are Lagrange multipliers determined from the constraint equations

$$I_m = \sum_{j=1}^{J} \hat{O}_j S(y_m, x_j) + \hat{N}_m - B, \quad m = 1, \cdots, M \tag{5}$$

$$P_0 = \sum_{j=1}^{J} \hat{O}_j \tag{6}$$

x_j and y_m are locations of the jth object cell and the mth image cell, respectively, S is the normalized point-spread function for the system, B is the bias on N_m, I_m is the mth measured image intensity value, P_0 is the total intensity, and ρ is a free parameter representing the signal-to-noise uncertainty which is acceptable. Solution of (3)–(6) requires digital computation, e.g., by using the Newton–Raphson method.

Actual examples of superresolution are provided by Frieden [45] and, earlier, by Biraud [46]. A striking example from astronomical optics is shown in Fig. 6. This figure shows an optical image of the "Bird" nebula, blurred by atmospheric turbulence. The 100×100 array of data was enlarged to 200×200 by the maximum-entropy method.

We believe that maximum-entropy processing will be of significant value in acoustic imaging, both as an application of optical imaging methods to acoustics and as an extension of the MLE techniques to more complex object or target distributions (see Section IV-A).

B. Range and Doppler Resolution

Because the velocity of sound is relatively low, signal gating or other temporal processing can readily provide good range resolution, a fact which has been used for many years in the field of sonar. For the same reason, substantial Doppler shifts can occur, which allow effective Doppler (or radial velocity) resolution to be obtained by appropriate processing.

Thus there are four different dimensions in which acoustic imaging or sonar systems can provide resolution and discrimination. Most acoustical imaging and sonar systems provide resolution in two of these dimensions and some provide three-dimensional resolution [47]. An example of three-dimensional imagery is shown in Fig. 7. A system with four-dimensional resolution is possible and in fact has been tested in the laboratory [48].

On the other hand, the simultaneous achievement of both range and Doppler resolution is not a simple matter. Range resolution requires relatively precise *time* information whereas Doppler resolution requires relatively precise *frequency* information. For a simple pulse, there is, of course, a sort of uncertainty principle

$$\text{TBW} = \Delta f \Delta t \sim 1 \tag{7}$$

which makes these two requirements conflict, where TBW is the time–bandwidth product for the pulse. In fact, in many practical systems which require both range and Doppler resolution, this problem is evaded by sending two pulses, a wide-band pulse (e.g., an FM chirp) to obtain range information and a long CW pulse to get the velocity information.

However, it is possible to obtain more elegant (though not always more efficient) solutions to this problem by using complex chirps or correlation processing and coded, large time–bandwidth product waveforms [47]–[50]. In this latter method, a coded waveform is transmitted and correlated with its replica after receipt. If the autocorrelation function has a single sharp peak, even when Doppler shifts are present, then simultaneous sharp range and Doppler resolution can be obtained. In general, however, there are several peaks and ambiguity problems arise. As a result, there is a whole literature on this subject in the radar field.

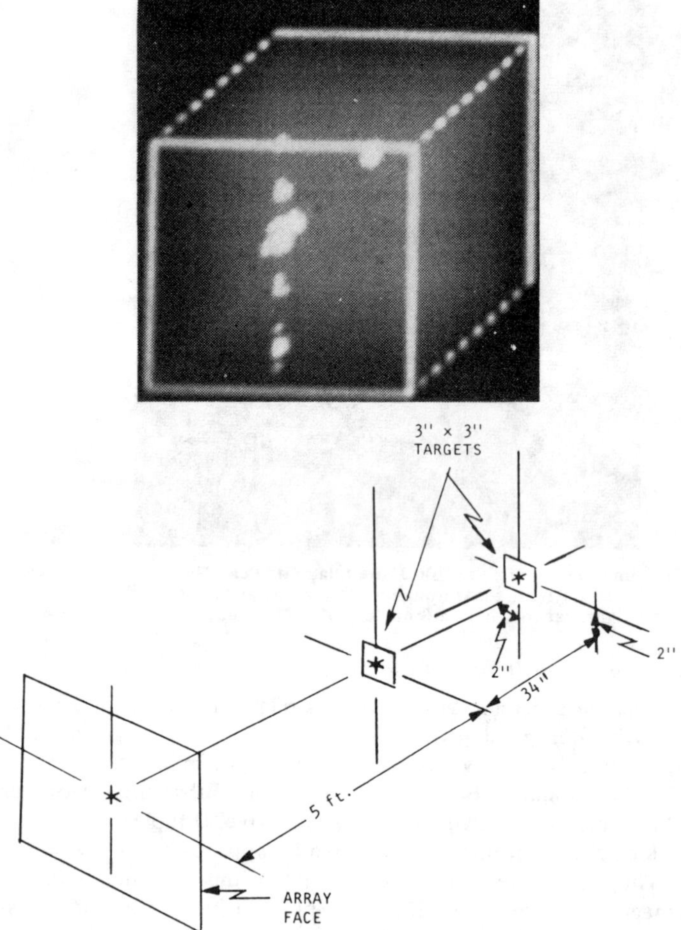

Fig. 7. Three-dimensional acoustic imaging. Top, geometry of acoustic array and two targets. Bottom, reconstructed image. Note that sidelobes of the front target are seen (after Koppelmann and Keating [47]).

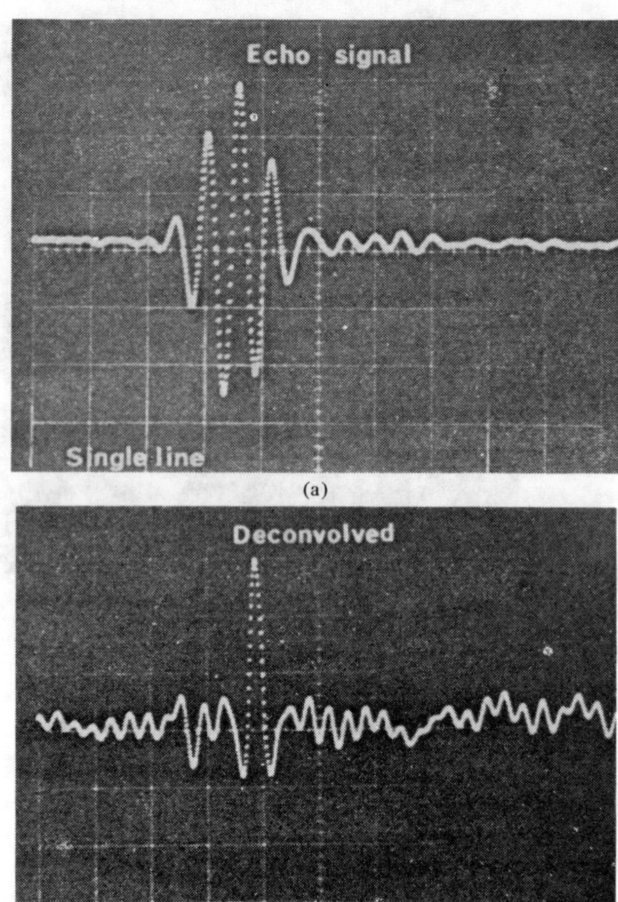

Fig. 8. Demonstration of deconvolution of A-scan signals: (a) the echo signal; (b) the output of the deconvolution filter (courtesy of D. E. Robinson and B. G. Williams [54]).

Doppler-only processing has been used primarily in medical imaging applications [51] and sonar [52]. Doppler resolution can be used to measure velocity (e.g., blood flow) or can be used to provide moving target (MTI) displays, where only moving objects or targets are presented in the display, and stationary interference is eliminated.

Range-only resolution can readily be obtained with minimal signal processing by using short pulses. It can readily be shown that the range resolution depends almost entirely on the signal bandwidth, even for complex, large time–bandwidth signals. The shorter a simple pulse, the larger the bandwidth, and the better the range resolution. The ultimate limitation on bandwidth is usually imposed by the bandwidth of the transmitter or receiver transducers, which are often resonant devices. For a given bandwidth, the resolution can be improved somewhat by nonlinear processing (e.g., thresholding) and deconvolution [53]–[56], as shown in Fig. 8. In this result, the original echo signal from a single reflector (stainless-steel wire) was spread more than 1 μs. On the other hand, the deconvolved signal was obtained through a filter which collapses the echo from a single target into a spike much narrower in width. The use of such simple pulses (with time–bandwidth products of around unity) is not, however, always the most effective approach. The peak transmitted power is often limited (e.g., by cavitation) and, therefore, so is the total energy if a short pulse is used. Using pulse-compression processing, a long wide-band signal can provide just as good range resolution as a simple short pulse. However, the long pulse allows the system to transmit a great deal more energy, thus improving the signal-to-noise situation considerably. Waveforms commonly used include FM chirps [57], Barker codes [20], pseudo-random codes [48], and Gaussian noise [50], [58].

It must be noted that in a system with lateral resolution, improved range resolution is not always obtained at zero cost. A short pulse incident on the receiver array at an angle does not reach all the elements at the same time. Unless time-delay beam-forming is used, the gating will result in some of the outer elements not "seeing" the pulse, resulting in reduced effective aperture and reduced resolution for off-axis objects. However, this effect has been analyzed [20], and does not impose serious problems in most cases. The B-scan system developed by Thurstone and Von Ramm [59], for example, is constructed to provide both high lateral resolution and high range resolution. In this system, a linear array is used to focus the transmitted beam and to scan the focus point longitudinally so that the return signal from the focus point, received with an appropriate time gating, forms an image point with high lateral and longitudinal resolution. Similarly, the results obtained by Koppelmann and Keating [47] show no observable degradation of the lateral resolution.

It should also be noted that better range resolution tends to mean that more information must be stored, handled, and displayed.

IV. STOCHASTIC SIGNAL PROCESSING

Many acoustic imaging systems utilize coherent acoustic radiation, usually via active techniques using either pulse-modulated CW, or broad-band coherent signals, such as FM chirps or even pseudo-random codes (see previous section). On the other hand, there are many usually passive[3] systems in which the received radiation is incoherent in the sense that it is not deterministic according to some model known by the system. Such systems frequently operate in a very poor signal-to-noise environment, and the extensive signal processing necessary to retrieve an acceptable version of the signal is a major area of concern and study.

Major applications of the imaging of stochastic signal sources include the diagnostics of machinery-generated noise and the passive acoustic surveillance of both underwater and surface vessels. Another area, which will not be considered here, is in the processing of seismic data. Two main topics will be considered in this section: a) the imaging of stochastic sources, and b) adaptive methods for handling nonstationary environments of stochastic interferences.

A. Stochastic Source Imaging

There are basically two widely used types of methods for imaging the sources of incoherent acoustic radiation. The first of these is basically one of cross correlation, with a number of quite sophisticated variations which are referenced in the next paragraph. The second, MLE, is an entirely statistical approach to the problem, and is of primary value for cases where the signal-to-noise situation is poor, as it frequently is in cases of interest.

In its simplest form, the cross correlation technique involves measuring the linear signal received at two hydrophones and finding the delay time between the signals which maximizes the cross correlate [60]. For a single far-field source, this will define a one-dimensional bearing, apart from an inversion ambiguity (i.e., ambiguity over which side of the line joining the detectors the signal came from). In general, of course, the source distribution is more complex and such a simple approach is no longer applicable. An extension of this approach to complex object distributions is provided by the Van Cittert–Zernike theorem [61], which relates the coherence between two different points within a frequency band to the distribution of sources of radiation in that band. This approach has been used experimentally in acoustic imaging [62], as well as an extension of it using polyspectra [63].

The second major technique, the MLE approach, can be introduced by noting that in a highly stochastic situation a high degree of uncertainty is present. Different measurements of, say, bearing made at different times, or use of different parts of the spectrum, will be different in such a stochastic situation. The MLE approach allows these different measurements or estimates to be integrated in an orderly fashion into an overall estimate. The basic principle [64] is to maximize the "likelihood function" $p(x|\theta)$, which

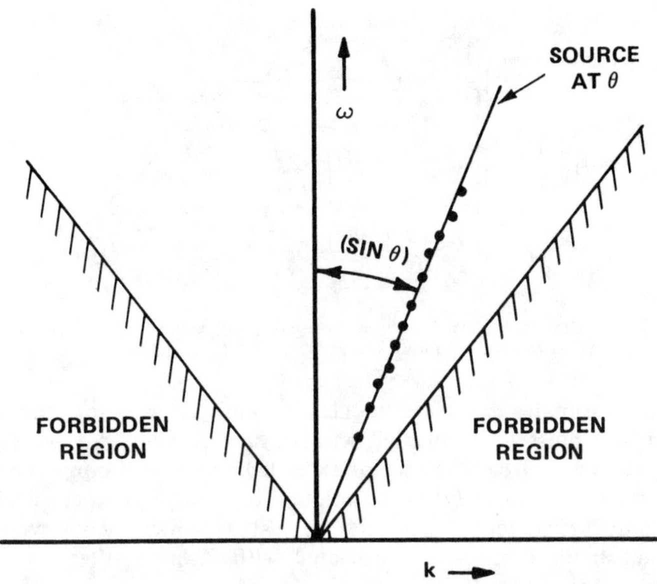

Fig. 9. Energy distribution in $k - \omega$ space. The forbidden region is unphysical because it would require either violation of the dispersion relation $\omega = ck$, where c is the velocity of sound, or of the inequality sin $\theta < 1$ (courtesy of R. K. Mueller).

is the conditional probability density of a measured input data vector x given a source at bearing θ.

A typical example follows from the simple two-sensor cross correlation approach mentioned in the second paragraph of this subsection. If we have an array of sensors whose number is significantly larger than two, then we will get a time-delay (and, therefore, bearing) estimate for each sensor-pair. The MLE approach is aimed at integrating all of these estimates into one 'good' estimate by maximizing the likelihood, or, more often, its logarithmn. The theory also shows that a lower bound, known as the Cramer–Rao bound, to the mean-square error in the final estimate is realizable. Further details of this technique may be found in [64]–[65] and in the bibliography there.

The basic MLE approach works best with a single object or target and fairly isotropic interference. If plane-wave interference is present, then the basic process must be modified so as to first eliminate the plane-wave interference [64]. However, one can imagine the MLE philosophy being extended to include a more complex target distribution, when it would become, in essence, the maximum-entropy approach discussed in Section II-A2. In this case, the plane-wave interference would probably not need to be removed. We believe that work in this direction will be very fruitful.

Another recent approach to optimum bearing estimation is the so-called $k - \omega$ approach [69], which utilizes peaks in the energy distribution in $k - \omega$ space generated via a two-dimensional Fourier transform from detector-position and time to wave-vector and frequency. In other words, estimates of the bearing of a source with a wide frequency spectrum or a multiple-line spectrum can be improved by finding a "best-fit" line through the distribution in $k - \omega$ space, the angle of this line giving the sine of the bearing. This is shown in Fig. 9. It has recently been noted [69] that the MLE approach is equivalent to forming a 'best' estimate by a linear combination of estimates obtained from the $k - \omega$ peaks.

A further extension of these ideas arises in the case of a moving source, when the problem becomes one of tracking,

---

[3] Of course, active systems tend to end up with incoherent radiation if the acoustic medium is highly nonstationary.

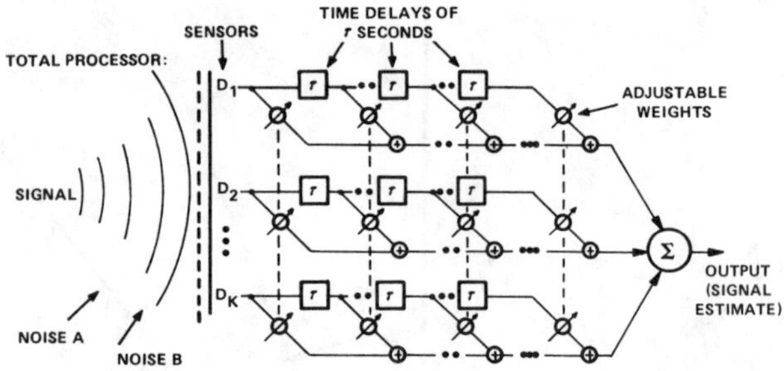

Fig. 10. Classical adaptive filter consisting of weights and delays in the time domain (after O. L. Frost, III, [73]).

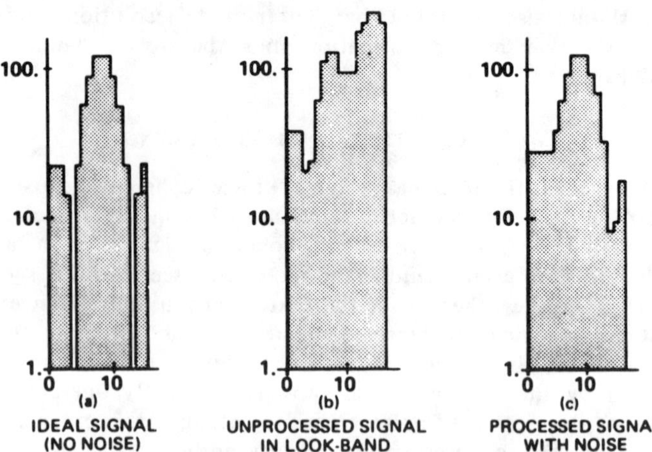

Fig. 11. Adaptive processing results for a simple four-element array (after Keating and Sawatari [77]).

and estimates must be updated as new information comes in and must be reconciled with earlier estimates. A widely accepted approach is that of extended Kalman filtering [68], but it has recently been pointed out [69] that classical, nonrecursive techniques may be just as advantageous when the stability problems associated with Kalman filtering are taken into account.

B. Adaptive Signal Processing

The processing of stochastic signals is frequently a battle against noise and interference, as indicated above. In a stationary noise/interference environment, the system can be optimized for that environment. However, most systems must operate in a changing noise/interference environment, and a system which can adaptively change to optimize itself to each noise environment is obviously advantageous. Most of the work in this area has been oriented toward sonar and radar systems. However, as microprocessor applications expend, it is very likely that adaptive processing will be utilized in medical and nondestructive testing applications as these areas grow.

The classical approach to adaptive processing [70] is known as optimal array processing, pioneered by Widrow and Griffiths [71] and based on the Wiener filter. The basis of this method is the minimization of the output power from a filter (see Fig. 10) consisting of weights and time delays in the different channels, followed by summing of the channel outputs.[4] The large number of degrees of freedom which can be inserted in this way allow excellent performance against a wide variety of noise situations, but result in a complex optimization problem. Formal solution gives the optimal power in a direction of interest in terms of the matrix inverse of the covariance matrix, formed from the expectation values of the cross correlations of signals from every pair of sensors.

In the frequency domain, one statement of the problem is to find the weights k which minimize the total power

$$P = \int \frac{d\omega}{2\pi} \; k^\dagger(\omega)\mathfrak{R}(\omega)k(\omega) \tag{8}$$

subject to the constraint that the processor has a specific finite response $f(\omega)$ in the direction of interest:

$$d_0^\dagger(\omega)k(\omega) = f(\omega). \tag{9}$$

In these equations, $\mathfrak{R}$ is the Fourier transformation of the co-

variance matrix (i.e., the cross spectral matrix),

$$\mathfrak{R}(\omega) = \langle x(\omega)x^\dagger(\omega)\rangle \tag{10}$$

and $x(\omega)$ is the vector of input signals in the frequency domain, $k(\omega)$ is the vector of weights, and $d_0(\omega)$ is the vector of input signals which would be obtained for a plane wave from the direction of interest. The symbol $\dagger$ represents the Hermitian conjugate and $\langle \; \rangle$ represents a statistical average. The formal solution to (8) and (9) is

$$k = \frac{f\mathfrak{R}^{-1}d_0}{d_0^\dagger\mathfrak{R}^{-1}d_0} \tag{11}$$

and

$$P = \int \frac{d\omega}{2\pi} \; \frac{|f|^2}{d_0^\dagger\mathfrak{R}^{-1}d_0}. \tag{12}$$

Except for small arrays, direct matrix inversion is usually impractical, and more indirect approaches, frequently gradient-descent methods [72], [73], are required. At any rate, classical optimal processing is often extremely complex and time-consuming and several suboptimal approaches (i.e., approaches which perform less well on the general problem) have been suggested. One approach is to use only part of the array to determine the adaptive parameters and all of the array to do the processing [74].

Another approach, which has been applied to several acoustic imaging problems [74], [75] is to design an adaptive method for specific, frequently occurring environmental situations, in this case consisting of both white noise and localized sources of interference [76]–[78]. Some results of computer simulation showing the performance of such an adaptive-processing technique are shown in Fig. 11. In this adaptive approach, all spectral bands are first examined, and the bearing of each interference source is estimated from data in the spectral band in which the radiation from that interference source is maximized. These estimated bearings are used to optimize the desired signal in a desired frequency band by spatially nulling the interferences in the manner explained below. The figures show logarithm of the intensity for each of 16 beams formed from the 4 detector signals. Fig. 11(a) is a baseline result which is the result of reconstructing, at the signal frequency, the ideal signal. Fig.

---

[4] The processing is often carried out in the frequency domain rather than the time domain, so that time delays become frequency-dependent complex weights.

11(b) is the conventional reconstructed result (at the signal frequency) of an input signal which contains the desired signal, white noise, and two nearby colored interferences. Fig. 11(c) is the result of adaptively processing the same input data.

Recently, it has been shown that classical adaptive processing reduces to the above simpler approach for the noise/interference environment considered [78]. The simpler approach [76]–[78] is equivalent to the removal, from the array data, of contributions from interferences in specific directions. This removal can be carried out quite efficiently by using a weight-vector having the form

$$k(\omega) = C(\omega)(I - \mathcal{P}(\omega))d_0(\omega) \tag{13}$$

for the direction corresponding to d_0, where $C(\omega)$ is a co-efficient involving $f(\omega)$ of (8), I is the identity matrix, and the matrix $\mathcal{P}$ is a projection operator, with rank equal to the number of localized interferences, which can be readily determined if the interference bearings are known. The directions of these interferences (and thereby $\mathcal{P}$) are then adjusted to optimize the performance in some sense. The same criterion, minimization of power in the direction of interest, which was used in classical optimal processing, can be employed. However, we have suggested minimizing the power summed over *all* directions instead [77], [78]. This has the important advantage of markedly reducing problems associated with cancelling out the signal of interest [78].

Finally, a recent paper in the medical imaging field describes a method which is more or less adaptive. This method [79], named interactive gain compensation, is intended for situations in which several interface reflections occur and is designed to compensate the deeper returns for the energy loss from earlier reflections.

V. IMAGE AND HOLOGRAM PROCESSING AND ENHANCEMENT

Many imaging approaches inherently involve aberrations, and all methods are prone to producing imagery degraded by deviations in system performance from the ideal. As a result, there has been considerable interest over the years in processing techniques designed to compensate for these failings. This section is intended to review a miscellany of such techniques.

A considerable literature [80], [81] has been developed on digital processing of imagery, primarily, of course, for optical imagery. Some of these techniques have been applied to acoustic imagery [82]–[85], primarily to Bragg images, which are subject to significant aberration. In one case, image processing has been applied [86] to the holograms, rather than the image.

Another common problem in acoustical imagery, worsened by the restricted apertures available, is the spurious detail which arises and which is closely related to "laser speckle." It has been demonstrated that this can be ameliorated by deliberately spoiling the coherence of the "illumination" source and averaging [87], [88]. Fig. 12 shows the effect of cancellation of spurious detail in a picture of the human elbow, taken by the SRI camera [87].

The small apertures common in acoustic imaging, as well as system errors, can also be responsible for the loss of small weak images in the image noise scattered from strong nearby images. A signal-processing approach known as the weak-

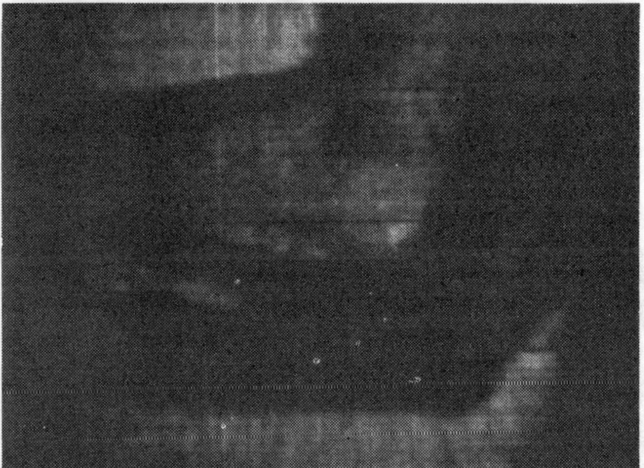

Fig. 12. Comparison of ultrasonic transmission images of the elbow formed with spatially coherent (top) and diffuse (bottom) insonification using the SRI-developed Ultrasonic Camera. Both images were focused at the midplane of the arm. High-contrast spurious patterns arising from out-of-focus superficial structures are evident in the coherently insonified image, but have been eliminated with diffuse insonification (courtesy of J. F. Havlice, P. S. Green, J. C. Taenzer, and W. F. Muller [87]).

signal enhancement technique (WSET) has been developed for this purpose [75], [88], [89]. This technique is most useful if phase errors are the dominant cause of noise in the image domain. Fig. 13 shows this characteristic of the WSET. The intensity of a weak source is 13.5 dB below the strong one and random phase errors are added deliberately. The WSET processed image (Fig. 13(b)) shows no evidence of noise due to phase errors. On the other hand, the intensified and clipped conventional reconstruction in Fig. 13(c) is extremely noisy and the desired weak image cannot be easily identified. However, the WSET does not work well for complex object distributions [75].

Another enhancement process which has been used on occasion to obtain more information from acoustic-imaging systems is the use of phase data. Metherell [90] has suggested the use of interferometric acoustic holography (see Fig. 14) while Kino's group have suggested the use of differential phase contrast images [91] obtained via their surface-acoustic-wave approach to image formation (Fig. 15).

System errors which are of concern include scanning errors [92], [93], channel electronics errors [94], [95], phase errors due to media turbulence [96], and errors due to quantization [97] or to deliberately ignoring either the phase or

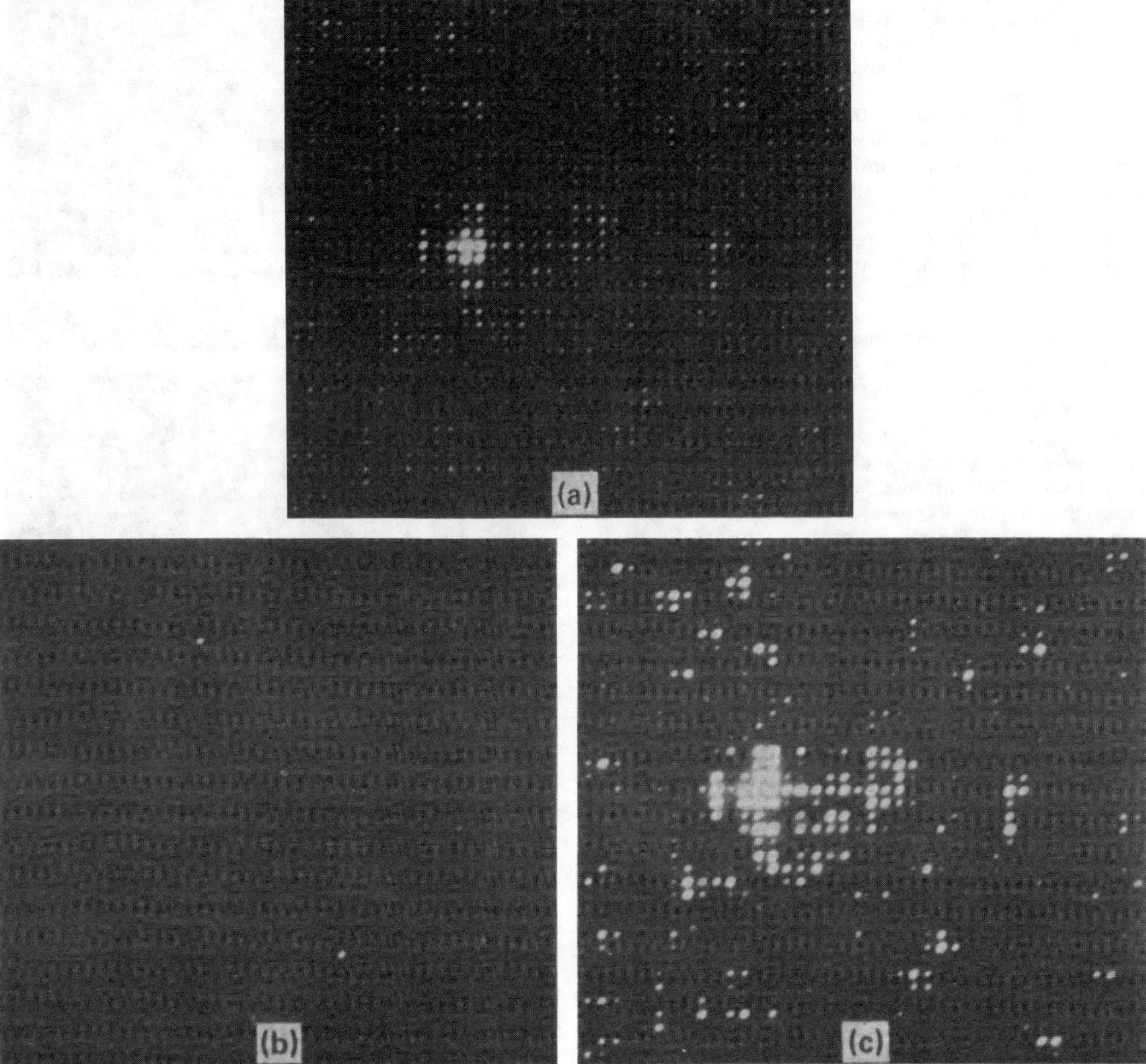

Fig. 13. Holographic image reconstructions of a strong wall reflection and a weak (−13.5 dB) point source, with random phase errors introduced in the hologram: (a) conventional reconstruction; (b) using WSET; (c) pseudo-enhancement using clipping (after Steinberg *et al.* [75]).

the amplitude information in a hologram [98], [99]. Some compensation for scanning errors has been suggested by Thijssen and Bakker [93], and Thorn has suggested the use of a phase and gain error-compensation map to reduce the channel errors [94]. Dallas and Lohmann have indicated that quantization errors should not be a serious problem and have shown how even 1-bit quantization can give relatively good results [97]. Ueda *et al.* have proposed that time-averaging the holographic data can significantly reduce turbulence effects, especially if the scale of the turbulence is larger than the object or target [96].

Interest in phase-only and amplitude-only holograms has been based on the idea that one might be able to reduce the processing needed to generate an image. The current consensus appears to be that amplitude-only holograms are more or less useless, but phase-only holograms might be of some use for far-field imaging [98], [99]. However, no one seems to have developed a system using phase-only holograms.

VI. Pattern-Recognition Processing

Pattern recognition has been investigated for many years and a great deal of literature exists [81], [100], mainly for speech recognition, optical character recognition, and target classification in radar and sonar. It is, of course, beyond the scope of this paper to review such literature, and the main purpose of this section is to describe how such techniques have been used in acoustic imaging.

In actual fact, there has not been a great deal of acoustic-imaging work employing these techniques, and the work which has been done has been preliminary in nature and

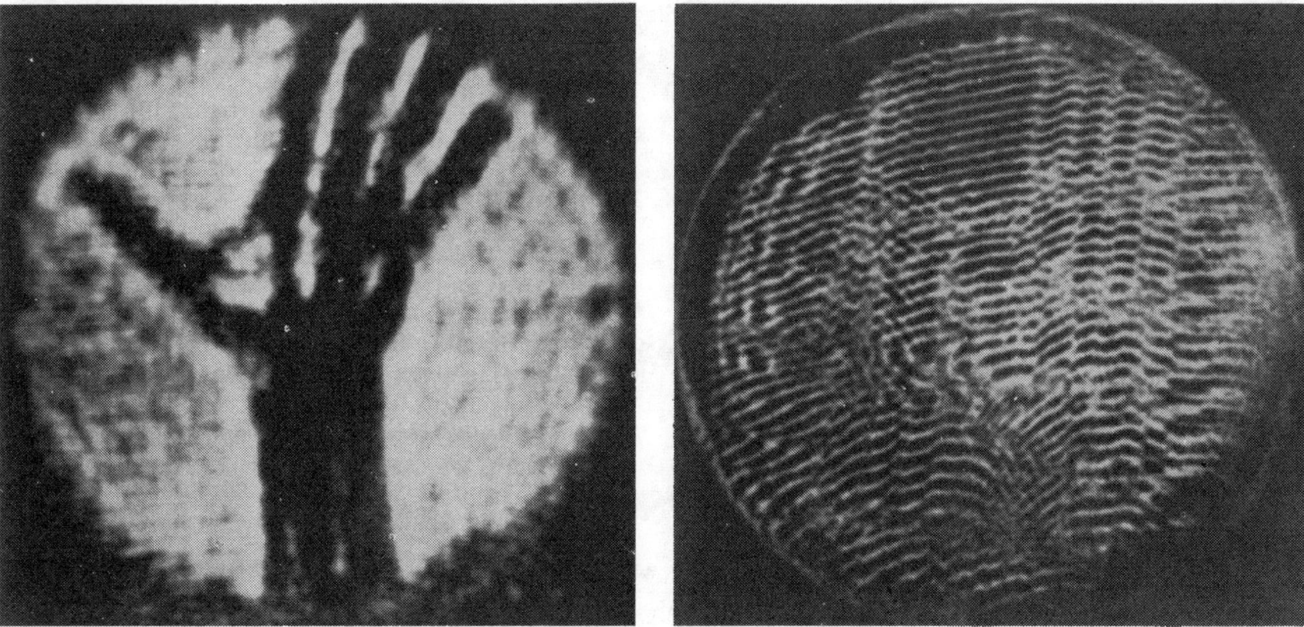

Fig. 14. A 12-inch aperture acoustical hologram (right) and reconstructed image of forearm (left) using the time-averaged linearized subfringe interferometry method of 1 MHz (courtesy of A. F. Metherell [90]).

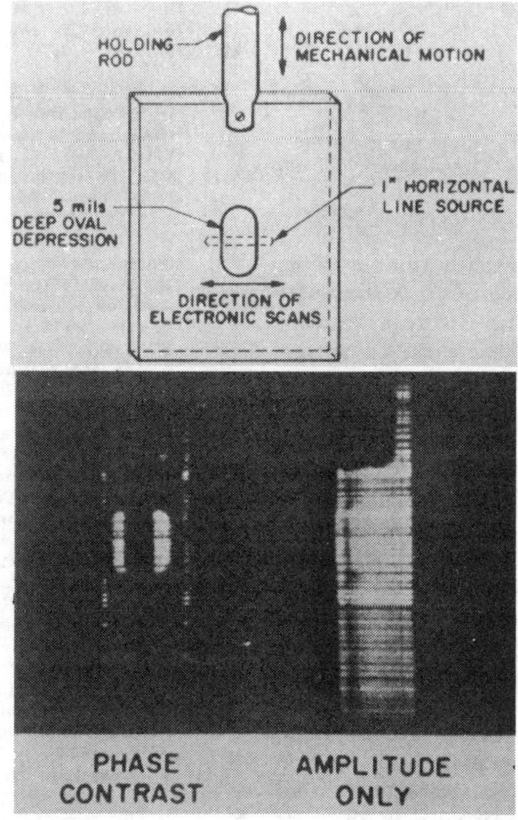

Fig. 15. Schematic and acoustic images showing a depression 5-mi deep on a piece of plexiglas. The phase shift introduced is about 40° (courtesy of G. Kino *et al.* [91]).

not very sophisticated. The earliest investigation which falls into the area of pattern recognition is the acoustic-matched-filter work reported by Pfeifer [101]. Pfeifer formed an acoustical hologram of a specific object and reproduced it on a thin metal sheet so that it could be reconstructed acoustically. He then allowed acoustic radiation scattered from similar objects to fall on the metal-sheet hologram, using an identical geometry. Under these conditions, the metal sheet hologram acts as a matched filter for the original object, and Pfeifer was able to show how the matched-filter output fell as the test object became more different from the original object [101], as demonstrated in Fig. 16. Matched-

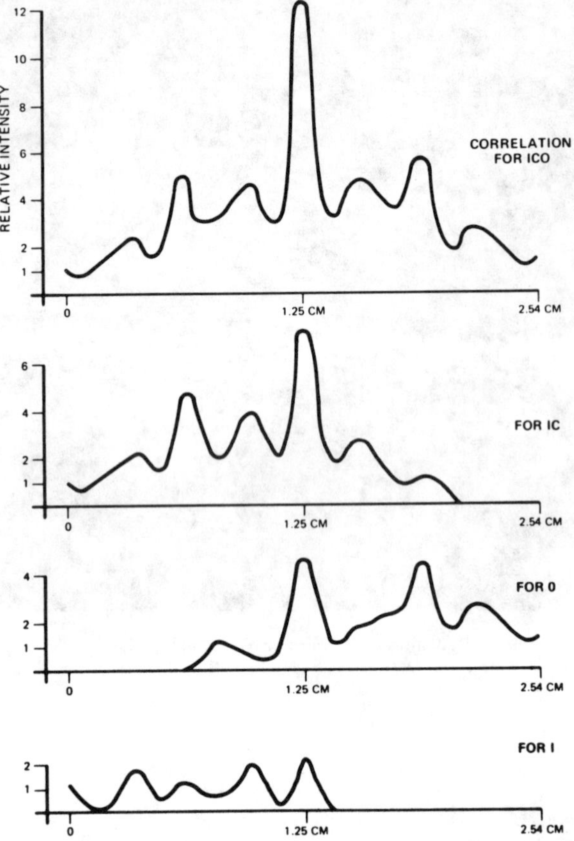

Fig. 16. Changes in correlation function for matched-filter correlation between hologram of the letters "ICO" and the field from different objects formed from these letters (after Pfeifer [101]).

filter techniques have also been used in ocean-bottom mapping [102], the matched filtering being carried out in a computer in this case. It is worth pointing out here that any current application of Pfeifer's work would probably use computer-matched filtering, rather than operating in the acoustical domain.

Other object recognition work has been carried out by Powers and Mueller [12], who used an intuitive edge-detection scheme for autofocusing, i.e., for finding the range at which the image reconstructed from a hologram is in focus, and by Preston [103], whose work is preliminary in nature and is concerned with medical applications.

It can be stated as a general comment that pattern-recognition techniques have not been applied in real situations to an extent at all commensurate with the amount of study which has been done. The main reason for this is the fact that these techniques are competing with the human brain, which is enormously successful as a pattern-recognition processor. Until our "artificial" methods are improved to the point where they are at least comparable with those of the animal kingdom, their widespread use will probably not occur. In this connection, it is interesting to note that Preston [103] has suggested reorganizing medical ultrasonic data so that human auditory analysis can be utilized for pattern recognition.

VII. CONCLUSIONS

Signal processing can markedly improve the effectiveness of acoustic-imaging systems, especially if the image-formation process is carried out digitally. Since the microprocessor is predicted to become a "zero-cost" item, the use of digital processing is likely to become even more widespread, and signal processing will become less expensive, and, therefore, cost-effective in a wider variety of equipment. An example of the revolutionary impact that can occur via digital processing is X-ray computerized axial tomography, which represents a considerable step forward in X-ray diagnostics.

The most important areas of future progress we see in application of signal processing to acoustic imaging are:

a) the use of resolution in three and four dimensions, with the associated additional information which is very valuable (but also difficult to handle);

b) the use of new less-noise-sensitive superresolution techniques to reduce array aperture limitations, and in particular, the use of maximum entropy techniques;

c) a greater use of adaptive processing in order to allow equipment to work efficiently in a wider variety of situations.

REFERENCES

Because many of the referenced papers are from the series *Acoustical Holography*, the following code will be used:

AH2 *Acoustical Holography*, vol. 2, A. F. Metherell and L. Larmore, Eds. New York: Plenum, 1970.
AH3 *Ibid*, vol. 3, A. F. Metherell, Ed. New York: Plenum, 1971.
AH4 *Ibid*, vol. 4, G. Wade, Ed. New York: Plenum, 1972.
AH5 *Ibid*, vol. 5, P. S. Green, Ed. New York: Plenum, 1974.
AH6 *Ibid*, vol. 6, N. Booth, Ed. New York: Plenum, 1975.
AH7 *Ibid*, vol. 7, L. W. Kessler, Ed. New York: Plenum, 1977.

[1] C. F. Vasile, "A numerical Fourier transform technique and its application to acoustic-surface-wave bandpass filter synthesis and design," *IEEE Trans. Sonics and Ultrason.*, vol. SU-21, pp. 7–11, Jan. 1974.

[2] F. L. Thurstone and H. E. Melton, Jr., "Biomedical ultrasonics," *IEEE Trans. Ind. Electron. Cont. Instrum.*, vol. IECI-17, pp. 167–172, 1970.

[3] D. L. Folds, "Focussing properties of solid ultrasonic cylindrical lenses," *J. Acoust. Soc. Amer.*, vol. 53, p. 826, 1973.

[4] K. T. Corbett, F. H. Middleton, and R. L. Steinberg, "Nonspherical acoustic-lens study," *J. Acoust. Soc. Amer.*, vol. 59, p. 1104, 1976.

[5] R. L. Whitman, M. Ahmed, and A. Korpel, "A progress report on the laser scanned acoustic camera," AH4, p. 11.

[6] R. Torguet, C. Bruneel, E. Bridoux, J. M. Rouvaen, and B. Nongaillard, "Ultrafast echotomographic system using optical processing of ultrasonic signals," AH7, p. 79.

[7] A. Hanafy and M. Zambuto, "Acoustic image converter for three-step acoustic holography," AH7, p. 117.

[8] K. R. Erikson, "Acoustical holography using temporally modulated optical holography," AH5, p. 59.

[9] A. L. Boyer, P. M. Hirsch, J. A. Jordan, Jr., L. B. Lesem, and D. L. Van Rooy, "Reconstruction of ultrasonic images by backward propagation," AH3, p. 333.

[10] P. N. Keating, R. F. Koppelmann, R. K. Mueller, and R. F. Steinberg, "Complex on-axis holograms and reconstruction without conjugate images," AH5, p. 515.

[11] Y. Aoki, "Image reconstruction by computer in acoustical holography," AH5, p. 551.

[12] J. P. Powers and D. E. Mueller, "A Computerized acoustic imaging technique incorporating automatic object recognition," AH5, p. 527.

[13] S. Winograd, "A new method of computing DFT," in *Rec. 1977 Int. Conf. on Acoust. Speech and Signal Processing*, p. 366.

[14] D. A. Gaubatz, "Fast beamforming processor," AH7, p. 495.

[15] J. F. Havlice, G. S. Kino, J. S. Kofol, and C. F. Quate, "An electronically focused acoustic imaging device," AH5, p. 317.

[16] R. D. Melen, J. D. Shott, B. T. Lee, and L. C. Granger, "Charge coupled devices for holographic and beam steering sonar systems," AH7, p. 461.

[17] J. F. Greenleaf, S. A. Johnson, S. L. Lee, G. T. Herman, and E. H. Wood, "Algebraic reconstruction of spatial distributions of acoustic absorption within tissue from their two-dimensional acoustic projections," AH5, p. 591.

[18] J. F. Greenleaf, S. A. Johnson, W. F. Samayoa, and F. A. Duck, "Algebraic reconstruction of spatial distribution of acoustic velocities in tissue from their time-of-flight profile," AH6, p. 71.

[19] J. F. Greenleaf, S. A. Johnson, R. C. Bahn, and B. Rajagopalan, "Quantitative cross-sectional imaging of ultrasound parameters," in *1977 IEEE Ultrason. Symp. Proc.*, pp. 989–995, 1977.

[20] P. N. Keating, R. F. Koppelmann, and R. K. Mueller, "Maximization of resolution in three dimensions," AH6, p. 525.

[21] R. K. Mueller, *Advances in holography*, vol. 1, N. H. Farhat, Ed. New York: Marcel Dekker, 1975, p. 45.

[22] G. Wade, M. Wollman, and K. Wang, "A holographic system for use in the ocean," AH3, p. 225.

[23] R. K. Mueller, "Acoustic holography," *Proc. IEEE*, vol. 59, pp. 1319–1335, 1971.

[24] T. Sato, M. Ueda, and S. Fukuda, "Synthetic aperture sonar," *J. Acoust. Soc. Amer.*, vol. 54, p. 799, 1973.

[25] L. Cutrona, "Comparison of sonar system performance achievable using synthetic-aperture techniques with the performance achievable by more conventional means," *J. Acoust. Soc. Amer.*, vol. 58, p. 336, Aug. 1975.

[26] M. L. Dick, D. E. Dick, F. D. McLeod, and N. B. Kindig, "Ultrasonic synthetic aperture imaging," AH7, p. 327.

[27] T. Iwasaki and Y. Aoki, "Ultrasonic holography in a source- and object-movable system," AH4, p. 653.

[28] W. H. Wells, "Acoustical imaging with linear transducer arrays," AH2, p. 87.

[29] E. Marom, R. K. Mueller, R. F. Koppelmann, and G. Zilinskas, "Design and preliminary test of an underwater viewing system using sound holography," AH3, p. 191.

[30] P. N. Keating, R. F. Koppelmann, T. Sawatari, and R. F. Steinberg, "Holographic aperture synthesis via a transmitter array," AH6, p. 485.

[31] K. Nitadori, "Synthetic aperture approach to multi-beam scanning acoustical imaging," AH6, p. 507.

[32] R. E. Williams, "Creating an acoustic synthetic aperture in the ocean," *J. Acoust. Soc. Amer.*, vol. 60, p. 160, 1976.

[33] K. Mano and K. Nitadori, "An experimental underwater viewing system using acoustical holography," *1977 IEEE Ultrason. Symp.*, p. 272, 1977.

[34] G. Toraldo Di Francia, "Resolving power and information," *J. Opt. Soc. Am.*, vol. 45, pp. 497–501, 1955.

[35] J. L. Harris, "Diffraction and resolving power," *J. Opt. Soc. Amer.*, vol. 54, pp. 931–936, 1964.

[36] C. W. Barnes, "Object restoration in a diffraction-limited imaging system," *J. Opt. Soc. Amer.*, vol. 56, pp. 575–578, 1966.

[37] B. R. Frieden, "Evaluation, design and extrapolation methods for optical signals, based on use of the prolate functions," *Progress in Optics*, vol. IX, E. Wolf, Ed. Amsterdam, Holland: North-Holland Publishing Co., 1971, (ch VIII, § 6.4).

[38] R. W. Gerchberg, "Superresolution through error energy reduction," *Opt. Acta.*, vol. 21, pp. 709–720, 1974.

[39] P. De Santis and F. Gori, "On an iterative method for superresolution," *Opt. Acta.*, vol. 22, pp. 691–695, 1975.

[40] T. Sawatari and P. N. Keating, "Superresolution for separating clustered images," presented at the Eighth Int. Symp. on Acoustical Imaging, May 30–June 1978, Key Biscayne, Florida.

[41] B. K. Gazey and D. J. Creasey, "A short-range high-resolution sonar using 'near-field' multiplicative array processing," *Ultrason. Int. 1975 Conf. Proc.*, pp. 261–265, 1975.

[42] O. E. Flynn and R. Kinns, "Multiplicative signal processing for sound source location on jet engines," *J. Sound Vibra.*, vol. 46, pp. 137–150, 1976.

[43] H. P. Brucker, "Cross-sensor beamforming with a sparse line array," *J. Acoust. Soc. Amer.*, vol. 61, pp. 494–498, 1977.

[44] E. T. Jaynes, "Prior probabilities," *IEEE Trans. Syst. Sci. Cybern.*, vol. SSC-4, pp. 227–241, 1968.

[45] B. R. Frieden, "Restoring with maximum likelihood and maximum entropy," *J. Opt. Soc. Amer.*, vol. 62, pp. 511–518, 1972.

[46] Y. Biraud, "A new approach for increasing the resolving power by data processing," *Astron. Astrophys.*, vol. 1, p. 124, 1969.

[47] R. F. Koppelmann and P. N. Keating, "Three dimensional acoustic imaging," presented at the Eighth Int. Symp. on Acoustical Imaging, May 30–June 1978, Key Biscayne, Florida.

[48] R. F. Koppelmann, T. Sawatari, and P. N. Keating, unpublished.

[49] R. A. Altes and W. D. Reese, "Doppler-tolerant classification of distributed targets—A bionic sonar," *IEEE Trans. Aerosp. Electron. Syst.*, vol. AES-11, p. 708, 1975.

[50] M. Siegel, M. Olinger, and B. Ho, "Doppler flow visualization using large time-bandwidth signals," AH7, p. 347.

[51] C. F. Hottinger and J. D. Meindl, "Real-time doppler imaging for unambiguous measurement of blood volume flow," AH6, p. 247.

[52] J. F. Bartram, "Transfer function model for a velocity measuring sonar system," in *Proc. EASCON, 76*, p. 123-A, 1976.

[53] D. H. McSherry, "Computer processing of diagnostic ultrasound data," *IEEE Trans. Sonics and Ultrason.*, vol. SU-21, p. 91, 1974.

[54] D. E. Robinson and B. G. Williams, "Computer acquisition and processing of ultrasonic data," in *Proc. 2nd European Congr. on Ultrason. in Med.* (Munich, Germany), p. 96, 1975.

[55] W. J. Sanders, "Computer processing of echocardiograph images," in *SPIE Seminar Proc. Cardiovascular Imaging and Image Processing*, vol. 72, p. 37, 1975.

[56] K. Willson and S. Leeman, "Simplified image processing for ultrasonic scans," *Phys, Med. and Biol.*, vol. 21, p. 447, 1976.

[57] M. H. Orr, R. C. Spindel, and R. P. Porter, "Long-range echo sounding with a chirp source," *J. Geophys. Res.*, vol. 81, p. 447, 1976.

[58] C. P. Jethwa, M. Kaveh, G. R. Cooper, and F. Saggio, "Blood flow measurements using ultrasonic pulsed random signal doppler system," *IEEE Trans. Sonics and Ultrason.*, vol. SU-22, p. 1–11, Jan. 1975.

[59] F. L. Thurstone and O. T. Von Ramm, "A new ultrasound imaging technique employing two-dimensional electronic beam steering," AH6, p. 249.

[60] See, for example, C. E. Ebbing and T. H. Hodgson, "Diagnostic tests for locating noise sources (Part II)," *Noise Control Eng.*, vol. 3, p. 30, 1974.

[61] M. Born and E. Wolf, *Principles of optics*. Oxford, England: Pergamon Press, 1970, p. 508.

[62] T. Sato and S. Wadaka, "Incoherent ultrasonic imaging system," *J. Acoust. Soc. Amer.*, vol. 58, p. 1013, 1975.

[63] K. Sasaki, T. Sato, and Y. Nakamura, "Holographic passive sonar," *IEEE Trans. Sonics and Ultrason.*, vol. SU-24, p. 193, 1977.

[64] W. J. Bangs and P. M. Schultheiss, in *Signal Processing*, J. W. R. Griffiths, P. L. Stocklin, C. Van Schooneveld, Eds. New York: Academic Press, 1973, p. 577.

[65] W. R. Hahn, "Optimum signal processing for passive sonar range and bearing estimation," *J. Acoust. Soc. Amer.*, vol. 58, p. 201, 1975.

[66] C. H. Knapp and G. C. Carter, "Generalized correlation method for estimation of time delay," *IEEE Trans. Acoust., Speech, Signal Processing*, vol. ASSP-24, p. 320, 1976.

[67] W. K. Fischer, "An alternate approach to optimum bearing estimation," NUSC Tech. Rep. 5439, 1976.

[68] See, for example, M. Boavista da Cunha, "Passive target tracking using non-linear estimation theory," M.S. thesis, Naval Postgrad. School, Monterey, CA, 1976.

[69] W. B. Adams, "Non-linear, non-recursive estimation for passive localization and tracking," in *Rec. 1977 Int. Conf. on Acoust., Speech, and Signal Processing*, p. 287, May 1977.

[70] A whole issue of *IEEE Trans. Antennas and Propagat.* was devoted to this field, vol. AP-24, Sept. 1976.

[71] B. Widrow, P. E. Mantey, L. J. Griffiths, and B. B. Goode, "Adaptive antenna systems," *Proc. IEEE*, vol. 55, p. 2143, 1967.

[72] L. J. Griffiths, "A simple adaptive algorithm for real-time processing in antenna arrays," *Proc. IEEE*, vol. 57, p. 1696, 1969.

[73] O. L. Frost, III, "An algorithm for linearly constrained adaptive array processing," *Proc. IEEE*, vol. 60, p. 926, 1972.

[74] N. L. Owsley, "A recent trend in adaptive spatial processing for sensor arrays: Constrained adaptation," in *Signal Processing*, J. W. R. Griffiths, P. L. Stocklin, and C. Van Schooneveld, Eds. New York: Academic Press, 1973, p. 591.

[75] R. F. Steinberg, P. N. Keating, and R. F. Koppelmann, "Experimental implementation of advanced processing in acoustic holography," AH6, p. 539.

[76] P. N. Keating, R. F. Koppelmann, R. K. Mueller, R. F. Steinberg, and G. Zilinskas, "Adaptive null-processing—A holographic approach and experimental results," *J. Acoust. Soc. Amer.*, vol. 59, p. 106, 1976.

[77] P. N. Keating and T. Sawatari, "Holographic adaptive processing—A comparison with LMS adaptive processing," AH7, p. 537.

[78] P. N. Keating, "A rapid approximation to optimal array processing for the case of strong locallized interferences," to be published in *J. Acoust. Soc. Amer.*

[79] A. K. Nigam and C. P. Olinger, "A large-aperture real-time equipment for vascular imaging," AH7, p. 65.

[80] P. Mengers and K. A. Wickersheim, "High speed digital image processing," *Research and Development*, p. 42, Oct. 1977.

[81] J. K. Aggarwal and R. O. Duda, in *Computer Methods in Image Analysis*, A. Rosenfeld, Eds. New York: IEEE, 1977.

[82] M. Takagi, N. B. Tse, G. R. Heidbreder, C. W. Lee, and G. Wade, "Computer enhancement of acoustic images," AH5, p. 541.

[83] J. C. Stamm and R. Priemer, "Image processing for aberration removal," AH7, p. 225.

[84] C. H. Lee, G. R. Heidbreder, G. Wade, and A. Coello-Vera, "On line interactive computer processing of acoustic images," AH7, p. 207.

[85] C. S. Clark and A. F. Metherell, "Digital processing of acoustical holograms," AH5, p. 471.

[86] A. Korpel, R. L. Whitman, and M. Ahmed, "Elimination of

spurious detail in acoustic images," AH5, p. 373.

[87] J. F. Havlice, P. S. Green, J. C. Taenzer, and W. F. Muller, "Spatially and temporally varying insonification for the elimination of spurious detail in acoustic transmission imaging," AH7, p. 291.

[88] P. N. Keating, R. K. Mueller, and R. R. Gupta, "Conventional and weak signal enhancement holography in the presence of measurement errors," AH4, p. 251.

[89] M. J. M. Clement, "A new processing technique for scanned ultrasonic holography," AH6, p. 557.

[90] A. F. Metherell, "Linearized subfringe interferometric holography," AH5, p. 41.

[91] G. Kino, W. Leung, H. Shaw, D. Winslow, and L. Zitelli, "Differential phase contrast imaging in the electronically focused acoustic system," AH7, p. 523.

[92] H. D. Collins and B. P. Hilderbrand, "The effects of scanning position and motion errors on hologram resolution," AH4, p. 467.

[93] J. M. Thijssen and J. H. Bakker, "Intensity modulation in B-scan systems: Correction of non-constant scanning speed and a device for suppression of reduplication artifacts," *2nd European Congr. on Ultrason. in Med.*, p. 115, May 1975.

[94] J. Thorn, "Gain and phase variations in holographic acoustic imaging systems," AH4, p. 569.

[95] J. L. Sutton, J. V. Thorn, and J. N. Price, "The effects of circuit parameters on image quality in a holographic acoustic imaging system," AH5, p. 573.

[96] M. Ueda, T. Sato, and O. Ikeda, "Ultrasonic holography free from phase turbulence," *J. Acoust. Soc. Amer.*, vol. 55, p. 1218, 1974.

[97] W. J. Dallas and A. W. Lohmann, "Influence of quantization and of other non-linear distortions of the holographic signal," AH4, p. 463.

[98] J. Powers, J. Landry, and G. Wade, "Computed reconstructions from phase-only and amplitude-only holograms," AH2, p. 185.

[99] O. K. Mawardi, "Amplitude-only and phase-only holograms," AH4, p. 519.

[100] D. Feucht, "Pattern recognition: Basic concepts and implementations," *Comput. Design*, p. 57, Dec. 1977.

[101] J. L. Pfeifer, "Acoustical reconstruction of holograms, and their potential use," AH4, p. 317.

[102] S. D. Morgera, "Signal processing for precise ocean mapping," *IEEE J. Ocean Eng.*, OE-1, p. 49, 1976.

[103] K. Preston, "Use of pattern recognition for signal processing in ultrasonic histopathology," NBS Special Publication 453, *Proc. Seminar on Ultrason. Tissue Characterization*, May 1975.

Medical Ultrasonic Imaging: An Overview of Principles and Instrumentation

JAMES F. HAVLICE AND JON C. TAENZER, MEMBER, IEEE

Abstract—Recent advances in electronics and digital processing techniques have significantly improved conventional ultrasonic imaging systems and allowed the development of new and sophisticated scanning methods. As a result, ultrasonic imaging devices have become an important modality for the clinical radiologist, complimenting the images obtained from X-ray and nuclear cameras. A particular advantage of ultrasonic waves is that they are nonionizing, thus presenting less risk to both patient and examiner. This paper presents some of the basic principles of ultrasonic propagation in tissue and how those principles impact the design of imaging devices. The characteristics of both the *B*-scan and *C*-scan techniques are described along with a summary of various scan formats that are currently available. Examples of *B*-scan and *C*-scan instruments are presented along with their relative advantages, limitations, and current usage; representative images are presented whenever possible. This paper concludes with a description of some new research developments in this rapidly emerging technology.

I. INTRODUCTION

THE ABILITY to "see" the internal organs of the human body in the form of an image, bearing a one-to-one correspondence to the anatomy involved, is a powerful diagnostic tool of modern medicine. Although tissue is opaque to visible light, the body is relatively transparent to other forms of radiation, such as X-rays, nuclear particles, and ultrasonic waves. Of these, only the ultrasonic waves are nonionizing, thus presenting much less risk of undesirable damage to both patient or examiner during exposure. Extensive investigations of the biological effects of ultrasound are currently in progress; however, no deleterious effects have been documented as a result of clinical examination by existing ultrasonic diagnostic equipment. As a result ultrasound is used for imaging adult reproductive systems and monitoring fetal viability, in addition to its more common uses, for example imaging the valve motion of the heart and the internal organs of the abdomen. These images are unique because they are obtained by ultrasonic waves interacting with the *mechanical* properties of tissue; hence, this modality has become complimentary to other diagnostic tools. In this paper, we present an overview of the physical principles of ultrasonic waves and a brief description of some of the imaging devices that have been developed. This paper is not intended to be comprehensive in its coverage of instrumentation; rather we have concentrated on those techniques that are in clinical use now or will be in the near future. In addition we have included a few instruments which, although unlikely to be used in a clinical setting, demonstrate an important feature of imaging with ultrasound.

Acoustic image formation is similar in many respects to optical image formation. It is even possible to record an acoustic image directly on photographic film [1], although this method is too insensitive, in current technology, to be useful for diagnostic purposes. Both the acoustical and optical techniques often employ refractive and reflective elements, such as lenses, prisms, or mirrors, to control the shape and direction of the beam; both are limited in image resolution by diffraction effects; both generally rely on changes in absorption or impedance to provide image contrast; both have phase contrast schemes available to provide additional image contrast when absorptive or impedance variations are insufficient to distinguish object structures; and both have developed holographic schemes for recording image data. In Section II we review the physical principles of acoustic wave propagation and their application to ultrasonic imaging.

There are also significant differences between the optical and acoustic techniques, the most obvious being that one cannot "see" sound directly. Hence, it is a characteristic of all acoustic-imaging schemes that some means be provided for converting the acoustical information to visible form. Although other physical phenomena have been employed, the most common scheme is to convert the acoustic signal to an electronic signal with an electromechanical transducer. The image is then processed and displayed in a manner very similar to television signals. In Sections III and IV, we examine a number of techniques for achieving this transfer of information and describe some of scanning techniques that have been developed. In Section V, we present a few techniques which are not currently in clinical use nor likely to be placed in use for at least a few years. However, they represent some of the current research and development efforts that may lead to further application of ultrasonic imaging for medical diagnosis. It is the goal of this paper to present an overview of the rich variety of available instrumentation and current research efforts that comprise the field of imaging with ultrasound.

II. PHYSICAL PRINCIPLES

A. Propagation

The sound energy used in medical diagnostic equipment travels through the body in the form of a longitudinal wave, that is, one in which the particle motion is in the same direction as the wave propagation. This type of wave is the same as the human ear hears as sound. Transverse waves, in which the particle motion is perpendicular to the direction of wave propagation, have not been used for medical diagnosis because of the extremely high attenuation of such waves in biological media.

Sound waves are generated and detected by a piezoelectric transducer [2], which is a device capable of converting electrical energy to acoustical energy and vice versa. A large number of natural and synthetic materials [3] have been discovered or developed which have a large piezoelectric effect, making it possible to achieve good efficiency in the transduction process.

Manuscript received June 16, 1978; revised January 11, 1979.
J. F. Havlice is with Diasonics, Inc., Sunnyvale, CA 94086.
J. C. Taenzer is with SRI International, Menlo Park, CA 94025.

The speed of propagation v of longitudinal waves in a liquid medium is determined by the "elastic" properties of that medium, specifically its mean density ρ and bulk modulus B, through the equation.

$$v = \sqrt{B/\rho}. \tag{1}$$

Although it is theoretically possible for the speed of sound to be frequency dependent (known as dispersion) [4], the small dispersion that has been measured for biological materials is not important for most imaging instruments available today. A list of the measured speed in some typical biological media is shown in Table I.

Another important physical aspect of sound waves is its attenuation as it propagates through a medium. As sound propagates its intensity I generally diminishes with distance of propagation z according to:

$$I = I_0 \exp{(-2\alpha z)}. \tag{2}$$

I_0 is the intensity at $z = 0$ and α is the amplitude attenuation coefficient, a few values of which are shown in Table I. Unlike the speed of sound, the attenuation coefficient is highly frequency dependent [4], a fact which has significant impact on equipment design and performance. As a rule of thumb, the attenuation coefficient increases approximately linearly with frequency. Referring to Table I, we see that a convenient average value of the attenuation coefficient of soft tissue is 1 dB cm^{-1} MHz^{-1}. Hence, a 3-MHz sound beam which has traveled a 20-cm distance through soft tissue is 60 dB below its initial intensity level; a sound beam at 10 MHz, traveling the same path, is 200 dB below its initial intensity level. Although this additional loss of signal could be compensated for by increasing the transmitted power, this would raise the intensity to a dangerous level. Hence, it is clear why 3 MHz (or lower frequency) sound rather than 10 MHz, is used for imaging structures deep in the body. However, if the body structures of interest lie near the skin surface or if the body itself is very small (as in an infant), higher frequencies may be used. This limitation on frequency impacts equipment performance because the frequency f, and sound speed v, determine the wavelength λ, of the sound beam through the equation

$$\lambda = v/f. \tag{3}$$

As we shall see, in a diffraction limited system, it is wavelength that determines the ultimate resolution of the imaging apparatus.

B. Contrast

In an optical image a structure distinguishes itself from surrounding structures by variations in reflectivity, attenuation, color, (frequency dependence), "texture," and when phase contrast is used, index of refraction. In acoustics, exactly the same sources of contrast are available although only attenuation, reflectivity, and texture are commonly employed in current instrumentation. Attenuation differences between various body structures are most important for those instruments which provide transmission images of the body (see Section IV). Reflectivity, the most important contrast agent for those instruments which provide reflection images of the body (see Section III), is used here in the narrow sense of an absolute reflection coefficient at a plane boundary between two different media. Reflectivity is determined, for structures larger than a few wavelengths, by the characteristic impedance of the two adjoining layers [5]. The characteristic impedance of a material

TABLE I

	Speed of Sound (m/sec)	Attenuation at 1 MHz (dB/cm)	Characteristic Impedance (10^6 kg m^{-2} s^{-1})
Water	1480	.0025	1.48
Air	330	12.000	0.0004
Amniotic Fluid	1510	.007	1.5
Fat	1410–1470	.35–.78	1.34–1.39
Soft Tissue (average)	1540	0.81	1.62
Liver	1550	0.95	1.66
Kidney	1560	1.1	1.63
Muscle	1590	with grain 1.5–2.1 against grain 1.8–3.3	1.71
Spleen	1550	0.52	1.65
Bone	4080	12	7.8
Vitreous of Eye	1520	0.1	1.52

Z, an acoustic concept analogous to the concept of impedance in electricity, is defined as the product of material density, ρ and sound speed v, as in

$$Z = \rho v. \tag{4}$$

Listed in Table I are some values of characteristic impedance for a variety of biological media. The power reflection coefficient R [6] for a normally incident sound beam traveling from a medium with impedance Z_1 into a medium with impedance Z_2 is given by

$$R = \left(\frac{Z_2 - Z_1}{Z_2 + Z_1} \right)^2. \tag{5}$$

The greater the difference of the impedances of the adjoining tissues, the greater the amount of energy reflected from the boundary. In soft tissues the reflection coefficient varies from -20 dB (between fat and muscle)[1] to -45 dB (between kidney and spleen). These are low-level reflections (less than 0.5 percent) so that most of the acoustic energy is transmitted through the interface and is available for imaging deeper structures. In some cases, however, a very-high-level reflection may take place, as in a bone/muscle interface which has a reflection coefficient of -4 dB. In such a case considerably less energy is transmitted, not very much is available for imaging deeper structures, and a "shadow" appears in a reflection-mode image. This "shadowing," when it occurs in a region where there is no normal anatomical reason for it, is an important indicator of abnormality. It has been used, for example, to distinguish between soft and calcified atherosclerotic plaque in the carotid arteries [7], [8] and to identify stones in the gall bladder or kidney.

The amount of sound and its spatial distribution reflected from an object depends not only on the difference between the acoustic impedance of the object and its surroundings but also on the physical size, orientation, and shape of the object. Objects much smaller than an acoustic wavelength reflect sound according to the Rayleigh scattering theory; hence, they exhibit a fourth power frequency dependence with a wide angular field distribution [9]. On the other hand, objects with dimensions larger than an acoustic wavelength (specular reflectors) reflect sound, independent of frequency, toward a direction which is dependent on the orientation of the object and with

---

[1] That is, the reflected signal is -20 dB from the incident signal.

an angular field distribution which is dependent on the incident sound field and the shape of the object. Although the theory of sound scattering and reflection from biological structures is not very well developed, it is experimentally observed that some body structures produce spatial echo patterns that have a different textural appearance than others and this difference acts as a contrast agent. For example: the wall of a blood vessel has a characteristic smooth specular appearance whereas a thyroid gland has a characteristic granular appearance. Other implications regarding specular reflectors will be discussed later in this chapter.

Ultrasonic images can be divided into two rather broad categories, "B-scan" images and "C-scan" images.[2] Each of these can be further divided and subdivided into classifications that are indicative of a scan technique (phased array, electronically stepped array, mechanical) and a scan modality (linear, sector, arc, compound). In general each scan technique has a full range of scan modalities. The situation is complicated by a further subdivision of each category into "real-time" or "non-real-time" scanners, "water path" or "contact" scanners, and "reflection" or "transmission" modes. We begin the discussion with the definition and illustration of the broadest category, B-scan techniques and C-scan techniques.

C. B-Scan

B-Scanning, or brightness mode scanning, provides a two-dimensional, cross sectional reflection image of the object that is scanned [10]. A B-Scan image is formed by sweeping a narrow acoustic beam through a plane and positioning the received echoes on a display such that there is a correspondence between the display scan line and the direction of acoustic propagation in the tissue. Generally the same transducer is used to both send and receive the acoustic signals. A fundamental feature of a B-Scan image is that one of the dimensions is inferred from the arrival time of echoes of a short acoustic pulse as they reflect from structures along a (presumed) straight-line path. Signals received from structures close to the transducer arrive earlier than signals received from structures far from the transducer [11]. The other (transverse) dimension is obtained by moving the transducer (either physically by mechanical means or apparently by electronic means) so that a different straight line path through the object is interrogated by another short acoustic pulse. This process is continued until the entire object region of interest is scanned. Some means of tracking the propagation path through the object is required in order to unambiguously define the image. A block diagram of a generalized B-Scanner is shown in Fig. 1. An electronic pulser excites a transducer so that a short burst of ultrasound is generated. Acoustic signals reflected from objects in the acoustic path impinge on the transducer, are converted to electronic signals, and processed for display. Very often the amplifier gain is increased with time in order to partially compensate for the attenuation experienced by signals reflected deeper in the body. This is known as time gain compensation (TGC). The position and angular direction of the ultrasound beam are determined by position monitoring electronics which keep track of where on the monitor the image signals should be displayed.

As the echoes are received by the transducer they are amplified, rectified, filtered, and the resulting signal is used to bright-

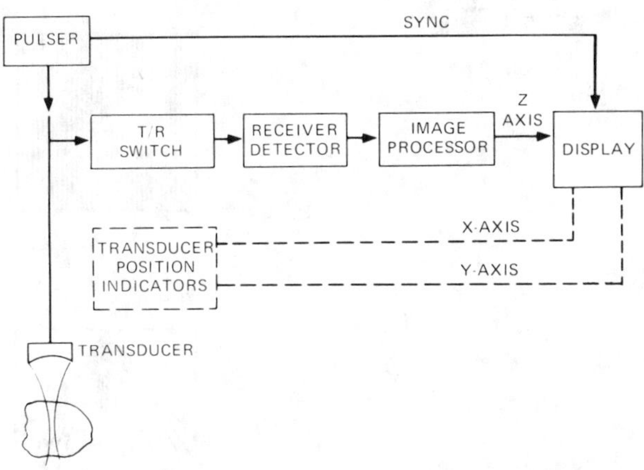

Fig. 1. A block diagram of a simple B-scan system.

ness modulate the display. Until a few years ago, the standard CRT monitor used in conjunction with ultrasonic receiving systems was a bistable unit with only an on or off condition. A threshold control allowed the user to vary the value of a critical signal level above which all received echoes were displayed (with the same brightness) and below which nothing was displayed. With such a display the resulting images were highly dependent on the threshold control and repeatability of images was difficult to achieve. In addition, since little more than contours were displayed, interpretation of the images was difficult.

One of the most important developments in acoustic imaging was the introduction of gray-scale display [35]. In a gray-scale display there are usually 10 or more distinct brightness levels. The imaging system assigns a given brightness level to a small range of echo intensities and distributes the brightness levels such that, for example, strong echoes are displayed brightest and weaker ones at progressively lower brightness levels. This type of display produces B-scan images which are less operator dependent and easier to interpret than the bistable images. Image repeatability also appears to be improved with gray-scale display. It is not surprising, therefore, that gray scale has become widely accepted. Color displays have also been used with different echo levels being displayed as different colors (36), (37). Although such images may appear quite dramatic, there is no more information in such a color display than in a gray-scale display with the same number of distinct levels.

Fig. 2 represents typical image formats for three scan modalities: linear, sector, and arc. For illustrative purposes the transducer size indicated in Fig. 2 is exaggerated; typically, the transducer diameter is only a small fraction of the scanned dimension. In a linear scan the transducer moves in a straight line. Note that the field-of-view in this direction is limited by the length of travel of the transducer. However, in the time (or depth) dimension, the field-of-view is limited only by the depth of penetration (i.e., the frequency and attenuation) or the physical size of the object being scanned. One advantage of this technique is that the image may consist of a uniform line density which results in a constant spatial sampling rate of the object and a pleasing display on the monitor. In the sector scan the transducer position remains fixed at a point on or above the object but is swept through an angular sector [12]. Note that in this case the field-of-view increases with depth of penetration. However, the line density diminishes as the field-of-view expands. This type of scan is particularly well suited

---

[2] We shall not discuss the "A-scan" technique since it does not provide an image in the normal sense.

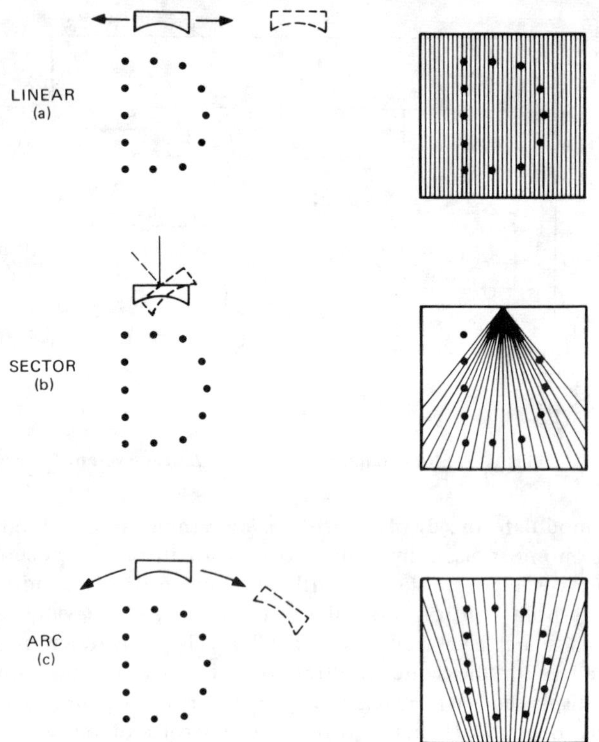

Fig. 2. Mechanical motion and image format for (a) linear, (b) sector, and (c) arc *B*-scans.

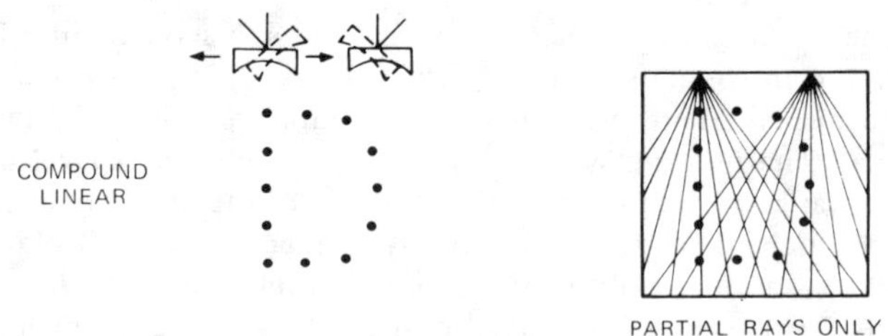

Fig. 3. Mechanical motion and image format for a compound linear scan. (Only two positions shown.) Note that in the compound region, object points are imaged with more than one acoustic ray.

for imaging through narrow apertures, such as for imaging the heart through the ribs. In an arc scan a transducer is moved along the arc of a circle, which gives rise to an image format that is the inverse of the sector scan [13]. Note that the field-of-view is largest near the transducer and decreases with depth of penetration. The arc scan (or a close approximation to it) is most often encountered in manual scans of the abdomen, the surface of which resembles the arc of a circle.

The compound scan [14], which is a combination of the sector scan with either a linear scan or an arc scan, is illustrated in Fig. 3. For illustrative purposes, only two positions in the linear travel and the respective sectors are shown. The sector is usually much smaller in compound scanning than in simple sector scanning where angles as large as ±45° are used. Note that in compound scanning, object points are imaged by more than one acoustic pulse along different ray paths. Compound scanning is used to overcome a major problem in *B*-scan imaging, namely the difficulty of imaging specular reflectors and objects lying behind specular reflectors. Recall that a specular reflector reflects sound toward a direction that is dependent on its orientation to the transducer. Hence, it is possible for an incident sound beam to reflect from a specular reflector in a direction such that the reflected sound beam does not return

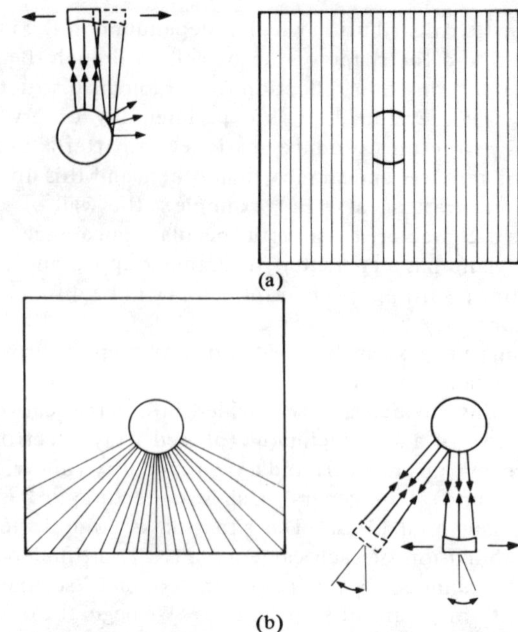

Fig. 4. (a) Linear scan and image of a specular cylindrical reflector. (b) Linear scan with compounding of the same object. Compounding "fills in" the nonimaged segments of the linear scan.

to the transducer. The imaging system (falsely) interprets this as the abscence of a reflector and does not display a signal even though a very strong reflecting interface may have been present. This is illustrated in Fig. 4(a) for a simple linear scan of a cylindrical object (a blood vessel, for example). The sound that impinges on the side of the object is reflected away from the transducer so that it is never received. In this simple case it is possible to mentally connect the two arcs to form a mental image of the true object shape; however, in a complex biological medium this is not always possible. The compound scan helps to "paint in" that part of the specular surface that was not imaged in the simple scan. This is illustrated in Fig. 4(b). Again, only two positions of the transducer are shown for the linear travel along with the particular sector angle that images part of the side of the vessel. The compound scan is also useful for imaging behind highly reflecting or attenuating structures (e.g., ribs) since hidden object points can be imaged from an unobstructed direction.

In Section III various diagnostic *B*-scan techniques will be discussed and compared. Each of the basic modalities has numerous embodiments encompassing manual, automatic mechanical, automatic electronic, and hybrid combinations. Some of the techniques work in "real time,"[3] that is, they are capable of acquiring and displaying dynamic images of organs that are in motion. One advantage of rapid image acquisition is that a large number of images and image planes may be inspected in a brief period of time. This is contrasted with "non-real time" scanners which require a few seconds to acquire and display the image, which means that they are not normally used for displaying organ motion.

Another distinction often applied to the general *B*-scan category is whether a system is a contact scanner or a water path scanner. In the former, the transducer contacts the skin surface directly; in the latter, the transducer first launches a sound beam into a liquid medium, usually water, before the

---

[3] Typically the images are obtained in a small fraction of a second.

sound beam enters the patient's skin through a membrane. The water path scanning technique is used principally in automatic mechanical scanners to isolate the mechanical motion from the patient. Usually the water path distance is made somewhat larger than the desired depth of penetration to eliminate artifacts that otherwise could appear due to reverberation between the skin and the transducer.

D. Resolution

Now that the general concepts of the B-scan have been defined, it is appropriate to consider the question of spatial resolution. There are two resolution factors in a B-scan: 1) Resolution in the direction of transducer motion, known as "lateral" or "transverse" resolution and 2) Resolution in the direction of acoustic pulse propagation, known as "axial" resolution. We begin by considering lateral resolution. In focused optical systems the resolution δ as defined by the Rayleigh criterion [15] is determined by the wavelength λ of the light and the numerical aperture of the focusing elements through the equation

$$\delta = \frac{1.22\lambda F}{D} \qquad (6)$$

where F is the focal length of the system and D the diameter of the circular entrance pupil. For two incoherent point sources this criterion places the center of the Airy disk (15) of one source onto the first zero of the Airy disk of the second source. The resulting intensity pattern has a 19 percent dip midway between the centers of the images of the two sources. Bringing the sources closer together will cause this dip to fill in until finally only a central maximum is present and no obvious feature of the intensity pattern allows one to distinguish the presence of one source from two sources.

Lord Rayleigh formulated his resolution criterion in order to predict the ability of an optical system to distinguish two *self-luminous* incoherent point sources (stars). Note that the optical system was operating in a "receive-only" mode, whereas an ultrasonic B-scan system operates in a transmit/receive mode. This means that the effective spatial response of the ultrasonic system to a point source reflector is the product of the transmitter field pattern with the receiver field pattern. Because the same transducer is usually employed for both transmit and receive, the effective spatial response pattern for a B-scan system is not an Airy pattern, but the *square* of the Airy pattern. This is illustrated in Fig. 5. The zeros of the two functions still coincide, but the squared response function is sharper than the unsquared response.

How does this affect resolution? It depends on what one wishes to define as the criterion for resolution. If, for example, the criterion is the distance to the first zero of the response function, then the "resolution" is identical to that calculated by Rayleigh (6). However, this is an arbitrary choice. For example, suppose we choose as our criterion that there be a 19 percent dip in the response function as was achieved in the receive only case. There is a rather good argument for using this criterion since an image is presented as a relative change of intensity of which some minimum variation is termed detectable.[4] Using this criterion it is easy to show that the

---

[4] Notice that even the 19 percent dip is an arbitrary number. In principle even a 1 percent dip or smaller is detectable. However, the "resolveable distance" is not very different for those two choices due to the rapidly varying response function.

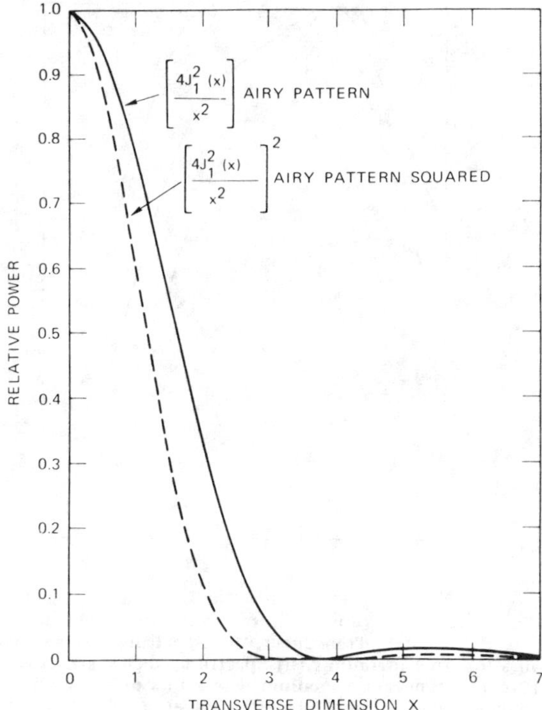

Fig. 5. Plot of the Airy pattern and the square of the Airy pattern. The "squared" response has steeper slopes than the usual Airy pattern, thus potentially increasing resolution.

"resolution" is better by about 25 percent than the Rayleigh estimate. For a 19-mm diameter 2.25 MHz focused transducer with a 12-cm focal length, the Rayleigh resolution in a homogeneous medium such as water is about 5 mm at the focal distance; if the 19 percent dip criterion is used the resolution is about 3.8 mm. The question of which criterion to choose is something of an academic one, since, as we shall soon see, there are many modifying factors for resolution in a complex biological medium.

It is important to understand that the above discussion applies only to the resolution in the transverse (transducer motion) dimension. Recall that the other dimension in a B-scan is inferred from the arrival time of sequentially reflected acoustic pulses. The resolution in this axial dimension is relatively unaffected by the presence or absence of focusing elements but is determined principally by the bandwidth of the transducer [16]; the larger the bandwidth, the shorter the acoustic pulse that can be generated and received, and the finer the definition along the axis of propagation. For a typical 2.25-MHz commercial medical transducer, it is possible to attain 70-percent bandwidth to provide a resolution of about 2 mm.

In the presence of a wide bandwidth signal, the application of (6) is not straightforward. Rather than simply having a single wavelength λ, there is a wide spectrum of wavelengths present. In a loss-free propagation medium the transverse resolution can be estimated by using the wavelength of the nominal center frequency of the transducer. The reason that this can be done is that, in the transverse dimension, the main effect of a broad-band signal is to change (or eliminate) the side-lobe structure of the transducer field pattern. However, the body is not a loss-free propagation medium and as a result of having frequency dependent absorption, the center frequency of the sound field is not constant with depth of penetration.

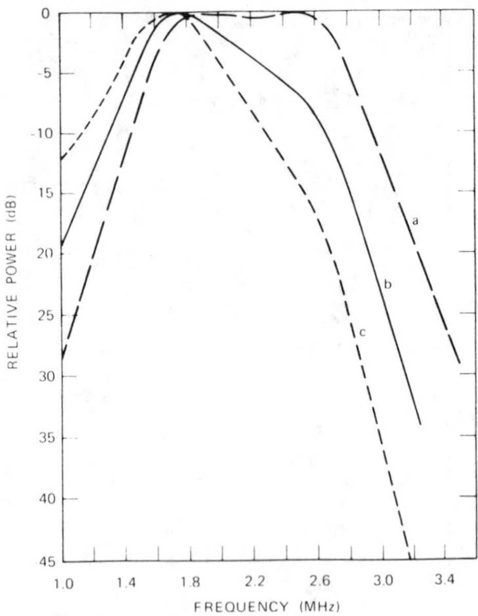

Fig. 6. Frequency spectrum of a transmitted/received echo from a broad band 2.25-MHz Transducer. (a) Spectrum when signal propagates in a loss-free medium. (b) Spectrum when a signal is reflected at a 10-cm distance in a medium with a loss of 1 dB cm^{-1} MHz^{-1}. (c) Spectrum when a signal is reflected at a 20-cm distance in a medium with a loss of 1 dB cm^{-1} MHz^{-1}.

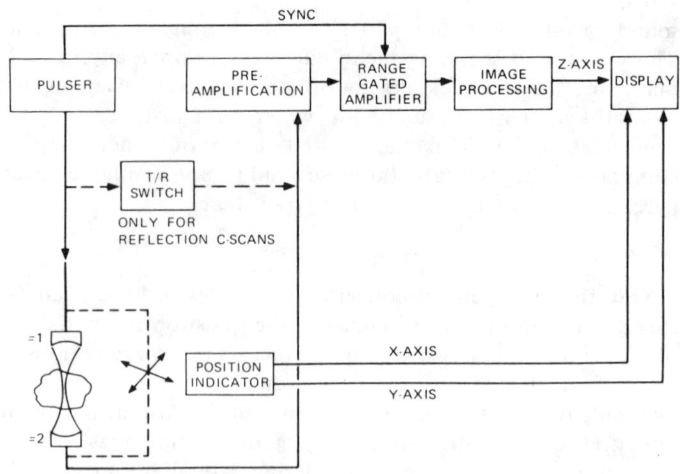

Fig. 7. A block diagram of simple C-scan system.

This is illustrated in Fig. 6 for a 2.25-MHz transducer. Curve "a" is the frequency spectrum (two-way response) for a pulse that was transmitted and received from a large plane reflector immersed in a nearly lossless medium (water). Curves "b" and "c" represent the calculated frequency spectrum of the same pulse after being reflected at a distance of 10 and 20 cm through tissue with an absorption coefficient of 1 dB cm^{-1} MHz^{-1}. Note that the center frequency decreases with increasing depth, thus adversely affecting the potential transverse resolution for deep structures.

There is another factor which negatively affects resolution. Most B-scanners achieve transverse resolution with fixed focus elements. Thus the resolution is poorer for structures both nearer to and farther from the transducer than the focal length of the fixed focus element. In addition, the designer is faced with the following compromise: resolution at the focal depth may be improved by increasing the aperture (D in (6)); however, the depth-of-focus, that region over which the optimum resolution is obtained, becomes smaller. It is a particularly unhappy compromise since the resolution improves only as the first power of the aperture whereas the depth-of-focus becomes smaller as the square of the aperture [17]. In other words one loses depth-of-focus much faster than one gains resolution. To minimize this effect only weak focusing is generally used in diagnostic instruments; even so, the resolution is noticeably poorer for points far from the focal distance whenever fixed focus elements are used. There are acoustic focusing elements that are not fixed in their focal distance, but which are electronically variable [18]-[20]. We shall not go into great detail in this chapter in describing the considerable variety of techniques that are available. In Section III we shall consider some of the more highly developed techniques and the images that they provide. However, we will consider the physical basis on which all of these techniques are based.

It is possible to construct an electronically variable focusing device because a piezoelectric transducer is sensitive not only to amplitude, but also to phase [21]. This is unlike the usual case of optics where images are made by power detectors that are phase insensitive.[5] Electronically variable focusing devices have two forms: the annular array [22], in which the phase is processed on the assumption of circular symmetry, and the linear array [23], [24], in which the phase is processed on the assumption of one dimensional symmetry. The former results in a focus similar to that obtained with a spherical lens; the latter results in a focus similar to that obtained with a cylindrical lens. A common denominator to both of these forms is that the transducer is subdivided into a number of independent units, the signals to and from which are independently processed before being combined for the final image. The process involves some type of phase modification, which is obtained either by differential time delay circuitry [25] or direct phase modulation [26]. The variable feature of the acoustic device arises from the ability to vary the electronic phase corrections as fast as the acoustic data is received. Using these techniques, it is possible, at least in principle, to obtain diffraction limited resolution throughout the entire field-of-view of a B-scan image. However, the complexity of such devices can be formidable.

E. C-Scan

C-scanning provides a two-dimensional orthographic image of an object. Unlike the B-scan, where one dimension of the image is inferred from the arrival time of an acoustic pulse, time plays no primary role in either of the two image dimensions of a C-scan. In a reflection C-scan, the time of arrival plays a secondary role in that it determines the distance of the image plane from the transducer; in a transmission C-scan, time plays no role whatsoever. A C-scan image resembles images obtained with X-ray fluoroscopy; hence, the images tend to look more familiar than a corresponding B-scan and are often more readily interpretable. There are, however, some serious difficulties with C-scan techniques that have limited their clinical usefulness. These techniques and their limitations will be discussed in Section IV of this paper.

Shown in Fig. 7 is a block diagram of a simple mechanically driven transmission C-scan system [27]. An electronic pulser

[5] In optical holography both amplitude and phase are encoded into the recording. However, the detection medium, usually film, is still phase insensitive. The hologram encodes the phase of the optical signal into power variations.

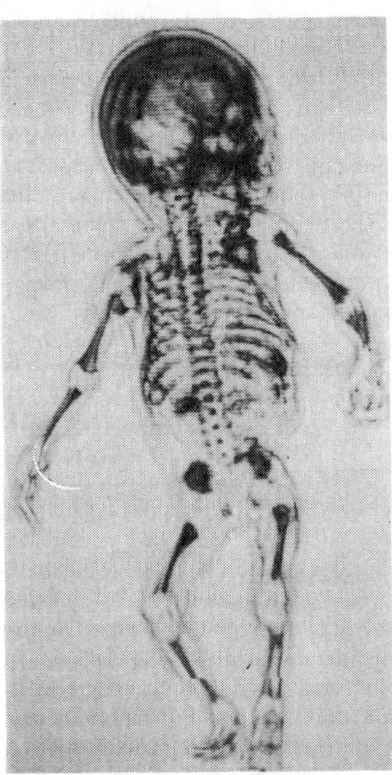

Fig. 8. *C*-scan transmission image of a full term still born fetus. (Picture courtesy of P. S. Green, SRI International.)

excites a transducer which generates a short burst of focused ultrasound that passes through an object-to-be-imaged. The perturbed sound field is converted to an electronic signal by a receiving transducer which is in incorrect spatial registration with the transmitter; the signal is pre-amplified before passing through a range gated amplifier which amplifies only the direct acoustic path signal. It should be noted that CW ultrasound could in principle be used; however, in the practical case multipath reverberations could cause severe image degradation. The combination of using pulsed insonification with a range-gated receiving system effectively eliminates this problem. The range gated signal is then processed for display by logarithmic compression and gray-scale mapping. The image of a full-term, still-born fetus shown in Fig. 8 is a good example of the potential of *C*-scan transmission imaging. The technique described is, however, impractical for clinical use since the image is generated over an extended period of time. Researchers in this field have developed a number of ingenious ways to produce images in only a fraction of a second; we will consider a few of these in Section IV. Note at this point that an image could also have been obtained by keeping the transmitter/receiver fixed and moving the *object* in a raster pattern or by flooding the entire object with a sound field (using a different type of transmitter than that shown in Fig. 7) and moving the receiver only.

The system described above could also be used to obtain a reflection *C*-scan image by using transducer #1 as both transmitter and receiver. The transducer could be scanned mechanically as before to obtain the two-dimensional image. In this case range gating not only removes multipath reverberations but also determines the distance of the image plane from the transducer.

Although the transmission and reflection *C*-scan techniques are similar, the images that result are quite different. The trans-

mission images depend for their contrast primarily on the differential attenuation properties of tissue; the reflection images depend for their contrast primarily on acoustic impedance variations. Reflection *C*-scans are particularly susceptible to specular reflection effects—small changes in object orientation often result in significantly different images. Transmission images are independent of specularity but are susceptible to coherent interference effects [28], [29].

Since the resolution in a *C*-scan system generally relies on the focusing properties of a lens for both displayed dimensions, equation (6), i.e., the Rayleigh criterion, is a good estimate for definition. The effective point response function may or may not be the square of the Airy function depending on the type of system used. This is in contrast to *B*-scans where the response function is almost always squared. The bandwidth of the transducer is not a factor in resolution since in a *C*-scan image both dimensions are "lateral" dimensions. As in *B*-scans, *C*-scan resolution suffers whenever ultrasound passes through tissue due to the frequency dependent absorption coefficient [30]. Depth-of-focus is not a major, direct factor in *C*-scan resolution but it has some significant indirect effects. For example, out of the focal plane objects may appear as out-of-focus artifacts in the images.

To summarize, acoustical and optical imaging systems are very similar in the basic physical principles upon which they are based. The differences between the two are related to difference in scan technique and the necessity of converting the acoustical information to visible form.

III. *B*-Scan Instrumentation

B-Scan instruments can generally be classified into two types.

1) Contact scanners—Those in which the transducers are in direct contact with the skin of the patient.

2) Water-path scanners—Those in which the transducers stand back from the skin with a contained liquid coupling medium being provided to conduct the sound from the transducers to the patient and back again.

Since these two types of instrumentation have their own advantage and disadvantages we shall discuss them separately.

A. Contact Scanners

In order to produce an ultrasonic image in the *B*-scan format, some means for moving the ultrasonic beam within the body must be employed. Many currently available contact *B*-scan instruments utilize some form of mechanical system for moving the ultrasonic transducer and thus the ultrasonic beam. These systems can be categorized into two types: those that are moved by hand and those that are moved by some form of motorized mechanism. The same effect can be accomplished by electronically switching or "phasing" stationary transducer elements of an ultrasonic array, and other currently available contact *B*-scan instruments use these techniques. Two methods of array scanning have been realized in diagnostic instrumentation: the linear stepped array and the linear phased array. In all cases, these systems employ transducers which are used in direct contact with the skin of the patient.

1) Manual Systems: The manual compound contact *B*-scan system has been the mainstay of diagnostic ultrasound imaging for many years. This form of ultrasound imaging system has evolved into sophisticated equipment capable of producing images with a significant degree of diagnostic information. Most often manual *B*-scan equipment is used for diagnosing ailments in the region of the abdomen such as cystic and

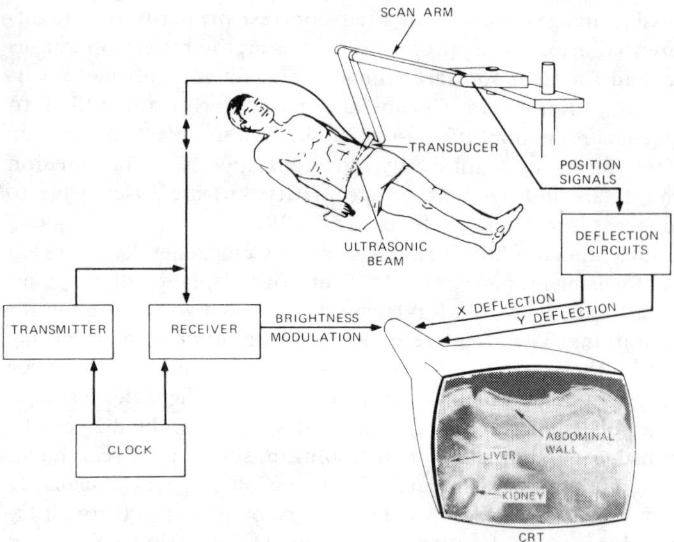

Fig. 9. A two-dimensional image of a cross section of the body can be produced with manual *B*-scan instruments. A typical system configuration includes the ultrasonic transducer which is mounted at the end of an articulated scan arm and which is moved by the technician or physician across the patient's body. The position of the ultrasound beam is sensed by resolvers in the scan arm and the resulting position signals determine the position of the electron beam on the CRT. In this way, the ultrasonic echoes sensed by the transducer are used to build up the image.

solid lesions [31], kidney and gall stones [32], carcinoma of the liver and uterus, cirrhosis of the liver, and for obstetrical applications such as placental localization [33] and the measurement of fetal biparietal diameter.

It is also beginning to be used for cardiac studies, imaging the thyroid gland and in the pancreas and stomach. Indeed, as time progresses and equipment improves, the number of uses for the manual contact *B*-scan imaging system is ever expanding.

Details of the operation of the compound contact *B*-scan imaging system are given elsewhere [34] so we will restrict this paper to a brief description. Contact *B*-scan imaging systems consist basically of three parts: 1) a scanning arm to control the travel of an ultrasonic transducer so that the ultrasound beam is always maintained in a single plane; 2) appropriate electronics for amplifying and detecting the returning echoes, monitoring the position and angle of the transducer, and driving and deflecting a display device; and 3) a display to convert the electronic signals into an image on a CRT device. A block diagram of a typical manual contact *B*-scan system is shown in Fig. 9. To use such an instrument, the ultrasonic technologist or physician grasps the transducer and places it against the patient. Ultrasonic coupling gel or mineral oil is used on the patient's skin (ultrasound is highly reflected and attenuated by air) and to provide a lubricated surface. As the operator guides the transducer across the skin, the electronic circuits sense the angle and position of the scan arm and, with that information, compute the angle and position of the ultrasound beam. As the transducer is moved, the electron beam in the CRT is deflected in a manner that makes each scan line in the image correspond in angle and position to the ultrasound beam in the patient. Thus an image is slowly built up of many scan lines. Depending on how the operator moves the transducer, linear, sector, arc, or compound scanning can be accomplished. However, one of the limitations of this technique is that image quality can be affected by the manner in which the

scanning is performed; hence, ultrasound technologists must be trained to develop good scanning technique.

Early equipment produced complete images only on film since just a few scan lines on the display were visible at a time due to the relatively short persistence of the CRT phosphor. By aiming a camera at the CRT and making an exposure during the entire scanning time, an entire image could be formed. Unfortunately, the operator of the equipment was essentially working blind and many trial-and-error attempts had to be made before satisfactory images could be produced.

The next step in the evolution of manual contact *B*-scan systems was the use of storage oscilloscopes as the display device. These scopes allowed the operator to see the image as it was being made and to make corrections more quickly. Unfortunately, storage oscilloscopes were not able to display a very wide range of gray levels and were best used to display bistable images. Thus ultrasound design engineers turned to a new device—the storage tube [38]. This cathode ray storage device contains a solid-state storage surface composed of many small diodes and an electron gun for addressing the diodes and reading the stored data. Since it is an electron beam device it offers great flexibility: the data can be written slowly and read quickly, allowing a standard television display to be used for producing the image. Selected areas of the storage surface can be enlarged providing a zoom feature. When properly adjusted, good gray-scale images can be produced with this device and compound contact *B*-scanners with gray scale capability soon became available. However, experience with the analog scan converter showed that memory nonuniformity (uneven image quality), drift (change of image, quality with time), and a limited writing rate (image quality variations with scanning speed) can be problems.

Several modern day scanners circumvent these problems by using a digital (solid-state) scan converter made up of semiconductor memory integrated circuits working in conjunction with electronic control circuits. In the digital scan converter the image is usually broken into a matrix of points or "pixels" and a memory "location" is assigned to each pixel. A number corresponding to the brightness of each pixel is stored in its corresponding location as the scan is being made. As many as 512×512 points each with as many as 64 shades of gray (a six bit code) are used so that the solid state memory may contain more than 1.5 million bits of information. The solid-state scan converter is fast enough to produce images on a standard television monitor while at the same time (from a human standpoint) storing the next image. This operation is accomplished by changing the data only in those memory locations corresponding to newly scanned areas of the image while retaining previously recorded data in all the other memory locations. Thus the operator is continuously presented with an image even though the scanning may take place slowly. The digital scan converter does not suffer from the memory nonuniformity and drift problems of the analog scan converter. Its major drawback has been its large cost; however, newer integrated circuits are quickly bringing the cost down. Some digital scan converters with limited numbers of pixels and shades of gray have suffered from quantization errors producing images which look contoured; however, this problem can be overcome by using more pixels and gray shades. The great flexibility of the solid-state approach makes it easy to achieve other capabilities such as zoom, gray-scale mapping changes, left/right image reversals, on screen notations for patient identification and date, and electronic calipers for measuring imaged structures. Two examples of

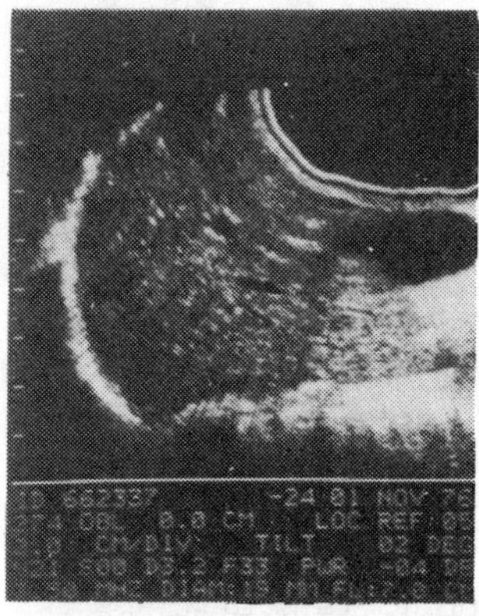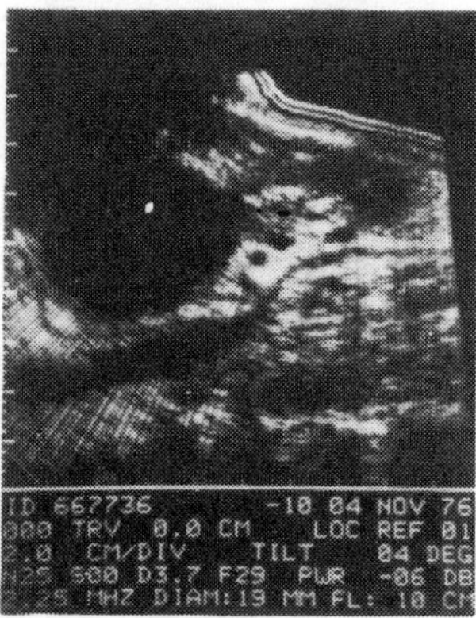

Fig. 10. These two images made with a manual compound contact *B*-scanner show cystic structures within the liver. (a) Along with a large cyst in the upper right, normal liver tissue with vascular and hepatic structures shows clearly in this image made at 3.5 MHz. (b) In contrast, a severely diseased liver shows as a significantly different image. Notice how patient, date, and system information as well as distance calibration (the row of marks along the left edge of the image) are displayed directly on the image in modern scanners. (Photos courtesy of Searle Ultrasound.)

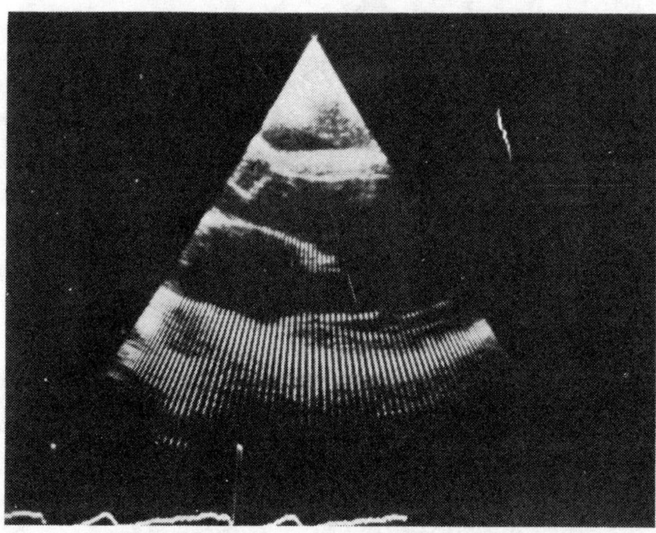

Fig. 11. By rocking a transducer rapidly back-and-forth, a mechanical cardiac scanner produces real-time cross sectional images of the heart. The piece-of-pie shaped image, seen in this figure, is typical of the sector format. (Photo courtesy of Picker Corporation.)

images obtained with a modern compound contact scanner with digital scan conversion are shown in Fig. 10.

The manual contact scanner presents certain problems due to its basic design. Since it works in contact with the patient, the skin and organs close to the skin are generally imaged poorly or not imaged at all because the receiver circuits require some time to recover from the large overload that occurs when the transmitter pulses the transducer. Typically the first centimeter of the image is artifact not actually related to the tissues that are present. Since the scan is manually controlled, image quality varies with the expertise of the operator, and this operator dependence can be a significant problem. Not only must operators be trained before they can produce quality images, but manual scanning is slow and relatively tedious; a patient procedure takes a considerable length of time considering the few diagnostic images that are produced. During the relatively long time (1 to 10 s) that it takes to scan out a single image, organs can move causing the image to be distorted which in turn may confuse the diagnosis. Lastly, manual contact *B*-scanners do not display organ motion in real time.

2) Real Time Systems: In certain diagnostic procedures, the accurate display of tissue motion can be important for a proper diagnosis, for example the detection of diseased heart valves or the determination of fetal viability. Instruments which can produce images rapidly enough to display such motion are called real-time systems. In addition to being able to display organ motion, real-time systems have another advantage: since the operator has nearly instantaneous positional feedback, patient procedures can be accomplished very rapidly since little time is wasted in locating the organ or tissue of interest. In real time systems the ultrasonic beam is either mechanically or electronically scanned.

Currently practical ultrasound equipment operates on the principle that only one acoustic pulse should be traveling in the field of interest at any instant in time. This puts a constraint on real-time equipment. The maximum frame rate, depth of field and number of scan lines in the image are related by the equation

$$R \cdot D \cdot N = \frac{V}{2} \tag{7}$$

where

$$R = \text{maximum frame rate } (\text{s}^{-1})$$
$$D = \text{depth of field (m)}$$
$$N = \text{number of scan lines}$$
$$V = \text{velocity of sound (m/s)}.$$

The velocity of sound is not significantly different for the various soft tissues of the body so that the product of frame rate, depth of field and number of scan lines is essentially a constant. In order to achieve an improvement in one factor, another must be sacrificed. For instance, to get more scan lines in the image, either the frame rate or the depth of field must be decreased. Therefore, high-quality real-time images are difficult to achieve for those organs (such as the liver) that require a large field of view.

3) Mechanical Scan: There are many types of real-time imaging systems currently in use. Perhaps the simplest technique for making real time images is to replace the human hand with a mechanical system that moves the transducer automatically. One such system is the mechanical sector scanner.

In this system a motorized mechanism automatically rocks or rotates the transducer while it is in contact with the patient's skin [39], [40]. Position sensors continuously detect the angle of the transducer and produce a signal used for determining the position of the displayed echoes in the image. Because the scanning is very rapid, there is no need for a scan arm, as in the manual scanner; but in other respects the system is essentially the same as that of a manual *B*-scanner (see Fig. 9).

The sector scan imaging technique is particularly suited for imaging the heart since the ultrasonic beam easily fits into the narrow entrance space between the ribs. Fig. 11 shows an image made with this type of system. Although the image is narrow at the top where skin contact is made, the wider image at the bottom shows a good portion of the heart lying behind the ribs. Images with good gray scale and of manual *B*-scan images quality showing motion of the heart muscle and valves can be made by the mechanical sector scanner. Abdominal organs can also be imaged by placing the transducer against the skin over the abdomen. Generally, however, sector-scan images of the abdominal organs are less useful than manual

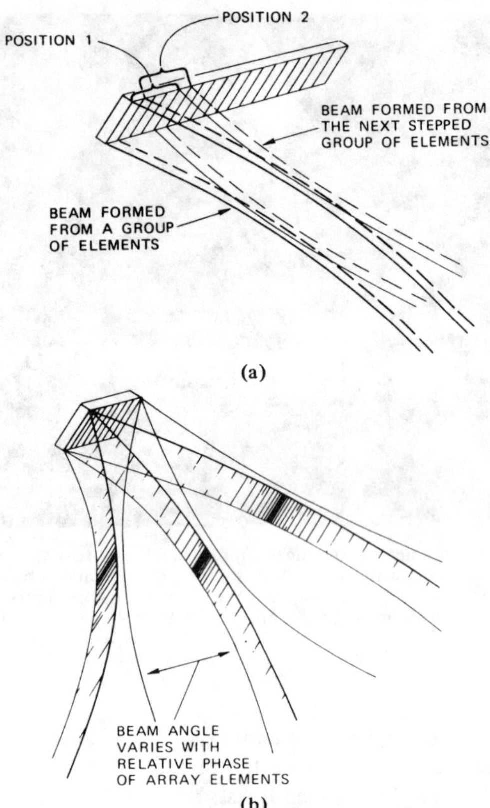

Fig. 12. Linear array ultrasound scanners operate on two different principles. (a) In the linear stepped array system, the beam produced by a small group of elements is moved rectilinearly by stepping the group of elements along the array one element at a time. (b) In the linear phased array system, all elements of the array are active; however the relative electronic delays associated with each element are varied, changing the beam angle so that a sector format is produced.

B-scans because of the small field of view of the sector format, especially near the abdominal wall. At the top of the image, the receiver overload recovery problem common to all contact scanners obliterates the image of the skin and structures near it. In addition, the oscillating or rotating motion of the contact sector scanner against the skin can be uncomfortable for the patient, especially when the transducer is moving over bone, such as a rib, and at times this motion causes the images to be blurred since the tissues may be moved by vibration. These motion caused problems, however, do not exist when the scanning is done electronically.

4) Electronic Scan: There are two distinctly different types of electronically scanned contact *B*-scan imaging systems: the linear stepped array (commonly called the "linear array") and the linear phased array (commonly called the "phased array"). The linear array requires a large number of small railroad-tie-shaped transducer "elements" to be arranged next to each other to form a line array, usually about 1-cm wide and 10- to 15-cm long. Fig. 12(a) shows a typical linear stepped array configuration. From one to four transducer elements are activated at a time and are sequentially stepped along the array so that the ultrasound beam is moved in a linear path even though the array is stationary. The phased array, while similar in construction, is quite different in operation. A phased array transducer is smaller (about 1-cm across and 1- to 3-cm long) and usually contains fewer elements, as shown in Fig. 12(b). Usually all the elements are active at the same time and the ultrasound beam angle is changed by proper phasing of the signals going to the elements for transmit and also by proper

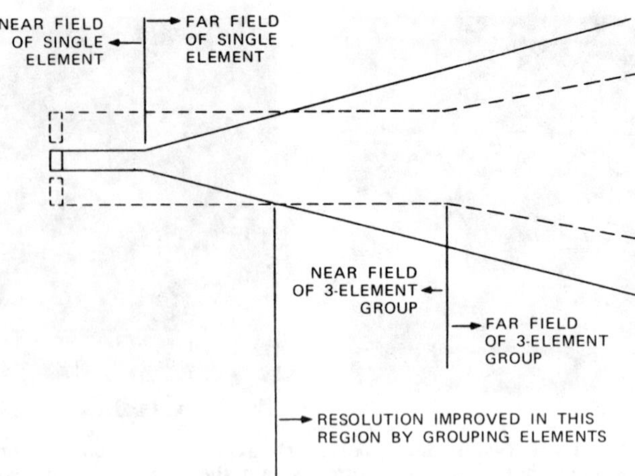

Fig. 13. By operating the narrow elements of a linear stepped array in groups, the resolution in the far field can be improved in comparison with the resolution obtained with only a single element.

phasing of the received signals from each element. This system is analogous to a phased array radar.

5) The Linear Array: Several systems are available which utilize a linear array design. Although images can be produced by activating only one element at a time to form the individual scan lines of the image, poor resolution and sensitivity prevent such a system from being viable. Instead the elements are connected in small groups, and by dropping the last element and connecting the next element of the array this small group of elements is stepped along one element at a time. By using a group of elements the active transducer area is increased which gives better sensitivity, and, in accordance with diffraction theory [5], the larger aperture gives better resolution in the far field. This occurs because the far field, where the beam starts to diverge, begins at a distance, x, given by

$$x = \frac{d^2}{4\lambda} \qquad (8)$$

where λ is the wavelength of the radiated ultrasonic energy and d is the width of the aperture. When comparing the field pattern of different numbers of grouped elements, the wavelength remains constant, and the distance to the far field varies as the square of the number of elements. Fig. 13 shows schematically the effect of increasing the group size from one element to three elements. In the three element case, the far field begins about nine times as far away from the transducer face and diverges at a smaller angle, as compared with the single element case. As can be seen, however, using a group of elements is detrimental to resolution in the near field.

When designing such a system, the resolution specifications for the instrument combined with the desired depth of field determines how many elements are connected together in the group. All elements in the group can simply be connected in parallel (i.e., all in phase) or in the individual elements can be relatively phased to improve the resolution in the imaged plane.[6] Since the phase profile across the active group of elements can remain the same no matter where the group of elements are located along the array, in-plane phased focusing to achieve better image resolution does not require much additional electronic complexity.

---

[6] Since the linear array is one-dimensional out-of-plane resolution cannot be improved by phasing but can be improved by the addition of a fixed cylindrical lens on the face of the array.

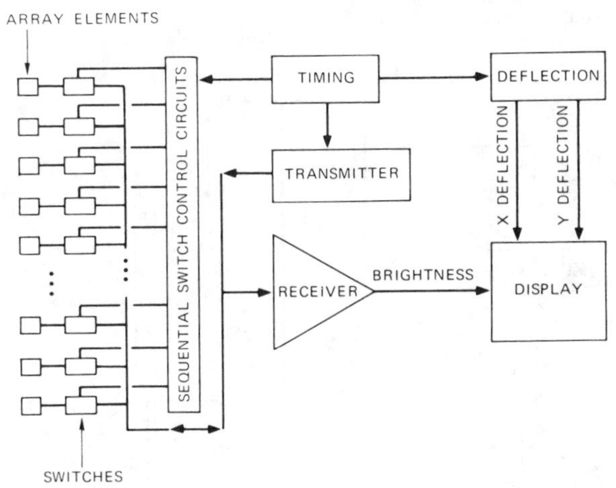

Fig. 14. Conceptually, the linear stepped array *B*-scan system is simple as is shown in this block diagram of a typical linear array system.

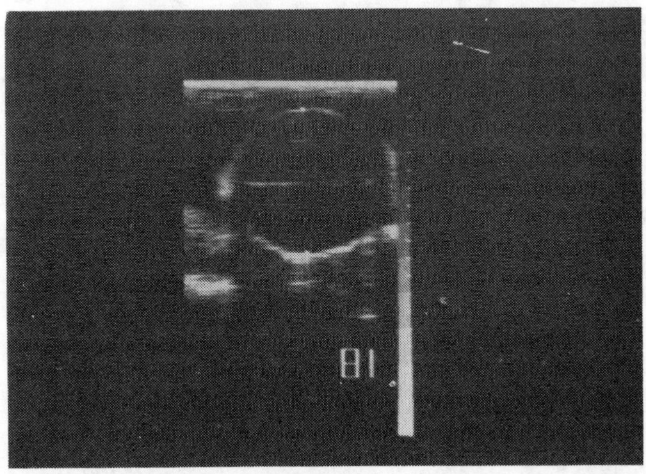

Fig. 15. In this cross sectional image of a fetal head made with a linear stepped array ultrasound scanner, the fetal skull and brain midline show clearly. The biparietal diameter is measured along the slightly brightened vertical scan line in the middle of the picture and displayed in the image above as 81 mm. (Photo courtesy of ADR Ultrasound.)

Fig. 14 shows a block diagram of a typical linear stepped array ultrasonic imaging system [41], [42]. Because most linear array systems do not use phased focusing, lateral resolution is generally inferior to that which can be achieved with a manual *B*-scanner even though the axial resolution (which is determined by the acoustic pulse length) can be similar to that realized by manual *B*-scan equipment. As in the mechanical real time system, there is a tradeoff between frame rate, depth of field, and number of acoustic scan lines; however, since lateral resolution is limited, a large number of scan lines would be redundant, and thus high frame rates are typically achieved. Most linear array scanners produce between 64 and 128 scan lines and run at 20 to 40 frames per second. These instruments are light weight and low cost due to the electronic simplicity of this technique.

The linear stepped array real time scanners have found acceptance in the field of obstetrics where they are especially useful in determining and following the state of a pregnancy [43]. Fetal age, an important factor of interest to the obstetrician, can be determined by measuring the biparietal diameter (BPD) (the distance across the skull) of the fetus [44]. Since the axial resolution of the linear array scanner is quite good, this device is well adapted to performing this measurement. Fig. 15 shows the image of a fetal head produced with a linear stepped array ultrasound scanner. The BPD which is measured along the slightly brightened vertical line in the middle of the image, is shown on the screen to be 81 mm indicating a gestational age of 33 weeks. The entire circumferential dimension of the fetal skull shows clearly because only slight ossification (calcification) of the bones occurs before birth.

The real-time aspects of this device make it well-suited to obstetrical work. Since the fetus frequently moves, especially during the last trimester of pregnancy, making accurate BPD measurements with a manual contact scanner can be difficult. The ultrasound beam must be oriented properly for accurate readings, and the rapid imaging of this type of instrument allows fetal motion to be noticed and corrections to be made. In addition, fetal viability, especially early in pregnancy, can be determined by observing motion of the fetal heart on the real time display.

6) The Phased Array: The other basic type of real-time contact array scanner, marketed by several manufacturers, is the linear phased array [45], [46]. By properly phasing the excitation signals to and from the individual elements of the array,

both beam steering (the angle relative to the face of the array at which the ultrasound beam propagates) and beam focusing can be achieved.[7] In this type of system, the scan produced is a sector, as shown in Fig. 12(b), and this kind of equipment is often used for cardiac imaging.

The term "phased array" is actually somewhat of a misnomer since for broad-band signals it is actually the relative *delay* of the signals from each element that determines the beam angle and focus. Two schemes are used for varying the signal delay: 1) a set of fixed delay lines that are switched into the signal path at appropriate times and in proper sequence, and 2) electronically variable delay lines where the delay is continuously adjusted by an appropriate control signal. Both schemes have been implemented in commercial equipment, but the electronically variable delay is somewhat more flexible. A block diagram of this type of linear phased array scanner is shown in Fig. 16. Because these systems require complex electronic delay line circuitry, the cost of a phased array scanner is high when compared with that of a linear stepped array.

Because there is only one transmitted pulse for each scan line, only a fixed focus at some preselected depth or focal line extending through a range of depths is possible on transmit. The received signals, in contrast, consist of many echoes, each from a different depth, arriving in time sequence. Hence, by varying the delays as the echoes are received it is possible to make the focus track the depth from which the echoes are returning [47]. In this way, the lateral resolution can be improved over that which would be achieved by a fixed focus system. Such a scheme could also be used to improve the focus of a linear stepped array system, but the added complexity defeats the purpose of the otherwise simple *B*-scanner. In the phased array system, the complex electronic delay circuits are already required for the beam steering function, and only slightly more complex control functions must be added to achieve focus tracking.

---

[7] As with the linear array, because the phased array is one dimensional, only in-plane focus can be electronically affected. However, in this case also, out-of-plane focus can be improved by the use of a cylindrical lens.

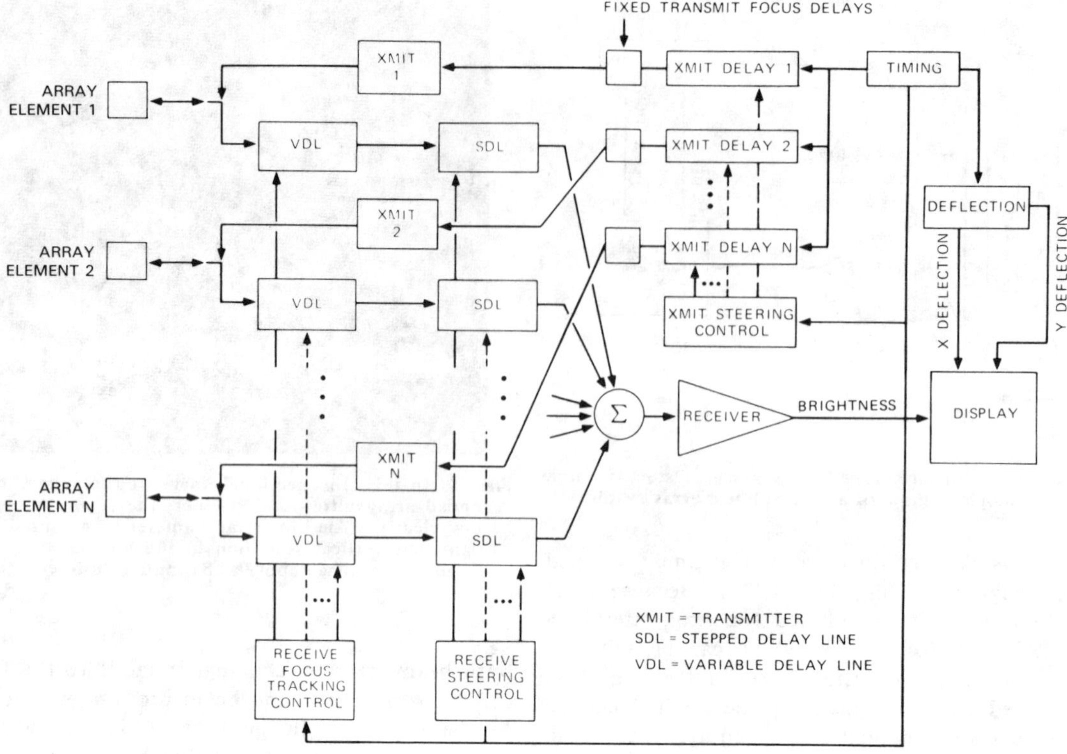

Fig. 16. Linear phased array *B*-scan systems require the most complex circuitry of any current ultrasonic imaging instrument. This block diagram of a typical system that uses variable delay lines indicates the compexity involved.

An abdominal image produced by a phased array scanner is shown in Fig. 17. This sagittal image of a normal adult liver clearly shows the portal vein and several of its branches. This picture was made with a system that employs electronic processing to remove the radial lines seen in Fig. 11 that are typical of many sector scan images.

Phased array imaging systems, as presently configured, have a basic limitation: because both the delays required for steering and the delays required for focusing are only stepwise approximated across the aperture (there are a finite number of non-infinitesimal elements), the far-field beam pattern may have relatively large sidelobes. The amplitude of these "grating" sidelobes requires that the dynamic range of the system be restricted if unambiguous images are to be produced. Since the dynamic range of a single transducer mechanical or manual scanner is not limited in this fashion, the tissue differentiation of a manual scanner is not currently achievable with a phased array system. Likewise, the delay profile required for optimum focus is only approximated and thus resolution is compromised. However, continuing research on the approximation problems may produce results that will allow future systems to nearly achieve manual *B*-scanner image quality. The phased array scanner offers a small and lightweight probe, high patient comfort, and a very rapid frame rate making this instrument quite attractive for cardiac and abdominal imaging.

B. Water Path Scanners

Thus far we have only discussed *B*-scan systems which require the ultrasonic transducer or array to be in direct contact with the patients skin. There is another class of scanners which utilize a liquid coupling medium between the transducer and

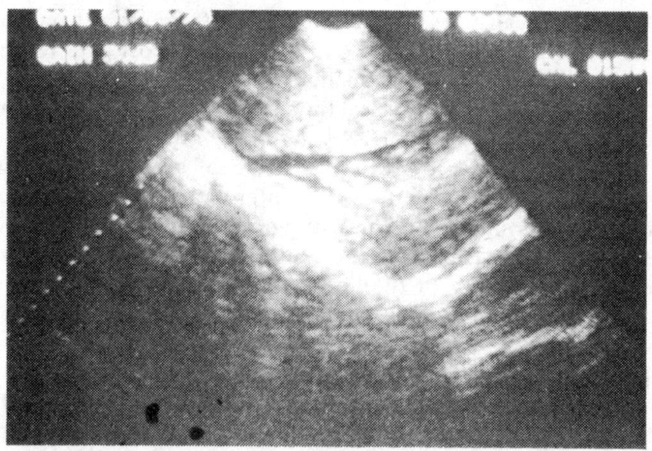

Fig. 17. The portal vein and normal liver are shown in this longitudinal abdominal image made with a phased array system. This system includes special processing to remove the "spoked" effect seen in many sector format images. (Photo courtesy of EMI Medical Inc.)

patient. By having an intervening medium, the transducer can be located away from the patient so that mechanical motion of the transducer is not transmitted to the patient. These are usually known as water path systems because the liquid medium is frequently water.

Most water path scanners operate on the principle that the distance between the transducer and the skin should be slightly greater than the depth of field so that multiple reverberations of sound between the skin surface and the front of the transducer do not cause artifacts in the image. In following this principle, the total path traveled by the ultrasound is at least twice as long as in contact scanners and either the frame

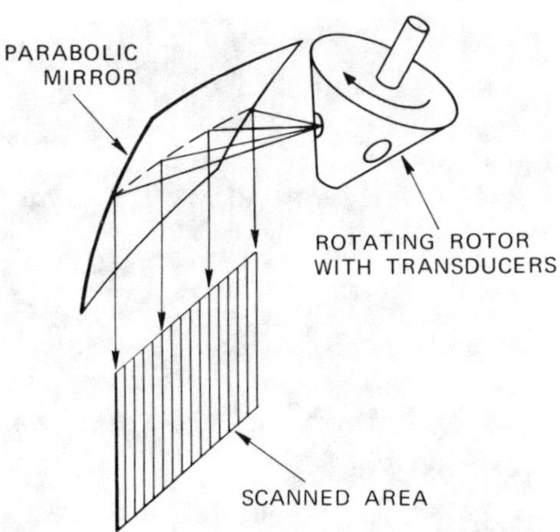

Fig. 18. This technique is used in one type of real time water path abdominal scanner for making high resolution *B*-scan images. A rotating rotor containing several transducers around its periphery scans the ultrasonic beam across a parabolic ultrasound mirror. After leaving the water filled housing in which the rotor and mirror are submerged, the reflected ultrasound beam forms a rectilinear scan.

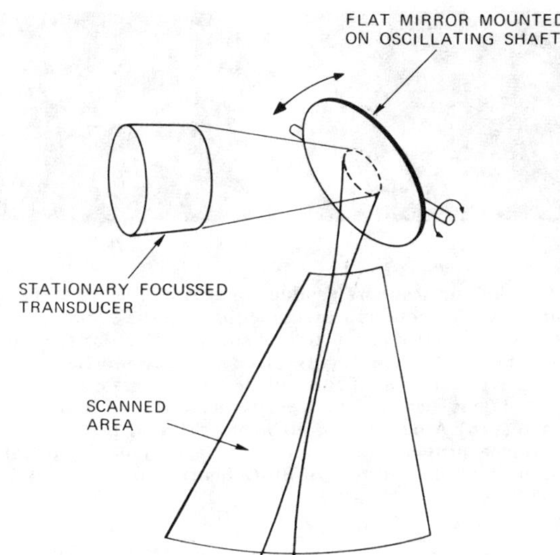

Fig. 19. Another technique used for a real time water path *B*-scan abdominal scanner, uses an oscillating ultrasonic mirror to direct the beam from a stationary transducer over a sector shaped area. The face of the transducer and the oscillating mirror are both submerged in a water filled housing.

rate or the number of scan lines must be halved in comparison to an equivalent contact scanner. Most water path scanners require rather bulky scan heads to contain fluid, but because of the water path, excellent images of the skin and structures just below the skin can be achieved. The water path also allows the use of nonsector mechanical scans as well as much larger transducers for improved resolution and sensitivity. Therefore, these systems have advantages that make them attractive for many applications. Although some experimental water path scanners require part or all of the patient to be submerged in a water tank in order to perform the scan, we will restrict this discussion to scanners which use a liquid filled bag or housing for patient coupling.

1) Abdominal Scanners: Several manufacturers currently have water path abdominal imaging equipment on the market. One such system produces real time rectilinear scans by reflecting the ultrasound beam from a transducer off of a parabolic ultrasonic mirror. A diagram of this concept is shown in Fig. 18. The transducer, mounted on the surface of a conically shaped rotor, rotates continuously, sweeping the ultrasonic beam across the patient in a recurrent fashion. By using more than one transducer on the rotor and selecting them sequentially, little time is wasted while waiting for the first transducer to complete a full revolution.

Another system also uses an ultrasonic mirror, as shown in Fig. 19; however, in this instrument the transducer is stationary and the mirror is moved with a rocking motion so that the area to be imaged is scanned by the reflected ultrasound beam [47]. With this system, the difficulties encountered in making electrical connections to a moving transducer are eliminated. This system can produce images at up to 12 frames per second.

Since in both of these systems the scanning mechanism is submerged in water and the water path equals the depth of field, these water path scanners contain a relatively large quantity of fluid and, therefore, have bulky and heavy scan heads. These are typically supported by a mechanical scan arm which is also quite large. Thus while these systems are electronically simple compared to the phased array, they are mechanically complex.

In yet a third system, the patient lies on a pliable membrane covering the surface of a water filled tank [48]. Submerged in the tank and facing toward the patient are eight focused transducers arranged along a line. A mechanical system causes all eight of the transducers to rock in synchronism so that

each transducer sequentially scans across the same plane. A complete scan takes about two seconds. By combining the eight resulting *B*-scans, each made from a slightly different angle, a compound *B*-scan image is produced. These images are of very high quality, and the system is well suited for imaging in obstetrics, the abdomen, breast and is especially useful for use with the neonati. Due to the relatively long scan time, however, images of moving organs, such as the neonatal heart, are blurred.

One of the major difficulties of a water path scanner is getting good coupling to the patient. Usually this is accomplished by making one surface of the water filled housing a very soft and compliant membrane so that the effect is similar to that of a water filled balloon. Abdominal scanners with large scan head surfaces must maintain contact over a large area and this can be difficult even with such a compliant coupling bag.

The greatest advantage of the water path abdominal scanner is the potential for manual contact scanner image quality in conjunction with real time imaging. Although this combination of features is very desirable the bulk and inconvenience of these scanners has so far restricted their acceptance by the medical community. Because of the limited experience with imaging the skin and structures just below the skin, current use of this information is quite limited, although there is thought to be future potential in burn studies.

2) Ophthalmic and Small-Parts Scanners: Up to this point we have been discussing *B*-scan equipment designed to produce images of large organs located in the abdomen or chest. There is another class of instruments which are primarily intended to make images of the eye and surrounding structures. These instruments are excellent for locating foreign objects located inside of the eye as a result of accident, of assessing the extent of traumatic damage to the eye and for determining and measuring detached retinas. Tumors of the eye and socket are also well imaged by such equipment [49]. These instruments are especially well suited for cases of eye trauma which causes internal bleeding and subsequent opacification of the vitreous [50]. Standard optical instruments become useless in such cases. Special ultrasound instruments have been developed for these and other ophthalmic applications.

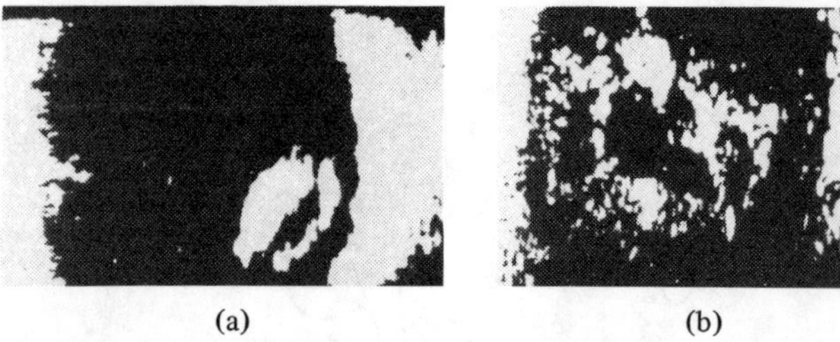

(a)   (b)

Fig. 20. Ophthalmic scanners produce images of the eye and surrounding structures. In these images, made through the eyelid, the front of the eye is to the left and the retinal surface shows as the curved demarcation between the normally black vitreous and the white retina seen in the right portion of the pictures. (a) An image of an eye with a dislocated lens, which can be seen near the back of the eye, is shown here. (b) A dense vitreous hemorrhage in this eye would prevent making a proper assessment of damage by using optical instruments alone. (Photo courtesy of Storz Instrument Company.)

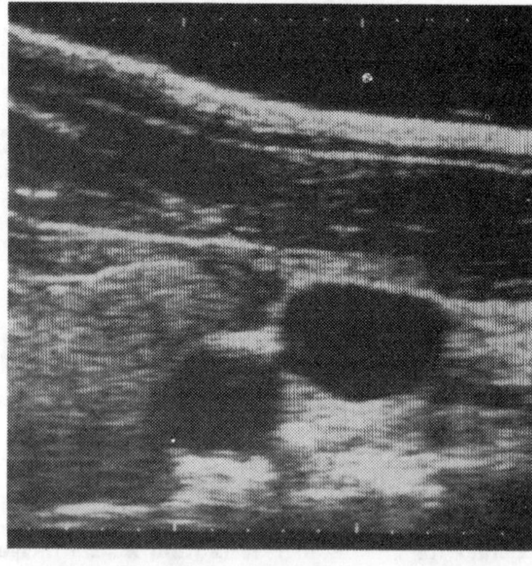

Fig. 21. In this cross sectional image of the neck made with a small parts scanner, a 3 cm by 3 cm area can be seen in detail. The right band at the top of the image is the skin, beneath which the sterno-cleido-mastoid muscle shows as a wide dark band. The oval cross section of the internal jugular vein and, to its left, the circular cross section of the carotid artery are shown. To the left of the carotid artery, the thyroid gland can be seen as a medium gray speckled area. To help in judging the size of these structures, the small white dots around the edge of the picture are spaced 2 mm apart. (Photo courtesy of Picker Corporation.)

An ophthalmic scanner uses a motor driven mechanical system to move a small high-frequency transducer rapidly back and forth producing a real time image of the eye, optic nerve, and orbit. Typically the depth of field covers the eyeball and part of the optic nerve. Because the attenuation coefficient of the vitreous, with which the eye is filled, is very low (Table I) and because the depth of field is short, frequencies between 10 and 20 MHz are used for good resolution. These scanners are generally compact; one ophthalmic unit is no larger than a portable television set. They can image the eye either through the closed eyelid or with the patient in the supine (lying on his back) position with the eye opened in a bath of eyewash-like liquid. Imaging through the eyelid provides the greatest patient comfort, but generally makes it difficult to image structures just behind the eyelid such as the cornea or iris. Since most diagnostic applications do not require that these structures be seen, this is not a major drawback. Fig. 20 shows two ophthalmic images made through the eyelid. Water bath imaging takes longer for a patient procedure, but provides superior imaging, especially of the cornea, iris, and lens.

Although these scanners are compact and can produce images with good resolution, in general the images have had poor gray scale which can make them somewhat hard to interpret. Of course, these scanners are designed for a very specialized purpose; However, some success is being achieved in using these instruments for other diagnostic purposes such as in the breast and thyroid gland.

Another type of water path real time B-scan instrument very much like the ophthalmic scanner is becoming available. It too is a mechanically scanned system, but it is designed to be a general purpose real time imaging system with many applications. This system is designed to produce manual B-scan quality images of a small field of view with excellent resolution [51]. Lateral and temporal resolution of better than 0.5 mm has been achieved. Any tissue or organ located within 4 to 5 cm of the skin can be imaged, so that many diagnostic applications become possible. These instruments are being assessed for use in the following diagnostic areas: testicular cancer, detecting and measuring atheromas and stenosis in carotid and femoral arteries [52], [53], the visualization of skin lesions and diseases, detecting certain thyroid and parathyroid diseases, assessing the extent of arthritic joint involvement, and visualizing the neonatal heart and spine. These instruments are also being investigated for imaging the eye and breast.

One small parts scanner [51] uses a 10-MHz single transducer which is mechanically oscillated along a straight line path. The resulting image is a linear scan with 200 scan lines

in a 3 cm field of view. The frame rate can be as high as 30 frames per second without sacrificing the number of scan lines since both the depth of penetration and the water path are short. Fig. 21 shows a transverse cross sectional image of the carotid artery and internal jugular vein made with this instrument.

Another instrument in this category has been specifically designed for imaging the carotid arteries in the neck [54]. It is primarily intended for use in assessing the extent of atherosclerotic plaque formation and produces both a B-scan image of a vessel and a Doppler shift auditory output from a selected area within the vessel [55]. For this reason it is called a duplex system. The Doppler section, which is integrated with but electronically separate from the imaging section, is designed to give an indication of blood flow velocity. This information can be very important for proper determination of vessel function.[8] The duplex scanner produces real time sector format images with the B-scan portion of the instrument. These images extend 4-cm deep and are made at 5 MHz. The scan head for this instrument is very small so that good patient coupling may be maintained for nearly all patients. The inclusion of the Doppler feature makes this system unique.

The field of diagnostic B-scan instrumentation has grown rapidly and continues to grow. New instruments and new B-scan techniques are frequently being announced. Also, new areas of clinical application are spawning new instrument designs, e.g. breast scanners. Because of the great variety of scanning techniques that are currently available and the rapid introduction of new techniques, we have, of necessity, limited our discussion to those techniques that we feel represent those with the greatest clinical acceptance or show some unique characteristic of interest. B-scan ultrasound is now a well established and extremely valuable procedure in many medical specialties.

---

[8] There are many Doppler instruments on the market; however, we have restricted this paper to B- and C- scan imaging instrumentation. Currently, the duplex system is the only unit which contains both B-scan imaging and Doppler capability.

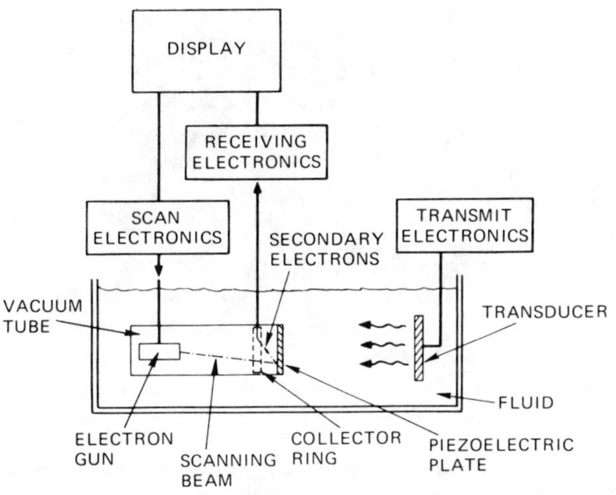

Fig. 22. A simplified block diagram of a Sokolov Tube as used in a transmission imaging system.

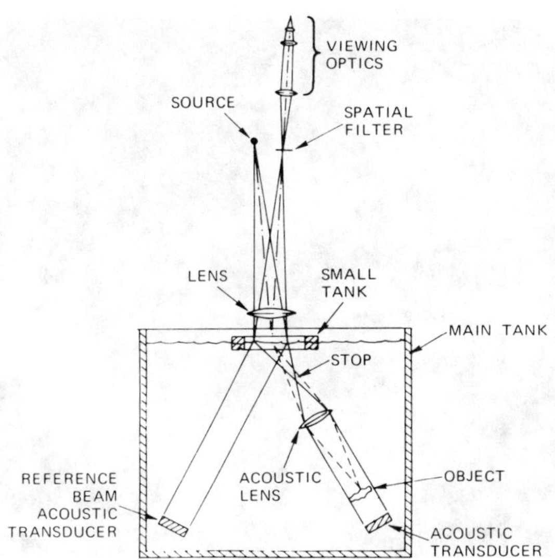

Fig. 23. Schematic of liquid-surface imaging system.

IV. C-Scan Instruments and Holography

Unlike the *B*-scan, which has been applied extensively to diagnostic medicine, the *C*-scan is virtually unused outside of research and development laboratories. This is in spite of the fact that the *C*-scan presents an image format similar to the obtained with X-ray fluoroscopy and, therefore, more familiar to clinical radiologists. In fact some of the first acoustic images were of the *C*-scan type. S. Ya. Sokolov, whose invention has come to the known as the Sokolov tube [56], proposed in 1929 to use a scanning electron beam to convert to an electronic signal the charge pattern image imposed on a piezoelectric plate by an incident acoustic beam. A schematic diagram of the device is shown in Fig. 22. The piezoelectric plate/scanning electron beam combination form the acoustic equivalent of a TV camera with the resulting images being displayed on a cathode ray tube. Although the promise of this technique spurred considerable development in Europe and the United States [57], [58], the device has so far found little application in diagnostic medicine due to its relatively poor sensitivity (10^{-7} to 10^{-8} W cm^{-2}) and poor resolution for other than normal acoustic incidence on the piezo-plate.

More recently, developments in ultrasonic holography [59]–[61], interferometry [62], [63], Bragg scattering of light by sound [64]–[66], one-dimensional [67], [68], and two-dimensional [69], [70], [71] acoustic arrays have been applied to the problem of producing *C*-scan images. It is impossible in a paper of this length to consider all the various techniques that have been reported; we have, therefore, chosen those techniques which in our opinion show the most promise for future clinical application or which best demonstrate a particular modality.

A. Ultrasonic Holography

In the mid-1960's there began an intense program to apply the principles of holography [72] to acoustic imaging. In those early years holography seemed like a natural solution to the many diverse problems facing the designers of ultrasound equipment. In acoustics one could directly measure and record not only the amplitude, but also the phase, of an acoustic signal through the piezoelectric effect. The recording could employ a multitude of scanning and encoding techniques which potentially had the advantages of large depth-of-field, three-dimensional reconstruction, close to single wavelength resolution, and lensless imaging. Unfortunately, the results obtained with most techniques were disappointing. The sensitivity was generally inferior to direct imaging techniques, the reconstructed images were often obtained many hours after the exposure, and the reconstructed images suffered from a 1000 to 1 perspective distortion [73]. This latter limitation meant that in order to view the images in true three-dimensional detail, a microscope would be required. Very little work on ultrasonic holography is being conducted now. However, one technique described below received considerable clinical study and became available commercially. The technique is called liquid surface holography [74]–[76], and it avoided the usual long delay between acoustic exposure and image reconstruction. Holography is a two-step process: first, the hologram, which is a coherent interference of the image signal with a reference signal, is "recorded" onto some medium; second, the image scene is reconstructed by "playing back" the hologram so that it becomes optically visible. Generally a laser is used for the second step, although computer reconstructions have been employed [77], [78]; the laser usually requires a film development time and the computer algorithms are usually too slow to provide the desired real time imaging. In the liquid-surface technique, illustrated in Fig. 23 the hologram is generated at the interface of a liquid medium and air; the pressure of the impinging sound waves causes a distortion of the normally plane liquid surface so that the interface becomes a dynamic hologram which does not require any further development or processing. The hologram is "played back" by the usual technique of laser illumination. Although an acoustic lens is in principle not required [75], the best images are obtained with a lens since it provides the largest numerical aperture and the highest sensitivity. A typical transmission image obtained with the liquid surface holographic technique is shown in Fig. 24. One can see alongside the humerus (black bone in center) the muscles and muscle attachments of the upper arm. The soft tissues are very apparent due to their different absorption coefficient from the surrounding medium.

Although this technique avoids some of the problems of acoustic holography, it suffers from one which is fundamental to all holographic schemes, namely, the requirement for highly coherent insonification in order to generate a distinct interference pattern. It has become apparent that incoherent in-

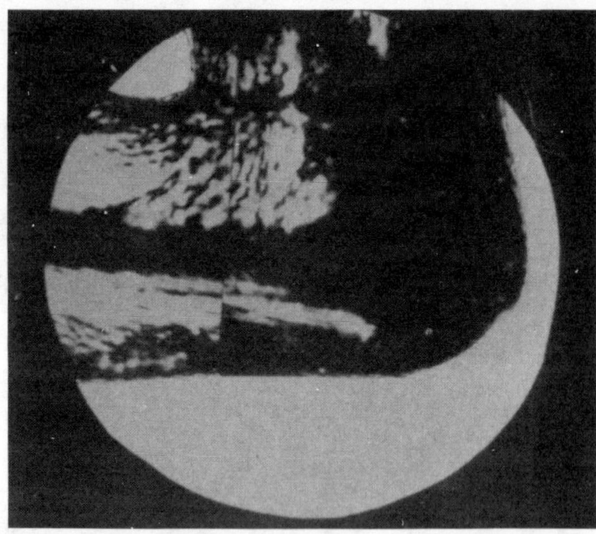

Fig. 24. Transmission C-scan image of the upper arm obtained with the liquid surface imaging system. Muscles and muscle attachments are showing especially the triceps, the biceps, and the attachments of the biceps to the radius and the attachments of some of the muscles in the forearm to the humerus. (Photo courtesy of B. Brendon, Holosonics, Inc.)

sonification produces images of greater fidelity with fewer spurious artifacts, particularly when imaging a large, inhomogeneous biological mass such as the abdomen. Nonetheless, the images are produced in real time, (an advantage that is significant) and with sufficient clarity and sensitivity to be potentially useful in some applications.

B. Ultrasonic Interferometry

As indicated in Section II, an ultrasonic wave is a mechanical displacement of the particles of the medium in which the sound propogates. This effect has been utilized in an instrument [79], [80], which allows not only the visualization of a sound field but also its quantitative measurement. A schematic diagram of the system, which has been named "Ultrasonovision," is shown in Fig. 25. Mounted in an acoustically transmissive fluid is a thin ($\sim$6 μm) metallized plastic film (called a pellicle) which is used as one of the mirrors of an optical Michaelson interferometer. Because it is so thin, the pellicle is sonically transparent for frequencies as high as 10 MHz and for angles of incidence from $0°$ to $40°$. As a result, the local pellicle displacement is equal to the displacement amplitude of the acoustic wave in the fluid. Although this displacement is very small[9] it is easily measured by the optical interferometer. In order to form an image, the interrogating laser beam must be scanned in a raster-like fashion over the surface of the pellicle. This can be accomplished by a mirror galvanometer or by acoustooptic deflection. As most interferometers the fundamental quantity measured is the phase difference between the signals in the information channel and a reference channel. On the one hand, it is the great advantage of such a system that it is extremely sensitive to small changes in signal; on the other hand, this sensitivity can be a disadvantage when the changes are due to spurious effects, such as mechanical or thermal drift. These spurious effects can be minimized by using a nonstationary reference mirror that is purposely "wiggled" through a distance corresponding to a $180°$ phase shift. It can be shown that the maximum output signal occurs for a $90°$ relative phase shift between the two signals; hence, by purposely changing the phase over $180°$ and at the same time

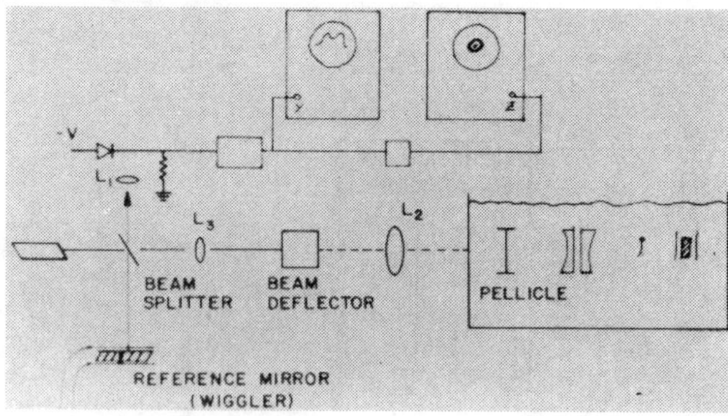

Fig. 25. Schematic representation of "Ultrasonovision", an interferometric detection scheme.

displaying only the *maximum* signal, the effects of nonultrasonic displacements can be essentially eliminated.

Images using this system are obtained by insonifying an object in a fluid bath and projecting the perturbed acoustic field onto the pellicle with acoustic lenses. The image projected onto the pellicle is read with the scanning interferometer, detected with a photodiode and displayed on a cathode ray tube. Alternatively, the deflection system may be programmed to scan a single line of the image repetitively and this signal displayed on an oscilloscope to quantitatively measure tissue parameters. Because the system can be calibrated against absolute standards and because it is linear over a range from 10^{-10} W/cm^2 to 1 W/cm^2, it is possible to measure *absolute* signal levels. An example of the utility of such a device is shown in Fig. 26 which shows an image of excised breast tissue with a malignant tumor. At the top is an optical photograph of the tissue, in the middle the acoustic image, and at the bottom a single line of the image through the malignant region. It has been found by such measurements that some types of malignant tissues have a lower transmission coefficient than normal tissues. Another example, shown in Fig. 27 is a composite picture of the human hand. The resolution of the interferometric system is in principle acoustic wavelength limited; however, if an acoustic lens is used, the numerical aperture of the lens will determine the resolution of the imaging system as a whole. With a frame rate of 4 frames per second, a total field-of-view of 150 mm diameter, and an 83-dB linear dynamic range, this relatively simple-to-construct instrument should find considerable application to the study of ultrasonic propagation and absorption, and transducer field patterns.

C. Bragg Diffraction Imaging

Light diffraction by sound waves was first predicted by L. Brillouin [81] in 1922 and verified experimentally by Debye and Sears (82) in the U.S. and Lucas and Biguard (83) in France in 1932. The phenomenon occurs because the mechanical displacement of particles due to a sound wave gives rise to local density variations in the medium. These density variations in a fluid may, in turn, be related to an optical refractive index variation through the Clausius–Masotti equation

$$\frac{1}{\rho} \frac{n^2 - 1}{n^2 + 1} = K \tag{9}$$

where ρ is the density, n is the refractive index, and K a material constant. As the sound wave propagates, therefore, a

[9] At 1.5 MHz with a sound intensity of 10^{-6} W/cm^2 in water the displacement amplitude is: 0.1 Å.

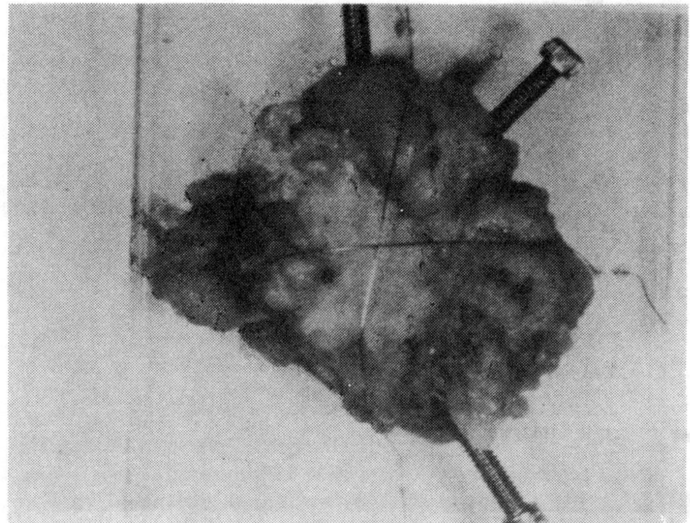

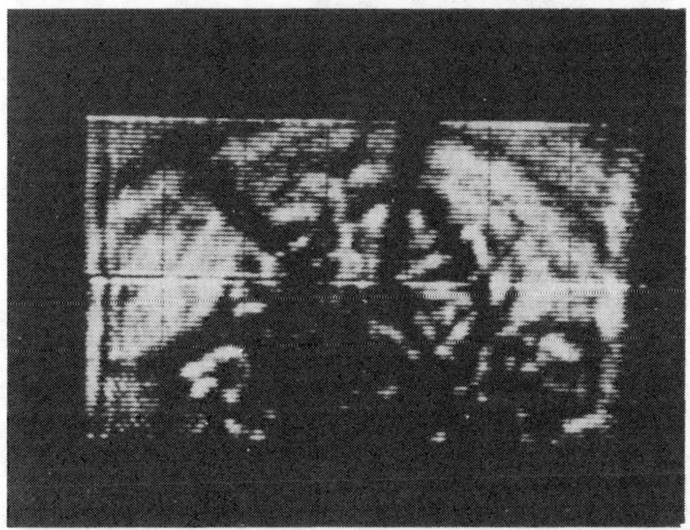

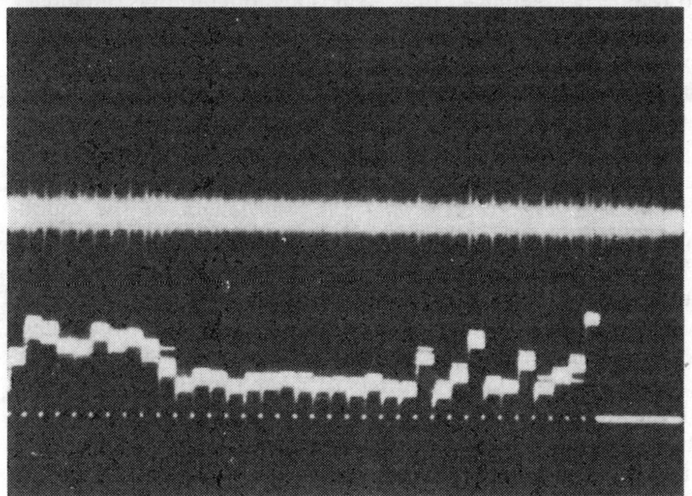

Fig. 26. Optical (top) and acoustic (middle) images of breast tissue with tumor taken by "Ultrasonovision." The bottom trace is video signal for a single line of the acoustic image, showing increased attenuation in the tumerous region. (Photo courtesy of R. Mezrich, Johnson & Johnson.)

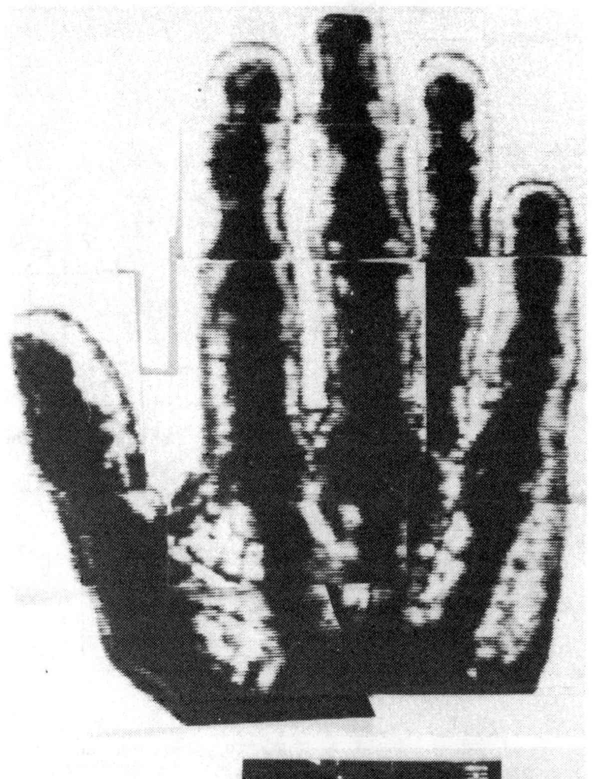

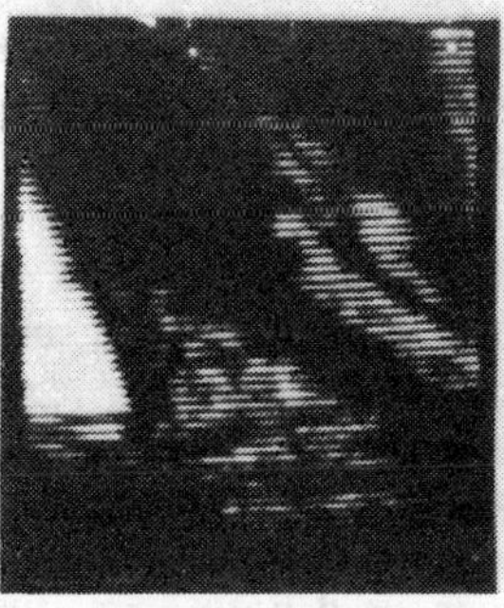

Fig. 27. Acoustic image of the adult hand. Lower picture shows detail of region of the palm near index finger, with a bifurcation of a blood vessel visible. (Photo courtesy of R. Mezrich, Johnson & Johnson.)

phase grating moving at the speed of sound is generated in the medium. Depending upon the frequency of the sound and the width of the sound beam in the direction of light propogation, this phase grating may be considered to be two dimensional (the Raman–Nath region) or three-dimensional (the Bragg region) [84]. When a beam of light is passed through this grating, diffraction occurs. In the first case many orders of diffracted light are generated; in the second case only one order is generated and only under the condition that the angle of incidence satisfies the equation

$$\sin \theta_B = \frac{\lambda}{2\Lambda} \tag{10}$$

where λ and Λ are the optical and acoustic wavelengths, respectively. The form of this equation is very similar to the Bragg equation relating the scattering of X-rays to the spacing of crystal planes. Hence, the phenomenon has come to be known as Bragg scattering of light by sound or, in its application to ultrasonic imaging, as Bragg diffraction imaging.

We shall not go into great detail on how this technique works or any of its special problems since other papers in this issue are devoted to the subject [85]. (A typical experimental arrangement is shown in Fig. 28.) Suffice it to say that the diffracted optical beam contains information about the amplitude and phase of the acoustic beam. Hence, an optical image of the acoustic field may be formed by properly processing the light

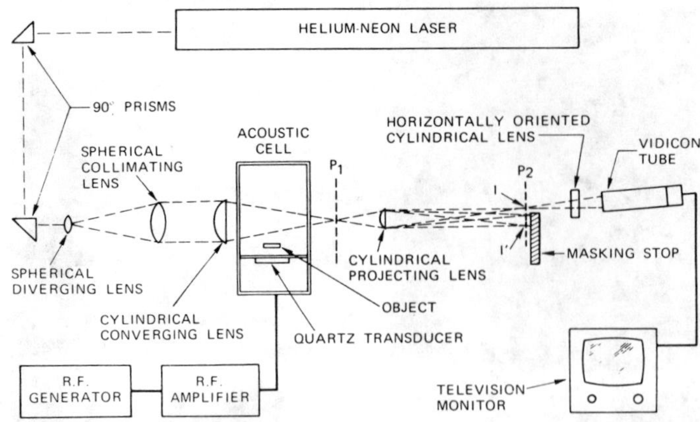

Fig. 28. Schematic diagram of a Bragg diffraction imaging system.

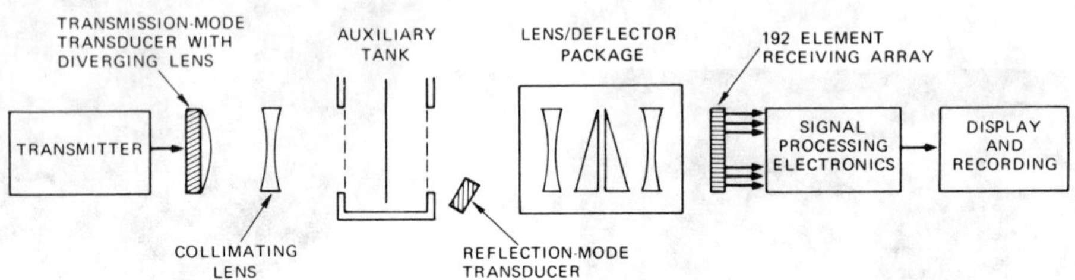

Fig. 29. Simplified block diagram of the SRI real-time imaging system.

beam. In principle, since both amplitude and phase are preserved in the interaction process, it is possible to image any acoustic cross section occurring ahead of the interaction region by slightly modifying the optical processing. In this sense Bragg diffraction imaging is very similar to a hologram and in fact theoretical analyses of the phenomenon are very similar to theoretical analyses relating to optical volume holography. To date practical embodiments have found little clinical application; however, Bragg diffraction imaging is remarkable in that it has been used both at relatively low frequencies (1–5 MHz) and at extremely high frequencies (800–1000 MHz) [86]–[88]. The higher frequencies provide images more akin to those made with a microscope than with a camera. We shall not consider acoustic microscopy in this paper since it is considered by a separate paper in this issue.

D. Piezoelectric Detection—Linear Array

Piezoelectric receivers are attractive principally because they are the most sensitive available detectors of ultrasound [89]. Because the C-mode requires the scanning of two spatial dimensions, imaging devices using the piezoelectric effect require a compromise between complexity and scanning speed. In Section II, for example, a very simple system was described in which a single transmitter and a single receiver were scanned in a raster fashion to develop the C-scan transmission image. However, the buildup time of the image was intolerably long for any clinical application. On the other hand, it is possible to conceive of a totally electronic, two-dimensional array of individual piezoelectric receivers each separately amplified and multiplexed to produce the image. Although the image can be produced in a very short time, the complexity of such a system is considerable. Even a minimal 200×200 element array is comprised of 4×10^4 transducers!

An interesting compromise between these two extremes is a hybrid system [90], [91], which is partially electronic and partially mechanical. Rather than constructing a 40 000 trans-

ducer two-dimensional array, a linear array of 200 elements is used to detect a single line of the image. The electronic read-out which can be as fast a $1\,\mu s$/element, is displayed on a CRT or read into a digital memory. Either the linear array or the image itself is then physically translated so that another line of the image can be obtained. In this way the image is "painted" onto the screen or into memory, a line at a time. Quite obviously, the ingenuity of such a system lies in how the mechanical scanning is achieved. Ideally, one would like 30 frames per second so that "real time" operation is obtained. An example of one scanning technique [90], [91] is shown schematically in Fig. 29. The heart of the mechanical system is a pair of counter-rotating polystyrene prisms which translate the two-dimensional acoustic image a line at a time across a stationary linear array of 192 piezoelectric elements. The resolution of the system is determined by the numerical aperture of the lens package and the wavelength of the sound beam; typically, at 2.25 MHz a resolution of 1.3 mm can be obtained. The detection sensitivity has been estimated at better than 10^{-11} W/cm^2, thus requiring an average intensity of less than 300 μW/cm^2 to image through the adult abdomen. Although only 15 frames per second has been achieved in the instrument, this frame rate is sufficient for dynamic viewing of the images, allowing the examiner to mentally reconstruct three-dimensional information from among two-dimensional images. Coupling to the patient can be achieved through immersion in a water tank or through the use of water bags.

Although the piezoelectric receiving array is capable of coherent detection, an interesting feature of this device is that the imaging does *not* rely on the use of coherent sound beams. In a sense, the linear array/acoustic lens combination can be thought of as an extremely sensitive film. Recent studies with this camera using highly diffuse insonification [92], [93], have indicated that a significant improvement in image quality results when the sound beam is neither spatially nor temporally coherent. Many spurious image artifacts that are present with

Fig. 30. Acoustic image obtained with the SRI *C*-scan system. Image of the colon in the adult abdomen. (Photo courtesy of P. S. Green, SRI International.)

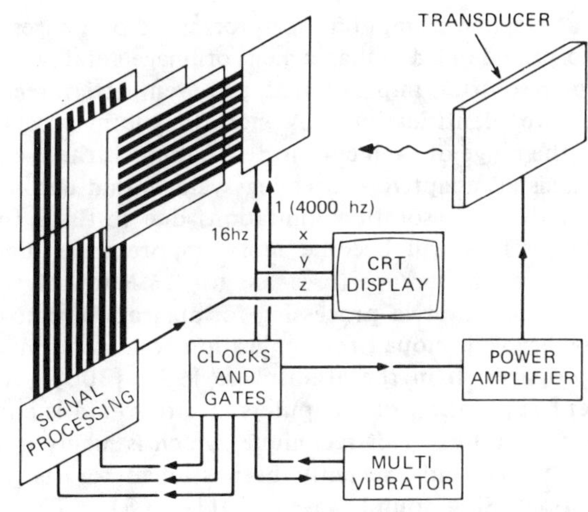

Fig. 31. Two-dimensional array requiring only $2N$ electronic components to form an N^2 array.

coherent beams are essentially eliminated, allowing repeatable, unambiguous interpretation of the attenuation images of soft tissue. Shown in Fig. 30 is a typical result.

E. Two-Dimensional Arrays

Perhaps the "conceptually ideal" image converter for acoustic *C*-scan imaging is a highly sensitive two-dimensional array of receiving elements, each with a high-gain amplifier, storage element, and commutation electronics. The unavailability of such a system, despite a number of efforts to produce such a system, has severly limited the clinical application of the two-dimensional array concept. To be sure, the task is a prodigious one; not only must one construct the 10^4 (or more) transducer elements and connect them to the 3 or 4×10^4 electronic components, but also one faces the practical design constraint that the system be stable over a long period of time and that all channels be balanced to one another. Whereas a small number of elements (in a linear array, for example) may be adjusted periodically, the work involved in adjusting such a large number of elements is prohibitive.

Piezoelectric [94], electret [95], and electrostatic transducer [96] elements have been employed for constructing two-dimensional arrays. An example of an imaginative scheme [96] for avoiding the N^2 number of components problem is shown in Fig. 31. In this case an electrostatic transducer array is formed by a set of intersecting metallized strips. By appropriate addressing and commutation schemes it is possible to use only $2N$ electronic elements to form an N^2 element image. Another approach [97] shown in Fig. 32 is to apply the principles of integrated circuitry and hybrid construction techniques to the fabrication of N^2 piezoelectric elements. More recently, the use of piezoelectric polyvinyl flouride plastic [98] film has been suggested to overcome some of the principal problems with these arrays, namely interelement crosscoupling, bandwidth, and sensitivity. To date no clinical results have been reported using these techniques. It is difficult, therefore, to anticipate whether the increased complexity and, of course, cost of such units will pay off in increased diagnostic information. However, the potential versatility of such systems, should they become practical, is a goal worth pursuing.

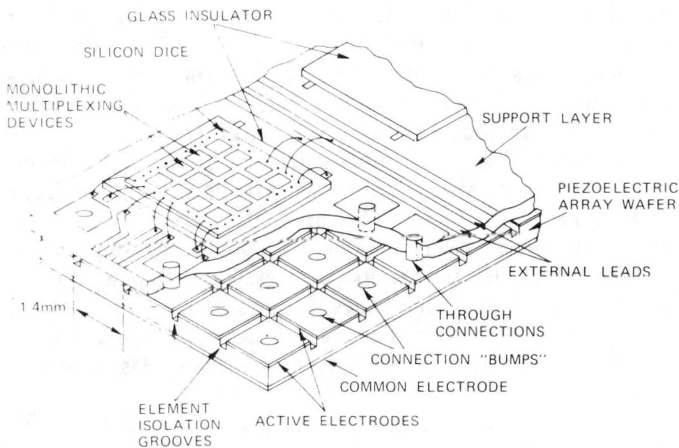

Fig. 32. Three layer integrated circuit approach to a two-dimensional array. (Courtesy of J. Meindl, Stanford University.)

V. A Sampling of Some Current Research Efforts

Progress in the development of sophisticated ultrasonic instrumentation has been rapid in the past ten years. Only a few years ago the standard ultrasonic examination was conducted with a manually scanned bistable-display *B*-scan unit. One reason for the rapid clinical acceptance of a new generation of imaging devices, particularly those with gray-scale capability, is that these new devices produce an image which is repeatable and which allows unambiguous interpretation of anatomical detail. Devices which produce images in real time partially remove the dependence of image quality on operator skill in addition to allowing a large number of scans in a short period of time.

A continuously developing digital technology promises to have a major impact on diagnostic equipment and its performance. Already the standard of excellence in display systems is the digital scan converter with all the flexibility for image acquisition that such a device allows. With the further growth of one- and two-dimensional array technology and its resulting complexity, it is reasonable to expect that the computer will serve an essential control function in future imaging systems. Furthermore, as the cost of computer systems falls, it is probable that on-line computer postprocessing of images will be used to provide edge enhancement of image detail, deconvolution for resolution improvement, and even pattern recognition for feature identification. A more long-term prospect, but within the range of even current technology, is the use of computer assisted adaptive processing systems that automatically compensate for resolution limitations due to tissue imhomogeneities. This will become more important as higher frequencies and larger apertures are used. Many of the basic concepts for adaptive processing for aberration removal have already been developed for application to astronomy and for laser propagation in the atmosphere [99], [100]. A totally different application of computers in ultrasound is computerized tomography. This technique, which is highly developed for X-ray, has only recently been studied for its potential application using sound waves [101]–[103]. The promise of this technique is that it may provide *quantitative* images of such fundamental parameters as tissue attenuation and sound speed.

The instrumentation developed to date has been based on amazingly little fundamental information about the ultrasonic scattering and absorptive properties of human tissue. In many ways designers of instrumentation have been lucky that the "try it and see if it works" approach has been so successful. In recent years a trend has developed toward a more analytical and quantitative determination of the mechanical properties of tissue and how it affects sound propagation [104], [105], [106]. This area, termed ultrasonic tissue characterization, is very new and the practical results, as they impact device design, are likely to be more than a couple of years away. But such studies are important since they may allow not only optimization of the design of current instrumentation, but also the design of whole new classes of ultrasonic devices.

There are many technical problems yet to be solved and many application areas of the body still to be explored. But ultrasound is now a major medical modality for the clinical radiologist; and it is likely to grow more important in the future as new and exciting technological advances are made. Sound waves provide a unique way of looking at the human body and how it functions, different from the images provided by X-rays or nuclear scans. We must continue to exploit this difference so that even more meaningful clinical instrumentation may be developed to benefit the human condition.

ACKNOWLEDGEMENT

The authors are indebted to W. Gilmartin and A. Waxman of Diasonics for a critical reading of this manuscript.

BIBLIOGRAPHY

[1] J. T. Dehn, "Interference patterns in the near field of a circular piston," *J. Acoust. Soc. Amer.*, vol. 32, no. 12, 1960.

[2] T. F. Hueter and R. H. Bolt, *Sonics*. New York: Wiley, 1955.

[3] D. Berlincourt et al., "Transducer properites of lead titanate zirconate ceramics," *IRE Trans. Ultrason. Eng.*, vol. UE-7, pp. 1–6, 1960.

[4] K. F. Herzfeld and T. A. Litovitz, *Absorption and Dispersion of Ultrasonic Waves*. New York: Academic Press, 1959.

[5] L. Kinsler and A. Frey, *Fundamentals of Acoustics*, 2nd ed. New York: Wiley, 1962.

[6] P. N. T. Wells, *Physical Principles of Ultrasonic Diagnosis*. New York: Academic Press, 1969.

[7] T. C. Evans, Jr., and J. C. Taenzer, "Ultrasound imaging of atherosclerosis in carotid arteries," *Appl. Radiology*, to be published.

[8] C. P. Olinger, and A. K. Nigam, "Application of high-resolution imaging to the detection and preliminary characterization of atherosclerosis," in *Ultrasound in Medicine, vol. 4*. New York: Plenum Press, 1978.

[9] J. M. Reed, "Challenges and opportunities in ultrasound," in *Ultrasonic Tissue Characterization*, M. Linzer, Ed. National Bureau of Standards Special Publication, #453, 1976.

[10] J. Reid and J. Wild, "Application of echo ranging techniques in determination of structure of biological tissues," *Science*, vol. 115, pp. 226–230, 1952.

[11] K. R. Erikson et al., "Ultrasound in medicine—A review", *IEEE Trans. Sonics Ultrason.*, vol. SU–21, no. 3, 1974.

[12] D. G. Tucker et al., "Electronic sector scanning," *Brit. Inst. Radio Eng.*, vol. 26, p. 465, 1958.

[13] G. Baum, "The current status of ultrasound mammography," in *Ultrasound in Medicine*, vol. 4. New York: Plenum Press, 1978.

[14] J. E. Fleming and A. J. Hall, "Two dimensional compound scanning—Effects of maladjustment and calibration," *Ultrasonics*, vol. 6, pp. 160–166, 1968.

[15] J. W. Goodman, *Introduction to Fourier Optics*. San Francisco, CA; McGraw-Hill, 1968, ch. 8.

[16] E. P. Papadakis and K. A. Fowler, "Broad-band transducers: radiation field and selected applications," *J. Acoust. Soc. Amer.*, vol. 50, pp. 729–745, 1969.

[17] A. Papoulis, *Systems and Transforms with Applications in Optics*. New York: McGraw-Hill, 1968.

[18] H. E. Melton, Jr., "Electronic focal scanning for improved resolution in ultrasound imaging," Ph.D. dissertation, Duke Univ. Durham, NC, 1971.

[19] J. F. Havlice et al., "An electronically focused acoustic imaging device," in *Acoustical Holography*, vol. 5. New York: Plenum Press, 1974, pp. 317–334.

[20] F. L. Thurstone and O. T. Ramm, "A new ultrasound technique employing two-dimensional, electronic beam steering," in *Acoustical Holography*, vol. 5. New York: Plenum Press, 1974.

[21] G. W. Stroke et al., *Ultrasonic Imaging and Holography*. New York: Academic Press, 1974.

[22] R. B. Bernardi et al., "A dynamically focused annular array," in *Ultrasonics Symp. Proc.* (IEEE Cat. #76, CH1120-55U), 1976.

[23] J. F. Havlice et al., "Electronically focused acoustic imaging device," *Appl. Phys. Lett.*, vol. 23, p. 581, 1973.

[24] F. L. Thurstone and O. T. Ramm, "A new ultrasound technique employing two-dimensional, electronic beam steering," in *Acoustical Holography*, vol. 5. New York: Plenum Press, 1974.

[25] R. E. McKeighen and M. P. Buchin, "New techniques for dynamically variable electronic delays for real time ultrasonic imaging," in *Ultrasonic Symp. Proc.* (IEEE Cat. #77, CH 1264-15V), 1977.

[26] J. F. Havlice, et al., "An electronically focused acoustic imaging device, in *Acoustical Holography*, vol. 5. New York: Plenum Press, 1974.

[27] P. S. Green, SRI International, Menlo Park, CA, private communication.

[28] P. S. Considine, "Effects of coherence on imaging systems," *J. Opt. Soc. Amer.*, vol. 56, p. 1001, 1966.

[29] A. Korpel et al., "Elimination of spurious detail in acoustic images," in *Acoustical Holography*, vol. 5. New York: Plenum Press, 1974, pp. 373–390.

[30] F. Dunn et al., "Absorption and dispersion of ultrasound in biological media," in *Biological Engineering* (Inter-University Electronic Series, vol. 9). New York: McGraw-Hill, 1969.

[31] C. C. Grossman et al., *Diagnostic Ultrasound*. New York: Plenum Press, 1966.

[32] F. G. M. Ross and P. N. T. Wells, "The principles and clinical applications of ultrasonic diagnosis," *J. Roy. Coll. Physicians London*, vol. 4, pp. 62–87, 1969.

[33] S. Campbell and E. I. Kohorn, "Placental localization by ultrasonic compound scanning," *J. Obstetrics and Gynaecology British Commonwealth*, vol. 75, pp. 1007–1013, 1968.

[34] P. N. T. Wells, *Physical Principles of Ultrasonic Diagnosis*. New York: Academic Press, 1969.

[35] G. Kossoff, "Improved techniques in ultrasonic cross-sectional echography," *Ultrasonics*, vol. 10, p. 221, 1972.

[36] M. Ide and N. Masazawa, "A color display for ultrasonotomography," *Excerpta Medica*, vol. 277, no. 95, 1973.

[37] H. Yokoi et al., "Quantized color ultrasonotomography," *Excerpta Medica*, vol. 277, no. 103, 1973.

[38] A. Waxman, "Image storage and image processing in gray scale ultrasound," in a book to be published, F. Winsberg, Ed., 1978.

[39] R. Eggleton et al., "Visualization of cardiac dynamics with real time B-mode ultrasonic scanner," *JCU*, vol. 2, p. 228, 1974.

[40] W. H. Schuette et al., "Real time two-dimensional mechanical ultrasonic sector scanner with electronic control of sector width," *SPIE*, vol. 96, pp. 345–348, 1976.

[41] N. Bom, "A multi-element system and its application to cardiology," *Excerpta Medica*, vol. 277, no. 2, 1973.

[42] D. L. King, "Real-time cross-sectional ultrasonic imaging of the heart using a linear array, multi-element transducer," *JCU*, vol. 1, p. 196, 1973.

[43] L. Findleton *et al.*, "Application of the multiple head transducer scanning device in early pregnancy," in *Proc. 20th Annu. Conf. AIUM*, Oct. 4–9, 1975.

[44] J. T. Queenan *et al.*, "Determination of fetal biparietal diameter as an index of growth," in *Proc. 20th Annu. Conf. AIUM*, Oct. 4–9, 1975.

[45] J. C. Somer, "Electronic sector scanning for ultrasonic diagnosis," *Ultrasonics*, vol. 6, p. 153, 1968.

[46] O. T. von Ramm and F. L. Thurstone, "Improved resolution in ultrasound tomography," in *Proc. 25th Annu. Conf. Engineering in Medicine and Biology*, p. 141, 1972.

[47] E. N. Carlsen *et al.*, "High resolution real time scanning of the abdomen," *Ultrasound in Medicine*, vol. 4, New York: Plenum Press, 1978, pp. 155–156.

[48] D. A. Carpenter and G. Kossoff, "The U.I. octoson-A new class of ultrasonic echoscopes," *Ultrasound in Medicine*, D. White and R. E. Brown, Eds., vol. 3B. New York: Plenum Press, 1977 pp. 1785–1786.

[49] G. Baum, "Problems in ultrasonographic localization and attempts at their solution," *Ophthalmic Ultrasound* (St. Louis, MO), 1969.

[50] L. Franzer, "An introduction to ophthalmic ultrasound," *Medical Ultrasound*, vol. 1, no. 4, pp. 20–25, Oct. 1977.

[51] P. S. Green *et al.*, "The SRI real-time ultrasonic artery imaging system," presented at 28th Annual ACEMB, New Orleans, LA, 1975.

[52] J. C. Taenzer, "Ultrasound imaging techniques in the evaluation of the peripheral arterial circulation," presented at 12th Annual Meeting of the Association of the Advancement of Medical Instrumentation, San Francisco, CA, March 13–17, 1977. Abstract published in *Medical Imaging*, vol. 2, no. 2, 2nd Quarter 1977, pp. 38–39.

[53] T. C. Evans and J. C. Taenzer, "Ultrasound imaging of atherosclerosis in carotid arteries," *Applied Radiology*, in press.

[54] F. E. Barber *et al.*, "Ultrasonic duplex echo-Doppler scanner," *IEEE Trans. Biomedical Eng.*, vol. BME-21, no. 2, pp. 109–113, Mar. 1974.

[55] D. J. Phillips *et al.*, "Ultrasound duplex scanning in peripheral vascular disease," *Radiology/Nuclear Medicine*, pp. 6–10, Jan.–Feb. 1978.

[56] S. Y. Sokolov, "Ultrasonic oscillations and their applications, *Tech. Physica USSR*, vol. 2, p. 522, 1935.

[57] J. E. Jacobs and Peterson, "Advances in the Sokolov tube," in *Acoustic Holography*, vol. 5. New York: Plenum Press, 1974, pp. 633–645.

[58] R. C. Addison, "A progress report on the Sokolov tube utilizing a metal fiber faceplate," in *Acoustical Holography*, vol. 5. New York, Plenum Press, 1974, pp. 659–670.

[59] B. P. Hildebrand and B. B. Brendon, *An Introduction to Acoustical Holography*. New York: Plenum Press, 1972.

[60] R. K. Mueller and P. N. Keating, "The liquid-gas interface as a recording medium for acoustical holography," in *Acoustical Holography*, vol. 1. New York: Plenum Press, 1969, pp. 49–55.

[61] B. B. Brenden, "Real-time acoustical imaging by means of liquid surface holography," in *Acoustic Holography*, vol. 4. New York: Plenum Press, 1973, pp. 1–10.

[62] R. S. Mezrich *et al.*, "System for visualizing and measuring ultrasonic wavefronts," *Acoustical Holography*, Vol. 6. New York, Plenum Press, 1975.

[63] R. Mezrich *et al.*, "Ultrasonic waves: Their interferometric measurement and display," *Appl. Optics*, vol. 15, p. 1499, 1976.

[64] A. Korpel, "Acoustic imaging by diffracted light I. Two-dimensional interaction," *IEEE Trans. Sonics Ultrason.*, vol. SU-15, pp. 153–157, 1968.

[65] J. Landry *et al.*, "Ultrasonic imaging of internal structure by Bragg diffraction," *App. Phys. Letts.*, vol. 15, p. 186, 1960.

[66] H. Keyani *et al.*, "Bragg-diffraction imaging: A potential technique for medical diagnosis and material Inspection, Part II", *Acoustical Holography*, vol. 5. New York: Plenum Press, 1974.

[67] P. S. Green *et al.*, "A new high-performance ultrasonic camera," *Acoustical Holography*, vol. 5. New York: Plenum Press, 1974, pp. 493–503.

[68] P. Alias and M. Fink, "Fresnel zone focusing of linear arrays applied to *B* and *C* echography," *Acoustical Holography*, vol. 7. New York: Plenum Press, 1977.

[69] P. Alais, "Real-time acoustic imaging with a 256 × 256 matrix of electrostatic transducers," *Acoustic Holography*, vol. 5. New York: Plenum Press, 1974, pp. 671–684.

[70] M. G. Maginness *et al.*, "An acoustic image sensor using a transmit-receiver array," *Acoustical Holography*, vol. 5. New York: Plenum Press, 1974, pp. 619–631.

[71] K. Erikson and R. Zuleag, "Integrated acoustic array," *Acoustical Holography*, vol. 7. New York: Plenum Press, 1977.

[72] G. W. Stroke, *An Introduction to Coherent Optics and Holography*. New York, Academic Press, 1966.

[73] A. F. Metherell *et al.*, "Introduction to acoustical holography," *J. Acoust. Soc. Amer.*, vol. 42, pp. 733–742, 1967.

[74] R. B. Smith and B. B. Brenden, "Refinement and variations in liquid surface and scanned ultrasound holography," *IEEE Trans. Sonics Ultrason.*, vol. SU-16, p. 29, 1969.

[75] P. Pille and B. P. Hildebrand, "Rigorous analysis of the liquid-surface acoustical holography system," *Acoustical Holography*, vol. 5. New York: Plenum Press, 1974.

[76] P. S. Green, "A new liquid surface-release method of acoustical image conversion," *Acoustical Holography*, vol. III, New York: Plenum Press, 1974, p. 173.

[77] J. W. Goodman, "Digital image formation from detected holographic data," *Acoustical Holography*, vol. 1. New York: Plenum Press, 1969.

[78] A. L. Boyer *et al.*, "Computer reconstructions of images from ultrasonic holograms," *Acoustical Holography*, vol. 2. New York: Plenum Press, 1970.

[79] R. S. Mezrich *et al.*, "System for visualizing and measuring ultrasonic wavefronts," *Acoustical Holography*, vol. 6. New York, Plenum Press, 1975.

[80] D. Vikomerson *et al.*, "An improved system for visualizing and measuring ultrasonic wavefronts," *Acoustical Holography*, vol. 7. New York: Plenum Press, 1977.

[81] L. Brillouin, "Diffusion de la lumiere et des rayons X par un corps transparent homogene," *Ann. Phys.* (France), 9th ser., vol. 17, p. 88, 1922.

[82] P. Debye and F. W. Sears, "On the scattering of light by supersonic waves," *Proc. Nat. Acad. Sci.* (US), vol. 18, p. 409, 1932.

[83] R. Lucas and P. Biquard, "Optical properties of solids and liquids under ultrasonic vibrations," *J. Phys. Rad.*, 7th Ser., vol. 3, p. 464, 1932.

[84] C. F. Quate *et al.*, "Interaction of light and microwave sound," *Proc. IEEE*, vol. 53, pp. 1604–1623, Oct. 1965.

[85] M. Ahmed and G. Wade, "Bragg diffraction imaging," this issue, pp. 587–603.

[86] J. Havlice *et al.*, "Visualization of sound beams in quartz and saffire near 1 GHz," presented at IEEE Symp. Sonics Ultrasonics, paper no. 14, Vancouver, Canada, Oct. 4–6, 1967.

[87] H. V. Hance *et al.*, "Optical imaging of a complex ultrasonic field by diffraction of a laser beam," *J. Appl. Phys.*, vol. 38, 1981–1983, 1967.

[88] C. S. Tsai and H. V. Hance, "Optical imaging of the cross section of a microwave acoustic beam in rutile by Bragg diffraction of a laser beam," *J. Acoust. Soc. Amer.*, vol. 41, pp. 1345–1347, 1967.

[89] D. H. R. Vilkomerson, "Analysis of various ultrasonic holographic imaging methods for medical diagnosis," *Acoustical Holography*, vol. 4. New York: Plenum Press, 1972, pp. 401–429.

[90] P. S. Green *et al.*, "A new high performance ultrasonic camera system," *Acoustic Holography*, vol. 5. New York: Plenum Press, 1974.

[91] K. W. Marich *et al.*, "Real-time imaging with a new ultrasonic camera: Part I, *In Vitro* experimental studies on transmission imaging of biological structures," *J. Clin. Ultrasound*, Mar. 1975.

[92] J. F. Havlice *et al.*, "Spatially and temporally varying insonification for the elimination of spurious detail in acoustic transmission imaging," *Acoustical Holography*, vol. 7. New York: Plenum Press, 1977.

[93] J. F. Havlice *et al.*, "Real-time acoustic transmission imaging using diffuse insonification," *Ultrasound in Medicine*, vol. 4. New York: Plenum Press, 1978.

[94] M. G. Maginness *et al.*, "An acoustic image sensor using a transmit-receive array," *Acoustical Holography*, vol. 5. New York: Plenum Press, 1974, pp. 619–631.

[95] A. K. Nigam *et al.*, "Foil electret transducer arrays for real-time acoustical holography," *Acoustical Holography*, vol. 4. New York: Plenum Press, 1972, pp. 173–194.

[96] P. Alias, "Acoustical imaging by electrostatic transducers," *Acoustical Holography*, vol. 4. New York, Plenum Press, 1972, pp. 237–249.

[97] J. D. Plummer *et al.*, "Two dimensional transmit/receive ceramic piezoelectric arrays—Construction and performance, to be published.

[98] J. Calierume *et al.*, "Comparison of ceramic and polymer transducers for medical imaging," presented at IEEE Ultrasonics Symposium, Cherry Hill, NJ, Paper L4, 1978.

[99] B. L. McGlamery, "Restoration of turbulence degraded images," *J. Opt. Soc. Amer.*, vol. 57, pp. 293–297, 1967.

[100] R. A. Muller and A. Buffington, "Real-time correction of atmospherically degraded telescope images through image sharpening," *J. Opt. Soc. Amer.*, vol. 64, pp. 1200–1210, 1974.

[101] J. F. Greenleaf *et al.*, "Algebraic reconstruction of spatial distributions of acoustic absorption within tissue from their two-dimensional acoustic projections," *Acoustical Holography*, vol. 5. New York: Plenum Press, 1974, p. 591.

[102] J. F. Greenleaf *et al.*, "Algebraic reconstruction of spatial distributions of acoustic velocities in tissue from their time of flight profiles," *Acoustical Holography*, vol. 6. New York: Plenum Press, 1975, p. 71.

[103] M. J. Jacobson *et al.*, "Perturbation method for determining acoustic rays in a two-dimensional sound speed medium," *J. Acoust. Soc. Amer.*, vol. 57, p. 843, 1975.

[104] R. C. Chivers and C. R. Hill, "A spectral approach to ultrasonic scattering from human tissue: Methods, objectives, and backscattering measurements," *Phys. Med. Biol.*, vol. 20, p. 799, 1975.

[105] R. C. Chivers *et al.*, "Frequency dependence of ultrasonic backscattering cross-section: An indicator of tissue structure characteristics," in *Ultrasonics in Medicine*, Amsterdam, The Netherlands: Excerpta Medica, 1974, p. 300.

[106] R. C. Waag and R. M. Lerner, "Tissue macrostructure determination with swept-frequency ultrasound," in *Proc. 1973 Ultrasonics Symp.*, p. 63 (IEEE Cat. No. 73 CHO 807-8 SU), 1973.

Acoustic Imaging for Nondestructive Evaluation

GORDON S. KINO, FELLOW, IEEE

Abstract—The application of acoustic imaging techniques to nondestructive testing (NDT) of materials is discussed. After a description of the standard NDT techniques employed in the field and some examples of mechanically scanned imaging devices, most of the paper is devoted to a description of electronically scanned and focused systems. As holographic techniques are described by Ahmed *et al.* [22] in an accompanying paper, they are not discussed here. It is shown that the use of imaging techniques makes it possible to locate the position of flaws quickly and accurately.

I. INTRODUCTION

AT THE PRESENT TIME a great deal of effort is employed in determining whether there are faults present in manufactured parts both during production and during their useful life. As the complexity and strength-to-weight ratio of structural materials is increased, the need for evaluation of defects becomes still more severe. Thus accurate methods are required which can determine the location, size, and type of flaw such as a crack or inclusion of foreign material. At a still more sophisticated level, there is interest in being able to measure the presence of residual stress in a weld, near a crack, or in a stressed part so as to be able to use fracture mechanics to predict the breaking point and useful life of a structure. As inspection techniques become more accurate and reliable and smaller and smaller defects become detectable, it then becomes more and more important to use fracture mechanics to determine the minimum size of defect which can affect the life of the structure.

A second type of problem which arises in such nondestructive evaluations of structures is the time and hence the cost of carrying out such assessments. As an example, it can cost $250 000 per day to take a nuclear reactor out of service and personnel may only be able to carry out measurements in the presence of residual radiation for a limited time, so it is vital to be able to carry out the inspection as accurately and as speedily as possible, and it is important to be able to evaluate the size and position of flaws reliably. Similarly, the Air Force routinely takes aircraft out of service and inspects them. The longer the inspection takes, the larger the proportion of aircraft out of service at any one time. If the inspection procedures are too costly, they are not worthwhile. For instance, as a precaution, turbine engine discs are replaced well before the end of their useful life. Cheap reliable and fast inspection procedures could therefore make a great deal of difference to costs in factory inspection, and could increase the useful life of expensive machines. In some cases they could make it possible to employ radically new structural materials. One example is the silicon nitride and silicon carbide structural ceramics proposed for automobile turbines; the reliability of such a material in a new application must, at least at first, be checked very thoroughly at every stage of manufacture and while in service.

Manuscript received June 30, 1978; revised October 20. 1978. This work was supported in part by the Rockwell International under Contract No. 74-20773 for the Advanced Research Projects Agency and in part by the Air Force Materials Laboratory under Contract F33615-74-C-5180, and in part by the Electric Power Research Institute under Contract RP609-1.

The author is with the Edward L. Ginzton Laboratory of the W. W. Hansen Laboratories of Physics, Stanford University, Stanford, CA 94305.

Reprinted from *Proc. IEEE*, vol. 67, pp. 510–525, Apr. 1979.

In this paper, we review the method of acoustic imaging, which uses acoustic waves to probe sample and produce a visual imaging of its internal structure. We confine ourselves mainly to nondestructive testing (NDT) examples rather than medical imaging because this latter subject is covered in other papers in this issue. As with medical imaging the procedure can be carried out in real time or near to real time, so it can be fast, and a great deal of information can be processed in a short time. The imaging devices have been used to search for various types of flaws and have been used in a phase contrast mode to measure stress. At the present time only relatively simple demonstrations of real time imaging have been carried out in the laboratory. But the techniques employed appear to hold great promise for future applications to NDT.

The standard techniques employed for inspection of solid parts have involved X-ray and radiographic methods, eddy current testing in metals, the use of dye penetrants, and acoustic methods. Radiographic techniques have some of the same disadvantages as they have in medicine. They require bulky apparatus particularly for thick metal parts. Furthermore, when large metal parts are being examined, very high energy beams must be employed which can involve clearing the area where the inspection is being carried out. This is a major disadvantage. On the other hand, just as in clinical practice, they provide familiar easily recognizable data and do not need any direct contact with the material being tested. With the advent of tomographic methods they are becoming an order of magnitude more sensitive to slight changes in material properties.

The eddy current techniques provide very useful information on near surface defects in metals and will, no doubt, be further improved in the next few years. The use of fluorescent dye penetrants is often a simple and effective way of detecting surface defects. Such methods are useful for evaluating the size of a surface crack, but do not necessarily evaluate its depth very accurately.

Acoustic techniques have the major advantage that they measure the elastic properties of the material. As we are normally interested in its mechanical properties, the acoustic measurement provides data most closely related to a determination of the viability and useful life of a material sample. In the past, the main thrust of acoustic measurement techniques has been to evaluate the position and size of fairly major defects such as cracks or debonded regions. It is only recently that acoustic techniques are beginning to be applied to measure more subtle characteristics such as the size and shape of a crack or defect, the strength of a bond, or the residual stress in a welded region or near a crack.

The basic acoustic techniques employed in NDT are very similar to those used in sonar and in medical applications, although there has been far less emphasis on obtaining acoustic images than there has been in the medical field. We shall first review some of the standard acoustic techniques for determining the presence of flaws in materials, and then discuss their advantages and disadvantages. The major part of this paper will then be devoted to a discussion of electronically scanned acoustic imaging techniques with the aim of providing real time or near to real time images of defect regions within a sample. We shall not deal in any detail with holographic techniques because these are covered by Ahmed *et al.* in another paper in this issue [22]. But it should be emphasized that acoustic holography was one of the earliest methods used for providing images of defect regions in materials, and in fact acoustic holography

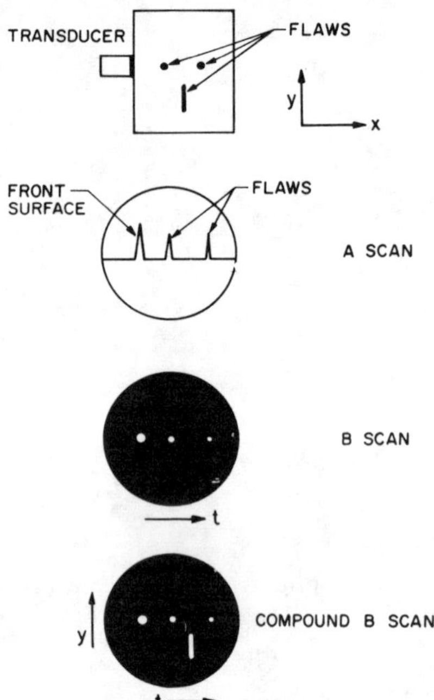

Fig. 1. A schematic of *A* and *B* scan operations.

apparatus is the only type presently available commercially to provide two- and three- dimensional images of defect regions.

II. *A*-Scan, *B*-Scan, and *C*-Scan Imaging

Before discussing imaging systems, it is worthwhile to review the standard acoustic techniques employed for nondestructive testing. In most NDT applications, a simple single piezoelectric transducer is used to excite an acoustic wave in the object being examined. Commonly, the transducer is placed in a water bath. In this case, the acoustic wave excited by the transducer propagates through the water, and into the object of interest, giving the advantage that it is easy to move the transducer around, but the disadvantage that the transducer may excite more than one type of wave in the medium. Because there is a large impedance mismatch between the water and the metal, the system may also be relatively inefficient.

A second technique illustrated schematically in Fig. 1 is to place the transducer directly against the solid material to be examined and make contact between the transducer and the sample with the use of grease or a thin layer of rubber.

Suppose now the acoustic transducer is excited by a short electrical pulse. If the transducer is correctly designed it will emit an acoustic pulse of length τ_p determined by its bandwidth ($\tau_p \approx 1/\Delta f$ where Δf is the bandwidth of the transducer). The generated acoustic pulse passes into the object and is reflected by the acoustic impedance discontinuities caused by the presence of flaws. The return echo signal arriving at the transducer is then received by the transducer, and amplified and displayed as a function of time on the oscilloscope. The time delay of the echo is $T = 2z/v_w$ where z is the distance of the flaw from the surface and v_w is the acoustic wave velocity in the material being examined. Thus from the time delay of the observed pulse on the oscilloscope one can determine the distance of the flaw from the surface. Furthermore, one might expect the amplitude of the return echo to depend on the size of the flaw, so that one could obtain rough information on the size of the flaw by measuring the amplitude of the return echo.

This technique is known as an A-scan (amplitude scan) technique.

By moving the transducer along the surface of the object being examined various flaws may be detected while the A scan information is being obtained. Thus one can detect the transverse position of the flaws, although the definition of the system in transverse direction will be dictated basically by the size of the transducer. If the distance z is such that $z \gg a^2/\lambda$ where a is the radius of the transducer and λ is the wavelength of the center frequency of the pulse, then one might expect that the flaw would be in the far field of the transducer and the beam diameter would be larger than that of the transducer. On the other hand, if the flaw is in the near field of the transducer, the transverse definition would be comparable to the radius of the transducer. Thus the best definition is obtained when the transducer diameter is chosen so that the flaw is located roughly at the boundary of the near and far field of the transducer. This typically limits definitions in the transverse direction to be relatively crude of the order of 1 cm at operating frequencies of a few megahertz.

On the other hand, the range definition of such an A scan system can be relatively accurate because as it is dictated by the length of the pulse, and is of the order of $v\tau_p/2$ where τ_p is the pulse length. Such devices are used at baseband, which is different from the normal radar system, with transducers whose bandwidth can be comparable to their center frequencies. At low frequencies, the definition is obviously poor. But as the frequency is increased to improve the definition, the attenuation of the signal in most solid materials typically increases as the square of the frequency, so that there is a limit to the upper frequency which can be used. Thus the larger the structures, the lower the frequency and the poorer the definition that must be employed. In materials like nuclear reactor steel where the walls may be as much as 25 cm thick, the operating frequencies employed are of the order of 2.25 MHz. As the acoustic velocity of longitudinal wave in such materials is 6×10^5 cm/s the best range definition that can be obtained is of the order of 3–5 mm and the transverse definition will be several times as poor as this. In aircraft materials such as titanium or aluminum, frequencies as high as 20 MHz may be used, with correspondingly better definitions, while with structural ceramics frequencies as high as 400 MHz have been employed. Still higher frequencies in the 2–3 GHz range have been used to image integrated circuits.

A disadvantage of this A-scan method is that it is slow and tedious. We observe one line of amplitude information at a time, and although one can invent mechanical means for moving the transducers relatively rapidly, large amounts of information must still be interpreted by a human operator.

An alternative technique is to use the so-called B-scan method in which the return echo signal is used to modulate the intensity of an oscilloscope spot, while time delay is represented by horizontal position, and the mechanical position along the surface of the object is represented by the vertical position on the oscilloscope. By this means a crude picture of the structure within the material can be presented as illustrated in Fig. 1. The problem here is that most structures are not flat and it is difficult to make contact over very large regions so that B-scan imaging has not been employed very much in NDT applications. The technique, on the other hand, has proved useful in the medical field because it is possible to make contact with the body very easily, and the body itself is flexible so the transducer itself can be moved around and tilted to direct the beam in an

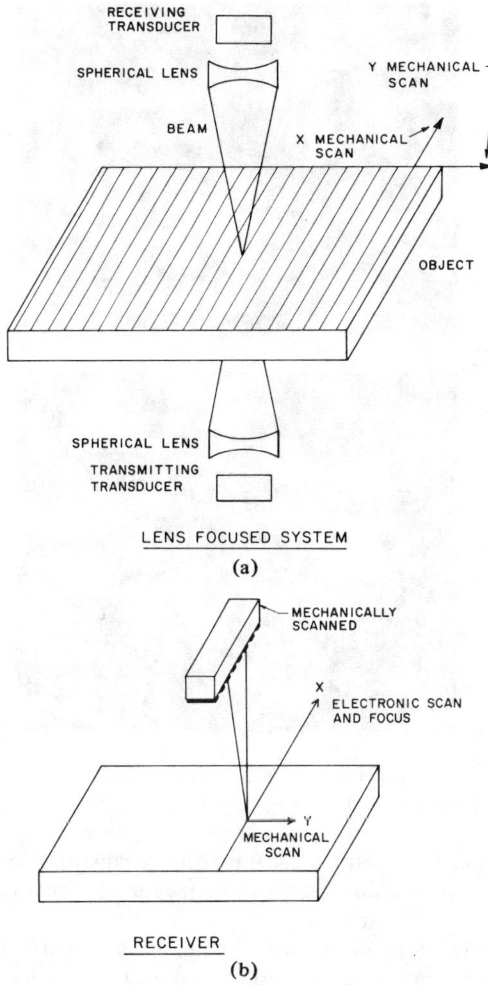

Fig. 2. (a) Mechanically scanned transmission system used for NDT. (b) A mixed electronically scanned and focused and mechanically scanned system.

arbitrary direction. By using a mechanical system with suitable electronic readouts to support the transducer, it has been possible to make the same spot within the body always occur at the same point on the oscilloscope and thus good B-scan images are regularly obtained with commercial medical instruments.

A third technique illustrated in Fig. 2(a) is to employ transmission imaging in a so-called C-scan method. Here, a focused transducer can be used to transmit an acoustic beam through the object of interest. If the object is thin, it may be placed at the focus of the acoustic beam and a second confocal focused receiving transducer can be used to receive the acoustic beam. The object of interest is then mechanically scanned across the beam while the beam itself is moved back and forth to create a raster scan. The results can be displayed and recorded either on a TV screen or on paper. The advantage of the method is that good definition can be obtained and a high quality transmission image of sheet metal and other objects can be observed.

A major development of this type of technique is the microscope of Quate et $al.$, which has been employed both in transmission imaging using this type of configuration, or in a reflection C-scan mode using one transducer as both transmitter and receiver [3]. The device operates in the gigahertz frequency range, and employs a thin film ZnO transducer deposited on a sapphire substrate, in which is machined a spherical lens. Contact is made to the sample through a thin layer of water. In

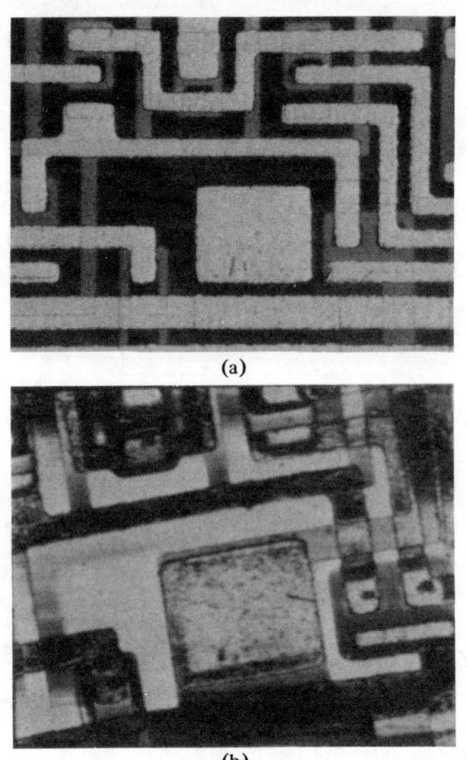

Fig. 3. Comparison of the optical (a) and acoustic (b) images of an integrated circuit. The aluminum linewidth is 7 μm [3].

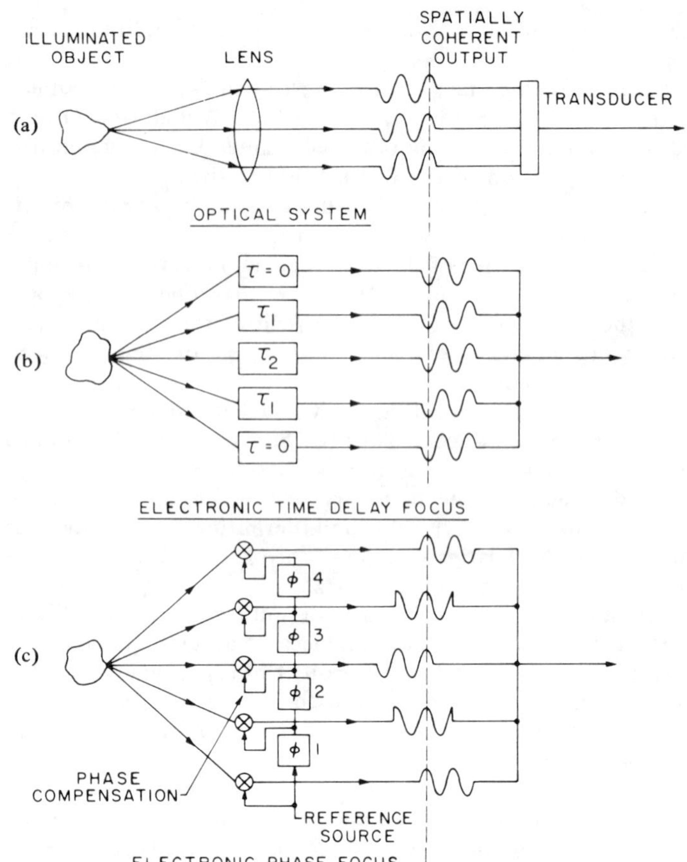

Fig. 4. (a) A schematic of rays passing through a physical lens to a plane transducer. (b) A schematic of a time delay system for focusing. (c) A schematic of a phase delay system for focusing.

this device, the sample is scanned by means of a loudspeaker movement in one direction and by means of a hydraulic piston in the perpendicular direction.

A picture of an integrated circuit obtained with this microscope operating in a reflection mode at a frequency of 2.4 GHz is shown in Fig. 3. In this case, the wavelength of the acoustic wave in the water medium is approximately 6000 Å, so the definition is comparable to or better than the best optical microscopes. This picture illustrates a very important property of acoustic nondestructive testing, the ability of acoustic waves to penetrate into an optically opaque object and measure subsurface properties. In this case, the aluminum gates of the MOSFET deposited on the substrate have a layer of SiO_2 approximately 1000 Å thick between the aluminum and the silicon; this region shows up as a bright spot. When no oxide is present the picture of the gate is dark.

It is apparent that two improvements are required in acoustic imaging techniques: First, there is a need to speed up the process by using electronic rather than mechanical scanning; secondly, there is a need to focus the acoustic beams so that both good transverse definition and range resolution through the depth of a thick sample can be obtained. The problem with focusing an acoustic beam is that a physical lens is normally required which must be immersed in a medium which can propagate acoustic waves. Typically this medium is water, so that for a low-frequency imaging system operating in the megahertz range the propagation path may be 10 cm or more; thus the imaging system tends to be very bulky and heavy. Furthermore, in many of these applications, good range definition as well as transverse resolution is required, so a lens is needed whose focal length can be varied as the pulse travels outwards from the transmitting transducer. This is a difficult problem and requires electronically variable focusing techniques rather than a physical lens.

If at the same time, one wants to provide electronic scanning over the face of the object rather than mechanical scanning, so as to speed up the process, it is necessary to replace the single mechanically scanned transducer with an array of small transducers in which the signal can be switched from one element to another.

We consider, as an example, the transmission system illustrated in Fig. 2(b), using an N-element array, which transmits a cylindrically focused beam with a similar focused N-element array as the receiver. If the system is mechanically scanned in a direction at right angles to the electronic scan, one might expect that the speed at which the scan could be carried out would be increased by a factor N, because the electronic scan would be virtually instantaneous, and now mechanical scanning would only have to be carried out in one direction rather than two. We shall show how such improvements in scan speed have in fact been obtained.

In order to understand what components are needed for an electronically focusing and scanning array, consider first the action of a physical lens which focuses the signal received from one point on an object onto the plane of a single large area transducer as shown in Fig. 4(a). The physical lens delays the rays passing through it so that all rays reaching the transducer from the focal point suffer the same phase and time delays. In order to carry out this process electronically, all the signals received by the individual array elements must be delayed in such a way so that they can be added to each other. The simplest way to do this conceptually is to connect delay lines to each element of the array so that a pulsed RF signal

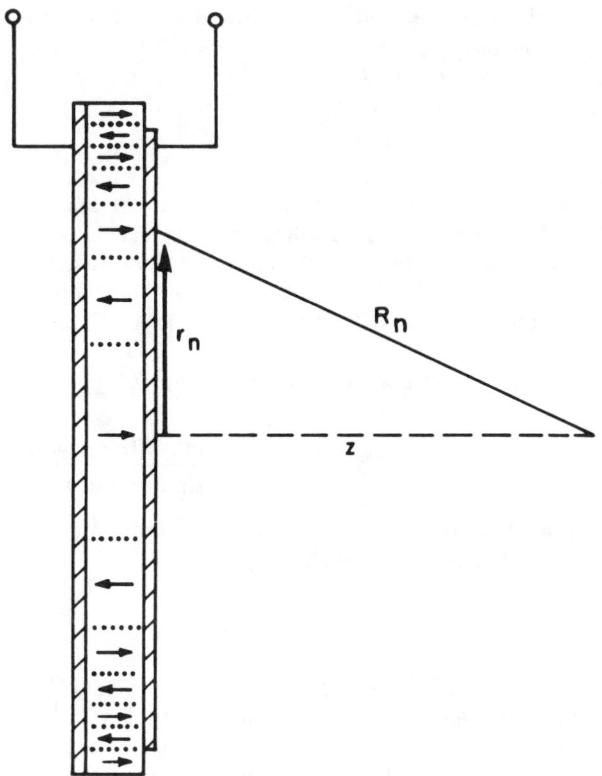

Fig. 5. A schematic of a Fresnel lens imaging system [4].

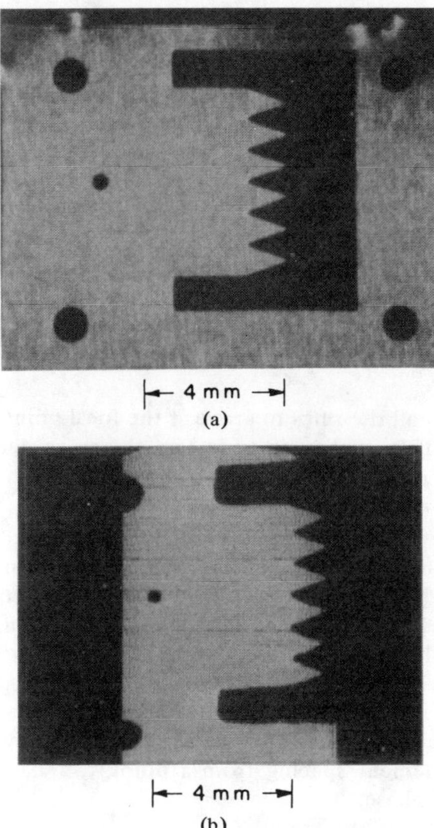

Fig. 6. Comparison of optical (a) and acoustic reflection (b) images of a sawtooth pattern punched in a 3-mil nickel sheet. The results were taken with a Fresnel lens at a frequency of 10 MHz [4].

emitted from a point on the object will arrive at the receiver with all pulses passing through each element of the array, arriving at the same time at the receiver, as illustrated in Fig. 4(b). Therefore, there will be a strong response from that particular point, but the signals from some other point would arrive at different times and be out of phase. We call this a time delay imaging system.

A simpler system to implement is the phase delay system illustrated in Fig. 4(c). In this case, an RF pulse several cycles long arriving from a point on the object passes through the individual transducer elements, and into a phase delay rather than a time delay system. In this case, the nth RF cycle from one element can be added to the $(n + 1)$th RF cycle from another array element. So all signals from the array elements could be added up to give a strong output corresponding to the point of interest. The rays emitted from any other point would give signals which would arrive out of phase. The disadvantage of such a phase delay system is that it is necessary to use an RF pulse several RF cycles long; therefore, the range definition of the system would tend to be deteriorated as compared to a system in which the time delays of the signals arriving from all elements are equal.

III. THE FRESNEL LENS

A simple example of an array system which uses phase delay rather than time delay is the Fresnel lens of Farnow and Auld [4]. Consider the system illustrated in Fig. 5 in which a disc-shaped transducer is divided into rings of radius r_n. Suppose a point on the object a distance z along the axis of the lens is a distance $R_n = \sqrt{r_n^2 + z^2}$ from the nth ring. Suppose the object is illuminated with a signal of frequency ω and wavelength λ. The phase delay of the ray reaching the nth ring will therefore be $2\pi R_n/\lambda$. Suppose we choose the $n = 0$ element, i.e., the center element, as the reference. The first element, $n = 1$ is chosen to have a radius r_2 such that the signal arriving is π out of phase with the signal on the axis. The $n = 2$ element is chosen so that the signal arriving at it is in phase and so on turn, i.e., all even elements are in phase and all odd elements are out of phase. Then all the signals arriving at the rings can be added if an extra π phase shift is introduced into the electronic signals picked up by the odd elements.

This aim has been accomplished by Farnow, by using a PZT ceramic transducer with ring radii r_n chosen so that

$$(\sqrt{r_n^2 + z^2} - z) = n\lambda/2. \tag{1}$$

The poling of the ceramic is reversed in sign at the appropriate positions, so the required π phase shift is automatically obtained. By using this system operating at 10 MHz either in reflection or in transmission with two such Fresnel lenses placed opposite each other, it is possible to mechanically scan the lenses across an object to form a C-scan image, and obtained good reflection and transmission pictures. A reflection image of a serrated metal sheet obtained with this system is shown in Fig. 6. We see that the definition is excellent, and in fact the definitions were very closely comparable to the predicted theoretical definitions.

The problem with such a simple Fresnel imaging system are of two kinds. First, the phases introduced are only 0 and π. Intermediate phases are required to obtain a perfect image with low sidelobes. The second problem is that if there are N rings, the total difference in length to the axial point between the outer and inner rings is $N\lambda/2$. Therefore, any RF pulses employed must be at least $N\lambda/2$ long spatially in order for

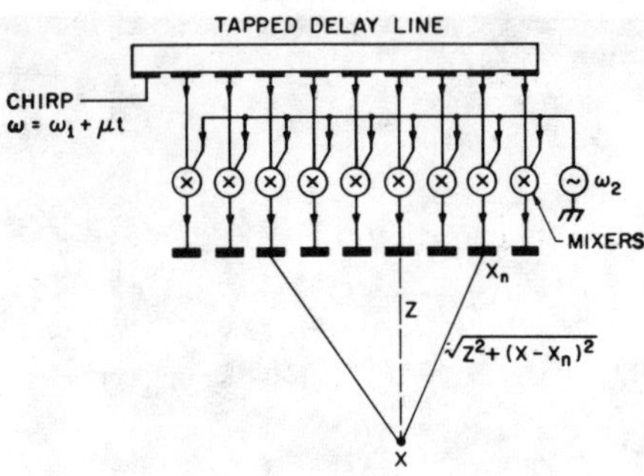

Fig. 7. A schematic of an acoustic surface wave tapped delay line system for acoustic imaging.

signals from all the rings to arrive at the focal point on the lens together. This implies, in turn, that the range definition will be dictated mainly by the depth of focus of the lens.

IV. CHIRP FOCUSED SYSTEMS

A useful method for NDT has been to provide an essentially continuous phase reference by the use of acoustic surface waves techniques [5], [6]. Consider the receiver system illustrated schematically in Fig. 7. Suppose the object is illuminated by a signal of frequency ω_s and wavelength λ in the medium. Then to the paraxial approximation of optics, the signal arriving at an element at position $x_n = nl$, $z = 0$ of the array where l is the array element spacing from a point x, z has a parabolic variation of phase:

$$\phi_n = -\frac{2\pi z}{\lambda} - \frac{\pi(x_n - x)^2}{z\lambda} + \omega_s t. \tag{2}$$

We suppose that the signal arriving from each array element is mixed with the signal from a corresponding tap on an acoustic surface wave delay line. The signal propagating along the acoustic surface wave delay line is chosen to have a parabolic variation of phase of the same magnitude but opposite sign to the signals arriving from the point x, z. When the two signals, one from the tap and one from the array element, are mixed, their frequencies add, as do their phases, so that by choosing the phase delay of the wave propagating along the delay line correctly, it is possible to cancel out the phase differences between the different rays arriving from the point x, z. Thus by this technique we can construct an electronically focused lens.

The correct signal to inject into the delay line is a linear FM chirp, one whose frequency varies linearly with time as $\omega = \omega_1 + \mu t$. This signal has frequency and phase at the nth tap given respectively by the relations

$$\omega = \omega_1 + \mu\left(t - \frac{x_n}{v}\right) \tag{3}$$

$$\phi_{Rn} = \omega_1\left(t - \frac{x_n}{v}\right) + \frac{\mu}{2}\left(t - \frac{x_n}{v}\right)^2 \tag{4}$$

where $v = l/\tau$ is the effective velocity of the acoustic wave between the array element connections, and τ the time delay of the acoustic wave from tap-to-tap of the delay line. The total output of the system is therefore of the form

$$V_{\text{out}} = \frac{K}{z^{1/2}} \sum w_n \exp\left[j(\phi_n + \phi_{Rn})\right] \tag{5}$$

where w_n is the amplitude weighting of the array elements, and K is a constant dictated by the sensitivity of the elements.

The variation in amplitude due to the different lengths of the ray paths is taken into account in the weighting w_n. By choosing the chirp rate μ such that

$$\mu = \frac{2\pi v^2}{\lambda z} = \frac{\omega_s v^2}{v_w z} \tag{6}$$

where v_w is the wave velocity in the medium, it can be shown that the terms varying parabolically as x_n^2 cancel out. Then with the weighting chosen such that $w_n = 1$ and the frequency ω_1 chosen to satisfy the relation $\omega_1 l/v = 2M\pi$, equation (5) may be summed to give the result

$$V_{\text{out}} = \frac{C}{z^{1/2}} \exp\left\{j[(\omega_1 + \omega_s)t + \mu(t^2 - (x/v)^2)/2]\right\}$$

$$\cdot \frac{\sin N\pi l(x - vt)/\lambda z}{\sin \pi l(x - vt)/\lambda z}. \tag{7}$$

We note that if N is large, the voltage output varies as sinc $[(x - vt)/d_x]$ where sinc $x = \sin \pi x/\pi x$, and

$$d_x = \frac{\lambda z}{Nl} = \frac{\lambda z}{D} \tag{8}$$

and D is the width of the array, and $C = K \exp -j2\pi z/\lambda$.

It follows from (7) that the maximum output $NC/z^{1/2}$ is proportional to the number of array elements and occurs at the time $t = x/v$. So the device behaves like a moving lens whose focal point moves at a velocity $v = dx/dt$ parallel to the array. From (6), it follows that the effective focal length $z = \mu\lambda/2\pi v^2$. The definition of the image or spacing between the 4-dB points is d_x. With uniform weighting ($w_n = 1$), the first sidelobe is approximately 13 dB down from the main lobe. Grating lobes or aliasing occurs when there is an extra $2\pi M$ phase shift between the rays reaching the neighboring elements. The spacing between the grating lobes and the main lobe follows from (7) to be where the denominator approaches zero, i.e., the Mth grating lobe is at a distance

$$d_{GM} = \frac{M\lambda z}{l} \tag{9}$$

from the main lobe. Thus the number of resolvable points in the image which are free from aliasing, i.e., free of regions where the image repeats itself, is just N the number of elements in the array.

This basic system is, in principle, simple. But, in practice, it typically requires mixers and amplifiers on each element and suitable summing networks. Furthermore, an acoustic surface wave delay line, with a total delay comparable to a TV line scan (64 μs), several inches long, with perhaps as many as 100 taps on it is required. Such delay lines are not necessarily simple to construct free of any defects. This is a serious problem because if M elements are missing, it can be shown that the maximum sidelobe amplitude due to the missing elements will be approximately M/N down from the main lobe.

The same systems can be used as a transmitter as well as a receiver by exciting the mixers from the delay line and from a separate oscillator so as to give an output signal centered about a frequency ω_s which can be used to excite an element of the array. In this case, of course, transmitter amplifiers are needed on each element.

When this device is used in the transmit mode, it behaves like a moving lens traveling at a velocity v parallel to the array.

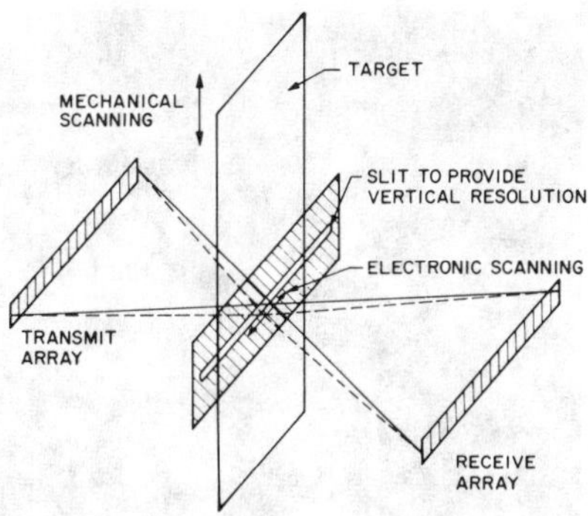

Fig. 8. A transmission imaging system with electronically scanned focused arrays. The mechanical scan provides scanning in the second dimension.

The time for which a single spot in the image is illuminated is approximately

$$\tau_x = d_x/v = \lambda z/Dv. \qquad (10)$$

But the time difference between the ray paths from the center and the outside of the beam is

$$\tau_R = D^2/8zv_w. \qquad (11)$$

In order for the spot to be illuminated by all the rays and hence for optimum definition to be obtained, it is apparent that there is a requirement that $\tau_R < \tau_x$. This, in turn, implies that with $\tau_R = \tau_x$ the minimum spot size is

$$d_x = (z\lambda^2 v/8zv_w)^{1/3} \qquad (12)$$

with

$$D = (8z^2 v_w \lambda/v)^{1/3} \qquad (13)$$

providing that the central axis of the beam is opposite the point of interest. If for instance the frequency ω_1 had been chosen so that the central axis of the beam was tilted, then the time difference between the rays would be much larger, and the system would not yield as good a definition. Thus the system is more suited for use with a long array, much longer than the spatial length of the chirp rather than a short array, shorter than the effective spatial length of the chirp; in this case the central axis of the beam would tilt during the scan.

A similar relationship holds for use of the system as a receiver when the transmitter is pulsed, i.e., when the point on the object is illuminated for a short time. The basic time for which the time the system must be illuminated then is dictated by the relations of (10) and (11).

This system has been constructed in several versions with as many as 80 array elements [7]. In the original system a receiver array was used to image a thin object illuminated from behind by a slit source. The object was mechanically scanned in the y direction while electronic scanning and focusing was carried out in the x direction. A later version of the device employed transmitting and receiving transducer arrays placed opposite each other, as illustrated in Fig. 8 with the object placed in between them and mechanically scanned up and down. Such a system has the advantage that it gives the speed and accuracy of electronic scanning, at least in one direction, thus speeding up the scan by approximately a factor of N. It also has the advantage that because both receiver and transmitter are focused on the same point the response of the system will vary as $[\mathrm{sinc}(x/d_x)]^2$. Thus the sidelobe level will be considerably reduced because the amplitude response function is

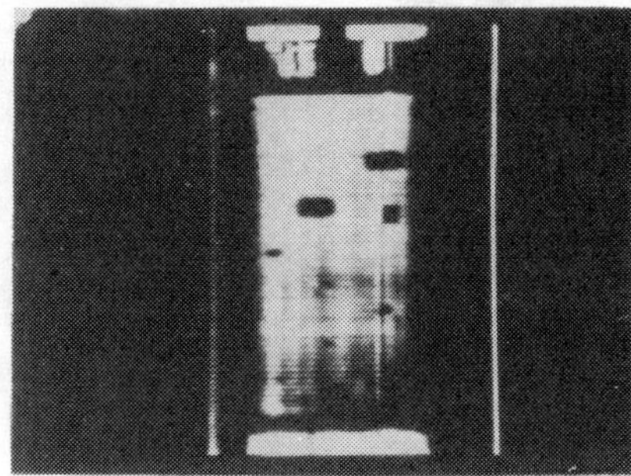

TRANSMISSION IMAGE OF BORON AND TITANIUM PANEL

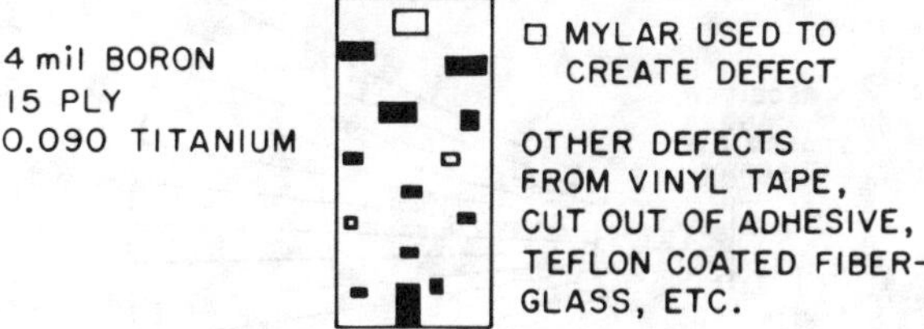

BORON TITANIUM LAMINATE PANEL

Fig. 9. A transmission image taken at 2.2 MHz with the system shown in Fig. 8 of a boron-reinforced epoxy sample on a titanium backing [5].

now squared, i.e. by a factor of 2 in dB. Because sinc x falls off approximately as $1 - \pi^2 x^2/6$ and $\mathrm{sinc}^2 x$ as $1 - \pi^2 x^2/3$, the definition, as measured by the -3-dB response, will be improved by approximately a factor of $1/\sqrt{2}$ yielding an effective spot size $d_x/\sqrt{2}$.

An example of such a scan used in a nondestructive testing application is shown in Fig. 9. In this case, a boron fiber reinforced epoxy laminate laid down on titanium was employed. The sample is approximately 22×7.5 cm in size and had defects deliberately introduced to it which can be clearly seen. The total scan took a few seconds, because the mechanical scanning was only in the vertical direction.

Systems of this type have also been used in a reflection mode. Here the same array is employed both as transmitter and receiver. In this case, the basic transverse definition obtained is, at best, like that in the transmission system, i.e., $d_x/\sqrt{2}$ [5]. The receiver is operated at a time $T = 2z/v$ later than the transmitter. Good range definition is obtained because the object point is only illuminated for a time $\tau_x = d_x/v$, so the range definition becomes

$$d_z \approx v_w \tau_x \approx \frac{v_w d_x}{v}. \qquad (14)$$

As the scan velocity v in such systems is comparable to the velocity v_w in the medium, the implication is that the range definition is comparable to the transverse definition. By using the relation that the total frequency excursion of the chirp is

$$\Delta f_c = \mu T/2\pi = \mu D/2\pi v \qquad (15)$$

where D is the width of the array, it can be shown

$$\tau_x \approx 1/\Delta f_c.$$

So the range definition turns out to be just would be expected from a pulse with approximately the same bandwidth as the chirp.

Systems of this kind have been used to observe objects in water and flaws in metal. A line parallel to the array is scanned;

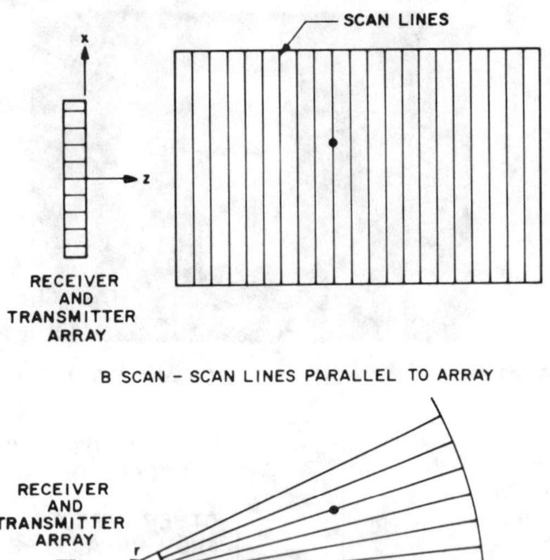

Fig. 10. Schematics of B scan imaging raster scans. The scan format used in the chirp focusing system has the scan lines parallel to the array.

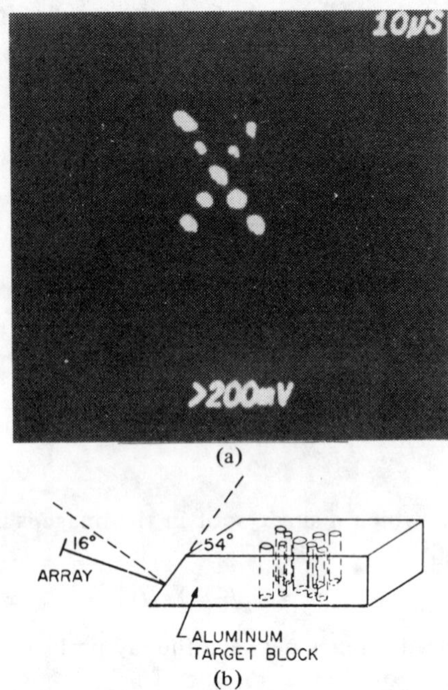

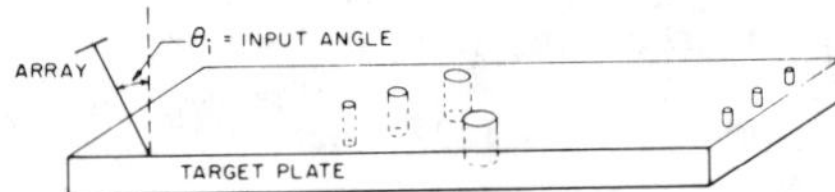

Fig. 11. (a) B-mode shear waves of 2-mm diameter holes in an aluminum block taken with $f_0 - 2.75$ MHz a scan velocity of 2 mm/μs. The central hole is 15 mm from the input end of the target block. (b) Schematic of a setup to excite shear waves in an aluminum block [5].

Fig. 12. A schematic of a setup to excite Rayleigh waves and Lamb waves in target plates from an array in water for Rayleigh waves in aluminum $\theta_i = 280$ [5]. Two sets of holes are shown, one set drilled through the body far from the end, and a second set 8 mm from the end.

then by altering the time delay between transmitter and receiver as well as the focal length electronically, a series of lines in the form of a raster in a plane perpendicular to the array is scanned, as illustrated in Fig. 10. We have constructed a 29-element system operating at a center frequency in the range from 1.5–2.5 MHz, with a field of view parallel to the array of approximately 4 cm and normal to array from 10 to 25 cm. A larger field of view could be obtained by the use of more elements. Shaw *et al.* have, for instance, obtained a 10-cm field of view with an 100-element transmission system [7]. The line time needed corresponds to a time delay $T = 2(z/v + L/v)$ where L is the length of the array. This time was varied with the range z in order to obtain the maximum frame rate; a frame rate of approximately 25 per second was obtained. The system has been used to observe objects in a water tank, as well as to observe various types of flaws in metals using various types of quasi-longitudinal and quasi-shear Lamb waves including flexural modes in thin plates, and Rayleigh waves on metal surfaces.

So far excitation of acoustic waves in metals has been carried out by using a transducer array immersed in water, and chirp bandwidths of the order of 1 MHz. Longitudinal waves are the least suitable to use because of their high velocity and hence poor definition. Shear waves can be excited by using an angled buffer on the substrate as shown in Fig. 11. If v_s is the velocity of the shear wave and v_w is the acoustic wave velocity in water, it follows from Snell's law that in the angles θ_w and θ_s the rays make the normal to the surface in the two materials respectively, and are related as follows:

$$\frac{\sin \theta_w}{\sin \theta_s} = \frac{v_w}{v_s}. \tag{16}$$

It follows from this relation that focusing can be obtained in the metal. Furthermore, to the paraxial approximation it can be shown that for the same initial beam angles at the array, the definition remains the same, but the focal length is decreased.

Rayleigh waves can be focused in much the same way using a wave incident from water at the correct angle to the surface, as shown in Fig. 12. However, it is entirely possible to construct suitable solid wedges for the purpose, as it would be to make shaped buffers fitted to the object of interest for direct shear or longitudinal wave excitation from an array of transducers.

An example of the results obtained with a focusing system using Rayleigh waves on aluminum is shown in Fig. 11. We observe that we can clearly pick out the lateral positions and range of several holes drilled in a metal sample. In nondestructive testing applications the problem with this and most other imaging systems is always that of sidelobes and grating lobes. By apodizing the amplitude weighting of the array elements it is possible to reduce the sidelobe level. In theory with such a rapidly scanned array, the sidelobe levels can be reduced by Hamming weighting to approximately 30 dB. In practice the sidelobe levels are considerably worse than this figure, and in most cases not better than 20 dB. One might expect that when operating in a transmit/receive mode, one would obtain the square of the individual focus array responses and therefore do considerably better. This is, in fact, true in transmission imaging, so that the sidelobe problem has essentially been eliminated in that case. On the other hand, in reflection mode imaging, it is possible to excite on a main lobe and receive

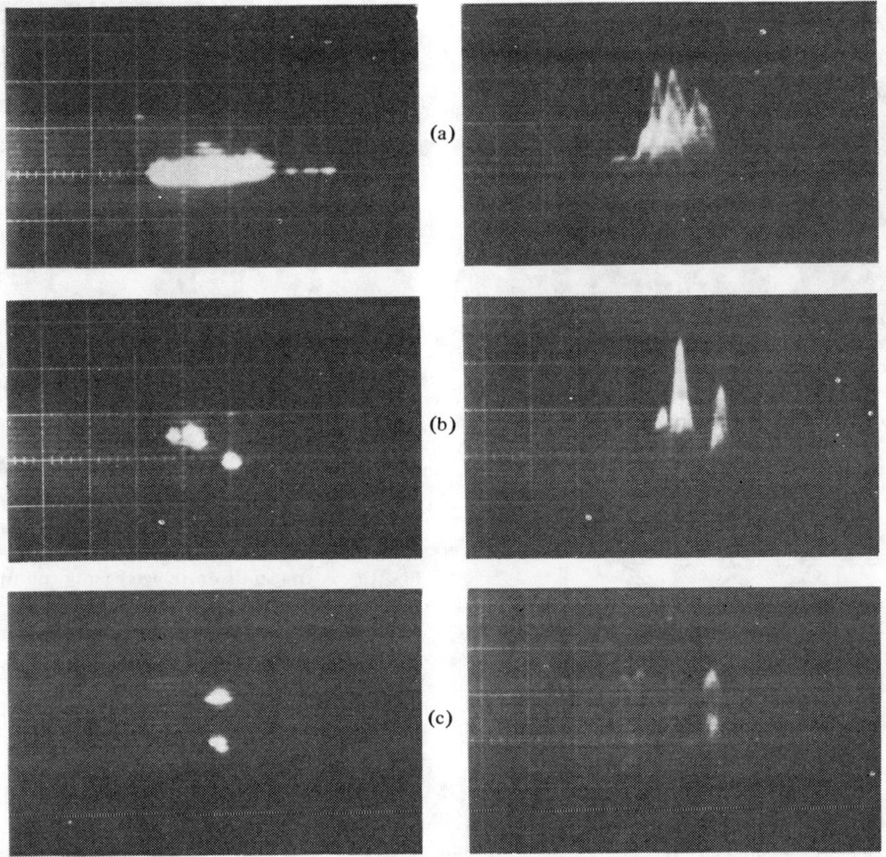

Fig. 13. Photographs of a surface crack taken in the gated mode with the crack facing the array (0°) at 45° to the array at 90° to the array. The configuration shown in Fig. 12 is used to excite Rayleigh waves [6]. A schematic of the alignment of the crack alignment relative to the transducer is shown in Fig. 14. (a) $\theta = 0°$.

on a sidelobe, and vice versa. Thus the ultimate sidelobe levels in a well adjusted system may not be adequate.

Unfortunately, we are often concerned with observing a small flaw in the neighborhood of a metal reflecting wall. Because of focusing, most of the beam energy illuminates the flaw; thus the response from the flaw is larger relative to that of the wall than it would be in a completely unfocused system. Nevertheless, the sidelobe signals received from a large scatterer may considerably exceed the signal from the flaw. As an example, if we consider excitation from a water bath, the reflection from the front surface of the object may be very high compared to that from a flaw buried deep within the object.

One way of eliminating this difficulty or at least decreasing it by a considerable margin, is to insure that the point of interest is only excited by the main lobe and received on a main lobe. To do this, we have gated the transmitter and receiver so they are only turned on when opposite a particular point. The gate times are then changed so as to scan the whole field of view in turn. The disadvantage of this technqiue is that the gate pulse times must be comparable to τ_x, so that only one spot is observed on each line. Thus if the number of resolvable spots is N, the frame time is increased by a factor of N. Typically the frame time for these kinds of images is of the order of 1/30th of a second. Thus now the scan time may take several seconds. For NDT purposes, this is not a major disadvantage, although not desirable, for it is still relatively fast compared to mechanical scanning. However it does provide high quality images over the whole field of view with very low sidelobe levels at all points.

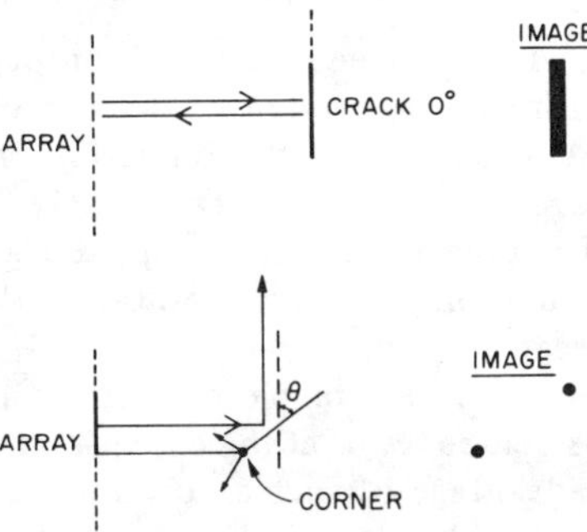

Fig. 14. Illustration of scattering from a crack head on and at an angle θ to a transducer array.

An example of such an image taken by Waugh is shown in Fig. 13 [6]. Here we observe the scattering from an artificial surface crack 1 cm long and 75 μm thick, as illustrated in Fig. 14. The surface crack is rotated to several positions relative to the array. When it is parallel to the array surface, it behaves as a specular reflector. The image shows the length of the crack with a thickness which depends on the definition of the imaging system. When the crack is rotated, the return beam does not hit the array. Therefore, the specular reflection from the crack is not observed, but only the scattering from its ends. Thus we observe two spots corresponding to the ends of the crack. Such results agree with theoretical predictions for scattering from a crack.

Another example is shown in Fig. 15 in which two small holes are observed at a distance 8 mm from the end of a sheet

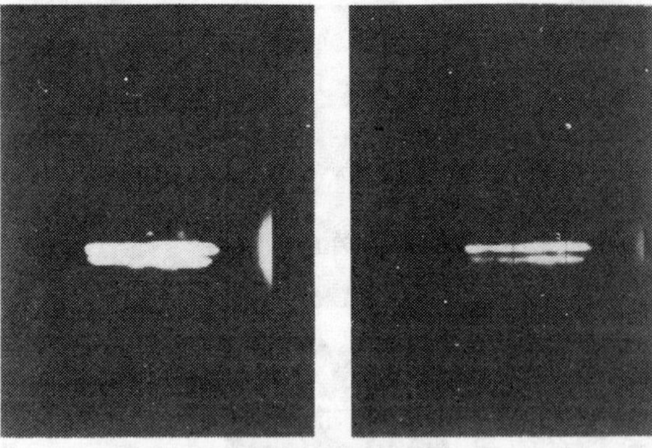

Fig. 15. Photographs of two small holes 8 mm from the end of a metal surface. The less intense image shows reflections from the two corners of the sample, as illustrated in Fig. 12 [6].

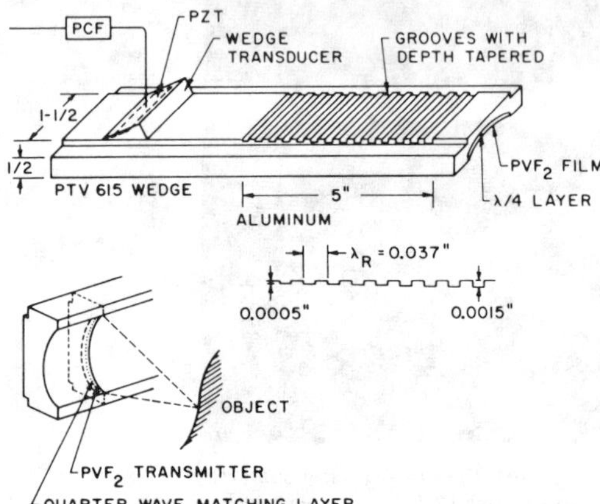

Fig. 16. Schematic of a grating array. In this example, the PVF$_2$ film is used as the receiver and transverse focusing is provided by shaping the lower surface.

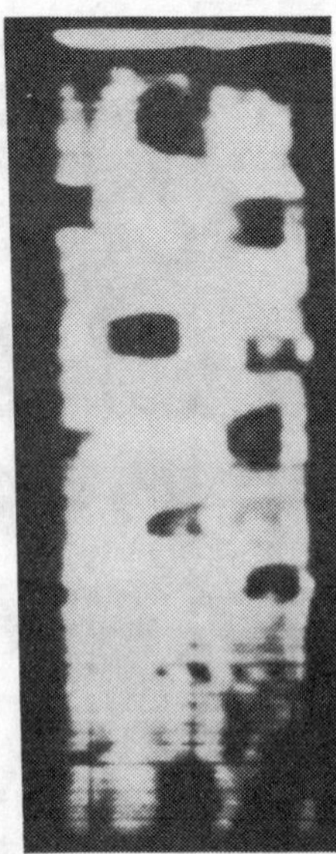

Fig. 17. A transmission image of a boron-fiber-reinforced epoxy bonds sample taken with the grating scanner of Shaw *et al.* [8].

of metal along which Rayleigh waves are propagating, as shown in Fig. 12. With sufficient intensity we can observe both the top of the metal sheet and the reflection from the surface wave passing around the end of the metal sheet to the next corner. As the intensity is turned up, the grey scale of the system is such that, one observes in addition, the holes in front of the metal sheet.

Thus this technique is capable of giving a considerable improvement in sidelobe levels at the expense of a relatively slow scan. The disadvantage of such a slow scan is not only that of speed; also the problem of display becomes more severe because each point in the image is only illuminated for a very small portion of the total time.

A. Grating Scanner

The advantage of a focused system is that the focused beam intensity is larger than that from a plane transducer by a factor $G = D/d_x = D^2/z\lambda$, where D is the width of the array. Its disadvantage is the complex electronics required. Shaw *et al.* have taken advantage of this improvement in sensitivity to construct an extremely simple imaging system [8]. This makes use of a metal substrate with a periodic array of cuts in its surface. A Rayleigh wave is excited on the surface of the metal by a wedge transducer, and is scattered by the grooves into a bulk wave in the substrate, as shown in Fig. 16. If the bulk wave in the substrate has a propagation constant $k_B = \omega/v_B$ and velocity v_B, while the surface wave has a propagation constant $k_R = \omega/v_R$ where v_R is the Rayleigh wave velocity, the bulk wave will be emitted at an angle θ given by the

relation

$$k_B \sin \theta = k_R - 2\pi/l \qquad (17)$$

where l is the spacing between the grooves. It will be observed that by varying the input frequency, the angle at which the bulk wave is emitted can be varied. In turn, it follows from (17), or a more detailed analysis of the type leading to (17), that by injecting a linear FM chirp along the delay line, a focused and scanned bulk wave may be emitted into the substrate. Similarly, by using the device as a receiver, a point source will give rise to an FM chirp which may be detected in a compression filter matched to the chirp rate.

Shaw *et al.* have made several versions of this device [8]. In the most recent type operating at a center frequency of 2.5 MHz, they employed a $\lambda/4$ matching layer of polyvinylidene fluoride (PVF$_2$) plastic on the lower surface of the substrate to efficiently excite a focused beam in water. This lower surface was shaped in the form of a cylinder to produce a cylindrical lens. This provides good definition over a limited depth range in a direction parallel to the grooves. The device was used to observe boron fiber reinforced materials of the type already described in both reflection and transmission modes. The beam was received with a separate PVF$_2$ transducer (the $\lambda/4$ matching layer) as shown in Fig. 16. Photographs of the flaws in this object taken both in transmission and in reflection are shown in Fig. 17. The basic principles of this device are scalable up to relatively high frequencies, and it is hoped that at a later time they will be able to operate at frequencies of the order of 100 MHz or more to obtain electronic imaging with a definition suitable for observing integrating circuits.

B. Digitally Produced Chirps

When more sensitivity and a variable focus is needed, it is possible to replace the acoustic delay line in the original system we have described with a digital system. On the basis of the theory already given, a reference signal of the form $\exp(j\pi(x_n - vt)^2/\lambda z)$ is required. An FM chirp can be sampled and the samples passed into a digital shift register. This yields plus or minus outputs at the taps of the form $\text{sgn}[\sin(\pi(x_n - vt)^2/\lambda z)]$. Thus the system behaves like a moving Fresnel lens

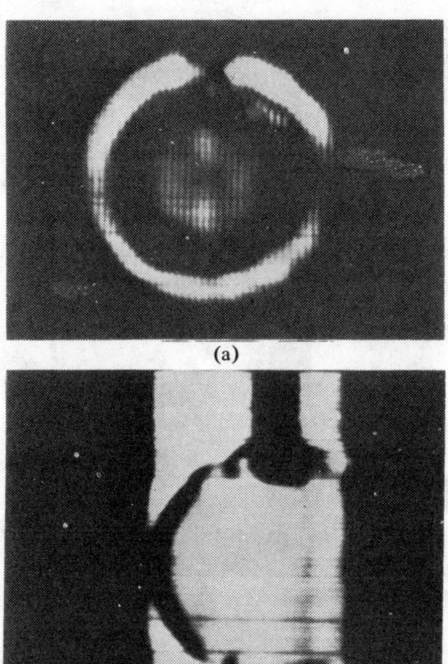

(a)

(b)

Fig. 18. Electronically scanned acoustic images of stress in a circular sample. (a) Double pulse technique. (b) Direct transmission mode.

with signals at the taps at time $t = 0$ of the form

$$V_R(x_n) = \frac{2}{\pi} \sum_{m=-\infty}^{m=\infty} \exp \frac{[j(2m + 1)\pi x_n^2/\lambda z]}{2m + 1} . \qquad (18)$$

The mth term of this series corresponds to a beam emitted from a real or virtual focus at $z_m = z/2m + 1$. A similar system has been demonstrated by Alais [9] and used for medical imaging with excellent results.

A multiple phase system of this type is being constructed by Bates and Shaw who use a digital shift register to switch 16 different phase references into individual elements of the array [10]. By this means, digital electronics can be employed in a quasi-analog system with the advantages that the FM chirp can be digitally programmed and need not be limited to the paraxial form, and the scan velocity can be chosen at will.

More generally following a treatment similar to that of Bates, [12] we can show that for an M phase system, the maximum phase error at the array is $\pm\pi/M$. If we write $u = \pi x^2/\lambda z$, a good approximation to the phase involves a simple sinusoidal error term:

$$\phi = u + \frac{8}{\pi^2} \frac{\pi}{M} \sin \frac{Mu}{2} . \qquad (19)$$

Following the analysis through by expanding $\exp j\phi$ in harmonics of Mu we find that the implication is that the main lobe is reduced in amplitude by a factor $J_0(8/\pi M)$. Furthermore, the two lowest order harmonics in Mu have an amplitude $J_1(8/\pi M)$ and the error voltage corresponding to this first harmonic at the phase z has the form [12]

$$\Delta V = J_1(8/\pi M) \exp (j\pi x_n^2 M/2\lambda z)$$

$$\cdot \exp (-2j\pi x x_n/\lambda) \exp (j\pi x^2/\lambda z). \qquad (20)$$

We note that in the worst case when

$$n^2 lM/2d_g = P \qquad (21)$$

$$2nx/d_g = Q \qquad (22)$$

where P and Q are integers, d_g is the grating lobe spacing; then if $d_g = lM/2$ there are sidelobes due to phase error at $x = \pm lM$ of amplitude

$$A_s = \frac{J_1(8/\pi M)}{J_0(8/\pi M)} \qquad (23)$$

relative to the main lobe. More generally these conditions cannot be satisfied and the sidelobe level is lower.

An interesting application of such systems is to phase contrast imaging. Recalling that the FM chirp behaves like a moving lens, it is possible to use the system in a phase contrast mode. In one case, such experiments are being carried out by using two chirps of frequencies $\omega = \omega_1 + \mu t$, $\omega = \omega_2 + \mu t$, respectively, inserted one after the other. Along the delay line these have frequencies $\omega = \omega_1 - \mu x/v + \mu t$, $\omega = \omega_2 - \mu x/v + \mu t$, respectively. So the chirps may either be in phase or out of phase, and spaced by a distance $\Delta x = (\omega_1 - \omega_2)/\mu$. The signals received by these lenses depend on the phase of the chirp signals relative to each other. So the system can be designed as a receiver in a dark field mode where the signals are out of phase, and a phase contrast differential image much like that of a Nomarski microscope can be obtained. Other gated modes of operation are also possible and have been used to scan inhomogeneous stress fields in metals. When stress is applied to a sample, the velocity of a wave passing through it changes and hence so does the phase delay of a wave passing through it.

Using mechanical scanning very accurate results based on this principle have been obtained but it can take several hours to scan an entire cross section of a metal sample. However, with an acoustic surface wave system of this type the first crude electronic images of stress have been obtained and are illustrated in Fig. 18. The digital imaging system of Bates and Shaw is being built for the purpose of obtaining better accuracy and obtaining better images of stress fields but at electronically scanned rates [10].

V. Time Delay Systems

At the beginning of this paper, we discussed the various types of scanned systems which could be employed. The time delay systems are very attractive because their range definition is not necessarily limited by the size of aperture as it would be in a phased focus system. However, the provision of variable time delay is a more difficult problem. Simple implementations of unfocused systems have already been employed in the nondestructive testing field. In one example, a group at the Watertown Arsenal have been employing a commercial Advanced Diagnostic Research (ADR) unfocused system to look at shell cases [11]. In this device an array of 64 elements in a line is employed. These elements are excited sequentially in groups of 4, with a short pulse, thus emitting a parallel beam of width approximately 1 cm. The beam is received by the same elements and displayed in the form of one line of a B scan. The device then moves on one element to the next group of 4 elements, and the process is repeated. Thus a 64 line image is obtained. In the NDT application, the device was used to obtain a C-scan reflection image of a shell casing by rotating it at a fixed distance from the array. It will be seen from Fig. 19 that good reflection images of defects in shell casings could be observed; these were taken at very high speeds relative to the normal mechanically scanned systems.

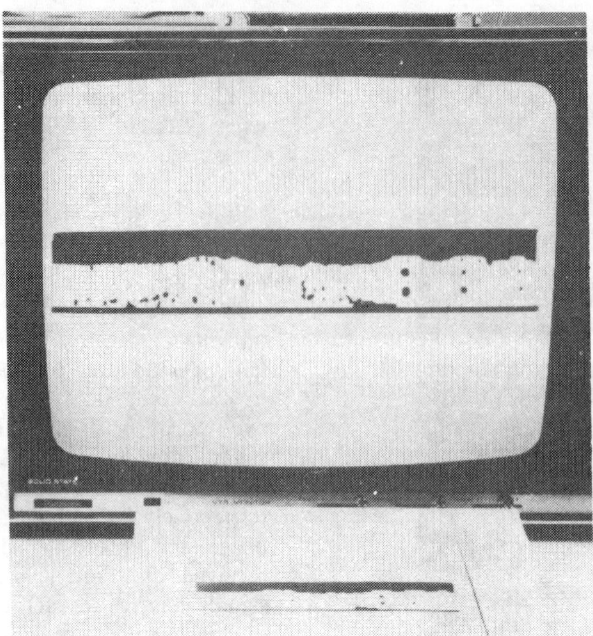

Fig. 19. A picture of flaws in the band around a shell casing taken with
an ADR system by Smith [11].

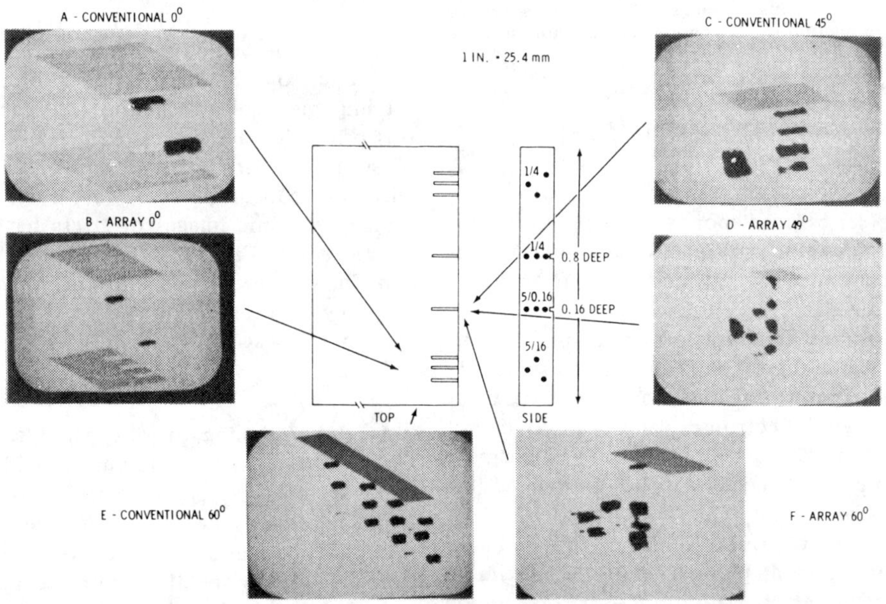

Fig. 20. Isometric images of side-drilled holes taken with the Battelle imaging system [13].

The ADR type of system is being worked on in several laboratories, and being applied mainly in medical applications. Because no delay lines are employed, it is possible to use this technique at relatively high frequencies. In our own laboratory, we have demonstrated a 16-element system operating with 2 ns pulses, for use in testing structural ceramics.

At the present time, several time delay focused systems are being constructed for NDT purposes. Several alternatives have been considered. One employed by Becker *et al.* at Battelle is to use 128 elements in a row exciting them sequentially in much the same manner already described in the ADR system [13]. However, by exciting the array elements with a programmed time delay between them, it is possible to excite a wave at an arbitrary angle to the array. The application is to look for faults in nuclear reactor walls. The ASMT regulations require that such observations must be made at several angles, so as to pick up specular reflectors. By using time delay techniques, the system can be scanned like the ADR system, except that now the scan can be carried out at several different angles. By mechanically scanning in the other direction, a large volume of material can be tested in a relatively short time. By using sophisticated display techniques, three-dimensional information can be obtained and an isometric projection display can be made which makes it relatively easy to interpret the results. A sample of an image obtained with this system is shown in Fig. 20.

The problem of carrying out the design for a full time delay system is a difficult one because of the necessity of providing adequate delay lines. In medical imaging systems, the best known example is the radial sector scan system constructed

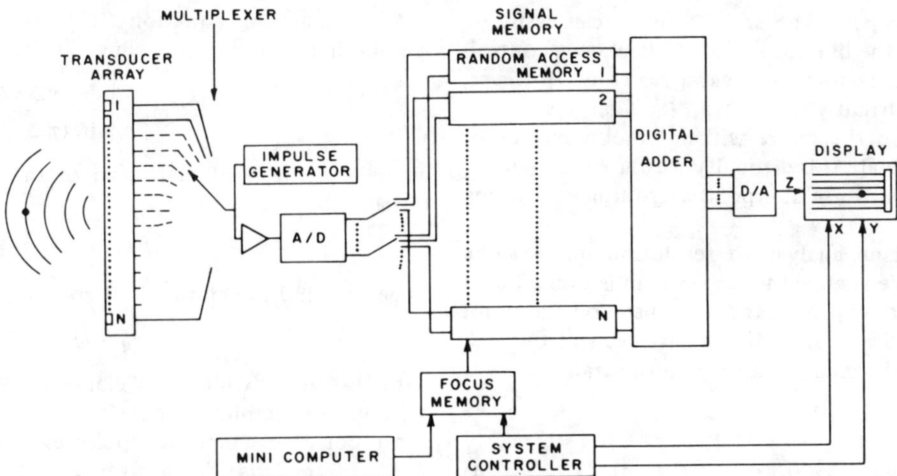

Fig. 21. A schematic of a synthetic aperture digital imaging system [16].

by Thurstone [14] with a scan along radial lines extending from the center of the transducer array, as illustrated in Fig. 10. In this system a beam is transmitted at an angle to the axis by delaying the signals which excite the elements appropriately. The signals received on the elements are passed through tapped electromagnetic delay lines. As the transmitted pulse travels out from the array, the focusing must be changed. To do this, Thurstone's system changes the delay time to each element by switching the taps on the delay lines and controlling the switching from a mini computer. The disadvantage of such a system is that the lumped delay lines take up a great deal of room, and it is only possible to work with a limited number of elements because of the complexity of the techniques required.

Another approach being actively pursued by Meindl *et al.* for a medical imaging system is to employ 20 or more CCD delay lines on one silicon chip for the purpose [15]. The problems that are involved are associated with the complexity of the control system, clock noise in the signal, limitations on dynamic range, and the difficulty of increasing the frequency to the higher ranges required by NDT. But it is expected that as these types of systems are developed, they will be employed in the NDT field as well as in medical imaging.

A third approach is to employ analog-to-digital (A/D) converters on each element and use digital delay systems. Such a system is not practical at the present time for the frequencies employed in the nondestructive testing fields because of the high cost of high speed A/D converters. But as such costs are decreasing rapidly, this will change. At present, it is necessary to employ some stratagem to decrease the number of A/D converters and the complexity of the system required.

The author and his co-workers are constructing a new synthetic aperture system for this purpose [16]. The basic system is illustrated schematically in Fig. 21. A short pulse is emitted from a single transducer and enters the object of interest. Reflected echoes are received on the same transducer, then passed through an amplifier and A/D converter into an 8 × 1000-bit RAM. The process is then repeated for the next element in the array, and the signals from that element are stored in a separate RAM. By using a clock rate, several times the signal frequency, several samples per RF cycle are obtained. Thus it is necessary to employ a relatively high frequency A/D converter. By the time the process is finished, information from the whole field of view is stored in the RAM memories and is available for reconstruction of an image. To image a

particular point in the field, signals are taken from the appropriate points in the RAM corresponding to the correct time delays. A basic system of this type has been demonstrated some time ago by Johnson *et al.* at the Mayo Clinic using a computer for storage and reconstruction of the image [17].

In our system high-speed RAM's are employed with a separate RAM focus memory to program, in turn, the registers from which the signals are read out. The digital signals are then added in a digital adder, passed to an A/D converter, and then used to intensity modulate the signal on the screen of a cathode ray tube. By carrying out these processes in turn, any line in the image can be scanned in any direction and a complete raster image constructed.

An important advantage of the synthetic focus approach is that it requires only a single front-end amplifier, regardless of the number of elements in the transducer array. This means that a great deal of effort can be put into the design of the front-end amplifier with little regard for its complexity, number of adjustments, expense, etc., all of which are important considerations in a system where an amplifier is required for each element of the array. As the signal emitted from an array element must travel to a point in the field and back, its effective length of travel is double that of an equivalent receiver system with a definition d_x with the object illuminated by an unfocused transmitter. Thus the transverse definition in this system would be $d_x/2$. But the sidelobe amplitude near to the focal point would vary as $\mathrm{sinc}(2x/d_x)$. On the other hand, as we have seen, a system with a focused transmitter and receiver has a $\mathrm{sinc}^2(x/d_x)$ response, and hence a much lower sidelobe level, but not such good definition as this system. A second interesting feature of such time delay systems is that only the sidelobes near the focal point have a $\mathrm{sinc}(2x/d_x)$ variation.

The range resolution is essentially determined by the pulse length (bandwidth) as with other imaging techniques. The system therefore provides the same improvement in transverse resolution as in scanned holographic imaging. But, in addition, as time delay rather than phase delay techniques are being used to reconstruct the image, excellent range resolution should also be obtained.

One problem with most electronically scanned acoustic imaging systems is that the line times and frame times are not usually compatible with a TV monitor. This is a disadvantage as the grey scale image quality of magnetically deflected cathode ray TV tubes is superior to that of the electrostatic deflection tubes used in oscilloscopes. The present design can easily be made compatible with the line time of a TV display by controlling the speed at which the focused lines are read out. However, the number of lines currently employed, 96, is far less than in a TV display, 525. So the image will not look continuous. One technique to eliminate this difficulty is to use only part of the screen. Another is to use interpolation routines for filling in.

We have carried out an analysis of resolution and sidelobe levels in the system. We assume that the system is excited by a pulse of the form $F(t) \exp j\omega t$, and is focused on the point (x_0, z_0). Then after suitable time delays have been introduced, the sum of the delayed signals returning to the transducers at $(x', 0)$ is of the form

$$G(t) = \int_{x_n} F(t - 2\Delta R/v) \exp j\omega(t - 2\Delta R/v) A(x') \, dx' \quad (24)$$

where v is the acoustic velocity in the medium, $A(x') \, dx'$ is the response of the transducer in the transmit–receive mode in the region between x' and $x' + dx'$, the $1/R$ amplitude variation has been reflected, or included in F, and

$$\Delta R = \sqrt{z^2 + (x' - x)^2} - \sqrt{z_0^2 + (x' - x_0)^2} \quad (25)$$

is the difference in range from $(x', 0)$ to (x, z) and (x_0, z_0).

By making the paraxial approximation that $(x' - x)^2 \ll z^2$, taking $x_0 = 0$, for simplicity we can write

$$\Delta R \approx \Delta z - x'\Delta x/z_0 \quad (26)$$

where $\Delta z = z - z_0$, $\Delta x = x - x_0$. It follows that the range resolution, i.e., the result with $\Delta x = 0$ is determined by the function $(F(t - 2\Delta z/v)$ for all transducers. So the range resolution is determined by the pulse shape and length.

On the other hand, the transverse definition of a line reflector and sidelobe levels at the focal plane $(\Delta z = 0)$ are determined by the integral

$$G(t) = \int F(t + 2x'\Delta x/z_0 v)$$

$$\cdot \exp j\omega(t + 2x'\Delta x/z_0 v) A(x') \, dx'. \quad (27)$$

It will be seen that at $t = 0$, $\Delta x = 0$ the output is

$$G(0) = F(0) \int A(x') \, dx. \quad (28)$$

So $G(0)$ is determined by the maximum amplitude of the pulse and the spatial integral of the transducer response.

More generally, it will be seen that at $t = 0$ the transverse response of the system as a function of Δx is the Fourier transform of the function $A(x')F(2x'\Delta x/z_0 v)$. In the special case when the pulse is many RF cycles long we regard $F(t)$ as constant and for simplicity take the transducer to consist of N infinitesimally thin elements l apart, excited uniformly. In this case $A(x')$ takes the form

$$A(x') = \sum_{0}^{N-l} \delta(x' - nl) \quad (29)$$

where $\delta(x)$ is a delta function.

After summing equation (27), $|G(t)|$ takes the same form we obtained for chirp focusing:

$$|G(t)| = \left| \frac{\sin(\pi\Delta x/d_x')}{\sin(\pi\Delta x/d_z)} \right| \quad (30)$$

where d_x', the 4 dB definiton of the system, is given by the relation

$$d_x' = \lambda z_0/2D \quad (31)$$

as before, and the grating lobe spacing d_g is

$$d_g = \lambda z_0/2l \quad (32)$$

with $D = Nl$ the width of N elements of the array.

Now, for simplicity, consider the situation when $F(t)$ is a short constant amplitude pulse extending from $-T/2 < t < T/2$. In this case for a given Δx the maximum value of x' at $t = 0$, for the array element at x' to be excited, is

$$x'_{max} = \pm z_0 vT/4\Delta x. \quad (33)$$

This implies that at the first grating lobe, where $\Delta x = d_g$, the number of elements excited is

$$M' = vT/\lambda = M \quad (34)$$

where M is the length of the pulse measured in cycles of the center frequency ω_0.

The implication is that the grating lobe amplitude is down by a factor M/N from the main lobe. So ideally an RF pulse only 1 RF cycle long should be employed to eliminate the grating lobe. Furthermore, for points further from the main lobe than d_g, the maximum value of the sidelobe amplitude is a factor $1/N$ down from the main lobe. More generally, if $\Delta x < d_x'M$ and the pulse is M RF cycles long $|G(0)|$ is given by (28). But for $\Delta x \gg Md_x'$ the sidelobe level approaches $1/N$. In the intermediate range of Δx the sidelobe level can only be accurately predicted if the pulse shape is known accurately. An assumption of a square topped pulse is not adequate, because this would assume a bandwidth much wider than the center frequency, thus leading to inaccurate results in this intermediate range of Δx. The more general case, therefore, still needs further study.

We may summarize these results by saying that beyond the first zero of the main lobe, not all the elements contribute, but the behavior of the focusing system near the main lobe is like that of a conventional lens operating with signals of wavelength $\lambda/2$. For Δx large, however, only one element contributes at a time, and so the response falls off by a factor $1/N$ where N is the number of elements. Thus by using only a short RF pulse grating lobes should be eliminated. We would therefore expect that with a 32 element system, the far out sidelobe level would be approximately -30 dB, and that because of the absence of grating lobes, relatively sparse wide aperture arrays can be used to give improved resolution.

Many of these conclusions hold for any imaging system which employs short RF pulses, such as the Thurstone [14] system or the Walker and Meindl system [15]. Grating lobes tend to be eliminated and a relatively sparse array can be used, while the far out sidelobes will be reduced in amplitude from the main lobe by a factor M/N.

The major disadvantage of a synthetic focusing system of this type is that its sensitivity will not be as good as a system which uses a focused transmitter and receiver, for only one element is excited at a time. On the other hand, as only one element is used at a time, in combination with a multiplexer to switch from element to element, the system is relatively simple and the single transmitter and receiver amplifier can be designed with special care. Thus it is possible to work with a higher voltage transmitter than is typically possible with multi-element system, to use a pulse train with a matched filter, and to design for the lowest possible amplifier noise figure. It is, of course, vital to use transducers with as high an efficiency as possible. Thus in our early experiments we are constructing transducers with quarter wavelength matching to water and a measured return loss of approximately 11 dB at 3.3 MHz, whereas our earlier focused array system had a return loss of the order of 40 dB.

Another problem with such systems is that of phase errors. One might expect to use three or four samples per RF cycle. On the basis of the theory already discussed for digital imaging systems, this would imply a reduction of the main lobe level by several dBs due to sampling. However, such considerations apply only to the main lobe; the far out sidelobe levels will still be reduced by a factor $1/N$ in a pulsed system of this type.

An interesting feature of such systems is that because of the flexibility of digital imaging, it is possible to construct two-dimensional focusing systems with a small number of elements. It is also possible to use very large arrays and focus with, say, 32 elements and move to the next 32 elements and image the same region. This gives the effect of a large aperture providing the focused images from both scans can be stored and added. Such a process is already carried out in unfocused medical B scan systems; the difference here is that electronic techniques would be used to move or tilt the beam rather than a mechanical scan, although mechanical scanning could be used too, with the advantage of partial focusing as compared to the standard mechanically scanned medical B scan system. By making such additions, the main lobe level can be increased in magnitude relative to the sidelobes so that one might expect to improve the performance of an imaging device by such stratagems. Another possibility demonstrated by the group at the Mayo Clinic, is to use several transmitter and receiver elements, in-stead of one [17]. By transmitting from M elements and receiving on N elements, there should be a sidelobe level reduc-tion comparable to MN. So far the early results obtained with an 8-element hardware system and 3-element software appear to bear out the basic theory that has been developed.

A third possibility is to use only a single transducer and move it mechanically from point to point in the x-y plane. Such a system has been constructed by Frederick *et al.* [18] who employed computer processing to form an image. They have obtained excellent results in thick metal samples.

It is apparent that digital techniques are extremely flexible, and that new methods and ideas can tried out almost at will by programming from a computer. The author therefore believes that such processing schemes are likely to be the most promising techniques to use in the future, especially as in the NDT field the speed necessary to observe extremely rapidly moving objects, as is required for observing a moving valve in a heart scan in medical imaging, is not really needed. Here the frame time can be more than adequate for real-time scanning. It is only when there will be a phase difference between the signals received by individual transducers, due to rapid move-ment of the object being observed, that there may be difficulty.

VI. Conclusions

We have described several types of electronically scanned imaging systems which have been employed in research applica-tions for nondestructive testing. The FM chirp focused system has been shown to operate extremely well in transmission imaging and would be very useful for fixed focal plane observa-tions in reflection imaging. Longitudinal waves, shear waves, and Rayleigh waves have been used for imaging in metals. By slowing up the scan and using a gated system it is possible to obtain extremely high quality B scan reflection images. New digital implementations of these systems are being constructed and should demonstrate very high performance capabilities both for B scan reflection mode imaging and phase contrast imaging.

CCD and lumped delay line systems are being developed for electronically scanned and focused time delay systems both for medical imaging and NDT applications. A promising and flexible approach is to use digitally focused and scanned systems. As digital technology is being developed so rapidly, such systems begin to look relatively practical, although there is a real need for cheap A/D converters so that more than one receiving element can be used at a time.

We have not discussed the problem of constructing acoustic arrays in any detail. The individual array elements for an imag-ing system must have a wide angle of acceptance, and in most cases a bandwidth of up to an octave. In a pulsed system, they must have, in addition, a good pulse response. Further-more there is a requirement for high transduction efficiency. So far most of the arrays that have been made for NDT pur-poses are made of PZT ceramics and are designed for operation in water; mode conversion is used to excite shear waves or Rayleigh waves in metals. A few contacting array transducers have been made for this purpose, and show good promise. In particular, the array elements normally have to be slotted, with a diamond saw so as to keep the cross coupling to a minimum. However, when an array is placed directly against a metal surface, early experimental results indicate that be-cause of the good matching to the acoustic impedance of the metal, slotted elements are not needed, so that the arrays may be constructed by photolithographic metal deposition tech-niques, to form the electrodes of the array elements [19]. By using a metal buffer shaped to the object being examined, it should be possible to use flat arrays. Such techniques have already been employed to examine ceramic ball bearings with a single flat transducer [20]. Finally, a new type of array material, PVF_2, a piezoelectric plastic with mechanical properties much like teflon is being worked on in several laboratories. Because it is easy to cut and handle, and has an acoustic impedance comparable to water, it may offer major advantages for the construction of arrays [21].

It is apparent that acoustic imaging is an extremely powerful method for finding flaws in materials rapidly and for observing their shape and size. Although the technology required is very sophisticated, the techniques are very speedy and provide by far, the most complete information on the nature of flaws that can be obtained.

Acknowledgment

The author would like to thank K. Bates, P. Grant, D. Corl, T. Waugh, and P. Khuri-Yakub for many stimulating discussions and use of some of their unpublished results. He would also like to thank B. A. Auld, C. F. Quate, J. Posakony, J. Shaw, and D. Smith for supplying me with photographs of images taken with their devices.

REFERENCES

[1] H. D. Collins, "Acoustical interferometry using electronically simulated variable reference and multiple path techniques," *Acoust. Holog.* (Plenum Press), vol. 6, pp. 597–619, 1975.

[2] B. P. Hildebrand and B. B. Brenden, *Introduction to Acoustical Holography*, New York: Plenum Press, 1972.

[3] V. Jipson and C. F. Quate, "Acoustic microscopy at optical wavelengths," *Appl. Phys. Lett.*, vol. 32, no. 12, pp 789–791, June 15, 1978.

[4] S. A. Farnow and B. A. Auld, "An acoustic phase plate imaging device," *Acoust. Holog.*, (Plenum Press), vol. 6, pp. 259–273, 1975.

[5] T. M. Waugh, G. S. Kino, C. DeSilets, and J. D. Fraser, "Acoustic imaging techniques for nondestructive testing," *IEEE Trans. Sonics Ultrason.*, vol. SU-23, pp. 313-316, Sept. 1976.

[6] G. S. Kino, T. M. Waugh, P. D. Corl, C. S. DeSilets, and P. M. Grant, "Acoustic imaging techniques for nondestructive testing," in *Proc. 1st Int. Symp. Ultrasonic Materials Characterization*, June 1978.

[7] W. P. Leung, H. J. Shaw, G. S. Kino, and L. T. Zitelli, "A new technique for high speed stress detection and imaging using a 100-element acoustic phased array," in *Proc. IEEE Ultrasonics Symp.*, pp. 255–258, 1977.

[8] A. Rønnekleiv, J. Souquet, and H. J. Shaw, "Grating acoustic scanners," in *Proc. Ultrasonics Symp.*, pp. 91–93, 1975.

[9] P. Alais and M. Fink, "Sonde multiple ultrasonore a focalisation et translation electronique," *Biocapt. 75*, pp. 481–486, Nov. 1975.

[10] K. N. Bates and H. J. Shaw, "Digitally controlled electronically scanned and focused ultrasonic imager," *Acous. Holog.* (Plenum Press), to be published.

[11] J. M. Smith, "Advanced acoustic imaging with linear transducer Arrays," Army Materials and Mechanics Research Center AMMRC TR 77-26, Dec. 1977.

[12] K. Bates, private communication.

[13] F. L. Becker, J. C. Crowe, V. L. Crow, T. J. Davis, B. P. Hildebrand, and G. J. Posakony, "Development of an ultrasonic imaging system for the inspection of nuclear reactor pressure vessels," Electric Power Research Institute EPRI RP 606-1, Sept. 1977.

[14] F. L. Thurstone and D. N. Von Ramm, "A new ultrasound imaging technique employing two-dimensional electronic beam steering," *Acoust. Holog.* (Plenum Press), vol. 5, pp. 249–259, 1974.

[15] J. T. Walker and J. D. Meindl, "A digitally controlled CCD dynamically focused phased array," *Proc. IEEE Ultrasonics Symp.* pp. 80–83, 1975.

[16] P. D. Corl, P. M. Grant, and G. S. Kino, "A digital synthetic focus acoustic imaging system for NDE," in *Proc. IEEE Ultrasonics Symp.*, Sept. 1978.

[17] S. A. Johnson, J. F. Greenleaf, F. A. Duck, A. Chu, W. R. Samaywa, and B. K. Gilbert, "Digital computer simulation study of a real-time collection, post-processing synthetic focusing ultrasound cardiac camera," *Acoust. Holog.* (Plenum Press), vol. 6, pp. 293–311, 1975.

[18] J. R. Frederick, C. J. H. Vandenbroek, R. C. Fairchild, and M. B. Elzinga, "Improved ultrasonic nondestructive testing of pressure vessels," U. S. Nuclear Regulatory Commission NUREG/CR-0135, Univ. Michigan, Ann Arbor, May 1978.

[19] C. DeSilets, "Transducer arrays suitable for acoustic imaging," Ph.D. dissertation. Stanford University, Stanford, CA, May 1978.

[20] A. G. Evans, G. S. Kino, B. T. Khuri-Yakub, B. R. Tittmann, "Failure prediction in structural ceramics," *Res. Suppl. J. Non-Destructive Testing*, vol. 35, no. 4, pp. 85–96, Apr. 1977.

[21] L. Bui, H. J. Shaw, and L. T. Zitelli, "Experimental broadband ultrasonic transducers using PVF_2 piezoelectric film," *Electron. Lett.*, vol. 12, no. 16, pp. 393–394, Aug. 5, 1976.

[22] M. Ahmed, K. Y. Wang, and A. F. Metherell, "Holography and its application to acoustic imaging," this issue, pp. 466–483.

Introduction to Computer Aided Tomography

HENRY J. SCUDDER, MEMBER, IEEE

Invited Paper

Abstract—In recent years, Computer Aided Tomography (CAT) has had a major impact on the medical fields of radiology and neurology and nuclear medicine. This paper introduces the basic physics and mathematics underlying the production of reconstructed tomographic images. It discusses the evolution and philosophies of different possible data collection and reconstruction schemes.

INTRODUCTION

COMPUTER AIDED Tomography (CAT) is causing a revolution in the medical field of radiology. By combining "ordinary" X-ray technology with sophisticated computer signal processing, it is possible to generate a display of the tissues of the body which is unencumbered by the shadows of other organs. An ordinary X-ray, system shown in Fig. 1, takes pictures by passing X-rays through the body and detecting them with a photographic emulsion. The different tissues in the body attenuate the X-ray beam differently, and the film responds to the intensity of the X-rays falling on it. The resulting image displays the accumulated attenuation of the original beam. Fig. 2 shows a typical ordinary X-ray plate.

CAT also passes X-rays through the body of a patient, but the detection method is usually electronic in nature, and the data is then converted from an analog signal to digital impulses in an analog-to-digital (A/D) converter. This digital representation of the X-ray intensity is fed into a computer, which then reconstructs an image.

Ordinary X-rays cover a plane in a single view, with height as well as width in the resulting picture. CAT restricts the thickness or height of the X-ray beam to about 1 cm or less, and scans a line in a single view. Many of these views are taken at different angles. A typical CAT setup is shown in Fig. 3 and 4, and a typical reconstructed image is shown in Fig. 5. The resulting CAT picture is a cross section of the patient. The usual method of doing tomography uses an X-ray detector which translates linearly on a track across the X-ray beam, and when the end of the scan is reached, the X-ray tube and detector are rotated to a new angle, and the linear motion is repeated. The latest generation CAT machines use a "fan-beam" geometry, with an array of detectors which simultaneously detect X-rays on a number of different paths through the patient. The relative merits and problems of the different schemes will be discussed later in the paper. Fig. 6 shows a block diagram of a typical CAT machine.

In medical nuclear imaging, images are formed of organs containing gamma-emitting radionuclides. Original imaging methods called scintillation cameras are analogous to conventional X-ray pictures. The usefulness of this technique is limited because 1) only organs with a high radionuclide concentration can be separated from their environment, 2) the resolution is limited by an absorbing collimator, so that improving resolution reduces the detector efficiency, 3) the radioisotopes widely used, such as ^{99m}Tc, have low-energy gamma radiation, which is subject to much absorbtion in the

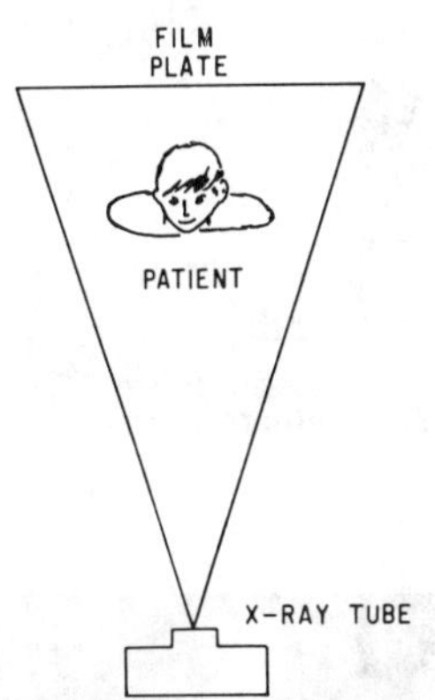

Fig. 1. Ordinary X-ray system.

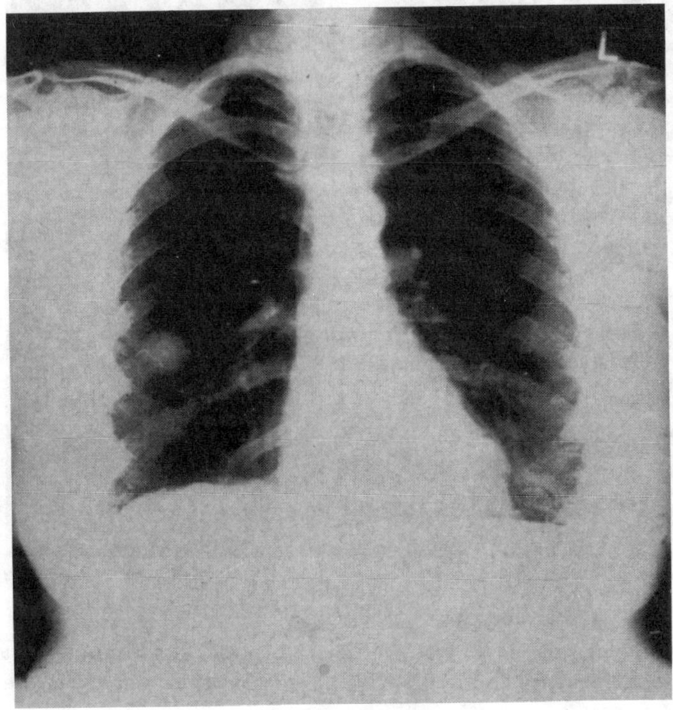

Fig. 2. Conventional chest X-ray.

Manuscript received January 14, 1978; revised March 1, 1978.
The author is with the General Electric Company, Corporate Research and Development Center, Schenectady, NY 12301.

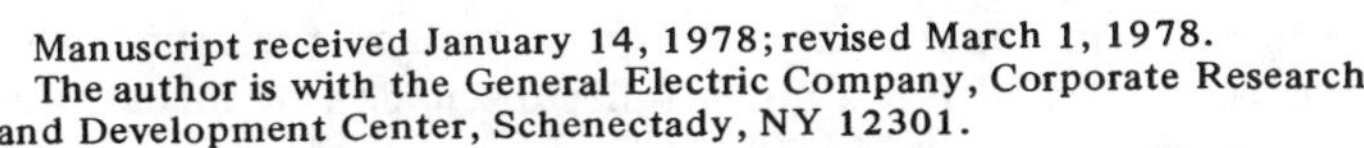

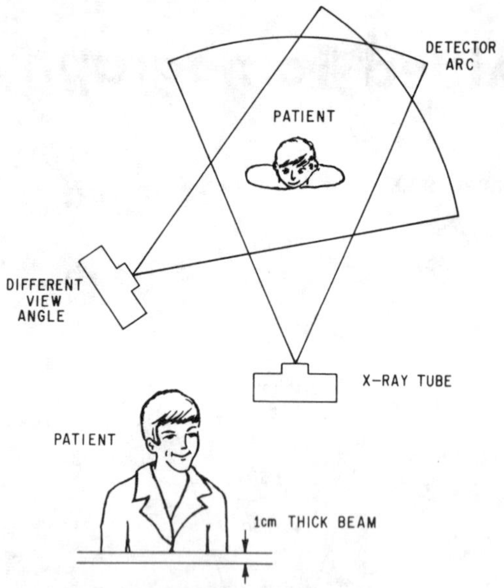

Fig. 3. Schematic tomographic system.

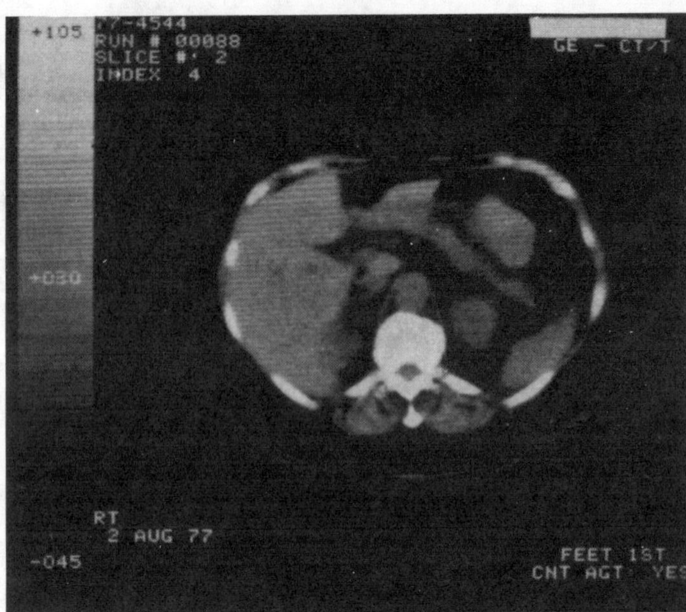

Fig. 5. Typical tomographic reconstruction of a CT scan showing liver and pancreas. Note the bile ducts in the liver (small low-density areas within the liver) and the small lymph nodes just above the vertebral body on either side of the aorta. Other organs seen are the spleen, kidney, and stomach (partially filled with gas).

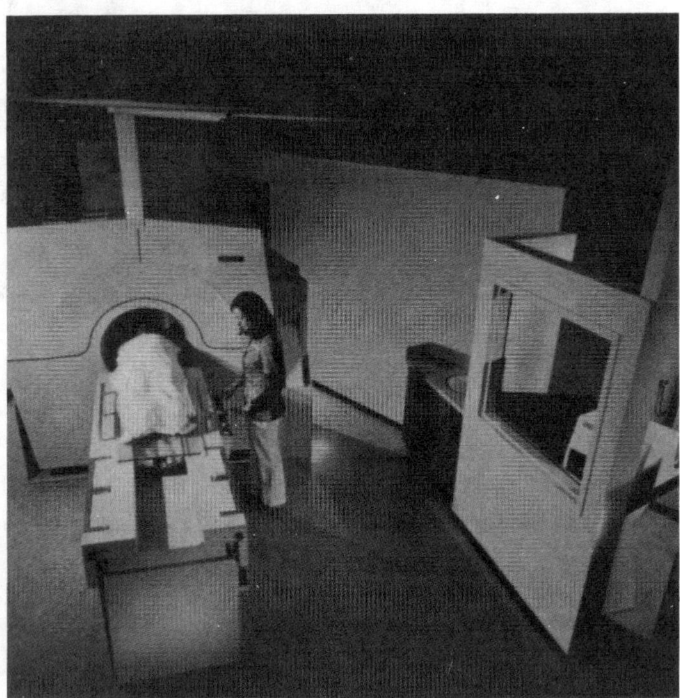

Fig. 4. Typical tomographic scanner and table.

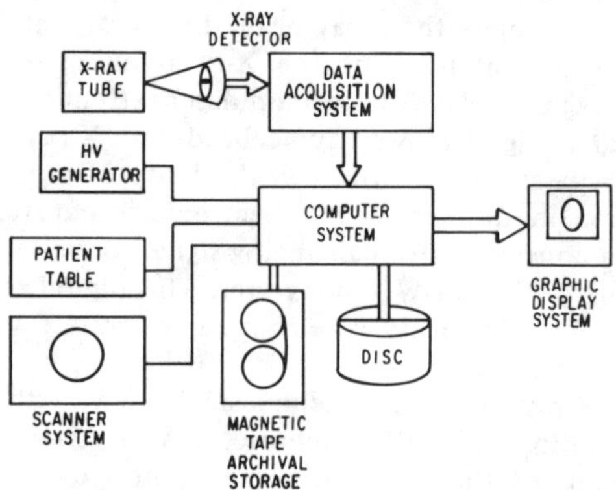

Fig. 6. Block diagram of tomographic system.

body causing the detector efficiency to vary significantly with depth, and to be affected by the presence of bone overlying the organ of interest.

Recent developments use tomographic reconstruction to provide a high-contrast image of organs and structures containing positron-emitting radioisotopes.

Positrons are annihilated by colliding with an electron which happens quite nearby the location of the emitting radioisotope atom. When this occurs two photons of 511 keV are simultaneously produced traveling in directions 180° apart. The occurrence of these annihilation events is determined by using time-coincidence detection, consisting of a set of scintillation detectors on each side of the patient, connected to single chan-

nel analyzers which only respond to 511 keV radiation photons. Only photons which occur within a few nanoseconds of each other in detectors on opposite sides of the body are counted. By offsetting the centers of the sets of detectors surrounding the patient, and by rotating the patient (or the detectors), a simultaneous set of view angles and detector translations occurs, giving the same type of geometry as in X-ray tomographic machines. A schematic diagram of such a system is shown in Fig. 7. The emission data must be corrected for the absorbtivity of the body. This is done by calibrating the body with a conventional X-ray tomograph and extrapolating the result to 511 keV absorbtivity, or by surrounding the body by an external ring of positron emitters, such as a solution of ^{64}Cu, and determining the count rate as a function of transverse and angular position. The same measurement is made with and without the patient in position, and the ratio yields the attenuation. For a much fuller discussion of this area of nuclear medicine see [16], [17].

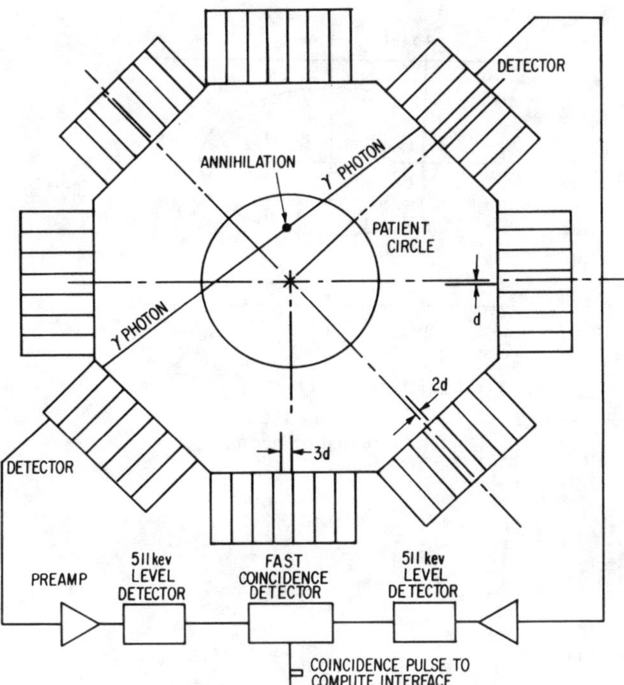

Fig. 7. Positron emission schematic diagram.

II. A Short History of Computer Aided Tomography

The eminent mathematician J. Radon [1] established the mathematical foundations of tomography in 1917, but the first practical reconstructions were done by Bracewell [2] in 1956. He was able to determine the regions of the sun which emit microwave radiation, although the microwave antennas available could only measure the intensity along a narrow ribbon in a given direction. He used a series of "strip sums" in different directions to reconstruct the image of the sun. Somewhat similar methods were developed by electron microscopists to determine the structure of small complex specimens.

Early image reconstruction work in the area of medical applications were carried out independently by Oldendorf [3], Kuhl and Edwards [4], and Cormack [5]. Important papers describing the modern convolution–back-projection method of reconstruction are by Shepp and Logan [10], Ramachandran and Lakshminarayanan [11], Merssereau and Oppenheimer [18], and King [19]. The first clinically useful tomographic equipment was a head scanner developed by G. Hounsfield [6] at the Center Research Laboratories of EMI Ltd. in 1970, and was installed at Atkinson Morley's Hospital in 1971. The first scanners in the U.S. were installed at the Mayo Clinic and Massachusetts General Hospital in 1973. In 1974 a whole body scanner was developed by Ledley, and installed at Georgetown University Medical Center. Since then a number of different companies have developed both head and body scanners, and a broadly based competitive market has developed. A comprehensive review is a paper by Cho and Burger [20].

III. Reconstruction Algorithms

The methods for reconstructing the tomographic image from the radiographic projections have developed in two different directions: 1) iterative algebraic reconstruction techniques and 2) Fourier transform techniques. The amount of data collected during the radiographic scans is generally on the order of 300 detectors and 300 views, resulting in about 10^5 data points. The number of picture elements (pixels) displayed is generally also about 300 × 300. If the projected data is represented by a 10^5 dimension vector X, and the absorption in each pixel element by a vector Y, then X and Y are related by a matrix A of 10^{10} elements:

$$X = A\,Y. \qquad (1)$$

The reconstruction problem amounts to inverting the matrix A, to obtain an image vector (if A^{-1} does not exist, some sort of a pseudoinverse can be taken, such as a least mean square error criterion)

$$Y = A^{-1} X \qquad (2)$$

from the data X. The number of operations involved in inverting a matrix is on the order of n^3 where n is the number of dimensions. The vectors X and Y have $n = 10^5$, so $(10^5)^3 = 10^{15}$ operations are required to invert A. Assuming each operation takes a microsecond, and there are about $\pi \times 10^7$ s/year, we would require $10^{15} \times 10^{-6}/\pi \times 10^7 \cong 31$ years to invert the matrix A for a given geometry. The iterative algebraic techniques approximate the vector Y by a series of vectors Y_i, and the closeness of the Y_i to Y is measured by forming pseudo data $X_i = A Y_i$ and seeing how close X_i is to the original data X. These operations are each done in a time proportional to n^2 instead of n^3, so the reconstruction time is significantly reduced. The original EMI machine is believed to have used an iterative type of algorithm, and much work has been done on developing this type of algorithm [7]–[9]. Bracewell's original technique was based on a Fourier transform approach, and most modern tomographic machines use a method based on this called the convolution–back-projection method. This will be discussed in some detail later in the paper.

The so-called third generation tomographic machines use a fan-beam geometry instead of a parallel-beam geometry. This necessitates a modification of the convolution–back-projection algorithm.

IV. Medical Aspects of Tomography

The first tomographic machines were head scanners. The patient's head is relatively easy to hold stationary during a scan, so the relatively slow scan speeds (2 min, typical) were not a major problem. If the patient moves during the course of a scan, strange streaks appear on the reconstructed image, called motion artifacts. To image the body of the patient, the scans must be done quickly. It is necessary for the patient to breathe, and the physiologic processes of the heart pumping blood and peristaltic digestive motions are not easily stopped. The second generation machines speeded up the linear and rotational motions of the machine, and used some parallelism by taking several views simultaneously by using more than one detector. The scan speeds of these machines are about 20 s. The patient is required to hold his breath during this time, which is quite a long time for sick people to attempt. If the patient breathes, the motion artifacts appear, and scan is probably spoiled. The third generation machines use a fan-beam geometry, taking many detector measurements simultaneously, and typically do a scan in about 5 s, which is well within a comfortable breath holding time. The effects of heart motion and peristalsis appear to be negligible at these speeds.

Other aspects of the design of tomographic systems are important. Because of the very large capital investment required to purchase one of these machines (typically about $500 000), the purchasing hospitals need to consider the problems of patient throughput and handling very closely. They often run at least two shifts of operation per day, 7 days per week. The more patients per day the machine can handle, the lower the cost per patient. In addition, the storage and retrieval of reconstructed images and the ability to have an archival storage is very important. A typical sequence involves the taking of several adjacent scans, to obtain a three-dimensional image for diagnostic purposes, followed by repeated scans at time intervals of several weeks to determine the progress of the patient's treatment. It is important to be able to compare these images with each other. Because of the large volumes of data required for each picture, a major software consideration is the design of a good image-retrieval system. The doctors should not need to be computer programmers in order to operate the system, and should not have to maintain photographic files in addition to the tomographic system.

The reliability and maintainability of the machines are also important. In a large throughput machine, the amount of "down time" becomes very important economically, both because of the cost of repairs and the loss of income during this time.

V. PHYSICS OF TOMOGRAPHY

X-ray photons interact with material in three principal ways: pair production, photoelectric absorption, and scattering. Pair production only occurs if the photon energy is greater than 1.022 MeV, which is much higher than the energies used in medical tomography (usually around 70 keV average). Photoelectric absorption occurs when the photon is completely absorbed, and transfers its energy to an electron. The electron then passes through the material giving up its energy until it comes to rest. Scattering has two components: coherent or Raleigh scattering in which the direction of the photon is changed, but it does not change frequency, or Compton, or incoherent scattering, where the photon gives up some of its energy to an electron and continues on in a different direction at a lower energy. The combined effects of scattering and absorption result in an exponential attenuation of a beam of photons as it passes through a material. A monoenergetic beam with an input intensity of I_0 photon/s, passing through a length x of material, has an output intensity of

$$I = I_0 e^{-\mu x}. \tag{3}$$

The attenuation μ depends on the energy of the X-rays and the particular material passed through. If the material is heterogeneous, as in the human body, the simple μx product is replaced by a line integral, and the intensity of the output becomes a function of the position.

Consider the geometry shown in Fig. 8. The attenuation in the patient's body is expressed as $\mu(x, y)$, and the output X-ray intensity $I(x)$ is expressed as

$$I(x) = I_0(x) \exp - \int_L \mu(x, y) \, dy. \tag{4}$$

The term

$$P(x) = -\ln\left(\frac{I(x)}{I_0(x)}\right) = \int_L \mu(x, y) \, dy \tag{5}$$

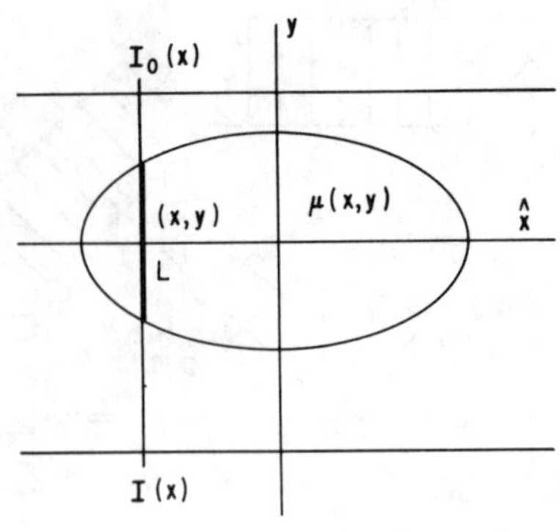

Fig. 8. Attenuation geometry.

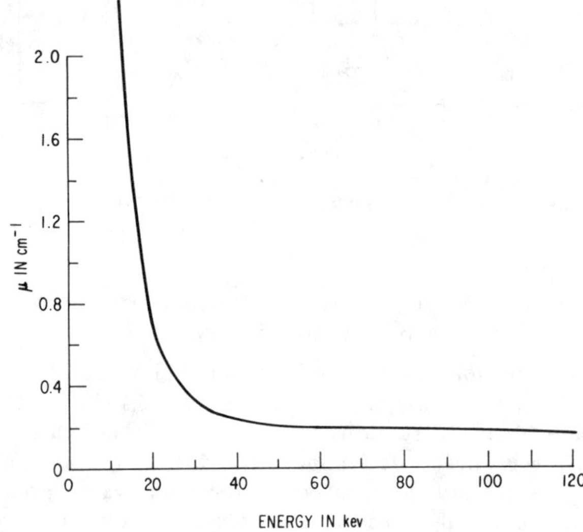

Fig. 9. Attenuation of water.

is known as the projection. In a radiographic image, such as an ordinary X-ray film, the projection is what you see. In tomography, numerous projections at different angles around the patient are taken, and the projections and the path of the X-ray through the patient are a function of the view angle θ.

Another important effect that must be considered in tomography is "beam hardening." The X-ray beams used in tomography in general are not monoenergetic, and the attenuation of most materials at X-ray energies act as a high-pass filter having a lower attenuation at higher energies than at low. The attenuation curve for water is shown in Fig. 9.

As the beam passes through the body, the relative amount of high energy photons becomes larger the further the beam continues. Since low energy photons do not penetrate material as well, they are considered "softer." Hence the phenomenon of "beam hardening." The net result is a signal change which is more complicated than the simple exponential above. It can be expressed as

$$I(x) = \int dE \, D(E) \, I_0(x; E) \exp - \int_L \mu(x, y; E) \, dy \tag{6}$$

where $D(E)$ is the detector response as a function of energy. One method of compensating for this beam hardening is to preharden the beam by passing it through an Al or Cu filter before it passes through the body. Hounsfield's original EMI scanner had a "water bag" surrounding the head so that the total path length for the X-rays was independent of the view angle. This works quite well since the attenuation of most parts of the body, except for bone, is near to that of water. However the patient-handling aspects of the water bag present a major problem. Most modern tomographic machines do not use a water bag, except for some head scanners.

The dynamic range of the intensity is another major problem. The largest patients' dimensions can be over 40 cm. The transmission of 40 cm of water at 70 keV is about $\exp(-0.19 \times 40) = 5 \times 10^{-4} \cong 2^{-11}$. The attenuation due to air is essentially negligible, so a signal dynamic range of 11 bit is required. A water bag would help a lot here also. In addition, the accuracy of the reconstruction requires on the order of 11 bit of data precision. If the system were linear, a 22-bit A/D converter would be needed to measure the intensity. An analysis of the effect of the logarithm, given in Appendix I, shows the dynamic range is reduced somewhat, but is still a major design consideration. Some possible solutions are to use an analog log amplifier before sampling the data, or to use a floating point A/D converter.

VI. Calibration

The projection $P(x)$ depends on measurements of both the transmitted X-ray intensity $I(X)$ and the incident X-ray intensity $I_0(X)$. Because of fluctuations in the X-ray beam and because of nonuniformity of the X-ray beam as a function of angle from the center of the beam, a calibration procedure is necessary. The different geometrical configurations produced by the different CAT manufacturers have different detailed calibration procedures, but a few general principles can be discussed. The intensity variations with time can be measured by putting a reference X-ray detector in a portion of the beam which does not intersect the patient, usually at the edge of the beam, and sampling this detector at the same time as the measurement of the beam transmitted through the patient is sampled. The spatial fluctuations can be measured during an initial calibration run using a known object, such as a water-filled cylinder in place of the patient. The theoretical attenuation of the cylinder is known so the distribution of the incident beam can be calculated by working backwards from the calibration data. The assumption is then usually made that the spatial effect is constant over a period of time, such as a day, so that calibration does not have to be repeated for each patient. We have

$$I_0(x) = I_c(x) \exp +y_c(x) \mu_c(x) \qquad (7)$$

where

$I_0(x)$ the incident intensity being determined;
$I_c(x)$ the measured calibration intensity;
$y_c(x)$ the known path length of the ray to x;
$\mu_c(x)$ the known attenuation of the calibration object.

The temporal variation is compensated for by multiplying the measured intensity $I(x)$ by the ratio I_{cr}/I_r, where I_{cr} is the reference intensity at calibration time, and I_r is the reference intensity during the measurement of $I(x)$. Another source of error is the accuracy of measurement of the incident is the drift of the electronic amplifiers used to raise the signal level of the detected X-ray intensities to the level needed to perform the A/D conversion. The amount of amplification needed is in general quite large, because the X-ray sources are limited in power, and because of the need to keep the dose to the patient as small as possible and still get an acceptable picture. Amplifiers with these large amplifications tend to be less stable over time than more usual amplifiers. One solution is to allow them to drift slowly, and calibrate them "on the fly," each time a group of measurements are taken, by switching in an electronic reference signal. The gains can then be compensated for in a similar manner to the variation in X-ray intensity measured above.

VII. Mathematics of Tomography

The basic idea of reconstruction of an image from a series of its projections appears to have been first discussed by Radon [1]. Consider the parallel geometry shown in Fig. 10. We have a fixed body centered coordinate system (x, y), and the X-ray tube and detector system rotate about the origin and translate across the patient. The rotation angle is designated by Θ, and a rotating coordinate system also centered at the origin $(\hat{x}, \hat{y})$ represents the detector position $\hat{x}$, and the distance along a ray $\hat{y}$. Any point on the body can be represented by either (x, y) or $(\hat{x}, \hat{y})$, and the coordinates are related by a rotational transformation.

$$\hat{x} = x \cos \Theta + y \sin \Theta$$

$$\hat{y} = -x \sin \Theta + y \cos \Theta \qquad (8)$$

or inversely

$$x = \hat{x} \cos \Theta - \hat{y} \sin \Theta$$

$$y = \hat{x} \sin \Theta + \hat{y} \cos \Theta. \qquad (9)$$

The body has an absorbtivity $\mu(x, y)$. If we express this in rotated coordinates, we have

$$\hat{\mu}_\Theta(\hat{x}, \hat{y}) = \mu(x, y) = \mu(\hat{x} \cos \Theta + \hat{y} \sin \Theta,$$

$$\hat{x} \sin \Theta + \hat{y} \cos \Theta). \qquad (10)$$

The two-dimensional Fourier transforms of these two functions are:[1]

$$U(X, Y) = \iint \mu(x, y) \exp[-j2\pi(xX + yY)] \, dx \, dy \qquad (11)$$

$$\hat{U}_\Theta(\hat{X}, \hat{Y}) = \iint \hat{\mu}_\Theta(\hat{x}, \hat{y}) \exp[-j2\pi(\hat{x}\hat{X} + \hat{y}\hat{Y})] \, d\hat{x} \, d\hat{y}$$

$$(12)$$

substituting (10) in (11), recognizing that $dx \, dy = d\hat{x} \, d\hat{y}$, the Jacobian is 1, and using (9) in (11) we get

$$U(X, Y) = \iint \hat{\mu}_\Theta(\hat{x}, \hat{y}) \exp -j2\pi[(\hat{x} \cos \Theta - \hat{y} \sin \Theta)X$$

$$+ (\hat{x} \sin \Theta + \hat{y} \cos \Theta)Y)] \, d\hat{x} \, d\hat{y}. \qquad (13)$$

Rearranging the exponent

$$U(X, Y) = \iint \hat{\mu}_\Theta(\hat{x}, \hat{y}) \exp - j2\pi[(X \cos \Theta + Y \sin \Theta)\hat{x}$$

$$+ (-X \sin \Theta + Y \cos \Theta)\hat{y}] \, d\hat{x} \, d\hat{y}. \qquad (14)$$

---

[1] An integral without limits means the limits are $\pm\infty$.

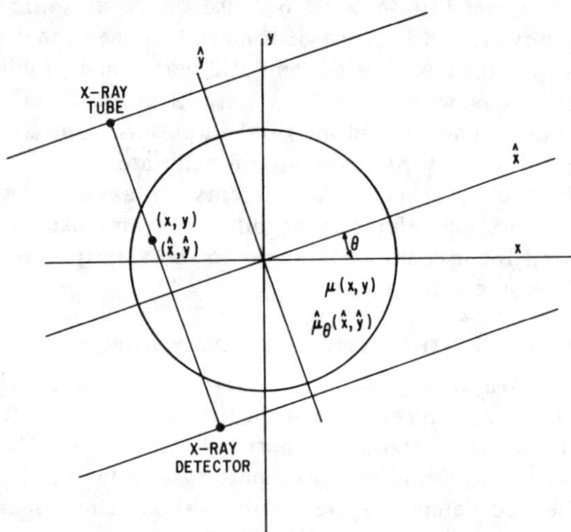

Fig. 10. Parallel geometry.

We see that if we set

$$\hat{X} = X \cos \Theta + Y \sin \Theta$$

and set

$$\hat{Y} = -X \sin \Theta + Y \cos \Theta \qquad (15)$$

then

$$U(X, Y) = \hat{U}_\Theta(\hat{X}, \hat{Y}). \qquad (16)$$

The two Fourier transforms are the same if axes $(\hat{X}, \hat{Y})$ are a rotation of $(X. Y)$ in the frequency domain by the view angle Θ.

The projection of the body at view angle Θ is

$$p_\Theta(\hat{x}) = \int_L \hat{\mu}_\Theta(\hat{x}, \hat{y}) \, d\hat{y} \qquad (17)$$

since $\hat{x}$ is the detector position and $\hat{y}$ is along a ray. Taking the one-dimensional Fourier transform of this at spatial frequency f

$$P_\Theta(f) = \int p_\Theta(\hat{x}) \exp[-j2\pi\hat{x}f] \, d\hat{x} \qquad (18)$$

and substituting (17) in (18)

$$P_\Theta(f) = \iint \hat{\mu}_\Theta(\hat{x}, \hat{y}) \exp[-j2\pi\hat{x}f] \, d\hat{x} \, d\hat{y}$$

$$P_\Theta(f) = \iint \hat{\mu}_\Theta(\hat{x}, \hat{y}) \exp[-j2\pi(f\hat{x} + 0\hat{y})] \, d\hat{x} \, d\hat{y}$$

and recognizing (12)

$$P_\Theta(f) = \hat{U}_\Theta(f, 0) = U(f \cos \Theta, f \sin \Theta). \qquad (19)$$

This result is commonly known as the projection theorem. The Fourier transform of a projection is a center-cross-section of the Fourier transform of the image. Most of the modern tomographic systems are based on this theorem. From here one can proceed in two directions. The whole operation can be done in frequency space directly, or the equivalent of these expressions can be transformed in the spatial domain.

The frequency space approach normally requires interpolation of the data, since the usual display medium is on a TV screen which requires a rectangular raster, and the projection (19) is in polar form. Most of the commercial machines work in the spatial domain, using what is known as the "convolution–back projection" approach. To derive this, consider the inverse transform of $U(X, Y)$ in polar coordinates

$$\mu(x, y) = \iint U(X, Y) \exp[j2\pi(xX + yY)] \, dX \, dY. \qquad (20)$$

The polar coordinates we will use are expressed by

$$x = r \cos \Phi \qquad X = R \cos \Theta \qquad R = \operatorname{sgn} Y \sqrt{X^2 + Y^2}$$

$$y = r \sin \Phi \qquad Y = R \sin \Theta \qquad \Theta - \arctan (Y/X) \bmod \pi$$

$$(21)$$

where

$$\begin{matrix} 0 < r < \infty & & 0 < \Phi < 2\pi \\ & \text{and} & \\ -\infty < R < \infty & & 0 < \Theta < \pi. \end{matrix}$$

The differential area $dX \, dY = |R| \, dR d\Theta$, and $U(R \cos \Theta, R \sin \Theta) = P_\Theta(R)$.

Substituting

$$\mu(x, y) = \int_0^\pi \int_{-\infty}^\infty P_\Theta(R) \exp[j2\pi(r \cos \Phi R \cos \Theta$$

$$+ r \sin \Phi R \sin \Theta)] |R| \, dR d\Theta \qquad (22)$$

$$\mu(x, y) = \int_0^\pi d\Theta \int_{-\infty}^\infty P_\Theta(R) |R| \exp[j2\pi Rr \cos(\Theta - \Phi)] \, dR.$$

$$(23)$$

The inner integral is the inverse transform of a product of two terms, the first of which is the transform of the projection at view Θ of the patient, and the second is the $|R|$. We will designate the inverse transform of $|R|$ by $k(x)$ and call it the kernel. The transform of a product of two functions is the convolution of the transforms of the functions, so we may write the inner integral of (23) the transform of the product of $|R|$ and $P_\Theta(R)$ as

$$g_\Theta(s) = \int_{-\infty}^\infty p_\Theta(s') k(s - s') \, ds' \qquad (24)$$

for the convolved detector readings at angle Θ. The outer integral is known as a back-projection. It represents the integral of the view contribution of $g_\Theta(r \cos(\Theta - \Phi))$ at each picture point (x, y) (or (r, Φ)). Equation (23) becomes

$$\mu(x, y) = \int_0^\pi g_\Theta(r \cos(\Theta - \Phi)) \, d\Theta. \qquad (25)$$

Equations (24) and (25) are relatively easy to approximate on a computer as one dimensional finite sums. The kernel "function" $k(x)$ needs some discussion. It falls in the class of "function" known as "generalized functions," a common example of which is the delta function $\delta(x)$ used casually by electrical engineers. In fact, it is easy to see that the second derivative of $|R|$ is $2\delta(R)$. The best way to understand the properties of one of these "functions" is to consider it as the limit of a "well behaved" function. Such a function is $Re^{-\epsilon|R|}$ which approximates $|R|$ as $\epsilon \to 0$. This is sketched in Fig. 11. Its

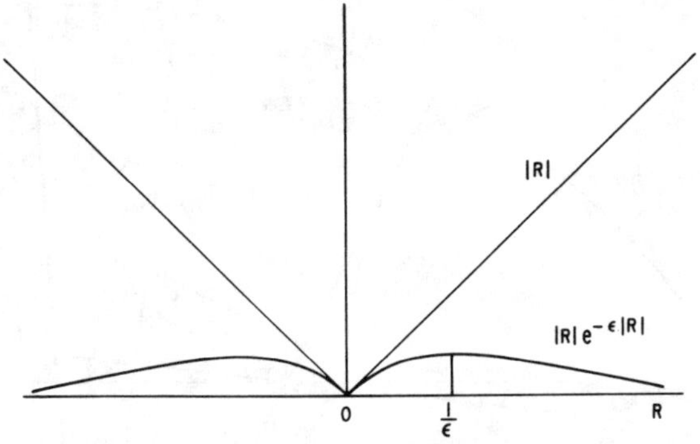

Fig. 11. Well-behaved kernel approximation in frequency domain.

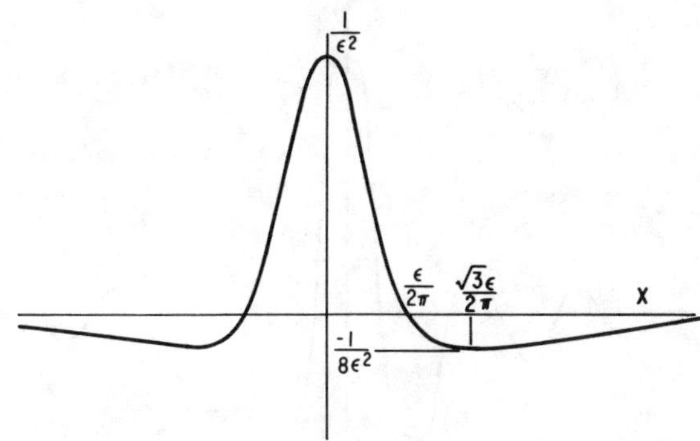

Fig. 12. Sketch of $\epsilon^2 - (2\pi x)^2/(\epsilon^2 + (2\pi x)^2)^2$. A well-behaved approximation to kernel function in spacial domain.

transform is

$$k_\epsilon(x) = \frac{\epsilon^2 - (2\pi x)^2}{(\epsilon^2 + (2\pi x)^2)^2}. \tag{26}$$

For large x, $k_\epsilon \cong -1/(2\pi x)^2$.

Near $x = 0$ the function changes sign, approaching $1/\epsilon^2$ as $x \to 0$ for any finite ϵ. A sketch of this kernel function for small ϵ is shown in Fig. 12. It is worth noting that the convolved detector readings $g_\Theta(x)$ are the derivative of the Hilbert transform of the projection functions $p_\Theta(x)$. This is shown in Appendix II, and provides an alternative approach to evaluating some theoretically interesting phantoms, such as those from a cylinder or ellipse (see [10, Appendix I]). In doing the calculation of the image from the measured projections, a number of approximations are necessarily made. The data available about the projections is necessarily discrete in both Θ and x, since only a finite number of views and detector positions can be sampled and stored in a computer system. In addition, one can make some assumptions about the behavior of the absorbtivity data. Two very common assumptions made are that $\mu(x, y)$ is bandlimited by a spatial frequency B cm^{-1} and that the data is collected at the Nyquist frequency, with a spacing of $a = 1/(2B)$ cm.

This leads to a kernel

$$k_L(x) = \int_{-\infty}^{B} |R|\, e^{j2\pi xR}\, dR \tag{27}$$

which can be expressed in the frequency domain as[2]

$$K_L(R) = B\, \text{rect}(R/2B) - \text{rect}(R/B) * \text{rect}(R/B). \tag{28}$$

Its Fourier transform is

$$k_L(x) = 2B^2 \,\text{sinc}\, 2Bx - B^2 \,\text{sinc}^2\, Bx. \tag{29}$$

A sketch of it is shown in Fig. 13.

Because the kernel is sampled at an $a = \frac{1}{2}B$ spacing only negative values or 0 values appear for $k_L(x)$ aside from $k_L(0)$

$$k_L(0) = B^2 = \tfrac{1}{4}a^2$$

$$k_L(l/2B) = 0, \quad \text{if } l \text{ even}$$

$$k_L(l/2B) = \frac{-B^2}{\left(\frac{\pi l}{2}\right)^2} = \frac{-1}{\pi^2 l^2 a^2}, \quad \text{if } l \text{ odd.} \tag{30}$$

This kernel was first discussed by Ramachandran and Lakshminarayanan [11]. Shepp and Logan [10] defined an alternative kernel function defined by

$$k_s(l/2B) = k_s(la) = \frac{-2}{\pi^2 a^2 (4l^2 - 1)} = \frac{-8B^2}{\pi^2 (4l^2 - 1)} \tag{31}$$

which is a sampled version of

$$k_s(x) = \frac{B}{\pi^2}\left[\frac{1 - \cos 2B(1/4B + x)}{1 \quad (1/4B + x)} + \frac{1 - \cos 2B(1/4B - x)}{(1/4B - x)}\right]. \tag{32}$$

This has a Fourier transform

$$K_s(R) = |R|\, \text{sinc}(R/2B) \cdot \text{rect}(R/2B). \tag{33}$$

Other kernels are possible and are sometimes used, but they all have properties similar to the ones described.

VIII. Modification to the Basic Algorithm for Fan-Beam Geometry

The more modern tomographic machines used a fan-beam geometry as shown in Fig. 14. The reconstruction of the image from this scheme requires a modification of the algorithm. The modifications were first analyzed by Herman *et al.* [14].

The point (x, y) in the patient is the point (r, Φ) in polar coordinate:

$$x = r \cos \Phi$$
$$y = r \sin \Phi.$$

Equations (24) and (25) for the parallel beam reconstruction can be put together:

$$\mu(x, y) = \int_0^\pi \int_{-\infty}^{\infty} p_\Theta(\hat{x})\, k(r \cos(\Theta - \Phi) - \hat{x})\, d\hat{x}\, d\Theta. \tag{34}$$

From the geometry of the fan beam shown in Fig. 14 we have[3]

$$\hat{x} = -\rho \sin \gamma$$
$$\Theta = \beta - \gamma \tag{35}$$

and from the Jacobian

$$\left|\frac{\partial(\hat{x}, \Theta)}{\partial(\beta, \gamma)}\right| = \rho \cos \gamma$$

where ρ is the source-to-body-center distance.

---

[2] We use the symbolism defined by Woodward, where rect $(x) = 1$, if $|x| < \frac{1}{2}$ and rect $(x) = 0$, if $|x| > \frac{1}{2}$, and sinc $(x) = \sin \pi x/\pi x$, rect and sinc are a Fourier transform pair.

[3] All angles are measured clockwise.

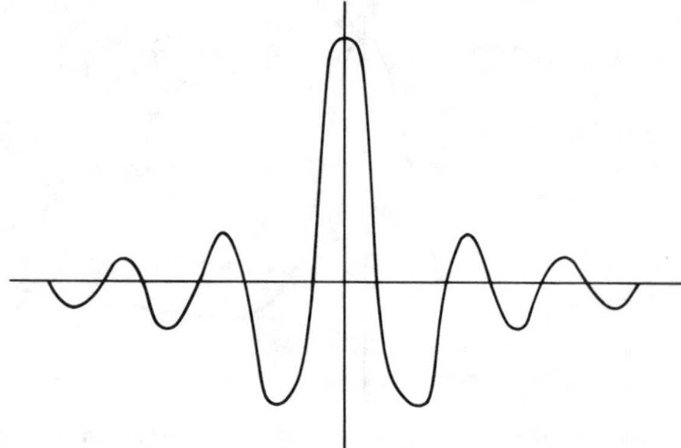

Fig. 13. Lakshminarayanan kernel.

Here γ is the detector angle in the fan beam, and β is the view angle of the fan beam (which is different from Θ, the view angle of an equivalent parallel beam). In practice $|\hat{x}| < T$ since any patient has only finite size, the integration limits for γ become $\pm\gamma_m$ with $\gamma_m = \arcsin(T/\rho)$. We have

$$\mu(x, y) = \int_0^\pi \int_{-\gamma_m}^{\gamma_m} p_{(\beta-\gamma)}(-\rho\sin\gamma)\, k(r\cos(\beta - \gamma - \Phi)$$

$$+ \rho\sin\gamma)\, p\cos\gamma\, d\beta d\gamma. \quad (36)$$

The first term $p_{(\beta-\gamma)}(-\rho\sin\gamma)$ is the projection data collected in the parallel geometry. In the fan-beam geometry the projection data collected we call $h_\beta(\gamma)$ and have

$$h_\beta(\gamma) = p_{(\beta-\gamma)}(-\rho\sin\gamma). \quad (37)$$

The projection data is multiplied by the term $\cos\gamma$. The argument of the kernel can be written $r\cos(\beta - \gamma - \Phi) + \rho\sin\gamma = r\cos(\beta - \Phi)\cos\gamma + (\rho + r\sin(\beta - \Phi))\sin\gamma$ and represents the orthogonal components of the vector from the source to the pixel at (x, y) being reconstructed.

We set

$$L\sin\gamma_0 = r\cos(\beta - \Phi) = \text{perpendicular component}$$
$$\text{of the vector}$$

$$L\cos\gamma_0 = \rho + r\sin(\beta - \Phi) = \text{parallel component of the vector}$$

where L is the source to pixel distance, and γ_0 is the detector angle of the ray through (x, y).

The argument of the kernel becomes

$$L\sin\gamma_0\cos\gamma - L\cos\gamma_0\sin\gamma = L\sin(\gamma_0 - \gamma).$$

The kernel k was defined as the Fourier transform of $|f|$

$$k(x) = \int |f|\exp[+j2\pi f x]\, df$$

which is a generalized function.

We have $k(L\sin\gamma)$, so

$$k(L\sin\gamma) = \int |f|\exp[+j2\pi f L\sin\gamma]\, df.$$

We define a new frequency variable $f' = fL\sin\gamma/\gamma$ and have

$$k(L\sin\gamma) = \int \left| \frac{f'\gamma}{L\sin\gamma} \right| \exp[j2\pi f'\gamma]\, \frac{\gamma df'}{L\sin\gamma}$$

so

$$k(L\sin\gamma) = \frac{\gamma^2}{L^2\sin^2\gamma} \int |f'|\exp[j2\pi f'\gamma]\, df.$$

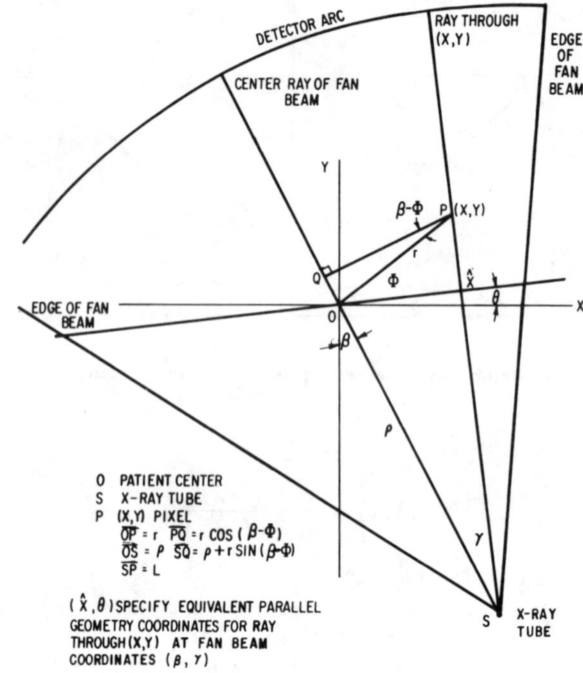

Fig. 14. Fan-beam geometry.

The integral is just $k(\gamma)$, so

$$k(L\sin\gamma) = \frac{\gamma^2}{L^2\sin^2\gamma}\, k(\gamma).$$

Define a fan-beam kernel

$$\hat{k}(\gamma) = \frac{\gamma^2}{\sin^2\gamma}\, k(\gamma)$$

and a fan-beam projection $\hat{h}_\beta(\gamma)$ for the data collected at angle γ in view β

$$\hat{h}_\beta(\gamma) = h_\beta(\gamma)\, \rho\cos\gamma.$$

The reconstruction algorithm (36) for the fan-beam case becomes

$$\mu(x, y) = \int_0^\pi \frac{d\beta}{L^2} \int_{-\gamma_m}^{\gamma_m} \hat{k}(\gamma_0 - \gamma)\, \hat{h}_\beta(\gamma)\, d\gamma \quad (39)$$

which is a "convolution–back-projection" algorithm as in the parallel geometry case, except for the additional weighting factor $1/L^2$ included in the back-projection operation. In summary, β = view angle, γ the detector angle

$$L = \sqrt{\rho^2 + r^2 + 2\rho r\sin(\beta - \Phi)} \;\text{(source to pixel distance)};$$

$$\gamma_0 = \arctan\left(\frac{r\cos(\beta - \Phi)}{\rho + r\sin(\beta - \Phi)} \right);$$

$$\Phi = \arctan(y/x), \quad r = \sqrt{x^2 + y^2}.$$

The practical reconstruction of tomographic pictures involves the approximation of these algorithms ((34) or (39)) so that the integrals can be calculated on a digital computer. The data usually is collected using discrete detectors, so $\hat{x}$ or γ is approximated with a step function, and the views are taken by rotating in discrete steps, so Θ or β are also discrete. The actual details of the reconstruction algorithms are considered confidential in the highly competitive tomographic industry, but some general principles can be discussed. The simplest form of approximation is the straightforward one of summing the discrete terms. Thus for pixel (x_m, y_n)

$$g_{\Theta_i}(\hat{x}_i) = \sum_{\Theta_j} k(\hat{x}_i - \hat{x}_j)\, P_{\Theta_i}(\hat{x}_j)\, \Delta x \qquad \text{convolution}$$

$$\mu(x_m, y_n) = \sum_{\Theta_i} g_{\Theta_i}(\hat{x}(x_m, y_n, \Theta_i))\, \Delta\Theta \qquad \text{back-projection.}$$

The computational advantage of the convolution–back-projection method is that the set of $g_{\Theta_i}(x_j)$ can be computed initially, one for each view, and stored. Then in the back-projection, the nearest value of $\hat{x}_j$ to the actual value of

$$\hat{x} = \sqrt{x_m^2 + y_n^2}\,\cos\,(\Theta_i - \arctan\,(y_n/x_m))$$

is chosen, and used to select the value of g_{Θ_i} to be added to the sum forming $\mu(x_m, y_n)$.

More generally, interpolation is often used to closer approximate the integral. In the above example, instead of choosing $\hat{x}_j$ close to $\hat{x}$, we select the values on either side of $\hat{x}$, x_j, x_{j+1} and form

$$g_{\Theta_i}(\hat{x}) = g_{\Theta_i}(\hat{x}_j) + [g_{\Theta_i}(\hat{x}_{j+1}) - g_{\Theta_i}(\hat{x}_j)] * \left[\frac{\hat{x} - x_j}{x_{j+1} - x_j}\right]$$

which is well known as linear interpolation. Interpolation can be viewed as the convolution of an interpolating function with the sampled data. In general, if we have a table of uniform samples of a continuous function of a real variable, $f(x)$, $x = n\Delta$, we form an approximation to intermediate values $\tilde{f}(x)$ by convolving the interpolating function $g(x)$ with $f_s(x)$

$$f_s(x) = \sum_k f(x)\,\delta\,(x - k\Delta)$$

$$f(x) \simeq \tilde{f}(x) = f_s(x) * q(x)$$

$$\tilde{f}(x) = \int \sum_k f(x)\,\delta\,(x - k\Delta)\, q(x - x')\, dx'$$

$$= \sum_k f(k\Delta)\, q(x - k\Delta).$$

For linear interpolation, $q(x)$ is a unit triangle

$$g(x) = \begin{cases} 1 - |x|/\Delta, & |x| < \Delta \\ 0, & |x| > \Delta \end{cases}$$

but it can be any function for other types of interpolation. For the nearest neighbor $q(x) = \text{rect}\,(x/\Delta)$.

Many types of interpolation are possible, depending on the particular problem. Recent work in numerical analysis has been in splines [13] which treats the interpolation problem rigorously. Since convolution in the space domain is a product of Fourier transforms in the spacial frequency domain, the operation of interpolation is equivalent to passing the convolved data through a "filter," the same as the projection data is passed through a "filter" of the kernel to create the convolved data. The two operations of interpolation and of convolving with the kernel can be combined into one, creating a new kernel which is the convolution of the original one with the interpolating function

$$\tilde{k}(x) = k(x) * q(x) = \int k(x - x')\, q(x')\, dx'$$

so only one convolution operation need be done. In addition,

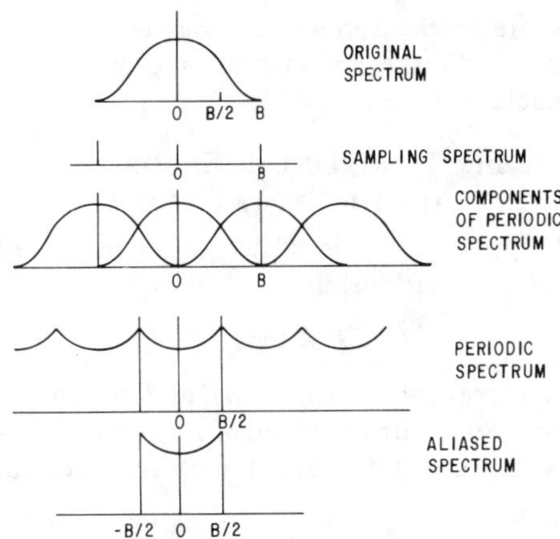

Fig. 15. Aliasing.

filtering of the projection data to remove noise or a known distortion of data, can also be combined with the convolution operation in a similar manner.

The operation of sampling the projection data, to put it into the computer, introduces the phenomenon of "aliasing" of the data. This idea is well understood by people working in the areas of digital signal processing [15], and image generation such as radar or infrared scanning. When data is sampled at a given rate, say every Δ, the spectrum of the resulting sampled data is periodic with a frequency of $1/\Delta$, and any information included in frequency components above $1/(2\Delta)$ is "folded back" and appears as if it occurred at a lower frequency. A pictorial representation of this is shown in Fig. 15. It can lead to artifacts in the image, such as the Moiré pattern generated by the plaid jackets sometimes worn by TV sportscasters. The classic solutions to this problem are to limit the bandwidth of the analog signal before sampling, or simply to increase the sampling rate.

The calculation of the reconstruction algorithm can be done in the digital computer in either fixed point or floating point arithmetic. Floating point has the advantage of being a better approximation to the continuum of real numbers than fixed point. It also automatically scales the calculation, and it often results in a much simpler program to understand and debug. Fixed point arithmetic has the advantage that in most digital computers it is faster than floating point, which is quite significant considering the number of operations performed in a 300×300 picture reconstruction. In the highly competitive tomography market, the speed of reconstruction is an important selling point, and is done nowadays in special-purpose hardware.

IX. Future Directions

The current trends in the industry appear to be to improve picture quality, primarily resolution improvement and artifact reduction, and to lower the cost with existing quality. In the future, there is much interest in developing a real time heart tomography machine, allowing radiologists to observe sequences of heart functioning throughout its cycle of operation.

Industrial tomography is another future direction in which tomography is heading. Tomography allows detailed inspection of complex and critical parts. Two important potential applications are inspection of jet engine and turbine parts, such as blades and disks, and inspection of welds and fuel rods in nuclear reactors.

APPENDIX I—NONLINEAR ERROR EFFECTS ON THE INPUT DATA

Ideally, the projection p is related to the measured intensity I by a logarithmic relationship

$$p = K \log I.$$

In practice, I is corrupted by noise n_I, and in particular the use of an A/D converter introduces quantization error. The actual log output is then corrupted by noise n_p also. We have:

$$p + n_p = K \log (I + n_I) = K \log I (1 + n_I/I)$$
$$\cong K \log I + K n_I/I \text{ if } n_I \ll I$$

so $n_p = K n_I/I$ is the noise on the projection. This has its largest value at the smallest values of I since the log is monotonic. In particular, if we are trying to achieve an accuracy of 10 bits, the smallest value of p would be 1024, and n_p would be $\frac{1}{2}$. The smallest value of I is then $\exp(1024/I)$, and if I is also digitally represented, $n_I = \frac{1}{2}$. We have $\frac{1}{2} = K/(2 \exp 1024/K))$ which is a transcendental equation for K. The solution is $K = 194.325$, and the smallest value of $I = 194.325$, which needs at least 8 bits to represent it. The dynamic range for I was 2000, which needs 11 bits to represent it so the total dynamic range of the input A/D converter for I is 19 bit, not 21 which was the linear assumption. The nonlinearity of the logarithm saves us two bits in this case.

APPENDIX II

The convolved detector readings $g(x)$ are proportional to the negative derivative of the Hilbert transform of the projection:

$$g_\Theta(x) = \frac{-1}{2\pi} \frac{d}{dx} H(p_\Theta(x)) = \frac{-1}{2\pi} \frac{d}{dx} \frac{1}{\pi} \int \frac{P_\Theta(x')}{x - x'} dx'$$

or

$$g_\Theta(x) = \frac{1}{2\pi j} \frac{d}{dx} \frac{1}{\pi j} \int \frac{P_\Theta(x') dx'}{x - x'}.$$

The integral is the convolution of $p_\Theta(x)$ and $1/x$.

We can write this as

$$g_\Theta(x) = \frac{1}{2\pi j} \frac{d}{dx} \frac{1}{\pi j} \int \pi j \operatorname{sgn} R \, P_\Theta(R) \exp [+j2\pi Rx] \, dR$$

since the Fourier transform of $1/x$ is $\pi j \operatorname{sgn} R$, and the Fourier transform of $p_\Theta(x)$ is $P_\Theta(R)$, and the convolution is the Fourier transform of a product. Taking the derivative

$$g_\Theta(x) = \frac{1}{j2\pi} \int \operatorname{sgn} (R) \, P_\Theta(R) \, j2\pi R \exp [j2\pi Rx] \, dR$$

cancelling the $j2\pi$, and recognizing $R \operatorname{sgn} R = |R|$

$$g_\Theta(x) = \int P_\Theta(R) \, |R| \exp [j2\pi Rx] \, dR$$

which is the inner integral of (23), except that (23) is evaluated at $x = r \cos (\Theta - \Phi)$. We thus have

$$g_\Theta(x) = -\frac{1}{2\pi} \frac{d}{dx} \int \frac{p_\Theta(x') \, dx'}{x - x'} = \int P_\Theta(x') \, k(x - x') \, dx'$$

or symbolically

$$g_\Theta(x) = \frac{-1}{2\pi} \frac{d}{dx} H(p_\Theta(x)) = p_\Theta(x) * k(x).$$

The taking of the derivative of the Hilbert transform of the projection is equivalent to convolving it with the kernel.

REFERENCES

[1] J. Radon, "(On the Determination of Functions from their Integrals Along Certain Manifolds)," *Ber. Saechs. Akad. Wiss. Leipzig, Math. Physics Kl.*, vol. 69, pp. 262–277, 1917.

[2] R. N. Bracewell, "Strip integration in radioastronomy," *Aust. J. Phys.*, vol. 9, pp. 198–217, 1956.

[3] W. H. Oldendorf, "Isolated flying spot detection of radiodensity discontinuities displaying the internal structural pattern of a complex object," *IRE Trans. Bio-Med. Elec.*, vol. BME-8, pp. 68–72, 1961.

[4] D. E. Kuhl and R. Q. Edwards, "Image separation radioisotope scanning," *Radiology*, vol. 80, pp. 653–661, 1963.

[5] A. M. Cormack, "Representation of a function by its line integrals, with some radiological applications," *J. Appl. Phys.*, vol. 34, pp. 2722–2727, 1963.

[6] G. N. Hounsfield, "A method of and apparatus for examination of a body by radiation such as X-ray or gamma radiation," British Patent No. 1283915, London, 1972.

[7] R. Gordon, R. Bender, and G. T. Herman, "Algebraic reconstruction techniques (ART) for three dimensional electron microscopy and X-ray photography," *J. Theor. Biol.*, vol. 29, pp. 471–481, 1970.

[8] G. T. Herman and S. W. Rowland, "Three methods for reconstructing objects from X-rays: a comparative study," *Comput. Graphics Process*, vol. 2, pp. 151–178, 1973.

[9] B. K. Vainshtein, "The synthesis of projecting functions," *Dokl. Akad. Nauk. SSSR*, vol. 96, pp. 1072–1075, 1971.

[10] L. A. Shepp and B. F. Logan, "The Fourier reconstruction of a head section," *IEEE Trans. Nucl. Sci.*, vol. NS-21, pp. 21–42, 1974.

[11] G. N. Ramachandran and A. V. Lakshminarayanan, "Three dimensional reconstruction from radiographic and electron micrographic application of convolutions instead of Fourier transforms," *Proc. Nat. Acad. Sci. U.S.*, vol. 68, pp. 2236–2240, 1971.

[12] R. B. Blackman and J. Q. Tukey, *The Measurement of Power Spectra from the Point of View of Communications Engineering.* New York: Dover, 1959.

[13] P. M. Prenter, *Splines and Variational Methods.* New York: Wiley, 1975.

[14] G. J. Herman, A. V. Lakshminarayanan, and A. Naparstek, "Reconstruction using divergent day shadowgraphs," *Compul. Biol. Med.*, vol. 6, pp. 259, 1976.

[15] R. Legault, "The Aliasing Problems in 2-Dimensional Sampled Imagery," in *Perception of Displayed Information*, L. M. Biberman, Ed. New York: Plenum Press, 1973, ch. 7, pp. 279–312.

[16] D. A. Chesler, "Positron tomography and three dimensional reconstruction techniques," in *Proc. Symp. Radionuclide Tomograph*, New York, NY, 1972.

[17] M. M. Ter-Pogossian, M. E. Phelps, E. J. Hoffman, and N. A. Mullani, "A positron-emission transaxial tomograph for nuclear imaging (PETT)," *Radiology*, vol. 114, pp. 89–98, Jan. 1975.

[18] R. M. Mersereau and A. V. Oppenheim, "Digital reconstruction of multidimensional signals from their projections," *Proc. IEEE*, vol. 62, pp. 1319–1338, 1974.

[19] R. King, "The harmony of reconstruction: A spectral theory of X-ray tomograph," General Electric 715 Monograph. 75CRD063, 1975.

[20] Z. H. Cho and J. R. Burger, "Construction, restoration and enhancement of 2 and 3 dimensional images," *IEEE Trans. Nucl. Sci.*, vol. NS-24, no. 2, pp. 886–899, Apr. 1977.

Physical Problems of Computerized Tomography

ALBERT MACOVSKI, FELLOW, IEEE

Invited Paper

Abstract—A cross-sectional image of an object can be accurately reconstructed if its projections or line integrals are known at all angles. This fundamental and exciting property has been applied to a variety of applications, primarily in the area of medical imaging. In many cases, however, the physical measurements fail to accurately define the complete set of line integrals. This leads to inaccuracies and distortions in the resultant reconstruction.

The physical measurements can be inadequate in a number of ways. These include nonlinearities, noise, and insufficient data. The nonlinearities can arise from a nonlinear detector process, or the inability to accurately extract the information in the exponent by taking logs. The noise can be the usual statistical uncertainty of the measurement or an interfering component such as scatter. The data can be insufficient in a number of ways including inadequate sampling or regions of missing data. Also, the measurements of a source distribution can be distorted by an unknown attenuation distribution, resulting in errors in the reconstruction.

I. BACKGROUND

COMPUTERIZED TOMOGRAPHY has had a profound impact on all branches of the applied and basic sciences, especially in medical imaging. Beginning with the introduction of the first EMI scanner [1] clinicians were astounded at the ability to visualize subtle structures that were heretofore invisible. The quality of the reconstructed images has continuously improved over the past decade, with the lastest instruments providing a degree of anatomical detail and freedom from artifact which leaves little to be desired.

During this same period, the fundamental techniques of reconstruction from projections were applied to other modalities of medical imaging. Nuclear medicine, involving the imaging of source distributions resulting from administered isotopes, saw the introduction of ECAT systems [2]–[4] where the emission function is reconstructed. Similarly, the distribution of administered positron-emitting isotopes were reconstructed in PET systems [5], [6] where use is made of the opposite-traveling photons produced by a positron annihilation.

In ultrasound, three-dimensional reconstructions were already being achieved without reconstruction from projections. Using pulsed excitation, the relatively slow velocity of propagation (1500 m/s) makes it convenient to use the time-of-flight information to map the reflectivity, at every point of interest. However, investigators were interested in images of parameters other than reflectivity including velocity and attenuation. These are obtained using classical reconstruction from projection techniques [7], [8] using measurements of transmission and time-of-flight.

Each of these imaging techniques is based on the fundamen-

Manuscript received July 26, 1982. This work was supported by National Institute of Health under Grant 5R01-25905-02 and the National Science Foundation under Grant ECS78-23307.

The author is with the Department of Electrical Engineering, Stanford University, Stanford, CA 94305.

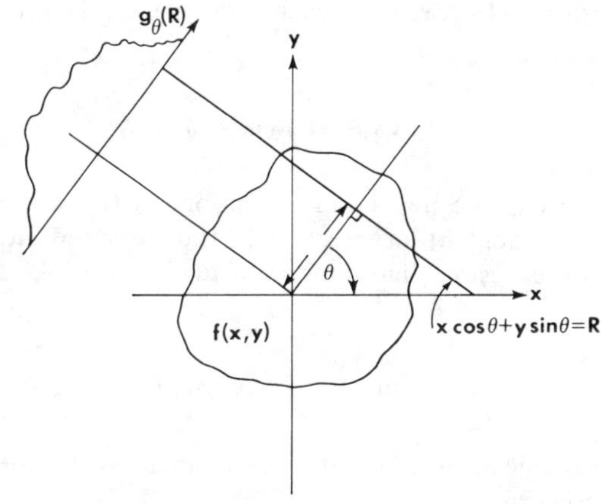

Fig. 1. Projection of a two-dimensional function.

tal methods of reconstruction from projections as first introduced by Radon [9]. A number of more tractable reconstruction procedures have been developed including ART [10], [11], and filtered back projection [12], [13]. Each of these assumes a complete set of accurate measurements of the projections or line integrals in order to reconstruct an artifact-free image.

In many physical systems, however, the measurements fail to accurately represent a complete set of projections. The inadequacy of the measurements can include nonlinearities, noise, and insufficient data. These inadequacies result in a variety of distortions of the reconstructed images. In this paper, we explore the various inadequacies in the physical measurements and their affects on the reconstruction.

II. DISCUSSION

In an ideal system, as shown in Fig. 1, a set of projections $g_\vartheta(R)$ are taken of a two-dimensional function $f(x, y)$ as given by

$$g_\vartheta(R) = \int_\vartheta f(x, y)\, dl \tag{1}$$

where R is measured at the angle ϑ, perpendicular to the projection direction along l, the line defined by $R = x \cos \vartheta + y \cdot \sin \vartheta$. Using any of the methods of reconstruction from projections, $f(x, y)$ is exactly restored, in the limit, from this continuous array of projection data.

The basic problem with the inadequacy of the physical measurements is that of the inadequacy of the projection data. We can assume ideal reconstruction methods which will provide a perfect rendition limited only by the available projection data.

A. Nonlinearities

A wide class of distortions results from projection measurements, or processed projection measurements, which include nonlinear functions of the desired line integral. A simple example of this phenomenon is a nonlinear detector used for measuring the projection data where, in addition to the desired projection $g(R)$, we obtain components of various powers of $g(R)$. When reconstructed, this produces a variety of distorting artifacts having distinctive shapes [14].

The most common cause of the nonlinearities is not nonlinear detection, but the inverting of the exponent in attenuation reconstructions. In X-ray CT, each measurement is of the general form

$$I = I_0 \exp - \int \mu(x, y)\, dl \tag{2}$$

where $\mu(x, y)$ is the desired cross-sectional attenuation function, I_0 is the incident intensity, and I the measured intensity. To achieve the desired line integral of $\mu(x, y)$ we take logs as given by

$$g(R) = \ln \frac{I_0}{I} = \int \mu(x, y)\, dl. \tag{3}$$

Again, this projection information at all angles will achieve the desired reconstruction.

The nonlinear problem arises on close inspection of (2). The attenuation coefficient, in addition to being a function of x and y, is also a function of z and of the photon energy or wavelength of the incident X-ray spectrum. Therefore, (2) inherently assumes that we are using a zero-width X-ray beam which is monoenergetic. Unfortunately, X-ray sources of these characteristics produce insufficient power to provide useful images. We, therefore, consider the nonlinearities produced by real sources having finite spectra and finite beam width. In the interest of avoiding undue notational complexity we will consider these phenomena separately.

1) Spectral Nonlinearities: In a measurement system where the measurement itself is the desired line integral, a linear averaging operation takes place. For example, assume we are measuring the projection of a distribution of sources, each radiating over a given spectrum. The resultant measurement will linearly represent the line integral of the source distribution at some average frequency determined by the source and detector spectra. Thus data can directly be used to reconstruct a distortion-free source distribution at the average frequency. In the X-ray case, we are reconstructing an attenuation distribution rather than a source distribution. Since the measurement is a nonlinear function of the attenuation, a finite spectrum results in nonlinearities in the projection information. These lead to reconstruction artifacts.

Using a finite X-ray spectrum, the measured intensity is given by

$$I = \int S(E) \exp \left[- \int \mu(x, y, E)\, dl \right] dE \tag{4}$$

where $S(E)$ is the source spectrum. Clearly, if we use a monoenergetic source where $S(E) = I_0 \delta(E - E_0)$, we would return to the formulation of (2) and, as in (3), be able to exactly specify the line integral. With a finite spectrum, however, we desire a projection of $\mu(x, y)$ at the average energy $\overline{E}$ as given by

$$g(R) = \int \mu(x, y, \overline{E})\, dl. \tag{5}$$

This desired result would be obtained if we directly measured the line integral of μ

$$\int \mu(x, y, \overline{E})\, dl = \int S(E) \left[\int \mu(x, y, E) \right] dE \Big/ \int S(E)\, dE. \tag{6}$$

When we take the log of the measured intensity given in (4), we get undesired nonlinear versions of the line integral, which can be structured as

$$\ln \left(\frac{I_0}{I} \right) = C_0 + C_1 \int \mu(x, y, \overline{E})\, dl$$
$$+ C_2 \left[\int \mu(x, y, \overline{E})\, dl \right]^2 + \cdots . \tag{7}$$

The constants C_i other than C_1 result from the solution of the nonlinear integral equation (4). If either the source were monoenergetic or μ were not a function of E, these constants would be zero. Thus the magnitude of these components depends on the spectral extent of $S(E)$ and $\mu(E)$, the degree to which the attenuation coefficient varies with energy.

These nonlinear components can cause relatively severe distortions [15]. This effect was first noticed in the early CT scans of the skull [1] as a "cupping" artifact inside the skull which was sometimes misinterpreted as representing white matter of the brain. It is interesting to note that this effect would be considerably more severe if lower energies were used where μ is a stronger function of energy. These lower energies are desirable since they have greater sensitivity to atomic number.

This spectral artifact has been dealt with in a variety of ways [16]. If the object consists of a single material, a one-to-one relationship exists between the measured intensity I and the desired line integral. Thus a simple nonlinear correction of the log of the intensity solves the problem. In medical imaging, however, we deal with varieties of bone, soft tissue, and sometimes air. The early scanners used a compensating water vessel to provide a constant path length through the object. In that case, the measurement indicates the relative amounts of bone and soft tissue in the path, assuming we are dealing with a portion of the anatomy devoid of air. This allows a reasonably accurate correction.

If the exponent could be linearized, where

$$\exp \left(- \int \mu dl \right) \cong 1 - \int \mu dl$$

we would have a formulation similar to (6) which avoids nonlinearities. This approximation is only valid for $\int \mu dl < 1$. Unfortunately, over most regions of the body, the line integral is approximately five, resulting from a μ of approximately 0.2 and a thickness of about 25 cm. Thus direct linearization cannot be accomplished. The linearization can be accomplished, however, through the subtraction of a known phantom whose dimensions, position, and material composition are comparable to the unknown object. In this process, the remaining differences are small enough to be linearized, eliminating the spectral artifact.

To illustrate the linearization of the line integral, assume

$L(x, y)$ is the known projection of the phantom. The difference of the measured intensities of the unknown object and the known phantom is given by

$$I - I_p = I_0 [e^{-\int \mu dl} - e^{-\mu L}]$$
$$= I_0 e^{-\mu L} [e^{-(\int \mu dl - \mu L)} - 1]. \qquad (8)$$

Assuming $|\int \mu dL - \mu L| \ll 1$, the exponential can be linearized giving

$$I - I_p = I_0 e^{-\mu L} \left(\mu L - \int \mu dl \right) \qquad (9)$$

where the unknown line integral has been linearized.

Another general approach involves multiple energy measurements. If we make an array of measurements at different energy bands, we can assume that μ is constant within each small spectral region. Taking the log of each measurement and summing the logs provides the desired line integral of the average attenuation coefficient. This approach is somewhat brute force, and requires energy selective detection which is not presently available.

A more effective approach makes use of the known physical mechanisms of attenuation. To a high degree of accuracy, the energy-dependent attenuation coefficient can be decomposed into basis functions [16]–[18] representing the photoelectric absorption and Compton scattering

$$\mu(E) = a_p f_p(E) + a_c f_c(E) \qquad (10)$$

where $f_p(E)$ and $f_c(E)$ are the energy dependence of the photoelectric and Compton attenuation phenomena and a_p and a_c are the energy-independent coefficients representing each material. We make two measurements, as indicated in (4), using two spectra $S_1(E)$ and $S_2(E)$. This gives us two equations and two desired unknowns, the unknowns being the line integrals of the coefficients

$$A_p = \int a_p \, dl \qquad (11)$$

$$A_c = \int a_c \, dl. \qquad (12)$$

We can solve the nonlinear integral equations for A_p and A_c using various numerical techniques involving the use of measurements of known materials to form polynomial solutions [17]. Once A_p and A_c are calculated at all angles and positions, they are used to reconstruct distortion-free images since the coefficients are energy independent. In addition to removing the spectral artifacts, this approach also provides separate reconstructions of $a_p(x, y)$ and $a_c(x, y)$ which can be used to identify the various materials.

An iterative approach [16] has also been implemented which makes use of the constrained values of attenuation which occur in body substances. An initial CT reconstruction is made which contains the nonlinear spectral errors. Each value is then restructured based on the assumed limited range of materials. The measured projection data are then corrected and the reconstruction repeated.

2) Beam-Width Nonlinearities: In addition to spectral shifts, (2) also assumes an infinitesimal beam width. In practice, however, the beam size is finite in order to have a finite power transmission. For simplicity we assume a collimated beam

having a cross-sectional distribution $s(x, z)$ with the beam in y direction at $\vartheta = 0$ providing a projection along x

$$g(R) = \iint s(x, z) \exp \left[- \int \mu(x, y, z) \, dy \right] dx \, dz. \qquad (13)$$

This expression can be expanded into the same power series as (7) resulting in similar distortions.

This distortion is at its greatest where the beam cross section includes large variations in the line integral. For example, assume that a high density bone partially occludes the beam. Ideally, the detected signal should represent the linear average of the line integrals of the portions of the beam with and without bone. Instead, the detected signal will represent the average of the exponents of the line integrals. Therefore, the region without bone will dominate, resulting in distortion.

Relatively little can be done to correct this nonlinearity [19], other than to use a very narrow beam. In theory, an array of very small detectors can be used transversing the beam. The incremental region covered by each detector $s_m(x, z)$ is sufficiently small to insure negligible variations in the line integral. The intensity received by each detector is, therefore, given by

$$I_m = \iint s_m(x, z) \exp \left[- \int \mu(x, y, z) \, dy \right] dx \, dz$$
$$= I_{0m} \exp \left[- \int \mu(x, y, z) \, dy \right] \qquad (14)$$

where $I_{0m} = \iint s_m(x, z) \, dx \, dz$, the effective source strength at each incremental detector position. The source function can be taken outside the integral under the assumption that the attenuation function has negligible variation within the incremental beam. The desired line integral of the average attenuation is then given by

$$\int \bar{\mu}(x, y, z) \, dy = \frac{1}{M} \sum_{m=1}^{M} \ln \left(\frac{I_{0m}}{I_m} \right). \qquad (15)$$

B. Insufficient Data

The reconstruction formulation relies on having a complete set of line integral or projection data. Every physical system must, therefore, depart from this model to some degree. An obvious example is the use of sampled data with the resultant potential for aliasing.

1) Aliasing: In general, all physical systems involving digital computers require samples of a continuous function. To satisfy the sampling theorem [20], and avoid aliasing we attempt to sample at a rate greater than twice the highest frequency. Our sampled estimate of the continuous projection function $\hat{g}(R, \vartheta)$ is given by

$$\hat{g}(R, \vartheta) = \sum_{m=1}^{M} \sum_{n=1}^{N} g(R, \vartheta) \, \delta(R - m\Delta R) \, \delta(\vartheta - n\Delta\vartheta) \qquad (16)$$

where $\Delta\vartheta$ and ΔR are the sampling intervals in angle and along each projection, respectively.

In some systems, a signal can be low-pass filtered prior to sampling to avoid aliasing. In CT this is difficult since the two-dimensional object is essentially unavailable. Sampling of the projection data is subdivided into angular or view sampling and projection sampling at each angle. View aliasing results where the view sampling is insufficient to cover the angular harmonics of the object. The only apparent solution is the use of more angular views.

Projection aliasing results primarily from the use of detector arrays. In the early "first generation" CT scanners the projection information was obtained by a scanning detector as given by

$$\hat{g}(t) = \int s(R - t)\, g(R)\, dR$$
$$= s(t) \star g(t) \tag{17}$$

where $\hat{g}(t)$ is the scanned estimate of the projection signal, $s(R)$ is the detector distribution, and the star $\star$ represents cross correlation. Thus the transform of the object projection $G(f)$ is low-pass filtered by the transform of the detector aperture $S(f)$. If additional low-pass filtering is desired to avoid aliasing, an additional electrical low-pass filter $H(f)$ can be used on the scanned signal. Since any desired filtering can be realized prior to sampling, aliasing errors are avoided.

In the interest of scanning time and more efficient source utilization most manufacturers have gone to detector arrays which simultaneously acquire an entire projection or view. In this case, the estimated projection $\hat{g}(R)$ is given by

$$\hat{g}(R) = [g(R) * s(R)] \; \sqcup\!\sqcup \left[\frac{R}{A}\right] \tag{18}$$

where, as before, $s(R)$ is the distribution of each detector in the array, A is the detector spacing, and the comb function $\sqcup\!\sqcup(x)$ is an array of delta functions given by

$$\sqcup\!\sqcup(x) = \sum_{n=-\infty}^{\infty} \delta(x - n). \tag{19}$$

Taking the Fourier transform of the sampled estimate of the projection we obtain

$$\hat{G}(f) = A[G(f)\, S(f)] * \sqcup\!\sqcup(Af) \tag{20}$$

which is a repetitive array of overlapping spectral islands. Unfortunately, unlike the case of the scanned detector, there is no apparent mechanism of using low-pass filtering to avoid the resultant overlap or aliasing.

The minimum overlap occurs with the widest possible detector aperture $s(R)$ corresponding to a detector of width of A as given by

$$s(R) = \text{rect}\left(\frac{R}{A}\right) \tag{21}$$

where the rect function is unity between $\pm\frac{1}{2}$ and zero otherwise. The resultant $S(f)$ is A sinc AF which has its first zero at $f = \pm 1/A$ and continues at higher frequencies with an envelope equal to $1/\pi f$. Since the spectrum is replicated at frequency intervals of $1/A$, the resultant spectra have significant overlap or aliasing.

Fig. 2 is an illustration of the spectrum of $\hat{g}(R)$ for a broadband "white" object. As is shown, there is no low-pass filter applied to $\hat{g}(R)$ which will eliminate the aliasing. One interesting approach to this problem has been the use of "offset" detector arrays which are used with rotary fan beam scanners [21]. The detector array is structured such that, after rotating 180°, the effective detector positions have moved half a detector width with respect to the object. Thus the effective sampling distance is cut in half to $A/2$. The resultant spectral dis-

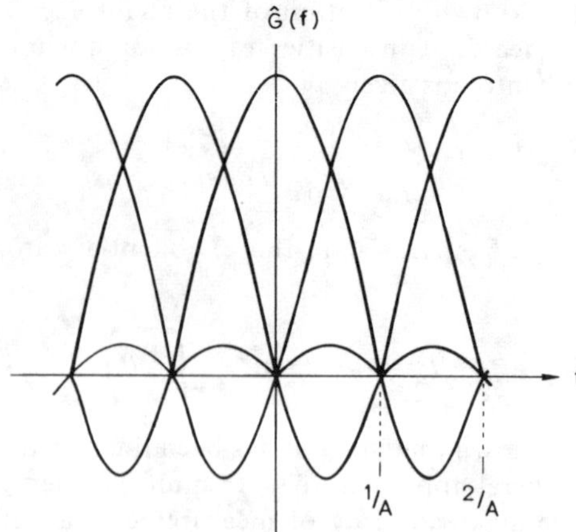

Fig. 2. Spectrum of detector array.

tribution is now replicated at frequency intervals of $2/A$ with the spectra centered at $\pm 1/A$ removed. Thus the same individual spectra shown in Fig. 1 are doubled in separation, significantly reducing the overlap and aliasing. A reasonable low-pass filter can then be found which is a compromise between resolution and aliasing.

2) Missing Data: A number of situations can arise where the set of sampled projection data is incomplete. The presence of a near-opaque object obliterates a portion of each projection. Similarly, on some occasions, a portion of the views may be unsuitable because of object motion, as with the beating heart. In these cases, attempts are made to reconstruct the object with the limited data.

Although commercial scanners have yet to provide reconstruction capability with limited data, many studies have been made to provide such reconstruction. These include analytic extension [22] and various approaches using estimation theory [23]–[25].

C. Interacting Parameters

In some cases, additional unknown or known parameters affect the measured projections, causing distortion. A widely studied example is that of attenuation in source distributions. In ECAT, or emission computerized axial tomography, the attenuation experienced by the source distribution causes significant distortion if not compensated for [26], [27]. The detectors are collimated to receive the source distribution along approximately a single line with the received intensity given by

$$I = \int s(l')\left[\exp - \int_l^L \mu(l)\, dl\right] dl' \tag{22}$$

where $s(l)$ is the source distribution along the line, $\mu(l)$ the attenuation distribution, and L the extent of the object.

The accurate reconstruction of s can only be accomplished if μ is known. One approach has been to assume a constant value of μ throughout the body so that only the outer boundaries of the body need to be measured. This is a reasonable assumption since, at the relatively high photon energies used in nuclear medicine, most body materials have comparable values of attenuation coefficient, the dominant mechanism being Compton scattering. A more accurate approach involves the use of an external isotopic source, at the same energy, to map $\mu(x, y)$ and use those values to correct the final reconstruction.

Another important case of interacting parameters occurs in

the reconstruction of cross-sectional images of the refractive index and the attenuation coefficient in ultrasound. In its classic form, the ultrasound system duplicates the X-ray geometry by sending a pulsed collimated sound beam through the body. The transmitted intensity I and the delay time T are measured and used to estimate the line integrals of the attenuation $\alpha(l)$ and the refractive index $n(l)$ as given by

$$\ln \frac{I_0}{I} = \int \alpha(l)\, dl \qquad (23)$$

$$T = \frac{1}{c_0} \int n(l)\, dl. \qquad (24)$$

These line integrals are then reconstructed to provide two-dimensional distributions of n and α. The problem is the assumption of straight-line propagation. The ultrasound beam is deflected by the gradient of the refractive index, and can experience a variety of distortions. This continues to be a serious problem. One general approach involves an iterative technique using an initial reconstruction which ignores the affects of refraction. Using this reconstruction, the beam paths are corrected using ray tracing to reduce the distortion. A more general approach involves the use of the wave equation where the reconstruction is approached as an inverse scattering problem [30].

D. Noise

In any physical system, the measurements are limited by some degree of uncertainty called noise. In radio frequency systems, where the energy per photon is relatively low, the additive Gaussian noise of thermal sources and amplifiers dominates the quantum noise. Here the number of quanta per information element is so high that the SNR is dominated by other effects. In X-ray systems, the reverse is true so that the noise is dominated by the number of photons per information element or pixel.

In CT systems, the noise in each reconstructed element is the sum of the noise due to each projection going through the pixel plus the noise coupled into that reconstructed pixel through the convolution kernel $h(R)$ [31], [32]. The resultant variance in the estimate of μ is given by

$$\sigma_\mu^2 = \frac{M}{\bar{n}t} \int_{-\infty}^{\infty} h^2(R)\, dR \qquad (25)$$

where M is the number of views, t the thickness of the section, and $\bar{n}$ the average transmitted photon density. The convolution kernel $h(R)$ has been normalized to provide the correct reconstruction of μ. Using this relationship we find a reconstructed SNR as given by

$$\text{SNR} = \frac{\Delta\mu}{\sigma_\mu} = K \Delta\mu \sqrt{\bar{N}M}\; w \qquad (26)$$

where K is a constant of order unity which depends on the reconstruction kernel, $\Delta\mu$ the change in attenuation coefficient in the region of interest, $\bar{N}$ the average number of transmitted photons per detector element, and w the width of the detector element along the section which is assumed to be inversely proportional to the cutoff frequency of the reconstruction filter.

We note with interest that, unlike the projection case, where the SNR depends solely on the number of photons per ele-

ment, we have an additional factor w, relating to the system resolution. Therefore, attempts to improve the resolution of CT systems suffer disproportionately, as compared to projection systems. If we assume uniform resolution in all dimensions, each detector element would be $w \times w$. In that case, $\bar{N}$ varies as w^2 so that the SNR varies as w^2 instead of w as in the projection radiography case.

In addition to the strong dependence on resolution, the element-to-element noise in CT systems is highly correlated [33] due to the convolution kernel. This accounts for its radial characteristic when scanning circular or elliptical structures of the body. Since the rays through the center are noisier than those off center, the predominant noise pattern is radial.

X-ray systems have an additive noise component due to scatter which results in both stochastic and deterministic errors [34]. The stochastic error is due to the increased number of photons per measurement, decreasing the SNR of each measurement by the factor $(1 + I_s/I_t)^{-1/2}$, where I_s is the scattered intensity and I_t the transmitted intensity per measurement. This factor is usually negligible in CT because of the collimation used.

The deterministic error is a nonlinearity similar to the previously described spectral and beam-width nonlinearities. The attempt to use logs to provide the desired line integral results in the nonlinear distortion as given by

$$I = I_0 \exp\left[-\int \mu dl \right] + I_s \qquad (27)$$

$$\ln \frac{I_0}{I} = C_0 + C_1 \int \mu dl + C_2 \left[\int \mu dl \right]^2 + \cdots. \qquad (28)$$

The resultant artifacts are similar to those of other nonlinearities. One potential solution to the problem is to estimate the scatter I_s and subtract it from the measured intensity I. The estimate can be made by assuming relatively uniform scatter intensity so that a separate detector, outside of the region of the collimated beam, can be used to provide the estimate.

III. Conclusions

The elegant mathematical formulation in computerized tomography provides flawless reconstructions if a complete set of line integrals are available. In physical systems, however, measurements of the line integral are often flawed by nonlinearities, insufficient data, and noise, causing various degrees of error and distortion in the reconstruction.

References

[1] G. N. Hounsfield, "Computerized transverse axial scanning (tomography): Part 1: Description of system," *Brit. J. Radiol.*, vol. 46, pp. 1016–1022, 1973.

[2] D. E. Kuhl and R. Q. Edwards, "Image separation radioisotope scanning," *Radiology*, vol. 80, pp. 653–661, 1963.

[3] A. R. Bowley, C. G. Taylor, D. A. Causer, *et al.*, "A radioisotope scanner for rectilinear arc transverse section and longitudinal section scanning," *Brit. J. Radiol.*, vol. 46, pp. 262–271, 1973.

[4] T. F. Budinger and G. T. Gullberg, "Three-dimensional reconstruction of isotope distributions," *Phys. Med. Biol.*, vol. 19, pp. 387–389, 1974.

[5] M. M. Ter-Pogossian, M. E. Phelps, E. J. Hoffman *et al.*, "A Positron-Emission Transaxial Tomograph for nuclear medicine imaging (PETT)," *Radiology*, vol. 114, pp. 89–98, 1975.

[6] M. E. Phelps, E. J. Hoffman, N. N. Mullani *et al.*, "Application of annihilation coincidence detection to transaxial reconstruction tomography," *J. Nucl. Med.*, vol. 16, pp. 210–224, 1975.

[7] J. F. Greenleaf, S. A. Johnson, S. L. Lee *et al.*, "Algebraic reconstruction of spatial distributions of acoustic absorption with tis-

sues from two-dimensional acoustic projections," in *Acoustical Holography*, vol. 5, P. S. Green, Ed. New York: Plenum, 1974, pp. 591-603.

[8] J. F. Greenleaf, S. A. Johnson, W. F. Samayoa *et al.*, "Algebraic reconstruction of spatial distributions of acoustic velocities in tissue from their time-of-flight profiles," in *Acoustical Holography*, N. Booth, Ed. New York: Plenum, 1975, pp. 71-90.

[9] J. Radon, "Uber die Bestimmung von Funktionen durch ihre Integralwerte langs gewisser Mannigfaltigkeiten," *Berichte Saechsische Akademie der Wissenschaften*, vol. 69, pp. 262-279, 1917.

[10] G. T. Herman and S. Rowland, "Resolution in ART: An experimental investigation of the resolving power of an algebraic reconstruction technique," *J. Theor. Biol.*, vol. 33, pp. 213-223, 1971.

[11] R. Gordon, "A tutorial on ART," *IEEE Trans. Nucl. Sci.*, vol. NS-21, pp. 78-93, 1974.

[12] R. N. Bracewell, "Strip integration in radioastronomy," *Aust. J. Phys.*, vol. 9, pp. 198-217, 1960.

[13] G. N. Ramachandran and A. V. Lakshminarayanan, "Three-dimensional reconstruction from radiographs and electron micrographs: Application of convolution instead of Fourier transforms," *Proc. Nat. Acad. Sci. U.S.*, vol. 68, pp. 2236-2240, 1970.

[14] A. J. Duerinckx and A. Macovski, "Classification of artifacts in X-ray CT images due to nonlinear shadows," *IEEE Trans. Nucl. Sci.*, vol. NS-26, pp. 2848-2852, 1979.

[15] R. A. Brooks and G. DiChiro, "Beam-hardening in x-ray reconstructive tomography," *Phys. Med. Biol.*, vol. 21, pp. 390-398, 1976.

[16] J. P. Stonestrom, R. E. Alvarez, and A. Macovski, "A framework for spectral artifact corrections in X-ray CT," *IEEE Trans. Biomed. Eng.*, vol. BME-28, pp. 128-141, 1980.

[17] R. E. Alvarez and A. Macovski, "Energy-selective reconstructions in x-ray computerized tomography," *Phys. Med. Biol.*, vol. 21, pp. 733-744, 1976.

[18] A. Macovski, R. E. Alvarez, J. L-H. Chan, and J. P. Stonestrom, "Correction for spectral shift in x-ray computerized tomography," in *Proc. on Image Processing for 2-D and 3-D Reconstruction from Projections*, paper MB1, Aug. 1975.

[19] G. H. Glover and N. J. Pelc, "Nonlinear partial volume artifacts in x-ray computed tomography," *Med. Phys.*, vol. 7, pp. 238-248, 1980.

[20] R. Legauet, "The aliasing problems in 2-dimensional sampled imagery," in *Perception of Displayed Information*, L. M. Biberman, Ed. New York: Plenum, 1973, ch. 7, pp. 279-312.

[21] T. M. Peters and R. M. Lewitt, "Computerized tomography with fan beam geometry," *J. Comp. Assist. Tomog.*, vol. 1, pp. 429-436, 1977.

[22] T. Inouye, "Image reconstruction with limited angle projection data," *IEEE Trans. Nucl. Sci.*, vol. NS-26, pp. 2666-2669, 1979.

[23] A. J. Rockmore and A. Macovski, "A maximum likelihood approach to transmission image reconstruction from projections," *IEEE Trans. Nucl. Sci.*, vol. NS-24, pp. 1929-1935, 1977.

[24] S. L. Wood, M. Morf, and A. Macovski, "Stochastic methods applied to medical image reconstruction," in *Proc. IEEE Conf. on Decision and Control* (New Orleans, LA), pp. 35-41, Dec. 1977.

[25] M. H. Buonocore, W. R. Brody, and A. Macovski, "Fast minimum variance estimators for limited angle CT image reconstruction," *Med. Phys.*, vol. 8, no. 5, pp. 695-702, Sept./Oct. 1981.

[26] O. J. Tretiak and C. Metz, "The exponential Radon transform," *SIAM J. Appl. Math.*, vol. 39, no. 2, pp. 341-354, 1980.

[27] G. T. Gullberg and T. F. Budinger, "The use of filtering methods to compensate for constant attenuation in single-photon emission computed tomography," *IEEE Trans. Biomed. Eng.*, vol. BME-28, pp. 142-157, 1981.

[28] J. F. Greenleaf, S. A. Johnson, and A. H. Lert, "Measurement of the spatial distribution of refractive index in tissues by ultrasonic computer assisted tomography," *Ultrasound Med. Biol.*, vol. 3, pp. 327-339, 1978.

[29] R. K. Mueller, M. Kaveh, and G. Wade, "Acoustical reconstructive tomography and applications to ultrasonics," *Proc. IEEE*, vol. 67, pp. 567-586, 1979.

[30] F. Stenger and S. A. Johnson, "Ultrasonic transmission tomography based on the inversion of the Helmholtz wave equation for plane and spherical wave insonification," *Appl. Math. Notes*, vol. 4, pp. 102-127, 1979.

[31] D. A. Chesler, S. J. Riederer, and N. J. Pelc, "Noise due to photon counting statistics in computed x-ray tomography," *J. Comp. Assist. Tomog.*, vol. 1, pp. 64-74, 1977.

[32] H. H. Barrett, S. K. Gordon, and R. S. Hershel, "Statistical limitations in transaxial tomography," *Comp. Biol. Med.*, vol. 6, pp. 307-323, 1976.

[33] R. E. Alvarez and J. P. Stonestrom, "Optimal processing of computed tomography images using experimentally measured noise properties," *J. Comput. Assist. Tomog.*, vol. 3, pp. 77-84, 1979.

[34] J. P. Stonestrom and A. Macovski, "Scatter considerations in fan beam computerized tomographic systems," *IEEE Trans. Nucl. Sci.*, vol. NS-23, pp. 1453-1458, 1976.

Mathematical Problems of Computerized Tomography

ALFRED K. LOUIS AND FRANK NATTERER

Invited Paper

Abstract—The data measured in computerized tomography; e.g., the X-ray attenuation in X-ray tomography or the resonance phenomena in nuclear magnetic resonance tomography, have to be processed to produce the pictures on which the diagnostic evaluation of the physician is based. This process consists of the solution of the following mathematical problem. The data depend on the searched-for distribution and this dependence can be described as an integral transform. To produce the final picture amounts to the inversion of the integral transform.

This paper is concerned with the description of the integral transforms modeling the different techniques in computerized tomography. Among other things, the following questions are treated. Which numerical problems do we have to encounter in inverting the transforms; e.g., what accuracy in the reconstruction can we expect in dependence on the accuracy of the data. To what extent is a distribution determined by a finite number of measurements. Is it possible to recover the distribution reliably if the data are incomplete.

I. Introduction

SPEAKING in mathematical terms, the problem of computerized tomography is simply to reconstruct a function in $\mathbb{R}^3$ from the values of its integrals over straight lines or planes. Although this reconstruction problem is only a rough model for the real problem, an adequate understanding of it is still one of the necessary prerequisites for any serious work in the field of computerized tomography.

From a mathematical point of view, our reconstruction problem is threefold: First of all, one has to find out to what extent the object is determined by the data. Secondly, one wants to know to what extent the object to be reconstructed is stable with respect to data errors. Finally, one has to devise algorithms which actually do the reconstruction.

The question of uniqueness is being dealt with in Section V by giving some uniqueness theorems for the relevant integral transforms. The stability problem is discussed in Section VI. Although we do not cover the development of numerical algorithms, we give explicit inversion formulas in Section IV. In Section VII we discuss three typical examples of problems for which the results of the preceding sections do not apply since only a part of the data are available, and we outline the computational procedure for the method of regularization which is applicable to many incomplete data problems. The theoretical foundations are laid in Section III where the relevant integral transforms are introduced and investigated in a mathematical fashion. In Section II we explain some mathematical tools which will be used throughout the paper.

Manuscript received April 20, 1982; revised September 15, 1982.

The authors are with the Institut für Numerische und Instrumentelle Mathematik, Universität Münster, D-4400 Münster, West Germany.

II. Mathematical Preliminaries

We will discuss the reconstruction problem in the framework of linear operators in normed linear spaces. For those readers who want a deeper treatment than the very short one we are giving below we recommend any textbook in functional analysis, e.g., [71].

The linear spaces we are dealing with are spaces of functions. For two functions f, g and real complex numbers α, β, the function $\alpha f + \beta g$ is defined by

$$(\alpha f + \beta g)(x) = \alpha f(x) + \beta g(x).$$

In order to measure the size of functions one uses norms. A norm is a real-valued function, usually denoted by $\| \cdot \|$, on a linear space, such that

$$\|f\| \geqslant 0, \quad \text{for all } f, \|f\| = 0 \text{ only for } f = 0$$

$$\|f + g\| \leqslant \|f\| + \|g\|$$

$$\|\alpha f\| = |\alpha| \, \|f\|.$$

Most of the time we will use the L_2 norm

$$\|f\| = \left(\int_\Omega |f|^2 \, dx \right)^{1/2}$$

for functions which are square integrable on some set Ω or other L_2-based norms, see Section III-B. If $\| \cdot \|_1$, $\| \cdot \|_2$ are norms on some linear space X, then $\| \cdot \|_1$ is said to be weaker than $\| \cdot \|_2$ if there is a constant c such that

$$\|f\|_1 \leqslant c \|f\|_2$$

for all f in X. If $\| \cdot \|_1$ is weaker than $\| \cdot \|_2$ and *vice versa*, the norms are said to be equivalent.

Let X, Y be linear spaces. A linear operator $R : X \to Y$ assigns to each $f \in X$ an element Rf in Y such that for all $f, g \in X$ and real (complex) α, β

$$R(\alpha f + \beta g) = \alpha Rf + \beta Rg.$$

The range of R is defined by range $(R) = \{g \in Y : g = Rf$ for some $f \in X\}$.

If X, Y are normed linear spaces (both norms being denoted by the same symbol) and if there is a constant c such that

$$\|Rf\| \leqslant c \|f\|$$

then R is called continuous. Note that the continuity depends on the norms chosen in X and Y.

If $Rf = 0$ implies $f = 0$, than R is invertible, i.e., for each $g \in$ range (R) there is precisely one element f, denoted by

Reprinted from *Proc. IEEE*, vol. 71, pp. 379–389, Mar. 1983.

$R^{-1}g$, such that $Rf = g$. $R^{-1} : Y \rightarrow X$ is also a linear operator. If there is some constant $c > 0$ such that

$$\|Rf\| \geqslant c\|f\|$$

then R^{-1} exists and is continuous.

An equation $Rf = g$ is said to be well posed, if R is invertible with R^{-1} continuous. Otherwise, $Rf = g$ is said to be ill-posed, see [63]. Note that ill-posedness depends on the norms used in X, Y. It is always possible to make $Rf = g$ well posed by replacing the norms in X, Y by weaker or stronger ones, respectively.

The difficulty with ill-posed problems is the following one: Either $Rf = g$ is not solvable or not uniquely solvable; this is the case if R is not invertible. Or, if R is invertible with R^{-1} not continuous, then $f' = R^{-1}g'$ need not be close to $f = R^{-1}g$ even if g' is close to g, i.e., $\|f - f'\|$ is not small if $\|g - g'\|$ is. Thus it is difficult to solve an ill-posed problem in the presence of errors, such as noise, imperfect modeling, or discretization.

III. The Transforms in Medical Imaging

In this section we introduce the transforms relevant in medical imaging: the Radon transform, the X-ray transform, the divergent-beam transform, and the attenuated Radon transform. (The Radon transform arises in two-dimensional (2D) tomography and in nuclear magnetic resonance (NMR) zeugmatography. Three-dimensional (3D) tomography gives rise to the X-ray transform. The divergent beam transform is used in 2D and 3D tomography for specific scanning modes. The attenuated Radon transform occurs in 2D emission tomography.) We then proceed to study the ranges and the continuity properties of some of these transforms. While knowledge about the ranges is useful for some incomplete data problems in Section VII, the continuity results solve the stability problem in Section VI.

A. Introduction of the Transforms

We first introduce some notation. We denote the N-dimensional real Euclidean space by $\mathbb{R}^N$, and we restrict ourselves here to $N = 2$ and $N = 3$. Let $|x|$ be the Euclidean length of the vector x in $\mathbb{R}^N$. The set of directions in $\mathbb{R}^N$ are the unit vectors in $\mathbb{R}^N$; they form the set

$$S^{N-1} = \{x \in \mathbb{R}^N : |x| = 1\}.$$

$V(a, r)$ is the ball around a with radius r.

Let f be a real-valued function in $\mathbb{R}^N$ which represents the sought after density distribution. We can assume that, after a suitable scaling, $f(x)$ is nonzero only for points x in the unit ball; i.e., supp $f \subset V(0, 1) = \Omega$.

The Radon transform Rf of f at the points $s \in \mathbb{R}$ and in the direction $\omega \in S^{N-1}$ is defined as the integral of f over the hyperplane perpendicular to ω and with signed distance s from the origin. In mathematical terms this reads as

$$Rf : Z \rightarrow \mathbb{R}, \qquad Z = \mathbb{R} \times S^{N-1}$$

with

$$Rf(s, \omega) = \int_{\omega_p} f(s\omega + \xi) \, d\xi. \qquad (3.1)$$

Here Z denotes the unit cylinder in $\mathbb{R}^{N+1}$ and ω_p is the subspace of vectors perpendicular to ω, i.e.,

$$\omega_p = \{x \in \mathbb{R}^N : x \cdot \omega = 0\}.$$

In X-ray tomography we consider a ray going through the point $x \in \mathbb{R}^N$ and having the direction $\omega \in S^{N-1}$. This leads to the X-ray transform Pf of f defined as

$$Pf(x, \omega) = \int_{-\infty}^{\infty} f(x + t\omega) \, dt. \qquad (3.2)$$

The value of $Pf(x, \omega)$ does not change if we move the point x along the direction ω because the integral is calculated over the whole real line. Therefore, it suffices to define Pf for values x in ω_p which leads to

$$Pf : T \rightarrow \mathbb{R}$$

where $T = \{(x, \omega) : \omega \in S^{N-1}, x \in \omega_p\}$ is, in the jargon of mathematics, the tangent bundle to S^{N-1}.

In two dimensions, we have with $\omega^\perp$ a unit vector in ω_p,

$$Rf(s, \omega) = Pf(s \cdot \omega, \omega^\perp). \qquad (3.3)$$

This means that in this case the two transforms differ only by the parametrization of the ray. Another way to label the straight lines in $\mathbb{R}^N$ leads to the divergent beam transform

$$Df(x, \omega) = \int_0^{\infty} f(x + t\omega) \, dt \qquad (3.4)$$

where x is thought of as the source of a ray with direction ω. If A is the set of sources, then

$$Df : A \times S^{N-1} \rightarrow \mathbb{R}.$$

In single-particle emission CT (SPECT), we consider two real-valued functions f and μ. Usually one denotes by μ the attenuation coefficient and by f the activity distribution. The transform which describes the data is the so-called attenuated Radon transform

$$R_\mu f : Z \rightarrow \mathbb{R}$$

where for $N = 2$

$$R_\mu f(s, \omega) = \int_{x \cdot \omega = s} f(x) \, e^{-D\mu(x, \omega^\perp)} \, dx. \qquad (3.5)$$

Note that in the special case $\mu = 0$ the attenuated Radon transform coincides with the usual Radon transform defined in (3.1). The data in positron-emission tomography (PET) pertain to the values of the product

$$e^{-R\mu} Rf$$

and do not give rise to new mathematical problems.

B. Continuity of the Transforms

In order to formulate the continuity result we introduce Sobolev spaces on Ω, Z, T. For more details see [67]. These spaces are defined with the help of the Fourier transform which we define to be

$$\hat{\psi}(\xi) = (2\pi)^{-M/2} \int_{\mathbb{R}^M} \psi(x) \, e^{-ix \cdot \xi} \, dx, \qquad \xi \in \mathbb{R}^M$$

for functions on $\mathbb{R}^M$. For any real number α we introduce the norm

$$\|\psi\|_\alpha = \left(\int_{\mathbb{R}^M} (1 + |\xi|^2)^\alpha \, |\hat{\psi}(\xi)|^2 \, d\xi \right)^{1/2}.$$

The Sobolev space H^α of order α on $\mathbb{R}^M$ consists of those distributions ψ on $\mathbb{R}^M$ for which $\|\psi\|_\alpha < \infty$.

It can be shown that for any integer $\alpha > 0$, H^α consists of functions whose (generalized) derivatives up to order α are square integrable. Hence the larger α the smoother are the functions in H^α; i.e., α is a measure for the smoothness of the functions in H^α. For instance, functions which are piecewise smooth with jumps only along smooth curves, i.e., densities of high-contrast pictures, are in H^α for $\alpha < \frac{1}{2}$. In particular, H^0 is simply the space of square integrable functions on $\mathbb{R}^M$.

For the following theorems, it is essential that the functions have compact support. Therefore, we introduce the Sobolev space

$$H_0^\alpha(\Omega) = \{f \in H^\alpha : \operatorname{supp} f \subseteq \Omega\}.$$

On the cylinder Z we use the norm

$$\|g\|_{\alpha, Z} = \left(\int_{S^{N-1}} \|g(\cdot, \omega)\|_\alpha^2 \, d\omega \right)^{1/2}$$

where the dot indicates the variable which is Fourier transformed.

On Z it replaces a one-dimensional (1D) variable, on T an $(N-1)$-dimensional variable

$$\|g\|_{\alpha, T} = \left(\int_{S^{N-1}} \|g(\cdot, \omega)\|_\alpha^2 \, d\omega \right)^{1/2}$$

on the tangent bundle T. The spaces $H^\alpha(Z)$, $H^\alpha(T)$ are made up of those (generalized) functions for which the respective norms are finite. For $\alpha = 0$, all spaces are simply spaces of square integrable functions with the natural L_2-norm.

Our continuity results read as follows:

Theorem 3.1: i) There exist constants $0 < \gamma_1 \leqslant \Gamma_1$ such that

$$\gamma_1 \|f\|_\alpha \leqslant \|Rf\|_{\alpha + (N-1)/2, Z} \leqslant \Gamma_1 \|f\|_\alpha$$

for all $f \in H_0^\alpha(\Omega)$.

ii) There exist constants $0 < \gamma_2 \leqslant \Gamma_2$ such that

$$\gamma_2 \|f\|_\alpha \leqslant \|Pf\|_{\alpha + 1/2, T} \leqslant \Gamma_2 \|f\|_\alpha$$

for all $f \in H_0^\alpha(\Omega)$.

The theorem tells us not only that R and P admit inverses but also that these inverses are continuous as operators from $H^{\alpha + (N-1)/2}(Z)$, $H^{\alpha + 1/2}(T)$, respectively, into $H_0^\alpha(\Omega)$, the order of the latter Sobolev space being best possible, in sense, that the result is wrong for any larger index. In particular, if α is such that the spaces on Z, T are simply the L_2-spaces (i.e., $\alpha = -(N-1)/2$ in the case of R and $\alpha = -\frac{1}{2}$ in the case of P), then $H_0^\alpha(\Omega)$ is a Sobolev space with negative order whose norm is weaker than the L_2 norm on $L_2(\Omega)$. This shows that neither R^{-1} nor P^{-1} are continuous in an L_2 setting, i.e., the reconstruction problem is ill posed. Fortunately, the ill-posedness is not pronounced very much.

The proof of Theorem 3.1 is based on a relation between the Fourier transform and P, R, respectively; namely, the so-called "projection theorem"

$$(Rf)^\wedge(\sigma, \omega) = (2\pi)^{(N-1)/2} \hat{f}(\sigma \cdot \omega) \qquad (3.6)$$

and

$$(Pf)^\wedge(\xi, \omega) = (2\pi)^{1/2} \hat{f}(\xi), \qquad \xi \in \omega^\perp. \qquad (3.7)$$

Both formulas, in which the Fourier transform on the left-hand side is taken with respect to the first variable, are easily derived by direct calculation.

Continuity results concerning the attenuated Radon transform are not known. For the divergent beam transform, continuity results are known only in the case $A = S^{N-1}$ where D coincides, up to differences in the notation, with P.

C. The Range of the Transforms

As motivated in Section II, we characterize in the following the range of the Radon transform, the X-ray transform, and give conditions for functions to be in the range of the attenuated Radon transform.

Theorem 3.2: A function $g \in H^{\alpha + (N-1)/2}(Z)$ is the Radon transform of a function $f \in H_0^\alpha(\Omega)$ if and only if

i) $g(s, \omega) = 0$ for all $|s| > 1$,
ii) g is even on Z, i.e., $g(s, \omega) = g(-s, -\omega)$,
iii) for each nonnegative integer m

$$\int s^m g(s, \omega) \, ds$$

is a polynomial in ω of degree less than or equal to m.

Theorem 3.3: A function $g \in H^{\alpha + 1/2}(T)$ is the X-ray transform of a function $f \in H_0^\alpha(\Omega)$ if and only if

i) $g(x, \omega) = 0$ for all $|x| > 1$,
ii) for each nonnegative integer m there exists a homogeneous polynomial P_m of degree m on $\mathbb{R}^N$ such that $P_m(\xi) = P_{m, \omega}(\xi)$ for each $\omega \in S^{N-1}$ and $\xi \in \omega^\perp$, where

$$P_{m, \omega}(\xi) = \int_{\omega^\perp} \langle \xi, x \rangle^m g(x, \omega) \, dx.$$

Whereas for these two transforms complete characterizations of the range are known this is presently not the case for the attenuated Radon transform. In order to formulate sufficient conditions which are satisfied by the functions in the range of R_μ we have to introduce the Hilbert transform

$$Hg(s) = -\frac{1}{\pi} \int \frac{g(t)}{s - t} \, dt. \qquad (3.8)$$

The integral is to be understood in the Cauchy principal value sense. Alternatively, we can define Hg by its Fourier transform

$$(Hg)^\wedge(\sigma) = -i \operatorname{sgn}(\sigma) \hat{g}(\sigma) \qquad (3.9)$$

with $\operatorname{sgn}(\sigma)$ the sign of σ.

Theorem 3.4: Let $N = 2$ and let μ be infinitely differentiable with support in Ω.

Let f be a distribution with support in Ω and let $g = R_\mu f$. Then g fulfills

$$\int_0^{2\pi} \int s^m e^{-ik\varphi} e^{(1/2)(I + iH) R_\mu(s, \omega)} g(s, \omega) \, ds \, d\varphi = 0$$

for $k > m \geqslant 0$, k, m integer. Here, $\omega = (\cos \varphi, \sin \varphi)$. The operator $\frac{1}{2}(I + iH)$ acts on the first variable of R_μ.

D. Notes and References

Motivations and relations to the physical background of the transforms introduced in this section can be found, e.g., in [20], [43], [44]. The Radon transform was originally studied by Radon in 1917 [54], in connection with hyperbolic differential equations, see also [23]. Radon transform and X-ray transform are special instances of the general k-plane transform introduced in [16] where integrals over k-dimensional hyperplanes are considered. Thus the Radon transform is the case $k = N - 1$ and the X-ray transform represents $k = 1$.

The attenuated Radon transform, also called exponential Radon transform, was introduced in connection with SPECT in [65].

The continuity results for the Radon transform and the X-ray transform are given in [59], [60] for weaker norms than in Theorem 3.1, there

$$|\Psi|_\alpha = \left(\int |\xi|^2 \, |\hat{\Psi}(\xi)|^2 \, d\xi \right)^{1/2}$$

was used. The isomorphy results of Theorem 3.1 are given in [38], [48].

The characterizations of the range of the Radon transform (Theorem 3.2) are known as Helgason–Ludwig consistency conditions, see [18], [40]. The corresponding result for the X-ray transform can be found in [60], for the attenuated Radon transform see [46].

IV. Inversion Formulas

The reconstruction of the searched-for desntiy from the measured data amounts to inverting the transform which describes the data. In the following we consider inversion formulas that use the complete set of data, e.g., $Rf(s, \omega)$ for all $\omega \in S^{N-1}$ and all $s \in \mathbb{R}$. Although complete data sets are never available in practice, it is important to study these formulas because they serve as a basis for the inversion algorithms. The procedures presently implemented are special discretizations of these formulas. Here we concentrate on the exact inversion and only make remarks concerning difficulties in the implementation.

A. The Radon Transform

To derive an inversion formula we use the relation (3.6) between the Fourier and the Radon transforms. Starting with the inverse Fourier transform in polar coordinates we get

$$f(x) = (2\pi)^{-N/2} \, 2^{-1} \int_{S^{N-1}} \int_{\mathbb{R}} |\sigma|^{N-1} \hat{f}(\sigma \cdot \omega) \, e^{i\sigma\omega x} \, d\sigma \, d\omega$$

$$= (2\pi)^{1/2 - N} \, 2^{-1}$$

$$\cdot \int_{S^{N-1}} \int_{\mathbb{R}} |\sigma|^{N-1} (Rf)^{\wedge} (\sigma, \omega) \, e^{i\sigma\omega x} \, d\sigma \, d\omega$$

$$= c_N R^* I^{N-1} Rf(x) \tag{4.1}$$

where $c_N = 2^{-1} (2\pi)^{1-N}$, R^* is the backprojection operator defined as

$$R^* q(x) = \int_{S^{n-1}} q(x \cdot \omega, \omega) \, d\omega \tag{4.2}$$

and

$$(I^{N-1} Rf)^{\wedge} (\sigma, \omega) = |\sigma|^{N-1} (Rf)^{\wedge} (\sigma, \omega). \tag{4.3}$$

In the implementation of this formula one uses a filtered version of the function $q = I^{N-1} Rf$, say, q_F, where

$$\hat{q}_F(\sigma, \omega) = F(\sigma) \, \hat{q}(\sigma, \omega). \tag{4.4}$$

Replacing q by q_F in (4.1) produces instead of f the function f

convolved with E, $f * E$, where $\hat{E}(\sigma \cdot \omega) = F(\sigma)$. This means that the choice of F is a tradeoff between a good approximation to f and a stabilization of (4.1). Implementations are known as filtered backprojections.

It is also possible to express $I^{N-1} Rf$ without using the Fourier transform. For $N = 3$, $I^2 Rf$ is $D_s^2 Rf$, the second derivative of Rf with respect to the first argument. In two dimensions, $I^1 Rf$ is equal to $HD_s Rf$, i.e., the Hilbert transform of the first derivative of Rf; for the definition of H see (3.8). Here the main difference between the inversion of the Radon transform in even and odd dimensions becomes clear. The differentiation and so the inversion in odd dimensions is local. This means that for the reconstruction of f at the point x it suffices to know $Rf(s, \omega)$ only for values of s near $x \cdot \omega$, i.e., to know the integrals over all hyperplanes in the neighborhood of x. In contrast, the Hilbert transform is not local and this means that in even dimensions Rf is needed for all s.

Using the Hilbert transform we can rewrite (4.1) for $N = 2$ as

$$f(x) = \frac{1}{2\pi^2} \int_0^\pi \int_{\mathbb{R}} D_s Rf(s, \omega) \, (s - x \cdot \omega)^{-1} \, ds \, d\varphi. \tag{4.5}$$

Putting $q = s - x \cdot \omega$, reversing the order of integration and integrating by parts we obtain

$$f(x) = \pi^{-1} \lim_{\epsilon \to 0} \left[\epsilon^{-1} F_x(\epsilon) - \int_\epsilon^\infty q^{-2} F_x(q) \, dq \right] \tag{4.6}$$

with

$$F_x(q) = (2\pi)^{-1} \int_0^{2\pi} Rf(x \cdot \omega + q, \omega) \, d\varphi.$$

This is the original inversion formula given by Radon in 1917. If we first backproject the data (i.e., if we compute $R^* Rf$) then the inversion formula (4.1) leads with the projection theorem to $g = R^* Rf$ where $\hat{g}(\xi) = |\xi|^{1-N} \hat{f}(\xi)$. We then have the inversion formula

$$f(x) = c_N I^{N-1} R^* Rf(x). \tag{4.7}$$

Note that in this formula one first backprojects the data and then applies I^{N-1}; here I^{N-1} acts on a function of N variables. Implementations of this formula are known as the rho-filtered layergram method.

Instead of inverting the Fourier transform in the projection theorem exactly one can use numerical inversion with the fast Fourier transform (FFT). This is the so-called Fourier method of reconstruction. Numerical difficulties arise in the approximation of $\hat{f}$ on a regular rectangular grid from the known values of $\hat{f}$ on a polar grid. The critical point here lies in the interpolation of $\hat{f}(\sigma \cdot \omega)$ in σ-direction.

A different type of inversion formula is produced by series expansions in terms of special functions. Here we use the Gegenbauer polynomials C_m^ν. These are polynomials of degree m, which are orthogonal over $[-1, 1]$ with respect to the weight function $w_\nu(s) = (1 - s^2)^{\nu - 1/2}$. They include as special cases the Legendre polynomials ($\nu = \frac{1}{2}$) and the Chebyshev polynomials of the first ($\nu = 0$) and second ($\nu = 1$) kind. Another set of orthogonal polynomials are the Jacobi polynomials $P_m^{(\alpha,\beta)}$. These are polynomials of degree m, which are orthogonal over $[-1, 1]$ with respect to the weight function $(1 - s)^\alpha (1 + s)^\beta$. Finally, the spherical harmonics are the eigenfunctions of the Laplacian on the unit sphere. Let us consider the 2D case. Then the Radon transform can be expanded in a Fourier series, where we use $\omega = (\cos\varphi, \sin\varphi)^T$

$$Rf(s, \omega) = \sum_{k=-\infty}^{\infty} g_k(s)\, e^{ik\varphi}$$

$$g_k(s) = (2\pi)^{-1} \int_0^{2\pi} Rf(s, \omega)\, e^{-ik\varphi}\, d\varphi. \qquad (4.8)$$

The function f is defined on the unit circle, therefore, we use polar coordinates r and θ and expand also f in a Fourier series

$$f(r, \theta) = \sum_{k=-\infty}^{\infty} f_k(r)\, e^{ik\theta}$$

$$f_k(r) = (2\pi)^{-1} \int_0^{2\pi} f(r, \theta)\, e^{-ik\theta}\, d\theta. \qquad (4.9)$$

Then the expansion coefficients of f can be expressed with the help of the expansion coefficients of Rf as

$$f_k(r) = -\frac{1}{\pi} \int_r^1 T_k\left(\frac{t}{r}\right) (t^2 - r^2)^{-1/2}\, g_k'(t)\, dt \qquad (4.10)$$

where T_k is the Chebyshev polynomial of the first kind.

Another type of inversion formula can be given when we expand Rf with respect to the first argument. Denoting by C_m^ν the Gegenbauer polynomial of degree m and index ν, we can represent in the N-dimensional case

$$Rf(s, \omega) = w_\nu(s) \sum_{m=0}^{\infty} C_m^\nu(s)\, q_m(\omega) \qquad (4.11)$$

where $w_\nu(s) = (1 - s^2)^{\nu - 1/2}$ and

$$q_m(\omega) = \int_{-1}^{1} Rf(s, \omega)\, C_m^\nu(s)\, ds \Big/ \int_{-1}^{1} w_\nu(s)\, [C_m^\nu(s)]^2\, ds.$$

Because of the consistency conditions for the Radon transform, the q_m are polynomials in ω which can be represented in the form (4.12) where the Y_λ are spherical harmonics of degree λ

$$q_m(\omega) = \sum_{\substack{\lambda=0 \\ \lambda + m \text{ even}}}^{m} d_{m\lambda} Y_\lambda(\omega). \qquad (4.12)$$

Using the coefficients $d_{m\lambda}$ in the expansion of Rf we can represent f at the point $x = s \cdot \theta$, $0 \leqslant s \leqslant 1$, $\theta \in S^{N-1}$ as

$$f(s \cdot \theta) = (1 - s^2)^{\nu - N/2}$$

$$\cdot \sum_{m=0}^{\infty} \sum_{\substack{\lambda=0 \\ m + \lambda \text{ even}}}^{m} c(N, m, \nu, \lambda)\, Q_{m,\lambda}^{\nu,N}(s)\, Y_\lambda(\theta)\, d_{m\lambda} \qquad (4.13)$$

where

$$c(N, m, \nu, \lambda) = 2^{1-2\nu}\pi^{1-N/2}$$

$$\cdot \frac{\Gamma(m + 2\nu)\, \Gamma((m - \lambda + 2)/2)}{\Gamma(m + 1)\, \Gamma(\nu)\, \Gamma((m - \lambda + 2 + 2\nu - N)/2)}$$

Γ denotes Euler's gamma function, and

$$Q_{m,\nu}^{\nu,N}(s) = s^\lambda P_{(m-\lambda)/2}^{(\nu-N/2,\lambda+N/2-1)}(2s^2 - 1)$$

with $P_k^{(\alpha,\beta)}$ the Jacobi polynomials.

The weight w_ν in the expansion of Rf corresponds to the weight $W_\nu(x) = (1 - |x|^2)^{\nu - N/2}$ in the expansion of f. Thus the selection of ν enables us to emphasize the interior of the domain ($\nu > N/2$), the boundary ($\nu < N/2$), or to put equal weight to the whole domain ($\nu = N/2$).

B. The X-Ray Transform and the Divergent Beam Transform

For the derivation of an inversion formula for the X-ray transform we proceed the same way as in the case of the Radon transform. This leads to

$$f(x) = C_N P^* I^1 Pf(x) \qquad (4.14)$$

where

$$C_N = \Gamma((N - 1)/2)\, \pi^{-N/2} 2^{-2}$$

$$(I^1 Pf)\,\hat{}\,(\xi, \omega) = |\xi|\, (Pf)\,\hat{}\,(\xi, \omega), \qquad \text{for } \xi \in \omega_p$$

and

$$P^* q(x) = \int_{S^{N-1}} q(E_\omega x, \omega)\, d\omega$$

with $E_\omega x$ the orthogonal projection of x onto ω_p. Again we can rewrite (4.14) as

$$f(x) = C_N I^1 P^* Pf(x). \qquad (4.15)$$

A similar formula can be obtained for the divergent beam transform. All these formulas are of limited practical value since they need complete data. Especially in the 3D case one is interested in the following situation. Assume the X-ray source is moved along a closed curve around the object and at each position there is a whole cone of rays emanating from the source and this cone covers the whole object. This is an open problem. For preliminary results see [45], [68].

C. The Attenuated Radon Transform

An inversion formula for the attenuated Radon transform is known only for constant attenuation. With

$$R_\mu^* g(x) = \int_{S^1} g(x \cdot \omega, \omega)\, e^{-D\mu(x, \omega^\perp)}\, d\omega$$

the backprojection operator for the attenuated transform, one obtains by direct calculation that

$$R_{-\mu}^* R_\mu f(x) = 2 \int_{\mathbb{R}^2} f(y) \cosh\left(\int_x^y \mu\, dt\right) |x - y|^{-1}\, dy.$$

If μ is constant, then the integral from x to y is simply $|x - y|\mu$, and the right-hand side is a convolution of f with the kernel

$$|x|^{-1} \cosh(\mu|x|).$$

By deconvolution we obtain an inversion formula which generalizes (4.7) and can be used to derive a reconstruction method of the rho-filtered layergram type. An inversion formula of type (4.1) and the corresponding filtered backprojection algorithm has been given in [66].

D. Notes and References

Inversion formulas for the Radon transform are given in most papers dealing with computerized tomography, for over-

183

views see, e.g., [20], [43]. The notation used here was introduced in [26]. The inversion formula given in (4.6) is Radon's original formula. Fourier series for the reconstruction problem have been studied in [5], the expansion of the Radon transform in terms of Gegenbauer polynomials has been used for $N = 2$ in [5], [42]; for the general case see [36]. Implementations of these formulas are treated in [55], a fast and accurate version for the Fourier method of reconstruction is given in [39], [61].

V. Uniqueness Problems

In this section, we treat the problem of the conditions on the data that are necessary to determine the searched-for function uniquely. Furthermore, we study the effects when these conditions are not fulfilled.

A. Complete Projections

First we consider the case of complete projections; i.e., we assume that for fixed $\omega \in S^{N-1}$ the function $Rf(s, \omega)$ is known for all s and $Pf(x, \omega)$ is known for all $x \in \omega_p$.

Theorem 5.1: A function f is uniquely determined by any infinite number of complete projections $Pf(\cdot, \omega)$. The same result holds for the Radon transform under the additional assumption that the directions ω must not be the zeroes of a polynomial on S^{N-1}. The divergent beam transform $Df(x, \omega)$ determines uniquely the function f if it is given for an infinite number of sources x outside Ω and for all directions ω.

Furthermore, Smith, Solmon, and Wagner stated in [59] that "a finite set of radiographs tells nothing at all." Here, "radiographs" means complete projections. They also showed that it was possible to construct a function which was arbitrary in the interior of the support of f and had the same projections as f if the number of the measurements were finite.

This is contrary, to some extent, to the experience obtained in practice, where CT scanners produce reliable pictures of cross sections through the human body although only a finite number of projections are used.

From a mathematical point of view this nonuniqueness of the reconstruction means that there are functions whose projections are zero in the considered directions. These functions are often called "ghosts" and they form the null space of the transform for finitely many projections.

Let $\omega_1, \cdots, \omega_p \in S^{N-1}$ be the given directions. Then we are interested in the functions f such that $Rf(s, \omega_i) = 0$ for $i = 1, \cdots, p$ and $s \in \mathbb{R}$. With the help of the series expansion (4.11) and the linear independence of the Gegenbauer polynomials we get the following result.

Theorem 5.2: Let $p \geq \binom{n+N-2}{N-1}$ for a nonnegative integer n and let p directions $\omega_1, \cdots, \omega_p$ be given, such that they are not the zeroes of a harmonic polynomial of degree $n-1$ over S^{N-1}. Then the Radon transform of any function f in $L_2(\Omega)$ which is a ghost in $L_2(\Omega)$ for these directions can be written as

$$Rf(s, \omega) = w_{N/2}(s) \sum_{m=n}^{\infty} C_m^{N/2}(s) \, q_m(\omega) \qquad (5.1)$$

where q_m is a polynomial of degree m with $q_m(\omega_i) = 0$ for $i = 1, \cdots, p$.

With the help of the inversion formula given in (4.13) we can give this result also for the function itself.

Theorem 5.3: Let the assumptions of Theorem 5.2 be fulfilled. Using the notation of (4.13), the ghosts have the form

$$f(s \cdot \omega) = \sum_{\substack{m=n}}^{\infty} \sum_{\substack{\lambda=0 \\ \lambda+m \text{ even}}}^{m} d_{m\lambda} Y_\lambda(\omega) \, Q_{m,\lambda}^{N/2,N}(s)$$

for $|s| \leq 1$, $\omega \in S^{N-1}$ and

$$\sum_{\substack{\lambda=0 \\ \lambda+m \text{ even}}} c(N, m, \nu, \lambda) \, d_{m\lambda} Y_\lambda(\omega_i) = 0, \qquad \text{for } i = 1, \cdots, p$$

$$\text{and} \quad m \geq n.$$

The fact that the series expansion of the ghosts starts with a polynomial of degree n indicates that they consist of highly oscillating functions. Further conclusions are given in Section VI.

B. Truncated Projections

Here it is assumed that $Rf(s, \omega)$ is known only for $|s| \leq a < 1$. This problem occurs, e.g., if one is interested only in the region $\Omega_a = \{x \in \Omega : |x| \leq a\}$. In this case, one does not want to waste radiation in the exterior of Ω_a. Let us consider $N = 2$.

A function f cannot possibly be reconstructed uniquely in this case. However, consider the function $g(s, \omega) = \rho(|s|)$ where ρ is a smooth function such that $\rho(s) = 0$ for $|s| \leq a$ and $|s| \geq 1$. According to Theorem 3.2, g is in the range of R, and the inversion formula (4.9) provides the function $f = R^{-1}g$, which turns out to be

$$f(x) = -\frac{1}{\pi} \int_{|x|}^{1} \rho'(s) \, (s^2 - |x|^2)^{-1/2} \, ds.$$

f is a function which does not vanish identically in Ω_a, but whose Radon transform vanishes for $|s| \leq a$. Thus there are functions in $K = \{f \in L_2(\Omega) : Rf(s, \omega) = 0 \text{ for } |s| \leq a\}$, and these functions are in no sense small.

For the divergent-beam transform, the truncation problem arises if for each source x only a certain cone C_x with vertex in x is scanned. In this case, we have the following nice uniqueness theorem, which is a simplified version of a result in [14].

Theorem 5.4: Let A be a smooth curve in the exterior of Ω, and let $S \subseteq S^{N-1}$ be a set of directions. Assume that for some source $x \in A$, the cone $C_x = \{x + t\omega : t \geq 0, \omega \in S\}$ does not meet Ω. Then, in the scanned region,

$$\bigcup_{x \in A} C_x \cap \Omega$$

f is determined uniquely by $Df(x, \omega)$ for $x \in A$, $\omega \in S$.

C. Hollow Projections

Now we study the opposite case: $Rf(s, \omega)$ is known only for $|s| \geq a$, i.e., only integrals outside Ω_a are taken. This problem arises, e.g., in X-ray tomography if a piece of metal is implanted in the tissue being scanned.

Theorem 5.5: The function f is uniquely determined in the exterior of Ω_a by $Rf(s, \omega)$ for $|s| \geq a$.

Corresponding theorems hold for P and D. Generally speaking, a function is uniquely determined outside some ball by its integrals which do not meet the ball, provided it tends sufficiently fast to zero at infinity.

D. Unknown Sources

Another type of uniqueness problem arises in emission-computed tomography (ECT): in order to correct for the attenuation by the tissue one has to find out the attenuation distribution μ. Ideally one would like to determine μ from the scanner output $g = R_\mu f$ without knowing the source distribution f.

It is tempting to try to compute μ from the consistency conditions given in Theorem 3.4, i.e.,

$$\int_0^{2\pi} \int s^m \, e^{-ik\varphi} \, e^{1/2(I+iH)} R\mu(s, \omega) \, g(s, \omega) \, ds \, d\varphi = 0 \quad (5.2)$$

for $k > m \geqslant 0$, k, m integer. Equation (5.2) constitutes a nonlinear system of equations for μ which can be set up without knowing f. To a certain extent, these equations determine μ uniquely.

Theorem 5.6: Let $N = 2$. Let $x_1, \cdots, x_n$ be sources at least one of which is outside Ω, and let

$$f = \sum_{k=1}^{n} f_k \, \delta(x - x_k)$$

i.e., the source distribution f is made up of finitely many sources x_k with activity f_k. Let $\mu = 0$ outside Ω. Then $D_\mu(x_k, \omega)$ is determined uniquely by (5.2) for all sources x_k and all $\omega \in S^1$.

The theorem reduces the uniqueness problem for unknown sources to the uniqueness problem for the divergent beam transform.

E. Notes and References

The uniqueness result in Theorem 5.1 is given in [59]. The proof of the mentioned nonuniqueness is not constructive; it uses existence theorems for solutions of partial differential equations. Further properties of the functions in the null space, the ghosts, are studied in [24], [32], [35], [48]. The construction of the ghosts with the help of series expansions are given in [36] and optimality conditions for the choice of directions in NMR are derived, see also [37].

The nonuniqueness of the reconstruction in the case of truncated projections was shown in [31], [14]. The uniqueness for hollow projections is a general theorem on the support of the Radon transform [17]. The material of Section V-D is taken from [46].

VI. RESOLUTION AND ACCURACY

In this section we seek answers to the following vague questions:

i) Suppose the smallest detail contained in the picture f has size d. How do we have to sample Rf in order to recover f reliably?

ii) Suppose we want to recover f with an accuracy δ. What accuracy is required for $g = Rf$?

The following may be considered to lead to an answer to the first question.

Theorem 6.1: Let $\omega_1, \cdots, \omega_p \in S^{N-1}$ and assume that there is no nonzero even harmonic polynomial of degree n with

$$p \geqslant \binom{n + N - 2}{N - 1}$$

which vanishes for $\omega_1, \cdots, \omega_p$. If $Rf(s, \omega_j) = 0$ for $j = 1, \cdots, p$ and $s \in \mathbb{R}^1$, then

$$\hat{f}(\xi) = |\xi|^{-N/2} \sum_{m=n}^{\infty} q_m \left(\frac{\xi}{|\xi|}\right) J_{m+N/2}(|\xi|)$$

where q_m is some even harmonic polynomial of degree m with $q_m(\omega_j) = 0$, $j = 1, \cdots, p$ and J_m is the Bessel function of the first kind.

This theorem follows from Theorem 5.2 and from the fact that the Fourier transform of $w_{N/2}(s) \, C_m^{N/2}(s)$ is a multiple of $\sigma^{-N/2} J_{m+N/2}(\sigma)$.

For the application of the theorem we have to make use of Debye's asymptotic formula

$$J_m(b) \sim \frac{e^{m(\tanh \alpha - \alpha)}}{\sqrt{2\pi m \tanh \alpha}}$$

for m, b large, and $\cosh \alpha = m/b$ fixed. Since $\tanh \alpha < \alpha$ for $\alpha > 0$ it follows that $J_m(b)$ is decaying exponentially for $m > b$ large. Thus $\hat{f}(\xi)$ is negligible for $|\xi| < n$ if f satisfies the conditions of the theorem.

We think of a function f with smallest detail d as having essentially the bandwidth $b = 2\pi/d$; i.e., $\hat{f}(\xi)$ is negligible for $|\xi| > b$. If such a function satisfies the hypothesis of the theorem with $n > b$, then $\hat{f}(\xi)$ is negligible for all ξ, i.e., essentially $f = 0$. It follows from (3.6) that Rf, as a function of s, has essential bandwidth b if this is true for f. Hence it follows from the sampling theorem that $Rf(s, \omega_j)$ can be reconstructed reliably from the values $Rf(s_l, \omega_j)$, $s_l = hl$, $h \leqslant d/2$, $l = 0, \pm 1, \cdots, \pm q = \pm[1/h]$, and it suffices to require that $Rf(s_l, \omega_j) = 0$ for all l and $j = 1, \cdots, p$ in order to conclude that essentially $f = 0$. Hence we arrive at the following conclusion, which is an answer to question i):

Let $\omega_1, \cdots, \omega_p$ satisfy the hypothesis of Theorem 6.1 with some n, and let s_l be as above. Then, a function with smallest detail d can be recovered reliably from the values $Rf(s_l, \omega_j)$, $l = 0, \pm 1, \cdots, \pm q$, $j = 1, \cdots, p$.

Now let's turn to question ii). Assume that Rf is known with an rms error ϵ; i.e., instead of Rf a function g has been measured such that

$$\|Rf - g\|_{0, Z} \leqslant \epsilon.$$

We want to compute a reconstruction f^* for f from g. In view of Theorem 3.2, g is not likely to be in the range of R, hence the equation $Rf^* = g$ is, in general, unsolvable. But even if $Rf^* = g$ is solvable, f^* need not be close to f in the sense of $L_2(\Omega)$, since R^{-1} is unbounded as an operator from $L_2(Z)$ into $L_2(\Omega)$, see Theorem 3.1. Problems of this type are called ill-posed in the mathematical literature, see, e.g., [63]. They can be solved by using *a priori* information, i.e., one assumes that the unknown function has certain properties, like smoothness, boundedness, etc. In view of the discussion in Section III we assume that $f \in H_0^\alpha(\Omega)$ for some $\alpha > 0$.

Theorem 6.2: Let $\|Rf - g\|_{0, Z} \leqslant \epsilon$ and $\|f\|_\alpha \leqslant \rho$. Then a reconstruction f^* to f can be computed from g, α, ρ, ϵ such that

$$\|f - f^*\|_0 \leqslant c(N) \, \epsilon^{(2\alpha)/(N-1+2\alpha)} \rho^{(N-1)/(N-1+2\alpha)}$$

where $c(N)$ is a constant depending only on the dimension N.

This theorem for which a proof is given in the Appendix, reveals that the sensitivity of pictures with respect to data errors depends largely on the smoothness of the picture. For high-contrast pictures, $\alpha \sim \frac{1}{2}$, hence the exponent of ϵ in the estimate for $\|f - f^*\|_0$ is close to $1/N$. This means that the number of significant digits in the reconstruction is roughly $(1/N)$th of the number of significant digits in the data. For smooth pictures, however, $\alpha \gg 1$, and the exponent of ϵ is close to 1, i.e., the numbers of significant digits in the reconstruction and in the data are roughly equal.

Theorem 6.2 is not realistic in as much that it assumes that Rf is sampled continuously. The next theorem deals with the case of discrete erroneous sampling.

Theorem 6.3: Let Rf be sampled at points $s_l = lh$, $l = 0$, $\pm 1, \cdots, \pm q = [1/h]$, and ω_j, $j = 1, \cdots, p$ such that for each $\omega \in S^{N-1}$ there is a j with $|\omega - \omega_j| \leq h$. Let ϵ_{lj} be the measurement error at (s_l, ω_j), and let

$$\epsilon = \left(\sum_{l,j} \epsilon_{l,j}^2 / 2pq \right)^{1/2}.$$

If $f \in H_0^\alpha(\Omega)$ and $\|f\|_\alpha \leq \rho$, then a reconstruction from the sampled values and the numbers α, ρ, ϵ can be computed such that

$$\|f^* - f\|_0 \leq c(N) \{h^\alpha + \epsilon^{(2\alpha)/(N-1+2\alpha)}\} (\rho + 1)$$

where $c(N)$ is some constant depending only on N.

This is the N-dimensional version of [48, Theorem 5.1]. As might have been expected, the exponents of ϵ in the last two theorems coincide. The latter theorem shows that the accuracy obtainable from finitely many samples of the data also depends basically on the smoothness of the picture, as can be seen from the appearance of the term h^α in that theorem.

A. Notes and References

Apparently, the first answer to the question of resolution has been given in [7] for $N = 2$ and uniform sampling in s and ω: In order to reconstruct a function with bandwidth b (where $b = 2\pi/d$, as defined earlier), one needs $p > b$ equally spaced projections, each sampled at the Nyquist rate $h = \pi/b$. While the proof basically depends on a somewhat loose application of the sampling theorem in polar coordinates, the proofs in [30] and [64] are based on an error analysis for reconstruction algorithms. Since $n = p$ for $N = 2$, Theorem 6.1 shows that this condition is, in fact, sufficient. However, the directions clearly need not be equally spaced. This follows also from [32], where a careful analysis in the transition region $p \sim b$ has been given.

The proof of Theorem 6.2 is patterned after [2]. That article also contains a general discussion of the ill-posedness of the Radon and other problems.

The error caused by using only a finite number of directions has also been considered in [8] and [41]. The latter paper contains an estimate which roughly corresponds to our Theorem 6.3 with $N = 2$, $\epsilon = 0$, and continuous sampling in s.

Theorems 6.2 and 6.3 rely heavily on the assumption that Rf is sampled (discretely or continuously) on all of $[-1, +1] \times S^{N-1}$. We do not know how the reconstruction error depends on ϵ if Rf is sampled only in a part of that region, see Section VII.

VII. Incomplete Data

A. The Limited Angle Problem

In practical applications, the problem often arises that the projection data are known only in a subset $S \subset S^{N-1}$. Let us consider the case $N = 2$ and denote again by $\omega = (\cos \varphi, \sin \varphi)^T$ the directions in S^1. We assume that the data $Rf(s, \omega)$ are missing for $|\varphi| \leq \theta < \pi/2$. Although Theorem 5.1 assures that f is uniquely determined, inversion formulas in the form of (4.1) do not exist.

Several attempts have been made to solve this problem. According to the projection theorem the Fourier transform of f is known for values $\sigma \cdot \omega$ where $|\varphi| > \theta$. Since f has compact support, the Fourier transform of f is an analytic function which can be computed for all of $\mathbb{R}^2$ by analytical continuation, see [22]. The backprojection of the data over $|\varphi| > \theta$ produces $B * f$ but $\hat{B}$ vanishes on a part of $\mathbb{R}^2$. Using the generalized inverse, one gets the minimum-norm solution in $L_2(\mathbb{R}^2)$ which does not have compact support, see [69]. The function computed in this way can be used as an initial point in an iteration. In each step, one forces the function to have compact support, to have the same Fourier transform as the searched-for density in the domain where it is known. Also other features can be included, see [11], [28], [62].

An approximate inversion formula patterned after (4.1) is given in [8]. Filter functions depending on the angles are developed such that the reconstruction $\Phi * f$ is a good approximation to the solution f.

Finally, we give an inversion formula based on the Helgason–Ludwig consistency conditions. The series expansion for the Radon transform given in (4.11) has here the form

$$Rf(s, \omega) = (1 - s^2)^{1/2} \sum_{m=0}^{\infty} U_m(s) q_m(\omega) \qquad (7.1)$$

where U_m is the Chebyshev polynomial of the second kind and q_m is

$$q_m(\omega) = \frac{2}{\pi} \int_{-1}^{1} Rf(s, \omega) U_m(s) \, ds$$

$$= \sum_{l=0}^{m} d_{m,l} e^{i(2l-m)\varphi}. \qquad (7.2)$$

The function $q_m(\omega)$ is computable from the data for $|\varphi| > \theta$. Using the orthogonality of the exponential function we get the system of linear equations for the $d_m = (d_{m,0}, \cdots, d_{m,m})^T$

$$(I - A_m(\theta)) d_m = Q_m \qquad (7.3)$$

where Q_m is the vector whose kth component is

$$Q_{m,k} = \frac{1}{\pi} \int_{\theta}^{\pi - \theta} q_m(\omega) e^{i(m - 2k)\varphi} \, d\varphi$$

and the matrix $A_m(\theta)$ is equal to the matrix $\rho(m + 1, \theta/\pi)$ studied in [58]

$$A_m(\theta)_{lk} = \frac{1}{\pi} \begin{cases} 2\theta, & \text{for } l = k \\ \dfrac{1}{l - k} \sin 2(l - k)\theta, & \text{for } l \neq k. \end{cases} \qquad (7.4)$$

It is shown in [58] that $I - A_m$ is invertible and that the spectrum of the matrix $A_m(\theta)$ splits into two subsets, some eigenvalues are close to 1 and the rest are close to 0. The number of eigenvalues close to 1 is proportional to $(\pi - 2\theta)/\pi$, i.e., the smaller the missing range the better is the condition number of the problem. Different methods for the study of the ill-conditioned nature of this problem have been used in [9].

Solving the system of equations in (7.3) we know the expansion coefficients of the Radon transform. In principle, it is possible to compute the function f with the help of (4.13) but this method is too slow for practical application. Fast implementations compute the g_m in (7.2) in the missing range and then use an inversion algorithm for the full-range problem. The extrapolation procedure for the data is as fast as the filtered backprojection. Algorithms are given in [33] and [34]. A careful solution of the system of equations is necessary due to the ill-conditioned nature of the problem; see also [51].

B. Truncated Projections

From Section V-B we know that f cannot, in general, be computed uniquely from truncated data. However, it turns out that the functions in the null space $K = \{f \in L_2(\Omega): Rf(s, \omega) = 0 \text{ for } |s| \leqslant a\}$ of the truncated Radon transform are almost constant in the interior of Ω_a. For, let $f \in K$ and $g = Rf$. Then, integrating by parts in the inversion formula (4.5) we obtain in the case $N = 2$ for $|x| < a$

$$f(x) = \frac{1}{4\pi^2} \int_{S^1} \int_{|s|>a} g(s, \omega) (s - x \cdot \omega)^{-2} \, ds \, d\omega.$$

Hence

$$|f(x) - f(a)| = \frac{1}{4\pi^2} \left| \int_{S^1} \int_{|s|>a} g(s, \omega) \right.$$
$$\left. \cdot \{(s - x \cdot \omega)^{-2} - s^{-2}\} \, ds \, d\omega \right|$$
$$\leqslant \|g\|_{0,Z} \, c(x, a)$$

$$c(x, a) = \frac{1}{2\pi^2} \left(\int_{S^1} \int_a^1 |(s - x \cdot \omega)^{-2} \right.$$
$$\left. - s^2|^2 \, ds \, d\omega \right)^{1/2}.$$

By numerical integration it has been shown (see [14]) that $c(x, a)$ is surprisingly small if x is well in the interior of Ω_a and if Ω_a is not too small, e.g., for $a = \frac{1}{2}$ and $|x| < \frac{1}{4}$.

Our conclusion is that truncated data determine f in the interior of Ω_a up to a function which is almost constant. In fact, the reconstructions done in [50] from truncated data with various algorithms are simply lifted versions of the original inside Ω_a. This means that density differences can be reconstructed reliably from truncated data.

If one is interested in the absolute values of the density, one has to preprocess the truncated data. This is done by estimating the values of $Rf(s, \omega)$ for $|s| > a$ from a priori information on the object, such as its size or boundary. How this can be done is described in [31].

C. Hollow Projections

From Theorem 5.5 we know that f is determined uniquely in the scanned region by the incomplete data. In the 2D case, f is given explicitly by Cormack's inversion formula (4.10): The angular Fourier coefficients f_k, g_k of f, $g = Rf$, respectively, are related by

$$f_k(r) = -\frac{1}{\pi} \int_r^1 T_k\left(\frac{t}{r}\right) (t^2 - r^2)^{-1/2} \, g_k'(t) \, dt.$$

Since this formula integrates only over $[r, 1]$, $f(x)$ can be computed for $|x| \geqslant a$ if $g(s, \omega)$ is known for $|s| \geqslant a$. However, we have a stability problem: For $u = t/r > 1$, $T_k(u)$ increases

exponentially as $k \to \infty$

$$T_k(u) = \cosh(k \cosh^{-1} u) \geqslant \tfrac{1}{2} (u + \sqrt{u^2 - 1})^k.$$

Hence we expect reconstruction from hollow data to be extremely sensitive with respect to noise and discretization errors.

A stable version of Cormack's formula has been derived in [52]. However, this formula integrates over $[0, 1]$ rather than over $[r, 1]$ and hence does not allow the reconstruction from hollow projections. As in the truncated case, projection completion methods can be used, as suggested in [31].

D. Regularized Least Squares Solutions

For many incomplete data problems, explicit inversion formulas are not known or difficult to use. Therefore, a more direct approach is advisable using only simple tools from linear algebra rather than the sophisticated analytical apparatus of Section IV. Since incomplete data problems are usually severely ill-posed we outline, in the following, the application of the well-known method of regularization to tomographic problems.

Denote by L_{jl}, $j = 1, \cdots, p$, $l = 1, \cdots, q$ a two-parameter family of strips or cones (or whatever satisfies assumption (7.8) below). We want to recover $f \in L_2(\Omega)$ from the integrals

$$R_{jl} f = \int_{L_{jl}} f(x) \, dx.$$

In order to allow for measurement errors in the $R_{jl} f$, we take as reconstructions f_δ^* for f the regularized least squares solution of this system, i.e., f_δ^* minimizes

$$\sum_{j,l} (g_{jl} - R_{jl} f)^2 + \delta^2 \|f\|_0^2 \qquad (7.5)$$

in $L_2(\Omega)$, where g_{jl} is the measured value for $R_{jl} f$ and $\delta^2 > 0$ is the regularization parameter. The choice of δ is crucial for the performance of the method. If δ is too big, then f_δ^* will look rather flat, no matter what the data are. If δ is too small, then f_δ^* will show large oscillations which have nothing to do with the true f, since in this case the method tries to fit $R_{jl} f_\delta^*$ to the erroneous g_{jl} too closely. There are some methods for computing an optimal value from the data [68]. A good value of δ can usually be found by reconstructing typical objects using a few values of δ.

Finding f_δ^* is a minimization problem in the Hilbert space $L_2(\Omega)$. It is easy to derive the following representation of its solution: f_δ^* is given by

$$f_\delta(x) = \sum_{x \in L_{jl}} r_{jl} \qquad (7.6)$$

where the r_{jl} are any solution of

$$\sum_{i,k} s_{jl,ik} \, r_{ik} + \delta^2 r_{jl} = g_{jl}.$$

$$s_{jl,ik} = \text{area} \, (L_{jl} \cap L_{ik} \cap \Omega). \qquad (7.7)$$

Formula (7.6) is essentially a backprojection as used in many reconstruction algorithms. In practical, applications the solution of the linear system (7.7) by standard methods would take an unacceptably long time on present-day computers. However, if the L_{jl} enjoy a certain rotational invariance, then (7.7) can be solved very efficiently. More precisely, we assume that there is an angle α such that

For $j = 0, \cdots, p - 1$, a rotation of L_{jl} by an angle α around the origin takes L_{jl} into $L_{j+1,l}$. (7.8)

Examples of scanning geometries satisfying (7.8) are the parallel and the fan-beam geometries, possibly with truncated and hollow projections and limited angle, and in three dimensions the cone-beam geometry if the sources are properly placed, e.g., if they are equally spaced on circles, as suggested in [25], [26], [13].

If condition (7.8) is met, then the $s_{jl,ik}$ depend only on $|j - i|$, and (7.7) reduces to

$$\sum_{i=0}^{p} S_{|i-j|} r_i + \delta^2 r_j = g_j, \quad j = 0, \cdots, p \quad (7.9)$$

where

$$r_i = \begin{pmatrix} r_{i1} \\ \vdots \\ r_{iq} \end{pmatrix} \quad g_j = \begin{pmatrix} g_{j1} \\ \vdots \\ g_{jq} \end{pmatrix}$$

and the k, l−element of the $q \times q$−matrix S_j is $(S_j)_{kl} = $ area $(L_{jk} \cap L_{0l} \cap \Omega)$.

The matrix S of (7.9) has the form

$$S = \begin{pmatrix} S_0 + \delta^2 I, & S_1, & \cdots, & S_p \\ S_1, & S_0 + \delta^2 I, S_1, & \cdots, & S_{p-1} \\ \vdots & \vdots & \vdots & \vdots \\ S_p, & S_{p-1}, \cdots, & S_2, & S_0 + \delta^2 I \end{pmatrix}.$$

I is the $q \times q$ unit matrix. A matrix of this type is called block-Toeplitz. S is invertible for $\delta^2 > 0$, and its inverse can be decomposed into

$$S^{-1} = L_1 U_1 + L_2 U_2$$

where L_i, U_i are lower and upper triangular block-Toeplitz matrices [3]. Once the L_i, U_i have been found and stored, (7.9) can be solved by performing four convolutions of length $p + 1$ (at most) on vectors of dimension q. This can be done very efficiently by means of FFT techniques. The number of arithmetic operation is of the order pq^2.

Exploiting rotational invariance is the underlying idea for many reconstruction algorithms ([1], [25], [13], [10]). The present algorithm, which has been suggested first in [27], differs from the others in that it does not use any discretization or series expansion of f. Numerical results for truncated and hollow projections have been obtained in [50].

APPENDIX

Proof of Theorem 6.2: For some $b > 0$ we define

$$\widehat{f}^*(\xi) = (2\pi)^{(1-N)/2} \widehat{g}(|\xi|, \xi/|\xi|)$$

$$\widehat{f}_b(\xi) = \widehat{f}(\xi)$$

for $|\xi| \leq b$ and $\widehat{f}^*(\xi) = \widehat{f}_b(\xi) = 0$ for $|\xi| > b$. From (3.6) we obtain for $|\xi| \leq b$

$$(f^* - f_b)^{\wedge}(\xi) = (2\pi)^{(1-N)/2} (g - Rf)^{\wedge}(|\xi|, \xi/|\xi|).$$

Hence, by Parseval's relation,

$$\|f^* - f_b\|_0^2 = (2\pi)^{1-N} \int_{|\xi| \leq b} |(g - Rf)^{\wedge}(|\xi|, \xi/|\xi|)|^2 \, d\xi$$

$$= (2\pi)^{1-N} \int_0^b \sigma^{N-1}$$

$$\cdot \int_{S^{N-1}} |(g - Rf)^{\wedge}(\sigma, \omega)|^2 \, d\omega \, d\sigma$$

$$\leq (2\pi)^{1-N} b^{N-1}$$

$$\cdot \int_0^b \int_{S^{N-1}} |(g - Rf)^{\wedge}(\sigma, \omega)|^2 \, d\omega \, d\sigma$$

$$\leq (2\pi)^{1-N} b^{N-1} \epsilon^2.$$

Also

$$\|f_b - f\|_0^2 = \int_{|\xi| \geq b} |\widehat{f}(\xi)|^2 \, d\xi$$

$$\leq b^{-2\alpha} \int (1 + |\xi|^2)^\alpha |\widehat{f}(\xi)|^2 \, d\xi$$

$$= b^{-2\alpha} \|f\|_0^2.$$

Combining the last two estimates yields

$$\|f^* - f\|_0 \leq \|f^* - f_b\|_0 + \|f_b - f\|_0$$

$$\leq (2\pi)^{(1-N)/2} b^{(N-1)/2} \epsilon + b^{-\alpha} \rho.$$

Balancing terms by putting $b = (\rho/\epsilon)^{1/(\alpha + (N-1)/2)}$ we obtain the theorem with $c(N) = (2\pi)^{(1-N)/2} + 1$.

REFERENCES

[1] M. D. Altschuler and G. T. Herman, "Fully-three-dimensional image reconstruction using series expansion methods," in *A Review of Information Processing in Medical Imaging*, A. B. Brill, Ed., Oak Ridge National Laboratory, Oak Ridge, TN, pp. 124–142.

[2] M. Bertero, C. De Mol, and G. A. Viano, "The stability of inverse problems," in H. P. Baltes, Ed., *Inverse Scattering Problems*. Berlin: Springer, 1980.

[3] R. R. Bitmead and B.D.O. Anderson, "Asymptotically fast solutions of Toeplitz and related systems of linear equations," Tech. Rep. EE 7915, Dep. Elec. Electron. Eng., James Cook Univ., Queensland, Australia, 4811.

[4] T. F. Budinger, G. T. Gullberg, and R. H. Huesman, "Emission computed tomography," in G. T. Herman, Ed., *Image Reconstruction from Projections*. Berlin: Springer, 1979.

[5] A. M. Cormack, "Representation of a function by its line integrals, with some radiological applications I," *J. Appl. Phys.*, vol. 34, pp. 2722–2727, 1963.

[6] ——, "Representation of a function by its line integrals, with some radiological applications II," *J. Appl. Phys.*, vol. 35, pp. 2908–2913, 1964.

[7] R. A. Crowther, D. J. De Rosier, and A. Klug, "The reconstruction of a three-dimensional structure from projections and its application to electron microscopy," *Proc. Roy. Soc. London*, vol. A 317, pp. 319–340, 1970.

[8] M. E. Davison and F. A. Grünbaum, "Tomographic reconstruction with arbitrary directions," *Commun. Pure Appl. Math.*, vol. 34, pp. 77–119, 1981.

[9] M. E. Davison, "The ill-conditioned nature of the limited angle tomography problem," to appear in *SIAM J. Appl. Math.*

[10] P.P.B. Eggermont, "Special discretization methods for the integral equations of image reconstruction and for Abel-type integral equations," Tech. Rep. MIP G 50, Medical Image Processing Group, SUNY, 1980.

[11] F. A. Grünbaum, "A study of Fourier space methods for limited angle image reconstruction," *Numer. Func. Anal. Opt.*, vol. 2, pp. 32–42, 1980.

[12] ——, "Reconstruction with arbitrary directions: Dimensions two and three," in G. T. Herman and F. Natterer, Eds., *Mathematical Aspects of Computerized Tomography*. Berlin: Springer, 1981, pp. 112–126.

[13] F. S. Ham, "Theory of tomographic image reconstruction: Proof that the reconstruction matrix reduces to block form in rotation-reflection symmetry," Gen. Elec., Tech. Rep.

[14] C. Hamaker, K. T. Smith, D. C. Solmon, and S. L. Wagner, "The divergent beam X-ray transform," *Rocky Mountain J. Math.*, vol. 10, pp. 253–283, 1980.

[15] C. Hamaker and D. C. Solmon, "The angles between the null spaces of X-rays," *J. Math. Anal. Appl.*, vol. 62, pp. 1–23, 1978.

[16] S. Helgason, "Differential operators on homogeneous spaces," *Acta Math.*, vol. 102, pp. 239–299, 1959.

[17] ——, "The Radon transform on Euclidian spaces, compact two-point homogeneous spaces, and Grassmann manifolds," *Acta Math.*, vol. 113, pp. 153–180, 1965.

[18] ——, *The Radon Transform.* Boston, MA: Birkhäuser, 1980.

[19] G. T. Herman, Ed., *Image Reconstruction from Projections: Implementation and Applications.* Berlin: Springer, 1979.

[20] G. T. Herman, *Image Reconstruction from Projections: The Fundamentals of Computerized Tomography.* New York: Academic Press, 1980.

[21] G. T. Herman and F. Natterer, Eds., *Mathematical Aspects of Computerized Tomography*. Berlin: Springer, LNMI 8, 1981.

[22] T. Inouye, "Image reconstruction with limited angle projection data," *IEEE Trans. Nucl. Sci.*, vol. NS-26, pp. 2666–2669, 1979.

[23] F. John, "Bestimmung einer Funktion aus ihren Integralen über gewisse Mannigfaltigkeiten," *Math. Ann.*, vol. 109, pp. 488–520, 1934.

[24] M. B. Katz, *Questions of Uniqueness and Resolution in Reconstruction from Projections.* Berlin: Springer, LNB 26, 1978.

[25] G. Kowalski, "Multislice reconstruction from beam scanning," *IEEE Trans. Nucl. Sci.*, vol. NS-26, no. 2, Apr. 1979.

[26] J. K. Leahy, K. T. Smith, and D. C. Solmon, "Uniqueness, non-uniqueness and inversion in the X-ray and Radon problems," to appear in *Proc. Int. Symp. on Ill-Posed Problems: Theory and Practice* (Univ. Delaware, Newark, Oct. 2–6, 1979).

[27] A. Lent, Seminar talk at the Biodynamic Research Unit, Mayo Clinic, Rochester, MN, 1975.

[28] A. Lent and H. Tuy, "An iterative method for the extrapolation of band limited functions," *J. Math. Anal. Appl.*, vol. 83, pp. 554–565, 1981.

[29] I. Lerche and E. Zeitler, "Projections, reconstructions and orthogonal functions," *J. Math. Anal. Appl.*, vol. 56, pp. 634–649, 1976.

[30] R. M. Lewitt, R.H.T. Bates, and T. M. Peters, "Image reconstruction from projections, II: Modified backprojection methods," *Optik*, vol. 50, pp. 85–109, 1978.

[31] R. M. Lewitt and R.H.T. Bates, "Image reconstruction from projections, III: Projection completion methods (theory)," *Optik*, vol. 50, pp. 180–205, 1978.

[32] B. G. Logan, "The uncertainty principle in reconstructing functions from projections," *Duke Math. J.*, vol. 42, pp. 661–706, 1975.

[33] A. K. Louis, "Picture reconstruction from projections in restricted range," *Math. Meth. in Appl. Sci.*, vol. 2, pp. 209–220, 1980.

[34] ——, "Approximation of the Radon transform from samples in limited range," in G. T. Herman and F. Natterer, Eds., *Mathematical Aspects of Computized Tomography*. Berlin: Springer, LNMI 8, 1981, pp. 127–139.

[35] ——, "Ghosts in tomography—The null space of the Radon transform," *Math. Meth. in Appl. Sci.*, vol. 3, pp. 1–10, 1981.

[36] ——, "Orthogonal function series expansions and the null space of the Radon transform, *SIAM J. Math. Anal.*, in press.

[37] ——, "Optimal sampling in nuclear magnetic resonance tomography," *Comput. Assist. Tomogr.*, vol. 6, pp. 334–340, 1982.

[38] ——, "Analytische Methoden in der Computer Tomographie," Habilitationsschrift, Münster Univ., 1981.

[39] K. H. Löw and F. Natterer, "An ultra-fast algorithm in tomography," Fachbereich der Universität des Saarlandes, 6600 Saarbrücken, Germany, Tech. Rep. A81/03.

[40] D. Ludwig, "The Radon transform on Euclidean spaces," *Commun. Pure Appl. Math.*, vol. 19, pp. 49–81, 1966.

[41] W. R. Madych, "Degree of approximation in computerized tomography," in E. W. Cheney, Ed., *Approximation Theory III*. New York: Academic Press, 1980.

[42] R. B. Marr, "On the reconstruction of a function on a circular domain from a sampling of its line integrals," *J. Math. Anal. Appl.*, vol. 19, pp. 357–374, 1974.

[43] ——, "An overview of image reconstruction," to appear in *Proc. Int. Symp. on Ill-Posed Problems: Theory and Practice* (Univ. of Delaware, Newark, Oct. 2–6, 1979).

[44] R. B. Marr, C. N. Chen, and P. C. Lauterbur, "On two approaches to 3D reconstruction in NMR zeugmatography," in G. T. Herman and F. Natterer, Eds., *Mathematical Aspects of Computerized Tomography*. Berlin: Springer, LNMI 8, 1981.

[45] G. N. Minerbo, "Convolutional reconstruction from cone-beam projection data," *IEEE Trans. Nucl. Sci.*, vol. NS-26, pp. 2682–2684, 1979.

[46] F. Natterer, "Computerized tomography with unknown sources," University Saarbrücken, Tech. Rep. TR A81/06, FB 10, 1981.

[47] ——, *Genauigkeitsfragen bei der numerischen Rekonstruktion von Bildern.* Basel, Switzerland: Birkhäuser, ISNM 49, 1979, pp. 131–146.

[48] ——, "A Sobolev space analysis of picture reconstruction," *SIAM J. Appl. Math.*, vol. 39, pp. 402–411, 1980.

[49] ——, "The identification problem in emission computed tomography," in: G. T. Herman and F. Natterer, Eds., *Mathematical Aspects of Computerized Tomography*. Berlin: Springer, LNMI 8, 1981, pp. 45–56.

[50] ——, "Efficient implementation of 'optimal' algorithms in computerized tomography," *Math. Meth. in Appl. Sci.*, vol. 2, pp. 545–555, 1980.

[51] A. Peres, "Tomographic reconstruction from limited angular data," *J. Comput. Assist. Tomogr.*, vol. 3, pp. 800–803, 1979.

[52] R. M. Perry, "Reconstructing a function by circular harmonic analysis of its line integrals," in *Image Processing for 2D and 3D Reconstruction from Projections*, Stanford, CA, 1975.

[53] E. T. Quinto, "Null spaces and ranges for the classical and spherical Radon transforms," *J. Math. Anal. Appl.*, vol. 90, pp. 408–429, 1982.

[54] J. Radon, "Über die Bestimmung von Funktionen durch ihre Integralwerte längs gewisser Mannigfaltigkeiten," *Ber. Verh. Sächs. Adad. Wiss. Leipzig*, vol. 69, pp. 262–277, 1917.

[55] S. W. Rowland, "Computer implementation of image reconstruction formulas," in G. T. Herman, Ed., *Image Reconstruction from Projections: Implementation and Applications*. Berlin: Springer, 1979, pp. 9–79.

[56] L. A. Shepp, "Computerized tomography and nuclear magnetic resonance," *J. Comput. Assist. Tomogr.*, vol. 4, pp. 94–107, 1980.

[57] L. A. Shepp and J. B. Kruskal, "Computerized tomography: The new medical X-ray technology," *Amer. Math. Monthly*, vol. 85, pp. 420–439, 1978.

[58] D. Slepian, "Prolate spheroidal wave functions, Fourier analysis and uncertainty—V: The discrete case," *Bell. Syst. Tech. J.*, vol. 57, pp. 1371–1430, 1978.

[59] K. T. Smith, D. C. Solmon, and S. L. Wagner, "Practical and mathematical aspects of the problem of reconstructing objects from radiographs," *Bul. AMS 83*, pp. 1227–1270, 1977.

[60] D. C. Solmon, "The X-ray transform," *J. Math. Anal. Appl.*, vol. 56, pp. 61–83, 1976.

[61] H. Stark, J. W. Woods, I. Paul, and R. Hingorani, "An investigation of computerized tomography by direct Fourier inversion and optimum interpolation," *IEEE Trans. Biomed. Eng.*, vol. BME-28, pp. 496–505, 1981.

[62] K. C. Tam, V. Perez-Mendez, and B. MacDonald, "Limited angle 3-D reconstruction from continuous and pinhole projection," *IEEE Trans. Nucl. Sci.*, vol. NS-27, pp. 445–458, 1980.

[63] A. N. Tikhonov and V. Y. Arsenin, *Solution of Ill-Posed Problems.* New York: Wiley, 1977.

[64] O. J. Tretiak, "The point-spread function for the convolution algorithm," in R. Gordon, Ed., *Image Processing for 2-D and 3-D Reconstruction from Projections*. Stanford, 1975.

[65] O. J. Tretiak and P. Delaney, "The exponential convolution algorithm for emission computed axial tomography," in *Proc. 5th Int. Conf. on Information Processing in Medical Imaging*, 1978.

[66] O. J. Tretiak and C. Metz, "The exponential Radon transform," *SIAM J. Appl. Math.*, vol. 39, pp. 341–354, 1980.

[67] H. Triebel, *Interpolation Theory, Function Spaces, Differential Operation.* Amsterdam: North-Holland, 1978.

[68] H. K. Tuy, "An inversion formula for cone-beam reconstruction," SUNY Buffalo, Tech. Rep. TR M1PG 57, 1981.

[69] ——, "Reconstruction of a three-dimensional object from a limited range of views," *J. Math. Anal. Appl.*, vol. 80, pp. 598–616, 1981.

[70] G. Wahba, "A new approach to the numerical evaluation of the inverse Radon transform with discrete, noisy data," in G. T. Herman and F. Natterer, Eds., *Mathematical Aspects of Computerized Tomography*. Berlin: Springer, 1981.

[71] K. Yosida, *Functional Analysis*, 6th ed. Berlin: Springer, 1980.

Reconstruction Algorithms: Transform Methods

ROBERT M. LEWITT, MEMBER, IEEE

Invited Paper

Abstract—Transform methods for image reconstruction from projections are based on analytic inversion formulas. In this tutorial paper, the inversion formula for the case of two-dimensional (2-D) reconstruction from line integrals is manipulated into a number of different forms, each of which may be discretized to obtain different algorithms for reconstruction from sampled data. For the convolution–backprojection algorithm and the direct Fourier algorithm the emphasis is placed on understanding the relationship between the discrete operations specified by the algorithm and the functional operations expressed by the inversion formula. The performance of the Fourier algorithm may be improved, with negligible extra computation, by interleaving two polar sampling grids in Fourier space. The convolution–backprojection formulas are adapted for the fan-beam geometry, and other reconstruction methods are summarized, including the rho-filtered layergram method, and methods involving expansions in angular harmonics. A standard mathematical process leads to a known formula for iterative reconstruction from projections at a finite number of angles. A new iterative reconstruction algorithm is obtained from this formula by introducing one-dimensional (1-D) and 2-D interpolating functions, applied to sampled projections and images, respectively. These interpolating functions are derived by the same Fourier approach which aids in the development and understanding of the more conventional transform methods.

I. Introduction

A. Scope

ALGORITHMS for image reconstruction from projections have extended our ability to visualize the internal structures of objects in a broad spectrum of physical applications, ranging from molecular dimensions (electron microscopy) to cosmic dimensions (radio astronomy). These algorithms are applicable when measured data have the form of line or strip integrals of the spatial distribution of a physical property of interest. In Computerized Tomography (CT), for example, reconstructed images enable us to visualize the distribution of X-ray attenuation coefficient within cross sections of the human body.

Accompanying papers in this special issue discuss the physics and engineering of data acquisition in CT, and the interpretation of the reconstructed images. This paper is intended as an introduction to the principles and implementation of a group of image-reconstruction algorithms which may be classified as 'transform" methods. The complementary class of algorithms, whose underlying principles are quite different, are discussed in a companion paper by Censor on "series expansion" methods [1.1].

This paper does not detail the historical development of the subject nor does it attempt to review all of the large and rapidly expanding body of literature relevant to image reconstruction by transform methods. Consistent with the tutorial aim of the paper, the list of references is representative rather than exhaustive, and most of the references are concentrated at the ends of the major numbered sections, together with supplementary notes.

It has been found appropriate to include in this paper two recent developments which have not been published elsewhere and which fit in naturally with the basic subject matter and theme of the paper. The first is a novel technique, introduced in Section IV-B, to improve the polar sampling in the Fourier domain with negligible extra computation. The second recent development is a new iterative reconstruction algorithm which is based on an existing inversion formula, sometimes known as "continuous ART." This algorithm is derived in Section VII.

We restrict the scope of this paper to the simplest examples of transform methods, namely, those algorithms for reconstruction of a two-dimensional (2-D) image from integrals along lines in a plane. These algorithms are of course useful in many applications involving three-dimensional (3-D) objects because such objects can be decomposed into a stack of thin 2-D slices. If line-integral data are available for each of these individual slices independent of the others, then the 3-D reconstruction problem may be decomposed into repeated 2-D reconstruction of serial cross sections of the object. When the data set cannot be decomposed on a slice-by-slice basis, the problem is fully 3-D—see, for example, Altschuler *et al.* [1.2]. Louis and Natterer [1.3] present the generalization to higher dimensions of some of the 2-D reconstruction formulas with which we are concerned in the present paper.

Section I presents basic concepts, terminology, and notation. The fundamental results derived in Section II are used to develop reconstruction formulas and the method of convolution-backprojection is derived and analyzed in Section III. Section IV discusses the inherent problems associated with the deceptively simple Fourier algorithm, and indicates ways in which its performance may be improved. The convolution–backprojection method is adapted for the fan-beam geometry in Section V. Section VI summarizes other reconstruction methods, including the rho-filtered layergram method, and methods involving expansions in angular harmonics. In Section VII, a new iterative reconstruction algorithm is derived from an existing inversion formula in a way that is comparable to the derivation of the other algorithms in this paper.

B. Preliminaries

We denote by $f(x, y)$ the function which represents the spatial distribution of some physical quantity in two dimensions. Although f is unknown *a priori*, in most applications it is known that the distribution is spatially bounded, so that f vanishes outside a finite region of the 2-D plane, which we

Manuscript received August 19, 1982; revised December 13, 1982. This work was supported by National Cancer Institute under Grant CA31843 and by the National Heart, Lung and Blood Institute under Grants HL28438 and HL4664.

The author is with the Medical Image Processing Group, Department of Radiology, Hospital of the University of Pennsylvania, Philadelphia, PA 19104.

Reprinted from *Proc. IEEE*, vol. 71, pp. 390–408, Mar. 1983.

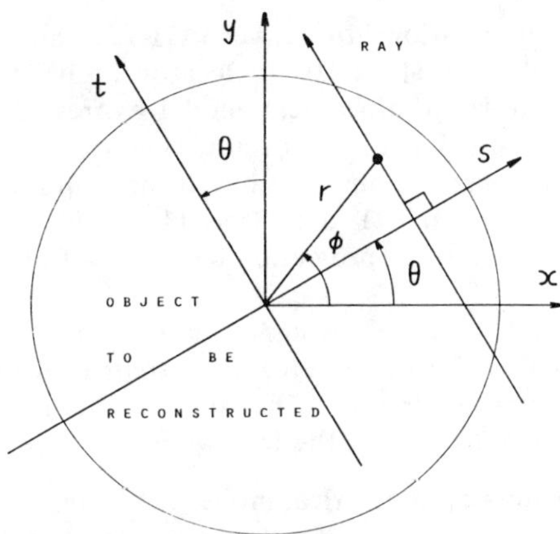

Fig. 1. The position of a point in the plane is specified by (x, y) or $(r \cos \phi, r \sin \phi)$. A ray is specified by its perpendicular distance (s) from the origin and its orientation (θ).

denote by Ω. Unless stated otherwise, we assume that f has been scaled and centered so that the corresponding Ω is a circle of unit radius centered at the origin of the coordinate system.

It is sometimes more convenient to express f in terms of polar coordinates (r, ϕ) rather than Cartesian coordinates (x, y). In this case we write

$$f(x, y) = f(r \cos \phi, r \sin \phi). \tag{1.1}$$

A line in the plane is specified by two parameters: its (signed) distance s from the origin and its angle θ with respect to the y-axis (see Fig. 1). We denote by $p(s, \theta)$ that function of two variables whose value for any (s, θ) is defined as the line-integral of f along the line specified by s and θ

$$p(s, \theta) = \int_{-T}^{T} f(s \cos \theta - t \sin \theta, s \sin \theta + t \cos \theta) \, dt$$

$$\tag{1.2}$$

where the limits of integration depend, in general, on s, θ, and Ω. For our standard case where Ω is the unit circle, we have

$$T(s) = (1 - s^2)^{1/2}, \qquad |s| \leqslant 1 \tag{1.3}$$

$$p(s, \theta) = 0, \qquad |s| > 1. \tag{1.4}$$

Note that for any s and θ, (s, θ) and $(-s, \theta + \pi)$ represent the same line in the plane, so that

$$p(s, \theta) = p(-s, \theta + \pi). \tag{1.5}$$

It is important to note that the arguments of the function $p(s, \theta)$ are *not* the familiar polar coordinates. To see this, consider two different straight lines through the origin, with angles θ_1 and θ_2. In general, the integrals of f are different for these two lines, so that $p(0, \theta_1)$ is not the same as $p(0, \theta_2)$, which does not make sense if the arguments are interpreted as polar coordinates. For this reason, some authors prefer to write $p(s; \theta)$ rather than $p(s, \theta)$.

At this point, it is convenient to collect together some of the terminology used in this paper. We refer to the *object* to be reconstructed (as represented by f), and a path of integration (specified by (s, θ)) is referred to as a *ray*. Further, when we relate theory to the geometry of typical scanning devices it is natural to refer to the "parallel-ray projection" of f at angle θ, that is, we consider the behavior of p as a function of s for a given, fixed, value of θ. In Section V we introduce the "diver-

gent-ray projection" of f, but in those parts of the paper preceding Section V we restrict our attention to the case of parallel-ray projections.

Both $p(s, \theta)$ and $f(r \cos \phi, r \sin \phi)$ are periodic functions of the angles θ and ϕ, respectively, so they may be represented using the following Fourier series expansions:

$$p(s, \theta) = \sum_{n=-\infty}^{\infty} p_n(s) \, e^{in\theta} \tag{1.6}$$

$$f(r \cos \phi, r \sin \phi) = \sum_{n=-\infty}^{\infty} f_n(r) \, e^{in\phi} \tag{1.7}$$

where the Fourier coefficients $p_n(s)$ and $f_n(r)$ may be found from

$$p_n(s) = \frac{1}{2\pi} \int_{0}^{2\pi} p(s, \theta) \, e^{-in\theta} \, d\theta \tag{1.8}$$

$$f_n(r) = \frac{1}{2\pi} \int_{0}^{2\pi} f(r \cos \phi, r \sin \phi) \, e^{-in\phi} \, d\phi. \tag{1.9}$$

In the following work we make frequent use of the Fourier transform in one and two dimensions. We use upper case letters for Fourier variables and a caret superscript for functions of these variables, so that $\hat{q}(X)$ denotes the function obtained by Fourier transformation of the function $q(x)$

$$\hat{q}(X) = \int_{-\infty}^{\infty} q(x) \, e^{-i2\pi Xx} \, dx. \tag{1.10}$$

In two dimensions

$$\hat{f}(X, Y) = \int_{-\infty}^{\infty} \int_{-\infty}^{\infty} f(x, y) \, e^{-i2\pi(Xx + Yy)} \, dx \, dy. \tag{1.11}$$

In terms of polar coordinates (R, θ) we have

$$\hat{f}(R \cos \theta, R \sin \theta) = \int_{0}^{2\pi} \int_{0}^{\infty} f(r \cos \phi, r \sin \phi)$$
$$\cdot e^{-i2\pi Rr \cos(\theta - \phi)} \, r \, dr \, d\phi \tag{1.12}$$

which can also be written as

$$\hat{f}(R \cos \theta, R \sin \theta) = \int_{0}^{\pi} \int_{-\infty}^{\infty} f(r \cos \phi, r \sin \phi)$$
$$\cdot e^{-i2\pi Rr \cos(\theta - \phi)} \, |r| \, dr \, d\phi. \tag{1.13}$$

The inverse Fourier transform corresponding to (1.10) is

$$q(x) = \int_{-\infty}^{\infty} \hat{q}(X) \, e^{i2\pi xX} \, dX \tag{1.14}$$

and the others follow a similar pattern.

If g and h are functions of one variable, the convolution of g and h, denoted by $g * h$, is

$$[g * h](x) = \int_{-\infty}^{\infty} g(x') \, h(x - x') \, dx'. \tag{1.15}$$

The convolution theorem for Fourier transforms may be

expressed as

$$[g * h]^{\wedge} = \hat{g}\,\hat{h}. \tag{1.16}$$

We denote by $\hat{q}_{\Sigma}(X)$ the function obtained by summing shifted versions of the function $\hat{q}(X)$ as follows:

$$\hat{q}_{\Sigma}(X) = \sum_{j=-\infty}^{\infty} \hat{q}(X + j/\Delta x) \tag{1.17}$$

where Δx is a specified constant. It is a well-known result of sampling theory that $\hat{q}_{\Sigma}(X)$ is the Fourier transform of the sampled version of the function $q(x)$, where the samples are spaced by Δx, from which it follows that

$$\hat{q}_{\Sigma}(X) = \Delta x \sum_{m=-\infty}^{\infty} \cdot q(m\Delta x)\, e^{-i2\pi X(m\Delta x)} \tag{1.18}$$

If $q(x)$ is zero outside an interval of finite extent, then $\hat{q}(X)$ is a particularly smooth function [1.4] which is infinite in extent. In other words, a function which is space-limited cannot also be band-limited. In the design of reconstruction algorithms using the transform approach it is often necessary to introduce a *window function* $W(X)$ which is zero for $|X| > C$, say, and which is used to multiply $\hat{q}(X)$ or $\hat{q}_{\Sigma}(X)$: the inverse transform of $[\hat{q}W](X)$ is a band-limited approximation to $q(x)$ and the inverse transform of $[\hat{q}_{\Sigma}W](X)$ is an *interpolated* version of $q(m\Delta x)$. If $q(x)$ is a band-limited function which is sampled with Δx small enough that $\hat{q}(X)$ is zero for $|X| \geq 1/(2\Delta x)$, then an appropriate choice for $W(X)$ is the following, with *cutoff frequency* C equal to $1/(2\Delta x)$:

$$W(X) = \begin{cases} 1, & |X| < C \\ 0, & |X| \geq C. \end{cases} \tag{1.19}$$

If $q(x)$ is not band-limited, then $\hat{q}(X)$ is overlapped by the "tails" of other components of $\hat{q}_{\Sigma}(X)$, namely, $\hat{q}(X + j/\Delta x)$ for $j \neq 0$. This phenomenon is called *aliasing*, and is a potential source of error when the function $q(x)$ (or its transform $\hat{q}(X)$) is to be recovered from its samples.

If $q(x)$ is not band-limited, then multiplication of $\hat{q}(X)$ or $\hat{q}_{\Sigma}(X)$ by a window function of the form (1.19) causes abrupt truncation of the function in the Fourier domain, which leads to oscillations in the spatial domain propagating from discontinuities in the original $q(x)$, analogous to the Gibbs phenomenon associated with truncation of a Fourier series. The amplitude of these oscillations may be reduced greatly by choosing a different window function whose value tapers less abruptly to zero at the cutoff frequency C.

C. The Problem, and Solution Methodologies

The problem of reconstruction from projections is the following: *given $p(s, \theta)$, find $f(x, y)$*. As a mathematical problem, where p and f are functions (known and unknown, respectively) finding f implies solving the integral equation (1.2). In fact, a solution was published by Radon in 1917 [1.5], with an inversion formula expressing f in terms of p.

The mathematical problem posed above, and solved by Radon, represents an idealized abstraction of the problem as it occurs in practical applications, that is: *given* discrete projection data in the form of estimates of p for a finite number of rays, *find* a 2-D image which is a reconstructed estimate of the unknown object. In addition to the discreteness and limited precision of measured data, we note in passing that a variety of physical problems [1.6], [1.7] can lead to significant non-

linearity in the relationship between CT data and the original object—see also [1.8]–[1.10]. Because of its mathematical tractability, however, the linear model expressed by (1.2) is the preferred starting point for the derivation of algorithms for image reconstruction, so that it becomes necessary to preprocess nonlinear CT data (see [1.6], [1.10]) into the form of estimates of p (projection data) for a finite number of rays.

Algorithms for image reconstruction from projection data may be classified into two categories: *transform methods* and *series expansion methods*. The approach used to derive a transform method involves the following sequence of steps:

1) formulate a mathematical model of the problem in which the known and unknown quantities are functions whose arguments come from a continuum of real numbers;
2) solve for the unknown function by producing an inversion formula;
3) adapt the inversion formula for application to discrete and noisy data.

In step 2), it is found that there are several formulas which are theoretically equivalent solutions to the problem posed in step 1). When each of these formulas is discretized (step 3)) it is found that the algorithms which result do not perform identically on real data, since different approximations have been introduced in step 3).

In contrast with step 1) above, the series-expansion approach to image reconstruction begins with a mathematical model of the problem which relates a finite set of known numbers (the projection data) to a finite set of unknown numbers, representing the image. This discrete formulation leads to a system of equations whose solution is found numerically, as opposed to the analytical solution obtained in step 2) of the transform approach.

Although the above classification of algorithms may appear to be clear-cut, in fact there exist algorithms of a "hybrid" nature, such as those discussed in Sections VI (B and C) and Section VII, which possess some of the characteristics of both transform and series-expansion approaches.

D. Sampled Projections and Images

In practical applications of reconstruction from projections, the measured data correspond to estimates of $p(s, \theta)$ for numerous discrete values of s and θ, and the reconstructed image is produced in the form of a 2-D array of numbers.

The principles involved in designing an algorithm for reconstruction from discrete data are illustrated most simply when p is sampled uniformly in both s and θ. We consider the case of projections which are measured at N angles $\Delta\theta$ apart, with M equispaced rays Δs apart for each of the angles of view, and we define the integers M^+ and M^- in terms of M as follows:

$$\left.\begin{array}{l} M^+ = (M - 1)/2 \\ M^- = -(M - 1)/2 \end{array}\right\} \quad M \text{ odd} \tag{1.20}$$

$$\left.\begin{array}{l} M^+ = M/2 - 1 \\ M^- = -M/2 \end{array}\right\} \quad M \text{ even.} \tag{1.21}$$

In order to ensure that the collection of rays specified by

$$\{(m\Delta s, n\Delta\theta): M^- \leq m \leq M^+,\ 1 \leq n \leq N\}$$

covers the unit circle (i.e., Ω) from a complete range of directions, we choose

$$\Delta\theta = \frac{\pi}{N} \qquad (1.22)$$

$$\Delta s = \frac{1}{M^+}. \qquad (1.23)$$

We refer to $p(m\Delta s, n\Delta\theta)$ as *parallel-ray data* to distinguish them from the *divergent-ray data* introduced in Section V. We consider a Cartesian grid of sample points in the image domain specified by $\{(k\Delta x, l\Delta y): K^- \leqslant k \leqslant K^+, L^- \leqslant l \leqslant L^+\}$, where K^- and K^+ are defined in terms of K, the number of points in the x-direction, analogous to (1.20), (1.21); L^- and L^+ are defined similarly in terms of L. A reconstruction algorithm is required to produce estimates of $f(k\Delta x, l\Delta y)$ at these $K \times L$ sample points from the $M \times N$ measurements $p(m\Delta s, \theta_n)$, where θ_n denotes $n\Delta\theta$. We denote by $\hat{p}(R, \theta_n)$ the 1-D Fourier transform with respect to s of the projection at angle θ_n, that is

$$\hat{p}(R, \theta_n) = \int_{-1}^{1} p(s, \theta_n)\, e^{-i2\pi Rs}\, ds. \qquad (1.24)$$

Consistent with (1.18) we define

$$\hat{p}_\Sigma(R, \theta_n) = \sum_{j=-\infty}^{\infty} \hat{p}(R + j/\Delta s, \theta_n). \qquad (1.25)$$

Now $p(s, \theta_n)$ is assumed to be zero for $|s| > 1$, so that this function is not band-limited, which implies that aliasing is present in the sampled data $p(m\Delta s, \theta_n)$ and in $\hat{p}_\Sigma(R, \theta_n)$. The aliasing may be reduced by filtering $p(s, \theta_n)$ before it is sampled and, in fact, the aperture of any physical measuring device has an averaging effect of this kind [1.6]. Even when aliasing is negligible, however, the sampled nature of the data implies that $\hat{p}(R, \theta_n)$ can be estimated only within the finite bandwidth $|R| < 1/(2\Delta s)$. It follows from the result stated in Theorem 2 below that when we reconstruct an image from sampled-projection data, it is unrealistic to expect a transform method to do better than estimate a function, denoted by $f_B(x, y)$, which is a band-limited approximation to $f(x, y)$. The Fourier transform of the function f_B may be expressed as the product of $\hat{f}$ and a window function $W(R)$, where R is the distance from the origin in Fourier space

$$\hat{f}_B(R \cos\theta, R \sin\theta) = \hat{f}(R \cos\theta, R \sin\theta)\, W(R). \qquad (1.26)$$

E. Notes and References

Image-reconstruction algorithms and their applications are discussed in a number of books [1.10]–[1.13], recent conference proceedings [1.14]–[1.19], special issues of journals [1.20]–[1.22], and review papers [1.2], [1.23]–[1.31]. Notes on early applications are contained in [1.32] and numerous current applications and future possibilities are described and classified in [1.33]. Mathematically oriented works include [1.34]–[1.36]; the latter contains a reprint of Radon's original paper [1.5]. Details of Radon's method of derivation may be followed more easily in [1.10, Sec. 16.2]. Radon's solution is not stated explicitly here—instead, we develop other inversion formulas (using the results in Section II) which are theoretically equivalent to Radon's.

Fourier transforms and sampling theory are discussed in many standard books, e.g., [1.37]. Sampling of projections is discussed in detail in [1.31], [1.38]. In this paper, we do not consider reconstruction from projection data which is incomplete, a situation that arises when the set of rays at a given angle does not span the whole object, or when a significant range of ray orientations (angles of view) is missing. Transform methods may be adapted to accommodate the former problem (hollow or truncated projections) [1.39]–[1.41], [1.2] and the latter problem (limited range of views) [1.42]–[1.45].

II. PROJECTION THEOREMS AND THEIR COROLLARIES

We refer to the following result as the *generalized projection theorem*.

Theorem 1: If $w(s)$ is any function of one variable for which the following integrals exist, then for all angles θ

$$\int_{-1}^{1} p(s, \theta)\, w(s)\, ds = \iint_\Omega f(x, y)\, w(x \cos\theta + y \sin\theta)\, dx\, dy.$$

$$(2.1)$$

Proof: Take the left side of (2.1), substitute for $p(s, \theta)$ from (1.2), and change variables of integration from rotated coordinates (s, t) to fixed coordinates (x, y).

Despite its simplicity, this result plays an important part in the derivation and understanding of many of the transform methods for image reconstruction. This result is useful because it shows that a specified operation on a projection at angle θ is equivalent to a related operation on the original object f. If the operation on f is invertible, such as Fourier transformation, for example, then we have at once a method for finding f, given p. This leads to an important special case of Theorem 1, the *projection theorem for Fourier transforms*.

Theorem 2: Let $\hat{p}(R, \theta)$ denote the 1-D Fourier transform of $p(s, \theta)$ with respect to the first variable, as defined in (1.24). Then

$$\hat{p}(R, \theta) = \hat{f}(R \cos\theta, R \sin\theta) \qquad (2.2)$$

Proof: In Theorem 1, substitute $\exp(-i2\pi Rs)$ for $w(s)$ in (2.1), and the result follows from the definitions of the 1-D and 2-D Fourier transforms in (1.24) and (1.11), respectively.

This result is sometimes called the *projection-slice theorem* or the *central-section theorem*, because of its physical interpretation. To see this, consider θ to be a given, fixed angle. Then the theorem says that as R varies, the value of $\hat{p}(R, \theta)$ is the same as the value of $\hat{f}$ at radius R and angle θ in Fourier space.

Another special case of Theorem 1 is the *projection-moment theorem*. We define $\mu^{(m)}(\theta)$, the mth moment of the projection at angle θ as

$$\mu^{(m)}(\theta) = \int_{-1}^{1} p(s, \theta)\, s^m\, ds. \qquad (2.3)$$

Theorem 3: Let $\mu^{(m)}(\theta)$ be as defined above, with m an integer and $m \geqslant 0$. Then for any such m there exist $2m + 1$ Fourier coefficients $\{\gamma_{m,n}, n = -m, \cdots, m\}$ such that

$$\mu^{(m)}(\theta) = \sum_{n=-m}^{m} \gamma_{m,n}\, e^{in\theta}. \qquad (2.4)$$

Proof: In Theorem 1, substitute s^m for $w(s)$ in (2.1). Then $w(\cos\theta + y \sin\theta)$ is a trigonometric polynomial and may be represented by a *finite* number of terms of an angular

Fourier series with coefficients denoted by $\alpha_{m,n}(x, y)$, that is

$$(x \cos \theta + y \sin \theta)^m = \sum_{n=-m}^{m} \alpha_{m,n}(x, y) \, e^{in\theta}. \qquad (2.5)$$

With the above substitutions in (2.1) we obtain the result of (2.4) with

$$\gamma_{m,n} = \iint_{\Omega} f(x, y) \, \alpha_{m,n}(x, y) \, dx \, dy. \qquad (2.6)$$

The significance of this result is that it tells us that the mth moment of the projection at angle θ does not change arbitrarily as θ varies: the mth moment varies no faster than $\cos (m\theta)$ or $\sin (m\theta)$. For example, the case $m = 0$ corresponds to the choice $w(s) = 1$ in (2.1), for which we find that the integral (over s) of $p(s, \theta)$ is independent of θ and its value is the double integral (over Ω) of $f(x, y)$.

It is easy to see that instead of considering moments, with $w(s) = s^m$, we would obtain a similar result by taking $w(s)$ as a polynomial of order m. In particular, if $w(s)$ is the Chebyshev polynomial of the second kind (order m), denoted by $U_m(s)$ [2.1], we have

$$\int_{-1}^{1} p(s, \theta) \, U_m(s) \, ds = \sum_{n=-m}^{m} c_{m,n} \, e^{in\theta} \qquad (2.7)$$

where the coefficients $c_{m,n}$ depend on f, as before. These coefficients can also be calculated from the projections using

$$c_{m,n} = \frac{1}{2\pi} \int_{0}^{2\pi} e^{-in\theta} \int_{-1}^{1} p(s, \theta) \, U_m(s) \, ds \, d\theta. \qquad (2.8)$$

If p is the projection of some object, as defined by (1.2), the coefficients calculated using (2.8) obey the following *consistency condition*:

$$c_{m,n} = 0, \qquad |n| > m. \qquad (2.9)$$

Also

$$c_{m,n} = 0, \qquad m + n \text{ odd} \qquad (2.10)$$

because of (1.5) and the fact that the even-(odd-) order Chebyshev polynomial is an even (odd) function of its argument.

If $w(s)$ is chosen as a member of a family of orthogonal polynomials, then the left side of (2.1) may be interpreted as the coefficient of an expansion of $p(s, \theta)$ in terms of these polynomials. For example, the $U_m(s)$ are orthogonal over $[-1, 1]$ with weight $(1 - s^2)^{1/2}$, that is,

$$\int_{-1}^{1} (1 - s^2)^{1/2} \, U_j(s) \, U_k(s) \, ds = \begin{cases} 0, & j \neq k \\ \pi/2, & j = k \end{cases} \qquad (2.11)$$

which leads, using (2.7), to the expansion

$$p(s, \theta) = \frac{2}{\pi} (1 - s^2)^{1/2} \sum_{m=0}^{\infty} \sum_{n=-m}^{m} c_{m,n} \, U_m(s) \, e^{in\theta}. $$

$$(2.12)$$

The results presented in this section express important properties of the projections and of their relationship to the original object. For a more complete and mathematically rigorous characterization, see [1.3] and [1.34]–[1.36].

III. Reconstruction by Convolution and Backprojection

A. Derivation of Reconstruction Formulas

The starting point for the derivation of this method is the projection theorem for Fourier transforms, but Fourier transforms do not appear explicitly in the final result. Taking the inverse Fourier transform of (2.2) we obtain

$$f(x, y) = \int_{0}^{\pi} \int_{-\infty}^{\infty} \hat{p}(R, \theta) \, e^{i2\pi R (x \cos \theta + y \sin \theta)} \, |R| \, dR \, d\theta.$$

$$(3.1)$$

When the definition (1.24) of $\hat{p}$ is substituted into (3.1) we obtain a reconstruction formula for $f(x, y)$, given $p(s, \theta)$.

For computations using sampled data, however, we need to introduce a window function in Fourier space, as explained in Section I-D, with the aim of reconstructing a function $f_B(x, y)$ which is a band-limited approximation to $f(x, y)$. Rewriting (3.1) in terms of $f_B(x, y)$, we find that

$$f_B(x, y) = \int_{0}^{\pi} \int_{-1/2\Delta s}^{1/2\Delta s} \hat{p}(R, \theta)$$

$$\cdot W(R) \, e^{i2\pi R (x \cos \theta + y \sin \theta)} \, |R| \, dR \, d\theta. \qquad (3.2)$$

We now substitute for $\hat{p}(R, \theta)$ from (1.24) and interchange the order of the integrations over s and R to obtain

$$f_B(x, y) = \int_{0}^{\pi} \int_{-1}^{1} p(s, \theta) \, q(x \cos \theta + y \sin \theta - s) \, ds \, d\theta$$

$$(3.3)$$

where

$$q(s) = \int_{-1/2\Delta s}^{1/2\Delta s} |R| \, W(R) \, e^{i2\pi Rs} \, dR. \qquad (3.4)$$

These equations form the basis of the method of reconstruction known as *convolution–backprojection* [3.1]–[3.4].

In order to see how this name arises, and how the method is implemented in practice, we decompose (3.3) into the following sequence of operations:

$$\tilde{p}(s', \theta) = \int_{-1}^{1} p(s, \theta) \, q(s' - s) \, ds \qquad (3.5)$$

$$f_B(x, y) = \int_{0}^{\pi} \tilde{p}(x \cos \theta + y \sin \theta, \theta) \, d\theta. \qquad (3.6)$$

The intermediate quantity $\tilde{p}(s', \theta)$, defined by (3.5), is the result of the convolution (over s) of the projection at angle θ and the function $q(s)$, defined by (3.4). We refer to $\tilde{p}(s, \theta)$ as the *convolved projection* at angle θ and we refer to $q(s)$ as the *convolving function*. Note that different convolving functions are obtained for different choices of the window function, since

$$\hat{q}(R) = |R| \, W(R). \qquad (3.7)$$

The operation represented by (3.6) is known as *backprojection*, and it has a simple geometrical interpretation. To see this, note that the arguments of $\tilde{p}$ in that equation are the parameters of a ray through the point (x, y) at angle θ, so that $f_B(x, y)$ is formed by the integration of the values of the convolved projections associated with all rays passing through the point (x, y).

B. Reconstruction Algorithm for Discrete Data

A reconstruction algorithm suitable for implementation using a digital computer is required to approximate $f_B(k\Delta x, l\Delta y)$, where $K^- \leqslant k \leqslant K^+$ and $L^- \leqslant l \leqslant L^+$, from $p(m\Delta s, \theta_n)$, where $M^- \leqslant m \leqslant M^+$ and $1 \leqslant n \leqslant N$ (recall the notation introduced in Section I-D). The simplest way to evaluate the backprojection integral is to use the trapezoidal rule

$$f_B(k\Delta x, l\Delta y) \simeq \Delta\theta \sum_{n=1}^{N} \widetilde{p}(k\Delta x \cos\theta_n + l\Delta y \sin\theta_n, \theta_n).$$

$$(3.8)$$

For each angle θ_n, we require the values of the convolved projection $\widetilde{p}(s', \theta_n)$ for $K \times L$ values of s'. One way to do this would be to perform a separate convolution for each individual value of s', using a trapezoidal approximation to (3.5) and appropriate samples $q(s' - m\Delta s)$ of the convolving function. Considering that $K \times L$ is usually between 256^2 and 512^2, this approach would be prohibitively expensive. A more practical approach is to evaluate $\widetilde{p}(m\Delta s, \theta_n)$ for $M^- \leqslant m \leqslant M^+$, and then use inexpensive interpolation to estimate the required $K \times L$ values of $\widetilde{p}$ from only M calculated values of the function. The convolution represented by (3.5) is therefore approximated by two operations on discrete data: a discrete convolution, the result of which is denoted by $\widetilde{p}_C$, followed by an interpolation operation, the result of which is denoted by $\widetilde{p}_I$. These operations are represented by the following pair of equations:

$$\widetilde{p}_C(m'\Delta s, \theta_n) = \Delta s \sum_{m=M^-}^{M^+} p(m\Delta s, \theta_n) q((m' - m)\Delta s),$$

$$M^- \leqslant m' \leqslant M^+ \quad (3.9)$$

$$\widetilde{p}_I(s', \theta_n) = \Delta s \sum_{m'} \widetilde{p}_C(m'\Delta s, \theta_n) I(s' - m'\Delta s) \quad (3.10)$$

where $I(s)$ is an *interpolating function* and the number of terms summed depends on the width of the nonzero part of $I(s)$. As an example, the function $I_L(s)$ corresponding to linear interpolation between adjacent samples is

$$I_L(s) = \begin{cases} \dfrac{1}{\Delta s}(1 - |s|/\Delta s), & |s| \leqslant \Delta s \\ 0, & |s| \geqslant \Delta s. \end{cases} \quad (3.11)$$

In this case, the sum in (3.10) has only two terms. Note that the discrete convolution (3.9) makes use of equispaced samples $q(m\Delta s)$ of the convolving function, which may be computed once for a particular choice of window function and stored. A possible candidate for the window function $W(R)$ is

$$W(R) = 1 - \epsilon|R|/C, \quad |R| \leqslant C$$

$$= 0, \quad |R| > C \quad (3.12)$$

where C is the cutoff frequency and the parameter ϵ takes values in the range $[0, 1]$. Putting $C = 1/(2\Delta s)$ and substituting into (3.4) we obtain

$$q(0) = \frac{3 - 2\epsilon}{12(\Delta s)^2} \quad (3.13a)$$

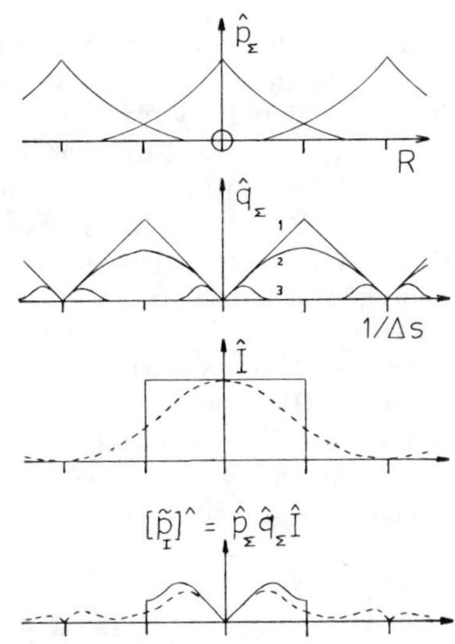

Fig. 2. Illustrative examples of the three functions of R (spatial frequency) whose product constitutes the Fourier transform of the convolved and interpolated projection data. See (3.15) and the text which follows it for details of these functions.

$$q(m\Delta s) = -\frac{\epsilon}{\pi^2(m\Delta s)^2}, \quad m \text{ even}, m \neq 0 \quad (3.13b)$$

$$q(m\Delta s) = -\frac{1 - \epsilon}{\pi^2(m\Delta s)^2}, \quad m \text{ odd}. \quad (3.13c)$$

The sequence corresponding to $\epsilon = 0$ is known as the Ramachandran–Lakshminarayanan [3.2] discrete convolving kernel; other useful kernels correspond to the choices $\epsilon = \frac{1}{2}$ and $\epsilon = 1$ in (3.13). Having chosen $q(m\Delta s)$ and $I(s)$, the convolution–backprojection algorithm is specified by (3.9), (3.10), and (3.8), where $\widetilde{p}_I$ is used in place of $\widetilde{p}$ in (3.8). We now examine in greater detail the relationship between these equations and (3.5) and (3.6) for which they are discrete approximations.

C. Analysis of Discrete Implementation of Convolution Formula

We now examine the relationship between the function $\widetilde{p}(s', \theta)$ given by (3.5) and the function $\widetilde{p}_I(s', \theta)$ given by (3.9) and (3.10). This is done most easily by examining the 1-D Fourier transforms of these functions, which we denote by $[\widetilde{p}]^\wedge(R, \theta)$ and $[\widetilde{p}_I]^\wedge(R, \theta)$, respectively.

From (3.5) and the convolution theorem for Fourier transforms (1.16), it is clear that

$$[\widetilde{p}]^\wedge(R, \theta) = \hat{p}(R, \theta)\hat{q}(R). \quad (3.14)$$

Although the convolutions expressed by (3.9) and (3.10) differ from (3.5) and from each other, it can be verified by straightforward manipulation that a similar convolution theorem for Fourier transforms exists in each case. For each sampled function appearing in these equations, its Fourier transform is a sum having the form of (1.18), so that the result for discrete convolution followed by interpolation is

$$[\widetilde{p}_I]^\wedge(R, \theta) = \hat{p}_\Sigma(R, \theta)\hat{q}_\Sigma(R)\hat{I}(R). \quad (3.15)$$

This result is important because it gives considerable insight into the factors affecting the choice of sampling increment Δs, window function $W(R)$ (which determines the convolving function $q(s)$), and interpolating function $I(s)$. The relationships between these parameters become clear on examination of the illustrative example shown in Fig. 2. The top line shows

$\hat{p}_{\Sigma}(R, \theta)$ as a function of R for a fixed θ. Note that $\hat{p}_{\Sigma}$ is the superposition of shifted versions of $\hat{p}$. Since $f(x, y)$ is zero outside a bounded region of the x–y plane, its Fourier transform is infinite in extent (see Section I-B). The same argument applies to $p(s, \theta)$ so $\hat{p}(R, \theta)$ is infinite in extent and overlaps the other components of $\hat{p}_{\Sigma}(R, \theta)$, namely, $\hat{p}(R + j/\Delta s)$ for $j \neq 0$. As usual, the overlapping (or "aliasing") can be reduced by reducing the sampling increment Δs or by low-pass filtering of $p(s, \theta)$ before sampling.

The second line in Fig. 2 shows $\hat{q}_{\Sigma}(R)$ for three different choices of $W(R)$ (see (3.7)). The graph labeled "1" corresponds to the window function specified in (1.19), with C equal to $1/(2\Delta s)$. The graph labeled "2" corresponds to the window function suggested by Shepp and Logan [3.4] for which

$$\hat{q}(R) = \begin{cases} \dfrac{1}{\pi \Delta s} \, |\sin(\pi R \Delta s)|, & |R| \leq \dfrac{1}{2\Delta s} \\[2ex] 0, & |R| > \dfrac{1}{2\Delta s}. \end{cases} \tag{3.16}$$

This choice of $\hat{q}(R)$ avoids the discontinuity in slope of $\hat{q}_{\Sigma}(R)$ which is evident on graph 1 at $R = 1/2\Delta s$, thereby reducing the severity of oscillations and overshoot error due to high contrast features in the original object. The graph labeled "3" corresponds to a window function which would be appropriate if $\hat{p}_{\Sigma}(R, \theta)$ were dominated by aliasing and noise for $1/4\Delta s < |R| < 3/4\Delta s$. The third line in Fig. 2 shows $\hat{I}(R)$ for two choices of $I(s)$, corresponding to the ideal low-pass filter (cf. (1.19)) and to linear interpolation, for which

$$\hat{I}_L(R) = \left(\frac{\sin(\pi R \Delta s)}{\pi R \Delta s} \right)^2. \tag{3.17}$$

The effect of interpolation is demonstrated by the graphs on the lowest line of Fig. 2 which show the product $[\tilde{p}_I]^{\wedge}(R, \theta)$ for both choices of interpolating function (and for the example of $\hat{q}_{\Sigma}(R)$ shown in graph 1). Comparing $[\tilde{p}_I]^{\wedge}(R, \theta)$ with $[\tilde{p}]^{\wedge}(R, \theta)$ (see (3.14)) we see that the former is corrupted by aliasing error which is an amplified version of the original aliasing in $\hat{p}_{\Sigma}$. The graph corresponding to linear interpolation shows that in this case $[\tilde{p}_I]^{\wedge}$ also contains spurious high-frequency components for $|R| > 1/2\Delta s$, which are due to the piecewise-linear nature of the corresponding $\tilde{p}_I(s, \theta)$. Note that both the aliasing error and the spurious high-frequency components are reduced very considerably by the use of the $\hat{q}_{\Sigma}(R)$ shown in the graph labeled "3," but, of course, high-frequency components of the original object are attenuated at the same time, thereby reducing the resolution of the reconstructed image.

This loss of resolution can be interpreted as the convolution of the image by a point-spread function, as we analyze in the following subsection.

D. Discrete Backprojection and the Point-Spread Function

We now examine the effect of evaluating the backprojection integral of (3.6) using the trapezoidal formula, as in (3.8). In the following analysis we consider $\tilde{p}(s', \theta_n)$ to be known precisely for arbitrary values of s', in order to separate the effect of sampling in the s parameter (described in Section III-C) and to focus attention on the effect of sampling in θ. Using this simplifying assumption, we derive the *point-spread function* of the reconstruction algorithm by examining the reconstruction

of an impulse object located at (ξ, η) in the plane. The object and its Fourier transform, denoted by $P(x, y)$ and $\hat{P}(X, Y)$, are

$$P(x, y) = \delta(x - \xi, y - \eta) \tag{3.18}$$

$$\hat{P}(X, Y) = e^{-i2\pi(X\xi + Y\eta)}. \tag{3.19}$$

Let $P_B(x, y)$ denote the *band-limited impulse* defined by

$$P_B(x, y) = \int_0^{\pi} \int_{-R_c}^{R_c} \hat{P}(R \cos \theta, R \sin \theta) \, W(R)$$

$$\cdot e^{i2\pi R (x \cos \theta + y \sin \theta)} \, |R| \, dR \, d\theta \tag{3.20}$$

where R_c is the cutoff frequency of the window. The function $P_B(x, y)$ represents the output of a reconstruction procedure of the kind given in (3.2). Substituting for $\hat{P}$ from (3.19) we find that

$$P_B(x, y) = \int_0^{\pi} \int_{-R_c}^{R_c} e^{i2\pi\rho R \cos(\theta - \gamma)} \, W(R) \, |R| \, dR \, d\theta \tag{3.21}$$

where

$$\tan \gamma = \frac{y - \eta}{x - \xi} \tag{3.22}$$

$$\rho = [(x - \xi)^2 + (y - \eta)^2]^{1/2}. \tag{3.23}$$

Interchanging the order of integration, the integral over θ is seen to be the integral representation of the Bessel function $J_0(2\pi\rho R)$ [2.1, formula 9.1.18] so we have

$$P_B(x, y) = \pi \int_{-R_c}^{R_c} J_0(2\pi\rho R) \, W(R) \, |R| \, dR. \tag{3.24}$$

Note that $P_B(x, y)$ depends only on ρ, the distance from (x, y) to the impulse location (ξ, η), and not on the direction of (x, y) relative to (ξ, η).

We are interested in the function, denoted by $P_N(x, y)$, which is obtained when the integral over θ in (3.21) is evaluated according to the trapezoidal rule, rather than analytically. By definition

$$P_N(x, y) = \Delta\theta \sum_{n=1}^{N} \int_{-R_c}^{R_c} e^{i2\pi\rho R \cos(\theta_n - \gamma)} \, W(R) \, |R| \, dR. \tag{3.25}$$

We now make use of the following identity, which may be obtained from the generating function for Bessel functions [2.1, formula 9.1.41]:

$$e^{iz \cos \theta} = \sum_{m=-\infty}^{\infty} i^m J_m(z) \, e^{im\theta}. \tag{3.26}$$

After interchanging the order of summation and integration, substituting the identity and summing over n, we find (after some manipulation) that

$$P_N(x, y) = \pi \int_{-R_c}^{R_c} \left[\sum_{k=-\infty}^{\infty} (-1)^{Nk} \, e^{-i2Nk\gamma} \, J_{2Nk}(2\pi\rho R) \right]$$

$$\cdot W(R) \, |R| \, dR. \tag{3.27}$$

Comparing this result with (3.24), we find that the $k = 0$ term of the sum gives $J_0(2\pi\rho R)$. The sum over the nonzero k, therefore, corresponds to an error introduced by the trapezoidal approximation of the integral over θ. Note that for each nonzero k, the corresponding term in the sum has a harmonic variation in γ with period π/Nk, so that the term has identical values on the $2Nk$ spokes of an imaginary wheel centered on (ξ, η). The most important conclusion from this analysis, which we now proceed to justify, is that these γ-dependent terms have a negligible effect on $P_N(x, y)$ within a certain radius of (ξ, η). This result follows from the behavior of the Bessel function $J_m(z)$ for large order m, which has its first maximum at argument $z > m$, and is negligible in comparison for $z \leqslant m - 2$, as can be deduced from its asymptotic expansion for large orders [2.1, formula 9.3.2]. Applying this to (3.27), we obtain

$$P_N(x, y) \simeq P_B(x, y), \qquad \rho \leqslant \rho_c \qquad (3.28)$$

where

$$\rho_c = \frac{N - 1}{\pi R_c}. \qquad (3.29)$$

Bearing in mind our original assumption, we conclude that it should be possible to reconstruct an image that is a band-limited replica of a given impulse object for those points of the image within a distance ρ_c of the location of the original impulse. If we consider a distributed object that is contained in a circle of diameter D_Ω to be a superposition of impulses, then we need $\rho_c > D_\Omega$ in order to avoid errors due to numerical approximation of the backprojection integral. Assuming that $D_\Omega = M\Delta s$ and $R_c = 1/2\Delta s$ we are led to the following condition relating the number of views (N) and the number of rays (M):

$$N - 1 > \frac{\pi M}{2}. \qquad (3.30)$$

This criterion provides a useful guideline for many applications, although in practice the function being backprojected is $\tilde{p}_I$ (see (3.10)) rather than $\tilde{p}$, as assumed in the preceding analysis, so that in reality the effects of the sampling in s and the sampling in θ interact in a complicated way. In particular, the point-spread function becomes position dependent: that is, $P_N(x, y)$ depends on (ξ, η) and not just on ρ and γ.

E. Notes and References

The method of convolution–backprojection was introduced in [3.1] and the simplicity of the discrete implementation was made clear in [3.2], [3.3]. The effects of interpolation and/or discrete backprojection are discussed in [3.4]–[3.11]. Some of these papers also discuss the effect of aliasing, which is considered in more detail in [3.12], [3.13].

The original inversion formula of Radon [1.5] may be obtained from (3.1) as follows. Take the definition (1.24) of $\hat{p}(R, \theta)$, and integrate by parts with respect to s to obtain $\hat{p}$ in terms of the partial derivative of $p(s, \theta)$ with respect to s. When this is substituted in (3.1), the R integral becomes the inverse Fourier transform of $|R|/R$, and the integral over s may be recognized as a convolution integral, known as the Hilbert transform [1.37], operating on the derivative of p. The integral over θ may be interpreted as backprojection of a modified version of p as before.

Radon's inversion formula may be derived from first princi-

ples [1.10, pp. 279–283] and used as the primary source of transform methods for image reconstruction. This approach is a popular and fruitful alternative to the approach followed in this paper, where we derive the various transform methods using Fourier transform identities and the results of Section II. The Radon formula must be "regularized" [1.10] to prepare it for numerical evaluation, a modification which is analogous to our use of a window function $W(R)$ in (3.2). Other, similarly motivated, modifications of the Radon inversion formula [3.14] may be more appropriate if the data do not correspond to uniformly spaced samples of $p(s, \theta)$, in which case the reconstruction algorithm involves shift-variant operations.

IV. RECONSTRUCTION BY FOURIER INVERSION

A. Reconstruction Algorithm for Discrete Data

This method for reconstruction follows directly from the relationship stated in Theorem 2 between the Fourier transform of a projection at angle θ and the Fourier transform of the object to be reconstructed. Taking the inverse Fourier transform of (2.2), we obtain

$$f(x, y) = \iint_{-\infty}^{\infty} \hat{p}((X^2 + Y^2)^{1/2}, \tan^{-1}(Y/X))$$
$$\cdot e^{i2\pi(xX + yY)} \, dX \, dY \qquad (4.1)$$

which is a reconstruction formula for $f(x, y)$, given $p(s, \theta)$. We refer to (4.1) as the Fourier inversion formula.

For practical applications, we require a reconstruction algorithm to perform numerical evaluation of (4.1) using sampled data, for which we need to restrict the domain of integration of the double integral to a finite region of the X–Y plane, denoted by Γ. We introduce a window function $W((X^2 + Y^2)^{1/2})$, as explained in Section I-D, and we attempt to find a function $f_B(x, y)$, which is a band-limited approximation to $f(x, y)$. Rewriting (4.1) in terms of $f_B(x, y)$ we have

$$f_B(x, y) = \iint_{\Gamma} \hat{p}((X^2 + Y^2)^{1/2}, \tan^{-1}(Y/X)) W((X^2 + Y^2)^{1/2})$$
$$\cdot e^{i2\pi(xX + yY)} \, dX \, dY. \qquad (4.2)$$

We now consider the evaluation of $\hat{p}(R, \theta_n)$, where the Fourier integral (1.24) is to be approximated by a finite sum over the samples $p(m\Delta s, \theta_n)$. From the relationship between (1.10) and (1.18), it is evident that the trapezoidal integration formula applied to (1.24) gives $\hat{p}_\Sigma$ rather than $\hat{p}$, where $\hat{p}_\Sigma(R, \theta)$ is related to $\hat{p}$ by (1.25). Numerical evaluation of (1.24) using the trapezoidal rule, therefore, yields

$$\hat{p}_\Sigma(R, \theta_n) = \Delta s \sum_{m=M^-}^{M^+} p(m\Delta s, \theta_n) e^{-i2\pi R(m\Delta s)} \qquad (4.3)$$

from which we may extract an approximation to $\hat{p}(R, \theta_n)$ within the finite bandwidth $|R| < 1/(2\Delta s)$.

Instead of evaluating $\hat{p}_\Sigma(R, \theta_n)$ according to (4.3) for arbitrary values of R, let us restrict our attention to $\hat{p}_\Sigma(\mu\Delta R, \theta_n)$, where μ is an integer and ΔR is a sampling increment in R. If we choose ΔR such that

$$\Delta R = \frac{1}{M\Delta s} \qquad (4.4)$$

then we obtain

$$\hat{p}_\Sigma(\mu\Delta R, \theta_n) = \Delta s \sum_{m=M^-}^{M^+} p(m\Delta s, \theta_n)\, e^{-i2\pi\mu m/M}. \quad (4.5)$$

A consequence of our choice of μ to be an integer is that the above formula gives only M distinct results. To see this, note that $\mu \pm lM$, l integer, will give the same result as μ. Although the formula has a well-defined and easily computed value in the general case where μ is an arbitrary real number, the advantage of restricting μ to integer values is that a family of efficient algorithms is available for producing the M distinct values of the sum corresponding to $\mu = 0, 1, \cdots, M-1$. These algorithms, generally known as the Fast Fourier Transform (FFT) [4.1], require on the order of $M \log_2 M$ multiplications and additions, whereas a straightforward evaluation of (4.5) for M values of μ requires on the order of M^2 such operations. The efficiency of these algorithms provides a strong incentive for approximating the double integral in (4.2) by sums which can be evaluated using the FFT. Unfortunately, evaluating both $\hat{p}$ and then f_B via the FFT introduces a problem of interpolation, which we describe in detail below.

For the moment, let us assume that we can interpolate from $\hat{p}_\Sigma(\mu\Delta R, \theta_n)$ to $\hat{p}((X^2 + Y^2)^{1/2},\ \tan^{-1}(Y/X))$ for arbitrary (X, Y) within the finite bandwidth Γ. Since, from (4.2),

$$\hat{p}((X^2 + Y^2)^{1/2}, \tan^{-1}(Y/X))\, W((X^2 + Y^2)^{1/2}) = \hat{f}_B(X, Y)$$

$$(4.6)$$

then $f_B(x, y)$ can be determined by a trapezoidal rule approximation to the inverse Fourier transform

$$f_B(k\Delta x, l\Delta y) \simeq \Delta X\, \Delta Y \sum_{u=U^-}^{U^+} \sum_{v=V^-}^{V^+} \hat{f}_B(u\Delta X, v\Delta Y)$$

$$\cdot\, e^{i2\pi[(k\Delta x)(u\Delta X)+(l\Delta y)(v\Delta Y)]} \quad (4.7)$$

where the double sum is over $U \times V$ samples of $\hat{f}_B$, using an obvious extension of the notation introduced in Section I-D. If we now put

$$\Delta x = \frac{1}{U\Delta X} \qquad \Delta y = \frac{1}{V\Delta Y} \quad (4.8)$$

we obtain

$$f_B(k\Delta x, l\Delta y) \simeq \Delta X\, \Delta Y \sum_{u=U^-}^{U^+} \sum_{v=V^-}^{V^+} \hat{f}_B(u\Delta X, v\Delta Y)$$

$$\cdot\, e^{i2\pi[ku/U+lv/V]}. \quad (4.9)$$

As in the 1-D case, the above formula gives only a finite number of distinct estimates of $f_B(k\Delta x, l\Delta y)$, for U different integers k and for V integers l. For these parameters the double sum may be evaluated efficiently using the FFT.

Analogous to the case of the 1-D forward transform, the nature of the approximation expressed in (4.9) may be made explicit: the right side is equal to the sum of shifted copies of f_B, where the shifts are in multiples of $1/\Delta X$ and $1/\Delta Y$ in the x and y directions, respectively.

Our approach to numerical evaluation of the Fourier inversion formula has been guided by an underlying motivation to use the FFT as much as possible. Fig. 3(a) shows the locations $(\mu\Delta R, \theta_n)$ in the X–Y (Fourier) plane at which we calculate $\hat{p}$

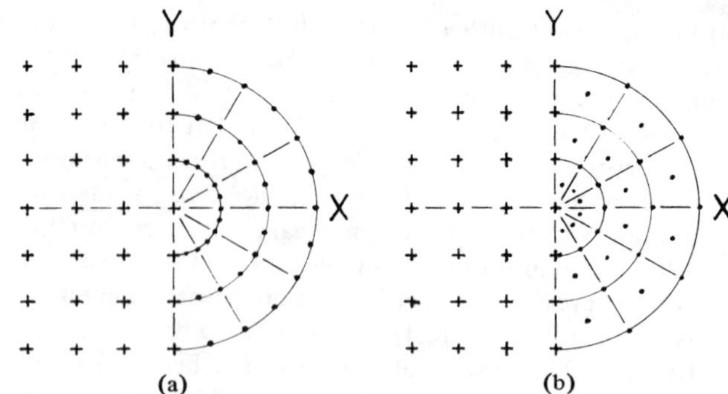

Fig. 3. Cartesian and polar sampling grids in Fourier space (for clarity, the two grids are illustrated in separate half-planes). (a) Conventional polar grid. (b) Modified polar grid with a radial offset of the samples at alternate angles.

using (4.5). These locations form a polar pattern of samples in the plane, characterized by uniform sample spacing in polar coordinates. The figure also shows as "+" those locations $(u\Delta X, v\Delta Y)$ at which we need to know the Fourier transform in order to evaluate $f_B(k\Delta x, l\Delta y)$ using (4.9). These locations form a Cartesian lattice of samples in the X–Y plane, so that some kind of interpolation is necessary to estimate the values at these sample points from the known values on the polar grid. Although there are many methods of interpolation which could be applied in this situation, we will consider two of the simplest as examples: nearest neighbor and bilinear interpolations. For any (X, Y), the *nearest neighbor estimate* of $\hat{f}(X, Y)$ is $\hat{p}(\mu\Delta R, \theta_n)$, where the integers μ and n are chosen to minimize

$$(X - \mu\Delta R \cos\theta_n)^2 + (Y - \mu\Delta R \sin\theta_n)^2$$

that is, the distance from the required sample point. For any (X, Y), the *bilinear interpolated estimate* of $\hat{f}(X, Y)$ is a weighted sum of the values of $\hat{p}(\mu\Delta R, \theta_n)$ at four neighboring sample points on the polar grid. We denote these points by $(\mu'\Delta R, \theta_{n'})$, $((\mu'+1)\Delta R, \theta_{n'})$, $(\mu'\Delta R, \theta_{n'+1})$, $((\mu'+1)\Delta R, \theta_{n'+1})$, where μ' and n' are chosen so that

$$\mu' \leqslant \mu^* = \frac{(X^2 + Y^2)^{1/2}}{\Delta R} \leqslant \mu' + 1 \quad (4.10)$$

and

$$\theta_{n'} \leqslant \theta^* = \tan^{-1}(Y/X) \leqslant \theta_{n'+1}. \quad (4.11)$$

To simplify notation, we introduce real numbers μ^* and θ^* defined in (4.10) and (4.11) above in terms of the given X and Y. For $n = n'$ and $n = n'+1$, compute

$$\hat{p}(\mu^*\Delta R, \theta_n) = (\mu' + 1 - \mu^*)\, \hat{p}(\mu'\Delta R, \theta_n)$$

$$+ (\mu^* - \mu')\, \hat{p}((\mu'+1)\Delta R, \theta_n) \quad (4.12)$$

then

$$\hat{p}(\mu^*\Delta R, \theta^*) = \frac{(\theta_{n'+1} - \theta^*)}{\Delta\theta}\, \hat{p}(\mu^*\Delta R, \theta_{n'})$$

$$+ \frac{(\theta^* - \theta_{n'})}{\Delta\theta}\, \hat{p}(\mu^*\Delta R, \theta_{n'+1}). \quad (4.13)$$

In summary, the reconstruction algorithm based on the Fourier inversion formula has three major subprocesses:

1) 1-D transforms of the projections at angles $\theta_n, n = 1, \cdots, N$;

2) interpolation from a polar to a Cartesian grid in Fourier space;

3) 2-D inverse transform to obtain the reconstructed image.

B. Some Refinements of the Basic Algorithm

It is clear from the derivation in the previous subsection that each step of the algorithm has its own potential sources of error, so that the overall result may be a rather weak approximation to the Fourier inversion formula. These sources of error include:

1) undersampling of the projections,
2) error in evaluation of $\hat{p}$,
3) error due to truncation of the Fourier domain,
4) interpolation error in the Fourier domain,
5) undersampling of the Fourier domain,
6) error in evaluation of f.

Obviously, these sources of error interact to a considerable extent. Rather than attempting to give a theoretical analysis of the approximation errors involved, which would be difficult and not particularly illuminating, we restrict ourselves to some general comments and indications of how these errors may be reduced in practice.

Undersampling of the projections (Δs too large) implies aliasing in the Fourier domain, which will corrupt estimates of $\hat{p}$ made using the trapezoidal integration rule (see (4.3), (1.25)). It is possible that the different kinds of interpolation implicit in other integration rules may lead to better estimates of $\hat{p}$ when aliasing is significant. Truncation of the Fourier domain implies the image will represent a smoothed version of the original object. If the truncation is too abrupt, however, high-contrast features in the original object will be reconstructed with considerable overshoot and ripple, and the Fourier domain will be undersampled (ΔX, ΔY too large in relation to the rate of change of the truncated function). This implies aliasing in the spatial domain, i.e., a high-contrast feature near a side of the image will cause "shadows" to appear near the opposite side of the image. If space-domain aliasing is significant, then the Fourier domain sampling increments (ΔX, ΔY) should be reduced or another integration rule should be used which can provide a better estimate of f.

In fact, one of the major problems with the algorithm specified in the previous section stems from the fact that the sampling increments in Fourier space are frequently such that the sampling theorem is only barely satisfied. Consider an image of $K \times L$ samples ($k\Delta x$, $l\Delta y$), where the rectangle having sides $K\Delta x$ and $L\Delta y$ is only just large enough to contain the nonzero part of $f(x, y)$, i.e., Ω. In theory, $1/(K\Delta x)$ is a sufficiently small value of ΔX to ensure that $\hat{f}(X, Y)$ is sampled adequately in X. In this case, however, the sample-to-sample variation of $\hat{f}(u\Delta X, v\Delta Y)$ is so large that the function could be regenerated from these samples only by interpolation with the classic "sinc" functions of sampling theory.

An example of this phenomenon which is more familiar in an engineering context would be a high-frequency sinusoidal signal which has been sampled at the minimum rate necessary to satisfy the sampling criterion; regeneration of the original signal would require a low-pass filter having ideal characteristics.

Returning to the image reconstruction example, we see from (4.4) and (1.23) that, for a circular region Ω, it appears reasonable to compute the transforms of the projections with $\Delta R = \Delta X = \Delta Y$. Unfortunately, the simple methods of interpolation stated in Section IV-A perform very poorly when ΔR is chosen according to (4.4) and $M\Delta s$ is only just sufficient for the rays to cover Ω, because the sampling criterion is only barely satisfied and these methods cannot reproduce the rapid variations of $\hat{f}(X, Y)$.

In order to ascertain the influence of $\Delta\theta$, note that the arc length, denoted by $A(R, \Delta\theta)$, from (R, θ) to $(R, \theta + \Delta\theta)$ is $R\Delta\theta$. Taking the cutoff frequency R_c to be $1/(2\Delta s)$, $\Delta R = 1/(M\Delta s)$ and $\Delta\theta = \pi/N$, we have

$$A(R_c, \Delta\theta) = \frac{\pi}{2} \frac{M}{N} \Delta R. \qquad (4.14)$$

When M and N are selected according to criterion (3.30), we find that $A(R_c, \Delta\theta)$ is approximately equal to ΔR, which seems intuitively reasonable. With these choices of parameters, then, $A(R, \Delta\theta)$ is less than ΔR for all R of interest, so that interpolation in the radial direction is likely to introduce larger errors, in general, than interpolation in the azimuthal direction, i.e., along an arc in Fourier space. In order to improve the accuracy of simple radial interpolation, it is common practice to decrease ΔR by increasing M (for Δs constant). When using the FFT, this is implemented by "padding" each projection with samples of zero value before transforming. Transform lengths of $2M$ or more are frequently used, which more than doubles the amount of computation involved in transforming the projection data, but the improvement in image quality is usually quite dramatic, due to the improvement in accuracy of the radial interpolation. Accuracy can be further improved by using higher order interpolating functions which involve more than the immediate neighbors of the sample to be interpolated. Interpolating functions of this kind may be derived by taking the inverse Fourier transform of a window function (see Section VII-C, also [4.2]).

Re-examining Fig. 3(a) from the point of view taken in this section, it becomes clear that the polar grid represents a very inefficient sampling of the Fourier domain. Close to the origin, where $\hat{f}(X, Y)$ is large, the polar samples are separated by only a very short distance in azimuth, yet they are far apart (ΔR) in radius. Some appreciation for this inefficiency can be gained from the observation that, within a radius R of the origin in Fourier space, the ratio of the number of Cartesian samples to the number of polar samples is approximately $(1/2)(R/R_c)$. This suggests that an attempt should be made to trade some of the unnecessarily fine angular sampling for an improvement in the marginal radial sampling. The "concentric squares" raster [1.25] is an example of this kind. Another approach, which has not been tried (to the author's knowledge) involves offsetting the samples from alternate projections to produce the pattern shown in Fig. 3(b). This pattern is produced by computing $\hat{p}(\mu\Delta R, \theta_n)$ for n even (say) and $\hat{p}(\mu + 1/2)\Delta R, \theta_n)$ for n odd. The samples of the latter kind, which are offset by half the radial sampling increment, can be computed using the FFT applied to the product $\exp(-i\pi m/M) p(m\Delta s, \theta_n)$.

Although this technique reduces considerably the average distance between samples in two dimensions, it should probably be combined with an overall reduction in the radial sampling increment, as suggested above, where $\hat{p}(\mu\Delta R/2, \theta_n)$ is computed for $0 \leqslant \mu \leqslant 2M - 1$ by padding $p(m\Delta s, \theta_n)$ with zeros before invoking the FFT. We now show how the corresponding offset samples $(\mu + 1/4)\Delta R$ and $(\mu + 3/4)\Delta R$ may be computed efficiently, for $0 \leqslant \mu \leqslant M - 1$. From (4.5)

$$\hat{p}_\Sigma((\mu + 1/4)\Delta R, \theta_n) = \Delta s \sum_{m=M^-}^{M^+} e^{-i\pi m/(2M)}$$
$$\cdot p(m\Delta s, \theta_n) e^{-i2\pi\mu m/M} \quad (4.15)$$

which may be evaluated for $0 \leqslant \mu \leqslant M - 1$ using the FFT. Note that $\hat{p}_\Sigma(R, \theta_n)$ is complex-valued, but in most applications $p(m\Delta s, \theta_n)$ is real, so that we have, from (4.5),

$$\hat{p}_\Sigma(\mu\Delta R, \theta_n) = \hat{p}_\Sigma^*((M - \mu)\Delta R, \theta_n) \quad (4.16)$$

where the asterisk denotes the complex conjugate, and μ could be any real number. In particular

$$\hat{p}_\Sigma((\mu + 3/4)\Delta R, \theta_n) = \hat{p}_\Sigma^*(\{(M - \mu - 1) + 1/4\}\Delta R, \theta_n) \quad (4.17)$$

which implies that $\hat{p}_\Sigma((\mu + 3/4)\Delta R, \theta_n), 0 \leqslant \mu \leqslant M/2 - 1$, can be inferred from the values $\hat{p}_\Sigma((\mu + 1/4)\Delta R, \theta_n)$, for $M/2 \leqslant \mu \leqslant M - 1$, computed using (4.15). Assuming that the projection data are real-valued, we see that the spectral offset of $(1/4)\Delta R$ in (4.15) causes half of the spectrum, which would otherwise be redundant due to conjugate symmetry, to be "folded back" to produce intermediate spectral samples. The result of using the M-point FFT is a set of spectral samples with a sampling increment of $\Delta R/2$, offset from the origin by half the sampling increment, as required.

It should be noted that those projection transforms which are not offset from the origin can also be calculated efficiently by eliminating redundancy in the transforms. One simple technique for doing this involves transforming two projections at once, with one (padded) projection forming the real component of complex-valued input data and the other projection forming the imaginary component. The output of the FFT is then decomposed into the original transforms of the projections by exploiting the odd–even symmetry of their respective real and imaginary parts. Using this technique, the amount of computation per projection turns out to be the same as that required by (4.15). An alternative technique involves packing a single projection into complex input data, and unraveling the resulting output; the 2-D version of this is often used to eliminate redundancy in the storage of $\hat{f}(X, Y)$ and in the computation of the image.

C. Comparison with Convolution–Backprojection

The algorithms discussed in Sections III and IV are both derived from the projection theorem for Fourier transforms. The 2-D inverse Fourier transform was expressed in polar coordinates to derive the convolution–backprojection algorithm and in Cartesian coordinates to derive the Fourier reconstruction algorithm. In view of their common ancestry, it may be somewhat surprising that these algorithms are utilized very differently in practice: the convolution–backprojection algorithm and its divergent-ray offspring of Section V are almost universally adopted in CT, to the exclusion of the Fourier (and other) reconstruction algorithms.

One reason for the dominance of the convolution–backprojection method is that the basic algorithm is straightforward to implement in software or hardware and produces sharp, accurate images from good-quality data. On the other hand, the Fourier method is not as straightforward to implement, due to the inelegant 2-D interpolation required, and the images produced by the basic algorithm (e.g., Section IV-A) are markedly inferior, again due to the interpolation. Recent

attempts [4.2], [4.3] to refine the basic algorithm by devoting careful attention to the sampling rates and to the interpolation in Fourier space appear to yield images comparable in quality to those of the convolution method, but the need remains for a thorough comparative study.

Since an apparently satisfactory algorithm (convolution–backprojection) exists, it is reasonable to question the need for investigating other algorithms, and the Fourier method in particular. One characteristic that the Fourier method has in its favor is that it requires potentially less computation to reconstruct the image, which will become increasingly important if the amount of data and the size of image matrices continue to increase in practical applications.

In order to compare the computation required by the two algorithms, we first note that an efficient implementation of the discrete convolution of (3.9) makes use of the FFT, with the projections padded out to twice their original length in order to avoid overlapping of the convolved data [3.6]. Since the Fourier algorithm of Section IV-B requires similar transforms, let us define a *unit of computation* to be the amount of computation required to perform an FFT of $2M$ samples. The discrete convolution of (3.9), implemented using the FFT, requires $2N$ units (N forward, N inverse transforms) plus multiplication of each transformed projection by $\hat{q}(R)$, which involves negligible extra computation.

The Fourier algorithm requires N units for the projection transforms, and the inverse transform on a $K \times K$ grid requires $2K$ transforms of length K, which is equivalent in computational work to $K(\log K/\log(2K))$ transforms of length $2K$, i.e., less than M units if we choose $K = M$, as is reasonable. With this choice, the forward and inverse transforms total less than $(N + M)$ units, compared with $2N$ units for the discrete convolution. Recall that the theoretically recommended (3.30) value for N is at least $(\pi/2)M$, so that the discrete convolution alone requires significantly more computation than the total of the projection transforms and the 2-D inverse transform.

We now need to compare the computation required for the interpolation and backprojection of the convolved data with the computation required for the 2-D interpolation in Fourier space. This comparison is not clear-cut, because both of these operations are highly implementation-dependent. Certainly, backprojection requires a large number (NK^2) of additions in the image matrix, and the interpolation, as specified in (3.10), would require a similar number of multiplications. However, it is common practice to implement the interpolation in two stages, where the first yields closely spaced samples of $\tilde{p}_I(s', \theta_n)$, thus creating a table from which the function value for any specified s' is approximated by selecting the nearest entry in the table. The advantage of this approach is that the number of multiplications per view is proportional to M, rather than K^2, and the backprojection over the K^2 image points requires only simple indexing and addition operations.

Similarly, in the Fourier algorithm, the interpolation of the projection transforms could be implemented with a number of multiplications per view which is proportional to M, but, in this case, a single view contributes to only a small fraction of the total of K^2 points in the 2-D transform.

In summary, the Fourier algorithm appears to have an advantage over the convolution method, in terms of the amount of computation required.

Unfortunately, the computational Fourier transforms whose efficiency makes the method attractive are also the source of some of its inherent disadvantages, compared to convolution–backprojection. Since the Fourier algorithm involves explicit evaluation of the complex amplitude of Fourier components of the image, an error in one such coefficient inevitably corrupts the whole image. One of the major causes of such an error is inexact interpolation, which affects the performance of the Fourier algorithm and that of the convolution backprojection algorithm in ways which are fundamentally different. Recall from Section III-C that when we attempt to regenerate a function from its samples by simple (e.g., linear) interpolation, the result differs from the original function in two ways: i) the result is a locally smoothed version of the original function and ii) the result also contains spurious rapid variations in its value or its derivatives. The effect of i) on the convolution method is relatively innocuous, since it amounts to a modification of the window function, resulting in additional smoothing of the image (in fact, Shepp and Logan [3.4] consider this an inherent part of the specification of a convolving function). The effect of ii) on the image is manifested by streaks radiating from sharp edges, comparable to the effect of too small a number of views (see Section III-D).

By contrast, the performance of the Fourier method is adversely affected by i), since the function being interpolated is in Fourier space, and smoothing (i.e., convolution) in the Fourier domain has the effect of multiplying the corresponding image by a function whose value decreases with increasing distance from the image-domain origin. This is a severe form of distortion, affecting in particular the reconstructed values corresponding to outer parts of the original object. This problem may be alleviated by increasing the sampling rate of the transforms of the projections, and by utilizing more accurate interpolation.

At first sight, it might appear that the performance of the Fourier method should not be affected adversely by ii), because rapid fluctuations in the Fourier domain (due to inexact interpolation) would ideally be transformed into spurious image features whose values become significant only at a considerable distance from the image origin, that is, outside the original object. Unfortunately, the discrete nature of the function in the Fourier domain implies that these rapid fluctuations are undersampled, so that the result of inverse transformation is an image which is corrupted everywhere, due to aliasing.

In order to exemplify these effects, we consider reconstruction of a simple object by the two methods. Let the object be described by the function which has value 1 inside a circle of radius a and is 0 outside. The Fourier transform of the object is an oscillatory function, with the oscillations becoming more rapid if the size of the object is increased, or if the object is moved away from the image origin. More rapid oscillations of the function imply, of course, more error introduced by simple interpolation between samples of that function. We now consider the convolution–backprojection method applied to projections of this object. In theory, when the projections are known for all s, it can be shown [3.6] that a convolved projection at angle θ has the same value for all s' corresponding to rays which intersect the circle of radius a. In practice, for sampled projections of this object, the convolved data are found to be in close agreement with the theoretical result. This implies that there is negligible interpolation error involved in reconstructing the values in the interior of the circle by convolution–backprojection, regardless of the size of the object or where it is positioned relative to the image origin. This

example illustrates, in its most extreme form, the underlying reason for the difference in performance of these two algorithms and serves to emphasize the power of the convolution–backprojection approach.

D. Notes and References

Image reconstruction by Fourier inversion was pioneered by Bracewell [4.4], who derived the projection theorem for Fourier transforms and applied it to a reconstruction problem in radio astronomy. The projection theorem itself was known earlier, but its potential uses in imaging were apparently not realized.

At present, radio astronomy is still the major application for the Fourier algorithm because in many experiments measured data correspond to samples of the Fourier transform of the spatial distribution of interest [4.5]. The algorithm is also well-suited to other applications, such as nuclear magnetic resonance (NMR) imaging [4.6], where the Fourier transforms of projections may be measured directly. A related algorithm has been derived for ultrasound-transmission CT, where the wave equation (with certain assumptions) leads to a generalization of the projection theorem for Fourier transforms [1.32]. In this case, the transform of a projection gives the 2-D transform on an arc through the origin.

The problems of interpolation in the Fourier domain have been addressed in [1.23], [4.2]–[4.5], [4.7]–[4.9]. A description of the FFT and the considerations involved in applying it are given in [4.10], and a well-documented package of programs is available [4.11]. It is worth noting that numerical integration formulas which are more sophisticated than the straightforward trapezoidal approximation may also be evaluated efficiently using the FFT [4.12]–[4.14].

V. Fan-Beam Reconstruction by Convolution and Backprojection

A. Derivation of Reconstruction Formulas

In medical applications of CT it is necessary to collect the projection data in as short a time as possible, in order to minimize the distortions due to patient movement. This is facilitated by using a fan beam of X-rays which diverge from an X-ray source, pass through the patient, and are intercepted by an array of detector elements. From these, the transmitted X-ray intensities are recorded as the source moves in a circular path around the patient.

The projection measurement geometry for divergent rays is illustrated in Fig. 4. Each ray, indexed by (s, θ) in the preceding sections, is now considered as one of a set of diverging rays (σ, β), where β determines the source position and σ is the angle of divergence of the ray from the source-to-center line. The line integral $p(s, \theta)$ is denoted by $g(\sigma, \beta)$ for $|s| < D$, where the locus of source positions is a circle of radius D. We assume that the source is always outside the object to be reconstructed, so that $g(\sigma, \beta) = 0$ for $|\sigma|$ greater than some acute angle, which we denote by δ.

In the spirit of Lakshminarayanan [5.1], we investigate how the parallel-ray reconstruction formulas of Section III can be adapted for the fan-beam measurement geometry. The following relationships are evident from Fig. 4:

$$s = D \sin \sigma \qquad \theta = \beta + \sigma \qquad p(s, \theta) = g(\sigma, \beta) \qquad (5.1)$$

$$r \cos (\theta - \phi) - s = U \sin (\sigma' - \sigma) \qquad (5.2)$$

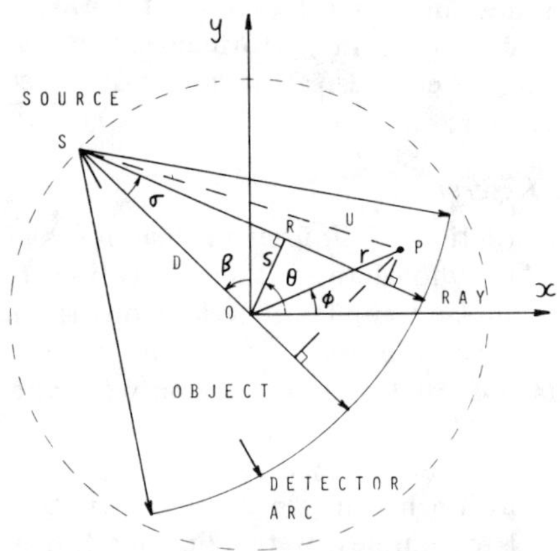

Fig. 4. Fan-beam geometry. A ray is specified by two parameters, σ and β. Let O be the origin and S be the position of the source, which lies on a circle of radius D around O. Then β is the angle the line OS makes with the y-axis, and σ is the angle the ray makes with SO. Such a ray is also one of a set of parallel rays, specified by the parameters s and θ. Let R be the point at which the ray meets the line through the origin which is perpendicular to the ray. Then θ is the angle OR makes with the x-axis and s is the distance OR.

where U is the distance from S to P in Fig. 4 and σ' is the angle between the line segments SO and SP. From the geometry, we have

$$U^2 = [r \cos (\beta - \phi)]^2 + [D + r \sin (\beta - \phi)]^2 \qquad (5.3)$$

$$\sigma' = \tan^{-1} \left[\frac{r \cos (\beta - \phi)}{D + r \sin (\beta - \phi)} \right]. \qquad (5.4)$$

From (1.24), (1.26), (2.2) it follows that the projection theorem may be written as

$$f_B(r \cos \phi, r \sin \phi) = (1/2) \int_{-\infty}^{\infty} \int_{-\infty}^{\infty} \int_{0}^{2\pi} p(s, \theta)$$

$$\cdot e^{i2\pi R[r \cos (\theta - \phi) - s]} W(R) |R| \, d\theta \, ds \, dR. \qquad (5.5)$$

We now change variables from (s, θ) to (σ, β) and obtain

$$f_B(r \cos \phi, r \sin \phi) = (D/2) \int_{-\infty}^{\infty} \int_{-\delta}^{\delta} \int_{-\sigma}^{2\pi - \sigma} g(\sigma, \beta) \cos \sigma$$

$$\cdot e^{i2\pi R U \sin (\sigma' - \sigma)} W(R) |R| \, d\beta \, d\sigma \, dR. \qquad (5.6)$$

Note that the integrand is periodic of period 2π in β, so that the limits of the β-integration may be replaced by 0 and 2π. The order of the integrations may be interchanged without difficulty and the reconstruction formula (5.6) may then be decomposed into two steps, as is done for the parallel-ray geometry (compare (3.5), (3.6))

$$\tilde{g}(\sigma', \beta) = \int_{-\delta}^{\delta} g(\sigma, \beta) \cos \sigma \, q(U \sin (\sigma' - \sigma)) \, d\sigma \qquad (5.7)$$

$$f_B(r \cos \phi, r \sin \phi) = (D/2) \int_{0}^{2\pi} \tilde{g}(\sigma', \beta) \, d\beta. \qquad (5.8)$$

B. Modification and Implementation of the Reconstruction Formulas

The major difference between (5.7) and (3.5) is the presence of U in the argument of the convolving function. From the

point of view of practical computation, it would be highly desirable to remove U from the integrand of the convolution integral, since U represents the distance between the source at coordinates $(D, \beta + \pi/2)$ and the point (r, ϕ) to be reconstructed. As a first step towards eliminating the U-dependence of the convolution integral, we express $q(U \sin \sigma)$ in terms of a family of convolving functions, denoted by $q_\chi(D\sigma)$, whose "cutoff frequency" χ is a function of C, U/D, and σ. Recall that $q(s)$ is derived from a window function $W(R)$ which is zero for $|R| > C$. After substituting in (3.4) with limits $\pm C$ for the R-integral, then changing the variable of integration from R to $R' = (RU \sin \sigma)/(D\sigma)$ we obtain

$$q(U \sin \sigma) = \left[\frac{D}{U} \frac{\sigma}{\sin \sigma} \right]^2 q_\chi(D\sigma) \qquad (5.9)$$

where

$$q_\chi(D\sigma) = \int_{-\chi}^{\chi} |R| \, W(RC/\chi) \, e^{i2\pi R (D\sigma)} \, dR \qquad (5.10)$$

and

$$\chi = \chi(C, U/D, \sigma) = C \frac{U}{D} \frac{\sin \sigma}{\sigma}. \qquad (5.11)$$

Equation (5.7) can now be implemented using a family of convolving functions q_χ appropriate for parallel-ray projections (compare (3.4)). As (5.10) shows, the specific *shape* of the window function $W(\cdot)$ is common to the whole family, although the cutoff frequency is variable. For computational economy, we require that

$$q(U \sin \sigma) = q^B(C, U) \, q^F(\sigma) \qquad (5.12)$$

so that the U-dependent component q^B of the overall convolving function may be implemented as a multiplicative weight in the backprojection operation, leaving the convolution operation independent of U. In addition, we would like the image to be reconstructed with uniform resolution. However, this implies that C be constant which would, in turn, force χ to vary with U, in which case it does not appear to be possible to design an appropriate convolving function which satisfies (5.12). Therefore, the most obvious way to design a convolving function satisfying (5.12) is to relax the above restriction on C and instead make χ constant, accepting that the resolution of the reconstructed image may not be uniform. While hardly justifiable in a mathematical sense, this tactic is not unreasonable when judged according to physical intuition. We note, as an aside, that the need to introduce reasoning of this kind shows merely that the operations which we are describing no longer have a simple interpretation in terms of Fourier transforms, and could probably be justified more plausibly by other approaches (see Section V-C). When we continue with our present approach by examining the consequences of setting χ constant (with C a dependent variable), we find that simple, efficient convolving kernels are obtained which are closely related to the corresponding parallel-ray kernels, and which agree with the results of other approaches for certain special cases. As an example, we take the convolving kernel of (3.13) and derive the corresponding divergent-ray kernel. We denote by χ^* a constant which we substitute for χ in (5.10) and we define a function q^* by (see (5.9))

$$q^*(U \sin \sigma) = \left[\frac{D}{U} \frac{\sigma}{\sin \sigma} \right]^2 q_{\chi^*}(D\sigma). \qquad (5.13)$$

By analogy with the derivation of (3.13), we put $\chi^* = 1/(2D\Delta\sigma)$, where $g(m\Delta\sigma, \beta)$ are the measured samples of $g(\sigma, \beta)$. Using the window function (3.12) in (5.10) we find from (5.13) that $q^*(U\sin(m\Delta\sigma))$ is given by

$$q^*(0) = \frac{1}{U^2} \frac{3 - 2\epsilon}{12(\Delta\sigma)^2}$$

$$q^*(U\sin(m\Delta\sigma)) = -\frac{1}{U^2} \frac{\epsilon}{\pi^2 \sin^2(m\Delta\sigma)}, \quad m \text{ even}, m \neq 0$$

$$q^*(U\sin(m\Delta\sigma)) = -\frac{1}{U^2} \frac{1 - \epsilon}{\pi^2 \sin^2(m\Delta\sigma)}, \quad m \text{ odd.} \quad (5.14)$$

The convolving kernel represented by (5.14) clearly satisfies our requirement for computational economy, namely (5.12). The reconstruction algorithm involves numerical evaluation of (5.7) and (5.8) with q^* in place of q. The factor $1/U^2$ which appears in the expression for q^* is most conveniently grouped with the backprojection step to form a *weighted backprojection* along divergent rays (recall that U is the distance from the point (r, ϕ) to the source position). Apart from this, and the factor $\cos\sigma$ appearing in (5.7), the derivation of an efficient algorithm from the reconstruction formulas differs very little in principle from the case for parallel-ray projections. The algorithm involves discrete convolution, interpolation, and fan-beam backprojection, where the considerations involved in implementing these operations are analogous to those discussed in Section III, and so we do not state the algorithm explicitly or discuss its implementation in more detail here.

C. Notes and References

The reconstruction formulas in Sections V-A and -B were derived for the case of detector elements distributed uniformly on a circular arc—see Fig. 4. The same approach can be used to obtain formulas for a linear detector irradiated by a fan beam. The starting point of this approach is the Fourier-transform equivalent of the "regularized" Radon inversion formula (see Section III-E) which is then adapted to the fan-beam geometry by a change of variables.

An alternative approach, also applicable to either kind of detector, performs the change of variables prior to regularization. This approach [1.10], [5.2] begins with the Radon inversion formula, from which an inversion formula for divergent rays is obtained by a change of variables. This formula is then regularized prior to numerical evaluation.

In general, the two approaches lead to different convolving functions (for equivalent choices of the window function) but the reconstructed images are likely to be indistinguishable in practice [5.3].

A third, and potentially more flexible approach [5.4] begins with what is effectively a regularized version of the Radon inversion formula, from which changes of variable can be made to accommodate an arbitrary measurement geometry.

Parallel-ray reconstruction algorithms can be used to reconstruct from fan-beam projection data using a data reorganization scheme known as *rebinning*, which involves 2-D interpolation in projection space [5.5]. A complete set of parallel-ray projections can be inferred from fan-beam data collected while the source moves through $180°$ plus the fan angle. This type of "short-scan" fan-beam data can be reconstructed using a modified convolution–backprojection algorithm [5.6], [5.7].

Unfortunately, it does not seem possible to modify the Fourier reconstruction method of Section IV for fan beams and still preserve its efficiency, so it is necessary to rebin the data in order to make use of this method. In contrast, the convolution–backprojection algorithm's advantages of accuracy and straightforward, efficient implementation carry over directly to the fan-beam geometry.

VI. Other Reconstruction Formulas

In this Section we outline some other algorithms for image reconstruction which may offer some advantages in special applications. Some of them are amenable to implementation using optical processors, as well as the customary digital computer—see also [6.1], [6.2].

A. Rho-Filtered Layergram Method

This method was introduced in an early paper of Bates and Peters [6.3], who used "ρ" as the radial variable in Fourier space (analogous to R in this paper). The method is based on the projection theorem for Fourier transforms and involves backprojection followed by 2-D spatial filtering. The operations are, therefore, similar to those of the convolution–backprojection method, but are performed in the reverse order [1.23]. We denote by $B(x, y)$ the image formed by backprojection of $p(s, \theta)$ as follows:

$$B(x, y) = \int_0^\pi p(x\cos\theta + y\sin\theta, \theta)\, d\theta. \quad (6.1)$$

Now

$$p(s, \theta) = \int_{-\infty}^\infty \hat{f}(R\cos\theta, R\sin\theta)\, e^{i2\pi Rs}\, dR. \quad (6.2)$$

Substituting for p in (6.1) we obtain

$$B(x, y) = \int_0^\pi \int_{-\infty}^\infty \hat{f}(R\cos\theta, R\sin\theta)$$

$$\cdot e^{i2\pi R(x\cos\theta + y\sin\theta)}\, dR\, d\theta. \quad (6.3)$$

We denote by $\hat{B}$ the Fourier transform of B, with a warning that $\hat{B}$ is not a function in the conventional sense since its value is undefined at the origin (mathematically, the Fourier transform of B is an example of a *generalized function*). Assuming for our purpose that $\hat{B}$ can be manipulated in the conventional manner, we find from (6.3) that (except for $R = 0$)

$$\hat{f}(R\cos\theta, R\sin\theta) = |R|\, \hat{B}(R\cos\theta, R\sin\theta). \quad (6.4)$$

Equations (6.1) and (6.4) indicate how $f(x, y)$ may be obtained from $p(s, \theta)$ by backprojection, Fourier transformation, multiplication by $|R|$ ("rho-filtering"), and inverse transformation. The value of $\hat{f}$ at the origin is simply the average density of the object, which may be found independent of B by integrating $p(s, \theta)$ with respect to s (see Section II).

There are a number of practical difficulties associated with this method, due to the fact that both B and $\hat{B}$ are of infinite extent, and must be truncated. Also, the array dimensions of the discrete transforms must be at least twice those of the final image in order to avoid aliasing, making the method rather inefficient on a digital computer, but the operations involved are well-suited to optical implementation [6.3]–[6.5]. The method is applicable to divergent-ray data, as shown by Gullberg [6.6].

B. Reconstruction Methods Using Angular Harmonics

Another reconstruction formula based on the projection theorem for Fourier transforms is obtained by decomposing the projections and image into angular Fourier series, as defined in (1.6)–(1.9). Taking the inverse Fourier transform in polar coordinates of (2.2) we have

$$f(r \cos \phi, r \sin \phi) = \int_0^{2\pi} \int_0^{\infty} \hat{p}(R, \theta)$$

$$\cdot e^{i2\pi rR \cos(\phi - \theta)} R \, dR \, d\theta. \quad (6.5)$$

We now use the identity (3.26) to expand the exponential after which we substitute for $\hat{p}$ from (1.24) and apply (1.6)–(1.9) to obtain

$$f_n(r) = 2\pi i^n \int_0^{\infty} J_n(2\pi rR) \int_{-1}^{1} p_n(s) \, e^{-i2\pi Rs} \, ds \, R \, dR. \quad (6.6)$$

Integrating by parts with respect to s, and interchanging the order of the R and s integrations, we obtain

$$f_n(r) = i^{n-1} \int_{-1}^{1} p_n'(s) \int_0^{\infty} J_n(2\pi rR) \, e^{-i2\pi Rs} \, dR \, ds \quad (6.7)$$

where $p_n'(s)$ is the derivative of $p_n(s)$. Now the integral over R corresponds to a known discontinuous integral of Bessel functions [2.1, formulas 11.4.37, 11.4.38] from which we obtain, after some manipulation,

$$f_n(r) = \frac{1}{\pi r} \int_0^{1} p_n'(s) \, Q_n(s/r) \, ds \quad (6.8)$$

where

$$Q_n(z) = \begin{cases} \dfrac{\sin(|n| \cos^{-1} z)}{(1 - z^2)^{1/2}}, & 0 \leqslant z < 1 \\[2ex] -(z^2 - 1)^{-1/2} [z + (z^2 - 1)^{1/2}]^{-|n|}, & z > 1 \end{cases} \quad (6.9)$$

This formula was obtained by Perry [6.7] and has been implemented optically by Hansen [6.8]. A related formula, derived by Cormack [6.9], is

$$f_n(r) = -\frac{1}{\pi r} \int_r^{1} \frac{p_n'(s) \, T_n(s/r)}{(s^2/r^2 - 1)^{1/2}} \, ds \quad (6.10)$$

where $T_n(z)$ denotes the Chebyshev polynomial of the first kind. Since $z = s/r \geqslant 1$ in (6.10), $T_n(z)$ is given by

$$T_n(z) = \cosh(n \cosh^{-1} z)$$
$$= \frac{[z + (z^2 - 1)^{1/2}]^n + [z + (z^2 - 1)^{1/2}]^{-n}}{2}. \quad (6.11)$$

Cormack's formula shows that it is possible, in principle, to reconstruct the outer part of an object from the outer parts of its projections. Unfortunately, a straightforward implementation of this formula is highly sensitive to errors in the data and in the numerical approximations [6.10], but it may be regularized [6.11] and has been applied to incomplete data by

Inouye [6.12]. The similarities and differences between Cormack's formula (6.10) and (6.8) are quite intriguing, and the relationships between these formulas have been studied recently by Hansen [6.13] and Verly [6.14].

C. Reconstruction by Polynomial Fit to Projections

The basic principles of this method are described in this section in terms of a specific family of polynomials, namely the Chebyshev polynomials of the second kind, which were used in the examples at the end of Section II. The formulas for the general case are given by Louis and Natterer [1.3]. We represent the projections $p(s, \theta)$ by a sum of functions of the form $(1 - s^2)^{1/2} U_m(s) \, e^{in\theta}$, as in (2.12), where the coefficients $c_{m,n}$ of the expansion may be calculated from the projections using (2.8). When this representation of $p(s, \theta)$ is substituted in a (linear) reconstruction formula, the result may be written as

$$f(x, y) = \sum_{n=-\infty}^{\infty} \sum_{m=|n|}^{\infty} c_{m,n} \Phi_{m,n}(x, y) \quad (6.12)$$

where the function $\Phi_{m,n}(x, y)$ has projections $(2/\pi)(1 - s^2)^{1/2} U_m(s) \, e^{in\theta}$. By substituting this projection into a reconstruction formula, we find that $\Phi_{m,n}$ is most conveniently expressed in polar coordinates

$$\Phi_{m,n}(r \cos \phi, r \sin \phi) = V_{m,n}(r) \, e^{in\phi} \quad (6.13)$$

where the $V_{m,n}(r)$ are functions related to the Zernike polynomials of optics. This method has been derived in a number of different ways by Cormack [6.15], Marr [6.16], Smith et al. [1.23], and Ein-Gal [6.17]. In practical implementations, only a finite number of coefficients can be used, so that the technique could be classified as a series-expansion method, as is done in [1.10]. The coefficients $c_{m,n}$ may be calculated using straightforward numerical integration of (2.8) or (6.15), but the summation over m of $c_{m,n} V_{m,n}(r)$ in (6.12) must be implemented carefully in order to avoid loss of precision for $|n|$ large.

D. Angular Harmonics and Divergent-Ray Data

We indicate here how the methods described in Sections VI-B and -C may be adapted for divergent-ray projections, using the notation of Section V. In Section VI-B we make use of the function $p_n(s)$ defined by (1.8). In order to express $p_n(s)$ in terms of fan-beam projections $g(\sigma, \beta)$, we use the identities (5.1) and change the variable of integration in (1.8) from θ to β, obtaining

$$p_n(D \sin \sigma) = \frac{e^{-in\sigma}}{2\pi} \int_0^{2\pi} g(\sigma, \beta) \, e^{-in\beta} \, d\beta. \quad (6.14)$$

Similarly, in order to express the $c_{m,n}$ of Section VI-C in terms of $g(\sigma, \beta)$, we use the identities (5.1) and change the variables of integration in (2.8) from (s, θ) to (σ, β), obtaining

$$c_{m,n} = \frac{1}{2\pi} \int_0^{2\pi} e^{-in\beta} \int_{-\delta}^{\delta} g(\sigma, \beta) \cos \sigma U_m(D \sin \sigma)$$

$$\cdot e^{-in\sigma} \, d\sigma \, d\beta. \quad (6.15)$$

A somewhat different way of adapting the method of Section VI-C to the fan-beam geometry is described in [1.10, sect. 13.2 and 13.3].

VII. An Iterative Transform Method

In this section we derive a reconstruction algorithm based on a novel discretization of a mathematical procedure for image reconstruction. The operations (on functions) specified by the reconstruction formula are simple and intuitively reasonable, and are repeated in an iterative manner. The way in which the algorithm for discrete data is derived from the reconstruction formula qualifies it as a transform method, but its iterative nature and its representation of the image give the algorithm much in common with iterative algorithms derived by the series-expansion approach.

A. The Reconstruction Formula

Herman and Lent [7.1] present an iterative reconstruction formula, which they call "Continuous ART" and which they show to be a particular example of a procedure (successive orthogonal projections in a Hilbert space) that is well known in mathematical analysis and optimization theory.

We consider functions f which are 0 outside a bounded region Ω in the plane, and we denote by $L(s, \theta_n)$ the length of intersection of the line (s, θ_n) and the region Ω. We wish to reconstruct a function f, given its projections $p(s, \theta_n)$ for all real numbers s and for a set of N discrete angles θ_n. The reconstruction formula operates on a "semidiscrete" function p of two variables, where one of the variables is restricted to a finite set of values and the other is not.

For integer $i \geq 0$, the $(i + 1)$th step of *continuous ART* (see, e.g., [7.1]) produces an image $f^{(i+1)}$ from the present estimate $f^{(i)}$ in the following way:

$$f^{(i+1)}(x, y) = \begin{cases} 0, & \text{if } (x, y) \notin \Omega \\ f^{(i)}(x, y) + \dfrac{p(s', \theta_n) - p^{(i)}(s', \theta_n)}{L(s', \theta_n)} \end{cases} \quad (7.1)$$

where

$$n = (i \bmod N) + 1$$

$$s' = x \cos \theta_n + y \sin \theta_n$$

$p^{(i)}(s, \theta_n)$ is the projection of $f^{(i)}(x, y)$, and $f^{(0)}(x, y)$ is a given function.

The sequence of images $f^{(i)}$ generated by this procedure is known to converge to an image which satisfies all the projections, if any such images exist (see, for example, [7.1], which may be consulted for more details). The rate of convergence and other properties of the process have been investigated theoretically in [7.2].

The physical interpretation of (7.1) is as follows. For a particular angle θ_n, find the projection at angle θ_n of the current estimate of the image, and subtract this function from the given projection at angle θ_n to form the *residual* projection as a function of s for this angle. For each s of the residual, apply a uniform adjustment to all image points (within Ω) that lie on the line (s, θ_n), where the adjustment is such that $p^{(i+1)}$

(s, θ_n) agrees with the given $p(s, \theta_n)$. The result of applying such an adjustment for all s is a new image which satisfies the given projection for this angle (but probably for none of the other angles). The process is then repeated for the next angle in the sequence. It is often useful to think of each step as a one-view backprojection of a scaled version of the residual.

B. Reconstruction Algorithm for Discrete Data

The formula stated in the previous subsection specifies operations on functions $p(\cdot, \theta_n)$. For practical computation we require an algorithm that operates on discrete data, for which we employ the measurement geometry and notation introduced in Section I-D.

In order to estimate $p(s, \theta_n)$ from its samples $p(m\Delta s, \theta_n)$ we introduce an interpolating function ψ of one variable such that

$$p(s, \theta_n) \simeq \sum_{m = M^-}^{M^+} p(m\Delta s, \theta_n)\, \psi(s - m\Delta s). \quad (7.2)$$

Similarly, in order to estimate $f(x, y)$ from its samples $f(k\Delta x, l\Delta y)$, we introduce a *basis function* $B(x, y)$ that acts as an interpolating function of two variables (the nomenclature here emphasizes the algorithm's affinity with the series expansion approach—see [1.1]).

$$f(x, y) \simeq \sum_{k = K^-}^{K^+} \sum_{l = L^-}^{L^+} f(k\Delta x, l\Delta y)\, B(x - k\Delta x, y - l\Delta y).$$

$$(7.3)$$

A natural criterion for interpolation is that it should lead to an interpolated function whose values at the sample points match the given data. This may be ensured by choosing interpolating functions that have value 1 when their arguments are 0 and have value 0 when their arguments are multiples of the sampling increment.

We now replace f by $f^{(i)}$ in (7.3) and substitute this expression in (1.2) to obtain

$$p^{(i)}(s, \theta) = \sum_{k, l} f^{(i)}(k\Delta x, l\Delta y)\, P_{k, l}^{(B)}(s, \theta) \quad (7.4)$$

where

$$P_{k, l}^{(B)}(s, \theta) = \int_{-\infty}^{\infty} B(s \cos \theta - t \sin \theta - k\Delta x,$$

$$\cdot\, s \sin \theta + t \cos \theta - l\Delta y)\, dt. \quad (7.5)$$

Note that $P_{k, l}^{(B)}(s, \theta)$ is simply the integral along the line (s, θ) of the basis function shifted to $(k\Delta x, l\Delta y)$.

The algorithm is derived by discretizing "continuous ART" according to the principles of interpolation stated above. Using (7.2) and (7.4), an approximation to (7.1) may be written in terms of discrete variables, where for conciseness we use an obvious subscript notation for $f(k\Delta x, l\Delta y)$ and $p(m\Delta s, \theta_n)$

$$f_{k, l}^{(i+1)} = \begin{cases} 0, & \text{if } (k\Delta x, l\Delta y) \text{ is not in } \Omega \\ f_{k, l}^{(i)} + \dfrac{\sum_m \left[p_{m, n} - \sum_{k', l'} f_{k', l'}^{(i)} P_{k', l'}^{(B)}(m\Delta s, \theta_n) \right] \psi(s_{k, l}'(\theta_n) - m\Delta s)}{L(s_{k, l}'(\theta_n), \theta_n)} \end{cases} \quad (7.6)$$

where

$$n = (i \bmod N) + 1$$

and

$$s'_{k,l}(\theta) = (k\Delta x)\cos\theta + (l\Delta y)\sin\theta.$$

C. Implementation of the Algorithm

In a practical implementation of the algorithm we need to specify appropriate functions ψ and B from the wide variety of interpolating functions which are available. In our implementation we find it convenient to use interpolating functions that do not fulfill the criterion specified following (7.3). Instead, we use an interpolation procedure that produces from the samples of f an approximation to a *smoothed version* of the original function. For 1-D interpolation, this procedure has the advantage that it is stable in the presence of error in the samples. More importantly, it permits the use of 2-D interpolating functions that are *rotationally symmetric*, in which case the projection of B is independent of angle. This angle independence of the projection leads to a welcome simplification in the implementation of the algorithm, compared with an implementation involving the traditional square pixel as the basis function.

Our selection of interpolating functions is based on an approach popular in digital signal processing. We first select a window function $W_1(S)$ in Fourier space, and derive ψ by taking the inverse Fourier transform of W_1. Because of its flexibility and its near-optimal properties, we choose the "Kaiser" window [7.3]

$$W_1(S) = \begin{cases} \dfrac{I_0(2\pi H_1\sqrt{C_1^2 - S^2})}{I_0(2\pi H_1 C_1)}, & |S| < C_1 \\[2mm] 0, & \text{otherwise} \end{cases} \tag{7.7}$$

where

$I_0(\cdot)$ Bessel function of the second kind, order 0;
S Fourier space variable (frequency);
C_1 cutoff frequency;
H_1 rolloff parameter.

We denote by $\psi_1(s)$ the inverse transform of the window function having parameters C_1 and H_1, from which we find

$$\psi_1(s) = \begin{cases} \dfrac{2C_1}{I_0(2\pi H_1 C_1)}\dfrac{\sin(2\pi C_1\sqrt{s^2 - H_1^2})}{2\pi C_1\sqrt{s^2 - H_1^2}}, & |s| \geq H_1 \\[3mm] \dfrac{2C_1}{I_0(2\pi H_1 C_1)}\dfrac{\sinh(2\pi C_1\sqrt{H_1^2 - s^2})}{2\pi C_1\sqrt{H_1^2 - s^2}}, & |s| \leq H_1. \end{cases} \tag{7.8}$$

Note that for $H_1 = 0$, $\psi_1(s)$ reduces to the familiar "sinc" function.

Similarly, we derive a 2-D rotationally symmetric interpolating function B_2 by taking the 2-D inverse transform of a 2-D rotationally symmetric window function $W_2(R)$, where R is the distance from the origin in Fourier space

$$W_2(R) = \begin{cases} \dfrac{I_0(2\pi H_2\sqrt{C_2^2 - R^2})}{I_0(2\pi H_2 C_2)}, & |R| < C_2 \\[2mm] 0, & \text{otherwise} \end{cases} \tag{7.9}$$

where parameters C_2 and H_2 are analogous to C_1 and H_1 of (7.7). From the projection theorem for Fourier transforms it

is evident that the projection of B_2 is independent of θ, and is equal to $\psi_2(s)$, where ψ_2 is the inverse Fourier transform of the 1-D window function of the form (7.7) and with parameters C_2 and H_2. In (7.5), $P_{k,l}^{(B)}(s, \theta)$ is the projection of a basis function B that has been shifted from the origin to the point (k, l) of the Cartesian grid. Replacing B by the function B_2 defined above, it is clear from the geometry that

$$P_{k,l}^{(B_2)}(s, \theta) = \psi_2(s - s'_{k,l}(\theta)) \tag{7.10}$$

where $s'_{k,l}(\theta)$ is defined following (7.6). Returning to the general statement of the algorithm (7.6), we replace $P_{k,l}^{(B)}$ and ψ by the particular functions ψ_2 and ψ_1, respectively, where both ψ_2 and ψ_1 are evaluated at the points $s'_{k,l}(\theta_n) - m\Delta s$, and are even functions of their arguments.

The algorithm requires that Ω and $f_{k,l}^{(0)}$ be specified, together with the following parameters:

$K, L, \Delta x, \Delta y$
$M, \Delta s$
$N; \theta_n, n = 1, 2, \cdots, N$
C_1, H_1 (or some alternative interpolating function $\psi(s)$)
C_2, H_2 (or some alternative basis function $B(x, y)$).

We denote by λ an additional parameter, known as the *relaxation factor*, which multiplies the correction term at each step i of the algorithm. The use of a λ in the range 0 to 2 has been found to be beneficial with conventional iterative algorithms [7.1].

The new algorithm described above has been implemented, and is found to produce images comparable in quality to those reconstructed by convolution–backprojection (these results will be published elsewhere). Since the algorithm involves iterative backprojection and reprojection operations, it requires a comparatively large amount of computer time on a general-purpose machine, a disadvantage that it shares with other iterative algorithms derived by the series-expansion approach. On the other hand, it also shares some of the significant advantages of these algorithms, namely, the ability to incorporate supplementary information (boundary contour, etc.) into the reconstruction process and the flexibility to adapt to applications where the data set is incomplete, or where closed-form inversion formulas cannot be found.

D. Notes and References

The present generation of iterative reconstruction algorithms search for an image which is piecewise constant on small squares (the pixels) and which is in reasonable agreement with the measurements. In this case, an image space basis function is simply that function which has value one inside a pixel and is 0 outside. In contrast to this, the basis functions introduced in Section VII-C are smooth and overlapping, and may be adjusted in a continuous manner to suit the problem at hand. Although these functions do not appear explicitly in our reconstruction algorithm (only their projections), it is of some interest to determine them by calculating the 2-D inverse Fourier transform of the rotationally symmetric window given by (7.9). This has been done in the context of antenna design by Hansen [7.4], with the help of a 1938 paper in the mathematical literature, and the result is just the 2-D analog of (7.8)

$$b(r) = \begin{cases} \dfrac{2\pi C_2^2}{I_0(2\pi H_2 C_2)}\dfrac{J_1(2\pi C_2\sqrt{r^2 - H_2^2})}{2\pi C_2\sqrt{r^2 - H_2^2}}, & |r| \geq H_2 \\[3mm] \dfrac{2\pi C_2^2}{I_0(2\pi H_2 C_2)}\dfrac{I_1(2\pi C_2\sqrt{H_2^2 - r^2})}{2\pi C_2\sqrt{H_2^2 - r^2}}, & |r| \leq H_2. \end{cases} \tag{7.11}$$

The 2-D transform pair (7.9)–(7.11) has a significance which extends beyond the context of image reconstruction. The Kaiser window (7.7) is in widespread use, and in many applications it is appropriate to derive a window function for two dimensions by rotating a 1-D window function about the origin, as is done throughout this paper. We make this point here because the closed-form expression (7.11) does not seem to be known as widely as it deserves.

VIII. Conclusion

The transform approach to image reconstruction from projections gives rise to a variety of algorithms, including those widely used in commercial CT scanners for medical imaging. The principles and implementation of these algorithms are outlined here using the tools of Fourier analysis which are familiar to electrical engineers. These techniques enable one to gain valuable insight, and an intuitive appreciation of the relationship between the discrete operations specified by the algorithm and the functional operations expressed by the inversion formula from which it is derived.

The inversion formulas which are usually employed apply specifically to the problem of image reconstruction from projections. A promising area for future research is the application of various general-purpose inversion techniques to the integral equation of image reconstruction. The iterative transform method described in Section VII is an example of this approach, which offers the flexibility to adapt to unconventional scanning modes for which it may not be possible to derive a closed-form inversion formula.

Acknowledgment

The author gratefully acknowledges numerous instructive and stimulating discussions with former and present members of two groups active in imaging research: Prof. R.H.T. Bates and his group at the University of Canterbury, Christchurch, New Zealand, and Prof. G. T. Herman and his group at the University of Pennsylvania, Philadelphia. In addition to the individuals named, Dr. T. M. Peters, Dr. Y. Censor, Dr. A. H. Lent, Dr. A. K. Louis, and Dr. H. K. Tuy have been especially helpful.

References

[1.1] Y. Censor, "Finite series expansion reconstruction methods," this issue, pp. 409–419.

[1.2] M. D. Altschuler, Y. Censor, G. T. Herman, A. Lent, R. M. Lewitt, S. N. Srihari, H. Tuy, and J. K. Udupa, "Mathematical aspects of image reconstruction from projections," in *Progress in Pattern Recognition*, vol. 1, L. N. Kanal and A. Rosenfeld, Eds. Amsterdam: North-Holland, 1981, pp. 323–375.

[1.3] A. Louis and F. Natterer, "Mathematical problems of computerized tomography," this issue, pp. 379–389.

[1.4] D. Slepian, "On bandwidth," *Proc. IEEE*, vol. 64, pp. 292–300, 1976.

[1.5] J. Radon, "Über die Bestimmung von Funktionen durch ihre Integralwerte längs gewisser Mannigfaltigkeiten," *Berichte Saechsische Akademie der Wissenschaften*, vol. 69, pp. 262–277, 1917.

[1.6] A. Macovski, "Physical problems of computerized tomography," this issue, pp. 373–378.

[1.7] P. M. Joseph, "Artifacts in computed tomography," in *Radiology of the Skull and Brain*, vol. 5, T. H. Newton and D. G. Potts, Eds. St. Louis, MO: C. V. Mosby, 1981, ch. 114, pp. 3956–3992.

[1.8] P. M. Joseph and R. D. Spital, "The exponential edge-gradient effect in X-ray computed tomography," *Phys. Med. Biol.*, vol. 26, pp. 473–487, 1981.

[1.9] G. Glover and N. Pelc, "The nonlinear partial volume artifact," *J. Comput. Assist. Tomog.*, vol. 3, pp. 573–574, 1979.

[1.10] G. T. Herman, *Image Reconstruction from Projections: The Fundamentals of Computerized Tomography*. New York: Academic Press, 1980.

[1.11] H. H. Barrett and W. Swindell, *Radiological Imaging: Theory of Image Formation, Detection and Processing*. New York: Academic Press, 1981.

[1.12] G. T. Herman, Ed., *Image Reconstruction from Projections: Implementation and Applications*. Berlin: Springer, 1979.

[1.13] T. H. Newton and G. Potts, Eds., *Radiology of the Skull and Brain*, vol. 5. St. Louis, MO: C. V. Mosby, 1981.

[1.14] M. M. Ter-Pogossian *et al.*, Eds., *Reconstruction Tomography in Diagnostic Radiology and Nuclear Medicine*. Baltimore, MD: Univ. Park Press, 1977.

[1.15] J. Raviv, J. F. Greenleaf, and G. T. Herman, Eds., *Computer Aided Tomography and Ultrasonics in Medicine*. Amsterdam: North-Holland, 1979.

[1.16] O. Nalcioglu, Z. H. Cho, and G. F. Knoll, Eds., "Workshop on physics and engineering in computerized tomography," *IEEE Trans. Nucl. Sci.*, vol. NS-26, pp. 2663–2909, 1979.

[1.17] G. T. Herman and F. Natterer, Eds., *Mathematical Aspects of Computerized Tomography*. Berlin: Springer, 1981.

[1.18] M. Z. Nashed, Ed., *Ill-Posed Problems: Theory and Practice*. Dordrecht: Reidel, to appear.

[1.19] O. Nalcioglu *et al.*, Ed., *International Workshop on Physics and Engineering in Medical Imaging* (IEEE Cat. 82CH1751-7). Silver Spring, MD: IEEE Comput. Soc. Press, 1982.

[1.20] Z. H. Cho, Ed., *IEEE Trans. Nucl. Sci.*, (Special issue on physical and computational aspects of 3-dimensional image reconstruction), vol. NS-21, pp. 1–93, 1974.

[1.21] ——, *Comput. Biol. Med.* (Special issue: Advances in picture reconstruction—Theory and applications), vol. 6, pp. 239–372, 1976.

[1.22] A. C. Kak, Ed., *IEEE Trans. Biomed. Eng.* (Special issue on computerized medical imaging), vol. BME-28, pp. 49–234, 1981.

[1.23] P. R. Smith, T. M. Peters, and R.H.T. Bates, "Image reconstruction from finite numbers of projections," *J. Phys. A: Math. Nucl. Gen.*, vol. 6, pp. 361–382, 1973.

[1.24] D. W. Sweeney and C. M. Vest, "Reconstruction of three-dimensional refractive index fields from multi-directional interferometric data," *Appl. Opt.*, vol. 12, pp. 2649–2664, 1973.

[1.25] R. M. Mersereau and A. V. Oppenheim, "Digital reconstruction of multi-dimensional signals from their projections," *Proc. IEEE*, vol. 62, pp. 1319–1338, 1974.

[1.26] R. Gordon and G. T. Herman, "Three-dimensional reconstruction from projections: A review of algorithms," *Int. Rev. Cytol.*, vol. 38, pp. 111–151, 1974.

[1.27] R. A. Brooks and G. Di Chiro, "Principles of computer assisted tomography in radiographic and radio-isotopic imaging," *Phys. Med. Biol.*, vol. 21, pp. 689–732, 1976.

[1.28] L. A. Shepp and J. B. Kruskal, "Computerized tomography: The new medical X-ray technology," *Amer. Math. Monthly*, vol. 85, pp. 420–439, 1978.

[1.29] H. J. Scudder, "Introduction to computer aided tomography," *Proc. IEEE*, vol. 66, pp. 628–637, 1978.

[1.30] A. C. Kak, "Computerized tomography with X-ray, emission, and ultrasound sources," *Proc. IEEE*, vol. 67, pp. 1245–1272, 1979.

[1.31] A. G. Lindgren and P. A. Rattey, "The inverse discrete Radon transform with applications to tomographic imaging using projection data," *Adv. Electron. Electron Phys.*, vol. 56, pp. 359–410, 1981.

[1.32] R. K. Mueller, M. Kaveh, and G. Wade, "Reconstructive tomography and applications to ultrasonics," *Proc. IEEE*, vol. 67, pp. 567–587, 1979.

[1.33] R.H.T. Bates, K. L. Garden, and T. M. Peters, "Overview of computerized tomography with emphasis on future developments," *Proc. IEEE*, this issue, pp. 356–372.

[1.34] D. Ludwig, "The Radon transform on Euclidean space," *Comm. Pure Appl. Math.*, vol. 19, pp. 49–81, 1966.

[1.35] K. T. Smith, D. C. Solmon, and S. L. Wagner, "Practical and mathematical aspects of the problem of reconstructing objects from radiographs," *Bull. Amer. Math. Soc.*, vol. 83, pp. 1227–1270, 1977.

[1.36] S. Helgason, *The Radon Transform*. Boston, MA: Birkhäuser, 1980.

[1.37] R. N. Bracewell, *The Fourier Transform and its Applications*. New York: McGraw-Hill, 1978.

[1.38] P. A. Rattey and A. G. Lindgren, "Sampling the 2-D Radon transform," *IEEE Trans. Acoust., Speech, Signal Processing*, vol. ASSP-29, pp. 994–1002, 1981.

[1.39] R. M. Lewitt and R.H.T. Bates, "Image reconstruction from projections: III: Projection completion methods (theory)," *Optik*, vol. 50, pp. 189–204, 1978.

[1.40] ——, "Image reconstruction from projections: IV: Projection completion methods (computational examples)," *Optik*, vol. 50, pp. 269–278, 1978.

[1.41] R. M. Lewitt, "Processing of incomplete measurement data in computed tomography," *Med. Phys.*, vol. 6, pp. 412–417, 1979.

[1.42] A. K. Louis, "Picture reconstruction from projections in restricted range," *Math. Meth. Appl. Sci.*, vol. 2, pp. 209–220, 1980.

[1.43] A. Lent and H. Tuy, "An iterative method for the extrapolation of band-limited functions," *J. Math. Anal. Appl.*, vol. 83, pp. 554–565, 1981.

[1.44] M. E. Davison and F. A. Grünbaum, "Convolution algorithms for arbitrary projection angles," *IEEE Trans. Nucl. Sci.*, vol. NS-26, pp. 2670–2673, 1979.

[1.45] K. C. Tam and V. Perez-Mendez, "Tomographical imaging with limited-angle input," *J. Opt. Soc. Amer.*, vol. 71, pp. 582–592, 1981.

[2.1] M. Abramowitz and I. A. Stegun, *Handbook of Mathematical Functions.* New York: Dover, 1965.

[3.1] R. N. Bracewell and A. C. Riddle, "Inversion of fan-beam scans in radio astronomy," *Astrophys. J.*, vol. 150, pp. 427–434, 1967.

[3.2] G. N. Ramachandran and A. V. Lakshminarayanan, "Three-dimensional reconstruction from radiographs and electron micrographs: Application of convolutions instead of Fourier transforms," *Proc. Nat. Acad. Sci. USA*, vol. 68, pp. 2236–2240, 1970.

[3.3] G. T. Herman and S. W. Rowland, "Three methods for reconstructing objects from X-rays: A comparative study," *Comput. Graphics Image Process.*, vol. 2, pp. 151–178, 1973.

[3.4] L. A. Shepp and B. F. Logan, "The Fourier reconstruction of a head section," *IEEE Trans. Nucl. Sci.*, vol. NS-21, pp. 21–43, 1974.

[3.5] P.F.C. Gilbert, "The reconstruction of three-dimensional structure from projections and its application to electron microscopy. II. Direct methods," *Proc. Roy. Soc. Lond.*, ser. B, vol. 182, pp. 89–102, 1972.

[3.6] R. M. Lewitt, R.H.T. Bates, and T. M. Peters, "Image reconstruction from projections II: Modified backprojection methods," *Optik*, vol. 50, pp. 85–109, 1978.

[3.7] S. W. Rowland, "Computer implementation of image reconstruction formulas," in *Image Reconstruction from Projections: Implementation and Applications*, G. T. Herman, Ed. Berlin: Springer, 1979, ch. 2, pp. 9–79.

[3.8] R. A. Brooks, G. H. Weiss, and A. J. Talbert, "A new approach to interpolation in computed tomography," *J. Comput. Assist. Tomog.*, vol. 2, pp. 577–585, 1978.

[3.9] P. M. Joseph, R. D. Spital, and C. D. Stockham, "The effects of sampling on CT images," *Comput. Tomog.*, vol. 4, pp. 189–206, 1980.

[3.10] P. B. Heffernan and R.H.T. Bates, "Image reconstruction from projections. VI: Comparison of interpolation methods," *Optik*, vol. 60, pp. 129–142, 1982.

[3.11] G. H. Weiss, A. J. Talbert, and R. A. Brooks, "The use of phantom views to reduce CT streaks due to insufficient angular sampling," *Phys. Med. Biol.*, vol. 27, pp. 1151–1162, 1982.

[3.12] R. A. Brooks, G. H. Glover, A. J. Talbert, R. L. Eisner, and F. A. DiBianca, "Aliasing: A source of streaks in computed tomograms," *J. Comput. Assist. Tomog.*, vol. 3, pp. 511–518, 1979.

[3.13] C. D. Stockham, "A simulation study of aliasing in computed tomography," *Radiology*, vol. 132, pp. 721–726, 1979.

[3.14] B.K.P. Horn, "Density reconstruction using arbitrary ray-sampling schemes," *Proc. IEEE*, vol. 66, pp. 551–562, 1978.

[4.1] A. V. Oppenheim and R. W. Schafer, *Digital Signal Processing.* Englewood Cliffs, NJ: Prentice-Hall, 1975.

[4.2] K.-H. Löw and F. Natterer, "An ultra-fast algorithm in tomography," Tech. Rep. A 81/03, Fachbereich Angewandte Mathematik und Informatik, Universität des Saarlandes, 6600 Saarbrücken, West Germany.

[4.3] H. H. Stark, J. W. Woods, I. Paul, and R. Hingorani, "Direct Fourier reconstruction in computer tomography," *IEEE Trans. Acoust., Speech, Signal Processing*, vol. ASSP-29, pp. 237–245, 1981.

[4.4] R. N. Bracewell, "Strip integration in radio astronomy," *Aust. J. Phys.*, vol. 9, pp. 198–217, 1956.

[4.5] ——, "Image reconstruction in radio astronomy," in *Image Reconstruction from Projections: Implementation and Applications*, G. T. Herman, Ed. Berlin: Springer, 1979, ch. 3, pp. 81–104.

[4.6] W. S. Hinshaw and A. H. Lent, "An introduction to NMR imaging: From the Bloch equation to the imaging equation," this issue, pp. 338–350.

[4.7] R. A. Crowther, D. J. DeRosier, and A. Klug, "The reconstruction of a three-dimensional structure from projections and its application to electron microscopy," *Proc. Roy. Soc. London*, vol. 317, pp. 319–340, 1970.

[4.8] A. R. Thompson and R. N. Bracewell, "Interpolation and Fourier transformation of fringe visibilities," *Astronomical J.*, vol. 79, pp. 11–24, 1974.

[4.9] R. M. Mersereau, "Direct Fourier transform techniques in 3-D image reconstruction," *Comput. Biol. Med.*, vol. 6, pp. 247–258, 1976.

[4.10] E. O. Brigham, *The Fast Fourier Transform.* Englewood Cliffs, NJ: Prentice-Hall, 1974.

[4.11] C. J. Weinstein *et al.*, Ed., *Programs for Digital Signal Processing.* New York: IEEE Press, 1979.

[4.12] F. Abramovici, "The accurate calculation of Fourier integrals by the Fast Fourier Transform technique," *J. Comp. Phys.*, vol. 11, pp. 28–37, 1973.

[4.13] ——, "The accuracy of finite Fourier transforms," *J. Comp. Phys.*, vol. 17, pp. 446–449, 1975.

[4.14] B. Einarsson, "Use of Richardson extrapolation for the numerical calculation of Fourier transforms," *J. Comp. Phys.*, vol. 21, pp. 365–370, 1976.

[5.1] A. V. Lakshminarayanan, "Reconstruction from divergent ray data," Tech. Rep. TR-92, Dept. Comput. Sci., State Univ. New York, Buffalo, NY, 1975.

[5.2] G. T. Herman, A. V. Lakshminarayanan, and A. Naparstek, "Convolution reconstruction techniques for divergent beams," *Comput. Biol. Med.*, vol. 6, pp. 259–271, 1976.

[5.3] R. M. Lewitt, "Ultra-fast convolution approximations for image reconstruction from parallel and fan beam projection data," Tech. Rep. MIPG25, Medical Image Processing Group, Dep. Comput. Sci., State Univ. New York, Buffalo, NY, 1979.

[5.4] B.K.P. Horn, "Fan-beam reconstruction methods," *Proc. IEEE*, vol. 67, pp. 1616–1623, 1979.

[5.5] T. M. Peters and R. M. Lewitt, "Computed tomography with fan beam geometry," *J. Comput. Assist. Tomog.*, vol. 1, pp. 429–436, 1977.

[5.6] A. Naparstek, "Short-scan fan-beam algorithms for CT," *IEEE Trans. Nucl. Sci.*, vol. NS-27, pp. 1112–1120, 1980.

[5.7] D. L. Parker, "Optimal short scan convolution reconstruction for fan beam CT," *Med. Phys.*, vol. 9, pp. 254–257, 1982.

[6.1] J. E. Greivenkamp, W. Swindell, A. F. Gmitro, and H. H. Barrett, "Incoherent optical processor for X-ray transaxial tomography," *Appl. Opt.*, vol. 20, pp. 264–273, 1981.

[6.2] T. Sato, K. Saski, Y. Nakamura, M. Linzer, and S. J. Norton, "Tomographic image reconstruction from limited projections using coherent optical feedback," *Appl. Opt.*, vol. 20, pp. 3073–3076, 1981.

[6.3] R.H.T. Bates and T. M. Peters, "Towards improvements in tomography," *New Zealand J. Sci.*, vol. 14, pp. 883–896, 1971.

[6.4] P. T. Gough and R.H.T. Bates, "Computer generated holograms for processing radiographic data," *Comput. Biomed. Res.*, vol. 5, pp. 700–708, 1972.

[6.5] T. M. Peters, "Spatial filtering to improve transverse tomography," *IEEE Trans. Biomed. Eng.*, vol. BME-21, pp. 214–219, 1974.

[6.6] G. T. Gullberg, "The reconstruction of fan-beam data by filtering the back-projection," *Comp. Graph. Image Process*, vol. 10, pp. 30–47, 1979.

[6.7] R. M. Perry, "Reconstructing a function by circular harmonic analysis of its Radon transform," in *Dig. Topical Meet. on Image Processing for 2-D and 3-D Reconstruction from Projections: Theory and Practice in Medicine and the Physical Sciences.* Washington, DC: Opt. Soc. of America, 1975, paper Th.A.6, pp. 1–4.

[6.8] E. W. Hansen, "Circular harmonic image reconstruction: Experiments," *Appl. Opt.*, vol. 20, pp. 2266–2274, 1981.

[6.9] A. M. Cormack, "Representation of a function by its line integrals, with some radiological applications," *J. Appl. Phys.*, vol. 34, pp. 2722–2727, 1963.

[6.10] R. M. Lewitt and R.H.T. Bates, "Image reconstruction from projections: I: General theoretical considerations," *Optik*, vol. 50, pp. 19–33, 1978.

[6.11] S. Alliney, "Digital reconstruction of images from their projections in polar coordinates," *Signal Process.*, vol. 3, pp. 135–145, 1981.

[6.12] T. Inouye, "Image reconstruction with limited view angle projections," in *Proc. Int. Workshop on Physics and Engineering in Medical Imaging* (IEEE Cat. 82CH1751-7), Silver Spring, MD: IEEE Comput. Soc. Press, 1982, pp. 165–168.

[6.13] E. W. Hansen, "Theory of circular harmonic image reconstruction," *J. Opt. Soc. Amer.*, vol. 71, pp. 304–308, 1981.

[6.14] J. G. Verly, "Circular and extended circular harmonic transforms and their relevance to image reconstruction from line integrals," *J. Opt. Soc. Amer.*, vol. 71, pp. 825–835, 1981.

[6.15] A. M. Cormack, "Representation of a function by its line integrals, with some radiological applications II," *J. Appl. Phys.*, vol. 35, pp. 2908–2913, 1964.

[6.16] R. B. Marr, "On the reconstruction of a function on a circular domain from a sampling of its line integrals," *J. Math. Anal. Appl.*, vol. 45, pp. 357–374, 1974.

[6.17] M. Ein-Gal, "The shadow transform: An approach to cross-sectional imaging," Rep. SEL-74-050, Information Systems Lab., Stanford Univ., Stanford, CA, 1974.

[7.1] G. T. Herman and A. Lent, "Iterative reconstruction algorithms," *Comput. Biol. Med.*, vol. 6, pp. 273–294, 1976.

[7.2] C. Hamaker and D. C. Solmon, "The angles between the null spaces of X-rays," *J. Math. Anal. Appl.*, vol. 62, pp. 1–23, 1978.

[7.3] L. R. Rabiner and B. Gold, *Theory and Application of Digital Signal Processing.* Englewood Cliffs, NJ: Prentice-Hall, 1975.

[7.4] R. C. Hansen, "A one-parameter circular aperture distribution with narrow beamwidth and low sidelobes," *IEEE Trans. Antennas Propagat.*, vol. AP-24, pp. 477–480, 1976.

Finite Series-Expansion Reconstruction Methods

YAIR CENSOR

Invited Paper

Abstract—Series-expansion reconstruction methods made their first appearance in the scientific literature and in the CT scanner industry around 1970. Great research efforts have gone into them since but many questions still wait to be answered. These methods, synonymously known as algebraic methods, iterative algorithms, or optimization theory techniques, are based on the discretization of the image domain prior to any mathematical analysis and thus are rooted in a completely different branch of mathematics than the transform methods which are discussed in this issue by Lewitt [51].

How is the model set up? What is the methodology of the approach? Where does mathematical optimization theory enter? What do these reconstruction algorithms look like? How are quadratic optimization, entropy optimization, and Bayesian analysis used in image reconstruction? Finally, why study series expansion methods if transform methods are so much faster? These are some of the questions that are answered in this paper.

I. Introduction

THE SERIES-EXPANSION approach to image reconstruction from projections differs fundamentally from the approach generally termed *transform methods* because the problem is discretized at the very beginning whereas with transform methods the continuous problem is handled until the very end when the final formulas are "discretized" for computational implementation.

This article is a tutorial on the series-expansion approach. It describes the methodology of the approach and takes the reader on a short tour of some reconstruction algorithms. We intentionally refrain from mathematical analysis and stay on a descriptive level trusting that readers with further interest will fill in by following the relevant literature. Such reading could start with Herman's book [33, chs. 6, 11–14] or with the survey [36]. Yet another suggestion would be to read our recent review [11] in conjunction with the present paper. The emphasis in [11] is on the mathematics of the so-called *row-action methods* which include many of the series-expansion reconstruction methods, whereas here the reconstruction problem itself is the central theme.

A reasonable coverage of series-expansion reconstruction methods could easily fill up a syllabus for an interesting one-semester course leading to the frontiers of theoretical and experimental research on the topic. Therefore, this tutorial can only introduce the subject and serve as a news-flash or an appetizer for further study. With both of these aims in mind the paper is laid out as follows. Section II describes a discretized model for an image-reconstruction problem; it is the simplest series-expansion model which deals with a grid of square pixels for transmission tomography. In Section III we

Manuscript received April 20, 1982; revised October 18, 1982. This work was supported by the National Institute of Health under Grant HL28438 and the National Science Foundation under Grant ECS-8117908.

The author is with the Medical Image Processing Group, Hospital of the University of Pennsylvania, Philadelphia, PA 19104, on leave from the Department of Mathematics, University of Haifa, Mt. Carmel, Haifa 31999, Israel.

formulate the methodology of the series-expansion approach and describe special features of the problem. Algebraic Reconstruction Techniques (ART) are presented in Section IV while Section V describes how the problem of solving equations may be converted to a feasibility problem of solving inequalities. Another route to handle the image-reconstruction problem is to introduce some extraneous criteria and appeal to optimization-theory techniques. We discuss in Section VI entropy optimization and describe, in Section VII, quadratic optimization in image reconstruction.

To fans as well as to critics of the series-expansion approach to image reconstruction we offer, in Section VIII, a discussion of some advantages and potential advantages of series-expansion methods.

In view of the present material, the wealth of row-action methods described in [11], and investigations reported elsewhere, we believe that the last word in series-expansion reconstruction methods is far from being said.

Besides presenting the principles of the series-expansion approach we admittedly concentrate on topics in which we are presently interested in our own research. No claim of exhaustiveness is made. In particular, we restrict ourselves to iterative techniques thereby leaving out the topic of non-iterative series-expansion methods. A good introduction to this subject may be found in [33, ch. 13].

Yet another pedagogical remark has to be discussed before we turn to the tutorial material itself. It is not unintentional that nowhere in this paper relative merits of the methods we present are discussed or any pictures produced by them are shown. It is not easy to conduct such a discussion in a responsible manner, particularly at the level of acquaintance with the methods acquired by a first time reader of this paper. Many of the papers cited in the references list given at the end of the paper include experimental results but all too often the experimental environment (e.g., test phantoms, level of discretization, amount and quality of projection data, amount of computational efforts invested, i.e., stopping rules, etc.) differ to such an extent that it is quite difficult to draw general conclusions. It is also generally true that there is no single method of choice and that some methods would perform better than others for particular application areas. For the readers' convenience we have marked with an asterisk those references which do contain experimental results and/or display reconstructed images. We advise readers interested in actual performance of the reconstruction methods presented here to consult the original sources of information.

II. A Discretized Model for an Image-Reconstruction Problem

The fundamental model in the series-expansion approach to the image-reconstruction problem of X-ray transmission is formulated in the following way: a Cartesian grid of square picture elements, called pixels, is introduced into the region

Reprinted from *Proc. IEEE*, vol. 71, pp. 409–419, Mar. 1983.

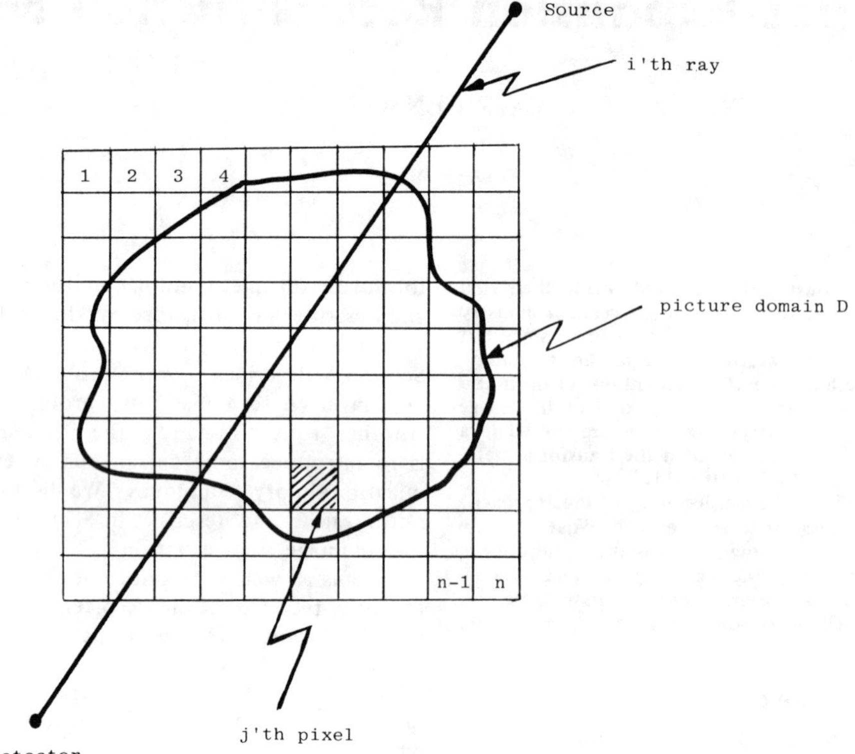

Fig. 1. The square pixels model for transmission tomography image reconstruction.

of interest so that it covers the whole picture that has to be reconstructed. The pixels are numbered in some agreed manner, say from 1 (top left corner pixel) to n (bottom right corner pixel) (see Fig. 1). The X-ray attenuation function is assumed to take a constant value x_j throughout the jth pixel for $j = 1, 2, \cdots, n$. Source and detector are assumed to be points and the rays between them—lines. Further, assume that the length of intersection of the ith ray with the jth pixel, denoted by a_{ij} for all $i = 1, 2, \cdots, m$, $j = 1, 2, \cdots, n$, represents the weight of the contribution of the jth pixel to the total attenuation along the ith ray.

The physical measurement of the total attenuation of the ith ray, denoted by y_i, represents the line integral of the unknown attenuation function along the path of the ray. Therefore, in this discretized model, the line integral turns out to be a finite sum and the whole model is described by a system of linear equations

$$\sum_{j=1}^{n} x_j a_{ij} \simeq y_i, \qquad i = 1, 2, \cdots, m. \qquad (2.1)$$

We may describe the above model in different words. Let $\{b_j(r, \phi)\}_{j=1}^{n}$ be the set of *basis functions*, in polar coordinates in plane, given by

$$b_j(r, \phi) = \begin{cases} 1, & \text{if } (r, \phi) \text{ belongs to the } j\text{th pixel} \\ 0, & \text{otherwise} \end{cases} \qquad (2.2)$$

and call

$$\hat{f}(r, \phi) = \sum_{j=1}^{n} x_j b_j(r, \phi) \qquad (2.3)$$

the *digitization* of $f(r, \phi)$ with respect to the basis functions

$\{b_j\}_{j=1}^{n}$ where x_j is constant within the jth pixel. Let $\{\mathcal{R}_i\}_{i=1}^{m}$ be a set of *linear* and *continuous* functionals which assign to any *picture* $f(r, \phi)$ a real number $\mathcal{R}_i f$. In our case, $\mathcal{R}_i f$ is the line integral of $f(r, \phi)$ along the ith ray. Now, y_i is only an approximation of $\mathcal{R}_i f$ because of the inaccuracy in the physical measurements. $\mathcal{R}_i f$ is close to $\mathcal{R}_i \hat{f}$ because of the continuity of $\mathcal{R}_i$ and since $\hat{f}$ is our approximation for f. Using the linearity of $\mathcal{R}_i$ we may then write

$$y_i \simeq \mathcal{R}_i f \simeq \mathcal{R}_i \hat{f} = \sum_{j=1}^{n} x_j \mathcal{R}_i b_j(r, \phi) = \sum_{j=1}^{n} x_j a_{ij} \qquad (2.4)$$

where $a_{ij} = \mathcal{R}_i b_j(r, \phi)$, thus arriving again at (2.1). In matrix notation we write (2.1) as

$$y \simeq Ax \qquad (2.5)$$

where $y = (y_i) \in \mathbb{R}^m$ (the m-dimensional Euclidean space) is the *measurement vector*, $x = (x_j) \in \mathbb{R}^n$ is the *image vector*, and the $m \times n$ matrix $A = (a_{ij})$ is the *projection matrix*.

The flexibility of the series-expansion approach can be appreciated from this description. First, the functionals $\mathcal{R}_i$ need not be the line integrals we used. They may be any other functionals which may arise in different reconstruction problems as long as their basic properties make them amenable to the modeling process. As an example, we mention the case of ECT (emission-computerized tomography) where the functionals $\mathcal{R}_i$ are the *attenuated line integrals* and the series-expansion approach leads to a system of nonlinear equations instead of the linear system (2.5). A description may be found in [12] and [4, sec. 4]. Secondly, the family of basis functions may be chosen differently than in (2.2). Some examples are discussed in [36, sec. 2] and a new idea is introduced by Buonocore *et al.* in [10].

In the remainder of the paper, we will restrict our attention to the model we have presented which yields a system of linear equations.

III. METHODOLOGY OF THE APPROACH AND SPECIAL FEATURES OF THE PROBLEM

To appreciate the enormous amount of work done on solving linear systems in general one may go back to take a look at [21] and remember that almost three decades of intensive work have passed since its publication. In image reconstruction, however, we have to bear in mind some special features of the problem. The system (2.1) is extremely large, with n (number of pixels) and m (number of rays) of the order of magnitude 10^5 each, in order to produce images with good resolution. The matrix A of the system is very sparse with about less than 1 percent of its entries nonzero because only few pixels have a nonempty intersection with each particular ray.

The system is sometimes underdetermined due to lack of information, often it is greatly overdetermined in which case it is most probably *inconsistent* (i.e., there does not exist a solution in the ordinary sense $x = A^{-1}y$, where A^{-1} is the inverse of A). Moreover, we might have reason to believe that the exact algebraic solution of the system, even if it would exist and we could compute it accurately, is no more desirable in terms of the reconstruction problem than some other, differently defined, "solution." Such a belief may stem from evidence about measurement inaccuracy or noise corruption of data and the fact that the original problem has undergone discretization.

The methodology of the series-expansion approach can be described in general terms as follows.

The original image-reconstruction problem has first to be formulated. At this stage, the physics of the particular problem (e.g., X-ray transmission, single-photon or positron-annihilation emission, ultrasound, etc.) is taken into account and some idealizing assumptions are usually made about it. Here is also where the scanning geometry has to be carefully recorded. The next step in the series-expansion approach is the discretization of the region of interest and it is here where the departure from the approach of transform methods occurs. In transform methods, the problem is handled in its continuous formulation right down to the implementation phase where the necessary approximations are made to the derived inversion formula, whereas here the discretization leads, as we described above, to a system of algebraic equations—linear for X-ray transmission image reconstruction and possibly nonlinear for other reconstruction problems.

In view of the special features of the system at hand, such as dimensions, sparsity, inconsistency, ill-conditioning, etc., one has to choose a *solution concept* according to which a solution for the system will be sought. Most often an optimization criterion is set up with the system of equations or some system of inequalities, derived from it, as the set of constraints over which the optimization has to be performed. This phase is most important since the decision taken here affects the set of "solutions" that will at all be considered for the image-reconstruction problem. The underlying idea is to use the information contained in the system (2.5) in a way that will reflect our limited faith in the equations. Generally, different routes are possible, each leading to a variety of solution concepts but the decision of which one to choose in any particular application rests with the solver and should usually be made with reference to the specific reconstruction problem at hand. The basic approaches are the following.

The Feasibility Approach: Here one seeks a solution which lies within a specified vicinity of all hyperplanes defined by the equations of (2.5). A description is given in Section V below.

The Optimization Approach: An objective function is pre-designated according to which a particular element will be singled out from the *feasible region* which is a set Q in $\mathbb{R}^n$. This feasible region may be composed from inequalities derived from (2.5) as described in Section V and additional inequalities describing *a priori* information about the desirable solution. Examples of optimization problems in image reconstruction are discussed in Sections VI and VII. The regularization approach described in Section VII also leads to an optimization problem.

The next step is the development of a reconstruction algorithm. Such an algorithm should be capable of handling the problem within the special mathematical environment of huge dimensions and sparseness. It should also be efficiently implementable on a computer.

The results of the computer implementation are then evaluated not only in the light of the mathematical problem but chiefly with respect to the original reconstruction problem. Fig. 2 describes the whole approach. The broken line square, numbered 9 in that figure, represents the mathematical efforts involved. The tools for these investigations come from linear algebra, optimization theory, and numerical analysis.

IV. ALGEBRAIC RECONSTRUCTION TECHNIQUES

ART (Algebraic Reconstruction Technique) was first published as a reconstruction algorithm in a 1970 paper by Gordon, Bender, and Herman [26] and was later recognized to be identical with Kaczmarz's algorithm for solving systems of linear equations [45]. Realizing how difficult it would be to handle directly the whole system of equations, Gordon *et al.* suggested an iterative process which starts from an initial approximation $x^0 \in \mathbb{R}^n$ to the image vector. In an iterative step, the current iterate x^k is refined (or say, corrected) to a new iterate x^{k+1} by taking into account only a single ray, say the ith, and changing only the image values of the pixels which intersect this ray. The discrepancy between the measurement y_i and the pseudo-projection data $\sum_{j=1}^{n} a_{ij} x_j^k$ obtained from the current image x^k is redistributed among the pixels along the ith ray proportionally to their weights a_{ij} in the whole ray. In this way, the pixel values along the ith ray are corrected to conform with the ith measurement without changing the rest of the image. Denoting $a^i = (a_{ij})_{j=1}^{n}$ as a vector in $\mathbb{R}^n$, this process is described by the following algorithm:

Algorithm 1. ART (Without Relaxation)

Initialization

$$x^0 \in \mathbb{R}^n \quad \text{is arbitrary.}$$

Typical Step

$$x^{k+1} = x^k + \frac{y_i - \langle a^i, x^k \rangle}{\|a^i\|^2} a^i. \tag{4.1}$$

Here we use the inner product notation and Euclidean norm

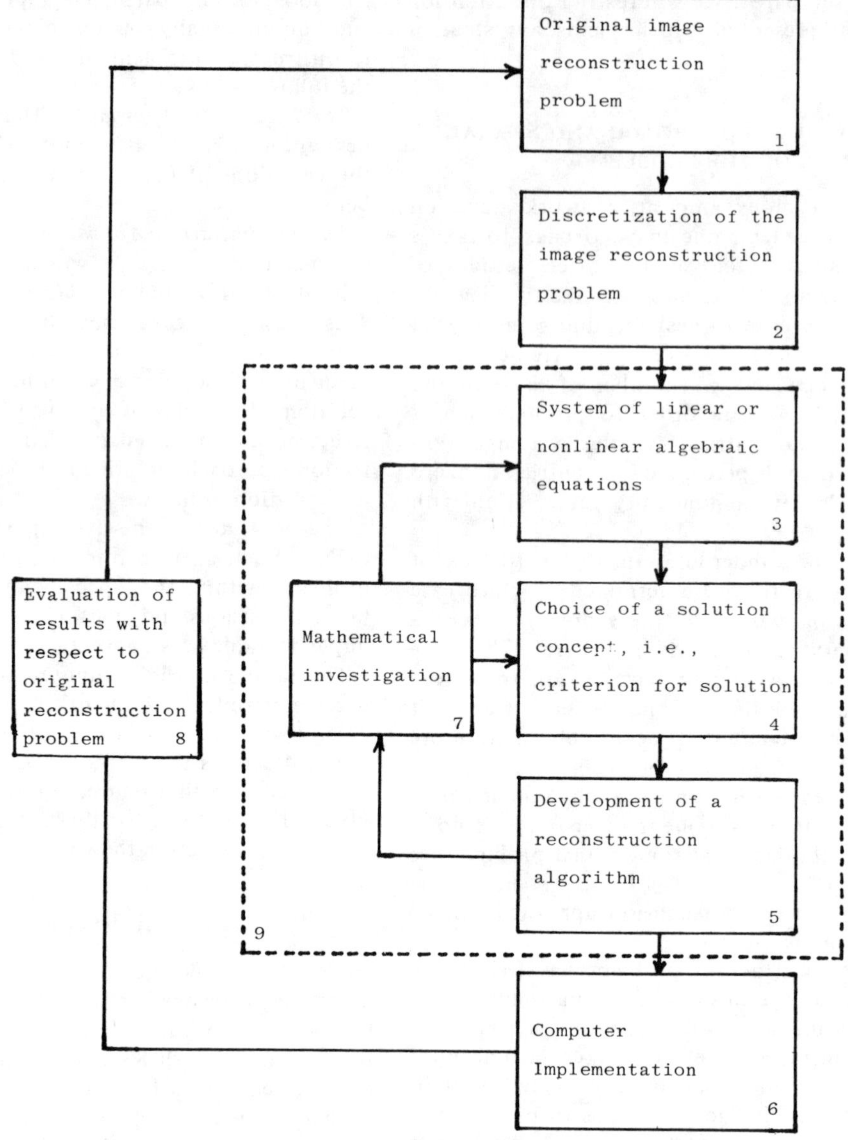

Fig. 2. Methodology of the series-expansion approach.

with the meaning that for every $u, v \in \mathbb{R}^n$

$$\langle u, v \rangle = \sum_{j=1}^{n} u_j v_j$$

and

$$\|u\|^2 = \langle u, u \rangle.$$

The rays are chosen cyclically, i.e.,

$$i = i_k = k \,(\mathrm{mod}\, m) + 1. \tag{4.2}$$

It turns out that besides the intuitive reasoning embodied in ART the algorithm has also the following geometrically meaningful interpretation in the space $\mathbb{R}^n$ of image vectors. The set

$$H_i = \{x \in \mathbb{R}^n | \langle a^i, x \rangle = y_i\} \tag{4.3}$$

composed of all solutions to the ith equation of (2.1) is a hyperplane in $\mathbb{R}^n$, whose normal vector is a^i. The point x^{k+1} (in $\mathbb{R}^n$) is nothing but the orthogonal projection of x^k onto the hyperplane H_i. Thus ART successively projects onto the hyperplanes H_i, represented by the equations of the system (2.1), taken up cyclically.

When considering an iterative process, some mathematical questions may be asked about the sequence of iterates $\{x^k\}_{k=0}^{\infty}$: i) does the sequence converge? ii) what is the nature of the limit vector $x^* = \lim_{k \to \infty} x^k$? iii) what is the rate of convergence to this limit? However, it is instructive to remember that these questions are concerned with the asymptotic behavior of the sequence of iterates produced by the iterative process at hand whereas, in practice, the algorithm is stopped after a finite number of iterations and a particular iteration is taken as an approximation to the desired (and usually unachievable) limit vector.

A question of supreme practical importance is the evaluation of the initial behavior of the infinite sequence of iterates. How "good" are the iterates themselves rather than the limit x^* as approximations to a desired image vector. Unfortunately, not much is known about this and it is always the case with iterative reconstruction methods that when we say that we use a reconstruction algorithm that "does so and so" we mean that we use as an approximate solution to the original image reconstruction problem an image which belongs to a sequence of images which converge (as vectors in $\mathbb{R}^n$) to a limit image which is supposed to have certain properties. This limit image is never achieved, thus "how much" of those desired properties is reflected in the approximate solution is a good question.

Another intriguing question is how does an algorithm like ART behave when applied to an inconsistent system of equations? In other words, is there a limit to the sequence of iterates produced by cyclically performing orthogonal projections onto hyperplanes which do not have points in common to all of them? Tanabe [66] answered this question for ART without the relaxation given above. The behavior of this algorithm for inconsistent systems when relaxation parameters are allowed was studied very recently by Eggermont et al. [16] and Censor et al. [14]. Relaxation parameters are a sequence $\{\lambda_k\}_{k=0}^{\infty}$ of real numbers, usually confined to the interval

$$\epsilon_1 \leqslant \lambda_k \leqslant 2 - \epsilon_2, \quad \epsilon_1, \epsilon_2 > 0 \tag{4.4}$$

which appear in the typical step of ART as

$$x^{k+1} = x^k + \lambda_k \frac{y_i - \langle a^i, x^k \rangle}{\|a^i\|^2} a^i. \tag{4.5}$$

They allow one to overdo or underdo the orthogonal projection prescribed by ART and are extremely important in practical implementation, see, e.g., [33, p. 197].

V. From Linear Equations to Linear Inequalities

In the search for an appropriate solution concept for the system of linear equations obtained by the series-expansion approach it has been suggested [31], [34], [39] to replace the system

$$\langle a^i, x \rangle = y_i, \quad i = 1, 2, \cdots, m \tag{5.1}$$

by a system of inequalities

$$y_i - \epsilon_i \leqslant \langle a^i, x \rangle \leqslant y_i + \epsilon_i, \quad i = 1, 2, \cdots, m \tag{5.2}$$

with ϵ_i, $i = 1, 2, \cdots, m$, some prescribed nonnegative "tolerances." This means that we do not strive to get an algebraic solution, which might not exist, of (5.1) but rather content ourselves with finding a solution for (5.2). Such a solution will be a point x which lies within the vicinities of all hyperplanes, defined by (5.1), as prescribed by the tolerances ϵ_i. Inequalities of the form (5.2) represent hyperslabs in $\mathbb{R}^n$ and the problem of finding a point in the intersection of such a finite family of hyperslabs may be called a *linear interval feasibility problem*.

Again, in view of the dimensionality and sparseness of the problem it seems advisable to use row action methods, [11]. Next we describe two such methods.

The first method disregards the fact that the inequalities in (5.2) come in pairs. By multiplying the left-hand side inequalities of (5.2) by -1 the system turns to be a twice as large (in number of inequalities) system of one-sided linear inequalities

$$\langle c^i, x \rangle \leqslant d_i, \quad i = 1, 2, \cdots, p. \tag{5.3}$$

ART for inequalities is the relaxation method of Agmon [2] and Motzkin and Schoenberg [57] as given in the following algorithm.

Algorithm 2

Initialization

$$x^0 \in \mathbb{R}^n \quad \text{is arbitrary.}$$

Typical Step

$$x^{k+1} = x^k + s_k c^i \tag{5.4}$$

where

$$s_k = \min \left(0, \lambda_k \frac{d_i - \langle c^i, x^k \rangle}{\|c^i\|^2} \right). \tag{5.5}$$

Here $\{\lambda_k\}_{k=0}^{\infty}$ are again relaxation parameters and to secure convergence of the algorithm to a solution of (5.3) they must be restricted as in (4.4).

The algorithm may be controlled by a cyclic sequence of indices, i.e., $i = i_k = k \pmod{p} + 1$.

Another reconstruction method applicable to (5.2) is ART3 due to Herman [31]. Here each hyperslab is enveloped by a larger hyperslab (see Fig. 3) and the following strategy is adopted.

i) If x^k is within the ith hyperslab then $x^{k+1} = x^k$.

ii) If x^k is outside the ith hyperslab but within its enveloping hyperslab then x^{k+1} is the *orthogonal reflection* of x^k with respect to the nearest boundary hyperplane of the hyperslab.

iii) If x^k is outside the enveloping hyperslab then x^{k+1} is the *orthogonal projection* of x^k onto the original ith hyperplane itself.

This gives rise to the following algorithm.

Algorithm 3: ART3

Initialization

$$x^0 \in \mathbb{R}^n \quad \text{is arbitrary.}$$

Typical Step

$$x^{k+1} = x^k + s_k \frac{a^i}{\|a^i\|^2} \tag{5.6}$$

where

$$s_k = \begin{cases} 0, & \text{if } |y_i - \langle a^i, x^k \rangle| \leqslant \epsilon_i \\ y_i - \langle a^i, x^k \rangle, & \text{if } |y_i - \langle a^i, x^k \rangle| \geqslant 2\epsilon_i \\ 2(y_i + \epsilon_i - \langle a^i, x^k \rangle), & \text{if } y_i + \epsilon_i < \langle a^i, x^k \rangle < y_i + 2\epsilon_i \\ 2(-y_i + \epsilon_i + \langle a^i, x^k \rangle), & \text{if } y_i - 2\epsilon_i < \langle a^i, x^k \rangle < y_i - \epsilon_i. \end{cases}$$

ART3 was successfully used as an image-reconstruction algorithm, see, e.g., Robb et al. [62] and Herman et al. [35].

VI. Entropy Optimization

The use of entropy is rigorously founded in several areas, as can be seen from [50], while in other situations entropy optimization is used on a more empirical basis. In image reconstruction from projections several authors advocate the maximum-entropy approach. Minerbo writes in [55]: "From the standpoint of information theory this approach [maximum entropy] is conceptually attractive: it yields the image with the lowest information content consistent with the available data [references]. Thus with this approach one avoids introducing extraneous information or artificial structure. The problem of reconstructing a source from a finite number of

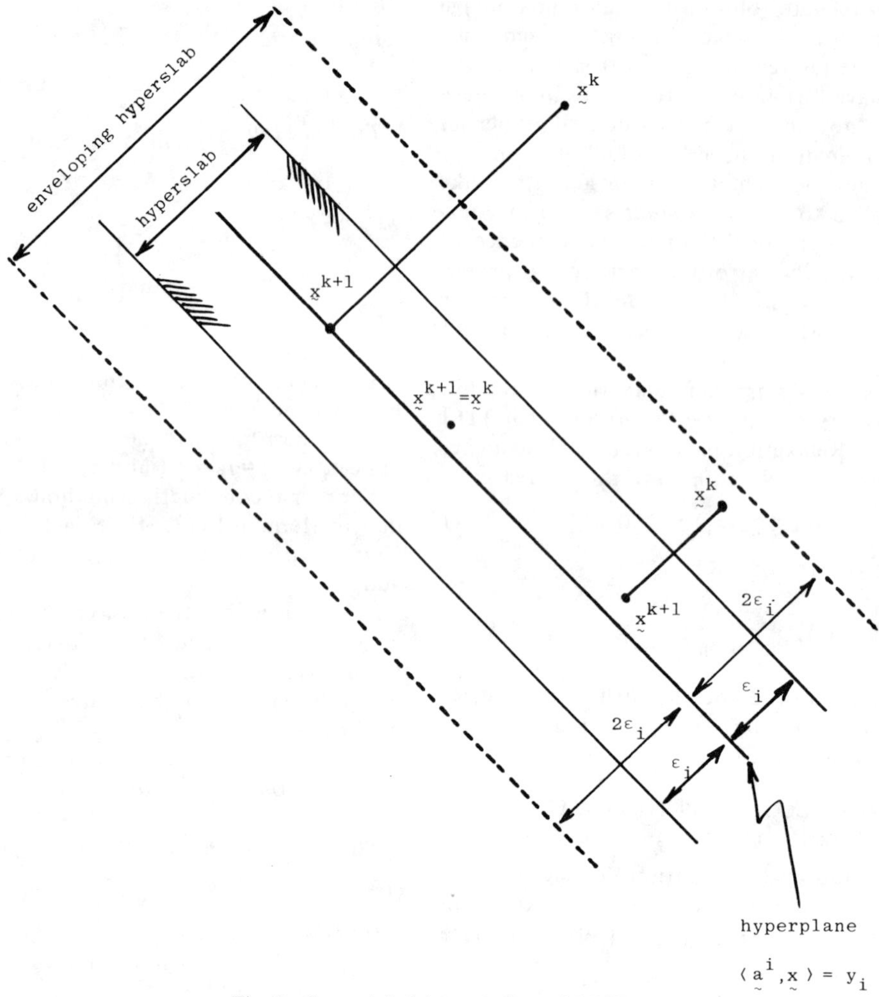

Fig. 3. Geometric interpretation of ART3.

views is known to be indeterminate [references]. A maximum entropy method thus seems attractive for this problem, especially when the available projection data are incomplete or degraded by noise errors." Frieden presents a communication-theory model for restoration of degraded images [23, p. 511]. By his model "the most likely object scene implied by given image data is found to obey a principle of maximum entropy." Frieden is concerned with *image restoration* but it is possible to argue along similar lines also for the *image-reconstruction* problem. Further information about the maximum-entropy approach to image reconstruction from projections might be obtained, e.g., from [6], [24], [28], [56], [63].

In spite of all this, we are obliged to say that the issue is still open for debate both theoretically and experimentally.

On the practical side it would be interesting to compare the performance of some entropy-optimization reconstruction techniques with other reconstruction methods in a way that will test the truth of the assertion that entropy-maximization reconstruction techniques are preferable in situations of information deficiency. Such situations will include reconstruction from incomplete data and might have practical significance towards dose-reduction studies.

It is interesting to note how entropy optimization enters in a variety of fields of applications besides image reconstruction from projections. Such fields include: i) transportation planning; ii) statistics; iii) numerical linear algebra; iv) chemistry, and v) geometric programming. Some further details about these and further references may be found in [17], [20], [47].

Entropy optimization refers to the mathematical problem of maximizing the functional

$$f(\boldsymbol{x}) = -\sum_{j=1}^{n} x_j \ln x_j$$

over various sets of constraints such as i) equality constraints $A\boldsymbol{x} = \boldsymbol{b}$; ii) inequality constraints $A\boldsymbol{x} \leqslant \boldsymbol{b}$; iii) box constraints $\boldsymbol{v} \leqslant \boldsymbol{x} \leqslant \boldsymbol{w}$, iv) interval constraints $\boldsymbol{c} \leqslant A\boldsymbol{x} \leqslant \boldsymbol{b}$, etc., or combinations of such.

In image reconstruction, the collected data and *a priori* information comprise the constraints over which entropy is maximized. A typical problem would be

$$\left.\begin{array}{ll} \text{maximize} & \left(-\sum_{j=1}^{n} x_j \ln x_j\right) \\[2mm] \text{subject to} & \langle \boldsymbol{a}^i, \boldsymbol{x} \rangle = y_i, \quad i = 1, 2, \cdots, m \\[2mm] \text{and} & \boldsymbol{x} \geqslant 0. \end{array}\right\} \quad (6.1)$$

The algorithm given below was first suggested as a reconstruction algorithm for this problem in [26]. Lent [48] proved that it actually converges, under some reasonable conditions, to the solution of this maximum-entropy problem.

Algorithm 4. MART (Multiplicative Algebraic Reconstruction Technique)

Initialization

$$x^0 = e^{-1}\,\mathbf{1}.$$

Typical Step

$$x_j^{k+1} = \left(\frac{y_i}{\langle a^i, x^k \rangle}\right)^{\lambda_k a_j^i} \cdot x_j^k, \quad j = 1, 2, \cdots, n. \quad (6.2)$$

Here e is the base of the natural logarithms, $\mathbf{1}$ is the vector with all ones, and λ_k are relaxation parameters such that $0 < \epsilon \leqslant \lambda_k \leqslant 1$. Equations are taken up cyclically, i.e., $i = i_k = k \,(\mathrm{mod}\, m) + 1$.

A necessary condition for the convergence of MART to the solution of (6.1) is that the feasible set be nonempty, i.e., that $Ax = y$ have a nonnegative solution. The behavior of the algorithm in the realistic situation when the equations are inconsistent is not known. We care to mention this because it so happens that for norm-minimization problems the behavior of ART (Kaczmarz's algorithm) when applied to inconsistent equations is much better understood (see Section IV and [14]).

The general optimization scheme of Bregman [8] was studied recently by Censor and Lent [13] who derived from it a row-action method for interval convex programming. This method applies, in particular, to entropy-optimization problems but has not yet been experimented with in image reconstruction. A new entropy-optimization iterative algorithm, called MENT, was recently introduced by Minerbo [55], [56].

Baba and Murata [6] consider the application of maximum entropy optimization to an image-reconstruction problem with restricted angular view. Some other sample references relevant to entropy optimization, though not concerned with image reconstruction, are Eriksson [19], Erlander [20], Lamond and Steward [47], and Agmon *et al.* [1].

VII. Quadratic Optimazation

Quadratic optimization techniques have been widely used in image reconstruction via series expansion. Under this heading fall norm-minimization methods, SIRT (Simultaneous Iterative Reconstruction Technique)-type methods, Bayesian reconstruction, block-iterative algorithms, and least squares regularization.

It has been argued, see, e.g., [34], that a desirable property of a reconstructed image is that the *variance*

$$\sum_{j=1}^{n} (x_j - \bar{x})^2$$

be small, where

$$\bar{x} = \frac{1}{n} \sum_{j=1}^{n} x_j$$

is the average attenuation of the digitized image. If $\bar{x}$ is considered fixed for all acceptable solutions then the minimum variance and minimum Euclidean-norm solutions coincide. In this way, we arrive at norm-minimization problems of the form

$$\text{minimize } \|x\|^2 \quad \text{subject to} \quad x \in Q \quad (7.1)$$

where $\|\cdot\|$ is the Euclidean norm

$$\left(\sum_{j=1}^{n} x_j^2\right)^{1/2}$$

and $x \in Q$ stands for the linear constraints which reflect the collected projection data and possibly some *a priori* information (see Section V above). Q is a subset of $\mathbb{R}^n$ called the *constraints set* of (7.1). As an example, we describe an algorithm due to Hildreth as discussed by Lent and Censor [49].

Hildreth's algorithm is an iterative procedure which produces a sequence of iterates $\{x^k\}_{k=0}^{\infty}$ which are known [49, theorem 3.1] to converge under certain resonable conditions to the solutions of (7.1) when

$$Q = \{x \in \mathbb{R}^n \,|\, Ax \leqslant b\} \quad (7.2)$$

with A some given $m \times n$ real matrix and b a vector in $\mathbb{R}^m$. The algorithm is a primal–dual algorithm (see, e.g., [53]) which keeps track during iterations of an additional sequence $\{z^k\}_{k=0}^{\infty}$ of dual variables.

Algorithm 5. Hildreth's Algorithm

Initialization

$z^0 \in \mathbb{R}_+^m$ is arbitrary ($\mathbb{R}_+^m$ is the nonnegative orthant of $\mathbb{R}^m$), and $x^0 = -A^T z^0$ (A^T is the transpose of the matrix A).

Typical Step

$$\begin{cases} x^{k+1} = x^k + c_k a^i & \text{and} \\ z^{k+1} = z^k - c_k e^i \end{cases} \quad (7.3)$$

with

$$c_k = \min\left(z_i^k, \lambda_k \frac{y_i - \langle a^i, x^k \rangle}{\|a^i\|^2}\right). \quad (7.4)$$

Here e^i is the ith standard basis vector with 1 in its ith coordinate and zeros elsewhere and a^i is the ith column of A^T. The control index i varies as iterations proceed so that $i \equiv i_k$ and the method may be cyclically controlled $i_k = (k \,\mathrm{mod}\, m) + 1$. A sequence $\{\lambda_k\}_{k=0}^{\infty}$ of relaxation parameters obeying (4.4) for all k is built into the algorithm.

For a geometric interpretation and more information see [49] or [11]. This algorithm underlies the series-expansion reconstruction method ART4 which minimizes norm over linear interval constraints. ART4, developed by Herman and Lent [40], takes advantage of the fact that constraints come as pairs of inequalities. It generalizes an earlier reconstruction algorithm called ART2 [34] and it motivated the development of a more general row-action method for interval convex programming, by Censor and Lent [13], which is based on Bregman's algorithm [8].

In the *least squares regularization approach* the problem

$$\text{``solve''} \ Ax = y \quad \text{such that} \quad x \in Q \quad (7.5)$$

where the linear system comes from (2.1) and the constraints set Q describes any additionally available information, is treated by interpreting it as

$$\text{minimize } (\|x\|^2 + \alpha^2 \|Ax - y\|^2) \quad \text{such that} \quad x \in Q. \quad (7.6)$$

The unique solution of (7.6) is referred to as the *regularized solution* of (7.5). By transforming (7.6) to a constrained norm-minimization problem over an auxiliary linear system of *consistent* equations, Herman *et al.* [42] have made ART-type norm-minimization methods applicable to the problem of finding constrained regularized solutions of large, *inconsistent* linear systems.

Several researchers were led by intuition and heuristics to propose various quadratic objective functionals other than the norm, as optimization criteria by which an acceptable reconstructed image should be chosen. It would be interesting to follow in detail the ideas underlying each individual study along this vein, however, instead, we will describe briefly the unifying work done recently by Herman and Lent [37] and Artzy *et al.* [5].

In [37] the authors identified a general quadratic optimization problem and formulated a general descent algorithm for it thus presenting a unified framework which contains several existing reconstruction methods as subcases. The general problem has the following form:

Problem 1: [5, eq. (5)]

minimize $\|D^{-1}x\|^2$ subject to

$$x \in K = \{x \in \mathbb{R}^n | k(x) \text{ is minimum}\}$$

where

$$k(x) = (y - Ax)^T W_1 (y - Ax) + (\bar{x} - x)^T W_2 (\bar{x} - x). \tag{7.7}$$

Here A is the $m \times n$ projection matrix, $y \in \mathbb{R}^m$ is the measurement vector. The matrices W_1 and W_2 are symmetric positive definite of the form

$$W_1 = aE \qquad W_2 = bB + cC^{-1} \tag{7.8}$$

where a, b, and c are nonnegative real numbers, E and B are symmetric positive definite matrices, and C is a symmetric positive definite matrix. C^{-1} is the inverse of the matrix C. D is some symmetric positive definite matrix, and $\bar{x}$ is a given vector.

Different choices of the matrix D and the functional $k(x)$ give rise to different optimization problems proposed for the image-reconstruction problem treated by the series-expansion approach. For such choices of D and $k(x)$ the general descent algorithm of [37] yields different reconstruction methods.

For example, the SIRT (Simultaneous Iterative Reconstruction Technique) is obtained as a special case of the general scheme. SIRT, proposed by Gilbert [25], is an iterative image-reconstruction method which treats all the equations of (2.1) simultaneously in each iterative step. Lakshminarayanan and Lent [46] showed that a particular version of SIRT strongly resembles the well-known Richardson least squares algorithm and by adopting the adjustable parameters of the latter they were able to produce generalized SIRT algorithms with improved convergence properties. A discussion of SIRT-type methods is given also in [36].

A completely different approach, with which we do not deal here at all, based on Bayesian analysis of the image-reconstruction problem, see [38], [41], [67] can be viewed, from the algorithmic aspect, as another special case of the general quadratic optimization approach given above.

We conclude this section with a description of the recent study of block-iterative algorithms done by Eggermont *et al.* [16]. Consider the system of linear equations

$$Ax = y \tag{7.9}$$

describing the discretized model of an image-reconstruction problem. The $m \times n$ matrix A may be partitioned in two ways as

$$A = \begin{bmatrix} a_1^T \\ \hline a_2^T \\ \hline \vdots \\ \vdots \\ \hline a_{LM}^T \end{bmatrix} = \begin{bmatrix} A_1 \\ \hline A_2 \\ \hline \vdots \\ \vdots \\ \hline A_M \end{bmatrix}. \tag{7.10}$$

Here a_i (elsewhere in this paper denoted by a^i) is an n-dimensional vector and its transpose a_i^T constitutes the ith row of A. Each submatrix A_i is an $L \times n$ block of rows of A and assuming there are M blocks of width L obviously means that $m = LM$ (the assumption that all blocks have equal size is only for convenience).

The n-dimensional vector y is partitioned as

$$y^T = (y_1, y_2, \cdots, y_{LM}) = (Y_1^T \mid Y_2^T \mid \cdots \mid Y_M^T) \tag{7.11}$$

where y_i is the ith coordinate of y and each subvector Y_i is a block of length L of elements of y. Note that in the special case $L = 1$, $A_i = a_i^T$ for $1 \leq i \leq M = m$.

The block–Kaczmarz algorithm of Eggermont *et al.* is the following group-iterative variation of (4.5):

Algorithm 6. Block-Kaczmarz, [16]

Initialization

$$x^0 \in \mathbb{R}^n \text{ is arbitrary.}$$

Typical Step

$$x^{k+1} = x^k + A_i^\dagger \Omega^k (Y_i - A_i x^k). \tag{7.12}$$

Here Ω^k is an $L \times L$ matrix called a *relaxation matrix*, $A_i^\dagger$ is the Moore–Penrose (generalized) inverse of A_i, and the blocks with respect to which the iteration is performed are chosen in a cyclic manner, i.e.,

$$i = i_k = k \,(\text{mod } M) + 1, \qquad k = 0, 1, 2, \cdots.$$

The case $\Omega^k = \lambda_k I$, with I standing for the $L \times L$ identity matrix, has, among other things, essentially been treated by Elfving [18]. In case $L = 1$, Algorithm 6 coincides with Algorithm 1 with a typical step as in (4.5). The relevance of the block–Kaczmarz algorithm to image reconstruction is twofold. First, partitioning the system (2.1) by rows and handling in each iterative step a subset of equations proves to be useful in image reconstruction. This is reflected in [16, sec. 4] where a problem of three-dimensional image reconstruction from X-ray cone-beam projection data is treated by the regularized least squares approach and a block–Kaczmarz (i.e., block–ART) algorithm is applied. The numerical results of that experiment are reported in [3]. Another example of a reconstruction method which employs groups of equations at each step is included in Oppenheim's work [60], this is also explained in [16, p. 52].

The second way by which the study of the block–Kaczmarz algorithm influences image reconstruction is by supplying a unifying framework for a wide class of iterative algorithms used in this field. The class of algorithms covered includes

Kaczmarz's and Richardson's methods for the regularized weighted least square problem with weighted norm, called Problem 1 above. The convergence theory presented in [16] for the block–Kaczmarz algorithm, therefore, contributes in a certain way to our understanding of various image-reconstruction algorithms.

VIII. Series Expansion versus Transform Methods

The first EMI head CT scanner invented by G. N. Hounsfield [44] used essentially ART and the series-expansion approach as its reconstruction method. For the pioneering achievement of building this scanner, including the mathematical approach and algorithm, Hounsfield shared the Nobel Prize with A. M. Cormack in 1979. Today, however, no commercially available CT scanner of X-ray transmission for medical purposes uses series-expansion reconstruction methods. The question why should series-expansion methods be studied at all in image reconstruction could be answered by saying that basic research should not be directed or judged according to its contemporary commercial merits (while apologizing for the analogy, we think of Radon's work back in 1917. Readers who are not familiar with Radon's work, and might therefore miss the point of this last remark, may wish to consult Lewitt's paper [51] or other papers in this issue).

Transform methods are as a rule faster image reconstructors than series-expansion methods since the latter are iterative algorithms notorious for their slow convergence. One can argue that time works in favor of series-expansion methods because future computer technology may increase the speed of computation, even on small machines, to a degree which would remove the advantage of transform methods in favor of series-expansion methods. However, there are some even better (in the practical sense) reasons that the reader should be aware of. Presently, the following points are worth mentioning.

1) Range of Applicability: New models for reconstruction problems are formulated either with new underlying physical principles or by introducing new geometries of data collection. It happens repeatedly that such models are handled by series-expansion methods because this approach lends itself more easily to adaptation to new geometries and new problems. Examples are the model for resistivity reconstruction described by Tasto and Schomberg in [68], image reconstruction from projections of ultrasonic travel times as studied by Schomberg [65] and Meyn [54], the simultaneous approach to the emission computerized tomography problem given by Censor *et al.* [12]. It seems that series-expansion methods are easily adjusted to handle new situations while transform methods are not that flexible.

2) High-Contrast Image Reconstruction: In [7] we read: "The most significant differences between medical and industrial applications of CT arise from the abrupt density changes often encountered in industrial objects. Our studies show that whereas one type of computational process (the convolution algorithm) is generally suitable for medical applications, another process (the ART algorithm or a derivative) is needed for the high contrast objects." Thus in nonmedical applications of CT, like nondestructive material testing, series-expansion methods seem to be of particular interest, see, e.g., [22].

3) Reconstruction from Few Directions: Reconstruction from few directions (less than 10) arises in several nonmedical applications. Some such applications are listed in [55] where we read the following: "Tests have shown [references] that,

with a small number of views, iterative methods generally perform better than two other widely used techniques, Fourier space inversion and convolutional backprojection. However, in ART-type algorithms "streaking" artifacts are a severe problem when the number of views is small [references]."

4) Emission Computerized Tomography: In single-photon emission computerized tomography (ECT), the basic mathematical problem is that of inverting the attenuated Radon transform, see, e.g., [9]. If both the attenuation and the activity distribution are unknown, the problem is inherently not uniquely determined because it calls for the solution of an integral equation the kernel of which is unknown (however, see, [58], [59]). Various methods for attenuation compensation are reviewed in [9, sec. 5.13] and it is beyond the scope of this paper to go into details on this subject. However, we read there [9, p. 218] that "the best results for the situation of *variable attenuation* coefficients encountered when imaging the thorax for lung and heart is the iterative least-squares method wherein *a priori* knowledge of the attenuation coefficients is introduced along with the geometrical weighting factor."

This approach, which falls into the category of series expansion, is carefully studied by Gullberg [29], [30].

A different idea for handling the ECT problem by calculating simultaneously attenuation and activity coefficients is proposed in [12]. It is definitely based on the series-expansion approach to image reconstruction and shows how flexible this approach is.

5) Three-Dimensional Reconstruction: Real three-dimensional image reconstruction, as opposed to three-dimensional reconstruction from consecutive reconstructed cross sections, is considered important for rapid data collection necessary for dynamic reconstruction of moving organs, see, e.g., [71, sec. 6.2] or [61]. In spite of their admitted slowness, various iterative reconstruction algorithms were applied to problems of real three-dimensional reconstruction because of the flexibility of the series-expansion approach mentioned above. Examples are Schlindwein's treatment of two-cone beam projections [64] and the work of Altschuler *et al.* [3] which shows the merits of an iterative refinement of real three-dimensional reconstruction obtained by plain backprojection. See also Colsher's work [15].

6) Incomplete Projections: X-ray dose reduction, speed-up of scan time, or other practical limitations which restrict the range of angles of projections or the density of rays in certain projections—all may lead to incomplete projection-data collection. For a thorough study of the application of some transform methods, through projection completion method, we refer the reader to a series of four papers by Lewitt, Bates, and Peters, the last of which (which includes also details about the preceding ones) is [52]. Oppenheim [60] has studied series-expansion reconstruction methods for tomography from incomplete projections and he writes: "The problem of reconstruction from incomplete projections highlights the basic difference between the convolution and the iterative methods for reconstruction. The convolution methods require that each projection be uniformly sampled, and that a value be assigned to each of the sampling points; hence incomplete projection must be completed. The iterative method, on the other hand, converts the reconstruction problem into one of solving a system of simultaneous linear equations by a relaxation technique, with missing projection values treated like missing equations, i.e., they are ignored."

Oppenheim's conclusions indicate the superiority of his series-expansion reconstruction method for reconstruction from limited field of view projections.

To summarize, we have mentioned here several aspects in which series-expansion methods differ from transform methods. See also [36] and [70, ch. 2] for relevant discussions. In doing so we have tried to make the point that although transform methods are faster and perform better in situations which are handled by present-day commercial scanners, there is accumulating evidence that the series-expansion approach has a potential of being useful in various important, perhaps less standard, situations.

ACKNOWLEDGMENT

Work on this paper was completed during the author's stay with the Medical Image Processing Group, Department of Radiology, Hospital of the University of Pennsylvania, Philadelphia.

REFERENCES

Remark: References marked with an asterisk contain experimental results and/or display reconstructed images.

[1] N. Agmon, Y. Alhassid, and R. D. Levine, "An algorithm for finding the distribution of maximal entropy," *J. Comput. Phys.*, vol. 30, pp. 250–258, 1979.

[2] S. Agmon, "The relaxation method for linear inequalities," *Can. J. Math.*, vol. 6, pp. 382–392, 1954.

*[3] M. D. Altschuler, Y. Censor, P.P.B. Eggermont, G. T. Herman, Y. H. Kuo, R. M. Lewitt, M. McKay, H. K. Tuy, J. K. Udupa, and M. M. Yau, "Demonstration of a software package for the reconstruction of the dynamically changing structure of the human heart from cone beam X-ray projections," *J. Med. Syst.*, vol. 4, pp. 289–304, 1980.

*[4] M. D. Altschuler, Y. Censor, G. T. Herman, A. Lent, R. M. Lewitt, S. N. Srihari, H. Tuy, and J. K. Udupa, "Mathematical aspects of image reconstruction from projections," in *Progress in Pattern Recognition*, L. N. Kanal and A. Rosenfeld, Eds., vol. 1. Amsterdam: North-Holland, 1981, pp. 323–375.

*[5] E. Artzy, T. Elfving, and G. T. Herman, "Quadratic optimization for image reconstruction, II," *Comput. Graph. Image Proces.*, vol. 11, pp. 242–261, 1979.

*[6] N. Baba and K. Murata, "Maximum entropy image reconstruction from projections," Tech. Rep., Dep. Appl. Phys., Hokkaido Univ., Sapporo 060, Japan.

[7] J. P. Barton, C. F. Barton, and K. Barley, "Computerized tomography for industrial applications," Tech. Rep. IRT 4617-011, Instrum. Res. Technol. Corp., San Diego, CA, Feb. 1979.

[8] L. M. Bregman, "The relaxation method of finding the common point of convex sets and its application to the solution of problems in convex programming," *USSR Computat. Math. Math. Phys.*, vol. 7, pp. 200–217, 1967.

*[9] T. F. Budinger, G. T. Gullberg, and R. H. Huesman, "Emission computed tomography," in G. T. Herman, Ed., *Image Reconstruction from Projections: Implementation and Applications* (vol. 32 in series *Topics in Applied Physics*). Berlin: Springer, 1979, ch. 5.

*[10] M. H. Buonocore, W. R. Brady, and A. Macovski, "A natural pixel decomposition for two-dimensional image reconstruction," *IEEE Trans. Biomed. Eng.*, vol. BME-28, pp. 69–78, 1981.

[11] Y. Censor, "Row-action methods for huge and sparse systems and their applications," *SIAM Rev.*, vol. 23, pp. 444–464, 1981.

*[12] Y. Censor, D. E. Gustafson, A. Lent, and H. Tuy, "A new approach to the emission computerized tomography problem: Simultaneous calculation of attenuation and activity coefficients," *IEEE Trans. Nucl. Sci.*, vol. NS-26, pp. 2775–2779, 1979.

[13] Y. Censor and A. Lent, "An iterative row action method for interval convex programming," *J. Optimization Theory Appl.*, vol. 34, pp. 321–353, 1981.

[14] Y. Censor, P.P.B. Eggermont, and D. Gordon, "Strong underrelaxation in Kaczmarz's method for inconsistent systems," to be published in *Numerische Mathematik*, also available as Tech. Rep. MIPG 62, Medical Image Processing Group, Dep. of Radiology, Univ. Pennsylvania, Philadelphia, Dec. 1981.

*[15] J. G. Colsher, "Iterative three-dimensional image reconstruction from tomographic projections," *Comput. Graph. Image Proces.*,

vol. 6, pp. 513–537, 1977.

[16] P.P.B. Eggermont, G. T. Herman, and A. Lent, "Iterative algorithms for large partitioned linear systems, with applications to image reconstruction," *Linear Alg. Its Appl.*, vol. 40, pp. 37–67, 1981.

[17] T. Elfving, "On some methods for entropy maximization and matrix scaling," *Linear Alg. Its Appl.*, vol. 34, pp. 321–338, 1980.

[18] ——, "Block-iterative methods for consistent and inconsistent linear equations," *Numerische Mathematik*, vol. 35, pp. 1–12, 1980.

[19] J. Eriksson, "A note on solution of large sparse maximum entropy problems with linear equality constraints," *Math. Program.*, vol. 18, pp. 146–154, 1980.

[20] S. Erlander, "Entropy in linear programs," *Math. Program.*, vol. 21, pp. 137–151, 1981.

[21] G. E. Forsythe, "Solving linear algebraic equations can be interesting," *Bull. Amer. Math. Soc.*, vol. 59, pp. 299–329, 1953.

*[22] J. S. Fraser, "Beam tomography or ART in accelerator physics," Tech. Rep. LA-7498-MS, Los Alamos Sci. Lab., Los Alamos, NM, Nov. 1978.

*[23] B. R. Frieden, "Restoring with maximum likelihood and maximum entropy," *J. Opt. Soc. Amer.*, vol. 62, pp. 511–518, 1972.

*[24] ——, "Statistical models for the image restoration problem," *Comput. Graph. Image Proces.*, vol. 12, pp. 40–59, 1980.

*[25] P. Gilbert, "Iterative methods for the three-dimensional reconstruction of an object from projections," *J. Theor. Biol.*, vol. 36, pp. 105–117, 1972.

*[26] R. Gordon, R. Bender, and G. T. Herman, "Algebraic reconstruction techniques (ART) for three-dimensional electron microscopy and X-ray photography," *J. Theor. Biol.*, vol. 29, pp. 471–481, 1970.

*[27] R. Gordon and G. T. Herman, "Three-dimensional reconstruction from projections: A review of algorithms," *Int. Rev. Cytol.*, vol. 38, pp. 111–151, 1974.

*[28] S. F. Gull and G. J. Daniell, "Image reconstruction from incomplete and noisy data," *Nature*, vol. 272, pp. 686–690, 1978.

*[29] G. T. Gullberg, "The attenuated radon transform: Theory and application in medicine and biology," Ph.D. dissertation, Tech. Rep. LBL-7486, Donner Lab., Univ. Calif., Berkeley, CA, June 1979.

*[30] ——, "The attenuated Radon transform: Application to single-photon emission computed tomography in the presence of a variable attenuating medium," Tech. Rep. LBL-10276, Donner Lab., Univ. Calif., Berkeley, CA, Mar. 1980.

*[31] G. T. Herman, "A relaxation method for reconstructing objects from noisy X-rays," *Math. Program.*, vol. 8, pp. 1–19, 1975.

*[32] G. T. Herman, Ed., *Image Reconstruction from Projections: Implementation and Applications* (vol. 32 in series *Topics in Applied Physics*). Berlin: Springer, 1979.

*[33] G. T. Herman, *Image Reconstruction From Projections: The Fundamentals of Computerized Tomography*. New York: Academic Press, 1980.

*[34] G. T. Herman, A. Lent, and S. W. Rowland, "ART: Mathematics and applications," *J. Theor. Biol.*, vol. 42, pp. 1–32, 1973.

*[35] G. T. Herman, A. V. Lakshminarayanan, and A. Lent, "The reconstruction of objects from shadowgraphs with high contrasts," *Pattern Recog.*, vol. 7, pp. 157–165, 1975.

[36] G. T. Herman and A. Lent, "Iterative reconstruction algorithms," *Comput. Biol. Med.*, vol. 6, pp. 273–294, 1976.

[37] ——, "Quadratic optimization for image reconstruction, I," *Comput. Graph. Image Proces.*, vol. 5, pp. 319–332, 1976.

*[38] G. T. Herman, H. Hurwitz, Jr., and A. Lent, "A Bayesian analysis of image reconstruction," in M. M. Ter-Pogossian *et al.*, Eds., *Reconstruction Tomography in Diagnostic Radiology and Nuclear Medicine*. Baltimore, MD: Univ. Park Press, 1977, pp. 85–104.

*[39] G. T. Herman, A. Lent, and P. H. Lutz, "Relaxation methods for image reconstruction," *Commun. ACM*, vol. 21, pp. 152–158, 1978.

*[40] G. T. Herman and A. Lent, "A family of iterative quadratic optimization algorithms for pairs of inequalities, with application in diagnostic radiology," *Math. Program. Study*, vol. 9, pp. 15–29, 1978.

*[41] G. T. Herman, H. Hurwitz, A. Lent, and H. P. Lung, "On the Bayesian approach to image reconstruction," *Informat. Contr.*, vol. 42, pp. 60–71, 1979.

*[42] G. T. Herman, A. Lent, and H. Hurwitz, "A storage-efficient algorithm for finding the regularized solution of a large, inconsistent system of equations," *J. Inst. Math. Appl.*, vol. 25, pp. 361–366, 1980.

*[43] G. T. Herman and F. Natterer, Eds., *Mathematical Aspects of Computerized Tomography* (*Lecture Notes in Medical Informatics*, vol. 8). Berlin: Springer, 1981.

[44] G. N. Hounsfield, "A method and apparatus for examination of a body by radiation such as X or gamma radiation," Patent

Spec. 1283915, The Patent Office, London, England.

[45] S. Kaczmarz, "Angenäherte Auflösung von Systemen Linearer Gleichungen," *Bull. Acad. Polon. Sci. Lett., A.*, vol. 35, pp. 355–357, 1937.

*[46] A. V. Lakshminarayanan and A. Lent, "Methods of least squares and SIRT in reconstruction," *J. Theor. Biol.*, vol. 76, pp. 267–295, 1979.

[47] B. Lamond and N. F. Stewart, "Bregman's balancing method," *Transp. Res.*, vol. 15B, pp. 239–248, 1981.

*[48] A. Lent, "Maximum entropy and multiplicative ART," in R. Shaw, Ed., *Image Analysis and Evaluation* (SPSE Conf. Proc.). Washington, DC: Soc. Photog. Sci. Eng., 1977, pp. 249–257.

[49] A. Lent and Y. Censor, "Extensions of Hildreth's row-action method for quadratic programming," *SIAM J. Contr. Optimiz.*, vol. 18, pp. 444–454, 1980.

[50] R. D. Levine and M. Tribus, Eds., *The Maximum Entropy Formalism.* Cambridge, MA: MIT Press, 1978.

[51] R. M. Lewitt, "Reconstruction algorithms: Transform methods," this issue, pp. 390–408.

*[52] R. M. Lewitt and R.H.T. Bates, "Image reconstruction from projections: IV: Projection completion methods (computational examples)," *Optik*, vol. 50, pp. 269–278, 1978.

[53] D. G. Luenberger, *Optimization by Vector Space Methods.* New York: Wiley, 1969.

*[54] K. H. Meyn, "A generalization of a theorem of Ostrowski and its application to a nonlinear extension of the method of Kaczmarz," Tech. Rep. MS-H 2466/80, Philips GmbH Forschunglaboratium Hamburg, W. Germany, 1980.

*[55] G. Minerbo, "MENT: A maximum entropy algorithm for reconstructing a source from projection data," *Comput. Graph. Image Proces.*, vol. 10, pp. 48–68, 1979.

*[56] ——, "Maximum entropy reconstruction from cone-beam projection data," *Comput. Biol. Med.*, vol. 9, pp. 29–37, 1979.

[57] T. S. Motzkin and I. J. Schoenberg, "The relaxation method for linear inequalities," *Can. J. Math.*, vol. 6, pp. 393–404, 1954.

[58] F. Natterer, "The identification problem in emission computed tomography," in G. T. Herman and F. Natterer, Eds., *Mathematical Aspects of Computerized Tomography* (*Lecture Notes in Medical Informatics*, vol. 8). Berlin: Springer, 1981, pp. 45–56.

*[59] ——, "Computerized tomography with unknown sources," Tech. Rep. A 81/06, Fachbereich Angewandte Mathematik und Informatik, Universtät Des Saarlandes, Saarbrücken, W. Germany, 1981.

*[60] B. E. Oppenheim, "Reconstruction tomography from incomplete projections," in M. M. Ter-Pogossian *et al.*, Eds, *Reconstruction Tomography in Diagnostic Radiology and Nuclear Medicine.* Baltimore, MD: Univ. Park Press, 1977, pp. 155–183.

*[61] E. L. Ritman, R. A. Robb, S. A. Johnson, P. A. Chevalier, B. K. Gilbert, J. F. Greenleaf, R. E. Sturm, and E. H. Wood, "Quantitative imaging of the structure and function of the heart, lungs, and circulation," *Mayo Clinic Proc.*, vol. 53, pp. 3–11, 1978.

*[62] R. A. Robb, J. F. Greenleaf, E. L. Ritman, S. A. Johnson, J. D. Sjostrand, G. T. Herman, and E. H. Wood, "Three-dimensional visualization of the intact thorax and contents: A technique for cross-sectional reconstruction from multiplanar X-ray views," *Comput. Biomed. Res.*, vol. 7, pp. 395–419, 1974.

*[63] R. Shaw, Ed., *Image Analysis and Evaluation* (SPSE Conf. Proc.). Washington, DC: Soc. Photog. Sci. Eng., 1977.

*[64] M. Schlindwein, "Iterative three-dimensional reconstruction from twin-cone beam projections," *IEEE Trans. Nucl. Sci.*, vol. NS-25, pp. 1135–1143, 1978.

*[65] H. Schoemberg, "Nonlinear image reconstruction from projections of ultrasonic travel times and electric current densities," in G. T. Herman and F. Natterer, Eds., *Mathematical Aspects of Computerized Tomography* (*Lecture Notes in Medical Informatics*, vol. 8). Berlin: Springer, 1981, pp. 270–291.

[66] K. Tanabe, "Projection method for solving a singular system of linear equations and its applications," *Numerische Mathematik*, vol. 17, pp. 203–214, 1971.

*[67] M. Tasto, "Reconstruction of random objects from noisy projections," *Comput. Graph. Image Proces.*, vol. 6, pp. 103–122, 1977.

*[68] M. Tasto and H. Schomberg, "Object reconstruction from projections and some nonlinear extensions," in *Pattern Recognition and Signal Processing*, C. H. Chen, Ed. Amsterdam, The Netherlands: Sijthoff and Noordhoft, 1978, pp. 485–503.

*[69] M. M. Ter-Pogossian *et al.*, Eds., *Reconstruction Tomography in Diagnostic Radiology and Nuclear Medicine.* Baltimore, MD: Univ. Park Press, 1977.

*[70] L. A. Weisberg, C. Nice, and M. Katz, *Cerebral Computed Tomography: A Text-Atlas.* Philadelphia, London, Toronto: W. B. Saunders, 1978.

*[71] E. H. Wood, J. H. Kinsey, R. A. Robb, B. K. Gilbert, L. D. Harris, and E. L. Ritman, "Applications of high temporal resolution, computerized tomography to physiology and medicine," in G. T. Herman, Ed., *Image Reconstruction from Projections: Implementation and Applications* (vol. 32 of series *Topics in Applied Physics*). Berlin: Springer, 1979, ch. 6.

A Tomographic Formulation of Spotlight-Mode Synthetic Aperture Radar

DAVID C. MUNSON, JR., MEMBER, IEEE, JAMES DENNIS O'BRIEN, STUDENT MEMBER, IEEE, AND W. KENNETH JENKINS, SENIOR MEMBER, IEEE

Abstract—Spotlight-mode synthetic aperture radar (spotlight-mode SAR) synthesizes high-resolution terrain maps using data gathered from multiple observation angles. This paper shows that spotlight-mode SAR can be interpreted as a tomographic reconstruction problem and analyzed using the projection-slice theorem from computer-aided tomography (CAT). The signal recorded at each SAR transmission point is modeled as a portion of the Fourier transform of a central projection of the imaged ground area. Reconstruction of a SAR image may then be accomplished using algorithms from CAT. This model permits a simple understanding of SAR imaging, not based on Doppler shifts. Resolution, sampling rates, waveform curvature, the Doppler effect, and other issues are also discussed within the context of this interpretation of SAR.

I. INTRODUCTION

BOTH computer-aided tomography (CAT) and synthetic aperture radar (SAR) are well-known techniques for constructing high-resolution images by processing data obtained from many different perspective views of a target area. The CAT scan, as it is familiarly termed now, is an X-ray technique which enables the imaging of two-dimensional cross sections of solid objects [1], [2]. In particular, tomography is used extensively for noninvasive medical examination of internal organs and in nondestructive testing of manufactured items. Although SAR is well known to a more exclusive community, it too is a well-developed technique for producing high-resolution images. In a SAR system, the desired image is a terrain map. The data are collected by means of an airborne or spaceborne microwave radar which illuminates the target area from different perspectives.

An early form of SAR, known as unfocused strip mapping, was demonstrated experimentally at the University of Illinois as far back as the early 1950's [3]. In strip-mapping SAR (both focused and unfocused), the position of the antenna remains fixed relative to the aircraft, thereby illuminating a strip of terrain as the aircraft flies. Proper processing of the returned signals allows the effective synthesis of a very large antenna, providing high resolution [3]–[6]. Extensive developmental work on optical processing of data collected in strip-mapping SAR was subsequently carried out by Brown and coworkers at what is now the Environmental Research Institute of Michigan. Walker [7], working with Brown, made a breakthrough in characterizing the requirements for optically processing coherent radar data collected from targets placed on a rotating platform, an experimental setup designed to simulate an airborne radar flying around a stationary ground patch—this was, in essence, the first spotlight-mode SAR. In this paper, we will focus on this latter type of SAR, in which the physical antenna is steered so that the same terrain area remains illuminated during a long data-collection interval [5], [7]–[9]. Spotlight-mode SAR is able to provide higher resolution of a more limited area than strip-mapping SAR, because the same terrain area is observed from many different angles.

The fact that CAT and spotlight-mode SAR have developed independently—CAT having attracted the interest of biomedical researchers, and SAR that of communications and radar specialists—has obscured a remarkable similarity of principle which they share. CAT processing has generally been characterized by the projection-slice theorem [1], [2], [10], [11], while spotlight-mode SAR processing has been described in the radar language of Doppler filtering [7], [8], [12]. A survey of published literature on SAR may not lead one to suspect that SAR is a distant cousin of CAT. The major objective of this paper is to demonstrate that CAT and SAR are, in fact, very similar concepts. It will be shown that spotlight-mode SAR can be interpreted as a tomographic reconstruction problem, and that the signal processing theory can be characterized in terms of the projection-slice theorem. The advantages in developing this connection are several. First, research into mathematical methods and algorithms developed in one field may be transferred to the other. Second, the tomographic interpretation simplifies the understanding of SAR, especially for those not versed in radar terminology. A third advantage is that the role of coherence is underscored and the speckle phenomenon is easily explained when SAR is interpreted as a narrow-band version of CAT.

Some of these concepts have been examined in relation to acoustic imaging using sources emitting short pulses or polychromatic continuous-wave (CW) illumination over circular apertures [13], [14]. Several authors have also discussed SAR utilizing polychromatic CW illumination over circular apertures (see, for instance, [15]). In practice, though, airborne radars are not coherent over extended flight trajectories due to unavoidable phase errors (caused by atmospheric granularity and motion error) and due to the angular dependence of the reflectors being imaged. Chen and Andrews [16] discuss the spotlight-mode SAR problem for sources emitting sinusoidal waveforms. Herman [2], [17] discusses related work in other fields, including radio astronomy.[1]

To introduce our basic approach, Section II reviews the projection-slice theorem and summarizes the fundamental principles of tomographic reconstruction. The mathematical formulation of SAR in Section III contains the significant contribution of this paper. If linear FM waveforms are transmitted during spotlight-mode operation, it is demonstrated that the demodulated wave-

Manuscript received July 6, 1982; revised March 28, 1983. This work was supported by the Joint Services Electronics Program under Contract N00014-79-C-0424. Portions of this manuscript were presented at the Fifteenth Asilomar Conference on Circuits, Systems, and Computers, Pacific Grove, CA, November 9–11, 1981.

The authors are with the Coordinated Science Laboratory and the Department of Electrical Engineering, University of Illinois, Urbana, IL 61801.

[1]Mensa *et al.* [18] also present some closely related work on microwave tomographic imaging. Reference [18] was published while this paper was still in review.

Reprinted from *Proc. IEEE*, vol. 71, pp. 917–925, Aug. 1983.

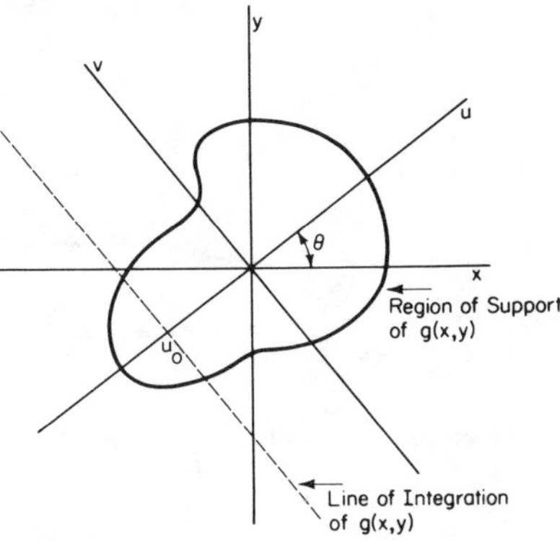

Fig. 1.   Line of integration for determining the projection $p_\theta(u_0)$.

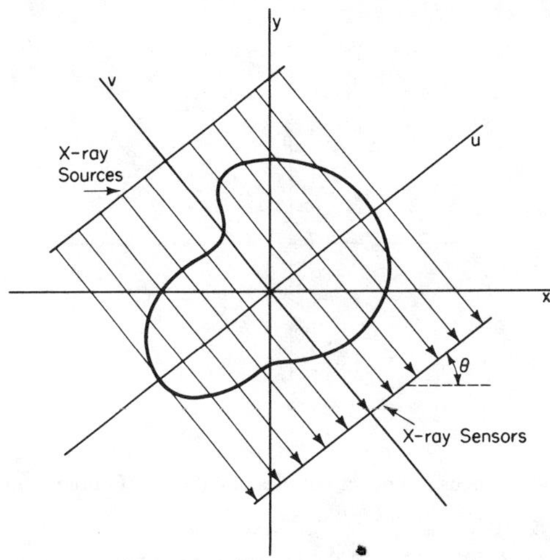

Fig. 2.   A parallel-beam X-ray tomography system.

form obtained at each look angle approximates a piece of the one-dimensional (1-D) Fourier transform of a central projection of the ground patch at a corresponding projection angle. A similar statement has been made by Brown [19] in his interpretation and generalization of the work by Walker [7]. Together with the projection-slice theorem, this enables SAR and the processing of SAR data to be viewed in terms similar to CAT, although the physical constraints and data-gathering limitations are somewhat different. SAR is then discussed as a narrow-band version of CAT and the possibility of using CAT processing algorithms, such as convolution backprojection, for SAR is presented. Finally, for completeness, Section IV addresses the issues of resolution, sampling rates, wavefront curvature, quadratic phase errors, effect of Doppler and time-varying range, and the modification of results for slant-plane geometry.

II. Brief Review of Computer-Aided Tomography

Computer-aided tomography is a technique for providing a two-dimensional (2-D) cross-sectional view of a three-dimensional (3-D) object through digital processing of many 1-D projectional views taken from different look angles. These projectional views are obtained by passing sets of narrow X-ray beams through the object and detecting their intensities using an array of sensors. If desired, a 3-D reconstruction may be obtained by this technique as a collection of parallel cross sections.

A. Projection-Slice Theorem

The principle underlying the theory of CAT is the projection-slice theorem [1], [2], [10], [11]. Let $g(x, y)$ be an unknown signal that is to be reconstructed from its projections. The Fourier transform of g is defined as

$$G(X, Y) = \int_{-\infty}^{\infty} \int_{-\infty}^{\infty} g(x, y) e^{-j(xX+yY)} \, dx \, dy$$

so that

$$g(x, y) = \frac{1}{4\Pi^2} \int_{-\infty}^{\infty} \int_{-\infty}^{\infty} G(X, Y) e^{j(xX+yY)} \, dX \, dY. \quad (1)$$

The projection of g at angle θ is formally given by

$$p_\theta(u) = \int_{-\infty}^{\infty} g(u\cos\theta - v\sin\theta, u\sin\theta + v\cos\theta) \, dv \quad (2)$$

where $p_\theta(u)$ evaluated at $u = u_0$ is simply a line integral in the direction of the v axis as illustrated in Fig. 1. Note that the u axis forms an angle θ with the x axis. The function $p_\theta(u)$ represents a series of such line integrals for each value of θ.

The 1-D Fourier transform of $p_\theta(u)$ is given by

$$P_\theta(U) = \int_{-\infty}^{\infty} p_\theta(u) e^{-juU} \, du.$$

Using this notation, the statement of the projection-slice theorem is simply

$$P_\theta(U) = G(U\cos\theta, U\sin\theta) \quad (3)$$

that is, the Fourier transform of the projection at angle θ is a "slice" of the 2-D transform $G(X, Y)$ taken at an angle θ with respect to the X axis.

B. Tomographic Reconstruction

In X-ray tomography, $g(x, y)$ is an unknown cross-sectional attenuation coefficient which is to be measured. Samples of the projection $p_\theta(u)$ are obtained in a parallel-beam system with an array of X-ray sources and detectors oriented at an angle θ with respect to the x axis, as shown in Fig. 2. Since the intensity of a received X-ray beam exhibits exponential dependence on the line integral of g [2], projections of g are found in terms of the logarithms of the measured intensities, i.e.,

$$p_\theta(u) = -\log \frac{I_\theta(u)}{I_0}$$

where I_0 is the intensity of the X-ray source and $I_\theta(u)$ is the received intensity at the detector. Projections $p_{\theta_i}(u)$ are obtained at equally spaced angles $\theta = \theta_i$ by rotating either the object or the array of X-ray sources and detectors through a set of discrete angles spanning 360°.

In present tomographic systems, it is common to reconstruct the attenuation coefficient $g(x, y)$ from the projections $p_{\theta_i}(u)$ via the convolution backprojection method [1]. This method will be described later in conjunction with a modification for SAR. An alternate method is direct Fourier domain reconstruction. It is the direct Fourier technique which is used primarily in SAR and it has also been considered for use in tomography [11], [20]. Using the direct Fourier technique, $g(x, y)$ is reconstructed from samples $p_{\theta_i}(u_j)$ of its projections as follows. For each angle θ_i, uniformly spaced samples of the Fourier transform $P_{\theta_i}(U)$ are computed from $\{ p_{\theta_i}(u_j) \}_{j=1}^{N}$ via the fast Fourier transform (FFT). From the projection-slice theorem, (3), the samples of $P_{\theta_i}(U)$ are samples of $G(X, Y)$ along a line at angle θ_i with the X axis. Thus the series of 1-D FFT's for the various θ_i provides samples of $G(X, Y)$ on the polar grid shown in Fig. 3. Interpolating the polar samples of G to a Cartesian grid allows the efficiencies of the 2-D inverse FFT to be utilized to approximate g on a

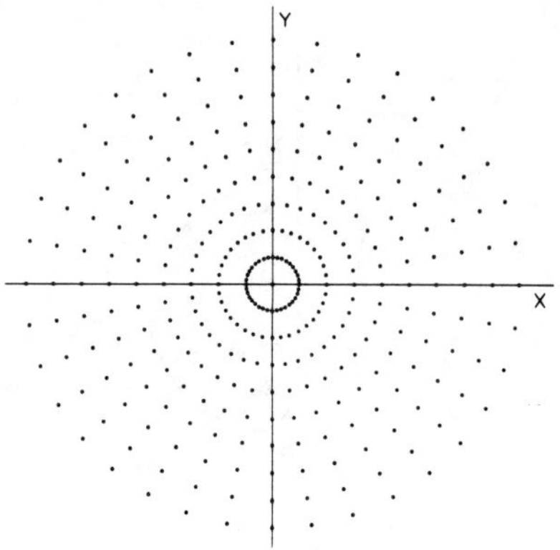

Fig. 3.   Locus of known samples of $G(X, Y)$ (Fourier domain).

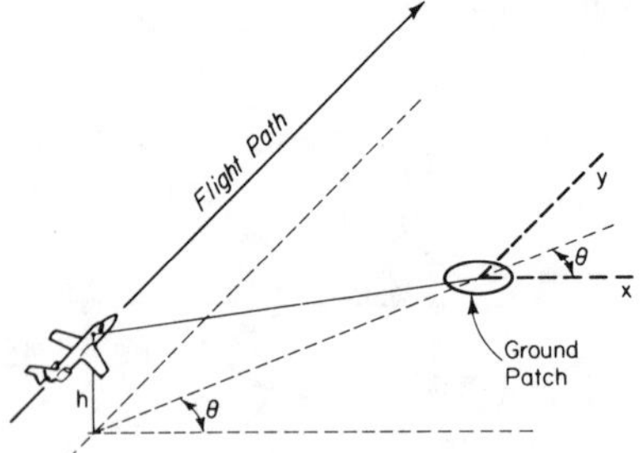

Fig. 4.   Geometry for data collection in spotlight-mode SAR.

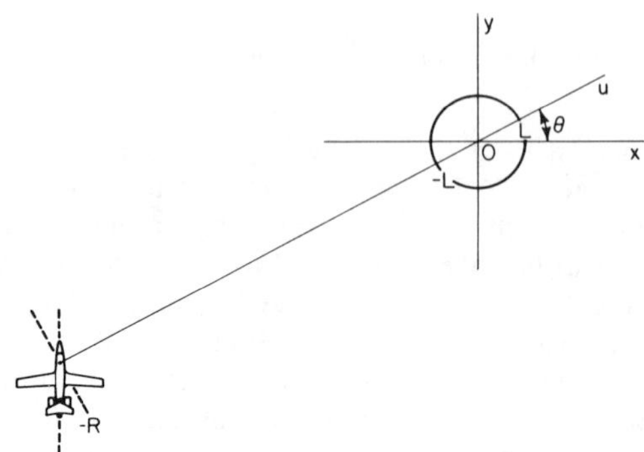

Fig. 5.   Ground-plane geometry for data collection in spotlight-mode SAR.

Cartesian grid [9], [11], [20]. It must be said, though, that no really "fast" algorithm has yet been devised to compute g from the polar samples of G (although this is an area of research [2], [11], [17], [20]–[23]); unless a time-consuming interpolation is carried out prior to employing the FFT, the image quality produced by the Fourier technique will be noticeably worse than that provided by the convolution backprojection method.

III.   Spotlight-Mode Synthetic Aperture Radar

A. Introduction

The limiting factor in the azimuthal (cross-range) resolving capabilities of an ordinary ranging radar is the antenna beamwidth in the distant field. For airborne operation, a narrow beamwidth requires an impractically large antenna. Spotlight-mode SAR effectively avoids this requirement by collecting radar returns from many different angular views of a target. By properly processing the return signals, very high resolution in azimuth can be achieved. High resolution in range may be achieved by transmitting high-bandwidth pulses as in a conventional radar.

The geometry for data collection in a spotlight-mode SAR is shown in Fig. 4. The x–y coordinate system (denoting *range* and *azimuth* coordinates, respectively) is centered on a relatively small patch of ground illuminated by a narrow RF beam from the moving radar. As the radar traverses the flight path, the radar beam, as operating in the spotlight mode, is continuously pointed in the direction (angle θ) of the ground patch. At points corresponding to equal increments of θ, high-bandwidth pulses (such as linear FM) are transmitted to the ground patch and echoes are then received and processed. The radar return yields a projectional view of the target, provided the phase front of the radio waves exhibits no significant curvature. This view turns out, in fact, to be a band-pass filtered projection of the ground-patch reflectivity, since the radio waves are narrow-band.

As the aircraft moves with respect to the target patch, the received signal undergoes a slight Doppler shift (to be discussed later) which varies according to the observation angle. The SAR imaging equations can be derived as a function of either the Doppler shift or the underlying change in viewing angle. It is important to emphasize, however, that the imaging principle employed in spotlight-mode SAR is tomographic, rather than Doppler based. That is, although the radar antenna must be moved from point to point to obtain different viewing angles, successful imaging is not dependent on a difference in relative velocity between the antenna and ground patch during pulse transmission and reception. As far as the imaging mechanism is concerned, the aircraft could completely stop at each transmission point in space and the SAR would still work properly.

B. Basic SAR Derivation

If it is assumed that the depression angle from the radar to the ground patch is zero, the geometry reduces to Fig. 5. Later, it will be indicated how the results can be modified for the case of a nonzero depression angle (i.e., the height $h \neq 0$). In Fig. 5, the reflectivity density of the ground patch is modeled by the complex function[2] $g(x, y)$ where a sinusoid reflected from a point (x_0, y_0) is scaled in amplitude by $|g(x_0, y_0)|$ and shifted in phase by $\angle g(x_0, y_0)$ where $g(x, y) = |g(x, y)| \exp(j\angle g(x, y))$. Furthermore, it is assumed that $g(x, y)$ is constant over the range of frequencies and range of viewing angles θ employed by the radar.

At angle θ, let the radar transmit a linear FM chirp pulse $\text{Re}\{s(t)\}$, where

$$s(t) = \begin{cases} e^{j(\omega_0 t + \alpha t^2)}, & |t| \leq \dfrac{T}{2} \\ 0, & \text{otherwise} \end{cases} \tag{4}$$

ω_0 is the RF carrier frequency and 2α is the FM rate. The return signal from a differential area centered on the point (x_0, y_0) at a distance R_0 from the radar will be

$$r_0(t) = A|g(x_0, y_0)|\cos\left(\omega_0\left(t - \frac{2R_0}{c}\right) + \alpha\left(t - \frac{2R_0}{c}\right)^2 \right.$$
$$\left. + \angle g(x_0, y_0) \right) dx \, dy$$

---

[2] The amplitude scaling occurs because only a fraction of the incident radiation is reflected back to the radar. The phase shift of the reflected wave may be caused by several factors; foremost is probably the shift at the air/target interface due to the difference between the dielectric constants of air and the target material. This effect is similar to that observed at the boundary of two waveguides having different characteristic impedances where at least one of the waveguides is dissipative [24]. The phase shift is also due to the tendency of the RF radiation to creep around target surfaces and its ability to penetrate soft objects and be reflected from within.

where A accounts for propagation attenuation, c is the speed of light, and $2R_0/c$ accounts for the two-way travel time from radar to target. The return $r_0(t)$ is written more simply as

$$r_0(t) = A \cdot \mathrm{Re}\left\{ g(x_0, y_0) s\left(t - \frac{2R_0}{c} \right) \right\} \, dx \, dy. \tag{5}$$

In Fig. 5, points in the ground patch equidistant from the radar lie on an arc, but for a typical system $R \gg L$, so that this arc is nearly a straight line. Therefore, taking $p_\theta(u)$ to be the line integral given by (2), it follows from (5), by superposition,[3] that the return signal from a differential line of scatterers normal to the u axis at $u = u_0$ is given by

$$r_1(t) = A \cdot \mathrm{Re}\left\{ p_\theta(u_0) s\left(t - \frac{2(R + u_0)}{c} \right) \right\} \, du.$$

If $R \gg L$, the attenuation A may be taken as a constant. Therefore, the return from the entire ground patch can be approximated by the integral of r_1 over u, given by

$$r_\theta(t) = A \cdot \mathrm{Re}\left\{ \int_{-L}^{L} p_\theta(u) s\left(t - \frac{2(R + u)}{c} \right) \, du \right\}. \tag{6}$$

This expression has the form of a convolution, thus the transform of p_θ can be obtained by Fourier methods over a range of frequencies determined by the bandwidth of $s(\cdot)$. For our case though, $s(\cdot)$ is a chirp pulse, and a different form of processing is customarily used. Substituting (4) into (6) gives

$$r_\theta(t) = A \cdot \mathrm{Re}\left\{ \int_{-L}^{L} p_\theta(u) \exp\left\{ j\left[\omega_0\left(t - \frac{2(R + u)}{c} \right) \right. \right. \right.$$
$$\left. \left. \left. + \alpha\left(t - \frac{2(R + u)}{c} \right)^2 \right] \right\} du \right\} \tag{7}$$

on the interval[4]

$$-\frac{T}{2} + \frac{2(R + L)}{c} \leqslant t \leqslant \frac{T}{2} + \frac{2(R - L)}{c}. \tag{8}$$

Letting

$$\tau_0 = \frac{2R}{c}$$

be the round-trip delay to the center of the ground patch and mixing (multiplying) $r_\theta(t)$ with the reference chirp

$$\cos\left[\omega_0(t - \tau_0) + \alpha(t - \tau_0)^2 \right] \tag{9}$$

yields

$$\tilde{r}_\theta(t) = \frac{A}{2} \mathrm{Re}\left\{ \int_{-L}^{L} p_\theta(u) \left[\exp\left\{ j\left[\omega_0\left(2t - \frac{2u}{c} - 2\tau_0 \right) \right. \right. \right. \right.$$
$$\left. \left. \left. + \alpha\left((t - \tau_0)^2 + \left(t - \tau_0 - \frac{2u}{c} \right)^2 \right) \right] \right\}$$
$$\left. \left. + \exp\left\{ j\left[\frac{4\alpha u^2}{c^2} - \frac{2u}{c}(\omega_0 + 2\alpha(t - \tau_0)) \right] \right\} \right] du \right\}.$$

The first term is centered on the RF carrier frequency ω_0, whereas the second term is not, so low-pass filtering $\tilde{r}_\theta(t)$ gives

---

$$\hat{r}_\theta(t) = \frac{A}{2} \mathrm{Re}\left\{ \int_{-L}^{L} p_\theta(u) \right.$$
$$\left. \cdot \exp\left\{ j\left[\frac{4\alpha u^2}{c^2} - \frac{2u}{c}(\omega_0 + 2\alpha(t - \tau_0)) \right] \right\} du \right\}.$$

Similarly, it can be shown that mixing $r_\theta(t)$ with

$$\sin\left[\omega_0(t - \tau_0) + \alpha(t - \tau_0)^2 \right]$$

and low-pass filtering gives the quadrature component

$$\tilde{r}_\theta(t) = \frac{A}{2} \mathrm{Im}\left\{ \int_{-L}^{L} p_\theta(u) \right.$$
$$\left. \cdot \exp\left\{ j\left[\frac{4\alpha u^2}{c^2} - \frac{2u}{c}(\omega_0 + 2\alpha(t - \tau_0)) \right] \right\} du \right\}.$$

The real signals $\hat{r}_\theta(t)$ and $\tilde{r}_\theta(t)$, therefore, determine the real and imaginary components of the complex signal

$$C_\theta(t) = \frac{A}{2} \int_{-L}^{L} p_\theta(u) \exp\left\{ j \frac{4\alpha u^2}{c^2} \right\}$$
$$\cdot \exp\left\{ -j\frac{2}{c}(\omega_0 + 2\alpha(t - \tau_0))u \right\} du. \tag{10}$$

The effect of the quadratic phase term in (10) will be considered later; for now let us assume that this factor can be removed to obtain

$$\overline{C}_\theta(t) = \frac{A}{2} \int_{-L}^{L} p_\theta(u) \exp\left\{ -j\frac{2}{c}[\omega_0 + 2\alpha(t - \tau_0)]u \right\} du.$$

This last expression can be identified as the Fourier transform of the projection $p_\theta(u)$, that is,

$$\overline{C}_\theta(t) = \frac{A}{2} P_\theta\left[\frac{2}{c}(\omega_0 + 2\alpha(t - \tau_0)) \right]. \tag{11}$$

The net result is that, at least within the time interval considered, the processed return signal $\overline{C}_\theta(t)$ is the Fourier transform of a projection.

According to the projection-slice theorem, $\overline{C}_\theta(t)$ is a slice at angle θ of the 2-D transform G of the unknown reflectivity density. From (8), the processed return $\overline{C}_\theta(t)$ is available for

$$-\frac{T}{2} + \frac{2(R + L)}{c} \leqslant t \leqslant \frac{T}{2} + \frac{2(R - L)}{c}.$$

So, from (11), $P_\theta(X)$ is determined for $X_1 \leqslant X \leqslant X_2$ with

$$X_1 = \frac{2}{c}\left(\omega_0 - \alpha T + \frac{4\alpha L}{c} \right)$$

$$X_2 = \frac{2}{c}\left(\omega_0 + \alpha T - \frac{4\alpha L}{c} \right). \tag{12}$$

Thus only the segment of width $X_2 - X_1$ of each slice of G is actually determined. Processing returns from angles satisfying $|\theta| \leqslant \theta_M$ provides samples of $G(X, Y)$ on the polar grid in the annulus segment shown in Fig. 6. Transform points at angle θ are determined from the radar return collected at angle θ. The inner and outer radii, X_1 and X_2, are proportional to the lowest and highest frequencies in the transmitted chirp pulse [7]. This observation follows easily since for a typical SAR, $\omega_0 \pm \alpha T \gg 4\alpha L/c$, so that (12) reduces to

$$X_1 = \frac{2}{c}(\omega_0 - \alpha T)$$

$$X_2 = \frac{2}{c}(\omega_0 + \alpha T). \tag{13}$$

---

[3] The assumption of superposition is properly questioned. The extent of its validity is carefully discussed by Rihaczek [25].

[4] For t not satisfying (8), the argument of $s(\cdot)$ in (6) can lie outside $\pm T/2$ so that $r_\theta(t)$ will not be correctly given by (7). It is possible, however, to process $r_\theta(t)$ over the slightly larger interval $-(T/2) + (2R/c) \leqslant t \leqslant (T/2) + (2R/c)$ to obtain somewhat improved resolution.

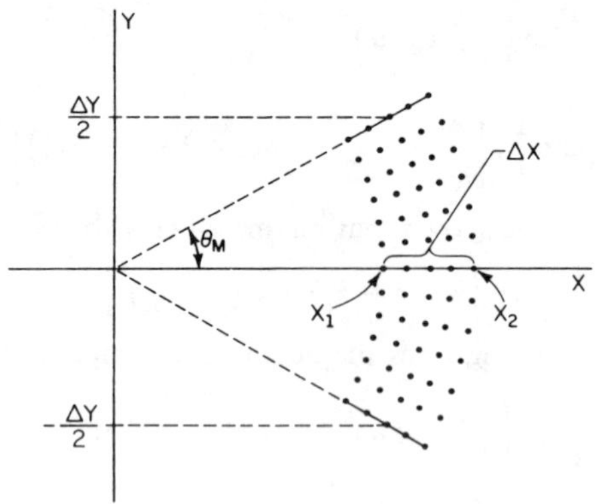

Fig. 6.   Annulus segment containing known samples of $G(X, Y)$.

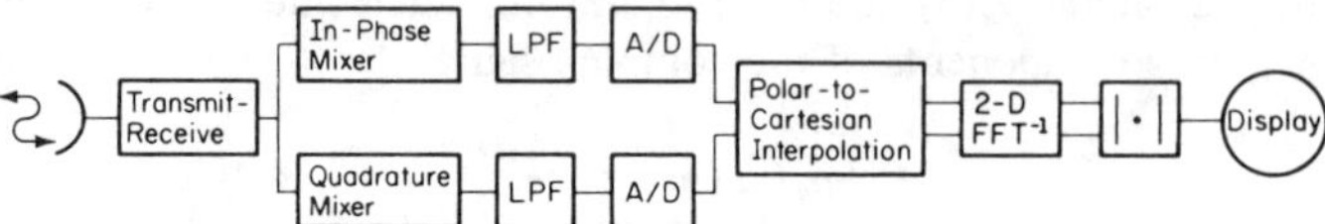

Fig. 7.   Required processing for spotlight-mode SAR.

From (4), the lowest and highest frequencies in the transmitted chirp pulse are $\omega_0 - \alpha T$ and $\omega_0 + \alpha T$ which are proportional to X_1 and X_2 in (13).

As remarked earlier, there is no known fast FFT-type algorithm for computing approximate samples of g from polar samples of G. In the case of SAR, an approximation to g is obtained by interpolating the known samples of G to a Cartesian grid, assuming unknown samples (those outside the annulus segment in Fig. 6) to be zero. This may be accomplished in a number of ways [11], e.g., by first linearly interpolating the samples of G on each radial line in Fig. 6 to a set of uniformly spaced vertical lines (resulting in a "keystone" grid [26]). These data are then linearly interpolated in the vertical dimension giving approximate samples of G on a Cartesian grid. After interpolation, an inverse 2-D FFT is employed and the amplitude of g is displayed for viewing [9], [26]. Before FFT processing, the samples of G are windowed to reduce sidelobe levels and are translated to the origin to save computation. The translation has no effect on the amplitude of the FFT output. The required processing for SAR is similar to that for tomography and is summarized in Fig. 7.

C. SAR as a Narrow-Band Version of CAT

The mathematical models for SAR and CAT bear enough resemblance to each other to allow both systems to be explained in terms of the projection-slice theorem. There are important differences, however. In SAR, the line integral involved in the projection is taken perpendicular to the direction in which the radio waves travel. This is in contrast to tomography, where the line integral is taken along the path of the X-rays. Also, a SAR system, utilizing a chirp waveform, determines the transform of the projection rather than the projection itself. Although it is not difficult to convert back and forth between the projection and its transform, this factor may partially explain why spatial domain reconstruction algorithms have not been considered for SAR.

The most striking difference between SAR and tomographic imaging is that SAR data are necessarily narrow-band. As we have seen, the transform domain data in a SAR system are restricted to lie in a small annulus segment with inner and outer edges that are determined by the frequency content of the transmitted chirp. Indeed, if the transmitted waveform is a sinusoid

(zero bandwidth) rather than a chirp, data are obtained at only a single ring in the transform domain [16]. However, if waveforms such as pseudo-random signals or even very short pulses are transmitted, the frequency content of the data in the transform domain is significant. (In fact, according to the model presented, if the SAR *could* transmit an impulse, $s(t) = \delta(t)$, with infinite bandwidth, the SAR imaging equation (6) would provide the projection $p_\theta(u)$ directly, as in tomography.) In general, the range information measured by a coherent SAR may be thought of as consisting of two parts: coarse range information providing the range resolution of the SAR, and fine range information (fractional wavelength range) that makes it possible to obtain high azimuth resolution through coherent processing.

Considering the narrow-band feature of SAR, it may seem surprising that acceptable imagery can be obtained. For example, an edge oriented at an angle $\theta_0 + 90°$ in the ground patch with real reflectivity will have significant frequency content in the transform domain along a line at an angle θ_0. If θ_0 does not fall within the look angle of the radar, such an edge will be obscured. Yet, unlike the attenuation coefficient in CAT, the reflectivity density in SAR is complex. Although the *magnitude* of the observed reflectivity density of resolution cells in the final processed image will not have significant frequency content within the annulus segment in Fig. 6, a random complex reflectivity can be attributed to an assumed distribution of point scatterers (each having random phase) in each resolution cell, giving rise to frequency components over much of the transform plane. Thus a segment of the transform plane displaced from the origin can contain significant information about the magnitude of the overall reflectivity density. This property is similar to holography, where a piece of a hologram contains the information essential for reconstructing a recognizable image. Indeed, a strong connection between SAR and holography has been established [27], [28].

Although SAR systems can produce high-quality imagery, various aberrations, such as coherent speckle, may be observed due to the narrow-band feature. For example, if the target is illuminated with a sinusoid of wavelength λ, then two point reflectors with approximately in-phase reflectivity and displaced in range by an odd multiple of $\lambda/4$ will result in destructive interference.[5] For the case of a transmitted chirp, interference can still occur. Here the response of the SAR system to a point reflector will be approximately a modulated 2-D sinc pulse having the width of a resolution cell (assuming an approximately rectangular region in Fig. 6); responses from adjacent point reflectors in the same resolution cell will thus overlap and interfere either constructively or destructively (see Fig. 8). At the expense of resolution, coherent speckle may be reduced by dividing the Fourier space into several sections and incoherently summing the magnitudes of the responses from each section.

Because SAR is essentially a narrow-band version of CAT, reconstruction algorithms used in one system may be used with only slight modification in the other. In the next section, a modification of the tomographic convolution-backprojection algorithm is introduced for use in SAR. This algorithm permits computation to proceed in step with data collection, since the final integration is performed over θ.

D. Reconstruction via the Backprojection Algorithm

The reconstruction of an image via convolution backprojection is accomplished on the basis of writing the Fourier integral (1) in polar form

---

[5] This factor is $\lambda/4$ rather than $\lambda/2$ due to two-way travel.

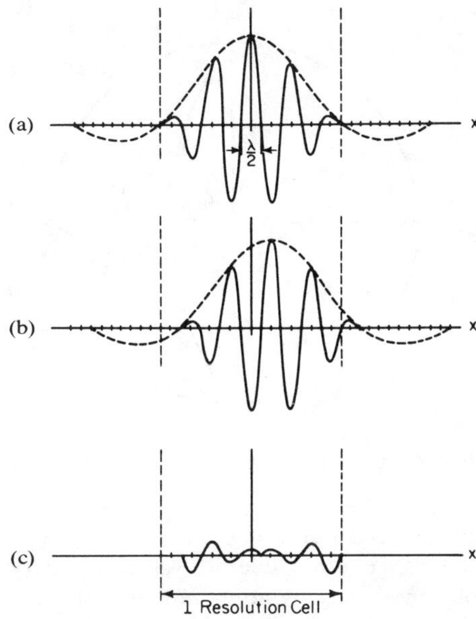

Fig. 8. One-dimensional example of destructive interference. (a) Real part of response from point target at $x = 0$. (b) Real part of response from point target at $x = \lambda/4$. (c) Sum of the responses. (Imaginary parts also destructively interfere.)

$$g(\rho\cos\phi, \rho\sin\phi) = \frac{1}{4\pi^2} \int_{-\pi/2}^{\pi/2} \int_{-\infty}^{\infty} G(r\cos\theta, r\sin\theta)|r|$$
$$\cdot \exp[jr\rho\cos(\phi - \theta)]\, dr\, d\theta$$
$$= \frac{1}{4\pi^2} \int_{-\pi/2}^{\pi/2} \int_{-\infty}^{\infty} P_\theta(r)|r|$$
$$\cdot \exp[jr\rho\cos(\phi - \theta)]\, dr\, d\theta \qquad (14)$$

where the second equality follows by the projection-slice theorem (3). The integral over r may be identified as an inverse Fourier transform with argument $\rho\cos(\phi - \theta)$, allowing (14) to be rewritten

$$g(\rho\cos\phi, \rho\sin\phi) = \frac{1}{2\pi} \int_{-\pi/2}^{\pi/2} [p_\theta * k](\rho\cos(\phi - \theta))\, d\theta$$
$$(15)$$

where

$$k = \mathcal{F}^{-1}[|r|].$$

The tomographic reconstruction algorithm evaluates the convolutions (possibly in the Fourier domain) for each θ, and then approximates the integral as a sum of these results.

In the case of SAR, we have available $P_\theta(r)$, the Fourier transform of the projection, so let us consider using (14) rather than (15). Notice that (14) requires $P_\theta(r)$ for all r, but from (12), the SAR system determines $P_\theta(r)$ over only a relatively small interval centered at $r = 2\omega_0/c$. Therefore, a window function vanishing outside this interval is applied before inverting $P_\theta(r)$ via an inverse FFT. Furthermore, since the known segment of P_θ is offset from the origin, P_θ is translated to the origin and the FFT result compensated accordingly. This is based on rewriting (14) as

$$g(\rho\cos\phi, \rho\sin\phi)$$
$$= \frac{1}{4\pi^2} \int_{-\pi/2}^{\pi/2} \left[\int_0^{X_2 - X_1} P_\theta(r + X_1)|r + X_1|W(r) \right.$$
$$\left. \cdot \exp[jr\rho\cos(\phi - \theta)]\, dr \right] \cdot \exp[jX_1\rho\cos(\phi - \theta)]\, d\theta \quad (16)$$

where X_1 and X_2 are given by (12) and W is a window function which tapers to zero on the interval $[0, X_2 - X_1]$. Finally, note that (16) requires that the inverse transform be evaluated at $\rho\cos(\phi - \theta)$ for various ρ, ϕ, and θ. Therefore, some interpolation of the FFT results is required before summing over θ. In addition, P_θ is available in a SAR system for only a restricted set of look angles as illustrated in Fig. 6. Thus it is desirable to apply a second window before integration over θ.

We have simulated the modified convolution–backprojection algorithm and compared it with the direct Fourier domain algorithm using linear interpolation in each dimension. Initial results show that the backprojection algorithm produces images of somewhat better quality—we hope to make this the subject of a future paper.

IV. Additional Considerations in SAR

A. Resolution and Required Sampling Rate

A SAR system provides transform domain data in the small polar region of the X–Y plane shown in Fig. 6. A definition of resolution in the image (spatial) domain can be motivated by considering the polar region to be approximated by a rectangle of width ΔX and height ΔY (see Fig. 6). The transform of a point reflector at (x_0, y_0) with reflectivity γ is

$$G(X, Y) = \int_{-\infty}^{\infty} \int_{-\infty}^{\infty} \gamma\delta(x - x_0, y - y_0)$$
$$\cdot \exp[-j(xX + yY)]\, dx\, dy$$
$$= \gamma\exp[-j(x_0 X + y_0 Y)]$$

so that the SAR system response to such a reflector is approximately

$$|\hat{g}(x, y)| = \frac{|\gamma|}{4\pi^2} \left| \int_{X_1}^{X_1 + \Delta X} \int_{-\Delta Y/2}^{\Delta Y/2} \right.$$
$$\cdot \exp[-j(x_0 X + y_0 Y)][\exp j(xX + yY)]\, dY\, dX \Big|$$
$$= \frac{|\gamma|}{4\pi^2} \left| \Delta X \,\mathrm{sinc}\left(\frac{1}{2}\Delta X(x - x_0)\right)\Delta Y \right.$$
$$\left. \cdot \mathrm{sinc}\left(\frac{1}{2}\Delta Y(y - y_0)\right) \right|.$$

The first zero crossings in the response occur at $x - x_0 = 2\pi/\Delta X$ and $y - y_0 = 2\pi/\Delta Y$. Therefore, as a rough guide, resolution of two point reflectors having equal reflectivity requires that the reflectors be separated by more than $2\pi/\Delta X$ in the x dimension and $2\pi/\Delta Y$ in the y dimension. From (13) and Fig. 6 we have, for $\theta_M \ll 1$, that $\Delta X \approx 4\alpha T/c$ and $\Delta Y \approx 2[(2\omega_0/c)\sin\theta_M]$. Thus the system resolution is defined as[6]

$$\delta_x = \frac{2\pi}{\Delta X} \approx \frac{\pi c}{2\alpha T} \qquad (17)$$

$$\delta_y = \frac{2\pi}{\Delta Y} \approx \frac{\pi c}{2\omega_0\sin\theta_M}. \qquad (18)$$

It is common in the SAR literature to refer to an area of size δ_x by δ_y in the reconstructed image as a *resolution cell*. Notice that the range resolution depends on only the bandwidth of the

[6]Although (17) and (18) are useful in practice, it requires more than a single pair of numbers (δ_x, δ_y) to precisely characterize resolution, because an actual target is composed of many interfering reflectors of varying intensities. See [25], [29] for further discussion.

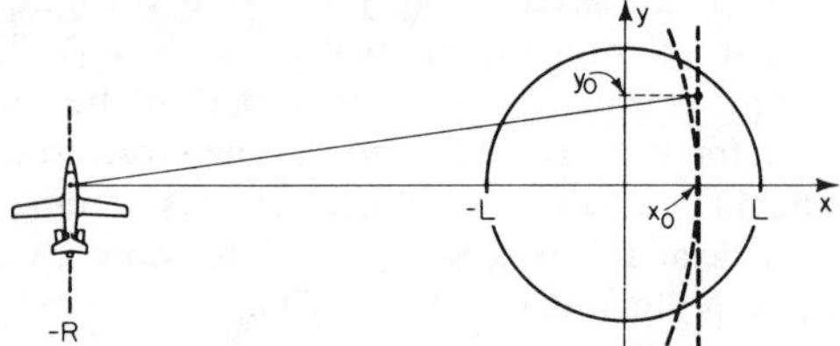

Fig. 9.   Wavefront curvature over the target field.

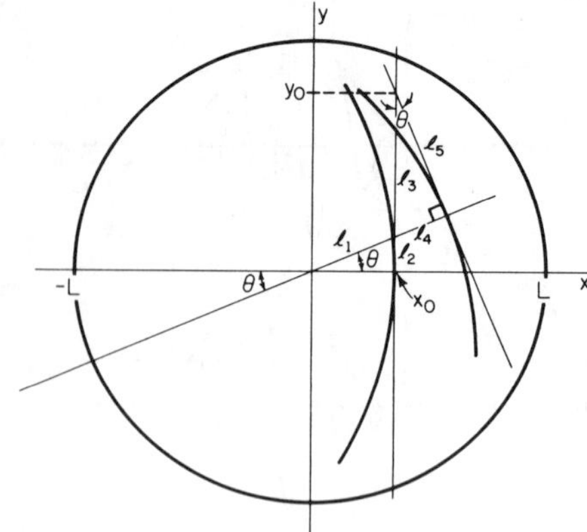

Fig. 10.   Wavefront curvature for projection angles 0 and θ.

transmitted signal, whereas the azimuth resolution depends on the center frequency and also on the range of look angles. Therefore, the resolving phenomena are entirely different in range and azimuth. Also, the necessary range of look angles to provide $\delta_y = \delta_x$ is actually quite small. For a typical SAR, ω_0 may be twenty times αT, giving $2\theta_M \approx 6°$.

Let us next consider an appropriate sampling rate for the transform in the polar region of Fig. 6. The usual sampling theorem will apply only if the inverse transform of the known segment of $G(X, Y)$ is spatially limited. Of course, this cannot be, since a signal cannot be both frequency limited and spatially limited. However, it is known that the true $g(x, y)$ is spatially limited by the radar antenna beam to a region of half-width L. Therefore, sampling rates in the X and Y directions should be *at least*

$$f_s = \frac{1}{2\pi}(2L) \text{ samples/rad.}$$

This corresponds to an image raster having

$$\left(\frac{L}{\pi} \cdot \Delta X = \frac{2L}{\delta_x}\right) \times \left(\frac{L}{\pi} \cdot \Delta Y = \frac{2L}{\delta_y}\right) = 4L^2/\delta_x\delta_y$$

samples or resolution cells in all. In practice, sampling rates somewhat higher than f_s are used.

B. Curvature of the Wavefront

As we have previously noted, SAR projections are not really taken over straight lines, but are taken over slight curves due to the outward propagation of waves from the transmitter. Two conditions must simultaneously be satisfied in order that this effect be neglected. First, the range error due to wavefront curvature over the target field must be less than a resolution cell, i.e.,

$$\frac{L^2}{2R} < \delta_x. \tag{19}$$

Condition (19) is obtained with the help of Fig. 9. The range error at a point (x_0, y_0) is

$$\left[(R + x_0)^2 + y_0^2\right]^{1/2} - (R + x_0)$$

$$= (R + x_0)\left\{\left[1 + \frac{y_0^2}{(R + x_0)^2}\right]^{1/2} - 1\right\}$$

$$\approx (R + x_0)\left\{1 + \frac{y_0^2}{2(R + x_0)^2} - 1\right\} \tag{20}$$

$$\approx \frac{y_0^2}{2R} \tag{21}$$

where the approximations hold since $R \gg x_0, y_0$. Evaluating (21) at the largest value of y_0 within the target patch gives (19).

A second condition arises since a SAR system coherently combines projections from many different angles. To preserve coherence, the range error due to wavefront curvature at a particular point must vary by no more than a small fraction of a wavelength through the full range of look angles. To analyze this effect, consider Fig. 10 which shows the wavefront curvature at the point (x_0, y_0) due to look angles 0 and θ. Evaluating the l_i gives

$$l_1 = \frac{x_0}{\cos\theta}$$

$$l_2 = l_1 \sin\theta = x_0 \tan\theta$$

$$l_3 = y_0 - l_2 = y_0 - x_0 \tan\theta$$

$$l_4 = l_3 \sin\theta = y_0 \sin\theta - x_0 \frac{\sin^2\theta}{\cos\theta}$$

$$l_5 = l_3 \cos\theta = y_0 \cos\theta - x_0 \sin\theta.$$

The range error at point (x_0, y_0) for a projection at angle θ is

$$\left[(R + l_1 + l_4)^2 + l_5^2\right]^{1/2} - (R + l_1 + l_4) \approx \frac{l_5^2}{2(R + l_1 + l_4)} \tag{22}$$

similar to (20). For a typical SAR system $R \gg l_1 + l_4$, so, from (21) and (22), the difference in wavefront curvature from a projection at angle 0 and a projection at angle θ is approximately

$$D = \frac{1}{2R}\left(y_0^2 - l_5^2\right)$$

$$= \frac{1}{2R}\left(y_0^2 \sin^2\theta + 2x_0 y_0 \sin\theta \cos\theta - x_0^2 \sin^2\theta\right). \tag{23}$$

Given the constraints $\theta \leqslant \theta_M$ and $x_0^2 + y_0^2 \leqslant L^2$, numerical optimization could be applied to (23) to obtain the maximum deviation. Instead, however, let us examine two special cases which would appear to yield large deviations:

$$1) \qquad x_0 = 0, \qquad y_0 = L$$

$$2) \qquad x_0 = y_0 = \frac{L}{\sqrt{2}}.$$

For case 1), the deviation (23) reduces to

$$D_1 = \frac{L^2 \sin^2\theta}{2R} \leqslant D_1^{\max} \triangleq \frac{L^2 \sin^2\theta_M}{2R}.$$

For case 2) we obtain

$$D_2 = \frac{L^2 \sin\theta \cos\theta}{2R} = \frac{L^2 \sin 2\theta}{4R} \leqslant D_2^{\max} \triangleq \frac{L^2 \sin 2\theta_M}{4R}$$

where the inequality assumes $\theta_M \leqslant \pi/4$. For θ_M in this range, we have $D_2^{\max} \geqslant D_1^{\max}$. Hence, to preserve coherency we require that $D_2^{\max}$ be much smaller than a fraction of a wavelength, i.e.,

$$\frac{L^2 \sin 2\theta_M}{4R} \ll \frac{c}{8\omega_0} = \frac{\lambda}{8}. \qquad (24)$$

Assuming $\delta_x = \delta_y$ in (17) and (18), condition (24) will be more severe than condition (19). If the target region to be mapped is too large to satisfy (24), the area may be mapped in smaller segments, using either antenna steering of a phased array or digital presumming methods [30]. Alternatively, the backprojection method may be applied even in the case of projections over curves in a manner described in [31].

C. Quadratic Phase Term

It was assumed earlier that the quadratic phase term in (10) can be removed. This can be partially accomplished by inverse transforming $C_\theta(t)$, multiplying by $\exp\{-j(4\alpha u^2/c^2)\}$, and then retransforming. However, there is some error in this procedure since $C_\theta(t)$ is not known for all t. If the step to remove the quadratic phase factor is omitted, the image suffers a consequent loss of resolution. However, if the inequality

$$\frac{4\alpha L^2}{c^2} \ll \frac{\pi}{2} \qquad (25)$$

is satisfied, then the loss of resolution will be small. We previously saw that the number of resolution cells in the reconstructed image will be

$$N^2 = \frac{4L^2}{\delta_x \delta_y}$$

where δ_x and δ_y are given by (17) and (18). Assuming $\delta_y \approx \delta_x$ and substituting from (17) gives

$$N^2 = \frac{16L^2\alpha^2 T^2}{\pi^2 c^2}. \qquad (26)$$

Defining the time–bandwidth product (TBW) of the transmitted chirp as

$$\text{TBW} = T \cdot \frac{2\alpha T}{2\pi} = \frac{\alpha T^2}{\pi}$$

and using (26), condition (25) becomes

$$N^2 \ll 2\,\text{TBW}. \qquad (27)$$

Condition (27) implies that the quadratic phase term can be neglected as long as the TBW is sufficiently large compared with N^2.

These relations show that neglecting the quadratic phase term imposes a limit on the resolution using SAR processing with chirp waveforms. Compensating for this term, as suggested above, is necessary for improved resolution.

D. Effect of Doppler and Time-Varying Range

Thus far, little mention has been made of the fact that the radar unit is moving as measurements are made—the radar unit was simply assumed to be placed at discrete positions along the flight path as projection data were gathered. Due to the motion of the aircraft, there is a Doppler effect which must be considered.

From Fig. 5 there is a radial component of the aircraft velocity $v_r = v \sin \theta$, where v is the speed of the aircraft. Therefore, the received signal, $r_\theta(t)$ in (6), is more accurately given by

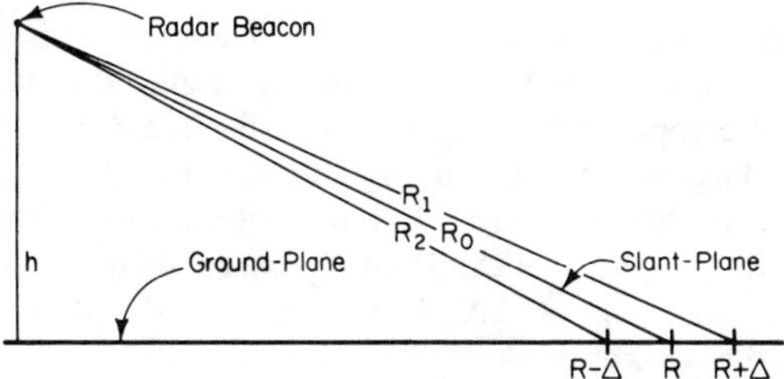

Fig. 11.   Side view of radar flown at height h.

$$r_\theta(t) = A \cdot \text{Re}\left\{ \int_{-L}^{L} p_\theta(u)\, s\left(at - \frac{2(R+u)}{c} \right) du \right\} \qquad (28)$$

with

$$a = \left(1 + \frac{v_r}{c} \right)^2 \approx 1 + \frac{2v_r}{c}$$

where the square is due to two-way travel. Instead of (9), the reference used for demodulation should then be

$$\cos\left[\omega_0(at - \tau_0) + \alpha(at - \tau_0)^2 \right]. \qquad (29)$$

Equations (28) and (29) give the correction for a target point at the center of the ground patch. The Doppler shift will vary slightly from point to point within the target patch since the angle from the radar and, therefore, the radial component of the aircraft velocity will vary slightly from the center to either side of the patch. Thus the reference waveform given by (29) cannot completely compensate for the Doppler effect. Assuming $\theta = 0$ in Fig. 5, and considering an extreme case, the radial component of the aircraft velocity for a point p^* at the top of the target patch at a distance R from the radar is approximately

$$v_r^* = v \sin\left(\tan^{-1} \frac{L}{R} \right) \approx v \frac{L}{R}.$$

The difference between the round-trip propagation times to the center of the target patch and to p^* is

$$\frac{2R}{c} - \frac{2R}{c + v_R^*} = \frac{2R}{c}\left(1 - \frac{1}{1 + \dfrac{vL}{cR}} \right) \approx \frac{2vL}{c^2}. \qquad (30)$$

To preserve the ability to measure fractional wavelengths (needed for high azimuth resolution), we require that c times (30) be less than one-quarter wavelength, i.e.,

$$\frac{2vL}{c} < \frac{\lambda_0}{4} \qquad \text{or} \qquad \frac{v}{c} < \frac{\lambda_0}{8L}$$

where $\lambda_0 = 2\pi c/\omega_0$. Thus for a given aircraft velocity, the variation in Doppler shift limits the target size. Notice that this condition is considerably different from the limitation (24) imposed by wavefront curvature.

Another factor that requires compensation is time-varying range. If the aircraft in Fig. 5 flies a straight path, the range to the center of the target patch will vary considerably. Thus R in (28) is actually a function of θ, and the demodulating waveform, (29), must be modified accordingly. Alternatively, a fixed high-frequency demodulator can be used, followed by a time-varying low-frequency demodulator that compensates for both time-varying range and Doppler. The second demodulator can be implemented digitally.

E. Modification of Results for Slant-Plane Geometry

In the previous analyses we have neglected the fact that the radar operates in the slant plane at some nonzero height h above the ground plane, as shown in Fig. 11. Therefore, it is necessary to modify our results by stretching the range dimension. The amount of compensation required is easily found by considering two point targets in the ground patch at distance R_1 and R_2 from the radar, as shown in Fig. 11. Let the locations in the ground plane be $R + \Delta$ and $R - \Delta$. The targets are, therefore, separated by a true distance of 2Δ. From the radar's point of view, however, the separation is

$$R_1 - R_2 = \sqrt{h^2 + (R + \Delta)^2} - \sqrt{h^2 + (R - \Delta)^2}$$
$$\approx \sqrt{h^2 + R^2 + 2R\Delta} - \sqrt{h^2 + R^2 - 2R\Delta}$$

for $R \gg \Delta$. This can be further approximated as

$$R_1 - R_2 = R_0\left[\sqrt{1 + \frac{2R\Delta}{R_0^2}} - \sqrt{1 - \frac{2R\Delta}{R_0^2}}\right]$$
$$\approx R_0\left[1 + \frac{R\Delta}{R_0^2} - \left(1 - \frac{R\Delta}{R_0^2}\right)\right]$$
$$= 2\Delta\frac{R}{R_0}.$$

Therefore, to obtain the true separation, 2Δ, it is necessary to stretch the range dimension by R_0/R. Taking this into account, the derivation in Section III can be easily modified, beginning with

$$r_\theta(t) = A \cdot \mathrm{Re}\left\{\int_{-L}^{L} p_\theta(u)s\left(t - \frac{2\left(R_0 + u\frac{R}{R_0}\right)}{c}\right) du\right\}$$

as a replacement for (6), where p_θ is the projection of the reflectivity density in the ground plane, R is the distance from the projection of the radar onto the ground plane to the center of the target patch, and R_0 is the true distance (in the slant plane) from the radar to the center of the target patch. Note that R/R_0 will vary as a function of range, and therefore as a function of θ for a straight-line flight path. Thus the modification required for each projection will, in general, be different.

V. Conclusion

A tomographic formulation of spotlight-mode SAR has been presented. We have shown that a chirped SAR operating in spotlight mode records a portion of the Fourier transform of a central projection of the ground patch at each look angle. This establishes that "polar format Doppler processing," used in SAR, is a form of tomographic reconstruction that may be conveniently described by the projection-slice theorem. The tomographic interpretation permits, we believe, a conceptually simpler understanding of SAR than an analysis based solely on Doppler concepts. An important benefit in making the connection between SAR and CAT is that algorithms and signal processing methods developed in one field may be applied to the other. For example, it was shown how the convolution-backprojection algorithm, that is widely used in commercial CAT scanners, can be modified for use in SAR.

Various issues concerning speckle, resolution, wavefront curvature, residual quadratic phase errors, and the effects of Doppler and time-varying range have been considered. In particular, it was shown that the terrain patch size is limited by the effects of wavefront curvature and Doppler.

Acknowledgment

The authors would like to thank the reviewers for making many helpful comments.

References

[1] H. J. Scudder, "Introduction to computer aided tomography," *Proc. IEEE*, vol. 66, pp. 628–637, June 1978.

[2] G. T. Herman, Ed., *Image Reconstruction from Projections*. New York: Springer, 1979.

[3] C. W. Sherwin, J. P. Ruina, and R. D. Rawcliffe, "Some early developments in synthetic aperture radar systems," *IRE Trans. Mil. Electron.*, vol. MIL-6, pp. 111–115, Apr. 1962.

[4] W. M. Brown and C. J. Palermo, "Theory of coherent systems," *IRE Trans. Mil. Electron.*, vol. MIL-6, pp. 187–196, Apr. 1962.

[5] W. M. Brown and L. J. Porcello, "An introduction to synthetic aperture radar," *IEEE Spectrum*, vol. 6, pp. 52–62, Sept. 1969.

[6] K. Tomiyasu, "Tutorial review of synthetic-aperture radar (SAR) with applications to imaging of the ocean surface," *Proc. IEEE*, vol. 66, pp. 563–583, May 1978.

[7] J. L. Walker, "Range-Doppler imaging of rotating objects," *IEEE Trans. Aerosp. Electron. Syst.*, vol. AES-16, pp. 23–52, Jan. 1980.

[8] W. M. Brown and R. J. Fredricks, "Range-Doppler imaging with motion through resolution cells," *IEEE Trans. Aerosp. Electron. Syst.*, vol. AES-5, pp. 98–102, Jan. 1969.

[9] "Advanced synthetic array radar techniques," First Interim Report, Radar and Optics Division, Environmental Research Institute of Michigan, unclassified excerpts, Mar. 1976, available from DTIC as Tech. Rep. AFAL-TR-75-87.

[10] R. M. Mersereau, "Recovering multidimensional signals from their projections," *Comput. Graph. Image Proc.*, vol. 1, pp. 179–195, Oct. 1973.

[11] R. M. Mersereau and A. V. Oppenheim, "Digital reconstruction of multidimensional signals from their projections," *Proc. IEEE*, vol. 62, pp. 1319–1338, Oct. 1974.

[12] M. I. Skolnik, *Introduction to Radar Systems*, 2nd ed. New York: McGraw-Hill, 1980, pp. 34–44.

[13] G. Wade, S. Elliott, I. Khogeer, G. Flesher, J. Eisler, D. Mensa, N. Ramesh, and G. Heidbreder, "Acoustic echo computer tomography," in *Acoustic Holography*, vol. 8, A. Metherell, ed. New York: Plenum, 1978.

[14] D. Mensa, G. Heidbreder, and G. Wade, "Aperture synthesis by object rotation in coherent imaging," *IEEE Trans. Nucl. Sci.*, vol. NS-27, pp. 989–998, Apr. 1980.

[15] D. Mensa and G. Heidbreder, "Bistatic synthetic-aperture radar imaging of rotating objects," *IEEE Trans. Aerosp. Electron. Syst.*, vol. AES-18, pp. 423–431, July 1982.

[16] C. Chen and H. C. Andrews, "Multifrequency imaging of radar turnable data," *IEEE Trans. Aerosp. Electron. Syst.*, vol. AES-16, pp. 15–22, Jan. 1980.

[17] G. T. Herman, *Image reconstruction from Projections*. New York: Academic Press, 1980.

[18] D. L. Mensa, S. Halevy, and G. Wade, "Coherent Doppler tomography for microwave imaging," *Proc. IEEE*, vol. 71, no. 2, pp. 254–261, Feb. 1983.

[19] W. M. Brown, "Walker model for radar sensing of rigid target fields," *IEEE Trans. Aerosp. Electron. Syst.*, vol. AES-16, pp. 104–107, Jan. 1980.

[20] H. H. Stark, J. W. Woods, I. Paul, and R. Hingorani, "Direct Fourier reconstruction in computer tomography," *IEEE Trans. Acoust., Speech, Signal Process.*, vol. ASSP-29, pp. 237–245, Apr. 1981.

[21] A. V. Oppenheim, G. V. Frisk, and D. R. Martinez, "An algorithm for the numerical evaluation of the Hankel transform," *Proc. IEEE*, vol. 66, pp. 264–265, Feb. 1978.

[22] A. J. Jerri, "Towards a discrete Hankel transform and its applications," *J. Appl. Anal.*, vol., 7, pp. 97–109, 1978.

[23] S. M. Candel, "Dual algorithms for fast calculation of the Fourier-Bessel transform," *IEEE Trans. Acoust., Speech, Signal Process.*, vol. ASSP-29, pp. 963–972, Oct. 1981.

[24] D. W. Dearholt and W. R. McSpadden, *Electromagnetic Wave Propagation*. New York: McGraw-Hill, 1973.

[25] A. W. Rihaczek, *Principles of High-Resolution Radar*. New York: McGraw-Hill, 1969, pp. 331–349.

[26] D. A. Schwartz, "Analysis and experimental investigation of three synthetic aperture radar formats," Coordinated Sci. Lab., Univ. of Illinois, Tech. Rep. T-94, Mar. 1980 (M.S. thesis).

[27] E. N. Leith, "Quasi-holographic techniques in the microwave region," *Proc. IEEE*, vol. 59, pp. 1305–1318, Sept. 1971.

[28] W. E. Kock, *Radar, Sonar, and Holography*. New York: Academic Press, 1973.

[29] R. O. Harger, *Synthetic Aperture Radar Systems: Theory and Design*. New York: Academic Press, 1970.

[30] J. C. Kirk, "A discussion of digital processing in synthetic aperture radar," *IEEE Trans. Aerosp. Electron. Syst.*, vol. AES-11, pp. 326–337, May 1975.

[31] B. K. P. Horn, "Density reconstruction using arbitrary ray-sampling schemes," *Proc. IEEE*, vol. 66, pp. 551–562, May 1978.

Reconstructive Tomography and Applications to Ultrasonics

ROLF K. MUELLER, SENIOR MEMBER, IEEE, MOSTAFA KAVEH, MEMBER, IEEE, AND
GLEN WADE, FELLOW, IEEE

Abstract—Computer technology has brought about a revolution in radiology. By combining the computer with X rays it is possible (in principle) to obtain tomographic images of any cross section in the human body. These techniques are now used for medical diagnosis in all the major hospitals of the world.

But X rays are not the only kind of radiation for which computer-assisted tomography is feasible. Microwaves, electron beams, ultrasound, fast subatomic particles from accelerators, gamma rays from such sources as positron annihilation, and even magnetic fields can also be used.

This paper is mainly concerned with ultrasound. Acoustic energy can often give a view of a cross section not available with X rays or other types of radiation. A mapping of acoustic and elastic discontinuities can be expected to give a basically different pattern than a mapping of X-ray absorption and scattering coefficients. Several methods of ultrasonic tomography are discussed including methods based on geometric optics and a Doppler-oriented approach. A major portion of the paper is concerned with introducing ways to take into account diffraction effects. Because of the wavelength differences, these effects are far more important for ultrasound than for X rays.

I. Introduction

A VERITABLE revolution in radiology has taken place with the use of computers in imaging internal organs within the human body. The computer is now an important factor for implementing diagnostic techniques in the major hospitals of the world. In computer tomography, ordinary X-ray technology has been combined with sophisticated computer signal processing. Using this approach it is possible in principle to obtain the image of any cross section within the body.

A tomogram is simply a picture of a slice. The word tomography is defined as " a diagnostic technique using X-ray photographs in which the shadows of structures before and behind the section under scrutiny do not show." Tomo comes from the Greek word tomos, meaning section, and graphy, of course, refers to a representation. In diagnostic medicine, a tomogram displays a cross section of the body at a desired location and with a desired orientation.

Although the use of computers for producing tomograms is relatively recent, tomography itself has been a flourishing diagnostic technique for a number of years. As early as 1921, radiologists [1], utilizing X-ray transmission, devised what we may call focal-plane tomography. The technique is illustrated in Fig. 1. As shown the X-rays pass through the entire body, and therefore through a continuum of parallel planes in body, such as the planes labeled A, B, and C, before exposing photographic film. The X-ray source moves in one direction along a straight line in an upper plane, the S plane, and the photographic film simultaneously moves in the opposite direction in a lower plane, the F plane. The body lies in between the two planes. It is rather easy to see that under these circumstances there is only one plane parallel to the two motions where the projected image remains stationary with respect to the moving film. The position of the plane depends upon the speed of the two motions. For example, if we wish the projection of point b to remain stationary on the film as the X-ray source moves over the distance $s - s'$, we must require that the film move simultaneously over the distance $f - f'$. Point b in plane B would then be sharply imaged on the film, but points a in Plane A and c in plane C would be smeared. Points b' and b'' would also stay in register on the film but not corresponding points in the A and C planes. Hence, only structure in plane B would be sharply recorded. All other structure would be blurred. The motion described produces an effect similar to that in a photograph where the camera has a narrow depth of field. The desired focal plane is registered sharply and objects on either side of that plane are blurred.

The use of this type of X-ray tomography is widespread. Other ways of employing these same principles are also being utilized but are not particularly popular. Focal-plane tomography has been used, for example, in imaging with radioisotopes [2] but on a strictly limited scale. In this application the radiation comes from a gamma- or positron-emitting radionuclide which has been injected into the patient. The process is properly referred to as emission imaging and is in contrast with the transmission imaging previously described where the source is external to the body. In radioisotope tomography, image information is detected by a scintillation counter. Tomographic effects can be produced by moving the patient and the detector in various ways or by using a focused collimator in front of the detector.

The main disadvantage of focal-plane tomography is the presence of blurred image elements from the unwanted object planes. Even so, an X-ray focal-plane tomogram provides a less ambiguous representation of internal bodily structure than does an ordinary X-ray image. With conventional procedures, the X rays diverge from the source and pass through the body, projecting the shadow of bones, organs, and tumors, etc. onto a sheet of film. X rays cannot be controllably deflected as, for example, light is deflected by a lens. Refraction, reflection, and diffraction are effects which are quite negligible with X rays. Absorption and scattering are the interactions used to form the images. The radiation is blocked and scattered away from the detector by the absorption and scattering centers within the object. Therefore, the radiographic images in ordinary X-ray pictures are actually shadow images.

Manuscript received October 3, 1978; revised December 3, 1978. The work of R. K. Mueller and M. Kaveh was supported by the National Science Foundation under Grant ENG76-84521.

R. K. Mueller and M. Kaveh are with the Department of Electrical Engineering, University of Minnesota, Minneapolis, MN 55455.

G. Wade is with the Department of Electrical Engineering and Computer Science, University of California, Santa Barbara, CA 93106.

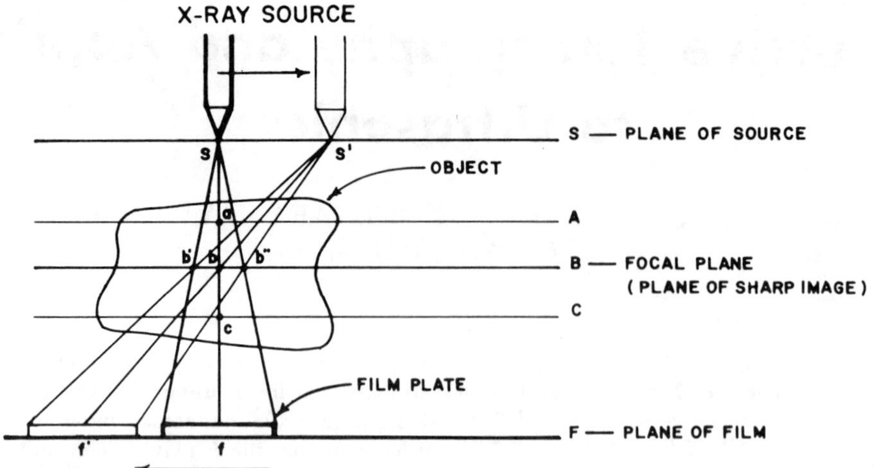

Fig. 1. Focal-plane tomography illustrating how the projection of point b onto plane F can be made to stay in register on moving film whereas point a and point c will not stay in register. If the X-ray source moves from s to s' at the same time the film plate moves from f to f', point b in plane B will be imaged sharply on the film but point a in plane A and point c in plane C will be blurred. Other points in plane B such as b' and b'' will also stay in register on the moving film.

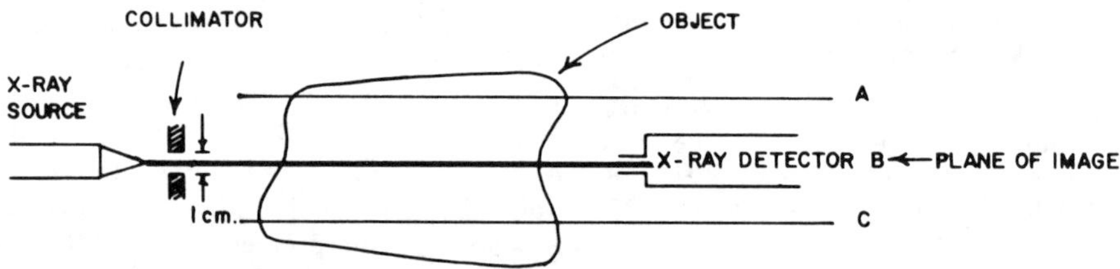

Fig. 2. Reconstructive tomography (RT) showing a collimated X-ray source which produces a pencil-like beam lying in plane B, the plane of the image. The X-rays traverse only the layer under examination so that unwanted planes are completely omitted. Thus points on planes A and C are never irradiated and do not show up in the reconstructed image.

Invaluable though these images are, they suffer from a major shortcoming: on the film, the internal structures of the body lap over each other to the extent that it is often difficult or impossible to distinguish between them. Thus the common X-ray image is by no means a complete and unambiguous representation of the X-ray transmission characteristics of the body being imaged. Like any other shadow image, it is a two-dimensional projection of three-dimensional structure. The image elements are contained within an infinite number of parallel planes in the body. All of these planes are collapsed onto the single plane containing the image. Depth information is completely lost and the confusion of the overlapping structure makes detection of subtle abnormalities difficult or impossible. Thus details in soft tissue are very difficult to discern in a conventional X-ray picture. This is particularly true when the X-ray density emerging from one structure differs only slightly from that from a neighboring one, a condition which often prevails with a tumor and the tissue in which it is embedded.

Obviously, focal-plane tomography is a partial solution to this problem. In a focal-plane tomogram, only a selected plane of the object is imaged in sharp focus; whereas in a conventional X-ray picture, all of the overlapping planes show up equally well. But even with focal-plane tomography, the other planes still show up. It is true that they are not imaged sharply, but they still appear as out-of-focus artifacts and are not completely eradicated. Image contrast may therefore continue to be low.

The ideal solution would be to image only a single selected plane without any interference from blurred image elements due to unwanted planes. Ideally, the blurred elements should be completely eliminated. What we really want is a sharp image of only the selected plane. We do not want interference from any other plane, whether in- or out-of-focus.

This condition is precisely the case in reconstructive tomography (RT), also referred to as computed tomography (CT), or computer-assisted tomography (CAT). With this approach, individual body layers are visualized in complete isolation. In RT the thickness and height of the X-ray beam is restricted by a collimator to one centimeter or less. The detected radiation passes through the desired anatomical plane in the form of a pencil beam without entering into other areas. This is illustrated in Fig. 2.

Imagine that the collimator of Fig. 2 effectively prevents the X rays from spreading, not only in the vertical direction as illustrated, but also in the direction perpendicular to the paper. Only a thin pencil-like region of the object, lying in plane B, is irradiated. The X-ray detector will measure the total radiation along a path defined by the thin region. After such a measurement is made for a single X-ray pulse, both the source and the detector are moved as a unit a short distance in the direction perpendicular to the plane of the paper. Another pulse is emitted and detected. This procedure is repeated over and over again. A complete X-ray projection in plane B is measured by sampling the output of the detector for each X-ray pulse at a large number of equally spaced positions (for example, 160 such positions) along a single scan direction. The sampled values are stored in the memory of a computer. Then the entire unit is rotated a small angle (for example, $1°$) while remaining in plane B and the process recurs. This is done repeatedly, with data being collected for all the scan directions

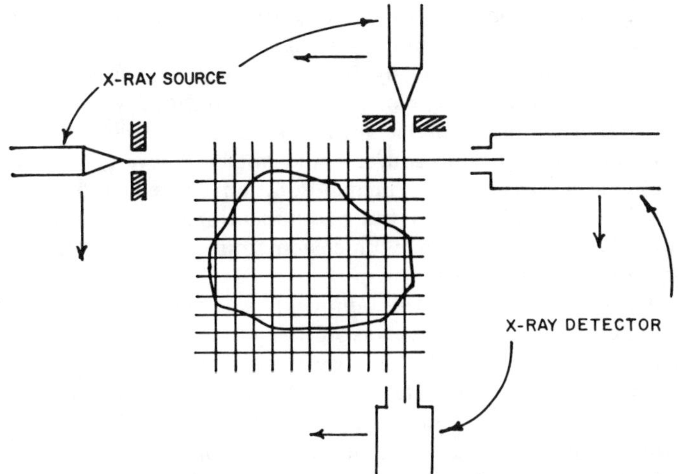

Fig. 3. Scanning pattern for the X-ray source and detector of Fig. 2 as it moves in the plane *B*. The detector samples the X-ray data for a large number of paths through the object along each projection. Successive projections are taken at small-angle intervals around the object. Eventually, projections around a 180° arc are taken. Only two projections are illustrated here, one at right angles to the other.

until the sum of the rotations of the unit adds up to 180°. When all the projections have been completed, the resulting information is processed by a computer to form a reconstruction of the cross section of the object at plane *B*. A typical scanning pattern is illustrated in Fig. 3.

As stated, the reconstruction is accomplished with a digital computer. The X-ray intensity data from the projections is converted from an analog signal to digital impulses in an analog-to-digital converter and fed into a computer which reconstructs the image. The resulting RT picture is a *B* plane cross section of the object.

A large number of projections are required before the image can be determined. Reconstruction from the projections is a mathematical process of substantial complexity and, in practice, necessitates the use of a digital computer. However, in principle, computer use is neither necessary nor unique to this method. Therefore, the term "reconstructive tomography" (RT) is more technically appropriate than either "computed tomography" (CT) or "computer-assisted tomography" (CAT).

The mathematical basis for a solution to the RT problem was solved more than 60 years ago by the Austrian mathematician Johann Radon [3]. He proved that any two-dimensional object can be reconstructed uniquely from an infinite set of its projections. This result has been independently rediscovered a number of times since then by other mathematicians, radio astronomers, electron microscopists, workers in optics, and medical radiologists. The first practical reconstructions of this kind were accomplished by the radio astronomer Ronald Bracewell in 1956 [4]. The same mathematical problem later arose in electron microscopy when workers attempted to reconstruct the molecular structure of complex biomolecules. A series of transmission micrograms were taken at various angles and methods for reconstructing images from them were arrived at independently of any of the earlier work [5], [6]. Similar techniques of image reconstruction were also independently developed for various optical applications [7], [8].

It is in the area of medical diagnosis, however, that the most excitement has been generated involving RT. In a recent tutorial article it was stated that these procedures may be bringing about a revolution in medicine comparable to that produced in the late 19th Century by the introduction of anesthetics and sterilization [9]. The first practical, clinically oriented solutions to reconstructive tomography appeared in the early 1960's, after Alan Cormack [10], [11] of Tufts University began to popularize and extend Radon's work. David Kuhl [12] and co-workers at the University of Pennsylvania built a transverse-section scanner for applications in nuclear medicine. Kuhl's scanner was the first tomographic device to isolate, for image reconstruction, a single plane transverse to the long axis of the patient's body. It completely eliminated information from other planes.

But the spark that ignited the greatest excitement in this field came from EMI, Ltd., in England. In 1971 that company announced the development of the EMI Scanner, involving X-ray scanning and digital computing [13], [14]. The system was largely the brainchild of Godfrey Hounsfield. It generated images of isolated slices of the brain with excellent contrast even for tissues with very small differences in their ability to absorb X rays. In 1974 a whole body scanner was developed by Ledley. Since then a number of different companies have manufactured both head and body scanners. A broadly based competitive market has by now been developed.

As indicated, X rays are certainly not the only kind of radiation for which reconstructive tomography can be useful. It has already been mentioned that microwaves, electron waves, and light waves can also be used. In addition, ultrasound, gamma rays from such sources as positron annihilation, fast subatomic particles from accelerators, and even magnetic fields can all be made to yield various kinds of projections from the internal structure of an object. Some of these techniques are inherently capable of discriminating between similar structures with greater sensitivity than X rays. With magnetic fields it may be possible to reconstruct images in which only blood flow is shown. The mathematical methods would be essentially the same as those that are being used for the case of X-ray radiation. This paper is mainly concerned with the use of ultrasound. But for historical interest, we will now make brief mention of applications to radio and radar astronomy, to electron microscopy, and to optics.

A. Application to Radio and Radar Astronomy

Although Radon, a mathematician concerned with gravitational theory, established the analytical foundation for tomography back in 1917 [3], the first practical tomographic reconstructions consistent with his work were not accomplished until almost 40 years later [4] by Ronald Bracewell, a radio astronomer. The problem was to map the regions of microwave radiation from the sun (or any other celestial entity) employing antennas that could only measure the intensity of the microwaves along narrow strips of the sky rather than at localized points. Bracewell used a series of so-called "strip sums," corresponding to strips of different orientations, to reconstruct a microwave image of emission from the sun.

Thus the radiation in this case was not from X rays but from microwaves. Bracewell wanted to reconstruct a solar map of such emission. His microwave antennas could not focus down to small patches on the sun's surface but only on thin strips crossing the surface like ribbons. The total emission from a single such strip could readily be measured and from a series of such measurements it was possible to construct a map of the local activity. It will be easy to see that this problem is precisely analogous to that of reconstructing a section of the body from its X-ray projections.

We can think of Bracewell's telescope as having the form of a long, narrow aperture and hence of detecting radiation from

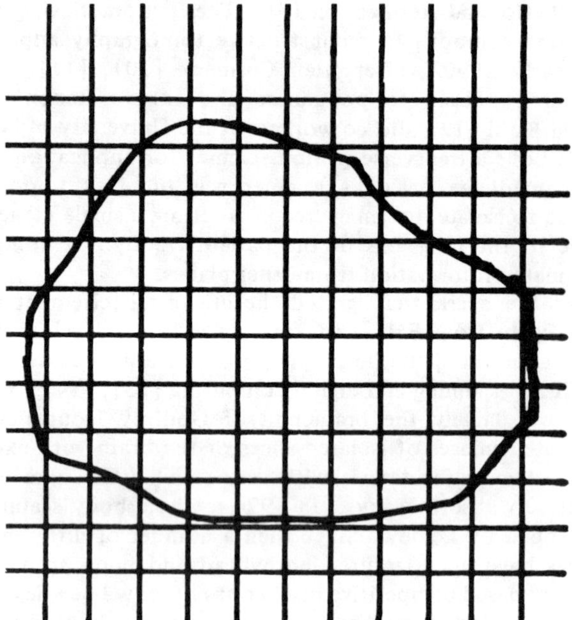

Fig. 4. The periphery of a region of intensity distribution for a hypothetical radio source is shown along with two sets of parallel lines representing strip scans. One set has vertical orientation and the other, horizontal orientation. Note that the geometry is the same as that in Fig. 3.

a long, narrow strip of the sky. As the earth rotated, the position of the strip would change and could be made to scan through the region of the sky containing the source of emission under consideration. The record of received power as a function of the position of the strip as it scanned with its orientation unchanged was given the name "strip scan" by Bracewell.

The essential problem of reconstructing a map from strip-scan data is obviously the same as that of reconstructing an image from X-ray projection data. This can be seen by examining Fig. 4. The figure shows the periphery of a region of brightness distribution over a hypothetical microwave radio source. To emphasize the similarity involved, the pattern has been deliberately drawn with the same shape as that in Fig. 3. The vertical and horizontal lines in Fig. 4 do not now represent X-ray beam paths but instead the narrow strips of sky through which Bracewell's radio telescope received its radiative input. The classical problem of data reduction for mapping the sky in radio astronomy is one of reconstructing a two-dimensional brightness distribution. A map of a radio-emitting or reflecting body can be reconstructed from strip scans just as an image of a cross section can be reconstructed from X-ray projections. Bracewell and various colleagues were the first to study and solve this problem [4], [15], [16].

Each of the lines in Fig. 4 represents, in its limiting form, a long strip of sky from which radiation is received by a radio telescope at a given instant of time. The earth's rotation, or adjustments to the radio telescope, may change the position of the line while the orientation in space remains fixed. As the position changes, the strip moves across the radio source and we can say that the source has been scanned. The record of received power obtained as the position of the strip changes is then precisely the strip scan.

A map of the radio source can be reconstructed by using data from the various strip scans corresponding to various orientations in space. In Fig. 4 only two such orientations

are indicated, one for which the strips run vertically and the other for which they run horizontally.

A study of the theory by Bracewell [4], [16] showed that: 1) only a finite number of position orientations were needed to obtain all the available information, 2) the brightness distribution of the radio source could not be recovered with infinite accuracy but a principal solution existed, and 3) the resolution obtainable in the two-dimensional reconstructions was that available in one-dimension from the radio telescope (that is, the width of the strip).

To show how well this approach worked, Bracewell and Riddle [16] used strip scans of the moon taken at position angles permitted by the east–west and north–south arrays of Stanford's 9.1-cm interferometer [15]. The data was gathered over a period from March 4, to April 1, 1961. They assumed that the lunar intensity distribution was symmetrical about the equator and were able to reconstruct the intensity pattern using only 14 position angles (orientations). The map they obtained served as a good test of their method. Although their results did not compare favorably with lunar observations using a high-resolution pencil-beam antenna, the general character of their reconstructed pattern was in good agreement with expectations.

Another type of tomographic imaging system that drew heavily from the early Bracewell work is one which combines the principles of tomography with Doppler techniques and has been useful in obtaining radar images of the moon [17]–[20]. At the earth's surface, the moon subtends an angle of only about 30 minutes. To produce a useful map of radio reflectivity over the moon's surface, a radar system employed for that purpose should achieve an angular resolution of less than one minute of arc. For typical radar frequencies, this would require an antenna with an aperture of the order of kilometers in size. Since apertures this large are not readily available, the radar observer as well as the radio astronomer has to employ special techniques to achieve the resolution needed. One such technique, involving a tomographic Doppler approach, has been used to obtain reflectivity maps of the moon at relatively long wavelengths.

The rotation of the moon, as seen from the earth, will cause the various elements of the moon's surface to have different line-of-sight velocity components and therefore to give different Doppler shifts. One way of getting a series of strip sums corresponding to narrow strips of surface on the moon is to irradiate the moon with continuous wave (CW) radiation and observe the reflected radiation at the various Doppler-shifted frequencies. Each elemental increment in the frequency spectrum contains the energy reflected from a strip parallel to the instantaneous apparent axis of rotation of the moon. Because of the Doppler effect, the radiation reflected from the surface of the moon in each of these parallel strips will be shifted in frequency by a different amount.

The technique that takes advantage of these principles is known as Radar Aperture Synthesis and was first described by Thomson [17]. The theory of the method was enunciated by Thomson and Ponsonby [18] who showed that two-dimensional tomographic reconstruction can be achieved due to the fact that the orientation of the moon's apparent axis of rotation, relative to features on the Moon's surface, changes with time. An unambiguous reconstructed image of the entire irradiated surface may be obtained if the spectra of the reflected radiation are observed as the direction of the moon's apparent rotation axis changes over a range of 180° with respect to the surface features. Since the strips are parallel to the apparent rotation axis, they also change in direction by a total of 180°. This technique requires only a relatively low-power CW radar with no degree of primary resolution from its antenna. The entire irradiated surface of the moon is observed at once so that the relative returns from widely separated regions can be compared directly.

It should be pointed out that this method will work only if the astronomical object has a relative motion with respect to the earth's surface such that the direction of its apparent rotation axis changes by 180° sufficiently fast so that the aspect of the object is not appreciably altered during the period of the change. Only then will it be possible to reconstruct a complete map from data obtained by a single antenna. The only astronomical object with such propitious behavior is the moon. On a favorable day, as viewed from the earth, the axis of the moon rotates through 180° in this manner between moonrise and moonset.

Although this method has been employed to map the moon at several wavelengths [19], other approaches are superior in terms of resolution. In practice the technique is of no use in planetary studies.

We have made no attempt to describe this system in sufficient detail so that a good understanding of how it works is available solely from the description. It is simply being mentioned here because of historical interest and also due to the fact that it is related to a type of ultrasonic tomographic system employing Doppler techniques that will be described in Section IV.

B. Application to Electron Microscopy

Another historically interesting area of application for reconstructive tomography is in electron microscopy. A problem arises because of the great depth of focus of an electron microscope, usually several thousand Angstroms in a standard high-resolution instrument. For an object shorter than this, the image produced will consist of a two-dimensional superposition of all the three-dimensional structure in the object. The focus for such a microscope cannot be adjusted to sharply image a selected cross section of narrow depth and the resulting pattern is frequently difficult to analyze. The problem is of precisely the same character as that in an ordinary X-ray image.

It might be thought that by using stereo-electron micrographs the difficulty could be surmounted. However, this is not entirely the case. Stereo microscopy does not reproduce structure in such a way that depth is determined quantitatively. In addition, even with ideal stereo pairs in which fine detail is clearly resolved, some points in a complex structure of substantial depth are bound to be obscured by others situated in front of them. To overcome this difficulty many stereo pairs have to be taken. For this reason stereoscopy is best suited for seeing details confined to the neighborhood of a single surface or for particularly simple objects.

As proposed in 1968 by De Rosier and Klug [5], these difficulties in distinguishing between overlapping structure can be overcome by reconstructive tomography. The details of the method they described are easy to understand in light of what we have previously discussed. They recognized that the typical image from an electron microscope is a two-dimensional projection of three-dimensional structure and that by collecting many different such projections, it would be possible to reconstruct the entire three-dimensional structure in the form of a

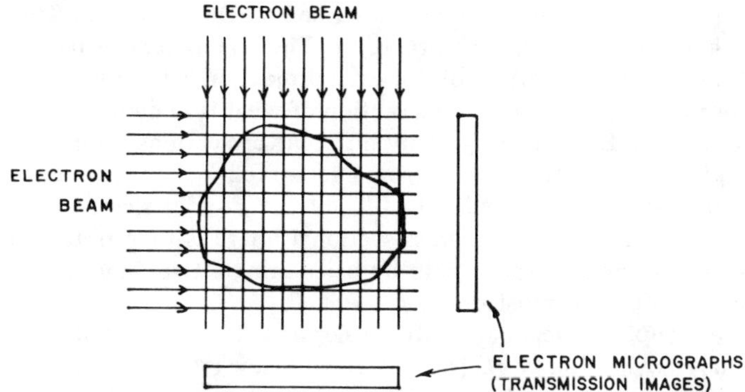

Fig. 5. The periphery of a cross section of a three-dimensional object under electron radiation in an electron microscope. The parallel lines represent paths of electrons. Two sets of parallel lines are shown, one with vertical orientation and the other with horizontal orientation. The two sets represent views of the object taken 90° apart.

stack of two-dimensional cross sections. They proposed obtaining the projections by rotating the object in small increments around a single axis. An electron micrograph would be made at each incremental position. In each micrograph, structure internal to the object lying in a selected plane perpendicular to the axis of rotation would be recorded along a single one-dimensional line through the micrograph. By measuring the density distribution along the corresponding line in each of the micrographs, it would be possible to isolate the information from the desired plane. In this fashion, one could reconstruct a number of two-dimensional cross sections and merely stack them together in the proper sequence to get a full three-dimensional picture. The key technique boils down to reconstructing a two-dimensional cross section from a large number of one-dimensional projections of that cross section.

Thus the essential problem of reconstructing a cross section in electron microscopy is basically the same as that of reconstructing a cross section in X-ray tomography. This point is illustrated in Fig. 5. The figure shows the periphery of a cross section under consideration. To emphasize the similarity with what we have already discussed, the cross section in Fig. 5 is deliberately sketched with the same shape as that in Fig. 3. The vertical and horizontal lines in Fig. 5 do not now represent X-ray beam paths, but rather the paths of the electrons which produce the projections.

De Rosier and Klug pointed out that the total number of projections needed to reconstruct a cross section can be small if the object under consideration has rotation or screw symmetry. They stated that for helical symmetry, as an extreme example, only one projection would be needed. It is not surprising therefore that they chose, as the first object to be reconstructed by their method, the tail of bacteriophage T4, which has good helical symmetry.

Although symmetry simplifies the process, nonsymmetrical objects can also be reconstructed, but more projections are needed. It is simply a matter of rotating the object in small increments and recording the two-dimensional projections. If all the necessary projections are collected regardless of object symmetry the process will reproduce a good image. In general, for a complete set of projections, the object must be rotated accurately in small increments through a total angle of 180°. Symmetry lessens the difficulty by reducing both the number of different projections required and the total angle of rotation. The authors estimated that a ribosome, with no symmetry whatsoever, would require about 30 different projections over a 180° angle.

The reconstruction process described by De Rosier and Klug is based on Fourier transformation. The one-dimensional electron intensity information for each projection is Fourier transformed to provide data for a section of what is known as Fourier space. By collecting many different projections (that is by taking many different electron micrographs) it is possible to gather all the data needed to fill out the Fourier space to the extent necessary. The cross sectional image is then obtained from the Fourier-space data by calculating a two-dimensional inverse Fourier transform.

A couple of years after De Rosier and Klug presented their analysis, Gordon *et al.* [6] described a new method for reconstructive tomography involving what they called algebraic reconstruction techniques (ART). Their method begins with an initial guess of the two-dimensional array of numbers that represents a reconstructed cross section and then it repeatedly modifies the guess in a systematic fashion until the density values stop changing. The method is so powerful that the authors estimated it would require substantially fewer electron micrographs (for example, five to ten) taken over a substantially smaller range of angles (for example, not exceeding about 60°) than the previous method. ART works for totally asymmetric objects and requires relatively little computer time or storage. To be able to get along with fewer micrographs is an important advantage. The authors pointed out that for a ribosome, the 30 projections needed with the De Rosier–Klug method, if taken by an ordinary electron microscope, would not only destroy the specimen, but would cover it with a thick layer of dirt from the microscope chamber.

The ART method is obviously applicable to X-ray photography as well as to electron microscopy. Gordon and colleagues observed that with this method of computed reconstruction, X-ray tomography would require considerably less total radiation than with the focal-plane approach.

C. Optical Applications

Similar techniques for reconstruction of cross-sectional images were also independently developed in the area of optics [7], [8]. Reconstructive tomography was suggested for use with both holographic interferometry and phase-contrast microscopy. We will consider these applications briefly and start with phase-contrast microscopy.

Many microscopic objects are nearly transparent but still can be imaged with good contrast by phase-contrast techniques. These objects absorb very little of the light passing through them but they often produce a spatially varying shift of phase in the transmitted light. Thus they do not primarily modulate the amplitude of the light, but rather its phase.

A phase-contrast imaging system need not be particularly complicated. One such system, originally proposed by Zernike [21], involves the use of a small quarter-wave plate through which the light, not scattered by the object, is focused and made to pass. The light which is scattered by the object follows a different path and is not affected by the plate. When these two beams of light are recombined to produce the image, one beam having been retarded by $\pi/2$ radians in the quarter-wave plate and the other having experienced no retardation, spatially varying amplitude modulation of the light takes the place of the original spatially varying phase modulation and good contrast in the image is made possible. The image may then display the phase-modulating regions of the object with excellent detail.

A problem arises because a phase-contrast microscope frequently has little depth resolution and the image is a two-dimensional superposition of the three-dimensional phase-modulating structure in the object. Such an image may be quite difficult to analyze. Berry and Gibbs [8] pointed out that when straight-line ray propagation may be assumed through the object, with the phase of the rays being controlled by line integrals along their paths, it is then possible to obtain data from the system to calculate the object's density function for phase modulation.

The technique proposed by Berry and Gibbs is identical in character with the techniques we have previously considered. The procedure is to take phase-contrast photographs over a range of incident directions for the light transmitted through the object. The authors derive an equation based on Fourier-transform techniques involving projections obtained by rotating the object in small increments around an axis through a total angle of 180°. The equation gives the density function for the phase-modulating regions in the object. As the authors state, the density function is overdetermined by the totality of possible photographs when this procedure is followed. The technique successfully accomplishes the inversion of data gathered by passing light through an object so that straight-line integrals of the density function are recorded.

Another area of application for roughly this same approach has one rather interesting variation involving holographic techniques. Rowley [7] noted that it was possible to produce a single holographic interferogram with sufficient information to permit the quantitative measurement of the index of refraction of a phase object as a function of position in three-dimensional space. He referred specifically to the type of holographic interferometry, frequently called double-exposure interferometry or time-lapse interferometry, produced by using a laser-illuminated diffuser as a temporally coherent but spatially extended diffuse source. A photographic plate in such a system is exposed twice and becomes the interferogram. For the first exposure there is no object in the system. The diffuse source provides one of the two interfering beams and a suitable reference beam becomes the other. For the second exposure, the object is placed between the diffuse source and the photographic plate. The reference beam is present as before. After the second exposure, the photographic plate is developed to produce an interferogram which yields the optical path-length differences between rays that pass through the phase object and similar rays that pass through the same space when the object is not present. Information contained in the holographic interferogram may then be used to find the spatial variation of the index of refraction of the phase object.

Note that in this application a series of exposures with rotation is not needed. The reason for this is that a holographic interferogram, by itself, provides a three-dimensional view of an object by reconstructing a replica of the original object beam. Therefore, a single such interferogram is equivalent to a large stack of photographs, each member of the stack viewing the object from a different perspective. An image of the object can be seen over a wide range of viewing angles, eliminating the necessity for making a series of exposures with rotation if the range is sufficiently wide.

Thus, in principle, a tomogram can be obtained from a single holographic interferogram. The quality of the tomographic reconstruction is determined primarily by the range of viewing angles involved, or in other words, by the effective field of view provided by the hologram-object-diffuser system. For the highest quality, the placement of the hologram film, the object and the diffuser should be such as to maximize the range of viewing angles afforded by the interferogram. The author suggested that additional information, that is information not actually contained in the hologram, may still be used in a somewhat artificial manner to improve the image quality if necessary. This information may consist of reasonable suppositions concerning the nature of the image of the object for perspectives outside the effective field of view.

The system is obviously unique in that it involves a combination of holography and tomography. Because of the holographic aspect, only one set of exposures, rather than many, need be made.

D. Outline of Sections to Follow

The above discussion was a review of tomography in its earlier and perhaps better-developed modes. This paper, however, is primarily concerned with ultrasound as the source of tomographic imaging, which we have not yet discussed. Although the authors do not consider the paper to be in any sense a survey of the state-of-the-art in computerized ultrasound tomography, they would like to point out that, in addition to the work reported here which they themselves are doing, important developments in various theoretical and experimental aspects of ultrasonic tomography have been made recently in a number of laboratories, principally in the United States. Places where this work is going on include the following.

1) Battelle Pacific Northwest Laboratories, where B. P. Hildebrand, D. E. Hufferd, T. P. Harrington, and associates have reconstructed acoustic velocity fields for the mapping of residual stress.

2) National Bureau of Standards, where M. Linzer, S. J. Norton and colleagues have worked on ultrasonic echo tomography.

3) Mayo Clinic, where J. F. Greenleaf, S. A. Johnson, C. R. Hansen, W. F. Samayoa, M. Tanaka, and associates have followed a number of approaches in the pursuit of clinical applications for ultrasonic tomography.

4) Purdue University, where A. C. Kak and colleagues have worked on ultrasonic tomography using attenuation data.

5) Washington University, where J. G. Miller and associates have worked on single-frequency tomography employing attenuation data.

6) University of Colorado, where P. L. Carson and colleagues have examined clinical applications of ultrasonic tomography.

7) General Electric Company, where G. H. Glover, J. C. Sharp, and associates have experimented with acoustic velocity-field reconstruction.

Even this list is not all inclusive, but it does indicate the wide variety of the research presently going on in an effort to push back the frontiers in this important field.

The early work in acoustic tomography was based on algorithms that were developed for X-ray and optical tomograms. Recently, it has become evident that more accurate models of the physical mechanisms generating the image are crucial in ultrasound for high resolution and correct reconstructions. A major portion of this paper will be concerned with introducing methods for ultrasonic tomography that include diffraction effects. This work can be characterized as a specialization for ultrasound of certain methods used for the solution of the wave equation [22]–[26].

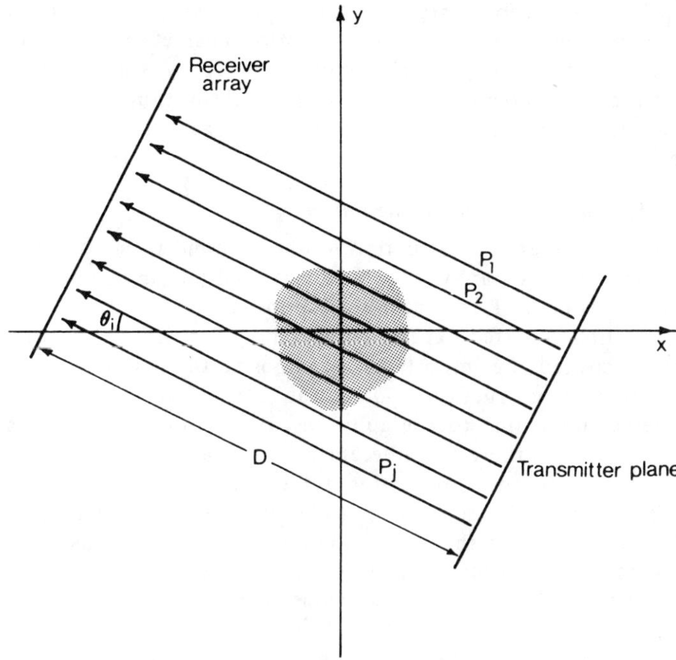

Fig. 6. Geometry of system for ultrasonic tomography using straight-path approximation.

This paper will continue with four major sections. In Section II, transmission methods based on geometrical optics are discussed. Section III introduces tomographic reconstruction of the velocity distribution founded on two perturbation solutions to the wave equation. Section IV discusses a Doppler-oriented method for ultrasonic tomography, and Section V details the validity of the models used in the methods based on the wave equation and geometrical optics.

II. GEOMETRICAL OPTICS-BASED METHODS

The methods currently in use in practical ultrasonic tomography are based on straight-path approximation. Fig. 6 shows the geometry of such systems. As indicated in this figure, the basic premise is that the transmitted wave travels in a straight line to the receiver. Thus the sensed wave at each point on the observation plane can be related to some characteristic of the medium only along the straight path connecting the receiver and the observation point. This obviously is a restrictive assumption, even though reasonably good tomograms have been obtained based on it [27], [28]. It should be mentioned that attempts have been made to include corrections to the straight-path approximation using geometrical optics and ray-tracing methods. These are generally time consuming and may not be suitable for near-real-time applications. Furthermore, all such methods neglect diffraction effects. In the following, several "straight-path" methods are briefly discussed, with emphasis on the ultrasonic sensing schemes.

Image reconstruction from projections falls into two basic categories: signal-space (or spatial domain) and Fourier-domain reconstruction. A multitude of schemes along these two general modes have been devised and their merits discussed in the literature. Theoretical and experimental investigations are especially numerous in the area of optical and X-ray image reconstruction as discussed previously, e.g., [3]–[7]. It so happens that the optimum parameter to be reconstructed is usually different for the ultrasonic and optical cases. For example, intensity shadows are the natural measurements on which the absorption characteristics of an opaque object are reconstructed from X-ray transmission. Ultrasonic tomography based only on absorption data however, has proven to be problematical [28], as will be discussed later.

A. Spatial Domain Reconstruction

This mode of reconstruction has been found most useful in ultrasonic tomography. The schemes used fall under the two categories of ART and the convolution method.

The first reported experimental tomograms with ultrasound demonstrated the importance of choosing the correct parameter for reconstruction. Greenleaf *et al.* [27] showed that whereas ultrasonic tomography based on absorption shadows were possible, there are inherently many inaccuracies. The inaccuracies are due to reflection, refraction, and diffraction. In this method, cross sections of the object are approximated by $N \times N$ grids, with the absorption assumed to be an unknown constant in each block of the grid. A number of projections are then used to solve simultaneous linear equations in the N^2 absorption values in each block.

As a remedy to the reflection and refraction problems in absorption-data reconstruction, the reconstruction of the distribution of the ultrasound velocity in the inhomogeneity was proposed [28]. This method is closely related to the reconstruction of index of refraction in optics [22], [23], [29]. The data-acquisition technique is via the measurement of the time of flight of ultrasound through the inhomogeneity. Fig. 6 shows the geometry of the imaging system. The waves impinging on the object are assumed to be along straight paths P_j. For each angle of incidence θ_i, the receiver array measures the time of arrival of the waves, for each ray, with respect to the time of transmission, and the time-of-flight T_{ij} is calculated. For an experimental measurement system see [28] and [30]. It is assumed that the velocity of propagation in the kth cell is a constant C_k. Thus

$$T_{ij} = \sum_{k=1}^{N} \frac{L_{kj}^{(i)}}{C_k} + \frac{D - \sum_{k=1}^{N} L_{kj}^{(i)}}{C_m} \tag{1}$$

where D is the distance between the transmitter and receiver, $L_{kj}^{(i)}$ is the length of the kth cell traversed by the jth ray at orientation i, C_m is the velocity in the medium surrounding the object and N is the number of object cells. If there are M rays considered, equation (1) represents a set of M equations in N unknowns with $M \ll N$. However, with a sufficient number of angles of incidence, one can obtain N' sets of linear equations in the N unknowns. Denoting $n_k = 1/C_k - 1/C_m$ as the parameter to be reconstructed the problem is now reduced to reconstructing n_k based on a set of measurement equations:

$$\sum_{k=1}^{N} L_{jk}^{(i)} n_k = \tau_{ij}, \qquad \begin{cases} i = 1, \cdots, I \\ j = 1, \cdots, M \end{cases} \tag{2}$$

where the definition of τ_{ij} is obvious from (1). In the following, two classes of spatial-domain methods for obtaining n_k based on (2) are discussed.

1) Algebraic Reconstruction Techniques (ART): The most straightforward method of finding n_k based on the linear degradation model of (2) is, of course, to solve the set of MI linear equations. The problem is that one is faced with the

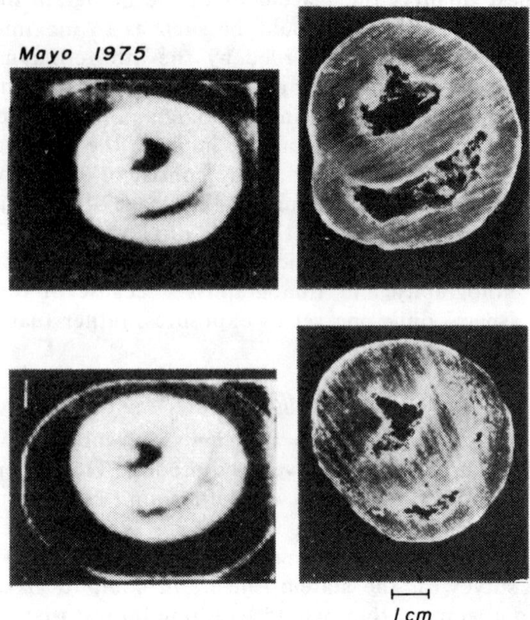

Fig. 7. Tomographic reconstructions of relative propagation delays within a canine heart (left) compared to photographs of cross-sections through corresponding levels (right). Taken from Greenleaf, *et al.* [28].

solution of very large, but sparse, and usually ill-conditioned and inconsistent sets of equations. Furthermore, these equations can be either underdetermined or overdetermined depending on the number of rays and profiles used. In addition, it is known that traditional methods of solving such equations could lead to unacceptably noisy solutions [31], [32]. Several methods have been applied to problems of image restoration given by equations such as (2). One of these, the projection method, tends to the minimum norm solution with respect to the initial guess for underdetermined systems. Since this method is iterative and *a priori* information about the solution can be included in the solution, one can obtain solutions that are a compromise in the output accuracy and noise [33]. Another method, based on the singular-value decomposition, gives the least squares solution to a set of overdetermined linear equations [34]. Application of this method to image restoration, which is similar to the problem at hand, with a compromise between accuracy and solution noise is given in [31]. This method, however, is computationally very time consuming.

Several methods of obtaining the solution to (2) with the specific application to this reconstruction problem as well as those of X-ray and electron micrographs have been developed under the generic name (ART) [6], [35]–[37]. These are computationally more efficient than normal methods of solving linear equations and the solutions that they approach are the same as the ones mentioned above. However, in these cases also, a compromise between accuracy and reconstruction noise has to be reached. Fig. 7 shows the reconstructed relative propagation delays within an excised canine heart obtained by Greenleaf *et al.* using time-of-flight data and an ART method.

2) Convolution Method in Tomography: Since the reconstruction of propagation delay or velocity has been found most reasonable and accurate in ultrasonic tomography, the convolution method is discussed with respect to profiles given by (2). The convolution method was formally suggested by Ramachandran and Lakshminarayanan [38], [39] for the reconstruction of radiographs and electron micrographs. The method is computationally more efficient than ART and is applicable to the solution of (2). The proof of the method is outlined below.

Note that (2) is a discrete version of the true equation describing the relative delay given by the following line integral

$$\tau_{\theta j} = \int_{\lambda_{\theta j}} n(x, y) \, d\lambda_{\theta j} \tag{3}$$

where $\lambda_{\theta j}$ denotes the path of the jth ray at angle θ from the x-axis and $n(x, y)$ is the continuous functional description of n_k. It is obvious that the same $\tau_{\theta j}$ results if the transmitter and receiver are kept constant, with rays parallel to the x-axis, and the object is rotated by $-\theta$. Denote the $n(x, y)$ rotated by $-\theta$ by $n_\theta(x, y)$ and its Fourier transform by $N_\theta(u, v)$. Then

$$\tau_{\theta j} = \int_{-\infty}^{\infty} n_\theta(x, y_j) \, dx.$$

Substituting for $n_\theta(x, y_j)$ in terms of $N_\theta(u, v)$ and integrating with respect to x and u results in

$$\tau_{\theta j} = \int_{-\infty}^{\infty} N_\theta(0, v) \exp(2\pi i y_j v) \, dv. \tag{4}$$

But the Fourier transform of the rotated object is the Fourier transform of the object rotated by the same angle. Thus

$$N_\theta(0, v) = N(W, \theta)|_{W=v}$$

where $W = \sqrt{u^2 + v^2}$ and the one-dimensional Fourier transform in (4) can be written in polar coordinates as:

$$\tau_{\theta j} = \int_{-\infty}^{\infty} N(W, \theta) \exp[2\pi i W r_j \cos(\alpha_j - \theta)] \, dW \tag{5}$$

where $y_j = r_j \sin \alpha_j$. If one makes the assumption that $N(W, \theta)$ is bandlimited to $[-B, B]$, the limits in (5) are changed to $-B$ and B. Furthermore, by the definition of Fourier transform:

$$n(r_j, \alpha_j) = \int_0^\pi \left\{ \int_{-B}^{B} N(W, \theta) \, |W| \right.$$

$$\left. \cdot \exp[2\pi i W r_j \cos(\alpha_j - \theta)] \, dW \right\} d\theta. \tag{6}$$

But the quantity inside the brackets is the convolution of $\tau_{\theta j}$ with the inverse transform of $|W|$ over $[-B, B]$, $h(r)$. And $n(r_j, \alpha_j)$ can be obtained by first convolving the measured profile $\tau_{\theta j}$ with the discrete inverse Fourier transform of $|W|$ over the band $[-B/2, B/2]$ and summing the results from all the profiles. Fig. 8 shows reconstructed sections of a breast using this technique and time-of-flight data.

The above reconstruction technique was based on deterministic considerations. That is, no random nature was assumed for the object and the profiles and measurement noise was not considered. Another method very closely related to the above, considers the optimum, in a Bayesian sense, inversion of the profiles into the reconstructed object [40]. Based on this, Glover and Sharp [41] have obtained ultrasonic tomograms using time-of-flight data and the convolution

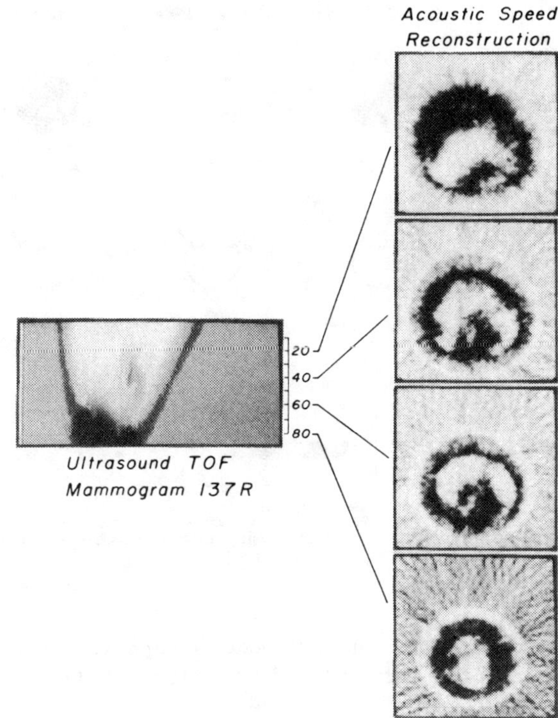

Fig. 8. An ultrasonic mammogram and four tomographic reconstructions of relative propagation delay or acoustic speed in a breast. (Courtesy of J. F. Greenleaf.)

method with a statistically derived kernel. This kernel is a modified version of the previously described one and is essentially an optimum inverse filter of the measurement aperture with noisy measurements. Thus the kernel is similar to the Wiener inverse filter described in [42].

B. Fourier Domain Reconstruction

Fourier domain reconstruction has been used extensively in optical image reconstruction, see for example [5], [29], [43]–[45].

The basis of the method is that the Fourier transform of the projection of an object is a slice of the Fourier transform of the object. Thus with enough projections, the Fourier transform of the object can be approximated and the object reconstructed. As an illustration of the ultrasonic case, in the following we consider the Fourier domain reconstruction of the relative inverse velocity distribution based on time-of-flight data.

Consider the continuous profiles at angle θ given as before by

$$\tau_\theta(y) = \int_{-\infty}^{\infty} n_\theta(x, y) \, dx. \tag{7}$$

Taking Fourier transforms of both sides of (7) with respect to y, results in

$$T_\theta(v) = \int_{-\infty}^{\infty} \int_{-\infty}^{\infty} n_\theta(x, y) \exp(-i2\pi v y) \, dx \, dy$$

$$= N_\theta(0, v) = N(W, \theta)|_{W=v}. \tag{8}$$

In practice there are only a finite number of angles θ_i and a finite sampling of the profile. Thus, the reconstructed Fourier transform is discrete. One has to interpolate between the

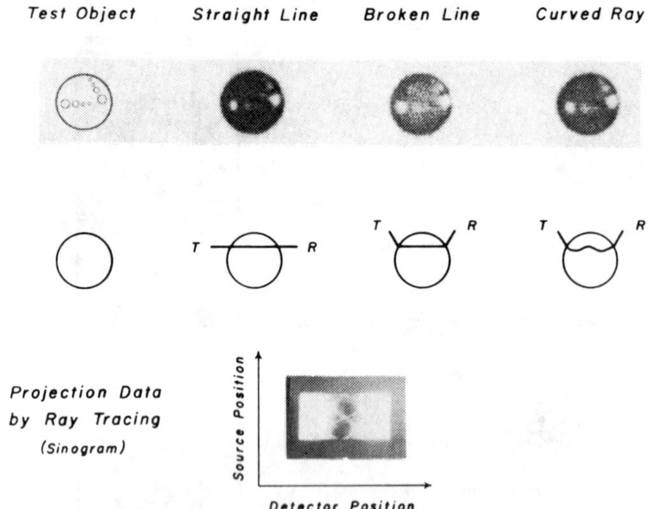

Fig. 9. Tomographic reconstructions using corrections to the straight-path model. Taken from Johnson *et al.* [47].

points especially for higher frequency components to obtain an estimate of the discrete Fourier transform of $n(x, y)$. This problem is discussed in detail in [44].

It is appropriate at this point to question the validity of the straight-path assumption in the above methods. This problem is addressed in detail in the section on the validity of the models. We note here, however, that as discussed in [46] all the above methods are based on the geometrical-optics arguments, that is, for $\lambda \ll$ size of scatterers. Although this is not true in the ultrasonic case, reasonably good images of the low-frequency portion of the disturbance are obtained. It is shown in a later section that the geometrical-optics assumption is not necessary for the validity of the time-of-flight method. It should be pointed out that even in the geometrical-optics limit, the straight-path approximation neglects refraction. Attempts have been made to correct this by calculating the actual ray through second-order approximations [46]. Then, since the algebraic reconstruction techniques do not depend on the straight-path approximation, the approximately calculated $L_{kj}^{(i)}$ can be used in (1) to partially account for refraction. This method has been used in an iterative fashion, where the straight-path solution is used as a starting guess for one based on ray tracing [47]. Fig. 9 shows reconstructions using corrections to the straight-path model. Even though these corrections eliminate some artifacts due to refraction, resolution is unaffected. This is due to the fact that diffraction is not considered, and the basic equations governing the propagation are those of geometrical optics.

A comparison of computation times for the convolution method and ART techniques is given in [32]. By their very nature the algebraic methods are computationally much less efficient than both the convolution and Fourier methods. Fourier-based methods can be made especially efficient by the use of now commonly available hardwired FFT processors. An advantage of algebraic techniques, however, is their ability to include *a priori* knowledge about the solution and their ready acceptance of modifications such as the non-straight-path approximations.

III. DIFFRACTION METHODS

In this technique the wave equation, which governs the propagation of sound through a medium with spatially varying material parameters, is solved approximately. The solution is then used to develop an algorithm to reconstruct one or more of these parameters from observed two-dimensional complex-amplitude distributions of sound waves propagated through the medium of interest.

In order to obtain an adequate equation of motion one can model the object of interest (biological tissue in our case) as a viscous liquid with inhomogeneous distributions of compressibility χ, density ρ, viscosity η, and compressional loss factor γ. An alternative model which leads to essentially the same equation of motion is a lossy inhomogeneous but isotropic solid with high enough attenuation of the transverse wave, so that all energy scattered into it is lost by absorption before it scatters back appreciably into logitudinal waves.

If one introduces a velocity potential ψ for the longitudinal motion, a vector potential $\vec{R}$ for the transverse motion, and assumes a single-frequency excitation with angular frequency ω, one obtains a set of coupled differential equations for the scalar ψ and the three components of the vector $\vec{R}$ given by

$$\omega^2 \rho^2 (\nabla \psi + \vec{R}) + \nabla \{(\chi + i\omega\gamma) \nabla^2 \psi\} - i\omega\eta\nabla \times (\nabla \times \vec{R}) = 0$$

and

$$\nabla \vec{R} = 0. \tag{9}$$

A reconstruction algorithm based on equations (9) with all four parameters ρ, χ, η, γ, all of which are treated as nonvanishing functions of position, is given in a forthcoming paper [48]. The purpose of the following discussion is to demonstrate this reconstruction process on a model which avoids unnecessary mathematical complexity, but is sufficient to demonstrate all aspects of the process, and allows us to compare the diffraction method of tomography with other transmission tomography approaches.

We consider an infinite space filled with a homogeneous loss-free acoustic medium with propagation velocity C_0. Imbedded in this medium is a loss-free object of constant density $\rho = \rho_0$ and a spatially varying velocity distribution $C(\vec{r})$. A sphere of radius 'a' completely encloses the object. The cartesian coordinate system x, y, z which we shall use in the following is centered in this sphere.

The assumption of a loss-free system implies $\eta = \gamma = 0$, which removes the coupling between the velocity potential ψ and the vector potential $\vec{R}$. The assumption of a constant density $\rho = \rho_0$ reduces the remaining equation for ψ to the Helmholtz equation:

$$\nabla^2 \psi + \frac{\omega^2}{C^2(\vec{r})^2} \psi = 0 \tag{10}$$

with

$$C^2(\vec{r}) = \frac{\chi(\vec{r})}{\rho_0}.$$

Equation (10) describes the desired simple model and serves as the basis for the following discussion of the diffraction method of tomography.

We can rewrite (10) as

$$\nabla^2 \psi + \frac{\omega^2}{C_0^2} \psi - \omega^2 \left(\frac{1}{C_0^2} - \frac{1}{C^2(\vec{r})} \right) \psi = 0. \tag{11}$$

Introducing the wavenumber $k = \omega/C_0$ and the function $F(\vec{r})$:

$$F(r) = k^2 \left(1 - \frac{C_0^2}{C^2(\vec{r})} \right) \tag{12}$$

we can write the wave equation as

$$(\nabla^2 + k^2)\,\psi = F(\vec{r})\,\psi. \qquad (13)$$

By definition the function $F(\vec{r})$ is zero for $|\vec{r}| > a$. We shall further assume that its mean is zero. This can always be achieved by appropriate choice of the sound velocity C_0 in the surrounding medium.

Equation (12) can be transformed into a Riccati equation in ∇u by introducing the new variable u by

$$u = \ln \psi \qquad (14)$$

and substituting into (12)

$$\nabla^2 u + (\nabla u)^2 + k^2 = F(\vec{r}). \qquad (15)$$

If one considers $F(\vec{r})$ as a small perturbation one can formally solve (13) and (15) by a perturbation method. The first-order approximation obtained by this method from (13) is known as Born's approximation [23]–[26]; the first-order approximation derived from (15) as Rytov's approximation [24]–[27].

A. Born and Rytov Approximations

We consider the function $F(\vec{r})$ in (13) and (15) as a small perturbation. To set this in evidence we introduce the fictitious variable ϵ and substitute $\epsilon F(\vec{r})$ for $F(\vec{r})$. The solutions ψ and u of (13) and (15) are then assumed to be developed into a power series of ϵ:

$$\psi = \psi_0(1 + \psi_1 \epsilon + \psi_2 \epsilon^2 + \cdots) \qquad (16)$$

and

$$u = u_0 + u_1 \epsilon + u_2 \epsilon^2 + \cdots \qquad (17)$$

and substituted back into (13) and (15). If one now collects equal powers of ϵ one obtaines an ordered set of inhomogeneous linear differential equations with forcing functions composed of the perturbation $F(\vec{r})$ and solutions of equations of lower order.

Combining (13) and (16) gives:

$$(\nabla^2 + k^2)\,\psi_0 = 0$$

$$\nabla^2 \psi_1 + 2\,\frac{\nabla \psi_0}{\psi_0} \cdot \nabla \psi_1 = F(\vec{r})$$

$$\nabla^2 \psi_n + 2\,\frac{\nabla \psi_0}{\psi_0} \cdot \nabla \psi_n = F(\vec{r})\,\frac{\psi(n-1)}{\psi_0} \qquad (18)$$

Combining (15) and (17) gives:

$$\nabla^2 u_0 + (\nabla u_0)^2 + k^2 = 0$$

$$\nabla^2 u_1 + 2(\nabla \mu_0 \cdot \nabla \mu_1) = F(\vec{r})$$

$$\vdots$$

$$\nabla^2 u_n + 2(\nabla u_0 \cdot \nabla u_n) = \sum_{\nu=1}^{n-1} \nabla u_{(n-\nu)}\,\nabla u_\nu. \qquad (19)$$

One can now identify the function ψ_0 with the wave which insonifies the test object and u_0 with the logarithm of this wave.

We shall in the following assume a plane-wave insonification:

$$\psi_0 = \exp\{i\vec{k} \cdot \vec{r}\} \qquad (20)$$

and

$$u_0 = i(\vec{k} \cdot \vec{r}) \qquad (21)$$

where $\vec{k}$ is the propagation vector of the impinging insonification wave.

With this insonification the first-order equations in (18) and (19) become identical:

$$\nabla^2 \psi_1 + i2\vec{k} \cdot \nabla \psi_1 = F(\vec{r}) \qquad (22)$$

and

$$\nabla^2 u_1 + i2k \cdot \nabla u_1 = F(\vec{r}). \qquad (23)$$

This does not mean, however, that the two approximations are identical. Equations (18) and (19) show that the higher order equations differ in the two approaches. This implies that the norm of the perturbation $F(\vec{r})$ which gives an acceptable first-order solution to our original wave equation (13) can be different for the Born or the Rytov approximation.

There is a wide literature discussing the relative merits of the two approximations as they apply to atmospheric scattering of light, radio waves and sound, with the result that most authors consider Rytov's approximation better for this application, e.g., [23]–[26].

In the case of ultrasonic tomography the situation is somewhat simpler because of the finite domain which the scatterer occupies. We shall present later some heuristic arguments which indicate that in the case of interest here the validity of both approximations require the same restrictions on the magnitude of the disturbance $F(\vec{r})$.

We obtain a formal solution of equation (22) by Fourier transformation. We define a radius vector $\vec{\Lambda}$ in the spatial-frequency space κ, μ, ν, and its absolute value $\Lambda = |\vec{\Lambda}|$ and let

$$S(\vec{\Lambda}) = \int \psi_1(\vec{r})\,\exp[-i(\vec{\Lambda} \cdot \vec{r})]\,d\kappa\,d\mu\,d\nu$$

$$T(\vec{\Lambda}) = -\int F(\vec{r})\,\exp[-i(\vec{\Lambda} \cdot \vec{r})]\,d\kappa\,d\mu\,d\nu. \qquad (24)$$

With this notation the Fourier transform of (22) becomes:

$$\Lambda^2 S(\vec{\Lambda}) + 2(\vec{k} \cdot \vec{\Lambda})\,S(\vec{\Lambda}) = T(\vec{\Lambda}) \qquad (25)$$

and we obtain

$$S(\vec{\Lambda}) = \frac{T(\vec{\Lambda})}{\Lambda^2 + 2\vec{k}\,\vec{\Lambda}}. \qquad (26)$$

Equation (26) is legitimate only for $\Lambda^2 + 2(\vec{k} \cdot \vec{\Lambda}) \neq 0$. In order to make (26) valid for all real values of $\vec{\Lambda}$ we assume that the propagation constant k of the undisturbed medium has an arbitrarily small but finite and positive imaginary part $k = k_0(1 + i\gamma)$. This assumption is physically reasonable as it represents loss in the medium and does not affect observable results; it can furthermore be removed after we have obtained the desired reconstruction by letting γ go to zero.

B. The Inversion Problem

We consider the measurement geometry shown schematically in Fig. 10. The insonifying field is a plane wave impinging on the object from an arbitrary direction. The scattered field is observed by a planar receiver array of finite aperture A, located a distance r from the origin. The limitations imposed on this geometry for the following considerations are that the radius vector $\vec{r}$ to the center of the array is perpendicular to the plane of the array and that its magnitude r is greater than the radius a (see Fig. 10).

One can accomodate all configurations possible under these limitations by putting the receive array center on the positive

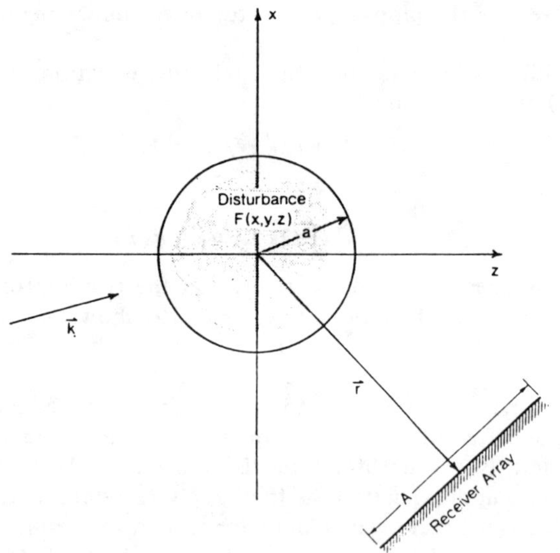

Fig. 10. Measurement geometry with plane-wave insonification.

z-axis at $z = z_0$ and permitting the test object to rotate around the origin. The field at the receiving aperture is a function of the space coordinates x, y, z, the propagation vector $\vec{k}$, and the rotation operator Θ which describes the orientation of the test object relative to the coordinate system.

In order to include this rotational degree of freedom into our notation we replace the function $F(\vec{r})$ by $F(\Theta \vec{r})$ and therefore $T(\vec{\Lambda})$ by $T(\Theta^{-1}\vec{\Lambda})$.

We can now express the field in the receive plane $\psi(x, y, z_0, \vec{k}, \Theta)$ in terms of our formal solution $S(\vec{\Lambda})$ and obtain for Born's approximation:

$$\psi(x, y, z_0, \vec{k}, \Theta) = \psi_0 \left(1 + \iiint \right.$$
$$\left. \cdot \frac{T(\Theta^{-1}\vec{\Lambda}) \exp [i(\kappa x + \mu y + \nu z_0)]}{(\Lambda^2 + 2\vec{k} \cdot \vec{\Lambda})} \, d\kappa \, d\mu \, d\nu \right) \quad (27)$$

and for Rytov's approximation:

$$\psi(x, y, z_0, \vec{k}, \Theta) = \psi_0 \exp \left\{ \iiint \right.$$
$$\left. \cdot \frac{T(\Theta^{-1}\vec{\Lambda}) \exp [i(\kappa x + \mu y + \nu z_0)]}{(\Lambda^2 + 2\vec{k} \cdot \vec{\Lambda})} \, d\kappa \, d\mu \, d\nu \right\}. \quad (28)$$

We can observe this function however only over the finite aperture A. Introducing an aperture function $g(x, y)$ one can rewrite (27) and (28) as

$$g(x, y) \iiint \frac{T(\Theta^{-1}\vec{\Lambda}) \exp [i(\kappa x + \mu y + \nu z_0)]}{\Lambda^2 + 2\vec{k} \cdot \vec{\Lambda}} \, d\kappa \, d\mu \, d\nu$$
$$= q(x, y, z_0, \vec{k}, \Theta) \quad (29)$$

where $q(x, y, z_0, \vec{k}, \Theta)$ is for Born's approximation:

$$q = g \cdot \frac{\psi - \psi_0}{\psi_0} \quad (30)$$

and for Rytov's approximation:

$$q = g \cdot \ln (\psi/\psi_0). \quad (31)$$

The objective of the inversion procedure is to express $T(\vec{\Lambda})$ in terms of the Fourier transform $U(\kappa, \mu, z_0, \vec{k}, \Theta)$ of the ob-

served function $q(x, y, z_0, \vec{k}, \Theta)$. Transforming (29) we obtain:

$$U(\kappa, \mu, z_0, \vec{k}, \Theta) = G(\kappa, \mu) * \int_{-\infty}^{+\infty} \frac{T(\Theta^{-1}\vec{\Lambda}) \exp (i\nu z_0)}{\Lambda^2 + 2\vec{k} \cdot \vec{\Lambda}} \, d\nu. \quad (32)$$

The function $G(\kappa, \mu)$ is the Fourier transform of the aperture function $g(x, y)$ and the star indicates convolution.

We have now to evaluate the integral I:

$$I = \int_{-\infty}^{+\infty} \frac{T(\Theta^{-1}\vec{\Lambda})}{\Lambda^2 + 2\vec{k} \cdot \vec{\Lambda}} \exp (i\nu z_0) \, d\nu \quad (33)$$

with given values for μ, κ, and Θ.

We consider first the denominator $(\Lambda^2 - 2\vec{k} \cdot \vec{\Lambda})$ of the integrand which is a quadratic function of ν and can be brought into the form

$$\Lambda^2 - 2\vec{k} \cdot \vec{\Lambda} = (\nu - \nu_1)(\nu - \nu_2) \quad (34)$$

with

$$\nu_{1(2)} = -k_z \underset{(-)}{+} \sqrt{k_z^2 - \kappa^2 - \mu^2 + 2\kappa k_x + 2\mu k_y}. \quad (35)$$

Due to our assumption that k is a complex number with a positive imaginary part, the two roots ν_1 and ν_2 are complex, with the imaginary part of ν_1 greater than zero and the imaginary part of ν_2 smaller than zero. The integral I can now be written in the form:

$$I = \int_{-\infty}^{+\infty} \frac{T(\Theta^{-1}\vec{\Lambda})}{(\nu - \nu_1)(\nu - \nu_2)} \exp (i\nu z_0) \, d\nu$$
$$= \int_{-a}^{+a} F(\kappa, \mu, z) \int_{-\infty}^{+\infty} \frac{\exp [i\nu(z_0 - z)]}{(\nu - \nu_1)(\nu - \nu_2)} \, d\nu \, dz \quad (36)$$

where $F(\kappa, \mu, z)$ is the partial Fourier transform of the rotated test object

$$F(\kappa, \mu, z) = \iint_{-a}^{+a} F(\Theta \vec{r}) \exp [-i(\kappa x + \mu y) \, dx \, dy. \quad (37)$$

The integral I_2 over ν:

$$I_2 = \int_{-\infty}^{+\infty} \frac{\exp [i\nu(z_0 - z)]}{(\nu - \nu_1)(\nu - \nu_2)} \, d\nu \quad (38)$$

can be integrated by considering the integral a contour integral in the complex plane $u = \nu + i\omega$ (see Fig. 11). We convert the integral, which extends originally over the real axis $u = \nu$, to a closed-loop integral by integrating over a circular arc $|u| = s$ in the upper half-plane and letting s go to infinity. One can show that the integral over the arc does not contribute to the contour integral provided that $(z_0 - z)$ is greater than zero. This however is always the case, since z is limited to $|z| < a$ and z_0 is by design greater than a. The only singularity inside the closed loop is a single pole at $\nu = \nu_1$ and we obtain therefore for the integral I_2:

$$I_2 = 2\pi i \frac{\exp [i\nu_1(z_0 - z)]}{(\nu_1 - \nu_2)}. \quad (39)$$

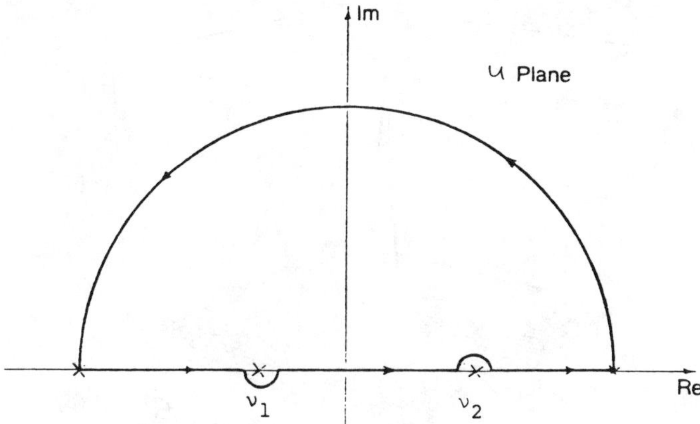

Fig. 11. Integration contour in complex u plane.

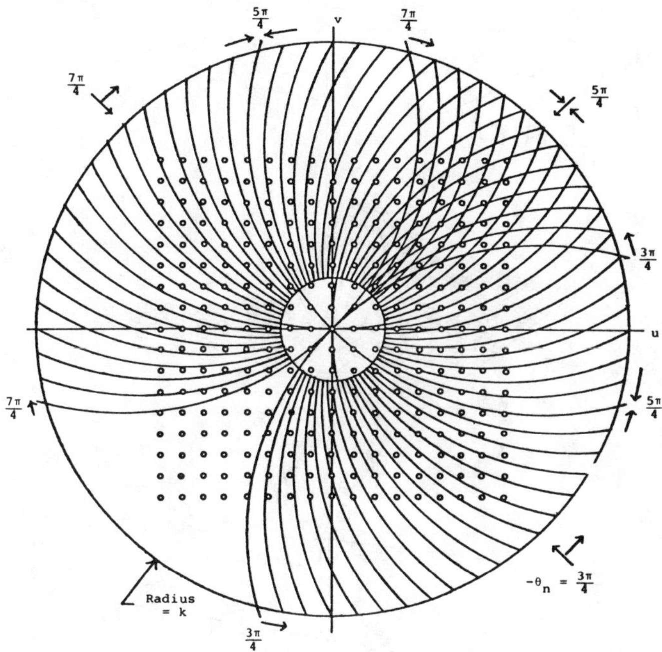

Fig. 12. Loci of available $\vec{\Lambda}$'s superimposed on a uniform grid of spatial frequencies.

Introducing this result into (36), we finally obtain in view of (37):

$$I = 2\pi i \, \frac{T(\Theta^{-1}\vec{\Lambda}_1)}{(\nu_1 - \nu_2)} \exp{(i\nu_1 z_0)} \qquad (40)$$

with $\vec{\Lambda}_1 = \{\kappa, \mu, \nu_1\}$. The roots ν_1 and ν_2 are given functions of κ, μ, and $\vec{k}$.

Introducing (40) into (32) gives

$$U = G * 2\pi i \, \frac{T(\Theta^{-1}\vec{\Lambda}_1)}{(\nu_1 - \nu_2)} \exp{(i\nu_1 z_0)}. \qquad (41)$$

The aperture transfer function G is a narrow pulse-like function with a width on the order of the reciprocal of the aperture diameter. It is therefore reasonable to assume that functions ν_1, ν_2 and the spectrum T of the disturbance do not vary appreciably over this width. One can therefore in good approximation replace (41) by

$$U \simeq 2\pi i \, \frac{T(\Theta^{-1}\vec{\Lambda}_1)}{(\nu_1 - \nu_2)} \, G * \exp{(i\nu_1 z_0)}. \qquad (42)$$

Equation (42) represents the basis for the reconstruction process. It follows from (42) that with every measurement of the scattered field over the aperture, one obtains a two-dimensional cut $T(\vec{\Lambda}_1)$ of the spectrum $T(\vec{\Lambda})$ of the disturbance. In order to reconstruct the function $F(\vec{r})$, however, one requires a sufficient three-dimensional sample of the spectrum $T(\vec{\Lambda})$. This can be achieved in a variety of ways.

One can leave the insonification fixed and rotate the test object. This results in a counter-rotating cut $T(\Theta_n^{-1}\vec{\Lambda}_1)$ of the spectrum which sweeps out the complete spectrum $T(\vec{\Lambda})$ in the spatial-frequency space.

One can, on the other hand, leave the test object fixed and rotate the insonification vector $\vec{k}$. This gives rise to a more complex process because not only are the roots ν_1 and ν_2 different functions of κ and μ for each measurement, but also the aperture function $G * \exp{(i\nu_1 z_0)}$ varies for each measurement.

Any combination of the two methods also can generate a sufficient sample of the spectrum $T(\vec{\Lambda})$.

C. Examples of the Perturbation Methods

In order to demonstrate the reconstruction methods given by (43), scattered waves from two-dimensional circular inhomogeneities were numerically calculated [49]. Thus the problem is specialized to the x-y plane with $\vec{\Lambda} = \{\mu, \nu\}$. Further-more, a sufficiently large aperture function was used and $G(\mu)$ in (42) was replaced by a Dirac delta function, resulting in the reconstruction equation

$$T(\Theta^{-1}\vec{\Lambda}) \simeq (\nu_1 - \nu_2) \cdot u \cdot \exp{(-i\nu_1 x_0)} \qquad (43)$$

where x_0 is the distance of the receiver line from the origin and $u = U/2\pi i$. Specifically for a finite number of profiles, the equations describing the values of $T(\vec{\Lambda})$ along the accessible measurement circles defined in analogy to (34) are given by [49], [50]

$$T(\Theta_n^{-1}\vec{\Lambda}) \simeq (\nu_1 - \nu_2) \, u_n \exp{(-i\nu_1 x_0)},$$

$$\text{fixed } \vec{k}, \text{ rotating object} \qquad (44)$$

and

$$T(\vec{\Lambda}) \simeq (\nu_1 - \nu_2) \, u_n \exp{(-i\nu_1 x_0)},$$

$$\text{rotating } \vec{k}_n, \text{ fixed object.} \qquad (45)$$

It should be noted again that in (44), ν_1 and ν_2 are independent of Θ_n. Thus $T(\vec{\Lambda})$ is derived from the calculated $T(\Theta_n^{-1}\vec{\Lambda})$ by simple rotation by Θ_n. On the other hand, $T(\vec{\Lambda})$ is directly obtained from (45). In this case ν_1 and ν_2 are functions of the wave-vector $\vec{k}_n$. For a finite observation window, the effect of the aperture transfer function in (41) is different for the two cases. Specifically, in terms of the effect on the reconstructed frequency components, the case given by (45) tapers the function $\psi(x_0, y)$ symmetrically about the axis of radiation, thus emphasizing the lower frequency components. In practice, equation (44) contains asymmetric shading of $\psi^{(n)}(x_0, y)$ depending on $\vec{k}_n$; for larger deviation of $\vec{k}_n$ from the normal, however, it contains more information about the higher frequency components of $\psi^{(n)}(x_0, y)$.

Another important aspect of these reconstruction techniques, in practice, is the Fourier domain evaluation of $T(\vec{\Lambda})$ based on discrete Fourier transformation. This has to be done in a computationally efficient manner. This implies the use

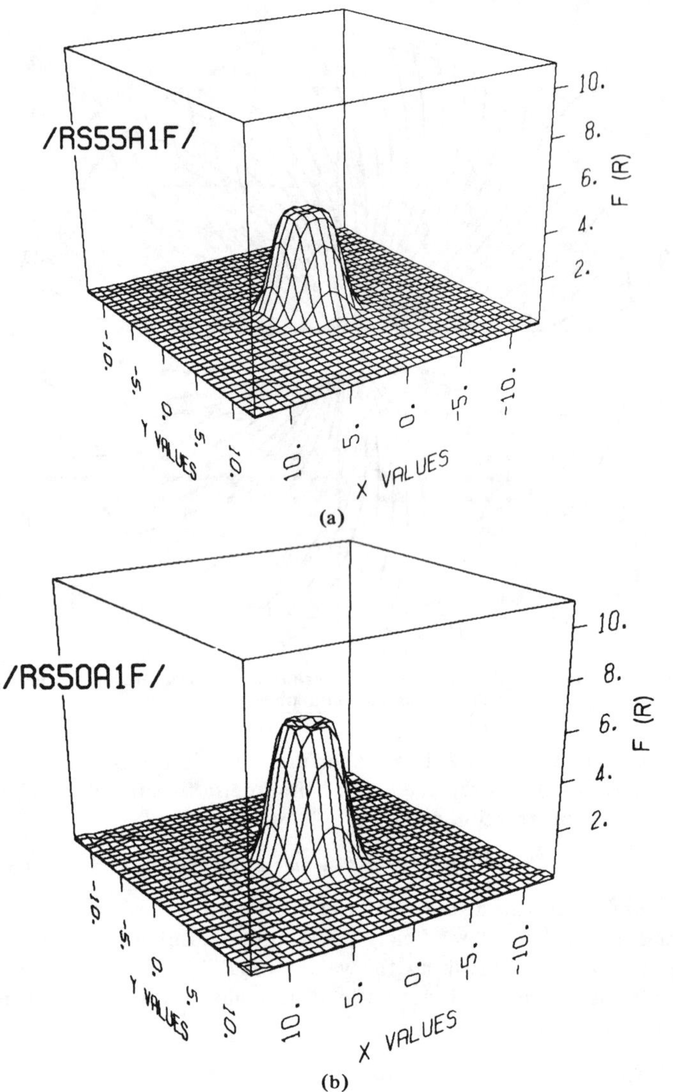

Fig. 13. (a) Reconstructed ΔC, filtered Born's approximation, radius = 3λ, $\Delta C = 0.05 C_0$. (b) Reconstructed ΔC, filtered Born's approximation, radius = 3λ, $\Delta C = 0.1 C_0$.

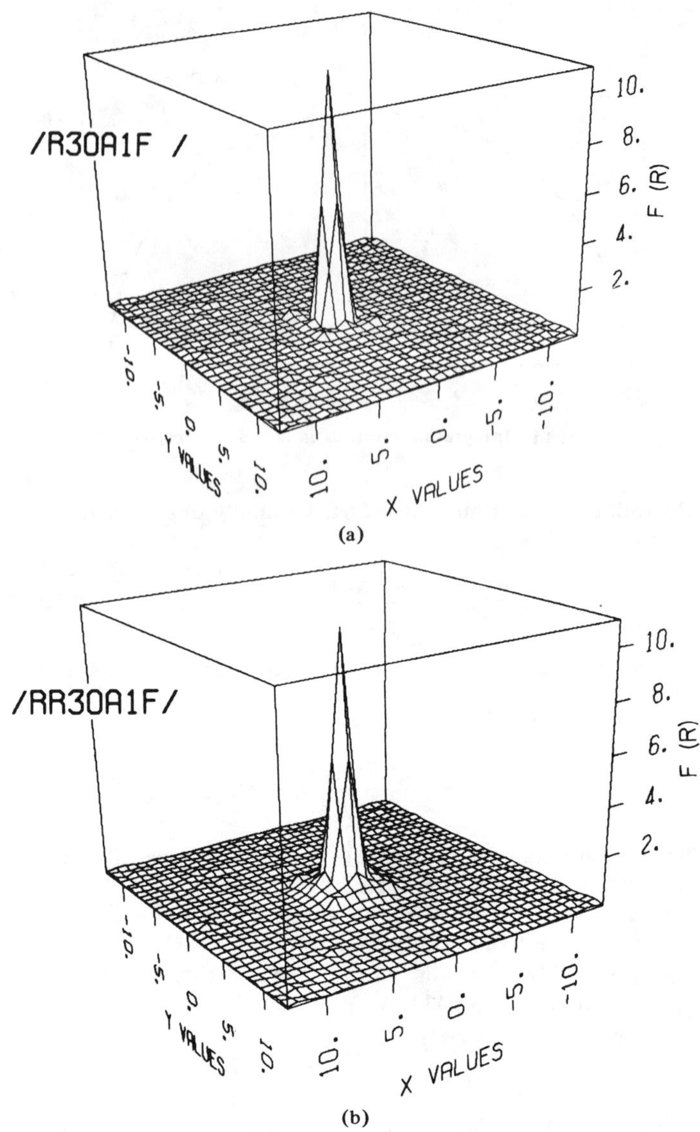

Fig. 14. (a) Reconstructed ΔC, Born's approximation, radius = λ, $\Delta C = 0.1 C_0$. (b) Reconstructed ΔC, Rytov's approximation, radius = λ, $\Delta C = 0.1 C_0$.

of fast Fourier algorithms, which require values of the function on a uniform, discrete lattice of frequencies. Since $T(\vec{\Lambda})$ is only obtained for frequencies on the accessible circles, the above requirement suggests interpolation of the irregularly-spaced frequency components onto the regular lattice. Fig. 12 shows the two-dimensional example considered. In this figure, the accessible circles in the spatial-frequency domain are superimposed on a lattice of frequencies required for fast Fourier transformation. It is obvious that with a sufficient number of profiles and accurate interpolation, the required frequency components can be obtained.

Figs. 13–15 show density plots of the reconstructed velocity disturbances ΔC for various uniform cylindrical inhomogeneities [50]–[52]. The reconstruction was based on a zeroth-order interpolation (nearest neighbor frequency assignment) of $T(\vec{\Lambda})$ onto a 64×64 grid at a spatial sampling period of $\Delta x = \Delta y = 0.2$. The receive array was at a distance x_0 indicated on the figures with a rectangular measurement taper of $P.\lambda$. Thirty-six profiles were used in all the reconstructions. The noise apparent on the reconstructed densities

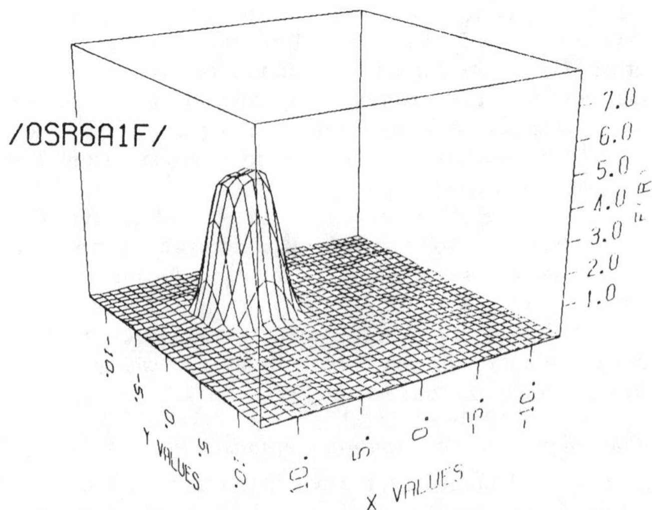

Fig. 15. Reconstructed ΔC, Born's approximation, radius = 3λ, $\Delta C = 0.05 C_0$, centered at $(4\lambda, 4\lambda)$.

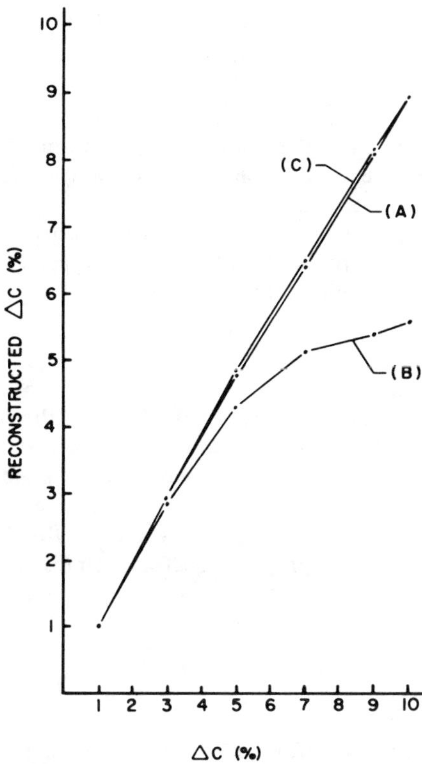

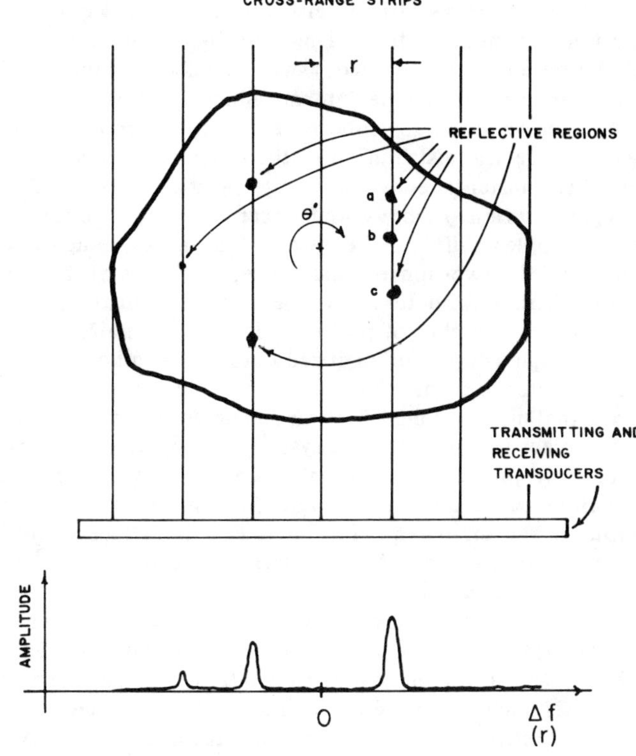

Fig. 16. Reconstructed peak value of the velocity variation as a function of the true peak value. Conditions for the plots: (a) radius = λ, Born's approximation. (b) radius = 3λ, Born's approximation. (c) radius = λ, Rytov's approximation.

Fig. 17. An outline of a cross section of an object with reflecting regions. The set of parallel lines represent cross-range strips for a tomographic system employing a Doppler technique. The cross-range distance r is shown for the three reflecting regions a, b, and c and $\dot{\theta}$ is the angular rotational velocity of the object. The plot below shows the amplitude of the ensemble of received signals as a function of Doppler frequency, and hence as a function of the cross-range position of the reflecting regions.

is due to interpolation and windowing of the profiles. It is obvious from Fig. 12 that the interpolation is more accurate for lower frequencies. Thus $T(\vec{\Lambda})$ may be windowed by a raised cosine of radius $|\vec{k}|$ to reduce the high-frequency noise as well as aliasing errors.

In order to investigate the quantitative accuracy of the methods, an investigation of the linearity of the reconstruction as a function of disturbance, magnitude, and geometry was made [51]. Fig. 16 shows plots of the reconstructed peak value of the disturbance as a function of the true value of the disturbance for two radii. It can be seen that the Born and Rytov approximations give identical results for a disturbance with radius equal to λ, and approximate linearity holds for $\Delta C/C$ in excess of 10 percent. It should be noted, however, that neither approximation is as valid for a larger radius of disturbance, pointing to the importance of both magnitude and geometry of the disturbance for the validity of the approximation used.

IV. Tomographic System Employing Doppler Techniques

As we have seen from the discussion in Section I on radar astronomy, the principles of tomography may be combined with Doppler techniques to produce a unique type of imaging. One ultrasonic embodiment of such a scheme, presented here not so much as a proven practicality but rather as a thought-provoking possibility, employs a transmitting and receiving transducer placed in a fluid adjacent to the body to be scanned [53], as shown in Fig. 17.

For ease of understanding the underlying principles, assume that the body is rotated at a constant angular velocity $\dot{\theta}$ about some center of rotation. (Alternatively, the transducer assembly could be rotated about a stationary body.) If we are interested in viewing a thin cross section of the object we would provide an ultrasonic sheet beam highly collimated in the direction normal to the plane of the cross section. Any specific reflecting region within the cross section located at a cross-range distance r from the rotational center (see Fig. 17) will have a component of linear velocity at right angles to the transducer length given by

$$V = r\dot{\theta} \qquad (46)$$

where r is the cross range of the reflecting region at that instant of time. Assume that the transmitting and receiving transducers occupy essentially the same position as indicated in the figure. If the transmitter emits a sinusoidal wave of frequency f_0, the wave scattered back toward the receiver from the reflecting region will be Doppler-shifted by an amount Δf such that

$$\Delta f = \frac{2Vf_0}{c} \qquad (47)$$

where c is the sound velocity in the medium.

Thus the cross-range distance of any reflecting region is proportional to the Doppler frequency shift. At any instance of time, the waves returning to the receiver from reflecting regions located along a single cross-range strip will all have the same Doppler-shifted frequency. The received signal at any frequency corresponds to the aggregate of all the reflected waves from a narrow strip intersecting the cross section in a direction perpendicular to the length of the transducer.

If the ensemble of received signals is passed through a frequency analyzer in a time interval which is short compared to the time required for rotating the object through a small angle, the spectral distribution of the ensemble will be a function of the instantaneous cross-range position of the reflecting regions within the body under scan. A plot of amplitude versus Doppler shift can be regarded as a one-dimensional projection of a two-dimensional image, the image of the cross section. This information must be digitized and the process repeated for a number of positions of the rotating body as it turns through $180°$. The digitized data can then be processed by a computer to obtain the final tomographic reconstruction.

Note that in the conceptual model described, the rotation of the object is inherent to the system and useful in two ways. It not only produces the Doppler Shift, but it also permits projections to be quickly taken at the appropriate angles for computing the tomogram. In principle, only half a revolution is needed to provide sufficient data for reconstructing the cross sectional image.

In order to get an idea of the various constraints inherent in the system, Gail Flesher of the University of California, Santa Barbara, has made some simple calculations. Consider an object that is enclosed in a circle of radius R and divided into N cross-range strips for the tomographic reconstruction. As a scattering center moves through a cross-range distance of width $2R/N$, it will reflect, on the average, an echo with a Doppler frequency at the value that corresponds to the strip through which it is moving. In order for the scattering center to stay within the boundaries of the strip during the measurement time Δt, the shortest allowable time for crossing the strip must be greater than the measurement time. Thus

$$\frac{2}{N\dot{\theta}} > \Delta t. \tag{48}$$

The Doppler frequency is highest for the strip with the greatest cross range on the side of the object advancing toward the receiver. There is no shift for the strip in the center. The frequency is lowest for the strip with the greatest cross range on the retreating side. The overall frequency range to be measured spans an interval of $4R\dot{\theta}/\lambda$ Hz. Dividing this by N gives the frequency difference between adjacent cross-range strips. The accuracy to which the frequency must be measured is, therefore,

$$\Delta f = \frac{4R\dot{\theta}}{\lambda N}. \tag{49}$$

For measuring to this accuracy, the measurement time must be greater than $1/\Delta f$,

$$\Delta t > \frac{1}{\Delta f} = \frac{\lambda N}{4R\dot{\theta}} \tag{50}$$

The above two inequalities set an upper and lower limit on Δt. Thus

$$\frac{\lambda N}{4R\dot{\theta}} < \Delta t < \frac{2}{N\dot{\theta}} \tag{51}$$

By forcing the two limits to be equal we can prescribe a value for N as follows:

$$\frac{\lambda N}{4R\dot{\theta}} = \frac{2}{N\dot{\theta}} \tag{52}$$

or

$$N = \sqrt{\frac{8R}{\lambda}}. \tag{53}$$

If $R = 20$ cm and $\lambda = 0.05$ cm, N will be about 57. This sets a rather severe restriction on the maximum number of pixels in the reconstructed image.

The number of projections necessary in a tomographic system is usually of the order of 100. Since each Δt gives one projection, this requirement yields

$$\Delta t < \frac{2\pi}{\dot{\theta}} 10^{-2}. \tag{54}$$

This inequality varies inversely with $\dot{\theta}$ as did the first one; but for $N = 57$, it is less restrictive and can be ignored.

To ensure that all scattered waves in a single cross-range strip arrive within a short enough period of time at the receiver to add together in the proper way during the measurement time Δt, the time of propagation for the most distant reflection and the least distant reflection must differ by less than about a tenth of the measurement time.

$$\frac{2R}{c} < \frac{\Delta t}{10}. \tag{55}$$

For $R = 20$ cm as before and $c = 1500$ m/s, the expression gives a Δt of about 3 ms. Consistent with this value of Δt is a rotation speed of about 2 r/s. Rotation that fast may at first appear to present a problem, but the "revolving" can be accomplished electronically by means of a circular array of transducers surrounding the object to be imaged.

V. The Validity of Models

As discussed in the previous sections, in ultrasonic tomography two basic approaches are used to obtain the information required to reconstruct the generally complex propagation velocity distribution. These approaches can be classified as ray-tracing methods and as wave-propagation methods.

Both methods are based on approximate solutions of the wave equation which governs the propagation of sound through media with inhomogeneous velocity distributions. The different assumptions made to derive these approximations distinguish the approaches and determine their range of validity.

It is the purpose of this section to examine these assumptions and discuss to some extent their effect on the resulting reconstruction.

We consider first the wave-propagation methods and then the ray-tracing methods. This is advantageous, since the basic equations for the ray-tracing method is obtained as a special case of one of the approximations used in the wave-propagation methods.

A. Wave-Propagation Methods

The wave equation which governs the propagation of ultrasound in inhomogeneous media was introduced in Section III. Two approximate methods for their solution were discussed.

The first method, known as Born's approximation, solves approximately the wave equation proper. In the second method, the wave equation is first transformed into a Riccati equation and then solved. This method is known as Rytov's approximation. Both approximations are based on perturbation methods where the deviation of the propagation velocity from its mean is considered a small disturbance. The magnitude of the disturbance F is measured by its norm $\|F\|$:

$$F = \frac{C(r)^2 - C_0^2}{C(\vec{r})^2} \quad \text{and} \quad \|F\| = \left[\frac{1}{V}\int_V FF^* \, dv\right]^{1/2} \quad (56)$$

where V is a suitably defined volume which completely contains the disturbance.

The perturbations (18) and (19) in Section III are derived under the assumption that the norm $\|F\|$ is small compared to unity. The perturbation equations however are not explicitly dependent on $\|F\|$. It is not immediately obvious therefore under what condition the formal solutions of (16) and (17) converge, nor how good an approximation the first-order solutions are.

A related question of particular interest here is whether Born's or Rytov's approximation represents a better solution for a disturbance of given magnitude.

A sufficient condition for the convergence of the perturbation solution is that the sequences

$$|\overline{\psi}_n| = \frac{1}{V}\int |\psi_n| \, dv \quad \text{and} \quad |\overline{u}_n| = \frac{1}{V}\int |u_n| \, dv \quad (57)$$

converge to zero with increasing n. The ψ_n and u_n are the nth-order terms for Born's and Rytov's approximation.

A practically useful indication for the quality of the first-order approximation is the magnitude of $|\overline{\psi}_2|$ and $|\overline{u}_2|$. In order to estimate $|\overline{\psi}_2|$ and $|\overline{u}_2|$, however, one has to have some knowledge or make some assumption about the spatial power spectrum $|T(\vec{\Lambda})|^2$ of the disturbance F.

A case discussed in [26] is the severely band-limited disturbance, where the spatial frequency spectrum $T(\vec{\Lambda})$ of F satisfies the condition

$$T(\vec{\Lambda}) = 0, \quad \text{for} \quad \Lambda > \Lambda_{\max} \ll k. \quad (58)$$

This case is of interest because Rytov's approximation is now closely related to the ray-tracing or "geometric optics" approximation of the wave equation and converges much faster than Born's approximation. We show this in the following for the two-dimensional case $\vec{\Lambda} \equiv \{\mu, \nu\}$ and $\vec{k} \equiv \{0, k\}$.

In order to evaluate $|\overline{\psi}_2|$ and $|\overline{u}_2|$ one has to find the first- and second-order solutions ψ_1, u_1 and ψ_2, u_2 inside the disturbance. In contrast to the solution outside the disturbance which was derived in Section III, one has to consider the contributions from both the forward-scattered and backscattered waves, that is from both the singularities ν_1 and ν_2 defined in Section III.

With the wave vector $\vec{k}$ of the impinging wave given by $\vec{k} \equiv \{0, k\}$ one obtains from (35) for the two singularities ν_1 and ν_2:

$$\nu_{1,(2)} = -k \underset{(-)}{+} \sqrt{k^2 - \mu^2} \quad (59)$$

which, because of (58), gives for the spatial frequency range where $T(\vec{\Lambda})$ is finite:

$$\nu_1 = -\frac{\mu^2}{2k} \simeq 0 \qquad \nu_2 = -2k + \frac{\mu^2}{2k} \simeq -2k. \quad (60)$$

Let S_n^B, S_n^R represent the spatial-frequency spectra of ψ_n and u_n, and T_n^B, T_n^R the spectra of the corresponding forcing functions f_n^B, f_n^R defined in (18) and (19). We then get

$$S_n^B = \frac{T_n^B}{\nu_1 - \nu_2}\left(\frac{1}{\nu - \nu_2} - \frac{1}{\nu - \nu_1}\right) \quad (61)$$

and correspondingly

$$S_n^R = \frac{T_n^R}{\nu_1 - \nu_2}\left(\frac{1}{\nu - \nu_1} - \frac{1}{\nu - \nu_2}\right). \quad (62)$$

For the first-order spectrum we obtain because of $T_1^B = T_1^R = T$:

$$S_1 = S_1^B = S_1^R = \frac{T}{\nu_1 - \nu_2}\left(\frac{1}{\nu - \nu_1} - \frac{1}{\nu - \nu_2}\right). \quad (63)$$

Since only the pole $\nu = \nu_1$ lies within the spatial frequency range where T is finite we obtain from (60) and (63)

$$S_1(\mu, \nu) = \frac{T(\mu, \nu)}{2k\nu} \quad (64)$$

and therefore for the first-order perturbation:

$$\psi_1 = u_1 = ik \int_{-a/2}^{y} F(x, \eta) \, d\eta . \quad (65)$$

This is equivalent to neglecting the second-order derivatives in the first-order perturbation (18) and (19).

The spatial-frequency range for which T_2^R and T_2^B are finite is twice as wide as the range for which T is finite. If we assume, however, that this spatial bandwidth is still sufficiently small compared to k to leave (60) valid, we obtain in analogy to (65)

$$\psi_2 = ik \int_{-a/2}^{y} f_2^B (x, \eta) \, d\eta \quad (66)$$

and

$$u_2 = ik \int_{-a/2}^{y} f_2^R (x, \eta) \, d\eta \quad (67)$$

with

$$f_2^B = - k^2 F(x, y) \int_{-a/2}^{y} F(x, \eta) \, d\eta \quad (68)$$

and

$$f_2^R = - k^2 (F(x, y)) + \left[\int_{-a/2}^{y} \frac{\partial F(x, \eta)}{\partial x} \, d\eta\right]^2 . \quad (69)$$

We can now derive an estimate of the means $|\overline{\psi}_2|$ and $|\overline{u}_2|$ over the disturbed area. Using the mean-value theorem of integration one obtains:

$$|\overline{\psi}_2| < ka\|F\|$$

$$|\overline{u}_2| < \|F\| + \|F\| (\mu_{\max}a) \frac{\mu_{\max}}{k} \quad (70)$$

$$|\overline{\psi}_1| = \|F\|.$$

Since $\mu_{\max}/k$ is, according to (58), very small compared to unity, we have the estimate

$$|\overline{\psi}_2| < ka\|F\|$$

$$|u_2| < \|F\|. \quad (71)$$

This estimate, expression (71), shows that Born's approximation requires for convergence not only a small norm but also a spatially confined disturbance, in contrast to Rytov's approximation, for which a small norm $\|F\|$ is sufficient to assume convergence.

One has to keep in mind that these conditions are sufficient conditions only, not necessary ones. They nevertheless give confidence in Rytov's approach, at least for a severely band-limited disturbance.

The model of a band-limited disturbance describes well the situation of light and sound transmission in a disturbed atmosphere [26], but it is not a good model for biological tissue. In biological tissue, the structure detail extends well below the wavelength of any ultrasound which is able to penetrate it. The spatial frequency spectrum therefore extends well beyond k. A better model for biological tissue is therefore one where the spatial frequency bandwidth is large compared to the wavenumber k of the probing ultrasound. For such a model the advantage of the Rytov approximation can be expected to disappear.

Some preliminary computer-model studies discussed earlier seem to indicate little difference between Born's and Rytov's approximations. These results however are very preliminary, and only show that the question of the relative merits of the two approximations for realistic models of biological tissue needs further exploration.

It is possible to extend the wave-propagation method to include higher order approximations. This would include the effect of multiple scattering which becomes increasingly important as the strength of the disturbance increases. The computational complexity for second-order approximation and higher with presently available algorithms is forbidding and has not been discussed in the literature.

The theoretical limit for the spatial-frequency range over which one can obtain information on the spectrum $T(\vec{\Lambda})$ of the disturbance is limited by the wavelength λ of the probing ultrasound:

$$0 < \Lambda < \frac{2}{\lambda}. \qquad (72)$$

The spatial-frequency range

$$0 < \Lambda < \frac{1}{\lambda} \qquad (73)$$

is accessible through forward-scattering or transmission measurements. A finite aperture in a fixed position (relative to the impinging wave vector) further limits the accessible frequency range. The spatial-frequency range

$$\frac{1}{\lambda} < \Lambda < \frac{2}{\lambda} \qquad (74)$$

can be obtained from backscatter or reflection measurements.

Frequency components in the spectrum of the disturbance beyond the range given by (74) generate evanescent waves which do not penetrate far beyond the disturbed area. Multiple-scattering transfers information from these spectral components to propagating waves which reach the receiving arrays, but it is doubtful whether this will ever be useful for enhanced resolution.

The actual resolution of the tomographic system is always less than the theoretically attainable resolution due to physical noise in the system and due to tradeoffs in the reconstruction algorithms. No systematic study of this problem is available in the literature.

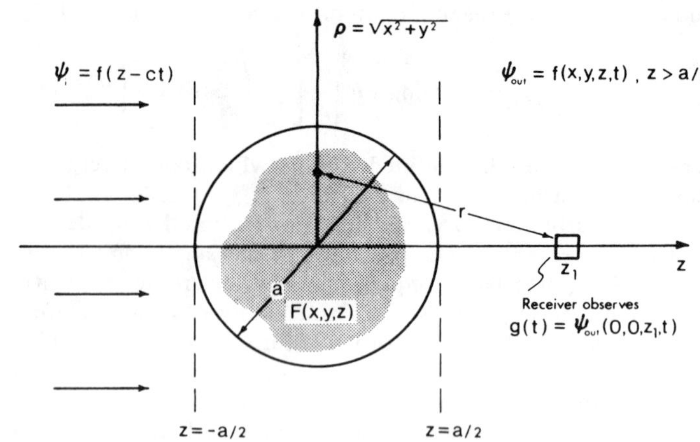

Fig. 18. Ray-tracing geometry.

B. Ray-Tracing Methods

The basic measurement geometry of the ray-tracing method is shown in Fig. 18. It is sufficient to consider the sampled ray along the z-axis. A plane wave ψ_{in} with arbitrary profile $f(z-ct)$ propagates along the z-axis and encounters a disturbed area $F(x, y, z)$ at $z > -a/2$. It then propagates through the disturbances and again enters a homogeneous medium at $z \geqslant +a/2$. The emerging wave $\psi_{out}(x, y, z, t)$ is sampled at $x = 0, y = 0, z = z_1$, giving rise to the time function

$$g(t) = (\psi_{out})\Big|_{\substack{x=0 \\ y=0 \\ z=z_1}} \qquad (75)$$

The objective of the time-of-flight method is to infer, from $g(t)$, structural information about the disturbance $F(x, y, z)$.

We shall first show that one obtains the desired relationship between g and F if one assumes a low spatial-frequency content for the disturbance F. With this assumption one can use the approximation discussed in Section V-A.

We assume that the incoming wave ψ_{in} is the following plane wave

$$\psi_{in} = \exp\left[ik(z - ct)\right]. \qquad (76)$$

The scattered wave ψ_{out} beyond the disturbance in Rytov's approximation is

$$\psi_{out} = \exp\left[ik(z - ct + u_1(x, y))\right] \qquad (77)$$

with

$$u_1(x, y) = \int_{-a/2}^{+a/2} F(x, y, z)\, dz . \qquad (78)$$

The observed function $g(t)$ (equation (75)) therefore becomes

$$g(t) = \exp\left[ik(z_1 + u_1(0,0) - ct)\right] . \qquad (79)$$

One obtains through a phase measurement the quantity $u_1(0, 0)$, which represents in this approximation a one-dimensional projection of the disturbance F:

$$u_1(0, 0) = \int_{-a/2}^{+a/2} F(0, 0, z)\, dz. \qquad (80)$$

This projection is then used as the basis of the reconstruction process discussed earlier.

If one uses pulse excitation:

$$\psi_{\text{in}} = \exp\left[-\left(\frac{z - ct}{c\tau}\right)^2\right] \qquad (81)$$

one obtains for the observed signal:

$$g(t) = \exp\left[-\left[\frac{z - u_1(0,0) - ct}{c\tau}\right]^2\right]. \qquad (82)$$

Equation (82) results from expanding ψ_{in} in (81) into its plane-wave components and superimposing the observed signals due to each component. One now obtains $u_1(0,0)$ by a time-of-flight measurement. Any other pulse shape or a ramp function for ψ_{in} gives a similar result.

This first approximation is known as the straight-path approximation. By including the second-order perturbation in (79), we get the path-bending correction.

The difficulty with this theoretical justification for the time-of-flight method is that the underlying assumption of a band-limited disturbance is questionable for biological tissue.

One can derive, however, directly from the time-dependent wave equation a first-order approximation for the observable function $g(t)$ which is similar to (75) but does not require any assumptions about the spatial-frequency spectrum of the disturbance. This approach has the additional advantage that it puts the obtainable resolution in evidence.

We refer again to Fig. 18 and assume as incoming wave ψ_{in} the pulse:

$$\psi_{\text{in}} = \exp\left[-\left(\frac{z - ct}{l}\right)^2\right] \qquad (83)$$

which satisfies the unperturbed wave equation

$$\left[\nabla^2 - \frac{1}{c^2}\frac{\partial^2}{\partial t^2}\right]\psi_{\text{in}} = 0 . \qquad (84)$$

Assuming in analogy to Born's approximations a perturbed solution $\psi = \psi_{\text{in}} + \psi_1$, one obtains as a first-order equation for ψ_1:

$$\left[\nabla^2 - \frac{1}{c^2}\frac{\partial^2}{\partial t^2}\right]\psi_1 = 2\frac{F(x,y,z)}{l^2}\left[1 + \frac{2(z - ct)^2}{l^2}\right]\psi_{\text{in}}. \qquad (85)$$

We solve this equation by the method of the retarded potential and obtain for $g(t)$:

$$g(t) = \exp\left[-\left[\frac{z_1 - ct}{l}\right]^2\right]$$
$$+ \int F \exp\left[-\left[\frac{r - ct + r}{l}\right]^2\right]\frac{1 + 2[(z - ct + r)/l]^2}{rl^2}\, dx\, dy\, dz \qquad (86)$$

where r is the distance from a point x, y, z in the disturbance to the receiver position at $(0, 0, z_1)$ and is given by

$$r = \sqrt{x^2 + y^2 + (z_1 - z)^2} . \qquad (87)$$

It is advantageous to introduce a cylindrical coordinate system ρ, ϕ, z with the z-axis as the cylinder axis. We can then write for r in the neighborhood of the z-axis:

$$r = (z_1 - z) + \frac{\rho^2}{2(z_1 - z)}. \qquad (88)$$

Neglecting terms of higher than second order in ρ and retaining ρ only in the exponent one obtains in good approximation

for $g(t)$

$$g(t) = (1 + \gamma)\exp\left[-\left[\frac{z_1 - ct}{l}\right]^2\right] \qquad (89)$$

with γ given by

$$\gamma \simeq \frac{2(z_1 - ct)}{l^2}\int_{-a/2}^{+a/2}\overline{F}(z)\, dz . \qquad (90)$$

The average $\overline{F}(z)$ is given by

$$\overline{F}(z) = \frac{1}{\beta^2}\int F(x,y,z)\exp\left[-\frac{x^2 + y^2}{\beta^2}\right]dx\, dy \qquad (91)$$

β is the effective radius of the smoothing function

$$\beta = l\sqrt{(z_1 - z)/(z_1 - ct)} . \qquad (92)$$

If one considers second-order terms in γ as negligible, one can write (89) in the form

$$g(t) = \exp\left[-\left(\frac{z_1 - ct - \int_{-a/2}^{+a/2}\overline{F}(z)\, dz}{l}\right)^2\right] \qquad (93)$$

which replaces the similar (80) and (82) derived by a geometric ray tracing model.

The resolution of the time-of-flight method is determined by the effective radius β of the smearing function given in (92). The parameters in (92) depend on the risetime $\tau = l/c$ of the probing pulse and the size of the object.

The factor $(z_1 - z)$ which ranges over the disturbance has a mean value of

$$\overline{(z_1 - z)} \geqslant a/2 \qquad (94)$$

and the factor $(z_1 - ct)$ which can be minimized by observing the leading edge of the pulse is limited by unavoidable noise in the system to a small multiple m of the pulse length l

$$(z_1 - ct) \simeq ml. \qquad (95)$$

Introducing these factors into (92) gives for the attainable resolution

$$\beta \simeq \sqrt{\frac{al}{2m}} \qquad (96)$$

which for practical systems is of the order of 10 wavelengths.

We have seen above that the geometric ray-tracing approach gives a relatively simple second-order approximation which takes into account the path bending caused by gradients in the velocity distribution. However, the actually measured distribution is, as we have seen, a severely smoothed version of the actual distribution. It is therefore not obvious that a correction based on this function, in which all higher spatial frequency components are filtered out, improves in general the resolution or reduces distortion.

VI. Conclusion

Several methods of ultrasonic tomography have been discussed. A review of well-known techniques for transmission tomography that are founded on geometrical optics has been included. More recent developments in this area based on wave equations and Doppler techniques were presented, and some new approaches for examining the validity of the models were introduced.

Improvements in methods involving geometric optics are basically in the area of algorithmic developments. This is a wholly numerical task. Research efforts in ultrasonic tomography can therefore benefit from general progress in the reconstruction techniques for X-rays and optics.

Improvements in resolution, however, and accuracy in the reconstructed parameters can only be obtained through the use of more exact models of the underlying physical processes. The wave-equation approach to the reconstruction of velocity distribution is a first step in this direction. Future work along this line will be to generalize diffraction methods for imaging with spherical-wave insonification and to include loss and variable density. Work to accomplish these ends is currently under way. Simultaneously with the theoretical and algorithmic developments, hardware feasibility studies must be made and tradeoffs between hardware and software must be considered. Furthermore, model validation has to be carried out to insure that the tomograms will be physically reasonable and accurate.

ACKNOWLEDGMENT

The authors would like to express great appreciation to Juliana L. Taylor for the important work, including technical editing, that she performed in processing this paper. They are also much indebted to Catherine Stadem, Charles Iverson, and Tracy H. Ricketts for the typing of this difficult manuscript and to Behzad Noorbehesht for its proofreading. Finally, the authors wish to state their indebtedness to unknown reviewers of this paper for the information and comments they provided, which has been used to strengthen the overall perspective in the presentation.

REFERENCES

[1] E. M. Bocage, French Patent 536 464, Paris, France, 1921. (Quoted in J. Massiot, "History of tomography," *Medica Mundi*, vol. 19, no. 3, pp. 106–115, 1974.)

[2] H. O. Anger, "Tomographic gamma-ray scanner with simultaneous readout of several planes," in *Fundamental Problems in Scanning*, A. Gottschalk, R. N. Beck, Eds. Springfield, IL: Thomas, 1968, pp. 195–211.

[3] J. Radon, "Uber die bestimmung von funktionen durch ihre intergralwerte langs gewisser mannigfaltigkeiten," ("On the determination of functions from their integrals along certain manifolds"), *Berichte Saechsische Akademie der Wissenschaften*, vol. 69, pp. 262–277, 1917.

[4] R. N. Bracewell, "Strip integration in radioastronomy," *Aust. J. Phys.*, vol. 9, pp. 198–217, 1956.

[5] D. J. De Rosier and A. Klug, "Reconstruction of three-dimensional structures from electron micrographs," *Nature*, vol. 217, pp. 130–134, Jan. 13, 1968.

[6] R. Gordon, R. Bender, and G. T. Herman, "Algebraic reconstruction techniques (ART) for three-dimensional electron microscopy and X-ray photography," *J. Theor. Biol.*, vol. 29, pp. 471–481, Dec. 1970.

[7] P. D. Rowley, "Quantitative interpretation of three-dimensional weakly refractive phase objects using holographic interferometry," *J. Opt. Soc. Amer.*, vol. 59, pp. 1496–1498, Nov. 1969.

[8] M. V. Berry and D. F. Gibbs, "The interpretation of optical projections," *Proc. Roy. Soc. Lond. A.*, vol. 314, pp. 143–152, Jan. 6, 1970.

[9] R. Gordon, G. T. Herman, and S. A. Johnson, "Image reconstruction from projections," *Scientific Amer.*, vol. 233, no. 4, 56–68, Oct. 1975.

[10] A. M. Cormack, "Representation of a function by its line integrals, with some radiological applications," *J. Appl. Phys.*, vol. 34, no. 9, pp. 2722–2727, Sept. 1963.

[11] ——, "Representation of a function by its line integrals with some radiological applications, II," *J. Appl. Phys.*, vol. 35, pp. 2908–2913, Oct. 1964.

[12] D. E. Kuhl and R. Q. Edwards, "Image separation radioisotope scanning," *Radiology*, vol. 80, pp. 653–661, 1963.

[13] G. N. Hounsfield, "A method of and apparatus for examination of a body by radiation such as X ray or gamma radiation," The Patent Office, London, Patent Specification 1 283 915, 1972.

[14] ——, "Computerized transverse axial scanning (tomography): Part 1. Description of system," *Brit. J. Radiol.*, vol. 46, pp. 1016–1022, Nov. 1973.

[15] R. N. Bracewell and G. Swarup, "The Stanford microwave spectroheliograph antenna, a microsteradian pencil-beam interferometer," *IRE Trans. Antennas Propagat.*, vol. AP-9, pp. 22–30, Jan. 1961.

[16] R. N. Bracewell and A. C. Riddle, "Inversion of fan-beam scans in radio astronomy," *Astrophys. J.*, vol. 150, pp. 427–434, Nov. 1967.

[17] J. H. Thomson, Talk presented at the Symposium on Planetary Atmospheres and Surfaces, Dorado, Puerto Rico, 1965.

[18] J. H. Thomson and J. E. B. Ponsonby, "Two-dimensional aperture synthesis in lunar radar astronomy," *Proc. Roy. Soc. A.*, vol. 303, pp. 477–491, Mar. 1968.

[19] J. E. B. Ponsonby, I. Morison, A. R. Birks, and J. K. Landon, "Radar images of the moon at 75 and 185 cm wavelengths," *The Moon*, vol. 5, pp. 286–294, Nov./Dec. 1972.

[20] T. Hagfors and D. B. Campbell, "Mapping of planetary surfaces by radar," *Proc. IEEE*, vol. 61, no. 9, pp. 1219–1225, Sept. 1973.

[21] F. Zernike, "Das Phasenkontrastverfahren bei der mikroskopischen beobacktung," ("The phase contrast method of microscopic observation"), *Z. Tech. Phys.*, vol. 16, p. 454, 1935.

[22] E. Wolf, "Three-dimensional structure determination of semitransparent objects from holographic data," *Optics Commun.*, vol. 1, pp. 153–156, 1969.

[23] K. Iwata and R. Nagata, "Calculation of three-dimensional refractive index distribution from interferograms," *J. Opt. Soc. Amer.*, vol. 60, pp. 133–135, 1970.

[24] L. A. Chernov, *Wave Propagation in a Random Medium*. New York: McGraw-Hill, 1969.

[25] V. I. Tatarski, *Wave Propagation in a Turbulent Medium*. New York: McGraw-Hill, 1961.

[26] J. W. Strohbehn, "Line of sight wave propagation through turbulent atmosphere," *Proc. IEEE*, vol. 56, pp. 1301–1318, Aug. 1968.

[27] J. F. Greenleaf, S. A. Johnson, S. L. Lee, G. T. Herman, and E. H. Wood, "Algebraic reconstruction of spatial distributions of acoustic absorption within tissue from their two-dimensional acoustic projections," in *Acoustical Holography*, vol. 5, P. S. Green, Ed. New York: Plenum Press, 1974, pp. 591–603.

[28] J. F. Greenleaf, S. A. Johnson, W. F. Samayoa, and F. A. Duck, "Algebraic reconstruction of spatial distributions of acoustic velocities in tissue from their time-of-flight profiles," in *Acoustical Holography*, vol. 6, New York: Plenum Press, 1975, pp. 71–90.

[29] D. W. Sweeney and G. M. Vest, "Reconstruction of three-dimensional refractive index fields from multidimensional interferometric data," *Appl. Optics*, vol. 2, 1973.

[30] P. L Carson, T. V. Oughton, and W. R. Hendee, "Ultrasonic transaxial tomography by reconstruction," *Ultrasound in Medicine*, vol. 2, D. White and R. Barns, Eds. New York: Plenum Press, 1976, pp. 341–350.

[31] H. C. Andrews and B. R. Hunt, *Digital Image Restoration*, Englewood Cliffs, NJ: Prentice-Hall, 1977.

[32] G. T. Herman and S. W. Rowland, "Three methods for reconstructing objects from X-rays: A comparative study," *Computer Graphics and Image Processing*, vol. 2, pp. 151–178, 1973.

[33] T. S. Huang, M. Kaveh, and S. Berger, "Some further results in iterative image restoration," presented at the Annual Meeting of the Optical Society of America, Boston, MA, Oct. 1975.

[34] C. Lanczos, *Linear Differential Operators*, London, England: Van Nostrand, 1964.

[35] R. Bender *et al.*, "ART and the ribosome: A preliminary report on the three-dimensional structure of individual ribosomes determined by an algebraic reconstruction technique," *J. Theor. Biol.* vol. 29, pp. 483–487, 1970.

[36] S. H. Bellman, R. Bender, R. Gordon, and J. E. Rowe, "ART is science, being a defense of algebraic reconstruction techniques for three-dimensional electron microscopy," *J. Theor. Biol.*, vol. 32, pp. 205–216, 1971.

[37] G. T. Herman and S. Rowland, "Resolution in art: An experimental investigation of the resolving power of an algebraic picture reconstruction technique," *J. Theor. Biol.*, vol. 33, pp. 213–223, 1971.

[38] G. N. Ramachandran and A. V. Lakshminarayanan, "Three-dimensional reconstruction from radiographs and electron micrographs: II. Application of convolutions instead of Fourier transforms," *Proc. Nat. Acad. Sci.*, vol. 68, no. 9, pp. 2236–2240.

[39] ——, "Three-dimensional reconstruction from radiographs and

electron micrographs: III. Description and application of the convolution method," *Indian J. Pure Appl. Phys.*, vol. 9, pp. 997-1003, 1971.

[40] H. Hurwitz, Jr., "Entropy reduction in Bayesian analysis of measurements," *Phys. Rev.*, vol. 12, pp. 698-704, 1975.

[41] G. H. Glover and J. L. Sharp, "Reconstruction of ultrasound propagation speed distribution in soft tissue: time-of-flight tomography," *IEEE Trans. Sonics Ultrason.*, vol. SU-24, July 1977.

[42] D. Slepian, "Linear least squares filtering of distorted images," *J. Opt. Soc. Amer.*, vol. 57, pp. 918-922, July 1967.

[43] O. Tretiak, "Recovery of multi-dimensional signals from their projections," *Computer Graphics and Image Processing*, vol. 1, pp. 179-195, Oct. 1973.

[44] R. M. Mersereau and A. V. Oppenheim, "Digital reconstruction of multidimensional signals from their projections," *Proc. IEEE*, vol. 62, Oct. 1974.

[45] R. M. Mersereau, "Recovering multidimensional signals from their projections," *Computer Graphics and Image Processing*, vol. 1, pp. 179-195, 1973.

[46] S. A. Johnson, J. F. Greenleaf, A. Chu, J. D. Sjostrand, B. K. Gilbert, and E. H. Wood, "Reconstruction of material characteristics from highly refraction distorted projections by ray tracing," in *Image Processing for 2-D and 3-D Reconstruction from Projections: Theory and Practice in Medicine and the Physical Sciences. A Digest of Tech. Papers*, (Stanford, CA) pp. TRB2-1-TUB2-4, Aug. 4-7, 1975.

[47] S. A. Johnson, J. F. Greenleaf, W. F. Samayoa, F. A. Duck, and J. D. Sjostrand, "Reconstruction of three-dimensional velocity fields and other parameters by acoustic ray tracing," in *1975 Ultrasonic Symp. Proc.* (IEEE Cat. No. 75, CHP994-1SU), 1975.

[48] R. K. Mueller and M. Kaveh, "Ultrasonic diffraction tomography," Internal Rep., Dep. Elec. Eng., Univ. Minnesota, Minneapolis.

[49] R. D. Iverson, M.S. thesis, Dep. Elec. Eng., Univ. Minnesota, Minneapolis.

[50] R. K. Mueller, M. Kaveh, and R. D. Iverson, "A new approach to acoustic tomography using diffraction techniques," in *Acoustic Holography*, vol. 8, A. Metherell, Ed. New York: Plenum Press, 1978.

[51] M. Kaveh, R. K. Mueller, and R. D. Iverson, "Ultrasonic tomography based on perturbation solutions of the wave equation," *Computer Graphics and Image Processing*, to appear.

[52] G. Wade, R. K. Mueller, and M. Kaveh, "A survey of techniques for ultrasonic tomography," in *Proc. of IFIP TC-4 Working Conf. Computer-Aided Tomography and Ultrasonics in Medicine*, J. Raviv, Ed. Amsterdam The Netherlands: North-Holland, 1978.

[53] G. Wade, S. Elliott, I. Khogeer, G. Flesher, J. Eisler, D. Mensa, N. S. Ramesh, and G. Heidbreder, "Acoustic echo computer tomography," in *Acoustic Holography*, vol. 8, A. Metherell, Ed. New York: Plenum Press, 1978.

Computerized Tomography with Ultrasound

JAMES F. GREENLEAF, MEMBER, IEEE

Invited Paper

Abstract —The mathematical basis for transmission computed tomographic imaging using straight-line reconstruction equations is discussed. Both narrow-band and broad-band solutions are described. The Born and Rytov methods are discussed and the Rytov inversion equation presented with some results. Problems with implementation of the method are mentioned. Backscatter reconstruction methods of seismology are discussed as to their strengths and weaknesses for use in tissue imaging.

INTRODUCTION

ULTRASOUND is the only imaging modality currently used in medical practice which is not electromagnetic. Ultrasound can be considered to be a propagating disturbance of the extrinsic properties (i.e., pressure, temperature, and particle position) of the tissue through which it travels. Unlike electromagnetic radiation which can exist in a vacuum, ultrasound must be supported by the material through which it propagates. This results in an extremely complex and strong interaction between the physical or intrinsic properties of the tissue, such as density and compressibility, and the extrinsic properties of the ultrasonic wave such as pressure and temperature [1]. The complexity of these interactions has resulted in great difficulty in solving accurately the governing wave equations for quantitative distributions of intrinsic tissue properties, although rather impressive results have been obtained in the echo backscatter mode as exemplified by the success of the two-dimensional (2D) echographic imaging industry [2] in which qualitative tomographic images are obtained with focused ultrasound without the need for a computer.

Many interactions of ultrasound with tissue such as scattering, absorption, nonlinearity, altered propagation speed, and Doppler shift due to tissue velocity can be used for generating contrast for making images of tissue [3]. The recent use of computerized tomography methods in medical X-ray imaging has, by analogy, generated some interest in quantitative imaging with ultrasonic energy [4]–[6].

The medical imaging hypothesis might be stated that the formation of an image having contrast which is related quantitatively to basic tissue properties allows visualization of the normal and abnormal intrinsic morphology of tissues and, therefore, provides potential for detection of pathology. Ultrasound is currently used in several qualitative modalities which image morphology. The most successful qualitative imaging method is the B-scan technique which obtains 2D images whose contrast is related to some measure of backscatter cross section. In utilizing the B-scan images, it is assumed that the backscatter varies with tissue character, certainly with tissue geometry. Many medically important decisions can be aided with information from B-scan images, and the method is now widely used [7].

Another qualitative method of imaging is to use the M-scan in which backscattered pressure amplitude is depicted as a function of time and thus defects in the motion of interfaces in organs such as the heart can be detected [8]. An orthographic C-scanner has been developed in which ultrasound is transmitted through the body and measured over a plane normal to the direction of propagation of sound in much the same way that a chest film is obtained with X-rays [9]. Orthographic ultrasound imagers have been used for visualization of soft tissues such as tendons, veins, and arteries which are difficult to image using X-rays although the ultrasound images are only qualitatively related to tissue parameters.

Quantitative imaging modalities using ultrasound have been confined mainly to computerized tomography. Currently, the most successful inversion of the wave equation for quantitative measurements of basic tissue properties such as speed and attenuation has been accomplished in the transmission mode using computerized tomography techniques [10]. The purpose of this paper is to describe the mathematical basis of the computerized transmission ultrasonic tomography methods and to describe their current limitations.

The paper will first describe the straight-line (SL) methods of reconstruction using the "Eikonal" method and will then derive the Born and Rytov approximations to the wave equation and the related solutions. Some results will be given for the SL methods and for the Rytov method. Finally, some seismic methods will be described.

EIKONAL METHOD

This approach attempts to develop an equation for the propagation of a pressure disturbance in a region given the distribution of refractive index within the region through which the disturbance is propagating. From the expression for the propagation of a disturbance, the "Eikonal equation" (Eikonal is Greek for "image" [11]), one attempts to obtain an expression for the intrinsic properties of the region. The problem with the Eikonal equation is that it is a geometric acoustic equation and, like geometric optics, ignores diffraction effects, an error to be discussed in the next section.

The equations of an acoustic field in an inhomogeneous medium have the form

$$\frac{\partial P}{\partial t} + \rho c^2 \, \text{div} \, V = 0 \tag{1}$$

Manuscript received April 19, 1982; revised December 2, 1982 and January 3, 1983. This work was supported in part under Grants CA 24085 from the National Cancer Institute, GM 24994 from the National Institutes of Health, and ECS 7926008 from the National Science Foundation.

The author is with the Departrment of Physiology and Biophysics, Mayo Foundation, Rochester, MN 55905.

Reprinted from *Proc. IEEE*, vol. 71, pp. 330–337, Mar. 1983.

$$\frac{\partial V}{\partial t} + \frac{1}{\rho} \operatorname{grad} P = 0 \qquad (2)$$

where P is the acoustic pressure, V is the particle velocity in the wave, ρ is the density, and c is the velocity of sound [12]. Equation (1) is the equation of continuity, and (2) is Euler's equation for force. Assuming sinusoidal excitation, that is, that pressure and velocity can be expanded in a Fourier series, i.e., $\partial/\partial t = -i\omega$, and eliminating V from (1) and (2) gives

$$\nabla^2 P + k^2 \rho - \frac{1}{\rho} \operatorname{grad} \rho \cdot \operatorname{grad} P = 0. \qquad (3)$$

Now define

$$\Psi = \frac{P}{\sqrt{\rho}} \qquad (4)$$

then we have

$$\nabla^2 \Psi + K^2(x, y, z)\Psi = 0 \qquad (5)$$

where

$$K^2(x, y, z) = k^2 + \frac{1}{2\rho} \nabla^2 \rho - \frac{3}{4}\left(\frac{1}{\rho}\operatorname{grad}\rho\right)^2. \qquad (6)$$

If we now express Ψ in a form which assumes the information to be in the *phase* part of an exponential form, where complex phase allows for spatial variation in both propagation velocity and attenuation, we use the form

$$\Psi(x, y, z) = \Psi_0 \exp\left[ik_0\phi(x, y, z)\right]. \qquad (7)$$

Substitution of (7) into (5) gives

$$ik_0^{-1}\nabla^2\phi - \nabla\phi \cdot \nabla\phi + A^2 = 0 \qquad (8)$$

where we have used $k_0^2 A^2 = k^2$, and we have also assumed constant ρ making

$$K = k = \frac{\omega}{c}.$$

Now if we remove diffraction by assuming $k_0 \to \infty$ or conversely, λ_0, the wavelength, goes to 0 (since k_0 is $2\pi/\lambda_0$), then we obtain

$$\nabla\phi \cdot \nabla\phi = A^2. \qquad (9)$$

This is the Eikonal equation [11], in which ϕ is the Eikonal, and is the basic equation of scalar geometric optics and acoustics.

We now let

$$A = 1 + \eta(x, y, z) \qquad (10)$$

and

$$\phi = \phi_0(x, y, z) + \phi_1(x, y, z)$$

where $\eta(x, y, z)$ is the change in refractive index, ϕ_0 is the unperturbed solution, and $\phi_1(x, y, z)$ is the solution when there is nonzero η. Substitution of (10) into (9) and ignoring terms of order $|\nabla\phi_1|^2$ and η^2 gives

$$\nabla\phi_0 \cdot \nabla\phi_1 = \eta \qquad (11)$$

since

$$\nabla\phi_0 \cdot \nabla\phi_0 = 1. \qquad (12)$$

The unperturbed solution (with plane-wave insonation) of (5) is

$$\Psi = \exp(ik_0\bar{k} \cdot \bar{r})$$

where $\bar{k}$ is the unit vector in the direction of propagation and $\bar{r}$ is $\bar{i}x + \bar{j}y + \bar{k}z$ in the Cartesian Coordinate System. This implies that

$$\phi_0 = \bar{k} \cdot \bar{r}$$

then (11) becomes

$$\bar{k} \cdot \nabla\phi_1 = \eta. \qquad (13)$$

This equation can be integrated along a line parallel to $\bar{k}$ giving

$$\phi_1(\bar{b}) - \phi_1(\bar{a}) = \int_0^{\left|\bar{b}-\bar{a}\right|} \eta \, ds \qquad (14)$$

where $\bar{a}$ is the beginning or entry point of the energy, i.e., the transmitter position, and $\bar{b}$ is the end point or the receiver position. The equation is complex and can be considered to be two reconstruction formulas, one for the speed of sound $C_0/[\eta(\bar{r})_{\mathrm{R(eal)}}]$ and one for the attenuation coefficient $(k_0 \eta(\bar{r})_{\mathrm{I(maginary)}})$.

These equations can be solved by obtaining measurements of ϕ_1 for a pleurality of insonification directions $\bar{k}$, through the object and solving for η using straight-line reconstruction algorithms that were developed for a variety of problems but are most well known for their use in X-ray computer-assisted tomography [13].

It must be remembered that these equations were obtained by 1) taking the high-frequency limit ($\lambda \to 0$) thus eliminating diffraction, 2) discarding higher order terms to obtain the Eikonal equations (9), and 3) assuming that density ρ is relatively constant in the scattering region.

We have recently demonstrated experimentally that diffraction is relatively strong at the relevant ultrasonic frequencies and should not be ignored [14]. This implies that at least some of the aberrations in images produced with (14) could be due to ignoring diffraction in the derivation.

The effect of ignoring the higher order terms will be felt more strongly the larger is η and $\nabla\phi$ but the extent to which this causes aberrations in tissue imaging is not yet characterized.

The effect of ignoring alterations in density is unclear. The density of tissues varies from about 1.06 in connective tissue to about 0.95 in fat. If we assume that the highest gradient in tissue occurs at an interface between fat and connective tissue within a distance of one wavelength (0.5 mm) at a typical frequency of 3 MHz then the gradient is

$$\nabla\rho \cong \frac{0.1}{0.5} = 0.2 \text{ in units of } \frac{\text{density}}{\text{mm}}. \qquad (15)$$

The term involving the second derivative of density in (6) is probably smaller than the term involving the gradient but if we assume it is the same, then for 3 MHz and for $\rho \sim 1.0$, we have

$$k^2 + \frac{1}{2\rho}\nabla^2\rho - \frac{3}{4}\left(\frac{1}{\rho}\operatorname{grad}\rho\right)^2$$

$$= \left(\frac{2\pi \times 3 \times 10^6}{1.5 \times 10^6}\right)^2 + \frac{1}{2}(0.2) - \frac{3}{4}(0.2)^2 \qquad (16)$$

$$= 157.9 + 0.1 - 0.03. \qquad (17)$$

Therefore, we see that ignoring density should cause little problem.

Equation (5) ignores mode conversion at interfaces (i.e., changes from longitudinal waves). The effects of such assumptions are also as yet unknown.

Of course, (14) can be solved by reconstruction for $\phi_1(r)$ measured at multiple frequencies thus obtaining a measure of attenuation for many frequencies. One would not expect $\eta_R(\bar{r})$ to vary strongly with frequency of insonation since velocity dispersion (variation of speed of sound with frequency) is not strong in tissues [15]. However, $k_0\eta_I(\bar{r})$ (attenuation coefficient) is known for its strong (virtually linear) dependence with frequency of insonation in tissues [16].

Attenuation can be split into two parts, that which is dependent on frequency (the slope) and that which is independent of frequency (the intercept at $\omega = 0$). Recently, we have reported some reconstructions of the frequency-dependent and frequency-independent parts of attenuation [17].

Dines *et al.* have described several methods for measuring the attenuation coefficient from wide-band signals [18]. Under the assumption that the Fourier spectral characteristics of the transmitted signal are Gaussian in shape and that attenuation per wavelength is relatively constant for the frequencies considered, then Dines *et al.* showed that there is a relationship between the shift in the center frequency of the received signal and the line integral of the attenuation coefficient. These methods, however, are derived under the assumption that the energy travels in a straight line and are, therefore, subject to the same problems as all straight-line methods.

In practice, the measurement of signal amplitude versus frequency using spectral analysis of the received pulse is very difficult because of the effect of multiple paths and the resulting phase interference at the transducer and in the medium. This causes scalloping or periodic variations in the amplitude of the Fourier transform of the signal. Kak *et al.* [19] have recently described methods of spectral filtering to allow accurate estimates of frequency spectra in transmission ultrasound. In practice, the arrival time and the log of the amplitude are measured from the received broad-band acoustic pulse and are used for estimates of the phase of the signal (ϕ_{1R}) required in (8), and the log amplitude (ϕ_{1I}) required in (9).

The clinical efficacy of images derived using the straight-line reconstruction equations (14) is being evaluated in a small trial [20] in which images of attenuation and speed are used for the detection of cancer in breasts. Some recent results are shown in Fig. 1 in which cancer has been imaged with a system described elsewhere [21]. The ray-like artifacts seen in the water are due to the low number of angles of view (60) compared to the number of pixels in the image (128×128). The exceptionally thick-appearing skin is due to the very high attenuation and associated reflection at the surface of the breast. Nonetheless, it is clear that one can discern high-speed regions in the area later found to have cancer. As yet it is unclear whether the SL method will prove to be clinically efficacious but certainly higher resolution imaging methods would be welcome.

DIFFRACTION TOMOGRAPHY METHODS

In the previous section, we developed the straight-line reconstruction formulas which ignored diffraction. In this section we will begin with the wave equation (5) and will approximate the equation using two well-known methods [Born (22) and Rytov (23)] which use perturbation techniques to transform the homogeneous wave equation (5), which has nonconstant coefficients, into a nonhomogeneous equation having constant coefficients that can be solved analytically and which includes the effects of diffraction.

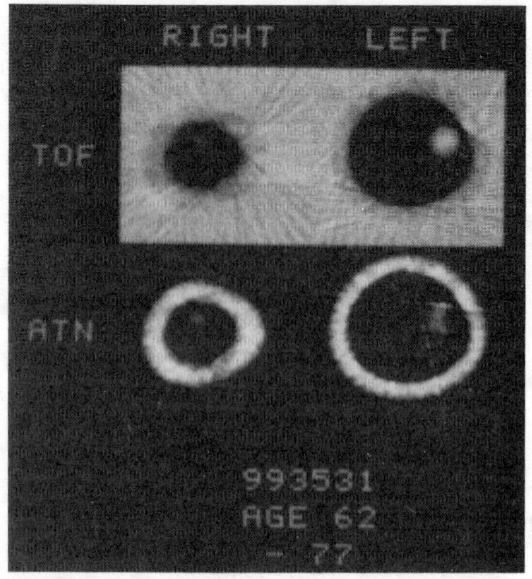

Fig. 1. Reconstruction of acoustic speed (upper) and attenuation (lower) in coronal planes through the right (left panels) and left (right panels) breasts of a patient with carcinoma in the right breast (at 2 o'clock). Image is 118×118 pixels obtained using straight-line reconstruction from 60 views.

BORN APPROXIMATION

The Born approximation begins with the Helmholtz equation (5). We then assume the total wave Ψ is made up of two terms, the incident wave Ψ^i and the scattered wave Ψ^s. Then (5) can be written

$$\nabla^2\Psi^s + k_0^2\Psi^s = F\Psi^i \tag{18}$$

if

$$F = -k_0^2(A^2 - 1)$$

and it is assumed

$$\Psi^s \ll \Psi^i. \tag{19}$$

Equation (18) is the first Born approximation to the Helmholtz equation and assumes that the amplitude of the scattered energy is much less than that of the incident energy. This, as we will see, is a tenuous argument for tissue media.

Equation (18) has been solved previously but before writing down the solution (which will not be derived in this paper), we will derive a similar equation from the Rytov approximation.

RYTOV APPROXIMATION

We also begin with the Helmholtz equation. The substitution into (5) of

$$\Psi(\bar{r}) = \exp(ik_0\phi(\bar{r})) \tag{20}$$

results in

$$ik_0^{-1}\nabla^2\phi - |\nabla\phi|^2 + A^2 = 0. \tag{21}$$

We let $\phi = \phi_0 + \phi_1$ and $A = \eta + 1$ where ϕ_0 is the phase component of the pressure distribution $\Psi(\bar{r})$ for no perturbation and where ϕ_1 is the phase perturbation due to the perturbation in the refractive index. Substituting the perturbations into (21) gives

$$ik_0^{-1}\nabla^2\phi_0 + ik_0^{-1}\nabla^2\phi_1 - |\nabla\phi_0|^2 - 2(\nabla\phi_0\cdot\nabla\phi_1) - |\nabla\phi_1|^2$$
$$+ 1 + 2\eta + \eta^2 = 0. \tag{22}$$

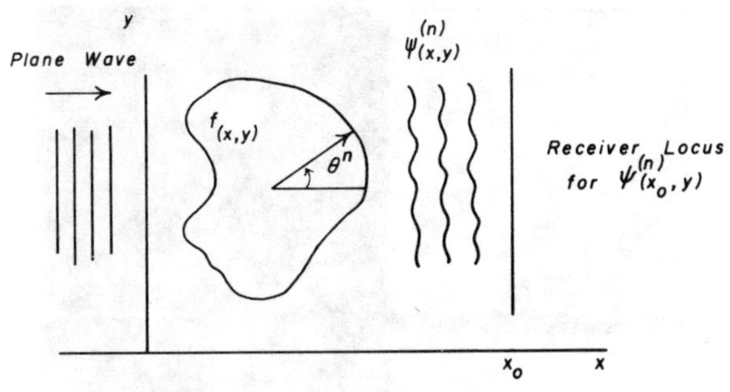

Fig. 2. Geometry for derivation of Rytov method of inverse scattering. Plane wave insonifies object and scattered wave is measured at X_0 for a plurality of angles of view. (Reproduced with permission from [10].)

If we ignore η^2 and $\nabla\phi_1{}^2$, we obtain

$$\nabla^2(\phi_1 \exp(ik_0\phi_0)) + k_0{}^2(\phi_1 \exp(ik_0\phi_0))$$

$$= i2k_0\eta \exp(ik_0\phi_0) \quad (23)$$

noting that $\nabla^2\phi_0 + k_0{}^2\phi_0 = 0$. Equation (23) has the same form as (18).

A method of obtaining the solution of (18) and (23) is by the use of a Green's function which is the solution of (18) when the inhomogeneous part (the right-hand side) is replaced with a spatial Dirac delta function, i.e.,

$$\nabla^2 G + k_0^2 G = \sigma(x - x_0)\, \sigma(y - y_0)\, \sigma(z - z_0).$$

The function G, which is the response of the system to a delta-function source term of unit amplitude at the point (x_0, y_0, z_0), is called the Green's function. For a good review of Green's functions see [24].

Since (18) and (23) are linear, their solution is a convolution of Green's solutions with the source terms for all space in which the source terms exist. The result (in two dimensions), using the geometry of Fig. 2, is [25]

$$\phi_1(x_0, y_0, \theta) = -\exp\left[-ik_0\phi_0(x_0, y_0, \theta)\right] \frac{k_0}{2}$$

$$\cdot \iint \eta(x, y) \exp\left[ik_0\phi_0(x, y, \theta)\right]$$

$$\cdot H_0(k_0\bar{r})\, dx\, dy \quad (24)$$

where

$$r = \sqrt{(x - x_0\cos\theta + y_0\sin\theta)^2 + (y - x_0\sin\theta - y_0\cos\theta_0)^2}$$

and where iH_0 is the Hankel function of the first kind and happens to be the Green's function for (23) in two dimensions. A similar equation results from applying the Green's function method to (18).

The problem now is to solve (24) for $\eta(x, y)$. This has been done by several other authors [1], [22], [23] and will not be done here in detail.

The result is

$$\hat{\eta}(U, V) = \frac{1}{2\pi} \frac{u}{k_0} \exp\left[i(k_0 - u)x_0\right] \hat{\phi}(x_0, u, \theta_i)$$

where

$$\hat{\eta}(U, V) = \frac{1}{(2\pi)^2} \iint \eta(x, y) \exp\left[-i(Ux + Vy)\right] dx\, dy \quad (25)$$

$$U = (u - k_0)\cos\theta_i - v\sin\theta_i$$

$$V = (u - k_0)\sin\theta_i + v\cos\theta_i$$

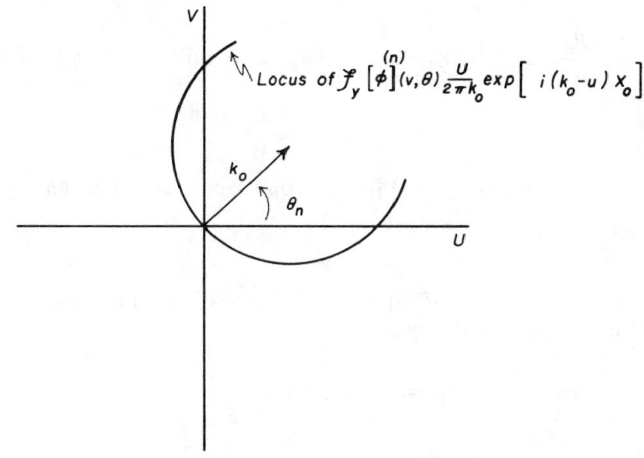

Fig. 3. Locus of the Fourier transform of $\Psi^{(n)}$ measured in Fig. 2 at X_0, in the 2D Fourier transform plane of the object. Rotation of the object rotates the center of the circular locus $\bar{k}_0$ and thus can fill in the plane for later inversion. (Reproduced with permission from [10].)

and

$$u^2 + v^2 = k_0^2.$$

We note that $\hat{\phi}_1(x_0, u, \theta_i)$ is the one-dimensional Fourier transform of $\phi_1(x_0, y)$ measured along the receiver locus shown in Fig. 2 for rotation angle θ_i. The values of the function $\hat{\theta}_1(x_0, u, \theta_i)$ are multiplied by a phasing factor $(\exp i(k_0 - u)x_0)$ and placed on a circular locus in the U, V plane of the Fourier transform of $\eta(x, y)$, i.e., $\hat{\eta}(U, V)$ as shown in Fig. 3. By rotating the object while keeping the insonifying plane and receiver locus constant, one can measure $\phi(x_0, y)$ for many values of θ_i and use the resulting series of $\hat{\theta}(x_0, u, \theta_i)\, i = 1, \cdots, N$ to "fill in" the U, V plane of the Fourier transform by rotating the circular locus of data points around the origin.

After "filling in" the Fourier domain, by using a suitable procedure for interpolating from the circular locus of $\hat{\phi}$ to the Cartesian coordinates of the Fourier plane, the inverse Fourier transform will result in the image of the function $\eta(x, y)$.

DATA-ACQUISITION CONSIDERATIONS

In practice, the measurable quantity is the pressure $P(\bar{r}, t)$ which is measured in the immersing liquid where $k = k_0$, thus

$$P(\bar{r}, t) = \text{Re}\left[P_0 \exp\left[i(\omega t + k_0\phi_1(\bar{r}))\right]\right] \quad (26)$$

where Re indicates the real part (measurements are always real) and where

$$P_0 = \exp(ik_0 D)$$

where D is the distance from the transmitter to the receiver.

To obtain the real (ϕ_R) and imaginary (ϕ_I) parts of ϕ_1, we multiply (in a modulator) the received signal which is proportional to $P(r, t)$ by $\sin \omega t$ and by $\cos \omega t$, obtaining two signals S_1 and S_2, thus

$$S_1 = P_0 \exp(-k_0\phi_I) \sin(\omega t) \cos(\omega t + k_0\phi_R(\bar{r}))$$

and

$$S_2 = P_0 \exp(-k_0\phi_I) \cos(\omega t) \cos(\omega t + k_0\phi_R(\bar{r})). \quad (27)$$

Then

$$S_1 = \frac{-P_0}{2} \exp\left[-k_0\phi_\mathrm{I}(\bar{r})\right]\left[\sin(k_0\phi_\mathrm{R}) - \sin(2\omega t + k_0\phi_\mathrm{R}(\bar{r}))\right]$$

and

$$S_2 = \frac{+P_0}{2} \exp\left[-k_0\phi_\mathrm{I}(\bar{r})\right]\left[\cos(k_0\phi_\mathrm{R}) + \cos(2\omega t + k_0\phi_\mathrm{R}(\bar{r}))\right].$$

$$(28)$$

Filtering out the high-frequency terms $\cos 2\omega t$ or $\sin 2\omega t$, and solving for ϕ_R and ϕ_I gives

$$\phi_\mathrm{R} = \frac{1}{K_0} \arctan\left(\frac{-\hat{S}_1}{\hat{S}_2}\right)$$

and

$$\phi_\mathrm{I} = \frac{1}{k_0}\left(\log\left(\frac{P_0}{2}\right) - \log\sqrt{(\hat{S}_1)^2 + (\hat{S}_2)^2}\right) \quad (29)$$

where the "hat" indicates low-pass filtered signals. These values can then be used in (14) to solve for the real and imaginary parts of $\eta(\bar{r})$.

Often, however, narrow-band signals are difficult to handle in the laboratory because of their propensity to generate standing waves. Therefore, broad-band pulses are generally used in which case the arrival time (suitably determined with an amplitude threshold device) and the log relative amplitude are used as estimates of $\phi_\mathrm{R}(\bar{b})$ and $\phi_\mathrm{I}(\bar{b})$, respectively [17].

Tone bursts, that is, single sinusoidal signals which are switched on for a period of several cycles then switched off, are very useful for obtaining narrow-band measurements while eliminating or at least providing control of standing waves by gating, i.e., measuring the signal before any reverberations in the water container occur.

The disadvantage of the coherent techniques is that for mathematical simplicity one is required to synthesize or to transmit a plane wave, something relatively difficult to achieve in practice since large-area transducers are difficult to make. In addition, the phase and amplitude of the received signal must be measured in such a way that the diffracting elements in the object move by less than approximately one quarter wavelength during the period of data acquisition. Currently, this obviates the use of the technique in the clinical environment because of the long period of time required to acquire the data, during which the patient is required to remain motionless. In addition, for the Rytov equation, the phase (ϕ_R in (29)) must be known in total radians not merely as the principle value of an arctan which is the measured variable. This requires "phase unwrapping" when the calculated phase jumps from -2π to $+2\pi$, for instance, and is also difficult to achieve in practice [25]. However, the extension of this technique to the utilization of broad-band pulses and to multiple path, parallel data-acquisition techniques may allow it to be implemented in a reasonable fashion [26].

We have recently used a variation of the above methods, based on the same wave equation (23) but cast in the form of a back-projection algorithm (called a back-propagation method by Devaney [27]), to obtain reconstructions of speed and attenuation within thin-walled rubber tubes filled with various fluids having different refractive indexes ($[\eta(x, y)$ in (24) is a refractive index). The Rytov reconstruction result is shown in Fig. 4 along with straight-line reconstructions of the same object.

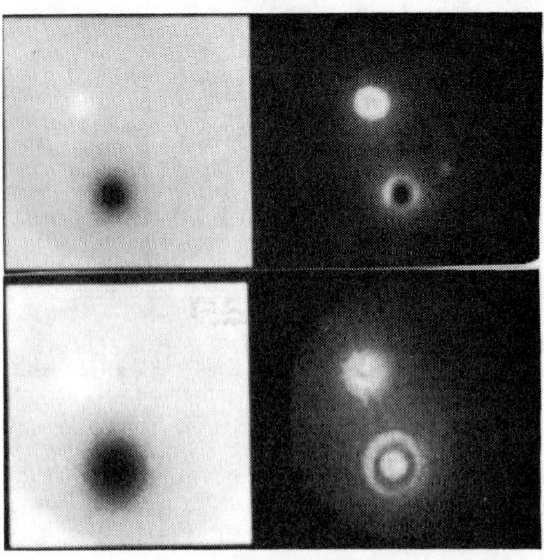

Fig. 4. Top, images of real (left) and imaginary (right) parts of $\eta(x, y)$ obtained using a modified Rytov method at 2.0 MHz. A plane wave was transmitted into the phantom and the scattered signal was received on the side of the phantom opposite to the transmitter. The phantom consisted of a finger cot filled with 0.9 percent saline (upper) and a finger cot filled with 50 percent isopropyl alcohol. In addition, there was a 1/2-mm stainless steel stylette which can be seen on the right. Reconstruction is 64 × 64 pixels from 100 views equispaced around 360°. Bottom, same format as top but reconstructed using straight-ray assumptions.

SEISMIC METHODS

To this point we have been describing computerized tomography methods that require transmission of the energy through the object. Currently, these are the only methods for obtaining quantitative images. However, it may be that images having higher resolution than common B-scans can be obtained using seismic methods applied to data obtained from backscattered energy.

Some backward wave propagation results for backscattered data have already been obtained by Burkhout *et al.* [28] using seismic methods in the Fourier domain and by ourselves and others using synthetic focusing methods in the time/space domain [29].

In addition to higher resolution in B-scan or echo modes, one might consider the backward propagation methods of seismology, to be described in this section, rather than the backward projection methods of straight-line reconstruction theory for increasing the fidelity of ultrasonic transmission tomography in the transmission mode [14].

In this section we will derive a backward propagation equation used in seismology and describe how it may be applied to both B-scan imaging and to transmission tomography.

Computer methods of migrating (focusing) seismic data have been used since the 1960's as an analog of manual methods developed in the 1940's for migrating waveform charts and tracings [28]. Migration methods can be derived from the scalar wave equation in which the boundary values at the surface of the volume being examined are the tracings or pressure waveforms measured from the returning backscattered waves resulting from reflection of the incident broad-band plane-wave pulse. Migration consists of two steps: first, the mathematical propagation backward into the media of the waveforms received at the surface; second, selection of the appropriate parts of the backward propagated signal which represent the reflectors in the media.

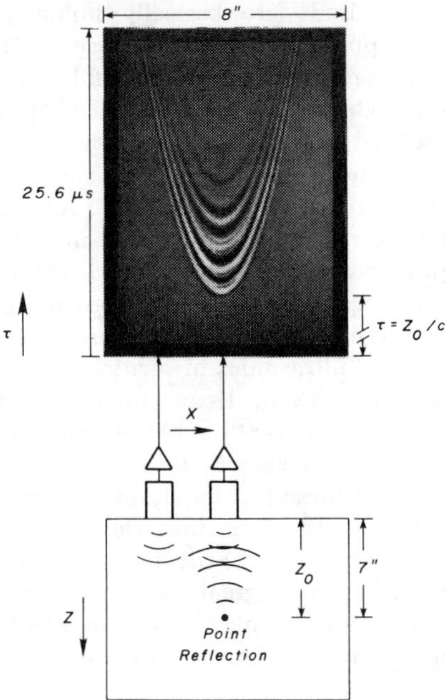

Fig. 5. Example of the reflection impulse response generated by transmitting into a volume having a single scatterer (air-filled straw). Transducer was scanned along the x-axis transmitting then receiving at each point. The response can be migrated using seismic methods, to image a point (see Fig. 7).

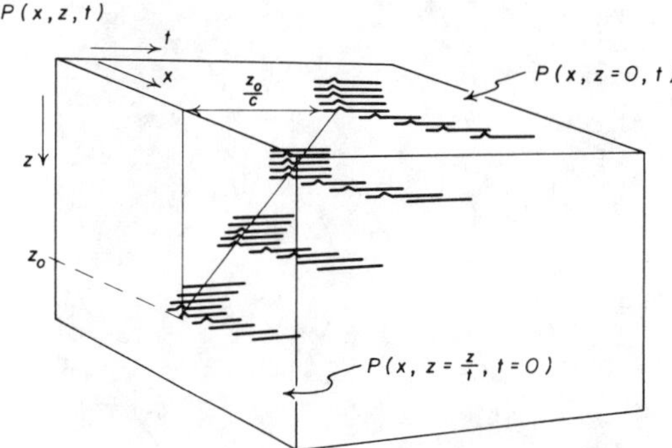

Fig. 6. Geometry of seismic reconstruction methods. The impulse from a point scatterer can be backward propagated into the volume and arrive at the ($x, z = z_0, t = 0$) plane when it is focused.

The geometry of the following discussion is such that the surface is the plane $z = 0$ and the x, y coordinates are the lateral (e.g., north) and down range (e.g., east) directions, respectively.

We will first derive the relationship between a 2D distribution of pressure $P(x, y, z = 0, t)$ at plane $z = 0$, and a 2D distribution of pressure at another plane $z = z_1$. We begin with the scalar Helmholtz equation (5) for loss-free homogeneous media

$$\frac{\partial^2}{\partial x^2} P + \frac{\partial^2}{\partial y^2} P + \frac{\partial^2}{\partial z^2} P + K^2 P = 0 \tag{30}$$

where K is not a function of space (but is a function of frequency), i.e., $K = \omega/c$. Taking the Fourier Transform of (30) with respect to x and y, we obtain

$$\frac{\partial^2}{\partial z^2} \hat{P} + (K^2 - K_x^2 - K_y^2) \hat{P} = 0$$

where

$$\hat{P} = \hat{P}(K_x, K_y, Z, \omega) \tag{31}$$

and where the boundary conditions are zero, for $y = x = 0$.

A solution of this equation is

$$\hat{P} = \exp(-iz\sqrt{K^2 - K_x^2 - K_y^2}) \tag{32}$$

from which we note

$$\hat{P}(K_x, K_y, Z_1, \omega) = \exp[-i(Z_1 - Z_0)\sqrt{K^2 - (K_x^2 + K_y^2)}]$$
$$\cdot \hat{P}(K_x, K_y, Z_0, \omega). \tag{33}$$

This equation allows us to calculate the pressure distribution over a plane $Z = Z_1$ given the pressure distribution over a plane $Z = Z_0$, given that speed c does not vary in the region. We can also calculate pressures along lines assuming the variation of pressure in y, say, was absent.

Fig. 5 illustrates the geometry and results of a seismic-like experiment, although done at ultrasonic frequencies. The data set $P(x, z = 0, t)$ was recorded by transmitting a cylindrical wave into the region (water with an air-filled straw reflector at $Z \cong 20$ cm) and receiving the reflected wave over the line $(x, z = 0)$.

The experimental details were that a 500-kHz transducer with a 3 mm $\times$ 19 mm aperture was scanned along the line $(x, z = 0)$ and pulsed every $\Delta x \cong \frac{1}{4} \lambda_0$ where λ_0 was the center wavelength of the pulse. At each position $(n\Delta x, n = 1, \cdots, 200)$ the returning pressure pulse $P(x, z = 0, t)$ was recorded.

The seismic imaging method [28] is 1) to take the 2D data set of Fig. 5, correct it for the fact that the transmitter and receiver were coincident giving

$$P_{c(\text{orrected})}(x, z = 0, \tau) = P_{\text{measured}}(x, z, = 0, t)$$

where

$$\tau = \frac{t}{2} + \frac{z}{c}$$

and 2) repropagate P_c downward, using (33), to each level of z, resulting in a three-dimensional data set $P_c(x, z, \tau)$, then 3) obtain an image $I(x, z)$ of the x, z plane in the object by taking $I(x, z) = P(x, z, t = 0)$.

One can understand why this gives a focused or "migrated" image by referring to Fig. 6. Notice that a point reflector will generate a hyperbola in the received signal space which, if backward propagated, will develop into an impulse (using (33) when $z = z_0$ and $t = 0$). Thus the image of the point scatterers is the front surface of the volume of data shown in Fig. 6, which is $I = P(x, z, t = 0)$.

Fig. 7 is a migrated image of the point response of Fig. 5, i.e., plane $P(x, z, t = 0)$. One can see the lateral resolution is about one-half wavelength (at 500 kHz) while the temporal resolution is degraded by reverberations in the transducer.

The assumptions used for this simple derivation of seismic imaging have been 1) constant speed (and density), 2) lossless media, and 3) no mode conversion (i.e., from bulk waves to shear waves) at the scatterers. Methods of compensating for variations in speed in the z direction are fairly well developed since this is mainly a layer-by-layer method and the velocity of each layer can be approximately taken into account. However, the effects of multiple reflection and variations in attenuation and speed in the lateral direction are difficult to account for, and are not yet fully understood [30].

The application of backward-propagation methods to transmission tomography is difficult since the time of arrival of

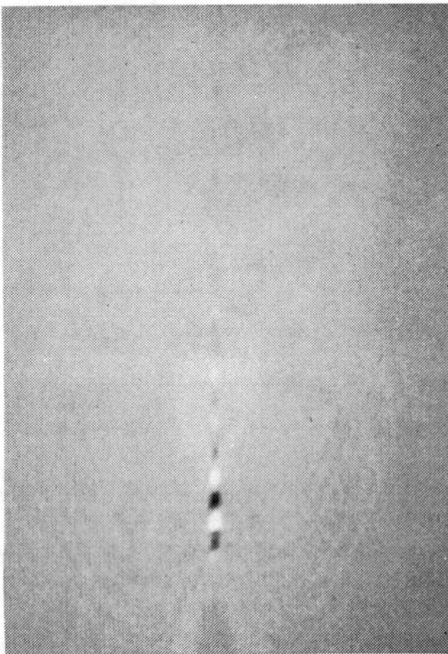

Fig. 7. Migrated response of single point reflector shown in Fig. 5. f_0 of pulse was 500 kHz. Width (lateral resolution) of reflector image is about one-half wavelength (at center frequency); length (axial resolution) is several wavelengths due to reverberations in transducer. Image represents dimensions 8 in. laterally and 1.5 in. in axial (verticle) extent.

the signals representing the individual scatterer does not correspond to the depth at which the scattering occurred. However, one could imagine backward propagating the signal received at $(x = x_0, y)$ to each line through the image in a manner similar to back projection in computed tomography. Then by repeating the procedure for a multiplicity of views, one would obtain a form of reconstruction. We have reported such a method and some results elsewhere [14], [31].

We have demonstrated good focusing using the seismic or synthetic focusing technique in a time-domain approach [29]. Recently, Ridder *et al.* [28] have shown very good results using the much faster Fourier domain, although still assuming constant speed of sound throughout the volume.

DISCUSSION

Although the straight-line reconstruction equations can be derived from the Helmholtz equation, the approximations required are too strong, resulting in images that are affected by aberrations due to diffraction and refraction. Several investigators are attempting to correct the straight-line reconstruction algorithms using various forms of multiple-frequency approximations [32], [33] and ray tracing [34]; however, the diffraction tomographies (Rytov especially) may result in better imaging. The Rytov approximation may give better images when diffraction is strong, and a modification by Bates *et al.* [35] may better account for refraction in the Rytov model.

The practical difficulties with measurement of data for the diffraction tomographies might be overcome with judicious choices of geometry and ultrasound transducers so that the coherent character of the transmitted and received waves can be maintained with little difficulty. Certainly the magnitude of the computational task for solving the diffraction tomographies can be handled by special hardware processors that are continually becoming more and more powerful and at the same time less expensive.

The seismic methods are basically holographic methods which have been applied to volume scattering. The aberrations due to variations in refraction index probably must be corrected iteratively, although the basic capabilities of the backward-propagation method as derived by Devaney in the modification of the Rytov method and the seismic migration technqiues derived by the oil prospecting industry are very similar.

Two major unsolved problems remain in the field of computed tomography—that of solving for distribution of anisotropic scalar values, and that of solving for distributions of vector-valued functions. Both of these problems have application in the field of ultrasonics in medicine and biology since the scattering properties of tissue are seldom isotropic and since properties such as velocity of blood flow can be considered functions that could be measured using tomography.

The application of these techniques in the clinical laboratory will require 1) demonstration that the resulting images are indeed useful diagnostically, 2) the design of a data-acquisition system which can acquire a great deal of data in a short period of time, and 3) acceptance by the radiologist of the relatively complex geometric and mathematical nature of the machine.

ACKNOWLEDGMENT

The author thanks D. Kasten for secretarial assistance and J. Lauer and S. Richardson for graphics and A. Chu and P. Thomas for technical assistance.

REFERENCES

[1] R. K. Mueller, "Diffraction tomography I: The wave equation," *Ultrason. Imag.*, vol. 2, pp. 213–222, 1980.

[2] J.O.S. Roelandt, "Practical echocardiography," in *Ultrasound in Medicine Series*, vol. 1, D. White, Ed. Forest Grove, OR: Res. Studies Press, 1977.

[3] M. Linzer and S. T. Norton, "Ultrasonic tissue characterization," *Annual Rev. Biophys. Bioeng.*, vol. 11, pp. 303–309, 1982.

[4] J. F. Greenleaf, S. A. Johnson, and A. H. Lent, "Measurement of spatial distribution of refractive index in tissues by ultrasonic computer assisted tomography," *Ultrasound Med. Biol.*, vol. 3, pp. 327–339, 1978.

[5] G. H. Glover and J. L. Sharp, "Reconstruction of ultrasound propagation speed distribution in soft tissue: Time-of-flight tomography," *IEEE Trans. Sonics Ultrason.*, vol. SU-24, no. 4, pp. 229–234, 1977.

[6] P. L. Carson, T. V. Oughton, W. R. Hende, and A. S. Ahuja, "Imaging soft tissue through bone with ultrasound transmission tomography reconstruction," *Med. Phys.*, vol. 4, no. 4, pp. 302–309, 1977.

[7] See for instance the *Ultrasound Med. Biol. J.* (New York: Pergamon, or *J. Ultrasound Med.* (Philadelphia, PA: W. B. Saunders).

[8] M. B. Sutton, A. J. Tajik, L-A. Mercier, J. B. Seward, E. R. Giuliani, and E. L. Ritman, "Assessment of left ventricular function in secundum atrial septal defect by computer analysis of the M-mode echocardiogram," *Circulation*, vol. 60, pp. 1082–1090, Nov. 1979.

[9] K. W. Marich, L. M. Zatz, P. S. Green, J. R. Suarez, and A. Macovski, "Real-time imaging with a new ultrasonic camera: Part I, In vitro experimental studies on transmission imaging of biological structures," *J. Clin. Ultrasound*, vol. 3. pp. 5–16, 1975.

[10] J. F. Greenleaf, "Computerized transmission tomography," in *Methods of Experimental Physics—Ultrasound*, vol. 19, P. D. Edmonds, Ed. New York: Academic Press, 1981, pp. 563–589.

[11] M. Born and E. Wolf, *Principles of Optics.* New York: Pergamon, 1964, p. 112.

[12] L. M. Brekhovskikn, *Waves in Layered Media.* New York: Academic Press, 1960, p. 171.

[13] G. T. Herman, *Image Reconstructions from Projections.* New York: Academic Press, 1980, p. 108.

[14] J. F. Greenleaf, P. J. Thomas, and B. Rajagopalan, "Effect of diffraction on ultrasonic computer-assisted tomography," in *Acoustical Holography*, vol. II. New York: Plenum, in press.

[15] M. O'Donnell, E. T. Jaynes, and J-G Miller, "Kramers-Kronig relationship between ultrasonic attenuation and phase velocity," *J. Acoust. Soc. America*, vol. 69, no. 3, pp. 696–701, Mar. 1979.

[16] S. A. Goss, R. L. Johnston, and F. Dunn, "Comprehensive compilation of empirical ultrasonic properties of mammilian tissues," *J. Acoust. Soc. America*, vol. 64, no. 2, Aug. 1978.

[17] J. F. Greenleaf and R. C. Bahn, "Signal processing methods for transmission ultrasonic computerized tomography," in *1980 Ultrason. Symp. Proc.*, pp. 966–972, Nov. 1980.

[18] K. D. Dines and A. C. Kak, "Ultrasonic attenuation tomography of soft tissues," *Ultrason. Imag.*, vol. 1, pp. 16–33, Jan. 1979.

[19] C. R. Crawford and A. C. Kak, "Multi-path artifact corrections in ultrasonic transmission tomography," in press.

[20] J. F. Greenleaf and R. C. Bahn, "Clinical imaging with transmissive ultrasonic computerized tomography," *IEEE Trans. Biomed. Eng.*, vol. BME-28, no. 2, pp. 177–185, Feb. 1981.

[21] J. F. Greenleaf and J. J. Gisvold, "A clinical prototype ultrasonic transmission tomographic scanner," presented at the 12th Int. Symp. on Acoustical Imaging. Acoustical Imaging '82, London, England, July 19–22, 1982 (abstract submitted for publication).

[22] E. Wolf, "Three-dimensional structure determination of semitransparent objects from holographic data," *Opt. Commun.*, vol. 1, no. 4, pp. 153–156, Sept. 1969.

[23] K. Iwata and R. Nagata, "Calculation of refractive index distributions from interferograms using Born and Rytov's approximation," *Jap. J. Appl. Phys.*, vol. 14, pp. 379–383, 1975.

[24] P. M. Morse and H. Feshbach, *Methods of Experimental Physics*, pt. II. New York: McGraw-Hill, 1953, p. 1361.

[25] J. M. Tribolet, "A new phase unwrapping algorithm," *IEEE Trans. Acoustics, Speech, Signal Proces.*, vol. ASSP-25, no. 2, pp. 170–197, Apr. 1977.

[26] S. K. Kenue and J. F. Greenleaf, "Limited angle multifrequency diffraction tomography," *IEEE Trans. Sonic Ultrason.*, vol. SU-29, no. 8, pp. 213–217, July 1982.

[27] A. J. Devaney, "A filtered backpropagation algorithm for diffraction tomography," *Ultrason. Imag.*, vol. 4, pp. 336–350, 1982.

[28] A. J. Berkhout, J. Ridder, and M. P. deGraaff, "New possibilities in data measurement, signal processing and information extraction: Philosophy and results," in *Pro. 12th Int. Symp. on Acoustical Imaging* (London, England, July 19–23, 1982), in press.

[29] S. A. Johnson, J. F. Greenleaf, M. Tanaka, B. Rajagopalan, and R. C. Bahn, "Quantitative synthetic aperture reflection imaging with correction for refraction and attenuation: Application of seismic techniques in medicine," in *Proc. San Diego Biomedical Symp.*, vol. 17, pp. 337–349, 1978.

[30] A. J. Berkout, "Wave field extrapolation techniques in seismic migration, a tutorial," *Geophysic*, vol. 46, no. 12, pp. 1638–1656, Dec. 1981.

[31] S. A. Johnson, J. F. Greenleaf, B. Rajagopalan, and M. Tanaka, "Algebraic and analytic inversion of acoustic data from partially or fully enclosing apertures," in *Acoustic Imaging*, A. F. Metherell, Ed. New York: Plenum, 1980, pp. 577–598.

[32] F. Stenger and S. A. Johnson, "Ultrasonic transmission tomography based on the inversion of the Helmholtz wave equation for plane and spherical wave insonation," *Appl. Math. Notes*, vol. 4, pp. 103–127, Dec. 1979.

[33] F. Stenger, "Asymptomatic ultrasonics inversion based on using more than one frequency," in *Acoustical Imaging*, J. P. Powers, Ed. New York: Plenum, 1982, pp. 425–444.

[34] H. Schomberg, "An improved approach to reconstructive ultrasound tomography," *J. Appl. D.. Appl. Phys.*, vol. 11, p. L181, 1978.

[35] R.H.T. Bates, W. M. Boerner, and G. R. Dunlop, "An extended Rytov approximation and its significance for remote sensing and inverse scattering," *Opt. Commun.*, vol. 18, no. 4, pp. 421–423, Sept. 1976.

An Introduction to NMR Imaging: From the Bloch Equation to the Imaging Equation

WALDO S. HINSHAW AND ARNOLD H. LENT

Invited Paper

Abstract —The emerging technology of NMR imaging is introduced here as a problem in system identification. We show how selected families of signals may be input into the system ("system," in this case, is almost synonymous with "patient") in order that the system's responses to these inputs may be directly interpreted in terms of the system parameters. Once identified, a raster display of the system parameters provides an internal image of the patient.

Inputs to the system are four-component functions of time. One component describes the strength of an RF signal, and the other three components govern the strength of three spatially varying, independently controlled magnetic fields (the *gradient* fields) in which the patient is immersed. In response to these inputs some of the protons in the patient, acting in concordance with the *Bloch equation*, give rise to local fluctuations in the magnetization which are detected with a tuned antenna and a sensitive receiver. The relationship between this output signal and the system parameters is summarized in the *imaging equation*.

I. INTRODUCTION

WE WILL TRY in this paper to introduce NMR (nuclear magnetic resonance) imaging to those who do not know NMR, but are somewhat familar with X-ray CT. Other articles in this issue should provide an adequate background. Here, we do not present all of the physical models and conceptual aids often used in introductory NMR papers, but present the mathematics in a reasonably accurate and consistent way. We do not discuss the complications resulting from departures from an ideal world, but do try to indicate where they occur. Finally, we stop short of discussing image reconstruction algorithms. This paper is intended as a resource for those who wish to develop their own reconstruction algorithms.

Even in a field as new as NMR imaging (the seminal paper appeared in 1973 [12]), subspecialties have already developed. In this paper we consider the imaging of protons (i.e., hydrogen nuclei) in stationary biological samples (people, mainly). We regretfully exclude from consideration the imaging of phosphorus, with its exciting potential for observing metabolism (but, for a review, see [11]), and dynamic imaging of the cardiovascular system (see, e.g., [18]). For introductory presentations of these (and other) clinical topics, as well as additional background reading in NMR, the recent conference proceedings [3] are recommended. Even more recent additions to the NMR tutorial literature are [21] and [22].

Before introducing the ideas of NMR imaging, we present a few representative NMR images. These images are intended to prove that the ideas, although sometimes subtle, are worth

Manuscript received October 5, 1982; revised December 15, 1982.
The authors are with the Technicare Corporation, Solon, OH 44139.

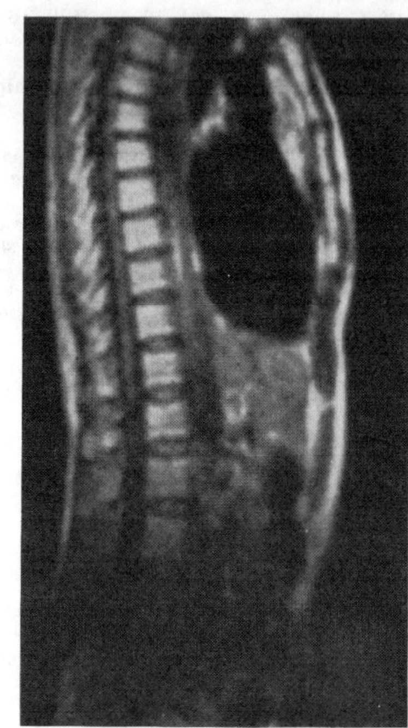

Fig. 1. This is a sagittal slice of the dorso-lumbar spine area. The image was obtained at 0.3 T using selective irradiation to define the slice, the saturation-recovery method to generate the NMR signal, and two-dimensional (2D) Fourier transformation to reconstruct the image. This image demonstrates the ability of NMR to provide views in any orientation.

studying. Fig. 1 is a 1.5-cm-thick sagittal image of the torso and is included to demonstrate the ability of NMR to generate views of any orientation. Fig. 2 is a transverse slice through the head which demonstrates the high spatial resolution possible with the technique. Fig. 3 is a set of three images showing a coronal slice through the brain. The only difference between the images of this set is the timing of the applied magnetic fields. This figure demonstrates the ability of NMR to produce images based on more than one single property of the tissue.

All of these NMR images were produced on an experimental prototype NMR imaging system built by the Technicare Corporation. The system, shown in Fig. 4, was operated at a field strength of 0.3 T and a frequency of 12.8 MHz.

Even without knowing precisely how the images were produced, it is clear that valuable information has been obtained; add in the knowledge that, unlike X-ray CT, no ionizing radiation was used in forming these images, and the mind boggles.

Reprinted from *Proc. IEEE*, vol. 71, pp. 338–350, Mar. 1983.

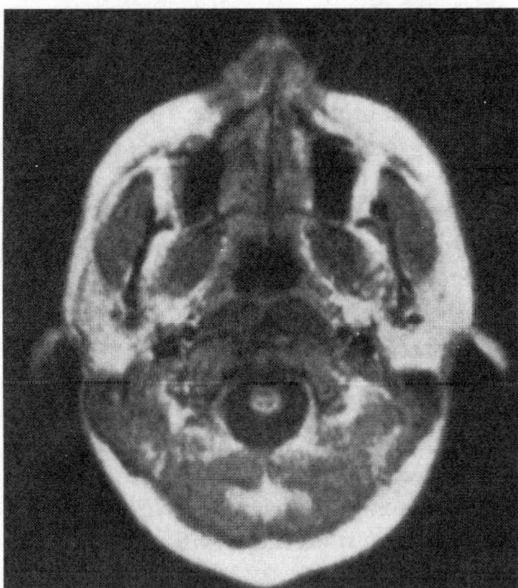

Fig. 2. This is a transverse slice of cranial anatomy at the level of the foramen magnum. It demonstrates the spatial resolution that can be obtained with NMR imaging. The methods used are the same as those for Fig. 1. The slice thickness is approximately 1 cm.

The remainder of Section I is devoted to introducing NMR imaging and comparing it with CT. Section II presents the Bloch equation, and Section III develops its consequences in an imaging system. Section IV discusses an idealized NMR receiver and its output signal $S(t)$. Finally, in Section V, the "imaging equations" of several different NMR imaging modalities are derived. At the end of Section I, for easy reference, is a partial list of symbols to aid the reader in sorting out notation.

A. CT and NMR: Physical Similarities

When one compares the NMR imaging system of Fig. 4 against a typical CT system, it is easy to be misled by their outward similarities. But CT relies on rotating mechanical gantries and the absorption of X-ray photons, while NMR is entirely electronic and is based on the interactions of small, rapidly varying, magnetic (the M of NMR) fields with loosely bound hydrogen nuclei (the N of NMR—R arrives in Section III) in the soft tissues of the body. Also, despite some brave attempts at three-dimensional reconstruction [20], CT is essentially a two-dimensional technology. NMR, on the other hand, seems to be intrinsically three-dimensional. One has a choice between collecting data from all of the three-dimensional objects and collecting data from only a single slice. In the first case, the data can be manipulated, using three-dimensional reconstruction techniques, to provide the image of a single slice. In the second case, special "slice-selection" techniques, which will be discussed later, are used to obtain data from only the selected slice. In either case, the slice can be in any orientation and at any level.

B. CT and NMR: Images

Let x stand for the vector of spatial coordinates. In CT, $\mu(x)$, the spatially varying X-ray attenuation coefficient, is the physical property being imaged. In NMR, *three* primary spatially varying physical properties (to be discussed), $M_0(x)$, $T_1(x)$, and $T_2(x)$, are necessary for a good description of an object. (In this sense, NMR resembles ultrasound imaging (see [6]) with its multiple imaging modalities.) However, these three properties are imaged differently. $M_0(x)$, which is

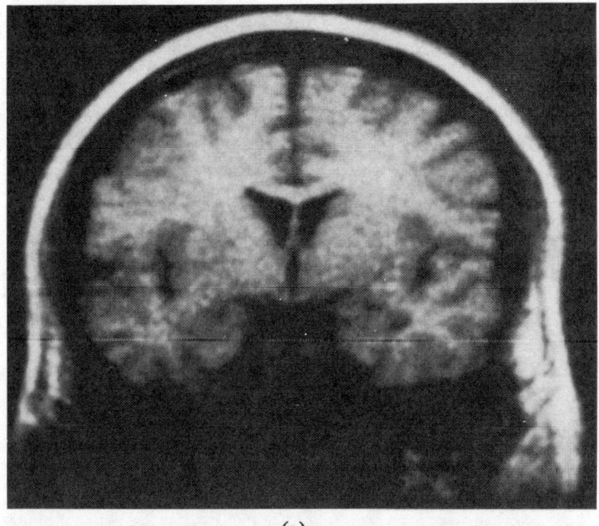

(a)

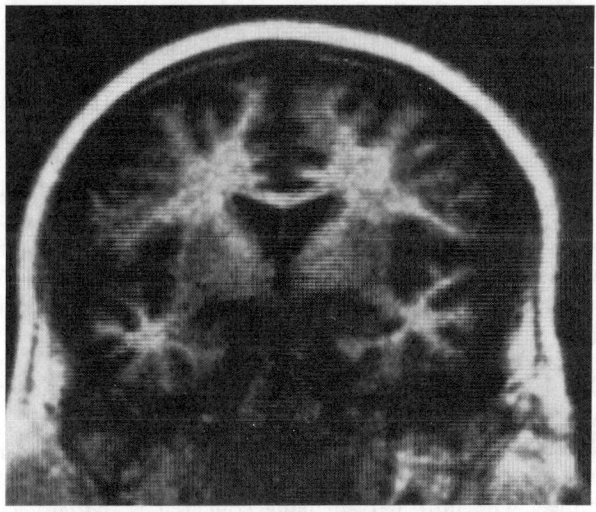

(b)

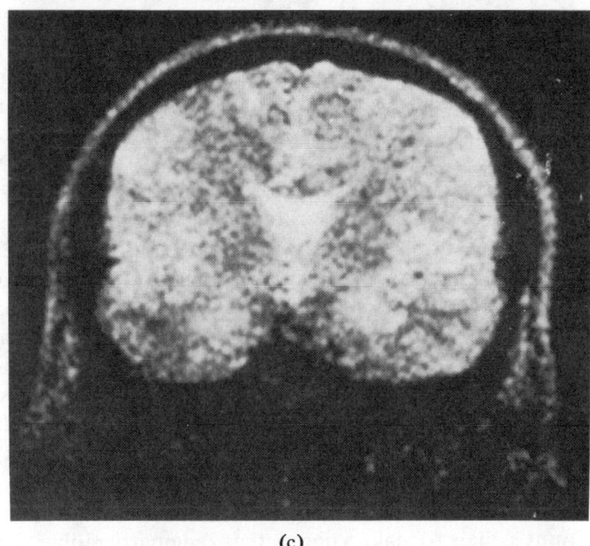

(c)

Fig. 3. This is a set of coronal head images showing the same slice with three different pulse sequences. Part (a) was obtained using the saturation-recovery method and part (b) using the inversion-recovery method. Note particularly the increased gray–white matter contrast in the inversion-recovery image. Part (c) was obtained using the same method as that used for (a) except that the data-acquisition interval occurred a significantly longer time after the first RF pulse. In this image, the material with long T_2 (the CSF) appears bright.

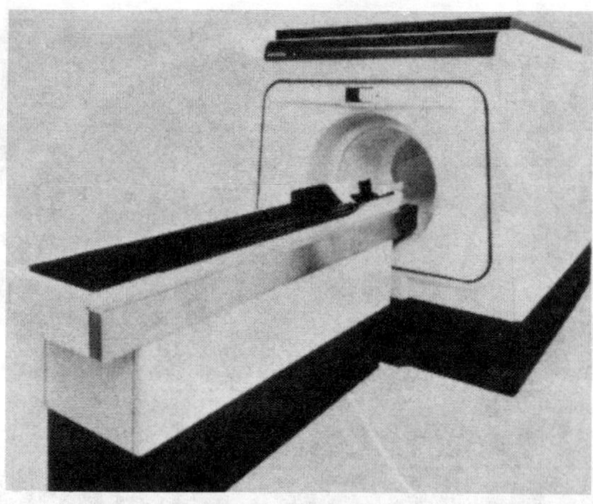

Fig. 4. Several NMR imaging systems, such as the one shown here, are now in use as clinical research tools. Note the deceptive resemblance to an X-ray CT scanner.

related to the distribution of "mobile" hydrogen nuclei (i.e., constituents of mobile molecules in liquid-like phases), has a role comparable to that of $\mu(x)$ in CT, in that it provides the overall image shape, while $T_1(x)$ and $T_2(x)$ (the "relaxation times") contribute significant local information. The distinction between gray matter and white matter in Fig. 3 is due almost entirely to T_1 differences, rather than to M_0 differences. It is possible (with considerable effort) to generate "pure" T_1 and T_2 images, but the usual NMR image is a composite combining M_0, T_1, and T_2; later, in Section V, we shall discuss some mechanisms for controlling their proportions.

C. CT and NMR: Input/Output Relationships

We are coming to some basic differences between CT and NMR.

1) In CT, as preceding articles have made clear, the inputs are X-ray pulses which are aimed at different parts of the sample. The information being collected is *spatially coded*. In NMR, a complicated signal $P(t)$ (a four-component vector function of time) is transmitted into the NMR system, and a complex (as opposed to "real") signal $S(t)$ emerges. Information about the sample is *temporally coded*. Although the Fourier integral can be used to go back and forth between the time domain and the space domain, this easy transfer is conceptual, rather than real, and it is dangerous to consider NMR and CT "pretty much the same sort of thing."

2) In every CT system built, the input signals necessarily have a similar form; the X-ray pulses are uniform in strength, and vary in direction. (We do not mean to slight the major advances made between the first-generation CT systems and present-day systems.) With NMR, the input signals can be *tailored* by the observer so that their interaction with the sample is *controlled*, to produce strikingly diverse images. To draw an analogy, think of a microscope with some of its attachments (polarizers, phase contrast, dark-field illumination) and of the variety of images it can produce. It takes an intimate working knowledge of the properties of the multitude of possible input signals to make a competent zeugmatographer. (*Zeugmatography* is Lauterbur's [12] coinage for NMR imaging.)

D. Basic NMR Components

Having warned the reader that NMR and CT are different, we name, but do not yet explain, the basic components of an NMR imaging system. These are as follows:

1) A *magnet*, which provides a strong (about 0.5 T), uniform, steady, magnet field H_0.

2) An *RF transmitter*, which delivers radiofrequency magnetic fields to the sample.

3) A *gradient system*, which produces time-varying magnetic fields of controlled spatial nonuniformity. The experimenter's controls for modulating the magnetic field experienced by the sample are lumped together in the vector $P(t)$, which will be formally defined in Section III.

4) A *detection system*, which yields the output signal $S(t)$.

5) An *imager system*, including the computer, which reconstructs and displays the images.

Our objective in this paper is to establish the "imaging equation," which shows, for a few different input signals, how the output signal is related to the sample properties $M_0(x)$, $T_1(x)$, and $T_2(x)$. To achieve this objective, we must look at the physical model which underlies NMR.

Partial List of Symbols

$\omega_0 = -\gamma H_0$	Larmor frequency corresponding to the static field.
$\omega'(x) = -\gamma(H_0 + G \cdot x)$	Larmor frequency at x when gradient G is applied.
ω	The irradiation frequency of the RF field.
$\omega_1 = -\gamma H_1$	The frequency of RF-induced rotation.
$\omega_h = -\gamma h(x)$	"Additional" rotation frequency caused by gradients.
H_0	Strength of the static magnetic field.
$H_0 = H_0 k$	The static magnetic field.
$H(t, x)$	Total magnetic field experienced at t, x.
$H_1(t)$	Modulation function for the RF field.
$H_1(t) = 2H_1(t) \cos \omega t i$	RF magnetic field.
$h(x) = G \cdot x$	Gradient magnetic field.
$M(t, x)$	Sample magnetization at t, x.
M_x, M_y, M_z	Components of M.
$M = M_x + iM_y$	(Complex) transverse magnetization.
$M_0 k$	The equilibrium nuclear magnetization.
$M^0(x)$	Sample magnetization at $t = 0$.
M_x^0, M_y^0, M_z^0	Components of M^0.
$M^0 = M_x^0 + iM_y^0$	Transverse magnetization at $t = 0$.

Arguments may be omitted (e.g., M) for brevity or added (e.g., $M(t, x)$) for clarity.

II. The Physical and Mathematical Model

The model of the spinning proton is as basic to NMR as the picture of absorbed and transmitted photons is to CT. In place of the Lambert–Beer law which describes photon absorption, NMR has the Bloch equation, which will be presented in this section and explored more fully in the next.

Physical Picture: Think of a top, spinning about its axis, which makes an angle α with the vertical. The rotation of the top's axis around the vertical is called *precession*. This spinning top is the simple, conceptual picture (the recent *Scientific*

American article on NMR imaging [16] has still more detail) of the proton and its spin, a subject treated rigorously only by quantum mechanics [1]. Under proper conditions, the proton (with its spin and associated magnetic field) precesses about a magnetic field (a *vector*, remember) as the top processes about the vertical.

In terms of this picture we can state some simple but important facts which, later, we derive from the Bloch equation.

Fact 1): The *rate* of precession (cycles per second) of a proton in a magnetic field is proportional to the *strength* of the field. (This is where the magnetic field H_0 comes in.)

Fact 2): There is *no* signal emitted by the proton when it is sitting at equilibrium, with its spin lined up with the magnetic field. There *is* a signal when the proton has been knocked out of alignment so that it makes some angle α with the magnetic field. (This is where the RF transmitter comes in—*it* does the knocking.)

Fact 3): If the magnitude field can be made nonuniform in a *controlled manner*, then, by Fact 1), protons at different points in space will precess at different frequencies. (The gradient system takes care of this spatial encoding.)

A. Mathematical Model—The Bloch Equation

We begin with the Bloch equation [2], which gives an accurate but phenomenological description of the time dependence of the *nuclear magnetization* $M(t)$ in the presence of an applied magnetic field $H(t)$. The nuclear magnetization $M(t)$ is the source of the "NMR signal" from which the image is ultimately constructed. We can think of the NMR sample as a black box with $H(t)$ as the input signal, or stimulus, and $M(t)$ as the output signal, or response. The black box is characterized by M_0, T_1, and T_2, and its behavior is governed by the Bloch equation.

$$dM/dt = \gamma M \times H - (M_x i + M_y j)/T_2 - (M_z - M_0)k/T_1.$$

$$(2.1)$$

Initially, in order to illustrate some basic properties of the Bloch equation, we will consider the equation as applied to an ensemble of identical nuclei, each experiencing the same field H. Then, fundamentals in hand, we will move on to heterogeneous samples and nonuniform fields.

B. Parameters of the Bloch Equation

The nuclear magnetization $M(t)$, induced in the sample by the magnetic field $H(t)$, is the local sum of the magnetic fields of the protons. The magnetization is a bulk property of the sample rather than a property of individual protons.

The *gyromagnetic ratio* γ is a physical property of the nucleus of the atom. Different chemical elements—in fact, different isotopes of the same element—exhibit significantly different gyromagnetic ratios. This makes it possible to observe protons and ignore phosphorus, for example. The gyromagnetic ratio of protons is 4.26×10^7 Hz$\cdot$T^{-1} (or 2.68×10^8 rad$\cdot$s$^{-1}\cdot$T^{-1}).

$H(t)$ is the magnetic field experienced by the nuclei being considered. We do not include in $H(t)$ the contributions to the magnetic field resulting from the local interactions and collisions experienced by the nuclei. The effects of these "internal" fields are included in the parameters T_1 and T_2.

There is another phenomenon which affects $H(t)$. The chemical electrons surrounding a given nucleus can shield the nucleus from the externally applied magnetic field by a very small amount. This shielding changes $H(t)$, shifts the resonant frequency, and as a result, is called a "chemical shift." These shifts, which for protons cover a range of about 10 ppm, are the substance of NMR spectroscopy. Although the Bloch equations may be generalized to include chemical shifts, the effect is ignored in the following development. Thus for our purposes, $H(t)$ is the field applied by the experimenter.

The coordinate system used in (2.1) is the *laboratory*, or *fixed*, reference frame. The k direction is taken to be parallel to H_0, where H_0 is the field of the large magnet. H_0 is often called the *static field*. By convention, k is the "longitudinal direction" and i and j define the "transverse plane."

The *equilibrium magnetization* $M_0 k$ is the nuclear magnetization which exists if the sample is maintained at the static field for a time long compared to T_1.

The "relaxation times," T_1 and T_2, represent the effect of the "relaxation" processes. The constant T_1 is the "longitudinal" or "spin-lattice" relaxation time and governs the evolution of M_z toward its equilibrium value M_0. The physical process involved in this relaxation is the dissipation of energy from the collection of nuclei, the "spin system," to the atomic and molecular environment of the nuclei, the "lattice." The process can be thought of as the reorientation of the spins into alignment with H_0.

The constant T_2 is the "transverse" or "spin–spin" relaxation time and governs the evolution of the magnitude of the transverse magnetization, $M_x i + M_y j$, toward its equilibrium value of zero. The physical processes which cause transverse relaxation include those which cause longitudinal relaxation, as well as the magnetic coupling between neighboring nuclei. The process can be thought of as the transverse orientation of the individual spins becoming randomized, or dephased, so that the sum of the transverse components of the fields of the nuclei in the collection goes to zero.

Although the Bloch equation accurately describes NMR imaging, it is, in fact, of limited validity. Perhaps the weakest assumption implicit in the equation is that the transverse relaxation is exponential. This assumption is fairly good for liquids, but is less valid for more "solid-like" samples. But solid-like samples have short T_2 values and, as a result, are not observed with the usual imaging methods.

C. The Bloch Equation as an Equation of Motion

The term $M \times H$ gives rise to the precessional motion mentioned earlier. To see how this comes about, we take $H = H_0 k$, assuming for the moment that H is static, and, for convenience, temporarily ignore the T_1 and T_2 terms of (2.1). Initially, the magnetization has components M_x^0, M_y^0, M_z^0. Then

$$dM/dt = \gamma M \times H_0 k. \qquad (2.2)$$

In coordinate form

$$dM_x/dt = \gamma H_0 M_y$$

$$dM_y/dt = -\gamma H_0 M_x$$

$$dM_z/dt = 0. \qquad (2.3)$$

These equations have the solution

$$M_x(t) = M_x^0 \cos \omega_0 t - M_y^0 \sin \omega_0 t$$

$$M_y(t) = M_x^0 \sin \omega_0 t + M_y^0 \cos \omega_0 t$$

$$M_z(t) = M_z^0$$

where ω_0 is the *Larmor*, or *resonant*, frequency of the spin system given by

$$\omega_0 = -\gamma H_0. \tag{2.4}$$

These equations validate Facts 1) and 2).

The inclusion of the T_1 and T_2 terms complicates matters only a little. The solution becomes

$$M_x(t) = e^{-t/T_2}(M_x^0 \cos \omega_0 t - M_y^0 \sin \omega_0 t)$$
$$M_y(t) = e^{-t/T_2}(M_x^0 \sin \omega_0 t + M_y^0 \cos \omega_0 t)$$
$$M_z(t) = M_z^0 e^{-t/T_1} + M_0(1 - e^{-t/T_1}). \tag{2.5}$$

The longitudinal component decays from its initial value of M_z^0 toward its equilibrium value of M_0. The transverse component rotates at frequency ω_0 and decays toward zero.

There is a compact, convenient expression for the transverse component of the magnetization. Define

$$M = M_x + iM_y. \tag{2.6}$$

Then

$$M(t) = M^0 \exp (i\omega_0 t - t/T_2) \tag{2.7}$$

where $M^0 = M_x^0 + iM_y^0$.

D. The Bloch Equation for Heterogeneous Samples and Nonuniform Fields

We now move on to the case of physical interest, heterogeneous samples and nonuniform magnetic fields. First consider the heterogeneity of the sample. Imagine the Bloch equation applied to a small volume of the sample at a given point x in the sample. Within this small volume we can assume that H is uniform, but there is a distribution of values of T_1 and T_2. There are interactions between nuclei which complicate the picture, but we will approximate the true situation by assuming that there are a finite number of different "types" of nuclei in the volume, each with its own value of T_1 and T_2. With each type, we associate a different magnetization for the volume, which is written $M_n(t, x)$, where x is the location of the small volume. Thus the total magnetization $M(t, x)$ for the volume is

$$M(t, x) = \sum M_n(t, x). \tag{2.8}$$

Rather than carry this notion through the following discussions, it is easier to re-introduce it after the final result is obtained and, until then, consider only one particular value for T_1 and for T_2. Since the output signal is a linear function of the sample magnetization (this will be shown in Section IV), we can do the summation after the signal processing is completed.

As for nonuniform fields, all we do is regard every variable of the Bloch equation (except γ, of course) as a function of both x and t. γ is determined once and for all by the choice of the nuclide to be imaged.

III. Solutions of the Bloch Equation—The Basic NMR "Toolkit"

In this section we introduce the most important NMR "stimulus" signals, and, for each stimulus $H(t,x)$, derive the resulting "response" magnetization $M(t, x)$ of the sample. We continue to confine ourselves to a simplified and idealized world, with occasional asides to mention important deviations from ideality. The uniform field H_0 has been introduced in earlier sections, so we begin with the gradient field and continue with the RF field. As we shall see, both of these fields contribute to the field $H(t, x)$ applied to the sample.

Both the gradient field and the RF field are under the control of the experimenter. The gradient field is governed by three input signals called $G_x(t)$, $G_y(t)$, and $G_z(t)$; the RF field is controlled by a signal called $H_1(t)$. We group these signals into a four-component vector $P(t)$. Conventionally, $H_1(t)$ is taken as the first component of P, followed by the three gradient controls. $P(t)$ is a full description of what is usually called a "pulse sequence." Section V presents several types of pulse sequences used in NMR imaging.

A. The Gradient Field

The gradient system includes a set of three independently computer-controlled coils which generate a spatially varying and time-varying magnetic field within the sample. These coils are referred to as the x-gradient, the y-gradient, and the z-gradient coils, names which are slightly misleading. We consider only the x-gradient in detail; the other gradients behave similarly. Fig. 5 diagrams these three gradient fields and their relationship to H_0 and the RF field.

The ideal x-gradient coil causes the z-component of the magnetic field to vary linearly with x as follows:

$$H(t, x) = H_0 k + G_x(t) x k.$$

The real x-gradient coil produces a field which has components in the x- and y-directions, but the uniform field in the z-direction is so strong that these components may be neglected by comparison. Thus we can call $G_x(t)$ the x-gradient and $G_x(t)x$ the x-gradient field even though the x-gradient coil produces other field components. When all three gradients coils are turned on, their superimposed fields yield

$$H(t, x) = H_0 k + G_x(t) x k + G_y(t) y k + G_z(t) z k.$$

The three gradients may be formally grouped into a gradient vector $G(t)$ with components $G_x(t)$, $G_y(t)$, and $G_z(t)$, which summarizes the temporal variation of the gradients. Thus we can write

$$H(t, x) = (H_0 + G(t) \cdot x) k.$$

It is this gradient field $G(t) \cdot x$ which induces the spatial coding of the resonance frequency that was alluded to in Fact 3). To see how this arises, take the special case of static gradients, $G(t) = G$. Then the Larmor frequency ω' of the infinitesimal sample at x is

$$\omega'(x) = -\gamma(H_0 + G \cdot x). \tag{3.1}$$

For a given, fixed G, two points in space which are displaced from each other by a vector which is orthogonal to G will have the same Larmor frequency, but, by transmitting a second stimulus signal with a different G, the two points may be made distinguishable. By transmitting enough different stimulus signals, *all* points may be made (almost) distinguishable, and this is what NMR imaging systems do.

We now take a quick look at two useful, simple gradient inputs. As we shall see, it is the transverse magnetization components M_x and M_y which determine the output signal and, hence, are of interest. The gradient fields have no effect on M_z.

The solution of the Bloch equation in complex notation, (2.7), becomes

$$M(t, x) = M^0(x) \exp (i\omega'(x) t - t/T_2(x)) \tag{3.2}$$

when we add the dependence upon x and change ω_0 to $\omega'(x)$.

1) The Readout Gradient: As we have just seen, if a static

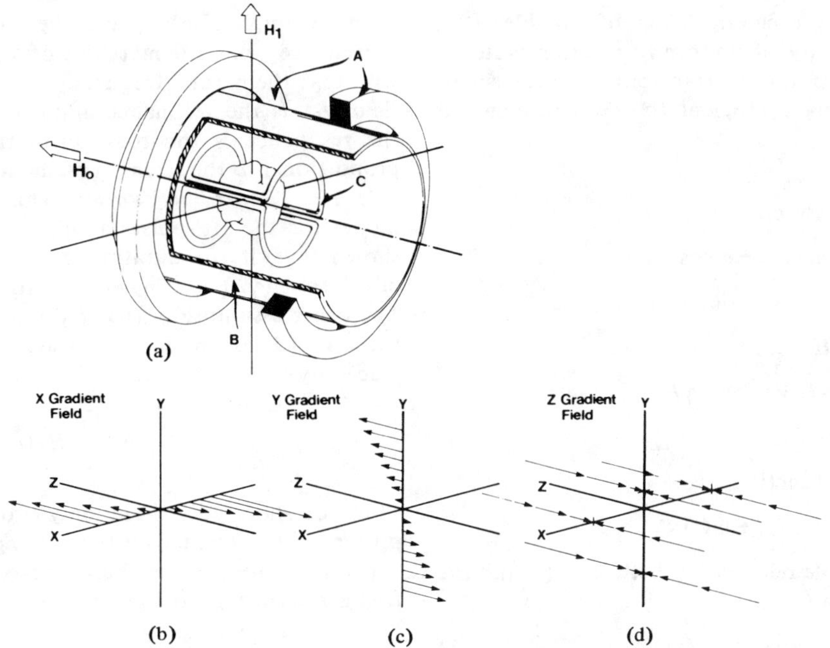

Fig. 5. This shows how the three major coil sets fit together, and indicates the geometry of their fields. The uniform static field H_0 is generated by the magnet A, drawn here as a large coil pair. The gradient field $G(x)$ is generated by a complex gradient coil set. In this drawing, they are shown as wound on the cylinder B. The RF field H_1 is generated by a "saddle coil" C. Part (b) is a representation of the x-gradient field. This field is parallel to H_0 and varies linearly with distance along the x axis but does not vary with distance along y or z. Parts (c) and (d) are similar representations of the y-gradient and z-gradient fields, respectively.

gradient G is applied while the signal is being observed, the frequency of the magnetization oscillations ω' becomes dependent upon x. This spatial dependence is reflected in the behavior of the output signal. The use of this tool, the "readout" gradient, will be introduced in Section V.

2) The Gradient Pulse: Another tool is the "gradient pulse," which consists simply of turning on a gradient for a short interval τ which is chosen to be much shorter than the relaxation times, so that we may consider the gradient constant during the time of the pulse. We drop the T_2 term from (3.2), to find that, after the pulse, we have

$$M(t, x) = M^0(x) \exp\left[i(\omega_0 - \gamma(G \cdot x))\tau\right]. \quad (3.2a)$$

B. The RF Field

In order to "activate" the nuclei so that they emit a signal, energy must be transmitted into the sample. That is what the RF transmitter does. The usual transmitter coil applies to the sample an RF magnetic field $H_1(t)$, where

$$H_1(t) = 2H_1(t) \cos \omega t\, i.$$

Such a field is said to be *linearly polarized*, since it oscillates in a single direction. We have taken this direction as the definition of i. ω is called the *irradiation frequency*; it is also the reference frequency of the RF transmitter and the detection system. A typical value for ω is 1.0×10^8 rad/s.

To discover how the RF field affects the magnetization, we would, in principle, just use the Bloch equation, setting $H = H_0 k + H_1(t)$. But if we do this, we find that the difficulty of the mathematics hides the phenomenon we are trying to examine. Fortunately, the physical insight of the early investigators [2] led them to a useful approximate solution. One writes

$$H_1(t) = H_1(t)\left[\cos \omega t\, i + \sin \omega t\, j\right]$$

$$+ H_1(t)\left[\cos \omega t\, i - \sin \omega t\, j\right].$$

The two expressions in square brackets describe *circularly polarized* fields of opposite polarization. It can be shown that the nuclei will respond to one of the fields, and will be almost unaffected by the other. (It is the sign of γ that determines which of the circularly polarized fields affects the nuclei.) Thus the effective field is

$$H_1(t) = H_1(t)\left[\cos \omega t\, i + \sin \omega t\, j\right].$$

We will look at the effect of this field on the nuclear magnetization using the simplifying assumption that the *modulation function* $H_1(t)$ turns the RF field on and off in a time short compared to both relaxation times. This is a fairly safe assumption for NMR imaging, where the shortest relaxation time observed is on the order of 40 ms and the longest RF pulse is on the order of 2 ms.

The Bloch equation, with the terms containing T_1 and T_2 omitted, is

$$dM/dt = \gamma M \times H.$$

During the RF pulse, the magnetic field is

$$H(t) = H_1(t) \cos \omega t\, i + H_1(t) \sin \omega t\, j + H k.$$

Here we take $H = H_0 + h$, where h is the contribution from the gradients. Thus the Bloch equation becomes

$$dM_x/dt = \gamma M_y H - \gamma M_z H_1(t) \sin \omega t$$

$$dM_y/dt = \gamma M_z H_1(t) \cos \omega t - \gamma M_x H$$

$$dM_z/dt = \gamma M_x H_1(t) \sin \omega t - \gamma M_y H_1(t) \cos \omega t.$$

We solve this equation by a clever change of variables [2], commonly used in the study of uniformly rotating systems. This change of variables is able to transform a linear set of equations with time-varying coefficient to one with constant coefficients.

Let

$$M_x = u \cos \omega t - v \sin \omega t$$

$$M_y = u \sin \omega t + v \cos \omega t. \tag{3.3}$$

Then the differential equation satisfied by u and v is

$$du/dt = (\gamma H + \omega) v$$

$$dv/dt = -(\gamma H + \omega) u + \gamma H_1 M_z$$

$$dM_z/dt = -\gamma H_1 v. \tag{3.4}$$

If we introduce a complex function

$$c(t) = u(t) + iv(t)$$

then (3.3) expresses a simple relationship between $c(t)$ and the transverse magnetization of (2.6)

$$M(t) = \exp(i\omega t) c(t). \tag{3.5}$$

1) The Rotating Frame: The u and v functions have an interesting interpretation. Consider an orthogonal set of unit vectors $i'(t)$ and $j'(t)$ such that

$$i'(t) = i \cos \omega t + j \sin \omega t$$

$$j'(t) = -i \sin \omega t + j \cos \omega t.$$

Using (3.3), one sees that

$$u(t) i' + v(t) j' = M_x i + M_y j.$$

The interpretation of this equation is that the functions $u(t)$ and $v(t)$ are the components of the vector $M_x(t) i + M_y(t) j$ with respect to the rotating axes $(i'(t), j'(t))$. A physicist, of course, would *start* with the rotating frame $(i'(t), j'(t))$ and *derive* the components of the magnetization in the rotating frame. We see now that the constant ω in the coordinate transformation (3.3) can be viewed as the rotation frequency of the rotating frame.

A convenient value to take for ω is ω_0, the Larmor frequency of the static field. Then, using the equality $\omega_0 = -\gamma H_0$, (3.4) becomes

$$du/dt = \gamma h v$$

$$dv/dt = -\gamma h u + \gamma H_1 M_z$$

$$dM_z/dt = -\gamma H_1 v \tag{3.6}$$

where h is the field contribution from the gradients.

If we look at the special case where $h = 0$ and H_1 is constant, the solution of (3.6) becomes transparent. It is

$$u(t) = u(0)$$

$$v(t) = v(0) \cos \omega_1 t - M_z(0) \sin \omega_1 t$$

$$M_z(t) = v(0) \sin \omega_1 t + M_z(0) \cos \omega_1 t \tag{3.7}$$

which says that the magnetization vector, as viewed in the rotating frame, rotates around the i' vector with angular frequency $\omega_1 = -\gamma H_1$. It is clear from this simple example, and true in general, that the Bloch equation is most simply solved and interpreted in the rotating frame.

This example also explains the <u>R</u> of <u>NMR</u>. The <u>R</u> stands for "resonance," and the matching of ω, the irradiation frequency, with ω_0, the natural frequency of precession of protons in the field H_0, is the resonance alluded to. The physical result of the resonance is the rotation of the nuclear spins at a rate proportional to the strength of the RF field.

2) The "Short" RF Pulse: This simple example is a good model for the RF pulses applied in NMR imaging. It can be shown that, if the duration of the RF pulse τ is short compared to $1/(\gamma h)$, setting h to zero is a good approximation. The other assumption, that H_1 is static, serves to simplify the form of (3.7). Without this assumption, $\omega_1 t$ would be replaced by

$$-\gamma \int_0^\tau H_1(t) \, dt.$$

Thus for short pulses, the only property of $H_1(t)$ that is important is its integral over time—the pulse *shape* has no effect.

The RF pulse can be characterized by two parameters. The first is the tip angle α given by

$$\alpha = \gamma \int_0^\tau H_1(t) \, dt$$

where τ is the length of the pulse. Thus α is the angle through which the RF field rotates the magnetization. The pulses most used in NMR imaging are the $90°$, or $\pi/2$ pulse, which rotates the magnetization from alignment with the main field H_0 into the transverse plane, and the $180°$, or π pulse, which inverts the magnetization, rotating it from alignment to antialignment with the main field. If we look at the magnetization just after a $\pi/2$ RF pulse at time τ, (3.7) becomes

$$u(\tau) = u(0)$$

$$v(\tau) = -M_z(0)$$

$$M_z(\tau) = v(0). \tag{3.8}$$

Just after a π pulse, we have

$$u(\tau) = u(0)$$

$$v(\tau) = -v(0)$$

$$M_z(\tau) = -M_z(0). \tag{3.9}$$

The second parameter characterizing the RF pulse is the orientation of the axis about which the magnetization is rotated. In this discussion, we considered only rotations about the i' axis in the rotating frame, but modern NMR transmitters can select any axis of rotation, and, in fact, many pulse sequences utilize more than one axis during the course of the sequence. It can be shown that selecting the axis in the rotating frame is the same as selecting the phase of the RF field in the lab frame.

3) Slice Selection: We would like to give a rough idea of the slice-selection, or tomographic, process. This process causes the magnetization within a selected slice to become activated and generate a signal, while the remainder of the sample remains quiet.

Two tomographic NMR methods have been proposed. One [8] involves applying time-dependent, or oscillating, gradients and using the steady-state-free-precession pulse sequence. It will not be discussed. The second is known as *selective irradia-*

tion or *selective excitation* and involves applying an RF pulse while a gradient is turned on and held steady. This method will be presented with the intention of showing only *how* it works—we will go out of our way to *avoid* the difficult and interesting mathematics associated with this technique.

As before, the RF pulse has the form

$$H(t) = 2H_1(t) \cos \omega t \, i$$

but this time we deal with a "long," or "shaped" pulse, and the variation of $H_1(t)$ with time is of special interest.

The gradient system contributes a field of the form $h(x)k$, where

$$h(x)k = (G \cdot x)k.$$

We shall see how, by choosing the vector G, a slice of any desired orientation may be selected.

Combining the RF field, the gradient field, and the static field

$$H(t, x) = (H_0 + h(x))k + 2H_1(t) \cos \omega t \, i.$$

The initial conditions are $M_x = 0$, $M_y = 0$, $M_z = M_0$. We simplify the analysis by assuming that $\omega = \omega_0$.

To analyze this experiment, we start with (3.6), which is the form the Bloch equation takes in the rotating frame. Such a system is difficult to analyze exactly. It has been the subject of a perturbation analysis by Hoult [9] and a simulation study by Locher [13]. What we shall do here is indicate what happens when a "weak" RF pulse is applied. This is the "small tip-angle approximation" and is reasonably valid as long as the RF field rotates the magnetization by less than about $30°$.

A second simplifying approximation, the dropping of the relaxation terms, was made in deriving (3.6), our starting point. Thus any analysis based on this equation is suspect if it extends into times comparable to the relaxation times. Also, we again approximate the linearly polarized RF field with its "effective" circularly polarized field.

If we are considering times short enough and H_1 weak enough, then M_z deviates little from its starting value M_0. This simplifies (3.6) considerably, to the point of permitting an analytic solution. The simplified equations are

$$du/dt = -\omega_h v$$
$$dv/dt = \omega_h u + \gamma H_1(t) M_0 \qquad (3.10)$$

where we have written ω_h for $-\gamma h(x)$.

We are now going to solve these differential equations using the proper initial conditions, $u = 0$ and $v = 0$. We use the now-familiar trick for converting (3.10) into a single differential equation. Reintroduce the complex function $c(t) = u(t) + iv(t)$. This function then satisfies the equation

$$dc/dt = i\omega_h c + i\gamma H_1(t) M_0$$

which has a simple integrating factor, $\exp(-i\omega_h t)$. Integrating

$$d(c \exp(-i\omega_h t))/dt = i\gamma M_0 \exp(-i\omega_h t) H_1(t).$$

The initial conditions specify the solution as

$$c(t) = i\gamma M_0 \exp(+i\omega_h t) \int_0^t \exp(-i\omega_h s) H_1(s) \, ds.$$

$$(3.11)$$

For ease of discussion, let us take $G_x = 0$, $G_y = 0$, and $G_z = G$, so that $(G \cdot x) = Gz$. When we reach the conclusion of the argument, it will be a simple matter to replace z with $(G \cdot x)/G$ in order to demonstrate slice selection in any orientation. It is important to make explicit the z-dependence of c.

$$c(t, z) = i\gamma M_0 \exp(-i\gamma Gzt) \int_0^t \exp(i\gamma Gzs) H_1(s) \, ds.$$

Also, recall that $H_1(t)$ is supposed to describe a pulse, so it must turn off (i.e., equal zero) at some time τ. Then, for $t > \tau$, $|c(t, z)| = |c(\tau, z)|$. Accordingly, we will attempt to choose $H_1(t)$ so that $c(\tau, z)$ describes a "slice." For concreteness, we will choose the slice around $z = 0$. (Experimentally, it is easy to move the slice to any other z level).

Our problem is now to

1) make $|c(\tau, z)|$ "large" for $|z| \leqslant a$
2) make $|c(\tau, z)|$ "small" for $|z| > a$. $\qquad (3.12)$

The solvability of the problem becomes more plausible if we write

$$|c(\tau, z)| = \gamma M_0 \left| \int_{-\tau/2}^{\tau/2} \exp(i\gamma Gzs) H_1(s + \tau/2) \, ds \right|$$

$$(3.13)$$

because then the right-hand side of (3.13) looks very much like a Fourier transform, and this guides our choice of pulse shape. For example, if we choose a Gaussian pulse shape

$$H_1(s + \tau/2) = \exp(-(sa\gamma G)^2/8)$$

then, providing τ is long enough so that the integrand is negligible at the ends of the region of integration, a table of integrals shows that $|c(\tau, z)|$ is proportional to $\exp(-2z^2/a^2)$. Standard statistics formulas show that this function has 95 percent of its area in the region $|z| \leqslant a$, which makes it adequately "slice-like." For a still sharper pulse, we could apply the theory of prolate spheroidal wave functions developed by Slepian, Pollak, and Landau [19], but such refinements are not necessary here.

Returning briefly to the slice at an arbitrary orientation, we replace z with $(G \cdot x)/G$, where $G^2 = G_x^2 + G_y^2 + G_z^2$. It is easy to verify that

$$|(G \cdot x)| \leqslant Ga$$

does indeed define a slice of thickness $2a$, and it is orthogonal to G.

IV. THE NMR DETECTION SYSTEM

In the previous section, we derived an expression for $M(t, x)$, the nuclear magnetization. It is the function of the NMR detection system, the receiver, to detect $M(t, x)$ and generate an output signal $S(t)$. In this section, we discuss, in terms of an idealized and simplified NMR receiver, how $S(t)$ is obtained. A block diagram of such a receiver is shown in Fig. 6.

A. The Receiver Coil

The receiver coil, which usually surrounds the sample, is an antenna which "picks up" the fluctuating nuclear magnetization of the sample and converts it to a fluctuating output voltage $V(t)$. (For this tutorial paper, we ignore the fine

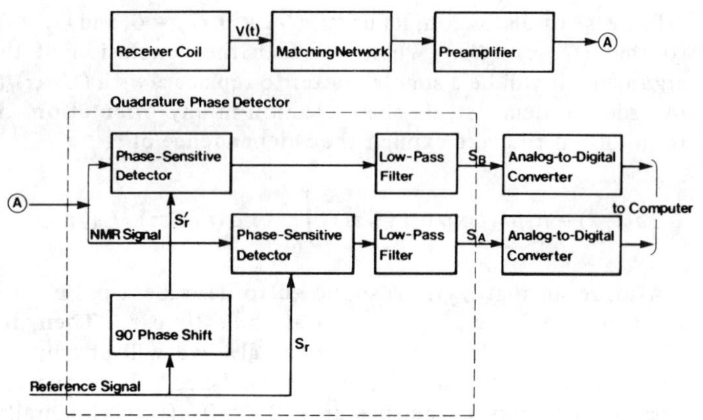

Fig. 6. Simplified block diagram of an NMR receiver system. The blocks are discussed in Section IV.

distinction between voltage and EMF.) Using some basic physics, it can be shown [10] that

$$V(t) = -\frac{d}{dt} \int M(t, x) \cdot B_c(x)\, dx. \tag{4.1}$$

The function $B_c(x)$ describes the sensitivity of the receiver coil at different points in space. More specifically, $B_c(x)$ is the ratio of the magnetic field produced by the receiver coil to the current in the coil. The function $B_c(x)$ can be measured in a given coil, or calculated from the placement of the wires in the coil.

The primary objective of receiver coil design is to prescribe wire placements so that $B_c(x)$ has the largest possible transverse component. The longitudinal component of $B_c(x)$ contributes little to the output voltage, and can be ignored. This is a result of the fact that the time derivative of $M_z(t, x)$ is much less than that of the transverse component. $M_z(t, x)$ decays exponentially with time constant T_1, typically 0.1 to 1 s, while the transverse component is oscillatory with a period of, typically, 0.05 to 0.2 μs.

In order to proceed with the minimum of complicating detail, we will assume a "perfect" receiver coil and take $B_c(x)$ to be

$$B_c(x) = ai + bj \tag{4.2}$$

where a and b are fixed, but unknown, constants. Equation (4.2) describes a coil which has uniform sensitivity over the sample, but whose direction of maximum sensitivity does not coincide with the direction of the applied RF field. Both of these assumptions are physically realistic: a carefully designed coil will not deviate from ideal uniformity by more than a few percent; however, in real coils, the direction of receiver sensitivity can be difficult to control and difficult to measure. But, as will become evident later, this indeterminacy in direction is absorbed into the "phase" of the output signal and causes little difficulty.

It is possible to use two receiver coils, one sensitive in the i direction and the other in the j direction, but a far more complicated receiver is required, and although this design provides a potential increase in signal strength, it does not change the relationship between the sample magnetization and the output signal of the receiver. Hence, we ignore this two-coil design.

With these simplifying assumptions, (4.1) becomes

$$V(t) = -\frac{d}{dt} \int (aM_x(t, x) + bM_y(t, x))\, dx$$

$$= -\frac{d}{dt} \int \mathrm{Re}\,((a - ib) M(t, x))\, dx. \tag{4.3}$$

This can be simplified further by using the special form of $M(t, x)$ appropriate to readout under steady gradients, (3.2). But, rewriting the (complex) transverse magnetization $M^0(x)$ in polar form

$$M^0(x) = A(x) \exp\,(i\theta(x))$$

and, making the replacements

$$a = k \cos \phi' \quad \text{and} \quad b = -k \sin \phi'$$

$$V(t) = -\frac{d}{dt} \int A(x) \exp\,(-t/T_2(x))$$
$$\cdot k \cos\,[\omega'(x)\, t + \theta(x) + \phi']\, dx. \tag{4.4}$$

We see that the receiver coil has modified $M_x(t, x)$ by a multiplicative factor k and by a *phase shift* ϕ'.

From here on, k is an arbitrary (fixed but unknown) constant, the *gain*, which depends upon the design of the receiver. Throughout the following development, we will retain the symbol k regardless of what factors it includes. Once a constant is arbitrary, it is *arbitrary*, and renaming it changes nothing. In practice, the absolute strength of the NMR signal, the numerical value of k, is difficult to obtain and is of little value.

We now simplify (4.4) still further by drawing on our knowledge of physical magnitudes. First, move the derivative inside the integral.

$$V(t) = k\omega_0 \int A(x) \exp\,(-t/T_2(x)) \{(1 + (\omega_h(x)/\omega_0))$$
$$\cdot \sin\,[\ ] + (1/(T_2(x)\,\omega_0)) \cos\,[\ ]\} \, dx.$$

Both the terms $\omega_h(x)/\omega_0$ and $1/(T_2(x)\,\omega_0)$ are on the order of 10^{-3}, so they are negligible compared to 1. Also, let $\phi' = \phi + \pi/2$. Then the working expression for $V(t)$ becomes

$$V(t) = k \int A(x) \exp\,(-t/T_2(x))$$
$$\cdot \cos\,[(\omega_0 + \omega_h(x))\, t + \theta(x) + \phi]\, dx \tag{4.5}$$

where we have absorbed all multiplicative constants into k.

Summarizing, the nuclear magnetization $M(t, x)$ has induced an output voltage $V(t)$ in the receiver coil. We call $V(t)$ the *NMR signal*.

B. The Matching Network

The matching network couples the receiver coil to the preamplifier in order to maximize energy transfer into the amplifier. The only effect the matching network has on the NMR signal is to change the value of k and to introduce an unknown contribution to the phase of the signal. The phase shifts introduced here and in subsequent circuits (as well as simple time delays, which, in the RF stages, are equivalent to phase shifts) are arbitrary in exactly the same way that the gain k is arbitrary. We will incorporate this arbitrary, equipment-generated, phase into ϕ.

C. The Preamplifier

The preamplifier is a low-noise first-stage amplifier. The effect on the signal is simply a change in k and ϕ.

Discussion of noise—the noise from the sample, the noise introduced by the amplifiers, etc.—would be appropriate here. But we move on.

D. The Quadrature Phase Detector

The quadrature phase detector accepts the RF NMR signal, which consists of a distribution of frequencies centered around or near the irradiating frequency ω, and shifts the signal down in frequency by ω. Thus the distribution of frequencies is unchanged except that it is now centered about zero. By reducing the center frequency we reduce significantly the demands on the analog-to-digital converter and the computer.

First, let us look at the operation of a single phase-sensitive detector. This circuit accepts two inputs, the NMR signal and a reference signal, and multiplies them, so that the output is the product of the two inputs. The signal input is $V(t)$, given by (4.5). The reference signal S_r can be taken to be

$$S_r = a \cos{(\omega t)}.$$

By choosing the frequency of the reference signal to be the same as that of the irradiating RF pulse, the receiver system is simplified considerably. Multiplying these two signals involves the product

$$\cos{(\omega t)} \cos{(\omega_0 t + \beta)}$$

which becomes

$$\tfrac{1}{2} \cos{[(\omega + \omega_0) t + \beta]} + \tfrac{1}{2} \cos{[(\omega_0 - \omega) t + \beta]}$$

where $\beta = \omega_h(x) t + \theta(x) + \phi$. But recall that the basic idea of resonance requires that ω and ω_0 are very close in value. Thus the output of the phase-sensitive detector consists of the sum of two components; one, a narrow range of frequencies centered at $2\omega_0$, and the other a narrow range centered at zero. (The output of nonideal detectors also includes a third component centered at ω_0.)

The low-pass filter following the phase-sensitive detector removes all components except those centered at zero. Then the signal $S_A(t)$ after the low-pass filter is

$$S_A(t) = k \int A(x) \exp{(-t/T_2(x))} \cos{[(\omega_0 - \omega) t + \beta]} \, dx.$$

The 90° phase-shift circuit accepts the reference signal $S_r(t)$ and has as output a signal $S_r'(t)$, which, without a great loss of generality, we can take to be

$$S_r'(t) = a \sin{(\omega t)}.$$

Following the same discussion for channel B, we obtain as the output of the low-pass filter

$$S_B(t) = k \int A(x) \exp{(-t/T_2(x))} \sin{[(\omega - \omega_0) t - \beta]} \, dx.$$

If we view the two output signals provided by the receiver as one complex output signal $S(t) = S_A(t) - iS_B(t)$ we have

$$S(t) = k \int A(x) \exp{(-t/T_2(x))}$$

$$\cdot \exp{[+i(\omega_0 - \omega + \omega_h(x)) t + i(\theta(x) + \phi)]} \, dx.$$

We can relate $S(t)$ to the magnetization by going back to (3.2), which gives the general form of the (complex) transverse magnetization under read gradients. This gives us

$$S(t) = K \int M(t, x) \exp{(-i\omega t)} \, dx \tag{4.6}$$

where $K = ke^{i\phi}$ is a complex "arbitrary constant," and

$$M(t, x) = M_x(t, x) + iM_y(t, x).$$

E. The Analog-to-Digital Converters

Since the usual computer is digital and not analog, it is necessary to convert the complex (two-channel) signal to two strings of digital numbers $\{S_n\}$ given by

$$S_n = K \int M(t, x) \exp{(-i\omega \, n\Delta t)} \, dx \tag{4.7}$$

where the sampling interval is Δt. With this equation, we connect the sampled output of the receiver S_n with the nuclear magnetization of the sample $M(t, x)$.

This sampling of the output signal is the chief obstacle to easy transfer between the time domain and the spatial domain. The Fourier integral is no longer available, and the errors of its discrete approximations are well known.

V. The NMR "Imaging Equation"

This section introduces some simple "pulse sequences" and uses the equations introduced earlier to obtain the "imaging equation" for a given pulse sequence; i.e., the expression for the NMR signal in terms of the properties of the sample. The imaging equation is a representation of what the reconstruction algorithm has as an input. The few pulse sequences we will consider in this section are simplified, but show the principal ways of obtaining a set of signals which contain enough information to permit reconstruction of an image. The actual reconstruction will be left as an exercise for the reader. (But should the reader wish to check his results, there are many interesting papers in the literature. See, for example, Shepp [17], Louis [14], Grunbaum [7], Marr et al. [15], and a long report by Cho et al. [4].)

A. 3D Backprojection

The simplest method in terms of collecting data, but perhaps the most complicated in terms of reconstructing the image, is three-dimensional (3D) backprojection. In this method, a single $\pi/2$ RF pulse is applied. After each such pulse, the gradient is turned on and the signal is recorded. This "read sequence" is repeated after the spins have been allowed to recover. But for each new read sequence, the *direction* of the gradient is changed, although the gradient strength is kept the same. This sequence in shown in Fig. 7. After G has pointed throughout one hemisphere, enough data exist to reconstruct the 3D image [14]. The NMR signal as a function of G can be obtained by using the tools of Section III.

Experimental Deviations from Ideality: The pulse sequence

discussed here is considerably simpler than would be practical. In particular, the read gradient cannot be turned on or off instantaneously. Any of several tricks can be used to overcome this particular problem. For example, the spin-echo method (see, e.g., [5]) can be incorporated into the pulse sequence in order to move the signal away from the gradient transient. Alternatively, the gradient can remain on and constant, even during the RF pulse, but this requires that the RF pulse be strong. Finally, the data sampling times can be spaced to compensate for the changing gradient strength.

In order to keep the discussion to a reasonable length, the experimental problems will be ignored in the remainder of this section.

Derivation of the Imaging Equation for 3D Backprojection: If we take the magnetization just before the RF pulse to be $M_0(x)\,k$, then, from (3.8), the magnetization just after the pulse in the rotating frame is $-M_0(x)\,j'$. From (3.3), if we take $t = 0$ to be at the end of the RF pulse, we have that the magnetization in the lab frame at $t = 0$ is

$$M(0, x) = -iM_0(x).$$

Whether the read gradient is turned on at $t = 0$ or at some time later causes the magnetization $M(t, x)$ to differ only in the phase angle, which, we have already agreed, is arbitrary. We assume the gradients are turned on and stable at $t = 0$.

The evolution of the magnetization in the presence of the read gradient is given by (3.2), and the signal obtained from that magnetization is given by (4.6). If we combine these equations we obtain

$$S(t) = -iK \int M_0(x) \exp\left[(i\omega'(x) - i\omega - 1/T_2(x))\,t\right] dx. \tag{5.1}$$

Using (3.1)

$$\omega'(x) = -\gamma G \cdot x + \omega_0$$

and incorporating $-i$ into K, we have

$$S(t) = K \int M_0(x) \exp\left[-(i\gamma G \cdot x + 1/T_2(x))\,t\right] dx. \tag{5.2}$$

We have assumed a detector operating at resonance, so $\omega = \omega_0$.

This is the imaging equation for the 3D backprojection method. The equation gives the signal $S(t)$ for a given gradient G. The constant K is independent of G.

If T_2 is long compared to the time interval $(0, \tau)$ over which we collect data we can neglect the T_2 term. The imaging equation then takes the form

$$S(t) = K \int M_0(x) \exp\left[-i\gamma t G \cdot x\right] dx. \tag{5.3}$$

We recognize the right-hand side of (5.3) as the Fourier transform of $M_0(x)$, sampled at the point $\gamma t G$. We are completely free to vary the vector G in any way that promises to give us sufficient data to approximate the inverse Fourier transform and, hence, $M_0(x)$.

One choice for a collection of pulse sequences is that of Shepp [17], who takes

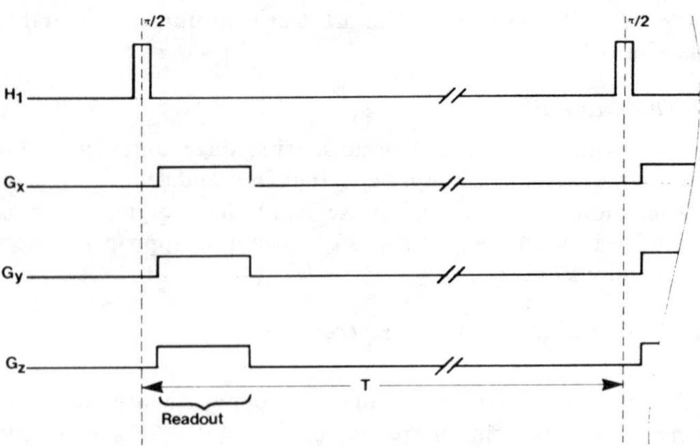

Fig. 7. Simplified timing sequence for the saturation-recovery method, using three-dimensional (3D) backprojection for image reconstruction. The sequence, consisting of an RF pulse followed by a gradient pulse, is repeated at intervals T. For each repetition, the direction of the gradient is changed. Data are collected during the time the gradient is applied.

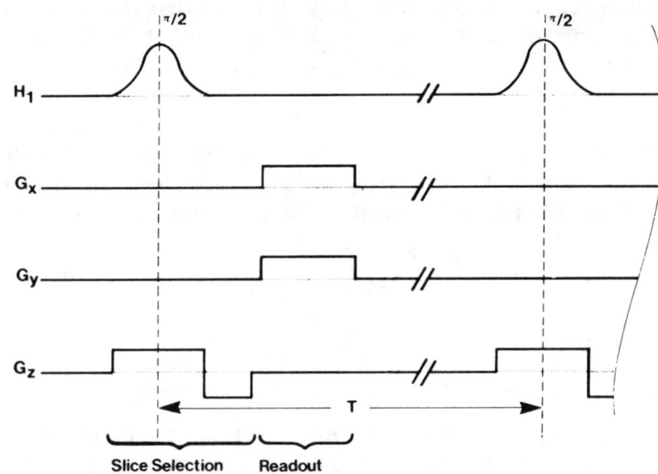

Fig. 8. Sequence for the saturation-recovery method using 2D backprojection for reconstruction. The sequence is the same as that in Fig. 7 with the short RF pulse replaced by the slice-selection RF and gradient pulses.

$$
\begin{aligned}
G_{x(jk)}(t) &= G \cos(\theta_j) \cos(\phi_k), && 0 \leqslant t \leqslant \tau \\
G_{y(jk)}(t) &= G \cos(\theta_j) \sin(\phi_k), && 0 \leqslant t \leqslant \tau \\
G_{z(jk)}(t) &= G \sin(\theta_j), && 0 \leqslant t \leqslant \tau. \\
\theta_j &= (j - \tfrac{1}{2})\,\pi/n, && j = 1, \cdots, n \\
\phi_k &= k2\pi/m, && k = 0, \cdots, m - 1
\end{aligned}
$$

and G is a fixed magnitude.

B. 2D Backprojection

If we modify the previous pulse sequence by using a *selective* $\pi/2$ RF pulse, we have a method for obtaining tomographic two-dimensional (2D) images. The pulse sequence is shown in Fig. 8. The data are collected as with 3D backprojection except that the direction of the gradient G stays in the plane of the selected slice.

As shown in Section III, the selective irradiation method, in a simple world, tips the magnetization within the slice into the x-y plane, leaving the magnetization in the remainder of the sample unaffected. For example, if the slice is normal to the z direction, we are concerned only with the distribution of the magnetization as a function of x and y. Thus the imaging equation is the same as in 3D backprojection except it is written for two dimensions:

$$S(t) = K \iint M_0(x, y)$$

$$\cdot \exp\left[-(i\gamma(G_x x + G_y y)t\right] dx\, dy. \qquad (5.4)$$

In this equation

$$M_0(x, y) = \int R(z) M_0(\boldsymbol{x})\, dz$$

where $R(z)$ is the response function resulting from the slice-selection pulse, and depicts the magnetization as a function of z. Essentially, $R(z)$ describes the shape of the slice carved out by the pulse.

Usually one samples data on a polar grid, using $\{P_k(t)\}$, $k = 0, \cdots, m - 1$, with $H_1(t)$ and $G_z(t)$ independent of k, but taking

$$G_{x(k)}(t) = G\cos(\phi_k) \qquad G_{y(k)}(t) = G\sin(\phi_k), \qquad 0 \leqslant t \leqslant \tau.$$

C. 3D Fourier

This method of collecting and reconstructing the data uses an additional tool, the gradient pulse. An idealized pulse sequence $P(t)$ is diagrammed in Fig. 9. There is a $\pi/2$ RF pulse, followed by a gradient pulse in the y–z plane, followed by a readout pulse with the x-gradient turned on. And then there is a recovery period before the next RF pulse. In the next pulse sequence, the y- and z-gradients are stepped slightly by the proper amount. We will show how this procedure can be used to sample Fourier space on a rectilinear grid.

As for the details, we draw heavily on the analysis leading to (5.2). Assume that the y- and z-gradients are on for a short time τ. Right after the pulse is turned off

$$M(\tau, \boldsymbol{x}) = -iM_0(\boldsymbol{x}) \exp\left[i(\omega_0 - \gamma(G_y y + G_z z)\tau)\right].$$

With the readout x-gradient turned on

$$M(t, \boldsymbol{x}) = M(\tau, \boldsymbol{x}) \exp\left[i(\omega_0 - \gamma G_x x)(t - \tau) - t/T_2(\boldsymbol{x})\right].$$

$$= -iM_0(\boldsymbol{x}) \exp\left[i(\omega_0 - \gamma(G_y y + G_z z)\tau\right)$$

$$- \gamma G_x x(t - \tau) - t/T_2(\boldsymbol{x})].$$

Therefore,

$$S(t) = K \int M_0(\boldsymbol{x}) \exp\left[-t/T_2(\boldsymbol{x})\right.$$

$$\cdot \exp\left(-i\gamma(G_y \tau y + G_z \tau z + G_x(t - \tau)x))\right] d\boldsymbol{x}.$$

If we ignore the T_2 term, $S(t)$ is just the Fourier transform of $M_0(\boldsymbol{x})$ sampled at the point $(\gamma G_x(t - \tau), \gamma G_y \tau, \gamma G_z \tau)$. To reconstruct $M_0(\boldsymbol{x})$, we might use a double-indexed collection of pulse sequences of the form $\{P_{jk}(t)\}$, where $-n \leqslant j \leqslant n$, $-n \leqslant k \leqslant n$. Each of these sequences would have the same $H_1(t)$ and $G_x(t)$, but

$$G_{y(jk)}(t) = j\Delta, \qquad 0 \leqslant t \leqslant \tau$$

$$G_{z(jk)}(t) = k\Delta, \qquad 0 \leqslant t \leqslant \tau.$$

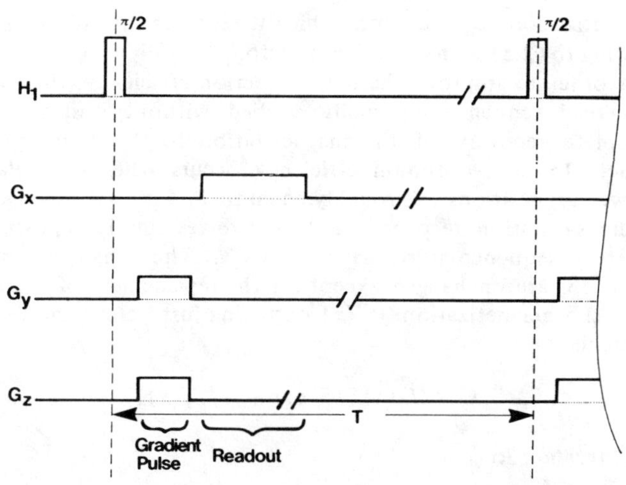

Fig. 9. Sequence for the saturation-recovery method using 3D Fourier transformation for image reconstruction. The direction and amplitude of the gradient pulse during the interval τ is different for each repetition. The data are collected during the time the x-gradient is applied.

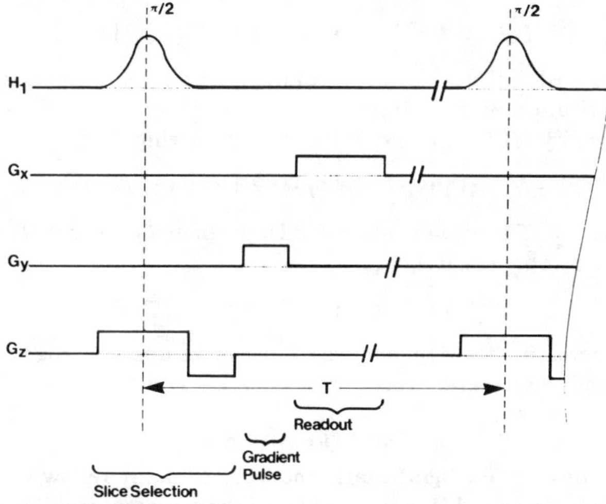

Fig. 10. Sequence for 2D imaging using Fourier transformation for image reconstruction. The amplitude of the y-gradient pulse is different for each repetition. The data are collected during the time the x-gradient is applied.

D. 2D Fourier

There are no surprises. The pulse sequence (Fig. 10) has a selective excitation pulse to delimit a z-slice, a y-gradient pulse, and an x-gradient readout pulse. A collection of pulse sequences $\{P_j(t)\}$, $-n \leqslant j \leqslant n$, is used. For the jth sequence

$$G_{y(j)}(t) = j\Delta, \qquad 0 \leqslant t \leqslant \tau.$$

Again, $S_j(t)$ is the 2D Fourier transform of the slice, sampled at $(\gamma G_x(t - \tau), \gamma j \Delta \tau)$.

E. Saturation Recovery

Saturation recovery is not a method of collecting data and forming an image, as are the four methods discussed earlier. Saturation recovery and, in fact, inversion recovery are methods of controlling the contribution of T_1 to the images and can be used with all of the four imaging methods.

The $\pi/2$ RF pulse in the read sequence sets the longitudinal magnetization to zero, from which it recovers toward M_0 according to (2.5) with M_z^0 taken as zero.

In order to improve the data-collection efficiency, the second read sequence is usually applied without waiting for complete recovery of the magnetization to its equilibrium value. In fact, optimum efficiency occurs when the delay between repetitions T is roughly equal to T_1.

The saturation recovery method involves simply repeating the read sequence at regular intervals T. The earlier imaging equations are unchanged except for the replacement of $M_0(x)$ with the magnetization $M^0(x)$ occurring just before the read sequence

$$M^0(x) = M_0(x) (1 - \exp [-T/T_1(x)]).$$

F. Inversion Recovery

This method is the same as saturation recovery except for the addition of a π, or inversion, RF pulse a time T_I before each read sequence. This has been found to increase the dependence of the image upon T_1.

At time T after the previous $\pi/2$ RF pulse, the sign of M_z is changed by the π RF pulse. Just after this pulse we have

$$M(T, x) = -M_0(x) (1 - \exp [-T/T_1(x)]).$$

Thus just before the next read sequence, the longitudinal magnetization is not $M_0(x)$, but is given by (2.5) with M_z replaced by $M(T, x)$ and t replaced by T_I, giving

$$M^0(x) = M_0(x) [\exp (-T_I/T_1) (-2 + \exp (-T/T_1)) + 1].$$

In practice, T is often made much larger than T_1 so that $M^0(x)$ becomes approximately

$$M^0(x) = M_0(x) (1 - 2 \exp (-T_I/T_1))$$

thus increasing the dependence of the image upon T_1 over that obtained in saturation recovery.

ACKNOWLEDGMENT

The authors are significantly indebted to many fellow workers. D. Kramer and H. Yeung provided the representative images and are responsible for their quality. J. Keller, R. Compton, E. Bomke, and others designed and built the imaging system. The referees, the editor, and other obliging readers of early versions of this paper contributed helpful comments.

REFERENCES

[1] A. Abragam, *The Principles of Nuclear Magnetization*. Oxford, England: Oxford Univ. Press, 1961.

[2] F. Bloch, "Nuclear induction," *Phys. Rev.*, vol. 70, pp. 460–474, 1946.

[3] Bowman Gray School of Medicine, *NMR Imaging* (Proc. Int. Symp. on Nuclear Magnetic Resonance Imaging; Winston-Salem, NC, 1981).

[4] Z. H. Cho et al., "Development of methods and algorithms for Fourier transform nuclear magnetic (NMR) imaging," Imaging System Science Lab., Dep. Elec. Sci., Korea Advanced Institute of Science, Seoul, Korea.

[5] C. T. Farrar and E. D. Becker, *Pulse and Fourier Transform NMR*. New York: Academic Press, 1971.

[6] J. F. Greenleaf, "Computerized tomography with ultrasound," this issue, pp. 330–337.

[7] F. A. Grunbaum, "Reconstruction with arbitrary directions: dimensions two and three," in *Mathematical Aspects of Computerized Tomography*, G. T. Herman and F. Natterer, Eds. Berlin, Germany: Springer, 1981.

[8] W. S. Hinshaw, P. A. Bottomley, and G. N. Holland, "Radiographic thin-section image of the human wrist by nuclear magnetic resonance," *Nature*, vol. 270, pp. 722–723, 1977.

[9] D. I. Hoult, "The solution of the Bloch equations in the presence of a varying B_1 field: an approach to selective pulse analysis," *J. Mag. Res.*, vol. 35, pp. 69–86, 1979.

[10] D. I. Hoult and R. E. Richards, "The signal-to-noise ratio of the nuclear magnetic resonance experiment," *J. Mag. Res.*, vol. 24, pp. 71–85, 1976.

[11] D. M. Kramer, "Imaging of elements other than hydrogen," in *Nuclear Magnetic Resonance Imaging in Medicine*, L. Kaufman, L. E. Crooks, and A. R. Margulis, Eds. Tokyo, Japan: Igaku-Shoin Med. Publ., 1981.

[12] P. C. Lauterbur, "Image formation by induced local interactions: Examples employing nuclear magnetic resonance," *Nature*, vol. 242, pp. 190–191, 1973.

[13] P. R. Locher, "Computer simulation of selective excitation in n.m.r. imaging," *Phil. Trans. Roy. Soc. London*, vol. 289, pp. 537–542, 1980.

[14] A. K. Louis, "Optimal sampling in nuclear magnetic resonance (NMR) tomography," *J. Comput. Assist. Tomog.*, vol. 6, pp. 334–340, 1982.

[15] R. B. Marr, C. Chen, and P. C. Lauterbur, "On two approaches to 3D reconstruction in NMR zeugmatography," in *Math. Aspects of Computerized Tomography*, G. T. Herman and F. Natterer, Eds. Berlin, Germany: Springer, 1981.

[16] I. L. Pykett, "NMR imaging in medicine," *Scient. Amer.*, May 1982.

[17] L. A. Shepp, "Computerized tomography and nuclear magnetic resonance," *J. Comput. Assist. Tomog.*, vol. 4, pp. 94–107, 1980.

[18] J. R. Singer, "Blood flow measurements by NMR," in *Nuclear Magnetic Resonance Imaging in Medicine*, L. Kaufman, L. E. Crooks, and A. R. Margulis, Eds. Tokyo, Japan: Igaku-Shoin Med. Publ., 1981.

[19] D. Slepian, H. O. Pollak, and H. T. Landau, "Prolate spheroidal wave functions, Fourier analysis, and the uncertainty principle, I and II," *Bell Syst. Tech. J.*, vol. 40, pp. 43–84, 1961.

[20] E. H. Wood, J. H. Kinsey, R. A. Robb, B. K. Gilbert, L. D. Harris, and E. L. Ritman, "Applications of high temporal resolution computerized tomography to physiology and medicine," in *Image Reconstruction from Projections: Implementations and Applications*, G. T. Herman, Ed. Berlin, Germany: Springer, 1979.

[21] P. Mansfield and P. G. Morris, *NMR Imaging in Biomedicine*. New York: Academic Press, 1982.

[22] Z. H. Cho, H. S. Kim, H. B. Song, and J. Cumming, "Fourier transform nuclear magnetic resonance tomographic imaging," *Proc. IEEE*, vol. 70, pp. 1152–1173, 1982.

Fourier Transform Nuclear Magnetic Resonance Tomographic Imaging

Z. H. CHO, SENIOR MEMBER, IEEE, H. S. KIM, STUDENT MEMBER, IEEE, H. B. SONG, STUDENT MEMBER, IEEE, AND JAMES CUMMING, MEMBER, IEEE

Invited Paper

Abstract—Nuclear Magnetic Resonance (NMR) tomographic imaging is a newly emerging, noninvasive, three-dimensional (3-D) imaging technique. Although similar to the well known X-ray Computerized Tomography (X-CT), it uses magnetic fields and RF signals to obtain anatomical information about the human body as cross-sectional images in any desired direction, and can easily discriminate between healthy and abnormal tissues.

This new technique is an interdisciplinary science which encompasses the latest technologies in electrical, electronics, computers, physics, chemistry, mathematics, and medical sciences. Principles of this new technique known as "Fourier transform nuclear magnetic resonance imaging" or simply "NMR imaging" are reviewed from the physics and engineering points of view to provide basic concepts and tools, which, hopefully, will be useful for the future development of this exciting new field. Along with the review of the basic principles and methods involved in NMR tomography, computer simulations and modelings are presented to clarify the complexity of the NMR imaging method and provide an insight into the method, especially image-formation aspects and processing, the central theme of NMR tomography. In this paper, four main types of imaging methods—namely, line-scan imaging, direct Fourier-transform (Kumar–Welti–Ernst method) imaging, line-integral projection reconstruction, and plane-integral projection reconstruction, as well as the possibility of relaxation time imaging, are discussed in detail. Methods of improving performance with respect to the statistical aspects of image quality and imaging times are also discussed.

I. INTRODUCTION

NUCLEAR MAGNETIC RESONANCE (NMR) tomography has recently gained great attention in the medical field because of its nonhazardous nature, high-resolution capability, and potential for chemical specific imaging. It compares well with other imaging modalities, e.g., X-ray or positron computerized tomography (CT). At the beginning of the 1970's, both Lauterbur [1] and Damadian [2] showed that NMR spectroscopic techniques can be applied to imaging of the human body and that the techniques have diagnostic uses similar to those of X-CT, but in three-dimensional (3-D) form. In 1978, Andrew *et al.* [3] demonstrated the very-high-resolution capability of NMR by obtaining a fine detailed image of the submillimeter septum of a small orange. More

recently, human head images shown by Moore [4] and Holland *et al.* [5] have definitively demonstrated the great potential of NMR tomography in medical imaging (see Fig. 1).

NMR tomographic images can be formed either by direct mapping or by projection reconstruction. To date, two potentially useful direct-mapping methods, namely, line-scan imaging [6] and direct Fourier imaging [7] have been suggested, along with the line-integral [8] and plane-integral [9] projection reconstructions.

An interesting aspect of NMR imaging is its diversity in image formation, data collection, and reconstruction. Many different imaging and data-processing methods are presently known and will be discussed in this paper relative to various factors such as imaging time, available field gradient, pulse strength and speed, signal-to-noise ratio (SNR), and artifacts associated with the restored-object image. Both the advantages and disadvantages of these various methods will be discussed as well as guidelines which may be useful for future NMR imaging system design and for improvement of currently available NMR imaging methods.

Great advances have been made in the development of instrumentation for whole-body NMR tomography. A magnet, gradient coils, an RF coil, and associated electronics are required to form an NMR tomographic system. A main-field strength of 500 G to 15 kG is expected to be used with field gradients of 0.01 to 1 G/cm, formed by X, Y, and Z gradient coils. With these strengths of magnetic field and gradients, the required RF range is approximately 2 to 70 MHz for proton resonance or density (hydrogen-density or water-content) imaging. Expected resolution in a conventional NMR imaging system depends on the field homogeneity and available strength of field gradients. For example, with a magnet of the static magnetic field of $H_0 = 5$ kG having homogeneity of $\Delta H = 4$ parts per million (ppm) (0.02 G) with field gradient of $G_{x,y,\text{or } z} = 0.4$ G/cm, the expected resolution limit is approximately 0.5 mm.

A typical NMR tomographic imaging system designed for human imaging is shown in Fig. 2(a) and (b). In this figure, a four-part air-core magnet with a bore hole diameter of 60–70 cm is surrounded by four pairs of field gradient coils (x and y), one pair of Helmholtz-type z gradient coils, and an RF coil, respectively. The configuration of magnet and gradient coil structure may differ depending on the design, but the basic concept will be similar to this for the majority of NMR imaging systems in the future. Although the physical arrangement of components and instrumentation is impor-

Manuscript received November 2, 1981; revised June 30, 1982. This work was supported in part by NIH under Grant 1PO1 CA 2881 for the Evaluation of High Field NMR Imaging, and in part under Grant from the Korea Science and Engineering Foundation for the Basic Study of Multidimensional Image Processing.

Z. H. Cho is with the Department of Electrical Science, Korea Advanced Institute of Science, Chongyangni, Seoul, Korea, and with the Department of Radiology, Columbia University, New York, NY.

H. S. Kim, H. B. Song, and J. Cumming are with the Department of Electrical Science, Korea Advanced Institute of Science, Chongyangni, Seoul, Korea.

Reprinted from *Proc. IEEE*, vol. 70, pp. 1152–1173, Oct. 1982.

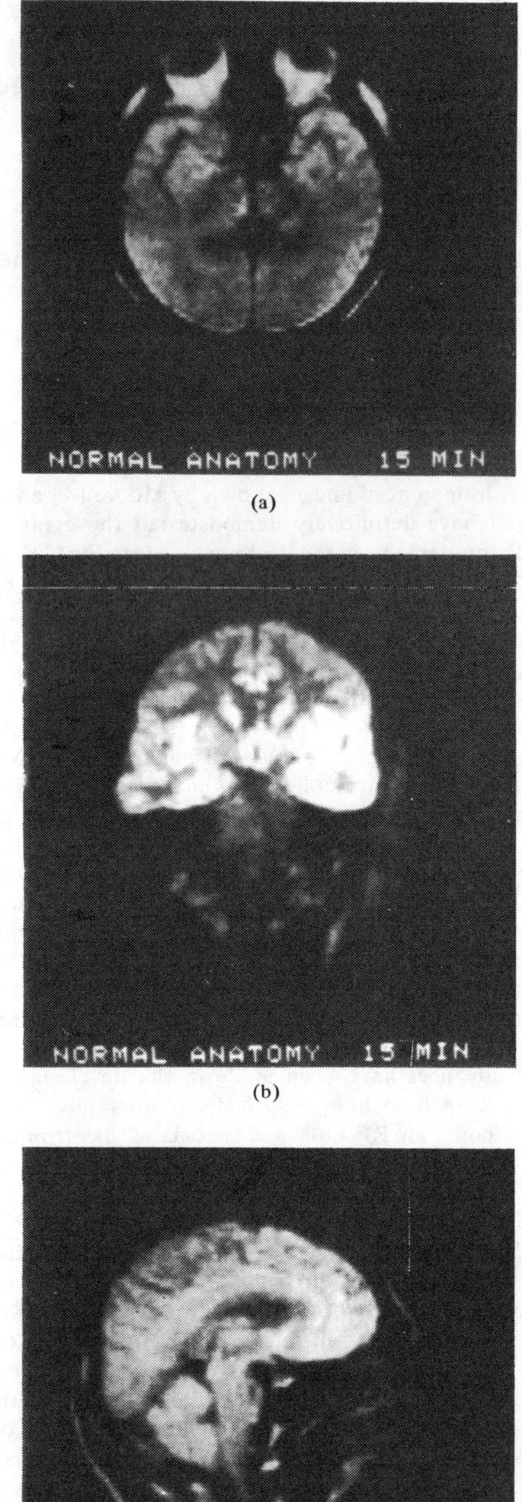

Fig. 1. NMR images of head. (a) Transverse axial view (similar to X-ray CT (X-CT) image). (b) Coronal view. (c) Sagittal view. (Courtesy of Siemens Central Research Laboratory, Erlangen, Germany, 1982).

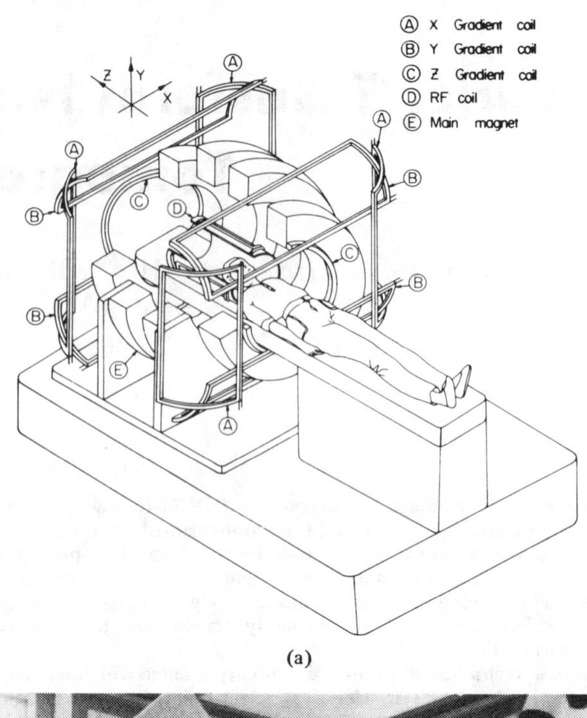

Fig. 2. (a) Sketch of actual NMR tomograph. Locations of gradient and RF coils are shown to illustrate the physical arrangement of an NMR imaging system. (b) An experimental 1-kG magnet for NMR tomography.

tant in NMR tomography, the main emphasis in this paper will be limited to basic imaging principles, modelings, and computer simulations of various potentially useful tomographic methods.

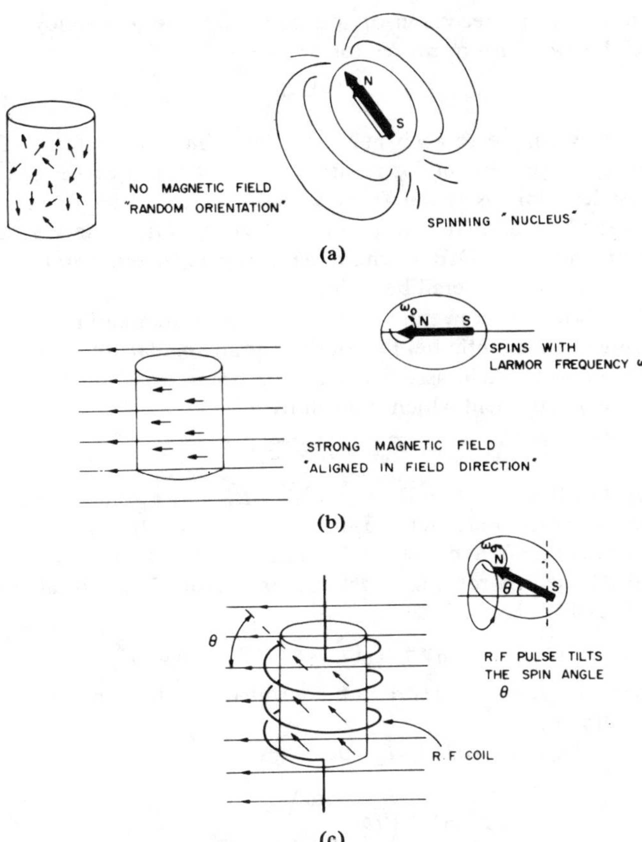

Fig. 3. Behavior of nuclear spins in various situations. (a) Without magnetic field. (b) With strong magnetic field. (c) Additional application of RF pulse with Larmor frequency.

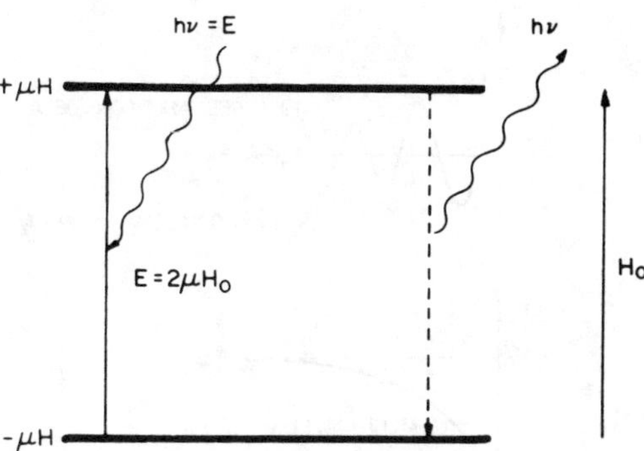

Fig. 4. Quantum mechanical description of NMR spin excitation and eventual emission of nuclear signal. Energy $h\nu$ is supplied by RF pulse through RF coil.

II. Principles of Image Formation in NMR Tomography [10]

A. Principles of NMR

NMR was discovered more than thirty years ago [11] and has become an indispensable analytical method and tool in chemistry and physics. Although the basic physics of NMR is well founded and discussions can easily be found elsewhere, we will describe a few topics necessary to the understanding of NMR as an imaging tool.

All materials, whether living or nonliving, contain nuclei that are either protons or neutrons or a combination of both [12]. Nuclei containing an odd number of protons or neutrons, or both in combination, possess a nuclear "spin" and a "magnetic moment." This situation is equivalent to an aggregation of many small magnets (see Fig. 3). In the real world, many materials are composed of several nuclei, and the most common nuclei are ^{1}H, ^{2}H, ^{7}Li, ^{13}C, ^{31}P, and ^{27}I. Although materials may be composed of nuclei with an even number of protons and neutrons which possess no spin or magnetic moment, they usually contain some nuclei with an odd number of protons or neutrons as well. Therefore, NMR is practically applicable to most solid- and liquid-phase materials. Among the 250 known stable nuclei, more than 100 nuclei have spin magnetic moment, and, in addition, another 800 radioisotope nuclei can also be targets of NMR.

When a material is placed in a magnetic field, some of the randomly oriented nuclei experience external magnetic torque which tends to align the nuclei parallel to the direction of applied magnetic field. The fraction of magnetized nuclei is limited by thermal agitation, and this small probability of magnetization at room temperature has been a difficulty in NMR imaging. The spinning nucleus responds to the external magnetic field like a gyroscope precessing around the direction of the field. The rotating or precession frequency of the spins is usually called the Larmor precession frequency $\vec{\omega}_0$ [12], [13]. Three distinct nuclear-spin states associated with surrounding magnetic field situations are illustrated in Fig. 3.

Another important phenomenon of NMR is that the applied external magnetic field creates an energy "absorption state," from a statistical point of view. The proton has intrinsic angular momentum or spin of $\hbar/2$, where $\hbar$ is Planck's constant divided by 2π. When proton nuclei are placed in a magnetic field, the nuclei will be in two energy states [12], [13], namely, $+\mu H$ and $-\mu H$ states (Zeeman splitting), where μ and H are the nuclear magnetic moment and applied magnetic field, respectively (see Fig. 4). For those nuclei or protons in $-\mu H$ energy state, irradiation of electromagnetic radiation of energy E equivalent to $2\mu H$ will raise the proton energy state up to $+\mu H$. This energy is usually supplied by an RF magnetic field H_1. In NMR, at room temperature, more protons are in a low-energy state than a high-energy state following the Boltzmann distribution. The excited proton tends to return or relax to its low-energy state which produces a "free induction decay" (FID) signal that is the fundamental form of the nuclear signal obtainable from an NMR system.

Two relaxation mechanisms are associated with excited nuclear spins, transverse or spin–spin relaxation, and longitudinal or spin–lattice relaxation. Transverse relaxation is faster than longitudinal relaxation so that the spin–spin relaxation time constant T_2 is always smaller than the spin–lattice relaxation time constant T_1. It is interesting to note that both these relaxation times (T_1 and T_2) are sensitive to the molecular structures and environments surrounding the nuclei. For instance, the mean T_1 values of normal and many malignant tissues vary substantially, allowing us to differentiate malignant tissues from normal tissue in many cases (see Fig. 5(c)). A similar tendency is observed for T_2 values. Imaging capabilities of these two important parameters, T_1 and T_2, together with the spin densities of the objects thus make NMR imaging a unique, versatile, and powerful technique in medical imaging. Let us now review the few fundamental processes involved in NMR tomographic imaging in a little more detail.

For convenience, a coordinate system is chosen as in Fig. 6, where the magnetic field vector $\vec{H}$ is taken in the z-axis direction. When the net magnetization vector $\vec{M}$ is at an angle θ to $\vec{H}$, the net energy of the system is [12], [13]

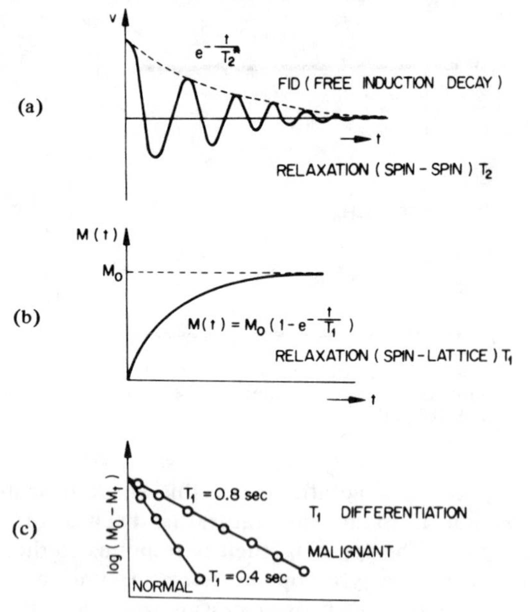

Fig. 5. Spin-relaxation mechanisms. (a) FID signals obtained show decaying modulated signal. The decay-time constant is T_2^*, the effective spin–spin relaxation time. (b) Spins also decay by dissipating energy to the surroundings. This energy-dissipation mechanism is usually slow and decays with spin–lattice relaxation time constant T_1. (c) These relaxation mechanisms are sensitive to the molecular structure and environment and are expected to be used for discriminating malignant and normal tissues in NMR tomograph.

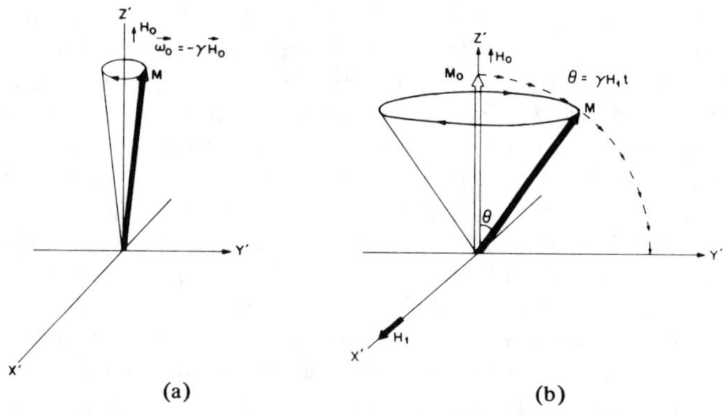

Fig. 6. Spin orientations with and without RF pulse. (a) Spin in the absence of RF pulse. (b) Spin with an application of suitable size of RF pulse. Usually RF pulse which could tilt the spins to 90° is used for the selection of a line or a slice (or slices) in NMR tomography.

$$E = -\vec{M} \cdot \vec{H} = -MH \cos \theta \tag{1}$$

and the equilibrium magnitude of the net magnetization is

$$M = N(-\gamma h)^2 H \cdot I(I + 1)/3KT_0 \tag{2}$$

where N is the number of spins, γ is the gyromagnetic ratio, I is the spin quantum number, K is Boltzmann's constant, and T_0 is the object temperature. The signal strength which is proportional to M may be increased by increasing the field strength H. Lowering T_0, which is usually not possible in medical applications, would also improve the equilibrium magnetization.

Spin precession can be observed by solving the differential equation of motion given by

$$\frac{d\vec{M}}{dt} = \gamma \vec{M} \times \vec{H}. \tag{3}$$

The resulting precession of spin as shown in Fig. 6 follows the well-known Larmor-precession frequency

$$\vec{\omega}_0 = -\gamma \vec{H} \tag{4}$$

which is unique to each nuclide. The minus sign indicates the clockwise precession for positive γ. The Larmor precession of a nuclear spin is taken from a classical mechanics viewpoint rather than a quantum theoretical viewpoint. The classical descriptions of NMR phenomena, however, often give a good insight into the overall behavior.

In NMR, it is convenient to use a rotating frame of reference, where the magnetic field is rotating at an angular frequency $\vec{\omega}$. The magnetic field associated in this frame is called the effective magnetic field which is given by

$$\vec{H}_{eff} = \vec{H} + \vec{\omega}/\gamma. \tag{5}$$

In the absence of an RF signal, $\vec{H} = \vec{H}_0$. At resonance, therefore, the fictitious field $\vec{\omega}/\gamma$ exactly cancels $\vec{H}$, and $\vec{H}_{eff}$ becomes zero. When the static magnetic field is in z direction and RF field is rotating clockwise in x–y plane, the total magnetic field $\vec{H}$ is

$$\vec{H} = H_0\hat{z} + H_1(\hat{x} \cos \omega t + \hat{y} \sin \omega t) \tag{6}$$

where $\hat{x}$, $\hat{y}$, and $\hat{z}$ represent coordinate vectors in Cartesian coordinates.

Inserting (6) into (5), $\vec{H}_{eff}$ becomes

$$\vec{H}_{eff} = \left(H_0 - \frac{\omega}{\gamma}\right)\hat{z}' + H_1\hat{x}' \tag{7}$$

where $\hat{x}'$ and $\hat{z}'$ are the coordinate vectors in the rotated coordinate. At resonance, once again $\vec{H}_{eff} = H_1\hat{x}'$. In this case, in a rotating frame, the only magnetic field is in the x' direction, and M precesses about x' axis or $\vec{H}_{eff}$ with frequency γH_1. The classical flipping angle or precession angle θ is given by

$$\theta = \gamma H_1 t_p \tag{8}$$

where t_p is the RF pulse duration. Application of an RF pulse which tips the magnetization $\vec{M}$ into the x–y plane results in excitation of the spin system (see Fig. 6). When H_1 is applied along the x' axis for a pulse period of t_p, the spin rotates or flips through an angle θ from the z axis toward the y axis. In general, θ is set to $\pi/2$ or π depending on the mode of excitation and type of NMR experiments. For the simplest case, $\theta = \pi/2$ is used to observe the maximum transverse component of magnetization.

After H_1 is turned off, the rotating magnetization induces a current into the pickup coil surrounding the object. The magnetization then relaxes, through neighboring spins and environment, to its thermal equilibrium so that the spins realign to the original H_0 field direction. On the other hand, the transverse component of magnetization which is related to the entropy of the system decays by a dephasing effect of spin–spin interaction.

In addition to the inherent spin–spin relaxation, there are other dephasing effects due to the magnetic-field inhomogeneity and field gradients which are deliberately added in NMR imaging to resolve the spatial distribution of spin density. In fact, they produce shifts in the Larmor frequencies throughout the sample, which results in a phase incoherency that eventually makes the composite sinusoidal signal decay faster than the inherent transverse relaxation time T_2. The effective transverse relaxation time resulting from field inhomogeneity

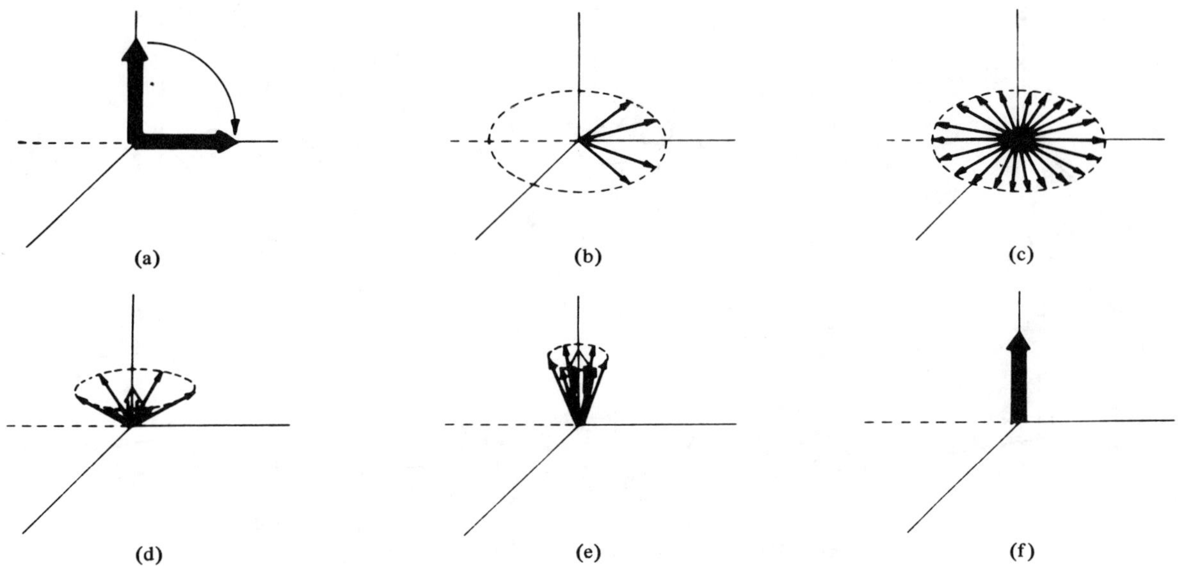

Fig. 7. Sequential illustrations of the spin-relaxation processes.

alone is given by [13]

$$\frac{1}{T_2^*} = \frac{1}{T_2} + \gamma \Delta H / 2 \tag{9}$$

where ΔH is the field inhomogeneity. When a field gradient is added to resolve the spatial distribution of spin density, T_2^* is further reduced and (9) becomes

$$\frac{1}{T_2^{**}} = \frac{1}{T_2^*} + \gamma G R \tag{9'}$$

where G (Gausses per centimeter) is a gradient and R (centimeters) is the object radius. The composite sinusoidal signal decaying with an effective transverse relaxation time T_2^{**} is known as FID, which is usually detected with a phase-sensitive detector, and results are similar to a decaying demodulated AM signal, as shown in Fig. 5(a).

Concurrently, longitudinal or spin-lattice relaxation forces the spins to realign in the H_0 (or z) direction since it is the lowest energy state or thermal-equilibrium state. Since it involves energy dissipation through the lattice, the longitudinal relaxation time T_1 is usually larger than T_2 and related to the z component of magnetization as (see Fig. 5(b))

$$M_z = M_0 (1 - (1 - M_z'/M_0) e^{-t/T_1}) \tag{10}$$

where M_z' is the z component of magnetization at the starting time of relaxation.

The two processes work simultaneously and vary greatly depending on the characteristics of the material. In the case of tissue, for instance, T_1 and T_2 are in the order of 0.5 s and 50 ms, respectively. T_1 cannot be smaller than T_2, since if all the spins are aligned in the z direction, there is no transverse component. In Fig. 7, sequential pictures of the relaxation processes are shown. In general, T_1, T_2, T_2^*, and T_2^{**} have the following relation:

$$T_2^{**} \leqslant T_2^* \leqslant T_2 \leqslant T_1. \tag{11}$$

When the two relaxation mechanisms are considered, the Bloch equation can be written as [12], [13]

$$\frac{dM_z}{dt} = \gamma (\vec{M} \times \vec{H})_z - \frac{M_z - M_0}{T_1}$$

$$\frac{dM_{xy}}{dt} = \gamma (\vec{M} \times \vec{H})_{xy} - \frac{M_{xy}}{T_2}. \tag{12}$$

Equation (12) indicates that the magnetization components M_z and M_{xy} are separately related to the relaxation times T_1 and T_2.

Spin echo techniques of several forms play a central and essential role in reducing data-acquisition time for NMR imaging for medical applications. There are two basic forms of the spin-echo technique applicable to NMR imaging, namely, the Hahn spin-echo technique and the Carr–Purcell Meiboom–Gill (CPMG) technique [12], [13]. The principle of the Hahn spin-echo technique is as follows (see Fig. 8): First, a 90° RF pulse with suitable pulse length is applied which flips the magnetization vector $\vec{M}$ to the y' axis. The spin magnetizations then dephase in time due to field inhomogeneity or added field gradients. Then a 180° pulse applied along the x' axis rotates the spins about the x' axis as shown in Fig. 8(c). The spin magnetizations now continue precessing but start rephasing. This process is equivalent to a regrowth of the FID signal at twice the dephasing time. At this instant, all the spins are completely rephased along the $-y'$ axis.

Instead of adding a 180° pulse along the x' axis, the CPMG method adds a 180° pulse along the y' axis which results in spin flips as shown in Fig. 8(h). Both these techniques are actively used in all the phases of NMR imaging to reduce the data-collection time, which is limited by T_1, as well as for the enhancement of the S/N ratio by signal averaging.

B. Theory of Fourier Transform NMR Tomographic Imaging and Effects of Spin Relaxation and Noise on the Images

In chemical applications, NMR requires a magnetic field as uniform as possible to reduce the averaging effect of many spatially dependent NMR spectra. In Fourier NMR imaging, however, a field gradient is deliberately added which makes the spatial distribution into Fourier-domain components. The basic form of 3-D Fourier transform NMR may be expressed as

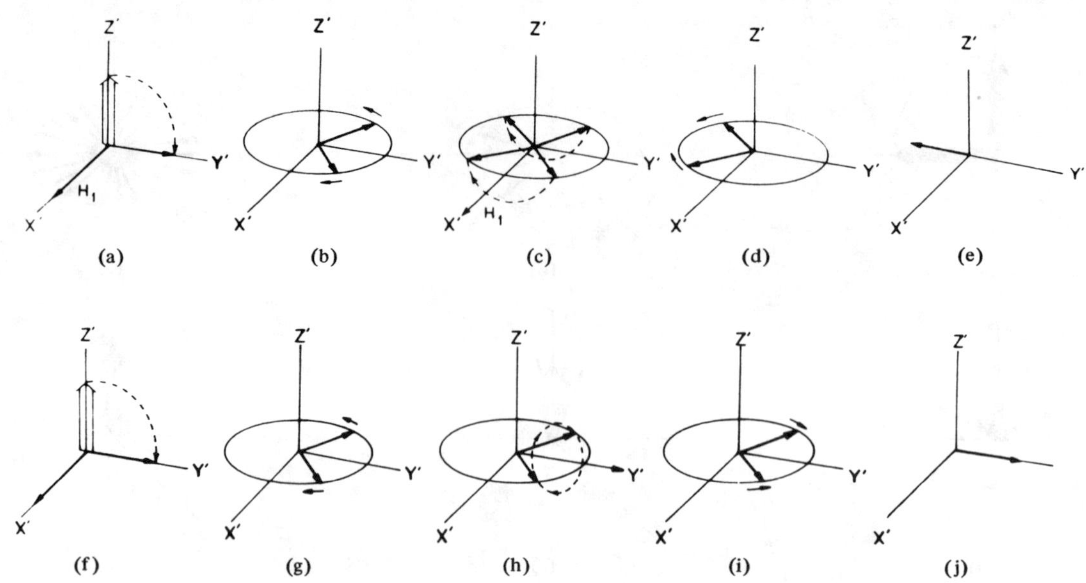

Fig. 8. Hahn spin echo. (a) The spins are rotated 90° by RF pulse. (b) Spin magnetizations dephase. (c) 180° pulse is applied along x' axis. (d) The spins are being refocused. (e) Spin echo is generated along −y' axis. Carr–Purcell and Meiboom–Gill (CPMG) spin echo. (f) The spins are rotated 90° by RF pulse. (g) Spins are dephased. (h) 180° pulse is applied along y' axis. (i) The spins are being refocused. (j) Spin echo is generated along y' axis.

$$s(t) = M_0 \iiint \rho(x, y, z) \exp\left[i\gamma \int_0^t \{x G_x(t')\right.$$

$$\left. + y G_y(t') + z G_z(t')\} \, dt'\right] dx \, dy \, dz \quad (13)$$

where $\rho(x, y, z)$ is 3-D spin density distribution and $G_x(t)$, $G_y(t)$, and $G_z(t)$ are the time-dependent field gradients along x, y, and z axes, respectively. The generated FID, $s(t)$, is, in effect, a Fourier-domain representation of the spin-density distribution. According to the well-known projection reconstruction technique [14]–[17] in X-CT, $s(t)$ is equivalent to $F(\rho, \theta)$ which is a Fourier transform of projection data or profile, i.e.,

$$s(t) \triangleq F(\rho, \theta). \quad (14)$$

The reconstructed image then can be represented as

$$f(r, \phi)_{\phi=\theta} = \frac{1}{4\pi^2} \mathcal{B}\{\mathcal{F}[F(\rho, \theta) \cdot |\rho|]\} \quad (15)$$

where $\mathcal{B}$ and $\mathcal{F}$ are the back projection and Fourier transform operator, respectively. In two-dimensional (2-D) NMR image reconstruction, line-integral projection data and FID are simply a Fourier transform pair, i.e.,

$$P(\omega_{x'}, \theta) \rightleftarrows \mathcal{F}[s(t); t \rightarrow \omega_{x'}]. \quad (16)$$

In rotated coordinates, (13) becomes

$$s(t) = M_0 \iint \rho(x', y') \exp\left[i\gamma x' G_{x'} t\right] dx' \, dy'. \quad (17)$$

Note that although $P(\omega_{x'}, \theta)$ is a function of $\omega_{x'}$ in NMR imaging, it represents the spatial-domain projection data with which the image can be reconstructed, e.g., by the well-known convolution–back-projection algorithm. Equations (16) and (17) are based on the assumption that a 2-D plane was selected.

If a line is selected by some means, as will be discussed later, application of a field gradient along the line will result in line scanning or mapping of spin density along the line [18]–[21]. Similarly, the entire volume of an object can be excited at a multiple of views, and the volume image can be reconstructed by the obtained data which represent plane integrals [9], [22], [24]–[26].

More than a dozen different NMR tomographic methods based on the above basic forms have appeared recently, each of which has advantages and disadvantages. NMR imaging can be divided into two broad groups; namely, nonreconstructive mapping and projection reconstruction, as shown in Table I. In the following sections, two other important subjects in NMR imaging, spin relaxation and noise, will be discussed in close relation to the image formation and data collection.

1) Spin-Relaxation Effects in NMR Imaging: Both spin–spin and spin–lattice relaxation times play an important role in NMR imaging, as we have seen from the previous discussions on T_1 variations in normal versus malignant tissue. In fact, both spin–spin and spin–lattice relaxation terms affect the FID signal. In conjunction with the line-integral projection discussed in the previous section, the FID appears as

$$s(t) = M_0 \int_x P_l(x) \exp\left(i\gamma x G_x t\right) \exp\left[-\left(\frac{1}{T_2^*}\right)t\right] f(T_1) \, dx$$

$$(18)$$

where $P_l(x)$ is a line integral of spin density along ω_x or x and $f(T_1)$ is the T_1-dependent decay term. Here note that $\omega_x = \gamma x G_x$. When $T_1 \gg T_2^*$, then the FID signal in (18) becomes

$$s(t) = M_0 \int_x P_l(x) \exp\left(i\gamma x G_x t\right) \exp\left[-\left(\frac{1}{T_2^*}\right)t\right] dx \quad (19)$$

where x is used instead of ω_x to show that the projection data $P_l(x)$ are explicit functions of x. Short effective transverse

TABLE I

Point Mapping	Non-reconstructive Imaging		Projection Reconstruction		Hybrid
	Line Scan Imaging (III-A-a)	Direct Fourier Transform (DFR) (III-A-b)	Line-Integral (LPR) (III-B-a)	Plane-Integral (PPR) (III-B-b)	
	Single Line (III-A-a-i)	2-D or 3-D KWE Method (III-A-b-i)	Single Slice (III-B-a-i)	Total Volume (III-B-b-i)	
	Full Line (Encoding) (III-A-a-iii)	Improved 2-D, 3-D KWE Method (III-A-b-ii)	Multislice (Encoding) (III-B-a-ii)	Total Volume with Spin Echo (II-B-b-ii)	
	Simultaneous Multislice (Encoding) (III-A-a-iv)	2-D KWE and Hutchison Method (III-A-b-ii)			
Multi-Points (Hinshaw et al)		Echo-Planar Method (Mansfield and Pykett)			Indirect Reconstruction (Lauterbur et al)

relaxation time T_2^* influences the line spread of the original projection data. The projection data can then be recovered by Fourier transform and the recovered data represent the line integral of spin density $P_l(x)$, broadened by a line-spread function which depends on the effective transverse relaxation time T_2^*. The Fourier transform of (19) which is the recovered projection data $P_r(x)$ is given by

$$P_r(x) = \int P_l(x') \frac{\dfrac{M_0}{T_2^*}}{(\gamma G_{x'} x' - \omega_x)^2 + \left(\dfrac{1}{T_2^*}\right)^2} \, dx'$$

$$= P_l(x) * \frac{\dfrac{M_0}{T_2^*}}{(\gamma G_x x)^2 + \left(\dfrac{1}{T_2^*}\right)^2} \tag{20}$$

where * denotes convolution operation. The broadening by transverse relaxation determines the ultimate resolution capability in NMR imaging.

2) Noise Consideration [12]: Noise in NMR is dependent on several factors such as the characteristics of the RF signal pickup coils and amplifier system, and the bandwidth of the nuclear signal. Signal strength can be improved by increasing the Larmor-precession frequency or lowering the object temperature T_0, or both, since the spin magnetization M_0 is related to f_0 and T_0 by

$$M_0 = N \gamma h^2 f_0 I(I + 1)/3KT_0 \tag{21}$$

where N is the number of spins. Following the application of

a 90° RF pulse, the magnetization precesses and decays or dephases with a time constant T_2^{**}. The magnetic flux through the receiver coil generated by this precession is given by

$$\Phi = \int_0^A M_0 \exp\left(-(t/T_2^{**}) - i2\pi f_0 t\right) da$$

$$= \xi M_0 \exp\left(-(t/T_2^{**}) - i2\pi f_0 t\right) A \tag{22}$$

where ξ is the coil filling factor and A is the coil cross section, respectively. It can be shown that in a practical system, the voltage generated in the coil by the magnetic flux can be written as [12]

$$s(t) = n\rho\xi QM_0 f_0 A \exp\left(-(t/T_2^{**}) - i2\pi f_0 t\right) \tag{23}$$

where n is the number of turns of coil, ρ is the ratio of coil inductance to the inductance of the system, and Q is the quality factor. The peak FID signal at $t = 0$ is given by

$$s_0 = n\rho\xi QM_0 f_0 A. \tag{24}$$

On the other hand, the noise signal generated in the signal pickup coil or detector is given by [12]

$$s_n = [8\pi KT_d f_0 L\rho Q(\Delta f)]^{1/2} \tag{25}$$

where L is the inductance of the detector coil, Δf is the bandwidth, and T_d is the detector or coil temperature. From (24) and (25), the SNR at a given temperature can be shown as

$$S/N \propto \frac{M_0 f_0^2}{f_0^{1/2}}$$

$$= M_0 f_0^{3/2}. \tag{26}$$

It should be noted that the S/N is sometimes given as proportional to $f_0^{7/4}$ in literature [27]. It is obvious that the S/N improves with higher magnetic field and larger spin magnetization M_0, which is inversely proportional to the object temperature. There are a few other factors which affect the S/N ratio as can be seen from (24) and (25). Noise factors employed in simulations were based on (24) and (25), and parameters were chosen as follows:

object size	$20 \times 20 \times 20$ cm^3
magnetic field H_0	5 kG
temperature T_0, T_d	300 K
cross section of coil A	60×60 cm^2
number of turns n	10
inductance ratio ρ	1
quality factor Q	100
coil filling factor ξ	$\frac{1}{9}$
bandwidth Δf	$\gamma \times G \times 20$ (cm).

C. Applications of the Spin-Echo Techniques in NMR Imaging [10]

Spin-echo techniques have a unique position in NMR applications. The Hahn spin-echo technique and the CPMG technique give accurate measurement of T_1 and T_2, and these techniques also provide signal averaging as well. As discussed earlier, the spin-echo technique can also be used for the selection of a line or lines to be mapped in the line-scanning method.

However, the most important application of spin echo in NMR imaging is to speed up data-collection times and also allow more efficient data collection from averaging. One of the serious drawbacks found in NMR imaging is the long data-collection time, mainly due to the spin–lattice relaxation time T_1. Each measurement necessitates a time period of the order of T_1, that is, about 0.5 s, for the system to relax, or return to equilibrium magnetization. For a slice-by-slice projection reconstruction, the minimum time for data collection is in the range of 50 s, which is somewhat larger than X-CT imaging time. For total volume imaging with plane-integral reconstruction, for example, a minimum data-collection time in the order of 5000 s will be needed if total angular views of 100×100 are to be collected. This unreasonably long minimum data-collection time, however, can be improved by the use of a multiple spin-echo repetition technique (as, for example, in line-integral projection reconstruction which will be discussed in detail in a later section—see Fig. 21).

In general, the time required in total volume imaging t is $T_1 \times N_\phi \times N_\theta$ where N_ϕ and N_θ are the numbers of views at ϕ and θ in spherical coordinates. Similarly, in the simple slice imaging, imaging time of $T_1 \times N_\phi \times N_s$ will be required for N_s slices.[1] Hence, in total volume imaging, FID's of $N_\phi \times N_\theta$ angular views must be obtained before image reconstruction starts. The absolutely necessary minimum time is, therefore, constrained by the above relations.

By use of spin-echo repetition in total volume imaging, a large number of spin echoes can be repeated within a T_1 or T_2 decay period, provided that T_2^{**} is much smaller than T_1 or T_2. In this way, the total data-collection time can be reduced to

$$t = \frac{T_1 \times N_\phi \times N_\theta}{N_{SE}} \qquad (27)$$

<hr>

[1]Generally, the minimum data-collection times required for whole volume imaging are about the same for all the imaging methods.

where N_{SE} is the number of spin echoes. For example, the measurement time of total volume data collection can be reduced from 5000 to 166 s if 30 spin echoes can be repeated within a T_1 period. This is an important indication that total volume NMR imaging is in the realm of realization if spin echoes are properly utilized. The number of spin echoes that can be obtained depends on the SNR and field gradient strength. A recent technique using a similar concept introduced by Mansfield and Pykett known as the Echo–Planar method may be useful for very fast imaging [60]. In this scheme, even a moving heart image is envisaged, provided there is a good SNR.

III. IMAGING METHODS AND TECHNIQUES IN NMR TOMOGRAPHY

A. Nonreconstructive Image Mapping Techniques in NMR Tomography

1) Line-Scan Imaging:

a) Basic principles of line-scan imaging: Line-scan imaging using spin-echo technique was first proposed by Maudsley [18], and the simplest form of line-scanning method is illustrated in Fig. 9. A plane is first selected, then a line is determined by the selection of an orthogonal plane, and finally points are mapped along the line by the application of RF pulses and field gradients as illustrated in Fig. 10. More specifically, a field gradient G_z and a $90°$ RF pulse select an x-y plane at z_0 of width Δz [28]. If a field gradient G_y is applied, then an FID of line integrals will appear. At time t', however, if a $180°$ RF pulse with a narrow bandwidth is applied, an x-z plane which is perpendicular to the x-y plane will select a line in the x direction that is the intersection of the two planes. Physically, the applied $180°$ RF pulse with a narrow band produces spin echoes or rephasing of the spins along the selected line. This is illustrated in Fig. 8(f)–(j), for the CPMG spin-echo technique [13]. At time $2t'$, spins along the line are rephased, and application of G_x will produce an FID which corresponds to the pixel (or voxels) spin densities along the line.

In this manner, any desired line can be selected and resolved. Variation of this basic line-scanning method using spin-echo technique leads to several interesting modified line-scanning methods.

An FID signal, which represents the spin density along a selected line is given by

$$s(t, y_0, z_0) = M_0 \exp\left(-\frac{t_y}{T_2}\right) \int_x \rho(x, y_0, z_0)$$

$$\cdot \exp(i\gamma x G_x t) \exp\left(-\frac{t}{T_2^*}\right) dx. \qquad (28)$$

A Fourier transform of the FID (28) gives the spin density profile along the x direction, i.e.,

$$S(\omega_x, y_0, z_0) = \int_{-\infty}^{\infty} s(t, y_0, z_0) \exp(-i\omega_x t)\, dt$$

$$= \exp\left(-\frac{t_y}{T_2}\right) \int_{-\infty}^{\infty} \rho(x, y_0, z_0)$$

$$\cdot G(\gamma x G_x - \omega_x)\, dx \qquad (29)$$

where $G(\omega_x)$ is the line-spread function and is given by

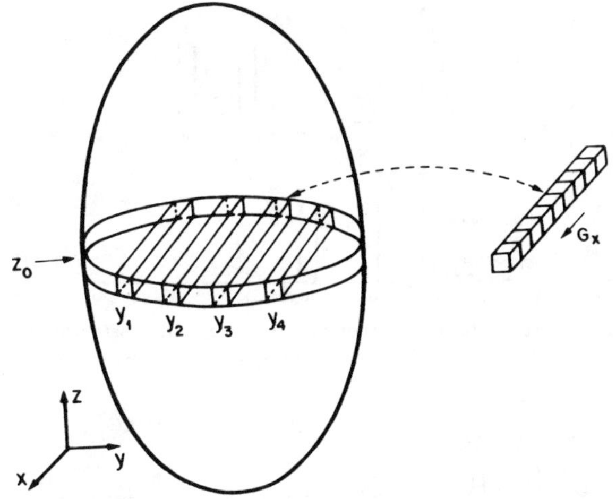

Fig. 9. Line selection process in multiple-line-scan imaging (line = 4).

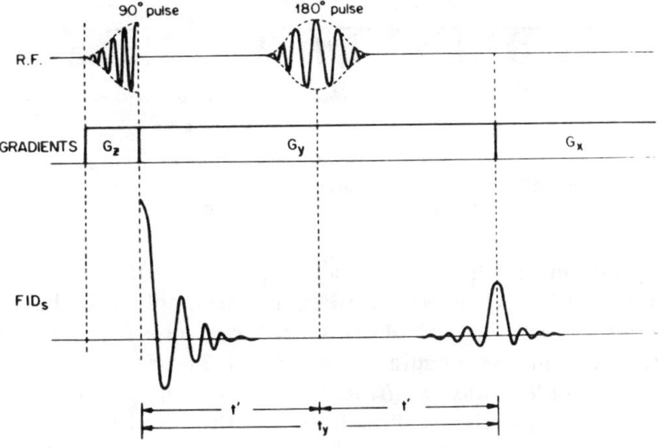

Fig. 10. Imaging scheme and pulse sequence of the basic line-scan imaging with spin echo.

$$G(\omega_x) = \frac{M_0/T_2^*}{(1/T_2^*)^2 + \omega_x^2}. \tag{30}$$

As is seen from (29), the spin density profile obtained by NMR line scanning is a convolution of actual spin density $\rho(x, y_0, z_0)$ and line-spread function $G(\omega_x)$. In most imaging applications, however, loss of resolution due to the line-spread function is not significant, and $G(\omega_x)$ will be treated as a delta function in this paper.

It is important to point out that, with single line-scanning NMR imaging, systematic artifacts exist due to the background signals arising from the preceeding FID (line integrals). During t_y period with field gradient G_y, large FID's arising from all the lines in the selected plane decay with an effective transverse relaxation time T_2^{**}, but the actual line of interest is only a small fraction of the total FID signal generated. In fact, the signal from rephasing spins along the selected line is actually riding on the tail of the previous FID signal and would naturally be influenced by the magnitude of this residue of the preceeding signal. Thus line artifacts appear on the image, and it is the most serious drawback of this method, especially in single line scanning.

Analytically, the FID signal obtained with spin echo can be expressed as

$$s(t, y_0, z_0) = M_0 \exp\left(-\frac{t_y}{T_2}\right)\left[\int_x \rho(x, y_0, z_0) \exp\left(i\gamma x G_x t\right) dx\right.$$

$$+ \int_x \left[\int_{y \neq y_0} \rho(x, y, z_0) \exp\left(i\gamma y G_y t'\right) dy\right]_{t'=t_y}$$

$$\left. \cdot \exp\left(i\gamma x G_x t\right) dx\right] \exp\left(-\frac{t}{T_2^*}\right)$$

$$= M_0 \exp\left(-\frac{t_y}{T_2}\right)\int_x \rho'(x, y_0, t_0) \exp\left(i\gamma x G_x t\right)$$

$$\cdot \exp\left(-\frac{t}{T_2^*}\right) dx \tag{31}$$

where

$$\rho'(x, y_0, z_0) = \rho(x, y_0, z_0)$$

$$+ \left[\int_{y \neq y_0} \rho(x, y, z_0) \exp\left(i\gamma y G_y t'\right) dy\right]_{t'=t_y}.$$

The first part of the second term in (31) is background, i.e., the tail signal of the unwanted preceding FID, and the significance of this term is clearly visible in single line-scan images. From (31), it can be seen that a large y field gradient makes T_2^{**} smaller for a given spin-echo duration, which reduces the tail influence. An increase of spin-echo duration also will reduce or eliminate this tail-signal effect.

Increase of spin-echo duration (t_y), however, reduces the FID signal of the selected line by simple T_2 decay and degrades the S/N ratio. This is an interesting tradeoff between signal decay and tail-signal effect for single line-scan imaging. Simulations indicate the possibility of choosing an optimum field gradient G_y and spin-echo duration depending on the noise levels and resolution of the NMR imaging system.

As expected, single-line scanning requires a large number of repeated data collections due to the poor S/N ratio. This drawback can partly be eliminated by multiple-line, full-line, or multislice full-line techniques using signal-encoding methods [20].

b) Multiple-line-scan imaging: Maudsley suggested a new extended single-line-scanning method by applying a multiple-line (composite frequency) spin-echo pulse with encoding so that several lines can be excited at each spin-echo RF pulse [20].

This method, however, still requires repetition of pulse excitation so that if n lines are to be excited simultaneously, then n pulse repetitions are required, and the gain is simply n times the signal average while it takes n times longer measurement time. The effect of n pulse repetitions is to increase the SNR by a factor of $\sqrt{n}$ in each of the n lines. For one particular line, statistical gain achieved by signal averaging is $\sqrt{n}$ improvement for n line encoding; however, it provides $(n-1)$ additional lines which have similar SNR gain. The difference between multiple-line scanning and single-line scanning is the frequency spectrum of the 180° RF spin-echo pulse. Let $S_1, S_2, \cdots, S_M$ be the measured composite FID signals, and let the signals from each line be $s_1, s_2, \cdots, s_M$, then the relation between $\boldsymbol{S}^M$ and $\boldsymbol{s}^M$ is given by

$$S^M = \begin{bmatrix} S_1 \\ S_2 \\ \cdot \\ \cdot \\ \cdot \\ S_M \end{bmatrix} = [H_M] \begin{bmatrix} s_1 \\ s_2 \\ \cdot \\ \cdot \\ \cdot \\ s_M \end{bmatrix} = [H_M] s^M \qquad (32)$$

where H_M is a Hadamard matrix given as

$$[H_M] = [H_{2N}] = \begin{bmatrix} [H_N] & [H_N] \\ [H_N] & -[H_N] \end{bmatrix} \qquad (33)$$

where

$$[H_N]_{N=2} = \begin{bmatrix} 1 & 1 \\ 1 & -1 \end{bmatrix} \quad \text{and} \quad [H_N]_{N=4} = \begin{bmatrix} 1 & 1 & 1 & 1 \\ 1 & -1 & 1 & -1 \\ 1 & 1 & -1 & -1 \\ 1 & -1 & -1 & 1 \end{bmatrix}.$$

The desired signal from each line can then be written as

$$s^M = \frac{1}{M} [H_M] S^M. \qquad (34)$$

As an illustration, let us consider a case with $M = 4$. FID S^M and desired signal s^M are related as

$$S_1 = s_1 + s_2 + s_3 + s_4$$
$$S_2 = s_1 - s_2 + s_3 - s_4$$
$$S_4 = s_1 + s_2 - s_3 - s_4$$
$$S_4 = s_1 - s_2 - s_3 + s_4. \qquad (35)$$

The desired line density function s^M can be obtained by coded addition and subtraction as indicated, i.e.,

$$s_1 = \tfrac{1}{4}(S_1 + S_2 + S_3 + S_4)$$
$$s_2 = \tfrac{1}{4}(S_1 - S_2 + S_3 - S_4)$$
$$s_3 = \tfrac{1}{4}(S_1 + S_2 - S_3 - S_4)$$
$$s_4 = \tfrac{1}{4}(S_1 - S_2 - S_3 + S_4). \qquad (36)$$

In this case, composite $180°$ RF pulse excitation is required which will result in negative and positive spin echoes, as illustrated in Fig. 11. Unless multiple-line scanning is extended to a full line, an unwanted signal-tail artifact is still present, but to a lesser degree than in single-line scanning.

c) Full-line-scan imaging and application of spin-echo repetitions: Full-line-scan imaging is a natural extension of multiple-line-scan imaging. Besides improvement against tail artifacts, additional spin-echo repetitions can be used for signal averaging or a reduction of the collection time [10].

In Fig. 12, full-line scanning using spin-echo repetition is illustrated. In this case, after selection of an x–y plane at z_0 by application of a $90°$ narrow-band RF pulse, two $180°$ spin-echo RF pulse sequences are added together with field gradients G_y and G_x. The t_y periods are used for rephasing the spins into the desired form and first half of t_s periods are assigned for FID signal readout. Repeating the spin echoes n times [10], total measurement times can be reduced from MT_1 to MT_1/n for M line scanning. An additional advantage of full-line scanning with a spin-echo technique is that two FID signals are obtained in each t_s period which are available for signal averaging. The total FID signals obtained in a T_1 period, therefore, are $2n$ when n spin echoes are repeated in

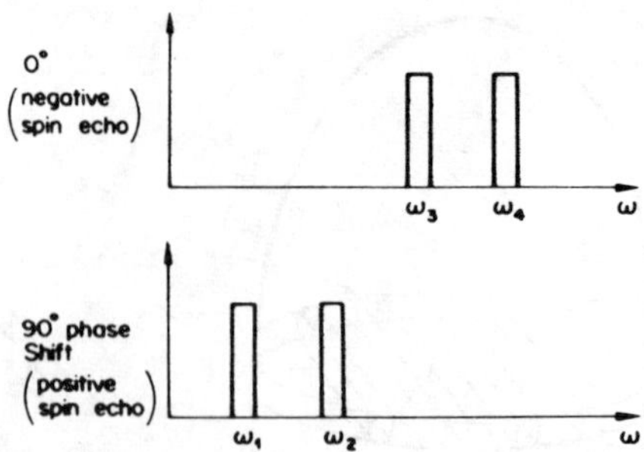

Fig. 11. An example of the spectrum of a $180°$ line selecting RF pulse in multiple-line-scan imaging method.

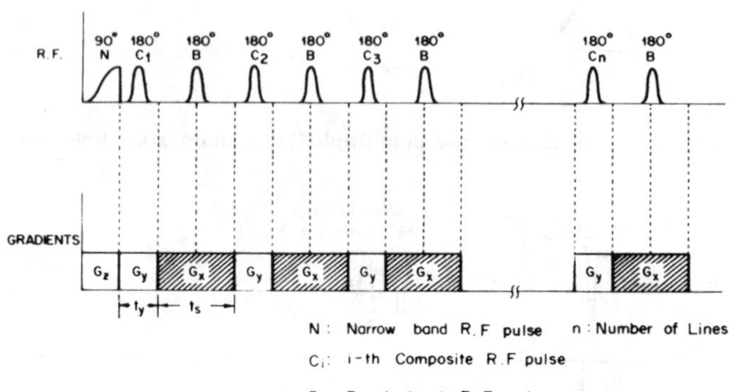

Fig. 12. RF and gradient-pulse sequences for full-line scanning with additional spin-echo repetitions.

a T_1 period. In this case, at each spin echo a different composition of $180°$ RF pulses (see Fig. 11) are applied so that the overall measurement time can be reduced by a factor equivalent to the number of spin echoes at each T_1 relaxation time.

d) Simultaneous multislice full-line-scan imaging with spin-echo repetitions: Principles of the multiple-line and full-line scanning with spin echoes can obviously be extended to multislice full-line scanning using additional spin-echo repetitions.

Selection of several slices can be made through the use of composite $90°$ RF pulse at the initial stage of the experiment, as is shown in Fig. 13.

First, a $90°$ RF pulse with l separate spectra selects desired layers along the z-direction together with field gradient G_z. Subsequently, similar to the case of multiline or full-line excitation, $180°$ composite pulse with M lines can be excited and rephased. Final readout by application of G_x will provide desired signals for extraction of m lines on l slices. To achieve fast data collection, spin-echo repetition is added, i.e., broadband $180°$ RF pulse at the G_x period provides spin rephasing as well.

Generalized formalism of the multislice multiple-line-scan imaging using spin echoes can be written as

$$\bar{S}^{LM} = \begin{bmatrix} S^{1M} \\ S^{2M} \\ \cdot \\ \cdot \\ S^{iM} \\ \cdot \\ S^{LM} \end{bmatrix} = [H_{LM}] \begin{bmatrix} s^{1M} \\ s^{2M} \\ \cdot \\ \cdot \\ s^{iM} \\ \cdot \\ s^{LM} \end{bmatrix} = [H_{LM}] \bar{s}^{LM} \qquad (37)$$

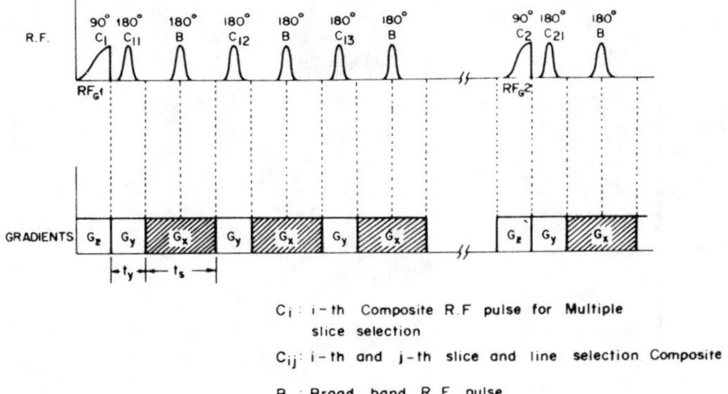

Fig. 13. RF and gradient-pulse sequences for multislice full-line scan imaging with additional spin-echo repetitions.

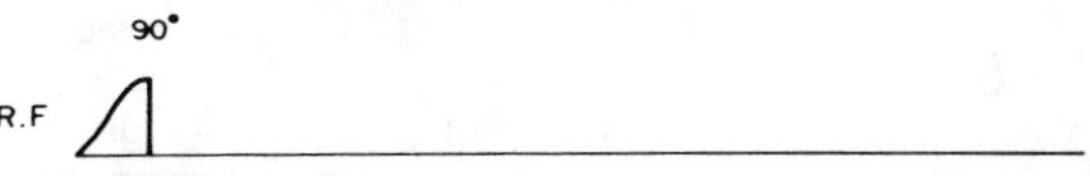

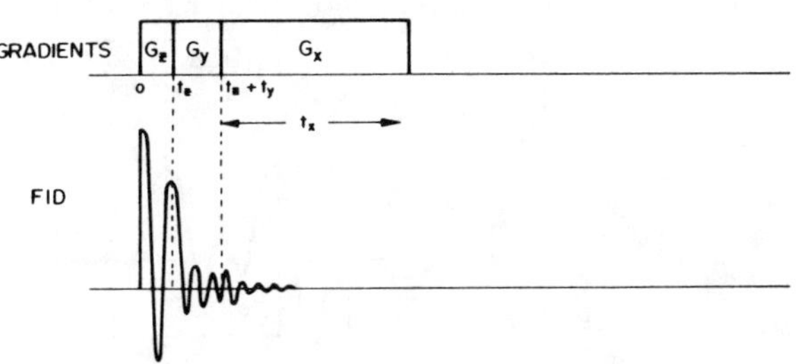

Fig. 14. Imaging sequences of original 3-D KWE direct Fourier imaging. $n\Delta t_z$ and $n\Delta t_y$ sequences are required for a complete 3-D volume imaging.

where H_{LM} is the Hadamard matrix

$$S^{iM} = \begin{bmatrix} S_{i1} \\ S_{i2} \\ \cdot \\ \cdot \\ S_{in} \\ \cdot \\ \cdot \\ S_{iM} \end{bmatrix} \quad \text{and} \quad s^{iM} = \begin{bmatrix} s_{i1} \\ s_{i2} \\ \cdot \\ \cdot \\ s_{in} \\ \cdot \\ \cdot \\ s_{iM} \end{bmatrix} \tag{38}$$

respectively. S_{in} is the composite FID obtained at ith and nth excitation, and s_{in} is the ith and nth slice and line component, respectively. The Hadamard matrix H_{LM} is

$$[H_{LM}] = [H_L] \otimes [H_M] \tag{39}$$

where $[H_L]$ and $[H_M]$ are the Hadamard matrices of slices and lines, and $\otimes$ is the Kroneker product, respectively.

As an example, in an $L = 4$ and $M = 4$ multislice–multiline scanning case, for each composite $90°$ RF pulse, four repeated excitations of $180°$ composite RF spin-echo pulses are needed. A total of 16 experiments are then performed and desired signals are extracted by encoding. Specifically, the Hadamard matrix for this case can be written as

$$[H_{44}] = \left[\begin{array}{cc|cc} [H_4] & [H_4] & [H_4] & [H_4] \\ [H_4] & -[H_4] & [H_4] & -[H_4] \\ \hline [H_4] & [H_4] & -[H_4] & -[H_4] \\ [H_4] & -[H_4] & -[H_4] & [H_4] \end{array} \right]. \tag{40}$$

Finally L and M can be extended to full lines and full slices. For this case, the amount of data-acquisition time will also increase L times compared with full-line scanning. Since the data-acquisition time increases rapidly, it is important to use spin-echo repetition as a means of reducing the data-acquisition times [10].

B. Direct Fourier-Transform Imaging

1) Basic Principles of the Kumar, Welti, and Ernst (KWE) Direct Fourier NMR Tomographic Imaging [7]: In the original article by Kumar, Welti, and Ernst (KWE), direct Fourier imaging was performed by total 3-D excitation of an object in three series of time sequences and 3-D Fourier transform of the data are considered as the 3-D spin density function.

In Fig. 14, a basic form of RF pulsing and field-gradient sequences of the 3-D KWE method is illustrated. In this case, three orthogonal field gradients G_z, G_y, and G_x are applied in sequence. The z-component of the local magnetic fields are, then, given as

$$H_z(x, y, z) = \begin{cases} H_0 + G_z z, & \text{for } 0 < t < t_z \\ H_0 + G_y y, & \text{for } t_z < t < t_z + t_y \\ H_0 + G_x x, & \text{for } t_z + t_y < t \end{cases} \tag{41}$$

where each time scale t_z and t_y is varied according to preassigned sequences, i.e., $t_z = 0 \sim t_a$, $t_y = 0 \sim t_a$, and t_a is the optimal observation time of FID. The series of the FID signals obtained in t_x periods, then will form a full 3-D FID signal set sufficient for reconstruction of the entire volume spin density.

Observed FID signal $s(t_x, t_y, t_z)$ is given by

$$s(t_x, t_y, t_z) = M_0 \int_x \int_y \int_z \rho(x, y, z)$$
$$\cdot \cos\{\gamma(G_x x t_x + G_y y t_y + G_z z t_z)\}$$
$$\cdot \exp(-(t_x + t_y + t_z)/T_2^*)\, dz\, dy\, dx. \tag{42}$$

Fourier transform of (42) results in spatial spin-density function $\rho(x, y, z)$. Fourier transform of (42) is given as

$$S(\omega_x, \omega_y, \omega_z) = \int_{t_x} \int_{t_y} \int_{t_z} s(t_x, t_y, t_z)$$
$$\cdot \exp\{-i(\omega t_x + \omega_y t_y + \omega_z t_z)\}\, dt_z\, dt_y\, dt_x$$
$$= \int_x \int_y \int_z \rho(x, y, z) \tfrac{1}{2} \{G(\gamma x G_x - \omega_x)$$
$$\cdot G(\gamma y G_y - \omega_y)\, G(\gamma z G_z - \omega_z)$$
$$+ G(-\gamma x G_x - \omega_x)\, G(-\gamma y G_y - \omega_y)$$
$$\cdot G(-\gamma z G_z - \omega_z)\}\, dz\, dy\, dz \tag{43}$$

where $G(\gamma x G_x - \omega_x)$, $G(\gamma y G_y - \omega_y)$, and $G(\gamma z G_z - \omega_z)$ are the line-spread functions.

Actual digital implementation of (43), however, requires some care. In applying a 2-D Fourier transform involving $N \times N$ image matrix, it is necessary to obtain $2N$ FID's and

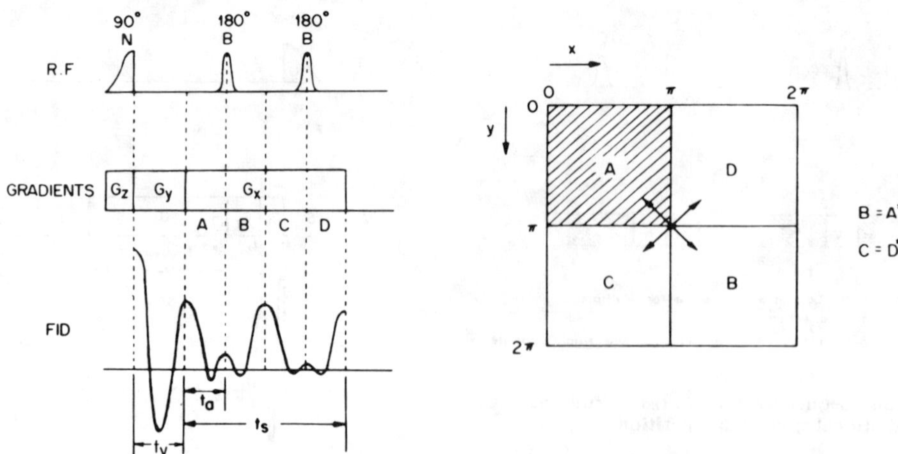

Fig. 15. Imaging sequences of single slice modified 2-D KWE direct Fourier imaging and corresponding Fourier transform frequency domain data sets. A and B, and C and D are the complex conjugates and, therefore, reproducible from one of the pairs. A and C (or vice versa) are sufficient, therefore, to generate a complete data set for 2-D FFT.

also $2N$ sample points in each FID in an angular period of $0 \sim 2\pi$ (see Fig. 15). In the original KWE method, only N FID's consisting of N samples each in an angular period of $0 \sim \pi$ were recorded. Image is then obtained through Fourier transformation. In the data, a set of N zeros is added into each N sample points in each digitized FID. After completion of the Fourier transformation of N FID's, only the real part of transformed values are stored in a matrix. In the second part, Fourier transform of the transposed matrix of the first Fourier transform matrix (real part only) is performed. Second Fourier transform operation is performed row by row with N zeros added to each row. Absolute values of the N^2 complex Fourier coefficients are then used for mapping of a 2-D NMR section image or Zeugmatogram.

Images obtained by this method, however, were relatively poor in quality and had symmetry artifacts mainly because of insufficient data. These drawbacks and the inherently slow data-collection procedure of the KWE method can be overcome by two improved KWE direct Fourier imaging methods described in the following section.

2) Improved Direct Fourier Transform Imaging—Improved KWE and Hutchison Methods [39], [58]:

a) Improved (modified) KWE direct Fourier imaging: Although the original KWE method can be used for both 2-D and 3-D direct Fourier imaging, in this section we will confine our discussion to 2-D imaging. The proposed methods overcome the inherent shortcomings of sampling and the data-collection problems of the original KWE method.

In this scheme, a single plane is first selected by application of a narrow-band $90°$ RF pulse [28] and field gradient G_z. 2-D FID sets are then obtained by varying the pulse length of G_y (see Fig. 15). During the G_x period, two spin echoes are produced by application of two broad-band $180°$ RF pulses. In effect, four FID's are obtained during this period, i.e., FID's labeled as A, B, C, and D. FID's (A, B) and (D, C) are complex conjugate pairs as shown in Fig. 15. Sampling intervals of t_x and t_y are determined by Nyquist sampling to avoid an aliasing effect. A series of FID sets are obtained as a function of t_y to form a complete set of 2-D FID signals. This data set will fill all the necessary data from 0 to 2π in both the x and y directions as is shown in Fig. 15. Note that in the original KWE method (Fig. 14), only A is obtained.

In the modified KWE method, generation of one FID signal requires a time period of

$$t = t_y + t_s \tag{44}$$

where t_s approximately equals to $4t_a$ (see Fig. 15).

The spin-echo technique employed in Fig. 15 is based on the CPMG spin-echo technique rather than the Hahn spin-echo method (see Fig. 8). In this method, the physical difference between CPMG spin-echo and Hahn spin-echo techniques is that the CPMG technique results in positive FID signals while Hahn spin-echo technique produces negative FID signals. The CPMG spin-echo process relevant to the present method is illustrated in Fig. 16. In Fig. 16(a), the spins are dephased with field gradient G_y. For simplicity, let us consider only one line with different phase in the y-direction. Within period A of Fig. 15, the spins in the selected plane are dephased with field gradient G_x, as shown in Fig. 16. After the first $180°$ spin-echo pulse in period B of Fig. 15, the spins are rotated about the y' axis and begin to rephase. The FID of period B has a conjugate relationship with that of period A. In period C, the spins are dephased in a different manner than in period A. After the second $180°$ spin-echo pulse, i.e., in period D the spins are again rotated about the y' axis and begin to rephase. Also the FID's in periods C and D have a conjugate relationship.

More specifically, the ideal FID's to be obtained with an assumption of quadrature detection[2] and the actual FID's in periods A, B, C, and D are given as

$$s(t_x, t_y; z_0) = M_0 \int_x \int_y \rho(x, y; z_0)$$

$$\cdot \exp\{i\gamma(xG_x t_x + yG_y t_y)\} \, dy \, dx \tag{45}$$

$$s_A = A_1 \cdot s(t_x, t_y; z_0) \tag{46}$$

$$s_B = A_2 \cdot s(\tfrac{1}{2} t_s - t_x, t_y; z_0) \tag{47}$$

[2] Also assume phase sensitive detection.

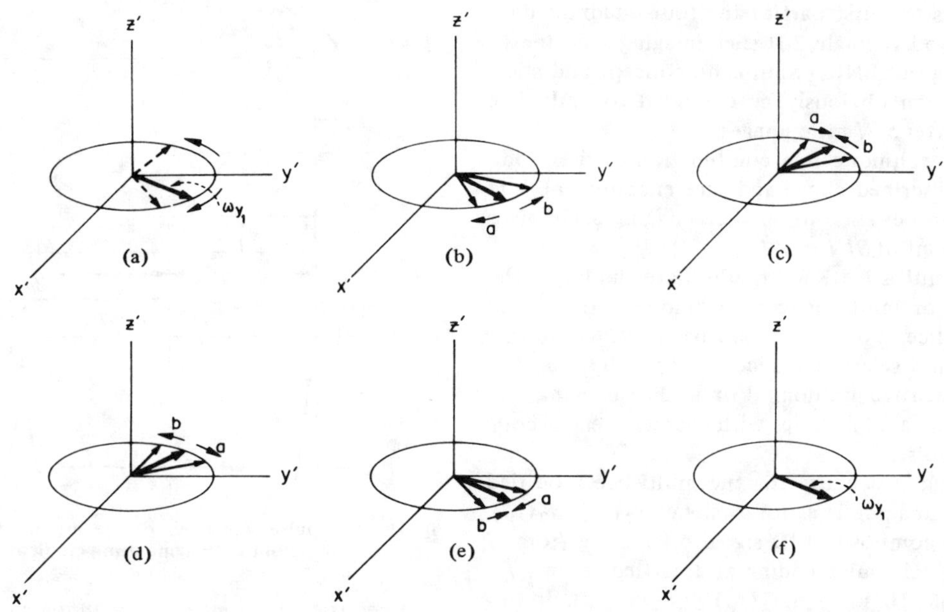

Fig. 16. Behavior of spin system in Fig. 15.

$$s_C = A_3 \cdot s(\tfrac{1}{2} t_s + t_x, t_y; z_0) \qquad (48)$$

$$s_D = A_4 \cdot s(t_s - t_x, t_y; z_0) \qquad (49)$$

where

$$A_1 = \exp\left\{-(t_x + t_y)/T_2^*\right\}$$

$$A_2 = \exp\left\{-(t_x + t_y)/T_2^*\right\} \exp\left\{-(\tfrac{1}{2} t_s - 2t_x)/T_2\right\}$$

$$A_3 = \exp\left\{-(t_x + t_y)/T_2^*\right\} \exp\left\{-\tfrac{1}{2} t_s/T_2\right\}$$

$$A_4 = \exp\left\{-(t_x + t_y)/T_2^*\right\} \exp\left\{-(t_s - 2t_x)/T_2\right\}$$

and t_x is restricted to $0 \leqslant t_x \leqslant t_s/4$. By simple attenuation corrections, (47)–(49) can now be placed to fill the required data sets in Fig. 15, i.e.,

$$B = s_B \exp\left\{(\tfrac{1}{2} t_s - 2t_x)/T_2\right\}$$

$$C = s_C \exp\left\{\tfrac{1}{2} t_s/T_2\right\}$$

and

$$D = s_D \exp\left\{(t_s - 2t_x)/T_2\right\} \qquad (50)$$

can be obtained. The conventional 2-D Fourier transform of the complete data set A, B, C, and D will result in a fully recovered 2-D spin-density image. An example of a 2-D FID set obtained from a phantom through improved KWE method is shown in Fig. 17.

The modified KWE method can be extended to a faster data-collection method by using spin-echo repetitions, as shown in Fig. 18. After one FID data set is obtained, the next FID data set can be obtained by a brief application of a y field gradient in a time interval of Δt_y at the end of first data collection. At this point, all the spins are rephased and returned to the state of the first t_y period plus Δt_y. This process can be repeated up to the point at which the FID signal is no longer useful due to noise. The example illustrated in Fig. 18 indicates that the kth regrown FID set can be given as

$$s^k(t') = \exp\left\{-t_s(k-1)/T_2\right\} s^1(t') \qquad (51)$$

where $\exp\left\{-t_s(k-1)/T_2\right\}$ is a compensation term for the kth

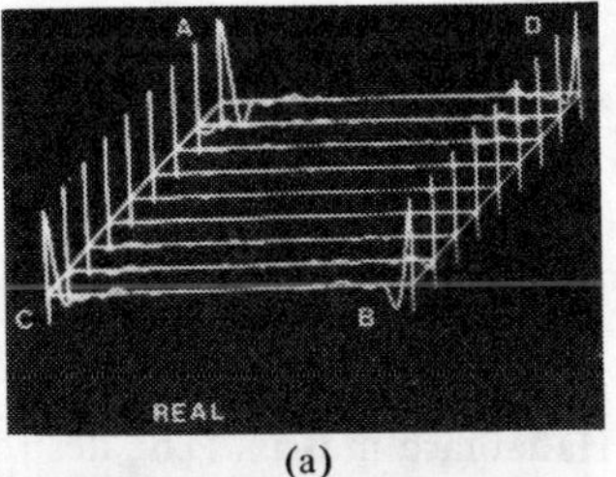

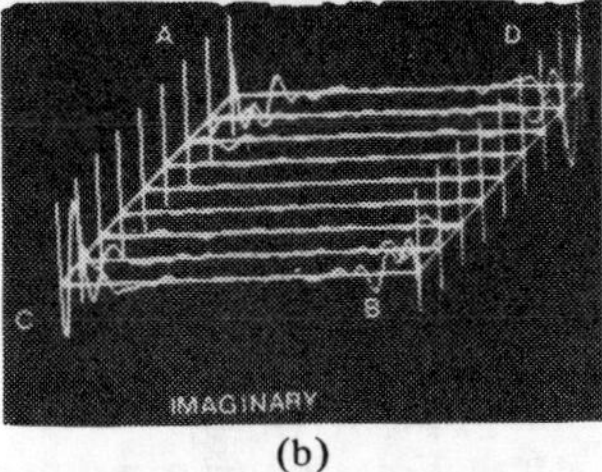

Fig. 17. FID sets obtained in 2-D space with the modified KWE method. (a) Real part. (b) Imaginary part.

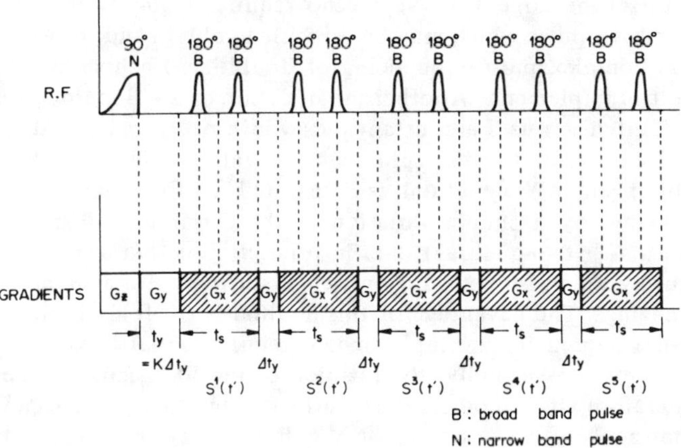

Fig. 18. Pulse sequences of single-slice modified KWE direct Fourier imaging (multiple spin-echo repetitions are applied to shorten the imaging time).

FID set, and $s^1(t')$ is the first part of the four-quadrant data set. Since this method is single 2-D slice imaging, it is inefficient and also gives poor SNR. Spin-echo concept and slice-encoding technique can obviously be extended to multislice imaging to obtain better S/N ratio images.

Multislice-imaging technique is a combination of the modified KWE method described above and slice-encoding method [20]. The total gain per slice for M-slice imaging again gives $\sqrt{M}$ times improvement of S/N ratio.

Principles of the multislice KWE method are similar to the previous multiplane or multiline-scan technique. First, as in the case of single-slice, $90°$ RF pulses having M composite spectra are applied and selected M slices either with some slice intervals or in consecutive fashion. For M slice imaging, the modified KWE are repeated M times with a larger spectral composition of $90°$ RF pulses.

The signal-encoding procedure for the multislice modified KWE direct Fourier imaging is as follows: Let $S_1(t_y)$, $S_2(t_y)$, $\cdots$, $S_M(t_y)$ be the composite FID signal originating from M slices with different RF pulse coding at a particular time t_y, i.e., a combination of FID's $s_1(t_y)$, $s_2(t_y)$, $\cdots$, $s_M(t_y)$. In vector notation of the FID's, $\boldsymbol{S}^M(t_y)$ and each slice data $\boldsymbol{s}^M(t_y)$ are related as

$$\boldsymbol{S}^M(t_y) = \begin{bmatrix} S_1(t_y) \\ S_2(t_y) \\ \cdot \\ \cdot \\ \cdot \\ S_M(t_y) \end{bmatrix} = [H_M] \begin{bmatrix} s_1(t_y) \\ s_2(t_y) \\ \cdot \\ \cdot \\ \cdot \\ s_M(t_y) \end{bmatrix} = [H_M]\,\boldsymbol{s}^M(t_y) \tag{52}$$

where H_M is the Hadamard matrix. The desired signal component from each slice can be obtained from (52) as

$$\boldsymbol{s}^M(t_y) = \frac{1}{M}[H_M]\,\boldsymbol{S}^M(t_y). \tag{53}$$

To obtain complete data sets for M slices with $N\Delta t_y$ sampling, it requires $N \times M$ repetitions of the experiment. With this procedure, noise statistics are improved in a similar way as in the multiple-line mapping with line or slice encoding.

b) Hutchison–KWE direct Fourier method: Although the KWE method enables us to obtain all the four quadrants of data unambiguously, it is often difficult to apply in some situations.

First, the large $180°$ spin echo requires high-power broadband RF pulse which may be difficult to obtain and, secondly, the complex pulse sequencing of double-spin echoes is difficult to implement. Another modification of KWE method due to Hutchison uses a constant pulsewidth of t_y and a gradient-pulse reversal for the spin-echo generation. This combined Hutchison–KWE method is illustrated in Fig. 19. In this scheme, by a simple variation of the amplitude of gradient pulse G_y, two-quadrant data in Fourier space can be obtained during the pulse period P_3 which is sufficient for artifact-free imaging. The advantage of this method is twofold. First, the pulse sequencing is simple since it requires variation of amplitude only. Secondly, the position of the FID signal is fixed; therefore, it is not seriously affected by the gradient-pulse transient effect. Several NMR imaging systems currently under development are considering this scheme as an alternative method for direct Fourier transform imaging in NMR tomography.

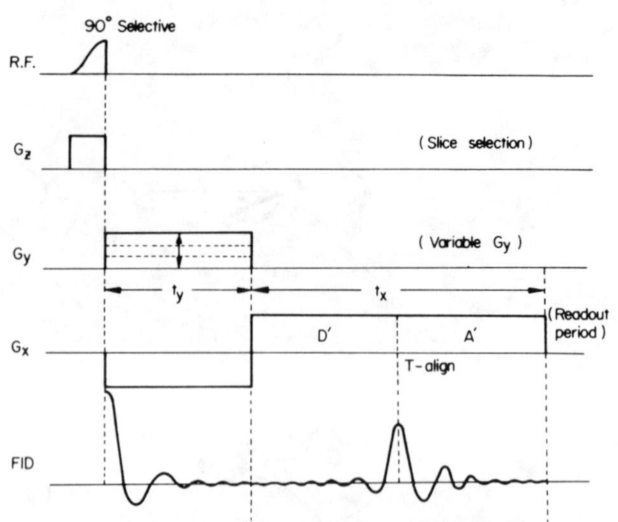

Fig. 19. The pulse sequences of the modified Hutchison–KWE direct Fourier imaging using gradient reversals.

B. Reconstructive Imaging Techniques from Projections in NMR Tomography

1) Line-Integral Projection Reconstruction (LPR):

a) Basic principles of LPR: Projection reconstruction using a 2-D and 3-D image reconstruction algorithm is well developed, especially in the areas of X-CT and radionuclide emission tomography [29]–[34]. Although there are several different ways of reconstructing the image, the basic form of the collected data is similar, i.e., line-integral projection data are obtained in angular steps. The most familiar and convenient method of reconstructing 2-D or 3-D images is the Fourier convolution method [14], [35], and total 3-D volume images are then obtained by stacking the 2-D images reconstructed from one-dimensional (1-D) projections. This Fourier convolution method may be summarized as follows. The reconstructed image $f(x, y)$ in 2-D coordinates is given by

$$f(x, y) = \int_0^\pi d\theta\, [P_l(x', \theta) * \xi(x')] \tag{54}$$

where $P_l(x', \theta)$ is projection data and $\xi(x')$ is the filter kernel which corrects for $1/r$ blurring that results from circular-symmetric linear superposition [14]. Fourier-domain representation of (54) is given as

$$f(r, \phi) = \frac{1}{4\pi^2} \int_{-\infty}^{\infty} \int_{-\infty}^{\infty} d\omega_y\, d\omega_x\, F(\omega_x, \omega_y)$$

$$\cdot \exp\,[-i(\omega_x x + \omega_y y)]$$

$$\cong \frac{1}{4\pi^2} \int_0^\pi d\theta \int_{\infty}^{\infty} d\rho\, F(\rho, \theta)\, \psi(\rho, \theta)$$

$$\cdot \exp\,[-i\rho r \cos(\theta - \phi)] \tag{55}$$

where

$$r = \sqrt{x^2 + y^2} \qquad x' = x\cos\theta + y\sin\theta \qquad \rho = \sqrt{\omega_x^2 + \omega_y^2}$$

and $\psi(\rho, \theta)$ is the filter function which is given by

$$\psi(\rho, \theta) = \psi(\rho) = |\rho|\, H(\rho). \tag{56}$$

$H(\rho)$ is the apodizing function for the optimization of the

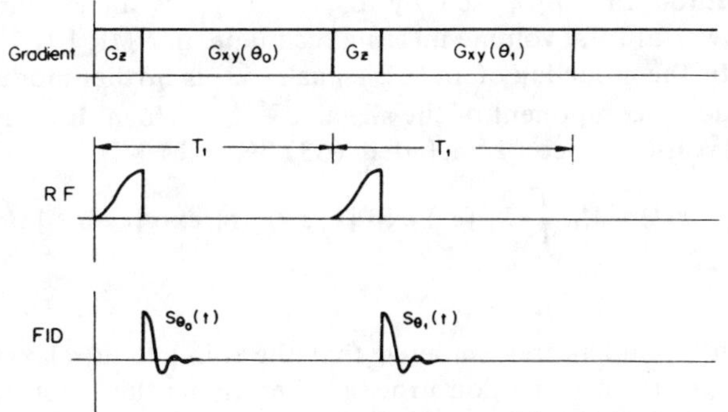

Fig. 20. FID, RF pulse timing, and field-gradient sequences in the basic single-slice line-integral projection reconstruction.

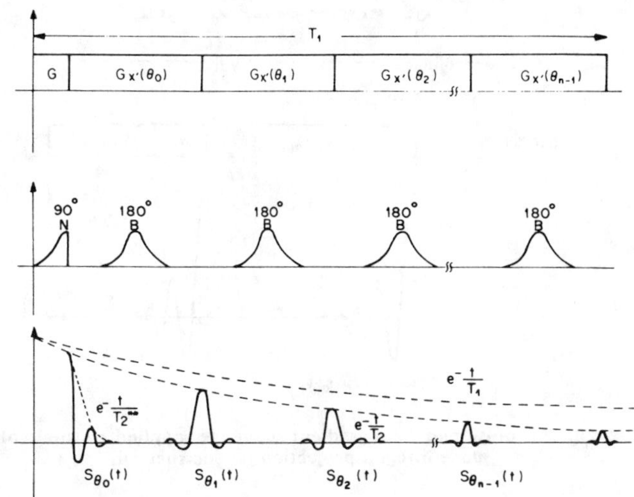

Fig. 21. Pulse and field-gradient sequences of the fast single-slice line-integral projection reconstruction imaging using series of spin-echo repetitions.

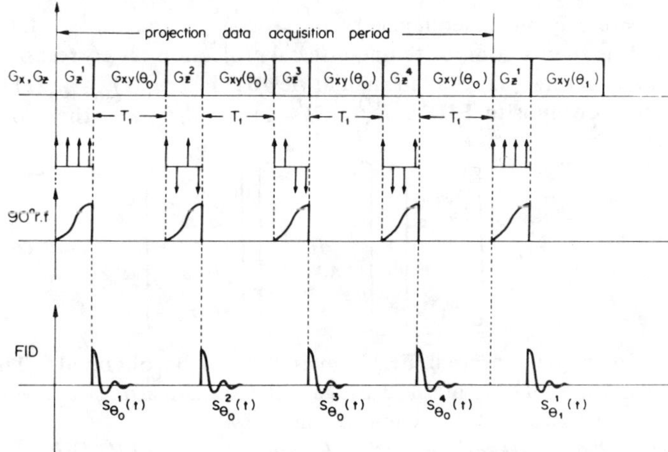

Fig. 22. Pulse and gradient sequences of the multiplane-line integral projection reconstruction using plane encoding (four-plane encoding).

density and spatial resolution under the given SNR [36]–[38]. It is easy to see that $F(\rho, \theta)$ and $P_l(x', \theta)$ are related as

$$\mathcal{F}^{-1}[P_l(x', \theta); x' \to \rho] = F(\rho, \theta). \tag{57}$$

From (54) and (55), therefore, reconstruction can be performed either by spatial-domain convolution (54) or Fourier-domain multiplicative operation (55). The central part of the Fourier convolution image reconstruction is, therefore, optimum filtering with a spatial-domain convolution kernel $\xi(x')$ or a frequency-domain filter function $\psi(\rho)$. The convolution kernel $\xi(x')$ and filter function $\psi(\rho)$ are related as

$$\xi(x') = \mathcal{F}[\psi(\rho); \rho \to x']. \tag{58}$$

In Fourier-transform NMR, the nuclear signal (FID) is the inverse Fourier transform of the spatial-domain spin density function by its own physical process, i.e., FID $s_\theta(t)$ at a given angular view θ is given by [10]

$$s_\theta(t) = M_0 \int_{x'} \int_{y'} \rho(x', y'; z_0) \exp[i\gamma x' G_{x'} t]\, dy'\, dx' \tag{59}$$

provided a plane at $z = z_0$ is selected. Although the FID signal $s_\theta(t)$ appears in time domain, it represents Fourier-domain projection data. When 2-D image reconstruction is required in the Fourier domain, FID signal $s_\theta(t)$ is simply replaced with $F(\rho, \theta)$ in (55). For the spatial-domain reconstruction (convolution reconstruction) projection data $P_l(x', \theta)$ is obtained through the Fourier transform of the FID signal, i.e.,

$$P_l(x', \theta) = \mathcal{F}[s_\theta(t); t \to x']. \tag{60}$$

The basic form of projection data obtainable in Fourier transform NMR is similar to the data obtained by X-CT. In Fig. 20, FID signals obtained at different angular views are shown together with the field-gradient and RF excitation sequences. The RF signal applied (see Fig. 20) contains only one frequency component in this case and satisfies the $90°$ spin flip. After $0 \sim \pi$ rotation of projection in an appropriate step by adjustment of the field gradients G_x and G_y, a complete projection-data set sufficient for reconstruction of a slice at the z_0 plane is obtained. At this point, 2-D image reconstruction can proceed according to (54) or (55). In the former case, each FID signal $s_\theta(t)$ is Fourier transformed, convolved with a filter kernel, and back-projected.

This simple basic form of the line-integral projection recon-

struction works well, and simulations, as well as some experimental images obtained, indicate excellent prospects of this method in NMR imaging [4], [5]. Disadvantages of this single-slice LPR method are somewhat slow data collection, a stringent requirement of field homogeneity, low sensitivity, and associated artifacts. Again, speed limitation can be partly overcome by use of spin-echo repetitions [10] (see Fig. 21). Another possibility of multislice imaging of a large volume is the multiple-slice excitation with encoding technique as will be discussed in the following.

b) Multiplane line-integral projection reconstruction by plane encoding [23]: This method is a combination of simple line-integral projection reconstruction and plane-encoding technique [20]. The principle of this method is illustrated in Fig. 22. It is similar to multiple-line-scan imaging with spin-echo repetitions which gives $\sqrt{n}$ times improvement in SNR for simultaneous n-slices imaging. As is shown in Fig. 22, for one data set at a view θ_i, the same G_z and G_x are applied n times each with a different frequency composition of RF pulses. To obtain a complete view data of n planes, data acquisition is repeated n times.

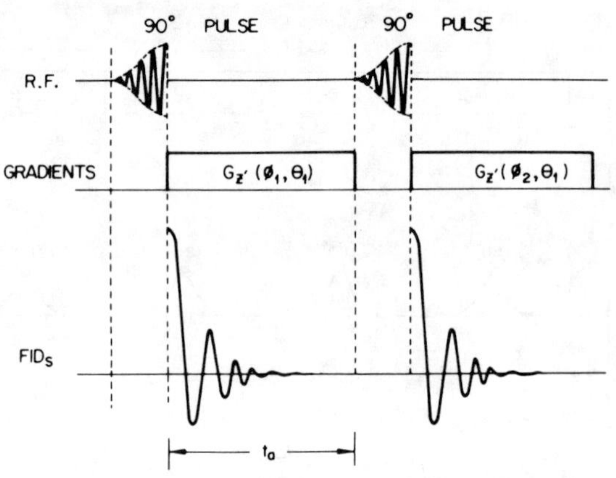

Fig. 23. RF pulse and field-gradient sequences applied to total volume plane-integral projection reconstruction.

The key to this method is the encoding of the signals according to the composite RF pulse sequence. Simple illustration of the encoding procedure using the Hadamard coding matrix can be given as follows. Let FID's obtained at each $90°$ composite RF pulse sequence be $S_{\theta_{1,1}}^{(t)}, S_{\theta_{1,2}}^{(t)}, \cdots, S_{\theta_{1,n}}^{(t)}$. Each FID is then a composite line-integral projection set corresponding to several planes at an angular view θ_1, i.e., $s_{\theta_1}(t)_{z_0}, s_{\theta_1}(t)_{z_1}$, etc. Composite FID's, $S_{\theta_{1,1}}^{(t)}, S_{\theta_{1,2}}^{(t)}, \cdots, S_{\theta_{1,n}}^{(t)}$ are, therefore, given as

$$
S_{\theta_1}^n = \begin{bmatrix} s_{\theta_1,1} \\ s_{\theta_1,2} \\ \vdots \\ s_{\theta_1,n} \end{bmatrix} = \begin{bmatrix} & \\ & H_n & \\ & \end{bmatrix} \begin{bmatrix} s_{\theta_1 z_0} \\ s_{\theta_1 z_1} \\ \vdots \\ s_{\theta_1 z_{n-1}} \end{bmatrix}.
\tag{61}
$$

From (61), desired FID signals S_{θ_i} can be obtained. The advantage of this method is again the statistical improvement with increase of total scanning time.

2) Plane-Integral Projection Reconstruction (PPR) [9]:

a) Basic principles of the total volume excitation and PPR: RF pulse and field-gradient sequences of the total volume PPR imaging are shown in Fig. 23. The FID signal of total volume plane-integral projection data in z'-direction can be expressed as

$$
s(t) = M_0 \int_{x'}\int_{y'}\int_{z'} \rho(x', y', z')
$$

$$
\cdot \exp\left[i\gamma(H_0 + z'G_{z'})t\right] dx'\, dy'\, dz'
$$

$$
= M_0 \int_{z'}\left[\int_{y'}\int_{x'} \rho(x', y', z')\, dx'\, dy'\right]
$$

$$
\cdot \exp\left[i\gamma(H_0 + z'G_{z'})t\right] dz'.
\tag{62}
$$

With phase-sensitive detection, the FID signal will be

$$
s(t) = M_0 \int_{z'} P_p(z') \exp\left[i\gamma z'G_{z'}t\right] dz'
\tag{63}
$$

where $P_p(z')$ is a plane integral. $s(t)$ are the projection data in the Fourier domain, and the Fourier transform of $s(t)$ are, therefore, spatial-domain plane-integral projection data with which reconstruction can be performed. This plane-integral

method first proposed by L. A. Shepp is an efficient and powerful total volume imaging technique in NMR [9].

In the modeling of an FID signal, (63) is further modified by a decay component of the signal, e^{-t/T_2^*}. When this transverse relaxation process is included, (63) becomes

$$
s(t) = M_0 \int_{z'} P_p(z') \exp\left[i\gamma z'G_{z'}t\right] \exp\left[-t/T_2^*\right] dz'.
\tag{64}
$$

It should be remembered that the spin-lattice relaxation or longitudinal relaxation process often limits the repetition rate of excitation of the spins or magnetization, especially so in total volume excitation where a large number of plane-integral projection data sets at different angular views are needed. If we adopt spherical coordinates, projection data sets of N_θ and N_ϕ are necessary. For clinical imaging, the number of views $N_\theta \times N_\phi$ approaches the order of 10 000 or more and also long measurement time. This drawback may be overcome by use of spin-echo repetitions, similar to the multiple-line or plane imaging (see the simulated results).

b) Algorithms for total-volume image reconstructions with plane-integral projection data [9]: 2-D image reconstruction from 1-D line-integral projection data is a well-known technique and has been successfully applied to X-CT. True 3-D volume image reconstruction of an object with 1-D plane-integral projection data is, however, relatively new [9].

From Fourier transform theory, it can be shown that the 3-D volume image $f(r, \theta, \phi)$ or $f(x, y, z)$ can be obtained if the object function $0(\omega_T, \theta_\omega, \phi_\omega)$ is known, i.e.,

$$
f(x, y, z) = \frac{1}{(2\pi)^3} \int_0^{2\pi} d\phi_\omega \int_0^{\pi} d\theta_\omega \int_0^{\infty} d\omega_T\, 0(\omega_T, \theta_\omega, \phi_\omega)
$$

$$
\cdot \exp\left[-i\omega_T T\right] \omega_T^2 \sin\theta_\omega
\tag{65}
$$

where $T = z\cos\theta + (x\cos\phi + y\sin\phi)\sin\theta$.

FID signal obtainable in NMR (64) and the basic form of the plane-integral projection data are related as

$$
s(t)_{\theta,\phi} = \mathcal{F}^{-1}\left[P_p(T, \theta, \phi); T \to \omega_T\, \theta \to \theta_\omega, \phi \to \phi_\omega\right]
$$

$$
\equiv \tilde{P}_p(\omega_T, \theta_\omega, \phi_\omega)
\tag{66}
$$

where $P_p(T, \theta, \phi)$ is the plane integral along T.

From (66), it is also easy to see that $P_p(T, \theta, \phi)$ is related to $\tilde{P}_p(\omega_T, \theta_\omega, \phi_\omega)$ as

$$
P_p(T, \theta, \phi) = \frac{1}{2\pi} \int_{-\infty}^{\infty} \tilde{P}_p(\omega_T, \theta_\omega, \phi_\omega) \exp\left[-i\omega_T T\right] d\omega_T.
\tag{67}
$$

Double differentiation of $P_p(T, \theta, \phi)$ by the Fourier differentiation theorem gives

$$
-P_p''(T, \theta, \phi) = \frac{1}{2\pi} \int_{-\infty}^{\infty} \tilde{P}_p(\omega_T, \theta_\omega, \phi_\omega)
$$

$$
\cdot \exp\left[-i\omega_T T\right] \omega_T^2 \, d\omega_T.
\tag{68}
$$

If we assume that $0(\omega, \theta_\omega, \phi_\omega)$ equals $\tilde{P}_p(\omega_T, \theta_\omega, \phi_\omega)$ in NMR, from (65) the reconstructed image function can be obtained by

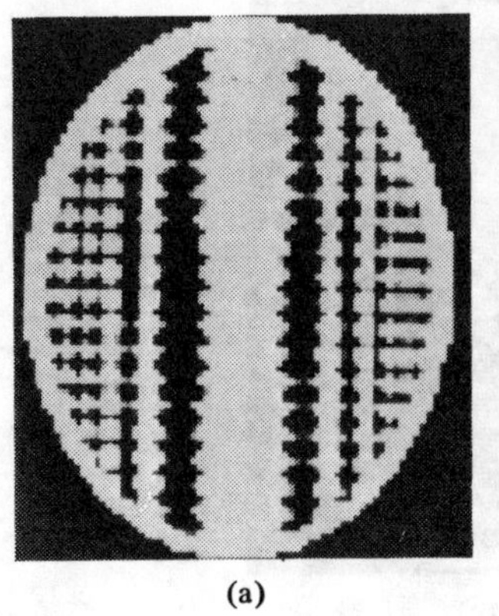
(a)

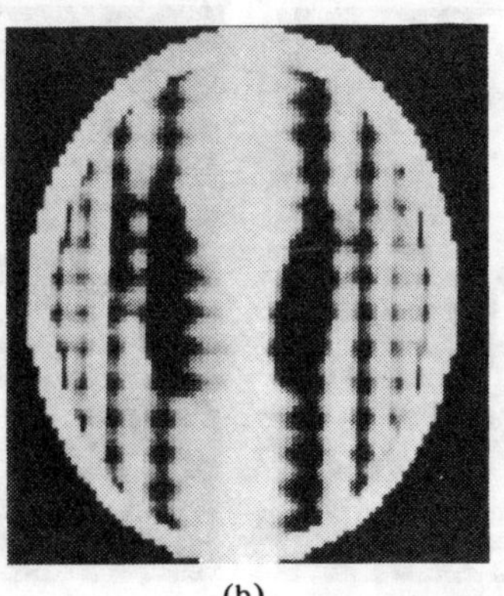
(b)

(c)

(d)

Fig. 24. Effects of field gradients. Images of single-line scan with various G_y with t_y = 50 ms, G_x = 0.1 G/cm, and no noise. (a) G_y = 0.1 G/cm. (b) G_y = 0.5 G/cm. (c) G_y = 1 G/cm. (d) G_y = 2 G/cm.

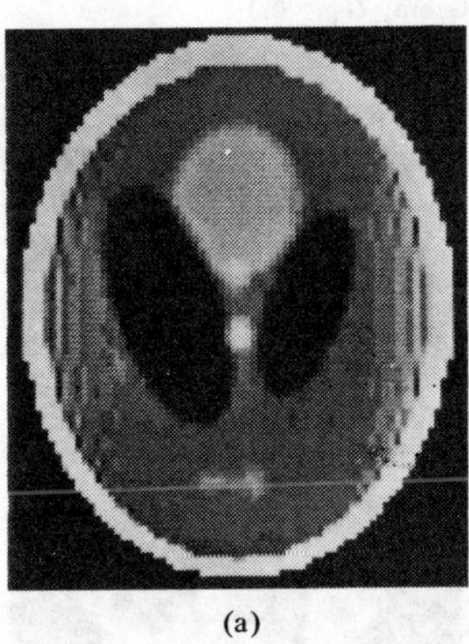
(a)

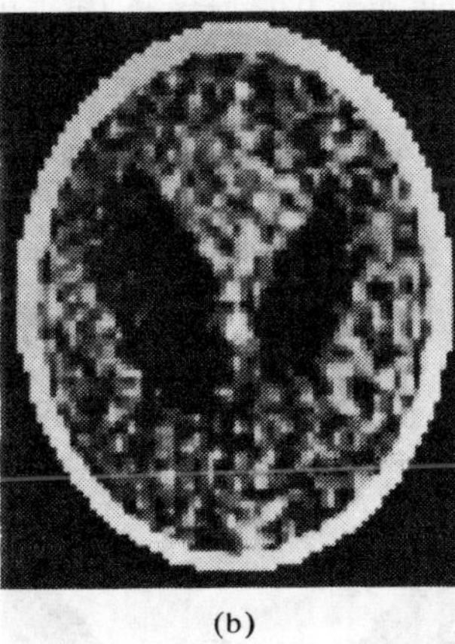
(b)

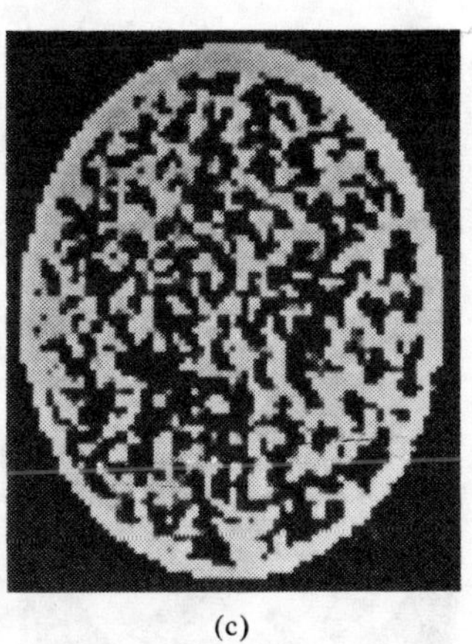
(c)

Fig. 25. Noise influences on images. Images of single-line scan with various levels of noise (G_x = 0.1 G/cm, G_y = 1 G/cm, and t_y = 0.1 s). (a) No noise. (b) Noise factor = 0.1. (c) Noise factor = 1. As expected, for single-line scan severe noise influence is seen on image even with noise factor of as little as 0.1.

$$f(x, y, z) = -\frac{1}{8\pi^2} \int_0^{2\pi} d\phi_\omega \int_0^{\pi} d\theta_\omega \, P_p''(T, \theta_\omega, \phi_\omega) \sin \theta_\omega.$$

(69)

This is Shepp's algorithm for direct total volume image reconstruction. It follows a simple format, i.e., at each ϕ and θ, FID is obtained, Fourier transformed, differentiated twice, and back-projected with respect to ϕ and θ.

The number of angular views, N_θ and N_ϕ, are found to be important and propagation of the artifact to entire volume images was also found. One important advantage of this algorithm is that the convolution operation is simple due to the short convolution kernel (spatial-domain filter kernel contains only two terms).

Another algorithm of indirect volume image reconstruction with plane integrals, due to Lauterbur [22], is based on well-known 2-D projection reconstruction with 1-D projection data. In this method, a number of plane-integral data are obtained for N_θ views at a given ϕ view. With this set of plane-integral data, a conventional X-ray film-like image is first obtained at a given ϕ. By obtaining N_ϕ views, multiples of chest film-like 2-D images are obtained, and any slice is then reconstructed using the corresponding 1-D projection data existing in the 2-D images. This method is indirect, but assures proper

reconstruction. This method was, however, not attempted in the present simulation study.

IV. COMPUTER SIMULATION AND DISCUSSION

Computer modeling and simulations are carried out with Shepp's 3-D phantom whose spin density varies from 1.0 to 1.04 [14]. To study the effect of noise of the image, random Gaussian noise is added to the FID. The noise level was based on the calculation given in Section II-B. The reconstructed phantom size was 64 × 64 pixels with a total of 32 slices.

In Fig. 24, the effect of field gradient G_y in the single-line-scan imaging is shown, i.e., the effect of T_2^{**} on the single-line-scan imaging. In this figure, the spin-echo time t_y was set to 50 ms. As expected, the effects of the signal tail due to the other lines are clearly visible (compare Fig. 24(b),(c), and (d) with (a)).

In Fig. 25, images of single-line scan with three different noise levels are shown.

In Fig. 26, for comparison images obtained by single-line, full-line, and multislice full-line scan are shown for the same noise level given in Fig. 25(c). As expected, image noise was progressively reduced from single-line toward full and multislice full-line scan.

In Fig. 27, the potential of spin-echo repetition for high-speed imaging is demonstrated for reducing the total measurement

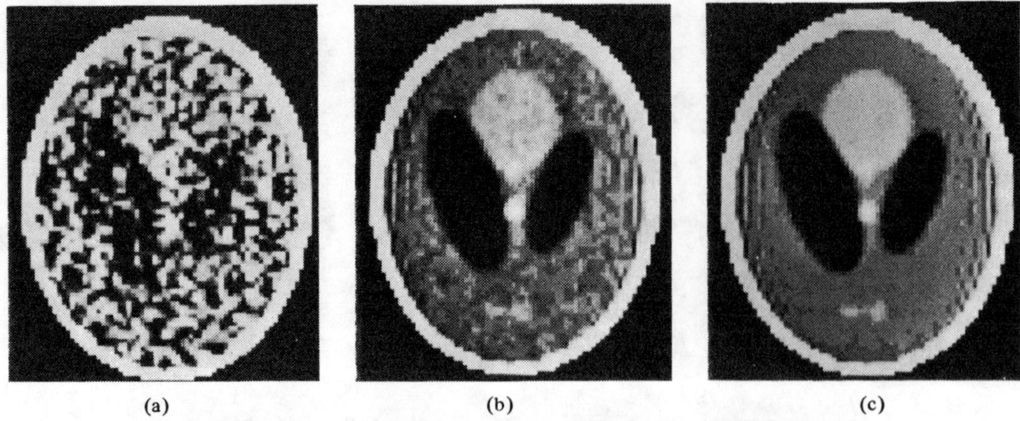

(a)   (b)   (c)

Fig. 26. Improvement of noise according to the different line-scan methods. Images of: (a) Multiple-line scan (16 lines G_x = 0.1 G/cm, G_y = 1 G/cm, t_y = 0.1 s, and noise factor = 1). (b) Full-line scan (64 lines G_x = 0.1 G/cm, G_y = 0.1, G_y = 0.1 G/cm, t_y = 0.1 s, and noise factor = 1). (c) Multislice full-line scan (G_x = 0.1 G/cm, G_y = 0.1 G/cm, t_y = 0.01 s, and noise factor = 1).

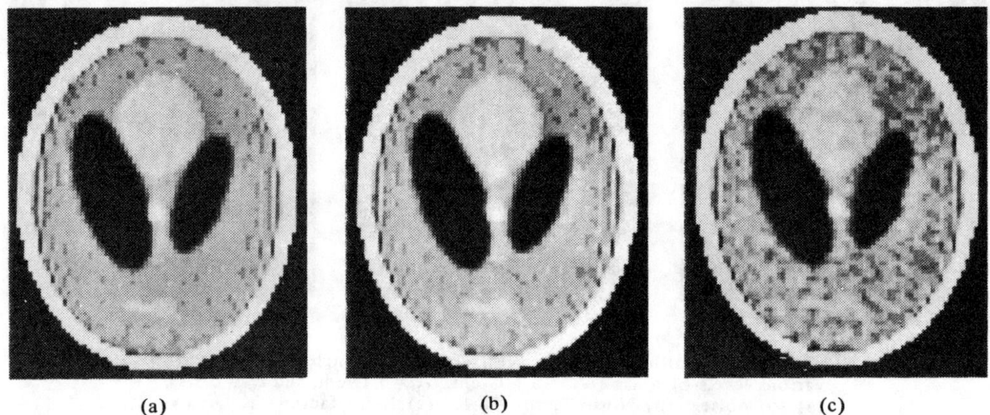

(a)   (b)   (c)

Fig. 27. Images of multislice full-line scan with three different numbers of spin-echo repetitions (G_x = 1 G/cm, G_y = 1 G/cm, t_y = 0.001 s, and noise factor = 1). (a) 16 spin echoes (t = 64 s). (b) 32 spin echoes (t = 32 s). (c) 64 spin echoes (t = 16 s), where t is the expected imaging times.

time, and images of multislice full-line scan with three different numbers of spin-echo repetitions are shown for an example.

In Fig. 28(a), the original phantom image is shown, and in Fig. 28(b) the image obtained by the original KWE method is shown. The latter shows a symmetry artifact due to the lack of data, i.e., missing data from π–2π in 2-D Fourier space. In Fig. 28(c) and (d), images of the modified KWE single slice and Hutchison–KWE are shown. Substantial improvements of image quality are noticed with both methods over original 2-D KWE technique. Note that the two images are identical in computer simulations due to the fact that both methods are essentially the same except RF and gradient-pulse sequences are different.

In Fig. 29, noise behavior of the line-integral projection reconstruction with several different noise factors is demonstrated. Images obtained by single-slice line-integral projection reconstruction with noise factors of 0, 1, 3, and 6 are shown.

Figs. 30 and 31 are images obtained by plane-integral reconstruction. In Fig. 30(a) and (b), the images are obtained by $N_\theta \times N_\phi$ of 50 × 50 and $N_\theta \times N_\phi$ of 100 × 100, respectively, with noise factors of 6. In Fig. 31, the images obtained with two different numbers of spin-echo repetitions are shown.

The gradient was set to 1 G/cm to obtain more spin echoes than the conventional NMR imaging systems which usually have field gradient of 0.1 G/cm. This high-field gradient may not be desirable from the noise point of view, since noise is proportional to the square root of bandwidth. With application of spin-echo repetitions, even with noise factor of 3, reasonable images are still obtained with a data-collection time of as short of 100 s (note that 32 slices are obtained simultaneously). Data-collection times can be further decreased at the expense of image quality.

Figs. 32–35 demonstrate propagation of artifacts for several different imaging modes when the object contains hot spots. In Figs. 32–34, images obtained at two different cut levels of the volume images by the multislice full-line scanning, multislice modified KWE direct Fourier imaging and 2-D line-integral projection reconstruction, respectively, are shown. It is interesting to observe and compare the effects of artifact propagation onto the other planes which actually do not contain hot objects. In Fig. 35, two images obtained by total volume plane-integral projection reconstruction with $N_\theta \times N_\phi$ of 50 × 50 and 100 × 100, respectively, are shown for comparison. At 50 × 50, a ring artifact due to the hot spots from other planes

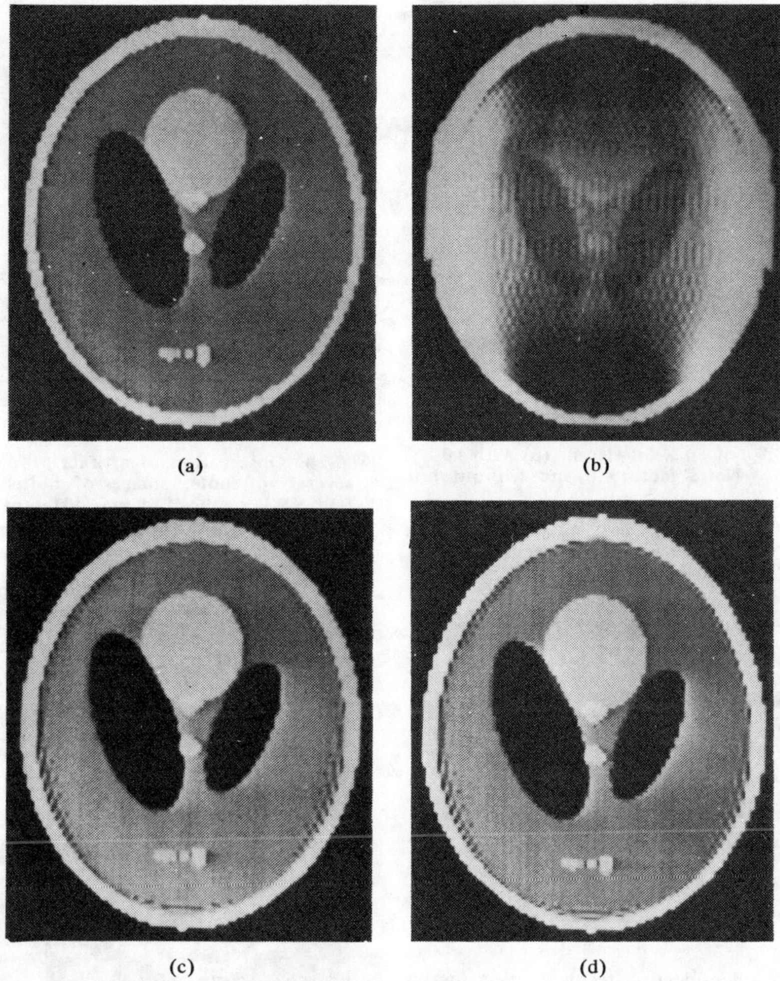

Fig. 28. Ideal and simulated images obtained by the original and improved KWE direct Fourier imagings. ($G_x = G_y$ = 0.1 G/cm with no noise). (a) Original phantom image. (b) Image obtained with original KWE method. (c) Image obtained with improved KWE method. (d) Image obtained with Hutchison–KWE method.

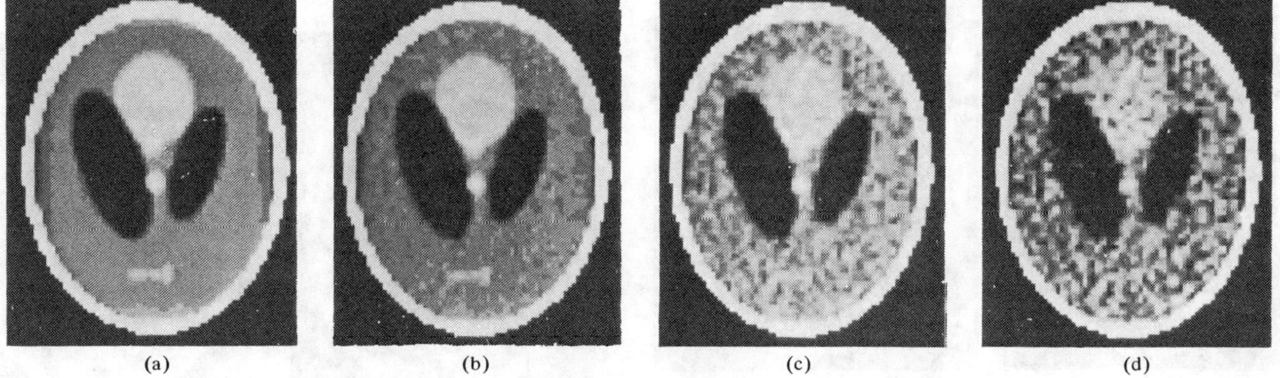

Fig. 29. Images obtained by line-integral projection reconstruction with different noise factors (100 views, G_{xy} = 0.1 G/cm). (a) No noise. (b) Noise factor = 1. (c) Noise factor = 3. (d) Noise factor = 6.

seriously affected image quality. Interestingly enough, both multislice modified KWE direct Fourier imaging and multislice full-line-scan imaging show the least artifact propagation. Even in the planes where the hot spots are contained, the ring artifact due to the hot spots was minimal with modified KWE imaging over other techniques—for example, total volume imaging with plane-integral projection reconstruction [9], [10].

V. CONCLUSION

The simple *single-line-scan method* can be extended to total volume imaging using spin-echo repetitions to enhance the SNR and be made comparable to other total volume imaging—for instance, total volume imaging with plane-integral projection data. Multislice full-line-scan imaging seems to be a potential candidate for NMR imaging.

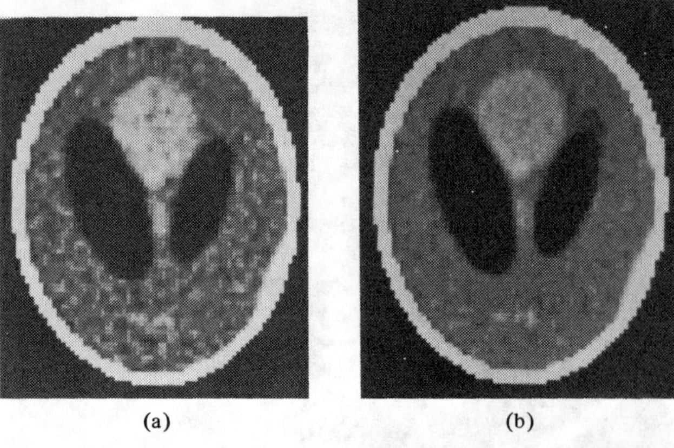

(a)   (b)

Fig. 30. Images obtained by total volume plane-integral projection reconstruction with: (a) $N_\theta \times N_\phi$ of 50×50 views. (b) With 100×100 views ($G_{xyz} = 0.1$ G/cm. Noise factor = 6 and without hot spots).

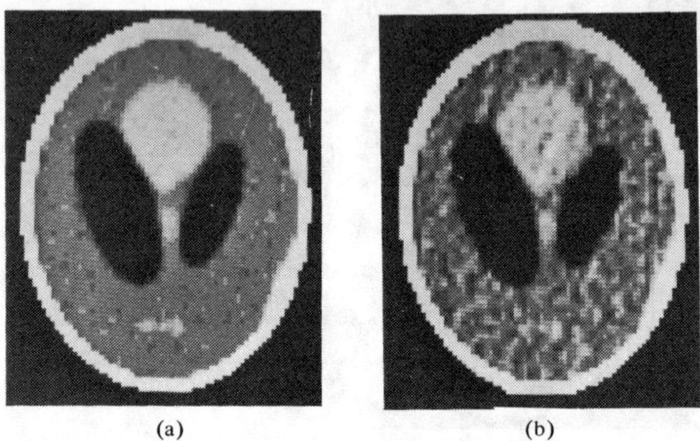

(a)   (b)

Fig. 31. Total volume plane-integral projection reconstruction images (without hot spots) obtained by spin-echo repetitions ($N_\theta \times N_\phi = 100 \times 100$, $G_{xyz} = 1$ G/cm). Images of: (a) 30 spin echoes ($t \simeq 167$ s). (b) 100 spin echoes ($t \simeq 50$ s), where t is the expected imaging times.

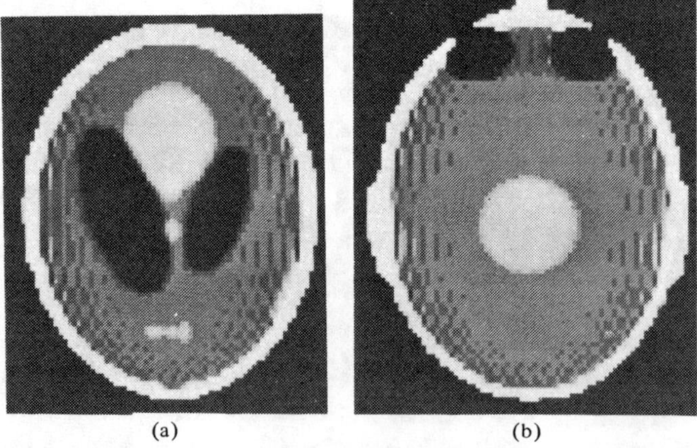

(a)   (b)

Fig. 32. Observation of artifact propagation when the object contains several hot spots. Images of multislice full-line scan at two different cut levels ($G_x = G_y = 0.1$ G/cm and no noise). (a) $z = 0.381$. (b) $z = 0$.

Obviously, single-line scan is inefficient and the large line artifact due to the unwanted FID signal tail degrades the image. A line-scan method with limited multislice–multiline imaging, however, might offer a unique possibility for rapid imaging of a small region.

Improved Kumar–Welti–Ernst direct Fourier imaging methods of both single and multislice with slice encoding give excellent artifact-free images.

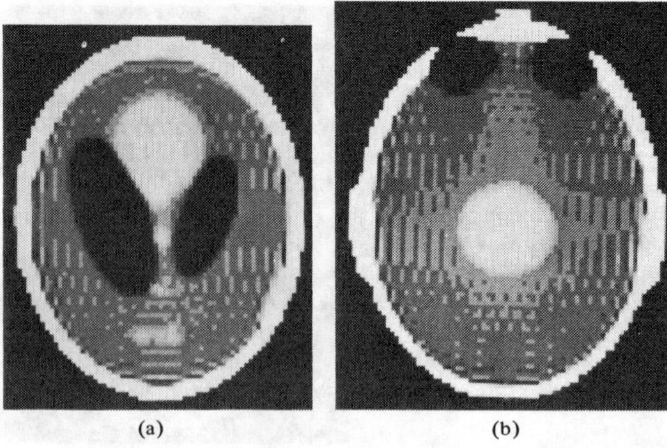

(a)   (b)

Fig. 33. Observation of artifact propagation when the object contains several hot spots. Images of multislice direct Fourier imaging (modified KWE method) at two different cut levels ($G_x = G_y = 0.1$ G/cm, and no noise). (a) $z = 0.381$. (b) $z = 0$.

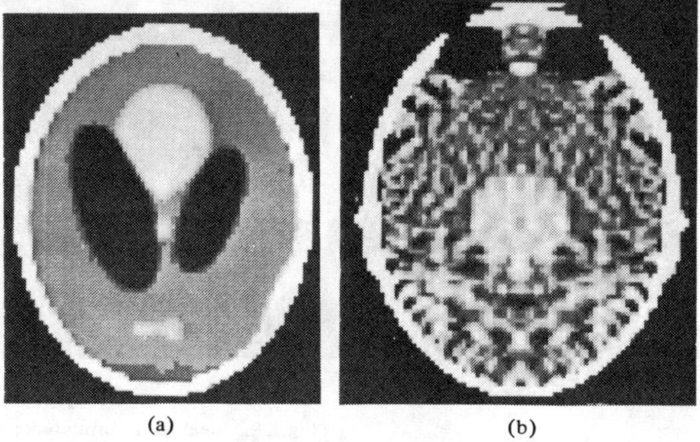

(a)   (b)

Fig. 34. Observation of artifact propagation when the object contains several hot spots. Images of 2-D line-integral projection reconstruction at two different cut levels (rays/view = 100, number of views $N_\theta = 150$, and no noise). (a) $z = 0.381$. (b) $z = 0$.

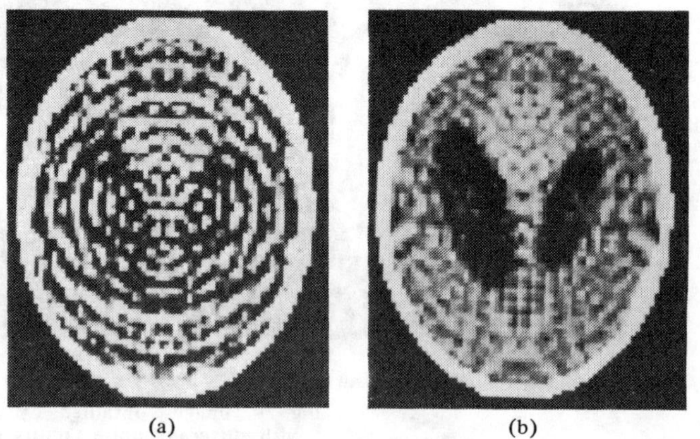

(a)   (b)

Fig. 35. Observation of artifact propagation when the object contains several hot spots. Images of total-volume plane-integral projection reconstruction (rays/view = 100, no noise and both at $z = 0.381$) with: (a) $N_\theta = N_\phi = 50$. (b) $N_\theta = N_\phi = 100$. Severe artifacts are observed due to the propagation of the streaks originated from some local hot spots.

Spin-echo technique employed in this method to obtain a full data set (four quadrants) is an improvement over the original KWE method and essentially fulfills the conditions necessary for 2-D Fourier transform and gives excellent quality images. It was also found that the Hutchison-KWE method is superior with respect to instrumental uncertainty, such as RF and gradient pulse timings.

Line-integral projection method has a reasonably high SNR and uses a reconstruction algorithm already developed for conventional X-CT. Data-collection time for a single slice is modest (about 50 s) when 100 views per slice are needed. Multiple spin-echo repetition technique can partly alleviate this problem and collection time can be reduced substantially.

Furthermore, by multiplane-encoding technique, higher SNR can be achieved and more spin-echo repetitions can be used. When all the planes of an object are encoded, this method converges to a total volume plane-integral projection method, which is considered the highest SNR NMR imaging method (requiring the longest data-collection time).

Total-volume plane-integral projection reconstruction gives the highest sensitivity among NMR imaging methods. The disadvantage of this method is its long minimum data-collection time but multiple spin echoes can reduce the total imaging time by a factor equivalent to the number of spin echoes applicable within T_1 decay. With a suitable field gradient and expected noise levels, application of 10 to 30 spin echoes appears possible in each T_1 period, and if the system noise is improved, the number of spin-echo repetitions can be increased further. By increase of the static magnetic field, it will also be possible to improve the imaging time in the total volume imaging.

In NMR imaging, it is reasonable to expect that a large number of new methods and techniques will be developed in the near future, especially in the areas of data-collection method and image processing.

In this paper, only a few potentially useful methods are analyzed and their perspectives are examined. Some of the more interesting aspects of NMR imaging are the potential for further improvement of the resolution and SNR with expected advances in hardware and software. NMR imaging has many unique properties which are "unconventional" both from traditional NMR chemistry and computer tomography points of view. NMR tomographic imaging seems a challenging new subject for many physical scientists; namely, electrical engineers, physicists, chemists, computer scientists, and medical researchers. From the evidence demonstrated by early investigations, it is not difficult to foresee that NMR may become a leading research topic in medical imaging and other physical sciences in the next decade, similar to X-CT development in the 1970's.

ACKNOWLEDGMENT

The authors would like to thank S. K. Hilal and A. Maudsley at Columbia University, New York, NY, and L. A. Shepp at Bell Laboratories, Murray Hill, NJ, for encouragement and many interesting discussions.

REFERENCES

[1] P. Lauterbur, "Image formation by induced local interactions: examples employing nuclear magnetic resonance," *Nature*, vol. 242, p. 190, 1973.
[2] R. Damadian, "Tumor detection by NMR," *Science*, vol. 171, p. 1151, 1971.
[3] E. Andrew, P. Bottomley, W. Hinshaw, G. Holland, and W. Moore, *Nature*, vol. 270, cover, 1977.
[4] W. Moore, G. Holland, and L. Kreel, "The NMR CAT scanner: A new look at the brain," *CT*, vol. 4, p. 1, 1980.
[5] G. Holland, R. Hawkes, and W. Moore, "Nuclear magnetic resonance (NMR) tomography of the brain: Coronal and sagittal sections," *J. Comput. Asst. Tomo.*, vol. 4, p. 429, 1980.
[6] P. Mansfield and A. Maudsley, "Fast scan proton density imaging by NMR," *J. Phys. E: Sci. Instrum.*, vol. 9, p. 271, 1976.
[7] A. Kumar, D. Welti, and R. Ernst, "NMR Fourier zeugmatography," *J. Mag. Res.*, vol. 18, p. 69, 1975.
[8] C-M. Lai, W. House, and P. Lauterbur, "Nuclear magnetic resonance zeugmatography for medical imaging," presented at Conf. Technology for Noninvasive Monitoring of Physiological Phenomena, session 30, IEEE and ERA Electro/78, Boston, MA, May 1978.
[9] L. Shepp, "Computerized tomography and nuclear magnetic resonance," *J. Comput. Asst. Tomo.*, vol. 4, p. 94, 1980.
[10] Z. H. Cho, S. K. Hilal, H. S. Kim, and H. B. Song, "Computer modeling and simulation of Fourier transform NMR tomography," in *NMR Imaging*. Philadelphia, PA: Saunders, in press.
[11] F. Block, "Nuclear induction," *Phys. Rev.*, vol. 70, p. 460, 1946.
[12] D. Shaw, *Fourier Transform NMR Spectroscopy*. New York: Elsevier, 1971.
[13] T. Farrar and E. Becker, *Pulse and Fourier Transform NMR*. New York: Academic Press, 1971.
[14] L. Shepp and B. Logan, "The Fourier resonstruction of a head section," *IEEE Trans. Nucl. Sci.*, vol. NS-21, p. 21, 1974.
[15] Z. H. Cho, J. K. Chan, Y. Chang, and E. Hall, "Comparative study of 3-D image reconstruction algorithms-with reference to number of projection and noise filtering," *IEEE Trans. Nucl. Sci.*, vol. NS-22, p. 344, 1975.
[16] H. Barrett and W. Swindell, "Analog reconstruction methods for transaxial tomography," *Proc. IEEE*, vol. 65, p. 89, 1977.
[17] H. J. Scudder, "Introduction to computer aided tomography," *Proc. IEEE*, vol. 66, p. 628, 1978.
[18] A. Maudsley, U.S. Patent applied for, P29, 36 465.6.
[19] J. Hutchison, W. Edelstein, and G. Johnson, "A whole-body NMR imaging machine," *J. Phys. E; Sci. Instrum*, vol. 13, p. 947, 1980.
[20] A. Maudsley, "Multiple-line-scanning spin density imaging," *J. Magn. Res.*, vol. 41, p. 112, 1980.
[21] L. Crooks, "Selective irradiation line scan technique for NMR imaging," *IEEE Trans. Nucl. Sci.*, vol. NS-27, p. 1239, 1980.
[22] P. Lauterbur, "Magnetic resonance zeugmatography," *Pure. Appl. Chem.*, vol. 40, p. 149, 1974.
[23] Z. H. Cho, J. B. Ra, Y. S. Kim, and H. S. Kim, "Line integral projection reconstruction (LPR) and its derivatives in Fourier transform NMR tomographic imaging," Korea Advanced Inst. Sci., ISSL Rep. 2, pp. 106, 1980.
[24] R. Marr, C-N. Chen, and P. Lauterbur, "On two approaches to 3-D reconstruction in NMR zeugmatography," in *Proc. Conf. en Mathematics Aspects of Computerized Tomography* (Mathematische Forschungsinstitute, Oberwolfach, West Germany, Feb. 10–16, 1980.
[25] H. S. Kim, "Fast total volume plane integrals projection reconstruction using spin echoes," Korea Advanced Inst. Sci., ISSL Rep. 2, pp. 137, 1980.
[26] P. Lauterbur and C-M. Lai, "Zeugmatography by reconstruction from projections," *IEEE Trans. Nucl. Sci.*, vol. NS-27, p. 1227, 1980.
[27] D. Hoult and R. Richards, "The signal-to noise ratio of the nuclear magnetic resonance experiment," *J. Magn. Res.*, vol. 24, p. 71, 1980.
[28] A. Garroway, P. Grannell, and P. Mansfield, "Image formation by a selective irradiative process," *J. Phys. C: Solid-State Phys.*, vol. 7, p. L457, 1974.
[29] G. Hounsfield, J. Ambrose, and J. Perry *et al.*, "Computerized transverse axial scanning," *Brit. J. Radiol.*, vol. 46, p. 1016, 1973.
[30] A. Cormack, "Reconstruction of densities from their projections, with applications in radiological physics," *Phys. Med. Biol.*, vol. 18, p. 195, 1973.
[31] Z. H. Cho, "General views on 3-D image reconstruction and computerized transverse axial tomography," *IEEE Trans. Nucl. Sci.*, vol. NS-21, p. 44, 1974.
[32] R. Brooks and G. Di Chiro, "Principles of computer assisted tomography (CAT) in radiographic and radioisotopic imaging," *Phys. Med. Biol.*, vol. 21, p. 689, 1976.
[33] M. M. Ter-Pogossian, "Basic principle of computed axial tomography," *Seminars in Nucl. Med.*, vol. 7, p. 109, 1977.
[34] Z. H. Cho, J. K. Chan, and L. Erikson, "Circular ring transverse axial positron camera for 3-D reconstruction of radionuclides distribution," *IEEE Trans. Nucl. Sci.*, vol. NS-23, p. 613, 1976.
[35] G. Ramachandran and A. Lakshminarayanan, "Three-dimensional reconstruction from radiographs and electron micrographs," *Proc. Nat. Acad. Sci. U.S.*, vol. 68, p. 2236, 1971.
[36] Z. H. Cho and J. Burger, "Construction, restoration, and enhancement of 2- and 3-dimensional images," *IEEE Trans. Nucl. Sci.*, vol. NS-24, p. 886, 1977.
[37] E. Tsui and T. Budinger, "A stochastic filter for transverse section reconstruction," *IEEE Trans. Nucl. Sci.*, vol. NS-26, p. 2687, 1979.
[38] W. Pratt, *Digital Image Processing*. New York: Wiley, 1978, 250 pp.
[39] H. B. Song, Z. H. Cho, and S. K. Hilal, "Direct Fourier transform

NMR tomography with modified Kumar–Welti–Ernst (MKWE) method," *IEEE Trans. Nucl. Sci.*, vol. NS-29, p. 493, 1982.
[40] J. R. Singer, "Blood flow measurements by NMR of the intact body," *IEEE Trans. Nucl. Sci.*, vol. NS-27, p. 1245, 1980.

Additional Bibliography on Projection Reconstruction and Related Topics

[41] H. H. Barrett, T. Bowen, R. S. Hershel, S. K. Gordon, and D. A. Delise, "Noise and dose considerations in transaxial tomography with X-rays and particles," in *Image Reconstruction for 2-D and 3-D Reconstruction from projections* (Tech. Dig., Opt. Soc. Amer.), Aug. 1976, publ. no. WB2.
[42] T. F. Budinger, K. M. Crowe, J. L. Cahoon, V. P. Elisher, R. H. Huesman, and L. L. Kanstein, "Transverse-section imaging with heavy charged particles; theory and applications," in *Image Reconstruction for 2-D and 3-D Reconstruction from Projections* (Tech. Dig., Optical Soc. Amer.), Aug. 1975, publ. no. MA 1.
[43] A. M. Cormack, "Representation of a function by its line integrals, with some radiological applications," *J. App. Phys.*, vol. 34, p. 2722, 1963.
[44] B.K.P. Horn, "Density reconstruction using arbitrary ray-sampling schemes," *Proc. IEEE*, vol. 66, p. 551, 1978.
[45] G. German, A. V. Lakshminaraynan, and A. Naparstek, "Convolution reconstruction techniques for divergent beams," *Comput. Biol. Med.*, vol. 6, p. 259, 1976.
[46] A. C. Kak, C. V. Takowatz, Jr., N. A. Baily, and R. A. Keller, "Computerized tomography using video recorded fluoroscopic images," *IEEE Trans. Biomed. Eng.*, vol. BME-24, p. 157, 1977.
[47] A. Macovski, "Ultrasonic imaging using arrays," *Proc. IEEE*, vol. 67, p. 484, 1979.
[48] R. M. Mersereau and A. V. Oppenheim, "Digital reconstruction of multidimensional signals from their projections," *Proc. IEEE*, vol. 62, p. 1319, 1974.
[49] J. Radon, "Über die Bestimmung von Funktionen durch ihre integral werte langs gewisser Mannig-faltigkeiten," *Ber. Saechsische Academie der Wissenschaften*," vol. 69, p. 262, 1917.
[50] R. K. Mueller, M. Kaveh, and G. Wade, "Reconstructive tomography and applications to ultrasonics," *Proc. IEEE*, vol. 67, p. 567, 1979.
[51] M. Ahmed and G. Wade, "Bragg diffraction imaging," *Proc. IEEE*, vol. 67, p. 587, 1979.
[52] Special Issue on Physical and Mathematiccal Aspects of 3-D Image Reconstruction (Z. H. Cho, Ed.), *IEEE Trans. Nucl. Sci.*, vol. NS-21, no. 3, 1974.
[53] Special Issue on Advances in Picture Reconstruction-Theory and Applications (Z. H. Cho, Ed.), *Comput. Biol. Med.*, vol. 6, no. 4, 1976.
[54] Special Issue on workshop on physics and Engineering in Computerized Tomography (O. Nalcioglu, Z. H. Cho, G. Knoll, Eds.), *IEEE Trans. Nucl. Sci.*, vol. NS-26, no. 2, 1979.
[55] Special Issue on Acoustic Imaging (K. Wang, Ed.), *Proc. IEEE*, vol. 67, no. 4, Apr. 1979.
[56] Special Issue on Computed Tomography (A. C. Kak, Ed.), *IEEE Trans. Biomed. Eng.*, vol. BME- Feb. (1981).

Additional References on NMR Imaging

[57] D. I. Hoult, "The NMR receiver: A description and analysis of design," in *Progress on NMR Spectroscopy*, vol. 12. New York: Pergamon, 1978, p. 41.
[58] J. Hutchison, R. Sutherland, and J. Mallard, "NMR imaging: Image recovery under magnetic fields with large non-uniformities," *J. Phys. E: Sci. Instrum.*, vol. 11, p. 217, 1978.
[59] L. Crooks, J. Hoenninger *et al.*, "Tomography of hydrogen with nuclear magnetic resonance and the potential for imaging other body constituents," *SPIE*, vol. 206, p. 120, 1979.
[60] P. Mansfield and I. L. Pykett, "Biological and medical imaging by NMR," *J. Magn. Res.*, vol. 29, p. 335, 1978.
[61] D. I. Hoult, "The solution of Bloch equations in the presence of a varying B_1 field—An approach to selective pulse analysis," *J. Magn. Res.*, vol. 35, p. 69, 1979.
[62] P. Bottomley, "A comparative evaluation of proton NMR imaging results," *J. Magn. Res.*, vol. 36, p. 121, 1979.
[63] A. Maudsley *et al.*, "Rapid measurement of magnetic field distributions using nuclear magnetic resonance," *Siemens Forsch. Entwickl.—Ber.*, vol. 8, p. 326, 1979.
[64] P. Mansfield, P. Morris, R. Ordidge, L. Pykett *et al.*, "Human whole-body imaging and detection of breast tumors by NMR," *Phil. Trans. Roy. Soc. Lond.*, vol. B289, p. 503, 1980.
[65] P. Bendel, C.-M. Lai, and P. Lauterbur," ^{31}P spectroscopic zeugmatography of phosphorus metabolites," *J. Magn. Res.*, vol. 38, p. 343, 1980.
[66] J. Hutchison, G. Johnson, and T. Redpath, "Spin warp NMR imaging and applications to human whole-body imaging," *J. Phys. E.: Sci. Instrum.*, vol. 13, p. 751, 1980.
[67] D. Kramer, "Imaging of elements other than hydrogen," in *NMR Imaging in Medicine*. Philadelphia, PA, Saunders, in press.
[68] D. Kramer, J. Schneider, A. Rudin, and P. Lauterbur, "True three dimensional nuclear magnetic resonance zeugmatographic images of a human brain," *Neuroradiology*, to be published.
[69] C.-M. Lai, "True three dimensional nuclear magnetic resonance imaging by Fourier reconstruction zeugmatography," *J. Appl. Phys.*, vol. 52, p. 1141, 1981.
[70] I. L. Pykett, "NMR imaging in medicine," *Sci. Amer.*, vol. 246, no. 5, vol. 78, May 1982.
[71] H. S. Kim, Y. S. Kim, Z. H. Cho, and S. K. Hilal, "Phase delay and attenuation corrections in Fourier transform NMR tomographic imaging," *IEEE Trans. Nucl. Sci.*, vol. NS-28, p. 142, 1981.
[72] T. F. Budinger, "Thresholds for physiological effects due to RF and magnetic fields used in NMR imaging," *IEEE Trans. Nucl. Sci.*, vol. NS-26, p. 2821, 1979.
[73] P. Mansfield and P. G. Morris, *NMR Imaging in Biomedicine*, Supplement 2 to *Advances in Magnetic Resonance*. New York: Academic Press, (1982).

Tutorial Review of Synthetic-Aperture Radar (SAR) with Applications to Imaging of the Ocean Surface

KIYO TOMIYASU

Invited Paper

Abstract—A synthetic aperture radar (SAR) can produce high-resolution two-dimensional images of mapped areas. The SAR comprises a pulsed transmitter, an antenna, and a phase-coherent receiver. The SAR is borne by a constant velocity vehicle such as an aircraft or satellite, with the antenna beam axis oriented obliquely to the velocity vector. The image plane is defined by the velocity vector and antenna beam axis. The image orthogonal coordinates are range and cross range (azimuth). The amplitude and phase of the received signals are collected for the duration of an integration time after which the signal is processed. High range resolution is achieved by the use of wide bandwidth transmitted pulses. High azimuth resolution is achieved by focusing, with a signal processing technique, an extremely long antenna that is synthesized from the coherent phase history. The pulse repetition frequency of the SAR is constrained within bounds established by the geometry and signal ambiguity limits.

SAR operation requires relative motion between radar and target. Nominal velocity values are assumed for signal processing and measurable deviations are used for error compensation. Residual uncertainties and high-order derivatives of the velocity which are difficult to compensate may cause image smearing, defocusing, and increased image sidelobes. The SAR transforms the ocean surface into numerous small cells, each with dimensions of range and azimuth resolution. An image of a cell can be produced provided the radar cross section of the cell is sufficiently large and the cell phase history is deterministic. Ocean waves evidently move sufficiently uniformly to produce SAR images which correlate well with optical photographs and visual observations. The relationship between SAR images and oceanic physical features is not completely understood, and more analyses and investigations are desired.

I. Introduction

A RADAR IS an electromagnetic wave sensor having a pulsed microwave transmitter, antenna, and receiver [1]. The antenna can be time-shared between transmitter and receiver by utilizing a circulator as shown in Fig. 1. The pulse transmitter signal is radiated by the antenna, reflected from the target, and sensed by the receiver. The reflected signal time delay is proportional to target range. The range resolution δ_r is determined by the effective radar pulse length τ, and $\delta_r = c\tau/2$ where c is light velocity. The azimuthal or cross-range direction of the target is established by the orientation of the antenna beam. The azimuthal or cross-range angular resolution is determined by the antenna beamwidth which is related to antenna size. In a synthetic aperture radar (SAR) to be described, the azimuthal resolution can be very significantly improved by the use of a phase coherent signal processing technique which integrates many transmitted pulses. Two-

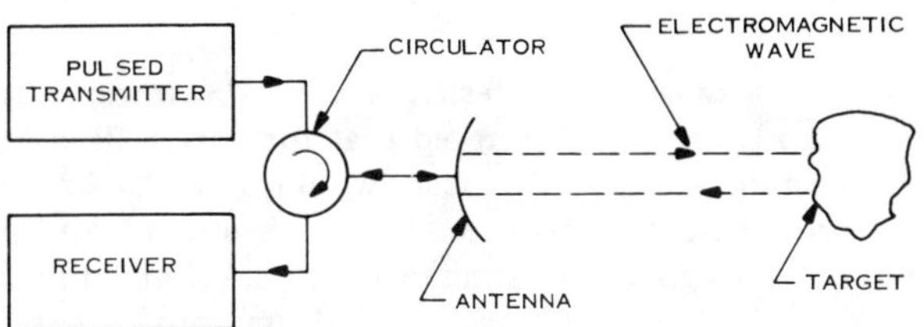

Fig. 1. Basic radar block diagram.

dimensional radar images of large areas can be produced with high spatial resolution.

This paper is intended for the student in SAR; as such, more sophisticated design details have been omitted intentionally. It is hoped that those working in related technologies will also find this paper of value to them. An attempt has been made to convey only the basic physical concepts involved in a SAR imaging the ocean surface.

Active and passive microwave sensors are being used to make remote observations of the earth during day or night, through cloud cover, and even through light rain [2]. A SAR operating at a microwave frequency can produce two-dimensional images of large area targets rapidly with the SAR mounted on an aircraft, and global coverage is potentially possible from spacecraft. Global observation of oceanic waves offer the potential of providing such useful data as surface wind speed, wind direction, significant wave height, etc., for meteorological forecasting and the prediction of disastrous oceanic storms.

High resolution in range is attained using transmitted pulses that are effectively of very short duration. In a conventional radar high range resolution is attained relatively easily; however, high resolution in azimuth becomes exceedingly difficult, especially at long ranges, because of the need for huge antennas. In a SAR, the radar platform moves along a straight path in a direction oblique (typically at right angles) to the target to be imaged as shown in Fig. 2. A coherent phase history of the pulsed return signal is generated, and, through a signal processing technique, extremely high resolution in the azimuth direction is attained without recourse to physically large antennas. In effect, a large aperture antenna is thus synthesized.

SAR began with an observation by Carl Wiley in 1951 that a radar beam oriented obliquely to the radar platform velocity vector will receive signals having frequencies offset from the radar carrier frequency due to the Doppler effect [3]. He noted that the Doppler frequency spread was related to the width of the antenna beam and could be split and filtered in

Manuscript received October 26, 1977; revised January 30, 1978.

The author is with the General Electric Co., Valley Forge Space Center, Philadelphia, PA 19101.

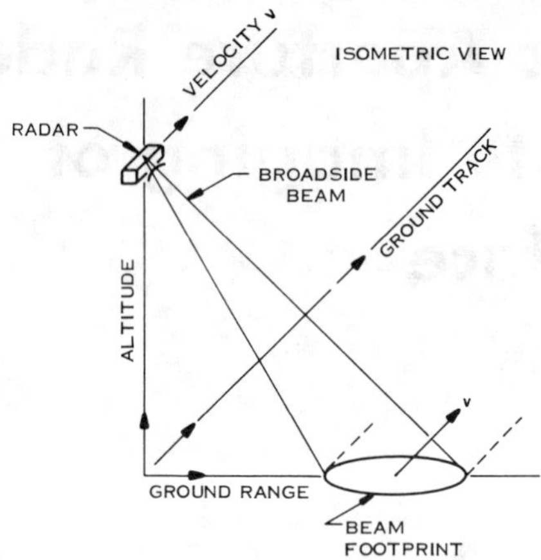

Fig. 2. Synthetic aperture radar (SAR) geometry.

the receiver, such that the desired antenna beamwidth could be made narrower. He also noted that for a given filter bandwidth, the narrowest angular beam would occur broadside to the platform velocity. In the ensuing years activity continued on analyses and signal processing techniques, refining the capabilities, and developing the hardware. Numerous papers have been written on this subject [4]. For background material the reader may find helpful the discussion by Cutrona [5] and the books written by Harger [6] and Rihaczek [7]. Kovaly [8] has recently published a collection of useful papers on SAR.

SAR processing entails the correlation of the return signal phase with that of a suitable reference signal. If the reference signal phase involves many cycles, this is called a focused synthetic aperture which is discussed in this paper. The formation of a synthetic aperture can be simplified by using a shorter history of return signal and a corresponding reduction in reference signal phase change. In this case the azimuth resolution will degrade. In the limit, the simplest synthetic aperture can be formed with a constant phase reference signal and a relatively short history of return signal. This is called an unfocused synthetic aperture [5] and will not be discussed.

The SAR image plane is defined by the radar platform velocity vector $\overline{v}$ and the radar antenna beam axis $\overline{R}$. The image coordinates are range, time delay, and range rate (Doppler). The SAR antenna beam can be pointed in any oblique direction relative to $\overline{v}$, however, there is a geometrical constraint involving the object scene plane normal $\hat{n}$. The constraint requires that $\hat{n}$ must not lie in the SAR image plane. In vector notation

$$(\overline{v} \times \overline{R}) \cdot \hat{n} \neq 0.$$

Other vector identities are $\overline{v} \cdot (\overline{R} \times \hat{n})$ and $\overline{R} \cdot (\hat{n} \times \overline{v})$. An equivalent constraint applies when SAR imagery is taken with a stationary radar platform and a moving object scene.

Assuming that the geometrical constraint is satisfied, a commonly used direction of $\overline{R}$ is perpendicular to $\overline{v}$. This is called "broadside," and this SAR geometry is assumed in this paper. If the direction is not broadside, it is called squint beam SAR [5], [9]–[11], and it offers a forward- or rearward-look capability. The signal processing becomes considerably more complex, and it requires a longer integration time or signal history for a given azimuth resolution. The squint beam SAR is not discussed in this paper. The basic principles of the SAR are discussed, as well as the physical significance of a synthetic aperture, the nature of range and azimuth ambiguities, imaging coverage rate, effects due to earth rotation and satellite-orbit

eccentricity, imaging of moving targets, various sources of errors, signal processing principles, radar frequency selection, signal-to-noise ratio, transmitter design, receiver design, and ocean wave images. Some design refinements and operational error corrections are also introduced.

II. The Synthetic Aperture

The resolution capability of a radar is specified in the range and cross-range (azimuth) directions. The range resolution δ_r of all radars depends on an effective transmitted pulse length τ or alternatively on a signal bandwidth. The angular cross-range or azimuth resolution depends on an equivalent antenna beamwidth. In a conventional radar the angular azimuth resolution is specified by the 3-dB or half-power beamwidth. The one-way 3-dB beamwidth θ_{13} is given nominally by

$$\theta_{13} = \lambda/L \text{ rad}$$

where λ is the radar wavelength, and L is the antenna aperture size.

Usually it is assumed that the antenna is focused to infinity, i.e., aperture with uniform phase, and the beamwidth is defined in the far zone. The linear azimuth resolution δ_{az} at a distance R is

$$\delta_{az} = R\theta_{13} = R\lambda/L.$$

For a given range R and given wavelength λ, if L is increased then δ_{az} is decreased. With very large values of L due consideration must be given to the far zone condition of the antenna. The far zone distance R_{fz} is given by

$$R_{fz} = 2L^2/\lambda.$$

From a point on the beam axis at R_{fz}, the path length variation across the antenna aperture is symmetrical and is $\lambda/16$ for a one-way path. The angular direction from the beam axis for half-power response is $\pm \theta_{13}/2 = \lambda/(2L)$ rad. When viewed in this direction at range R_{fz}, the one-way phase across the aperture will appear to have a linear slope with a total phase change of π radians.

In a SAR application, which is a phase coherent system, the antenna beamwidth and phase must be considered over a two-way path so that the net two-way 3-dB beamwidth θ_{23} is narrower than θ_{13} by one-half, and it is given approximately by

$$\theta_{23} = \lambda/(2L_{sa})$$

where L_{sa} is the aperture length. The subscript "sa" anticipates synthetic aperture.

A. Near-Zone Focused Long Array

At an arbitrary range R_0, the linear azimuth resolution can be made arbitrarily fine by utilizing a large value of L_{sa}. With very large L_{sa} it is possible for R_{fz} to exceed R_0, and the antenna is then focused in the near zone [12], [13] to achieve a linear azimuth resolution given by

$$\delta_{az} = \theta_{23}R_0 = \frac{\lambda R_0}{2L_{sa}}.$$

B. Close Target Separability

The spatial resolution of a long focused array can also be defined by its capability of resolving two close targets [7]. This can be achieved if the difference in the path lengths equals one-half wavelength. By referring to Fig. 3, the long array has

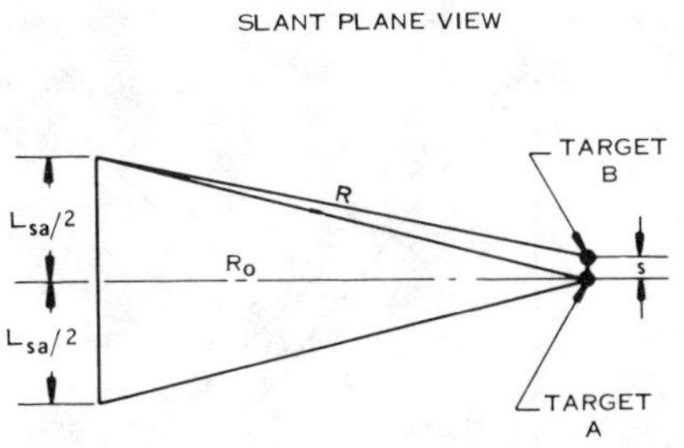

Fig. 3. Close target separability.

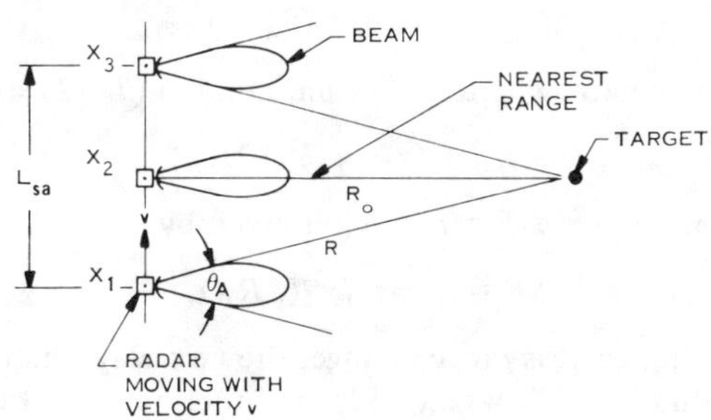

Fig. 4. Radar-target geometry.

a length L_{sa}, and the mid-array range to the target is R_0. The array tip range R to the target is given by

$$R = \sqrt{R_0^2 + (s - L_{sa}/2)^2}$$

where s = separation between two targets. The derivative is

$$\frac{dR}{ds} = \frac{s - L_{sa}/2}{R_0}.$$

At $s = 0$, the derivative is

$$\frac{\Delta R}{\Delta s} = \frac{-L_{sa}}{2R_0}.$$

A one-half wavelength total path difference is equivalent to $\Delta R = \lambda/4$, so that the spatial resolution Δs which is equal to the azimuth resolution δ_{az} becomes

$$\delta_{az} = \frac{R_0 \lambda}{2L_{sa}}.$$

C. Synthesized Antenna Array

To illustrate the previous discussion, consider the following: to achieve δ_{az} = 15 m at a target range of $R_0 = 10^6$ m with λ = 0.1 m, the aperture length L_{sa} is 3.333 × 10³ m and θ_{23} = 1.5 × 10⁻⁵ rad. For this example, $R_{fz} = 2.222 \times 10^8$ m, so that the target is in the near zone of this large aperture antenna. Such an antenna array, 3.33 kilometers long, is impractical for aircraft or spacecraft. Fortunately, the array need not necessarily be continuous, but can be composed instead of numerous small elemental radiators placed sufficiently close together to prevent grating lobes in the angular directions of interest, and properly phased to focus the aperture at range R_0. Further, it is not necessary for all elements to radiate simultaneously since each of the elements can be excited in sequence provided an orderly coherent phase relationship is maintained. Hence, a physically smaller radiator can be carried aboard a platform moving at a constant velocity v with the radar transmitting pulses periodically as the radiator is laterally displaced by a proper amount. In this manner, the equivalent of a very long antenna array with length L_{sa} is synthesized from a number of small elements equal in number to the pulses transmitted and integrated coherently. This synthesized antenna array is called a synthetic aperture. There are critical limits on the pulse repetition frequency discussed later under ambiguities.

The time that the target is illuminated by the radar beam, or dwell time, is $T_D = L_{sa}/v$, where v is the radar platform velocity. For an aperture length of $L_{sa} = vT_D$, the linear azimuth resolution δ_{sa} is given by

$$\delta_{az} = R_0 \frac{\lambda}{2L_{sa}} = \frac{\lambda R_0}{2vT_D}.$$

For a specified azimuth resolution δ_{az} the required dwell time $T_D = \lambda R_0/(2\delta_{az}v)$. A radar illumination time of T_D (which is typically in the order of one second) can be provided with a one-way radar antenna beamwidth $\theta_R = L_{sa}/R_0$. This beamwidth requires a small radiator (radar antenna) length $L_R = \lambda/\theta_R$. An equation involving L_{sa} and L_R can be obtained from

$$\theta_R = \frac{L_{sa}}{R_0} = \frac{\lambda}{L_R}$$

or

$$\lambda R_0 = L_R L_{sa}.$$

The azimuth resolution can be written as

$$\delta_{az} = \frac{\lambda/2}{\theta_R} = \frac{\lambda/2}{L_{sa}/R_0} = \frac{L_R}{2}.$$

The azimuth resolution of a focused SAR is equal to one-half the radar-antenna length L_R, and this resolution is independent of radar frequency and range. The azimuth resolution δ_{az} is also equal to one half the radar wavelength ($\lambda/2$) divided by the radian viewing angle either of the target by the radar (θ_R) or the radar from the target (L_{sa}/R). Very fine resolution images can, in principle, be produced with a small low-gain radar antenna (small L_R), but because of the low antenna gain, very high power transmitters are required for target detection.

D. Doppler Frequency

The SAR involves phase coherent signal processing, and, for an isolated target, the phase history during the integration time follows a quadratic phase function, as will be shown. The slant-plane radar geometry is illustrated in Fig. 4. It is assumed that the radar antenna beam axis is oriented at right angles (broadside) to the radar platform velocity vector. The antenna beam illuminates the target when the platform reaches position x_1 but not before. It continues to illuminate the target for a distance L_{sa} until it reaches x_3. The range to the target is R given by

$$R = \sqrt{R_0^2 + (x - x_0)^2}$$

where

R_0 nearest range to target;
x position of radar platform;
x_0 platform position corresponding to R_0 (x_2 in Fig. 4).

The azimuth beamwidth θ_A and L_{sa} are related by

$$L_{sa} = 2R_0 \tan(\theta_A/2).$$

By assuming a narrow antenna beam, i.e., $\tan(\theta_A/2) \doteq \theta_A/2$

$$R \doteq R_0 + (x - x_0)^2/(2R_0).$$

The change in range $\Delta R = R - R_0$ is given by

$$\Delta R = (x - x_0)^2/(2R_0).$$

Corresponding to this range change, the two-way phase change as a function of x follows a quadratic function given by

$$\phi(x) = (x - x_0)^2/(\lambda R_0) \text{ wavelengths.}$$

It is desired to change from the independent position parameter x to time t. By assuming a constant velocity v for the radar platform, the displacement $x - x_0 = v(t - t_0)$, and the two-way phase change as a function of t becomes

$$\phi(t) = v^2(t - t_0)^2/(\lambda R_0) \text{ wavelengths}$$

where t is the time variable corresponding to position x.

A time rate of change in phase causes a frequency shift, and the two-way Doppler frequency f_D is given by the first derivative of the phase change:

$$f_D = 2v^2(t - t_0)/(\lambda R_0).$$

It is noted that the Doppler frequency changes linearly with time, and the total change during the target illumination period is $2v^2 T_D/(\lambda R_0) = v/\delta_{az}$.

In this section it has been shown that an extremely long antenna capable of very fine angular resolution can be synthesized from processing the coherent radar signals received by a relatively smaller antenna that is periodically pulsed while the radar is moving obliquely to the antenna beam.

III. Ambiguities

As stated, the synthesized antenna consists of numerous radiating elements whose separation is established by the radar-pulse repetition frequency and platform velocity. There are limiting values on the pulse repetition frequency (PRF) imposed by geometry. Thus, if the PRF is so high that return signals from two successive transmitted pulses arrive simultaneously at the receiver, there will be ambiguity in the response. Conversely, if the PRF is so low that the reflected signal phase of any target changes by 2π radians or more between two successive pulses, there will again be ambiguity in the response.

A. Range Ambiguity

The high PRF limit is governed by the elevation beamwidth geometry and radar-pulse propagation time [14]. An elevation view of the radar beam geometry is depicted in Fig. 5(a). The beam intercepts the ground at near range R_n and far range R_f. The ground swath width $W_g = (R_f - R_n)/\sin \phi_i$, where ϕ_i is the incidence angle. In Fig. 5(b) a timing diagram is illustrated with a transmitted pulse of length τ and a received pulse signal starting at $t = 2R_n/c$ and ending at $t = 2R_f/c + \tau$. The high PRF limit of receiving simultaneous return signals from two successive pulses is given by

$$\text{PRF}_{\text{high}} = 1/[2\tau + 2(R_f - R_n)/c].$$

This upper PRF limit is commonly called the range ambiguity limit. In practice the highest operating PRF is set lower than that limit. In some applications the received pulse length

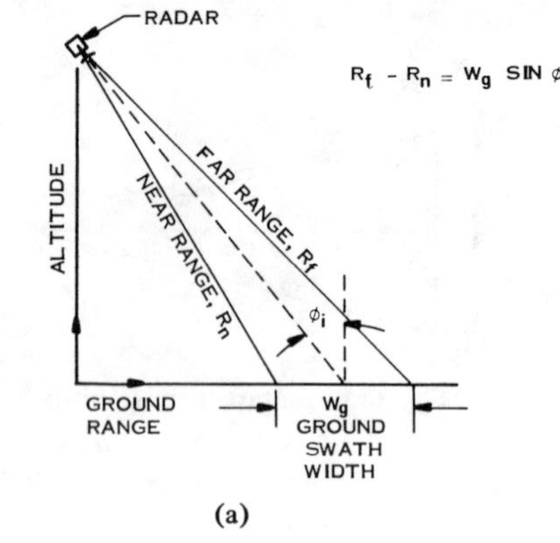

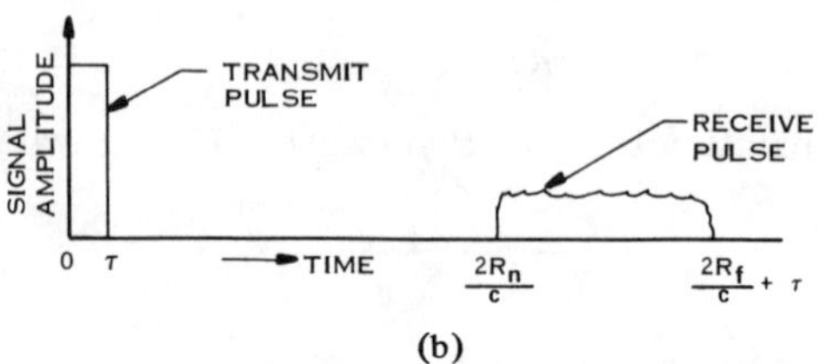

Fig. 5. Radar range characteristics. (a) Elevation view. (b) Pulse characteristics.

$2(R_f - R_n)/c$ is considerably shorter than the round-trip pulse time $2R_f/c$. Thus it is possible to transmit pulses in rapid succession, to have several pulses in transit simultaneously, and to avoid eclipsing the reflected signals by temporal interlacing with the transmitted pulses. Another problem that can potentially cause a range ambiguous response is a radar return from the nadir direction. Frequently the radar cross section in the nadir direction is very strong. Its effects can be reduced substantially be orienting a radar beam null towards nadir.

B. Azimuth Ambiguity – 2π Radian Shift Between Pulses

The low PRF limit is governed by the geometry that causes a maximum phase shift of 2π rad from pulse-to-pulse of any target illuminated by a broadside oriented radar beam. The targets of principal concern occur at beam edge in the azimuth plane. If a 2π-rad phase shift occurs, there will be ambiguity in distinguishing these targets from other targets at the same range that cause zero phase shift (zero Doppler). The zero phase shift targets lie on a plane that is oriented at right angles to the radar platform velocity vector or at the center of the broadside beam. There are different approaches to establishing the low PRF limit, and four are presented here. It is instructive to examine these approaches for the insight they afford into the SAR concept. In all cases, it is shown that $\text{PRF}_{\text{low}} = v/(L_R/2)$ where v is radar platform velocity and L_R is radar antenna size. The first approach considers a maximum of 2π-rad shift during a pulse-repetition period. The second approach stipulates that the PRF must exceed the maximum Doppler frequency. The third approach is based on the requirement that the number of pulses integrated must exceed the number of azimuth resolution cells across the radar linear beamwidth. Finally, the low PRF limit is examined in terms of a synthesized linear array antenna that places the array grating lobes in the directions of nulls of the element pattern.

In the first approach to a lower PRF limit, the tolerable two-way phase shift during the interpulse period is 2π rad for a target at azimuthal beam edge. The slant plane geometry is shown in Fig. 6, and the radar range R to a target at beam edge

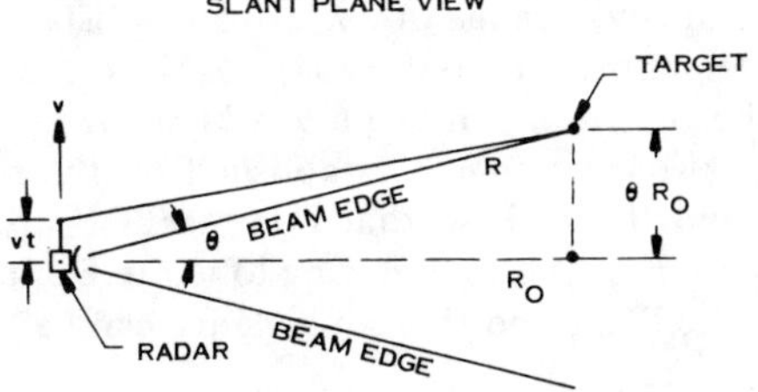

Fig. 6. Beam edge target geometry.

is given by

$$R = \sqrt{R_0^2 + (\theta R_0 - vt)^2}$$

where θ is the angle from beam axis and t is the time from nearest range (R_0) location. By taking the time derivative of R and noting that R is approximately equal to R_0

$$\frac{dR}{dt} = v\theta.$$

A 2π-rad two-way phase shift at beam edge is equivalent to $\Delta R = \lambda/2$. The direction of beam edge is arbitrarily chosen to be the first null of the one-way radar beam pattern so that $\theta = \pm\lambda/L_R$, where L_R is radar-antenna size. This direction is selected to minimize the azimuth ambiguity response. In this calculation the time interval Δt is the interpulse period, so $\mathrm{PRF} = 1/\Delta t$. The lower PRF limit is given by

$$\mathrm{PRF}_{\mathrm{low}} = \frac{v\theta}{\Delta R} = \frac{v(\lambda/L_R)}{\lambda/2} = \frac{v}{L_R/2}.$$

This equation implies that the transmitter must be pulsed before the radar platform moves a distance equal to one-half the antenna size. For high-quality imagery, the lowest operational PRF should be perhaps 25 percent greater than this $\mathrm{PRF}_{\mathrm{low}}$.

C. Azimuth Ambiguity–PRF Equal to Doppler Frequency

In the second approach, the PRF must equal or exceed the maximum Doppler shift of the return signals. The transmitted signal has spectral components separated in frequency from the carrier by an amount equal to the PRF. The received signal has additional spectral components separated in frequency from the carrier determined by the Doppler shift from the targets illuminated by the antenna beam. Targets at the center of the broadside beam will return signals with zero Doppler shift. Targets ahead of broadside center are characterized by a positive Doppler and those behind by negative Doppler frequencies. If the return of a target is shifted in frequency by an amount equal to the PRF, the receiver will be unable to distinguish the pulsed return signal from that of a target on broadside center. Thus the PRF has to be sufficiently high to exceed the maximum Doppler shift of targets located at beam edge. The Doppler shift f_D due to a radial velocity v_r is given by

$$f_D = \frac{2v_r}{c}f$$

where f is the radar frequency and c is the light velocity.

By referring to Fig. 7, $v_r = v \sin \theta \doteq v\theta$. The angle θ to the first null of the one-way radar illumination beam is $\theta = \pm \lambda/L_R$. Thus the lower limit of the PRF is

$$\mathrm{PRF}_{\mathrm{low}} = f_D = \frac{v}{L_R/2}.$$

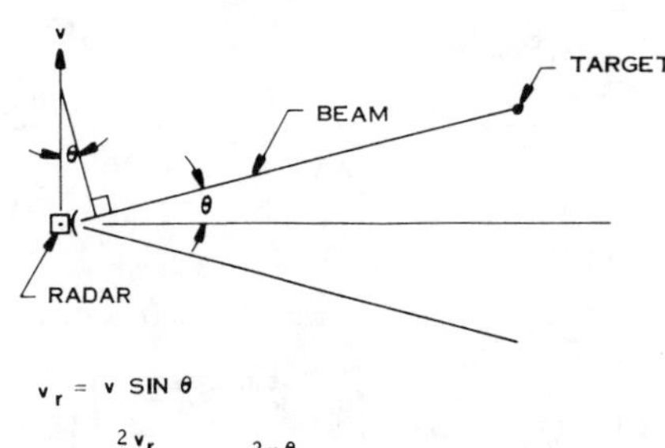

Fig. 7. Doppler frequency geometry.

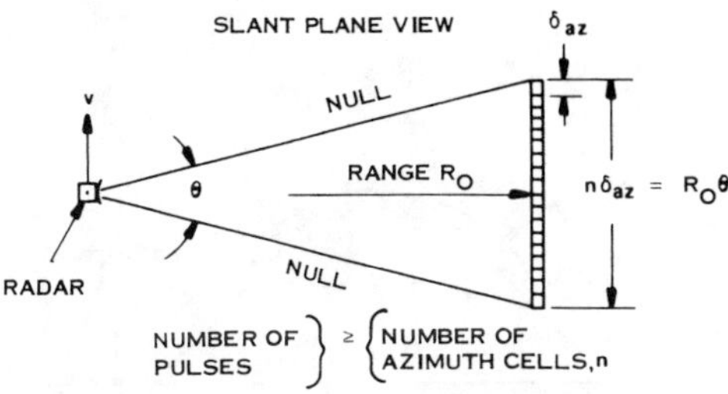

Fig. 8. Azimuthal cells within linear beamwidth.

D. Azimuth Ambiguity–Integrated Pulses Equal to Azimuth Cells

The third approach is based on the stipulation that n pulsed measurements are necessary to solve n unknowns. The number of pulsed measurements is equal to the product of the PRF and integration time T_D, i.e., $n = \mathrm{PRF} \times T_D$. The n unknowns of interest are the total number of azimuth resolution cells at range R_0 which occupy the linear beamwidth $\theta R_0 = R_0 2\lambda/L_R$ where θ is the one-way null–null angular beamwidth. This is shown in Fig. 8. The total signal $\overline{E}_R(t)$ at the receiver is the complex sum of the reflected signals from n resolvable scatterers at range R_0. This can be written as

$$\overline{E}_R(R_0, t) = \sum_n \overline{E}_i(R_0, t)$$

where $\overline{E}_i$ is the complex reflected signal from scatterer i. The azimuth resolution δ_{az} is $R_0\lambda/(2vT_D)$ so that the number of resolvable cells is $\theta R_0/\delta_{az} = 4vT_D/L_R$. The number of pulsed measurements is $\mathrm{PRF} \times (\theta R_0)/v = \mathrm{PRF} \times (2R_0\lambda)/(L_R v)$. Thus the lower PRF limit is

$$\mathrm{PRF}_{\mathrm{low}} = \frac{v}{\delta_{az}} = \frac{v}{L_R/2}.$$

E. Azimuth Ambiguity–Array Grating Lobe at Element Null

In the last approach the synthesized linear array antenna is analyzed. The overall array pattern is configured so that a low response occurs in the angular direction of the first grating lobe where the Doppler frequency is equal to the PRF. The usual normalized linear antenna array pattern E_{LA} is given by the product of a normalized array factor E_{AF} and a normalized element pattern E_{EP}, that is, $E_{\mathrm{LA}} = E_{\mathrm{AF}}E_{\mathrm{EP}}$ [15]. The normalized synthesized array pattern for a SAR differs in the following way. The normalized array factor is modified to account for the two-way coherent phase effect, and this is accomplished by doubling the element spacing D_{PP} that ap-

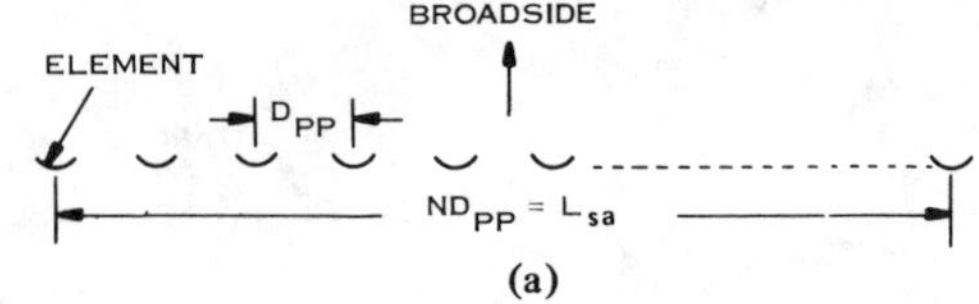

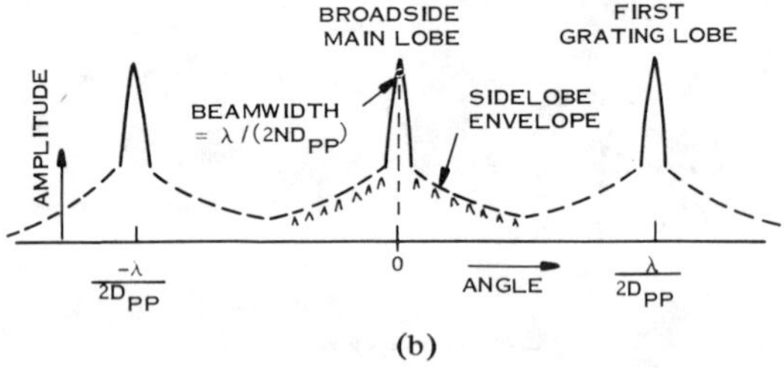

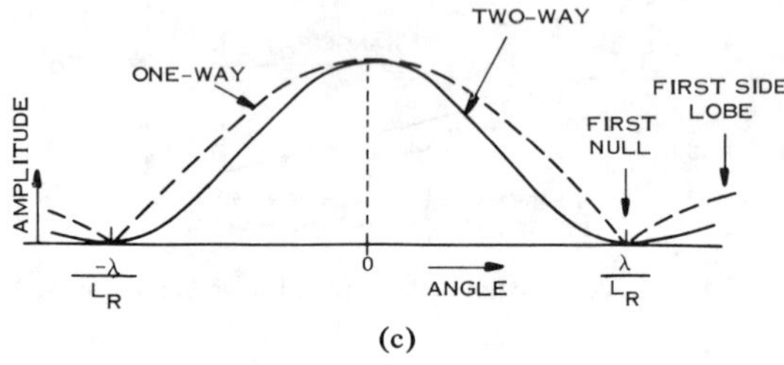

Fig. 9. Linear-array pattern. (a) N-element array configuration. (b) Two-way array factor, in-phase excitation. (c) Element pattern.

pears in the argument of the sine terms. The normalized element pattern is also modified in that the gain has to be considered in two directions. See Fig. 9. Thus, the normalized synthetic array pattern $E_{sa}(L_{sa}, \theta)$ of array length L_{sa} is the product of a normalized two-way array factor $E_{2a}(2D_{PP}, \theta)$ and the normalized two-way element pattern $E_{2e}(L_R, \theta)$ where L_R is the element length. Thus

$$E_{sa}(L_{sa}, \theta) = E_{2a}(2D_{PP}, \theta) E_{2e}(L_R, \theta).$$

The normalized two-array factor E_{2a} is derived from the one-way array factor with element spacing D_{PP} by merely doubling the element spacing to $2D_{PP}$ to obtain

$$E_{2a} = \frac{\sin[2D_{PP}N(\pi/\lambda)\sin\theta]}{N\sin[2D_{PP}(\pi/\lambda)\sin\theta]}$$

where

D_{PP} distance between elemental radiators, or pulse-to-pulse displacement of radar antenna;

θ angle from array broadside;

N number of pulses integrated.

For a long array, ND_{PP} is large, and the angular values of interest become small. Thus, an approximate value of E_{2a} can be written

$$E_{2a} \doteq \frac{\sin(ND_{PP}\, 2\pi\theta/\lambda)}{N\sin(D_{PP}\, 2\pi\theta/\lambda)}.$$

The two-way 3-dB beamwidth is $\lambda/(2ND_{PP}) = \lambda/(2L_{sa})$ where $N = \text{PRF} \times T_D$, and the synthetic array length $L_{sa} = vT_D$. The first one-way sidelobe level is -13.2 dB relative to the main lobe, and it occurs at an angle of $\pm 3\lambda/(4ND_{PP})$ from the main-lobe center. The two-way sidelobe level is 26.4 dB below the mainlobe level. The first two-way grating lobe occurs where a

differential one-way range of $\pm\lambda/2$ from a distant target occurs between elements separated by D_{PP}. Thus, the first two-way grating lobe occurs at an angle $\theta = \pm(\lambda/2)/D_{PP} = \pm\lambda/(2D_{PP})$. The element spacing D_{PP} is established by the radar platform velocity v and the PRF so that $D_{PP} = v/\text{PRF}$ or $\text{PRF} = v/D_{PP}$. In the direction of the first grating lobe the Doppler frequency is equal to the PRF, and this equivalence can be readily shown. The Doppler frequency

$$f_D = \begin{cases} 2v_r/\lambda = 2v\theta/\lambda \\ \dfrac{2v}{\lambda} \cdot \dfrac{\lambda}{2D_{PP}} = \dfrac{v}{D_{PP}} \end{cases}.$$

The Doppler frequency is v/D_{PP} and this is also PRF.

The overall synthesized array configuration must suppress these grating lobes to eliminate azimuth ambiguity. The grating lobe response can be minimized by matching the angular direction of a grating lobe to the direction of a null in the element-illumination pattern. The one-way normalized element-radiation pattern of an element large in size relative to wavelength is given by [15]

$$E_{1e} = \frac{\sin(\pi L_R\theta/\lambda)}{L_R\theta/\lambda} \text{ and } E_{2e} = \frac{\sin^2(\pi L_R\theta/\lambda)}{(L_R\theta/\lambda)^2}.$$

Both one-way and two-way element patterns are shown in Fig. 9(c). The first null occurs where $\pi L_R\theta/\lambda = \pm\pi$, so that the null direction is

$$\theta = \pm\lambda/L_R.$$

By equating angular directions

$$\theta = \frac{\lambda}{2D_{PP}} = \frac{\lambda}{L_R}$$

or

$$D_{PP} = \frac{L_R}{2}.$$

This means that the PRF must be sufficiently high so that the transmitter is pulsed again by the time the antenna moves by one half its length. This is equivalent to

$$\text{PRF}_{\text{low}} = \frac{v}{L_R/2}.$$

All of the four approaches to establish the lower limit of PRF have yielded the same value, and the four concepts are physically equivalent. These approaches to avoid azimuth ambiguity can be summarized by stating that the first is a maximum 2π-rad phase-shift limit between pulses, the second is equating the PRF to the maximum Doppler frequency, the third is equating the number of pulsed measurements to the number of azimuth resolution cells, and the fourth provides a very low synthetic array pattern response in the direction of array grating lobes.

F. Minimum Antenna Area

To avoid range and azimuth ambiguities, PRF design margins are required for reasonably high quality SAR images from realistic hardware. For instance, the PRF may be constrained by the following inequality:

$$1.25\, \text{PRF}_{\text{low}} < \text{PRF} < 0.75\, \text{PRF}_{\text{high}}.$$

Since the PRF limits are established by the geometry, a minimum radar antenna size can be derived by considering only the ratio of the PRF limits. The ratio of the PRF limits is given by

$$\frac{\mathrm{PRF}_{\mathrm{low}}}{\mathrm{PRF}_{\mathrm{high}}} = \frac{2v(2\tau + 2(R_f - R_n)/c)}{L_R}.$$

The following quantities are now defined: 1) ground swath width $W_g = (R_f - R_n)/\sin \phi_i$, where ϕ_i = incidence angle; 2) radar beamwidth in the elevation plane is $\lambda/H_R = (W_g \cos \phi_i)/R_0$, where H_R is the radar antenna height and R_0 = radar range; 3) radar antenna area $A_R = L_R H_R$.

If it is assumed that the transmit-pulse length $\tau \ll 2(R_f - R_n)/c$, then the antenna area A_R required to satisfy the two ambiguity constraints is given by

$$A_R = \frac{\mathrm{PRF}_{\mathrm{high}}}{\mathrm{PRF}_{\mathrm{low}}} \frac{4v\lambda R_0}{c} \tan \phi_i.$$

The antenna area is related to the ratio $\mathrm{PRF}_{\mathrm{high}}/\mathrm{PRF}_{\mathrm{low}}$, and this ratio is always greater than unity. If the ratio is near unity there exists a minimum antenna area that will assure simultaneous compliance with both ambiguity constraints. Operationally, a ratio too near unity is undesirable since this provides no allowance for design and hardware margins. Note that the required antenna size increases with v, λ, R_0, and $\tan \phi_i$. Additional discussion of antenna size requirements to avoid both ambiguities can be found in the literature [14], [16].

There are upper and lower limits on the SAR pulse-repetition frequency to avoid ambiguities, and these limits have a dominant effect on the mapping rate to be discussed in Section VI.

IV. SIGNAL PROCESSING

A two-dimensional image scene of a radar-mapped area can be produced by coherently processing the phase history of the signals received by a SAR. The image plane is defined by the radar platform velocity vector and the radar antenna beam axis. The two orthogonal axes of the processed image are range and cross-range (azimuth). The position along the range axis is determined by time delay of the received pulse, and the position along the cross-range axis is determined by range rate of the target distance or the Doppler frequency of the return signal from the target. Three-dimensional physical features of the mapped surface are projected by the processing technique into this two-dimensional plane. A method of obtaining three-dimensional images using a dual-channel vertical interferometric receiver has been reported [17].

As stated previously, the SAR image has high resolution in both range and cross range directions. High resolution in range is achieved by the use of very short transmitted pulses and wide bandwidths. In the cross range direction high resolution is achieved by the use of a synthesized antenna and coherent processing of the phase history of the return signals from many successive pulses. This process of achieving high resolution in the cross range direction is sometimes called azimuth compression. The total phase and amplitude history of a target must be collected for the duration of the integration or dwell time before signal processing can commence. The integration time involved is on the order of a second, depending on the application.

Two signal processing techniques are discussed in the literature. The optical method requiring photographic equipment [18] is quite mature and numerous processed images have been reported. Digital methods utilizing computers have been

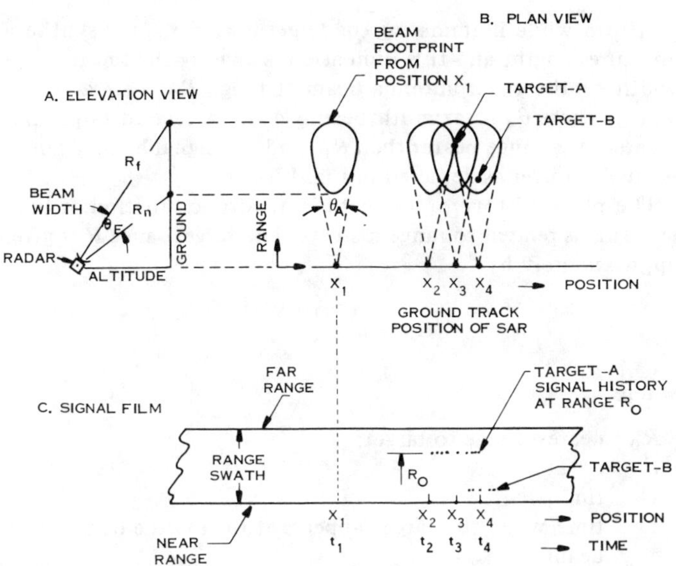

Fig. 10. Pulsed SAR and signal film.

recently discussed [11], [19], [20], and these approaches offer the potential of near real time imaging.

A. Target Phase History

In this paper, only the optical method of signal processing will be discussed since it can readily convey the physical principles involved. To simplify the discussion, a single target geometry is examined first, followed by a multiple target example. In Fig. 10(a) an elevation view is shown of a SAR at an altitude H with radar antenna beam of width θ_E which intercepts the ground at near range R_n and far range R_f. In Fig. 10(b) a plan view of the geometry is shown with the abscissa axis depicting the ground-track position of the radar platform moving at a constant velocity. Thus, the abscissa can be considered as either position or time. The ordinate axis in Fig. 10(b) is ground range, and targets A and B are shown at different ranges. The radar-antenna beam axis is oriented at right angles to the radar-platform velocity vector, and the azimuth beamwidth is θ_A. At time t_1, the radar is located at ground position x_1. The beam is yet at some distance from the first target A so that no signal is received. At a later time t_2 the radar is at position x_2. Now the radar beam first illuminates the target, and a reflected signal is detected. In Fig. 10(c), a portion of a signal film strip is shown. The width of the signal film corresponds to the ground swath illuminated by the radar beam. The film width is shown related to the time Δt required for a radar pulse to sweep across the beam footprint on ground, i.e., $\Delta t = 2(R_f - R_n)/c$. The received phase history from each transmitted pulse is recorded across the width of the signal film. Between pulses the film is advanced by small increments. Thus, a position across the film width corresponds to range position, and a position along the film length corresponds to along-track position of the radar platform. In Fig. 10(b), the target is first illuminated when the radar platform travels to position x_2, and in Fig. 10(c), a target response is depicted at range R_0. Thereafter, until time t_4 or radar platform position x_4 each transmitted pulse will produce a detected signal; this is illustrated in Fig. 10(c). The target is illuminated between time t_2 and t_4, and this interval is called the integration or dwell time. It is noted that the distance traversed by the radar platform while illuminating the target is $x_4 - x_2$, the synthetic aperture length, and this dimension is exactly the linear beamwidth of the radar antenna beam at range R_0, i.e., $x_4 - x_2 = \theta_A R_0$ where θ_A is azimuth beamwidth. A second target B is located at a range nearer than R_0, and the signal history length is much shorter as depicted in Fig. 10(c).

The phase history of a target is a quadratic function of time, and this is related to range history. The target range R is given approximately by

$$R \doteq R_0 + \frac{1}{2}\frac{(vt')^2}{R_0}$$

where

R_0 nearest range to target;
t' $t - t_3$;
t time;
t_3 time when the target appears at the middle of the radar beam.

The relative two-way phase history is a quadratic function given by

$$\phi = \begin{cases} 2(R - R_0)/\lambda \text{ wavelengths} \\ \dfrac{(vt')^2}{\lambda R_0} \text{ wavelengths.} \end{cases}$$

The maximum amount of phase shift depends on illumination time and, hence, on azimuth resolution δ_{az}. Thus,

$$\phi_{max} = \frac{(vT_D)^2}{4R_0\lambda} = \frac{\lambda R_0}{16\delta_{az}^2} \text{ wavelengths.}$$

It is noted that ϕ_{max} is proportional to target range R_0 and inversely to δ_{az}^2.

A lens to focus the phase history is found to be proportional to R_0. A thin lens has a focal length given approximately by $D^2/(8\Delta z)$ where D is lens diameter and Δz is the optical path difference between rays passing through the lens center and lens edge. In the present example $D = vT_D$ and $\Delta z = \lambda\phi_{max}$. The focal length is $R_0/2$, and this type of lens is called a "conical" lens.

B. Depth of Focus

The accuracy with which a given quadratic phase function must be matched to the range depends on the tolerable phase error across the aperture L_{sa}. This is called depth of focus [7]. It is assumed that two-way and one-way phase errors of $\lambda/4$ and $\lambda/8$, respectively, can be arbitrarily allowed at the ends of the aperture. The nearest range to the target is R_0, and the range from aperture ends is $R = \sqrt{R_0^2 + (L_{sa}/2)^2}$. The derivative $dR/dR_0 = R_0/R$. The one-way phase error across the aperture caused by improper positioning of the quadratic function is $|\Delta R - \Delta R_0| = \pm\lambda/8$. The total depth of focus (DOF) is $2\Delta R_0$ and

$$\text{DOF} = \frac{2\lambda R_0^2}{(L_{sa})^2}$$

or

$$\text{DOF} = \frac{8\delta_{az}^2}{\lambda}.$$

The depth of focus becomes shallower or the focus becomes more critical as δ_{az} is made smaller. For example, if $\lambda = 0.1\,\text{m}$,

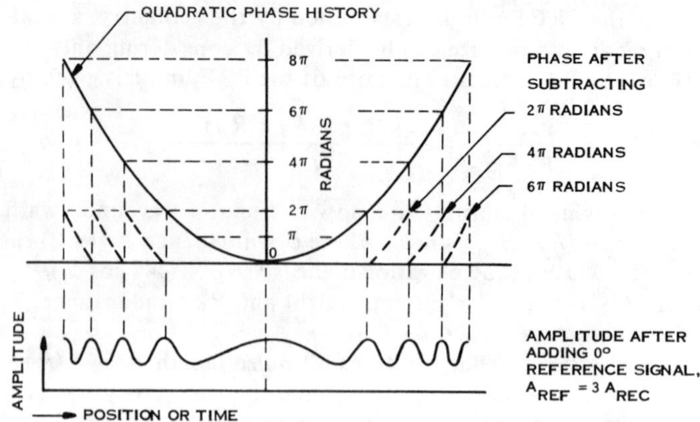

Fig. 11. Coherent addition of receiver and reference signals.

$R_0 = 10^6$ m, $v = 7.6 \times 10^3$ m/s, and $T_D = 0.439$ s, then $\delta_{az} = 15$ m, and the depth of focus is 1.8×10^4 m. With coarse azimuth resolution and a narrow range swath a single quadratic phase function may be adequate for signal processing the entire image.

C. Signal Film

The signal amplitude and phase history is recorded on film after phase coherent addition of the received signal with a reference signal. When two signals are in phase a higher combined level is obtained than when out of phase. The quadratic phase history of a single target is shown in Fig. 11. The abscissa can be either time or platform position. The ordinate represents phase or time after the pulse is radiated. After subtracting multiples of 2π rad the dashed line phase function in Fig. 11 is obtained. When the receiver and reference signals are coherently added, the resultant amplitude response is shown by the bottom curve in Fig. 11. It is assumed that the ratio of reference (A_{REF}) to receive (A_{REC}) signal amplitudes is 3. The spatial pattern is similar to that of a Fresnel zone plate in optics. When recorded on a signal film with the use of a narrow beam of light there will be a series of bright (or dark) spots that are aligned parallel to the film direction with the spots closer together at the two ends than in the middle of the series. The length of the spot series corresponds to the synthetic aperture length or the signal integration time. An example of raw-data signal film is shown in Fig. 12. The ordinate and abscissa axes are range and along-track directions, respectively. When a suitable Fresnel zone plate or a lens is aligned over the series of spots, and when a parallel beam of coherent light is passed through both the lens and the signal film, the light beam is brought to a focus. This is a Fourier transformation process. The physical registration of the lens is important since any misalignment will destroy the focus. It should be noted that a smaller diameter lens with the same focal length will also focus the beam, but the azimuth resolution will degrade inversely with the diameter.

D. Optical Processing

To properly focus the signal history of a target at any range, the lens must meet certain requirements. For a given azimuth resolution δ_{az} the lens width corresponds to the synthetic-aperture length or signal integration time and, hence, it is proportional to target range. The lens thickness is proportional to ϕ_{max} and, hence, to target range. These two physical constraints make the lens appear conical in shape. See Fig. 13. The focal length of the lens is also proportional to target range.

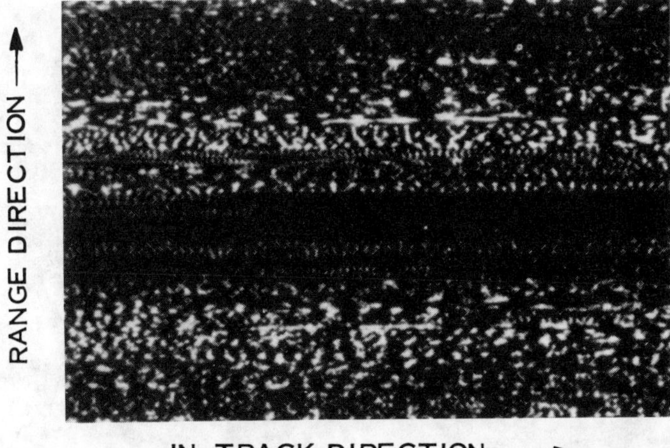

Fig. 12. Raw data signal film. (Courtesy of A. Kozma, Environmental Research Institute of Michigan.)

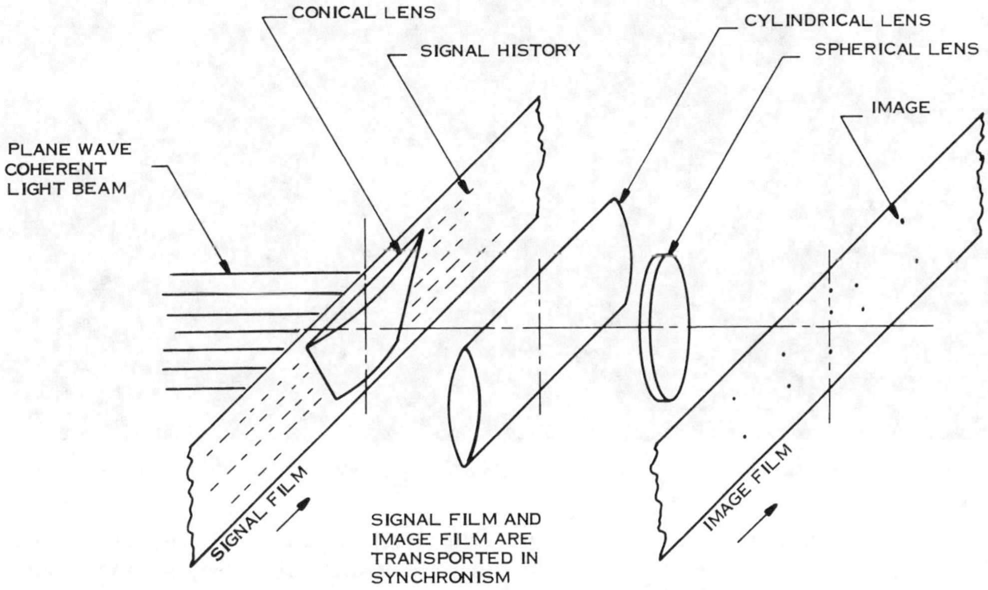

Fig. 13. Optical processing of signal film.

This conical lens will produce images of all targets differing in range but lying in one azimuth or cross-track direction. These images will appear on one line across the width of the image film. The conical lens is then shifted in the direction of the film strip by one azimuth resolution distance to produce the next line of images in the range direction. Auxiliary optics composed of cylindrical and spherical lenses are used to project the target images onto the image film [5]. An example of a SAR image is shown in Fig. 14. By using an X-band SAR with five-foot range resolution and seven-foot azimuth resolution, the Environmental Research Institute of Michigan has taken a radar image of a scene along the Huron River near Detroit, MI, and this image is shown in Fig. 14. An enlargement of the radar image of an orchard along the Huron River is shown in Fig. 15. The radar subtrack is parallel to the ordinate and is below the images.

E. Multiple Targets

The presence of a multiplicity of targets at the same range but differing in azimuthal position is discussed. From each transmitted pulse the total return signal $\overline{E}_r$ for a particular range resolution bin is the complex addition of all reflected signals $\overline{E}_i$ from targets at that range illuminated by the radar antenna beam. Each target is characterized by a separate quadratic phase function. Mathematically the return signal is

$$\overline{E}_r = \sum_n \overline{E}_i$$

where $\overline{E}_i$ = reflected wave from target i.

In general, $\overline{E}_r$ will change from pulse to pulse due to a change in the relative geometry. The $\overline{E}_r$ amplitude and phase history is processed and recorded on film in the same manner as that for a single target example discussed above. Fourier transformed images of the targets will appear at their proper relative positions as the conical lens and auxiliary optics are moved along the length of the signal film.

As mentioned earlier a uniformly weighted long array has nearest one-way sidelobe levels that are 13.2 dB below the mainlobe, and the signal processed two-way sidelobe level will thus be 26.4 dB below the mainlobe. In some applications 26.4-dB sidelobes may not be sufficiently low. The sidelobes can be reduced further by amplitude weighting the signal his-

Fig. 14. SAR image of a scene along Huron River near Detroit, MI. (Courtesy of A. Kozma, Environmental Research Institute of Michigan.)

tory across the synthetic aperture in exactly the same manner as tapering the illumination of an antenna aperture [21]. The mainlobe width or azimuth resolution will degrade when weighting the aperture.

In an elementary optical processor, a troublesome direct light beam will impinge on the image film which can be eliminated by shifting the range and azimuth spectra by an "offset" frequency [6], [7].

V. Phase Errors

Since a SAR is a phase-coherent system, the production of high-quality radar images assumes that: 1) the radar generates accurate target phase histories, and 2) the signal processor utilizes the correct correlative phase functions. These two assumptions may not always be valid. In this section the sources and effects of these phase errors are discussed. In some instances, the phase errors can be compensated, in others not. The subject of phase errors and their effects is very complicated, hence, in this tutorial paper only a simplified discussion will be given to convey the concepts. The interested reader can pursue the topic further by referring to the literature [22]-[28].

In treating phase errors there are three aspects to the data, viz. nominal (expected) values, known deviations, and residual uncertainties. The principal portion is the expected or as-

sumed value, such as velocity of the radar platform. Where deviations are anticipated, provisions can be made for precise determinations, and these corrections or compensations can be applied to the data. However, as with all measurements, there will still remain a small residual error. These aspects of phase errors are discussed in this section.

A. Range Curvature

The principal sources of phase errors are imperfections in the system such as radar-platform velocity deviations, targets in motion, electromagnetic path length fluctuations, and electronic equipment instabilities. In addition to these system imperfections there is a phase error present in a perfect system that is a consequence of a high resolution geometry. High resolution applications require long integration times, and the target range may change so much that the time delay variation during the integration time may be comparable to or exceed that associated with the range resolution. This effect is called range curvature [28]. The geometry for analysis is the same as that used for describing the quadratic phase history. The nearest range to the target is R_0, and the maximum radar range R_m during the integration time is

$$R_m = \sqrt{R_0^2 + (vT_D/2)^2}$$

Fig. 15. Enlargement of radar image of an orchard in Fig. 14. (Courtesy of A. Kozma, Environmental Research Institute of Michigan.)

and

$$R_m - R_0 \doteq \frac{1}{8} \frac{(vT_D)^2}{R_0} = \frac{\lambda^2 R_0}{32\, \delta_{az}^2}.$$

The range curvature (RC) is $R_m - R_0$, and it increases rapidly as δ_{az} decreases. Relative to range resolution δ_r the ratio of RC to δ_r is

$$\frac{\text{RC}}{\delta_r} = \frac{\lambda^2 R_0}{32\, \delta_r \delta_{az}^2}.$$

For an example, let $\lambda = 0.1$ m, $R_0 = 10^6$ m, $\delta_r = \delta_{az} = 15$ m, then RC/δ_r is 0.09 which is a negligible amount. Ratio values in excess of 0.3 will probably cause image degradation, and this must be either avoided by design or compensated during the signal processing.

B. Radar-Platform Instability

For an illustration of phase errors in an imperfect SAR system, the uncertainty or instability of the radar platform velocity is considered. A nominal value can be obtained for an airborne radar from a wind-speed indicator or an inertial navigation system; for a satellite-borne radar, from ephemeris data. An aircraft is apt to encounter turbulence so that linear accelerometers are used to determine deviations in aircraft velocity and position to provide inputs for corrections to the signal processor [23], [24]. Deviations that are fairly gradual can be measured and used relatively easily to compensate for phase errors. Rapid fluctuations which are difficult to measure and utilize are called residual phase errors. The problem becomes more acute with high-resolution applications since it is difficult to maintain constant aircraft velocity for long time periods. This requirement is discussed later.

C. Effects of Phase Errors

Qualitative effects of various error sources are shown in Table I. The radar platform errors are divided into the three principal component directions, i.e., along-track (along the assumed flight vector), altitude, and cross-track. Thus, for example, an error in platform altitude may result in image mis-

TABLE I
EFFECTS OF PHASE ERRORS

Source of Error		Image Misregistration	Image Shift	Azimuth Defocus	Range Defocus	Range Walk	Azimuth Walk	Image Main Lobe loss	Image Sidelobe Increase
Platform									
Along-track	x	X							
	$\dot{x}$			X				X	X
	$\ddot{x}$			X			X	X	X
	higher derivatives			X			X	X	X
Altitude	H	X							
	$\dot{H}$		X			X			
	$\ddot{H}$			X	X			X	X
	higher derivatives			X	X			X	X
Cross-track	y	X							
	$\dot{y}$		X			X			
	$\ddot{y}$			X	X			X	X
	higher derivatives			X	X			X	X
Target									
Range	R	X							
	$\dot{R}$		X			X			
	$\ddot{R}$			X	X			X	X
	higher derivatives			X	X			X	X
Along track	x	X							
	$\dot{x}$			X				X	X
	$\ddot{x}$			X			X	X	X
	higher derivatives			X			X	X	X
Propagation Path									
	phase jitter			X	X			X	X
Electronic Stability									
	phase jitter			X	X			X	X

registration since the radar is configured to operate on a range basis so that an altitude error will result in ground range error. An error in along-track platform velocity, if appreciable, can result in defocusing in azimuth. A derivation of the tolerable uncertainty in along-track velocity is presented later. Because of azimuth defocus there will be a loss in the main lobe response of the image and an increase in image sidelobe level. The synthetic aperture radar platform is assumed to travel at a constant velocity. If there is acceleration, it may cause azimuth defocus, azimuth resolution-cell walk, image main lobe loss, and increased image sidelobe level. An aircraft altitude rate caused by air turbulence, or a satellite altitude rate due to orbit eccentricity, may cause the image to shift in the cross-range direction. A derivation of this image shift is presented in a later paragraph. Altitude change and earth rotation may displace a given target by an amount comparable to or exceeding one range resolution cell, called range walk. Second and higher order derivatives of the altitude, if of sufficient magnitude, cause azimuth defocus, range defocus, image main lobe loss, and increase in image sidelobe level. The effects due to radar platform cross-track errors are similar to those for altitude errors.

D. Earth Rotation Effects

Errors in range and range derivatives due to target-location instabilities can cause a multitude of degrading effects. For an airborne SAR, terrestrial targets are regarded as being stable. For a satellite-borne SAR the satellite orbit planes are referenced to space, and terrestrial targets move at earth rotational rates which cause various errors such as image shift and azimuth defocus. The errors are greatest when the satellite is crossing the equator and least at the highest latitude of the orbit. Earth rotational speeds can be calculated accurately, and the residual uncertainty may be negligible.

A spaceborne radar offers the potential of viewing the global ocean surface. The satellite velocity is constant, and satellite ephemeris can be accurately predicted; however, Doppler frequency shifts and received signal phase errors introduced by earth rotation, satellite orbit eccentricity, ionospheric granularity, and moving targets will affect the image [26]. The SAR antenna beam is assumed to be oriented at right angles to the satellite velocity vector. If the relative velocity vector between radar and target has a radial (or range) component in addition to that due only to satellite velocity, it will cause the image to shift along-track (or cross-range) position unless compensated. Furthermore, if the product of the radial component of velocity and the radar illumination time is greater than the range resolution distance, range walk occurs as discussed [22], [28], which has to be compensated during signal processing. If the relative-velocity vector has a significant component parallel to satellite track, the image will defocus unless compensated. Numerical examples of earth rotational and orbit eccentricity effects are discussed in the following paragraphs.

The equatorial earth-surface speed is 463 m/s and its effect on SAR performance depends on satellite position, satellite velocity, and orbit inclination angle. Earth rotation can cause image shift, range walk, and defocusing effects. A radar radial component of earth rotation will shift the angular direction of zero Doppler frequency and hence shift along-track positions of the images unless compensated. Images may be restored to

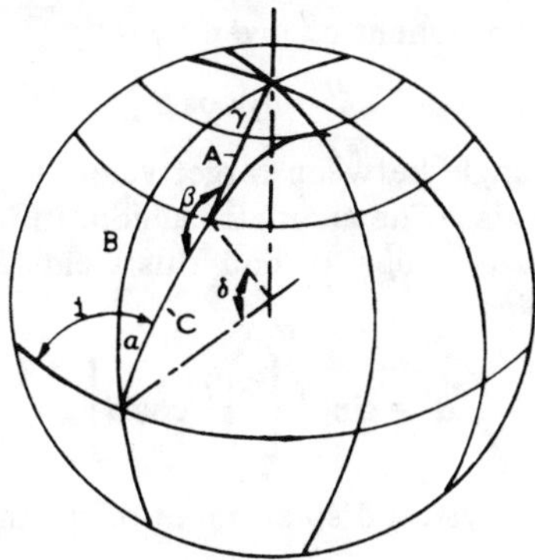

Fig. 16. Spherical geometry. A, B, C, are sides of a spherical triangle. B is an arbitrary meridian.

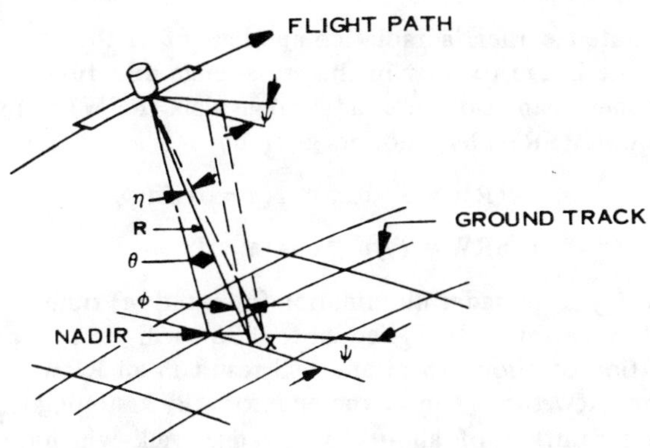

Fig. 17. Radar geometry. θ: cone angle, η: cross cone angle, ψ: satellite yaw angle, R: slant range from satellite to earth, ϕ: incidence angle (from local vertical).

their proper positions within the antenna beamwidth by either 1) trimming the receiver local oscillator frequency, or 2) rotating the antenna beam in yaw about satellite nadir to include the zero Doppler frequency direction [6]. The amount of compensation for either method is varied along the satellite orbit with peak compensation at equatorial crossing and zero compensation at the highest latitude. An along-track component of earth rotation may cause image defocusing from a long integration time.

Fig. 16 illustrates the geometry needed to analyze the effect of earth rotation. The arc C represents satellite travel along its ground track, related to the angle from ascending node δ. The spherical angle is $(i{-}90)$ where i is the orbit inclination angle. Spherical angle β is used to calculate the component of earth rotation velocity in the radial direction. Over one-fourth of the orbit it can be seen that β varies from $3\pi/2{-}i$ at the equator, to $90°$ at maximum latitude. The radial velocity component due to earth rotation is

$$v_r = (v_{eq} \sin A) \cos (\pi - \beta) \sin \phi_i$$

where

v_{eq} equatorial earth rotational velocity;
A arc distance from the pole;
ϕ_i incidence angle.

Hence, v_r varies from a maximum at the equator to zero at maximum latitude.

The Doppler frequency shift f_D caused by the rotating earth is

$$f_D = (2f/c)v_{eq} \sin \phi_i \sin A \cos (\pi - \beta) \tag{1}$$

where f is radar frequency, and c is the speed of light. With $f = 3000$ MHz, $\phi_i = 22.67°$, and $\beta = 162°$, f_D is 3394 Hz at the equator. If the receiver local oscillator frequency is shifted in amount equal to the Doppler frequency, the image will be properly processed. Alternately, the antenna boresignt can be redirected to restore the image. This is discussed in the following paragraphs.

Fig. 17 shows the radar geometry. The Doppler frequency in the radar return signal caused by satellite motion over a stationary earth is

$$f_D = (2f/c)v \sin \eta \tag{2}$$

where v is satellite velocity and η is the cross-cone angle. If the 3-dB azimuth beamwidth of the radar antenna is $1°$, and a satellite velocity of 7.499 km/s is assumed for an 808-km-

altitude satellite, the Doppler frequency for a cross-cone angle of $0.5°$ is 1300 Hz. Thus, the Doppler frequency due to earth rotation is about 2.6 times (3394/1300) higher, and received signals appear to be reflected from targets in a direction about $1.3°$ from the antenna-beam boresight. Without compensation, the processing of these target returns will not normally produce images since the apparent targets are outside the antenna beamwidth.

An equivalent yaw bias angle of the radar antenna beam to compensate this effect is computed. Referring again to Fig. 17, it can be seen that for a ground arc length X

$$X = R \sin \eta = (R \sin \theta) \sin \psi. \tag{3}$$

By equating Doppler equations (1) and (2) and cancelling $2f/c$ terms

$$v \sin \eta = v_{eq} \sin A \cos (\beta + \psi) \sin \phi_i. \tag{4}$$

Dividing (3) by (4) gives

$$\cot \psi = \tan \beta + \frac{v \sin \theta}{v_{eq} \sin \phi_i \cos \beta \sin A}.$$

For the cited example with $\theta = 20°$, an antenna yaw bias angle $\psi = 3.736°$ is required at the equator to compensate for earth rotation. The yaw bias must be varied along the orbit because of the β and A parameters. The amount of antenna yaw is independent of radar frequency.

An along-track component of earth rotation may cause image defocusing. Defocusing becomes significant when the quadratic phase history over the synthetic aperture deviates in excess of about one-quarter radar wavelength. From symmetry, the phase error is considered over one-half of the synthetic aperture length $vT_D/2$. The radar range at the extremities of the synthetic aperture is $\sqrt{R_0^2 + (vT_D/2)^2}$. If this range is differentiated with respect to v, a velocity difference Δv that causes a range error of $\lambda/16$ can be calculated. The tolerable along-track velocity component Δv is given by

$$\Delta v = \frac{4R_0}{T_D^2 v} \frac{\lambda}{16} = \frac{v\delta_{az}^2}{R_0 \lambda} \tag{5}$$

where R_0 is the slant range. Note that the tolerable Δv becomes more critical as the azimuth resolution is improved. For the cited example of $\delta_{az} = 15$ m and $R_0 = 858$ km, $\Delta v = 19.7$ m/s. Inasmuch as the maximum along-track component of earth rotation is 143 m/s, there will be a significant amount of defocusing that must be compensated.

As stated earlier, a radial component of earth rotation will cause the image to shift in the cross-range direction. A radial component can also cause radar range walk (RRW) and surface range walk (SRW) by amounts given by

$$RRW = T_D v_{eq} \cos(\pi - \beta) \sin \phi_i$$

$$SRW = T_D v_{eq} \cos(\pi - \beta)$$

where T_D is the radar illumination (integration) time on target. An illumination time T_D equal to 0.38 s will yield an azimuth resolution of about 15 m and will result in an RRW of about 64 and SRW of 167 m at the equator. By assuming a surface range resolution of about 15 m, range walk will have to be compensated in the signal processing.

E. Orbit Eccentricity

Orbit eccentricity causes an altitude rate and displaces images in the track direction. With descending altitude, the velocity vector will dip below the local horizon. The zero Doppler frequency direction is perpendicular to the satellite velocity vector [6] so that the image will shift rearward relative to the subsatellite point. The image shift z is given by

$$z = \frac{H\dot{H} \cos \theta}{v}$$

where H is satellite altitude and θ is beam angle from satellite nadir. By considering a finite residual orbit eccentricity $\epsilon = 0.002$ for a near perfect circular orbit and also earth gravity zonal harmonics, calculations have shown that the altitude rate may be as large as 20 m/s [29]. The entire image frame will shift a maximum of 2400 m, and this is negligible when viewing waves with an antenna beamwidth of about $1°$ or wider. It should be noted that since the orbit perigee will migrate, the orbital position for maximum altitude rate will also migrate. Similar to the earth rotation effect, compensation for altitude rate can be accomplished by trimming the receiver local-oscillator frequency or by rotating in yaw the antenna-boresight axis about the local satellite nadir. With an integration time T_D of about 0.38 s, the range will change by $\dot{H} T_D \cos \theta$, and the surface range will change by $\dot{H} T_D \cos \theta / \sin \phi_i$. For the example cited with $\delta_{az} = 15$ m, the surface range will change by 18.5 m, and this requires compensation. The effect of orbit eccentricity on image focusing is negligible.

F. Target Motion

The discussion has considered targets that are stationary on the earth's surface but with the earth rotating around its own axis. The phase errors due to earth rotation can be compensated using deterministic approaches. Phase error is also caused by targets moving on the earth's surface. The target motion can be resolved into an along-track component and a cross-track radial component. An along-track component will cause azimuth defocusing and (5) can be used to quantify the effect. A radial component will cause image shift as stated earlier. For a reference in this discussion, a stationary target will show a radial velocity component v_r' at an angle θ from broadside direction given by

$$v_r' = v \sin \theta$$

where v is the radar platform velocity. Conventional SAR signal processing will place the image of this stationary target at $\theta = 0°$ where the Doppler frequency is zero. If the target is now considered to be moving with a velocity v_t, there will be a radial velocity component v_r'' given by

$$v_r'' = v_t \cos \beta$$

where β is the angle between target velocity vector and radar antenna beam axis. The geometrical condition for zero Doppler occurs when $v_r'' + v_r' = 0$, and this yields for the direction θ' of zero Doppler

$$\theta' = \sin^{-1}\left[\frac{-v_t}{v} \cos \beta\right].$$

The cross-range physical displacement of the image $\Delta x'$ is

$$\Delta x' = -R_0 \frac{v_t}{v} \cos \beta \qquad (6)$$

where R_0 is the target range. As to the direction of image shift, a radial target-velocity component towards the radar will cause the processed image to appear at a location rearward in the cross-radial direction relative to the location of the processed image of a stationary target. As an example, if $R_0 = 10^6$ m, $v_t = 10$ m/s, $v = 7.6 \times 10^3$ m/s, and $\beta = 65°$, the image shift is 556 m.

In addition to radial velocity, radial acceleration will cause image distortion, such as azimuth defocus, range defocus, range walk, and azimuth walk. The most sensitive effect is azimuth defocus. Thus, if an arbitrary one-half wavelength, two-way phase error is allowed during the integration time T_D, then the tolerable uncompensated radial acceleration $\ddot{R}$ corresponds to a radial position error of $(\frac{1}{2})\ddot{R} T_D^2$. This error can have a maximum of $\lambda/4$ for a one-way path. Thus

$$\frac{\ddot{R} T_D^2}{2} \leqslant \frac{\lambda}{4}$$

and

$$\ddot{R} \leqslant \frac{\lambda}{2T_D^2} = \frac{2v^2 \delta_{az}^2}{R^2 \lambda}.$$

As an example, if $R = 10^6$ m, $\lambda = 0.1$ m, $v = 7.6 \times 10^3$ m/s, $\delta_{az} = 15$ m, then the radial acceleration $\ddot{R}$ must be less than 0.26 m/s².

G. Ionospheric Granularity

Another source of phase error is variations in phase velocity along the beam propagation path between radar and target. The ionosphere is composed of layers of free electrons that exhibit an index of refraction of less than unity, and the ionosphere affects phase velocity and, hence, phase coherence. For a microwave beam traversing the ionosphere, the physical quantity of interest is the total columnar electron content (TCEC) along the path given in units of electrons per square meter of cross section. The TCEC at midlatitudes typically varies diurnally between 0.2×10^{17} and 1×10^{17} e/m² with the higher values prevailing during afternoons and early evenings. Above equatorial regions and at high latitudes, the TCEC is typically 10^{18} e/m². During magnetic storms TCEC values of 10^{19} e/m² have been measured [30]. With a TCEC as high as 10^{19} e/m² and a radar frequency above 1000 MHz, calculations show that Faraday rotation of a linearly polarized signal and the amount of dispersion across about a 5-percent bandwidth are both negligible.

Amplitude and phase scintillations have been observed on signals traversing an inhomogeneous ionosphere [31]–[33].

Phase perturbations caused by ionospheric irregularities have been reported on a communication link at frequencies of 162 and 324 MHz from a 1100-km-altitude satellite beacon to ground [34]. Experiments conducted during traveling ionospheric disturbances show up to 3-percent variations in TCEC [35]. In other experiments the sizes of ionospheric granularity cells have been estimated to be as small as 150 m [36] or smaller [37]. If these values of granularity are realistic, SAR performance can be degraded. While both amplitude and phase scintillations can affect SAR imagery, it is likely that phase scintillations will be more detrimental than amplitude scintillation.

The phase granularity can be calculated from time-delay formulations given by Burns and Fremouw [38]. The two-way excess phase delay is derived

$$\Delta\phi = 1.68 \times 10^{-6} \, (\text{TCEC})/f \text{ rad}$$

where f is the radar frequency in hertz.

The phase granularity $\Delta\Delta\phi$ caused by fractional ionospheric granularity (GR) is $\Delta\Delta\phi = 1.68 \times 10^{-6} \, (\text{TCEC})(\text{GR})/f$. If TCEC $= 2 \times 10^{17}$, GR $= 0.03$, $f = 3000$ MHz, then $\Delta\Delta\phi = 3.36$ rad or 0.54 wavelengths. To achieve an azimuth resolution of 15 m, an integration time of about 0.38 s, and a synthetic aperture length of about 2.83 km is required. The tolerable number of granular cells and the phase variation across each granular cell are governed by the integrated sidelobe level of the processed image. If ionospheric granularity cells are as small as 150 m, a tolerable phase variation across each cell is less than 1/20 wavelength which in turn specifies the tolerable TCEC granularity. The foregoing calculation of 0.54 wavelength phase granularity, if indeed it occurs, will result in a significant degradation in image quality.

Ionospheric density variations cannot be reliably predicted but statistical magnitudes have been investigated. Phase fluctuations on the order of $\lambda/4$ rad of the RF cycle are deemed undesirable. For a satellite-borne L-band SAR, imagery over Alaskan territories may be seriously degraded a fair fraction of the time [39]. At midlatitude regions, it is probable that on the average, ionospheric granularity will not affect L-band imagery of the ocean surface.

The radar beam propagation path between radar and target during the integration time may be subject to variations. For an airborne SAR, inhomogeneities in the troposphere may be a problem [40], [41]. For a satellite-borne SAR, inhomogeneities in both the troposphere and the ionosphere may pose problems. For a relatively coarse azimuth resolution, the integration time is relatively short, and variations in the electromagnetic wave path may be negligible. The presence of rain [42] can cause attenuation, and hence loss of signal, and scatter the transmitted pulse which can contribute to noise and possibly range ambiguity.

Phase errors may also be introduced by instabilities in the SAR electronics, e.g., due to oscillator drift or jitter in the timing of the transmitted pulses. Phase jitter in excess of $\pi/8$ rad of the RF cycle is undesirable in most applications.

VI. Mapping Rate

The paper so far has covered the principles and design constraints of the synthetic aperture radar as well as the signal processing techniques for generating two-dimensional radar images. The mapping or coverage rate of the radar based on geometrical constraints imposed by ambiguity limits [14], [16] and not by radar signal-to-noise is of considerable inter-

est and this is now discussed. In a previous section on ambiguities the following equation was given applicable to a broadside viewing geometry:

$$\frac{\text{PRF}_{\text{low}}}{\text{PRF}_{\text{high}}} = \frac{2v}{L_R} [2\tau + 2(R_f - R_n)/c]$$

where τ is the transmitted pulse length.

By assuming $R_f - R_n = W_g \sin \phi_i$ and a negligibly small value of τ relative to $(R_f - R_n)/c$

$$\frac{\text{PRF}_{\text{low}}}{\text{PRF}_{\text{high}}} \doteq \frac{4v}{cL_R} W_g \sin \phi_i$$

where W_g is the ground swath width and ϕ_i is the incidence angle.

The desired ground-mapping rate is the product of radar platform velocity or radar-beam footprint speed v and the ground swath width W_g. Thus, the areal mapping coverage rate vW_g is given by

$$vW_g = \frac{cL_R}{4} \frac{1}{\sin \phi_i} \frac{\text{PRF}_{\text{low}}}{\text{PRF}_{\text{high}}}$$

or

$$vW_g = \frac{c\delta_{\text{az}}}{2} \frac{1}{\sin \phi_i} \frac{\text{PRF}_{\text{low}}}{\text{PRF}_{\text{high}}}.$$

The areal mapping rate can be increased by degrading azimuth resolution. This results from the minimum antenna-area constraint that a longer radar antenna (larger δ_{az}) results in a shorter antenna height which broadens the elevation beamwidth and hence increases the ground swath width W_g. The mapping rate is inversely proportional to the sine of the incidence angle. As the incidence angle approaches normal to the surface, $\sin \phi_i$ becomes smaller and the areal mapping rate increases due to an increase in W_g for a given elevation beamwidth of the radar antenna. Under theoretical conditions the PRF ratio may approach unity for the maximum mapping rate, however, considering practical antenna patterns and SAR operational parameters, the PRF ratio should be nearer 0.5. Note that the mapping rate equation is independent of radar altitude and target range because it was assumed that $\tau \ll (W_g/c) \sin \phi_i$. At low altitudes this assumption may not be valid. While the PRF ratio may not vary much with altitude, the individual values of PRF_{low} and PRF_{high} do vary with altitude.

The mapping rate based on ambiguity limits is independent of range resolution δ_r since δ_r is dependent on the instantaneous RF bandwidth of the SAR electronics and not on geometry. There is an exception to this; if high resolution δ_r is obtained by a long duration linear FM swept transmitted pulse, then the general equation should be used.

The areal mapping rate given here is that constrained by geometry and temporal factors, and it is proportional to azimuth resolution. Other factors which affect mapping rate are signal-to-noise ratio, probability of detection, false alarm rate, etc.

VII. Signal-to-Noise Ratio

The generation of high-quality two dimensional radar images by a SAR requires a sufficiently high signal-to-noise ratio (SNR). In this section the SNR equation is derived from fundamental radar principles.

The basic pulsed-radar equation that gives the SNR is [5]

$$\frac{S}{N} = \frac{P_t G_t A_r \eta \sigma}{(4\pi)^2 R^4 k T_r \overline{NF} B L_s} \tag{7}$$

where

P_t transmitted peak power
G_t transmitter-antenna gain
A_r receiving-antenna gain
η antenna efficiency
σ radar cross section
R slant range
k Boltzmann's constant
T_r absolute receiver temperature
$\overline{NF}$ relative-noise figure
B receiver-noise bandwidth
L_s total system loss.

To achieve fine range resolution it is necessary to use transmitter pulses of short duration which in turn requires high peak power for a given SNR. This peak power requirement can be reduced by the use of frequency-dispersive, linear FM sweep, and pulse-compression techniques. The peak power can be reduced by the ratio of τ_i/τ_c where τ_i is the initial uncompressed pulse length and τ_c is the compressed pulse length.

In a conventional SAR the boresight of the antenna beam is perpendicular to the radar platform velocity vector. As mentioned above, the azimuthal resolution for the focused case in the limit is equal to one-half the physical length of the antenna in the flight vector direction. In this geometry the target is illuminated for a time T_D given by

$$T_D = \frac{R \theta_R}{v}$$

where

R slant range
θ_R radar antenna azimuth beamwidth
v radar platform velocity.

In a coherent radar system where azimuth resolution is derived from a synthesized antenna, there is an SNR advantage due to pulse integration. The SNR improvement factor for the SAR is

$$\text{Improvement Factor} = \frac{\tau_i}{\tau_c} (\text{PRF}) \, T_D \tag{8}$$

where PRF is the pulse repetition frequency and T_D is the target illumination time.

By combining (7) and (8) the following equation is obtained:

$$\frac{S}{N} = \frac{P_t \tau_i \text{PRF} \, T_D G_t A_r \sigma \eta}{(4\pi)^2 R^4 k T_r \overline{NF} B \tau_c L_s} \tag{9}$$

The product $P_t \tau_i$ PRF is the average power transmitted P_{ave}. For an optimally designed receiver $B \tau_c = 1$, i.e., the matched-filter case. The gain G_t of the antenna is given by $G_t = 4\pi A_r \eta / \lambda^2$. The radar cross section σ of a resolution cell is $\sigma = \delta_{az} \delta_r \sigma^0$ where δ_{az} and δ_r are azimuth and range resolutions respectively and σ^0 is the normalized radar cross section. With these substitutions, (9) can be rewritten as

$$\frac{S}{N} = \frac{P_{\text{ave}} T_D A_r^2 \eta^2 \delta_{az} \delta_r \sigma^0}{4\pi R^4 k T_r \overline{NF} \lambda^2 L_s}. \tag{10}$$

The dwell time T_D on a target is governed by the azimuth resolution δ_{az}, and hence, it is related to synthetic aperture length $L_{sa} = v T_D$. Thus

$$T_D = R\lambda/(2v\delta_{az}). \tag{11}$$

By combining (10) and (11)

$$\frac{S}{N} = \frac{P_{\text{ave}} A_r^2 \eta^2 \delta_r \sigma^0}{8\pi R^3 k T_r \overline{NF} \, v\lambda L_s}.$$

This SNR equation is given by Cutrona [5]. The SNR improves with degradation in range resolution, i.e., with increase in δ_r, since the RF bandwidth decreases. The SNR is independent of azimuth resolution δ_{az} since δ_{az} is a consequence of the amount of signal integration time T_D. The SNR decreases with the radar wavelength λ, platform velocity v, and cube of the range (R^3).

For target detection, two additional factors need to be considered, viz. probability of detection and false alarm rate. In many respects the received signal resembles noise in character so that the radar system is designed to assure detecting the target in the presence of noise with a high degree of probability, such as 95 percent. Furthermore, noise characteristically contains spikes in its spectra so that the radar system is designed to assure that noise spikes are not to be mistaken as real targets no more often than a given rate, such as 1 pulse in 10^5 pulses. Detection probability and false alarm rate are discussed in the literature [43].

VIII. Simplified Block Diagram of a Synthetic Aperture Radar

A SAR is a phase-coherent sensor that repetitively transmits high-power pulses and detects the return signals. See Fig. 18. These signals are processed coherently to produce two-dimensional radar images.

The typical SAR transmitter is designed to overcome limitations of peak power in components and to satisfy stringent azimuth and range resolution requirements. High resolution in azimuth requires stringent phase stabilities from pulse-to-pulse and over the integration time. High range resolution requires wide RF bandwidths. To meet the signal-to-noise ratio and target detection requirements, a high average radiated power can be obtained by a high transmit pulse duty cycle. These requirements on the transmitter can be satisfied by transforming short wide-band pulses into long pulses with the same swept bandwidth utilizing a frequency dispersive delay line [44]. Alternately, electronic circuits using a voltage contolled oscillator can also provide the desired transmit pulse [45]–[47]. The output from the high power amplifier passes through a circulator and is radiated by the radar antenna. The received signal passes through the same circulator, is amplified and pulse compressed. The pulse compression circuit can use a frequency dispersive delay line which converts a wideband linearly swept FM long pulse into a short pulse signal with same bandwidth. The phase of the short pulse is measured by the phase coherent detector, and the resultant signal is delivered to the signal processor.

The SAR is mounted on a platform moving at a constant velocity. The PRF must be sufficiently high to avoid azimuth ambiguity. This criterion requires that the radar platform displacement cannot exceed one-half the antenna size between successive transmit pulses. This geometrical constraint on the pulse-to-pulse displacement of the antenna beam is indicated by dashed lines in Fig. 18.

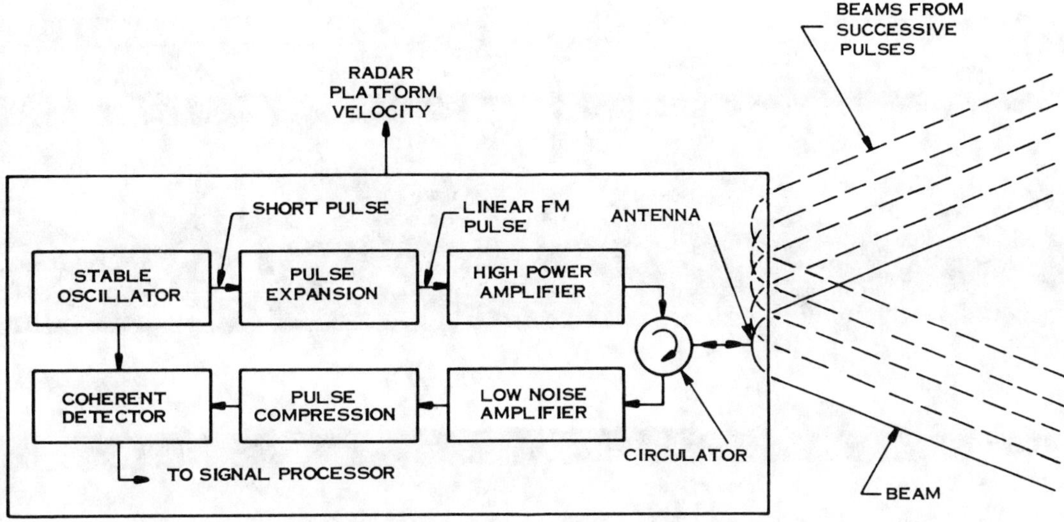

Fig. 18. Simplified block diagram of SAR.

In a SAR, phase stability is exceedingly important. The prime oscillator which provides the signal for the transmitter as well as the reference for the receiver must be very stable. The timing of the transmit pulses must be very precise with respect to the prime oscillator. If the radar platform velocity is not constant, the deviations must be measured and this data used to compensate either the incoming signal or passed on to the signal processor as a correction [23], [24], [48].

IX. RADAR IMAGE OF OCEAN WAVES

The preceding discussion dealt with two-dimensional radar images of isolated targets. In this section, radar images of ocean waves which are dynamic and not usually moving uniformly are discussed. The formation of oceanic waves due to wind, their physical characteristics, electromagnetic wave scattering behavior, and signal response to a SAR, are all complex and not adequately understood. Much work has been done and reported on the problem, and more work is required. Examples of SAR images of ocean waves are shown in Fig. 19. These *L*-band images were reported by Brown *et al.*, and good correlation has been found with visual observations and optical photographs [49]. The bright line across the top of each of the four 30-km-long strip photos is the radar subtrack. The measurements were taken over the Central Atlantic Ocean, and the airborne radar was flown in a large square box pattern to view the same area of ocean surface from four different headings. The data was processed to achieve a 15-m resolution. The waves observed have 200-m wavelengths. It is noted that the directions of the images of the wave "crests" rotate by about 90° between successive image film strips. Other examples of SAR images have been reported [50]–[54].

The oceanic scattering of conventional (i.e., non-SAR) radar signals has usually been reported in terms of integrated characteristics of the signal return [55], [56]. The oceanic patch has been typically on the order of kilometers to tens of kilometers, and the size of the area selected to be sufficiently large so that the normalized radar cross section will not change if a still larger area were illuminated. The ocean surface "roughness", which is related to the radar cross section, or scattering coefficient increases with wind speed and varies with bearing with the highest and lowest cross sections in the upwind and crosswind directions, respectively. The measurements are insensitive to wave motion *per se*. A microwave scatter-

meter to be borne by a satellite is being built to perform radar cross section measurements of the ocean surface from which wind speed and wind direction can be inferred on a global basis [57].

In contrast, the measurement or observation of oceanic waves by SAR relies upon a different characterization of the oceanic surface. Thus the independent patch of sea being considered has a size on the order of meters instead of kilometers, and the presence of wave motion is vitally important to the phase history of the return signal. At present there is relatively little known about the radar signal response of a small patch of dynamic sea with dimensions equal to the SAR resolution cell size, yet the information required by a SAR are radar cross section (amplitude), phase, phase rate (Doppler), range, and range rate (radial velocity) for each small oceanic resolution cell of sea illuminated by the radar antenna beam.

Factors which influence the oceanic surface are wind speed history, wind direction history, fetch distance, depth of water, amount of pollution [58], and others. The ocean surface includes small capillaries, gravity waves, swell, orbital motion, wave speed, capillary speed, wave slope, wave direction, specular surface area, specular surface curvature, etc. Orbital motion [59], [60] has a significant effect on SAR images. For each of these surface descriptors, the average or median magnitude is desired as well as spread of values and distribution. The ocean wave velocity vector direction relative to radar platform velocity vector and antenna beam direction influences the radar response. The radar signal response appears in terms of signal amplitude, phase, Doppler, time delay, etc. The signal-integration time period is on the order of a second.

Ocean-wave motion relative to the radar beam can be resolved into three velocity components, viz. satellite along-track, satellite cross-track cross-radial, and satellite cross-track radial. An along-track component may cause image defocusing. A cross-track cross-radial component has no effect on the radar. A cross-track radial component causes a Doppler frequency shift in the radar return signal, and the processed image may shift in the track direction.

The spatial-resolution cell area is the product of $\delta_r \delta_{az}$, and within this area numerous independent radar-scattering points may physically exist. The radar, however, is insensitive to this large number since the smallest resolvable cell is $\delta_r \delta_{az}$. Because of this limitation, the radar will assign to each $\delta_r \delta_{az}$ cell

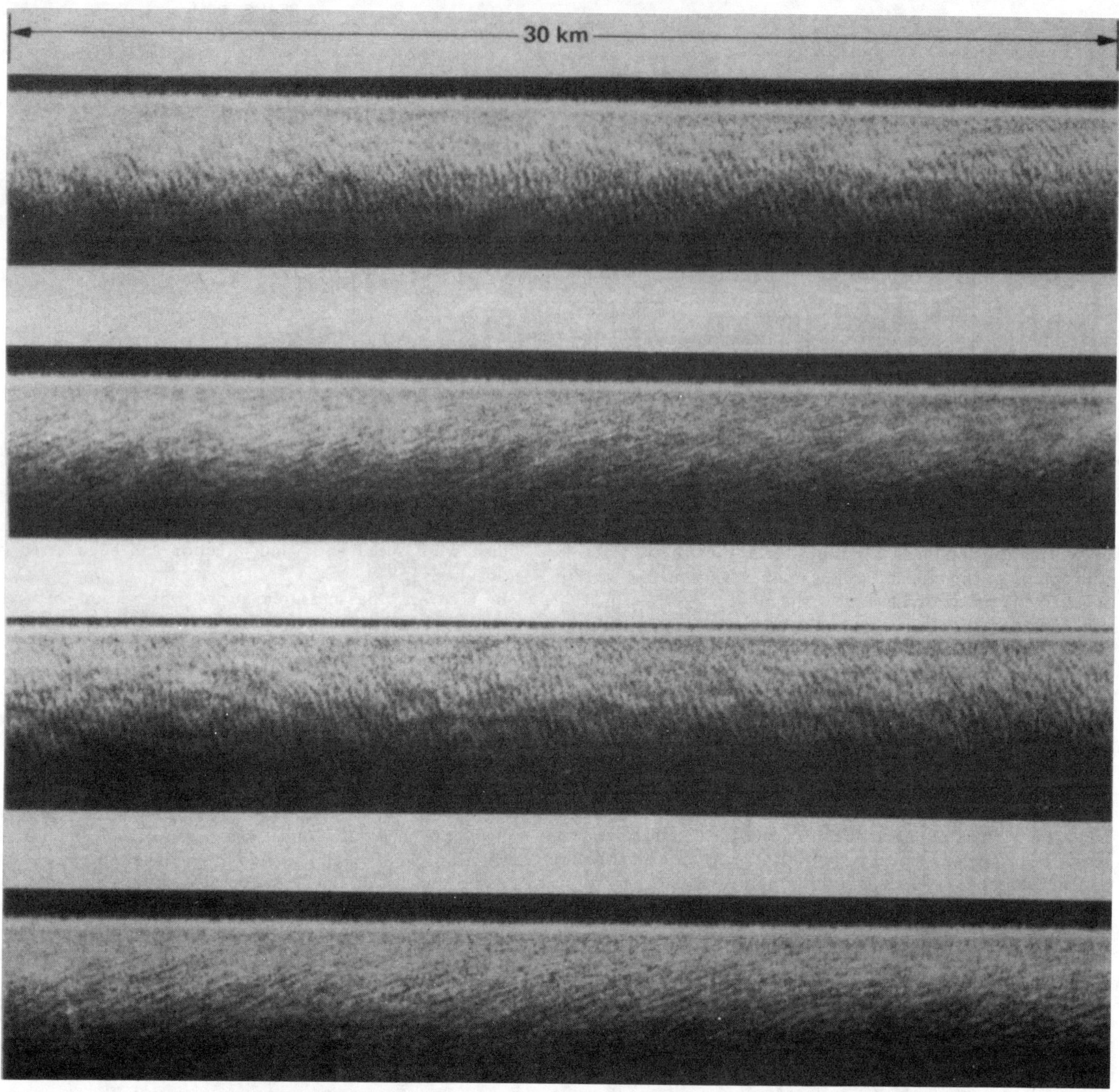

Fig. 19. SAR images of ocean waves. (Courtesy of Walter E. Brown, Jr., Jet Propulsion Laboratory.)

a single integrated value of phase and amplitude to the scattered signal, and these are the input data to the SAR signal processor. In the processor it is assumed that the scattered phase and amplitude of each resolvable cell will not change during the integration time of about one second. The ocean surface decorrelation time has been reported to be in the order of 0.010 s [61], but apparently the amount of decorrelation is not very significant since radar images have been produced. Further, if the signals from all cells in a scene change essentially in unison, good images will be processed. The signal response from each $\delta_r \delta_{az}$ cell will depend on incidence angle, heading, radar wavelength, RF bandwidth, polarization, etc. Large specular surfaces that are flat or nearly so, whose normals are oriented toward the SAR, do not produce strong images [62] due to rapid spatial migration of the phase center

of the reflected radar signal during the integration time. Furthermore, this configuration violates the SAR geometrical constraint mentioned in the Introduction.

The entire radar antenna beam will illuminate perhaps thousands of $\delta_r \delta_{az}$ resolution cells in a scene. The radar data from all of the cells are accumulated from pulse to pulse, and after collecting the data for the total integration time period, signal processing can be initiated. A signal processor based on optical techniques assumes that the scene comprising numerous resolution cells can be treated uniformly. Earlier, it was stated that a small component of target radial velocity will cause a small cross-range shift of the image position. If all resolution cells in the scene were to move radially in unison, there would be no concern. If, on the other hand, the radial velocities of all cells were slightly different from each other, there may be considerable image smear which cannot be compensated. In the other direction, if the scene were moving parallel to the radar platform velocity vector and all cells were moving together, the scene would be initially defocused but this can be compensated. However, if the cells have slightly different along-track velocities, there may be considerable distortion which cannot be compensated.

Other signal processing problems may be caused by acceleration and high component velocities of the ocean surface cells. Radial acceleration may cause azimuth and range defocusing, and an along-track acceleration may cause azimuth walk. A high radial velocity will cause range walk.

Ocean wave motion may be described, perhaps simplistically, in terms of a physical displacement of gravity waves with capillaries and orbital motion of the ocean surface. Elachi *et al.* [51] suggest that in SAR images of the ocean surface, "three sources of cross section modulation seem to play an important role: change of the local tilt angle, variation of the surface roughness, and the waves' orbital velocity." They further state that not all of their measurements support this suggestion. Larson *et al.* [53] suggest that wave height might be inferred from image depth of focus which depends on radial acceleration of the wave. It is observed that of the wave images reported by Larson *et al.* [53] most wave crests are oriented essentially parallel to the aircraft velocity vector. The effects of random phase changes have been discussed by Elachi *et al.* [63]. A complete understanding of these mechanisms and their effect on image formation does not appear to be available.

From the analyses presented in this paper it appears that the resolution in the azimuth direction is limited in part to the spread of the along-track component of the wave velocity. An examination of (5) indicates that a shorter wavelength radar is less sensitive to along-track velocity spread. A radial velocity causes image shift in the cross-radial (azimuthal) direction, and a spread in radial velocities within a scene will cause smearing in the azimuthal direction. For a radar system with δ_{az} = 15 m, a maximum tolerable azimuthal smear Δx may be 5 m. Thus, from (6), $\Delta x = 5$ m $= R \Delta v_r (\cos \beta)/v$. If $R = 10^6$ m, $v = 7.6 \times 10^3$ m/s, and $\beta = 65°$, the tolerable spread in radial velocity $\Delta v_r = 0.09$ m/s. This seems to be a very stringent requirement to be expected from oceanic waves.

It should be noted that if stationary targets such as shoreline, towers, buildings, etc., are included in the same scene as oceanic waves, the best focus conditions for radar images of the oceanic waves may cause the stationary targets to defocus.

There is a great deal of interest in obtaining the directional spectra of oceanic waves. A SAR appears to yield the spatial features [49], and perhaps wave amplitude can be inferred as well. An *L*-band SAR is planned for the NASA SEASAT satellite scheduled to be launched in May 1978 at an orbit altitude of about 800 km [49].

X. Radar Frequency Dependence

The choice of the frequency of a synthetic aperture radar depends on many factors, some of which favor high and some low microwave frequencies. These are listed qualitatively in Table II. It is assumed that the resolution is fixed. *X*-band and *L*-band are regarded as approximate high and low frequency boundaries, respectively. In general, the higher frequency shows more advantages than disadvantages, however, this must be compared with hardware advantages of the lower frequency. Another consideration is target reflection as a function of radar frequency.

TABLE II
Frequency Dependence (For a Given Azimuth Resolution)

Factor	Favor High Microwave Frequency	Favor Low Microwave Frequency
High range resolution $\delta_r = c/(2\Delta f)$	smaller % bandwidth	
High azimuth resolution $\delta_{az} = L_R/2$		greater antenna surface tolerance
Integration time, T_D $T_D = \lambda R_0/(2v\delta_{az})$	shorter T_D	
Radar antenna area, A_R $A_R \propto \lambda$(ambiguity limited)	smaller A_R	
Depth of focus, DOF DOF = $8\delta_{az}^2/\lambda$	greater depth	
Range curvature, RC RC $\propto \lambda^2/\delta_{az}^2$	less curvature	
Along-track velocity error $\Delta v_i \propto \delta_{az}^2/\lambda$	more tolerant	more sensitive
Radial acceleration, $\ddot{R}$ $\ddot{R}_{max} \propto \delta_{az}^2/\lambda$	more tolerant	
Signal-to-noise ratio	slightly better	
Transmitter efficiency		better
Receiver noise temperature		better
Ionospheric granularity	much less effect	

An airborne simultaneous *X*- and *L*-band dual polarization synthetic aperture radar has been developed by ERIM [64]. Comparative radar images of ocean surfaces were taken at the Marineland Test Site off the coast of Florida on December 15, 1975 [65].

XI. Conclusions

A SAR, can produce high resolution two-dimensional images of radar-mapped areas. The radar is carried by a constant velocity moving platform such as an aircraft or satellite. The antenna beam is typically at right angles to the velocity vector. High resolution in range is attained by the use of wideband transmitted pulses and high resolution in cross range (azimuth) is achieved by signal processing the coherent phase history of the signals reflected by the targets, collected for the integration time period. Range and azimuth ambiguities restrict the pulse-repetition frequency to certain bounds. High quality images require accurate knowledge of the range histories to the targets and residual range uncertainties result in image degradation.

SAR images of ocean waves have been reported and these correlate well with optical photographs and visual observations. Despite these correlations, the relationship between SAR images and the dynamic ocean surface is not well understood. Detailed radar signal response of a small patch of sea with dimensions of range and azimuth resolutions is required in terms of reflected amplitude, Doppler shift, Doppler spread, range rate, etc., as functions of incidence angle, heading, radar wavelength, RF bandwidth, polarization, etc. A more complete characterization of the ocean surface in terms of those physical parameters remains to be done. A SAR does offer a possibility of measuring the directional spectra of oceanic waves.

NOMENCLATURE

A	spherical arc
A_r	receiving antenna area
A_R	radar antenna area
A_{REC}	received signal amplitude
A_{REF}	reference signal amplitude
B	receiver noise bandwidth
c	light velocity
D	lens diameter
D_{PP}	pulse-to-pulse displacement of radar antenna
DOF	depth of field
e/m^2	electrons per square meter
E_{AF}	normalized array factor
E_{EP}	normalized element pattern
E_{LA}	normalized linear array pattern
E_{sa}	normalized synthetic array pattern
E_{2a}	normalized two-way array factor
E_{1e}	normalized one-way element pattern
E_{2e}	normalized two-way element pattern
$\overline{E}_R(t)$	total complex signal
$\overline{E}_i(t)$	complex reflected signal from a scatterer
f	frequency
f_D	Doppler frequency
FM	frequency modulation
GR	granularity
G_t	transmitter antenna gain
H	satellite altitude
H_R	radar antenna height
Hz	Hertz
i	orbit inclination angle
k	Boltzmann's constant; fraction
km	kilometer
L	antenna length
L_R	radar antenna length
L_s	total system loss
L_{sa}	aperture length (synthetic aperture)
m	meter
MHz	megahertz
n	number of unknowns
N	noise power; number of array elements
$\overline{NF}$	relative noise figure
P_{ave}	average transmitter power
P_t	peak transmitted power
PRF	pulse repetition frequency
PRF_{high}	upper limit of PRF
PRF_{low}	lower limit of PRF
R	range
R_f	far range
R_{fz}	far zone range
R_m	maximum range
R_n	near range
R_0	nearest range of target
RC	range curvature
RF	radio frequency
RRW	radar range walk
s	target separation
S	signal power
SAR	synthetic aperture radar
SNR	signal-to-noise ratio
SRW	surface range walk
t	time
T_D	dwell (integration) time

T_r	absolute receiver temperature
TCEC	total columnar electron content
v	radar platform velocity
v_{eq}	earth equatorial rotational velocity
v_i	along-track velocity
v_r	radial velocity
v_t	target velocity
W_g	ground swath width
x	radar platform position
X	ground arc length
y	cross-track position
z	distance
β	spherical angle, target angle
δ	ascending node angle
δ_{az}	azimuth (cross range) resolution, linear
δ_r	range resolution, linear
ϵ	orbit eccentricity
η	antenna efficiency, cross cone angle
θ	angle, cone angle
θ_A	azimuth beamwidth
θ_E	elevation beamwidth
θ_R	one-way radar antenna beamwidth
θ_{13}	one-way 3-dB beamwidth
θ_{23}	two-way 3-dB beamwidth
λ	wavelength
σ	radar cross section
σ^0	normalized radar cross section
τ	pulse length
τ_c	compressed pulse length
τ_i	initial uncompressed pulse length
ϕ	phase
ϕ_i	incidence angle
ψ	satellite yaw angle

ACKNOWLEDGMENT

The author wishes to thank M. Berkowitz, Manager of Communication and Navigation Engineering, General Electric Space Division, for carefully reviewing the manuscript and making numerous helpful comments.

REFERENCES

[1] M. I. Skolnik Ed., "An introduction to radar," in *Radar Handbook*. New York: McGraw-Hill, 1970, ch. 1.

[2] K. Tomiyasu, "Remote sensing of the earth by microwaves," *Proc. IEEE*, vol. 62, pp. 86–92, Jan. 1974.

[3] C. W. Sherwin, J. P. Ruina, and R. D. Rawcliffe, "Some early developments in synthetic aperture radar systems," *IRE Trans. Mil. Electron.*, vol. MIL-6, pp. 111–115, Apr. 1962.

[4] W. M. Brown and L. J. Porcello, "An introduction to synthetic-aperture radar," *IEEE Spectrum*, vol. 6, pp. 52–62, Sept. 1969.

[5] L. J. Cutrona, "Synthetic aperture radar," in *Radar Handbook*, M. I. Skolnik, Ed. New York: McGraw-Hill, 1970, ch. 23, pp. 23.1–23.25.

[6] R. O. Harger, *Synthetic Aperture Radar Systems, Theory and Design*. New York: Academic Press, 1970.

[7] A. W. Rihaczek, *Principles of High-Resolution Radar*. New York: McGraw-Hill, 1969.

[8] J. J. Kovaly, *Synthetic Aperture Radar*. Dedham, MA: Artech House, 1976.

[9] R. C. Heimiller, "Theory and evaluation of gain patterns of synthetic arrays," *IRE Trans. Mil. Electron*, vol. MIL-6, pp. 122–129, Apr. 1962.

[10] J. L. Farrell, J. H. Mims, and A. Sorrell, "Effects of navigation errors in maneuvering SAR," *IEEE Trans. Aerosp. Electron. Syst.*, vol. AES-9, pp. 758–776, Sept. 1973.

[11] J. C. Kirk, Jr., "A discussion of digital processing in synthetic aperture radar," *IEEE Trans. Aerosp. Electron. Syst.*, vol. AES-

11, pp. 326–337, May 1975.

[12] J. W. Sherman, III, "Properties of focused apertures in the Fresnel region," *IEEE Trans. Antennas Propagat.*, vol. AP-10, pp. 399–408, July 1962.

[13] L. J. Ricardi, "Near-field characteristics of a linear array," in *Electromagnetic Theory and Antennas, Proceedings of a Symposium held at Copenhagen, Denmark, June 1962*, E. C. Jordan, Ed. New York: Pergamon Press, 1963, pt. 2, pp. 1301–1305.

[14] R. W. Bayma and P. A. McInnes, "Aperture size and ambiguity constraints for a synthetic aperture radar," in *Record IEEE 1975 Int. Radar Conf.*, pp. 499–504, 1975.

[15] T. C. Cheston and J. Frank, "Array antennas," in *Radar Handbook*, M. I. Skolnik, Ed. New York: McGraw-Hill, 1970, ch. 11, pp. 11.1–11.71.

[16] L. J. Cutrona, "The role of synthetic aperture radar in earth resource monitoring," AIAA Paper no. 70–315, AIAA Earth Resources Observations and Information Syst. Meeting, Annapolis, MD, Mar. 2–4, 1970.

[17] L. C. Graham, "Synthetic interferometer radar for topographic mapping," *Proc. IEEE*, vol. 62, pp. 763–768, June 1974.

[18] L. J. Cutrona, E. N. Leith, L. J. Porcello, and W. E. Vivian, "On the application of coherent optical processing techniques to synthetic-aperture radar," *Proc. IEEE*, vol. 54, pp. 1026–1032, Aug. 1966.

[19] J. C. Kirk, Jr., "Digital synthetic aperture radar technology," in *Record IEEE 1975 Int. Radar Conf.*, pp. 482–487, 1975.

[20] D. E. Dudgeon, "Fundamentals of digital array processing," *Proc. IEEE*, vol. 65, pp. 898–904, June 1977.

[21] J. W. Sherman, III, "Aperture-antenna analysis," in *Radar Handbook*, M. I. Skolnik, Ed. New York: McGraw-Hill, 1970, ch. 9, pp. 9.1–9.40.

[22] R. K. Raney, "Synthetic aperture imaging radar and moving targets," *IEEE Trans. Aerosp. Electron. Syst.*, vol. AES-7, pp. 499–505, May 1971.

[23] J. H. Mims and J. L. Farrell, "Synthetic aperture imaging with maneuvers," *IEEE Trans. Aerosp. Electron. Syst.*, vol. AES-8, pp. 410–418, July 1972.

[24] J. C. Kirk, Jr., "Motion compensation for synthetic aperture radar," *IEEE Trans. Aerosp. Electron. Syst.*, vol. AES-11, pp. 338–348, May 1975.

[25] K. Tomiyasu, "Ocean-wave cross-radial image error in synthetic aperture radar due to radial velocity," *J. Geophys. Res.*, vol. 80, p. 4555, Nov. 20, 1975.

[26] ——, "Phase and Doppler errors in a spaceborne synthetic aperture radar imaging the ocean surface," *IEEE J. Oceanic Eng.*, vol. OE-1, pp. 68–71, Nov. 1976.

[27] C. A. Greene and R. T. Moller, "The effect of normally distributed random phase errors on synthetic array gain patterns," *IRE Trans. Mil. Electron.*, vol. MIL-6, pp. 130–139, Apr. 1962.

[28] E. N. Leith, "Complex spatial filters for image deconvolution," *Proc. IEEE*, vol. 65, pp. 18–28, Jan. 1977.

[29] J. H. Chestek, General Electric Company, private communication.

[30] J. Aarons (Ed.), *Total Electron Content and Scintillation Studies of the Ionosphere*, AGARDograph No. 166, Mar. 1973.

[31] J. Aarons, H. E. Whitney, and R. S. Allen, "Global morphology of ionospheric scintillations," *Proc. IEEE*, vol. 59, pp. 159–172, Feb. 1971.

[32] R. K. Crane, "Ionospheric scintillation," *Proc. IEEE*, vol. 65, pp. 180–199, Feb. 1977.

[33] W. E. Brown, III, G. G. Haroules, and W. I. Thompson, III, "Mid-latitude ionospheric scintillation fading of microwave signals," *Nature*, vol. 259, pp. 294–296, Jan. 29, 1976.

[34] L. J. Porcello and L. R. Hughes, "Observed fine structure of a phase perturbation induced during transauroral propagation," *J. Geophys. Res.*, vol. 73, pp. 6337–6346, Oct. 1, 1968.

[35] K. C. Yeh, "Traveling ionospheric disturbance as a diagnostic tool for thermospheric dynamics," *J. Geophys. Res.*, vol. 77, pp. 709–719, Feb. 1, 1972.

[36] R. Sagalyn, AFCRL, private communication.

[37] J. P. McClure, Univ. of Texas, Dallas, private communication; see also J. W. Wright, J. P. McClure, and W. B. Hanson, "Comparisons of ionogram and OGO-6 satellite observations of small-scale F-region inhomogeneities," in *Digest 1975 USNC/URSI Annual Meeting*, Boulder, CO, Oct. 20–23, 1975, pp. 58–59.

[38] A. A. Burns and E. J. Fremouw, "A real-time correction technique for transionospheric ranging error," *IEEE Trans. Antennas Propagat.*, vol. AP-18, pp. 785–790, Nov. 1970.

[39] W. D. Brown, "Ionospheric effects on the SEASAR synthetic-aperture radar based on wideband satellite data," in *Program and Abstracts of 1977 USNC/URSI Meeting*, Stanford, CA. June 22–24, 1977, p. 186.

[40] L. J. Porcello, "Turbulence-induced phase errors in synthetic-aperture radars," *IEEE Trans. Aerosp. Electron. Syst.*, vol. AES-6, pp. 636–644, Sept. 1970.

[41] W. M. Brown and J. F. Riordan, "Resolution limits with propagation phase errors," *IEEE Trans. Aerosp. Electron. Syst.*, vol. AES-6, pp. 657–662, Sept. 1970.

[42] R. K. Crane, "Prediction of the effects of rain on satellite communication systems," *Proc. IEEE*, vol. 65, pp. 456–474, Mar. 1977.

[43] L. V. Blake, "Prediction of radar range," in *Radar Handbook*, M. I. Skolnik, Ed. New York: McGraw-Hill, 1970, ch. 2, pp. 2.16–2.29.

[44] E. C. Farnett, T. B. Howard, and G. H. Stevens, "Pulse-compression radar," in *Radar Handbook*, M. I. Skolnik, Ed. New York: McGraw-Hill, 1970, ch. 20.

[45] J. R. Klauder, A. C. Price, S. Darlington, and W. J. Albersheim, "The theory and design of chirp radars," *Bell Sys. Tech. J.*, vol. 39, pp. 745–808, July 1960.

[46] W. J. Caputi, Jr., "Stretch: a time-transformation technique," *IEEE Trans. Aerosp. Electron. Syst.*, vol. AES-7, pp. 269–278, Mar. 1971.

[47] ——, "Stabilized linear FM generator," *IEEE Trans. Aerosp. Electron. Syst.*, vol. AES-9, pp. 670–678, Sept. 1973.

[48] K. A. Graf and H. Guthart, "Velocity effects in synthetic apertures," *IEEE Trans. Antennas Propagat.*, vol. AP-17, pp. 541–546, Sept. 1969.

[49] W. E. Brown, Jr., C. Elachi, and T. W. Thompson, "Radar imaging of ocean surface patterns," *J. Geophys. Res.*, vol. 81, pp. 2657–2667, May 20, 1976.

[50] C. Elachi, "Wave patterns across the North Atlantic on September 28, 1974 from airborne radar imagery," *J. Geophys. Res.*, vol. 81, pp. 2655–2656, May 20, 1976.

[51] C. Elachi and W. E. Brown, Jr., "Models of radar imaging of the ocean surface waves," *IEEE Trans. Antennas Propagat.*, vol. AP-25, pp. 84–95, Jan. 1977; also *IEEE J. Oceanic Eng.*, vol. OE-2, pp. 84–95, Jan. 1977.

[52] L. I. Moskowitz, "The feasibility of ocean current mapping via synthetic aperture radar methods," in *Proc. Amer. Soc. Photogrammetry Fall Conv.*, Part II, pp. 760–771, Oct. 2–5, 1973.

[53] T. R. Larson, L. I. Moskowitz, and J. W. Wright, "A note on SAR imagery of the ocean," *IEEE Trans. Antennas Propagat.*, vol. AP-24, pp. 393–394, May 1976.

[54] T. R. Larson, L. I. Moskowitz, and J. W. Wright, "Correction to a note on SAR imagery of the ocean," *IEEE Trans. Antennas Propagat.*, vol. AP-24, p. 905, Nov. 1976.

[55] N. W. Guinard and J. C. Daley, "An experimental study of a sea clutter model," *Proc. IEEE*, vol. 58, pp. 543–550, Apr. 1970.

[56] W. L. Jones, L. C. Schroeder, and J. L. Mitchell, "Aircraft measurements of the microwave scattering signature of the ocean," *IEEE Trans. Antennas Propagat.*, vol. AP-25, pp. 52–61, Jan. 1977; also *IEEE J. Oceanic Eng.*, vol. OE-2, pp. 52–61, Jan. 1977.

[57] W. L. Grantham, E. M. Bracalente, W. L. Jones, and J. W. Johnson, "The Seasat-A satellite scatterometer," *IEEE J. Oceanic Eng.*, vol. OE-2, pp. 200–206, Apr. 1977.

[58] R. O. Pilon and C. G. Purves, "Radar imagery of oil slicks," *IEEE Trans. Aerosp. Electron. Syst.*, vol. AES-9, pp. 630–636, Sept. 1973.

[59] W. C. Keller and J. W. Wright, "Microwave scattering and the straining of wind-generated waves," *Radio Science*, vol. 10, pp. 139–147, Feb. 1975.

[60] ——, "Modulation of microwave backscatter by gravity waves in a water tank," U. S. Naval Research Lab. Report 7968, Mar. 29, 1976.

[61] M. I. Skolnik, "Sea echo," in *Radar Handbook*, M. I. Skolnik, Ed. New York: McGraw-Hill, 1970, ch. 26, p. 26.25.

[62] E. L. Johansen, "The synthetic-array radar image of a flat plate," *IEEE Trans. Aerosp. Electron. Syst.*, vol. AES-6, pp. 395–398, May 1970.

[63] C. Elachi and D. D. Evans, "Effects of random phase changes on the formation of synthetic aperture radar imagery," *IEEE Trans. Antennas Propagat.*, vol. AP-25, pp. 149–153, Jan. 1977.

[64] R. Rawson, F. Smith, and R. Larson, "The ERIM simultaneous X- and L-band dual polarization radar," in *Record IEEE 1975 Int. Radar Conf.*, pp. 505–510, 1975.

[65] R. A. Schuchman, R. F. Rawson, and E. S. Kasischke, "Analysis of synthetic aperture radar ocean wave data collected at Marineland and Georges Bank," Environmental Research Institute of Michigan Report no. 123000-11-F, Apr. 1977.

Spaceborne Synthetic-Aperture Imaging Radars: Applications, Techniques, and Technology

CHARLES ELACHI, MEMBER IEEE, T. BICKNELL, ROLANDO L. JORDAN, AND CHIALIN WU

Abstract—In the last four years, the first two Earth-orbiting, spaceborne, synthetic-aperture imaging radars (SAR) were successfully developed and operated. This was a major achievement in the development of spaceborne radar sensors and ground processors. The data acquired with these sensors extended the capability of Earth resources and ocean-surface observation into a new region of the electromagnetic spectrum. This paper is a review of the different aspects of spaceborne imaging radars. It includes a review of: 1) the unique characteristics of spaceborne SAR systems; 2) the state of the art in spaceborne SAR hardware and SAR optical and digital processors; 3) the different data-handling techniques; and 4) the different applications of spaceborne SAR data.

I. INTRODUCTION

IN JUNE 1978, the Seasat satellite was put into orbit around the Earth with a synthetic-aperture imaging radar (SAR) as one of the payload sensors [12]. The Seasat SAR provided, for the first time, synoptic radar images of the Earth's surface with a resolution of 25 m. The success of this complex sensor was a major technological advance, and it opened up a new dimension in our capability to observe, monitor, and study the Earth's surface [31], [39]. In November 1981, the second imaging radar was successfully operated from space on the Shuttle [33]. The Shuttle Imaging Radar-A (SIR-A) acquired images over a variety of regions around the world with an imaging geometry different from the one used by the Seasat SAR.

Spaceborne photography became available in the early 1960's with the advent of the space age. This was followed in the late 1960's and 1970's with the acquisition of multispectral visible and infrared (IR) imagery, thermal imagery, and passive microwave imagery. These sensors allowed us to acquire information about the surface by studying its emitted energy in the microwave and IR regions of the spectrum and the reflected energy in the visible and near-IR regions. All these sensors are passive in nature, i.e., they detect the energy which is generated by the sun or the surface.

The SAR imaging sensor provides information about the surface by measuring and mapping the reflected energy in the microwave region, thus extending the capability of sensing the surface properties into a new dimension. In addition, because it uses its own energy and operates at a relatively long wavelength, it acquires surface imagery at all times, i.e., day or night and through cloud cover. Thus it has the unique capability required for continuous monitoring of dynamic surface phenomena.

The imaging resolution of passive sensors is equal to their angular resolution (i.e., observing wavelength over aperture size) multiplied by the range between the sensor and the area

or object being imaged. Thus the size of the resolution element increases linearly with the observing wavelength and sensor altitude, and is inversely proportional to the aperture size. In the optical and IR regions, very high resolution is achievable from orbit with reasonable size apertures because of the short operating wavelength. In the microwave region, the operating wavelength is relatively large, and apertures of many hundreds of meters to many kilometers are required to achieve high resolution of tens of meters or less. This, of course, is impractical at the present time.

The SAR sensor circumvents this limitation by using the ranging and Doppler tracking capability of coherent radars to acquire high-resolution images of the surface from orbital altitudes. Two neighboring targets are separated by their differential time delay and Doppler history, neither of which is a function of the distance to the sensor. Thus the resolution of a SAR system is independent of the sensor altitude. This unique advantage does impose some restrictions on the sensor imaging swath, antenna size, and power requirements. The basic properties of spaceborne SAR systems are discussed in Section II and the technological aspects of the sensor are presented in Section III.

Because the SAR uses the Doppler history to achieve high resolution in one of the spatial dimensions, each pixel is generated by processing a large number of successive echoes. This leads to a large number of arithmetic operations in order to generate the image. This arithmetic complexity is beyond the present capability of real-time processors. The development of digital processors for spaceborne SAR data is a very active and challenging research field. This aspect of the SAR system is the subject of Section IV.

A very elegant way of executing a large number of the types of calculations required for SAR data processing can be achieved with optical techniques. In actuality, the first airborne SAR systems used optical processors. In Section V, we discuss how these types of processors have been adapted to handle the unique aspects of spaceborne SAR data.

Once the image has been formed, a number of post-image-formation processing steps are used to maximize the usefulness of the information in the radar imagery. These include, among others, radar image registration to multispectral visible/IR images, automatic textural analysis, and speckle statistical analysis. These techniques are addressed in Section VI.

Section VII addresses interpretation techniques and applications of spaceborne SAR data. We review the techniques and image features that an interpreter uses in extracting information about the surface, and we present a variety of specific examples in the different areas of the Earth Sciences—geology, oceanography, glaciology, and agriculture.

At the end of each section, we briefly discuss the developments expected in the near future. In Section VIII, we present

Manuscript received February 1, 1982; revised July 29, 1982. The research described in this paper was performed under Contract with the National Aeronautics and Space Administration. The submission of this paper was encouraged after the review of an advance proposal.

The authors are with the Jet Propulsion Laboratory, California Institute of Technology, Pasadena, CA 91109.

Reprinted from *Proc. IEEE*, vol. 70, pp. 1174–1209, Oct. 1982.

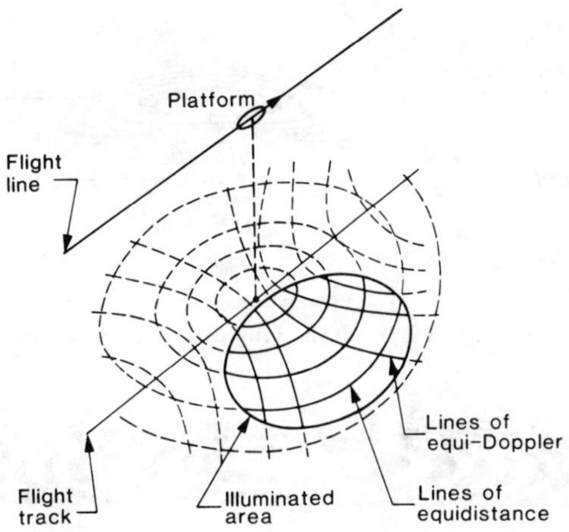

Fig. 1. Coordinate system for SAR image formation. A set of circles and hyperbolas define the equirange and equi-Doppler lines, respectively.

our opinion of the major challenges in the field of SAR remote sensing for the 1980's and briefly review the development being planned for spaceborne SAR systems during this decade.

II. SPACEBORNE SAR PRINCIPLE

In the synthetic-aperture technique, the Doppler information in the returned echo is used simultaneously with the time-delay information to generate a high-resolution image of the surface being illuminated by radar [16], [70], [26], [44], [52]. The radar usually "looks" to one side of the moving platform—to eliminate right–left ambiguities—and perpendicular to its line of motion. It transmits a short pulse of coherent electromagnetic energy toward the surface. Points equidistant from the radar are located on successive concentric spheres. The intersection of these spheres with a flat surface gives a series of concentric circles centered at the nadir point (see Fig. 1). The backscatter echoes from objects along a certain circle will have a well-defined time delay but different Doppler characteristics.

Points distributed on coaxial cones, with the flight line as the axis and the radar as the apex, provide identical Doppler shifts of the returned echo but different delays. The intersection of these cones with a flat surface gives a family of hyperbolas (Fig. 1). Objects on a specific hyperbola will provide equi-Doppler returns. Thus if the time delay and Doppler information in the returned echoes are processed simultaneously, the surface can be divided into a coordinate system of concentric circles and coaxial hyperbolas (Fig. 1), and each point on the surface can be uniquely identified by a specific time delay and specific Doppler. The brightness that is assigned to a specific pixel (picture-resolution element) in the radar image is proportional to the echo energy contained in the time-delay bin and the Doppler bin, which corresponds to the equivalent point on the surface being imaged. The resolution capability of the imaging system is thus dependent on the measurement accuracy of the differential time delay and differential Doppler (or phase) between two neighboring points on the surface.

In actuality, the situation is somewhat more complicated. The radar transmits a pulsed signal in order to obtain the time-delay information. To obtain the Doppler information unambiguously, the echoes from many successive pulses are required with a pulse-repetition frequency (PRF) which meets the Nyquist sampling criterion. Thus as the moving platform passes

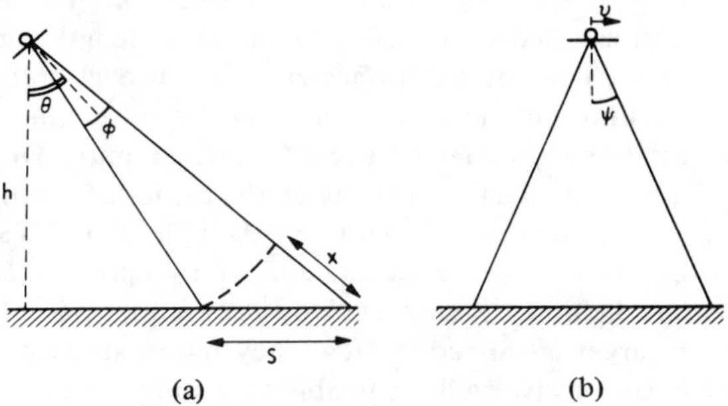

Fig. 2. Imaging radar viewing geometry: (a) in the range plane, (b) in the azimuth plane.

over a certain region, the received echoes contain a complete Doppler history and range-change history for each point on the surface that is being illuminated. These complete histories are then processed to identify uniquely each point on the surface and to generate the image. This is why a very large number of operations are required to generate each pixel in the image. Such is not the case with optical sensors. A simplified comparison is that the radar sensor generates the equivalent of a hologram of the surface, and further processing is required to obtain the image. This processing can be done either optically or digitally.

One unique feature of the synthetic-aperture imaging radar is that its resolution capability is independent of the platform altitude. This is a result of the fact that the image is formed by using the Doppler history and the differential time delays, none of which is a function of the range from the radar to the surface. This unique capability allows the acquisition of high-resolution images from satellite altitude as long as the received echo has sufficient strength above the noise level.

In this section, we will discuss the main features of spaceborne SAR systems. These include: azimuth and range ambiguities, range walk, the effects of Earth's rotation and orbital characteristics, surface interactions, SAR image characteristics, key tradeoff parameters influencing the sensor design, and nonconventional SAR systems.

A. Ambiguities

There will be ambiguity in the response if the PRF is so high that return signals from two successive transmitted pulses arrive simultaneously at the receiver. This is called range ambiguity. Conversely, if the PRF is so low that the return is not sampled at the Nyquist rate, there will be Doppler azimuth ambiguity.

The upper limit of the PRF is fixed by the range or elevation beamwidth of the SAR antenna. A view of the beam geometry in the range plane is shown in Fig. 2. In order to avoid the situation in which the far edge echo arrives at the receiver simultaneously with the near edge echo from the following pulse, it is necessary that

$$T > 2X/c \qquad (1)$$

i.e.,

$$T > \frac{2h}{c} \frac{\tan \theta}{\cos \theta} \phi = \frac{2\lambda h}{cW} \sin \theta / \cos^2 \theta \qquad (2)$$

or

$$\text{PRF} < cW \cos^2 \theta / 2\lambda h \sin \theta \qquad (3)$$

where T is the time between successive pulses, λ is the radar wavelength, W is the antenna width, θ is the look angle, h is the platform height, c is the speed of light, X is the slant range swath, and ϕ is the beamwidth (see Fig. 2(a)). The above equations assume that ϕ is small and the pulse length is much smaller than T. The Earth's surface curvature is neglected.

The lower limit of the PRF is imposed by the requirement that the PRF must equal or exceed the maximum Doppler shift of the return signals. Targets at the center of the broadside beam will return signals with zero Doppler shift. Targets ahead of broadside center are characterized by a positive Doppler and those behind by negative Doppler frequencies. If the return of a target is shifted in frequency by an amount equal to the PRF, the receiver will be unable to distinguish the pulsed return signal from that of a target on broadside center. Thus the PRF has to be sufficiently high to exceed the maximum Doppler shift of targets located at beam edge. The Doppler shift f_D due to a radial velocity v_r is given by

$$f_D = \frac{2v_r}{c} f \tag{4}$$

where f is the radar frequency. By referring to Fig. 2(b), $v_r = v \sin \psi \simeq v\psi$. The angle ψ to the first null of the one-way radar illumination beam is $\Psi = \lambda/L$ where L is the antenna length. Thus the lower limit of the PRF is

$$\mathrm{PRF}_{\mathrm{low}} = f_D = \frac{2v}{L}. \tag{5}$$

The two limitations derived above give

$$\frac{cW \cos^2 \theta}{2\lambda h \sin \theta} > \mathrm{PRF} > 2v/L \tag{6}$$

which can be rewritten as

$$WL > \frac{4v\lambda h \sin \theta}{c \cos^2 \theta}. \tag{7}$$

This condition imposes a minimum size on the antenna area (WL) which is required to avoid ambiguities. Equation (7) should be used only in preliminary calculations. In actual design, the Earth curvature should be taken into account.

B. Point-Target Response

The simplest way to understand the SAR image-formation mechanism and the necessary processing is to consider the case of a bright point target on the surface. Let us consider the case of a linearly phase-modulated waveform $W(t)$.

$$W(t) = A(t)e^{i[\omega_0 t + (a/2)t^2]}$$

where

$$A(t) = 1, \quad \text{for } nT - \tau < t < nT + \tau$$

$$A(t) = 0, \quad \text{otherwise} \tag{8}$$

where T is the pulse repetition period, 2τ is the pulse length, ω_0 is the carrier frequency, a is the chirp rate, and n is an integer. While the target is within the antenna beam, the returned echo $E(t)$ will be modulated by the antenna pattern (which is neglected here) and by a phase shift proportional to the round-trip delay; i.e.,

$$E(t) \sim A(t)e^{i[\omega_0 t + (a/2)t^2 + r(t)]} \tag{9}$$

where

$$r(t) = \sqrt{h^2 + X^2 + v^2 t^2}.$$

If the successive echoes are frequency shifted down to video and their instantaneous amplitude (not envelope) is used to modulate the light intensity of an optical film scanner, the

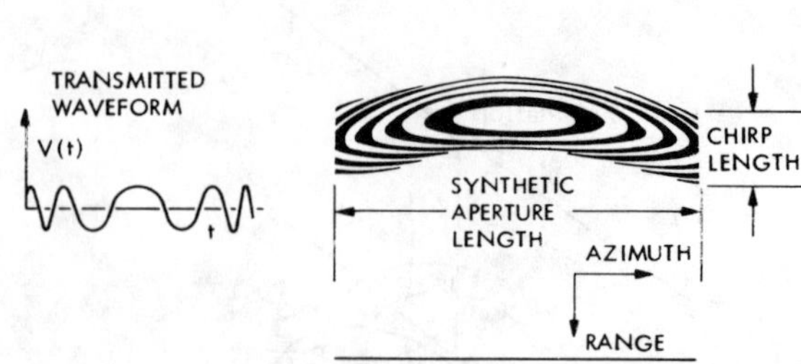

Fig. 3. Point-target response showing the range-curvature effect.

Fig. 4. Point-target response for an airborne system when the range curvature is negligible.

corresponding record will be what is shown in Fig. 3. Each vertical line corresponds to one echo which has a chirp behavior (see insert in Fig. 3). Successive echoes are slightly shifted in phase relative to each other because of the platform motion and the resulting Doppler shift. The whole pattern is also bent because of the large change in the distance from the spaceborne platform to the target while the target is in the beam. This bending in the pattern is called range curvature. In the case of aircraft systems, this bending is negligible (see Fig. 4).

In reality, the point-target response is even more complex. Because of the Earth's rotation, which adds an additional Doppler component, the orbit ellipticity, and errors in the spacecraft attitude, the point-response pattern is asymmetric (as shown in Fig. 5).

In its simplest form (Fig. 4), the synthetic-aperture point response can be easily compressed into the image point. This can be done optically or digitally. In the optical processing approach, the modulated signal film acts like a Fresnel lens and will focus incident laser light into a focal point which is the image. In the digital processing case, a two-dimensional correlation, or two successive one-dimensional (one along each axis) correlations with a reference function, will compress the signal data to form the image. In the real case (Fig. 5), the range walk and range curvatures have to be taken into account and corrected for. These can be estimated from knowledge of the spacecraft state vector. However, some feedback mechanism is usually required to achieve accurate compression. The compression techniques are discussed in detail in Section IV.

C. Orbital and Environmental Factors

The satellite orbital plane is fixed in space. Targets on the Earth's surface move with a linear velocity which is dependent on their latitudes. It is maximum at the equator and zero at the poles. The resulting Doppler effect leads to an asymmetry in the point response as discussed above. Three methods can be used to compensate for this effect [77]: i) rotating the antenna beam in yaw about the satellite nadir to include the zero Doppler-frequency direction. (Because the rotation angle varies with latitude, this requires the satellite attitude to be continuously adjusted.); ii) continuously adjusting the receiver local-oscillator frequency with respect to the transmitted frequency to cancel the effect of the Doppler from the Earth rotation; and iii) subtracting the Doppler due to Earth rotation from the received signal during processing. The last approach was used by the Seasat SAR.

In a similar way, orbit eccentricity causes an altitude change

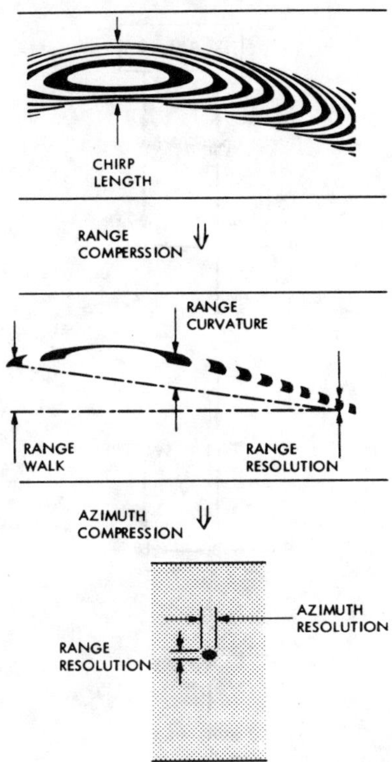

Fig. 5. Point-target response showing the spaceborne SAR case where range curvature and range walk are present. Also illustrated are the processing steps as well as other parameters discussed in the paper.

and displaces the image in the track direction. With descending altitude, the velocity vector will dip below the local horizon. The zero Doppler-frequency direction is perpendicular to the satellite-velocity vector so that the image will shift rearward relative to the subsatellite point [44], [77]. The image shift is given by

$$s = \frac{h}{v} \frac{dh}{dt} \cos \theta. \tag{10}$$

Similar to the Earth-rotation effect, compensation for altitude change can be accomplished by rotating the antenna boresight axis in yaw about the local satellite nadir, by trimming the receiver local-oscillator frequency, or during processing. It should be noted that since the orbit perigee will migrate, the orbital position of maximum altitude change rate will migrate.

The orbital effects (ellipticity and attitude errors) are deterministic and well behaved. Therefore, they can be estimated directly or by analyzing the data using clutterlock feedback. However, undeterministic effects could be encountered with spaceborne radar systems. Amplitude and phase random scintillations are caused by ionospheric irregularities [1], [21]. The phase scintillation would degrade the radar image if the granularity along a synthetic-aperture length leads to phase shifts in excess of a small fraction of a radian. The magnitude of the phase granularity can be calculated from time-delay formulations given by Burns and Friemouw [17], and it is expected to be of appreciable impact only for systems operating at frequencies lower than 1 GHz.

D. Range Curvature and Range Walk

During integration along the synthetic-aperture length, the target range does change in excess of the range resolution, as illustrated in Fig. 3. This effect is called range curvature [56]. If R_0 is the nearest range to the target and R_m is the maximum range at the edge of the synthetic aperture, then

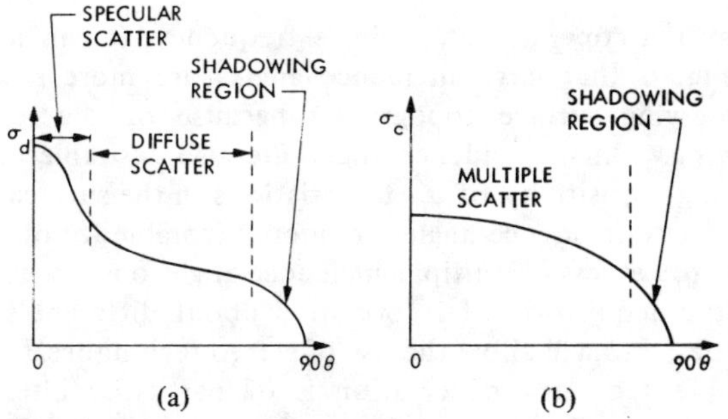

Fig. 6. Simplified sketch of the backscatter cross section behavior as a function of incidence angle and polarization: (a) direct backscatter, (b) depolarized backscatter. The two curves are not to the same scale.

$$R_m = \sqrt{R_0^2 + \left(\frac{v\zeta}{2}\right)^2} = R_0 + \frac{1}{8}\frac{(v\zeta)^2}{R_0} \tag{11}$$

where $\zeta = \lambda R_0/2vr_z$ = integration time, and r_z is the azimuth resolution. The range curvature is given by

$$R_C = R_0 - R_m = \frac{1}{8}\frac{(v\zeta)^2}{R_0} = \frac{\lambda^2 R_0}{32 r_z^2}. \tag{12}$$

Relative to the range slant resolution r_r, then

$$\frac{R_c}{r_r} = \frac{\lambda^2 R_0}{32 r_r r_z^2}. \tag{13}$$

For the Seasat SAR system, $r_r = r_z = 7$ m, $\lambda = 0.25$ m, and $R_0 = 850$ km. The range curvature is equal to

$$\frac{R_c}{r_r} = 4.3.$$

This implies that a point migrates through 4.3 resolution elements during the formation of the synthetic aperture. This effect must be taken into account during processing (see later).

The range walk is defined as the difference in the range to a point target when it leaves the illumination beam relative to when it enters the beam (see Fig. 5). The range walk is a function of attitude errors, orbit ellipticity, and linear velocity of the target. It can be one to two orders of magnitude larger than the range resolution.

Range curvature and range walk are called range migration.

E. Surface Interaction Mechanisms

The brightness of an individual pixel in a radar image is a direct representation of the backscatter cross section of the corresponding area on the surface being imaged. The backscatter cross section is mainly dependent on the physical (e.g., slope, roughness, and near-surface inhomogeneities) and electrical (e.g., dielectric constant) properties of the surface, as well as the radar wave characteristics—incidence angle, frequency, and polarization state. A number of interaction mechanisms contribute to the backscattered energy [47]. Bragg scattering is dominant at relatively large incidence angles and for relatively well-organized surfaces. Rayleigh scattering is dominant in the case of discrete objects. Specular reflection is of particular importance at near-vertical incidence, and multiple scattering plays a key role in depolarization of the incident wave.

In its most simplified form, the behavior of the backscatter cross section σ as a function of incidence angle is shown in a sketch form in Fig. 6. Because of the numerous surface parameters which influence the backscatter cross section, a complete description of the surface properties will most likely require multiple observations with different radar parameters. If the radar system operates at a single frequency, it can be seen from Fig. 6 that large incidence angles are more favorable for observing surface topography because of the resulting shadowing. Small incidence angles are also desirable because of the high sensitivity of σ_d to variations in the surface slope. Intermediate incidence angles are more favorable for observing surface roughness. Multiple incidence-angle observation will allow the acquisition of information about different surface properties, and will allow the use of stereo techniques.

Multiple-frequency observation is of particular interest at intermediate angles in order to acquire a measure of the spectral characteristics of the surface roughness. Multiple-polarization observations provide information about volumetric and multiple scattering, and will tend to supress the effects of the large-scale topography (i.e., slope changes).

F. Noise in SAR Systems: Thermal and Speckle Noise

If we neglect the quantization noise, the two types of noise to be considered in a radar design are the thermal noise and the speckle noise.

The thermal noise is an additive noise which is due to the noise temperature at the input of the receiver. The signal-to-thermal noise ratio can be improved by increasing the transmitted peak power or decreasing the receiver temperature. This is the type of noise encountered in real-aperture radar systems.

The speckle noise is due to the coherent nature of the SAR image-formation process. This noise gives the radar image a fine texture similar to what is observed when a scene is illuminated with laser light. The speckle noise is proportional to the reflected signal power. Thus it is a multiplicative noise which cannot be reduced by increasing the transmitted power. The speckle noise can only be reduced by averaging independent looks.

Before detection, the speckle noise is assumed to be a zero-mean Gaussian noise on each of the in-phase and quadrature components. After detection, the intensity in an image pixel has then an exponential probability distribution of the form

$$p(I) = \frac{1}{I_0} e^{-I/I_0} \tag{14}$$

where I_0 is the average return in the absence of speckle. As multilooks are coherently added, the speckle variance is reduced and becomes chi-squared (χ^2) distributed with $2N$ degrees of freedom where N is the number of independent looks. This gives a probability density function for the intensity of an image pixel as

$$p(I) = \frac{1}{\Gamma(N)} \frac{1}{I_0} \left(\frac{I}{I_0}\right)^{N-1} e^{-I/I_0}. \tag{15}$$

This distribution has a mean of $\mu = NI_0$ and a standard deviation $\Sigma = \sqrt{N}\, I_0$.

One measure of an image radiometric resolution, for a stationary scene, is

$$Q = 10 \log \left(\frac{\mu + \Sigma}{\mu - \Sigma}\right) = 10 \log \left(\frac{\sqrt{N} + 1}{\sqrt{N} - 1}\right) \tag{16}$$

which clearly shows that higher values of N are desirable. However, for $N \geq 25$ (e.g., $Q = 1.8$ dB), large increases in N give only small improvement in Q. This should be traded off with the fact that increasing N immediately degrades the image resolution in a proportional way.

A detailed theoretical study with experimental verification of the speckle noise property was given by Bennett and McConnell [8].

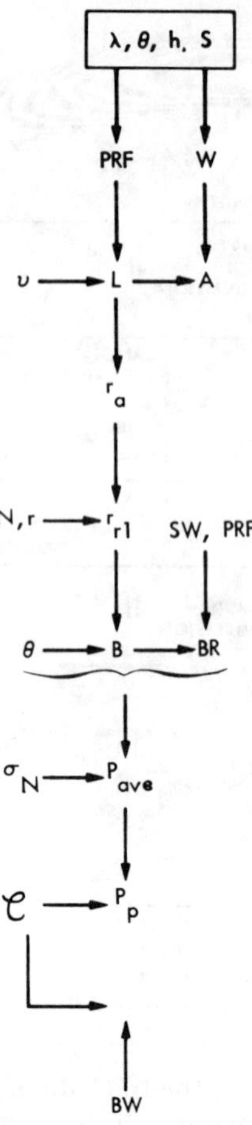

Fig. 7. Sketch showing the steps of one procedure to determine the different parameters for a spaceborne SAR system.

G. Key Tradeoff Parameters

In defining and optimizing the design of a radar system, a large number of parameters have to be determined and traded off. Sophisticated computer programs have been developed at the Jet Propulsion Laboratory (JPL), Pasadena, CA, in connection with the development of the Seasat SAR and SIR-A, and with the planning of Venus orbiting–imaging radar (VOIR) and future Shuttle and free-flying SAR sensors.

For illustrative purposes, a simplified step-by-step parameters estimation procedure is described here. Other procedures could be equally well used. The most involved steps are not included, such as integrated ambiguities or sidelobes level, image-calibration parameters, pixel-brightness statistics, Earth ellipticity, spacecraft-attitude effects, system nonlinearities, sample-digitization level, effect of data-link bit error rates, sampling noise, etc.

We assume that the radar wavelength λ, illumination incidence angle θ, and image swath width S are fixed by the scientific objective. We also assume that the orbit altitude h and platform velocity v are given, and we neglect the surface curvature. In a complete design procedure, these parameters λ, θ, S, and h are usually input variables which can also be varied to optimize the design.

The steps of the procedure are given in a schematic form in Fig. 7. The pulse-repetition frequency is derived from the requirement that the echoes from successive pulses should not overlap. Thus (see Fig. 2)

$$\text{PRF} \leq CS \sin \theta / 2 \tag{17}$$

and the antenna width is given by

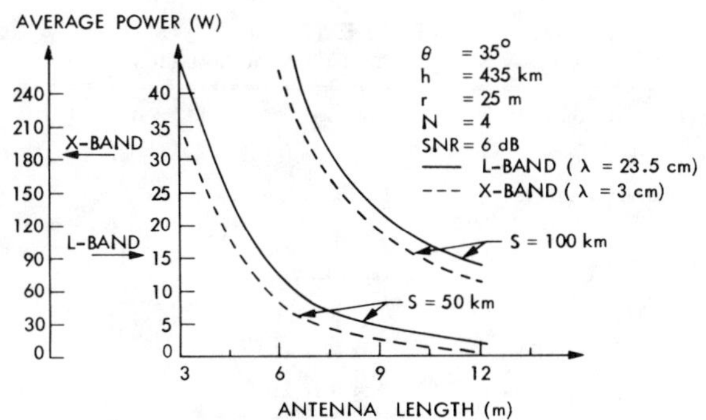

Fig. 8. Illustrative examples of tradeoff curves.

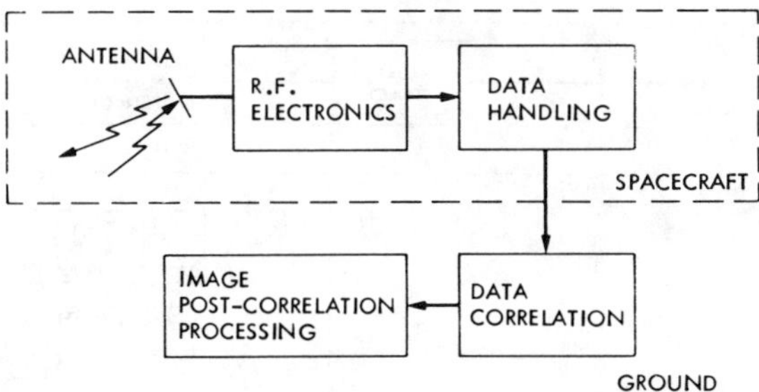

Fig. 9. Simplified block diagram of a typical SAR system showing its main elements.

$$W = \lambda h / S \cos^2 \theta. \tag{18}$$

From the maximum PRF, we can then determine the minimum antenna length such that the Doppler shift is sufficiently sampled by the PRF.

$$L > \frac{2v}{\mathrm{PRF}}. \tag{19}$$

The antenna width and minimum length give the minimum antenna area $A = WL$. The one-look azimuth resolution is theoretically equal to half the antenna length for a fully focused system [16]. Thus

$$r_{al} = L/2. \tag{20}$$

If we assume that the desired resolution r (assumed to be the same in azimuth and range) and total number of looks N are given, then the one-look range resolution is

$$r_{rl} = r^2 / N r_{al}. \tag{21}$$

The bit rate is then determined by the bandwidth, the sampling duty cycle, and the number of bits per sample.

The next key parameter is the average transmitted power required to achieve a noise-equivalent backscatter σ_N. This is the surface backscatter cross section which will give a thermal signal-to-noise ratio (SNR) of unity (i.e., 0 dB).

$$P_{\mathrm{ave}} = \frac{8\pi k T \lambda B h^3 \, \mathrm{PRF}}{\sigma_N c L W^2 \cos^3 \theta} \tag{22}$$

and the peak transmitted power is

$$P_p = \frac{8\pi k T \lambda B^2 h^3}{\sigma_N c L e W^2 \cos^3 \theta} \tag{23}$$

where e is the compression ratio. The dispersed pulse length is equal to

$$\tau = e/B. \tag{24}$$

The above equations give the simplified relationships between the radar parameters. In defining a SAR system, the designer can change a number of input parameters to optimize the system. Fig. 8 gives some illustrative examples of tradeoff curves.

H. Nonconventional SAR Systems

A number of coherent imaging radar systems have been proposed which use a slight variation relative to the conventional synthetic-aperture technique discussed above. Some of these systems were proposed in order to get around the limitation imposed on the swath width by the ambiguities; others have the capability of surface imaging at a constant incident angle (but variable azimuth angle). Some of these systems are discussed here briefly. These include the burst-mode SAR, the scan SAR, the geosynchronous SAR, and the bistatic SAR. All of these systems basically use the concept of range-Doppler processing to generate two-dimensional images.

In the conventional SAR, a continuous array along the flight is synthesized to achieve the high resolution. Repetitive subarrays can also be used to improve resolution relative to a real-aperture system. These can be achieved by turning on the radar for a predetermined time period and then turning it off for another time period, and so on. This is called the burst-mode SAR. With this approach, the power consumption is reduced by the turnoff duty cycle; however, there is a proportional loss in the resolution or number of looks.

One variety of the burst mode is to keep the radar turned on all the time, sequentially stepping the beam position, however, to illuminate neighboring swath track on the ground. The physical beam of the antenna initially illuminates one subswath long enough to synthesize a radar image covering the entire area of the beam. The beam is then pointed to the neighboring subswath for an equal length of time, and so on. The whole cycle is then repeated when the spacecraft moves about the length of the antenna footprint. This mode was proposed and studied by Moore, Classen, and Lin (see [62] and [76]). In effect, a burst mode is being used for each subswath. Cutrona [26] proposed the use of a wide-beam illuminator and simultaneous narrow receiving beams for the different subswaths. Classen and Eckerman [18] proposed a variant of this idea in which a constant incident angle, but variable illumination direction, could be achieved by illuminating the surface with a wide conical beam and by using narrow sub-beams for reception.

To synthesize a long aperture, the radar platform must be moving relative to the target. Thus a geostationary orbiting radar cannot use the synthetic-aperture technique. However, a geosynchronous radar in an inclined orbit will undergo a mutating motion which would allow aperture synthesis. The geosynchronous SAR was studied by Tomiyasu [76], [77]. The main advantage of such a SAR is that it could map a large limited area (such as the U.S. and Central America) repetitively every 24 h. However, the power requirements and antenna size are relatively large though feasible.

In a bistatic SAR, the transmitter and receiver are not collocated. A synthetic aperture can be achieved with either the receiver, or transmitter, or both in motion. A number of configurations have been studied [76] and Elachi *et al.* [35].

III. Spaceborne SAR Sensors

A SAR system can be divided into five major elements (Fig. 9). The antenna is the interface between the on-board RF electronics and free space. It radiates the electromagnetic energy toward the object to be sensed, and it collects the backscattered energy. The RF electronics consists of the transmitter subsystem which generates the RF signal and the receiver

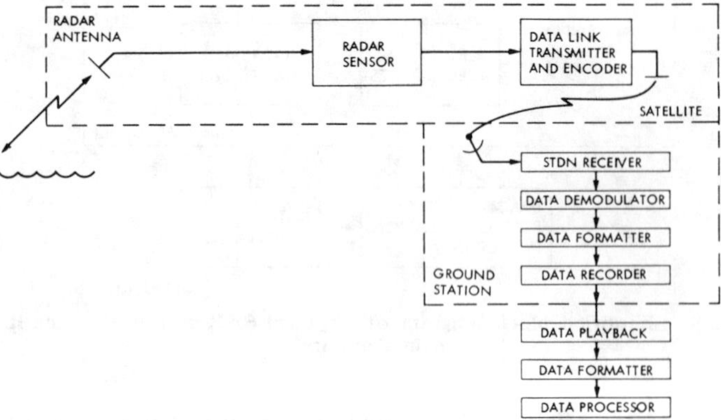

Fig. 10. Simplified block diagram of the Seasat SAR.

TABLE I
Seasat-A SAR System Characteristics

Satellite altitude	800 km
Wavelength	0.235 m
Theoretical resolution	25 x 25 m on the surface at 4 looks
Swath width	100 km
RF bandwidth	19 MHz
Transmit pulse length	33.4 µsec
Pulse repetition range	1463 to 1640 pps
Transmit time bandwidth product	634
Radar transmitter peak power	1000 W
Sensitivity time control range	9 dB
Data recorder bit rate	110 Mbits/sec (5 bits per word)
Radar DC power	500 W
Radar antenna dimensions	10.7 by 2.16 m
Radar antenna gain	35 dB

subsystem which detects the returned energy and converts it into a form which can be handled by the data-handling element. This element, in turn, reformats the data and transmits them to the data correlator. The output of the data-handling element could be either a digital tape with a digital record of the returned echoes or an optical film with an analog record of the returned echoes. This record contains what is commonly called the "signal data." These first three elements are referred to as the "SAR sensor." They are discussed in this section.

The data-correlator element transforms the "signal record" into an "image record" which is a two-dimensional representation of the surface reflectivity. This is the stage at which a recognizable image is acquired. These image data are then processed by an image post correlation processor for geometric and radiometric calibration, and for registration with other data sets acquired with similar (other radar data acquired at different frequency, polarization, or incidence angle) or different (visible or IR) imaging sensors. These last two elements are the subjects of Sections IV, V, and VI.

The first spaceborne SAR system was flown on the Apollo 17 spacecraft around the Moon. It was intended for subsurface sounding of the lunar crust [67], [66]. This sensor, called the Apollo Lunar Sounder Experiment (ALSE) radar was not specifically designed for surface imaging, and, therefore, will be only briefly discussed in this paper.

The first spaceborne SAR which was specifically designed to acquire synoptic high-resolution images of a planetary surface is the Seasat SAR which operated in orbit around the Earth during a 100-day period in the summer of 1978 [12]. The Seasat SAR [49], [48] incorporated some of the most advanced sensor technology of the late 1970's, and it is described here in detail. More recently, an imaging SAR was flown on the second Shuttle flight in November, 1981 [30]. This sensor [42], called the SIR-A, is very similar to the Seasat SAR as far as the electronics are concerned. Only its unique and additional features are discussed here.

A. The Seasat SAR

The Seasat SAR sensor system, shown in Fig. 10, consists of a planar array antenna, a transmitter/receiver RF sensor, an analog data link, a data formatter, and a high-density digital recorder subsystem which outputs the "signal record." The characteristics of the sensor are summarized in Table I. It was designed to provide continuous strips of radar imagery with a 100-km swath at a resolution of 25 m from an orbital altitude of 800 km. During its 100 days of operation, it acquired a voluminous set of images of the Earth's surface corresponding to a total imaged area of about 126 million square kilometers

(including multiple coverage). Because the radar data were directly linked to a limited number of specially equipped ground stations, the coverage was limited to the central and northern American hemisphere, western Europe, the North Atlantic, the North Pacific, and the northern polar regions.

Antenna: The Seasat-A antenna system consists of a 10.74- by 2.16-m phased-array system deployed after orbit insertion. This deployed antenna is configured to fly with the long dimension along the spacecraft-velocity vector and bore-sighted at an angle of 20.5° from the nadir direction in elevation (cone) and 90° from the nominal spacecraft-velocity vector (clock). The antenna dimensions (10.74 m X 2.16 m) are dictated by a desire to limit range and Doppler ambiguities to acceptably low levels (see (6), (17)–(19)). At a nominal 20.5° look angle from nadir, a total beamwidth in elevation of 6.2° is required to illuminate a 100-km swath on the Earth's surface from an 800-km-high orbit. Thus the antenna cross-track dimension is 2.16 m to limit the radiation to these sets of angles (see (18)). The area illuminated on the surface of the Earth is from 240 to 340 km to the right of the subspacecraft point. The antenna elements in elevation are weighted to limit sidelobes in the cross-track direction. The minimum antenna along-track length is limited by a desire to keep azimuth sampling ambiguities to an acceptably low level (see (19)) while the maximum along-track length is determined by the requirement to illuminate a sufficiently large patch of terrain to allow processing of the data to achieve 25-m resolution in azimuth with four looks.

These two requirements limit the antenna length along the velocity vector to between 10.5 and 14 m. The 10.74-m antenna length was dictated by the available volume within the satellite shroud. The level of integrated ambiguities in azimuth was estimated to be between −18 and −24 dB, depending on the selected PRF and processor bandwidth in azimuth.

The antenna subsystem consists of eight mechanically deployed, electrically coupled, flat microstrip panels. This array is shown in Fig. 11 in both stowed and deployed configurations. The construction of the microstrip is depicted in Fig. 12, and the deployment and extension mechanization is shown in Fig. 13.

RF Sensor: The radar RF sensor provides the antenna with

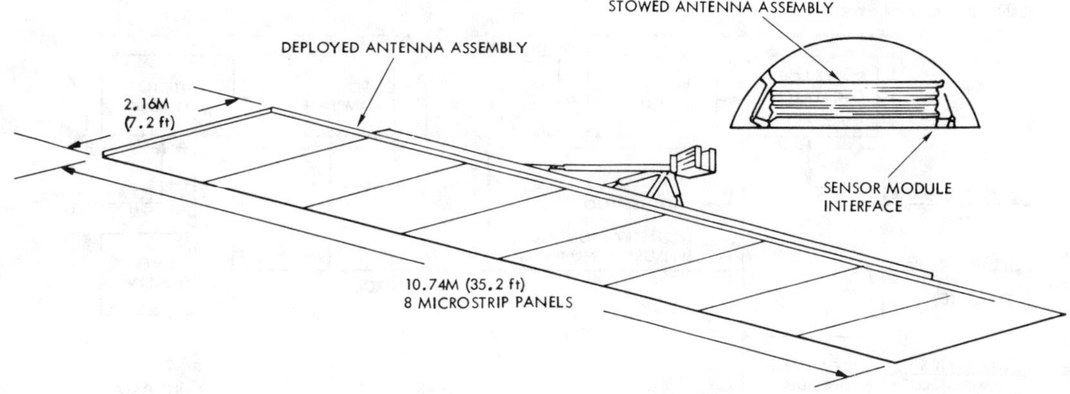

Fig. 11. Seasat SAR antenna shown in its stowed and deployed configurations.

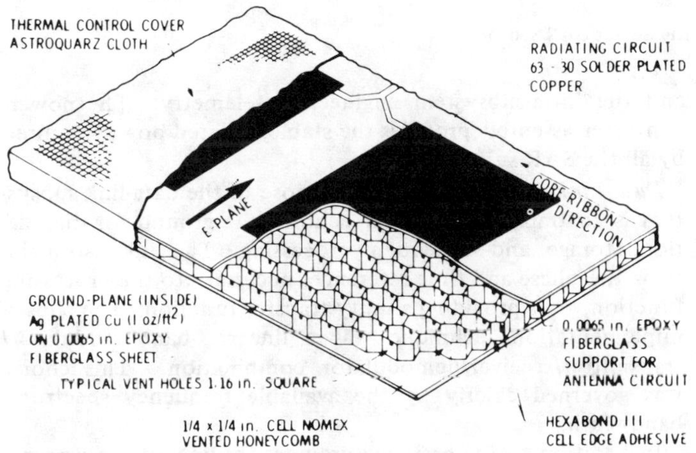

Fig. 12. Construction of the microstrip honeycomb pannels which were used in the Seasat and SIR-A antennas.

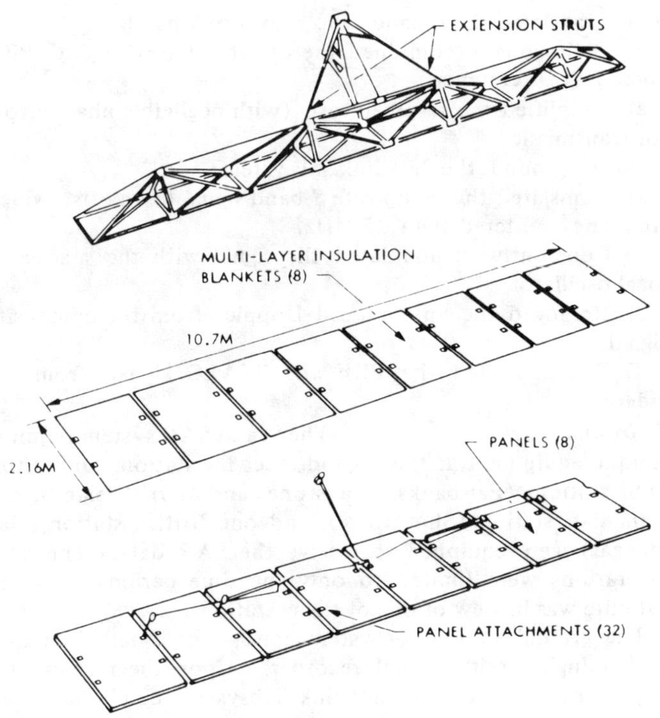

Fig. 13. Seasat SAR antenna mechanical components and assemblies.

a series of high-power coherent pulses of energy at L-band and amplifies the weak return echoes collected by the antenna. The radar sensor consists of four subassemblies: transmitter, receiver, logic and control, and power converter. A diagram of the sensor is shown in Fig. 14, and the principal sensor parameters are tabulated in Table II.

To obtain an adequate SNR from a system whose range resolution is 25 m on the surface and which utilizes a solid-state transmitting device, it is necessary to use a long transmitted pulse and pulse-compression techniques to reduce the peak-power requirement. The output of the transmitter assembly is, as a result, a linearly swept frequency-modulated pulse (or chirp) having a 634:1 compression ratio. It is generated in a surface acoustic wave (SAW) device located in the chirp generator subassembly of the transmitter assembly. The output of the transmitter is coupled to the antenna subsystem through an output combiner. A portion of the output (leakage) is also impressed on the receiver input where a load is placed in the circuit each time the transmitter operates. This prevents the leakage pulse from burning out the input stage of the receiver.

Echo returns are coupled into the receiver assembly through the output network in the transmitter. Because the echo's intensity is expected to vary in proportion to the variation of antenna gain with angle, a sensitivity time control (STC) has been incorporated in the receiver. The STC action, initiated by satellite stored commands, linearly decreases the receiver gain by 9 dB during the first half of the return-echo period, and then increases the gain until the end of the echo has been received. The application of the STC results in a nearly uniform signal (echo) return for a uniform scattering field, and, as a result, the dynamic range required to transmit the resultant data to Earth is reduced by 9 dB.

The sensor-receiver output is sent to the data link along with timing and frequency references derived from the SAR system local oscillator (STALO). The STALO generates a very stable (in frequency) signal at a nominal frequency f_s (f_s = 91.059 MHz), a portion of which is delivered to the multiplier assembly. Another portion of this signal is used to derive both square-wave clock and sine-wave signals at $f_s/3$, which are used in synchronizing other sensor electronics subsystem functions. The frequency multiplier assembly provides signals at $3f_s$, $9f_s$, and $18f_s$. The $3f_s$ and $18f_s$ signals are delivered to the chirp generator where, along with a portion of the STALO signal, f_s, they are used to generate the linear FM pulse (chirp) signal at the carrier frequency of $14f_s$. The signal at $9f_s$ and a por-

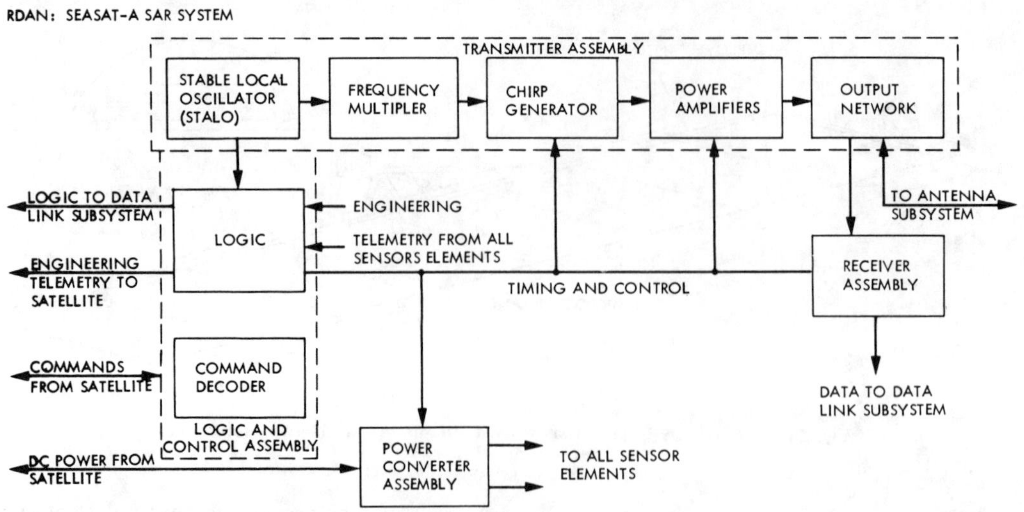

RDAN: SEASAT-A SAR SYSTEM

Fig. 14. Block diagram of the Seasat SAR sensor.

TABLE II
SENSOR ELECTRONICS SUBSYSTEM IMPLEMENTATION

Electronics	Implementation
Center frequency	1274.8 ± 0.31 MHz
Bandwidth	19.05 ±.05 MHz
STALO frequency	91.059 ±.0022 MHz
STALO stability	3 parts/10^{10} in 5 milliseconds
Pulse width	33.9 ±0.8 μsec
Peak power	1000 W nominal
Pulse envelope rise time	90 nsec
Pulse envelope fall time	90 nsec
Pulse repetition frequencies	1464, 1540, 1580, 1647 ±.1PPS
Noise temperature	650 Kelvin, nominal
Receiver gain control steps	8
Gain control step spacing	3 ±0.3 dB
Gain control range	77 to 98 dB
STC gain variation	9
Receiver gain flatness	±0.33 dB
Receiver gain stability (0 – 60°C)	±1.0 dB
Receiver bandwidth (3 dB)	22 ±0.2 MHz
Receiver phase ripple	4.0° dev. from quadratic
Transmitter FM slope	0.5622 MHz/μsec
Transmitter phase response	3° rms

tion of the signal at f_s are delivered directly to the data-link subsystem along with a signal derived from the PRF event which divides the interpulse interval into 4096 sectors.

The remaining two assemblies in the sensor electronics subsystem are the logic and control as well as the power converter. They provide the primary electrical interface with the satellite. The logic and control assembly receives commands from the satellite, decodes them, and causes the sensor electronics subsystem to assume one of a number of operating modes. In addition, the logic and control interfaces between the satellite and the intra-subsystem engineering telemetry. The power-converter assembly provides the stable, isolated power required by all the SAR subsystems.

Data-Link Subsystem: The purpose of the data-link subsystem is to transmit the radar echo to the ground for digitization, storage, and subsequent processing. The link also maintains the phase and time references necessary to the processing function, thus providing a unity transfer function. The chosen implementation technique was a linear S-band modulator/transmitter/receiver/demodulator combination. This choice was governed chiefly by the available frequency spectrum/bandwidth.

In addition to the basic requirement for linearity to preserve the SAR coherent information, the inclusion of necessary phase and timing signals placed an additional burden on the linear property of the link. The data-link subsystem performed the following functions:

a) Translated the L-band echo return to S-band.

b) Orthogonally combined the offset video with both PRF and STALO reference.

c) Amplified the result linearly (with negligible phase error) for transmission.

On the ground, the data-link subsystem:

a) Translated the composite S-band signal to an offset video frequency centered at 11.25 MHz.

b) Coherently demodulated the signal with the spacecraft local oscillator.

c) Removed the link-induced Doppler from the composite signal,

d) Reconstructed the PRF and STALO signals from the video.

Ground Station Subsystem: The Seasat SAR system required unique equipment at the ground receiving station. Only three U.S. stations (Fairbanks, Goldstone, and Merritt Island), one Canadian station (Shoe Cove), and one British station (Oak Hangar) were equipped to receive the SAR data. The SAR operations were limited to only the time periods when the satellite was in view of one of those stations.

The ground station subsystem consists of a data formatter and a high-density digital recorder. Upon the receipt of a trigger signal from the data-link subsystem demodulator as-

Weight: 128 kg
Size: 120 x 85 x 26 cm
Peak Power Transmitted: 1100 watts
Average Power: 650 watts
Frequency: 1278 MHz
Bandwidth: 6 MHz
Pulse Length: 30.4 μsec (chirped)
PRF: variable between 1464 Hz and 1824 Hz

Weight: 70 kg
Size (envelope): 108 x 65 x 43 cm
Average Power: 135 watts
Film Capacity: 1100 meters
Film Speed: 36 mm/sec
Operation Time: 8 hours

Weight: 200 kg
Radiating Area Dimensions: 9.44 x 2.09 meters
Polarization: HH
Gain: 33 dB
3-dB Beamwidth: 6.2° x 1.2°

Fig. 15. Photographs of the SIR-A sensor and antenna.

sembly, the data formatter accepts and digitizes the analog offset video signal furnished by the demodulator. Digitization occurs only during the period ($\sim$300 μs) when the SAR video return is expected. The resulting 13 680 samples, which are generated at a rate of 227 Mbits/s, are temporarily stored within the data formatter. Information on the operational status of the data formatter and the demodulator is also collected and retained.

The video samples, the status information, and the GMT time are formatted and sent to the high-density digital recorder (HDDR) at a rate of about 113 Mbits/s. The HDDR records this high-rate stream on 1-in width magnetic tape. Recording uses 40 (of 42) parallel tracks on the tape at a recording speed of 150 in/s. Parity is included on each track and timing information is carried on one of the remaining tracks.

The output "signal" tape is then used in the correlator element to obtain the final image.

B. Shuttle Imaging Radar-A (SIR-A)

The SIR-A was flown on the second flight of the Columbia in November 1981. The flight lasted for three days, and the radar acquired data during a total time period of $7\text{-}\frac{1}{2}$ h. Even with a brief time period, images were acquired over selected regions in North, Central, and South America, Africa, Asia, and Australia. The total area covered was about 10 million square kilometers.

The SIR-A sensor is a modified, but similar, version of the Seasat sensor, and it used some of the residual Seasat hardware. The main differences in the SIR-A sensor were the following: a narrower bandwidth (6 MHz versus 18 MHz for Seasat), a larger incidence angle (50° versus 20°), a narrower swath (50 km versus 100 km), a slightly lower resolution (38 m versus 25 m), but a higher number of looks (6 versus 4). The SIR-A data were optically recorded on an on-board recorder. This allowed acquisition of data at any desired location around the world within the limitation of the orbital coverage. The "signal film" was retrieved after the Shuttle landing and was processed in an optical correlator (see Section V) to generate the two-dimensional imagery. The orbital altitude was 245 km. Fig. 15 shows photographs of the SIR-A sensor and antenna.

C. Apollo Lunar Sounder (ALSE)

The design of the ALSE was dominated by the primary objective of subsurface detection [67]. The potential of depth penetration of a radar wave is proportional to the wavelength of the wave. Since deep penetration was desired, the frequen-

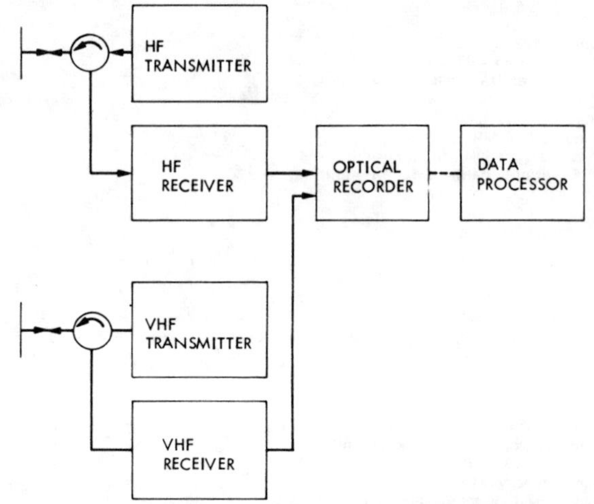

Fig. 16. Apollo Lunar Sounder Experiment system configuration.

TABLE III
LUNAR SOUNDER SYSTEM CHARACTERISTICS

	HF Mode		VHF Mode
	HF1	HF2	
Wavelength (m)	60	20	2
Center frequency (MNz)	5.266	15.8	158
RF bandwidth (MHz)	0.5333	1.6	16.0
Pulsewidth (µs)	240	80	8.0
Time–bandwidth product	128	128	128
Range resolution, free space (m)	300	100	10
Transmitter peak power (W)	130	118	95
Transmitter average power (W)	12.4	3.7	1.5
Effective antenna gain (dB one-way, including efficiency)	-0.8	-0.7	+7.3
Noise figure (dB)	11.4	11.4	10.0
Pulse repetition rate (s^{-1})	397*	397*	1984
Recording duration (µs)	600	600	70

*Interlaced on HF1 and HF2.

cies used in the Apollo system were very low. The ALSE system was operated in three frequency ranges: 5 MHz (HF-1), 15 MHz (HF-2), and 150 MHz (VHF). The two HF frequencies were operated simultaneously and were designed for deep sounding. The VHF system was designed for shallow sounding and for surface imagery. The flight ALSE system had four major hardware components (Fig. 16). At the heart of the system was the coherent SAR (CSAR) sensor containing the transmitters and receivers.

Separate transmit/receive antennas were provided for the HF and VHF ranges. The received signal was recorded by an optical recorder. The receiver also monitored the average reflected electromagnetic power and transmitted these data together with other engineering data by way of a 51.2-kbit/s telemetry channel. The average reflected power data were used for calibration purposes as well as for aid in data interpretation.

Since no internal access from the Command Module to the optical recorder was available, the photographic film on which the recorder stored the radar data was retrieved by an astronaut during an extra-vehicular activity (EVA); this was carried out toward the end of the Apollo 17 mission, during the trans-Earth phase. The basic parameters of the ALSE radar are given in Table III. Each of the three frequency bands utilizes a linear frequency-modulation (FM) transmitter pulse. An FM bandwidth of 10 percent of the carrier frequency is employed at each frequency band, as limited by the antenna subsystems. The linear FM pulse is generated by a voltage-controlled

oscillator which, at the start of each pulse, is phase-locked to a stable local oscillator. The duration of the FM sweep in each system is set to maintain a time–bandwidth product of 128. Upon reception of the echo, the signals are offset in frequency while maintaining phase coherence. The transmitted waveform envelope had a linear rise and fall for all three channels in order to limit the sidelobes caused by the Fresnel ripples.

Automatic gain control was incorporated at both HF and VHF. To avoid undue complexity in the data processing, the gain setting was allowed to change no more often than once every 30 s and then in discrete steps. During the flight of Apollo 17, the power return did follow predicted specular values on the average; however, significant variations in return power were observed over some regions of the lunar surface. The VHF subsystem incorporated a 12-dB increase in gain 13 µs after arrival of the specular pulse. The initial gain of the radar system was set so that the specular pulse would have a received amplitude close to the saturation point of the optical recorder in order to achieve a wide dynamic range. However, shortly after arrival of the specular return, the level of the received signal was expected to drop significantly and rapidly as a result of weak diffuse off-nadir scattering. Consequently, additional gain was required in order to obtain a radar image of the lunar surface.

The HF-1 and HF-2 systems used a dipole antenna of 0.4 and 1.2 wavelengths, respectively. To achieve an antenna tip-to-tip length of 24 m, two extendable/retractable elements were required. A retracted element was spooled as two flat metallic ribbons, which, upon extension, curled together into a circular rod. To match the complex antenna impedance to the radar, an electrical network was constructed and mounted in the antenna housing. A hybrid unit mounted in the scientific-instrument module provided the power division and the appropriate electrical phase to feed the antenna elements as a dipole. To maintain low side lobes, the antennas were designed with extreme amplitude and phase linearity across the bandwidth. This was done at the expense of antenna efficiency; the minimum efficiency across the band was 65 percent for the HF-1 system and 43 percent for the HF-2 system.

The VHF antenna was designed to satisfy a linear amplitude and phase response as well as a directionality requirement. The antenna was a Yagi of five directors and one reflector. The Yagi, mounted at the rear of the service module, was erected by a spring mechanism. The antenna had a beamwidth of 70° in the plane containing the antenna elements and a beamwidth of 50° in the orthogonal plane. To suppress ambiguity between terrain returns on the left and right sides of the spacecraft in the imaging mode, the antenna axis was pointed 20° off nadir.

The optical recorder was required to accept input data over the video bandwidths of the radar and to have adequate storage capacity to permit the radar to operate for nearly six orbits of the Moon. The video bandwidth is largest—16 MHz—during VHF operation. The decision to use a CRT/film-type optical recorder was based both upon the ease with which such a recorder would meet the input and storage requirements, and upon the compatibility of the film-storage medium with coherent optical processing.

D. Future Development

A number of spaceborne SAR systems are presently under development or are being designed for flight in the 1980's. These include the German Spacelab radar system (flight in

1983), the U.S. Shuttle Imaging Radar-B (in 1984), the Shuttle Active Microwave Experiment (SAMEX) radar (series of flights in 1986–1988), the Venus Radar Mapper (in 1988), and a number of free-flying systems for the late 1980's under study by the U.S., the European Space Agency (ESA), Japan, and Canada. The Shuttle-borne systems are expected to be more flexible with emphasis on scientific research, while the free-flying systems are planned for long-term semioperational observation with minimum variation in the operating parameters. The main emphasis in the next ten years is on multiparameter (i.e., multiple-frequency, multipolarization, variable observation geometry) and long-lifetime sensors. The Seasat and SIR-A sensors were all solid state. Going to higher frequencies (C- and X-band) requires the use of traveling-wave tubes (TWT's) or the development of high-frequency solid-state transmitters with peak-power capability between 2 and 10 kW and average transmitted power of a few hundred watts. New development in field-effect transistors (FET's) and electron-bombarded semiconductors (EBS's) should make it feasible to develop such high-power transmitters. TWT transmitters are capable of achieving the power requirements; however, they are less attractive than solid-state systems because of the need of high-voltage power supplies and their lower reliability for multiyear missions.

Another approach is to use a distributed array of low-power solid-state transmit–receive elements. These elements will be directly coupled to the antenna radiating elements. Such a distributed SAR approach will allow the radiation of a high-power signal, which is the superposition of the radiated signals from hundreds, or even thousands, of low-power elements. This technique is commonly used with ground-based radar systems.

The distributed SAR approach has another advantage. By using phase shifters, the beam can be controlled in both dimensions, allowing variable incidence angle and spotlight observation. It can also compensate for any mechanical distortions in the large SAR antenna, allowing a relaxation of the structural requirement which could be challenging at X-band frequencies.

IV. Digital Processing of Spaceborne SAR Data

The SAR image formation process, as described in Section II, is to use coherent phase information in an array of radar echoes to synthesize an effective antenna aperture which is much larger than the size of the physical antenna. This approach enables high-spatial-resolution radar images to be attained with a practical-size antenna. Digital processing for SAR image formation involves sampled and quantized SAR echo data and represents a numerical evaluation of the synthetic-aperture beam-formation process. A large number of arithmetic computations are involved. The process, nevertheless, can be very accurate in representing the radiometric reflectivity of the target surface being imaged. The inherent flexibility in a sequential execution of digital SAR processing functions also allows users to extract special information such as Doppler spectra and pixel phases at various intermediate stages of the SAR correlation process. The added accuracy and flexibility of digital SAR processing relative to that of analog optical processing represent an appreciable advantage, which is considered rather significant as computer equipment is increasingly involved in performing quantitative analysis of remotely sensed data.

The arithmetic computation requirement for digital SAR image formation corresponds to the product of the number of computations involved to produce an output pixel and the pixel-throughput rate required for the system. For SAR image formation in real time, both the pixel rate and the per-pixel computation increase with the resolution capability. For a typical spaceborne SAR operating at L-band, such as Seasat SAR, the computation rate required for real-time processing exceeds 10^9 operations/s. Conventional digital computers support a rate of approximately only 10^6 operations/s. Such a high rate of computation indeed represents one major bottleneck in realizing an economical digital SAR processing system. For this reason, high-speed digital processors for airborne SAR sensors [50], [63] became possible only in the early- to mid-1970's with the availability of integrated circuits, which is two decades after the development of analog optical SAR processors.

The large number of arithmetic computations characterizes one part of the digital SAR correlation task. The numerical nature of the digital correlation process calls for the formulation of an accurate mathematical procedure, which is often referred to as the SAR correlation algorithm, to manipulate the sampled echo signals to accomplish the SAR correlation process. Design of this procedure is a two-step process. The first step involves an accurate modeling of the SAR response to a point target as well as a continuous field of reflecting targets. This modeling is required to formulate an inversion process and to provide all the necessary functions for reconstructing the target scene from the received echo signals. The model is also essential in evaluating the performance of a SAR System with respect to its attainable limit. The second step is to implement the processing functions of the SAR image reconstruction process in a clearly defined, mathematical computation procedure. Because digital processing is a sequential procedure, a computationally efficient algorithm often implies savings in computing time or hardware logics and may dictate the selection of a specialized hardware architecture. Besides the computational efficiency of the algorithm, the related costs of software and hardware implementation and the maintainability of the system are all of practical concern.

Digital processing for spaceborne SAR data concerns the general algorithmic and implementation issues described briefly above. Analysis of the response of a target to a spaceborne SAR has shown a number of differences relative to the treatment of a conventional airborne SAR. The focus of the first part of this section is thus on the computational algorithm for SAR image formation and the associated techniques in accommodating a number of peculiarities relating to data gathered by a spaceborne SAR. The different hardware architectures and several existing ground-based SAR processors and possible approaches for future development will be described in the later part of the section.

A. Modeling of SAR Response to a Target Field

Analysis of target response to an airborne SAR and the signal-processing principle was presented by Cutrona [26] and Leith [57]. As presented in Section II, spaceborne SAR involves a more complicated sensor–target relative-motion problem than the airborne SAR. A recent effort to provide a detailed modeling of target response to a spaceborne SAR sensor and the associated representations for signal processing was reported by Wu *et al.* [85]. Briefly, SAR echo response to a point target is a series of pulses, each of which is a replica of the original transmitted waveform, but is associated with a time or phase delay proportional to the round-trip distance to the target. This one-to-one correspondence between the echo time and phase delay is a result of the use of coherent wave-train in generating the radar carrier and in demodulating it at reception. The ensemble of returned echo signals can be assembled into a rectangular format with spatial range delay, r, along one axis and the along-track or azimuth position, x, for the other axis. The echo response to a point target can therefore be written as

$$h(x, r) = h_1(x, r) \otimes h_2(x, r) \qquad (25)$$

where $\otimes$ denotes a two-dimensional convolution, and

$$h_1(x, r) = W(x) \exp\left(-j\,\frac{4\pi r_1(x)}{\lambda}\,\delta(r - r_1(x))\right). \qquad (26)$$

$$h_2(x, r) = \frac{2}{cV}\,\delta(x)\,A(r)\,\exp(-j\psi(r)) \qquad (27)$$

where

$r_1(x)$ round-trip distance from target to sensor at x
$\psi(r)$ phase encoding of radar transmitted pulses
$W(x)$ radar illumination at sensor position x
$A(r)$ amplitude waveform of the transmitted pulses
$\delta(t)$ Dirac's delta function
V surface projection of the along-track speed of the sensor
c speed of light.

The function $h_2(x, r)$ is one dimensional, representing the waveform of the radar-transmitted pulse. Function h_1 is a curved response function, representing the locus of the target delay with a phase angle proportional to its range distance.

Radar echo return and reception is a physical process. The key issue in SAR imaging is the coherency of the carrier wave in the transmission–modulation and receiving–demodulation process, which results in a deterministic phase variation of the echo response from a point target. Equation (25) also shows that the transmitted waveform is preserved in the one-dimensional time or range dimension; however, it is associated with a varying range and phase delay as the sensor changes its position in the X-dimension. This is clearly illustrated in Figs. 3–5.

For extended target with reflectivity $\sigma(x, r)$, the signal received by an idealized radar receiver represents a linear superposition of echoes from a continuous field $\sigma(x, r)$. The echo response $S(x, r)$ can be written as the following convolution:

$$S(x, r) = \sigma(x, r) \otimes h(x, r). \qquad (28)$$

Substituting (25) into the above, we have

$$S(x, r) = \sigma(x, r) \otimes h_1(x, r) \otimes h_2(x, r). \qquad (29)$$

Equation (29) describes the SAR echo response to an extended target $\sigma(x, r)$. The reconstruction of the scene can be accomplished by a two-step matched filtering involving the time-reversed range transmitted waveform h_2 and azimuth response h_1. Imaging radar systems often use a linear FM-phase-encoded waveform; however, other coding schemes can also be used. For a linear FM waveform, deconvolution of $S(x, r)$ or (29) with the reverse of the $h_2(x, r)$ function results in a sinc-function ($\sin a/a$) type of response in the range di-mention [20].

The waveform of h_1 depends mainly on the range delay function $r_1(x)$. For the Seasat SAR sensor in a near-circular

orbit, the range or phase delay can be approximated by a second-order power series [85]. It is also clear that the (x, r) coordinates are interchangeable with (τ, t) for the pair of along-track elapsed time, τ, and range echo delay time, t, respectively. Using the notation τ, the phase angle of $h_1(x, r)$ in (26) becomes

$$\phi(\tau) \cong \phi(0) + 2\pi(f_D\tau + \tfrac{1}{2}\dot{f}_D\tau^2) \qquad (30)$$

where f_D and $\dot{f}_D$ can be referred to as the Doppler center frequency and frequency rate, respectively. The phase delay $\phi(t)$ is proportional to the range delay $r_1(t)$ multiplied by 4π over the radar wavelength. An additional factor of 2 accounts for the round-trip traveling of the radar transmitted wave. The polynominal expression in (30) is a convenient way to characterize the SAR Doppler phase response for digital SAR processing, and the functional expressions for f_D and $\dot{f}_D$ factors in terms of sensor and target position and velocity vectors are derived by Wu *et al.* [85]. For Seasat SAR, the orbit geometry is such that magnitudes of the higher order terms in the series expansion of the phase function are indeed negligible.

By properly determining the numerical values of the Doppler parameters f_D and $\dot{f}_D$ through the sensor orbit and attitude predicts and the SAR echo data, the function h_1 is now defined. A matched filtering of the range-compressed echo signals with the time-reversed h_1 completes the SAR image reconstruction process. Using $\hat{\sigma}(x, r)$ as the reconstructed scene, the expression of $\hat{\sigma}(x, r)$ is

$$\hat{\sigma}(x, r) = [S(x, r) \otimes h_2^{-1}(x, r)] \otimes h_1^{-1}(x, r). \qquad (31)$$

Substituting (29) into (31), $\hat{\sigma}(x, r)$ can be expressed as

$$\hat{\sigma}(x, r) = \sigma(x, r) \otimes [(h_1 \times h_1^{-1}) \otimes (h_2 \otimes h_2^{-1})] \qquad (32)$$

where h_1^{-1} denotes the time-reversed response of the h_1 function. The quantity given in the square bracket of (32) is now the response of the SAR-sensor system to a point target. As mentioned previously, a quadratic echo phase function results in a sinc type of response in the matched filtering process. Using linear FM pulse for radar transmission, the SAR sensor response to a point target resembles a two-dimensional sinc function. The half-power width of the main lobe is the resolution of the imagery. A detailed treatment of the resolution function in terms of the Doppler parameters is given by Wu *et al.* [85].

B. SAR Correlation Algorithms and Correlator Architecture

The previous subsection establishes the functional basis for reconstructing a scene from the SAR received echo signals. The algorithm development for digital SAR processing now deals with the formulation of an efficient computational procedure for implementing the matched filtering process given in (31). The compression of the range response h_2, which is a replica of the radar-transmitted waveform, is a one-dimensional correlation operating on the sequence of sampled echo signals. This process is considered straightforward and is common practice in pulsed radars with amplitude or phase encoding of transmitted waveform. A common technique is to use SAW devices to perform the pulse compression. The focus of this section is on the compression of the SAR azimuth response h_1.

There are currently two categories of concepts in realizing the azimuth correlation function described in the previous subsection. The first one uses a cross-correlation process where a waveform which is an estimate of the target response

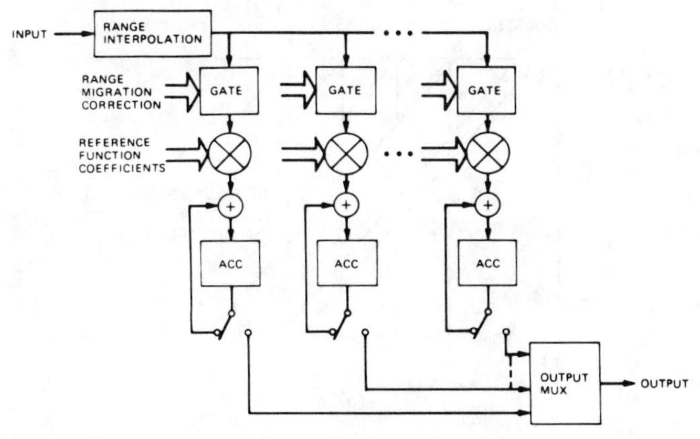

Fig. 17. Azimuth correlator architecture using distributed accumulator approach.

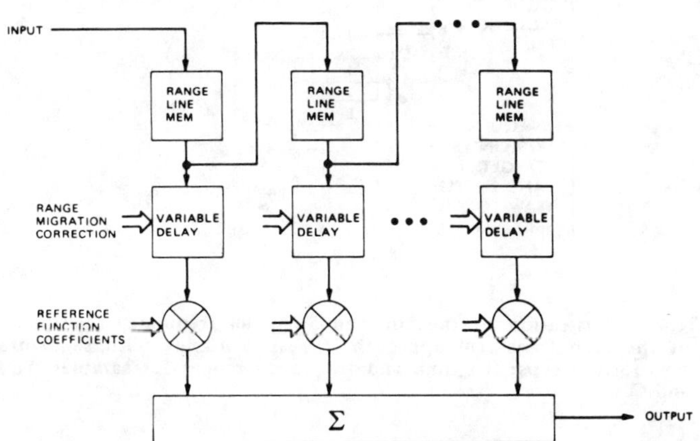

Fig. 18. Azimuth correlator architecture using tapped shift-register approach.

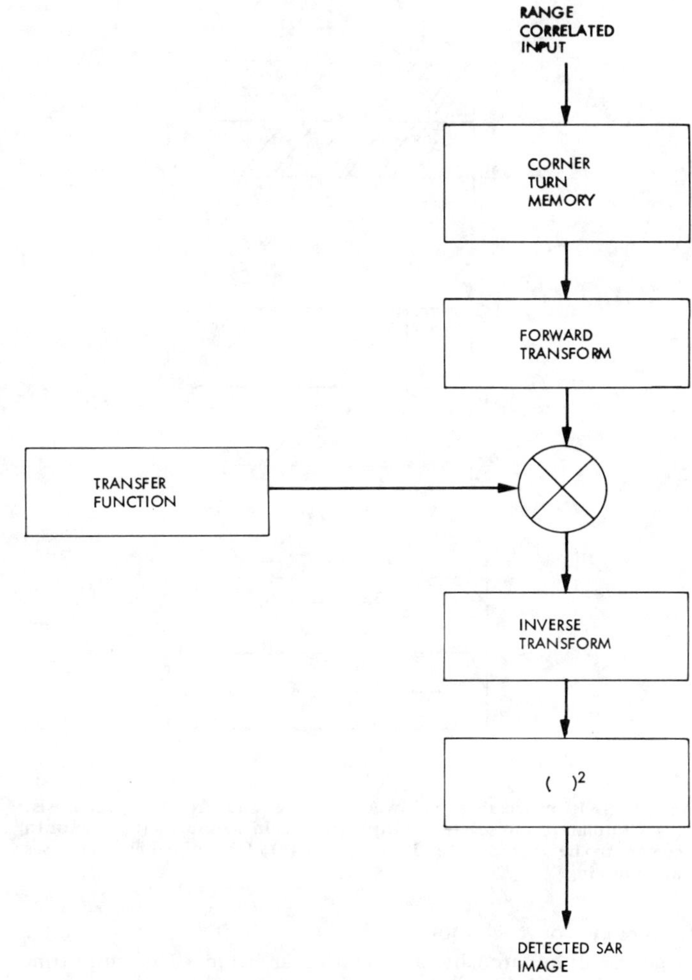

Fig. 19. Frequency-domain convolver for SAR azimuth correlation.

is generated to serve as the correlation reference function. The other category treats the SAR processing much as the signal processing for echo data received from a linear-phase-array radar. The ultimate long synthetic apertures are formed by several stages of array processing, each forming a longer aperture from outputs of shorter ones. In this approach, pulse compression is accomplished without the generation of the explicit target response waveform.

The correlation between signal data and reference can be accomplished by either a time-domain convolution process or a frequency-domain fast correlation approach. A usual time-domain convolver for one-dimensional signal correlation can assume either of two alternative forms: the distributed accumulator or the tapped-shift register, as shown in Figs. 17 and 18. For SAR data with severe range-curvature effect [69], both correlators illustrated in Figs. 17 and 18 incorporate appropriate compensation to accommodate such a curved two-dimensional SAR response. The configuration in Fig. 17 incorporates gating control to select the appropriate data samples. The configuration in Fig. 18 incorporates extra shift-register cells and control to enable selection of the appropriate sets of data samples. The two configurations shown in Fig. 18 exhibit the following differences: 1) the dynamic range requirement for the accumulator memory cells is greater than that for the tapped shift-register data sample memory cells; and 2) the accumulator approach involves the passing of coefficients from channel to channel whereas the shift-register approach involves the passing of radar data

samples from channel to channel. Considerations on large-scale integration (LSI) implementation of such a correlator were discussed by Tyree [79].

The SAR correlation can also use the fast Fourier transform (FFT) as a means of reducing the number of arithmetic operations relative to the direct time-domain approach. After the range correlation is accomplished, a range "corner-turn" operation is done which changes sequential data access from the range dimension to the azimuth dimension. A functional block diagram of this approach is shown in Fig. 19. Note that the transform involved can be any efficient linear transformation that exhibits the convolutional property. Applications of the FFT for SAR correlation were reported by Wu [82], Cumming [22], and Vant [81], and the polynominal transform by Truong [78].

The other approach to SAR processing, which does not involve azimuth response waveform in an explicit manner, generally makes use of the fact that the Doppler response given in (30) is quadratic. Synthetic-aperture processing thus resembles the compression of such a linear FM or chirp signal. In this section, we briefly describe two such digital SAR-processing algorithms.

A time derivative of the phase history in (30) provides a linear frequency and time relationship of the target response. The Doppler frequency response versus time for multiple targets which are separated in azimuth but are at the same range is shown in Fig. 20(a). The finite response in time and

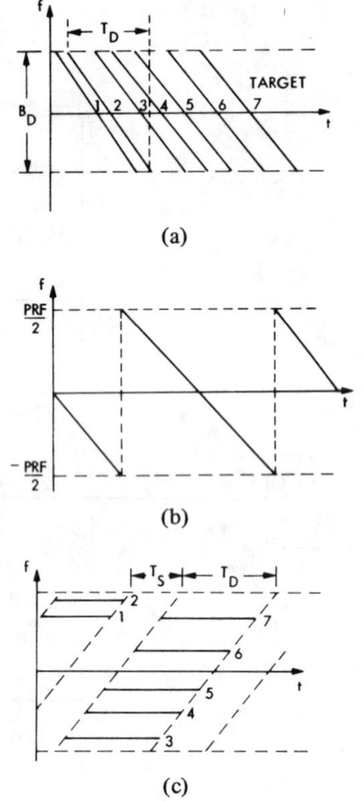

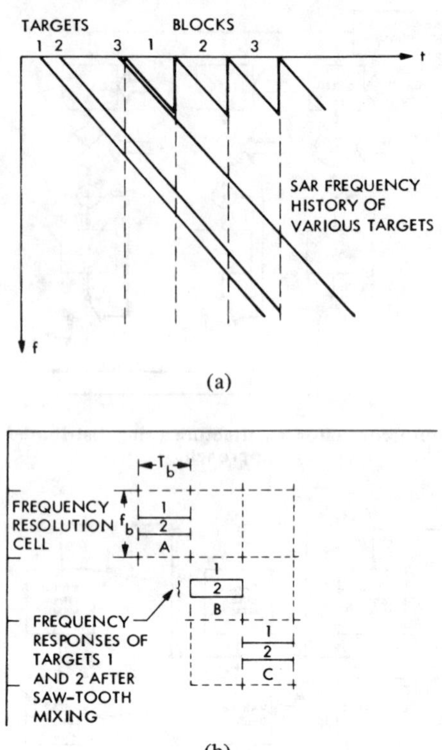

Fig. 21. Illustration of the time and Doppler frequency relationship of the step transform approach: (a) auto mixing with segmented sawtooth sweeps; (b) time and frequency ranges for samples A, B, and C.

Fig. 20. SAR processing by sweep mixing and frequency analysis: (a) Doppler responses to multiple targets in azimuth; (b) sawtooth sweep to be mixed with the signal in (a); (c) frequency responses after mixing.

frequency for each point reflects the finite duration that a target is illuminated by the main radar beam. The finite time duration and Doppler bandwidth are indicated by T_D and B_D, respectively, in the figure. The composite signal return when mixed by a coherent frequency-sweep waveform, which is shown in Fig. 20(b), results in a signal represented in Fig. 20(c). SAR responses to targets at different locations are now resolved into different frequency and time intervals. The frequency sweep covers a range over the radar PRF, which is always designed to be greater than the Doppler bandwidth B_D. The oversampling margin, which provides a corresponding time separation T_S between two responses of the same frequency, allows unambiguous resolution of such targets by selecting a proper data block for the frequency analysis. The block size must be between T_D and the sum of T_S and T_D. Using the maximum allowable size, a fraction $T_S/(T_S + T_D)$ of the frequency-transformed results is valid. Overlapped blocks are then necessary to provide continuous output in the azimuth dimension. A two-dimensional radar map is produced by repeating this process for samples at different range positions. The technique described here is often referred to as the "deramp" approach and was reported by Brown *et al.* [15].

One method, which is often referred to as the step-transform [59], or the subarray [80], can be used to simplify the arithmetic operations of the deramp method described above. Instead of using a block size which is greater than the synthetic-aperture length T_D, the procedure is multistage and operates on a much smaller block of data at each stage. The idea is shown in Fig. 21(a). Small data blocks and segmented sweeps are used. The frequency resolution which is directly related to the spatial resolution of targets is very coarse due to the small number of signal samples contained in a data block

(frequency resolution is PRF/N in the first step of frequency analysis, where N is the size of block). Fine frequency and target resolution can be obtained by performing another level of analysis on data samples from different blocks but carrying the coherent Doppler information of the same target area (see Fig. 21). Fig. 21(a) shows the frequency histories of several targets and segmented sawtooth sweeps. The points used for the second step of analysis are labeled A, B, and C in Fig. 21(b). Special conditions must be met for a good time-and-frequency correspondence to perform frequency transform and analysis in the second step of operation. The dashed grid in Fig. 21(b) provides that the fine frequency of a given target, e.g., target 1 or 2, is fixed over the blocks. This condition is met when there are equal numbers of blocks over the full synthetic aperture and numbers of frequency-resolution elements over the maximum Doppler bandwidth. This implies that the size of the time block equals the square root of the product of the full aperture duration and the corresponding Doppler bandwidth [59]. Note that points A, B, and C in Fig. 21(b) can be in the same band of frequency resolution rather than in the stepped bands as shown, if a continuous long sweep such as the one in Figs. 20(b) is applied.

The subarray type of processing approach reported by Van de Lindt [80] is similar in principle to the multistaged approach shown above. The interpretation is viewed through the array-antenna synthesizing. At each stage of operation, a longer antenna aperture is synthesized based on the shorter ones produced from the previous stage. It is required that the arrays in order to be synthesized in a higher level must all be pointing toward the same patch of target area in both the azimuth and range distance directions.

The approaches described above differ in the number of

arithmetic computations and the complexity in processing control. In general, for the case of large time–bandwidth product, the time-domain correlation is associated with the highest degree of arithmetic computation and parallelism. The frequency-domain fast correlation has potentially the simplest control function for high-resolution processing. The multistage frequency analysis or subarray approach involves the least amount of arithmetic computation. The processing complexity issues are discussed in the next subsection.

C. Processor Complexity Issues

The general correlation and architectural concepts for digital SAR processing have been described above. A major difficulty in realizing a digital SAR processing system for high-resolution and high-swath imaging is mainly associated with the requirement for a very large amount of data memory for line storage/corner-turn or accumulation and a very-high-speed arithmetic computation requirement. The curvature effect is, in general, more severe for a spaceborne SAR than an airborne SAR because of the larger value of V^2/R, which is equivalent to the centrifugal acceleration of the sensor relative to the target. The range curvature requires that the azimuth response h_1 must be treated as a two-dimensional function.

The variation of Doppler parameters is caused by the changing of the tangential velocity of targets on Earth or planetary surfaces due to the rotation of the planet. The change of tangential velocity affects both the Doppler variation over the swath because of the varying angle of incidence over the swath and the variation over different orbit positions or latitudes where the target surface speed is a function of latitude. The rate of change of Doppler parameters is inversely proportional to the radar frequency. Rapid change of correlation reference functions is therefore required in order to obtain high-quality SAR imagery.

The large number of memory storage and arithmetic units, and the added procedures to accommodate the severe-range curvature and Doppler-variation effects, both significantly impact the complexity of a digital SAR processor. A brief and simplified assessment of the arithmetic calculations requirement is given here.

The complexity of a specific digital SAR processing approach is characterized by arithmetic complexity and control-function complexity. The arithmetic complexity depends on a number of factors, the most predominant being the throughput rate, the pulse-compression ratio, and the number of looks. The arithmetic-processing rate can be measured by the product of the pixel rate at the output of the processor and the number of arithmetic operations required to produce each pixel. The pulse-compression factor of SAR azimuth correlation is equal to the ratio of the synthetic-aperture length to the corresponding azimuth resolution. This is equal to the number of complex arithmetic operations K_t

$$K_t = \frac{\mathcal{L}}{r_a} = \lambda R / 2(r_a)^2 \tag{33}$$

where $\mathcal{L}$ is the azimuth footprinted on the surface. For a near-optimal SAR system, the echo window is nearly equal to the separation between pulses, and r_a is equal to half the physical aperture. The pixel rate P is very close to the bandwidth B of the radar transmitted pulses. Thus

$$P \simeq B = \frac{c}{2r_r \sin \theta}. \tag{34}$$

The arithmetic-complexity measure A_T is the product of K_T and P, and is given by

$$A_T = \frac{\lambda R c}{4 r_r (r_a)^2 \sin \theta}. \tag{35}$$

For the frequency-domain processing approach using the FFT multistage processing, the number of arithmetic operations per pixel is approximated by

$$K_f = \log_2 K_t \tag{36}$$

and the complexity measure A_f is given by

$$A_f = \frac{c}{2r_r \sin \theta} \log_2 \left| \frac{\lambda R}{2r_a^2} \right|. \tag{37}$$

Equations (35) and (37) are useful for a quick assessment of the arithmetic complexity of the processor for various SAR systems.

The control-function complexity is not easily quantifiable. In general, the control complexity increases as the system-performance requirements (resolution, sidelobe levels, etc.) become more stringent. The SAR processor must include a controller which determines accurately the parameters required for processing. These include exact description of the range history between the radar and the target, which requires precise knowledge of the orbital and attitude characteristics, as well as the surface curvature and surface velocity at the point of observation. Fig. 22 summarizes the control functions. Predictions of SAR Doppler processing parameters can be obtained from the spacecraft state vectors, which are part of the ephemeris. Refinement of the processing parameters is then obtained by a feedback loop (clutterlock and autofocusing). Rapid updating of the azimuth correlation reference functions and range-curvature compensation coefficient increases the complexity of the overall processor.

D. Clutterlock and Autofocusing

Clutterlock and autofocusing refer, respectively, to the estimation of the instantaneous Doppler frequency f_D and Doppler frequency $\dot{f}_D$ at the center of antenna azimuth beam based on the SAR received echo data. These two parameters define the basic response of the SAR system to a point-target according to (30), and are crucial in computing the SAR correlator response to obtain high-quality SAR imagery. Since SAR response waveform based on a quadratic phase function which has a linear frequency response over the time span represents the typical linear FM waveform, compression of such waveform, and the distortion due to mismatch in the frequency and rate coefficients are well known in radar signal processing, e.g., Cook [20]. Quantitatively, a mismatch in the center frequencies f_D of the echo response and the correlator parameter results in an apparent shift in the target position as well as a loss in the output SNR; and a mismatch in $\dot{f}_D$ results in a degraded radar resolution.

These Doppler parameters are solely determined by the relative-motion characteristics between the SAR sensor and the targets. They can be estimated accurately provided that precision orbit and attitude data of the spacecraft are given. The clutterlock and autofocusing are used primarily in cases where the available orbit and attitude predicts are not accurate enough to maintain a reference phase function that meets the requirements on image quality.

The clutterlock techniques in general make use of the fact

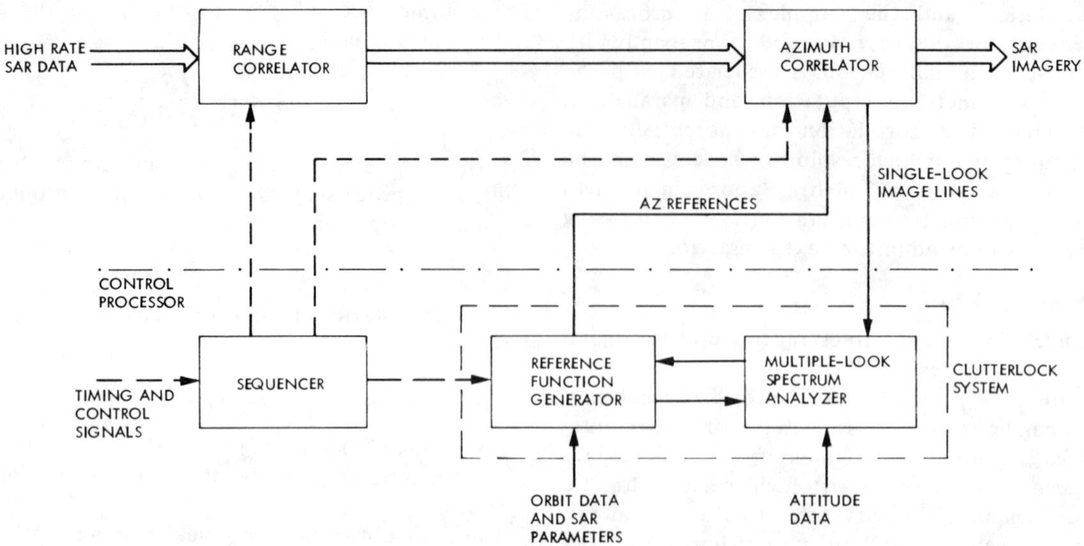

Fig. 22. Real-time SAR processor control block diagram.

that the SAR antenna response in azimuth is nearly identical to the SAR Doppler spectral response due to a one-to-one relationship between the radar perspective angle in the along-track direction and the instantaneous Doppler frequency of a target. The Doppler frequency at the center of the antenna along-track beamwidth can be obtained by evaluating the Doppler spectral pattern of the echo. This method is subject to error because the Doppler spectral pattern obtained over a short period of time can be affected by the presence of strong targets in the leading or trailing part of the antenna beam. More sophisticated approaches based on the response from the same target area can attain an accuracy on Doppler frequency estimate over a finite target area to within a few hertz ([83], [24]).

SAR systems are often designed to have a Doppler bandwidth measured over half-power points within 80 percent of the radar PRF. Since the Doppler spectral pattern varies smoothly, an estimation accuracy of the Doppler center frequency to within a few percents of the PRF is adequate to meet most of the image-quality requirements. Accurate estimates are most promising for possible information-extraction applications, such as the determination of the SAR platform attitude from SAR data [84], and ocean currents.

The autofocusing technique estimtes the Doppler frequency rate from SAR echo data. The mismatch in $\dot{f}_D$ induces image blurring that can be detected by measuring the effective spatial bandwidth of the processed image. In a multiple-look SAR correlator, the mismatch in $\dot{f}_D$ can also be detected from the misregistration of the different single-look scenes. As a result of the linear FM waveform, it is easily derived that the amount of misregistration between looks is linearly proportional to the mismatch of $\dot{f}_D$. This method through multiple-look registration is very effective but is subject to the existence of clearly discernible targets to obtain the registration measures [63].

E. Existing Ground-Based Digital Processors for Spaceborne SAR's

Seasat SAR has been the only available spaceborne high-resolution imaging radar for remote-sensing applications with digital data handling. The tremendous interest in obtaining high-quality SAR imagery and in quantitative data analysis using computers prompted the development of digital processors for producing Seasat SAR imagery. Digital SAR correlators capable of producing imagery at a near-real-time data-acquisition rate were not possible due to the need of a high-throughput processor that met the stringent computation and control requirements discussed before. Software-based SAR processors using programmable peripheral array processors were first developed in the U.S. (Jet Propulsion Laboratory) and Canada (MacDonald, Detwiller and Associates), and then in Europe (Royal Air Force, England) and Japan (Nippon and Mitsubishi). A frequency-domain fast-correlation algorithm was the main approach in compressing the dispersed range and azimuth responses into a narrow pulse. The commercially available peripheral array processors such as the AP-120B manufactured by the Floating Point System are used in computing the FFT and other vector processing at a much faster rate than that of a conventional general-purpose computer. The commercial array processors in general have an adder and a multiplier in parallel. The hardware is designed to allow pipelined operations in those multipliers and adders as well as in other storage memory units. For vector processing where the procedure is highly repetitive and the data storage in memory is in form or arrays, this parallel and pipelined execution of data access and arithmetic units at a rate of one set of such operations per machine-clock period allows a very high-throughput capability. A review of those array processors for vector data processing is reported in a special issue of the IEEE COMPUTER magazine (Sept. 1981).

The digital correlator currently existing at JPL applies three parallel AP-120B array processors in performing the FFT fast correlation to produce Seasat SAR imagery [86]. This system is called the Interim Digital SAR Processor (IDP). The IDP throughput is currently one five-hundredths of the real-time data-acquisition rate. Noting the fact that Seasat SAR calls for a compression ratio (number of samples required to be coherently integrated to compress the pulse and produce one output sample) of approximately 700 in range correlation and 200 per each of the four looks in azimuth to produce a final pixel, and the pixel rate in real-time acquisition is approximately 2.4 million pixels/s, the current system is, nevertheless, still a very cost-effective approach. The IDP System currently produces a digital 100-km × 100-km Seasat SAR frame in about 2 h. Some of the digital products are shown in this paper.

The Canadian processor, developed by MacDonald Detwiller and Associates (MDA) is described by Bennett [8]. The FFT fast correlation in conjunction with an AP-120B array processor is applied in the MDA system. Software implementations of frequency-domain fast correlation were also made on the CRAY-1 computer [65] and other general-purpose computers [9], [64], [58]. A summary of various SAR processor development was reported by Guignard [43].

F. Future Developments

Digital data processing for spaceborne SAR sensors generally requires a large number of arithmetic computations and very involved processing control functions to produce a meaningful size of image. Future spaceborne SAR flights certainly require a fast throughput and accurate processing system to support experiments aimed at applications for real-time environment observation, especially ocean and ice. A real-time digital SAR processor thus is the development goal, and is being pursued in the U.S., Canada, the European Space Community, and Japan.

SAR processing algorithms and knowledge of peculiarities in the control functions for spaceborne SAR data are much better established now than prior to the launch of Seasat SAR. Implementation of a real-time SAR processor involves trade-offs between cost and functional flexibility, arithmetic accuracy, and other performance requirements. We expect the cost-effectiveness of a digital SAR processor will continuously benefit from advancement in electronics technology. Specific areas that are applicable to future SAR processor development include: the computer-aided design (CAD) techniques for custom very-large-scale integrated circuits (VLSI) and gate-array logics, faster and more compact memory devices as well as peripheral array processors, distributed processing techniques, etc. This list covers a wide spectrum of advanced electronics technology development, even though the quantity of SAR processors that may be manufactured is quite limited. Real-time digital SAR processor development would definitely contribute in the area of electronics applications and distributed system techniques. A discussion on the trend of radar-signal processing development is more thoroughly presented by Brookner [13].

Development in the next decade may still be focused on ground-based SAR processors. A real-time spacecraft on-board SAR processor is feasible provided that 1) the processing operations can be handled by a system within the speed, volume, and power constraints; and 2) the required applications and the range of flexibility are well defined.

V. Optical Processing of Spaceborne SAR Data

Optical techniques for processing SAR data were developed primarily in the 1960's. Since that time, there have been no major developments of new techniques. One reason for the lack of further development has been the emphasis on digital techniques, with the inherent advantages of accuracy and adaptability. Another reason is that the state of the art in the optical technology used in conventional processors has not progressed significantly, and major improvements did not

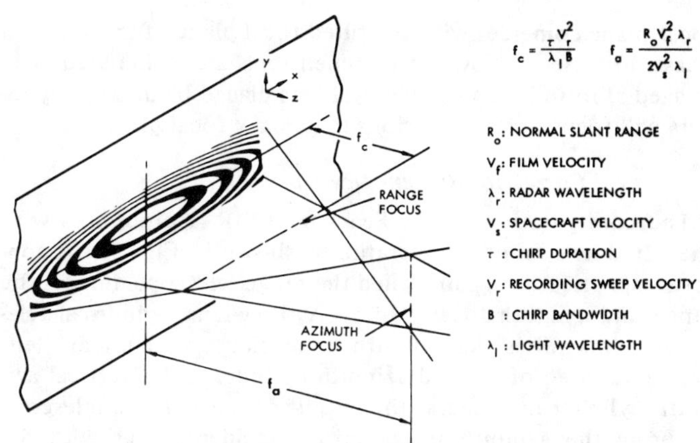

Fig. 23. Focal properties of a point-target phase history.

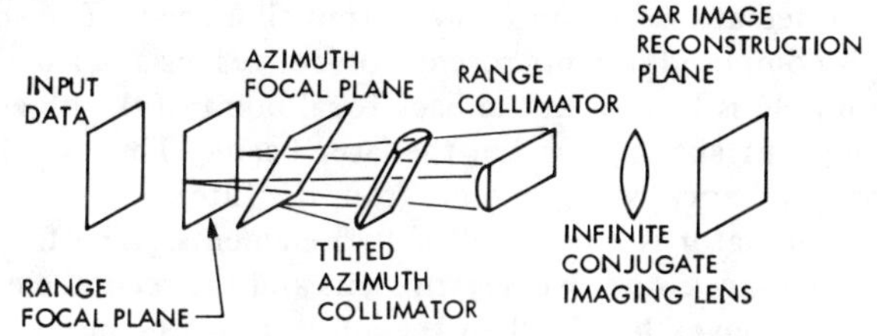

Fig. 24. Configuration of a simplified optical correlator system.

appear feasible. However, recent interest in the applications of spaceborne SAR, has led to renewed emphasis on SAR data processor development, both digital and optical. The primary effort in digital techniques is centered on throughput improvement, while the emphasis in optical systems is the reduction of size, weight, and power consumption for remote-site or on-board processing applications.

A. Conventional Optical Processing

The phase history generated by a point target (Figs. 3–5) is similar to a Fresnel-zone plate. This fact makes SAR data natural candidates for optical processing. A basic introduction to optical processing of SAR data is given by Goodman [41]; see also [51]. Since the phase function is quadratic in both dimensions, it diffracts a coherent plane wave, illuminating it into a converging beam that will focus at a point. Unfortunately, the converging wave will come to a focus at different distances from the zone plate for the range and azimuth directions. These distances are referred to as the range and azimuth focal lengths, respectively. They are shown graphically in Fig. 23, and they are expressed in terms of the radar system parameters.

An important point to note is the dependence of the azimuth focal length on range. Not only is the azimuth focal length different from the range focal length, but it varies linearly with range dimension. This linear variation can be compensated for by using a conical lens. Manufacturing such lenses is difficult, however, and a cylindrical lens rotated about the horizontal axis leads to the same compensation. One of the simpler configurations for an optical correlator is shown in Fig. 24. A cylindrical lens in range is placed so that its input focal plane occurs at the zone-plate range focus, thereby collimating the wavefronts of all targets. A second cylindrical lens is used in a similar manner in azimuth. The lens is rotated so that its input focal plane coincides with the tilted focal plane of the azimuth phase histories. Now both dimensions are collimated, i.e., imaged at infinity, and a spherical lens placed behind the cylinders will focus both dimensions in its back focal plane.

B. Optical Correlator System Description

The configuration of the Seasat and SIR-A processors with the tilted-lens mode of operation is shown in Fig. 25. A confocal, spherical lens pair, called the range telescope, images the range and azimuth focal planes. A three-lens cylindrical telescope demagnifies the azimuth dimension. An auxiliary lens pair composed of a tilted azimuth cylinder and a vertical azimuth cylinder are used at the output of the azimuth telescope to bring the azimuth image into coincident focus with the range image. Frequency filtering and range-migration correction are done at the back focal plane of the first spherical lens by a combination of cylindrical lenses. A relay lens magnifies an intermediate image onto the output film drive. The spatial filter is composed of a microscope objective lens and a pinhole. The pinhole is located at the back focal point of the objective, blocking out spatial noise in the laser beam. Thus a "clean" diverging spherical wave emerges from the filter.

The collimator is composed of two elements. The first element is a convex–concave negative lens and the second element is a plano-convex lens. When the aperture of the input lens is illuminated by the diverging wave from the filter, the output will be a plane wave which is then reflected through a 90° bend by mirror M_1 toward mirror M_2, the first element of the primary optical system. Mirror M_2 bends the beam through another 90° angle and can be adjusted to provide an offset illumination angle in range and/or azimuth. It is desirable to have the center frequency of the spatial frequency band in both dimensions aligned with the optical axis to insure optimum use of the lens apertures. Thus if a signal film has equal positive and negative frequencies in both range and azimuth, the center of the band is zero frequency in both dimensions. Hence, the film should be illuminated with an on-axis beam. However, if the data have equal positive and negative frequencies in azimuth but run from 0 to some positive frequency in range, a range offset would be used. This case is the normal mode of operation.

The input film drive transports the signal film to be processed. The optical axis position of the film drive is determined by the range focal length of the signal film. The range telescope is a confocal spherical lens pair. Spatial frequency spectrum of the data occurs at the back focal plane. An expanded view of the frequency plane optics is shown in Fig. 26.

The frequency plane filter is used to block all light outside the bandwidth of the data to be processed. Two pairs of knife edges in range and azimuth are adjusted to the rectangular aperture corresponding to the range and azimuth bandwidth. Since illumination offset is used to bring the center of the bandwidth along the optical axis, the rectangle will, in general, be centered about the optical axis.

The shift lens, also located at the frequency plane, is a cylindrical lens with power in the azimuth direction. It is used for films with azimuth focal lengths that are too long to allow processing (without the shift lens). The shift lens does not reduce the tilt angle of the azimuth focal plane but translates it in the negative direction (opposite the direction of light) along the optical axis. Rotation of the shift lens about the optical axis introduces positive or negative range walk depend-

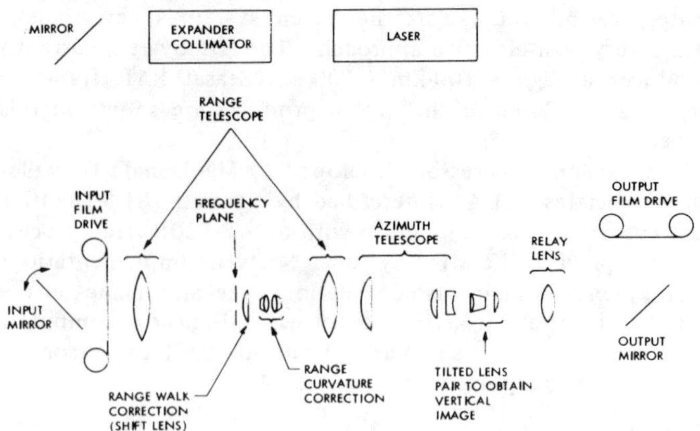

Fig. 25. Details of the Seasat SAR and SIR-A optical correlator.

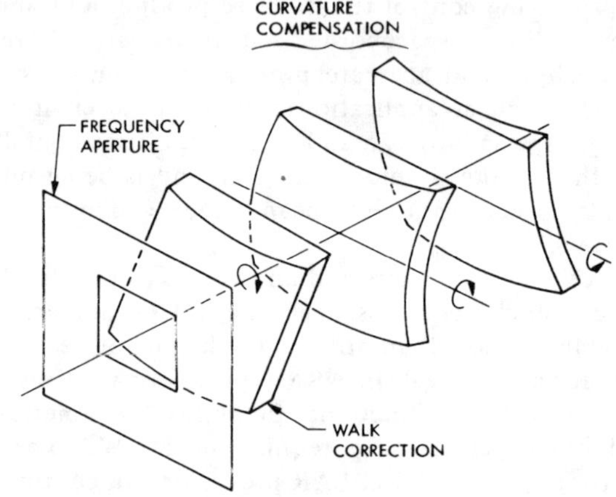

Fig. 26. Frequency plane optics showing the frequency filter, the curvature compensation, and the walk correction elements.

ing on the direction of rotation. This adjustment is used to remove range walk. A positive and negative azimuth cylindrical lens pair is located immediately after the shift lens. The lenses will introduce positive or negative range curvature when rotated in opposite directions about the horizontal axis perpendicular to the optical axis. This adjustment is used to remove range curvature.

The second range telescope lens is identical to the first with its orientation with respect to light direction reversed. It is located so that its input focal plane coincides with the output focal plane of the first lens. This combination forms a telescope with one-to-one magnification.

The azimuth telescope is a three-lens cylindrical telescope used to demagnify the azimuth image. The azimuth image will usually occur within a few inches of the output focal plane of the last lens. The demagnification setting is adjusted so that the azimuth scale factor of the image center matches the range scale factor.

A cylindrical lens pair is located immediately after the azimuth telescope. The first is tilted about the horizontal through its center perpendicular to the optical axis. The angle corresponds to the angle of the azimuth focal plane. This lens collimates the azimuth phase histories, removing the focal-length variation with range. The second lens refocuses the phase histories to its back focal plane which is coincident with the range focus. This plane contains an intermediate image of the SAR focused data.

A relay lens is used to magnify the intermediate image onto the output film drive. The magnification factor is normally set so that the output image will have a specified scale factor.

C. Special Considerations for Spaceborne SAR Data Processing

1) Extensive Phase Histories in Range and Azimuth: In order to reduce peak power, spaceborne radars usually transmit frequency-modulated long pulses, resulting in a high time-bandwidth product of the chirp to be recorded. Since the data record will eventually be recorded in a two-dimensional raster format, a high sweep linearity will be required in the range dimension. The accuracy is approximately the reciprocal of the time–bandwidth product. In the case of Seasat, the accuracy required was approximately 1 part in 1000. Only the highest precision type of recorder can normally achieve such accuracy. The CRT type of recorder used for Seasat required the addition of a digitally controlled correction signal to the basic sweep signal.

The large slant range at which spaceborne SAR's operate gives rise to a large azimuth phase history with a high time-bandwidth product. As in the case of the range dimension, the azimuth dimension must be recorded linearly to an accuracy approximately equal to the reciprocal of the time–bandwidth product. In the case of Seasat, this number was about 1 part in 4000 for a single-look resolution of 6 m.

The linearity of the recording in azimuth must be such that the focal length for a given slant range remains constant as the spacecraft velocity changes. Since the orbit is circular, the radar is accelerating toward the target as it passes over it. This causes the effective velocity to be lower than the actual tangential or orbital velocity. It can be shown that the effective velocity is proportional to the orbital velocity according to the relationship

$$V_{\text{eff}} = \sqrt{\frac{\text{Earth radius}}{\text{orbit radius}}} \times V_{\text{orb}}. \tag{38}$$

This poses an interesting problem when we try to maintain accurate focus simultaneously with a constant azimuth scale factor since the ground velocity (of the antenna footprint)

$$V_{\text{ground}} = \frac{\text{Earth radius}}{\text{orbit radius}} \times V_{\text{orb}}. \tag{39}$$

The differences in focus and scale factor are usually small enough to ignore. The long phase histories have long focal lengths in range and azimuth, requiring unreasonably long optical path lengths or the addition of shift lenses. A combination range- and azimuth-shift lens was required for Seasat to reduce the optical path lengths to an acceptable level. The shift lens was also used as the range-walk correction lens. Corrections for severe range walk cause focal shifts which must be compensated for.

The combination of large phase histories and large numbers of range-resolution cells leads to a requirement for large optical apertures at high resolution. The number of input data points in range was approximately 13 000 for Seasat, several times that of the best CRT recording systems. Such resolutions are obtainable by laser-beam recording techniques. However, not many coherent optical correlators are capable of processing such a high space–bandwidth product (6000). The system for processing Seasat data described earlier does have a 10 000

space–bandwidth product in each dimension, but the recorder used was a CRT recorder with only about a 1500 product.

2) Range Curvature and Walk Corrections: While only very-high-resolution or long-wavelength airborne SAR systems require range-migration (combination of curvature and walk) compensation, spaceborne SAR systems generally will because of the long slant range involved. The Seasat SAR range curvature was on the order of 5 resolution cells, and the walk was sometimes over 100 resolution cells. The basic technique for correction of range curvature and range walk was described earlier. Since the relative change in slant range for spaceborne SAR systems is usually small, a single curvature correction is usually accurate for a near-circular orbit. However, range-walk compensation may have to be updated several times within the range swath. This update rate will increase with attitude errors, resolution improvements, and slant-range increase.

3) Doppler Tracking: Since spacecraft velocities are so great compared to aircraft velocities, it is desirable to use narrower beamwidths to reduce the Doppler bandwidth and hence the PRF. This narrowing of beam usually necessitates some type of Doppler tracking system since attitude changes and planet rotation will cause Doppler shifts that are significant when compared to the bandwidth. At higher frequencies, such as X-band, the Doppler shifts may often be an order of magnitude greater than the bandwidth, or many times the PRF. While Doppler tracking in an optical system is conceptually easy, the system becomes very complicated when trying to maintain accurate focus and location.

The actual Doppler spectrum is displayed in the frequency domain of the range telescope. Energy centroid detectors or a pair of detectors placed on either side of Doppler centroid peak may be used to determine the center, or at least detect when the spectrum is centered. As the spectrum drifts off center, an error signal could be generated to drive the input mirror so that the illumination angle would change and recenter the spectrum. Such a system would have to be capable of following a Doppler drift out to PRF/2 and then rapidly shift back a whole PRF to the next ambiguity spectrum coming into the bandpass of the optical system. The system should have a time constant of several synthetic apertures so that it will be insensitive to terrain changes. Furthermore, to prevent blurring of the output image, the output mirror must be shifted synchronously in the opposing direction to maintain the tracking velocity of the output film drive.

4) Geometric Correction and Location Determination: The conversion of slant range to ground range is not as difficult for spaceborne SAR systems as it is for airborne systems for a given swath width. A much smaller beam covers a given swath width on the ground. In the case of Seasat, the total incidence angle change was about $6°$, resulting in a relative ground range scale change of about 28 percent. Breaking the data up into four swaths resulted in an error of about ± 3.5 percent at each quarter-swath edge when the ground range scale at the center was correct. The use of a nonlinear output film plane or distortion optics could conceivably be used to compensate for the residual error, but loss of resolution would most likely occur.

Doppler centroid drifts from zero Doppler cause a parallelogram-type skew in azimuth proportional to the Doppler angle. A rectangular pattern on the ground will be imaged to a parallelogram where the cross-track sides are not perpendicular to the swath direction. Compensation for such skew can be compensated for as part of the Doppler tracking system, but the restrictions on mirror positions and angular positional accuracy are severe.

Accurate location is a difficult problem for spaceborne SAR's in general, and there are additional problems in the conventional optical systems. Usually, there are no positional references. Thus relative positions of input data, output recording film, and all optical elements must be precisely maintained. The ability to accommodate image shifts caused by orbital variations, timing changes, and attitude errors is very complex. A very precise and adaptable timing transfer system is required to maintain accurate reference of the input data to a time base during the processes of film recording and correlation to imagery. Some type of reference fiducial must be generated in the imagery, and a computer-generated list of locations of the marks must be made. The experience with Seasat has shown that it is difficult to obtain absolute location—to within a few kilometers—in this type of system.

5) Calibration: There are several potential error sources in an optical processing system which can contribute to calibration problems for a SAR system. In film recording, the diffraction efficiency is highly sensitive to recording spot size, exposure, and development process. All of these parameters must be maintained constant to provide reasonable calibration. Within the correlator itself, spatial and temporal variations of illumination intensity will contribute errors. The development process of the output image film and subsequent copies, again, contributes errors. The use of reference calibration signals can help reduce the errors from the above sources. If a known signal is input into the system, it should undergo the same transfer function as the data, and thus variations due to the processing system could be removed from the output imagery. Unfortunately, it is difficult to make a reference signal with characteristics identical to those of the radar data. Noise can be bandwidth limited in range to simulate the chirp spectrum, but azimuth filtering to simulate the antenna pattern is a complex process. Efforts to calibrate Seasat data using a series of calibrated noise steps resulted in errors of up to 2 dB contributed by the processor. These errors were in addition to those of the sensor, data link, and data-recording system.

D. Areas of Current Research and Development in Optical Processing

As mentioned previously, the primary emphasis in optical processing system research and development has been placed on size, power, and weight reduction. Conventional optical systems have the capability of running at real-time rates, but the use of film as an input and output medium makes the processors large, nonrepeatable, and slow with respect to real-time turnaround. Recent developments of spatial light modulators (SLM's) have supplied an acceptable replacement for film as the input medium to the system. Two basic types of processors are described below. The first type simply uses a two-dimensional SLM as the input, and employs the simple range cylinder with tilted azimuth cylinder correlator described earlier. The second type is quite different, using a one-dimensional acoustic–optic cell input with a charge-coupled device (CCD) array detector at the output.

1) Two-Dimensional, Spatial Light Modulator Correlator: A schematic representation of a two-dimensional correlator using an SLM input is depicted in Fig. 27. The system shown uses a

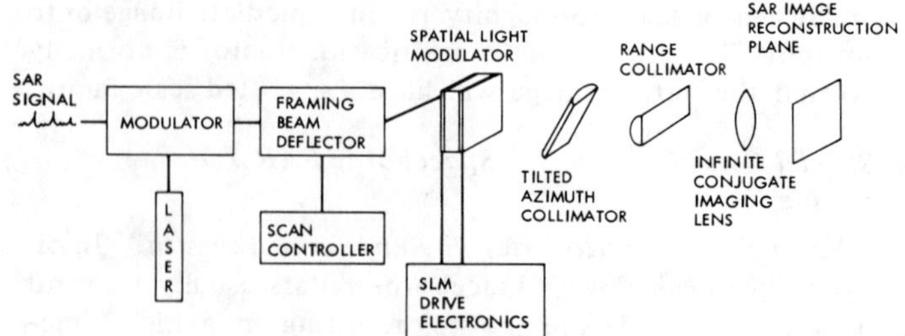

Fig. 27. Schematic of a one-dimensional SAR correlator using spatial light-modulator input.

laser scanning system to write the data in raster format on the SLM. Other types of writing systems could be used such as a CRT or an LED array with a slow mirror scan in azimuth. Such write systems are complex and limit the reduction of system power, weight, and size.

A number of SLM's have been developed by industry, but the prime candidates are the Itek PROM (Pockel's readout optical modulator) and the Hughes LCLV (liquid-crystal light valve). At this point in time, the PROM appears to be more useful because of its higher storage time (tens of seconds as opposed to about 100-ms decay time for the LCLV). The higher storage time is necessary to obtain sufficient synthetic-aperture buildup. A CCD-addressable LCLV is currently under development at Hughes. Such a device would eliminate the need for the input scanning system. A full frame of data is directly inputted into a CCD storage array which is part of the LCLV structure and subsequently strobed onto the liquid-crystal material. It must then be processed before decay occurs. This two-dimensional approach is especially attractive for systems requiring additional data processing such as image spectrum analysis or feature recognition. A coherent two-dimensional image is present at the output, and subsequent processing operations can be easily added.

2) Hybrid Acoustooptic/CCD Correlator: Recent development of two key components have made possible a very small, lightweight, low-power, yet high-performance data-processing system. Psaltis [68] at the California Institute of Technology has developed a conceptual design for a two-dimensional data processor using laser diode illumination, acoustooptic (A-O) cell data input, and a CCD detector array for the output. Recent development of the laser diodes and CCD array detectors has made the scheme feasible and attractive for various applications. The A-O cell technology has been well developed for some time.

The processing scheme is a hybrid approach in that range correlation is performed spatially as in a conventional system while azimuth correlation is performed temporally as in a time-domain convolution processor. The operation of the system is shown in Fig. 28. A radar echo or PRF line is launched into the A-O cell. The length of cell (in microseconds) corresponds to the length of the range line to be processed. When the echo is fully in the cell, the laser diode is strobed with a pulse short enough to "freeze" the echo. The light is collimated in the range dimension so that range compression occurs through diffraction, much the same way it does in a conventional optical correlator. The range focal plane, which occurs at some distance from the cell, is imaged in range onto the CCD array with the light uniformly dispersed in the vertical or azimuth direction. Each vertical column of the CCD array

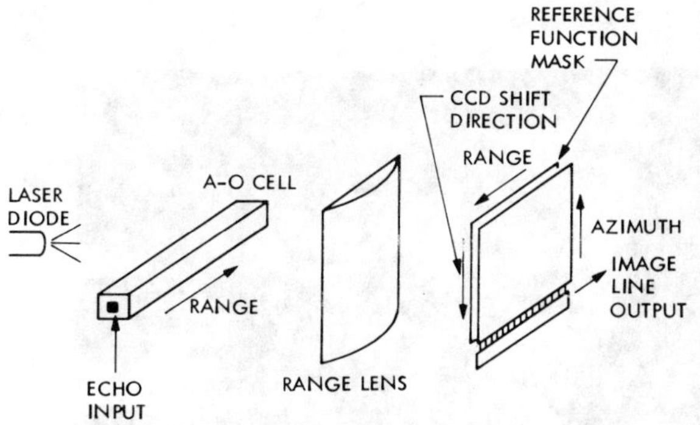

Fig. 28. Schematic of a possible optical SAR processor using a one-dimensional acoustooptical input and a CCD array output.

corresponds to a line of constant range (neglecting range curvature). As new range lines come in, rows of data are shifted downward. The transmission mask in front of the CCD array contains the azimuth reference function. The mask and the detector are analogous to a time-domain azimuth correlator. Each CCD detector element, in conjunction with its corresponding value of the reference function, is a multiplier/accumulator. Thus a 300-by-500 array performs 150 000 multiplies and adds every PRF line. By the time a particular target shifts from the top to the bottom of the array, it has been fully correlated with the reference function and hence "compressed."

Once the mask is generated (the mask can be computer generated and written on a film recorder), the nominal reference function has been fixed. However, adjustments for "focus" can be made over quite a large range by simply changing the shift rate in the CCD array so that the FM rate of incoming data will match the mask.

Furthermore, Doppler offsets, range walk, and range curvature can be easily accommodated. Since the input video data are placed on a carrier (the center frequency of the A-O cell is usually in the 70- to 80-MHz region), the carrier frequency can be offset to null out the Doppler frequency. A given Doppler offset will correspond to a specific range walk. Range walk is caused by targets shifting slightly (in the horizontal direction) as they pass through the antenna beam. This causes the targets to cross range cell columns in the detector. A simple rotation of the array will afford exact tracking of the target trajectories. Although range curvature does not usually occur in the azimuth integration period that current CCD devices can accommodate, it can be easily corrected for by rotated cylindrical lenses in much the same way it was done in the Seasat optical processor.

The above architecture is also highly modular in every dimension. Arrays can be stacked in range for increased swath width. Since the output is complex, they can be stacked in azimuth to provide either higher resolution or more looks. They can also be stacked in operating-bias level to provide increased dynamic range.

Research and development in the detector array field is quite active in industry, and the system performance will improve along with CCD array improvements. Texas Instruments is expecting to have a 1200-by-1200 device on the market within the next two years. This device, which is essentially a single chip a few centimeters on a side, would be performing well over 10^9 multiplies/s in the above system and could accommodate 10^{11} multiplies/s if required.

VI. POST-IMAGE-FORMATION PROCESSING

After the correlation step, the radar data are in a two-dimensional image format, similar to a regular photograph. However, a number of processing steps are still required to achieve radiometric and geometric calibration. The radiometric-calibration step involves corrections for antenna pattern shading, range-to-surface variation, and other known nonlinear processes in the sensor and correlator. The purpose of this step is to have the intensity of each pixel directly proportional (or related by a known function) to the surface backscatter cross section. The geometric calibration step involves adjustment of the spatial location of each pixel in the image such that it could be superimposed on a well-defined cartographic grid.

A number of other post-image-formation processing techniques have also been used as a first step to facilitate information extraction. Some of these techniques are reviewed in this section. They are texture analysis, speckle statistics, registration to visible and IR images, color coding, and stereo imaging. Some of these techniques are still at an early stage of development; however, they seem to have good potential.

A. Geometric Calibration

The SAR uses the time delay and the Doppler (or phase) history to locate a particular target on the surface relative to the satellite orbit. These two measurements are not dependent on the satellite attitude, which is the case with passive sensors. For the SAR, the determination of pixel location is mainly dependent on the accuracy of knowledge of the spacecraft location, on the internal timing of the signals, and on the characterization of the processing algorithm. A detailed analysis of the effects of the different error sources was given by Curlander and Brown [25] and Curlander [23]. Based on the analysis of Seasat SAR data over a number of sites, they concluded that pixels can be located with an absolute accuracy better than 200 m (i.e., 8 resolution elements). This is definitely not a basic limit. With a more favorable illumination geometry (larger incidence angle) and tighter requirements on the ephemeris accuracy, absolute accuracy down to about a few tens of meters or a few resolution elements is definitely feasible.

B. Radiometric Calibration

Radiometric calibration involves correction to the image such that the surface backscatter cross section can be derived directly from the image pixels' intensity. Depending on the application, different levels of calibration are desired. In some cases, only relative calibration of pixels in a scene or relative calibration between images taken at different times is needed. In other cases absolute calibration is necessary.

Errors due to the sensor elements can be corrected by: 1) continuously monitoring the level of the transmitted signal and the transfer function of the receiver; 2) measuring the antenna radiation pattern before launch and making ground receiver measurements during the flight; and 3) measuring the transfer function of the ground processor. Preliminary analysis conducted using the Seasat SAR data indicates that rms relative temporal calibration between different passes over the same area is ±0.5 dB [Held and Croft, private communication]; however, more research in this area is still required.

Another factor which plays an important role in the SAR calibration is the presence of speckle. The coherent noise will add uncertainty to the measured intensity of a specific pixel as

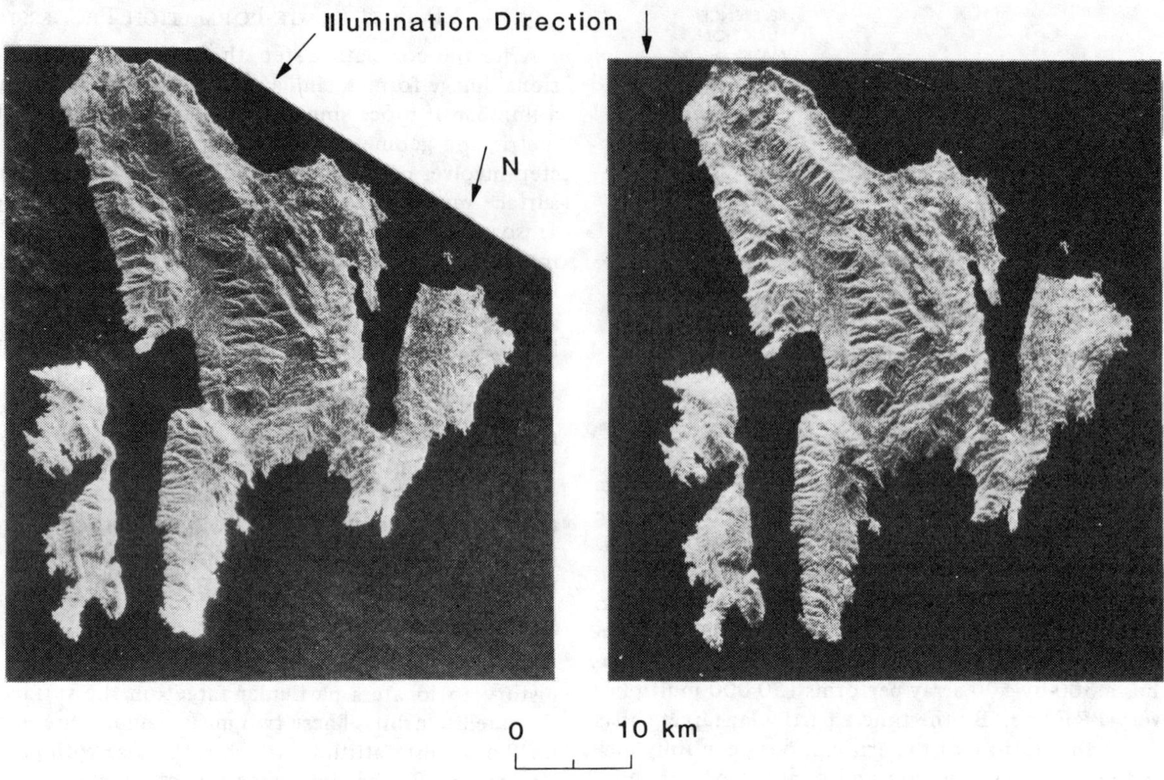

Fig. 29. Stereo pair images of the island of Cephalonia in Greece, acquired with the SIR-A. The angle of convergence is only 5°. This still allows stereo observation.

discussed earlier. In order to minimize the ratio of the standard deviation to the mean intensity, a large number of looks must be acquired. This, in turn, will degrade the resolution. Thus a tradeoff must be made between spatial resolution and "radiometric resolution." This has been discussed by Moore [61].

C. Texture Analysis

One of the features which is used in the analysis of an image is its texture. The texture is defined as the spatial variation in the image brightness on the scale of a few tens of resolution elements.

A number of researchers have developed and used analytical techniques to study and classify texture in radar images. Shanmugan *et al.* [75] and Blom and Daily [10] used spectral analysis to classify geologic units based on their texture in the radar image. Blom and Daily [10] used a processing technique of splitspectrum to enhance the identification of geologic structures in radar images. In this technique they generated a false-color image where the hue is proportional to the low-frequency spatial components of the image spectrum and the intensity is proportional to the high-frequency spatial components.

D. Speckle Statistical Properties

The speckle in the radar image is a result of the interaction of the coherent electromagnetic wave with a rough surface. It is basically the interference pattern resulting from the combination of the returns from the different scattering points on the surface. Thus the statistical properties of the speckle as a function of the observing frequency are dependent on the surface roughness.

In his paper, Jain [46] used the decorrelation properties of the speckle as a function of the radar frequency to derive the rms height of ocean waves imaged with the SAR. If the wave height is small, a slight change in the observing frequency will induce only slight change in the speckle pattern, i.e., high correlation. If the wave height is large, a slight change in the observing frequency will completely change the speckle pattern, implying strong decorrelation. This technique is of particular interest because it will extend the capability of SAR use in observing ocean-surface wave patterns.

E. Multisensors Registration

The radar provides an image of the surface scattering properties in the microwave region. Thus the combination of radar images with visible/IR images will provide us with a more complete picture of the surface scattering and emission properties over most of the electromagnetic spectrum which is accessible to spaceborne remote sensors.

The digital registration of radar data (airborne and spaceborne) to Landsat data was reported by Daily *et al.* [27] and Blom and Daily [10]. This required a good deal of effort for a number of reasons: 1) the data were taken from different platforms, and 2) the two types of sensors have different imaging geometry (i.e., radar uses a range–time format, while Landsat uses an angle–angle format in the image formation). The foreshortening in the radar images makes it particularly complicated to register accurately images of surfaces with extensive topographic change.

The analysis of the combined Seasat–Landsat images provided encouraging results. Blom and Daily [10] analyzed the combined images of the San Rafael Swell region in eastern Utah. They found that the addition of the Seasat data im-

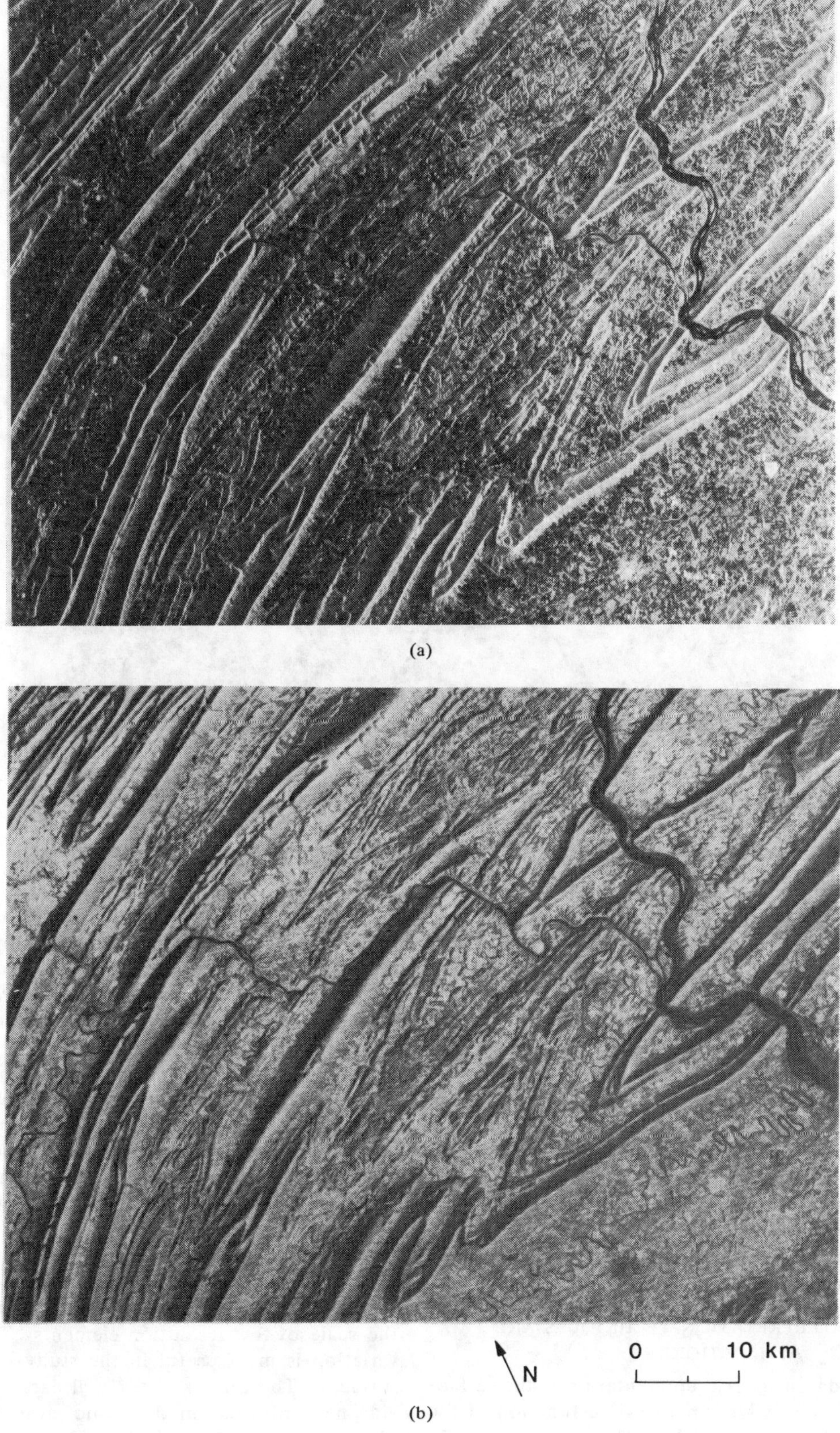

Fig. 30. Seasat (a) and Landsat (b) images of the Appalachians near Harrisburg, PA. The Susquehanna River is visible in the upper right corner. The pattern of "noses" formed by the mountains and valleys represents plunging structures formed by the folded layers.

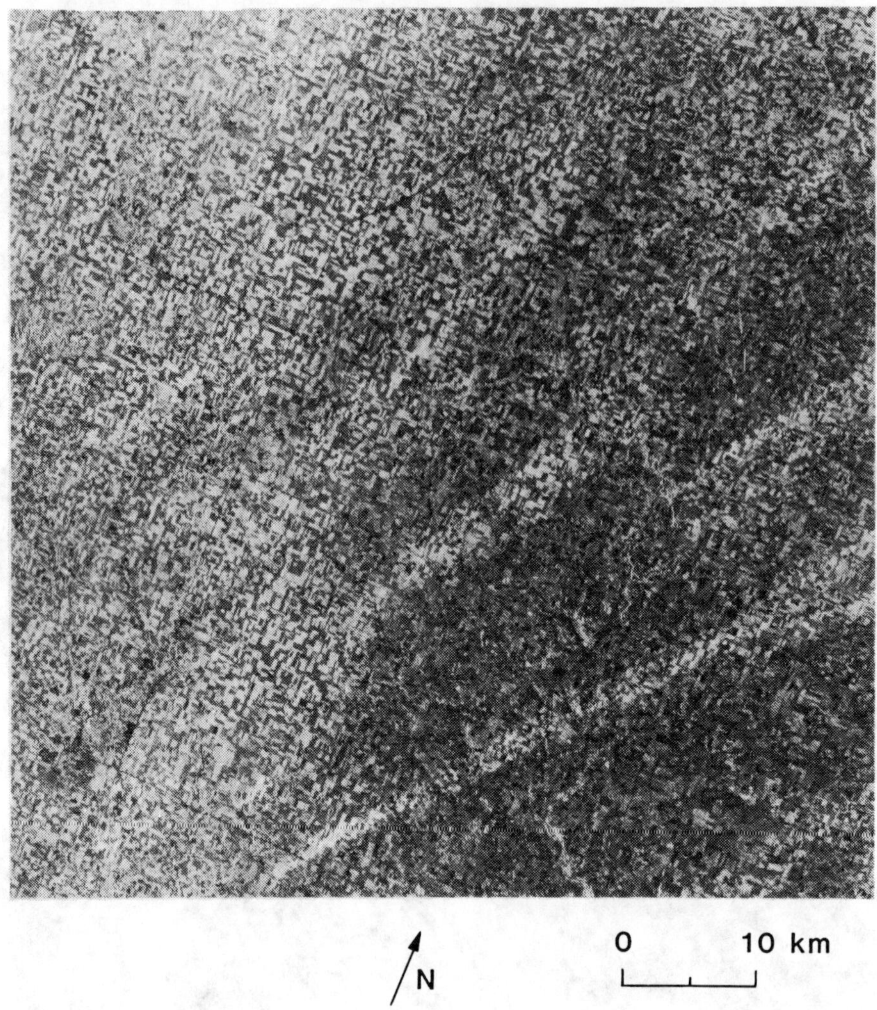

Fig. 31. Seasat image of cultivation fields around Ames, IA.

proved the lithographic classification capability from 59 percent with Landsat alone to 72 percent with the combined data set.

F. Stereo Imaging

The radar sensor can provide stereo images in a manner similar to visible sensors. In this case, two orbital passes are required such that two images of the same area can be acquired with two incidence angles.

In the case of Seasat and SIR-A, only limited stereo capability was possible. Because the look angle was fixed, small convergence-angle stereo was acquired in limited cases when a certain area was observed in the far edge of the swath on one orbital pass and in the near edge of the swath on another orbit. Fig. 29 shows such a pair of images.

VII. Data Interpretation Techniques and Applications

The tone of the radar image is a representation of the surface backscatter cross section, which in turn is a function of the surface slope, its roughness at the scale of the radar wavelength, and its complex dielectric constant. For relatively long radar wavelengths, the volumetric properties of the near-surface region also play a role in the backscatter return.

The interpretation of the SAR images and raw data is based on three types of information: 1) geometric patterns, forms, and shapes; 2) image tone and texture; and 3) coherency properties, such as speckle statistics and Doppler shift. Examples of the first one are lineaments, folds, dunes, drainage patterns, cultivation fields boundaries, ocean-wave patterns, current boundaries, ice flows, etc. These patterns, forms, and shapes are interpreted in a way similar to that used with regular photography. Fig. 30 shows a Seasat SAR and a Landsat image of the folded Appalachians near Harrisburg, PA. The folded structures, a series of anticlinal and synclinal features, are clearly recognizable on both images for the same reason, i.e., a recognizable variation of image tone in an organized pattern which, from field experience, is usually associated with folding of geologic strata.

Image tone and texture are primarily a function of the surface roughness and subresolution small-scale topography, the surface complex dielectric constant, and surface variations on the scale of few resolution elements. The dielectric constant variation is most useful in the study of vegetated and moist surfaces. The tonal and textural data on the radar image provide new information that is not available with optical or IR photography. Interpretation of the data requires an understanding of the interaction of microwaves with natural surfaces [74], [11]. Fig. 31 shows a Seasat SAR image of cultivation fields in Central Iowa. The tonal variations in the SAR image are not directly correlated with the tonal variations observed on Landsat images. This shows that the surface properties

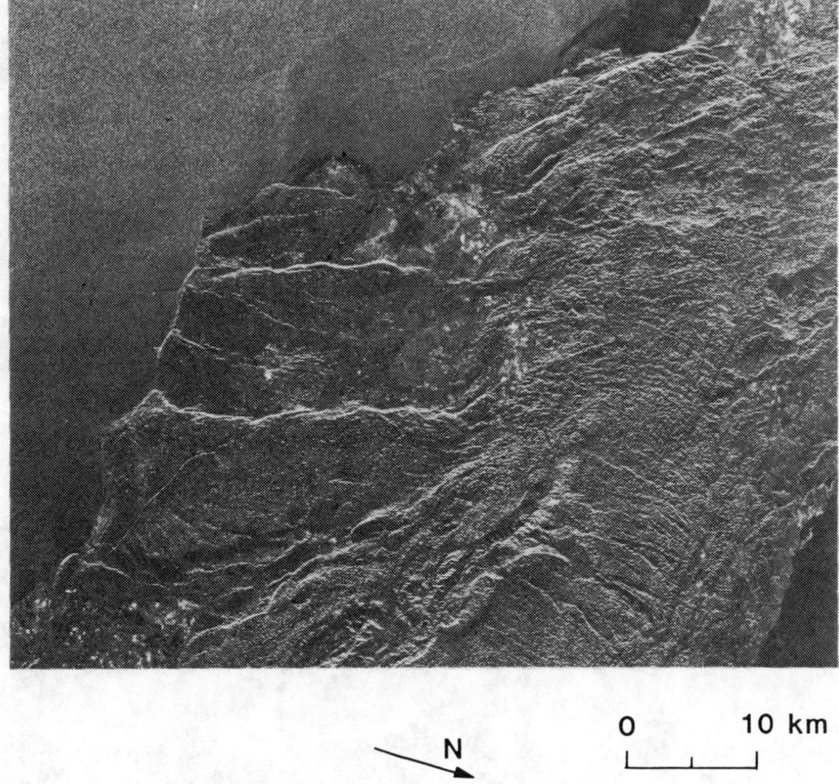

Fig. 32. Seasat image of Central Jamaica. The Blue Mountains in eastern Jamaica represent a pre-Eocene igneous and metamorphic complex. They show as coarse texture. Younger limestones cover most of the rest of the island and form karst topography which shows as fine denture.

have different effects on the response of each sensor. Work is presently ongoing, mostly at the University of Kansas and JSC, on how to use these two types of data in a complementary way to improve the discrimination and identification of crops.

Fig. 32 is a Seasat SAR image of Jamaica. The area in the image is completely covered by vegetation. Variations in the image texture are clearly visible. These variations correlate well with the surface geology [28]. The fine texture corresponds to limestone areas where the karst topography is well developed. The coarse texture corresponds to areas with igneous or metamorphic rocks. The topographic texture is visible on the radar image because of the strong sensitivity of the backscatter intensity to variations in the surface slope.

The third type of information is unique to coherent radar sensors. The surface roughness and texture of the subresolution scale leads to interference patterns which are represented by the speckle in the radar image. The statistical properties of the speckle are related to the surface geometric properties, and recent research has been conducted on deriving surface height statistics, particularly for ocean waves [46], using the speckle decorrelation properties as a function of observation frequency.

The target motion (for example, ocean currents and waves, vessels, man-made objects, etc.) also has an effect on the Doppler shift of the echo. Research is ongoing to measure the surface motion magnitude and spatial distribution from the radar data.

The Seasat SAR data, and the recently acquired SIR-A data, are being used in a number of applications related to the Earth and Ocean Sciences. In this section, we present a brief overview of the main research results in the fields of geology,

oceanography, glaciology, and agriculture with some discussion about future potentials of the SAR sensor.

A. Geologic Mapping Applications

In geologic mapping applications, the SAR images are used to detect, delineate, map, and identify features, patterns, shapes, albedo variations, and texture variations, and their relative spatial relationship. The image brightness, which is a direct representation of the intensity of the radar backscatter, is mainly an effect of the surface slope, roughness (surficial and volumetric), and dielectric constant.

On a qualitative basis, radar images are interpreted in a way similar to that used with regular photography [60], [5], [72]. The radar sensor has the advantage that the angle of illumination, and to some extent the direction of illumination, are selectable. This is not the case with spaceborne visible and IR sensors where the geometry is completely fixed by the position of the Sun and the time of data acquisition. Proper illumination geometry is of particular importance for structural mapping. Thus the radar and visible IR sensors will complement each other by providing different spectral signatures and illumination geometry.

Quantitative analysis of the radar imaging albedo is somewhat more involved. Models have been developed, and to some extent tested, to relate surface roughness and dielectric constant to the radar return. However, there is still a need for appreciably more work to be able to interpret quantitatively the albedo in radar images.

Fig. 33 is a SAR image of the central part of the Dominican Republic. Fig. 34 shows simplified interpretation maps of the

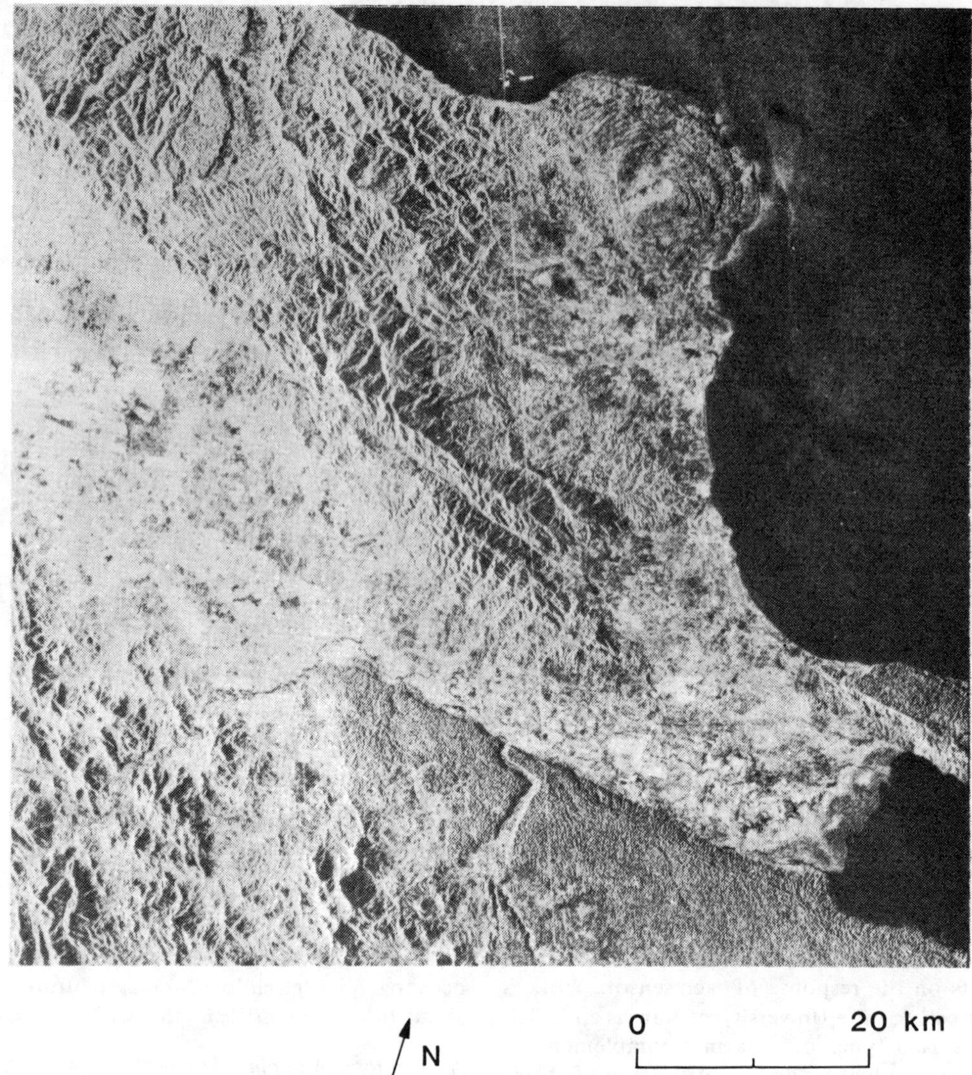

Fig. 33. Seasat image of the northeast part of the Dominican republic. Three major topographic units are visible. The youngest deposits of flat-lying soils and grounds occupy the central region. Tertiary lime-stones that give rise to karst topography (fine texture) cover the lower right region in the image. Cretaceous and older volcanic rocks underlie the more rugged mountainous basement in the rest of the image.

lineaments and the texture in the radar image. Lineaments are visible as an abrupt, spatially linear, change in image brightness [73], in texture (see Fig. 33), in drainage-flow direction (see Fig. 33), or topography (see Fig. 32). Linear features mapped on a radar image must be verified on the ground to determine their exact nature. Large-scale linear features are usually associated with faulting. Variation in texture is usually associated with change in lithology. In Figs. 32 and 33, the fine texture corresponds to Tertiary limestone units which formed karst topography. The very coarse texture corresponds to igneous and metamorphic units. The rest of the area corresponds to Quaternary alluvium.

In a detailed comparative analysis of the Seasat SAR and Landsat images of the Pine Mountain thrust region near Knoxville, TN, Ford [37] concluded that these two sensors are complementary for lineament mapping. The Seasat SAR seems to be superior because of the sensitivity of radar backscatter to surface slope change, and because it allows at least two different illumination directions. However, the use of both sensors does allow a more complete mapping capability.

The spatial relationship of surface features is an important geologic indicator. Fig. 35(a) shows the radar image of Central Ireland. This is a region covered with drumlins (elongated, well-defined hills) which are remnants of the glacial period. The alignment of these hills reflects the retreat pattern of the ice sheet ([38]; see Fig. 35(b)).

Fig. 36 shows a simpler and more direct case of identification based on spatial relationship. A very bright region is seen emanating from the bottom of a cone-shaped feature with a circular crater at the top. This occurs in a volcanic region north of Flagstaff, AZ. This can be immediately interpreted as a very rough, recent lava flow emanating from a well-defined cinder cone. A detailed analysis of radar images of volcanic fields is given by Schaber *et al.* [74].

More subtle features could be enhanced by special processing. Blom and Daily [10] used color enhancement of slight albedo and texture variations to detect and delineate a geologic structure in the Patrick Draw, WY. The geologic feature, a subsurface arch, was almost invisible on the surface. However, the surface texture, which is mainly controlled by the drainage

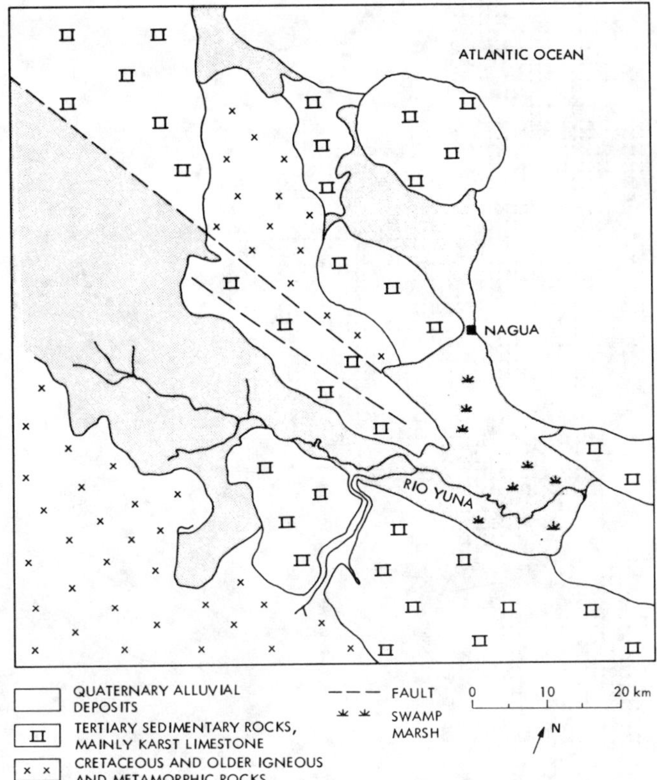

Fig. 34. Simplified map of lineaments and texture observed in Fig. 33. (Courtesy of T. Dixon.)

patterns, and the surface albedo, which is mainly affected by the vegetation cover, were slightly affected by the regional sub-surface structure. Blom and Daily [10] used a digital combination of Seasat and Landsat images of the San Rafael Swell region to enhance the capability of classifying the lithologic units in that region.

Another type of geologic feature, sand dune fields, was studied by Blom and Elachi [11]. In this case, the surface consists of a number of smooth tilted facets, and the scattering occurs primarily in the specular mode; that is, strong echoes are returned from the dunes' facets that are properly oriented (e.g., normal or near normal) relative to the radar illumination.

The effect of the illumination geometry is illustrated in Fig. 37, which shows the Seasat and SIR-A images of the Santa Ynez Mountains. Because of the near-vertical illumination of the Seasat SAR, the foldover effect leads to extensive distortions in the mountainous area, making interpretation very difficult. In the case of the SIR-A data, the large incidence-angle illumination allows a much better view of the layered structure in the mountainous terrain. However, in the flat areas, the Seasat image seems to contain additional useful information on the surface drainage. Thus it seems that a dual- (or multiple-) incidence angle illumination will be required to acquire a full picture of the surface structure.

B. Oceanographic Applications

In oceanographic applications, the imaging radar sensor has a unique and essential characteristic—the capability to acquire high-resolution images of the surface regardless of cloud cover and at any time of the day or night. This characteristic is essential because of the dynamic nature of almost all the features on the ocean surface. A review of spaceborne imaging radar applications in oceanography is given by Beal *et al.* [6].

The radar sensor provides an image that is representative of the surface backscatter characteristics. In the case of the ocean, the backscatter is completely controlled by the small-scale surface topography: the short gravity and capillary waves which scatter the radar energy by the Bragg scattering mechanism, and the local tilt of the surface, which is due to the presence of large waves and swells. Thus the SAR is capable of imaging surface and near-surface phenomena that affect the surface roughness directly or indirectly. These phenomena include surface waves, internal waves, currents, weather fronts, wind or oil slicks, and eddies. In this section, we discuss examples of ocean features that have been observed with Seasat SAR. Some of these observations have not been verified by simultaneous ground truth; however, we will present the most logical interpretation. The Seasat SAR provided for the first time a synoptic high-resolution view of large ocean areas; and in some cases, it provided repetitive observations of the same region every three days. Some of the observed features were never observed before, and their interpretation is controversial at the present time. Other features were observed to occur much more commonly than had previously been thought.

Surface waves are visible on the radar image as a periodic regular change in the image tone (Fig. 38). The spatially periodic change in the surface–coherent backscatter cross section is a result of three surface effects that are modulated by the presence of a propagating surface wave or swell: 1) local slope; 2) the intensity and bunching of small gravity and capillary waves; and 3) the wave orbital velocity, which affects the phase of the returned echo. The relative importance of these three effects is not yet well understood [36], [29], [3], [71], [2].

Fig. 38 shows a Seasat image of ocean surface waves acquired over the northeastern Atlantic, near the Shetland Islands. The surface waves had a wavelength of about 300 m, and the refraction patterns near the coast are clearly visible. This Seasat image was acquired in 14 s. Thus it represents an almost in-

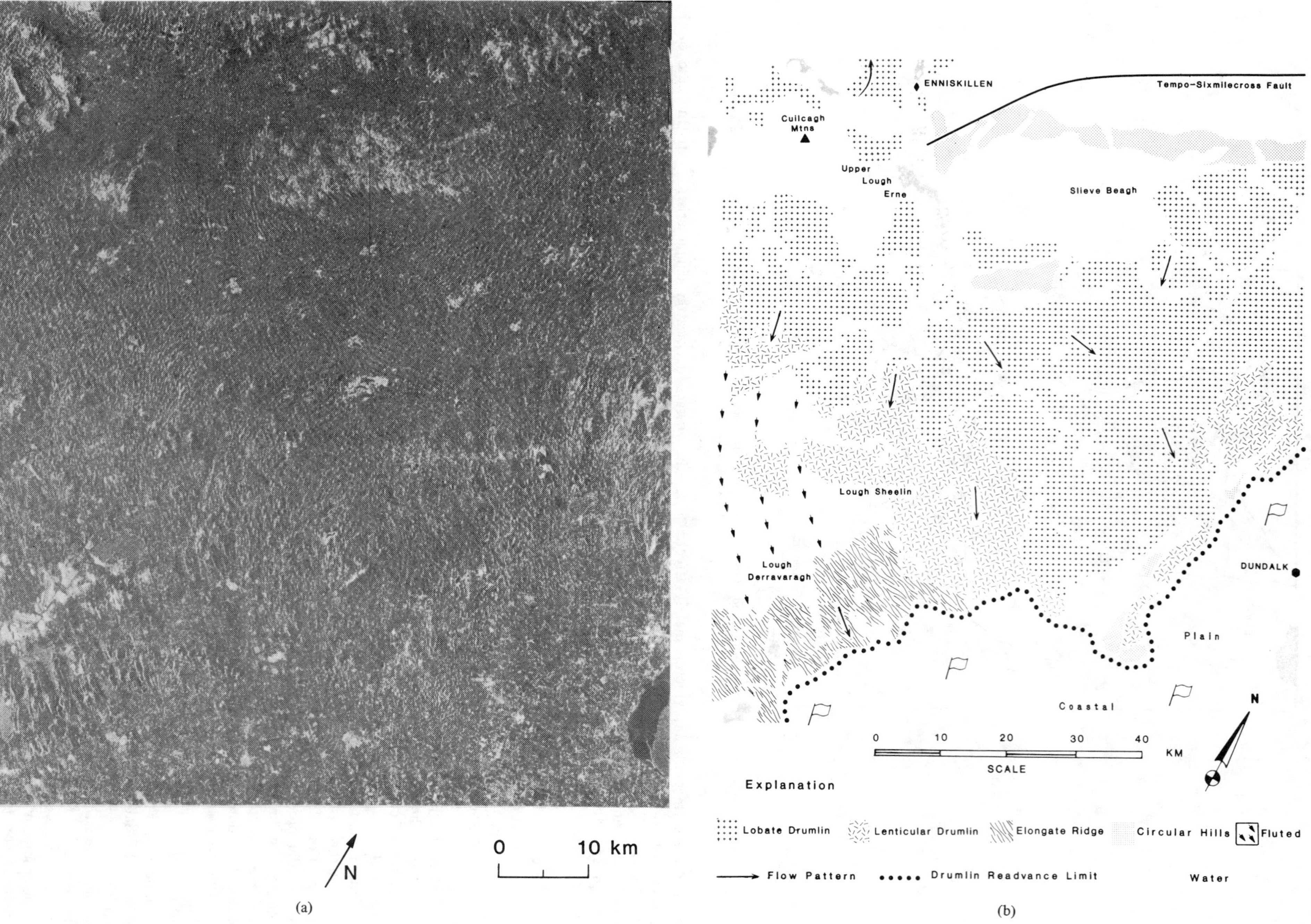

Fig. 35. Seasat image of Central Ireland. (a) This area contains thousands of drumlins which were formed by the flow patterns of the glacial ice in prehistoric times. (b) Simplified sketch illustrating some of the features seen in (a). (Courtesy of J. Ford.)

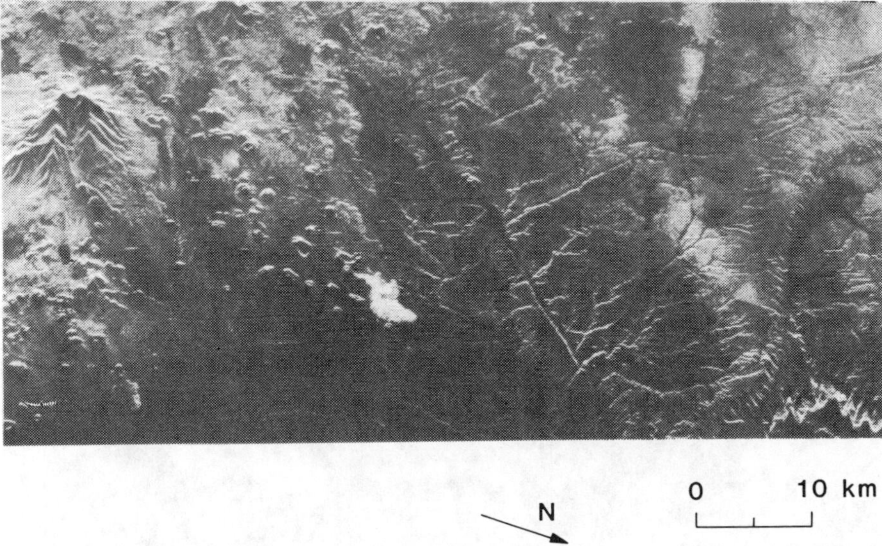

Fig. 36. Seasat image of the San Francisco volcanic field, north of Flagstaff, AZ. Numerous cinder cones and craters are visible. The brightest area corresponds to the lava flow emanating from the SP cinder cone.

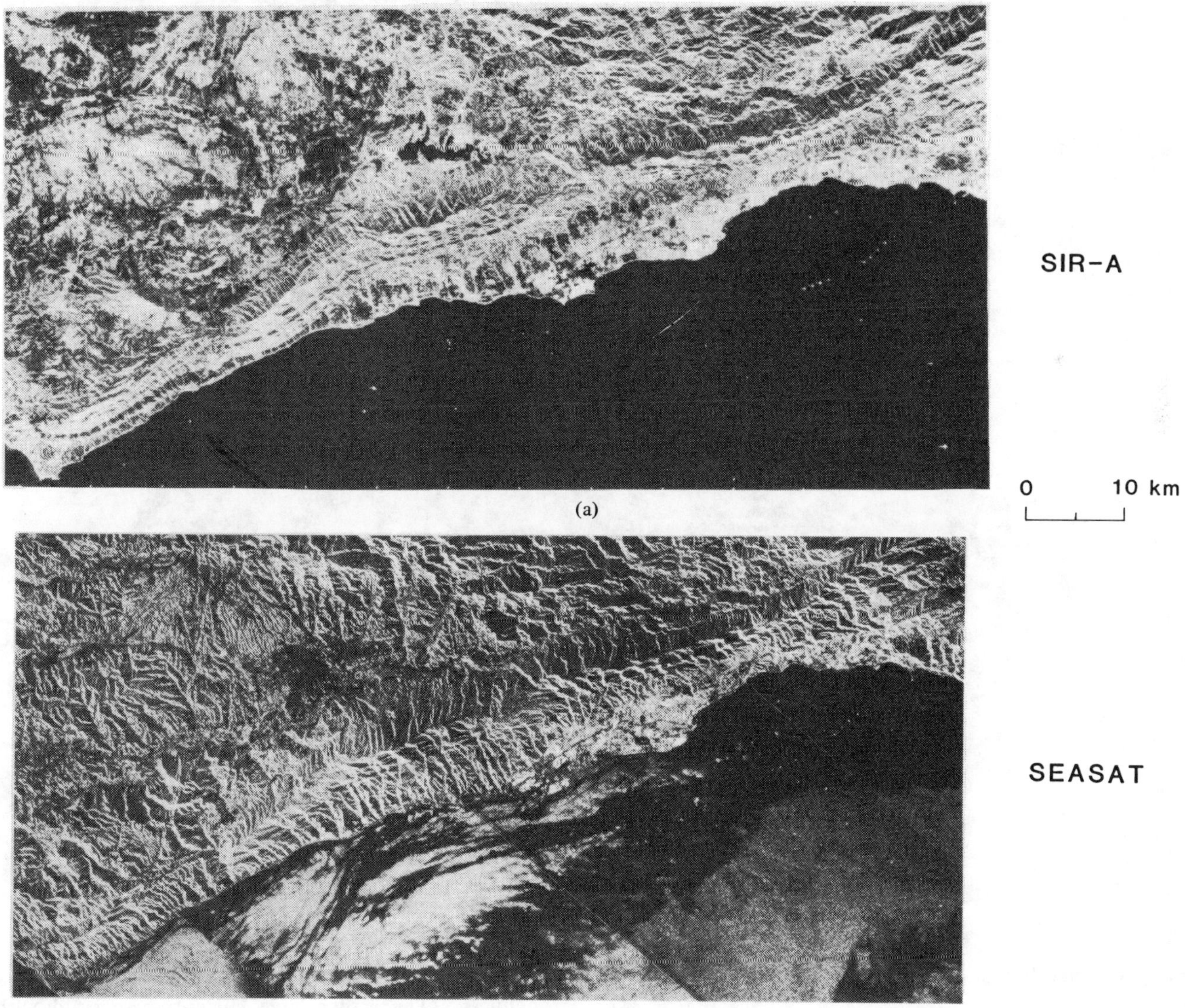

(a)

(b)

Fig. 37. Seasat (a) and SIR-A (b) images of the Santa Ynez Mountains along the California coastline near Santa Barbara. The SIR-A image is clearly superior to study the structure in the mountainous region. The Seasat image provides additional information in relatively flat regions.

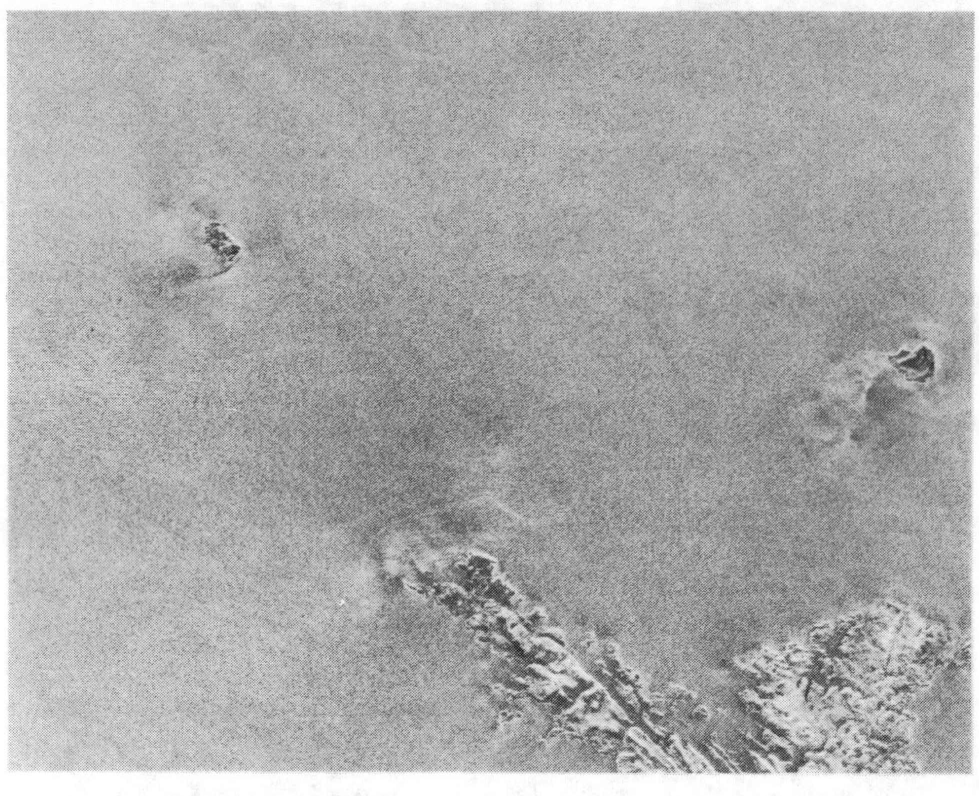

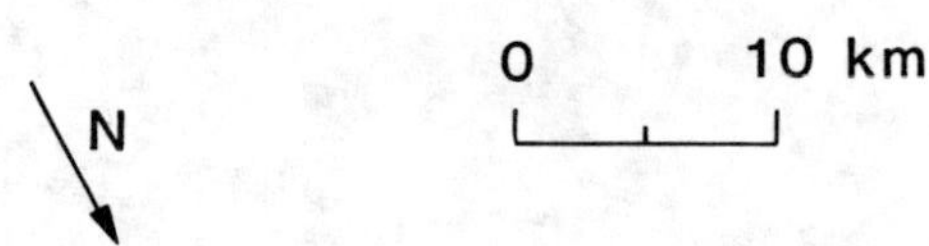

Fig. 38. Seasat image of surface ocean waves near Shetland Island, England. The swell had a wavelength of 300 m. The two small islands are Foule and Fair Isle. Observe the refraction and diffraction of the swell near the coast.

Fig. 39. Seasat image of internal waves near the island of San Nicolas off the coast of California.

stantaneous snapshot of the wave pattern over this 100×100 km region.

Fig. 39 shows internal waves in the western Atlantic just east of Manhattan Island. These waves are observed as a result of their surface manifestations and their effect on the surface roughness. The rather large currents associated with these waves modify the capillary–ultragravity surface-wave spectrum overlying the oscillations. The exact mechanisms by which

Fig. 40. Seasat image of the Nantucket Island region. The island is
visible in the upper left corner of the image. Most of the other
patterns observed on the ocean surface reflect the bottom topography
in this shallow region.

the modifications take place are still the subject of discussion, but at least two hypotheses have been advanced [40]. According to the first hypothesis, the high velocity of surface water arising from the internal wave amplitude can sweep surface oils and materials together to form a smooth strip near regions of surface water convergence. The second mechanism predicts that capillary and ultragravity wave energy is concentrated in the convergence zone by surface-current stress, which then becomes a region of enhanced roughness rather than a smooth area as with the first hypothesis. When such smooth and rough regions are illuminated away from normal incidence and then viewed at nonspecular angles, the smooth region would appear darker and the rough one brighter than the normal sea surface. This geometry is the same for both imaging radar and multispectral (including optical) sensors.

Internal waves are usually observed on the radar image as a wave packet that consists of a series of convex strips, with the spatial periodicity becoming shorter toward the center of curvature. The length of the crest may range up to many tens of kilometers. The leading wavelengths are on the order of 1 to 2 km and decrease monotonically toward the rear. They usually occur in groups or packets, and they have been observed in numerous places along the western and eastern coasts of North America. Similar observations have been conducted with aircraft SAR [34] and optical sensors [4]. On some Seasat single swaths, more internal waves could be observed than the total number observed during dozens of aircraft flights over a period of five years. This illustrates the new insight that resulted from the Seasat SAR experiment on the extent and rate of occurrence of certain dynamic ocean phenomena.

An interesting phenomenon which was observed for the first time with the Seasat radar is shown in Fig. 40. The different patterns observed in the shallow waters around Nantucket Island correlate very closely with the bottom bathymetry. The radar waves do not penetrate the ocean surface sufficiently to sense the bottom topography. The most likely interpretation is that the change in the thickness of the water column modulates the velocity of the near-surface current. This in turn modulates the ocean surface roughness which is the main physical parameter that the radar is sensing. Thus indirectly, the radar image reflects the bottom topography.

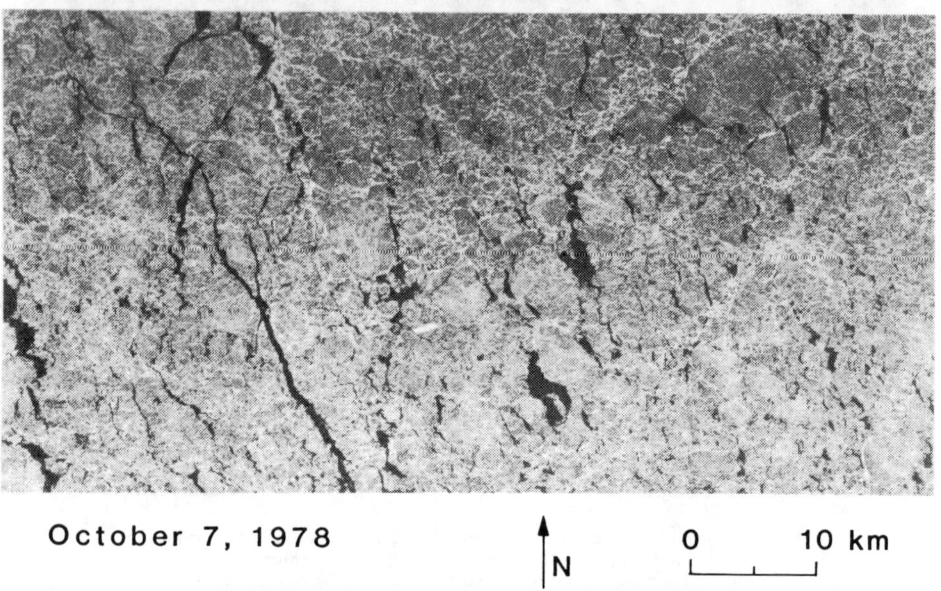

Fig. 41. Seasat image of polar ice floes in the Beaufort Sea acquired six days apart. The bright section is most likely a stranded iceberg.

Other features which were observed on radar images include current boundaries, eddies, and vessels.

C. Polar Ice and Glaciology Applications

Spaceborne imaging of the polar ice cover is of particular interest in two areas: 1) mapping of the ice-cover motion and extent and spatial distribution of the open water channels, and 2) determination of the ice floes' age.

A spaceborne imaging SAR is the ideal sensor for mapping the ice spatial distribution, extent, and motion. The all-time capability of the radar allows repetitive observation all through the year. Global coverage every three to four days can be easily achieved at the polar regions. For this application, the main observable characteristics are the shape, size, and distribution (including accurate spatial location) of the ice features [55]. Leberl et al. [54] have shown that the polar ice motion can be mapped with the Seasat data to an accuracy of 150 m or better and that furture systems should be able to achieve a location accuracy of better than 50 m. Fig. 41 shows an example of a Seasat image of an ice region which was observed over a period of about two months in the summer of 1978. Fig. 42 shows the motion of that region during that time period.

To be able to determine the ice type and age, a better understanding of the wave–surface interaction mechanisms is required. At the present time, it seems that a multiparameter radar system might be necessary in order to classify uniquely which ice floes are recently formed, one year old, or many years old.

Fig. 43 is the Seasat SAR image of the Malaspina Glacier in southeastern Alaska. The ice-floe patterns are observed because of the folded moraines, which usually have different roughness characteristics from the surrounding ice.

D. Renewable Resources

Landsat data are being used to observe, identify, estimate the extent of, and monitor the growth of different crops on a regional scale. The use of the surface cover reflection in the visible and near-IR spectral regions has been very successful; however, it is limited by the clouds which, over many world regions, could last for many weeks at a time. Thus a combina-

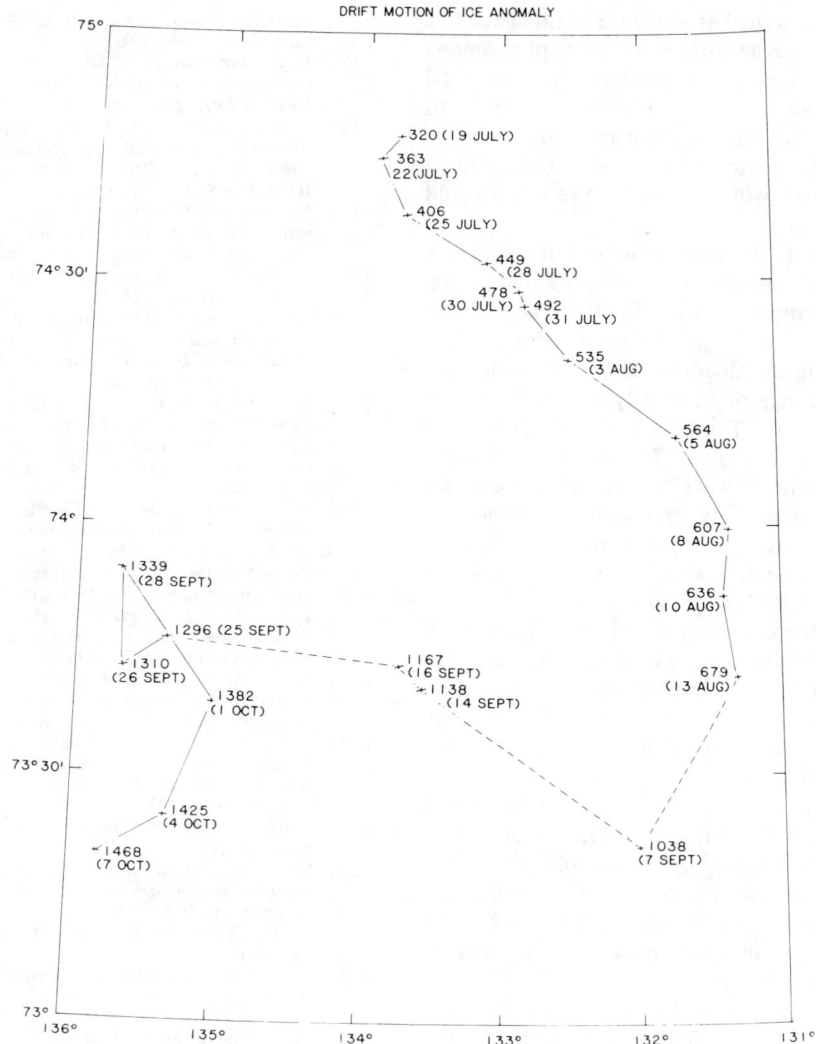

Fig. 42. Long-term motion of the bright feature in Fig. 41. (Courtesy of B. Holt.)

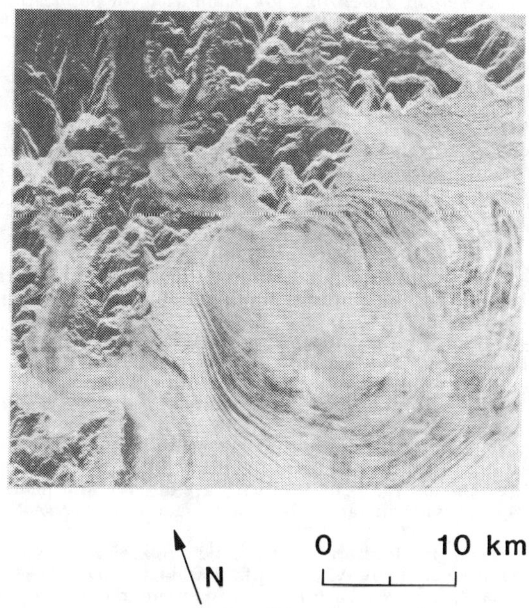

Fig. 43. Seasat image of the Malispina glacier, AK. The ice-floe pattern is visible as a series of bright and dark curvilinear regions. These correspond to the areas of different roughness.

tion of visible/IR and microwave imaging sensors will allow a continuous monitoring capability where the radar sensor will be used mainly to observe changes during the cloudy periods, and the visible/IR sensor will provide identifications at the pre- and post-cloudiness times.

Fig. 31 is a Seasat SAR image over Ames, IA. The distribution of the cultivation fields is clearly visible. Different fields have different albedo; however, it is not yet well understood how the radar albedo relates to the nature and properties of the surface and the surface cover. An interesting effect is observed on this image—an increase of the albedo over the upper half of the image and over streak-like areas in the lower half. The most likely interpretation is that this increase in the average albedo is due to an increase in the soil moisture as a result of a rainstorm which occurred just a few hours before the data were acquired. This same effect was observed in numerous other places where post-rain images showed bright albedo streaks while pre-rain images of the same areas did not.

VIII. The Next Decade

The Seasat SAR demonstrated that high-resolution synoptic radar images can be acquired from space and can be used to continuously monitor the Earth's surface. The analysis of the

Seasat SAR data clearly showed that spaceborne radar sensors are essential for monitoring ocean-surface dynamic phenomena and for improved structural mapping, particularly in tropical and arid regions. They also play a complementary role to Landsat-type sensors for lithologic mapping and crop monitoring. Thus the imaging radar sensor is an important element of the spaceborne sensors that will be used in the 1980's and beyond for Earth observation.

The success of the Seasat SAR experiment and of the SIR-A has led to an international interest in developing and flying more sophisticated spaceborne SAR's. In 1983 an X-band SAR, will be flown by the Germans on Spacelab. For the mid 1980's, the U.S. is planning multiparameter Shuttle radar systems which have a wide range of flexibility and will be used mainly for research purposes. The SIR-B (1984 flight) will have a controllable incidence angle. The SAMEX (Shuttle Active Microwave Experiment, 1987–1990 flights), will operate at L- and C-band at all polarizations, and with a variable incidence angle. The data handling and processing will be completely digital. This sensor could also be operated from an orbiting platform for long-duration missions.

For long-term observations, a number of free-flying SAR systems are under study by the U.S., Japan, Canada, and the ESA. These systems will have less flexibility; however, their main challenge is in the fast turnaround of the data. They all will require a real-time digital correlator system, which is a major technological development.

In the area of data analysis, a number of research topics will be of particular interest during the next decade. These include the use of speckle statistics to classify surface unit, use of the Doppler information to map ocean currents, use of multispectral multipolarization radars for lithologic and surface cover classification, and the use of multi-incidence angle imaging for structural mapping and stero imaging.

Finally, a mission to map the cloud-hidden surface of Venus is planned for the late 1980's. This mission, called Venus Radar Mapper, will use an orbiting synthetic-aperture imaging radar very similar to the ones used by Seasat and SIR-A. Later, in the 1990's, there are plans to image the surface of Titan with an orbiting radar.

Acknowledgment

The work reported in this paper would not have been possible without the help of many of our colleagues who are involved in the radar remote sensing program at JPL. They are too many to list here, but they all contributed in some way or other to this work. We would also like to acknowledge the excellent support of Ms. Olivia Tyler and Ms. Sue Conrow in preparing the artwork and typing the manuscript.

References

[1] J. Aarons, H. E. Whitney, and R. S. Allen, "Global morphology of ionospheric scintillations," *Proc. IEEE*, vol. 59, pp. 159–172, 1971.

[2] W. R. Alpers, D. B. Ross, and C. L. Rufenach, "On the detectability of ocean surface waves by real and synthetic aperture radars," *J. Geophys. Res.*, vol. 86, pp. 6481–6498, 1981.

[3] W. R. Alpers and C. L. Rufenach, "The effect of orbital motion on synthetic aperture imagery of ocean waves," *IEEE Trans. Antennas Propagat.*, vol. AP-27, pp. 635–690, 1979.

[4] J. P. Apel, H. M. Byrne, J. R. Proni, and R. L. Charnell, "Observations of oceanic internal and surface waves from the Earth Resources Technology Satellite," *J. Geophys. Res.*, vol. 80, pp. 865–881, 1975.

[5] T. E. Avery, *Interpretation of Aerial Photographs*, 3rd. ed. Minneapolis, MN: Burgess, 1977.

[6] R. C. Beal, P. S. Deleonibus, and I. Katz, *Spaceborne Synthetic Aperture Radar for Oceanography*. Baltimore, MD: John Hopkins Univ. Press, 1981.

[7] J. R. Bennett, I. G. Cumming, and R. A. Deane, "The digital processing of SEASAT synthetic radar data," in *Proc. IEEE Int. Radar Conf.*, pp. 168–175, Apr. 1980.

[8] J. R. Bennett and P. R. McConnell, "Considerations in the design of optimal multilook processors for image quality," presented the SAR Image-Quality Workshop, paper ESA SP-172, Frascati, Italy, December 11, 1980.

[9] M. Benson, "Digital processing of SEASAT-A SAR data using linear approximations to the range cell migration curves," in *Proc. IEEE Int. Radar Conf.*, pp. 176–181, Apr. 1980.

[10] R. Blom and M. Daily, "Radar image processing for rock type discrimination," *IEEE Trans. Geosci. Remote Sensing*, vol. GE-20, pp. 343–351, July 1982.

[11] R. Blom and C. Elachi, "Spaceborne and airborne imaging radar observation of sand dunes," *J. Geophys. Res.*, vol. 86, pp. 3061–3070, 1981.

[12] G. Born, J. A. Dunne, and D. B. Lowe, "SEASAT mission overview," *Science*, vol. 204, pp. 1405–1406, 1979.

[13] E. Brookner, "Present and future trends in radar signal processing," *Trends and Perspectives in Signal Processing*, vol.I, no. 4, Oct. 1981.

[14] W. E. Brown, Jr., C. Elachi, and T. W. Thompson, "Radar imaging of ocean surface patterns," *J. Geophys. Res.*, vol. 31, pp. 2657–2667, 1976.

[15] W. M. Brown, G. G. Houser, and R. G. Jenkins, "Synthetic aperture processing with limited storage and presuming," *IEEE Trans. Aerosp. Electron. Syst.*, vol. AES-9, pp. 166–176, 1973.

[16] W. M. Brown and L. J. Porcello, "An introduction to synthetic-aperture radar," *IEEE Spectrum*, vol. 6, pp. 52–62, 1969.

[17] A. A. Burns and E. J. Fremouw, "A real-time correction technique for transionospheric ranging error," *IEEE Trans. Antennas Propagat.*, vol. AP-18, pp. 785–790, 1970.

[18] J. P. Claassen and J. Eckerman, "A system concept for wide swath constant incidence angle coverage," in *Proc. Synthetic Aperture Radar Technology Conf.* (New Mexico State Univ., Mar. 8–10, 1978).

[19] *IEEE Computer* (Special Issue on Array Processors), vol. 15, Sept. 1981.

[20] C. Cook and M. Bernfeld, *Radar Signals: An Introduction to Theory and Application*. New York: Academic Press, 1967, sec. 6.3 and 7.3.

[21] R. K. Crane, "Ionospheric scintillation," *Proc. IEEE*, vol. 65, pp. 180–199, 1977.

[22] I. G. Cumming and J. R. Bennett, "Digital processing of Seasat SAR data," in *Proc. IEEE Int. Conf. Acoustic, Speech, Signal Process.* (Washington, DC, Apr. 1979), pp. 710–717.

[23] J. C. Curlander, "Location of spaceborne SAR imagery," *IEEE Trans. Geosci. Remote Sensing*, vol. GE-20, pp. 359–364, July 1982.

[24] J. Curlander, F. Li, and C. Wu, "Estimate of Doppler parameters for spaceborne synthetic aperture radar processing," *IEEE Trans. Aerosp. Electron. Syst.*, submitted for publication, 1982.

[25] J. C. Curlander and W. E. Brown, "A pixel location algorithm for spaceborne SAR imagery," presented at the IGARSS Conf., Washington, DC, June 8, 1980.

[26] L. J. Cutrona, "Synthetic aperture radar," in *Radar Handbook*, M. I. Skolnik, Ed. New York: McGraw-Hill, 1970.

[27] M. Daily, C. Elachi, T. Farr, R. Stromberg, S. Williams, and G. Schaber, "Application of multispectral radar and landsat imagery to geologic mapping in Death Valley, California," Jet Propulsion Lab., Pasadena, CA, Tech. Rep. 78-14, 1978.

[28] T. Dixon, private communication, 1982.

[29] C. Elachi, "Radar imaging of the ocean surface," *Boundary Layer Meteorol.*, vol. 13, pp. 154–173, 1977.

[30] ——, "Shuttle imaging radar: Research sensor for earth resources observation," presented at the IGARSS Conf., Washington, DC, June 1981.

[31] ——, "Spaceborne imaging radar: Geologic and oceanographic applications," *Science*, vol. 209, pp. 1073–1082, 1980.

[32] ——, "Wave patterns across the North Atlantic on September 28, 1974 from airborne radar imagery," *J. Geophys. Res.*, vol. 81, pp. 2655–2656, May 20, 1976.

[33] C. Elachi *et al.*, "The shuttle imaging radar (SIR-A): Preliminary results," *Science*, submitted for publication, 1982.

[34] C. Elachi and J. Apel, "Internal wave observations made with an airborne synthetic aperture imaging radar," *Geophys. Res. Lett.*, vol. 3, pp. 647–650, 1976.

[35] C. Elachi, R. Goldstein, and D. Held, "Spaceborne bistatic SAR," presented at the IGARSS Conf., Washington, DC, 1981.

[36] C. Elachi and W. E. Brown, "Models of radar imaging of the ocean surface waves," *IEEE Trans. Antennas Propagat.*, vol. AP-25, pp. 84–95, Jan. 1977; also *IEEE J. Oceanic Eng.*, vol. OE-2, pp. 84–95, Jan. 1977.

[37] J. Ford, "Seasat orbital radar imagery for geologic mapping: Tennessee–Kentucky–Virginia," *Amer. Assoc. Pet. Geologists*,

vol. 66, p. 2064, 1980.

[38] ——, "A contrast in landform mapping from Seasat radar images," *Quaternary Geology*, to be published, 1982.

[39] J. Ford, R. Blom, M. L. Bryan, M. Daily, T. Dixon, C. Elachi, and H. Xenos, *Seasat Radar Views America, the Caribbean and Western Europe*, Jet Propulsion Lab., Pasadena, CA, publication 80-67, 1980.

[40] H. E. Garrett and B. A. Hughes, "On the interaction of surface and internal waves," *J. Fluid Mech.*, vol. 52, pp. 179-191, 1972.

[41] J. W. Goodman, *Introduction to Fourrier Optics.* New York: McGraw-Hill, 1968.

[42] J. Granger, "Shuttle imaging radar—A," presented at the IGA RSS Conf., Washington, DC, June 1981.

[43] J. P. Guignard, "Overview of digital processing of SAR data," in *Proc. 15th Int. Symp. on Remote Sensing of Environment* (Ann Arbor, MI, May 1981).

[44] R. O. Harger, *Synthetic Aperture Radar Systems: Theory and Design.* New York: Academic Press, 1970.

[45] D. Held and N. Mehta, "Calibration of synthetic aperture radars: The effects of nonlinearities," presented at the IGARSS Conf., Washington, DC, June 1981.

[46] A. Jain, "Determination of ocean wave heights from synthetic aperture radar imagery," *Appl. Phys.*, vol. 13, pp. 371-382, 1977.

[47] F. Janza, "Interaction mechanisms," in *Manual of Remote Sensing*, R. G. Reeves Ed. Falls Church, VA: Amer. Soc. of Photogrammetry, 1975, ch. 4.

[48] R. L. Jordan, "The Seasat—A synthetic aperture radar system," *IEEE J. Oceanic Eng.*, vol. OE-5, pp. 154-163, 1980.

[49] R. L. Jordan and B. L. Huneycutt, "Seasat—A synthetic aperture radar performance," presented at the Int. Conf. Communications, Boston, MA, ICC'79, June 10-13, 1979.

[50] J. C. Kirk, "A discussion of digital processing for synthetic aperture radar," *IEEE Trans. Aerosp. Electron. Syst.*, vol. AES-11, pp. 326-337, May 1975.

[51] A. Kozma, E. M. Leith, and N. G. Massey, "Tilted plane optical processor," *Appl. Opt.*, vol. 11, pp. 1766-1777, 1972.

[52] J. J. Kovaly, *Synthetic Aperture Radar.* Dedham, MA: Artech House, 1976.

[53] T. R. Larson, L. I. Moskowitz, and J. W. Wright, "A note on SAR imagery of the ocean," *IEEE Trans. Antennas Propagat.*, vol. AP-24, pp. 393-394, May 1976.

[54] F. Leberl, J. Raggam, C. Elachi, and W. Campbell, "Sea ice motion measurements from Seasat SAR images," *J. Geophys. Res.*, submitted for publication, 1982.

[55] F. Leberl, M. L. Bryan, C. Elachi, T. Farr, and W. Campbell, "Mapping of sea ice measurement of its drift using aircraft synthetic aperture radar images," *J. Geophys. Res.*, vol. 84, pp. 1827-1835, Apr. 20, 1979.

[56] E. N. Leith, "Complex spatial filters for image deconvolution," *Proc. IEEE*, vol. 65, pp. 18-28, 1977.

[57] ——, "Quasi-holographic techniques in the microwave region," *Proc. IEEE*, vol. 59, pp. 1305-1318, Sept. 1971.

[58] F. Li and H. Zebker, "A digital Seasat SAR correlation-simulation program," in *Dig. 1981 Geoscience and Remote Sensing Symp.*, *Vol. II*, IEEE Geoscience and Remote Sensing Society, pp. 548-554.

[59] L. Martinson, "A programmable digital processor for airborne radar," in *IEEE 1975 Int. Radar Conf. Rec.*, pp. 186-191, Apr. 1975.

[60] V. C. Miller, *Photogeology.* New York: McGraw-Hill, 1961.

[61] R. K. Moore, "Tradeoff between picture element dimensions and noncoherent averaging in side-locking airborne radar," *IEEE Trans. Aerosp. and Electron. Syst.*, vol. AES-15, pp. 697-708, 1979.

[62] R. K. Moore, J. P. Claassen, and Y. H. Lin, "Scanning spaceborne synthetic-aperture radar with integrated radiometer," *IEEE Trans. Aerosp. Electron. Syst.*, vol. AES-17, pp. 410-419, 1981.

[63] R. E. Morden and F. Powell, "SAPHIRE design and development," Goodyear Aerospace Corporation, Arizona Division, Litchfield Park, AZ, paper GERA-2177, Rev. A, Sept. 1977.

[64] N. Nohmi, N. Ito, and S. Hanaki, "Digital processing of spaceborne SAR data," European Space Agency Rep. SP-172, Dec. 1980.

[65] M. Ono *et al.*, "Digital processing of SEASAT SAR data using CRAY-1," European Space Agency, Rep. ESA SP-172, (SAR Image Quality), pp. 45-46.

[66] W. J. Peeples, W. R. Sill, T. W. May, S. H. Ward, R. J. Phillips, R. L. Jordan, E. A. Abott, and T. J. Killpack, "Orbital radar evidence for lunar subsurface layering in mare serenitatis and crisium," *J. Geophys. Res.*, vol. 83, pp. 3459-3468, 1978.

[67] L. J. Porcello, R. Jordan, J. S. Zelenka, G. F. Adams, R. J. Phillips, W. E. Brown, S. H. Ward, and P. Jackson, "The Apollo lunar sounder radar system," *Proc. IEEE*, vol. 62, pp. 769-783, 1974.

[68] D. Psaltis, private communication, 1981.

[69] R. K. Raney, "Synthetic aperture imaging radar and moving targets," *IEEE Trans. Aerosp. and Electron. Syst.*, vol. AES-7, no. 3, pp. 499-505, May 1971.

[70] A. W. Rihaczek, *Principles of High-Resolution Radar.* New York: McGraw-Hill, 1969.

[71] C. L. Rufenach and W. R. Alpers, "Imaging ocean waves by SAR with long integration times," *IEEE Trans. Antennas Propagat.*, vol. AP-29, pp. 422-428, 1981.

[72] F. F. Sabins, *Remote Sensing: Principles and Interpretation.* San Francisco: Freeman, 1978.

[73] F. F. Sabins, R. Blom, and E. Elachi, "Seasat radar image of the San Andreas Fault, California," *Amer. Assoc. Pet. Geol.*, vol. 64, p. 614, 1980.

[74] G. G. Schaber, C. Elachi, and T. Farr, "Remote sensing data of SP lava flow and vicinity in North Central Arizona," *Remote Sensing of the Environment*, vol. 9, p. 169, 1980.

[75] K. S. Shanmugan, V. Narayanan, V. S. Frost, J. A. Stiles, and J. C. Holtzman, "Textural features for radar image analysis," *IEEE Trans. Geosci. Remote Sensing*, vol. GE-19, pp. 153-156, 1981.

[76] K. Tomiyasu, "Conceptual performance of a satellite borne, wide swath SAR," *IEEE Trans. Geosci. Remote Sensing*, vol. GE-19, pp. 108-116, 1981.

[77] ——, "Tutorial review of synthetic aperture radar with application to imaging of the ocean surface," *Proc IEEE*, vol. 66, pp. 563-583, 1978.

[78] T. K. Truong, I. S. Reed, R. G. Lipes, and C. Wu, "On the application of a fast polinominal transform and the Chinese remainder theorem to compute a two-dimensional convolution," *IEEE Trans. Acoust., Speech, Signal Processing*, vol. ASSP-29, no. 1, pp. 91-97, Feb. 1981.

[79] V. C. Tyree, "Custom large scale integrated circuits for spaceborne SAR processors," in *Proc. Synthetic Aperture Radar Technology Conf.*, paper V-4 (New Mexico State Univ., Las Cruces, NM, Mar. 1978).

[80] W. J. Van de Lindt, "Digital technique for generating synthetic aperture radar image," *IBM J. Res. Develop.*, pp. 415-432, Sept. 1977.

[81] M. R. Vant, R. W. Herring, and E. Shaw, "Digital processing techniques for satellite borne synthetic aperture radars," *Can. J. Remote Sensing*, vol. 5, no. 1, 1979.

[82] C. Wu, "A digital system to produce imagery from SAR," in *Proc. AIAA Systems Design Driven by Sensors*, paper no. 76-968, Oct. 1976.

[83] C. Wu, "Electronic SAR processors for space missions," in *Proc. SAR Technology Conf.* (New Mexico State Univer., Las Cruces, NM, 1978).

[84] C. Wu, J. Curlander, and A. DiCenzo, "Determination of spacecraft attitude using synthetic aperture radar data," in *Proc. Conf. AIAA Sensor System for the 80's*, AIAA paper 80-1922, pp. 57-60, 1980.

[85] C. Wu, K. Y. Liu, and M. Jin, "Modeling and a digital processing algorithm for spaceborne SAR signals," *IEEE Trans. Aerosp. Electron. Syst.*, to be published, Sept. or Nov. 1982.

[86] C. Wu, B. Barkan, W. Karplus, and D. Caswell, "Seasat SAR data reduction using parallel array processors," *IEEE Trans. Geosci. Remote Sensing*, vol. GE-20, no. 3, pp. 352-358, July 1982.

Developments in Radar Imaging

DALE A. AUSHERMAN, Member, IEEE

ADAM KOZMA, Member, IEEE

JACK L. WALKER, Member, IEEE
Environmental Research Institute of Michigan

HARRISON M. JONES

ENRICO C. POGGIO
M.I.T. Lincoln Laboratory

Using range and Doppler information to produce radar images is a technique used in such diverse fields as air-to-ground imaging of objects, terrain, and oceans and ground-to-air imaging of aircraft, space objects, and planets. A review of the range–Doppler technique is presented along with a description of radar imaging forms including details of data acquisition and processing techniques.

Manuscript received March 13, 1984; revised June 26, 1984; released for publication July 9, 1984.

This work was supported by the U.S. Air Force, the U.S. Army, and the U.S. Navy. The U.S. Government assumes no responsibility for the information presented.

Authors' addresses: D.A. Ausherman, A. Kozma, J.L. Walker, Environmental Research Institute of Michigan, P.O. Box 8618, Ann Arbor, MI 48107; H.M. Jones and E.C. Poggio, Lincoln Laboratory, Massachusetts Institute of Technology, P.O. Box 73, Lexington, MA 02173.

I. INTRODUCTION

The purpose of this paper is to discuss various types of imaging radars. These radars take a number of forms according to the intended application. The forms range from synthetic aperture radars (SARs) carried on moving platforms, which are intended to be used to image strips or patches of terrain, to stationary radars for imaging objects placed on rotating platforms, objects moving by the radar such as aircraft or orbiting objects, or celestial objects like the Moon and planets.

Although these radars take different forms and have various applications, all are coherent radars which utilize the range–Doppler principle to obtain the desired image. That is, the image is made using conventional techniques to obtain fine-range resolution and using the Doppler frequency gradient generated by the rotation of the object field relative to the radar to obtain a cross-range resolution that is much finer than that obtainable by the radar's beamwidth.

In this tutorial paper, we give an introduction to range–Doppler radar imaging and briefly describe various forms this technique takes. A historical perspective of the development of the imaging technique, along with a number of examples, is given in Section II. In Section III, we develop the fundamentals of range–Doppler imaging in detail and discuss various processing approaches which deal with motion through resolution cells. We treat the general three-dimensional case, including the concept of three-dimensional processing. In Section IV, we include a detailed discussion of radar imaging techniques, including the data acquisition and details of the data-processing techniques.

A. Introduction to Radar Imaging Concepts

The Doppler frequency gradient required to obtain fine cross-range resolution is generated by the motion of the object relative to the radar; this motion is generated in a variety of ways which can be related to the simplified case of a stationary monostatic radar illuminating a rotating object. Fig. 1 portrays a three-dimensional object as projected into the $x-y$ plane, with the object rotating with a uniform angular motion about the z axis. However, as discussed in the following paragraphs, such restrictive assumptions can be removed and three-dimensional bodies rotating about an *arbitrary* axis with *nonuniform* rotation rates can be imaged. In addition, bistatic radar operation also can be accommodated.

If the object, contained within the beam of the radar, is rotating about the point A at ω radians per second and the coherent radar is located a distance r_a from the object, then the range to an object point with initial ($t = 0$) coordinates (r_0, θ_0, z_0) is given by

$$r = [r_0^2 + r_a^2 + 2r_a r_0 \sin(\theta_0 + \omega t) + z_0^2]^{1/2}. \tag{1}$$

If the distance to the object is much larger than the size of the object ($r_a \gg r_0, z_0$), a good approximation is

Reprinted from *IEEE Trans. Aerosp. Electron. Syst.*, vol. AES-20, pp. 363–398, July 1984.

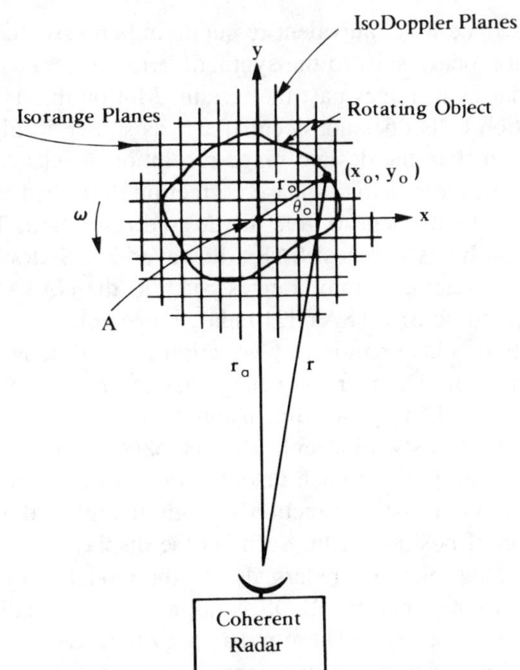

Fig. 1.   Range–Doppler imaging.

$$r \approx r_a + x_0 \sin \omega t + y_0 \cos \omega t. \qquad (2)$$

Similarly, the Doppler frequency f_d of the returned radar signal is

$$f_d = \frac{2}{\lambda}\frac{dr}{dt} = \frac{2x_0\omega}{\lambda}\cos \omega t - \frac{2y_0\omega}{\lambda}\sin \omega t \qquad (3)$$

where λ is the radar wavelength.

If the radar data are processed over a very small time interval centered at $t = 0$, (2) and (3) can be approximated as

$$r = r_a + y_0 \qquad (4)$$

$$f_d = 2x_0\omega/\lambda. \qquad (5)$$

Therefore, by analyzing the returned radar signal in terms of range delay and Doppler frequency, the (x_0, y_0) components of the position of the point scatterer can be estimated. The surfaces of constant range are parallel planes perpendicular to the radar line of sight (RLOS), and the surfaces of constant Doppler are parallel planes parallel to the plane formed by the rotation axis and the RLOS. This constitutes the usual range–Doppler imaging procedure. The presence of the object rotation rate ω in (5) implies that in order to obtain a properly scaled image of the object, the magnitude of ω must be known. Most techniques for estimating the rotation rate depend on a priori knowledge and/or analysis of periodicities in the radar signal level. Another implicit assumption is that the distance r_a from the radar antenna to the center of the object is constant and known. In applications where r_a is a function of time, the effects of time-varying range must be removed from the received signal in the radar receiver and/or processor.

The resolution in range is achieved by conventional means using a train of short or long coded pulses which provide a range resolution ρ_r determined by the bandwidth B_W of the pulse. Hence

$$\rho_r = c/2B_W \qquad (6)$$

where c is the velocity of propagation of the radar energy.

We see from (5) that we can achieve a cross-range resolution $\Delta x = \rho_a$ if we can measure Doppler frequencies with a resolution of

$$\Delta f_d = 2\omega\rho_a/\lambda. \qquad (7)$$

Since a frequency resolution Δf_d requires a coherent processing time interval of approximately $\Delta T = 1/\Delta f_d$, cross-range resolution is given by

$$\rho_a = \lambda/2\omega\Delta T = \lambda/2\Delta\theta \qquad (8)$$

where $\Delta\theta = \omega\Delta T$ is the angle through which the object rotates during the coherent processing time.

Fine cross-range resolution implies coherent processing over a large $\Delta\theta$; however, (2) and (3) indicate that both the range and Doppler frequency of a particular point scatterer can vary greatly over a large processing interval. This means that during a processing time interval sufficiently long to give the desired cross-range resolution, points on the rotating object may move through several resolution cells. Therefore, the usual range-delay measurement and Doppler-frequency analysis implied by (4) and (5) will result in degraded imagery for the large processing interval case.

To avoid image degradation caused by motion through resolution cells while using the simple range–Doppler analysis described above, we must limit the size of the coherent processing time ΔT. In the special case described above (constant rotation rate and RLOS perpendicular to the axis of rotation), no motion through a range resolution cell and a Doppler resolution cell will occur if

$$\Delta T < 2\rho_r/\omega D_a \qquad (9)$$

and

$$\Delta T < \omega^{-1}(\lambda/D_r)^{1/2} \qquad (10)$$

respectively, where D_r and D_a are the maximum range and cross-range dimensions, respectively, of the object. Consequently, one must limit the resolution of the imaging system such that

$$\rho_a^2 > \lambda D_r/4 \qquad (11)$$

$$\rho_a\rho_r > \lambda D_a/4. \qquad (12)$$

In general, the image scene dimensions are not the only parameters regulating the extent of the coherent processing interval—and hence the cross-range resolution of conventional range–Doppler images. When the angular rate is variable and/or the radar range directions are not coplanar in a coordinate system that rotates with the object, the constraint of no motion through a Doppler resolution cell (10) may have to be modified to a more stringent one, leading to even smaller values of ΔT.

IEEE TRANSACTIONS ON AEROSPACE AND ELECTRONIC SYSTEMS   VOL. AES-20, NO. 4   JULY 1984

Often, a finer cross-range resolution is desired, and hence points in the object move through range and/or Doppler resolution cells during the coherent integration time. In this case, simple frequency analysis will yield degraded imagery; the effect of motion through resolution cells must be compensated. Several techniques of compensating for this motion through cells have been developed over the years. These range from linear piecewise approximations to account for the motion, to sophisticated "extended" methods, to elegant methods of formatting the data prior to the image formation processing. Some of these methods are discussed in Sections III and IV.

B. Applications of Radar Imaging

Application of these principles has yielded various forms of range–Doppler radars as stated above. The well-known stripmap SAR technique [1] is a special case where the Doppler gradient is achieved by the relative rotation produced by scanning an antenna fixed to a moving platform over a strip of terrain. This is illustrated in Fig. 2. Here a coherent radar carried on a moving platform at a velocity v illuminates a stationary point 0 on

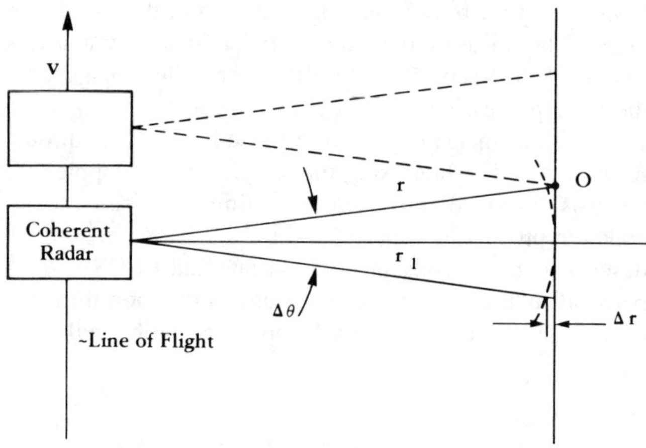

Fig. 2. Stripmap synthetic aperture radar.

the terrain at broadside range r_1 from the flight line. The point 0 is first illuminated by the forward edge of the antenna beam and is last illuminated when the aft edge of the beam passes by the point. The apparent total rotation of the object in the neighborhood of point 0 is equal to the angle subtended by the radar's antenna beam, which is approximately $\Delta\theta = \lambda/L$, where L is the length of the radar antenna in cross range. Using this relation in (8) yields the well-known formula for the cross-range resolution of an SAR, namely, $\rho_a = L/2$.

With the stripmap SAR, the apparent rotation rate of the object (i.e., the relative rotation between the object and the RLOS) is not constant and hence the Doppler frequency produced by a scatterer is a function of time. To achieve a fine cross-range resolution, it is necessary to make a correction for the change in frequency. Such a correction is often called "focusing the synthetic aperture

array" since it is equivalent to supplying an essentially quadratic phase shift to the synthetic array generated by the radar as it moves past the terrain. Motion through resolution cells does not occur if Δr, as shown in Fig. 2, is smaller than the desired range resolution. Under this condition, the quadratic phase correction described above is by itself sufficient to give the desired resolution. This condition holds for most SARs; however, for SARs [2] which operate at extreme ranges, such as the NASA satellite-borne SEATSAT [3] radar, range cell migration correction is also required. Correction for both range cell migration and Doppler frequency change of scatterers can be accomplished by two-dimensional correlation of the received signals with a replica of the expected return from a fixed point in each resolution cell in the scene. This cross-correlation function's magnitude plotted as a function of position in the scene is the displayed image.

Rotating platform radars also fit the model shown in Fig. 1 (except that the RLOS is not always perpendicular to the rotation axis). These radars are often used to obtain radar cross-section measurements and to produce images to obtain radar signatures [4, 5]. Processing to eliminate the effects of migration through resolution cells is almost always required. A form of airborne terrain mapping radar, called the spotlight radar, also fits this simple model [6–10] (except that the relative rotation rate can vary). In this form, the radar is carried in a moving vehicle and the antenna illuminates a fixed spot on the terrain from a continuously changing look angle, as shown in Fig. 3. If the gross Doppler due to the change of distance from the aircraft to the center of the spot is compensated, it can be shown that the spot of terrain can be treated as a rotating object field illuminated by a distant stationary radar.

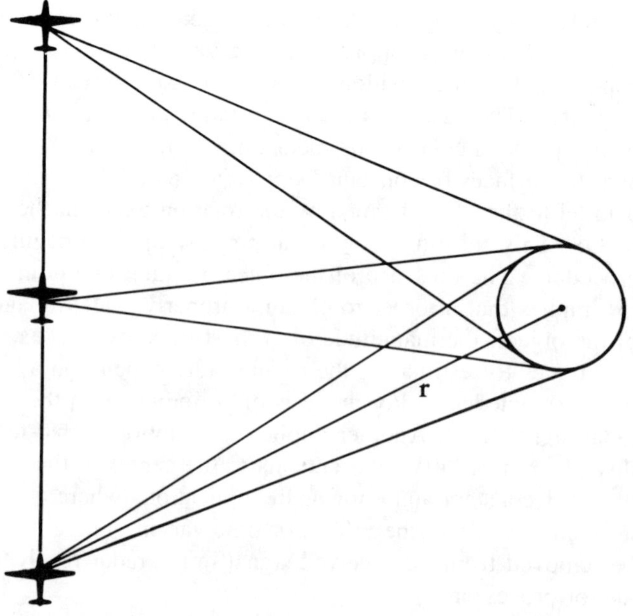

Fig. 3. Spotlight synthetic aperture radar.

Ground-based radars [11] which image moving vehicles such as aircraft or objects moving in orbit also fit the model, provided the radar tracks the object in its trajectory. The gross Doppler due to the trajectory is removed and the Doppler gradient appears as if the motion were due only to the rotation of the object relative to the RLOS. This relative rotation is caused by the translational motion of the target along its trajectory and by the rotational motion of the target itself (both rotations must be described in the same coordinate system). The trajectory and rotational motions which provide the Doppler gradient are not always known a priori, and one of the main problems in the image formation is to correctly estimate these motions from the radar data.

An important ground-based application of range–Doppler radar is to image the Moon or planets in radar astronomy [12]. The technique is called delay-Doppler imaging in astronomy. The radar is located at a fixed site on the Earth and illuminates the Moon or a planet. Contours of constant delay appear as annuli on the planet, as shown in Fig. 4. Contours of constant Doppler appear

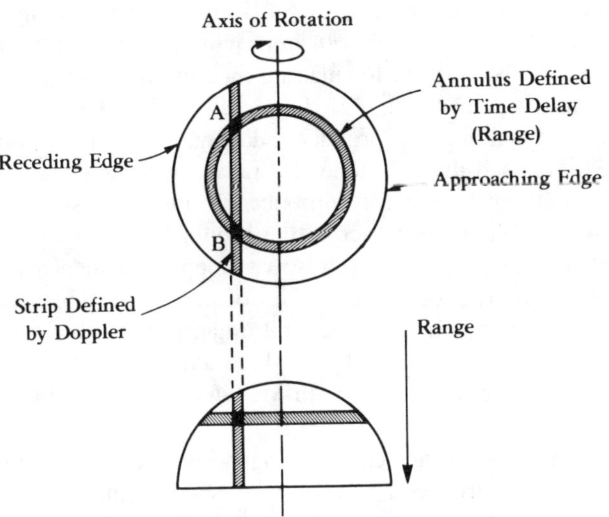

Fig. 4.   Delay-Doppler imaging in radar astronomy, after Green [32].

as straightline strips parallel to the rotation axis of the planet. The intersection of an annulus and a strip define the delay-Doppler resolution patches, as shown in black in the figure. The size of the resolution patches are determined by the bandwidth of the pulse modulation and the Doppler-frequency resolution, or by the coherent integration time. The image obtained using this technique is ambiguous since the returns from A and B at the intersection of an annulus and a strip cannot be distinguished from each other. However, using an interferometer, one patch can be nulled with respect to the other and the reflectivity of a patch can be isolated.

It is also possible to form images of objects which have no appreciable trajectory motion relative to the radar. Instead, the natural undulation of the object, such as a rocking motion of a ship due to wave action, is used to create the Doppler gradient. In this type of imaging,

which has been called inverse synthetic aperture radar (ISAR) [13], it is also necessary to make an estimate of the magnitude and direction of the undulation from the data since these parameters are unknown.

II. HISTORICAL PERSPECTIVE

A. Synthetic Aperture Radar

The earliest statement that Doppler-frequency analysis could be used to obtain fine cross-range resolution is attributed to Carl Wiley of the Goodyear Aircraft Corporation in June 1951. At the same time, a group at the University of Illinois [14] was conducting experimental studies which revealed that radar returns from certain terrain samples produced frequency spectra containing sharp lines. In a report dated March 1952, they noted these lines were due to strong fixed targets within the beam of the observing radar and concluded this effect could provide a radar system with greatly improved angular resolution. This group constructed an X-band radar and in early 1953 used it to produce a radar map using frequency analysis techniques to obtain high resolution in cross range. The radar that produced this map was an unfocused system; that is, there was no phase correction provided to compensate for the changing Doppler frequency [9].

In 1953, an Army summer study, called Project Wolverine, was convened at the University of Michigan for the purpose of recommending research and development programs leading to better battlefield surveillance techniques. As a part of this study, the Doppler-frequency technique was examined in more detail. Participants in this study included representatives from universities and industry, including the Universities of Illinois and Michigan, Goodyear, Philco, General Electric, and Varian. The result of this study was a development program which proceeded, under Army sponsorship, to further develop the range–Doppler radar principle.

A part of this program was to develop a practical data processor which could accept wideband signals and carry out the necessary Doppler-frequency analysis at each resolvable range interval so that a useful image could be produced. A group at the Willow Run Laboratories of the University of Michigan, under L.J. Cutrona, was assigned the problem of developing an optical computer for this purpose. Processing techniques considered by other groups included electronic processors, recirculating delay lines, and storage tubes.

In the ensuing years, the Willow Run group constructed an X-band radar and built an optical computer. The equipments were completed in the summer of 1957 and the first, fully focused SAR map was produced in August 1957. Very soon after this, the Army requested that a demonstration system be constructed. This system, the AN/UPD-1, was produced by the

Willow Run group in conjunction with Texas Instruments. Five radar systems were built and various demonstration flights were conducted in the spring of 1960 [1].

In subsequent years, the state of the art of SAR for the military was further developed by a number of organizations. Currently, a SAR is used as a standard reconnaissance tool by the Air Force. This radar system, called the UPD-4, was built by Goodyear Aerospace [15]. In late 1972, a three-wavelength SAR was included in the Apollo 17 lunar mission. The objectives of the Apollo 17 Lunar Sounder Experiment (ALSE) were to detect subsurface geologic structures, to generate a continuous lunar profile, and to image the Moon at radar wavelengths. A great deal of important data on the surface and subsurface features were gathered during this experiment [16]. During the last decade, SAR has also been applied to such diverse civilian applications as terrain mapping [17, 18], oceanography [19–21], and ice studies [22, 23]. In 1978, NASA launched the SEASAT satellite which carried an *L*-band SAR. During its relatively short life, it imaged many parts of the world and provided a great deal of important data to oceanographers and other scientists [24–26]. An example of the type of image produced by this instrument is shown in Fig. 5. NASA is continuing to develop SAR for

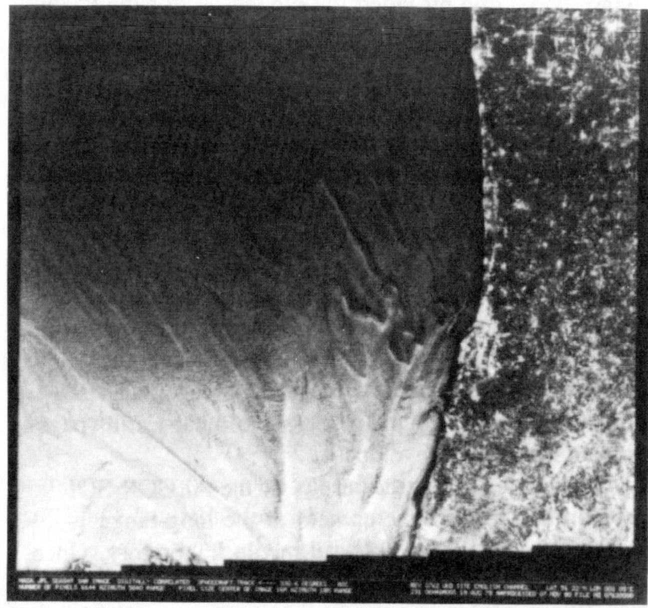

Fig. 5. A 100-km by 100-km frame from the *L*-band SEASAT SAR collected on August 19, 1978. It shows the English Channel (Strait of Dover) between Rams Gate Head on the left and the French coast in the vicinity of Dunkerque and Calais on the right. The linear features in midchannel and the distinctive surface patterns around Rams Gate Head both are the result of tidal currents flowing over sand ridges at the bottom of the channel. The ground resolution of the image is 25 × 25 m (courtesy of NASA/JPL).

space applications with its shuttle imaging radar (SIR) series. SIR-A was carried aboard the shuttle flight in November 1981 [27] and plans for subsequent flights for SIR-B and SIR-C are being carried out. In addition, the European Space Agency [28], Canada [29], and Japan [30] have announced intentions to place SARs in orbit during the next decade.

Recently, ERIM[1] has built a SAR designed to support engineering operations in the Arctic. This system, called the sea ice and terrain assessment radar (STAR), is currently being operated by Intera, Ltd., in support of two Canadian oil companies drilling in the Beaufort Sea. A block diagram of this radar and a picture of the equipment is shown in Figs. 6 and 7, respectively. The system is installed in a light twin-engine aircraft and flies mapping missions of the ice fields surrounding the drilling rigs. The data is processed in real time in the aircraft by an analog/digital processor, and the ice map is telemetered to a ground station where a mosaic of the area surrounding the drill rig is assembled. This map is used by ice experts aboard the rig to assess the ice conditions. A sample of the type of imagery produced by this system is shown in Fig. 8.

B. Radar Astronomy

Independent of the work that was being done in SAR, Green formulated the concept of delay-Doppler imaging in the 1950s with the aim of improving the resolution of the radars being used for making measurements of the Moon and planets [31, 32]. In the late 1950s, Pettingill used the technique to produce radar images of the Moon [33]. He used the Millstone Hill radar, operating coherently at 440 MHz, to produce 26 range cells of 75-km resolution each across the Moon. In each range cell, Pettingill was able to resolve Doppler frequencies to $\pm 1/10$ Hz by processing a series of pulses existing over a 10-s duration. In 1961, several organizations obtained radar echos from Venus [34–38]. In addition, radar contacts have been made with Mercury and Mars [39–42].

The planet Venus can be imaged with good sensitivity only near inferior conjunction, i.e., when Venus is approximately between the Earth and the Sun. At this distance, even the narrow beam of the National Astronomy, and Ionosphere Center's Arecibo radar, produced by the 300-m dish, has about twice the diameter of the planet; so Doppler is needed to obtain good cross-range resolution. An image of Venus using Arecibo data taken in 1975, 1977, and 1980, is shown in Fig. 9.

C. Imaging of Orbiting Objects

In the early 1960s, it was recognized that the range–Doppler technique could be applied to imaging of orbiting objects. A radar for this purpose, called the synthetic spectrum radar, was built by Westinghouse under Defense Advanced Research Projects Agency (DARPA) sponsorship. This radar was an instantaneously narrowband radar which used frequency stepping

[1]In 1973, the Willow Run Laboratories separated from the University of Michigan and became the Environmental Research Institute of Michigan (ERIM), a not-for-profit research organization.

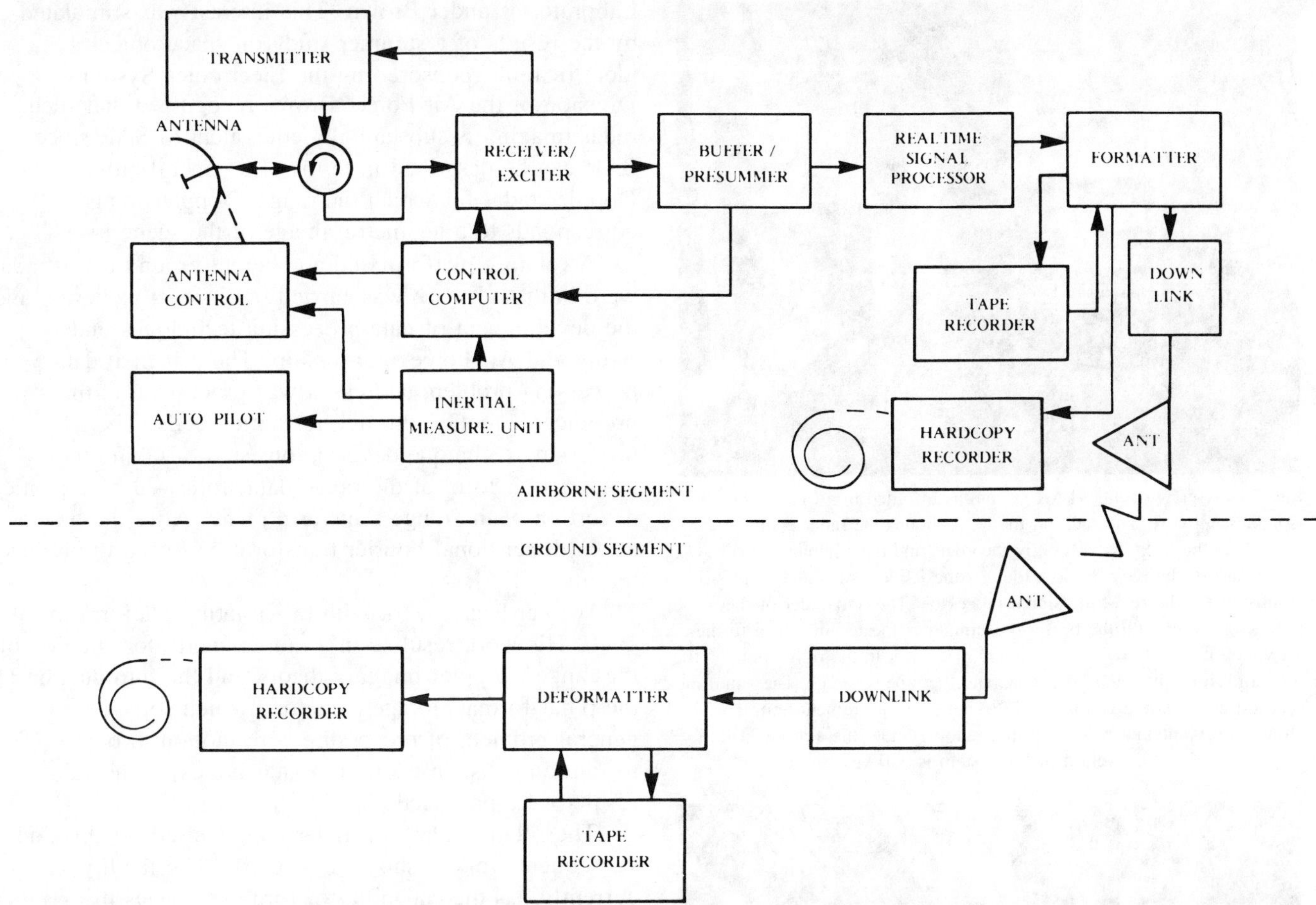

Fig. 6. Block diagram of the STAR system. The radar operates at *X* band and uses a swept YIG oscillator to generate a linear frequency-modulated pulse for transmission. The bandwidth of the pulse over 30 μsec is 15 MHz and 30 MHz for 6- and 12-m resolution, respectively. The returned pulse is compressed by a separate SAW device for each resolution. The range swath covered is 22.4 km and 44.7 km at 6- and 12-m range resolution, respectively. The azimuth compression is performed by the digital real-time signal processor which produces seven 6-m resolution images which are incoherently superimposed. These data are sent via a downlink to a ground station where the stripmap is recorded on film and on a tape recorder. The image data are also recorded aboard the aircraft.

techniques to achieve a wide bandwidth. In the late 1960s, Rome Air Development Center (RADC) developed the Floyd Site radar for imaging orbiting objects. This radar was built by General Electric and the processing techniques were developed by Syracuse Research Corporation.

A 94-GHz radar for space object identification (SOI) was constructed by Aerosapce Corporation in the 1960s. This radar has a 1-GHz bandwidth and produces a time–bandwidth of 10^6 using a 1-ms pulse length [43].

The first high-quality images of near-Earth space objects were obtained in the early 1970s using data collected by the ARPA, Lincoln Laboratory, *C*-band, observables radar (ALCOR). These data were processed by Lincoln Laboratories and the Syracuse Research Corporation. Even though ALCOR was not designed for radar imaging, successful results were made possible by the 50-cm range resolution, by coherent data recording, and by sufficient sensitivity to image low altitude satellites.

In the middle 1970s, the success of the early ALCOR results persuaded DARPA to sponsor an SOI program at Lincoln Laboratories. Included in this program were

upgrades to the ALCOR radar, such as an increase in PRF to 200 Hz and the ability to record pulse compressed data in up to three adjacent 30-m range windows. Data acquisition procedures and range–Doppler image processing efforts for many classes of near-Earth space objects were fully developed.

In the late 1970s, the results of the ALCOR SOI program led to the development of the long-range imaging radar (LRIR) [11] at Lincoln Laboratory. Once the LRIR became operational, significant image processing developments were achieved. The LRIR is an *X*-band radar with a bandwidth which is 10 percent of the center frequency. It was specifically designed to be able to image satellites at synchronous range. The wide bandwidth allows for 25-cm range resolution, and the maximum PRF of about 1000 Hz allows for imaging of rapidly rotating space objects and provides added imaging sensitivity.

Significant progress was made in the late 1970s and early 1980s in processing data from the LRIR. A technique called extended coherent processing (ECP) was developed. ECP is an efficient general imaging technique which speeds up processing of image data and allows

Fig. 7. A view of the STAR system as installed in a Cessna 441 Conquest aircraft. The rack on the left contains the radar control computer, the VISOR hard copy recorder, and the antenna control. The lower part of the rack in the middle is the RF and mounted atop is the controller for the real-time signal processor. The remainder of the processor along with the buffer/presummer is located in a rack further aft which is not shown in the picture. The rack to the right contains the downlink formatter, the downlink, and the tape recorder. The small rack forward contains the Litton LTN-76 inertial measurement unit. The slotted array antenna is located in a radome under the aircraft. Total weight of the system is 340 kg.

Fig. 8. STAR imagery of an area in western Pennsylvania, south of Altoona, shows the radar's 6- by 12-m resolution wide swath mode (44.7 km). The sensor was flown at a 26 000-ft altitude. Evitts Mountain and Dunning Mountain are the ridges running south to north on the left; to the right (east of these) is the Juniata River.

carrying out new applications such as wide-angle imaging, stroboscopic imaging, and three-dimensional imaging.

D. Rotating Platform Imaging

In the early 1960s, work began in the development of techniques for imaging rotating objects at the Willow Run

Laboratories under Brown. This interest was stimulated by the results of a summer study on space object identification sponsored by the Electronics Systems Division of the Air Force. Brown recognized that such radar imaging is substantially equivalent to SAR since SAR can be described in terms of a general pulse-Doppler radar for which the range–Doppler image corresponds to a geometric image of the scene [44].

A rotating platform and a coherent ground-based radar were built and work was carried out in data gathering and the development of data-processing techniques under Army and Air Force sponsorship. The principal data-processing problem addressed was processing in the presence of motion through resolution cells. The processing technique devised consisted of taking the Fourier transform of the range data, followed by a gentle distortion of the range transform plane. After these steps, a two-dimensional Fourier transform was used to produce the image [45].

Walker began work with this rotating platform in 1970. His work resulted in a more general formulation of the range–Doppler imaging theory and the introduction of the polar-format storage technique which solved the general problem of processing with motion through resolution cells. In addition, extensive experimental results were produced [5].

The rotating platform radar facility used for this and subsequent work is shown in Fig. 10. The facility currently has the capability of forming images using radar illumination at a center frequency of 10 GHz, 35 GHz, and 94 GHz. A radar image of a vehicle produced by the facility, along with an optical image, is shown in Fig. 11 [46].

In addition to the work just discussed, Mensa et al. [47, 48] at the pacific Missile Test Center and a group under Wehner at Naval Ocean Systems Center have worked on imaging of rotating objects [49], as have Chen and Andrews [50, 51]. Recently, a number of authors have studied the relation between techniques used in tomography and range–Doppler imaging [52–54]. Their conclusion is that range–Doppler imaging can be analyzed using the projection-slice theorem from computer-aided tomography (CAT). Conversely, it has been suggested that processing techniques borrowed from tomography may advance the state of radar processing techniques [55].

III. RANGE–DOPPLER IMAGING FUNDAMENTALS

In Section I, we introduced the basic concept of using range and Doppler (range–rate) time signals to provide two-dimensional images of a rigid object field. In this section, we develop in more detail the principles of range–Doppler imaging of rotating objects to serve as a background for subsequent discussions of general imaging radar configurations. The fundamentals presented here involve a three-dimensional imaging geometry with separate (bistatic) transmitting and receiving antennas moving along arbitrary trajectories. Important special

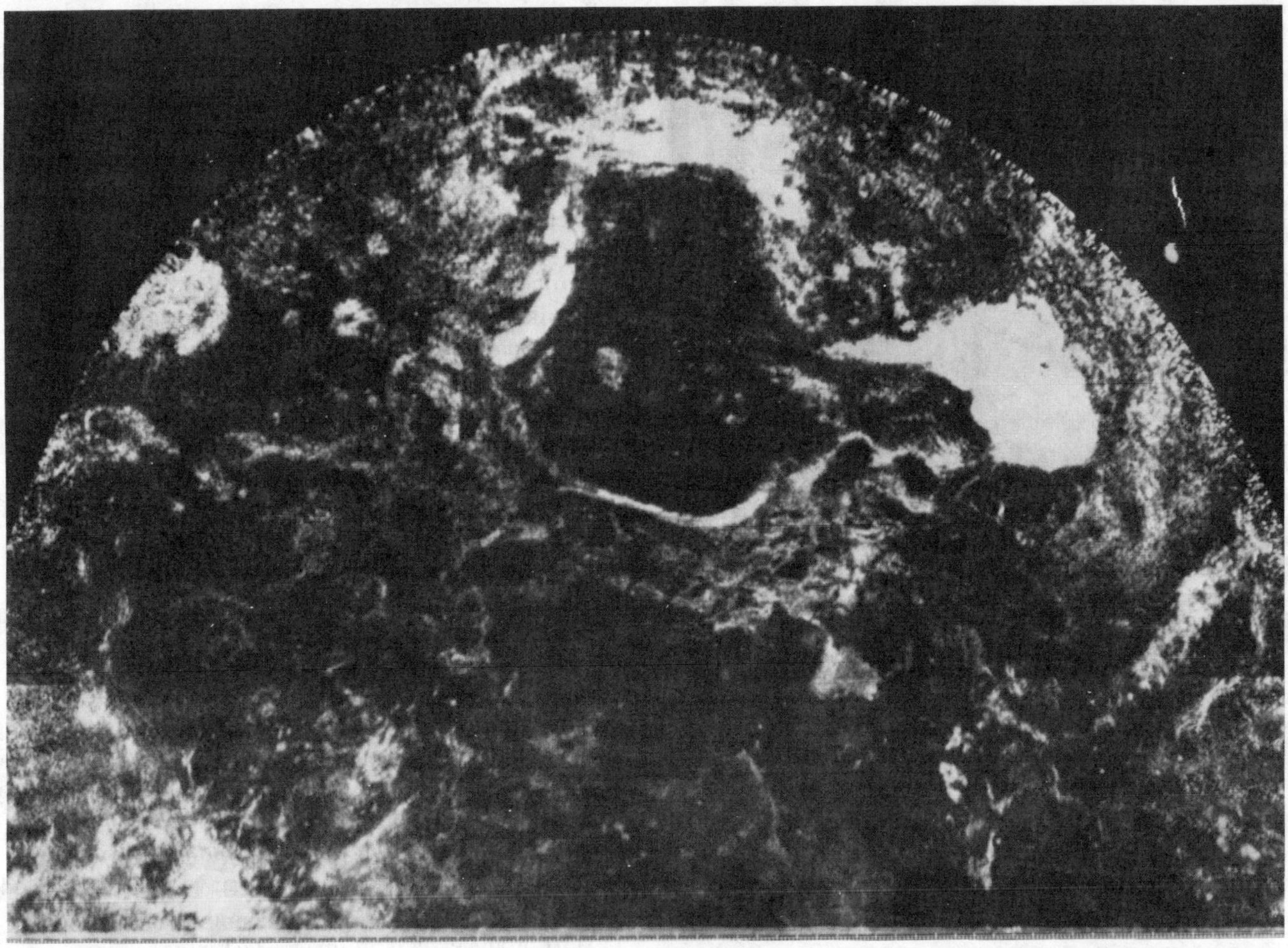

Fig. 9. Radar imagery of the surface of Venus reveals the varied and complex nature of its surface terrain. This mosaic was obtained with the 12.6-cm radar interferometer of the National Astronomy and Ionosphere Center and covers the area from 30°N to 70°N latitude and from 100°W to 40°E longitude. The large radar-dark pear-shaped feature at top center is Planum Lakshmi, a broad flat plateau surrounded by steep scarps. The very bright feature to its right is Maxwell Montes, which measures 750 km north to south and includes the planet's highest evaluation, 11 km above the planetary mean (courtesy D.B. Campbell, NAIC).

Fig. 10. Rotating platform radar facility uses separate transmitting and receiving horns shown located on the tower. The tower is located about 40 m from the platform which is about 6 m in diameter and has a rotation period of 168 s. The radar transmitter and receiver are located inside the building.

cases such as stripmap SAR, spotlight SAR, and space-object imaging with a fixed radar are treated in Section IV.

A. General Three-Dimensional Radar Imaging

In this section, we consider a more general range–Doppler imaging situation involving a bistatic transmitter/receiver configuration and a three-dimensional rigid object as shown in Fig. 12. Both the object and the antennas can have arbitrary motion, although only the relative motion of the scatterers with respect to the antennas is important for the radar imaging methods considered here. For vehicle-borne terrain imaging radars, this motion is often measured by means of inertial navigation-based systems and supplemented by data-derived motion estimates as required. For ground-based space-object imaging radars, the motion is usually derived by fitting radar data to obtain precise models which describe the object's orbital and rotational motion.

The fundamental task of a radar imaging system is to estimate the reflectivity σ of each element of the object as a function of the spatial coordinate r_0. That is, the

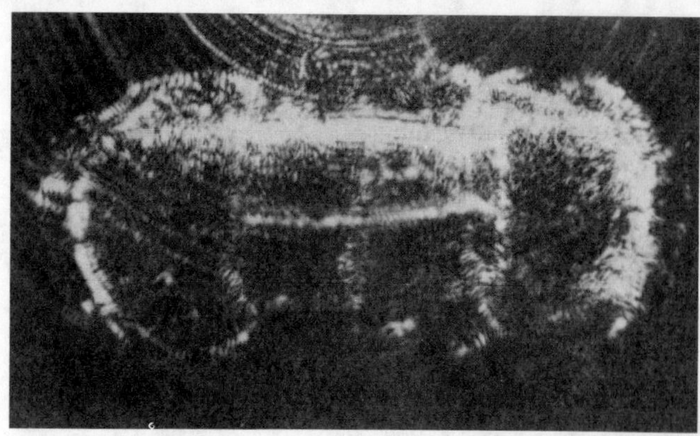

Fig. 11. Rotating platform radar image and optical image of a Volkswagen. The radar image is a superposition of data obtained over a 360° rotation of the table.

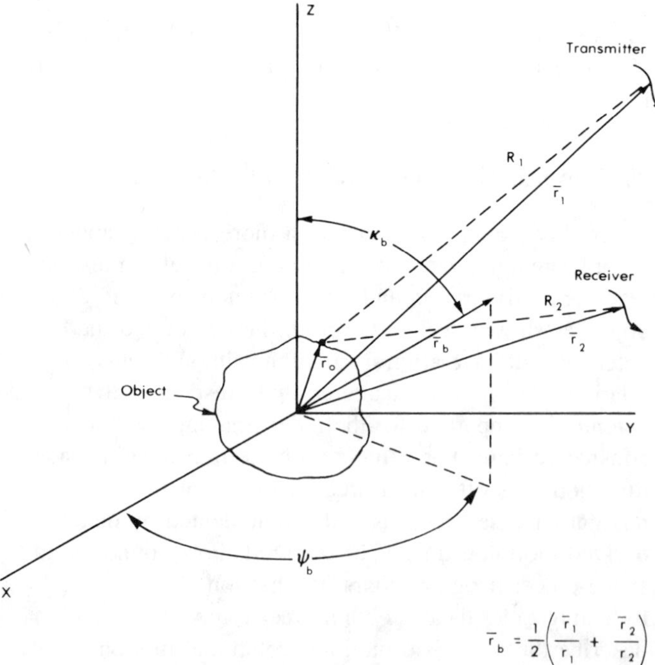

$$\bar{r}_b = \frac{1}{2}\left(\frac{\bar{r}_1}{r_1} + \frac{\bar{r}_2}{r_2} \right)$$

Fig. 12. Three-dimensional radar imaging geometry showing bisector vector. (Symbols with overbars correspond to boldface symbols in text.)

reflectivity function is to be approximated by an image function $G(r_0)$ which is calculated from the returned radar signals. Because of the limitations of the radar data, the function $G(r_0)$ will be a blurred representation of $\sigma(r_0)$. This blurring is characterized by the "point target response" function, $h(r_0)$, which is the image function $G(r_0)$ calculated from the signal returned from an isolated point scatterer.

To achieve good image quality, it is important that $|h|$ have its maximum value over r_0 corresponding to the location of the point scatterer and have as sharp a peak as possible with low sidelobes. In general, objects of interest contain many elemental scatterers and, under the assumption of linearity, the image G can be represented as a superposition of point target response functions.

For a transmitted signal $s(t)$, the signal received from a point scatterer is

$$s_r(t) = \sigma s \left(t - \frac{R_1 + R_2}{c} \right) \tag{13}$$

where $R_1 + R_2$ is the time-varying two-way range to the object point, and σ is the reflectivity associated with the point. An image of the object can be achieved if $R_1 + R_2$ is a different function of time for each point on the object. In principle, the total received signal from all scattering elements of the object can be cross correlated with a set of reference functions of the form given by (13) to produce such an image, $G(r_0)$.

In practice, various approximations and limiting assumptions are often made which have led to a number of different methods for processing the received radar data to form an image of the scene. For example, in Section I, we discussed the conventional range–Doppler approximation for a two-dimensional rotating scene (where the RLOS was perpendicular to the rotation axis) and showed that y_0 and x_0 were directly related to range and range–rate measurements made over sufficiently small time intervals which leads to a relatively simple range and Doppler-frequency analysis type of signal processor.

In this section, we consider larger coherent processing time intervals in order to achieve fine resolution over large scenes, and therefore, more general image formation methods are required. All of the image formation methods described are based on the same fundamental process of measuring range and changes in range to produce image resolution. Some are distinguished from one another by virture of the different approximations which are made to minimize hardware complexity and/or maximize processing speed. Others are merely different mathematical formulations of the same fundamental technique such as time-domain (spatial-domain) versus frequency-domain analysis. We have not attempted herein to provide a complete taxonomy of radar image formation techniques but will review four representative methods to serve as a background for the more detailed description of radar imaging techniques in Section IV.

(1) *Pulse-by-Pulse Correlation Imaging.* The cross-correlation image function $G(r_0)$, calculated over a set of discrete pulses of radar data, using (13) as the reference signal, can be written as a sum of single-pulse cross-correlation functions. The cross-correlation function for the pth pulse can be expressed very simply as a phase-corrected pulse-compressed radar return sampled at the bistatic range $R(r_0, p) = (R_1 + R_2)/2$ to the point r_0 in the object (see Fig. 12). To permit this simple calculation, the pulse-compression system should be configured to give a response from a point scatterer located at r_0 which has the constant phase $[4\pi R(r_0, p/\lambda + \text{constant}]$ across the main peak of the response. The additive constant can be ignored. From such a pulse-compression system, the response from a point scatterer at range R_s would have the form $S[R] = A(R - R_s)$ $\exp[j4\pi R_s/\lambda]$, where $A(R - R_s)$ is a real function with its peak at $R = R_s$. The usual practical implementation of pulse compression for a chirp waveform results in a weak quadratic dependence of phase on the sampling range R. We assume such effects to be negligible. For convenience, the pulse-compressed signal is calibrated so that a point scatterer's radar cross section (RCS) is given by the peak value of A^2.

Under the above circumstances, the cross-correlation function over the set of pulses $\{p\}$ is given by

$$G(r_0) = \sum_{\{p\}} W(p)S[R(r_0, p)] \exp[-j4\pi R(r_0, p)/\lambda]. \qquad (14)$$

For each point r_0, the range is calculated from the known motion of the object, the transmitter, and the receiver at the time on target $t(p)$ of the pth pulse. The symbol $S[R(r_0, p)]$ denotes the pulse-compressed return sampled at the calculated range $R(r_0, p)$. This calculated range also determines the phase correction in (14). The real weights $W(p)$ can be used in various ways to optimize the image quality. They can be used to suppress cross-range sidelobes. If data from multiple target rotations are used, they can, in some cases, be selected to suppress cross-range ambiguous images. The weights are normalized $\sum W(p) = 1$ so that in the image of a point scatterer, the peak value of $|G|^2$ is the scatterer's RCS.

Except for the effects of sidelobe suppression weights used in pulse compression and the possibly nonuniform weights $W(p)$ in (14), this function $G(r_0)$ optimizes the signal-to-noise ratio for detecting a scatterer at r_0. It also does well in separating scatterers from each other if the point target response function $h(r_0)$ has low sidelobes and a single sharp peak within the extent of the object. Since the function $G(r_0)$ is linear in the received signal, the effects of the scatterers in the target are linearly superposed in the complex function G. If signal saturation is avoided and the signal quantization step is small compared with the noise, the only nonlinear effects to confuse the image are those that occur physically in the scattering of the signal from the object, such as shadowing and multiple scattering.

For image processing, it is convenient to rewrite (14) in terms of the relative range

$$D(p) = D(r_0, p) = R(r_0, t) - R(0, t) \qquad (15)$$

where 0 is the origin of the displacement vector r_0. In Fig. 12, 0 is the origin of the x, y, z coordinate system, and $R(0, t) = (|r_1| + |r_2|)/2$. This coordinate system origin can be any convenient point in the object. In terms of $D(p)$, (14) becomes

$$G(r_0) = \sum_{\{p\}} W(p)\tilde{S}[D(p)] \exp[-j4\pi D(p)/\lambda] \qquad (16)$$

where

$$\tilde{S}[D(p)] = S[R(r_0, p)] \exp[-j4\pi R(0, p)/\lambda]. \qquad (17)$$

The formulation of $G(r_0)$ in terms of the relative range separates out the phase corrections depending on ranges to the origin of the coordinate system origin (17) from those depending on aspect (16). The term *aspect* denotes an orientation of the RLOS relative to the target. If the radar is bistatic, the aspect depends on the orientations of both lines of sight relative to the target, i.e., the orientation of the bisector vector r_0 shown in Fig. 12. The remainder of this paragraph discusses only the monostatic case, but similar conclusions can be reached in the bistatic case. That the phase corrections in (16) depend only on aspect can be understood by noting that, since imaging object sizes are usually much smaller than radar ranges, the far-field approximation of electromagnetic scattering theory is valid. In this case, the relative range $D(r_0)$ is given, to an excellent approximation, by the scalar product between the vector (r_0) and the unit vector along the RLOS direction. Consequently, for a given point (r_0), $D(r_0)$ depends only on aspect.

Furthermore, it is well known that radar returns at one far-field range and at a given target aspect can be predicted from returns measured at other far-field ranges, at the same aspect, by making a phase correction for the range difference. The calibration of $|S(p)|^2$ to give the RCS includes the usual range-squared amplitude correction. Thus the returns $\tilde{S}(p)$ obtained from calculating (17) would be the same regardless of the ranges at which the returns $S(p)$ were obtained. Consequently, one can conclude that the properties of $G(r_0)$ depend mainly on the target aspects sampled by the data and (to a lesser extent) on the weights $W(p)$ used in calculating the image.

It can be shown that the formulation of the image function in (14) is equivalent to the backprojection processing method [54], a common tool in the field of CAT. The backprojection algorithm applied to a coherent imaging system forms an image via a coherent summation (for each resolvable image element) of samples of multiple functions representing the total reflectivity of the scene as projected onto the line of sight to the scene.

Thus the backprojection algorithm is equivalent to the operation implied by (16), where $S(p) \exp[-j4\pi D(p)/\lambda]$ is the projected reflectivity of the scene. The phase adjustment is required to account for the propagation effects associated with measuring projected reflectivity from a remote location.

(2) *Multiple-Subaperture Processing.* Equation (14) can be used in principle to calculate well-focused images of scenes or objects of arbitrary dimensions, using arbitrarily long coherent data intervals. In many practical applications, however, the pulse-by-pulse correlation imaging method, which is computationally inefficient, can be reliably replaced by a more efficient method known either as subaperture image processing in spotlight SAR applications, or as extended coherent processing in rotating space-object applications.

In this method, the sum over pulses is replaced by a coherent sum of conventional range–Doppler images calculated over smaller subintervals of the total coherent processing data. The size of these subintervals (subapertures) is chosen to be sufficiently small that no motion through resolution cells occurs for their duration. With subintervals of such size, the range–Doppler images can be calculated by FFT processing, which is at least one order of magnitude faster than pulse-by-pulse processing.

The subimages are subsequently aligned in range and range–rate to account for the relative motion of scatterers occurring between separate subintervals. The extended image is obtained by coherently summing all aligned subimages.

A more detailed description of the structure of such an algorithm is presented in Section IVB dealing with imaging of rotating space objects.

(3) *Multiple-Subpatch Processing.* As was described previously, the migration of points through resolution cells can be avoided if one chooses sufficiently small coherent processing time intervals and/or if the object size is sufficiently small. The previously described multiple subaperture method relies on a sequence of conventional range–Doppler processing operations over short time intervals followed by a coherent summation to form the final image. Similarly, one can achieve fine resolution over scenes larger than those permitted by the inequalities (11) and (12) if the large scene is divided into an array of smaller subpatches. We then compensate for the motion between the radar and the center of each subpatch, and the situation reduces to the case of an array of smaller rotating scenes.

The division of the large scene into smaller scenes involves dividing the range extent of the target field into a number of subswaths and partitioning the total Doppler spectrum into a number of frequency sub-bands followed by the usual Doppler-frequency analysis of each sub-band to form the final set of subimages. One particular implementation of this method has been called a two-stage FFT [56] or, more generally, the multiple-subpatch approach. In any case, by choosing the diameter D of the subpatches to be

$$D \le 4\rho^2/\lambda \tag{18}$$

an image of the entire scene with resolution ρ can be achieved by a final mosaicking operation.

In practice, the multiple-subpatch method is most applicable to vehicle-borne radar imaging of large scenes. An example of how this method can be implemented for processing spotlight mode radar data is described in Section IV.

(4). *Polar Format Processing.* Another method [5] for dealing with the problem of motion through resolution cells involves interpreting the radar data in an appropriate three-dimensional spatial frequency space. The radar pulses are first converted to a range-frequency form (Fourier transform of compressed range data) which correspond to polar line segments in the three-dimensional frequency space of the target. Each segment is oriented according to the angular coordinates of the radar at the time of transmission. Depending on the relative motion of the radar and target during the time that a sequence of pulses is transmitted, a portion of the three-dimensional frequency space is collected (usually a curved surface). An image of the target can then be formed by taking a three-dimensional Fourier transform of the collected data.

The fundamental features of this method can be derived by observing that for each compressed range pulse $u(t)$, the complex signal received from a target field is given by

$$s_r(t) = \int_v \sigma(r_0) u\left(t - \frac{R_1 + R_2}{c}\right) dr_0 \tag{19}$$

where $R_1 + R_2$ is the two-way range to the differential scattering volume element dr_0, located at r_0, as shown in Fig. 12, and where $\sigma(r_0)$ is the reflectivity density and, for convenience, includes two-way propagation effects and various system gains. The integration is carried out over the volume of the target.

If we take the Fourier transform of this range data,

$$S_r(f) = \int s_r(t) \exp[-j2\pi ft] \, dt \tag{20}$$

we obtain

$$S_r(f) = \int_v \sigma(r_0) U(f) \exp\left[-j\frac{2\pi f}{c}(R_1 + R_2)\right] dr_0 \tag{21}$$

where $U(f)$ represents the non-negative frequency response in range. Furthermore, we have assumed that $R_1 + R_2$ does not change significantly during a range pulse.

The time-varying effects of the two-way range ($r_1 + r_2$) to the origin can be removed by multiplying the received signal with a reference function proportional to

$$M_{\text{ref}} = \exp\left[+j2\pi f\left(\frac{r_1 + r_2}{c}\right)\right]. \tag{22}$$

This represents the fundamental motion compensation step of the radar imaging system and, as is discussed later, must be performed with great precision to produce high-quality imagery. If the ranges to the transmitter and receiver (r_1 and r_2) are large compared with the size of the object, we can let

$$R_1 = |\mathbf{r}_1 - \mathbf{r}_0| \approx r_1 - \mathbf{r}_0 \cdot \frac{\mathbf{r}_1}{r_1} \qquad (23)$$

$$R_2 = |\mathbf{r}_2 - \mathbf{r}_0| \approx r_2 - \mathbf{r}_0 \cdot \frac{\mathbf{r}_2}{r_2} \qquad (24)$$

and the resulting range-frequency data can then be expressed as

$$S_r(f) \exp\left[+j2\pi f\left(\frac{r_1 + r_2}{c}\right)\right]$$

$$= U(f) \int_v \sigma(\mathbf{r}_0) \exp\left(+j\frac{4\pi f}{c}\mathbf{r}_b \cdot \mathbf{r}_0\right) d\mathbf{r}_0 \qquad (25)$$

where $\mathbf{r}_b$ is the transmitter/receiver bisector vector as indicated in Fig. 12 and is given by

$$\mathbf{r}_b = \frac{1}{2}\left(\frac{\mathbf{r}_1}{r_1} + \frac{\mathbf{r}_2}{r_2}\right). \qquad (26)$$

We have assumed that the antennas are moving relative to the object and that therefore $\mathbf{r}_b$ varies slowly from pulse to pulse.

An examination of (25) indicates that each radar pulse produces a polar line segment of the three-dimensional Fourier transform of the target reflectivity function $\sigma(\mathbf{r}_0)$ by proper interpretation of frequency space. That is, we can define a three-dimensional spatial frequency variable $\mathbf{f}$ as

$$\mathbf{f} = \frac{2f}{c}\mathbf{r}_b. \qquad (27)$$

This implies that the radar data for a sequence of pulses can be represented in three-dimensional frequency space as

$$S(\mathbf{f}) = H(\mathbf{f}) \int_v \sigma(\mathbf{r}_0) \exp[+j2\pi\mathbf{r}_0 \cdot \mathbf{f}] d\mathbf{r}_0 \qquad (28)$$

where $H(\mathbf{f})$ is the three-dimensional aperture function. The effective length of each polar line segment of the aperture is determined by the bandwidth of the transmitted signal $U(f)$. As the radar observes the target from different aspects (ψ_b, κ_b), indicated in Fig. 12, $\mathbf{f}$ maps out a surface in three-dimensional space which constitutes the complete three-dimensional aperture function of the imaging system.

The bistatic path shown in Fig. 13(a) is determined by the pointing direction of the bisector vector $\mathbf{r}_b$ as the transmitting and receiving antennas move along their trajectories. For the monostatic spotlight mode case, the bistatic path then reduces to the path of the vehicle carrying the spotlight radar and $\mathbf{r}_b$ corresponds to the RLOS.

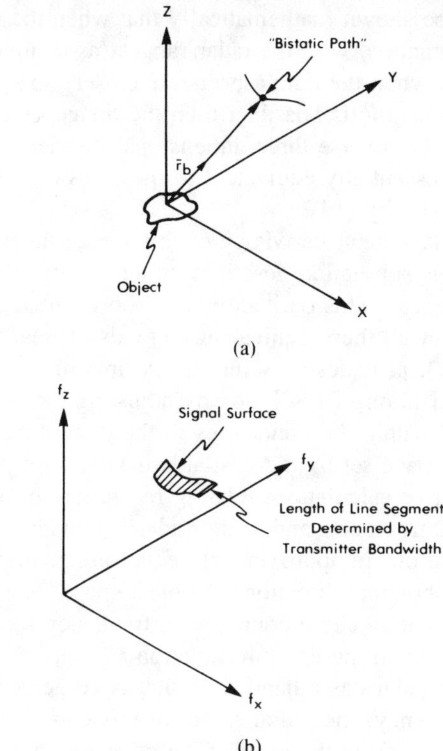

Fig. 13. Signal surface in frequency space corresponding to changes in aspect angle during radar data collection. (a) Object space. (b) Frequency space.

An image of the target, i.e., an estimate of $\sigma(\mathbf{r}_0)$, is achieved by carrying out an inverse Fourier transform of $S(\mathbf{f})$. The image G resulting from this operation was indicated previously as being characterized by the point target response function h which is the three-dimensional Fourier transform of $H(\mathbf{f})$. Ideally, h should have a very narrow extent in all three dimensions, i.e., a three-dimensional delta function which would imply that the aperture function H should be unity over the entire frequency space. This occurs only in the limit where an infinite bandwidth signal is transmitted and returns are collected over all aspect angles ($0 \leq \psi_b \leq 2\pi$, $0 \leq \kappa_b \leq \pi$).

In practical cases, only a small portion of the frequency space is observed, as is depicted in Fig. 13(b), with the attendent limitation on the point target response in each dimension. For example, straight line flight paths produce planar data collection surfaces and the general three-dimensional processing problem reduces to a two-dimensional Fourier transformation with a resulting two-dimensional image of the object, i.e., no resolution in the direction normal to the collection plane. A wide variety of radar configurations [57] can be envisioned for observing other portions of the three-dimensional frequency space; e.g., a stationary two-dimensional array of mutually coherent wideband radars would generate samples in a volume and a single moving continuous wave (CW) radar would sample the frequency space only along a curve.

It can be shown mathematically that when the object is small comapred with the radar ranges (as assumed above) and when the data aspects are closely spaced so that good imaging is possible, then the image function, defined as the inverse three-dimensional Fourier transform of $S(f)$, is essentially equivalent to the cross correlation function given by (14).

The independent derivation of this image function given in this subsection describes an alternative way to form the image. This derivation also shows the resolution properties of all these equivalent methods of image formation. It provides a useful context in which to deal with optimization of resolution by adjusting the weighting function H within the boundaries in the three-dimensional frequency space set by the available data. It also permits quick iterative calculations relating resolution to the available data aspects and to the radar bandwidth. For example, to obtain approximately equal image resolutions in three orthogonal directions in object space, one needs an approximately cubic boundary in frequency space outside of which the aperture function H vanishes. If a monostatic radar has a bandwidth that is 10 percent of the center frequency, the radial extent of this cube is a tenth of its distance from the origin. The other two dimensions of the cube must correspond approximately to a solid angle of aspects measuring 0.1 rad by 0.1 rad.

As an illustration of the three-dimensional processing concept for the rotating object case (mathematically equivalent to a fixed object and moving antenna), let us consider an object consisting of three point scatterers as indicated in Fig. 14(a). The resulting "three-dimensional image" for the three object points is also indicated in Fig. 14(c) as three cone-like distributions whose points of concentration correspond to the locations of the object points (2 on the x,y plane and 1 above). If we project the data stored on the conical surface onto the f_x, f_y plane in frequency space as shown in Fig. 14(d) and follow with a two-dimensional Fourier transform, we obtain the image shown in Fig. 14(e). By the projection-slice theorem [54], this is equivalent to an x,y plane slice in three-dimensional image space.

Although a three-dimensional data collection and processing approach can be used to obtain images of three-dimensional objects free from degradations caused by motion through resolution cells even in very general radar configurations, two-dimensional processing approaches are often desirable for practical implementations. This stems in part from processing speed considerations and the operational difficulty in obtaining video signal samples over a large volume of processor space.

Two-dimensional processing is optimum when the relative radar/object motion is such that the bistatic vector r_b remains in a plane and/or if the object points to be imaged lie on a plane. In the latter case, the three-dimensional data are projected onto the plane containing the object points selected for optimum focus, as shown in Fig. 14(d). Scattering centers of the object which are located out of the selected compensation plane sometimes called the focused target plane (FTP) will be degraded in the final image. This degradation is expected from projection-slice considerations or by observing that the

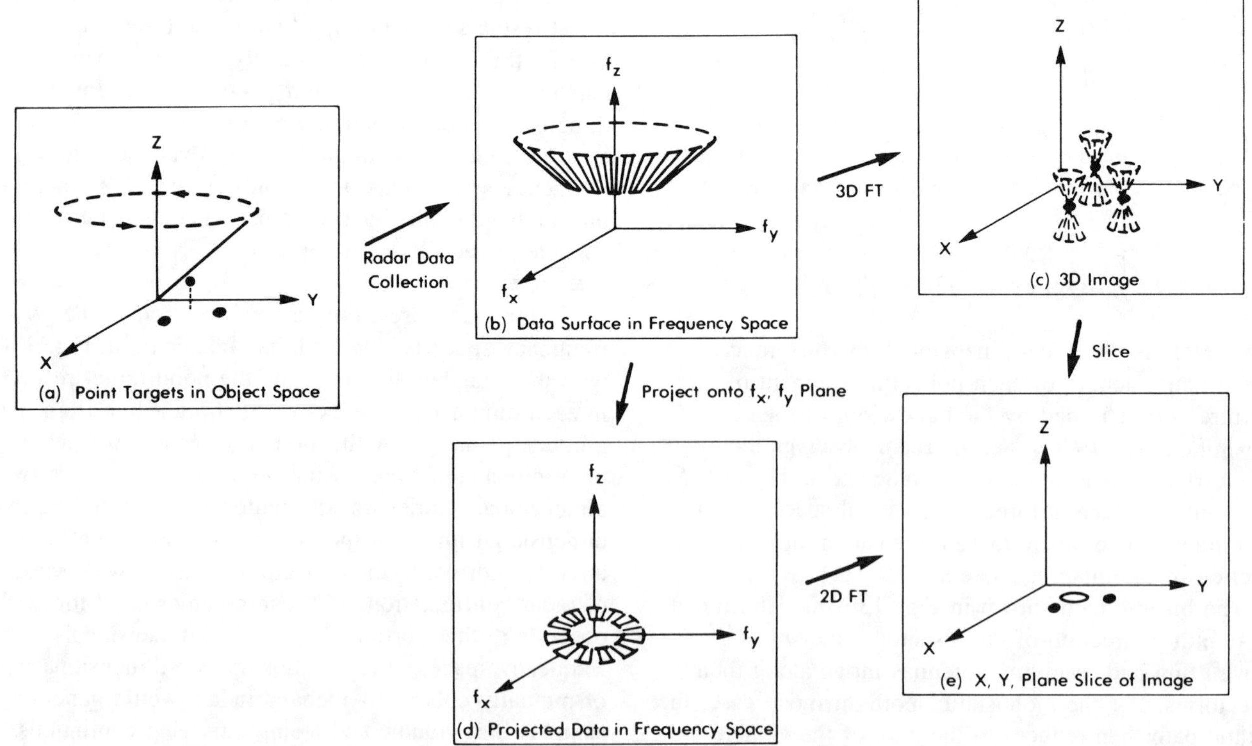

Fig. 14. Illustration of the three-dimensional processing concept. (a) Point targets in object space. (b) Data surface in frequency space. (c) Three-dimensional image. (d) Projected data in frequency space. (e) $X - Y$ plane slice of image.

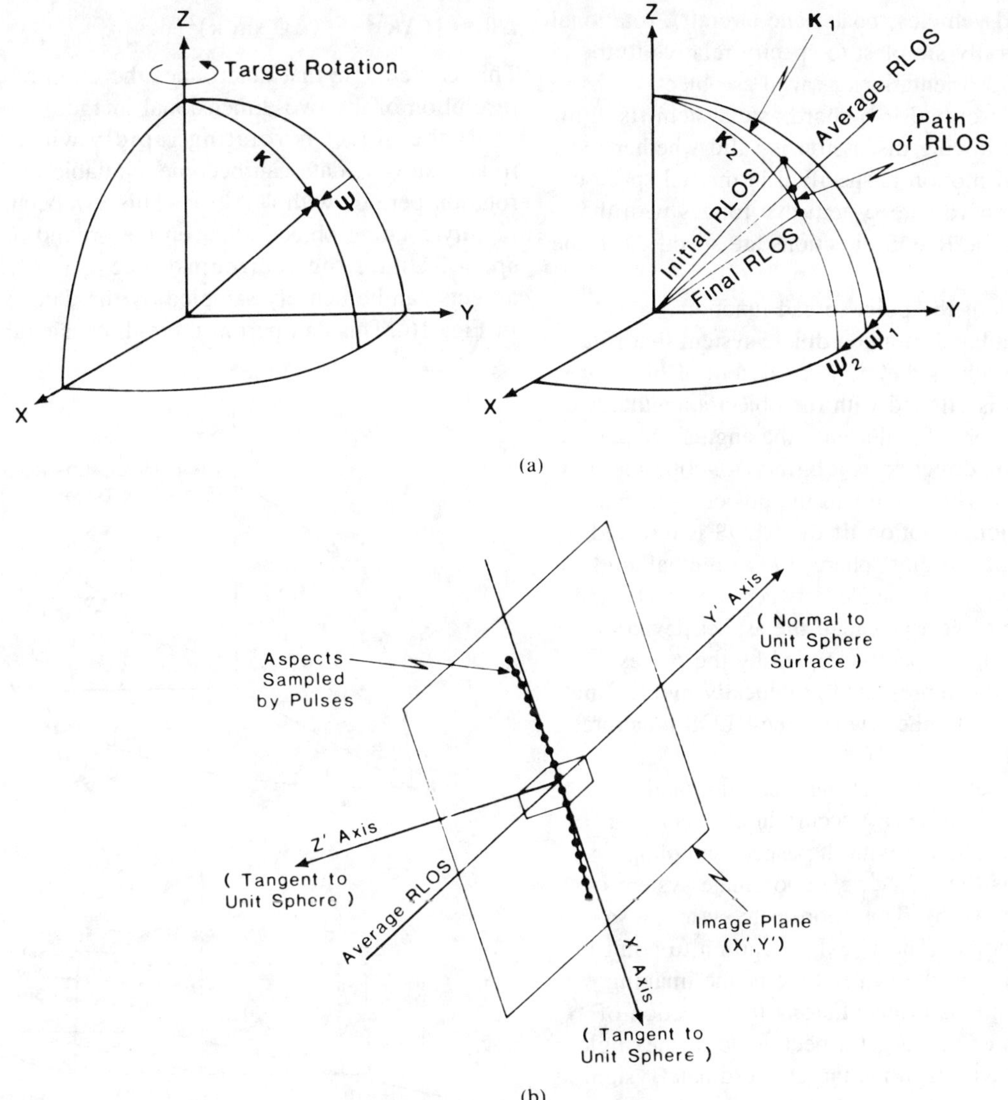

Fig. 15. (a) Target aspects sampled by RLOS when both κ and ψ change a few degrees. $\Delta\kappa = \kappa_2 - \kappa_1$, $\Delta\psi = \psi_2 - \psi_1$, $\Delta\theta = [(\Delta\kappa)^2 + (\Delta\kappa \sin\kappa)^2]^{1/2}$. (b) Detail enlargement from Fig. 16(a) at aspects sampled on surface of unit sphere. Dots represent pulse aspects.

relative spacing of the three-dimensional fringe structure in frequency space associated with each object point is preserved after projection only for points located on the compensation plane.

B. Properties of Three-Dimensional Radar Images

In this subsection, we discuss in more detail some of the important properties of radar images calculated using the methods described above. Specifically, we emphasize the dependence of the point spread function on the target aspects which are sampled by the radar pulses. Important properties include cross-range resolution and the spacing of cross-range ambiguous images. The results are applicable to monostatic radars or to bistatic radars with small bistatic angles. For small bistatic angles, the equivalent monostatic RLOS bisects the bistatic angle. This subsection also assumes the object to be small compared with the radar range.

(1) Dependence on Observed Target Aspects. As emphasized previously, the properties of an image depend mainly on aspects sampled by the pulses used in calculating the images. When the radar samples a planar angle of target aspects, the image will necessarily be two dimensional. When the radar densely samples a solid angle of target aspects, the image will be three dimensional. The aspects sampled depend on the rotational motion (if any) of the object as well as on the orientation of the RLOS and its variation with time. They also depend on the subsets of radar pulses chosen for imaging.

For a space object, it is generally convenient to deal with object rotations and RLOS rotations relative to the distant stars, i.e., relative to "inertial space." Artificial satellites as well as natural objects in the solar system generally rotate with a constant angular velocity vector in inertial space. For objects in the Earth's atmosphere (including stationary scenes, objects on rotating platforms, ground vehicles, boats, and aircraft), rotational motions are generally simplest to specify relative to the Earth. Thus RLOS orientations as well as object orientations are described in a coordinate system fixed in the Earth. The following discussion is valid whether the object's rotational motion is specified in inertial space or in a background coordinate system that rotates with the Earth, as long as the RLOS directions are specified in the same way.

The properties of the point spread function h are conveniently calculated in a coordinate system that rotates with the object, such as the (x, y, z) system of Fig. 15(a). The z axis is aligned with the object's angular velocity vector. (For a fixed scene, the angular velocity is zero and the z-axis direction is arbitrary.) Define the unit sphere to be fixed with respect to the object so it shares the object's rotational motion. If the RLOS is directed along the radius of the unit sphere, the azimuthal angle ψ and the polar angle κ, the angle between the RLOS and the angular velocity vector, called the aspect deviation angle, will define the aspects sampled by the pulses. Also, aspects can be represented graphically by drawing the points on the unit sphere where the RLOS punctures the spherical surface.

The simplest description of the resolution and ambiguity properties of h (r_0) occurs in a rectangular coordinate system aligned with the aspect sampling geometry, such as the (x', y', z') coordinate system of Fig. 15(b) or Fig. 16(b). This coordinate system also rotates with the target. The y' axis is chosen to point in the RLOS direction at the center time of the imaging interval. The x' axis is oriented along the direction of increasing values of the target aspect angle θ, the angle swept out by the RLOS in the target coordinate system at the image center time. The rate of change of θ, $\dot{\theta}$, equals the magnitude of the RLOS angular velocity vector relative to the target

$$\dot{\theta} = [(\dot{\kappa})^2 + (\dot{\psi} \sin \kappa)^2]^{1/2} \qquad (29)$$

where $\dot{\kappa}$ and $\dot{\psi}$ are the rates of change of the angles κ and ψ, respectively.

The (x', y') plane is thus tangent to the surface swept out in the target coordinate system by the RLOS. The second cross-range direction is chosen perpendicular to this plane so as to complete a right-hand coordinate system.

The RLOS's are approximately coplanar with respect to the object if the changes in the angles ψ and κ, $\Delta\psi \approx \dot{\psi} \Delta T$ and $\Delta\kappa \approx \dot{\kappa}\Delta T$, respectively, are small. When the RLOS directions are coplanar with respect to the object, the images will necessarily be two dimensional in nature. The radar returns will not be affected by the z' coordinate of any scatterer so the function $G(r_0)$ cannot depend on z'. For the two-dimensional case then, the cross-range axis x' will be oriented along the direction of increasing values of the angle θ, such that during the imaging interval ΔT, from (29),

$$\Delta\theta \approx [(\Delta\kappa)^2 + (\Delta\psi \sin \kappa)^2]^{1/2}. \qquad (30)$$

This is the angle that determines the cross-range (x') resolution of the two-dimensional image.

If the object is rotating rapidly while the RLOS rotates slowly, data can become available over many rotation periods with $\dot{\psi} >> \dot{\kappa}$. This can occur with a rapidly rotating object either on the ground or in deep space. Under these circumstances, a solid angle of aspects can be densely sampled by the data, as illustrated in Fig. 16. This can permit three-dimensional imaging if

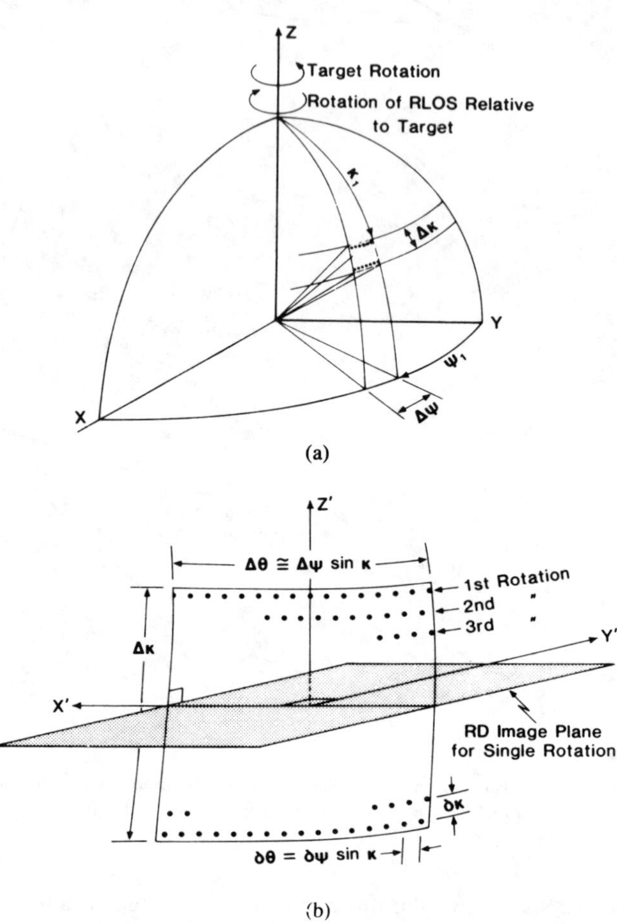

Fig. 16.   (a) Target aspects sampled for a three-dimensional image ($\dot{\psi} >> \dot{\kappa}$). (b) Detail enlargement from Fig. 17(a) at aspects sampled on unit sphere. Dots represent pulse aspects.

the aspects are sampled densely enough. In such cases, $\dot{\theta} \approx \dot{\psi} \sin \kappa$ and $\Delta\theta \approx \Delta\psi \sin \kappa$. The x' cross-range axis as defined above lies along the direction of increasing ψ, while the z' cross-range axis is in the direction of decreasing κ, as shown in Figs. 16(a) and (b). These figures are drawn with a small positive value for $\dot{\kappa}$. Fig. 16(b) is an enlargement of a portion of Fig. 16(a).

In Fig. 16(b), target rotation causes the RLOS to rapidly sweep in the ψ direction. Successive pulses during such a sweep sample the aspects shown by a row of dots. Pulses that do not fall within the $\Delta\psi$ interval are not used in the image. The slow change in κ due to RLOS rotation causes the sampled aspects to be displaced downward to the next row of dots on the next target rotation. Over many tens of rotations, this process densely samples a solid angle of aspects. The image will be three dimensional with resolution in the x' direction determined by the aspect change $\Delta\theta = \Delta\psi \sin\kappa$. Resolution in the z' direction is determined by the aspect change $\Delta\kappa$.

If $\dot\kappa$ is too small to give a significant change $\Delta\kappa$ over the available data, an image using data from the interval $\Delta\psi$ over many target rotations will be two dimensional since the RLOS are approximately coplanar. This class of images is known as "stroboscopic" and is discussed in Section IVB.

(2) *Cross-Range Ambiguous Interval and Cross-Range Resolution.* When an approximately coplanar set of aspects is sampled, as illustrated in Fig. (16), the cross-range ambiguous images are separated in the x' direction by $\mathrm{amb}(x') = \lambda/(2\delta\theta)$, where $\delta\theta$ is the change in aspect between pulses. To calculate $\delta\theta$, divide θ given by (29) by the radar's PRF. If the radar's PRF is too low, cross-range ambiguous images will overlap the true image. The resolution in the x' direction is proportional to $\lambda/(2\Delta\theta)$, where $\Delta\theta$ is given by (30). Since the image function does not depend on z', one can say that the resolution in the z' direction is "infinite."

When a solid angle of aspects is densely sampled as in Fig. 16(b), the resolutions in the two cross-range directions x' and z' depend on the extent of aspect change, $\Delta\theta$ and $\Delta\kappa$, respectively. In addition, the discrete sampling of aspects with steps $\delta\theta$ (per pulse) and $\delta\kappa$ (per rotation) causes cross-range ambiguous images in the x' and z' directions, respectively. If either $\delta\theta$ or $\delta\kappa$ is too large (because of the values of PRF, ψ and $\dot\kappa$), then the cross-range ambiguous images may overlap the true image of the target, making the image difficult or impossible to interpret.

The cross-range ambiguous interval in the x' direction, $\mathrm{amb}(x')$, and that in the z' direction, $\mathrm{amb}(z')$, are given by

$$\mathrm{amb}(x') = \lambda/(2\delta\theta) \tag{31}$$

and

$$\mathrm{amb}(z') = \lambda/(2\delta\kappa) \tag{32}$$

respectively.

If the values of $\mathrm{amb}(x')$ and $\mathrm{amb}(z')$ are larger than the corresponding maximum cross-range extents of the targets, the images will be unambiguous. For calculating $\mathrm{amb}(x')$, one can use

$$\delta\theta \approx \psi \sin\kappa = \dot\psi \sin\kappa/\mathrm{PRF}$$
$$= 2\pi \sin\kappa/(T\,\mathrm{PRF}) \tag{33}$$

where T is the target's rotation period and PRF is the radar pulse repetition frequency. Similarly, to get $\mathrm{amb}(z')$, one can use

$$\delta\kappa = T\dot\kappa = 2\pi\dot\kappa/\dot\psi. \tag{34}$$

When producing three-dimensional images, the impulse response (IPR) widths (sometimes loosely referred to as resolution) in the three dimensions follow from the principles given previously. That is, the range resolution is determined by the transmitted radio frequency (RF) bandwidth (BW),

$$\rho(y') = k\,c/2\mathrm{BW} \tag{35}$$

and the two cross-range dimensions have resolution given by

$$\rho(x') = k\,\lambda/2\Delta\theta \tag{36}$$

and

$$\rho(z') = k\,\lambda/2\Delta\kappa \tag{37}$$

respectively. Here k is a parameter which encompasses both the definition of resolution in terms of IPR width, i.e., IPR width at 3 dB down versus 6 dB down, and the effect of IPR mainlobe broadening due to the aperture weighting function selected for IPR sidelobe control.

C. Motion Measurement Requirement

These coherent radar imaging techniques all require precise knowledge of the time-varying position of the radar relative to the target scene in order to form good quality images. Ideally, the relative range to each image grid point must be known to some fraction of a wavelength over the integration period being used to obtain fine cross-range resolution. Since we are correlating range-derived phase information over some coherent aperture, any error in knowledge of relative position R_ϵ will give rise to a phase error given by

$$\phi_\epsilon = 4\pi R_\epsilon/\lambda \tag{38}$$

which will cause perturbations in the cross-range IPR of the radar in a manner analogous to antenna pattern perturbations caused by mechanically or electrically induced phase errors across a real antenna aperture.

The effects upon image quality of such phase errors depend upon the form of the errors, as is determined by standard antenna theory. For example, motion-measurement errors which give rise to phase errors which vary linearly across the aperture cause shifting of the position of the image response. Errors which vary quadratically across the aperture cause mainlobe broadening. Higher order errors cause perturbations further out on the impulse response sidelobes. For example, errors which vary sinusoidally cause discrete paired-echo sidelobes some distance from the mainlobe. Wideband random phase errors cause noiselike sidelobes distributed across the entire scene. Energy scattered into the sidelobes by any of these errors comes at the expense of mainlobe energy, and hence these errors all cause apparent loss of target RCS. Further, these effects can be scene position invariant, or position invariant, depending upon whether the motion errors are applicable to the entire scene or target or are dependent upon individual resolution cell under consideration.

It is not possible to set a universal threshold on motion determination accuracy. Such a limit depends upon the quality required of the image, as well as upon the form, or frequency content, of the phase error function. In some cases, the effects of low frequency errors, which manifest themselves in the relatively high signal-to-noise mainlobe, can be extracted from the image data and used to derive a correction to the collected data. Often several wavelengths of quadratic error can be corrected in this manner. On the other hand, higher frequency errors are not only detrimental for a given amplitude but are also more difficult to measure from the image data. Thus, high frequency errors, and hence the position measurement errors which cause them, are often restricted to be less than some small fraction of a wavelength.

In the case of airborne systems observing stationary objects on the ground, the relative motion must be measured onboard the aircraft using some type of motion-sensing equipment such as an inertial measurement unit (IMU), perhaps augmented by ground-based aids to navigation such as beacons. In the case of Earth-fixed systems observing space objects, the relative motion is determined by appropriate modeling and tracking of the object's orbit, along with using radar derived data regarding rotational motion of the object. Much of the technical challenge in implementing coherent imaging radars is in accomplishing these accurate determinations of relative position, and substantial effort has been directed toward this problem. An adequate treatment of these techniques is beyond the scope of this paper.

IV. RADAR IMAGING TECHNIQUES

The previous section described the fundamental processes required to form images from radar signals using knowledge of target and sensor vehicle motion. Various specific implementations of these principles vary significantly in detail depending upon the application, even though the underlying fundamentals are the same. This section reviews various generic implementations in order to highlight similarities between applications. Where possible, specific examples are provided.

Implementations involving imaging of fixed targets or scenes from moving sensor-bearing vehicles are considered first. Conventional wide-area stripmap mode SAR and the spotlight mode SAR are both described. The second part of the section provides a look at implementations which utilize the same principles in providing multidimensional images of moving or rotating objects from Earth-fixed coherent radar sensors.

A. Vehicle-Borne Imaging of Fixed Objects

Radar systems designed to provide images of the Earth's surface are generally airborne or spaceborne sensors. The motion of the sensor-bearing vehicle provides the relative motion between sensor and target required to perform imaging.

There are two generic types of fixed-target imaging systems. The conventional stripmap mode SAR provides for wide-area coverage by producing imagery of a strip of terrain illuminated by an antenna whose boresight angle is nominally fixed with respect to the vehicle velocity vector. For such a system, vehicle travel over time, in conjunction with antenna ground-range coverage, determines total image coverage. Cross-range resolution is determined by the effective scene rotation during illumination as determined by the antenna azimuth beamwidth. The alternative approach is to decouple antenna boresight angle from the vehicle velocity vector in order to provide longer illumination dwell on the area of interest. This approach provides for finer cross-range resolution at the expense of total image coverage. This latter approach is commonly referred to as spotlight mode SAR.

(1) Conventional Stripmap Mode SAR. The fundamentals of conventional stripmap mode synthetic aperture radar has been extensively documented in available literature [44, 59, 60, 61]. We provide a quick review here in order to note its relationship to other forms of range–Doppler imaging.

The data acquisition geometry associated with stripmap SAR is depicted in Fig. 17. In such a system,

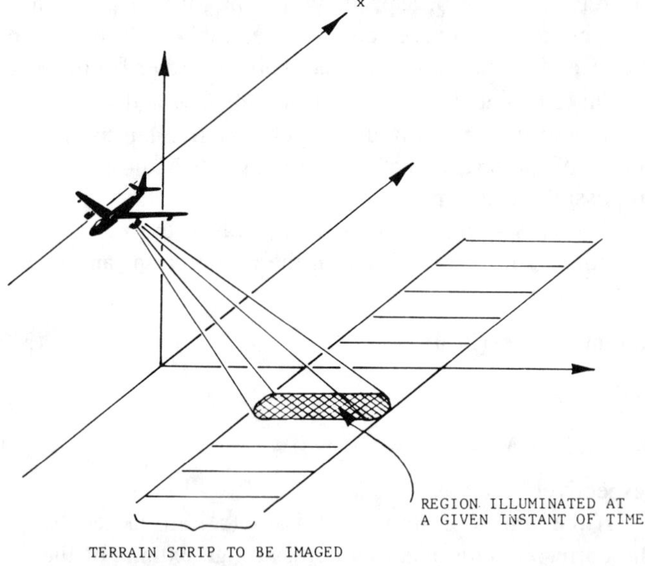

Fig. 17.   Schematic representation of stripmap mode imaging radar.

range resolution is achieved through accurate time-delay measurement obtained by transmitting dispersed pulses and applying pulse-compression techniques to the returned pulses. As indicated previously, azimuth or along-track resolution is obtained by recording the Doppler frequency (range–rate) as scattering elements migrate through the antenna beam. Knowledge of the Doppler frequency versus time relationship for a scatterer at a known range, which is computed based on measurements or a priori knowledge of vehicle motion, allows one to precisely locate the scatterer in a manner analogous to the pulse compression applied to the range direction.

Stripmap SAR Data Acquisition. The form of a typical stripmap mode SAR system is shown in Fig. 18. A coherent waveform generator (WFG) provides a wideband signal for periodic transmission, at the pulse repetition frequency (PRF), through a "fixed" antenna in order to illuminate the terrain strip of interest. The transitted signal has the form

$$s(t) = a(t) \exp\{j2\pi[f_0 t + \phi(t)]\} \tag{39}$$

where f_0 is the RF carrier frequency, $a(t)$ is the amplitude weighting of the pulse, and $\phi(t)$ is the phase modulation used to obtain resolution in range.

During the imaging time, the antenna pointing direction must be adjusted slightly to compensate for angular excursions made by the sensor platform. Steering commands are usually derived from information obtained from the aircraft inertial navigation system (INS) and from real-time analysis of the Doppler spectrum of the received signals. Unlike a real aperture side-looking radar system, antenna pointing for an SAR does not effect output image geometry. Rather, pointing impacts SNR of the image by virtue of achieving adequate signal power from the image area during coherent integration.

Returned signals from the terrain strip are received via a coherent receiver and are frequency converted to baseband for analog to digital (A/D) conversion in preparation for digital processing. After baseband conversion, the signal received from a single point scatterer at along-track position x_0 and cross-track range (broadside) r_0 is given by

$$S(x,y,x_0,r_0) = \sigma \exp\left\{ j2\pi \left[\frac{-2f_0 R(x - x_0, r_0)}{c} + \phi\left(\frac{2y}{c} - \frac{2R(x - x_0, r_0)}{c} \right) \right] \right\} \tag{40}$$

where the complex-valued weight σ is determined by transmitted pulse weighting, the antenna pattern, attenuation with distance, propagation phase effects, scatterer complex radar reflectivity, and $R(x - x_0, r_0)$ is the one-way range to the scatterer of (x_0, r_0) for along-track position x. One-dimensional samples of this function are obtained at along-track positions $X = n\Delta x = nv/\text{PRF}$, where v is the platform velocity and n represents pulse number. The signal in the fast-time dimension is represented in cross-track spatial coordinates y, where $y = ct/2$. The arguments x_0 and r_0 in the form of S reflect the scatterer-position-variant nature of S.

As part of the process of baseband conversion, compensation for turbulence-induced antenna phase center motion away from the desired straight path flight line must be applied. Such compensation takes the form of phase shifts, and in some cases time shifts, of the received signal. This is usually the case for airborne systems flying in a turbulent atmosphere, rather than for spaceborne systems such as SEASAT and SIR-A whose motion is generally accurately predictable using ephemeris information and spacecraft models. It is also possible to record the measured motion information and to take it into account as part of the correlation processing operation. However, the latter approach can prevent the use of more efficient means of implementing the image formation processing step.

In general, the motion compensation process adjusts

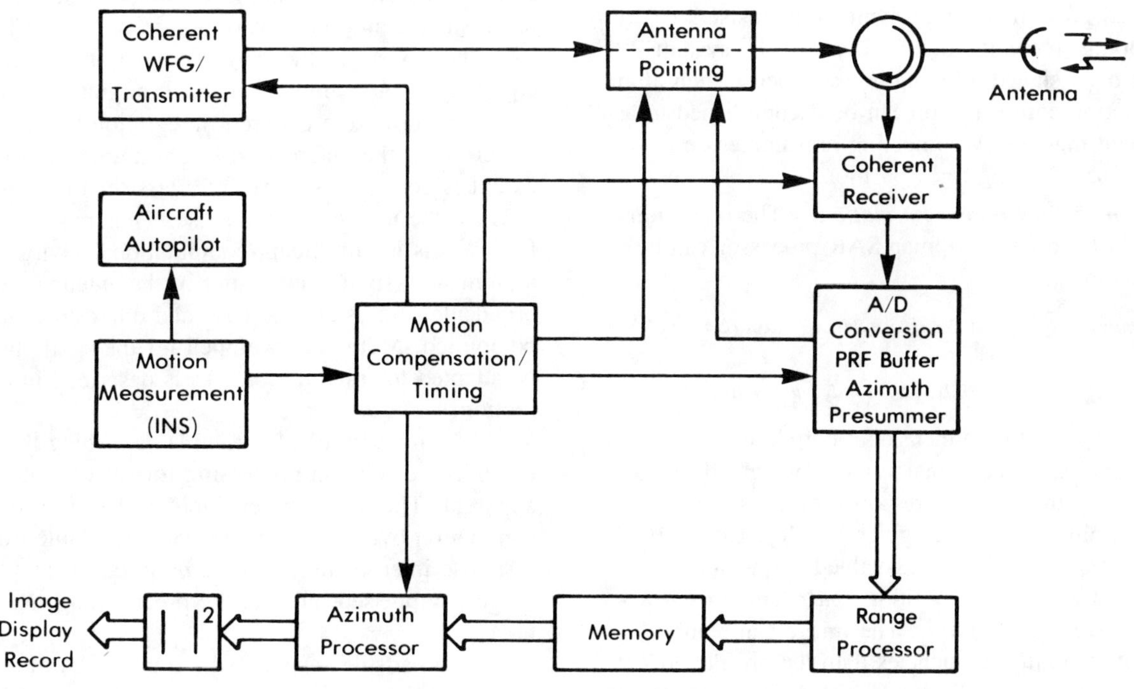

Fig. 18. Typical stripmap mode SAR system.

the phase and time delay of the signals to remove the effects of aircraft displacement on a pulse-by-pulse basis. In cases where the depression angle change over the image swath is sufficiently small, a single correction applied to the returns from all ranges will be adequate. For wide-swath-width systems, range-dependent correction schemes are required to apply corrections which are dependent upon the depression angle to the range of interest.

To correct for variations in along-track position, the system PRF can be slaved to vehicle velocity. Alternatively, the knowledge of along-track motion can accompany the signal data and be accounted for as part of the image-formation process.

Following conversion to baseband and assuming that digital processing techniques are to be used in forming the image, the received signals are converted to quantized discrete sampled data. For cases involving significantly less than unity duty cycle, a PRF buffer serves to spread the digital samples over the entire interpulse period in order to minimize the peak data rate.

An azimuth presummer is then usually employed to low-pass-filter and downsample the data in the azimuth dimension to the minimum Doppler bandwidth required to support the desired along-track resolution. This step is taken to minimize the amount of data to be digitally processed. The original azimuth sample rate (the PRF) must be high enough to unambiguously sample the Doppler spectrum associated with the antenna beamwidth. This beamwidth is often greater than the minimum required to achieve the desired azimuth resolution due to antenna size constraints associated with the sensor platform. Also, such excess beamwidth is often used to provide noncoherent averaging in order to reduce the effects of coherent microwave speckle in the final image. The usual presummer implementation consists of multiple overlapping, recursive digital filters. If the system PRF has not been slaved to along-track velocity, then along-track motion compensation can be accomplished in an equivalent manner by computing presummer outputs at equally spaced along-track positions.

Stripmap SAR Image Formation. The operation required of a digital stripmap SAR processor can be expressed as

$$O(ndx, mdy) = \sum_i \sum_j s(i\Delta x, j\Delta y)w(i\Delta x - ndx, j\Delta y - mdy)$$

$$\hat{S}(i\Delta x - ndx, j\Delta y - mdy, ndx, mdy) \qquad (41)$$

representing the two-dimensional correlation of the two-dimensional sampled signal s with a weighted complex conjugate of the sampled response of the system to an isolated point scatterer, as given by (40). Here, $O(ndx, mdy)$ represents the complex-valued output image sampled at along-track positions, ndx, and cross-track positions (range bins) mdy. The image can exhibit different sampling frequencies than the prefiltered sampled signals as indicated by the difference between Δx and dx, and Δy and dy. Also, $w(x, y)$ is the weighting

function applied to control the sidelobes of the system point-target response. The extent of summation over the range direction for each output sample is determined by the time duration of the transmitted pulse. The extent of summation in along track is determined by the illumination interval, which in general is a function of range as determined by the antenna cross-range beamwidth.

In simpler notation, this process an be denoted by

$$O(n, m) = \sum_i \sum_j s(i, j)w(i - n, j - m)$$

$$\hat{S}(i - n, j - m, n, m). \qquad (42)$$

The form of reference function $\hat{S}$ denotes the range dependence of the system reference function. Theoretically, a different $\hat{S}$, as indicated by the fourth argument m, must be used when correlating each range bin of interest. In practice, however, a single reference function will suffice over a considerable number of range bins.

In most systems, the signals are range-compressed prior to the azimuth correlation process. For example, in the STAR system described in Section II, the received signals are pulse-compressed prior to A/D conversion using a surface acoustic wave (SAW) device. In this case, the final azimuth correlation process is given by

$$O(n, m) = \sum_i \sum_j s'(i, j)w(i - n)$$

$$\hat{S}'(i - n, j - m, n, m) \qquad (43)$$

where $s'(i, j)$ is the range-compressed signal, $w(m)$ is the weighting applied in azimuth, and $\hat{S}'$ is the range-compressed system reference function which in general has a $\sin x/x$ amplitude variation in the range dimension [62]. The extent of the range summation (in j) in (43) is equivalent to the amount of range migration of a point scatterer during the coherent integration time. For a system with the antenna boresight pointed broadside, this extent is generally significantly less than that implied by (42) for the uncompressed pulse. Thus range compression first results in significant computational savings. For a system with significant squint of the antenna away from broadside, this is not the case and other procedures must be applied. Methods developed for the spotlight case may be adapted for this purpose, as is described in a later section.

The similarity of (43) to (14) describing the general extended correlation processing for rotating objects is apparent. The range-dimension correlation of (43), the summation over j, may be viewed as a finite impulse response interpolation process required to sample the range-compressed pulse at the precise range $R(r_0, p)$ for (14).

For broadside systems where the range migration during the integration time (so-called range walk) is less than on the order of 1/2 of a range resolution cell, the image formation process simplifies further. This condition is achieved if

$$\rho_a^2 \rho_r \geq \lambda^2 R / 16 \tag{44}$$

where ρ_a and ρ_r are the azimuth and range resolutions, respectively, and R is the operating range [63]. In such a case, the system reference function becomes separable in range and azimuth and the image formation process becomes a sequence of two one-dimensional processing steps [64].

(2) Spotlight Mode SAR. Spotlight SAR [6–10, 54, 56, 65] has as its objective the production of imagery exhibiting resolution finer than that associated with the limits imposed by a fixed antenna, or to produce imagery with a great deal of angular diversity with which to understand the directional characteristics of the scene reflectivity of interest. Benefits which may accrue through use of the spotlight mode come at the expense of area coverage since longer dwell times are required.

Spotlight Data Acquisition. The collection geometry for the spotlight mode SAR is shown in Fig. 19. As the vehicle carrying the SAR sensor moves past the area of interest, the antenna boresight is continually realigned so as to point at the center of the scene. The antenna beamwidth must be large enough to adequately illuminate the desired area to be imaged, and the duration of the illumination must be long enough to obtain sufficient

effective rotation of the scene to obtain the desired cross-range resolution, as given by $\Delta\theta = \lambda/\rho_a$. The scene may be three dimensional in nature and the sensor may not precisely follow a straightline path. A motion-sensing system must be used to determine the required antenna pointing angles and to provide knowledge of relative motion between the vehicle and the scene, knowledge which must be used during the image formation processing step.

Fig. 20 shows a possible configuration for a spotlight mode SAR system. The diagram assumes the use of a linear frequency modulation (FM) waveform for use in obtaining fine range resolution, although such an assumption is not necessary in order to perform spotlight imaging. As before, an inertial measurement system can provide pointing angles for the antenna, although for the spotlight case, the illumination follows a fixed point on the ground rather than following a strip of terrain parallel to the flight track as was the case for stripmap.

The first step in preparing for range–Doppler imaging is to remove the effects of the gross range changes to scene center on a pulse-by-pulse basis over the coherent illumination time. In the system of Fig. 20, this is accomplished by multiplying the returned signals with a replica of the transmitted signal, only delayed by precisely the round-trip delay to scene center. This delay is determined by real-time computation of the range to the scene center r_a using INS-supplied information.

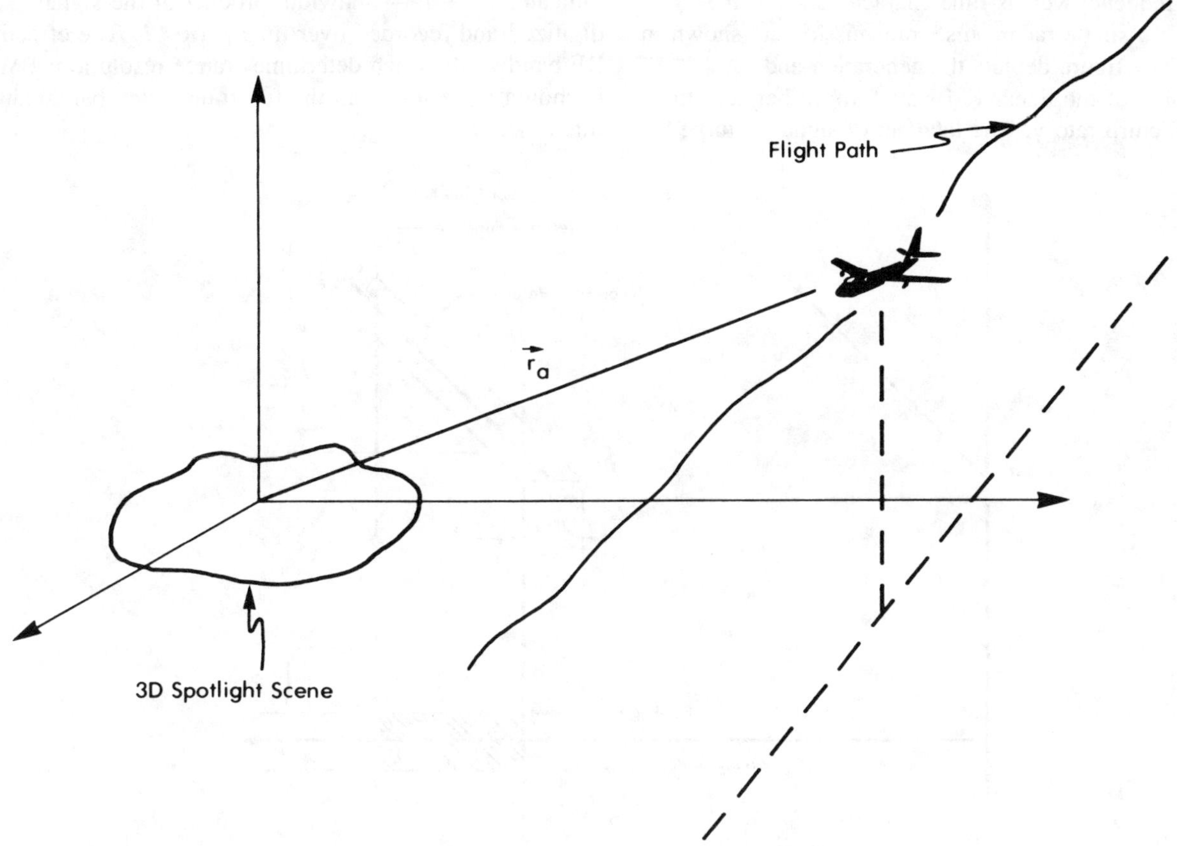

Fig. 19.   Spotlight mode SAR collection geometry. (Symbol with overbar corresponds to boldface symbol in text.)

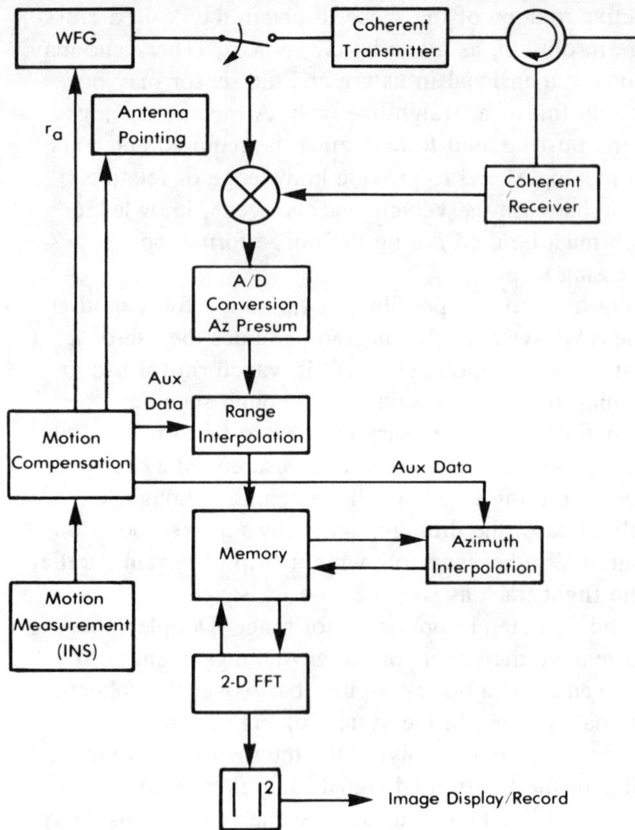

Fig. 20.   Simplistic spotlight SAR system with polar-format processing.

The frequency-versus-time characteristics of the signals for a single radar pulse transmission are shown in Fig. 21. The figure depicts the generation and transmission of the linear FM waveform to begin at time zero with chirp rate γ. The total set of signals returned from the desired area, beginning with the near-edge return and ending with the far-edge, are shown occurring with appropriate delay associated with round-trip propagation. Mixing with a replica of the original transmission delayed by the round-trip time to scene center produces a constant frequency signal for each return from a point scatterer. The frequency of this signal is proportional to the range of the scatterer.

The entire set of constant-frequency signals associated with the scene to be imaged are shown centered about zero frequency in Fig. 21. These video signals would thus be encoded as complex-valued (I and Q) data. The figure depicts a direct conversion of RF to I and Q data. With practical considerations given to filtering of signals from terrain which is illuminated but not desired in the final image, there might be several intermediate-frequency processes required to produce the desired result.

The total set of video signals have bandwidth BW_v related to total range swath width (SW) by the scale factor $2\gamma/c$. The duration of the signals is now proportional to the original sweep time and hence to the bandwidth to be used to obtain range resolution. Note that the signals from all ranges do not completely overlap in time, although chirp rates and pulse lengths may be chosen to minimize this effect. In such cases, only the central overlapped region is A/D converted and recorded to avoid the inefficiencies associated with storing and processing of digital data whose time–bandwidth product is not wholly occupied. The shaded area in Fig. 21 indicates the time–bandwidth product of the signal digitized and recorded over time period T. The effective RF bandwidth which determines range resolution, BW_{rf}, is shown to be less than the full transmitted bandwidth in this case.

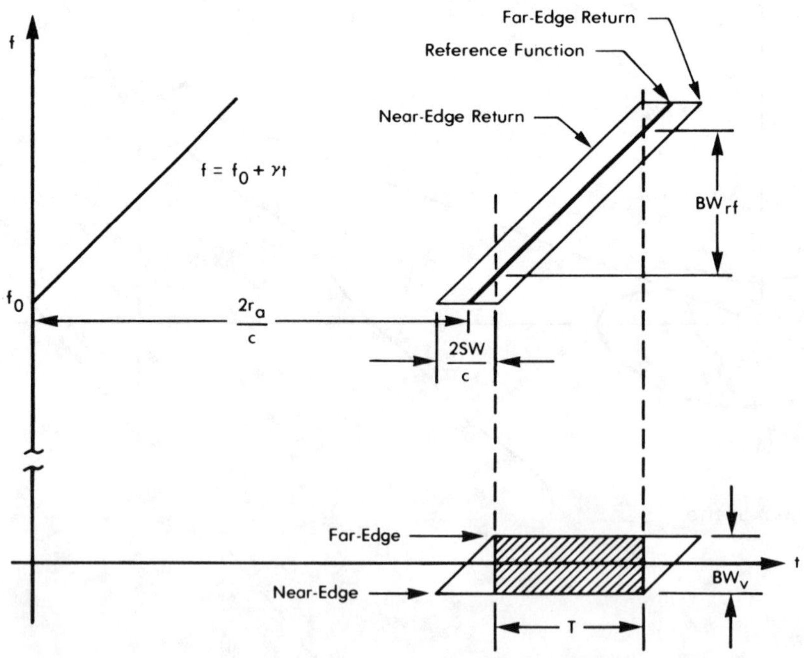

Fig. 21.   Spotlight range tracking to produce video.

Use of linear FM waveform in this deramping scheme on a pulse-by-pulse basis has resulted in signals with frequency and starting phase determined by the relative range of a scatterer to scene center, thus establishing the conditions required to perform frequency-domain range–Doppler imaging. In instances where other transmitted waveforms are desired, it is still possible to achieve this condition by first pulse-compressing the received signals to achieve fine range resolution (while retaining the phase information) and then Fourier-transforming the signal such that point scatterers give rise to signals with frequency and starting phase proportional to relative range to scene center.

Spotlight Image-Formation.   As described in Section III, there are at least four fundamental ways of accomplishing the image-formation process of such signals: (1) subaperture linear range–Doppler processing; (2) multiple-subpatch linear range–Doppler processing; (3) whole-scene polar-format processing; and (4) backprojection or general correlation processing. The relative advantages and disadvantages of these approaches are dependent upon the particular system parameters at hand and would have to be determined on an ad hoc basis.

The subaperture linear range–Doppler processing approach is analogous to the extended correlation processing (ECP) algorithm described in Section IVB for efficient processing of extended correlation data. The two-dimensional signals are arrayed in a simple linear fashion and multiple azimuth subapertures are two-dimensional Fourier-transformed to form complex-valued, coarse azimuth-resolution images. The subapertures are chosen to be small enough such that there is insignificant range-cell migration during the subaperture interval. Each of the images formed within subapertures are then compensated in phase and spatial rotation to compensate for the scene rotation which occurs between subapertures, are upsampled in azimuth to accommodate the eventual finer azimuth resolution, and coherently summed and detected to form the final image. Because of the analogy to the ECP algorithm, discussion of the approach is deferred to Section IVB.

The backprojection processing method is common to the field of computer-automated tomography (CAT). Various analogies have been drawn between CAT processing and spotlight SAR processing [54]. As was mentioned in Section III, the backprojection processing approach is essentially the same as the pulse-by-pulse correlation approach as it is applied to the imaging of rotating objects and thus will not be discussed in further detail here.

The multiple-subpatch processing method and the polar-format processing method are described in more detail below.

Multiple-Subpatch Processing.   If the spotlight SAR signals are simply rectilinearly formatted and two-dimensionally Fourier-transformed over the entire collection duration, then the point scatterer migration

effects described in Section III will limit the useful portion of the final scene to a region about the central compensation point with approximate diameter $D = 4\rho^2/\lambda$. The multiple-subpatch image-formation approach accepts this limitation and in an efficient manner applies the same process multiple times at different locations to obtain full quality over the entire scene. The full scene is essentially divided into several smaller scenes of diameter less than the limit imposed by scatterer migration, each scene being compensated for motion relative to its center.

An efficient process for accomplishing this method is depicted in Fig. 22. The input to the process is the video signal which has been compensated to the center of the scene by mixing with the reference function $R_a(t)$. This function, which changes on a pulse-by-pulse basis according to the pulse-by-pulse changes in range, has caused any signal received from the center of the scene to exhibit zero frequency and phase over the entire coherent integration period. The full scene signal is passed through a bank of bandpass filters which filter the data in the fast-time dimension into some number N of frequency sub-bands corresponding to range subswaths across the scene. The frequency content of each subswath has been reduced nominally by a factor of $1/N$ such that the N output channels can each be downsampled (reduced sampling frequency) by an equivalent amount. In practice, however, some excess subswath BW is required to prevent ambiguities due to nonideal bandpass filters.

Each of the signals corresponding to the range subswaths are then recompensated using reference function $R_i(t)$ such that the nominal center of each range subswath exhibits zero frequency and phase over the integration time. The reference function is generated on the basis of differential range, on a pulse-by-pulse basis, between the center of the subswath and the center of the entire scene. This process "stabilizes" the azimuth Doppler frequency content within each subswath in preparation for filtering in the azimuth, or slow time, dimension to form image subpatches.

The azimuth bandpass filters for each subswath partition the Doppler spectrum into some number M of sub-bands corresponding to multiple subpatches in the cross-range direction within each subswath. The outputs of this process are downsampled in slow time to the minimum allowed to unambiguously represent the signals. The outputs of each of the $N \times M$ filters is additionally compensated to set the center of each subpatch to zero frequency and phase over the integration time by multiplying by reference functions $R_{nm}(t)$, which are formed on the basis of differential ranges between subpatch centers and range subswath centers on a pulse-by-pulse basis.

Each of the $N \times M$ channels which have been created by this process now provide signals for multiple subpatches covering the entire scene, with each channel compensated in frequency and range to the center of the associated subpatch. The data within each channel is then

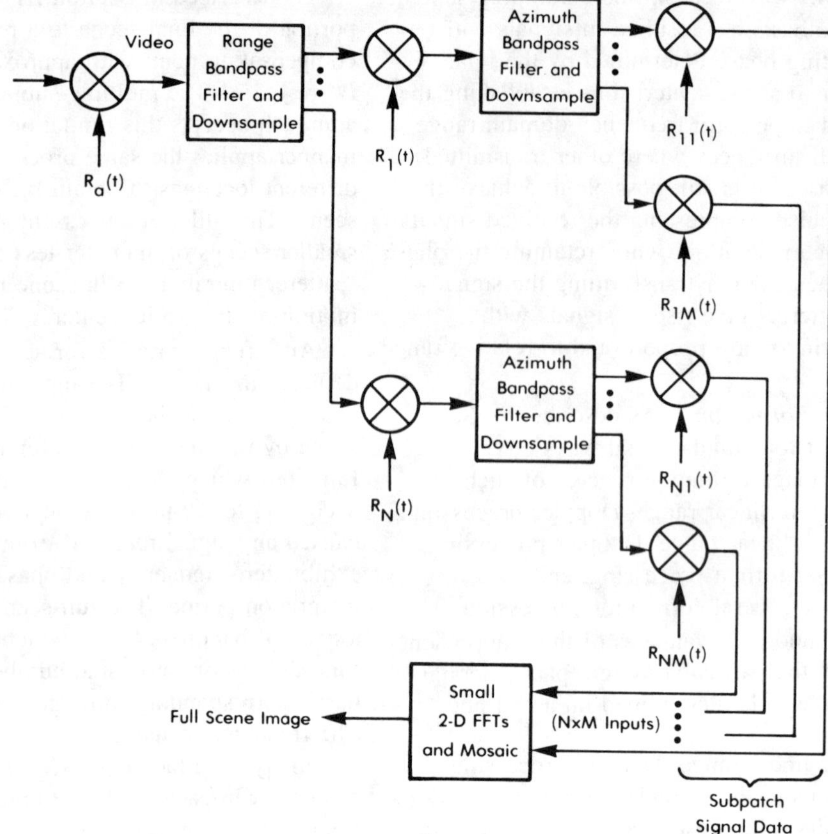

Fig. 22.   Multipatch range–Doppler processing.

two-dimensionally Fourier-transformed to form the subpatch images, which may then be mosaicked to form the full scene image. The processing within each subpatch relies entirely on linear range–Doppler analysis since each subpatch scene dimension was limited in extent to prevent relative range walk greater than some fraction of a resolution cell during the required integration time.

Polar-Format Processing.   The formulation of Section III provides a sound basis for application of the polar-format processing approach to spotlight SAR data. Section III determines that each individual radar transmission and reception which is appropriately compensated for range to scene center and which is processed such that frequency and starting phase become proportional to relative range to a scatterer can be thought of as viewing a linear one-dimensional segment of the three-dimensional Fourier transform of the (in general) three-dimensional scene. Taken as a whole, the total set of such observations over the flight path in Fig. 19 corresponding to the coherent illumination period, one is essentially observing a two-dimensional curved surface within the three-dimensional transform. This surface is known as the collection signal surface.

Although one can theoretically perform a three-dimensional transform of a volume containing this surface to form a three-dimensional image of the scene, the obtainable sensor vehicle excursion in the third dimension is usually not sufficient to provide meaningful resolution in the third dimension. Thus, two-dimensional approaches normally suffice. (The resultant two-dimensional output is also compatible with current two-dimensional display technology.)

As implied in Section III, when applying two-dimensional processing to form a two-dimensional image, one must account for the noncoplanar excursions of the sensor vehicle in order to obtain a correctly focused image. Even then, correct focus can be obtained only for collections of scatterers which lie in a common plane. This plane is called the focus target plane and can be arbitrarily chosen prior to processing but would usually be made to correspond to the nominal ground plane within the scene of interest.

The method for accounting for noncoplanar motion of the collection vehicle is illustrated in Fig. 23. The signal values corresponding to the collection signal surface must be projected in a direction normal to the chosen focus plane until they intersect the desired processing plane. Projection of the signal values in this particular direction preserves the correct relative phase of the samples for signals which result from scatterers lying in the focus plane, as was described in Section III. The intersecting plane is known as the reference plane, or alternatively, the output image plane.

Selection of the reference plane determines the perspective, or point of view, associated with the final

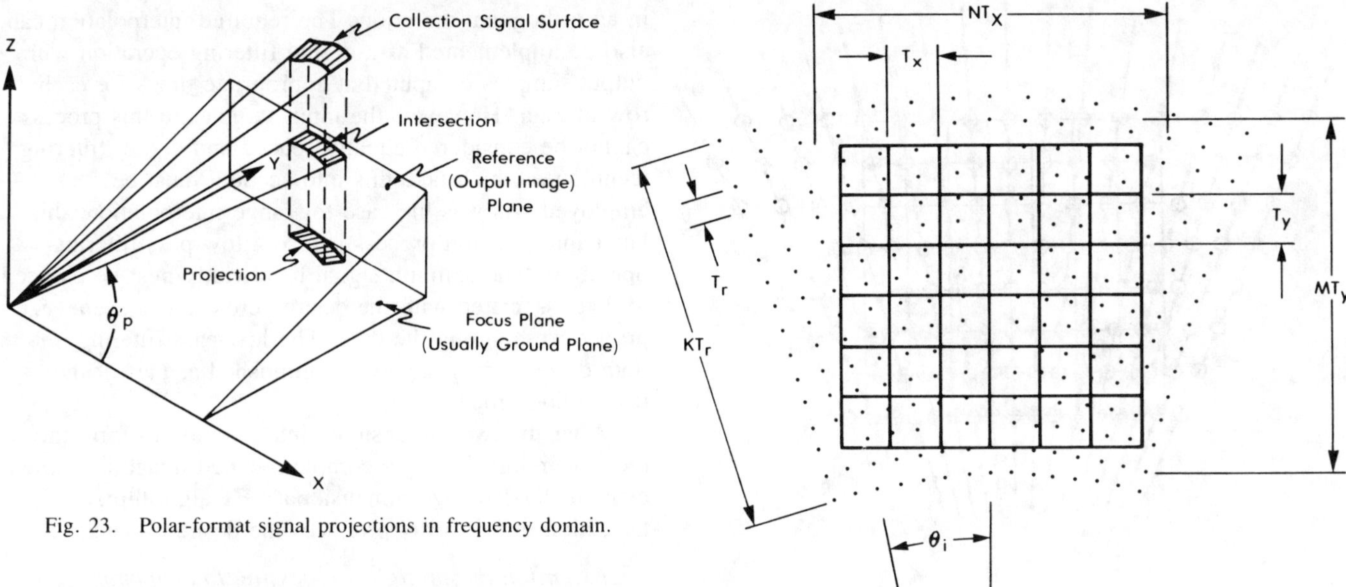

Fig. 23.   Polar-format signal projections in frequency domain.

Fig. 24.   Digital polar-format geometry.

image. If one wishes the image to appear as if the viewer were looking straight down upon the scene, then the ground plane itself is selected as the reference plane (possibly synonymous with the focus plane in this case). Conventional SAR images for the stripmap case have the perspective normal to the ''SAR plane,'' which is defined to be the plane formed by a central point within the scene and the velocity vector of the sensor vehicle. To affect a similar appearance for the spotlight case, the reference plane might be selected to nominally coincide with the curved collection signal surface. It must be pointed out that the concept of point of view is correct only for scene elements lying within the focus plane. Point scatterers out of this plane will image at positions which do not correctly follow from rules of perspective, an effect known as range layover.

Once the focus and reference planes have been selected, the polar-formatting operation is straightforward. Based upon the projection of collection surface signal sample positions in a direction normal to the focus plane, positions of the samples in the intersected reference plane are computed. Auxiliary data describing the pulse-to-pulse position of the antenna phase center relative to the scene center and knowledge of the frequency-versus-time relationship for the transmitted pulse are used in this geometrical computation. Once these positions have been determined, the collected signal data is appropriately described in Fig. 24.

Fig. 24 shows the relative positions of the data samples as they have been projected into the reference plane. The samples, represented as black dots, are shown arrayed along radial lines at angles θ_i corresponding to the line-of-sight angles to scene center for each radar transmission, as projected into the reference plane. The spacing between samples T_r is determined by the original video signal sampling period as projected into the reference plane. The original video sampling frequency must be high enough to unambiguously sample the video spectrum whose bandwidth is dependent upon the range extent of the illuminated scene.

The number of samples along each radial line K is determined by the effective duration of the video signal as given by T in Fig. 21. By virtue of the linear FM deramping operation, this duration is directly proportional to the effective RF bandwidth used to obtain range resolution.

To form an image, the geometric array of samples in Fig. 24 must be Fourier-transformed in two dimensions. In order to take advantage of the efficiency of a two-dimensional FFT and to produce an image which is sampled on a two-dimensional grid, one must resample the data of Fig. 24 to produce new samples occurring at the intersections of a two-dimensional rectilinear grid as depicted in Fig. 24. The range and azimuth sample spacings associated with this grid, T_y and T_x, determines the extent of the output image in the range and azimuth dimensions, respectively. The number of grid samples, and hence the extent of the grid, in the range and azimuth dimensions determines the output sample spacing in both dimensions of the image. This interpolated grid is often increased in size prior to the two-dimensional FFT by the padding of zeros in order to increase the image sampling rate on output, although the system resolution is dependent only on the portion of the grid filled with actual signal data. The grid values might also be weighted in range and azimuth prior to FFT in order to lower the sidelobes of the Fourier transform process.

The original system concept depicted in Fig. 20 indicated that the formation of the new sample grid may be performed as two separate one-dimensional interpolation steps. The first step, illustrated in Fig. 25, is known as range interpolation. For this stage, each individual radar pulse is simply resampled such that the new samples fall on positions along the horizontal lines making up the interpolation grid. This operation may be viewed as a digital filtering technique where the input function is a discrete set of uniformly spaced samples and

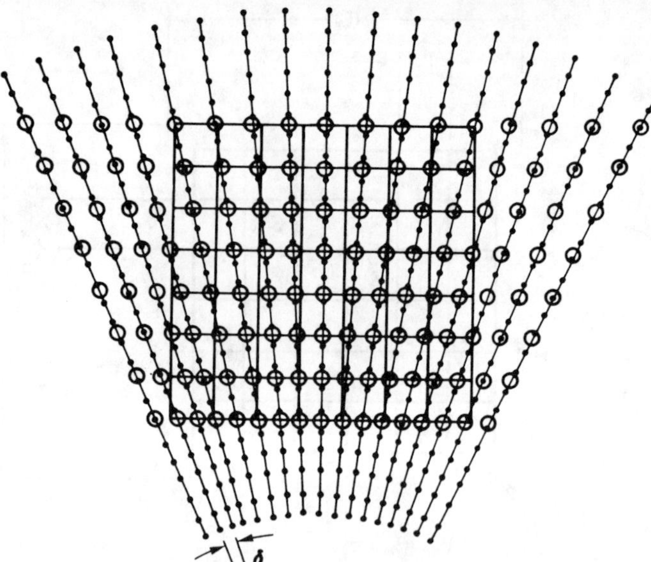

Fig. 25. Polar-format range interpolation. (Key: ● indicates range interpolated samples (input); ○ indicates azimuth interpolated samples (equally spaced in x and y.)

the output samples are computed at a lower sampling rate and with some specified delay with respect to the first sample within each radar pulse. Since, in general, the output samples from this operation occur with lower frequency than the input samples (due to the likelihood of overillumination of the desired scene), one must perform low-pass filtering of the original data to ensure that aliasing effects do not occur. For range interpolation, this low-pass digital filter may be thought of as a range prefilter which limits the video frequencies present to those associated with the final desired range extent of the imaged scene.

The second stage of polar-format interpolation is shown in Fig. 26. The azimuth interpolation operates on the samples produced from the range interpolation, only

in an orthogonal direction. The required interpolation can also be implemented as a digital filtering operation with output samples computed at appropriate times for each row of data. However, the input samples to this process cannot be considered equally spaced and digital filtering techniques which take this into account must be employed. As was the case for range interpolation, this latter interpolation process is also a low-pass filtering operation. The azimuth signal bandwidth must be reduced to that associated with the desired cross-range scene size prior to resampling the data. The low-pass filtering in both dimensions is easily accomplished as part of the resampling process.

After the two-dimensional interpolation to form the rectilinear signal grid, a complex-valued image is formed using a standard two-dimensional FFT algorithm. Detection of this array produces the desired image.

Extension of Spotlight Processing to Stripmap SAR. Practical implementations of the stripmap processing algorithm noted above are restricted to situations where the radar illumination is primarily in the broadside direction, and where the amount of range cell migration of scatterers is minimal (on the order of a few cells). However, the aforementioned spotlight SAR image formation processes may be beneficially applied to stripmap cases which do exhibit squinted antenna since the algorithms, in combination with the preprocessing compensation for gross pulse-to-pulse range changes, inherently compensate for the associated range walk effects.

The approach to accomplishing "spotlight" production of stripmap data is shown in Fig. 27. The desired stripmap scene is envisioned as being partitioned

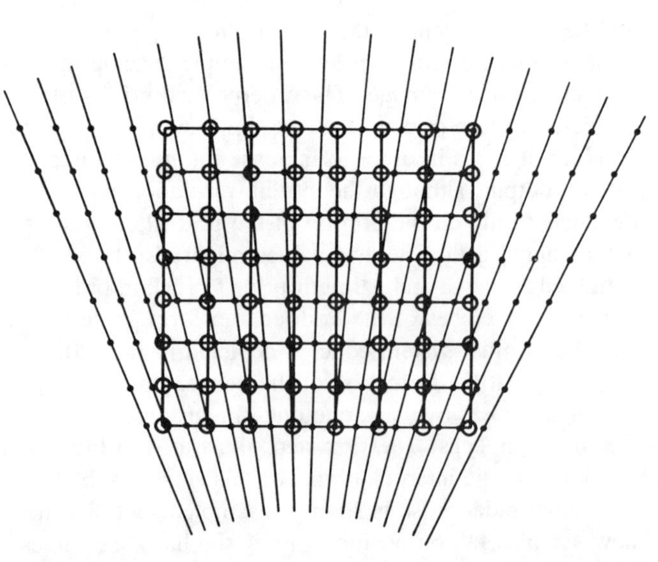

Fig. 26. Polar-format azimuth interpolation. (Key: ● indicates raw data samples (input); ○ indicates range interpolated samples (equally spaced in y.)

AUSHERMAN ET AL: DEVELOPMENTS IN RADAR IMAGING

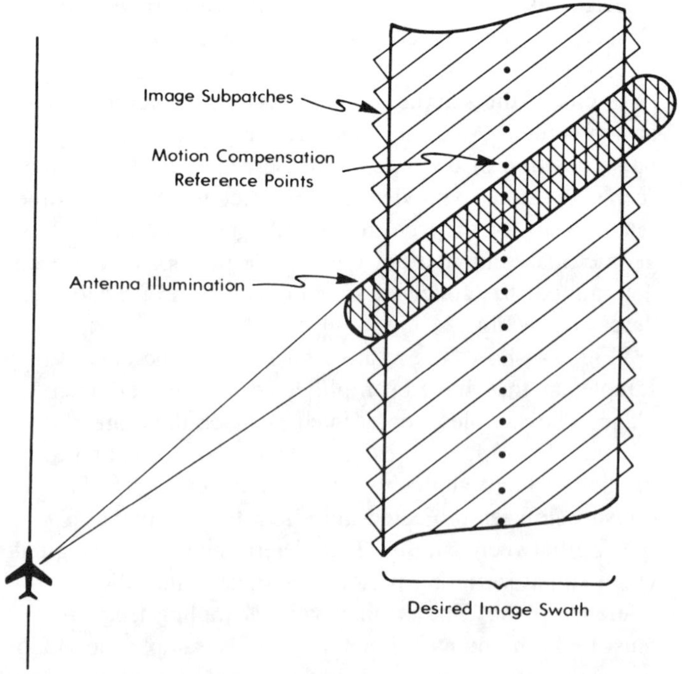

Fig. 27. Spotlight image formation applied to squinted stripmap SAR.

into many subpatches in a manner analogous to the spotlight subpatch processing approach mentioned earlier. As the fixed antenna beam migrates over each of these subpatches, the signal data for each subpatch is isolated by motion-compensating to the center of the cell (removing range changes to subpatch centers) and low-pass-filtering to remove signal data which does not contribute to the desired subpatch scene. The data within each cell is then processed by any of the given spotlight algorithms, and the final full-strip image is formed by mosaicking of the individual subpatches after resampling in the along-track and cross-track dimensions.

Although this approach is robust in terms of compensating for severe range walk, there are various factors which could limit the practicality of a given implementation. Since the antenna beam is not slewed to illuminate the individual subpatches, the subpatch must be limited in size such that the entire patch can be illuminated simultaneously over the coherent integration period required to achieve the desired cross-range resolution. To achieve reasonably sized patches, this requires excess antenna beamwidth over the minimum required to achieve the cross-range resolution. Also, a fair amount of processing overhead is entailed in filtering the data into subpatches and in resampling and mosaicking the results to form the full image. In the event that FFT methods are involved in forming subpatch images, the smaller patch sizes resulting from the antenna beamwidth limits also begin to limit the efficiency of the FFT algorithm itself.

B. Ground-Based Imaging of Moving Objects

In this section, we discuss useful image types and imaging applications for the case of a ground-based, fixed radar with moving object targets, such as the solar system's bodies and artificial Earth satellites. Because of their possible varied motion characteristics, these objects can provide a wide spectrum of illustrative and important imaging cases and applications.

Many of the imaging methods discussed here apply, or can be appropriately modified, for other moving targets such as rotating platforms, aircraft, ships, and ground vehicles.

(1) FFT Range–Doppler Images. In Section I, it was pointed out that if the coherent processing interval ΔT is sufficiently small, one can perform conventional range–Doppler processing to calculate images. Here, we demonstrate that $G(r_0)$ can be efficiently calculated using the (FFT) method if ΔT strictly satisfies the constraint of no motion through resolution cells. In this case, $G(r_0)$ will be known as an FFT range–Doppler image.

In many space object imaging applications, useful results often can be obtained by FFT range–Doppler imaging. This can be understood from (9) and (10), since artificial satellites typically have limited dimensions and planetary imaging requires resolutions on the order of 10 km.

The constraints on ΔT can be more precisely stated by requiring that during this interval

(i) the relative range to every scatterer not change by more than a fraction of the range resolution,
(ii) the relative range rate to every scatterer remain within 1 range–rate resolution cell.

It will be shown that condition (i) is necessary to use the full efficiency available from the FFT method. When condition (ii) is satisfied, it can be shown that the relative range to every scatterer varies linearly with time to a precision of a small fraction of the wavelength. Furthermore, in this case, it can also be shown that for three-dimensional objects, it is necessary for all RLOS during the imaging interval to be very close to coplanar.

Specific expressions for image intervals that meet the range–Doppler imaging conditions, analogous to those in (9) and (10), are stated for typical applications.

Range–Doppler Imaging Coordinate System. Range–Doppler images can be most conveniently calculated in the (x',y',z') "imaging" coordinate system of Section IIIB. In this coordinate system, the RLOS directions are specified by the angles θ and η shown in Fig. 28. Fig. 28 is a local view of the surface of the unit sphere including all RLOS positions during ΔT. The angle between the x',y' plane and the RLOS is denoted by η. This is the

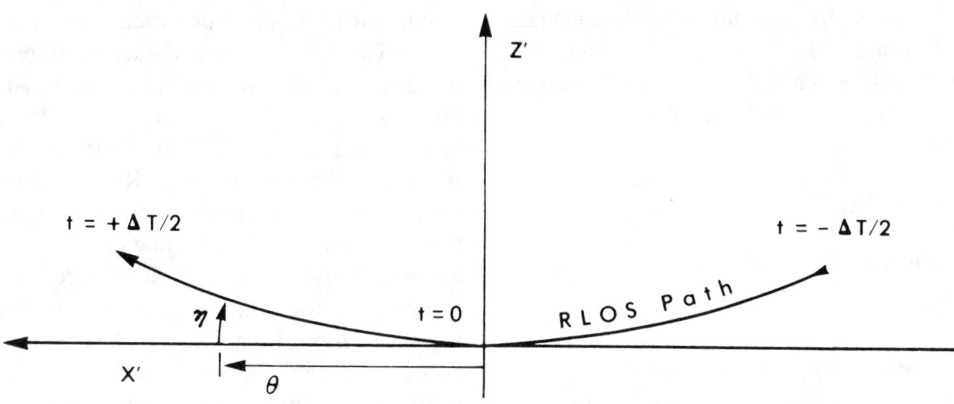

Fig. 28.   Aspects sampled for linear range–Doppler imaging on surface of unit sphere.

complement of a conventional polar angle measured from the z' axis. The azimuthal angle of the RLOS about the z' axis is θ, with $\theta = 0$ at $t = 0$, θ increasing with time.

With this geometry, the relative range to point (x', y', z'), defined by (16), can be written

$$D(t) = x' \cos \eta \sin \theta + y' \cos \eta \cos \theta + z' \sin \eta. \quad (45)$$

From this one gets

$$D(0) \equiv D_0 = y' \quad (46a)$$

$$\dot{D}(0) \equiv \dot{D}_0 = x' \dot{\theta}_0 \quad (46b)$$

$$\ddot{D}(0) \equiv \ddot{D}_0 = x' \ddot{\theta}_0 - y' \dot{\theta}_0^2 + z' \ddot{\eta}_0. \quad (46c)$$

Range–Doppler Image Function. If the radar's PRF is constant and if condition (ii) for FFT range–Doppler imaging is satisfied, one can approximate $D(t)$ over the interval ΔT by a linear function of the pulse number p

$$D(x', y', z', t) \equiv D(p) \approx D_0 + \dot{D}_0 p / \text{PRF} \quad (47)$$

where p is defined to be zero at $t = 0$, the center of ΔT. The error in this linear approximation can be estimated by $\ddot{D}_0 t^2 / 2$.

With (46) and (47), equation (15) becomes

$$G(x', y', z') \approx \exp(-4\pi j y' / \lambda) P(x', y') \quad (48a)$$

where

$$P(x', y') = \sum_p W(p) \tilde{S}(p) \exp(-4\pi j \dot{\theta} x' p / \text{PRF}) \quad (48b)$$

is the range–Doppler image function. The summation extends over the pulses in the interval ΔT. Because of (46a) and (46b), the calculated image function $P(x', y')$ is also available as a function of D and $\dot{D}_0$, $P(D_0, \dot{D}_0)$.

The function $P(x', y')$, as expressed in (48b), has the form of a discrete Fourier transform to be calculated at each value of y'. This form has some advantages in computational speed. However, without an additional approximation, it cannot be evaluated with the full efficiency available from the FFT. The quantity $\tilde{S}(p)$ [(17) and the definition of $S(p)$] comes from the radar return sampled at the range $R(\mathbf{0}, t) + D(t)$, where $D(t)$ depends on both x' and y' by (46) and (47). To evaluate (48b) efficiently with the FFT, $S(p)$ cannot depend on x'. However, if condition (i) is satisfied, i.e., if the change in relative range is small compared with the range resolution, then $S(p)$ sampled at

$$R(\mathbf{0}, t) + y' + x' \dot{\theta} p / \text{PRF}$$

is approximately equal to $\tilde{S}(p)$ sampled at

$$R(\mathbf{0}, t) + y'.$$

With this approximation, $\tilde{S}(p)$ becomes independent of x' and (48b) can be evaluated as an FFT at each value of relative range, y'.

In this more general context, the relation between the relative Doppler frequency of the scatterer f_D and the scatterer's cross-range displacement x' is given by

$$f_D = 2\dot{D}_0(x', y', z') / \lambda = 2x' \dot{\theta} / \lambda$$

as compared with (5).

Determination of Range–Doppler Imaging Intervals. The first condition limiting the interval ΔT for range–Doppler imaging (that the relative range to a scatterer change less than the range resolution) can be written

$$\Delta\theta \approx \dot{\theta}\Delta T < \rho_r / |x'|_{\max}. \quad (49)$$

Here, $|x'|_{\max}$ is the largest cross-range displacement of any scatterer in the target. This is a more general version of the expression in (9).

A similar limiting expression for ΔT from condition (ii) is given by

$$\Delta T < C \, (\lambda / |\ddot{D}_0|_{\max})^{1/2} \quad (50)$$

where $|\ddot{D}_0|$ is the maximum value of $|\ddot{D}_0(x', y', z')|$ for any scatterer in the target and C is a dimensionless numerical constant.

In most cases where range–Doppler imaging is used, the $(\dot{\theta}_0)^2$ contribution to $\ddot{D}_0$ predominates. In such cases, the angular rate of the RLOS relative to the target is approximately constant, and the RLOS are approximately coplanar relative to the target. Then (50) can be written

$$\Delta\theta \approx \dot{\theta}\Delta T < C \, (\lambda / |y'|_{\max})^{1/2} \quad (51)$$

where $|y'|_{\max}$ is the maximum range displacement from the origin to a scatterer. This expression is a more general version of (10).

If the range–Doppler image is to have equal range and cross-range resolution, $\rho_a = \rho_r = \rho$, then to satisfy (49) and (51), respectively, $|x'|_{\max}$ and $|y'|_{\max}$ must each be less than $4\rho^2/\lambda$. Outside these limits one can see a slight smearing of the scatterer's image. The smearing gradually becomes more pronounced the farther the scatterer is from the origin.

Fig. 29 shows this smearing as a function of the target's location. This range–Doppler image was calculated from simulated radar data, assuming that $\lambda = 3$ cm. The true location of each scatterer is at the center of its image area. It should be noted that as a scatterer's image is smeared over a larger area, the peak RCS falls below the actual RCS of the scatterer. For a few of the scatterers, the loss in image RCS is shown in dB. The integral in square meters over the scatterer's image area remains constant. Total "power" is conserved between data input and range–Doppler image output.

In some important cases, the contribution of $\ddot{\theta}_0$ or $\ddot{\eta}$ to (46c) cannot be neglected. The first class of cases consists of stable or very slowly rotating targets in low Earth orbit near the beginning or end of a pass when the satellite's velocity vector is directed almost toward or

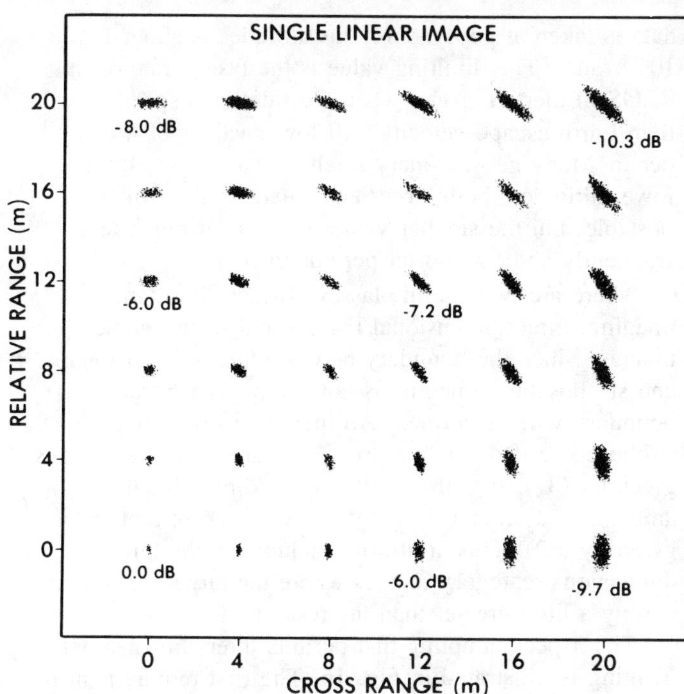

Fig. 29. Range–Doppler image over 7.2° of aspect change with too large an interval (θ = constant; simulated data λ = 3 cm).

coherent data that spans a time significantly greater than the interval ΔT which can be used in linear range–Doppler imaging. This set of data need not be continuous. It can, for example, be made up of many widely separated intervals. Two particular classes of data sets are discussed.

The first class of data sets, associated with wide-angle imaging, uses one continuous interval of data ΔT, where ΔT is larger than can be used in linear range–Doppler imaging, but is a fraction of the target's rotation period. The second class, associated with multiple rotation imaging, uses many equal intervals selected synchronously from successive target rotation periods. This second class includes stroboscopic and three-dimensional imaging.

Wide-Angle Imaging. In wide-angle imaging, the continuous data interval used ΔT is significantly larger than the interval that can be used in range–Doppler imaging, i.e., ΔT severely violates (49) and (50) so that simple Fourier transform processing cannot be used. These larger values of ΔT correspond to larger aspect changes $\Delta\theta$. Point scatterer-like features that give persistent returns during this interval image with a sharper cross-range resolution according to (8). Also, the boundaries of specular surface are more sharply defined. More specular surfaces are included in the image because of the wider range of aspects covered by the data. The image SNR will improve for small persistent point scatterers, thus yielding in some cases otherwise unobtainable information about some of the low RCS features of the target.

When the aspect rate $\dot\theta$ is constant, Fig. 29 shows the smearing of a range–Doppler image that results when

away from the radar. In these cases, $\ddot\theta_0$ is important. In the second class of cases, $\ddot\eta_0$ is predominant. These involve very rapidly rotating targets where the angle κ between rotation axis and the RLOS is small or close to 180°. Other cases where these second derivatives cannot be neglected must be expected, but the above two classes are known to occur frequently.

(2) *Extended Images.* An extended correlation image is obtained by evaluating $G(r_0)$ over a set of

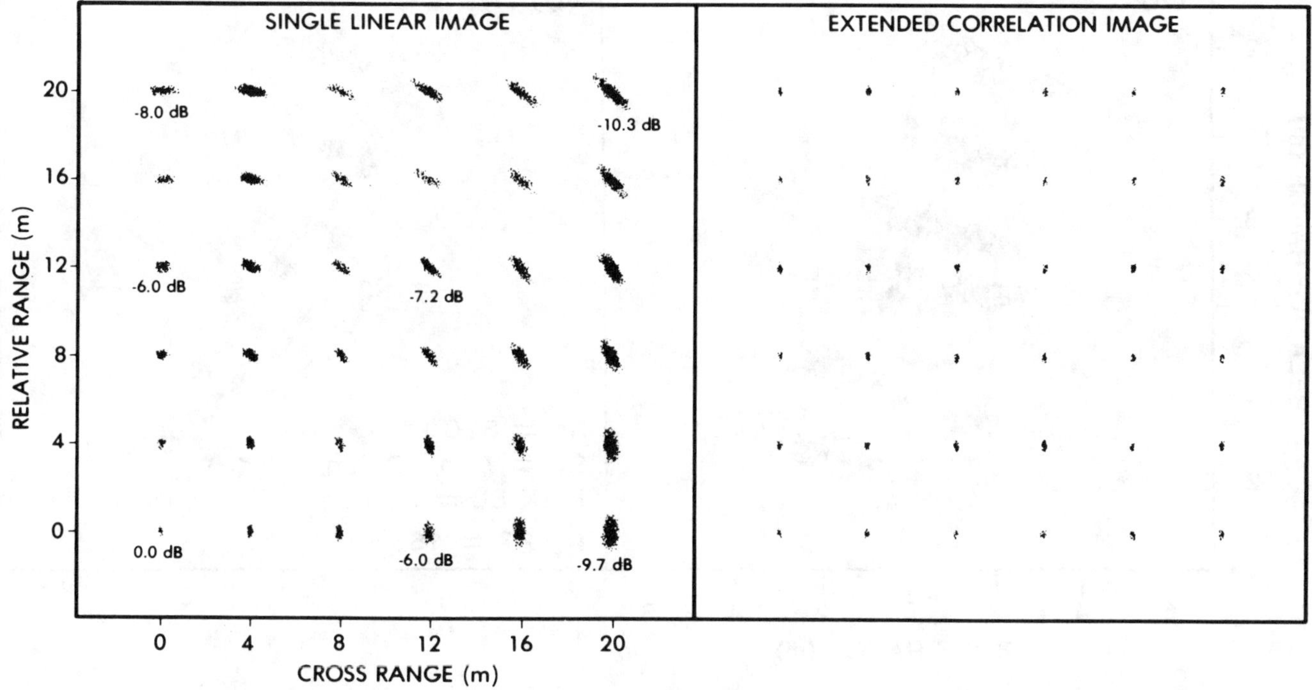

Fig. 30. Comparison of range–Doppler with correlation image over 7.2° of aspect change (θ = constant; simulated data).

both constraints on range–Doppler imaging are violated by an extraordinarily large target. (The radar data is simulated.) Fig. 30 shows the same range–Doppler image beside a correctly calculated correlation image. The correlation image correctly focuses, with no loss of RCS, all scatterers in this large target.

Near the end of subsection IV B-1, a not unusual case was described where a linear range–Doppler was limited in cross-range resolution by $\ddot{\theta}_0$. This occurs because early (and late) in a near overhead pass of an Earth-stable target, the aspect rate, $\dot{\theta}$, is small and rapidly varying. Fig. 31(a) shows a range–Doppler image calculated using a $\Delta\theta$ that violates (49) by a factor of 7. (Again, radar data is simulated.) The actual scatterer locations can be seen in Fig. 31(b) which was calculated by correlation imaging using the same data interval. The nature and location of the smearing on the range–Doppler image confirms that the $\ddot{\theta}_0 X'$ contribution to $\ddot{D}_0$ in (46c) is the dominant source of smearing. Again, on the correlation image, each scatterer is correctly focused. Similar image improvement in these cases has been obtained with real data.

Multiple Rotation Imaging. The data used in multiple rotation images covers the same interval $\Delta\psi$ (Fig. 16) on each of many successive rotations. According to the discussion in Subsection IIC, useful multiple rotation images require that the rotation rate $\dot{\psi}$ be much larger than the rate of change κ of the aspect deviation angle. For satellites in orbit about the Earth, it can be shown that the largest possible value of $\dot{\kappa}$ when data is taken at geosynchronous altitudes is about 1.3×10^{-4} rad/s. This limiting value is the fastest rate of the RLOS in inertial space, when the satellite's speed is less than Earth escape velocity. All lower values of $\dot{\kappa}$ can occur. Many geostationary satellites have $\kappa = 0$. At lower altitudes, both larger and smaller values of $\dot{\kappa}$ are possible, but the smaller values of $\dot{\kappa}$ occur much less frequently and for shorter periods of time.

There are two useful classes of multiple rotation imaging: three-dimensional images and stroboscopic images. Since the boundary between three-dimensional and stroboscopic imaging is not sharp, an arbitrary boundary will be defined. An image will be called stroboscopic if $\rho(z') > z'$ extent of target, where $\rho(z')$ is given by (37). It will be called three dimensional if $\text{amb}(z') > z'$ extent of target $> \rho(z')$, where $\text{amb}(z')$ is given by (32). This arbitrarily includes in the three-dimensional category images where the target's z' extent is only a little greater than the resolution.

The aspect sampling that permits three-dimensional imaging is illustrated in Fig. 16. The first requirement in the selection of data for three-dimensional imaging is to ensure that $\text{amb}(x')$, given by (31), is greater than the x' extent of the target and that $\text{amb}(z')$, given by (32), is greater than the z' extent. At X band with typical satellite dimensions, this generally requires that both $\delta\theta$ and $\delta\kappa$ be a small fraction of a degree. The second requirement is that enough data be used to give the desired resolution in both the x' and the z' directions. At X band, this generally requires $\Delta\theta \approx \Delta\kappa \approx$ a few degrees.

For stroboscopic imaging, the aspect deviation angle κ effectively remains constant over the entire data set

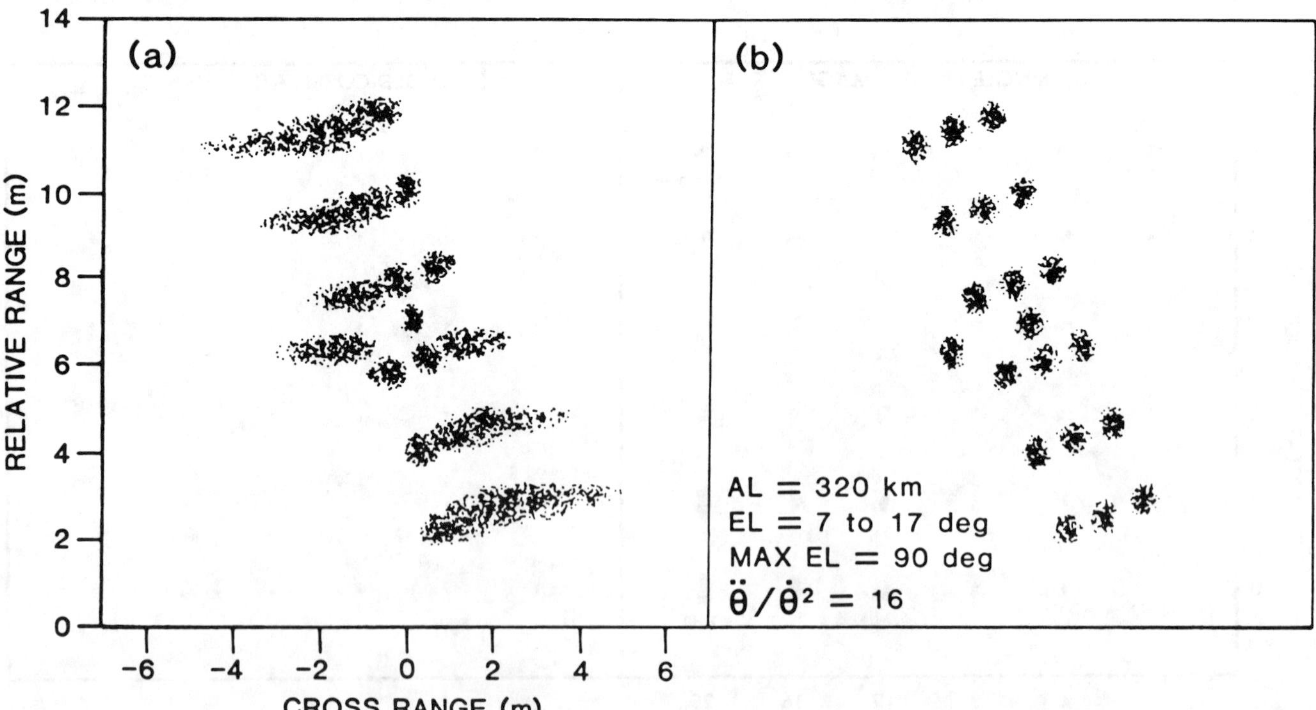

Fig. 31. (a) Range–Doppler image of Earth-stable target at low elevation from overhead pass ($\dot{\theta}$ = rapidly changing; $\Delta\theta \approx 6°$; simulated data). (b) Correlation image from same data used to calculate (a).

AUSHERMAN ET AL: DEVELOPMENTS IN RADAR IMAGING

used in the image. The same arc of a κ = constant small circle on the unit sphere in the target coordinate system is sampled again and again on successive target rotations. This redundant sampling of the same arc of aspects is useful mainly because it permits coherent integration to suppress the noise. With uniform weighting, correlation imaging is the optimum process for this coherent integration over rotation periods. With each rotation weighted the same, the noise power level in the correlation image is suppressed by the factor of $1/N$, where N is the number of rotations used. Because the weights are normalized, the target RCS in the image remains the same.

If the RLOS used are approximately coplanar, the stroboscopic image, like a single rotation image using the same ψ interval, is two dimensional. The image function $G(\mathbf{r}_0)$ need only be calculated over the $z' = \mathbf{0}$ plane.

An additional important property of stroboscopic imaging is that it can be used to suppress the cross-range ambiguous images that occur with PRF limited data. With a large rapidly rotating target, $\delta\theta$, the change in aspect between the pulses used in an image calculated from a single rotation may be so large that the x' extent of the target exceeds the ambiguity interval amb(x') given by (31). This would cause the ambiguous images on each side to overlap the true image. If the apparent rotation period of the satellite is not an integral multiple of the radar's interpulse period, the aspects sampled by the pulses on successive rotation periods are not precisely the same and the sampled aspects are interleaved. This interleaving of aspects, which usually occurs, causes the ''ghost'' (i.e., ambiguous) images in successive single rotation correlation images to be misaligned in phase, while the true images are correctly aligned in phase with each other. With coherent summing over rotation periods, the ghost images are partially suppressed. Optimal suppression of the ghost images can be achieved with proper selection of nonuniform weights between rotation periods. The nonuniform weights usually cause a modest reduction in the SNR gain for the true image.

Any rapidly rotating geostationary satellite whose rotation axis has a constant orientation relative to the Earth will have a constant κ so stroboscopic imaging can be done. At geostationary ranges, the improved image SNR is needed. Other deep space targets may possibly be found with the rapid rotation and extremely slow $\dot{\kappa}$ needed for stroboscopic imaging.

(3) Data Acquisition: Ground-Based

Radars. Ground-based radars for imaging of man-made moving objects require, among other attributes, sufficient sensitivity for the objects' range, good frequency stability for phase measurements, a PRF capability greater than the greatest Doppler frequency spread of the objects to be imaged, and a PRF control system to insure that transmitted pulses will not interfere with the received pulses.

The long range imaging radar (LRIR) is an example [11]. It was designed to meet these requirements for artificial satellites out to geosynchronous ranges. Some of its design parameters are listed in [11]. In deep space, coherent integration over a large number of pulses is generally required for adequate image signal-to-noise ratio. At a PRF of 1200, unambiguous images of objects with cross-range extents exceeding 4 m can be obtained with rotation periods as short as 2 s.

These ground-based radars, like (spotlight) SAR radars, can use time–bandwidth exchange techniques to pulse-compress a wideband FM waveform. Fig. 32, which is similar to Fig. 20, shows a possible simplified radar system configuration. The most essential difference from Fig. 20 is that the real-time tracking system with its input measurements of range, azimuth, and elevation replaces the motion measurement system of the airborne SAR. The other major, but not essential, difference is that the steps that represent polar-format processing are omitted. Instead, in Fig. 32, the pulse-compressed radar data, along with auxiliary data, are recorded for separate image processing. Fig. 21, which shows the signals from the transmitter, from the receiver, and from the correlation mixer of a (spotlight) SAR also applies to the ground-based radar. However, the small range extents of typical man-made moving targets causes the two parallelograms on the figure to become extremely slender. Essentially, the full length of the chirp pulse can be used.

The recorded pulse-compressed signals and auxiliary data are used to calculate FFT images (see Section IVB-1). Because of the small size of the objects, single FFT images with cross-range resolution equal to the range resolution often are well focused over the full extent of the target. If extended images are required, they also can be calculated. Since the extended images require better trajectory and rotational models of the objects, human intervention would normally be required.

The recorded auxiliary data contains metric information which can be used along with the pulse-compressed signal data to improve the trajectory estimate. The ''predicted range'' which is recorded gives the precise range to one of the range recording bins (i.e., to one of the range FFT outputs). This allows the range to every range bin to be accurately calculated at every pulse.

Dynamical Modeling for Space Object Imaging. Dynamical models describing the orbital motion of the target center of mass and the rotational motion of the target relative to the distant stars are essential inputs in the calculation of the correlation image function of (16). The orbital model is needed to perform the overall center of mass Doppler component phase correction of (17). Both the orbital and the rotational motion model are needed to determine the extent of the integration time (number of pulses) required to sample the aspects necessary to provide a good resolution image and to determine the correct relative range rate (frequency to cross-range conversion scales).

Precision Requirements for Dynamical Models. As previously indicated (Section IIIC), in order to obtain

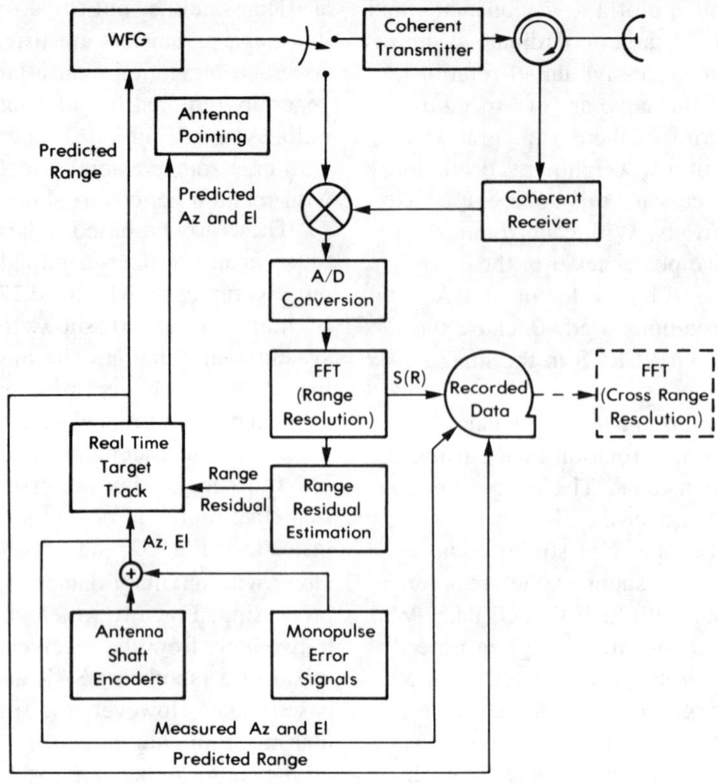

Fig. 32. Simplified ground-based radar systems.

quality images from the calculation of (16), the combined dynamical model parameters should be determined to sufficient precision that they determine range variations to any point r_0 in the object to a precision of a small fraction of a wavelength over the data interval of the image calculation. Experience has shown that in many cases orbital and rotational motion parameters determined from radar data can give on the order of $\lambda/30$ range precision or better. In particular, one can demonstrate that when one is estimating orbital parameters, the calculated range variation error due to orbital parameter errors can often be estimated by

$$R_\epsilon \lesssim \sigma(R_{obs}) \, \Delta T/\mathrm{DT} \qquad (52)$$

where $\sigma(R_{obs})$ is the rms range observation error. Typically, $\sigma(R_{obs})$ is on the order of several centimeters to a meter. DT is the data time interval over which the trajectory fit is calculated. It is typically 10 min or longer. ΔT is the coherent imaging interval. For an Earth-stable target, ΔT may be typically one or two orders of magnitude smaller than DT (which is limited by the duration of the pass) and consequently the $\lambda/30$ precision requirement may or may not be achieved. For rapidly rotating targets, ΔT is usually sufficiently smaller than DT that the precision requirement is easily reached. Also for some of these rapidly rotating targets, techniques using phase-derived ranges have been developed for calculating orbit fits with rms range observation errors, $\sigma(R_{obs})$, on the order of 1 mm. With phase-derived ranges, the $\lambda/30$ precision is achievable for $\Delta T \approx \mathrm{DT}$

and thus all the recorded data can be used in one coherent interval.

Rotational model parameters, such as the target's angular velocity and the orientation of its rotation axis, often cannot be determined as reliably as the orbital parameters. The development of techniques to determine rotational motion parameters is a crucial and still very active endeavor. The successful techniques depend critically on the nature of the data, such as the extent of change of the orientation of the target. Refinement of rotational motion parameters using phase-derived range measurements has been successfully achieved for a few selected targets. In every case, a preliminary approximate rotational model must be obtained before refinements with phase-derived ranges can be performed. Often the preliminary model, however, may be difficult to determine.

Except at low elevations or over very long time intervals, a propagation model that is a standard troposphere model for the radar site is adequate. The troposphere model errors and the ionospheric effects do not change rapidly enough to defocus the resulting images. In the exceptional cases, orbit fit range residuals from phase-derived ranges have been fitted to smooth functions of time. These smooth functions have been used for additional propagation corrections.

Extended Coherent Processing (ECP). Here we discuss an algorithm called ECP which has been developed for the purpose of efficiently calculating, analyzing, and displaying the pulse-by-pulse correlation image function defined by (14). The method used by ECP is basically of the multisubaperture processing type discussed in Section IIIB-2.

This program estimates $G(\boldsymbol{r}_0)$ for arbitrarily long sets of data by means of a coherent summation of linear images evaluated over shorter segments of the data intervals. Like all correlation imaging, ECP requires orbital and rotational models that give precise estimates of range variations at all the input data times. These precise models are used to correctly account for the nonlinear motion of scatterers in a wide-angle image, and/or the rotation-to-rotation relative motion in a multiple rotation image. The ECP image is an excellent approximation to $G(\boldsymbol{r}_0)$. Furthermore, its evaluation is also very efficient, being at least an order or magnitude faster than the pulse-by-pulse calculation of $G(\boldsymbol{r}_0)$.

The ECP Algorithm. To calculate a correlation image using (14) or (15)–(17), it is necessary to calculate the quantity $W(p)S(p)\exp[-j4\pi R(p)/\lambda]$ (or the equivalent quantity from (16)) once for every $\boldsymbol{r}_0$ grid point in the image and to repeat these calculations for every pulse. These repetitive calculations, although straightforward, require about an order of magnitude more computer time than calculating a linear range–Doppler image using (48b) over the same set of pulses. This fact suggests that it would be worthwhile to reformulate extended correlation imaging so as to use range–Doppler image functions, $P(D,\dot{D})$, calculated over subintervals of the total data set.

In order to do this reformulation, it is necessary to replace (46a) and (46b) by a calculation of D_0 and $\dot{D}_0$ as a function of (x,y,z) for a more general fixed orientation of the (x,y,z) coordinate system with respect to the target. The y' axis can be aligned with the range direction at the center time of only one range–Doppler subinterval. Thus (46a) and (46b) cannot be used for any other subintervals. Fortunately, the calculation of D and $\dot{D}$ from (x,y,z) is straightforward given any rectangular coordinate system that rotates with the target.

Let the time-varying unit vector $\boldsymbol{u}(t)$ be aligned with the RLOS at all times. This unit vector, and its time derivative $\dot{\boldsymbol{u}}(t)$ can be calculated in the target's coordinate system $\boldsymbol{r}_0 = (x,y,z)$ using the target's orbital and rotational models. The equations needed are commonplace tools in applied satellite dynamics. They will not be given here. If the radar range is much larger than the target, the relative range to an $(\boldsymbol{r}_0)$ grid point is given in terms of this unit vector by the dot product

$$D(\boldsymbol{r}_0) = \boldsymbol{u} \cdot \boldsymbol{r}_0 \tag{53a}$$

and the relative range rate is given by

$$\dot{D}(\boldsymbol{r}_0) = \dot{\boldsymbol{u}} \cdot \boldsymbol{r}_0. \tag{53b}$$

Equation (53b) is obtained by differentiating (53a), holding $\boldsymbol{r}_0$ constant. These relative ranges and relative range rates need only be calculated at the center times of the range–Doppler subintervals. The calculations are further shortened by calculating $\boldsymbol{u}(t)$ and $\dot{\boldsymbol{u}}(t)$ only once for each subinterval. The simple dot products, (53a) and (53b), are all that must be repeated for each $(\boldsymbol{r}_0)$ grid point in the image.

If the radar range is not much larger than the object, the dot product approximation of (53) cannot be used. Instead, the instantaneous position of the radar in the target's coordinate system is given by

$$\boldsymbol{r}_r = -R(\boldsymbol{0},t)\boldsymbol{u} \tag{54}$$

and the exact relative range is given by

$$D(\boldsymbol{r}_0) = |\boldsymbol{r}_0 - \boldsymbol{r}_r| - |\boldsymbol{r}_r|. \tag{55}$$

The relative range rate $\dot{D}$ is obtained by differentiating the expression for D, holding $\boldsymbol{r}_0$ constant. These exact calculations require a modest increase of computer time over the time required by the dot product approximation. For a bistatic system, the relative range would be the average between relative ranges calculated for the transmitter and the receiver.

Let $D(n) \equiv D(\boldsymbol{r}_0,n)$ and $\dot{D}(n) \equiv \dot{D}(\boldsymbol{r}_0,n)$ denote the calculated values of D_0 and $\dot{D}_0$ at the center time of the nth range–Doppler image subinterval to be used in calculating the correlation image. With this notation, the linear approximation equivalent to (47) gives the relative range at pulse p in the nth subinterval as

$$D(\boldsymbol{r}_0,p) \approx D(\boldsymbol{r}_0,n) + \dot{D}(\boldsymbol{r}_0,n)p/\text{PRF} \tag{56}$$

where, as in (47), $p = 0$ at the center time of the nth range–Doppler subinterval. When (56) is used in (16), the contribution to $G(\boldsymbol{r}_0)$ from the nth subinterval becomes

$$G(\boldsymbol{r}_0,n) \approx \exp[-4\pi jD(n)/\lambda]P[n,D(n),\dot{D}(n)] \tag{57}$$

where

$$P[n,D,\dot{D}] = \sum_{\{p\}_n} W(p)\tilde{S}(p)\exp[-4\pi j\dot{D}/(\lambda\,\text{PRF})]. \tag{58}$$

The summation in (58) is over the set of pulses $\{p\}_n$ contained in the nth subinterval. In (58), as in (48b), the phase-corrected signal $\tilde{S}(p)$ is sampled at the approximate range $[R(\boldsymbol{0},t) + D]$, instead of at the more precise range $[R(\boldsymbol{0},t) + D + \dot{D}\,p/\text{PRF}]$, in order to permit FFT evaluation of the Fourier transform.

The ECP approximation to the correlation image function $G(\boldsymbol{r}_0)$ is obtained by summing (57) over the N subintervals.

$$G_{\text{ECP}}(\boldsymbol{r}_0) = \sum_{n=1}^{N} \omega(n)\exp[-4\pi jD(n)$$

$$/\lambda]P[n,D(n),\dot{D}(n)]. \tag{59}$$

For flexibility and convenience, a new set of weights $\omega(n)$ has been introduced here, controlling the relative contribution from the various range–Doppler image functions. To closely approximate the original correlation image, the original weights $W(p)$ would be used in (58) and the new weights $\omega(n)$ would be uniform.

Effective calculation of (58) using FFT methods, as in Subsection IVB-1, will give the function $P[n,D,\dot{D}]$ only at a discrete set of $(D,\dot{D})$ grid points. In general, the calculated points $[D(r_0 n), \dot{D}(r_0,n]$, where the function P is needed for (59), will fall between the $(D,\dot{D})$ grid points at which the function P has been calculated. The calculated function $P(n,D,\dot{D})$ is stored in a two-dimensional array or table containing the real and imaginary parts of P. Bivariate linear interpolation is used to extract $P[n,D(r_0,n), \dot{D}(r_0,n)]$ from this table. The interpolation is, in effect, performed separately on the real and imaginary parts of P. The table or array in which $P(n,D,\dot{D})$ is stored is called the nth ''periodogram.''

When (59) is used to approximate the original correlation image, one is effectively modeling the smoothly varying actual relative range $D(r_0,p)$ by a piecewise linear function of time where it is used to calculate the phase corrections in (58) and (59). When $D(r_0,p)$ is used in extracting $\tilde{S}(p)$ from the radar data for (58), it is approximated by a step function that takes a new constant value for each range–Doppler subinterval. This modeling is illustrated in Fig. 33 for one r_0 grid

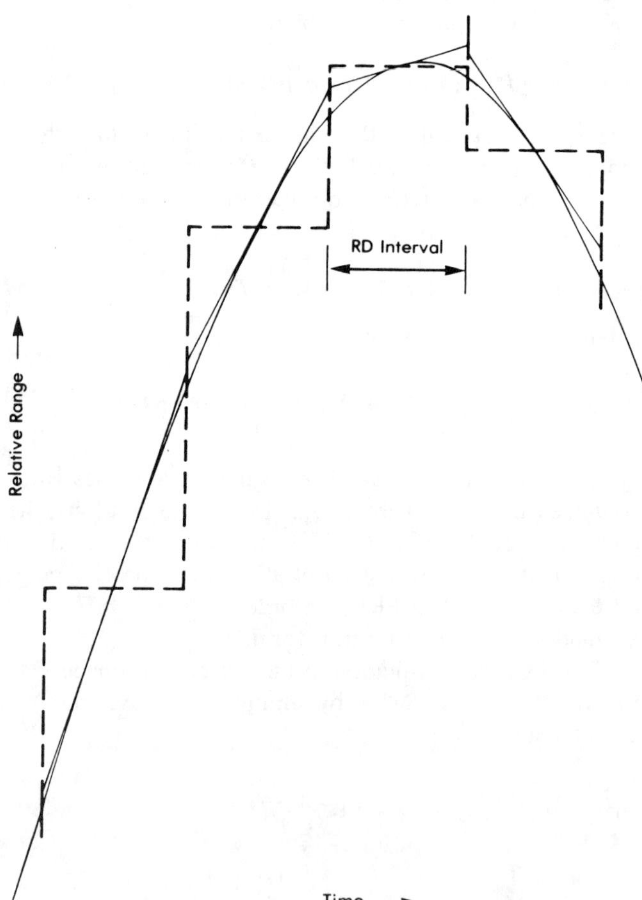

Fig. 33. Relative range to a scatterer versus time. Piecewise linear approximation shown for phase (solid lines) and step function approximation for range sampling (dashed lines). The length of the FFT processing interval is exaggerated to make the errors visible.

point in a rapidly rotating target. The sloping lines tangent to the smooth curve are the piecewise linear approximations used in phase corrections. The horizontal and vertical dashed lines are the step function approximation used for the relative range in sampling the radar data.

The ECP Algorithm: Numerical Considerations. To ensure that the preceding approximations do not cause significant errors, both constraints on range–Doppler imaging expressed by inequalities (49) and (50) must be satisfied by every range–Doppler subinterval used.

Low cross-range sidelobes in the periodogram images are desirable if they can be obtained without degrading the extended image. Using a sidelobe suppression set of tapered weights $W(p)$ in calculating the periodograms accomplishes this.

The radar returns $S(p)$ must be extracted from the recorded pulse-compressed radar signals at the desired range $R_d = R(0,t) + D$ without introducing harmful errors. Interpolation is required. If the signals are recorded at a range spacing of $c/(4BW)$, where c is the speed of light and BW is the bandwidth, then linear interpolation is adequate. This sample spacing is half the maximum spacing allowed by the sampling theorem. It is obtained by padding half the pulse compression FFT inputs with zeros.

If the PRF is much greater than the Doppler bandwidth of the object, then a number of successive pulses can be presummed into each FFT input at a given value of D. Prior to this presumming, the signals must be phase-corrected (17) and interpolated to the range R_d. If the number of pulses presummed is less than the number of pulses between FFT inputs, it is best to select for presumming a cluster of adjacent pulses centered on the time of each FFT input.

We call the Fourier transform in (58) ''symmetric'' because the reference phases in the exponential function are all zero at the center time of the range–Doppler interval, since p is zero at this time. The FFT calculation of $P(D_0,\dot{D}_0)$ must be arranged to calculate such a symmetric Fourier transform in order for (57) and (59) to be valid.

After the periodograms, $P[n,D,\dot{D}]$ are correctly calculated and stored, a possible source of error in calculating (59) is the bivariate linear interpolation used to get $P[n,D(n),\dot{D}(n)]$ from the periodogram tables. Errors here are controlled by calculating and storing the periodograms over a sufficiently fine grid in both the range and range rate directions.

A grid spacing in relative range D of $c/(4BW)$ is sufficiently small to give reasonably accurate range interpolation. The grid spacing required in relative range rate $\dot{D}$ depends on the periodogram sidelobe level. If the sidelobes in the periodograms are low, a grid spacing of $\lambda/(4\Delta T)$ in $\dot{D}$ gives reasonably accurate range–rate interpolation. This too is half the maximum grid spacing allowed by the sampling theorem. This requires padding about half the FFT input array with zeros for Doppler imaging. If the sidelobes in the periodograms are large, then a finer $\dot{D}$ grid is required. The relative weights $\omega(n)$ to use between periodograms depend on the type of imaging. For three-dimensional imaging, a sidelobe suppression taper, as a function of κ suppresses sidelobes in the second cross-range direction z'. For stroboscopic imaging, uniform weights between periodograms give optimum SNR improvement, but the nonuniform weights discussed in Section IVB-2 may be needed to suppress ambiguous images in the original cross-range x' direction.

For wide-angle imaging, it has been found best to use periodograms that overlap 50 percent, i.e., half the pulses used in the nth periodogram are reused in the $(n + 1)$th periodogram. A sidelobe suppression weighting $W(p)$ is used in calculating these periodograms, and similar weighting $\omega(n)$ is used between periodograms in calculating (59).

V. SUMMARY

In this paper we have presented a general treatment of range-doppler radar imaging techniques and have given detailed discussions of some of the most prominent and illustrative applications, such as airborne SAR imaging and space object (planets, artificial satellites) imaging from ground-based wideband radars. We have also stated the general properties of, and the necessary requirements for, useful radar images. The different image processing algorithms required to perform particular imaging tasks have been introduced and outlined.

We have stressed that all these imaging techniques are basically equivalent and can be developed from a common theoretical background, which is, in fact, also common with tomographic imaging applications.

These techniques have been conceived and developed to deal with the problem of the scatterer's motion through resolution cells, thus permitting a much wider spectrum of applications than allowed by obeying the stringent requirements of linear range–Doppler imaging. These techniques, in order to handle the data-intensive applications, have also been developed to be computationally efficient.

The differences among the various computational algorithms are affected by the approximations that are valid in specific applications and also by tradeoffs between image quality and computational efficiency.

ACKNOWLEDGMENT

The developments reviewed in this paper are the result of significant contributions over nearly three decades by various researchers too numerous to list. The references provide partial documentation of these contributions.

REFERENCES

[1]   Cutrona, L.J., Vivian, W.E., Leith, E.N., and Hall, G.O. (1961)
      A high-resolution radar combat-surveillance system.
      IRE Transactions on Military Electronics, MIL-5, (Apr. 1961), 127.

[2]   Leith, E.N. (1977)
      Complex spatial filters for image deconvolution.
      Proceedings of the IEEE, 65, 1 (Jan. 1977), 18.

[3]   Jordan, R.L. (1980)
      The Seasat—A synthetic aperture radar aperture.
      IEEE Journal of Oceanic Engineering, OE-5, 5 (Apr. 1980), 154.

[4]   Marlow, H.C., Watson, D.C., Van Hoozer, C.H., and Freeny, C.C. (1965)
      The RAT SCAT cross-section facility.
      Proceedings of the IEEE, 53 8 (Aug. 1965), 946.

[5]   Walker, J.L. (1980)
      Range-Doppler imaging of rotating objects.
      IEEE Transactions on Aerospace and Electronic Systems, AES-16 1 (Jan. 1980), 23–52.

[6]   Kirk, J.C., Jr. (1975)
      A discussion of digital processing in synthetic aperture radar.
      IEEE Transactions on Aerospace and Electronic Systems, AES-11 (May 1975), 326–337.

[7]   Kirk, J.C., Jr. (1975)
      Digital synthetic aperture radar technology.
      In *IEEE 1975 International Radar Conference Record,* p. 482.

[8]   Kirk, J.C., Jr. (1975)
      Motion compensation for synthetic aperture radar.
      IEEE Transactions on Aerospace Electronic Systems, AES-11 3 (May 1975), 338–348.

[9]   Kovaly, J.J. (1977)
      High resolution radar fundamentals
      In Eli Broakner (Ed.), *Radar Technology.*
      Dedham, Mass.: Artech House, 1977.

[10] Brookner, E. (1977)
      Synthetic aperture radar spotlight mapper.
      In Eli Brookner (Ed.), *Radar Technology*
      Dedham, Mass.: Artech House, 1977.

[11] Bromaghim, D.R., and Perry, J.P. (1980)
      A wideband linear FM ramp generator for the long-range imaging radar.
      IEEE Transactions on Microwave Theory and Techniques, MTT-26, 5 (May 1980), 322.

[12] Shapiro, J.J. (1968)
      Planetary radar astronomy.
      IEEE Spectrum, 5, 3 (Mar. 1968), 70.

[13] Prickett, M.J., and Chen, C.C. (1980)
      Principles of inverse synthetic aperture radar (ISAR) imaging.
      IEEE 1980 EASCON Record, p. 340.

[14] Sherwin, C.W., Ruina, J.P., and Rawcliff, R.D. (1962)
      Some early developments in synthetic aperture radar systems.
      IRE Transactions on Military Electronics, MIL-6 (Apr. 1962), 111.

[15] Jolley, J.H. and Dotson, C. (1981)
      Synthetic aperture radar improves reconnaissance.
      Defense Electronics, 13 9 (Sept. 1981), 111.

[16] Porcello, L.J., et al. (1974)
      The Apollo lunar sounder radar system.
      Proceedings of the IEEE, (June 1974), 768–783.

[17] Daily, M., Elachi, C., Farr, T., and Schaber, G. (1978)
      Discrimination of geologic units in Death Valley using dual frequency and polarization radar data.
      Geophysical Research Letters, 5 (1978), 889.

[18] Shuchman, R.A., Davis, C.F., and Jackson, P.L. (1975)
      Contour stripmine detection and identification with imaging radar.
      Bulletin of the Association of Engineering Geology, X-11 (1975), 99.

[19] Brown, W.E., Jr., Elachi, C., and Thompson, T.W. (1976)
      Radar imaging of ocean surface patterns.
      Journal of Geophysical Research, 81 (1976), 2657.

[20] Shemdin, O.H., Brown, W.E., Jr., Staudhammer, F.G., Shuchman, R., Larson, R., Zelenka, J., Rose, D.B., McLeish, W., and Berles, R.A. (1978)
      Comparison of in situ and remotely sensed ocean waves off Marineland, Florida.
      Boundary Layer Meteorology, 13 (1978), 173.

[21] Shuchman, R.A. (1981)
      Processing synthetic aperture radar data of ocean waves.
      In J.F.R. Gower (Ed.), *Oceanography from Space.*
      New York: Plenem, 1981, p. 477.

[22] Gray, A.L., Hawkins, R.K., Livingstone, E.E., Arsenault, Drapier, and Johnstone, W.M. (1982)
      Simultaneous scatterometer and radiometer measurements of sea-ice microwave signatures.
      IEEE Journal of Oceanic Engineering, OE-7, (1982), 20.

[23] Luther, C.A., Lyden, J.D., Shuchman, R.A., Larson, R.W., Holmes, Q.A., Nuesch, D.R., Lowry, R.T., and Livingstone, C.E. (1982)
      Synthetic aperture radar studies of sea ice.
      In *IEEE International Geoscience and Remote Sensing Symposium,* Munich, Germany, (1982), pp. TA-8 1.1–1.9.

[24] Beal, R.C., DeLeonibus, P. and Katz, I. (eds.). (1981)
      Spaceborne Synthetic Aperture Radar for Oceanography.
      Baltimore, Md.: Johns Hopkins Press, 1981.

[25] Gonzalez, F.I., Beal, R.C., Brown, W.E., Jr., DeLeonibus, P.S., Gower, J.F.R., Lichy, D., Ross, D.B., Rufenach, C.L., Sherman, J.W., III, and Shuchman, R.A. (1979)
      SEASAT synthetic aperture radar: Ocean wave detection capabilities.
      Science, 204 (1979), 418.

[26] Gower, J.F.R. (Ed.). (1981)
      Oceanography from Space.
      New York: Plenum, 1981.

[27] Elachi, C., et al. (1982)
      Shuttle imaging radar experiment.
      Science, 218 (1982), 996.

[28] Duchossors, G., and Honvault, C. (1981)
      The first ESA remote sensing satellite system ERS-1.
      Presented at the 15th International Symposium on Remote Sensing of the Environment (Ann Arbor, Mich., May 1981).

[29] Raney, R.K. (1982)
      The Canadian RADARSAT program.
      In *Proceedings of the 1982 International Geoscience and Remote Sensing Symposium* (IGARSS '82), IEEE Catalog 82CH14723-6.

[30] Matsumoto, K., Kishida, H., Yamada, H., and Hisoda, Y. (1982)
      Development of active microwave sensors in Japan.
      In *Proceedings of the 1982 International Geoscience and Remote Sensing Symposium* (IGARSS '82), IEEE Catalog 82CH14723-6.

[31] Green, P.E., and Price, R. (1960)
      Signal processing in radar astronomy.
      Technical Report 234, Lincoln Laboratory, Massachusetts Institute of Technology, Cambridge, Oct. 1960.

[32] Green, P.E. (1978)
      Radar measurements of target scattering properties.
      In J.V. Evans and T. Hagfors (Eds.), *Radar Astronomy.*
      New York: McGraw-Hill, 1978, pp. 1–75.

[33] Pettengill, G.A. (1960)
      Measurements of lunar reflectivity using the Millstone radar.
      Proceedings of the IRE, 48 (1960), 933.

AUSHERMAN ET AL: DEVELOPMENTS IN RADAR IMAGING

[34] Pettengill, G.A., et al. (1982)
A radar investigation of Venus.
Astronomical Journal, 67 (1982), 181.

[35] Smith, W.B. (1963)
Radar observations of Venus 1959 and 1961.
Astronomical Journal, 68 (1963), 15.

[36] Muchleman, D.O., Black, N., and Holdridge, D.B. (1962)
The astronomical unit determined by radar reflections from Venus.
Astronomical Journal, 67 (1962), 191.

[37] Thompson, J.H., et al. (1961)
A new determination of the solar parallax by means of radar echoes from Venus.
Nature, 190 (1961), 519.

[38] Kotelnikov, V.A., et al. (1962)
Radar system employment during radar contact with Venus.
Radiolekhnika i Electronika, 7 (1962), 1715.

[39] Carpenter, R.L., and Goldstein, R.M. (1983)
Radar observations of Mercury.
Science, 142 (1983), 381.

[40] Pettengill, G.H. (1965)
Recent Arecibo observations of Mars and Jupiter.
Journal of Research of the National Bureau of Standards D, 69 (1965), 1627.

[41] Dyce, R.B. (1965)
Recent Arecibo observations of Mars and Jupiter.
Journal of Research of the National Bureau of Standards D, 69 (1965), 1628.

[42] Evans, J.V., et al. (1965)
Radio echo observations of Venus and Mercury at 23 cm wavelength.
Astronomical Journal, 70 (1965), 486.

[43] La Hoffneon, R A., Hurlbut, R.H., Kind, D.E., and Wentroub, H.J. (1969)
A 94-GHz radar for space object identification.
IEEE Transactions on Microwave Theory and Techniques, MTT-17 12 (Dec. 1969), 1145.

[44] Brown, W.M. (1967)
Synthetic aperture radar.
IEEE Transactions on Aerospace and Electronic Systems, AES-3 (1967), 217.

[45] Brown, W.M., and Fredericks, R.J. (1969)
Range-Doppler imaging with motion through resolution cells.
IEEE Transactions on Aerospace and Electronic Systems, AES-5 (Jan. 1969), 98.

[46] Walker, J.L., Carrara, W.G., and Cindrich, I. (1973)
Optical processing of rotating-object radar data using a polar recording format.
Technical Report RADC-TR-73-136, AD 526 738, Rome Air Development Center, Rome, NY, May 1973.

[47] Mensa, D., Heidbreder, G., and Wade, G. (1980)
Aperture synthesis by object rotation in coherent imaging.
IEEE Transactions on Nuclear Science, NS-27 (Apr. 1980), 989.

[48] Mensa, D. (1982)
High resolution imaging.
Dedham, Mass.: Arctech House, 1982.

[49] Wehner, D.R., Prickett, M.J., Rock, R.G., and Chen, C.C. (1979)
Stepped frequency radar target imagery, Theoretical concept and preliminary results.
Technical Report 490, Naval Ocean Systems Center, San Diego, CA, Nov. 1979.

[50] Chen, C.C., and Andrews, H.C. (1980)
Target-motion-induced radar imaging.
IEEE Transactions on Aerospace and Electronic Systems, AES-16 (Jan. 1980), 2–14.

[51] Chen, C.C., and Andrews, H.C. (1980)
Multifrequency imaging of radar turntable data.
IEEE Transactions on Aerospace and Electronic Systems, AES-16 (Jan. 1980), 15–22.

[52] Mensa, D.L., Halevy, S., and Wade, G. (1983)
Coherent Doppler tomography for microwave imaging.
Proceedings of the IEEE, 71 (Feb. 1983), 254.

[53] Munson, D.C., and Jenkins, W.K. (1981)
A common framework for spotlight mode synthetic aperture radar and computer-aided tomography.
In *Proceedings of the 15th Asilomar Conference on Circuits, Systems, and Computus* (G.L. Pacific Grove, Calif., Nov. 9–11, 1981), p. 217.

[54] Munson, D.C., O'Brien, J.D., and Jenkins, W.K. (1983)
A tomographic formulation of spotlight-mode synthetic aperture radar.
Proceedings of the IEEE, 7 (Aug. 1983), 917–925.

[55] Aleksoff, C.C., LaHaie, I.J., and Tai, A.M. (1983)
Optical-hybrid backprojection processing.
In *Proceedings of the 10th International Computing Conference* (Apr. 6–8, 1983), IEEE Catalog 83 CH 1880-4.

[56] Mims, J., and Farrell, J.L. (1972)
Synthetic aperture imaging with maneuvers.
IEEE Transactions on Aerospace and Electronic Systems, AEA-8 (July 1972), 410–418.

[57] Brown, W.M. (1980)
Walker model for radar sensing of rigid target field.
IEEE Transactions on Aerospace and Electronic Systems, AES-16 (Jan. 1980), 104–107.

[58] Lewitt, R.M. (1983)
Reconstruction algorithms: Transform methods.
Proceedings of the IEEE, 71 (Mar. 1983), 390–408.

[59] Brown, W.M., and Porcello, J.L. (1969)
An introduction to synthetic aperture radar.
IEEE Spectrum, 6 (Sept. 1969), 52–62.

[60] Leith, E.N. (1971)
Quasi-holographic techniques in the microwave region.
Proceedings of the IEEE, 59 (Sept. 1971), 1305–1318.

[61] Kozma, A., et al. (1972)
Tilted-plane optical processor.
Applied Optics, 11 (Aug. 1972), 1766–1777.

[62] Wu, C. (1980)
A digital fast correlation approach to produce SEASAT SAR imagery.
In *Proceedings of the IEEE 1980 International Radar Conference*, pp. 153–160.

[63] Leith, E.N. (1973)
Range-azimuth-coupling aberrations in pulse-scanned imaging systems.
Journal of the Optical Society of America, 63 (Feb. 1973), 119–126.

[64] Ausherman, D.A. (1980)
Digital versus optical techniques in synthetic aperture radar (SAR) data processing.
Optical Engineering, 19 (Mar./Apr. 1980), 157–167.

[65] Skolnik, M.I. (1980)
Introduction to Radar Systems, 2nd ed.
New York: McGraw-Hill, 1980, pp. 34–44.

Passive Microwave Remote Sensing of the Earth from Space—A Review

ENI G. NJOKU, MEMBER, IEEE

Abstract—During the past decade, microwave radiometry from space has developed into a powerful technique for remote sensing of the earth's atmosphere and surface. Passive microwave sensors on earth-orbiting satellites are beginning to make significant contributions to the fields of operational meteorology and oceanography. This paper reviews the development of microwave radiometry from space as a tool for several atmospheric and surface remote-sensing applications. The basic spacecraft radiometer system concepts are discussed and a description of the key individual sensors launched prior to 1981 is provided along with their significant results. Recent studies on new instrument designs and potential applications are summarized, and indicate the unique possibilities for future implementation of passive microwave techniques.

I. INTRODUCTION

IN RECENT YEARS there has been growing interest in the use of microwave and millimeter-wave radiometry for remote sensing of the earth from space. Some applications have become well established, such as temperature sounding for meteorological purposes and sea-ice mapping for navigation in polar regions. Other applications are still in the demonstration phase, such as measurements of surface temperature and wind speed over the oceans. The potential applications of radiometry from space have proliferated rapidly in the past decade, and include observations of surface features over ocean, land, and ice regions, and the monitoring of phenomena in the lower and upper regions of the atmosphere. To develop these applications for scientific, government, and commercial requirements a number of microwave radiometer systems have been designed over the past several years and successfully operated in space, and other more advanced systems are in the planning stages. Staelin [1], [2] and Tomiyasu [3] have reviewed the progress in development of techniques for passive microwave earth observations. The present paper reviews the progress to date in implementation of these techniques using satellite sensors. A brief discussion of the historical development of microwave radiometry from space is provided followed by a review of radiometer system concepts as applied to spacecraft platforms. The microwave radiometric sensors launched on the Nimbus satellites, Skylab, and Seasat are discussed with a summary of the important results from each sensor. Finally, future development concepts are discussed with reference to new applications and operational demonstrations.

II. BACKGROUND

A. Historical Development

Subsequent to the early ground-based passive microwave observations of the atmosphere by Dicke *et al.* [4] it was realized that the use of radiometers in space for microwave observations of the earth's emitted radiation was a valuable means for studying global properties of the earth's atmosphere and surface. The first test however of a spacecraft microwave radiometer was on the Mariner 2 Venus flyby mission of December 1962. The microwave radiometer aboard the spacecraft successfully measured emission from the planet at frequencies of 15.8 and 22.2 GHz on three scans of the planetary disk [5]. Results showed that the planetary emission was characterized by limb-darkening, and confirmed the high surface temperature of Venus.

The application of microwave radiometry from space to remote sensing of the earth began with observations from the Soviet satellite Cosmos 243 which was launched into an elliptical orbit around the earth on September 23, 1968. Measurements were made at frequencies of 3.5, 8.8, 22.2, and 37.5 GHz in a nonscanning, nadir-viewing mode, from which estimates of atmospheric water vapor, liquid water, sea temperature, and ice cover were made [6]. This was followed by a series of earth-viewing radiometers on both U.S. and Soviet satellites. The most extensive observations to date have been made by radiometers on the Nimbus series of satellites. Microwave radiometers launched prior to 1981 are listed in Table I with brief descriptions of their characteristics. These radiometers, and a well-established program of supporting research and aircraft radiometer flights, have helped to demonstrate the growing potential of microwave radiometry for operational remote sensing from space.

In progressing toward the development of operational spaceborne remote sensors, two kinds of system have evolved. Atmospheric sounders provide information about vertical profiles of temperature and molecular constituents in the atmosphere by making measurements near the molecular resonance frequencies. Surface sensors, on the other hand, operate primarily at window frequencies, where atmospheric absorption is low and surface features can be imaged or measured quantitatively. For most of these surface features high spatial resolution is desirable. For both sounders and surface sensors the microwave instruments have a distinct advantage over their counterparts at infrared or visible wavelengths in that the presence of most cloud cover does not significantly degrade the measurement accuracy. Thus microwave measurements from orbit provide a global, day or night, nearly all-weather remote-sensing capability. These advantages, together with the unique signatures of some surface and atmospheric features at microwave wavelengths, have encouraged the development of spacecraft passive microwave sensors in recent years.

Fig. 1 shows the microwave absorption spectrum of the earth's atmosphere [7]. The two curves give the zenith opacity, calculated using the 1962 U.S. Standard Atmosphere, for the primary absorbing constituents: water vapor, oxygen, and ozone. The lower curve is for no water vapor, while the upper curve is for 2-g/cm^2 total water vapor (assuming a water vapor density of 10 g/m^3 at the surface, decreasing exponentially with

Manuscript received September 4, 1981; revised March 19, 1982. This research was carried out by the Jet Propulsion Laboratory, California Institute of Technology, under Contract with the National Aeronautics and Space Administration.

The author is with the Jet Propulsion Laboratory, California Institute of Technology, Pasadena, CA 91103.

TABLE I
HISTORY OF MICROWAVE RADIOMETRY ON SPACECRAFT
(Adapted from Staelin [2].)

Year of Launch	Spacecraft	Instrument Acronym	Frequencies (GHz)	Antenna Type	Swath Width of Scan (km)	Smallest Resolution Element (km)	Principal Parameters Measured or Inferred
1962	Mariner 2 (Venus flyby)	–	15.8, 22.2	Mechanically scanned parabola	Planetary	1300	Limb darkening of planetary emission, temperature
1968	Cosmos 243	–	3.5, 8.8	Nadir-viewing parabola	–	13	Atmosphere: Water vapor content, liquid water content
1970	Cosmos 384		22.2, 37				Surface: Sea temperature, sea ice concentration
1972	Nimbus-5	ESMR	19.3	Electrically scanned array	3000	25	Atmosphere: Rain rate Surface: Sea ice concentration, ice classification
		NEMS	22.2, 31.4, 53.6, 54.9, 58.8	Five lens-loaded horns, nadir-viewing	–	200	Atmosphere: Temperature profile, water vapor content, liquid vapor content Surface: Ice classification, snow cover
1973	Skylab	S-193	13.9	Mechanically scanned parabola	180	16	Surface: winds, precipitation
		S-194	1.4	Nadir-viewing array	–	115	Surface: soil moisture
1974[†]	Meteor	–	37	Dual polarization 35° from nadir	–	–	Atmosphere: liquid water content
1975	Nimbus-6	ESMR	37	Electrically scanned array, dual-polarization	1300	20 x 43	Same as Nimbus-5 ESMR
		SCAMS	22.2, 31.6, 52.8, 53.8, 55.4	Three rotating hyperbolic mirrors	2700	150	Same as Nimbus-5 NEMS
1978[†]	Block 5D	SSM/T	50.5, 53.2, 54.3, 54.9, 58.4, 58.8, 59.4	Single rotating mirror	1600	175	Atmosphere: Temperature profile
1978[†]	Tiros-N (2 satellites)	MSU	50.3, 53.7, 55.0, 57.9	Dual rotating mirrors	2300	110	Atmosphere: Temperature profile
1978	Seasat	SMMR	6.6, 10.7, 18, 21, 37	Offset-fed oscillating parabola, dual-polarization	600	18 x 28	Atmosphere: Water vapor content liquid water content, rain rate
1978	Nimbus-7				800	22 x 35	Surface: Sea temperature, wind speed, sea ice concentration, ice classification, snow cover, soil moisture

[†] Additional launches in subsequent years.

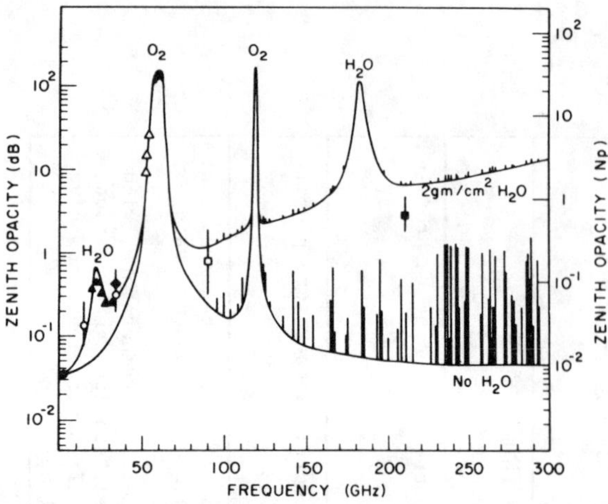

Fig. 1. Microwave absorption spectrum of the earth's atmosphere for constituents water vapor, oxygen, and ozone (after Waters [7]).

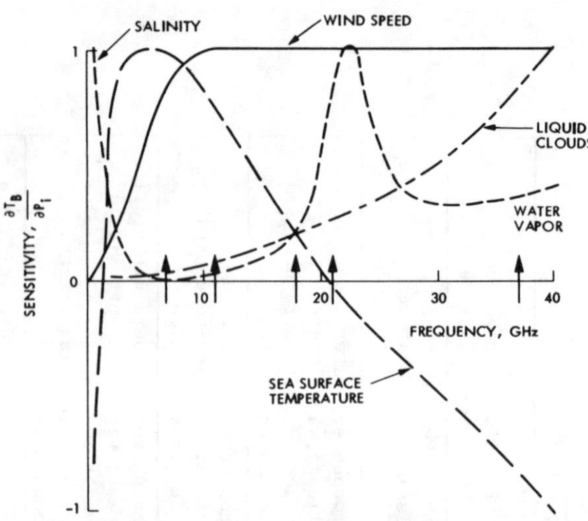

Fig. 2. Normalized sensitivity of brightness temperature (T_B) to various geophysical parameters (P_i) as a function of frequency (schematic). Arrows indicate SMMR frequencies (after Wilheit *et al.* [19]).

a scale height of 2 km). Also shown are some measured values as discussed in [7].

B. Atmospheric Sounding

One of the earliest meteorological applications of spaceborne radiometry was in global atmospheric temperature sounding. The mixing ratio of oxygen in the atmosphere is quite uniform and time-invariant, thus measurements of atmospheric emission at frequencies around the oxygen resonance complex (centered near 60 GHz) are proportional to atmospheric temperature at altitude levels defined by temperature weighting functions [8], [9]. By choosing frequencies whose weighting functions peak at different altitudes, retrieval techniques can be used to estimate vertical temperature profiles by inversion of the microwave data [10], [1].

The Nimbus-5 Microwave Spectrometer (NEMS) was the first instrument of this type, with three oxygen channels for temperature sounding. Since the weighting functions are weakly dependent on atmospheric water content and surface reflectivity, two additional channels were added, one on the water vapor absorption line (22.2 GHz) and one at a window frequency (31.4 GHz). Results from NEMS have been reported by Waters *et al.* [11], and Staelin *et al.* [12], [13]. A second instrument of this type, the Scanning Microwave Spectrometer (SCAMS), was flown on Nimbus-6. SCAMS provided global maps of atmospheric temperature structure and further demonstrated the feasibility of the technique for studying meteorological phenomena [14], [15]. The success of these two experimental sensors led to the development of microwave temperature sounders for operational use in synoptic meteorology. One of these is the four-channel Microwave Sounding Unit (MSU) launched on the TIROS-N satellite series. Another is a seven-channel microwave temperature sounder (SSM/T) operated on the Defense Meteorological Satellite Program (DMSP) Block 5D satellite.

Techniques are presently being studied to use resonances other than the oxygen 60-GHz complex for atmospheric temperature and composition sounding. The oxygen line at 118 GHz shows promise for temperature sounding from geosynchronous orbit, since the higher frequency reduces the antenna size required to achieve satisfactory spatial resolution from that altitude. The 183-GHz water vapor line is sensitive to changes in atmospheric water vapor gradients above about 2 km. Thus measurements around this frequency may be used to study the

vertical distribution of water vapor. Measurements of temperature and water vapor profiles from geosynchronous orbit are necessary for future operational severe-storm monitoring from space [16].

Another approach to monitoring atmospheric constituents, particularly in the upper atmosphere, is the limb-sounding technique. This technique can provide substantially improved sensitivities and vertical resolution over downward-looking systems. Ozone in particular, among other molecular species, is known to have a marked effect on the earth's environment, and there is considerable incentive for measuring its spatial and temporal distribution. Limb-sounding radiometers operating at microwave and millimeter wavelengths are currently under development, and will enable global measurements of these species to be made [17].

C. Surface Sensing

Surface-sensing applications can be divided into three main categories: Ocean, Ice, and Land. In general, atmospheric window frequencies are used to study the surface phenomena. However, measurements at these frequencies are affected to some extent by tropospheric water vapor, clouds, and rainfall. Hence most surface-sensing radiometer systems include frequency channels sensitive to atmospheric water vapor and liquid water, to measure global distributions of these parameters and to correct for their effects on the measurement of surface parameters. Microwave radiation from atmospheric liquid water and the earth's surface is by the mechanism of nonresonant thermal emission, thus the precise frequencies chosen to observe these parameters are usually noncritical. Frequencies are generally chosen to maximize sensitivity to particular parameters under different environmental conditions and to operate in regions of the spectrum free of interference from ground-based or earth-to-space radars and communication links.

For example, the SMMR (discussed in Section IV-G) is a five-frequency radiometer system designed primarily to measure sea-surface temperature, wind speed, and atmospheric water vapor and liquid water. Fig. 2 shows the sensitivities of the radiometer measurements (brightness temperatures, T_B) to these four parameters and salinity, as functions of frequency. These curves are based on physical models of ocean and atmosphere microwave emission, as reviewed by Wilheit [18], [19], and have been normalized for representation on the same scale. The SMMR frequencies are indicated on the frequency axis, and provide good sensitivity to and discrimination of the four required parameters while not being affected by variations in salinity. (Further discrimination is obtained by utilizing the polarization properties of the received radiation.) Physical models of microwave emission from ocean, ice, and land surfaces have been reviewed elsewhere in the literature [18]–[23] and will not be discussed at length here.

Radiometers on the Cosmos satellites, and the two low-frequency channels on NEMS and SCAMS, made the first measurements of atmospheric water vapor and cloud liquid water over the oceans [6], [13]. These measurements were possible due to the contrast between the warm radiative temperature of atmospheric water against the cold radiative background of the ocean. Against the warm background radiation over land, these measurements cannot be accurately made. The radiometers also measured sea-ice concentration, ice type, and snow cover [23]. The sea-ice measurements were substantially improved by measurements from the 19.35-GHz Electrically Scanning Microwave Radiometer (ESMR) on Nimbus-5 and the 37-GHz ESMR on Nimbus-6. The ESMR's provided medium resolution (~35 km) images of the polar ice, containing information on the variations of the ice packs on time scales ranging from several days to seasons [24]. The technique uses the large differences in emissivity and polarization properties of the various ice types, and of the neighboring sea water. Applications of such data for ship navigation and offshore engineering in polar regions and for climatological studies appear promising.

The ESMR instruments have also been used for global measurement of rainfall over the oceans. Rain has an enhanced effect on brightness temperature, over nonprecipitating liquid water, due to the larger droplet sizes than found in nonraining clouds, and due to the greater total water content in rain clouds. While quantitative measurements are difficult at present due to the complicated modeling problems involved, precipitation areas in the vicinity of storm systems have been identified, and relative global distributions of precipitation have been obtained [25], [26].

During 1973 and 1974 two microwave radiometers at 13.9 and 1.4 GHz were operated aboard the orbiting Skylab space station. Three short-duration missions during this period permitted earth observations by the two sensors, designated S193 and S194, respectively, between latitudes of $\pm 50°$. Real-time adjustments in operating modes were made possible by communication between ground investigators and crew members on the spacecraft. The S193 sensor was a combined radiometer/scatterometer/altimeter instrument, enabling comparisons to be made between passive and active microwave responses to a variety of land and ocean surfaces [27]. The S194 sensor made coarse spatial resolution brightness temperature measurements, which have shown correlations with large-scale phenomena, such as soil moisture over the central and western portion of the U.S. [28].

The latest in the series of spaceborne surface-sensing radiometers is the Scanning Multichannel Microwave Radiometer (SMMR). This instrument was launched on both the Nimbus-7 and Seasat satellites in 1978. The instrument has been described in detail by Gloersen and Barath [29], and Njoku *et al.* [30]. The additional capabilities of the SMMR over previous radiometers are primarily in the measurement of sea-surface temperature and wind speed. However, the five-frequency dual-polarization instrument also measures atmospheric water vapor, liquid water and rain rate, sea-ice concentration, ice type, snow cover, and can provide information on soil moisture. The effect of surface temperature on the emissivity and brightness temperature of the ocean is well understood [31], [32]. Wind speed, however, affects the surface emissivity only indirectly through the generation of ocean waves and foam. The complexity of this indirect relationship has made it difficult to develop precise models of brightness temperature dependence on wind speed [33]–[36]. Techniques for inverting data from the ten brightness temperature channels to obtain the ocean and atmospheric parameters, and determinations of the accuracies of the retrieved parameters, are currently being evaluated.

The success of the Seasat oceanographic satellite mission, which operated a number of active microwave and infrared sensors in addition to the SMMR, has generated interest within NASA, NOAA, and the military for future development of operational ocean-monitoring satellites, in which passive microwave sensors will undoubtedly play a major role. Operational ice-monitoring satellites with microwave radiometers aboard can also be expected to receive impetus in the years ahead. The outlook for operational spaceborne radiometers in earth resources and land applications is less clear. Although spacecraft radiometer experiments for the land applications will most likely be continued in the coming years, much research and experimental analysis remain to be done to understand the complex terrain electromagnetic interactions before the microwave data can become of operational use.

III. SPACEBORNE RADIOMETER SYSTEM CONCEPTS

Spaceborne radiometer systems may have a variety of characteristics related to their specific applications. However, there are certain basic features common to most systems which can be broadly classified into radiometer system features and features related to the spacecraft platform. These general features will be discussed here, prior to a more detailed discussion of individual sensors in the next section.

A. Radiometer System Description

Radiometer systems for microwave remote sensing typically consist of three basic subsystems: 1) an antenna and scan subsystem, which receives incoming radiation from specified beam-pointing directions; 2) a radiometer receiver and electronics subsystem, which detects and amplifies the received radiation within a specified frequency band; and 3) a data and control subsystem, which provides timing and sequencing signals for the antenna and radiometer subsystems, and performs digitizing, multiplexing, and formatting functions on the radiometric and housekeeping data to form the output digital data stream. In spaceborne applications, the microwave radiometer may be only one of a number of different sensor types on the spacecraft. Thus the radiometer output is typically interfaced with data from the other sensors and transmitted to ground via the spacecraft data system. On the ground, data from each sensor are separated and combined with ancillary spacecraft data such as ephemeris and timing data to form the basic sensor data record. For the microwave radiometer, the sensor data record forms the input to three stages of data processing: 1) radiometer calibrations, in which the radiometer digital output voltages are converted into units of antenna temperature; 2) antenna pattern corrections, in which effects of radiation entering the antenna sidelobes are accounted for; and 3) geophysical parameter retrievals, in which brightness temperatures measured by the radiometer system are interpreted in terms of the corre-

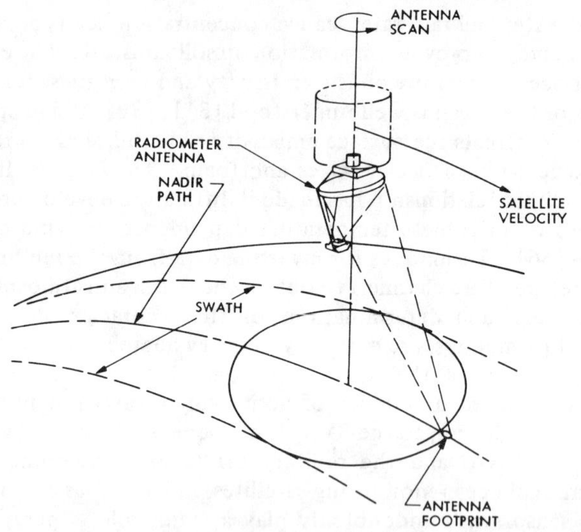

Fig. 3. Conical scan configuration, illustrating constant earth-incidence angle feature over wide swath.

sponding surface or atmospheric features. Stages 1) and 2) are usually considered as instrument-related stages in the data processing, with brightness temperatures as the final processed sensor outputs, whereas stage 3) involves modeling of the surface and atmospheric emission characteristics and the use of various data-inversion techniques. For some applications, not all of these data-processing steps are necessary. For example, brightness temperature images of the polar regions are sufficient to show the variations in extent and type of sea ice, by virtue of the large brightness temperature contrasts between ice and water and between the different ice types.

To provide global coverage with adequate spatial resolution from earth-viewing remote sensors in orbit, scanning antennas are required. Microwave antennas may be scanned either mechanically as in rotating reflectors, or electrically as in phased-array antennas. Whichever type is used, scanning is generally in the cross-track dimension, and coverage in the other dimension is provided by the spacecraft motion (the situation is somewhat different at geosynchronous altitude, where the spacecraft remains fixed over a given point on the earth). One particular scan geometry which has become popular for both scanned reflector antennas and phased arrays is the conical scan, in which the beam is offset at a fixed angle from nadir and scanned about the vertical (nadir) axis. The beam thus sweeps out the surface of a cone. This is illustrated by the diagram in Fig. 3. If the full 360° of a scan is utilized, double coverage fore and aft of the spacecraft is obtained. The main advantage of this type of scan is that the angle of incidence of the antenna beam at the earth's surface is constant, independent of scan position. This significantly increases the accuracy with which the brightness temperature data can be interpreted in terms of surface parameters.

For spaceborne applications, most experience to date has been achieved using radiometers of the Dicke-switched superheterodyne type. An example of this type of system is shown in Fig. 4. Prior to the receiver portion of the radiometer is a network of switches. The first of these determines which of a number of signals are to be fed into the receiver, either a signal from the vertical or horizontal antenna ports, or from one of the two calibration targets. Measurements of the calibration targets are used later in the data processing to calibrate the radiation received via the antenna in units of antenna temperature. The Dicke switch switches periodically at a high rate be-

tween the incoming signal and a known reference source. A synchronous detector at the other end of the receiver demodulates the signal. By these high-frequency comparisons of the signal with a known reference source, the effect of low-frequency gain variations in the amplifiers and other active devices is minimized. The local oscillator (LO) frequency is at the center of the desired radiometer passband and is mixed with the input signal to produce an intermediate-frequency (IF) signal which is then amplified and detected. In this system, the critical noise component is the mixer, and considerable effort is made to keep this as low noise as possible to improve the receiver sensitivity. After demodulation, the signal is integrated and sampled, and output to the data system. The critical receiver parameters in determining the temperature sensitivity (ΔT_{rms}) of the radiometer are the receiver noise temperature T_R, the receiver predetection bandwidth B, and the integration time τ. For a Dicke radiometer with square-wave demodulation the sensitivity can be expressed as

$$\Delta T_{\mathrm{rms}} = \frac{2(T_A + T_R)}{\sqrt{B\tau}}$$

where T_A is the antenna temperature [37]. As available integration time becomes smaller in advanced systems designed for high surface spatial resolution, total-power radiometers can be considered. Total-power radiometers are simpler in concept since they have no Dicke switch and demodulator. This results in approximately a factor-of-two improvement in sensitivity. The disadvantage is that variations in output level caused by changes in gain and bandwidth of the amplifiers are not compensated for. Recent advances, however, in component technology and circuit design have improved stability to the point where total-power radiometers are now being implemented in designs for future satellite radiometer systems [38]. The development of low-noise RF amplifiers may in the future also eliminate the requirements for LO/mixer heterodyne systems at the lower microwave frequencies, thus resulting in a reduction in receiver noise temperature. Other radiometer systems than described above have also been used in the past for various applications with varying degrees of success [39].

The instrument data processing usually occurs in the ground segment and consists of data calibrations and antenna pattern corrections. The data are calibrated using an equation which converts radiometer output voltage levels to antenna temperatures referenced to the antenna input ports. This equation makes use of radiometric data from the two radiometer calibration targets of known microwave temperature. The form of the equation is derived from prelaunch instrument calibration in a thermal-vacuum chamber which simulates space conditions. The equation is essentially linear, but nonlinearities in instrument performance over the range of operating conditions may require nonlinear terms to be added to the calibration equation. The calibrated data must also be corrected for effects due to the antenna. The antenna receives radiation from regions of space defined by the antenna pattern. The antenna pattern is usually strongly peaked along its beam axis, and when pointing at the ground its spatial resolution or footprint is generally defined by the angular region over which the antenna power pattern is less than 3 dB down from its value at beam center. Contributions to the antenna temperature from regions outside the footprint region are accounted for by inversion of the antenna pattern equation. This inversion procedure rapidly becomes complex as increasing accuracy is sought in deriving brightness temperatures for the 3-dB footprints. A tradeoff usually occurs between data-processing complexity and bright-

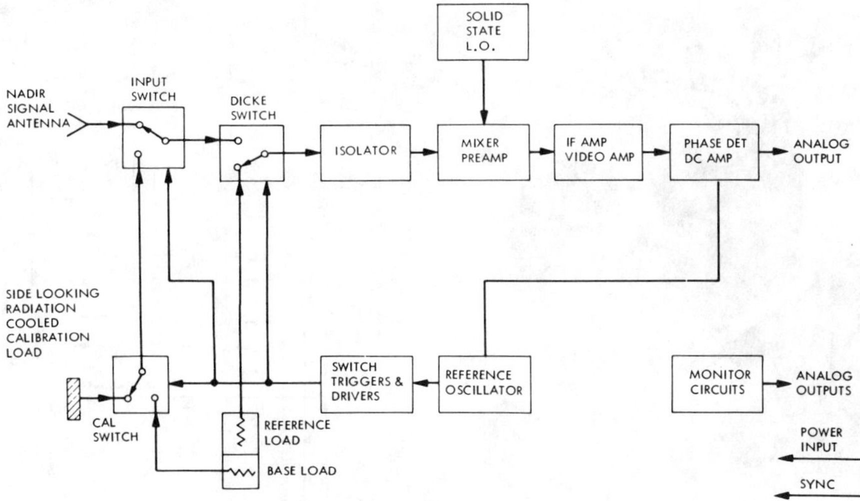

Fig. 4. Typical Dicke-switched superheterodyne radiometer configuration as implemented in NEMS (Nimbus-5).

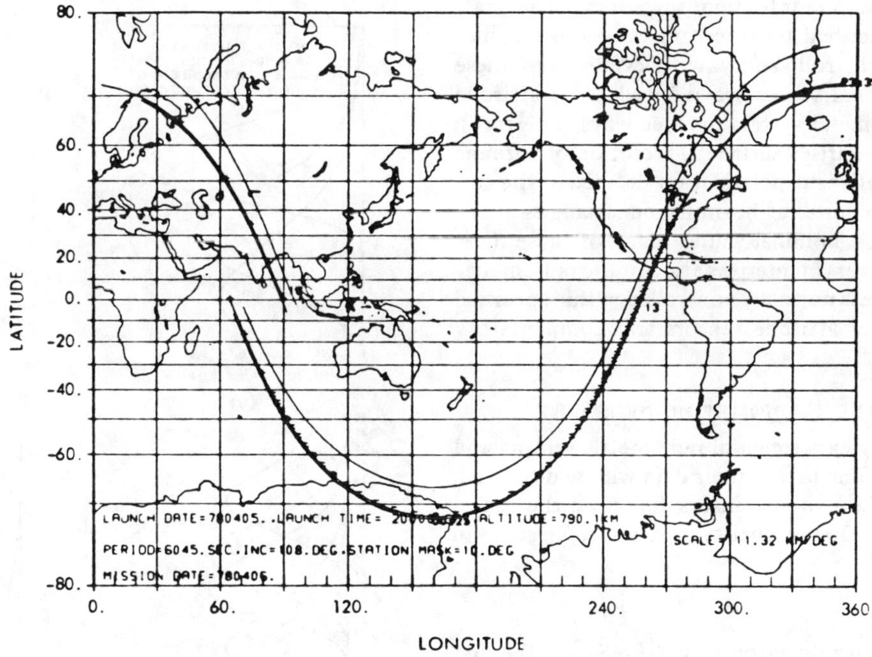

Fig. 5. Mercator projection of Seasat SMMR swath coverage for a single orbit. Asymmetry is due to offset scan.

ness temperature accuracy. The situation can be improved considerably by the design of antennas with high beam efficiency and low sidelobes.

The remaining data processing consists of interpreting the brightness temperatures in terms of the desired geophysical variables. This involves physical models of microwave emission from the earth's atmosphere and surface and the use of various data inversion techniques. Since these techniques depend on the particular application, further discussion will be delayed until the description of specific spacecraft sensors in the next section.

B. Spacecraft Considerations

Microwave radiometers are typically one of several sensors flown together on a spacecraft to form a combined remote-sensing payload. Besides being a platform used to place the microwave radiometer system in orbit, certain aspects of the spacecraft or satellite mission design can influence the utility of the radiometer data. These are 1) orbit design, 2) attitude control, and 3) the data processing and transmission network.

For the nongeosynchronous, circular earth orbits most commonly used in microwave remote sensing, the orbital parameters of importance are altitude, inclination, and the related ground trace pattern. The orbital altitude and the sensor scan geometry together determine the swath width on the earth's surface. The orbit inclination determines the latitude range of coverage. The altitude and inclination together determine the nodal precession rate and the ground trace pattern. As an example, Fig. 5 shows a Mercator projection of the Seasat SMMR swath coverage for a single orbit. The Seasat orbit was approximately circular, with an altitude of 800 km, inclination of 108°, and period of 101 min. The orbit was chosen as a compromise between the requirements of the various active and passive sensors on the spacecraft. For further discussion of orbit considerations see King [40]. The spacecraft attitude (i.e., stability in

Fig. 6. Photograph of NEMS instrument (Nimbus-5) showing separate
H_2O and O_2 modules and power supply module.

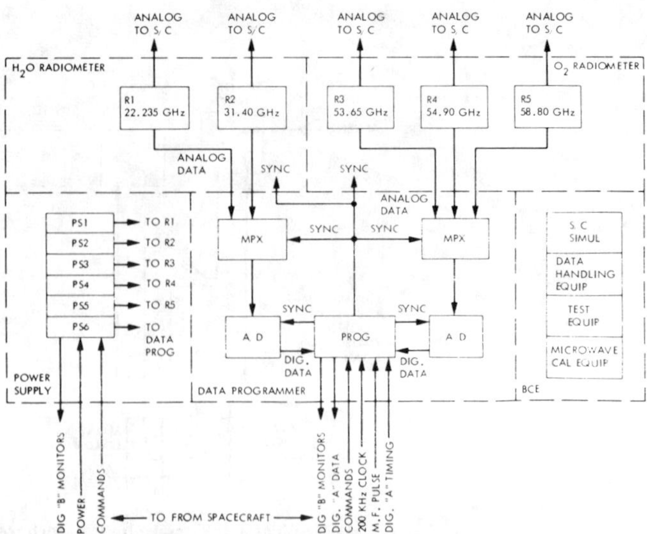

Fig. 7. NEMS (Nimbus-5) functional block diagram.

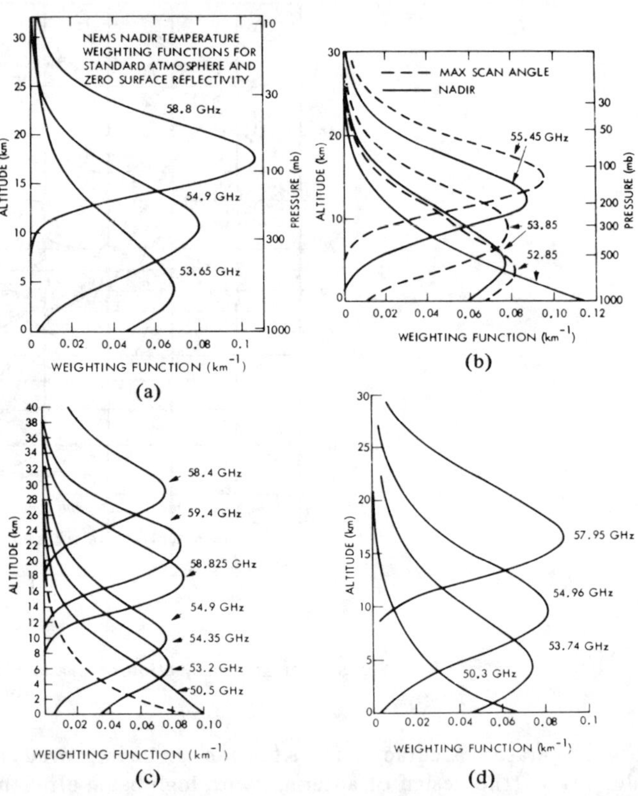

Fig. 8. Atmospheric temperature weighting functions viewing earth
from space: (a) NEMS (Nimbus-5); (b) SCAMS (Nimbus-6); (c)
SSM/T (Block-5); (d) MSU (Tiros-N). Calculations assumed a calm
sea background for (b), (c), and (d), and zero surface reflectivity for
(a).

orbit) is also an important factor for remote sensors. Spacecraft
attitude is normally described by three angles in a rectangular
coordinate system: pitch, roll, and yaw. Deviations of these
angles from their nominal values are referred to as attitude
errors and affect a radiometer system in three ways: 1) error in
footprint location at the earth's surface; 2) rotation of antenna
polarization vectors relative to polarization defined at the surface; and 3) deviation of antenna beam incidence angles at the
earth's surface from their nominal value. Each of these three
effects can give rise to errors in interpretation of the radiometric
data. Spacecraft attitude is normally controlled within specified
tolerances by the use of attitude sensors and compensatory
mechanisms.

IV. Spaceborne Radiometric Sensors

In this section the key experimental radiometric sensors and
the scientific results obtained from their data will be discussed.
The discussion emphasizes those sensors flown on the spacecraft listed in Table II. Operational sensors are referred to in
the next section.

A. NEMS (Nimbus-5)

The Nimbus-5 Microwave Spectrometer (NEMS) was the first
microwave temperature sounder flown in space [41]. The instrument could be considered as composed of two parts: 1) three
channels at center frequencies 53.65, 54.9, and 58.8 GHz for
measuring primarily the atmospheric temperature profile; 2)
two channels at 22.234 and 31.4 GHz, sensitive over the oceans
to water vapor and liquid water, and indicating emissivity and
surface temperature over land. Although these two parts could
operate separately, performance was improved by using data
from all channels simultaneously in the profile and parameter
estimations. A photograph of the NEMS instrument is shown
in Fig. 6. The instrument comprised four main functional units
as shown in the functional block diagram (Fig. 7). These were:
1) the H_2O radiometer unit, 2) the O_2 radiometer unit, 3) the
data/programmer unit, and 4) the power supply unit.

The H_2O radiometer unit consisted of channels R_1 (22.235
GHz) and R_2 (31.4 GHz), which were completely independent.
Each was fed by a lens-loaded circular horn, nadir-viewing,
with a 3-dB beamwidth of $10°$. This provided a surface footprint of about 190-km diameter. The O_2 radiometer unit consisted of channels R_3, R_4, and R_5 (53.65, 54.9, and 58.8 GHz),

which were also independently operating radiometers. The
five radiometer channels were functionally identical and of the
Dicke-switched, superheterodyne type, with two-point calibration system as shown in Fig. 4.

The NEMS channels 3, 4, and 5 atmospheric temperature
weighting functions are shown in Fig. 8(a). These enabled
atmospheric temperature to be sensed in the troposphere and
lower stratosphere. To determine the atmospheric temperature
profile at a number of discrete points using data from the three

TABLE II
U.S. EARTH-ORBITING SPACECRAFT WITH EXPERIMENTAL
PASSIVE MICROWAVE SENSORS

Satellite Characteristics	Nimbus-5	Skylab Earth Resources Experimental Package (EREP)	Nimbus-6	Seasat	Nimbus-7
Launch date	December, 1972	May, 1973	June, 1975	June, 1978	October, 1978
Main Program Objectives	Development of measurement techniques for atmospheric processes related to meteorology and general circulation.	Development of visible, infrared, and microwave sensors, and data evaluation techniques for Earth resource applications from space.	To sound the atmosphere using advanced techniques extending measurement capabilities demonstrated on previous Nimbus satellites.	Proof-of-concept mission to demonstrate: (1) techniques for global monitoring of oceanographic phenomena; (2) key features of an operational ocean monitoring system.	To conduct experiments in the pollution, oceanographic and meteorological disciplines. Refine atmospheric measurement capabilities demonstrated on previous Nimbus satellites.
Sensor Payload	Temperature Humidity Infrared Radiometer Surface Composition Mapping Radiometer (SCMR) Electrically Scanning Microwave Radiometer (ESMR) Infrared Temperature Profile Radiometer (ITPR) Selective Chopper Radiometer (SCR) Nimbus-E Microwave Spectrometer (NEMS)	Multispectral Photographic Cameras (S190A) Earth Terrain Camera (S190B) Infrared Spectrometer (S191) Multispectral Scanner (S192) Microwave Radiometer/ Scatterometer and Altimeter (S193) L-band Radiometer (S194)	THIR ESMR High Resolution Infrared Radiation Sounder (HIRS) Scanning Microwave Spectrometer (SCAMS) Earth Radiation Budget (ERB) Limb Radiance Inversion Radiometer (LRIR) Pressure Modulator Radiometer (PMR)	Radar Altimeter (ALT) Seasat-A Satellite Scatterometer (SASS) Synthetic Aperture Radar (SAR) Scanning Multichannel Microwave Radiometer (SMMR) Visible and Infrared Radiometer (VIRR)	THIR SMMR ERB Coastal Zone Color Scanner (CZCS) Limb Infrared Monitor of the Stratosphere (LIMS) Stratospheric Aerosol Measurement (SAM II) Stratospheric and Mesospheric Sounder (SAMS) Solar Backscatter Ultraviolet and Total Ozone Mapping Spectrometer (SBUV/TOMS)
Orbit Characteristics: Altitude Inclination	Circular sun-synchronous 1100 km 99°	Circular 438 km 50°	Circular sun-synchronous 1100 km 99°	Circular 800 km 108°	Circular, sun-synchronous 955 km 99.2°
Attitude Stabilization: pitch roll yaw	±1.0° ±0.5° ±0.5°	±2.0° ±2.0° ±2.0°	±0.5° ±0.5° ±1.0°	±0.5° ±0.5° ±0.5°	±0.7° ±1.0° ±1.0°

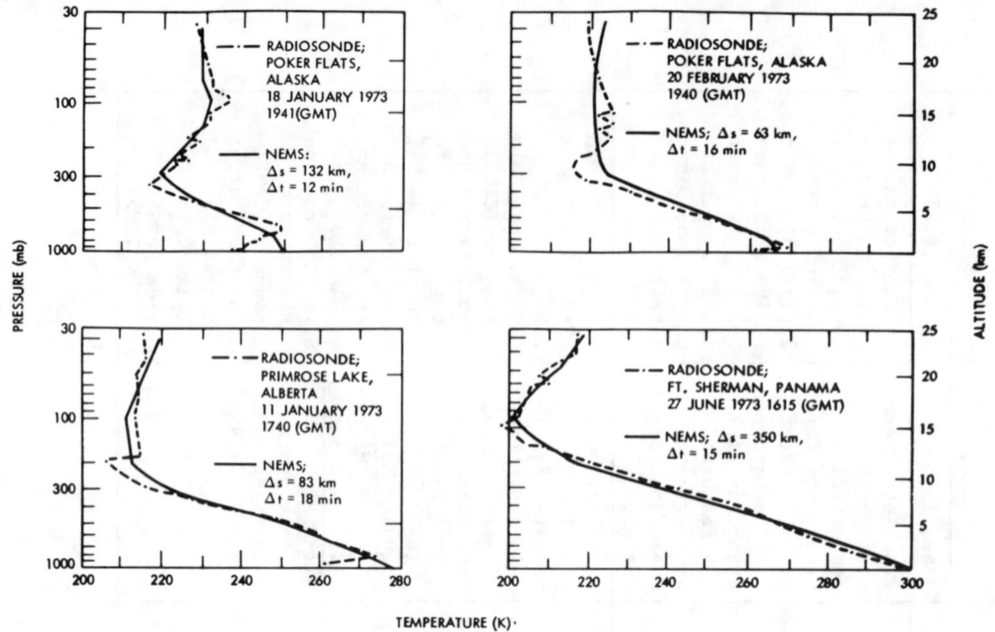

Fig. 9. Comparisons of individual temperature soundings by NEMS and coincident radiosondes. The spatial difference Δs and time difference Δt of the NEMS sounding relative to the radiosonde are indicated for each sounding (after Waters *et al.* [11]).

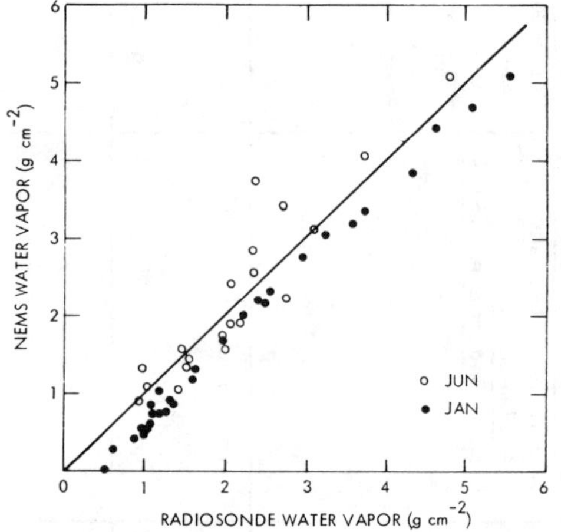

Fig. 10. Comparisons of NEMS water vapor retrievals with radiosonde water vapor measurements (after Staelin *et al.* [13]).

brightness temperature channels, a statistical retrieval approach was used, incorporating *a priori* statistics from radiosonde data and atmospheric model calculations. Results from NEMS using this approach are illustrated in Fig. 9. These show the NEMS-retrieved profiles compared with radiosonde data in four different situations. The errors are largest where sharp changes in profile occur, showing the limitations in vertical resolution imposed by the width of the weighting functions. Comparisons using the most reliable NMC temperature profiles indicated that the NEMS rms temperature accuracy averaged over the profile was about 2°C. The effects of clouds on the profile retrieval accuracy were investigated by Staelin *et al.* [12]. Clouds were observed to affect less than 0.5 percent of the temperature profile soundings. Most such effects occurred in the intertropical convergence zone (ITCZ) and altered the inferred temperature profile by less than a few degrees centigrade. Furthermore, these large clouds could be detected by NEMS channels 1 and 2 and thus could be accounted for in applications of the data.

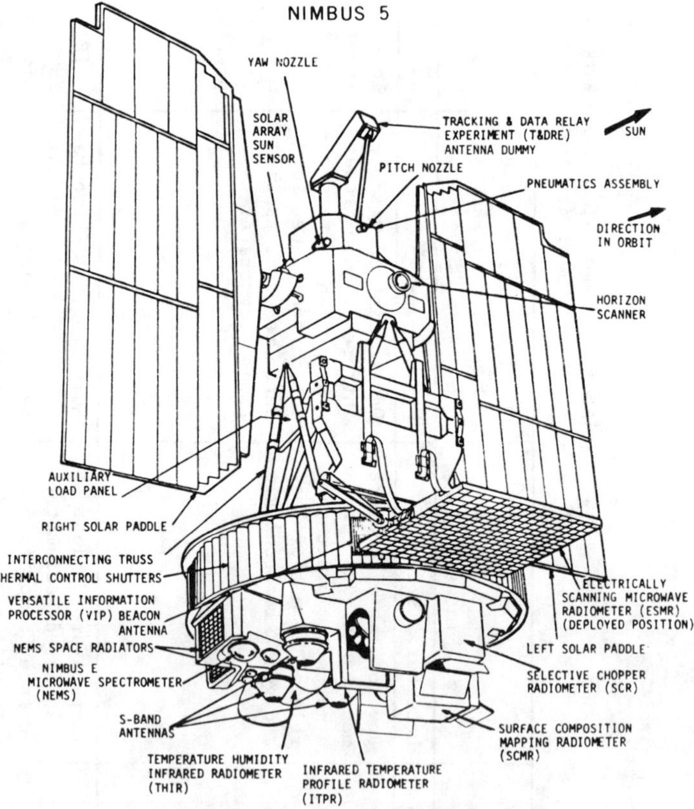

Fig. 11. Nimbus-5 satellite, launched December 1972, showing placement of NEMS and ESMR sensors.

The NEMS channels 1 and 2 were used for determining columnar atmospheric water vapor and liquid water abundances using simple regression approaches [13], [42]. The accuracy of NEMS water vapor estimates was tested by comparison with radiosondes launched from ships and islands. The results are shown in Fig. 10 and indicate an overall rms accuracy of about

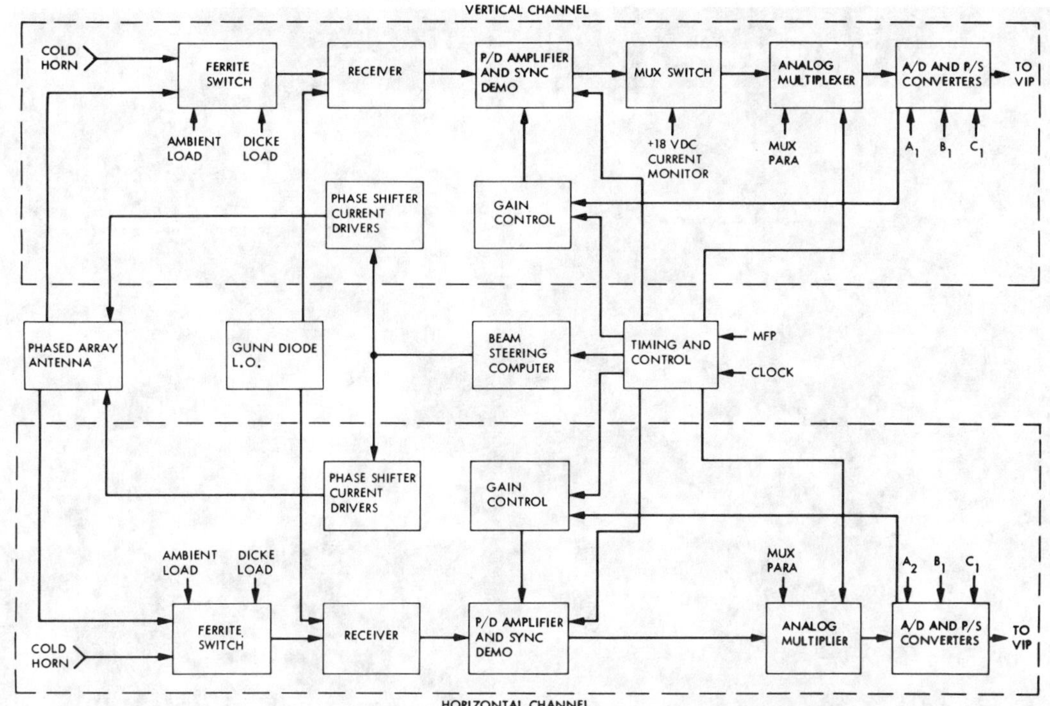

Fig. 12. System block diagram of ESMR (Nimbus-6).

0.4 g/cm^2. Accuracy for the NEMS liquid water estimates was difficult to determine experimentally since there were no reliable sources of comparison data. Theoretical rms accuracies were estimated as 0.01 g/cm^2.

Whereas NEMS channels 1 and 2 could be used for atmospheric water determinations over the oceans, they also provided information on the global distribution and character of various types of snow and ice. Seasonal variations in the ice and snow, and different types of sea ice and firn, could clearly be distinguished from observations in the polar regions [23].

B. ESMR (Nimbus-5)

The Electrically Scanning Microwave Radiometer (ESMR) was first launched aboard the Nimbus-5 satellite in December 1972. Its objective was to map surface features of the earth by means of received radiation at 19.35 GHz, particularly the distribution of polar ice and precipitating clouds over ocean areas [43].

The instrument consisted of four major components: 1) a phased-array microwave antenna consisting of 103 waveguide elements each having its associated electrical phase shifters; 2) a beam-steering computer which determined the coil current for each of the phase shifters for each beam position; 3) a microwave receiver with center frequency 19.35 GHz; and 4) timing control and power circuits. The instrument is shown diagrammatically on the Nimbus-5 spacecraft in Fig. 11. The block diagram is similar to one channel of the ESMR on Nimbus-6 (shown in Fig. 12). The radiometer was of the Dicke-switched superheterodyne type.

The aperture area of the phased-array antenna was 83.3×85.5 cm, with polarization linear and parallel to the spacecraft velocity vector. The antenna beam was scanned cross-track (i.e., perpendicular to the spacecraft velocity vector) in 78 steps, $\pm 50°$ from nadir, every 4 s. Scanning was achieved by means of the electric phase shifters in series with each waveguide element and controlled by timing commands via a beam-steering

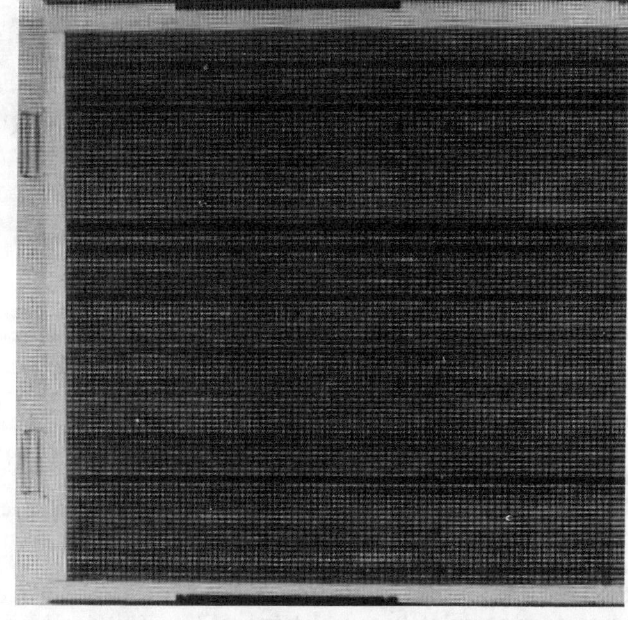

Fig. 13. Photograph of ESMR waveguide phased array antenna.

network. A photograph of waveguide array is shown in Fig. 13. The antenna beamwidth was $1.4° \times 1.4°$ near nadir, and degraded to $2.2°$ crosstrack $\times 1.4°$ down-track at the $50°$ scan extremes. From a nominal orbit of 1100-km altitude the footprint resolution was 25×25 km near nadir, degrading to 160×45 km at the ends of scan. The swath width generated by the $\pm 50°$ cross-track scan was 1570 km, with overlap extending to the equator crossings for successive orbits. Thus complete global coverage, including the polar regions, was obtained within 12 h, counting both day and night portions of the orbit. To account for effects of antenna sidelobes a simple one-dimensional correction was applied to the antenna temperatures. This was sufficient due to the low antenna sidelobe levels in the plane

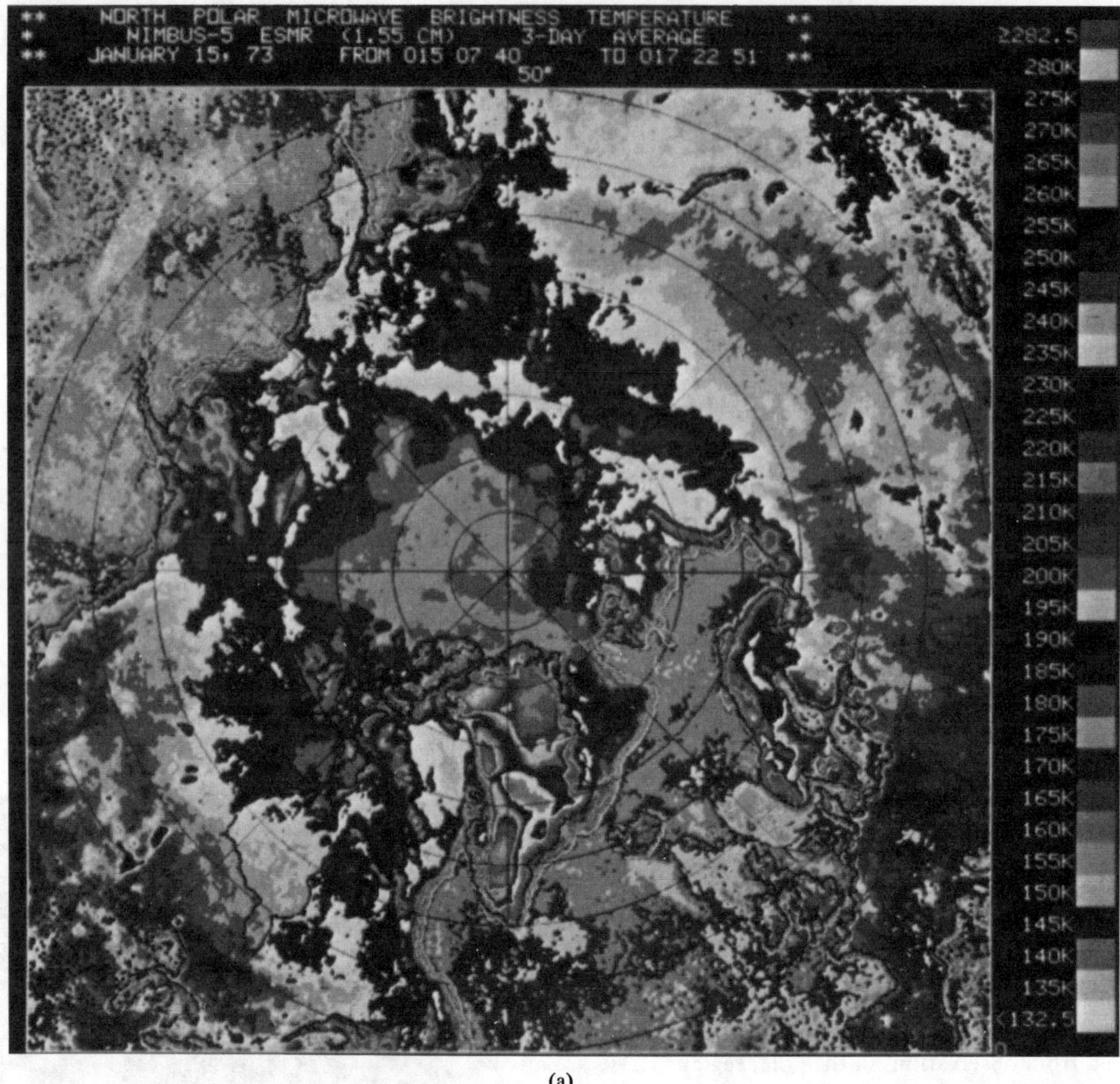

(a)

Fig. 14. Images of north polar region generated from brightness temperatures measured by the Nimbus-5 ESMR: (a) winter (January 1973) (after Zwally and Gloersen [24]).

Note: Fig. 14(a) and (b) appeared in color in the original publication.

parallel to the waveguide elements. A matrix operation on the 78 antenna temperatures in each scan performed the necessary corrections for each beam position.

The ESMR capability for providing images of the polar ice-caps, through clouds, and both day and night, has found important applications in polar research and marine operations. There is a large contrast in brightness temperature between open sea water and completely consolidated sea ice. Thus intermediate brightness temperatures occurring within the ~35-km ESMR footprint could be ascribed to mixtures of open water and ice, whose percentage concentrations could be estimated to an accuracy of about 15 percentage points. This accuracy is affected to some extent by the existence of three radiometrically distinct sea ice types: first year, multiyear, and first year thin sea ice. These ice types each have characteristic emissivities due to their surface and internal structure. Fig. 14 shows two ESMR images of the arctic at different seasons. The winter (January 15, 1973) image shows the ice canopy to be composed of two general types of ice: the principally multiyear ice covering the main portion of the Arctic Ocean, with brightness temperatures ranging from 209 to 223 K, and either first-year or first-year/multiyear mixtures with higher brightness temperatures covering the southern portions of the marginal seas. By the end of the

summer melt season, the ESMR image for the late summer (September 9, 1973) shows that most of the ice that covered the marginal seas has melted. Detailed examination of year-round images such as these has provided a wealth of information on the complex morphology and dynamics in the artic and antarctic regions [24], [44]–[47].

Over the oceans the ESMR has been shown to be capable of detecting precipitation areas. These appear in the ESMR images as regions of high brightness temperature caused by the larger droplet sizes and total water content in precipitating clouds [26]. Meteorological applications of these images compared to images from infrared and visible sensors have been discussed by Wilheit et al. [25]. Similar studies by Allison et al. [48] and Adler and Rodgers [49] have used the ESMR data to provide semi-quantitative rainfall characteristics of oceanic tropical cyclones and to study convergence phenomena in regions not often detectable with other satellite sensors.

ESMR measurements have also been shown to be responsive to soil-moisture conditions over large land areas [50]. At the ESMR frequency (19.35 GHz), correlations with soil moisture are limited to predominantly bare soil and low vegetation density areas. Because of this limitation, and the relatively coarse spatial resolution, current applications of this

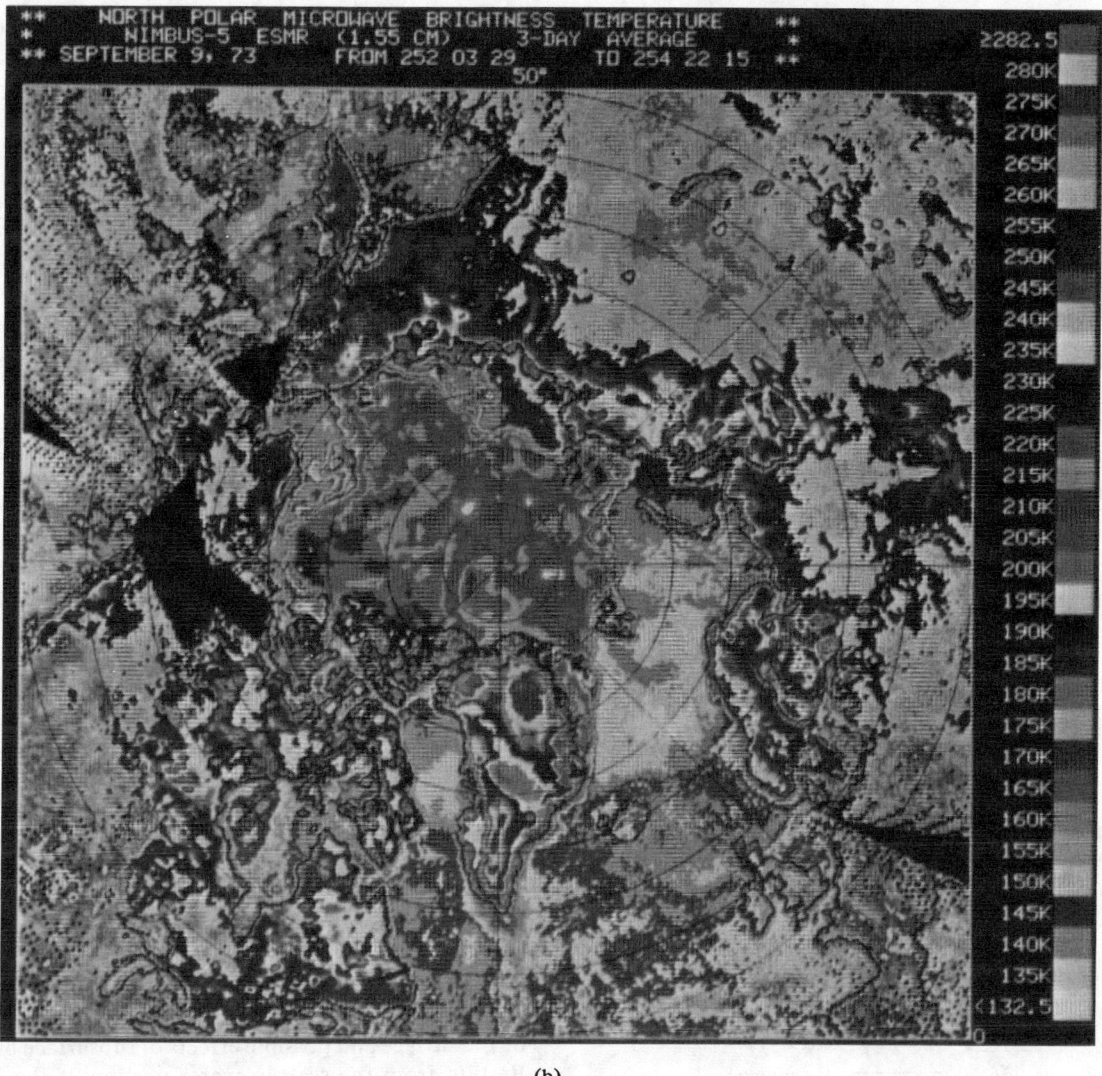

(b)

Fig. 14. Images of north polar region generated from brightness temperatures measured by the Nimbus-5 ESMR: (b) summer (September 1973) (after Zwally and Gloersen [24]).

kind of data are limited. These studies do indicate future potential, however, for instruments designed specifically for soil-moisture applications.

C. S-193 (Skylab)

The Skylab microwave radiometer/scatterometer and altimeter instrument, designated S-193, was one of six experimental remote sensors making up the Earth Resources Experimental Package (EREP), operated on Skylab missions between May 1973 and February 1974. The three instrument components operated at the same frequency (13.9 GHz) and shared a common antenna and scan system. Certain electronic subsystems were also shared to minimize weight and power requirements. The instrument objectives were to make simultaneous measurements of radar backscatter and radiometric brightness temperature from orbit, in a number of scanning modes, primarily for the purpose of studying winds and precipitation over the oceans. The instrument has been described by Potter *et al.* [51] and Moore *et al.* [52], and is shown on the spacecraft in Fig. 15.

The (S-193) antenna was a 115-cm-diameter mechanically scanned parabolic reflector, with dual polarization and a 2° beamwidth. The antenna was gimballed, permitting antenna scanning both along and across the flight path, and at the nadir position provided a circular footprint of 16-km diameter. Drive commands were received from an antenna controller which could follow any of four preset scan modes. A block diagram of the system is shown in Fig. 16. The signal from the antenna was preamplified using a tunnel-diode amplifier, and the IF signal generated by the mixer was split between the radiometer and scatterometer receivers. After detection and integration, the output was digitized and recorded on an EREP 10-kbit/s tape-recorder channel. The calibration source box contained two calibration sources, used for temperature reference and to set the automatic gain control of the radiometer receiver. Three choices of receiver integration times were available in an effort to accommodate the different scan modes of the antenna. Complete calibration of the system including the antenna was not performed prior to launch. Instead, the antenna insertion loss and the system transfer function were computed in orbit, based on measurements with the antenna pointed towards cold space of assumed microwave temperature 2.7 K.

Analysis of the radiometric data was directed towards studying correlations between the active and passive data over a variety of surface types. These correlations were studied using

Fig. 15. Skylab, launched May 1973, showing location of EREP sensors on the multiple docking adaptor.

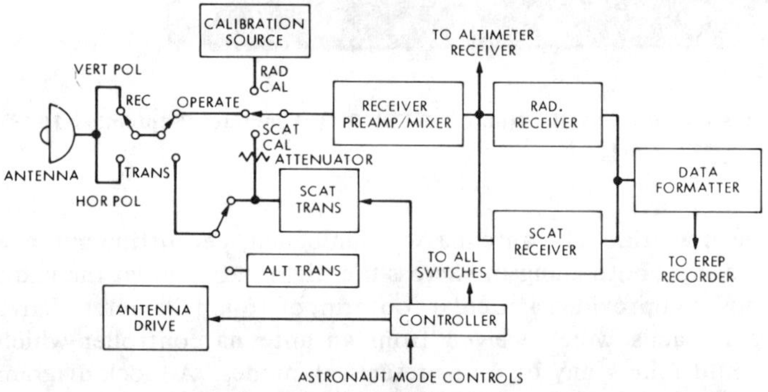

Fig. 16. Skylab S-193 system block diagram.

data measured at antenna scan angles between $0°$ and $48°$ from nadir. Lowest correlations were found between active and passive data at vertical polarization and $30°$ nadir angle [27]. Effects of clouds and weather, however, probably significantly affected the results, making conclusions about surface effects difficult. Studies of the effects of soil moisture on the radiometer response were reported by Moore *et al.* [53]. Since soil-moisture surface measurements were difficult to obtain, a related antecedent precipitation index (API) was used instead. Although a trend was evident towards lower emissivities with higher API, the correlation was relatively low, probably due to the many assumptions in the API model and the significant effects of surface roughness and vegetation at 13.9 GHz. Another study by Ulaby *et al.* [54] compared data from the S-193, S-194 (1.4-GHz), and ESMR (19.35-GHz) sensors, over the Utah Great Salt Lake Desert. Within this region, large decreases in brightness temperature and increases in backscattering coef-

ficients were observed, as a result of the smooth, bare nature of the surface and possible effects of subsurface brine sediments. Results from the scatterometer portion of the instrument are discussed in more detail by Moore and Young [55].

D. S-194 (Skylab)

The S-194 was an *L*-band (1.4-GHz) radiometer system flown as part of the EREP remote-sensing payload on Skylab. The objective was to measure radiation from the earth at this frequency, with application to earth resources and in particular soil moisture. The instrument consisted of a fixed, nadir-viewing, phased-array antenna, and receiver, calibration, and data subsystems [51]. The antenna beamwidth was $15°$, providing a surface footprint of 115-km diameter. The radiometer was a modified Dicke type, with tuned RF receiver and gain modulation. The instrument is shown on the spacecraft in Fig. 15.

In addition to comparisons with S-193 and ESMR data (described above), the data from S-194 were studied for correlations with soil moisture by Eagleman and Lin [28]. Due to the large footprint size, water balance models were used to extrapolate point measurements of surface soil moisture for comparison with the spacecraft data, Fig. 17. The observed correlations with soil moisture in the top 2.5 cm were quite high. However, the data points used were not strictly independent since they represented footprints with significant amounts of overlap. Studies by McFarland [55] using the antecedent precipitation index showed similar results.

E. SCAMS (Nimbus-6)

The Scanning Microwave Spectrometer (SCAMS) on Nimbus-6 had similar objectives to the NEMS instrument, i.e., to deter-

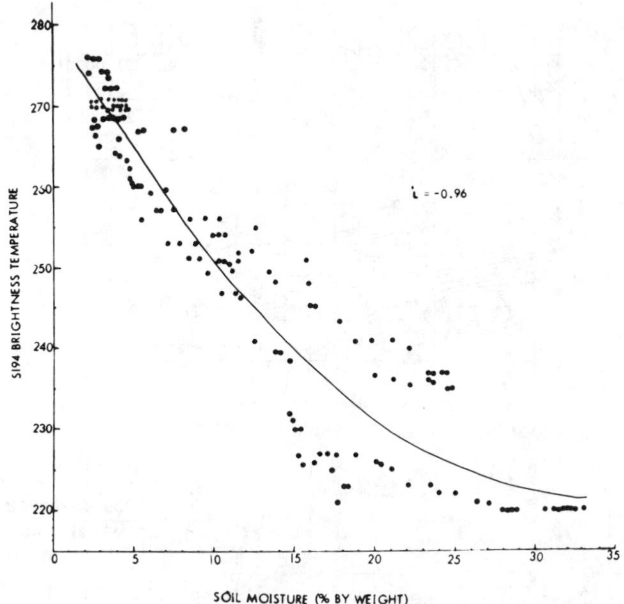

Fig. 17. Skylab S-194 brightness temperature relationship with soil moisture over Kansas and Texas sites, 1973 (after Eagleman and Lin [28]).

Fig. 18. Photograph of SCAMS instrument (Nimbus-6).

mine atmospheric temperature profiles and, over ocean surfaces, the abundances of water vapor and liquid water in the atmosphere [57]. Whereas NEMS observed atmospheric parameters at nadir, along the subsatellite track, SCAMS operated by scanning to either side of this track to produce maps of these parameters with nearly full earth coverage. SCAMS was intended to provide a unique global data set for research and trial operational use in meteorological applications, and for use in the Global Atmospheric Research Program (GARP).

A photograph of the SCAMS instrument mounted in its assembly fixture is shown in Fig. 18. There is one eantena each for the two H_2O channels and a single antenna for the three O_2 channels. Scanning was achieved by stepping a reflector in front of each antenna. Each reflector, inclined at $45°$ to its antenna, scanned the antenna beam in a left-handed sense with respect to the spacecraft velocity vector, and a complete $360°$ scan took 16 s. Thirteen earth-data samples, each separated by

a $7.2°$ scan step, were recorded between $\pm43.2°$ from nadir. 3 s at the end of each earth scan were reserved for reflector rotation and system calibration, which took place by 1-s views of cold space and of an instrument blackbody source. The antenna beamwidths of $7.5°$ gave ground resolutions of 145 km at nadir and 220×360 km at the edges of the scan ($43.2°$ from nadir). The $\pm43.2°$ scan covered a swath width of 2400 km, which provided nearly full earth coverage every 12 h. The polarization vector rotated as the beam scanned. At nadir, polarization was parallel to the satellite velocity vector for all channels except channel 5 (55.45 GHz), for which it was perpendicular.

The functional operation of the SCAMS was similar to that described for the NEMS instrument. The 22.2- and 31.6-GHz channels shared no components in common, whereas the three O_2 channels shared a common antenna and calibration target. A channelizing filter separated the frequencies of the two O_2 channels with like polarizations; the third O_2 frequency was separated by a polarization transducer. The radiometers were of the Dicke-switched superheterodyne type and, from the Dicke switchback, were identical in operation to those used on the NEMS. The use of external calibration targets viewed by the antennas was an improvement in the calibration design. By this means a more accurate system calibration was achieved for the orbital radiometric data. After calibration in the ground processing, the data were deconvolved to remove the antenna sidelobe contributions. The high beam efficiencies of the SCAMS antennas ($\gtrsim 97$ percent) enabled this to be done fairly simply.

Weighting functions for the three temperature-sounding channels are shown in Fig. 8(b). These provided theoretical retrieval accuracies comparable to NEMS. SCAMS-derived temperatures profiles were compared with radiosonde temperatures for several European frontal systems by Grody and Pellegrino [14]. Fig. 19(a) shows a cloud image from the NOAA-4 VHRR for a case study region over Europe, with two adjacent SCAMS grid patterns for January 26 and 27, 1976. The temperature field at the 700-mbar level in the atmosphere derived from available radiosonde reports is shown in Fig. 19(b), revealing a deep trough with strong temperature gradients. Fig. 19(c) shows the 700-mbar SCAMS-derived result in which the positions of the major trough and ridge are well defined, although the amplitudes are somewhat underestimated. The rms temperature accuracies at this level for the SCAMS retrievals are about 2 K. A more stringent test of SCAMS cloud-penetrating capabilities was presented by Rosenkranz *et al.* [15], in which the instrument was used to study the development of Typhoon June over the Pacific. Results showed the possibility of deriving cloud liquid water content and sea surface winds around the typhoon from the 22- and 31-GHz channels. The 55.45-GHz channel displayed the typhoon's warm core temperature structure at the 200-mbar level. Improved spatial resolution would have increased the impact of these measurements. Kidder *et al.* [58] have also investigated the use of SCAMS data for estimation of tropical cyclone central pressure and outer winds. Fig. 20 shows SCAMS-derived columnar water vapor contours in the western Pacific, compared to local radiosonde observations. Knowledge of these large variations in water vapor within the tropical environment is of utmost importance in understanding the development of tropical cyclones and cloud clusters (see also [59]).

F. ESMR (Nimbus-6)

The successful operation of the ESMR on Nimbus-5 laid the basis for a second ESMR which was launched on the Nimbus-6

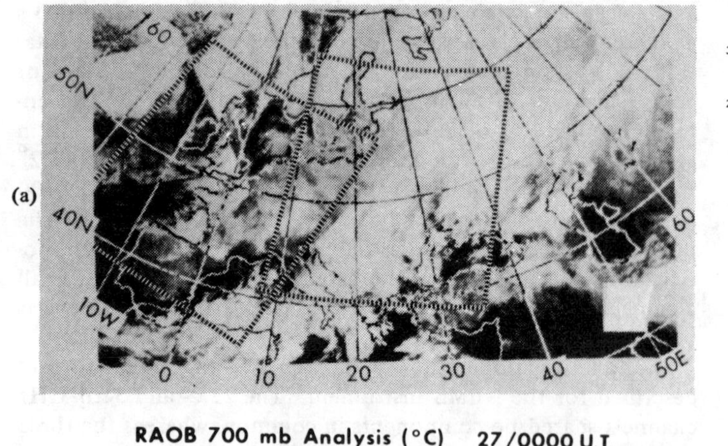

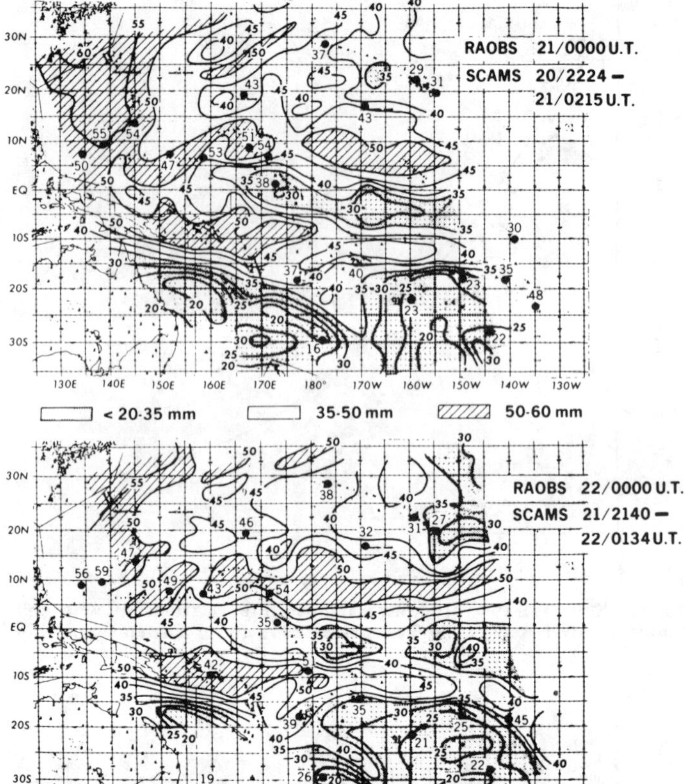

Fig. 20. Comparisons between SCAMS retrieved precipitable water (mm) and radiosonde measurements (●), August 20–22, 1975 (after Grody [10]).

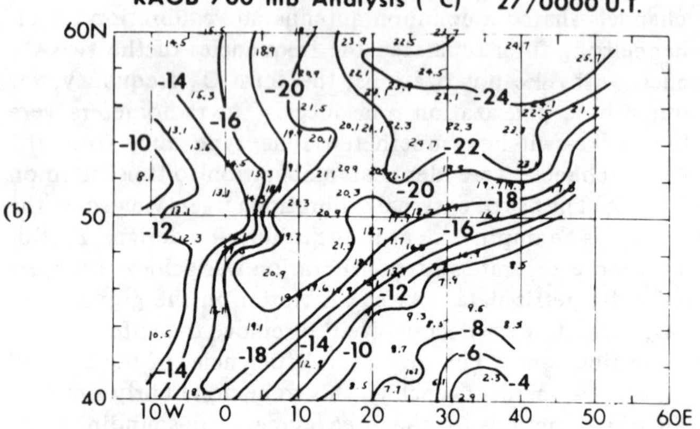

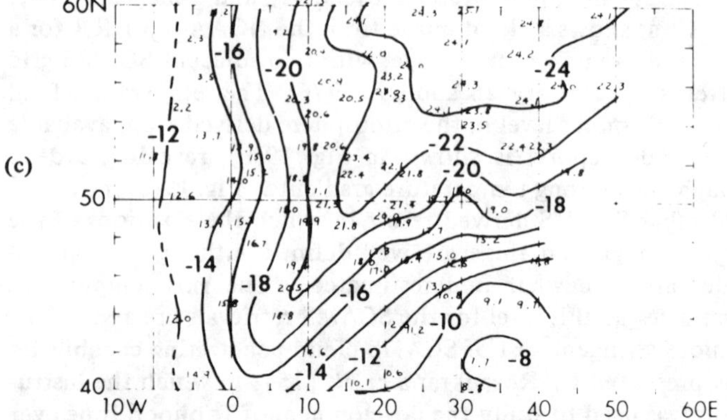

Fig. 19. Comparisons between SCAMS 700-mbar retrieved temperature measurements and radiosonde data, January 26/27, 1976: (a) NOAA-4 VHRR satellite image showing cloud features and SCAMS grid coverage; (b) analysis of 0000 UT radiosonde temperatures; (c) analysis of 2248-0038 UT SCAMS retrieved temperatures (after Grody and Pellegrino [14]).

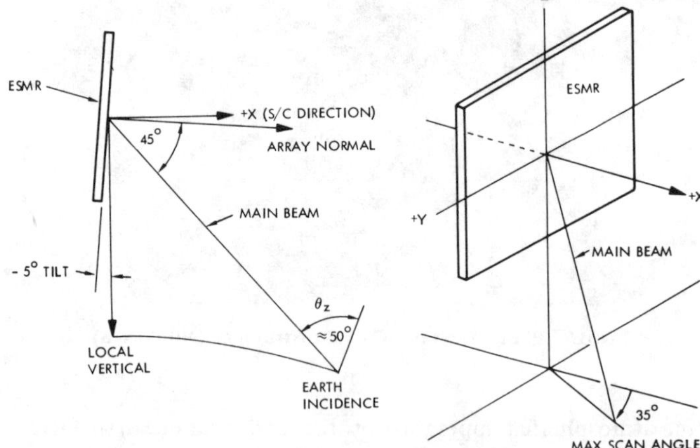

Fig. 21. ESMR (Nimbus-6) antenna scan geometry (after Wilheit [60]).

satellite in June 1975 [60]. The operating wavelength for the Nimbus-6 ESMR (ESMR-6) was 37 GHz (as opposed to 19.35 GHz for ESMR-5). This frequency change had the effect of tripling the instrument's sensitivity to water droplets while keeping its sensitivity to water vapor essentially the same, thus making it easier to distinguish light rain areas from areas of high water vapor. A secondary effect was to roughly double the contrast between first-year and multiyear ice, although some increase in ambiguity of ice concentration determination occurred. Snowfield mapping capability was also expected to improve.

The ESMR-6 measured both horizontally and vertically polarized radiation at the 37-GHz frequency, as opposed to horizontal only for ESMR-5. The polarization information facilitated quantitative interpretation of the radiometric measurements, and provided information on winds over the oceans.

The antenna beam of the ESMR-6 scanned ahead of the spacecraft along a conical surface, with a constant angle of 45° with respect to the antenna axis (Fig. 21). The beam scanned in azimuth ±35° about the forward direction in 71 steps. The 3-dB beamwidth varied from $0.95° \times 1.0°$ at scan center to $1.17° \times 0.85°$ at the scan extremes. The antenna axis was tipped forward 5° from the vertical axis of the spacecraft (as a design tradeoff), which resulted in the antenna beam intersecting the earth at a nearly constant incidence angle throughout the scan. The variation of incidence angle across the scan was about $\pm 0.6^\circ$. The 3-dB footprint on the earth's surface had dimensions approximately 20×43 km. The scan pattern resulted in a swath width of 1300 km, which allowed polar coverage up to latitudes of 85.7°.

The radiometer section of the instrument was similar in operation to that of ESMR-5. However, there were two separate receivers, one for each polarization, with common Gunn-diode LO's (Fig. 12). Radiation of both polarizations was received and separated in the phased-array antenna before being fed into the radiometers.

The dual-polarization capability of ESMR-6 was used to study its effectiveness for improved measurements of wind speed over the ocean and rainfall rate, in addition to continuation of the polar ice studies begun with ESMR-5. Wilheit [61] analyzed coincident ESMR-6 brightness temperatures and wind measurements from NOAA data buoys to get an improved understanding of the effect of ocean emissivity on wind speed. ESMR-6 data were also used by Weinman and Guetter [62] to show the potential for using dual-polarization measurements to determine rainfall over land as well as ocean.

G. SMMR (Seasat and Nimbus-7)

The Scanning Multichannel Microwave Radiometer (SMMR), launched on the Seasat and Nimbus-7 satellites in 1978, is currently the state-of-the-art instrument for passive microwave surface sensing. It measures dual-polarized radiation from the earth at frequencies of 6.6, 10.7, 18, 21, and 37 GHz. The SMMR data provide information on sea surface temperature, wind speed, atmospheric water vapor, cloud and precipitating liquid water, and sea ice type and concentration. Information on soil moisture and terrain snow cover properties is also obtainable. The SMMR instrument has been described in detail by Gloersen and Barath [29], and Njoku et al. [30].

A front view of the SMMR is shown in Fig. 22. There are six independent Dicke-type superheterodyne radiometers, fed by a single antenna and a calibration subsystem. Fig. 23 shows the system block diagram. At 37 GHz, two radiometers simultaneously measure two orthogonally polarized components of the received signal. At the other four frequencies, the radiometers alternate between the two polarizations during successive scans. In this manner ten data channels, corresponding to five dual-polarized signals, are provided by the instrument.

The SMMR has a scanning antenna system, consisting of an offset parabolic reflector with a 79-cm-diameter collecting aperture and a multifrequency feed assembly. The antenna reflector is mechanically scanned about a vertical axis, with a sinusoidally varying velocity, over a $\pm 25^\circ$ azimuth angle range. The antenna beam is offset 42° from nadir, thus the beam sweeps out the surface of a cone and provides a constant incidence angle at the earth's surface. Calibration is achieved by alternately switching in a "cold horn" viewing deep space and a "calibration load" at instrument ambient temperature, at the scan extremes.

The Seasat SMMR data processing is shown schematically in Fig. 24. The SMMR digital bit stream is extracted from the satellite data stream in the early stages of ground processing to form the Sensor Data Record (SDR). This contains the SMMR radiometric, engineering, and housekeeping data, in addition to satellite and footprint location data. The SDR is input to the calibration processing, which converts the digital radiom-

Fig. 22. Photograph showing front view of SMMR instrument (Seasat and Nimbus-7).

eter output data into antenna temperatures [63]. The antenna temperatures are input to the antenna pattern correction algorithms, which reformat the data, compensate for antenna sidelobe and cross-polarization effects, and perform a number of other supplementary operations such as corrections for spacecraft attitude and data quality flagging [64]. The brightness temperature data are then passed on to the final stage of data processing in which the geophysical parameters are derived.

The ocean-parameter retrieval algorithms are based on physical models of the effects of surface temperature and wind speed on brightness temperature [18]. The 6.6-GHz frequency was chosen for sensitivity to sea-surface temperature (SST). At 10.69 GHz, there is increased sensitivity to wind speed but little contamination by atmospheric effects. The 18-, 21-, and 37-GHz frequencies collectively provide information on atmospheric water vapor, cloud liquid water, and rainfall, and make corrections for these effects at the lower frequencies (see Fig. 2). Dual polarization is used at all frequencies to provide additional discriminatory capability. In practice, combinations of particular brightness temperatures are used in the derivation of each parameter, as determined by regression analyses or other retrieval techniques. The dual-polarization multifrequency capability is also used for improved discrimination of ice types and measurement of snow properties.

Initial results of comparisons between Seasat SMMR measurements and data from other sources have been described by Lipes et al. [65], [72] and Hofer et al. [66]. Fig. 25 shows the results of point comparisons between Seasat SMMR and conventional SST measurements in the Pacific Ocean. The

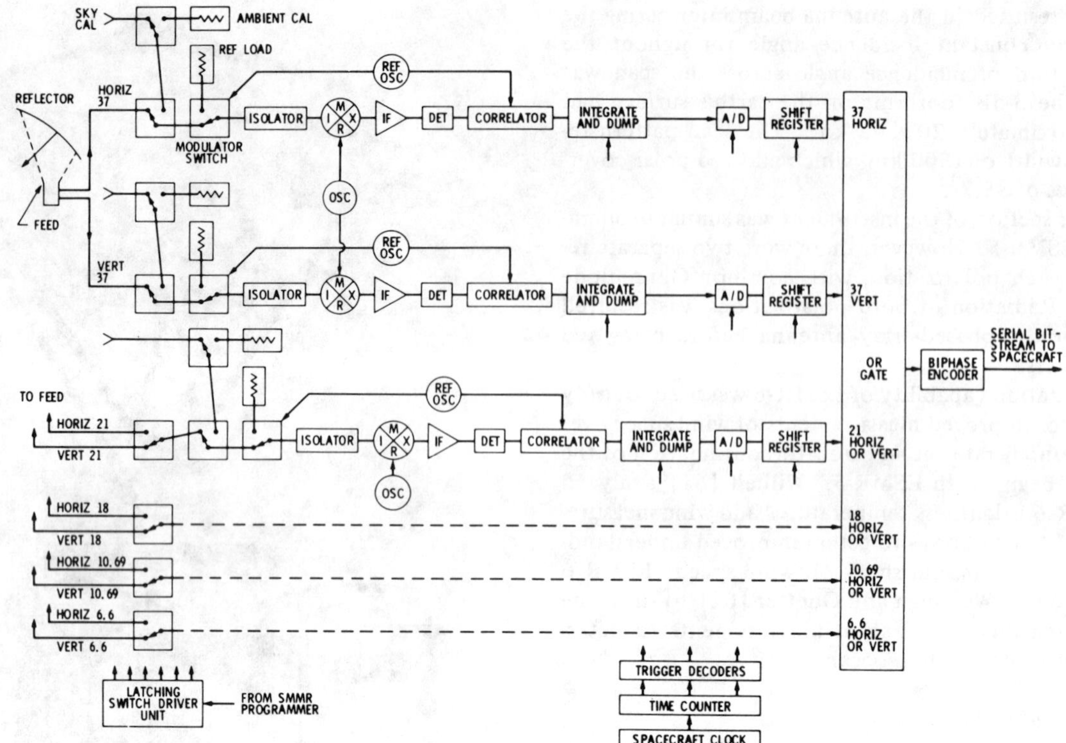

Fig. 23. SMMR instrument functional block diagram.

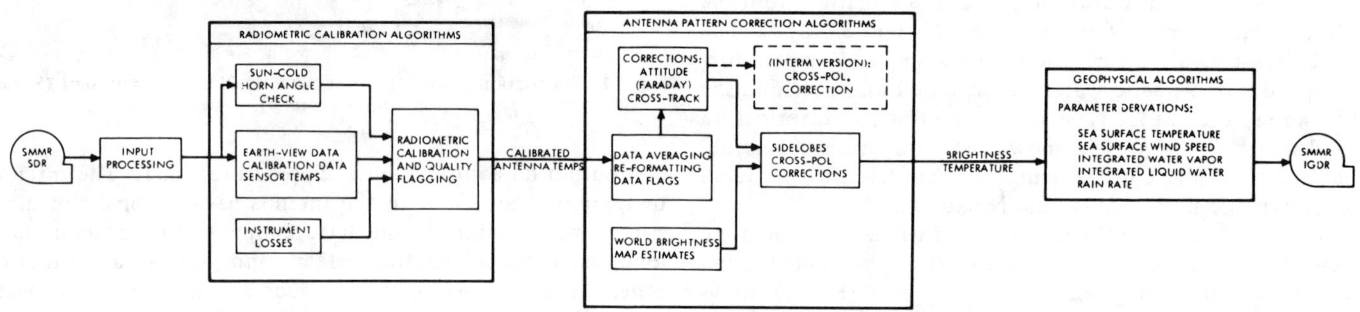

Fig. 24. Seasat SMMR data processing flow diagram (after Njoku *et al*. [30]).

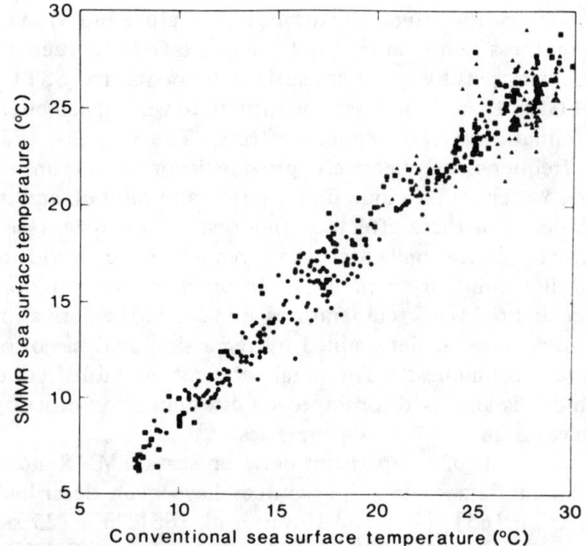

Fig. 25. Comparisons of Seasat SMMR retrieved sea surface temperature measurements and conventional XBT and ship measurements in the Pacific Ocean (after Hofer *et al*. [66]).

rms discrepancy between the two data sets is approximately 1.2 K. A 12-day-average SMMR global SST map for July, 1978 is shown in Fig. 26. Contours near coastal regions and inland waters may be unreliable, but in open ocean areas (∼600 km from land) the map is believed accurate to about 1 K. A scatter plot of SMMR wind-speed measurements versus winds derived from surface observations in the N.E. Pacific is shown in Fig. 27. The rms discrepancy is approximately 2 m/s which is close to the expected accuracy of the surface measurements themselves. Continuing analysis of SMMR data from both Seasat and Nimbus-7 satellites will enable studies of a global nature to be performed for oceanography, weather, and climate applications.

H. Other Sensors

In addition to progress made in the U.S. represented by the evolution of sensors described above, other nations, notably the U.S.S.R., Europe, Japan, and India have also developed plans for the utilization of microwave radiometry from space. As shown in Table I, the radiometers aboard the Soviet Cosmos-243 and -384 satellites provided the first microwave views of

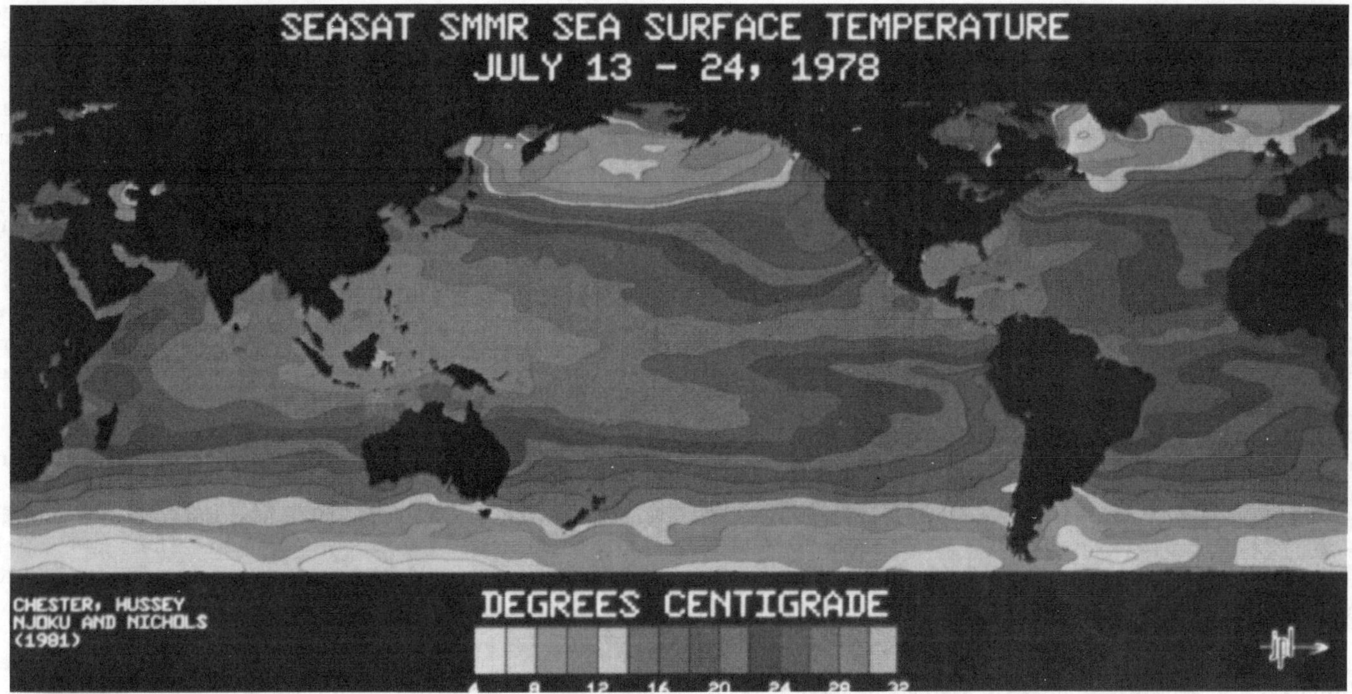

Fig. 26. Global sea surface temperature contour map derived from Seasat SMMR data, July 13–24, 1978.
Note: This figure appeared in color in the original publication.

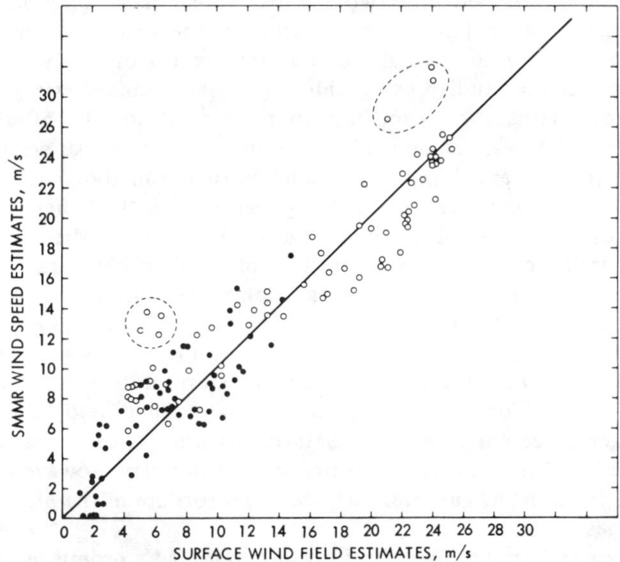

Fig. 27 SMMR retrieved wind comparisons with surface truth winds derived by kinematic analysis. Comparisons are for two satellite passes over the Gulf of Alaska region. (Circled points correspond to unreliable surface truth.) (After Lipes [72].)

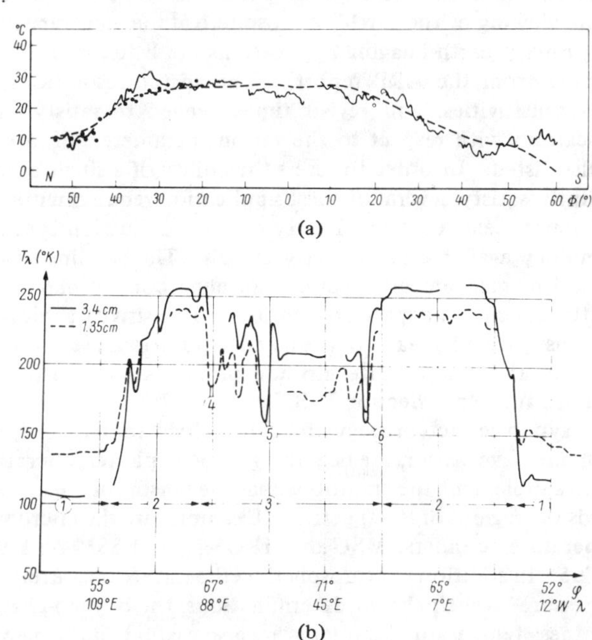

Fig. 28. Results from Cosmos-243 radiometers. (a) Surface temperature estimates in the Pacific Ocean compared with climatology (dashed line) and ship reports (circles). (b) Brightness temperature variations over the Antarctic continent, showing ① open sea, ② sea ice, ③ continental ice (including ④, ⑤, and ⑥: Western, Amery, and Lasarev barrier glaciers, respectively). (After Basharinov et al. [6].)

the earth from space. The two lower frequencies on Cosmos-243, 3.5 and 8.8 GHz, provided information on surface conditions, while the two higher frequencies, 22.2 and 37 GHz, were used to estimate atmospheric water vapor and liquid water [6]. Results from Cosmos-243 are shown in Fig. 28. Fig. 28(a) shows estimates of surface temperature in the Pacific Ocean as compared with mean climatic data and with ship reports at the higher latitudes. Fig. 28(b) shows brightness temperature variations over the Antarctic, and indicates the contrast observed at frequencies of 8.8 and 22.2 GHz between the open ocean, floating sea ice, and various regions of continental ice. The Cosmos-384 satellite, launched two years after Cosmos-243 in 1970, carried the same frequencies and had similar objectives [67]. The U.S.S.R. launched its Intercosmos-20

satellite in 1980, which had a microwave radiometer on board for making oceanographic measurements including surface temperature and wind speed [68].

India launched its first remote-sensing satellite "Bhaskara" in June 1979, which included a Satellite Microwave Radiometer (SAMIR) operating at frequencies of 19.1 and 22 GHz. Objectives of SAMIR were primarily to monitor atmospheric water vapor and liquid water in relation to studies of the Indian Monsoon. The instrument and initial results have been described by Pandey et al. [69]. A second, similar instrument was launched in November, 1981.

V. Future Developments

During the past decade, passive microwave remote sensing from space has made dramatic progress. For several applications, spaceborne microwave sensors have demonstrated their potential for becoming beneficial components of global monitoring systems. This potential will quite possibly be realized during the 1980's, and new applications will be advanced, as technology and data utilization capabilities continue to develop. As the applications proliferate and new sensor types evolve, it is clear that some coordination is required to design efficient sensors that can satisfy broad groups of satellite data users in a way that is economic and yet satisfies the various foreseeable government and commercial program objectives. In an attempt to provide insight into some of these issues a panel comprising instrument scientists, researchers, and operational data users was assembled by NASA in 1977 to review the current state of the art, and to make recommendations on directions which future system developments should take. This Applications Review Panel (ARP) produced a final report [70] whose contents are highly relevant to the discussion in this section and which will be referred to as appropriate.

A. Applications

Applications of passive microwave systems in space may be divided into two broad groups, those that require imaging of the earth and atmosphere beneath the satellite, and those that require viewing of the earth's atmosphere at the planetary limb. The primary earth-imaging applications are listed in Table III (adapted from the ARP report). The spatial resolutions, receiver sensitivities, and revisit times needed to satisfy these applications with respect to the various parameters of interest are also listed. In order to assess the ability of a single system to jointly satisfy several of these application requirements, the ARP report selected a baseline system for discussion based on technology available in the early 1980's. The baseline system had a 4-m mechanically scanned antenna compatible with a Shuttle launch. The spatial resolution and sensitivity achievable with this system for each of the listed applications are also given in Table III for a satellite altitude of 900 km. The table is discussed further in Section V-B.

For synoptic meteorology and climatology applications, passive microwave sensors are beginning to be exploited operationally to supplement the traditional passive sensors in the infrared and visible regions of the spectrum. Examples are the microwave temperature sounders: MSU on TIROS-N, and SSM on DMSP Block 5. In addition to atmospheric temperature measurements or pressure-level thickness determinations, the oxygen-channel brightness temperature gradients are also useful in deriving wind fields at different levels in the atmosphere, particularly for geostrophic winds. To date, the temperature sounding instruments have had horizontal resolutions in excess of 100 km, making them useful only for observing synoptic-scale meteorological systems. Such sensors would be of even greater value if instruments having smaller fields of view were available to probe cloud-shielded subsynoptic and mesoscale weather situations. Within the tropical environment, knowledge of the large variations in water vapor are of great importance in understanding the development of tropical cyclones and cloud clusters. Most numerical prediction models require at least two vertical layers of water vapor amounts in the atmosphere rather than the total (integrated) amounts derived from previous microwave instruments. Utilization of the 183-GHz water vapor line in addition to the line at 22.2 GHz may improve the ability to derive water

vapor profile information. For operational use in these applications, satellite data with complete global coverage approximately every 6 h are desirable.

In severe storm applications the time scales of interest are short ($\sim$1 h) and the spatial scales are small ($\sim$10 km); thus the use of geostationary platforms and higher frequencies such as the 118-GHz O_2 line and the 183-GHz H_2O line become desirable. Key measurement parameters, in addition to atmospheric temperature profile and water vapor, are precipitation and sea-surface winds. Precipitation has been observed over the oceans using ESMR data at 19.35 and 37 GHz, although the measurements suffer from modeling difficulties and coarse spatial resolution with respect to dimensions of typical rain cells. The use of frequencies above the 60-GHz oxygen complex shows promise for more quantitative rain measurements over both ocean and land areas. Studies of hurricanes and tropical cyclones using microwave data from Nimbus-5 and -6 sensors have shown much potential in storm forecasting studies and in understanding storm development. These applications will be much improved by sensors with better time and spatial resolution.

Ocean remote-sensing applications using microwave radiometers are in an early stage of development. The primary measurement requirements are for surface temperature, surface winds, and salinity. Oil slick detection and pollution monitoring are further possibilities [71]. The applications can be broadly classified into two groups. Open-ocean phenomena typically have large-scale features on the order of tens of kilometers with variabilities on time scales of a few days. These can be studied using wide-area observational coverage by spacecraft sensors at medium spatial resolutions (10–50 km). The results can be applied to medium- to long-range weather forecasting, and large-scale modeling of ocean dynamics and air–sea interactions. Coastal applications, on the other hand, focus on localized currents and smaller scale eddies which generally require spatial resolutions of less than 5 km, and on salinity and pollution monitoring, typically requiring resolutions of less than 1 km. The low microwave frequencies (1 to 10 GHz) necessary for making the ocean-surface measurements combined with the need for high spatial resolution in some of the applications is a driving force towards the development of larger space antennas. The SMMR instruments on Seasat and Nimbus-7 have provided the first steps in ocean microwave sensing from orbit, and more advanced sensors are in the planning stages.

Sea and land ice applications have received a promising start from measurements made by NEMS, SCAMS, and the ESMR's on Nimbus-5 and -6, and more recently by the SMMR on Nimbus-7 and Seasat. The principal measurement goals are the determination of temporal and spatial variations of sea-ice concentration and type, and horizontal and vertical temperature distributions and snow-accumulation rates on the ice sheets of Greenland and Antarctica. These measurements are important in advancing the understanding of ice dynamics, improving maritime operations and ship navigation in polar regions, and in climate modeling studies. For these applications, improved spatial resolutions of less than 5 km would aid in the location of specific large leads in the ice pack and enable more accurate ice-concentration determinations to be made.

Passive microwave sensing of land parameters, such as soil moisture and snowpack water equivalent, is far from maturity. This is mainly due to the variable nature of terrain surfaces and the poor spatial resolutions of current space sensors for

TABLE III
APPLICATIONS AND OBSERVABLE PARAMETERS FOR HIGH-RESOLUTION PASSIVE MICROWAVE SATELLITES
(Adapted from [70].)

In the FREQUENCY (GHz) group, columns 1.4–37 are under SMMR and columns 55, 90, 183 are under TIROS-N.

APPLICATION AREAS AND OBSERVABLE PARAMETERS	SPOT SIZE (KM)	ΔT_rms	REVISIT TIME (HR)	SPOT SIZE (KM) AT CRITICAL FREQUENCY, HEIGHT (KM) 900	ΔT_rms AT DESIRED RESOLUTION, HEIGHT (KM) 900	[SPOT SIZE ⊕V / DESIRED SIZE], HEIGHT (KM) 900	[ΔT_rms (AVAILABLE)V / ΔT_rms (REQUIRED)], HEIGHT (KM) 900	1.4	3.0	6.6	10.7	18	21	37	55	90	183
SYNOPTIC METEOROLOGY & CLIMATOLOGY																	
Temperature Profile	50	0.3	3-12	3.3	0.3	0.06	1.1							·	⊕		
Water Vapor Profile	15	0.5	3-12	8.6	0.6	0.6	1.2					+	⊕	+			+
Water Vapor Profile (Non-Tropical)	15	0.5	3-12	1.0	3.0	0.06	6.0									+	⊕
Liquid Water Abundance, Rain Rate	2-10	2	3-12	4.9	1.3	0.5	0.6		·	·	·	+	+	⊕	·	+	
Sea Surface Temperature	50	0.3	6-36	28	0.1	0.6	0.4	·	+	⊕	·	+	·	+			
Sea Surface Wind (Magnitude)	50	1	3-12	17	0.1	0.3	0.1	+	·	+	⊕			+			
Sea Surface Wind (No Precipitation)	50	1	3-12	4.9	0.2	0.1	0.2					+	+	⊕			
SEVERE STORMS																	
Temperature Profile	3-30	0.3	1-6	3.3	0.6	0.11	1.9							·	⊕		
Water Vapor Profile	3-15	0.5	1-6	8.6	0.6	0.4	1.2					+	⊕	+			+
Water Vapor Profile (Non-Tropical)	3-15	0.5	1-6	1.0	3.0	0.06	6.0									+	⊕
Liquid Water Abundance, Rain Rate	2-10	2	1-6	4.9	1.3	0.5	0.6		·	·	·	+	+	⊕	·	+	
Sea Surface Temperature	3-30	0.3	2-6	28	0.2	0.9	0.6	·	+	⊕	·	+	·	+			
Sea Surface Wind (Magnitude)	3-30	1	1-6	16.9	0.2	0.6	0.2	+	·	+	⊕			+			
Sea Surface Wind (No Precipitation)	3-30	1	1-6	4.9	0.4	0.2	0.4					+	+	⊕		+	
OCEAN SURFACE																	
Surface Wind Velocity	2-50	1	3-12	16.9	0.1	0.3	0.1	+	·	+	⊕			+			
Surface Wind Velocity (No Precipitation)	10-15	1	3-12	4.9	0.2	0.1	0.2					+	+	⊕		+	
Sea Surface Temperature	1-50	0.3	6-36	28	0.1	0.6	0.4	·	·	⊕	·	+	·	+			
Salinity	0.5-10	0.3	3-12	130	0.5	13.0	1.6	⊕	·	+	·	+		+			
Oil Slicks, etc. (No Precipitation)	0.5	0.3	1-12	4.9	25	9.8	84	·	·	+		+		⊕		+	
LAND PARAMETERS																	
Soil Moisture (Low Frequency)	3-25	1	6-36	130	0.2	5.2	0.2	⊕		+							
Soil Moisture (Higher Frequency)	3-25	1	6-36	28	0.2	1.1	0.2	·		⊕				·			
Snow Cover and Type, Frozen Ground	3-25	1	6-12	4.9	0.5	0.2	0.5		·	+		+		⊕		+	
SEA AND LAND ICE																	
Sea Ice Concentration	1-5	2	3-12	4.9	2.5	1.0	1.3					+		⊕		·	
Sea Ice Type	1-5	1	6-12	4.9	2.5	1.0	2.5		·	·	+	+		⊕		·	
Land Ice Properties (e.g., Firn)	10-50	1	12-36	4.9	0.2	0.1	0.2		·	·	+	+		⊕		·	

making these measurements. In water resources applications, soil-moisture information can be applied in hydrological models for predicting runoff and flood conditions. Similarly, snowpack measurements can be used to estimate spring runoff and melt water. Both applications require data with resolution on the order of less than 3 km. For agricultural applications, where soil-moisture information is used in crop yield forecasting models and large-area resource planning, spatial resolutions of about 10 km are desirable. For studies of the effects of soil moisture and snow cover on climate, somewhat larger spatial resolution is acceptable. Soil moisture is best measured using low frequencies in the 1- to 3-GHz range, where depth penetration on the order of centimeters can be achieved, and confusing effects of surface vegetation and roughness are minimized. For snowpack monitoring, a multifrequency approach is most promising, using several frequencies in the range 3 to 90 GHz.

Microwave sensing of the earth's upper atmosphere (stratosphere, mesosphere, and lower thermosphere) is a relatively new application. Global measurements in the upper atmosphere of the abundances of several molecular species, and measurements of temperature, winds, magnetic field, and reference pressure levels, will assist in understanding the complex chemistry and transport processes of that region. Limb-sounding techniques are best suited to these measurements since they provide substantially improved sensitivities and vertical resolutions over downward-looking experiments. With such techniques, several important measurements can be made using existing technology. The extension of microwave technology to submillimeter wavelengths will allow many more important measurements to be made.

B. Technology Advancement

The improvement in characteristics of the various spacecraft sensors described in previous sections, and the expanding applications and requirements discussed above, lead naturally to a discussion of the technological capabilities for meeting these requirements in the 1980's. In addition, as pointed out in the ARP report [70], there are substantial economic benefits to be gained in satisfying a large number of applications by using a few versatile system designs. This is especially true of applications that require improved spatial resolutions and hence larger and more costly antennas. A suggested possibility for the near term is the use of a 4-m offset-fed parabolic reflector antenna which could be stowed for launch within the Shuttle payload bay, and when deployed in space could be scanned mechanically at a rate of up to about 60 r/min. This type of antenna was used as a baseline for deriving the performance characteristics presented in Table III. An off-axis feed location was chosen to avoid blockage and to provide high beam efficiency. The antenna would scan about a vertical axis causing the beam to sweep out a conical surface, with a constant incidence angle at its intersection with the earth. For the purpose of the calculations in Table III an incidence angle of $55°$ was assumed, the sum of the receiver noise temperature and the antenna temperature was assumed to be $(400 + 20\nu)$ K, where ν is the radiometer frequency in gigahertz, and the receiver bandwidth for each channel was assumed to be 100 MHz. These numbers may vary in actual systems but are good baseline approximations. The table also suggests a range of frequencies which could be used to serve the listed applications. These frequencies are indicated by three symbols: + indicates frequencies that are of primary importance, · indicates helpful secondary frequencies, and ⊕ indicates the "critical" frequency

for which the spatial resolution was determined for the purposes of the analysis.

By studying Table III it can be seen that the critical frequency spot size is significantly greater than the maximum desired spot size only for the salinity, oil slick, and soil-moisture measurements. To meet the requirements of these applications, much larger antenna systems are required. A number of other parameters appear to have marginal resolutions, but useful information could nevertheless be obtained. High spatial resolution implies short integration times, and certain applications may, therefore, require receiver sensitivities that are unobtainable. With a foreseeable future doubling of receiver sensitivities, only the water vapor determinations using 183 GHz appear to have serious problems for lack of sensitivity. Cryogenic receivers could solve this problem.

The ARP study report suggested four classifications of systems for future passive microwave sensing from orbit: 1) A system of the kind described above, providing full earth coverage and satisfying the majority of applications; 2) large, specialized antenna systems designed for low-frequency high-resolution applications such as salinity and soil moisture; 3) geosynchronous atmospheric sounders operating around the O_2 and H_2O resonance frequencies; 4) limb-scanning systems for upper atmospheric studies. Development of such systems will depend largely on the priorities assigned to the various applications.

VI. Discussion

This paper has reviewed the development of passive microwave remote sensors as applied to earth observations from space. In the temperature sounding application the technique has reached the operational stage with the implementation of the MSU. An advanced version of this instrument with extended capabilities, the AMSU, is currently being planned by NOAA and NASA. A limited-operational sensor for oceanographic applications has also been discussed by the U.S. Navy, NOAA, and NASA, to meet the growing needs for continuous global oceanographic data sets. However, an increasingly careful scrutiny is being placed on new developments in these areas due to the high operational costs. It is hoped that continuing emphasis can be maintained on the experimental and operational demonstrations in order that the momentum gained during the past decade of microwave radiometry from space is not lost.

References

[1] D. H. Staelin, "Passive remote sensing at microwave wavelengths," *Proc. IEEE*, vol. 57, no. 4, 1969.

[2] ——, "Passive microwave techniques for geophysical sensing of the earth from satellites," *IEEE Trans. Antennas Propagat.*, vol. AP-29, pp. 683–687, July 1981.

[3] K. Tomiyasu, "Remote sensing of the earth by microwaves," *Proc. IEEE*, vol. 62, no. 1, 1974.

[4] R. H. Dicke, R. Beringer, R. L. Kyhl, and A. B. Vane, "Atmospheric absorption measurements with a microwave radiometer," *Phys. Rev.*, vol. 70, p. 340, 1946.

[5] F. T. Barath, A. H. Barrett, J. Copeland, D. E. Jones, and A. E. Lilley, "Mariner 2 microwave radiometer experiment and results," *Astron. J.*, vol. 69, no. 1, 1964.

[6] A. E. Basharinov, A. S. Gurvich, S. T. Yegorov, A. A. Kurskaya, D. T. Matveyev, and A. M. Shutko, "The results of microwave sounding of the earth's surface according to experimental data from the satellite Cosmos 243," in *Space Research XI*. Berlin: Akademie-Verlag, 1971.

[7] J. W. Waters, "Absorption and emission by atmospheric gases," in *Methods of Experimental Physics*, vol. 12, p. B, M. L. Meeks, Ed. New York: Academic Press, 1976, pp. 172–176.

[8] M. L. Meeks and A. E. Lilley, "The microwave spectrum of oxygen in the earth's atmosphere," *J. Geophys. Res.*, vol. 68, p. 1683, 1963.

[9] W. B. Lenoir, "Microwave spectrum of molecular oxygen in the mesosphere," *J. Geophys. Res.*, vol. 73, p. 361, 1968.

[10] J. W. Waters and D. H. Staelin, "Statistical inversion of radiometric data," Quart. Progr. Rep. 89, MIT Research Lab. of Electronics, Cambridge, MA, 1968.

[11] J. W. Waters, K. F. Kunzi, R. L. Pettyjohn, R. K. L. Poon, and D. H. Staelin, "Remote sensing of atmospheric temperature profiles with the Nimbus-5 microwave spectrometer," *J. Atm. Sci.*, vol. 32, no. 10, 1975.

[12] D. H. Staelin, A. L. Cassel, K. F. Kunzi, R. L. Pettyjohn, R.K.L. Poon, P. W. Rosenkranz, and J. W. Waters, "Microwave atmospheric temperature sounding: effects of clouds on the Nimbus-5 satellite data," *J. Atm. Sci.*, vol. 32, p. 1970, 1975.

[13] D. H. Staelin, K. F. Kunzi, R. L. Pettyjohn, R.K.L. Poon, R. W. Wilcox, and J. W. Waters, "Remote sensing of atmospheric water vapor and liquid water with the Nimbus-5 microwave spectrometer," *J. Appl. Meteorol.*, vol. 15, no. 11, 1976.

[14] N. C. Grody and P. P. Pellegrino, "Synoptic-scale studies using Nimbus-G scanning microwave spectrometer," *J. Appl. Meteorol.*, vol. 16, p. 816, 1977.

[15] P. W. Rosenkranz, D. H. Staelin, and N. C. Grody, "Typhoon June (1975) viewed by a scanning microwave spectrometer," *J. Geophys. Res.*, vol. 83, no. C4, 1978.

[16] T. T. Wilheit, R. R. Adler, R. Burpee, R. Sheets, W. E. Shenk, and P. W. Rosenkranz, "Monitoring of severe storms," in *High Resolution Passive Microwave Satellites*, D. H. Staelin and P. W. Rosenkranz, Eds., MIT Research Lab. of Electronics, Cambridge, MA, 1978.

[17] J. W. Waters and S. C. Wofsy, "Applications of high resolution passive microwave satellite systems to the stratosphere, mesosphere, and lower thermosphere," in *High Resolution Passive Microwave Satellites*, D. H. Staelin and P. W. Rosenkranz, Eds., MIT Research Lab. of Electronics, Cambridge, MA, 1978.

[18] T. T. Wilheit, "A review of applications of microwave radiometry to oceanography," *Boundary-Layer Meteorol.*, vol. 13, pp. 277–293, 1978.

[19] T. Wilheit, A.T.C. Chang, and A. S. Milman, "Atmospheric corrections to passive microwave observations of the ocean," *Boundary-Layer Meteorol.*, vol. 18, pp. 65–77, 1980.

[20] C. T. Swift, "Passive microwave remote sensing of the ocean—A review," *Boundary-Layer Meteorol.*, vol. 18, pp. 25–54, 1980.

[21] P. Gloersen, H. J. Zwally, A.T.C. Chang, D. K. Hall, W. J. Campbell, and R. D. Ramseier, "Time-dependence of sea-ice concentration and multiyear ice fraction in the arctic basin," *Boundary-Layer Meteorol.*, vol. 13, pp. 339–358, 1978.

[22] T. J. Schmugge, "Microwave approaches in hydrology," *Photogramm. Eng. Remote Sensing*, vol. 46, pp. 495–507, Apr. 1980.

[23] K. F. Kunzi, A. D. Fisher, D. H. Staelin, and J. W. Waters, "Snow and ice surfaces measured by the Nimbus-5 microwave spectrometer," *J. Geophys. Res.*, vol. 81, no. 27, 1976.

[24] H. J. Zwally and P. Gloersen, "Passive microwave images of the polar regions and research applications," *Polar Rec.*, vol. 18, no. 116, 1976.

[25] T. T. Wilheit, J. S. Theon, W. E. Shenk, L. J. Allison, and E. B. Rodgers, "Meteorological interpretations of the images from the Nimbus-5 electrically scanned microwave radiometer," *J. Appl. Meteorol.*, vol. 15, p. 166, 1976.

[26] T. T. Wilheit, A.T.C. Chang, M.S.V. Rao, E. B. Rodgers, and J. S. Theon, "A satellite technique for quantitatively mapping rainfall rates over the oceans," *J. Appl. Meteorol.*, vol. 16, p. 551, 1977.

[27] A. Sobti and R. K. Moore, "Correlation between microwave scattering and emission from land and sea," *IEEE Trans. Geosci. Electron.*, vol. GE-14, no. 2, 1976.

[28] J. R. Eagleman and W. C. Lin, "Remote sensing of soil moisture by a 21-cm passive radiometer," *J. Geophys. Res.*, vol. 81, no. 21, 1976.

[29] P. Gloersen and F. T. Barath, "A scanning multi-channel microwave radiometer for Nimbus-G and Seasat-A," *IEEE J. Oceanic Eng.*, vol. OE-2, no. 2, 1977.

[30] E. G. Njoku, J. M. Stacey, and F. T. Barath, "The Seasat scanning multichannel microwave radiometer (SMMR): Instrument description and performance," *IEEE J. Oceanic Eng.*, vol. OE-5, no. 2, 1980.

[31] L. A. Klein and C. T. Swift, "An improved model for the dielectric constant of sea water at microwave frequencies," *IEEE Trans. Antennas Propagat.*, vol. AP-25, p. 104, 1977.

[32] H. C. Blume, B. M. Kendall, and J. C. Fedors, "Measurements of ocean temperature and salinity via microwave radiometry," *Boundary-Layer Meteorol.*, vol. 13, p. 295, 1978.

[33] W. Nordberg, J. Conaway, D. B. Ross, and T. Wilheit, "Measurements of microware emission from a foam-covered, wind-driven sea," *J. Atm. Sci.*, vol. 28, p. 429, 1971.

[34] J. P. Hollinger, "Passive microwave measurements of sea surface roughness," *IEEE Trans. Geosci. Electron.*, vol. GE-9, p. 165, 1971.

[35] W. J. Webster, T. T. Wilheit, D. B. Ross, and P. Gloersen, "Spectral characteristics of the microwave emission from a wind-driven, foam-covered sea," *J. Geophys. Res.*, vol. 81, p. 3095, 1976.

[36] T. T. Wilheit, "A model for the microwave emissivity of the ocean's surface as a function of wind speed," *IEEE Trans. Geosci. Electron.*, vol. GE-17, pp. 244–249, 1979.

[37] J. D. Kraus, *Radio Astronomy*. New York: McGraw-Hill, 1966.

[38] Hughes Aircraft Co., "Special sensor microwave/imager (SSM/I), overall preliminary design review," Hughes Aircraft Co., El Segundo, CA, Nov. 1979.

[39] R. M. Price, "Radiometer fundamentals," in *Methods of Experimental Physics*, vol. 12, pt B, M. L. Meeks, Ed. New York: Academic Press, 1976, pp. 210–222.

[40] J. C. King, "Quantization and symmetry in periodic coverage patterns with applications to earth observation," *J. Astro. Sci.*, vol. XXIV, no. 4, 1976.

[41] D. H. Staelin, F. T. Barath, J. C. Blinn, and E. J. Johnston, "The Nimbus-E microwave spectrometer (NEMS) experiment," in *The Nimbus-5 User's Guide*. Greenbelt, MD: NASA/Goddard Space Flight Center, 1972.

[42] N. C. Grody, "Remote sensing of atmospheric water content from satellites using microwave radiometry," *IEEE Trans. Antennas Propagat.*, vol. AP-24, no. 2, 1976.

[43] T. T. Wilheit, "The electrically scanning microwave radiometer (ESMR) experiment," in *The Nimbus-5 User's Guide*. Greenbelt, MD: NASA/Goddard Space Flight Center, 1972.

[44] P. Gloersen, T. T. Wilheit, T. C. Chang, W. Nordberg, and W. J. Campbell, "Microwave maps of the polar ice of the earth," *Bull. Amer. Met. Soc.*, vol. 55, no. 12, 1974.

[45] P. Gloersen and V. V. Salomonson, "Satellites—New global observing techniques for ice and snow," *J. Glaciology*, vol. 15, no. 73, 1975.

[46] W. J. Campbell, P. Gloersen, W. J. Webster, T. T. Wilheit, and R. O. Ramseier, "Beaufort sea ice zones as delineated by microwave imagery," *J. Geophys. Res.*, vol. 81, no. 6, 1976.

[47] P. Gloersen, H. J. Zwally, A.T.C. Chang, D. K. Hall, W. J. Campbell, and R. O. Ramseier, "Time-dependence of sea-ice concentration and multiyear ice fraction in the Arctic basin," *Boundary-Layer Meteorol.*, vol. 13, p. 339, 1978.

[48] L. J. Allison, E. B. Rodgers, T. T. Wilheit, and R. W. Fett, "Tropical cyclone rainfall as measured by the Nimbus-5 electrically scanning microwave radiometer," *Bull. Amer. Met. Soc.*, vol. 55, no. 9, 1974.

[49] R. F. Adler and E. B. Rodgers, "Satellite-observed latent heat release in a tropical cyclone," *Mon. Weather Rev.*, vol. 105, p. 956, 1977.

[50] T. J. Schmugge, J. M. Meneely, A. Rango, and R. Neff, "Satellite microwave observations of soil moisture variations," *Water Resources Bull.*, vol. 13, no. 2, 1977.

[51] A. E. Potter, C. K. Williams, A. L. Grandfield, K. J. Demel, M. C. Trichel, T. L. Barnett, R. D. Juday, W. E. Hensley, N. M. Hatcher, W. E. McAllum, J. T. McGoogan, J. C. Jones, O. N. Brandt, J. G. Braithwaite, R. H. McLaughlin, R. Collins, W. H. Peake, and R. K. Moore, "Summary of flight performance of the Skylab earth resources experimental package (EREP)," in *Proc. 9th Int. Symp. on Remote Sensing of the Environment* (Ann Arbor, MI), p. 1803, 1974.

[52] R. K. Moore, J. P. Claassen, A. C. Cook, D. L. Fayman, J. C. Holtzman, A. Sobti, W. E. Spencer, F. T. Ulaby, J. D. Young, W. J. Pierson, V. J. Cardone, J. Hayes, W. Spring, R. J. Kern, and N. M. Hatcher, "Simultaneous active and passive microwave responses of the earth—The Skylab Radscat experiment," in *Proc. 9th Int. Sym. on Remote Sensing of Environment* (Ann Arbor, MI), p. 189, 1974.

[53] R. K. Moore, F. T. Ulaby, and A. Sobti, "The influence of soil moisture on the microwave response from terrain as seen from orbit," in *Proc. 10th Int. Symp. on Remote Sensing of Environment* (Ann Arbor, MI), 1975.

[54] F. T. Ulaby, L. F. Dellwig, and T. Schmugge, "Satellite microwave observations of the Utah Great Salt Lake Desert," *Radio Sci.*, vol. 10, no. 11, 1975.

[55] R. K. Moore and J. D. Young, "Active microwave measurements from space," *IEEE J. Oceanic Eng.*, vol. OE-2, no. 4, 1977.

[56] M. J. McFarland, "The correlation of Skylab L-band brightness temperatures with antecedent precipitation," in *Proc. NASA Earth Resources Symp.*, NASA TMX-58168, p. 2243, 1976.

[57] D. H. Staelin, A. H. Barrett, P. W. Rosenkranz, F. T. Barath, E. J. Johnston, J. W. Waters, A. Wouters, and W. B. Lenoir, "The scanning microwave spectrometer (SCAMS) experiment," in *The Nimbus-6 User's Guide*. Greenbelt, MD: NASA/Goddard Space Flight Center, 1975.

[58] S. Q. Kidder, W. M. Gray, and T. H. Vonder Haar, "Estimating tropical cyclone central pressure and outer winds from satellite microwave data," *Mon. Weather Rev.*, vol. 106, p. 1458, 1978.

[59] N. C. Grody, A. Gruber, and W. C. Shen, "Atmospheric water content over the tropical Pacific derived from the Nimbus-6 scanning microwave spectrometer," *J. Appl. Meteorol.*, vol. 19, p. 986, 1980.

[60] T. T. Wilheit, "The electrically scanning microwave radiometer (ESMR) experiment," in *The Nimbus-6 User's Guide*. Greenbelt, MD: NASA/Goddard Space Flight Center, 1975.

[61] T. T. Wilheit, "The effect of wind on the microwave emission from the ocean's surface at 37 GHz," *J. Geophys. Res.*, vol. 84, pp. 4921–4926, 1979.

[62] J. A. Weinman and P. J. Guetter, "Determination of rainfall distributions from microwave radiation measured by the Nimbus-6 EMSR," *J. Appl. Met.*, vol. 16, pp. 437–442, 1977.

[63] P. N. Swanson and A. L. Riley, "The Seasat scanning multichannel microwave radiometer (SMMR): Radiometric calibration algorithm development and performance," *IEEE J. Oceanic Eng.*, vol. OE-5 no. 2, 1980.

[64] E. G. Njoku, E. J. Christensen, and R. E. Cofield, "The Seasat scanning multichannel microwave radiometer (SMMR): Antenna pattern corrections—development and implementation," *IEEE J. Oceanic Eng.*, vol. OE-5, no. 2, 1980.

[65] R. G. Lipes, R. L. Bernstein, V. J. Cardone, K. G. Katsaros, E. G. Njoku, A. L. Riley, D. B. Ross, C. T. Swift, and F. J. Wentz, "Seasat scanning multichannel microwave radiometer: Results of the Gulf of Alaska workshop," *Science*, vol. 204, no. 4400, 1979.

[66] R. Hofer, E. G. Njoku, and J. W. Waters, "Microwave radiometric measurements of sea surface temperature from the Seasat satellite: First results," *Science*, vol. 212, p. 1385, 1981.

[67] A. E. Basharinov, A. S. Gurvitch, A. K. Gorodezky, S. T. Egorov, B. G. Kutuza, A. A. Kurskaya, D. T. Matveev, A. P. Orlov, and A. M. Shutko, "Satellite measurements of microwave and infrared radiobrightness temperature of the earth's cover and clouds," in *Proc. 8th Int. Symp. on Remote Sensing of Environment* (Ann Arbor, MI), pp. 291–296, 1972.

[68] A. M. Shutko, private communication, 1980.

[69] P. C. Pandey, A. K. Sharma, and B. S. Gohil, "A simulation technique for the determination of atmospheric water content with Bhaskara satellite microwave radiometer (SAMIR)," *Proc. Indian Acad. Sci.*, vol. 90, pp. 105–110, 1981.

[70] D. H. Staelin and P. W. Rosenkranz, Eds. *High Resolution Passive Microwave Satellites; Applications.* Review Panel Final Rep., MIT Research Lab. of Electronics, Cambridge, MA, 1978.

[71] J. P. Hollinger and R. A. Mannella, "Oil spills: Measurement of their distributions and volumes by multifrequency microwave radiometry," *Science*, vol. 181, pp. 54–56, 1973.

[72] R. G. Lipes, "SMMR Panel Report," in Seasat-JASIN Workshop Rep., Publ. 80-62, vol. 1, pp. 5–51, Jet Propulsion Laboratory, Pasadena, CA, 1980.

Seismic Signal Processing

LAWRENCE C. WOOD AND SVEN TREITEL

Invited Paper

Abstract—Seismic prospecting for oil and gas has undergone a digital revolution during the past decade. Most stages of the exploration process have been affected: the acquisition of data, the reduction of this data in preparation for signal processing, the design of digital filters to detect primary echoes (reflections) from buried interfaces, and the development of technology to extract from these detected signals information on the geometry and physical properties of the subsurface. The seismic reflection is generally weak, and it must be strengthened by the use of signal summing (stacking) procedures. The determination of depths to a target horizon requires knowledge of the propagational velocities of seismic stress waves, and a wealth of technology has evolved for this purpose. More recently, it has been possible to relate signal amplitude to the physical properties of the medium traversed and, in particular, to make inferences about the oil and gas content of the buried rocks. Much of the exploration effort occurs in offshore areas, where reverberations in the water layer mask reflections from below. The method of predictive deconvolution has been most effective in its ability to attenuate these reverberations, making it possible to detect reflections from structures at depth. Seismic signal processing is neither pure science nor pure art, and offers a continuing challenge to the practitioners of both cultures.

I. INTRODUCTION

MASSIVE AMOUNTS of seismic data are recorded and processed on a routine basis by the oil industry. Seismic surveys are carried out on a surface grid in order to build up a three-dimensional picture of the subsurface geology in a region, and each survey mile contains around 50 million bits of information, making modern data processing impossible without high-speed digital computers. Domestic oil companies acquired and processed around 390 000 line miles of data in the United States alone during 1973, at a total cost of about $370 million [1]. These figures do not include a similar international exploration effort.

Seismic signal processing can be divided into three categories: 1) data acquisition, 2) data processing, and 3) data interpretation. Though this paper will deal mainly with data processing, data acquisition and interpretation will be treated where necessary. Only modern reflection seismology methods are discussed as they are presently used to explore for hydrocarbon reserves. We shall not deal with processing techniques used in earthquake seismology, nuclear detection, earth crustal studies, and architectural engineering. General exploration objectives include the mapping of subsurface geological structures, the detection of hydrocarbon accumulations, and the estimation of total energy reserves in an area. As shown in Fig. 1, most reservoirs [2] are associated with geological formations having convex upward structures (anticlines) and linear displacements (faults) rather than with concave upward structures (synclines). Many deposits also relate to lateral changes in composition (stratigraphic traps). Time differences between reflected seismic signals map structural deformation, whereas amplitude changes

Manuscript received September 26, 1974; revised November 11, 1974.
The authors are with the Research Center, Amoco Production Company, Tulsa, Okla. 74102.

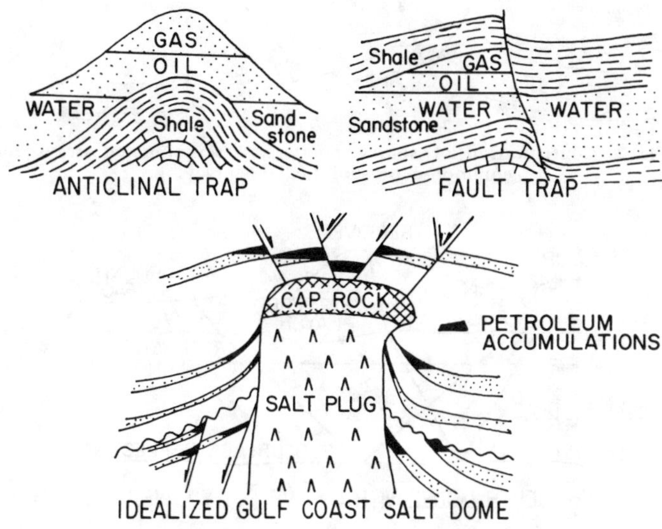

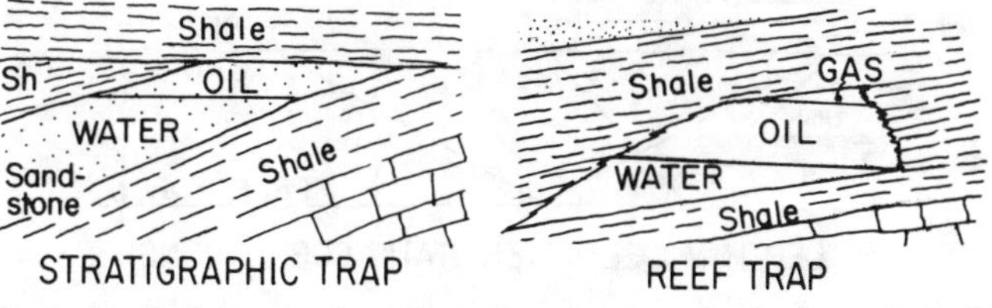

Fig. 1. Typical structural configurations for trapping hydrocarbons [2], [18].

of reflected signals may indicate the presence of hydrocarbons. The first part of this paper describes some basic time and amplitude adjustments, while the latter part deals with design of digital filters.

II. DATA ACQUISITION

Readers unfamiliar with exploration methods must acquire a rudimentary knowledge of seismic field procedures [3], energy sources [4], and recording instruments [5], before seismic signal processing can be fully understood. Only those procedures currently employed in common-depth-point (CDP) surveying [6] will be reviewed in this paper. "Split-spread" methods [7]–[9] are not treated. A brief review of data acquisition practices precedes discussion of seismic processing methods.

Fig. 2 shows the essence of a seismic data gathering system. Elastic disturbances created by seismic energy sources propagate through the earth, where interfaces between geological strata reflect spreading wavefronts. Arrival times of single-bounce echoes (primary reflections) at surface receivers permit the determination of depths and inclination angles of reflectors when subsurface velocities are known. The receivers shown in Fig. 2 actually represent a composite array (group) of

Reprinted from *Proc. IEEE*, vol. 63, pp. 649–661, Apr. 1975.

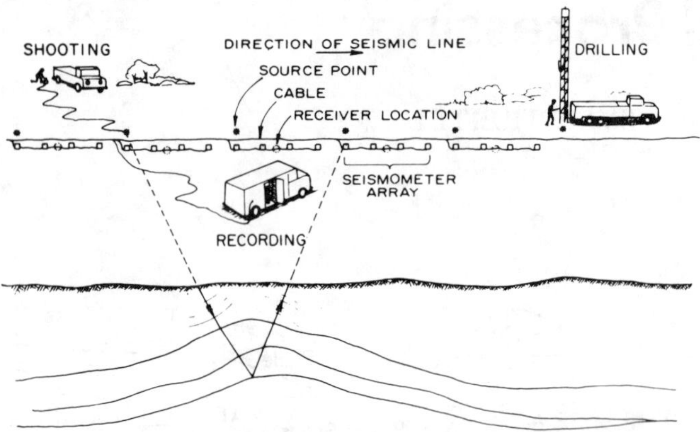

Fig. 2. Configuration of source points and seismometer arrays for common-depth-point (CDP) surveying.

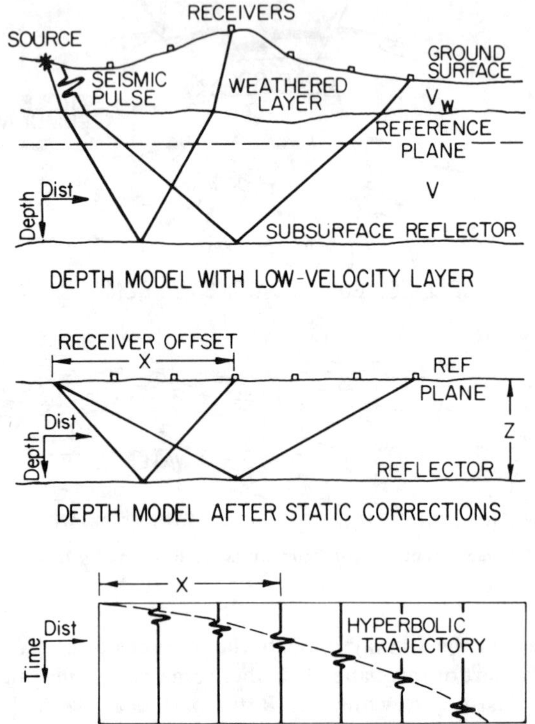

Fig. 3. Basic models of a reflection seismograph system.

transducers (seismometers) as illustrated in Fig. 3. These groups may consist of up to 100 individual geophones laid out in various linear and spatial patterns with group intervals (distance between groups) ranging from 50 to 900 ft. Each time a source is activated it is common practice to record either 24, 48, or 96 group arrays (traces) on digital tape simultaneously as a single recording. The seismic "master" cable joining these groups typically ranges from 1 to 3 mi in length. Seismic surveys are conducted along parallel straight lines and individual lines may extend for distances of 1 to 100 mi for total survey distances of 1 to 1000 mi or more.

Many different types of energy sources are used to generate seismic waves. Dynamite and other high energy explosive sources provide the simplest and most efficient means of releasing energy, but environmental considerations have led to the development of many alternate sources: implosive air guns, electrical sparkers, vibrating chirp systems [10], [11], etc.

A seismic source must provide good reflection signal-to-noise ratios at all times of interest. Weak sources are, therefore, laid out in arrays similar to receiver arrays, and signals generated by multiple source arrays are summed (stacked) together in a process called "vertical stacking." Vertical stacking should not be confused with "horizontal stacking" that sums traces lying in a common-depth point plane. Source and receiver arrays cancel unwanted ambient noise, attenuate surface waves, smooth time variations caused by surface irregularities, and discriminate against scattered energy. Many authors [12]–[14], [20] have studied optimum design of arrays, and an important problem in acquiring data in a new prospect is to relate array configurations and vertical stacks with reflection quality.

Modern instruments and data acquisition systems record fairly accurate facsimiles of the ground's response to incoming reflected energy. Many references [5], [15], [16] cover this subject in good detail; consequently, we review only those aspects most relevant to signal processing. Seismometers convert particle velocity to electrical voltages for land surveys, whereas in marine work they convert pressure variations to voltage. As mentioned in the preceding, an array may have up to 100 transducers with the array signal recorded on a single channel. A total of 24, 48, or 96 array signals are multiplexed and recorded digitally on magnetic tape (a single seismic record) by an instrument truck as shown in Fig. 2. Seismic traces seldom exceed 6 s in length because hydrocarbon reservoirs rarely occur below 30 000 ft in geologic basins, where velocities average around 15 000 ft/s. Special chirp systems [10], [11], however, may record 15 s of data. Reflected signals contain frequencies from a few hertz to a few hundred hertz, and field data is usually sampled at 1, 2, or 4 ms rates with alias frequencies (half the sampling frequencies) of 500, 250, or 125 Hz, respectively.

Digital seismic-recording systems have dynamic ranges around 80 dB. Exploration geophysicists define a decibel as $20 \log_{10} (A/A_0)$, where A/A_0 is the amplitude ratio. Signals, however, may rise 100 dB above ambient noise levels. Digital processing is able to recover another 20 or 30 dB of signal lying within the noise. Reflection amplitudes decay about 100 dB in the first 4 s of recording, primarily due to attenuation losses along the travel path. Consequently, amplifier gain levels change many times during recording in order to preserve signal amplitude for subsequent processing. Modern gain systems include instantaneous-floating-point and binary-gain control. Binary-gain amplifiers record the times of gain changes to allow recovery of signal amplitude. Field instruments record 16 bits. Most processing programs require only 12 bits, while final plotter output displays use the most significant 8 bits. A 24-trace seismic record contains around 1 million bits of information, and a typical marine crew may acquire 200 such records a day. Having discussed the rudiments of seismic data acquisition, we now consider processing these gigantic data sets on a computer.

III. Preliminary Corrections

Signal processing begins with the demultiplexing of field records. This results in a work tape with signal traces in sequential order. Trace data is preceded on tape by header information giving elevations, seismometer group intervals, sampling rate, word size, trace length, and similar information. The creation of a work tape in a format compatible with central computing center requirements is one of the largest and most frustrating processing tasks, despite industry attempts [17] to standardize tape formats. Adjustment of times and amplitudes

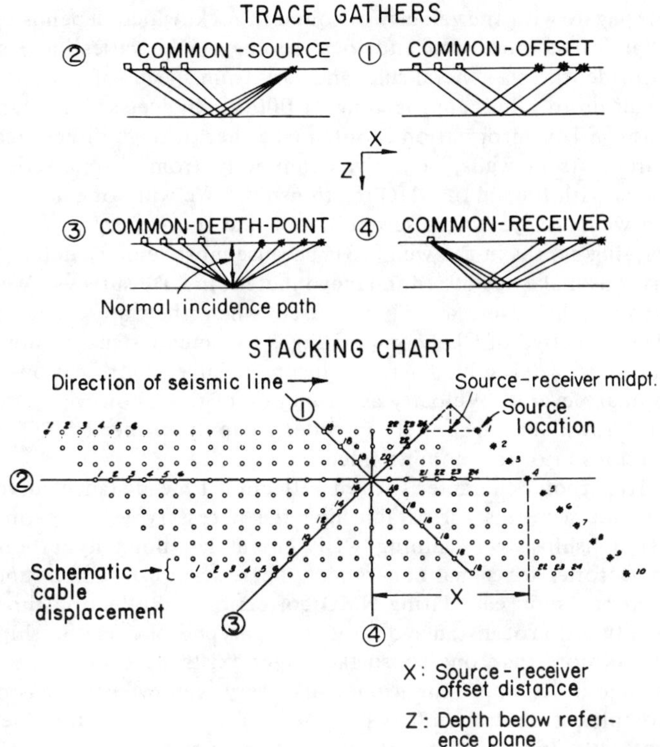

Fig. 4. Source and receiver positions corresponding to four principal planes used for sorting seismic traces [19].

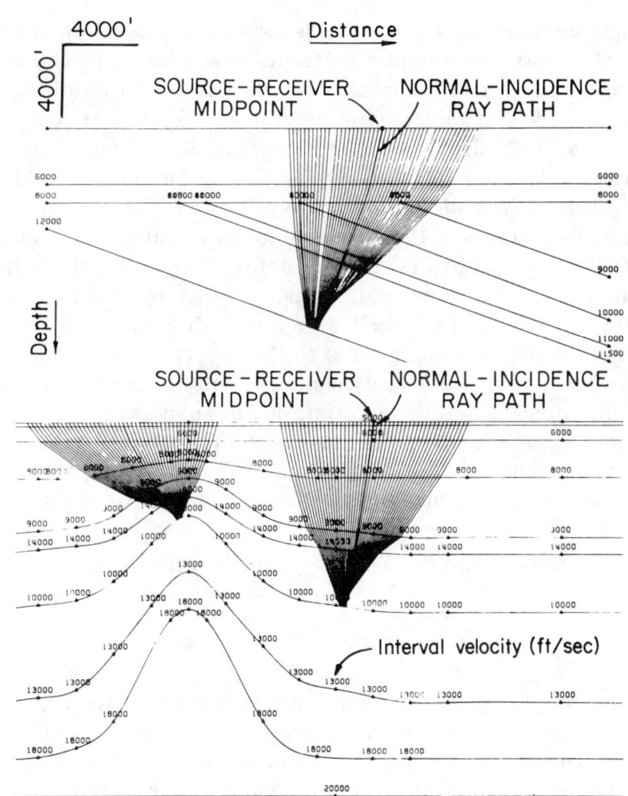

Fig. 5. Ray-path diagrams for CDP traces. Normal-incidence ray paths correspond to ideal CDP compositing.

to correct for various physical phenomena follows demultiplexing and reformatting. We briefly discuss time adjustments before proceeding to the important topic of relative amplitude preservation.

Geophysicists divide time corrections into static and dynamic categories [18]. A "static correction" consists of the application of a time shift, or translation, to an entire trace. In other words, a constant time correction term is added or subtracted from all reflection times, regardless of record time or reflector depth. "Dynamic corrections," on the other hand, vary with record time and therefore depend on reflector depth. Elevation changes and near-surface inhomogeneities severely degrade trace-to-trace continuity and the purpose of automatic static computations is to remove time variations caused by anomalous conditions at the earth's surface.

A region of very low velocity extends from the earth's surface to a depth of several tens to hundreds of feet; at this point velocities change either gradationally or abruptly from values near 2000 to 5000 ft/s or more. Time delays associated with this "weathered layer" disrupt reflection continuity (i.e., trace-to-trace alignment) and pose a major obstacle to successful processing of data acquired on land. Seismic lines recorded at sea, however, do not usually require static adjustments because of the uniform water layer of constant elevation.

An assumption underlying all automatic correction programs [19] is that a simple translation of a trace converts it into a model trace that would have been recorded had sources and receivers been vertically displaced downward to a reference plane with no weathering material present (see Fig. 3). This time delay is assumed to be "surface consistent," that is, to be a sum of an "initiation" or source related component and a contribution characteristic of a given surface or "receiver" position. The validity of these two assumptions is confirmed by the great success of modern static correction programs [19], al-

though near-surface layers behave as complicated filters whose impulse responses distort amplitude and phase characteristics of seismic wavefronts. Further discussion of static and dynamic corrections requires knowledge of seismic trace sorting procedures.

Traces are usually collected into one of four kinds of data sets [19] or "gathers," depending on different objectives. For this purpose a diagram called a "stacking chart" is used (see Fig. 4). Sources are activated sequentially in the field (Fig. 2) with each initiation creating a "common-initiation" record. Surface positions of sources and receivers are displaced vertically on a stacking chart for clarity. Fig. 4 illustrates common-initiation gathers of 24 traces. These diagrams define four principal trace gathers called "common-initiation," "common-receiver," "common-offset," and "common-depth-point." Common-initiation gathers consist of traces having the same source, common-receiver gathers consist of traces having identical surface locations and common-offset gathers are traces with the same source-receiver distance ("offset").

IV. HORIZONTAL (CDP) STACKING

Traces with a CDP have a common midpoint [6] between source and receiver (Fig. 4); in the case of horizontal interfaces they also have common points on reflecting interfaces called "common-reflection-points" (CRP). Otherwise, common subsurface reflection points, however, migrate laterally and spread apart as structures become more complicated; nevertheless, complex geometries frequently cause small dispersion [21] of CRP locations (Fig. 5), so that CDP trace compositing is still successful. The last two decades have shown that horizontal (CDP) stacking is the single most important step in seismic signal processing. Stacking consists of the simple sum of traces contained in a CDP plane to produce a single composited trace. The latter's surface position is then equated with the common source-receiver midpoint. The summing of CDP traces succeeds because primary CRP reflections are in phase and add constructively, whereas ambient noise and other seismic signals not in phase cancel. Compositing increases reflection signal-to-noise ratios by factors approaching $\sqrt{N}$, where N is the number ("fold") of CDP traces summed. Horizontal stacks of 12, 24, and 48 fold are routinely produced.

CDP traces must be corrected for travel-time differences caused by varying ray path distances prior to stacking. This latter correction [18], called "normal-move-out" (NMO), depends on depth (record time) to the reflecting horizon and is, therefore, classified as a dynamic correction. NMO is defined as the increase in reflection time due to an increase in distance from source to receiver for a horizontal reflecting interface in a homogeneous medium of constant velocity. A simple expression for an NMO time increment can be derived from Fig. 3:

$$\Delta T_{\mathrm{NMO}} = T_x - T_0 = \frac{1}{V}\sqrt{4Z^2 + X^2} - T_0 \qquad (1a)$$

$$\Delta T_{\mathrm{NMO}} \sim \frac{X^2}{4VZ} \qquad (1b)$$

where $T_0 = 2Z/V$ is the two-way reflection time for the zero-offset trace, T_x is the two-way reflection time for a trace of offset distance X, V is the velocity of the medium, Z is the depth to the reflecting horizon, and X is the source-receiver separation (offset).

NMO correction involves the subtraction to a time increment ΔT_{NMO} from each record time T_x, with interpolation as necessary. This correction converts a trace of offset distance X into a zero-offset trace that would have been initiated and recorded at a common source-receiver midpoint (Fig. 4). Equations (1) show the dynamic nature of the NMO correction, because even in this most elementary case it is a function of depth, velocity, and offset.

Two facts contribute greatly to the success of CDP stacking. First, reflection time–distance curves (T_x versus X) from complicated structures are approximated well by a hyperbolic relationship [21] of the form,

$$T_x^2 = (T_0 + \Delta T_{\mathrm{NMO}})^2 = T_0^2 + \frac{X^2}{V^2}. \qquad (2)$$

Second, the purpose of NMO corrections is to align single-bounce ("primary") reflections prior to summing. Multiple-bounce ("multiple") reflections travel at lower average velocities than primary reflections with the same arrival times, since velocity usually increases with depth. Therefore, multiple reflections having greater NMO are misaligned and attenuated in CDP stacking.

NMO corrections and CDP compositing create new traces [21] called "normal-incidence traces" (NIT). These correspond to identical source and receiver positions (i.e., zero offset). The zero-offset traces also have identical incident and reflected ray path segments, as shown in Fig. 5. The NIT ray paths form right angles with reflecting horizons at points of reflection called "normal-incident points" (NIP). Thus CDP stacking produces a suite of NIT traces with reflection travel paths normal to subsurface horizons (Fig. 5).

V. VELOCITY ANALYSIS

The most important variable in seismic prospecting is velocity, because distances to subsurface reflectors are calculated from observed travel times and known velocities. Seismic waves propagate with the velocity of sound in rock, which depends on chemical composition and local geology. Velocities increase with depth as a general rule, and vary from speeds of 1100 ft/s in air up to values approaching 21 000 ft/s in deep sedimentary basins. This information is obtained either through direct measurements in wells, or derived indirectly from seismic reflections with the aid of NMO relationships. We will not elaborate on well surveys where seismometers and sources are placed at varying depths in the well [18], because most velocity determinations make use of redundancy inherent in CDP surveys. Well surveys, however, are always used when they are available. The objective of CDP compositing is to increase signal-to-noise ratios to a level sufficient to insure reliable identification of primary events. Velocity as a function of time, however, must be known very accurately in order to apply proper NMO corrections prior to summing traces.

Hyperbolic characteristics of reflection time–distance curves provide a means for establishing the necessary velocity–time relationships by scanning CDP ensembles along hyperbolic trajectories for signal coherence. These scans establish a function to use in calculating NMO corrections. Reflection times as a function of distance do not satisfy hyperbolic relationships when more than one subsurface layer exists; nevertheless, this second-order approximation works very well even in areas of complex structural geology provided parameters are determined correctly [21]. Only reflections from a single interface in a homogeneous medium have a truly hyperbolic time–distance curve (see (1)).

Reflection times for a horizontal reflector below a sequence of N horizontal layers with constant interval velocities can be described by an infinite power series of the form [21],

$$T_{X,N}^2 = C_1 + C_2 X^2 + C_3 X^3 \cdots. \qquad (3)$$

A hyperbolic approximation analogous to the single-layer case results from retention of the first two terms,

$$T_{X,N}^2 = T_{0,N}^2 + \frac{X^2}{V_{\mathrm{rms}}^2} \qquad (4a)$$

where

$$T_{0,N} = \sum_{k=1}^{N} \frac{2Z_k}{v_k} \qquad (4b)$$

$$V_{\mathrm{rms}} = \left(\frac{1}{T_{0,N}} \sum_{k=1}^{N} v_k^2 t_k\right)^{1/2} \qquad (4c)$$

and X is the offset distance, N is the number of layers overlying the reflecting horizon, Z_k is the thickness of the kth layer, v_k is the interval velocity of the kth layer, t_k is the two-way travel-time in kth layer, $T_{0,N}$ is the two-way traveltime to the bottom of the Nth layer for the NITth trace, and V_{rms} is the rms velocity. In the limit, (4) reduce correctly to describe a single-layer, and then there is no difference between rms and interval velocity.

An expression can be derived [22] from (4c) for calculating interval velocities v_N in the multilayered situation when rms velocities are known. Velocity spectra described below are one way of measuring rms velocities. These average velocities $\bar{V}_N$ are calculated in succession beginning from $\bar{V}_1 = v_1$ using the following relationship:

$$v_N = \left(\frac{\bar{V}_N^2 T_{0,N} - \bar{V}_{N-1}^2 T_{0,N-1}}{T_{0,N} - T_{0,N-1}}\right)^{1/2} \qquad (5)$$

where $\bar{V}_N$ is the rms velocity to the bottom of the Nth layer, and $\bar{V}_{N-1}$ is the rms velocity to the top of the Nth layer. Hyperbolic approximations (4) are accurate within 2 to 5 percent in geologic areas of simple structural deformations, that is where inclination angles of interfaces do not exceed about $15°$; and interval velocities (5) are often estimated with accuracies between 5 and 10 percent for use in stratigraphic studies and for detection of hydrocarbon accumulations.

A velocity versus time display called a "velocity spectrum" [21] is generally used to determine hyperbolic parameters, which are calculated from CDP traces assuming that travel-times of reflections from a CRP lie along a hyperbola. The determination of velocity becomes a matter of scanning various hyperbolic trajectories for maximum reflection coherency. Spectra are generated by incrementing normal incidence travel-times $T_{0,N}$ and keeping them constant while incrementing V_{rms} at regular intervals between some minimum and maximum value. Each $(T_{0,N}, V_{rms})$ pair defines a hyperbola, and coherency of data contained in a gate about this curve (Fig. 6) is measured. Traces are scanned with various hyperbolas whose apexes are fixed at the origin (i.e., $X = 0$ and $T_{0,N}$ = constant). A velocity spectrum consists of a three-dimensional surface of coherency as a function of normal incidence time $T_{0,N}$ and rms velocity V_{rms}.

This spectrum may be displayed as contour lines which represent the intersection of level planes of constant coherency with the coherency surface. Interpretation of velocity spectra requires skill and experience, because multiple reflections and other seismic events in addition to primary reflections tend to align themselves along hyperbolic trajectories. A spectral interpretation consists of the location of peaks on the coherency surface that correspond to primary reflections. These peaks are then suitably joined to obtain an average stacking velocity (V_{rms}) versus time ($T_{0,N}$) function display.

Coherence measurements are a crucial part of the determination of effective stacking velocities from multifold seismic data, and they have received considerable attention in [22]. The basic problem is to establish the similarity that exists between various time gates centered about hyperbolic trajectories (see Fig. 6). The main task is to measure alignment. Cross correlation and semblance are two commonly used statistical measures.

Cross correlation functions may or may not be sensitive to amplitude changes between time gates, this sensitivity depending on normalization procedures. The following normalized coherency function [23] employing zero-lag values of auto-correlation and cross correlation functions is not sensitive to rms signal amplitude variations between channels:

$$S = \frac{2}{M(M-1)} \sum_{i=1}^{M} \sum_{i>i'} \frac{R_{ii'}(0)}{\sqrt{R_{ii}(0) R_{ii'}(0)}} \tag{6}$$

where M is the number of CDP traces, $R_{ii}(0)$ is the zero-lag value of the autocorrelation function of the ith trace, and $R_{ii'}(0)$ is the zero-lag value of the cross correlation function between the ith and i'th traces. This cross correlation measure varies between -1 and 1, where 1 corresponds to perfect signal coherency.

Another useful quantity for measuring multichannel coherence is semblance, which is defined [23] as the normalized output/input energy ratio. Output energy is measured on a composited time gate obtained by summing input time gates. The semblance coefficient S_c is sensitive to channel amplitude differences and varies between 0 and 1, with 1 denoting identical signals. It, too, can be expressed in terms of zero-lag

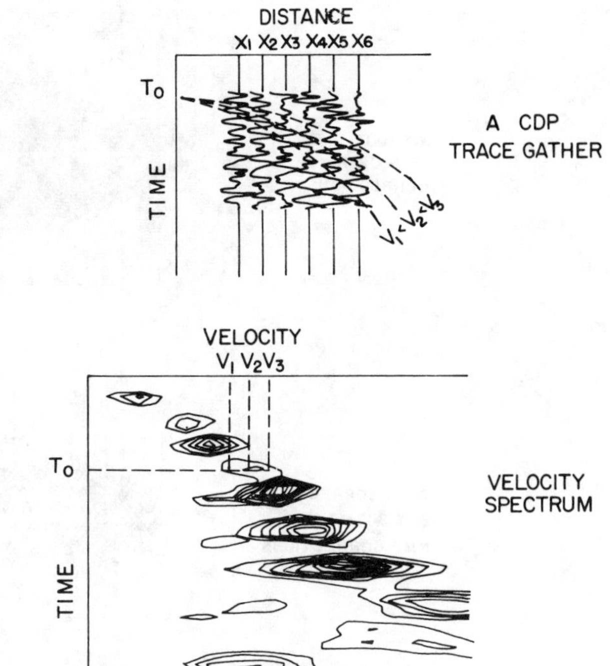

Fig. 6. A velocity spectrum displaying coherency as a function of reflection time and rms velocity.

values of correlation functions,

$$S_c = \frac{\sum_{i=1}^{M} \sum_{i'=1}^{M} R_{ii'}(0)}{M \sum_{i=1}^{M} R_{ii}(0)}. \tag{7}$$

These coherence measures are closely related, and the optimum statistic for extracting velocity information from CDP trace gathers may not yet have been found.

VI. Relative Amplitude Preservation

Prior to 1970, seismic amplitudes were used almost exclusively as a qualitative tool for identifying seismic events. A recent development [24]–[26] relating large amplitude anomalies, called "bright spots," with the possible presence of hydrocarbon accumulations has added a new and significant dimension to the search for oil and gas deposits. Exploration has been generally restricted to the location of structural features such as anticlines, faults, and salt domes (Fig. 1) delineable with trace-to-trace differences in reflection time arrivals. Structural traps favoring the accumulation of hydrocarbons are drilled successfully about 20 percent of the time; however, amplitude information increases these percentages by helping to pinpoint changes in rock composition, layer thickness and stratigraphic conditions. The approach is successful [26] about 70 percent of the time in locating gas accumulations in young, unconsolidated Pleistocene (not over 12 million years in age) deposits in offshore Nigeria, Indonesia, and the U.S. Gulf Coast [29]. The "bright-spot" technology is being refined in the hope that it can treat amplitude anomalies observed in older, petroliferous sediments around the world in areas such as Alaska, the North Sea, California, and the continental United States.

Porous rocks at depth are usually filled with salt water, but may contain oil or gas. The new technology works best in lo-

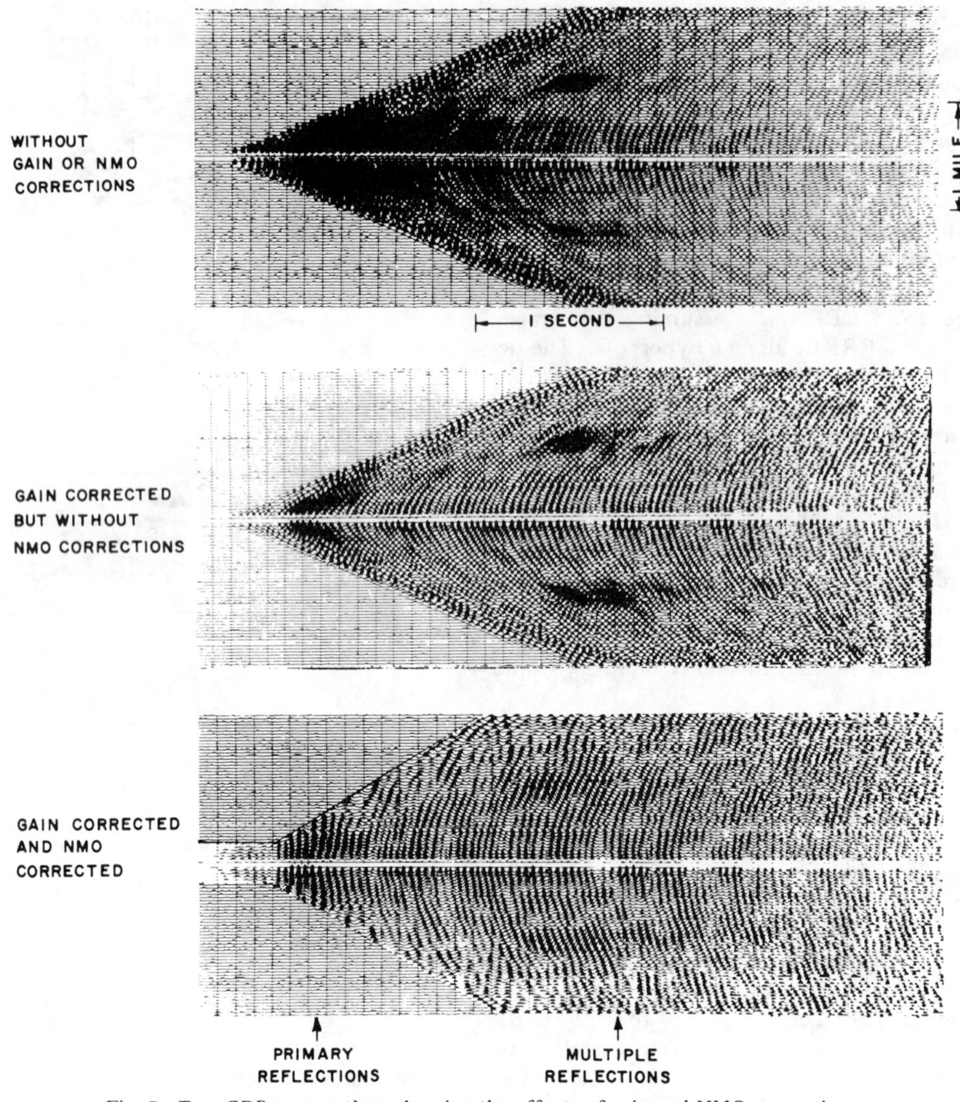

Fig. 7. Two CDP trace gathers showing the effects of gain and NMO corrections.

cating gas reservoirs because they cause a greater variation of reflection amplitudes. The amount of energy reflected at an elastic interface depends on the change in acoustic impedance (i.e., velocity–density product) across the interface. Gas-filled rocks have much lower velocities and, therefore, greater acoustic contrasts than either oil or brine saturated rocks, thereby reflecting a greater percentage of incident energy.

A simple expression [27] relates reflected and refracted amplitudes across an interface for the special case of plane waves incident on plane interfaces at normal incidence. In general, compressional (P) and shear (S) wave modes propagate in an elastic medium. Snell's law and Fermat's principle of minimum-time paths govern refraction at an interface, where incident energy splits into reflected and refracted P and S modes. No mode conversion occurs for normal incidence, and a simple normal-incidence reflection coefficient relates incident and reflected amplitudes,

$$A_r = \frac{\rho_2 v_2 - \rho_1 v_1}{\rho_2 v_2 + \rho_1 v_1} \qquad (8)$$

where 1 is the medium containing the incident wave, 2 is the medium containing the transmitted wave, ρ is the density, and v is the interval velocity. A corresponding transmission coef-

ficient relates incident and transmitted amplitudes,

$$A_t = \frac{2\rho_1 v_1}{\rho_1 v_1 + \rho_2 v_2}.$$

Appropriate equations for oblique incidence are much more complicated [28], because mode conversion must be taken into account. Nevertheless, normal incidence coefficients are very useful and quite accurate for stacked traces in areas having simple geological structures.

Gas has a much larger effect on reflected amplitudes than oil, so that amplitude anomalies associated with gas/brine contacts are greater than those related to oil/brine and gas/oil interfaces. Normal incidence reflection coefficients for gas-filled sandstones encased in slow-velocity shales may approach 40 percent, as compared to 10 percent or less for brine-charged sandstones. Coefficients for oil-bearing sands exhibit intermediate values. Thus hydrocarbons may produce amplitude anomalies around 12 dB. Polarity reversals also characterize hydrocarbon accumulations, because acoustic impedances across the upper interface of gas and, to a lesser extent, oil reservoir sands encased in shale decrease (negative $\rho_2 v_2 - \rho_1 v_1$ differences). In contrast, velocities and densities associated across the upper interface of a brine-filled reservoir sand encased in shale usually increase with depth (positive $\rho_2 v_2 - \rho_1 v_1$ differences). Thus rapid lateral increases in amplitude and sudden changes in polarity as shown in Fig. 8 may indicate a hydrocarbon accumulation at depth.

Trace amplitudes may vary 100 dB during the first four seconds of recording. Hence current digital instruments with dynamic ranges around 80 dB may be insufficient, but nevertheless they represent a significant improvement over the 40-dB analog systems in use several decades ago. The industry neglected amplitudes prior to the discovery of the "bright-spot" technique, and tended to destroy relative reflection amplitude relationships by improper use of automatic gain control (AGC) and trace average amplitude equalization procedures. Reflection amplitudes require some kind of time-dependent adjustment after corrections for gain recording functions have been made. This is because the human eye cannot assimilate dynamic ranges of 80 dB. The main factors contributing to reflection amplitude decay include attenuation caused by reflection and transmission coefficients, diverging wavefronts and frequency-selective absorption.

Techniques for the design of inverse gain functions to preserve relative reflection amplitude variations within and between traces fall into statistical and deterministic categories. Both approaches attempt to correct traces for average attenuation rates while preserving instantaneous variations caused by changes in subsurface acoustical impedances. Deterministic approaches define general models to describe many of the possible factors affecting amplitudes such as diverging wavefronts, frequency-selective absorption, reflection and transmission losses, source and receiver array effects and so on. Statistical approaches, on the other hand, produce average gain functions based on collections of traces sorted by common range, source, receiver, etc.

These average gain curves may be exponential functions of the form $a_0 \exp(a_1 t)$ and $(a_0/t) \exp(a_1 t)$, or polynomials of the form, $a_0 + a_1 t + a_2 t^2 + \cdots + a_N t^N$.

Arbitrary constants $a_i (i = 0, N)$ are determined by statistical regression. Trace amplitudes are then corrected by multiplication with an inverse gain function $g^{-1}(t)$.

$$G(t) = \frac{a(t)\bar{g}}{g(t)}$$

where $a(t)$ is the instantaneous trace amplitude (including polarity) corrected for recording gain, $g(t)$ is the gain function consisting of an average instantaneous trace amplitude (e.g., absolute value) obtained through statistical regression, and $\bar{g}$ is some desired average absolute-value of trace amplitude (e.g., 307 for 12-bit data, where 2047 is the maximum possible value).

In this manner, all traces have similar absolute amplitudes over all time gates, and they can be displayed conveniently (Fig. 7). Relative trace-to-trace reflection amplitude variations caused by changing subsurface conditions are thus preserved. The statistical approach is used most often, but sometimes gives poor results in areas of low signal-to-noise ratio, where the regression coefficients $(a_0, a_1, \cdots, a_N)$ tend to be affected by noise. Deterministic models often yield better results in such noisy areas.

The "bright-spot" technique is used to locate hydrocarbons, to determine reservoir dimensions [29], and to establish fluid content, either oil or gas. These estimates ultimately provide reserve figures used in economic evaluations of prospects prior to lease sales. Bright spots possess diagnostic features in addition to their large reflection amplitudes and to their polarity reversals, all of which serve to pinpoint hydrocarbon indicators (HCI) as well as lithologic change indicators (LCI). Large amplitude events of limited lateral extent having no inclination or dip on a stacked section sometimes correspond to reflections from gas/brine, gas/oil, or oil/brine interfaces (Fig. 8). These "contact events" constitute an important HCI. They are essentially horizontal on a stacked section because fluids tend to align themselves along gravitational equipotential surfaces regardless of the complexity of geological structures. Contact events may indicate the presence of hydrocarbons and help to define reservoir dimensions. Slow velocities also characterize hydrocarbon accumulations. Their effect is to delay reflections from fluid contacts. Contact events from thick reservoirs often have a convex downward appearance ("velocity pulldown") on a stacked section. Consequently, many bright spots have a "fisheye" appearance, as shown in Fig. 8. This effect occurs because reflections from the top of the reservoir are convex upward in accordance with the geological structure, whereas slower reservoir velocities cause contact events to be concave downward. Diffracted wavefronts from edges of reservoirs where hydrocarbons terminate add to this "fisheye" effect, and provide an additional HCI. Another criterion is the marked attenuation of amplitudes of reflections originating from horizons beneath reservoirs. Large transmission losses and strong reverberations associated with shallow accumulations attenuate or "mask" reflections from underlying strata and deeper reservoirs.

Modeling is still another important aspect of bright spot interpretation [29]. Here the objective is to assist geophysical

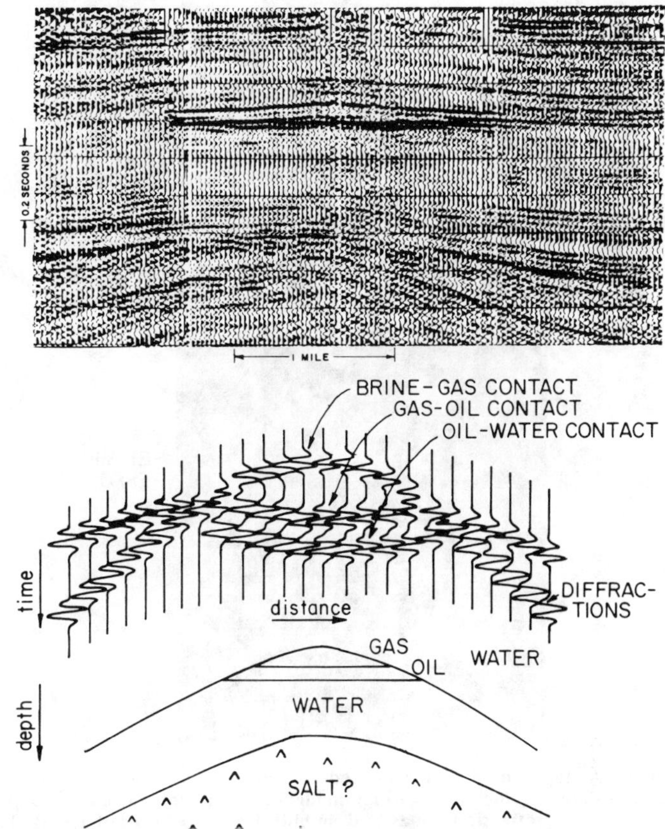

Fig. 8. An amplitude anomaly exhibiting many seismic features of an idealized "bright-spot" associated with a hydrocarbon reservoir.

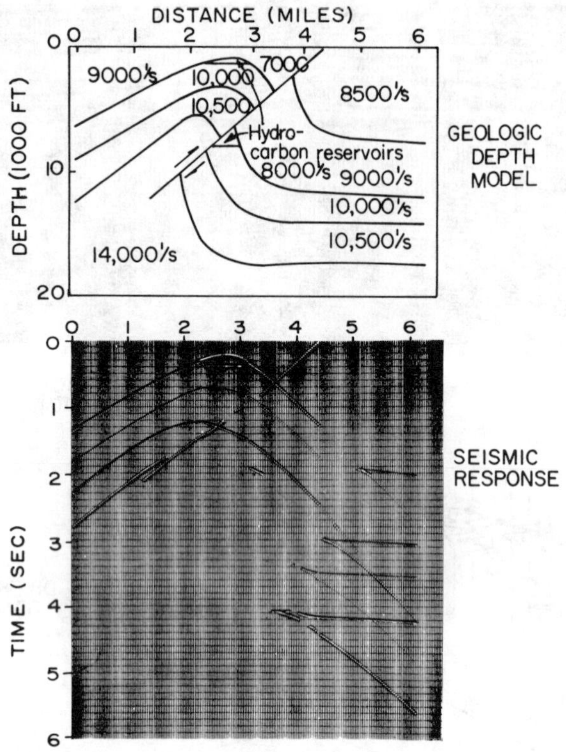

Fig. 9. A depth model of a faulted anticline structure with hydrocarbon reservoirs. Idealized normal-incidence traces show the corresponding seismic reflection times and amplitudes. (Courtesy of Dr. B. T. May and Dr. F. Hron.)

interpretation by means of computer simulated reflection amplitude anomaly patterns. This is done with synthetic traces computed from geological depth models (Fig. 9). Sophisticated modeling procedures produce synthetic records, and model parameters such as layer thicknesses and velocities are varied iteratively until times and amplitudes match observations within specified tolerances. Success depends on the ability to record as many high-frequency components as possible in the field, so that subsequent deconvolution (see Section VII) and source pulse-compression techniques can improve the resolution of thin layers.

Amplitude anomalies do not always indicate hydrocarbon accumulations. Reflected signal strengths depend on subsurface impedance contrasts, and many factors other than hydrocarbon accumulation can cause large impedance contrasts. Thin lenses of lava and tightly cemented layers of silt, lime and lignite known as "hard streaks" give rise to bright spots similar to those associated with hydrocarbon reservoirs [30]. Low-saturation gas sands [31] and rocks deposited in shallow water environments also produce large amplitude reflections. Furthermore, by no means are all hydrocarbon deposits commercial, and careful interpretations must be made to establish thicknesses, fluid content, saturation levels, areal extent and other similar variables.

The bright-spot method works best in outlining gas reservoirs in unconsolidated sand reservoirs at depths not exceeding 6000 ft. Amplitude anomalies associated with older rocks at greater depths are exceedingly difficult to interpret because rocks are more indurated, have less pore space and, therefore, smaller impedance changes across elastic interfaces. Multiple reverberations as well as geological complexities tend to become more bothersome with depth. Onshore surface conditions further complicate interpretations because of changes in

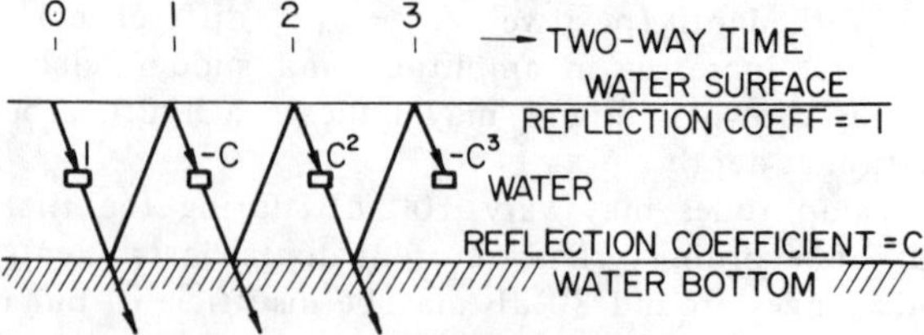

Fig. 10. Reverberations in the water layer where ray paths have been drawn as slanted lines in order to illustrate time dependence [33].

the shallow layers, topography, and variations in source and receiver coupling. Despite these many difficulties, amplitude anomalies have defined many new oil and gas fields throughout the world, and many unexpected benefits have resulted from attempts to extract meaningful information from seismic amplitudes.

VII. The Method of Predictive Deconvolution

A substantial fraction of the globe's deposits of oil and gas is buried in subsurface rocks overlain by water. Typically, a seismic source imparts a pulse of energy into the water just a few feet below the surface. This source pulse travels from the water into the rock formations below it, where it is split into a large number of waves traveling along various paths determined by the material properties of the medium. Whenever such a wave encounters a change in acoustic impedance (which is the product of rock density and rock propagation velocity), a certain fraction of the incident wave is reflected upwards. Seismic detectors situated on the water surface record the continual motion of the water under the impact of seismic waves impinging from below. This recording is performed digitally at a fixed sampling increment. The resultant set of discrete observations is called a "marine seismic trace", and constitutes a sample of a time series.

The interpreter of such marine recordings is faced with the task of extracting the direct reflections which give him information about the subsurface geometry from a recording which contains a wealth of background interference and noise. One of his several problems is the presence of the so-called "multiple reflections" or "reverberations." These slowly decaying wave trains usually arise in the water layer, which tends to act as a strong waveguide because it is bounded above and below by media of radically differing acoustic impedances. The water reverberation phenomenon came to light when it was observed that seismic traces recorded in water depths greater than 10 ft or so exhibit a marked sinusoidal, or "ringing" appearance.

During the past two decades very significant strides have been made in a continuing effort to remove reverberations from marine data. One of the more successful approaches is based on a rather simple theoretical model of a reverberating trace. The treatment given below is an abbreviated version of a discussion by Robinson [33].

Consider an ideal source located on the water surface emitting a unit spike (or unit pulse) at time $t = 0$, and assume that a detector just below the water surface responds only to downward motion (see Fig. 10). Both the air water and water rock interfaces are strong reflectors. We restrict ourselves to plane wave fronts whose raypaths are perpendicular to the interfaces, although for the sake of clarity these paths have been drawn as slanting lines in Fig. 10. Under such so-called "normal incidence" conditions, we may associate a reflection coefficient of -1 with the lower surface of the air–water inter-

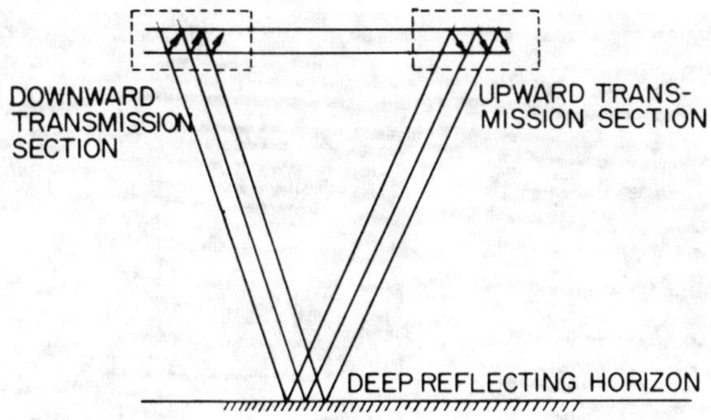

Fig. 11. The cascading effect of the water layer on a reflection from great depth [33].

face, while we let the water-bottom reflection coefficient be c, whose magnitude must be less than unity from physical considerations. A source pulse generated in the water layer will reverberate between these two strong reflectors, although part of the energy will be propagated into the underlying rocks. Let the integer n represent one roundtrip, or two-way travel-time in the water layer. Then the downgoing unit spike, which occurs at time $t = 0$, is followed at intervals of n time units by successive downgoing spikes whose values are $-c$, $+c^2$, $-c^3$, and so on. The z transform[1] of such a water-confined reverberation spike train is

$$C(z) = 1 - cz^n + c^2 z^{2n} - c^3 z^{3n} + \cdots. \tag{9}$$

Since $|c| < 1$, this convergent geometric series can be summed to yield

$$C(z) = \frac{1}{1 + cz^n}.$$

An inverse filter to remove the water reverberations is therefore

$$A(z) = \frac{1}{C(z)} = 1 + cz^n.$$

Because $|c| < 1$, it follows that both the water reverberation spike train $C(z)$ as well as the corresponding "dereverberation" filter $A(z)$ are minimum-delay [32].

In actuality, a part of the energy originally present in the downgoing unit spike travels into the medium below the water layer, in which it continues to propagate until it encounters a deep reflector. At this point, some of the incident energy is reflected upwards, and when this reflected pulse enters the water layer from below, it in turn becomes partially trapped and causes reverberations (see Fig. 11). In other words, the water layer affects the deep reflection returns twice—once on the way down, and once on the way up. To a good approximation, the z transform of the resulting spike train can be obtained by merely cascading the response (9) with itself [32] and thus

$$C(z) = (1 - cz^n + c^2 z^{2n} - c^3 z^{3n} + \cdots)^2$$

$$= \frac{1}{(1 + cz^n)^2}. \tag{10}$$

This reverberation spike train is also minimum delay. An inverse filter to remove the cascaded set of reverberations is

[1] Geophysicists define the z transform as $C(z) = \sum_{n=-\infty}^{+\infty} c_n z^n$ rather than as $C(z) = \sum_{n=-\infty}^{+\infty} c_n z^{-n}$, as electrical engineers do.

now given by

$$A(z) = \frac{1}{C(z)} = (1 + cz^n)^2$$

$$= 1 + 2cz^n + c^2 z^{2n} \tag{11}$$

or

$$A(z)C(z) = (1 + 2cz^n + c^2 z^{2n})(1 - cz^n + c^2 z^{2n} - c^3 z^{3n} + \cdots)^2$$

$$= 1.$$

We see that the filter $A(z)$ *deconvolves* the reverberation spike train $C(z)$ to the unit spike at zero delay.

The deconvolution method just described is of slight practical value because the reverberation patterns encountered in petroleum exploration are far more involved. Now it turns out that the minimum-delay property of the reverberation spike train $C(z)$ is quite general in the sense that the unit spike response of an arbitrary system of horizontally stratified layers also is minimum delay [35]. In practice, the source pulse is a broader time function, say b_t, rather than merely a unit spike. If this source pulse is reasonably sharp, as will be the case for an explosion of dynamite, then we may expect b_t to have most of its energy concentrated near its front end, i.e., to be "front loaded." Front-loaded time functions tend to be approximately minimum delay, and for the moment we assert that the source pulse b_t does in fact have this property.

We assume that the reverberation *pulse* train, say r_t, is the convolution of the reverberation spike train c_t of (10) with the pulse b_t,

$$r_t = c_t * b_t$$

where the asterisk denotes convolution. We imagine that the marine seismic trace x_t arises from the linear superposition of a large number of deep reflections, each of which has the characteristic shape of the pulse train r_t. Let ϵ_t be a series of spikes whose amplitudes represent the values of the deep reflection coefficients, and whose times represent the two-way travel time to these reflectors. Our model of the marine seismic trace x_t is, therefore,

$$x_t = c_t * b_t * \epsilon_t$$

$$= r_t * \epsilon_t.$$

Next, we assume that the series ϵ_t is uncorrelated and random. In particular, this means that the series ϵ_t is totally unpredictable, in the sense that knowledge of the amplitudes and arrival times of the first k deep reflections does not permit us to make any deterministic statement about the amplitude and arrival time of the $(k + 1)$th reflection. Of course, we cannot prove that the actual earth has this property (and there are some demonstrable cases for which it does not), but the practical success of a deconvolution approach based on this model suggests that the random and uncorrelated representation of the series ϵ_t is generally reasonable.

On the other hand, the reverberation pulse train r_t is predictable if we assume, as we do here, that both the source pulse b_t as well as the reverberation spike train c_t are minimum delay [36]. Let ϕ_τ be the autocorrelation of the marine trace x_t. Then we have,

$$\phi_\tau = E\{x_t x_{t+\tau}\} = E\{r_t r_{t+\tau}\} * E\{\epsilon_t \epsilon_{t+\tau}\}$$

where E is the expectation operator. But since ϵ_t is random and uncorrelated,

$$E\{\epsilon_t \epsilon_{t+\tau}\} = E\{\epsilon_t^2\} = P\delta_{\tau 0}$$

where P is the power in the series ϵ_t, and where $\delta_{\tau 0}$ is the Kronecker delta. Therefore,

$$\phi_\tau = P\, E\{r_t r_{t+\tau}\}$$

and P is a scale factor which does not affect the final result and will thus be neglected. We conclude that the trace autocorrelation ϕ_τ is equal to the autocorrelation of the reverberation pulse train r_t within an arbitrary scale factor. Furthermore, the minimum-delay property of r_t enables us to predict its reverberation component c_t if we compute a prediction operator for prediction distance n, where we recall that n is two-way travel time in the water layer. If we delay the output of such a prediction operator by n time units and subtract it from r_t, we obtain the nonreverberatory component of r_t, namely, the source pulse b_t. The linearity of the prediction operator allows us to apply it to the entire trace x_t, suppressing from the data the reverberatory components c_t.

Let a_t be such a prediction operator. For the simplest case, this operator is given by (11), but in practice a far more general approach results from the use of Wiener theory [34]. Minimization of the mean square error between a desired output and an actual output yields a set of normal equations involving the trace autocorrelation coefficients ϕ_t. If we identify the desired output with an input advanced by n time units, the $(m + 1)$ length least squares prediction operator a_t is the solution of the system,

$$
\begin{bmatrix}
\phi_0 & \phi_1 & \cdots & \phi_m \\
\phi_1 & \phi_0 & & \\
 & & \cdot & \\
 & & \cdot & \\
 & & \cdot & \\
\phi_m & \phi_{m-1} & \cdots & \phi_0
\end{bmatrix}
\begin{bmatrix}
a_0 \\
a_1 \\
\cdot \\
\cdot \\
\cdot \\
a_m
\end{bmatrix}
=
\begin{bmatrix}
\phi_n \\
\phi_{n+1} \\
\cdot \\
\cdot \\
\cdot \\
\phi_{n+m}
\end{bmatrix}. \quad (12)
$$

The autocorrelation matrix of this system contains only the $(m + 1)$ independent elements $\phi_0, \phi_1, \cdots, \phi_m$, and these are arranged in such a manner that all elements on the main diagonal as well as any super- or subdiagonals are equal. This so-called Toeplitz structure enabled Levinson [37] to obtain an efficient recursive algorithm for the solution of the normal equations. It is of interest to note that the case $n = 1$ leads to a set of normal equations arising in the linear prediction approach to speech compression [38].

The prediction operator coefficients $a_0, a_1, \cdots, a_m$ can be used to construct the prediction error operator for prediction distance n,

$$1, \underbrace{0, 0, \cdots, 0}_{n-1 \text{ zeroes}}, -a_0, -a_1, \cdots, -a_m.$$

This prediction error operator is then convolved with the marine trace x_t to yield,

$$z_t = x_t - a_0 x_{t-n} - a_1 x_{t-n-1} - \cdots - a_m x_{t-n-m}.$$

The series z_t, therefore, represents the deconvolved marine trace, from which the reverberation spike train c_t has been removed. Alternatively, z_t is the prediction error series associated with the prediction error operator for prediction distance n, where n is two-way travel time in the water layer.

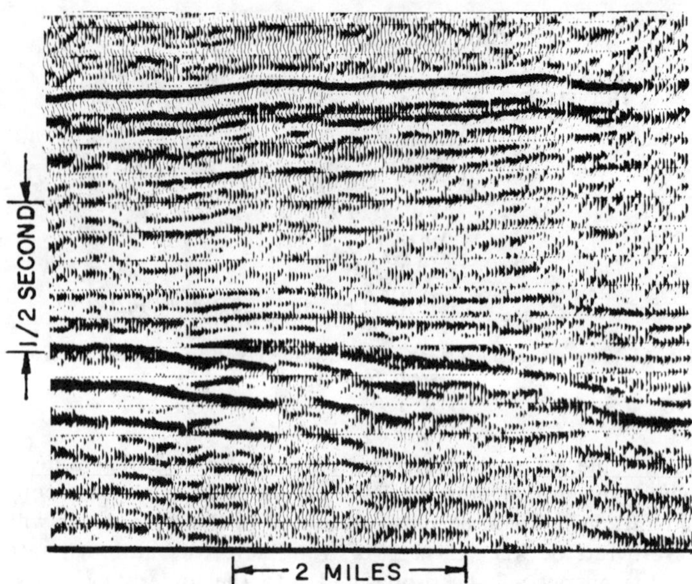

Fig. 12. An example of composited (CDP) marine data.

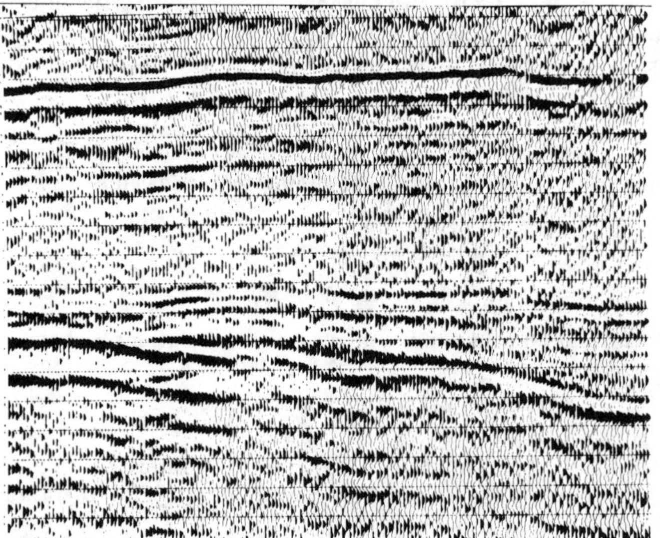

Fig. 13. The seismic data shown in Fig. 12 after application of predictive deconvolution.

The approach we have described is called the method of predictive deconvolution, which dates back to the work of Geophysical Analysis Group (GAG) at Massachusetts Institute of Technology between 1952 and 1957 [39]. Fig. 12 shows a selected portion of a marine seismic line which has been stacked. The vertical scale is two-way travel time, while the horizontal scale represents distance. In Fig. 13 we may observe the output after every trace has been filtered with a predictive deconvolution operator. We note that a significant amount of reverberating energy has been removed from the input data. It is customary to follow the dereverberation procedure with a number of further digital filter applications designed to compress the source pulse and to provide greater emphasis to the deeper reflections. This goal is accomplished with Wiener shaping filters (see Section VIII), which are designed for a selected number of gates on each trace. The variations in source pulse shape with travel time can be accounted for and, in effect, the Wiener shaping filters are applied in a time-varying manner (see Fig. 14).

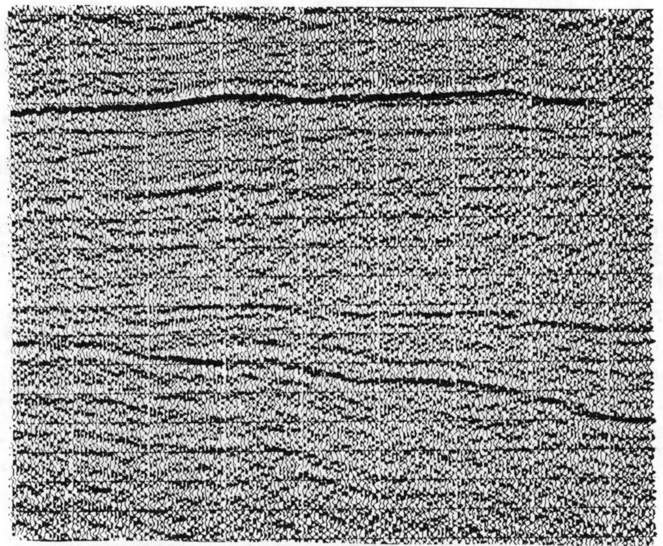

Fig. 14. The seismic data shown in Fig. 12 after Wiener filtering and time-varying pulse compression.

Query: Very nice indeed, but how often does real data respond to such treatment?

Answer: To the extent that it obeys our model's assumptions, namely that:

1) the layered earth is a linear system;
2) the reverberation spike train and the source pulse are minimum delay;
3) the deep reflector reflection coefficient series is random and uncorrelated.

In actuality, of course, these assumptions may or may not be upheld. All we can say is that widespread application of the predictive deconvolution technique has demonstrated its ability to remove reverberations, and thereby to permit the identification of reflections from depth. In instances for which assumption 2) is inappropriate, viable alternatives exist, of which the homomorphic deconvolution approach [40], [41] is one.

Our treatment of the method of predictive deconvolution has necessarily been quite brief. Unmentioned here is a wealth of implementational detail, such as the choice of proper lag windows for the autocorrelation coefficients ϕ_t, the determination of "good" values for the operator length, $(m + 1)$ and the two-way travel time in the water layer (n), etc. The interested reader must be referred to the cited references for further discussion of these by no means negligible points.

VIII. WIENER SHAPING FILTERS

We have already seen how the method of predictive deconvolution is based on Wiener's least mean-square error criterion. In geophysical work the need to alter the shape of a given signal pulse often arises. The problem can be attacked with zero-phase bandpass filters in the frequency domain. However, the amount of control one has on the shape of the output pulse is limited, and we have found it more expedient to design such shaping filters in the time domain.

We consider the problem of finding an $(m + 1)$-length filter $f_t = (f_0, f_1, \cdots, f_m)$, which shapes an $(n + 1)$-length input pulse $b_t = (b_0, b_1, \cdots, b_n)$ into an $(m + n + 1)$-length desired output pulse $d_t = (d_0, d_1, \cdots, d_{m+n})$ in such a way that the error energy between the desired output d_t and the actual $(m + n + 1)$-length output $c_t = (c_0, c_1, \cdots, c_{m+n})$ is minimized.

The actual output is the convolution of the filter with the input

$$c_t = \sum_{s=0}^{m} f_s b_{t-s}.$$

The error energy I is

$$I = \sum_{t=0}^{m+n} (d_t - c_t)^2 = \sum_{t=0}^{m+n} \left(d_t - \sum_{s=0}^{m} f_s b_{t-s}\right)^2. \quad (13)$$

The preceding error energy is at its minimum value if its partial derivatives with respect to each of the filter weighting coefficients $f_0, f_1, \cdots, f_m$ equal zero. We have,

$$\frac{\partial I}{\partial f_j} = \sum_{t=0}^{m+n} 2\left(d_t - \sum_{s=0}^{m} f_s b_{t-s}\right)(-b_{t-j}) = 0$$

which gives

$$-\sum_{t=0}^{m+n} d_t b_{t-j} + \sum_{t=0}^{m+n} \left(\sum_{s=0}^{m} f_s b_{t-s}\right) b_{t-j} = 0$$

or

$$\sum_{s=0}^{m} f_s \sum_{t=0}^{m+n} b_{t-s} b_{t-j} = \sum_{t=0}^{m+n} d_t b_{t-j}, \quad j = 0, 1, \cdots, m.$$

Now

$$\sum_{t=0}^{m+n} b_{t-s} b_{t-j} = \phi_{j-s}$$

and

$$\sum_{t=0}^{m+n} d_t b_{t-j} = g_j$$

where r_j is the autocorrelation of the input pulse b_t, g_j is the cross correlation between the input pulse b_t and the desired output pulse d_t. We thus obtain,

$$\sum_{s=0}^{m} f_s \phi_{j-s} = g_j, \quad j = 0, 1, \cdots, m. \quad (14)$$

This system of $(m + 1)$ linear simultaneous equations in the unknowns $f_0, f_1, \cdots, f_m$ can also be written in the matrix form

$$
\begin{bmatrix}
\phi_0 & \phi_1 & \cdots & \phi_m \\
\phi_1 & \phi_0 & & \\
 & & \cdot & \\
 & & \cdot & \\
 & & \cdot & \\
\phi_m & \phi_{m-1} & \cdots & \phi_0
\end{bmatrix}
\begin{bmatrix}
f_0 \\
f_1 \\
\cdot \\
\cdot \\
\cdot \\
f_m
\end{bmatrix}
=
\begin{bmatrix}
g_0 \\
g_1 \\
\cdot \\
\cdot \\
\cdot \\
g_m
\end{bmatrix}
\quad (15)
$$

where $\phi_{-j} = \phi_j$ because b_t is real valued. We note that the normal equations (15) for the Wiener shaping filter reduce to the normal equations (12) for the predictive deconvolution filter if we identify the crosscorrelation vector $(g_0, g_1, \cdots, g_m)$ with the vector $(\phi_n, \phi_{n+1}, \cdots, \phi_{n+m})$. This is so because in the case of predictive deconvolution the desired output $d_t =$

r_{t+n}, where r_t is reverberation pulse train. Hence,

$$g_j = \sum_t d_t r_{t-j} = \sum_t r_{t+n} r_{t-j}$$

$$= \sum_t r_{t+(n+j)} r_t = \phi_{n+j}, \quad j = 0, 1, \cdots, m.$$

The method of predictive deconvolution is accordingly seen to constitute a particular realization of the Wiener shaping filter. Solutions of the more general system (14) are again readily obtained with Levinson's algorithm.

An expression for the normalized minimum square error, E_N, results when the normal equations (14) are substituted into the error energy relation (13),

$$E_N = 1 - \sum_{t=0}^{m} f_t g_t'$$

where g_t' is the normalized cross correlation coefficient [42],

$$g_t' = \frac{g_t}{\sum_{t=0}^{m+n} d_t^2}.$$

It follows that

$$0 \leqslant E_N \leqslant 1$$

and the extreme cases $E_N = 0$ and $E_N = 1$ correspond, respectively, to perfect agreement and to no agreement between the actual output c_t and the desired output d_t.

Space unfortunately precludes the presentation of numerical examples illustrating these principles, and the reader is referred to the afore cited references for further details.

IX. Conclusions

In this paper, we have outlined how seismic data are acquired, interpreted, and processed. One of the major problems we have omitted, however, is the processing sequence, that is, the order in which the corrections are made and the filters applied. For example: Should static corrections be estimated before or after NMO? Should predictive deconvolution be applied before or after CDP stacking? Should Wiener filters be applied before or after velocity analysis? Unique answers to such questions do not appear to be available.

Processing sequences depend on geological conditions and vary from area to area. Geophysical objectives tend to determine a particular sequence, while geological factors cannot always be considered. Land data require static corrections to adjust for surface irregularities, and therefore tend to undergo more complicated processing sequences than marine data. As a general rule, however, both land and marine records are sorted into CDP trace gathers, subjected to velocity analysis, NMO corrected and composited. Scaling, static corrections and digital filtering alter this basic flow. A typical marine sequence might consist of the following steps:

demultiplexing

reformatting

gain recovery

sorting for relative amplitude scaling

bandpass filtering

predictive deconvolution

Wiener filtering

CDP sorting

velocity analysis

NMO correction

CDP stacking

Wiener filtering

modeling, migration, and interpretation.

Static corrections complicate the processing of data acquired on land. The NMO correction procedure requires the use of an initial average velocity function in order to reduce trace-to-trace time variations of reflections. Automatic static correction programs cannot handle large time increments between traces, and this fact necessitates the use of an initial gross, average velocity function. Once static corrections have been determined, they can be applied before the NMO corrections to produce a final processed seismic line. If an average velocity function is used for preliminary NMO estimation, a typical land processing sequence might consist of the following steps:

demultiplexing

reformatting

gain recovery

sorting for relative amplitude scaling

bandpass filtering

predictive deconvolution

Wiener filtering

NMO correction

automatic static correction.

A final seismic line on land might consist of the following steps after demultiplexing, reformatting, and amplitude scaling:

static corrections

bandpass filtering

predictive deconvolution

Wiener filtering

CDP sorting

velocity analysis

NMO correction

CDP stacking

Wiener filtering

modeling, migration, and interpretation.

New technology continually alters and modifies the flow of these sequences. Such innovations present a never-ending challenge to the ingenuity of geophysicists involved in the processing of exploration seismic data.

Acknowledgment

The authors wish to thank S. N. Domenico for helpful discussions, G. Bard for preparing the illustrations, and Amoco Production Company for permission to publish. Appreciation is also extended to K. L. Peacock, R. C. Heiser, P. W. Johnson, B. T. May, F. Hron, R. D. Bjerstedt, and P. F. Barron for help with the data processing required for the illustrations.

References

[1] "Outlay for U.S. seismic work hits record high, SEG reports" *Oil and Gas J.*, vol. 72, no. 32, p. 64, Aug. 1974.

[2] A. I. Levorsen, *Geology of Petroleum*. San Francisco, Calif.: Freeman, 1958.

[3] N. A. Anstey, "Seismic prospecting instruments: Signal Characteristics and instrument specifications," *Geoexploration Monog.*, ser. 1, vol. 1, no. 3 (Gerbrüder Borntraeger, 1 Berlin 38), 1970.

[4] F. S. Kramer, R. A. Peterson, and W. C. Walter, Eds., *Seismic Energy Sources 1968 handbook*. United Geophysical Corp. (Bendix Corporation subsidiary), 1968.

[5] B. S. Evenden and D. R. Stone, "Seismic prospecting instruments: Instrument performance and testing," *Geoexploration Monog.*, ser. 1, vol. 2, no. 3 (Gebrüder Borntraeger, 1 Berlin 38), 1971.

[6] W. H. Mayne, "Common reflection point horizontal data stacking techniques," *Geophysics*, vol. 27, no. 6, pp. 927–938, Dec. 1962.

[7] L. L. Nettleton, *Geophysical Prospecting for Oil.* New York: McGraw-Hill, 1940.

[8] C. A. Heiland, *Geophysical Exploration.* Englewood Cliffs, N.J.: Prentice-Hall, 1940.

[9] J. J. Jakosky, "Exploration geophysics," Trija, 2nd edition, 1950.

[10] J. M. Crawford, W. E. N. Doty, and M. R. Lee, "Continuous signal seismograph," *Geophysics,* vol. 25, no. 1, pp. 95–105, Feb. 1960.

[11] R. L. Geyer, "The VIBROSEIS system of seismic mapping," *J. Canadian Soc. Explor. Geophys.,* vol. 6, no. 1, pp. 39–57, Dec. 1970.

[12] L. V. Lombardi, "Notes on the use of multiple geophones," *Geophysics,* vol. 20, no. 2, pp. 215–226, Apr. 1955.

[13] M. K. Smith, "Noise analysis and multiple seismometer theory," *Geophysics,* vol. 21, no. 2, pp. 337–360, Apr. 1956.

[14] M. Holzman, "Chebyshev optimized geophone arrays," *Geophysics,* vol. 28, no. 2, pp. 145–155, Apr. 1963.

[15] A. J. Hermont, "Design principles for seismic reflection amplifiers," *Geophys. Prospect.,* vol. 4, no. 3, pp. 279–293, Sept. 1956.

[16] R. L. Gray, J. H. Leitinger, and J. C. Hollister, "Determination of seismic system distortion and its compensation using digital filters," *Geophysics,* vol. 33, no. 2, pp. 285–301, Apr. 1968.

[17] E. J. Northwood, R. C. Weisinger, and J. J. Bradley, "Recommended standards for digital tape formats," *Geophysics,* vol. 32, no. 6, pp. 1073–1084, Dec. 1967.

[18] C. H. Dix, *Seismic Prospecting for Oil.* New York: Harper & Brothers, 1952.

[19] M. T. Taner, F. Koehler, and K. A. Alhilali, "Estimation and correction of near-surface time anomalies," *Geophysics,* vol. 39, no. 4, pp. 441–463, Aug. 1974.

[20] J. O. Parr, and W. H. Mayne, "A new method of pattern shooting," *Geophysics,* vol. 20, no. 3, pp. 539–564, July 1955.

[21] M. T. Taner, E. E. Cook, and N. S. Neidell, "Limitations of the reflection seismic method; lessons from computer simulations," *Geophysics,* vol. 35, no. 4, pp. 551–573, Aug. 1970.

[22] M. T. Taner, and F. Koehler, "Velocity spectra-digital computer derivation and applications of velocity functions," *Geophysics,* vol. 34, no. 6, pp. 859–881, Dec. 1969.

[23] N. S. Neidell, and M. T. Taner, "Semblance and other coherency measures for multichannel data," *Geophysics,* vol. 36, no. 3, pp. 482–497, June 1971.

[24] C. I. Craft, "Detecting hydrocarbons—for years the goal of exploration geophysics," *Oil and Gas J.,* vol. 71, no. 8, pp. 122–125, Feb. 1973.

[25] "Lithology and direct detection of hydrocarbons using geophysical methods," in *Symp. Rec. Geophys. Soc. Houston,* Oct. 1973.

[26] A. L. Hammond, "Bright spot: Better seismological indicators of gas and oil," *Science,* vol. 185, no. 4150, pp. 515–517, Aug. 1974.

[27] F. S. Grant, and G. F. West, *Interpretation Theory in Applied Geophysics.* New York: McGraw-Hill, 1965.

[28] W. M. Ewing, W. S. Jardetsky, and F. Press, *Elastic Waves in Layered Media.* New York: McGraw-Hill, 1957.

[29] J. P. Lindsey, and C. I. Craft, "How hydrocarbon reserves are estimated from seismic data," *World Oil,* vol. 177, no. 2 pp. 23–25, Aug. 1973.

[30] D. McNabb, "Bright-spot warning: it's not infallible," *Oil and Gas J.,* vol. 72, no. 34, pp. 50–51, Aug. 26, 1974.

[31] S. N. Domenico, "Effect of water saturation on seismic reflectivity of sand reservoirs encased in shale," *Geophysics,* vol. 39, no. 6, pp. 759–769, Dec. 1974.

[32] S. Treitel and E. A. Robinson, "The stability of digital filters," *IEEE Trans. Geosci. Electron.,* vol. GE-2, pp. 6–18, Nov. 1964.

[33] E. A. Robinson, "Multichannel z-transforms and minimum-delay," *Geophysics,* vol. 31, pp. 482–500, June 1966.

[34] K. L. Peacock and S. Treitel, "Predictive deconvolution: theory and practice," *Geophysics,* vol. 34, pp. 155–169, Apr. 1969.

[35] E. A. Robinson, *Multichannel Time Series Analysis with Digital Computer Programs.* San Francisco, Calif.: Holden-Day, 1967.

[36] E. A. Robinson, *Random Wavelets and Cybernetic Systems.* London, England: Charles Griffin, 1962.

[37] N. Levinson, "The Wiener rms error criterion in filter design and prediction," *J. Math. Phys.,* vol. 25, pp. 261–278, Jan. 1947.

[38] J. Makhoul, "Linear prediction: a tutorial review," this issue, pp. 561–580.

[39] Issue on the MIT Geophysical Analysis Group reports, *Geophysics,* vol. 32, pp. 441–525, June 1967.

[40] A. V. Oppenheim, R. W. Schafer, and T. G. Stockham, "Nonlinear filtering of multiplied and convolved signals," *Proc. IEEE,* vol. 56, pp. 1264–1291, Aug. 1968.

[41] T. J. Ulrych, "Application of homomorphic deconvolution to seismology," *Geophysics,* vol. 36, pp. 650–660, Aug. 1971.

[42] S. Treitel and E. A. Robinson, "The design of high-resolution digital filters," *IEEE Trans. Geosci. Electron.,* vol. GE-4, pp. 25–38, June 1966.

Seismic Imaging by Holography

GERALD L. FITZPATRICK

Abstract—During the last half century, seismic imaging techniques have seen steady improvements. With the recent advent of relatively cheap and readily available computers, many complicated algorithms for obtaining seismic images that were formerly only theoretical curiosities can now be implemented. This paper reports on the applications of yet another imaging technique, namely holography, with particular emphasis on Fourier transform holography. A variety of laboratory, field, and computer experiments are described together with several anticipated practical applications, and it is shown among other things that certain image enhancement techniques based on holography can significantly improve siesmic images and image-related data.

I. Introduction

IN A 1967 article entitled "Introduction to Acoustical Holography" [1] by Metherell *et al.*, there were suggestions to the effect that the techniques of acoustic holography might possibly be applied to the case of seismic waves in the earth. Suggestions to this effect had also been made by Farr [2] and Silverman [3] and were also implicit in the early work of various investigators in acoustic and optical holography [4]. Eleven years after the publication of Metherell's paper, we are apparently entering a period where such "3-D" techniques are being seriously explored by oil companies and others as another possible tool in their search and evaluation of oil and other mineral deposits. At least two oil company sponsored research groups in the U.S. are currently pursuing the application of holography and related techniques to these problems. Beyond the applications involving mineral resource location and mapping, consideration is also being given by a number of investigators to the possible application of these techniques to mapping major structural features of the earth itself [5] using, for example, natural earthquakes or power plant noise as sources.

Another anticipated application of holography involves the development of an acoustic holography based system for "seeing" ahead of large tunnel-boring machines [6], [7].

The present review article will address some of these developments; however, it will not be primarily bibliographical in nature. The approach will be to cover a variety of selected topics including some new material, ranging from small-scale laboratory experiments to large-scale applications in the mining and oil industries.

Because there are so many techniques that are similar to holography or are "holographic" in nature, the meaning of the term holography as it is used in this paper needs further clarification. Many of the experiments reported here result in what we will call conventional holograms by which we mean that an effective reference wave is mixed with the received signals to produce a true interference pattern or hologram. Furthermore, in such conventional holographic techniques, it is the analysis of this hologram and its reconstruction rather than an analysis of individual time traces that leads to a reconstructed image. Most conventional holograms also usually involve an effective two-dimensional recording array; however, the applications discussed here are not limited in any way to two-dimensional recording arrays. The more conventional one-dimensional recording array used in the oil industry for surface prospecting and in borehole geophysics applications may also be used in making holograms.

Finally, it will be considered within the scope of this article to introduce new material wherever it seems appropriate to do so or where it will stimulate interest.

II. Why Holography?

For many readers of this journal and certainly for the authors, it probably goes without saying that the reason why a considerable effort has gone into the application of holography to problems in acoustic and related imaging problems is

Manuscript received June 1, 1978.

This paper was prepared while the author was at Holosonics Inc. of Richland, WA. He is now with the Seismic Acoustics Laboratory, University of Houston, 4800 Calhoun Blvd., Houston, TX 77004.

"self-evident." Nevertheless, it is worth repeating, why a technique like holography is so appealing, especially in the context of seismic data gathering and interpretation.

This question is especially relevant here since it is not necessary, as it is in optical holography, to employ holographic recording strategies to obtain the phase information in seismic data; i.e., geophones are linear detectors, not square law detectors, and as a consequence amplitude and phase information have always been readily available in seismic data.

Thus the traditional problem has not been to store phase information, rather, it has been to find some way to extract from this information and the amplitude data, information regarding the scattering targets and other structural features of interest. In the very early applications of seismic techniques, the only practical way to do this was to perform a pulse-echo type of analysis in which certain structural features or characteristics were identified by eye on the geophone traces themselves and these features were used to obtain a map of the geologic structure.

Current day wave equation "migration" techniques and related approaches provide considerably more information than these early approaches and have proven their value in the successful search for minerals. However, these techniques still require that a full-time trace for each geophone detector or group of detectors be recorded and stored in some way. The advantage of the recording of seismic data by conventional holography is not only that it opens up new possibilities for reconstructing and interpreting the data, but it also means that no recording of time traces per se is required. All that is required is that the time-dependent record signal, call it $S(X, Y, Z, t)$, be mixed in real time with a local oscillator reference wave, call it $R(t)$ and the time average intensity taken to produce the hologram value $H(X, Y, Z)$

$$H(X, Y, Z) = \frac{1}{T} \int_0^T |S(X, Y, Z, t) + R(t)|^2 \, dt. \qquad (1)$$

In the special circumstance that a monochromatic vibrator source is being used, the signals are continuous so that the H value is merely proportional to the integrand. All such holographic detection schemes and/or analog devices such as "mixers" used to achieve such detection, yield a hologram value given essentially[1] by $H \sim \cos \phi$ where ϕ is the phase difference between the local oscillator reference signal and the signal being recorded at the position of the geophone detector. It is important to point out that continuous waves are not necessary in making the holograms. The basic prescription for making holograms expressed by (1) is equally valid for impulse signals or continuous signals. If impulse signals are being used one need only ensure that the proper analog detection devices are employed and that sufficient integration time be allowed so that all of the important returns have arrived. In effect a local oscillator reference wave at a given frequency merely picks out of the impulse the Fourier frequency component at that same frequency.

The foregoing method of recording seismic data holographically can have great practical advantages, not the least of which is the savings in the amount of data that needs to be stored for each geophone location. Furthermore, with the data readily available in the field as an array of a relatively

<hr>

[1] In expanding the integrand of (1) constant or slowly varying (with position) terms are dropped.

small number of hologram values and with the current day availability of microcomputers and like devices for performing hardwired reconstructions, the distinct possibility of reconstructing preliminary geologic cross sections in the field asserts itself.

We are not suggesting here that the practice of recording complete time traces be abandoned and that all of the many successful techniques based on this practice be discarded. We are suggesting that there are many applications especially small-scale applications where the traditional techniques for taking data and interpreting that data are no longer strictly necessary or desirable in order to obtain good images of geologic structure.

Once the data have been recorded holographically, a large variety of schemes for analyzing, interpreting, and reconstructing the data become possible. Holograms may be added, subtracted, filtered, correlated and so on before being reconstructed. This capability allows one to take advantage of a large variety of existing computer assisted techniques originally suggested by developments in modern optics and optical data processing for improving and interpreting reconstructed images of geologic structure.

III. Field Experiments

The three earliest known field experiments in holography are those of Leriwell [8], Mueller, Steinberg, and Farr [9], and Fitzpatrick [10]. Although the early results of these experiments were certainly not spectacular successes, the experience gained in attempting these experiments proved to be a valuable aid in suggesting improvements. This aptly describes the authors' work, since data gathered in his 1969 field experiment [10] has been available for use in testing a variety of new theoretical data taking techniques, data reconstruction techniques, and image enhancement techniques. These new techniques have significantly improved the analyses and interpretation of this field data.

A. One-Dimensional Holography Arrays

Both the experiments of Leriwell [8] and Mueller et al. [9], at least in the early phases, were exercises in creating one-dimensional holograms. Such holograms consist of a line, or at most, several parallel lines of detectors instead of two-dimensional arrays of detectors. Although information on Leriwell's work is sketchy, it appears that he employed a 90-Hz mechanical vibrator source and a line of detectors 4350-ft long with spacings of 25 ft. It is not known to what extent the reconstructed data could be correlated with known structures present at the site.

A somewhat more ambitious experiment in 1969 in which a one-dimensional hologram was made was performed in a joint effort by Mueller and Steinberg (Bendix Research Laboratories of Southfield, MI) and Farr (Pan American Oil Company of Tulsa, OK, now known as Amoco [9]). Sufficient data was actually taken using crossed array techniques to allow a two-dimensional hologram to be reconstructed. However, this was not reported until much later [11]. This later data analysis will be discussed in more detail in the next section.

The experiment in question took place in the Gulf of Mexico over a thoroughly mapped salt-dome structure. Both the seismic source and the receivers were towed by a ship. The maximum frequency employed in the experiment was about 70 Hz, the active line of hydrophone detectors measured 1350 ft and the spacing was about 8 ft between individual hydrophones. Spatial location of the detectors was determined by constant updating of information from several microwave navigation buoys. The entire scan length was about 2.5 mi.

The received signals were mixed with local oscillator signals ninety degrees out of phase producing so-called phase-quadrature intensities. That is, two hologram values $A \cos \phi$ and $A \sin \phi$ were produced and recorded[2] where A is the amplitude of the mixed signals and ϕ is the phase difference between the local oscillator and the recorded signal. To obtain the reconstructed images, a cross correlation imaging technique [11] was used instead of the conventional wavefront reconstruction techniques using a laser or a computer algorithm such as fast Fourier transformation. To obtain the "correlator" needed to form the image, a velocity versus depth model for the area of interest was first constructed using other available data.

An imaginary point scatterer was then located at some point at depth Z below the hologram array where the image value was to be computed. The "response" expected from this single point scatterer, i.e., the expected hologram values in the surface line (or the surface array), was then computed using the velocity versus depth model. This synthetic "correlator" $H_c(Z)$ also consists of real and imaginary parts in quadrature just as the full hologram H_s measured at the surface was a complex hologram.

$$H_s = A \cos \phi + i A \sin \phi. \qquad (2)$$

To obtain the "correlation" image intensity at the point Z, one simply cross correlates H_s (the entire hologram) with $H_c(Z)$, i.e.,

$$I = \int H_s H_c^*(Z)\, ds \qquad (3)$$

where the integration takes place over the hologram surface. Thus in this type of reconstruction technique, one interrogates the full hologram to find out to what extent it is made up of individual hypothetical holograms arising because of the presence of various point scatterers. This reconstruction technique has a number of advantages not the least of which is the fact that one can, in principle, improve on the velocity-depth model by providing sufficient feedback to improve the model. A successful model is obtained when the correlation integrals, "I" are at their maximum values.

It should be stressed that in spite of the apparent differences, between this "correlation" imaging approach and conventional holographic reconstruction, there are also significant similarities. The integral in (3) clearly involves every point of the hologram H_s just as the reconstruction of the hologram H_s would involve information from each point of H_s.

B. Two-Dimensional Hologram Arrays

Although the data taken by Bendix and Pan Am were essentially sufficient to make two-dimensional holograms, this was only done much later. The interesting paper by Farr [11] presents this analysis together with the aforementioned analysis of the one-dimensional data. All things considered, the initial field tests of Bendix–Pan Am were very encouraging. Structural details related to the known geology at the site

were seen in addition to features not apparently seen in conventional pulse-echo and migration analyses. The experimental results seem to support the idea that the superior lateral resolution characteristics[3] of any two-dimensional array (holographic or otherwise) make it an excellent imaging system in complex geological situations compared with the conventional seismic reflection techniques involving only one-dimensional uncrossed arrays. It should be stressed, however, that these results, encouraging though they are, have by no means exhausted the possible advantages of holographic data taking or holographic data processing.

These authors limited their reconstruction algorithms to the "correlation" imaging technique described above. It is not known whether or not any actual wavefront reconstruction using holography was attempted. There are also many possibilities for enhancing data that could eventually be tried with data of this type. As Farr indicates in his concluding remarks [11], "conventional seismic data processing has had nearly a half-century to perfect its techniques so that one should not be too quick to judge these early steps in processing of seismic data using holographic techniques."

A completely different type of two-dimensional hologram on a moderately large scale was produced in a 1969 experiment by the present author [10] at Rock Springs, WY, in a U.S. Bureau of Mines experiment. Here, we present some of the results of that experiment to show how these data were originally analyzed and how the originally poor images have been improved.

As an example of what can be done to aid in delineating a fixed geological object being imaged in a seismic hologram arrangement, consider the experiment illustrated in Fig. 1. The object to be imaged in this experiment was an explosively formed rubble zone in oil shale. The source of seismic energy was a 150-g explosive charge (unrelated to the fracturing explosives) at a depth of 195 ft. Data was collected using geophones that occupied positions in a 21×21 array on the ground surface. The full details of this experiment and the manner in which the data were processed are given elsewhere [10]. It should be pointed out that the data were not recorded holographically in this experiment, that is, a reference wave was not supplied at the time data was being recorded but was supplied at a later time via computer. Complete time traces were recorded so that a variety of methods of making holograms from the data could be tested. However, the same holograms could have been formed directly if a reference wave had been supplied in the field. In that case it would not have been necessary to record individual time traces.

Since the wavelength of the seismic wave (50 ft) was roughly half the size of the object in this experiment the image resolution in this system is extremely poor. Furthermore, owing to severe anisotropy of the pressure wave velocity, wavefronts from the source were not spherical but ellipsoidal. Added to these difficulties is the fact that the medium was not uniform nor homogeneous. Clearly, this site and the experimental situation fall under the category of a real-world situation.

Fig. 2(a) illustrates a Fourier transform hologram which is a hologram made with the synthetic reference source at the same average depth as the object or region to be imaged. The location of the point source reference is shown in Fig. 1. The

---

[2] If only a single real hologram $A \cos \phi$ were used the reconstruction yields an unwanted conjugate image. It will be shown later that when the complex hologram $Ae^{i\phi} = iA \cos \phi + A \sin \phi$ is reconstructed only a single image is reconstructed.

[3] A line array cannot resolve image detail perpendicular to the line, whereas a circular two-dimensional array for example can resolve in any lateral direction equally.

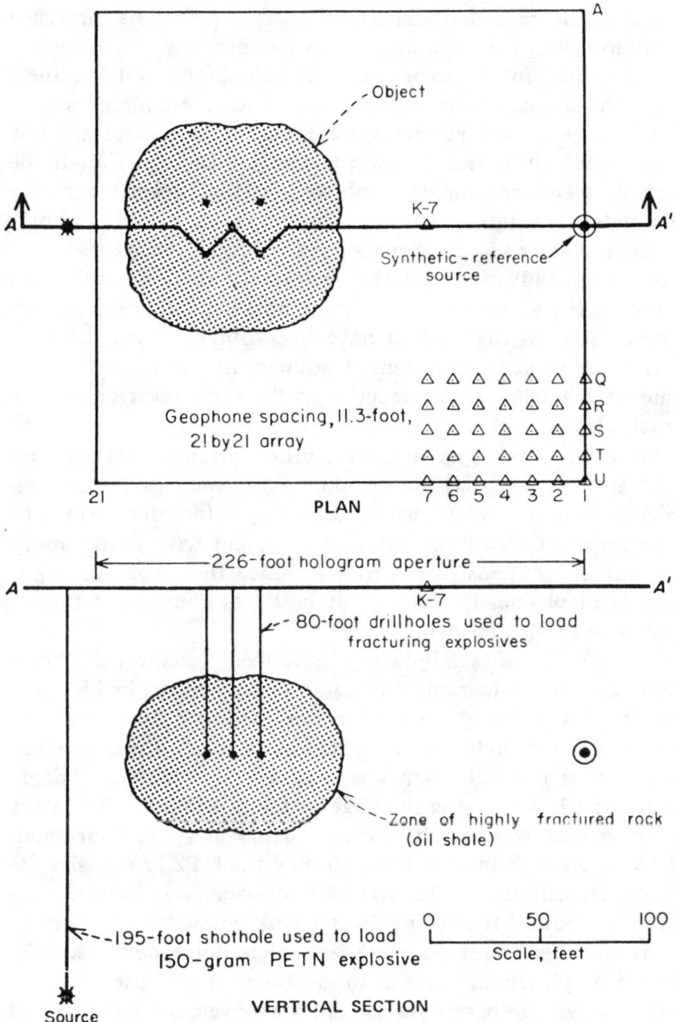

Fig. 1. Experimental arrangement used to produce a seismic hologram of an artificially produced fracture zone in oil shale. The true source and a synthetic reference source are shown. A more detailed account of this experiment is reported in [10].

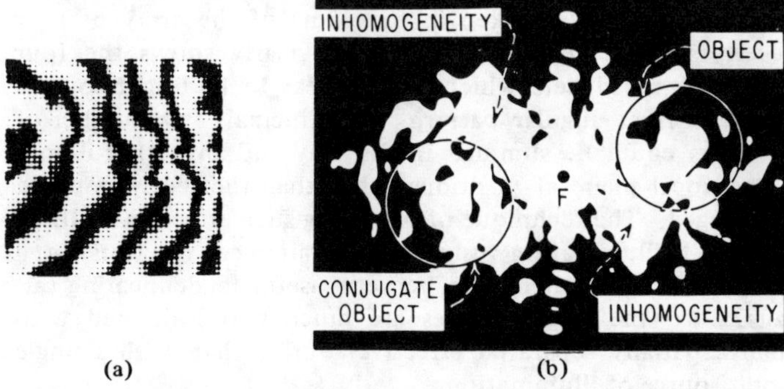

Fig. 2. Reconstruction of field data. (b) is laser reconstruction of (a). The reconstruction shows a roughly circular object at the position of the fracture zone. The quality of the image is very poor, owing principally to the low resolution of the system and the fact that a laser instead of a computer was used to reconstruct the image. Computer reconstruction removes the conjugate image and information surrounding the focal point of the lens. However, other features such as the anisotropic nature of the rock at this site also conspire to degrade the images.

laser reconstruction is also shown in Fig. 2(b). A crude circular object is visible in the reconstruction at the expected position of the object and what was originally called a "nonuni-

formity" is also present. This "nonuniformity" was apparently an artifact due to optical noise since it does not appear in the computer reconstructed images of the same data (see Fig. 18).

Now examine Figs. 13 and 18 for some of the latest results obtained from this same original data. In these latter figures we illustrate two entirely different kinds of imaging techniques. In Fig. 13, a technique called interferometric imaging which is vaguely similar to the correlation imaging idea used by Mueller, Steinberg, and Farr [9], [11] was used in conjunction with a new image enhancement technique both of which will be discussed later in this paper. In Fig. 18 an actual computer reconstruction of the hologram using a fast Fourier transform algorithm is shown. In Fig. 13 a zone of fractured rock of the expected four lobed configuration is clearly delineated. Similarly, in the computer reconstruction (Fig. 18) with no enhancement of any kind, the same zone is delineated. The quality of these images is considerably better than the laser reconstructed images of Fig. 2.

Finally, in this section we would like to mention the results of an interesting experiment recently completed by Hildebrand and Fandneff [12]. These authors were attempting to obtain images of debris buried in shallow trenches at the Hanford Works near Richland, WA. The conditions at this site surely rank it among the poorest from a technical standpoint, that one is likely ever to encounter in such work. Although these authors did not record their data holographically but recorded full time traces, they used only the first arrivals which, as we show later, is equivalent to recording the phase argument of the hologram rather than the hologram itself. This technique, like holography, has the advantage that full time traces need not be recorded except in so far as they are needed in obtaining the time of flight data.

The filled trenches in question were roughly 12 ft wide at the top tapering to a 4-ft width at a depth of 12 to 15 ft and extended over a considerable area. The actual sampling aperture measured roughly 50 ft by 40 ft. There were two different velocity layers not including the trenches. There was a layer having a velocity of 1250 ft/s extending to a depth of 7 ft and another layer below this with a velocity of 1875 ft/s. The experimental arrangement for taking the data consisted of a series of 30-ft deep water-filled drill holes and a source array at the surface. Detectors were placed in the bottom of the drill holes and the surface source (a plate and sledge) was "scanned" to synthesize the data in a reciprocity arrangement.[4]

The authors were able to use a backward-wave reconstruction algorithm, which will be discussed in more detail later, to reconstruct this near-field data and obtained an excellent image showing the boundaries of the trenches. No debris was seen in the trenches however, owing to the wavelength (7–9 ft).

Small-scale experiments of this type are relatively easy and inexpensive to perform and are surprisingly successful considering the near surface conditions which suggest that techniques of this kind will find increasing acceptance in a wide variety of problem areas where current techniques may have failed.

C. Past Proposals

In addition to the field experiments that were discussed above, there have been some interesting and ambitious proposals. Notable among these was the plan by Bendix under Advanced Research Projects Agency (ARPA) funding [13] to

---

[4] Source and receiver exchanged.

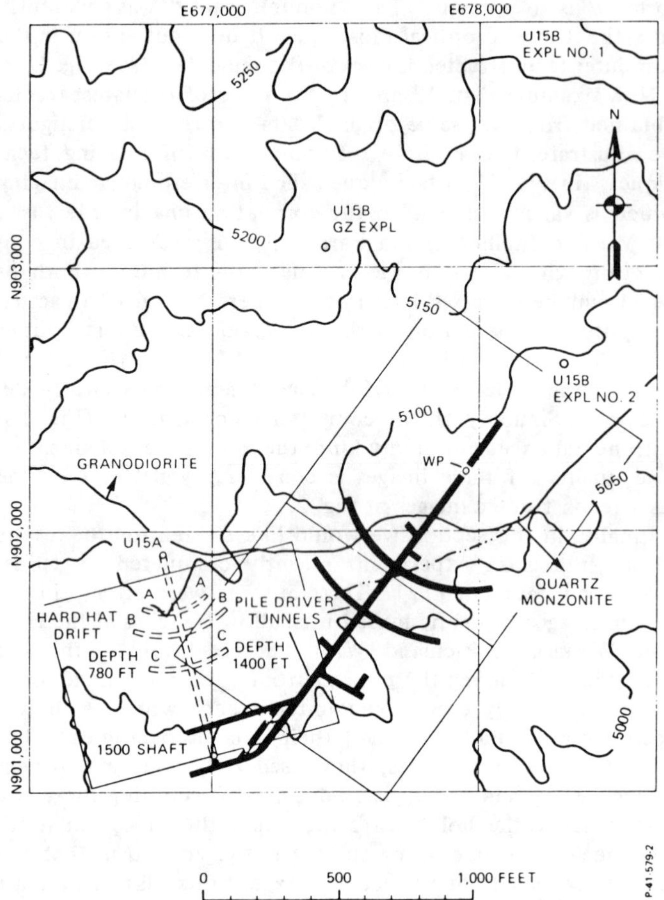

Fig. 3. Map showing location of pile driver holographic aperture with respect to Nevada test site. (Proposed (ARPA) experiment by Bendix Research Laboratories.)

map the tunnel complexes and the fracture cavity at the Pile Driver experiment at the Nevada test site (Fig. 3). This imaging experiment was unfortunately never funded.

It should be noted, however, that there is considerable current interest by organizations such as the Defense Nuclear Agency in finding ways of evaluating the effects of nuclear blasts on underground structures. It is not unlikely that some of these early proposals will again see the light of day. In any case, plans of this type make it clear that a considerable amount of unpublished background work has already been done in many areas.

IV. TECHNIQUES FOR GATHERING DATA

There are two basic problems associated with the application of holography to the earth sciences. First, there is the problem of obtaining a sufficient amount of data to make an acceptable hologram of the targets to be imaged and secondly, there are problems associated with processing these data to obtain interpretable images. Although these problems are always present in any application of holography or indeed in any conventional seismic technique, they are especially significant in the present application owing to the potentially large scale of the experiments and the complexity of the targets being imaged.

A. Reciprocity Arrangements

The reciprocity theorem [14] states essentially that any source-receiver pair may be exchanged without in most cases

changing the recorded signals. This fact gives one increased flexibility when designing seismic holography experiments. For example, in the experiment of Hildebrand and Fandneff [12], the actual source was a scanned surface-coupled struck plate. The actual receivers were placed in several shallow water filled drillholes below the base of the trenches to be imaged. The combination of well-coupled receivers and a reasonably energetic surface source (even though poorly coupled) resulted in good signals at the buried receivers.

By taking advantage of the reciprocity theorem, this data was essentially the same, as far as phase information is concerned, as data that would have been obtained had these investigators used several buried sources in the drillholes and scanned a single surface receiver at the same locations as the struck plate.

One clear advantage of the reciprocal arrangement used by these authors was that they could employ small diameter drillholes for the passive receivers. Had they attempted instead to use a series of downhole sources this might have been a more difficult and expensive experiment since these sources might have been physically large or at best less convenient than a downhole passive receiver.

An example of a laboratory produced "reciprocal" holograms are the holograms and the reconstructions in Fig. 8(a) and (b). The hologram and reconstruction of Fig. 8(a) are particularly instructive of the reciprocity technique in general. In Fig. 8(a) the hologram was produced by scanning a single source at 125 kHz using the large scanner of Fig. 5. The target to be imaged was a right angular planar array of four small (9/16 of an inch in diameter, 20 mils thick PZT5) passive receiving transducers. The array of receivers was located at a depth of about 9 ft in a large water tank below the scanner.

The outputs of the four receivers were combined in a summation amplifier and this composite signal was used to produce a single hologram value and was given the same spatial address for plotting purposes as the single scanning source. Thus the reciprocal hologram obtained in this way looks as if it were made with four sources and a single scanned receiver.

This situation is well illustrated by the computer reconstruction of the reciprocal hologram (Fig. 8(a)) where the reconstructed image was taken in the plane of the array of four receivers. The reconstructed image clearly shows the four receiving transducers which now appear to be bright sources in the correct angular pattern. In principal, any number of receivers could be summed in this way and any other illuminated focal plane at positions other than the receivers could be imaged. The technique of providing such effective multiple "source" illumination using many summed receivers in a reciprocal arrangement can be very useful in delineating targets since the target images are much better defined with many spatially separated effective sources than with a single point source of illumination.

The pulse-echo hologram of Fig. 8(b) was made with a single stationary passive receiver located slightly outside a circularly scanned source array consisting of a single circularly scanned source using the scanner of Fig. 5 located over a concrete test block. The output of this stationary receiver was stored at the spatial address of the moving source and hologram values produced. The reciprocity theorem states that this is essentially the same as an "ordinary" hologram made by using a single stationary source, and circularly scanning a single passive receiver. The successful reconstruction of the buried styrofoam targets (Fig. 8(b)) bears out this supposition.

One is clearly not limited to a single source any more than one is limited to a single receiver. Thus in general, one may have an array of sources and an array of receivers either one of which or both may be scanned to obtain the necessary data [15].

B. Crossed Linear Arrays

A particularly useful scanning technique from a practical standpoint has been described by Milder and Wells [17] and Wells [16]. These authors show that sufficient data for constructing a hologram consisting of N^2 elements can be obtained by using a single linear array of N receivers (sources) and scanning a single source (receiver) through N stations located along a line perpendicular to the detector array. This approach has great practical value when one is attempting to construct large two-dimensional holograms. The Bendix–Pan Am experiment discussed earlier [9], [11] in which a salt-dome in the Gulf of Mexico was being mapped employed this strategy to great advantage in making large two-dimensional holograms.

C. First-Arrival Holography

The reciprocity theorem and crossed-array techniques provide methods for reducing the number of actual detectors, amplifiers, and associated apparatus required to make holograms; and, under the proper experimental conditions, this can greatly reduce the time and effort required to obtain the hologram. In the introduction we also pointed out that the very process of taking data holographically greatly reduces the amount of data needed since complete time traces need not always be recorded. It was also pointed out in the introduction that impulses in addition to continuous waves could be used in making holograms. If impulses are used and if one integrates over these entire incoming time traces (1) there will be other unwanted contributions to the hologram besides the early arriving scalar waves. That is, the later arriving shear waves and some surface wave information contribute and these can act as undesirable sources of hologram noise.

Thus it can be advantageous in certain situations such as through-transmission experiments or refraction experiments to eliminate these difficulties when impulses are used by recording the phase argument ϕ of the hologram $H = A \cos \phi$ using first arrivals rather than the hologram itself. In this way one still has the advantage of "holographic recording techniques" in that only one piece of wave information need be recorded per geophone, but information from unwanted later arrivals is excluded.

The technique of examining only the first arrival times or the relative arrival times of signals transmitted through a region of interest to the hologram detector array has been shown to be a workable concept both in the laboratory (see Fig. 14) and in the analysis of field data [18]. In this regard, the recent experiment of Hildebrand and Fandneff [12] discussed earlier is also interesting since shallow debris-filled trenches at the Hanford site in Richland, WA, were successfully imaged using only information from the first arrivals.

In the first-arrival technique, the time of arrival of a transmitted signal (call it t_A) is multiplied by a circular frequency ω_0 characteristic of the typical rise-time associated with the arriving signals (see Fig. 4).

Thus the arrival time can be used to compute a phase angle $\phi = \omega_0 t_A$ for each geophone detector location in the array. Defining some reference wave phase ϕ_R characteristic of an

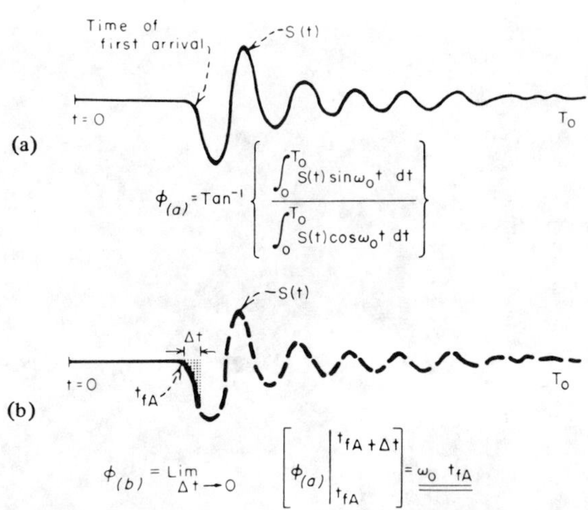

$$\phi_{(a)} = \mathrm{Tan}^{-1} \left\{ \frac{\int_0^{T_0} S(t) \sin \omega_0 t \; dt}{\int_0^{T_0} S(t) \cos \omega_0 t \; dt} \right\}$$

$$\phi_{(b)} = \lim_{\Delta t \to 0} \left[\phi_{(a)} \Big|_{t_{fA}}^{t_{fA} + \Delta t} \right] = \underline{\underline{\omega_0 \, t_{fA}}}$$

Fig. 4. Calculation of phase angles of a given Fourier component within an idealized impulse by: (a) carrying out integrations over full records and (b) limiting integrations to the interval preceding the arrival of the signal.

arbitrary reference wave, one may compute hologram values from the simple formula[5]

$$H = \cos(\phi_R - \phi). \qquad (4)$$

These holograms contain a considerable amount of information about the objects through which the wave was transmitted, since this information is principally phase information. Therefore, in spite of the fact that apparently only one piece of information t_A needs to be recorded for a given time trace, the holograms produced in this way are perfectly acceptable.

The savings in the amount of data required for a given trace can have considerable practical significance in situations where exotic apparatus is not available for recording and storing large quantities of data. Basically, all that is required to make such first-arrival holograms is apparatus to measure the time of flight. This can be accomplished in simple small-scale applications with a single geophone-amplifier arrangement and a counter timer or oscilloscope for measuring time of flight of an appropriate source pulse.

Fig. 14 illustrates a laboratory scale hologram and its computer reconstruction produced from first arrival data (a simple pulser and counter-timer was used). Fig. 18 is a first arrival hologram and its computer reconstruction of the field data taken in the arrangement of Fig. 1.

It should also be clear from the success of the shallow near surface work of Hildebrand and Fandneff [12] and the complications that would have resulted if a near surface pulse-echo experiment had been tried instead, that the first-arrival technique can be very useful and possibly crucial to be the success of certain kinds of small scale near surface experimental situations.

V. LABORATORY MODELING

When the scale of the problems with which one is dealing is potentially very large, as it often is in geophysical applications, modeling over the years and it was this type of activity, two-models of actual or anticipated field situations provide valuable insights into the design of improved experiments, they

---

[5] As mentioned earlier, we usually compute an imaginary hologram $H = A \cos \theta + iA \sin \theta$ in order to remove the conjugate image.

Fig. 5. A large-scale circular (5-ft diameter) scanner mounted over concrete test block. Two to four inches of water cover the concrete block.

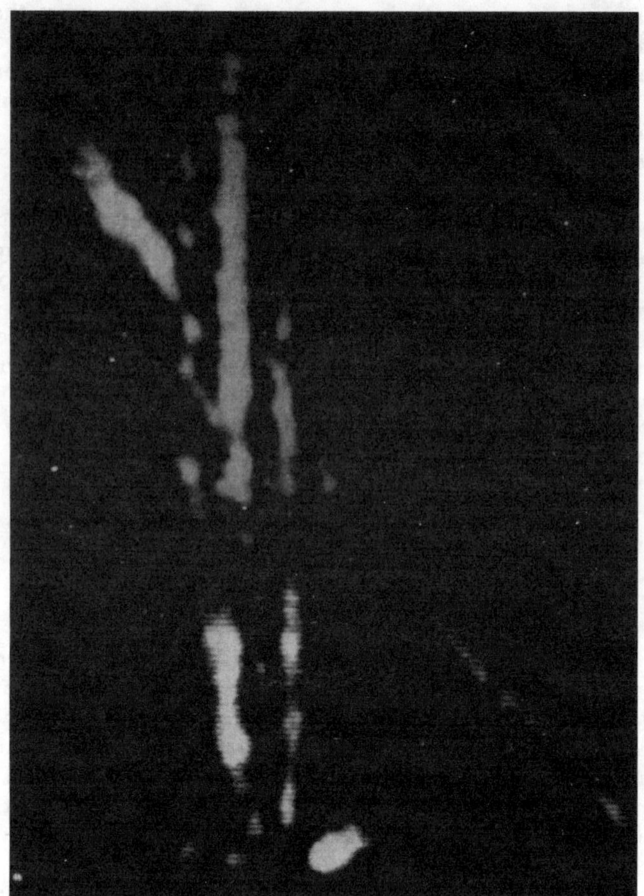

Fig. 6. The holographic image of three small ($\frac{3}{4}$ in diameter) steel rods, 54 in from transducer in the water tank. A fourth rod just below cuts the three at an angle (frequency 125 kHz).

can also provide valuable data for insertion into interpretive computer programs and other data analysis procedures. Without this data even a well-understood problem of data taking and data reduction is difficult to apply in the field.

Numerous investigators have experimented with seismic modeling over the years and it was this type of activity, two-dimensional seismic modeling, that first raised the possibility in the author's mind of doing three-dimensional modeling using holographic data reduction. One of the first investigators to set up laboratory experiments for the purpose of testing the potential application of holography to the seismic case was Farr [19].

A. Examples

For an example of imaging in models on a somewhat larger scale and in both water and elastic materials, consider the following experiments performed by the author and illustrated in Fig. 5 through 10. In these recent experiments a large circular scanner was used to take data from a concrete test block [6], [7]. A smaller test block was used in 1974 by the author at the U.S. Bureau of Mines to obtain similar data (Fig. 11).

It is worth pointing out that little is to be gained by building larger models than those indicated since most of the principals of data taking and reduction can be amply studied with these experimental arrangements. That these experimental arrangements are much larger than actually necessary, however, does not follow. The size of an experimental model system is often keyed to the device or devices required to take the data. In the case of the large concrete block being used as a data producing system at our laboratory in Richland, WA the data taking system as previously mentioned was a large five-foot diameter circular scanner (Fig. 5). This scanner or its subsequent versions may eventually have some commercial significance and so must be tested in an environment of the proper scale even though the principals involved in taking data could and have been adequately studied using smaller scale systems.

B. Field "Modeling"

Another example where the apparatus dictates the size of the experimental "model" is afforded by some recent experiments of Lovhaugen and Stamnes [20]. These investigators

are studying the imaging characteristics of a seismic array and associated data processing system that will soon be put to the test in field exploration work. To accomplish these goals they are performing experiments in a Norwegian fjord attempting to image sources and source arrays placed on the seabed.

VI. METHODS FOR IMPROVING IMAGES

There are a variety of techniques in holography where the spatial frequency content of the hologram is altered in order to achieve some desirable result. This alteration usually consists in selectively filtering or phase shifting various spatial frequency components in the hologram, but it may also involve the addition, subtraction, etc., of various holograms to produce the desired results. The flexibility that holography provides in altering the original data in novel ways to improve or enhance certain aspects of the reconstructed image is one of the principle advantages of holographic data processing.

A. Weak Signal Enhancement

A difficulty commonly encountered in processing conventional seismic data and one to be expected in holographic processing as well is the problem of extracting a weak return signal from some dominant nearby background signal. A typical example of this would be a point "diffuse" scatterer located just above a plane reflector. Keating et al. [21] have developed a technique called "weak signal enhancement" that involves an effective filtering or "damping" of those spatial frequency components on the hologram that are characteristic of the target information to be suppressed.

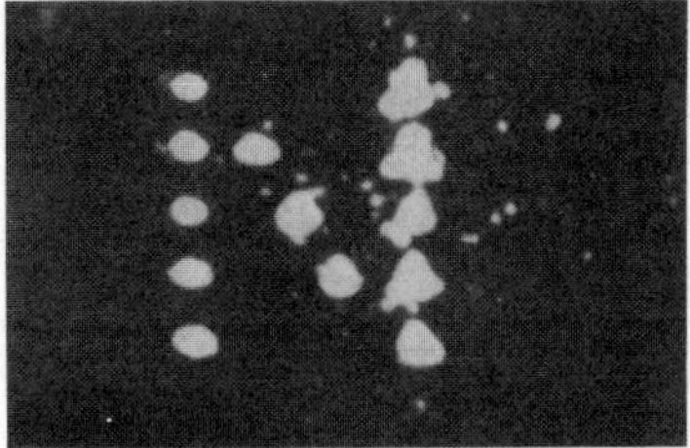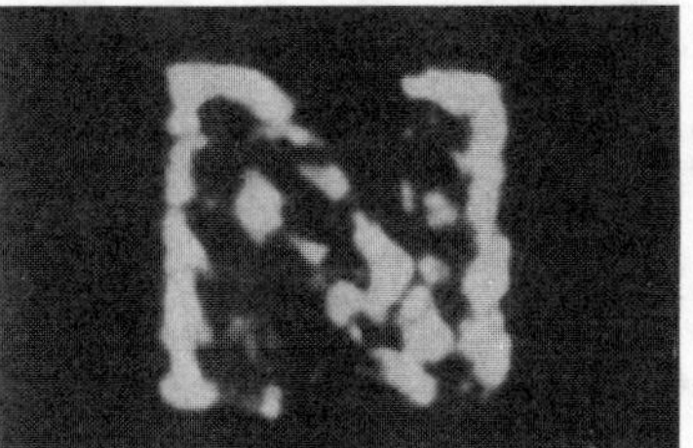

Fig. 7. Laser reconstruction of test objects at a depth of 4 ft in a water tank. Left—Reconstruction of 17-in high styrofoam letter "*N*" with corner reflectors cut in the surface. Right—Reconstruction of 17-in high letter "*N*" with styrofoam spheres attached to the surface (frequency 125 kHz).

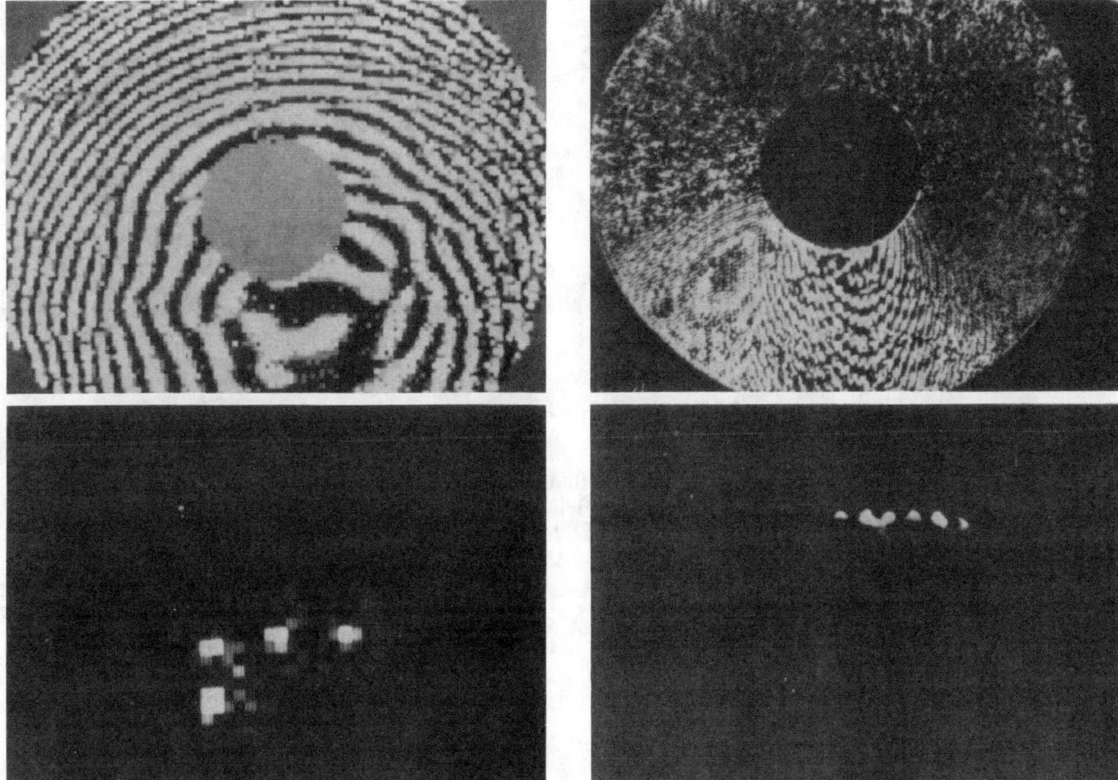

Fig. 8. Left—The hologram above was scanned using the large scanner shown in Fig. 5 operating at 125 kHz. Data was transmitted to a minicomputer for storage and reconstruction. The "target" was an array of four small receiving transducers in a right angular pattern. The spacing between transducers was roughly 4.5 in. The outputs from these four receiving transducers were summed and this signal used to produce the plane wave reciprocal 128 × 128 hologram shown above. This reciprocal hologram was "rotated" and reconstructed using a computer to produce the image of the receiving transducers which now appear to be sources owing to the reciprocal geometry. Right-Hologram and laser reconstruction of six 6-in diameter styrofoam resolution spheres 4 feet deep in concrete (top) the hologram, (botton) optical reconstruction—six spheres.

In the above situation of the point target scatterer and plane reflector, the desired target information from the point scatterer is scattered through a wide angle and so tends to produce hologram fringes with a high spatial frequency. The plane reflector produces hologram fringes with a lower spatial frequency.

It is certainly possible in principle to eliminate the low-spatial-frequency components by conventional optical filtering techniques where appropriate masks are inserted in the focal plane of a transforming lens element in order to block out information regarding the plane reflector. It is also possible to perform all of these transformations and the masking by using a computer. This is essentially the approach of Mueller and Keating. (See also the review article by these authors in this journal for further details.) These authors have demonstrated that where applicable, techniques of this type lead to dramatic improvements in the images reconstructed from holograms [21]. In the foregoing example the "roughness" or diffraction features of the reflector would be enhanced while the more slowly varying spatial surface features that usually give large returns would be suppressed in the reconstructed image. There are yet other possibilities for enhancing images that do not involve filtering of hologram data. These techniques, broadly referred to as interferometric techniques, involve superimposing various holograms and reconstructing the composites to achieve desired improvements [22].

B. Phase Contrast Enhancement Techniques

It has been shown, for example, that the image-background contrast of the phase object images reconstructed from acoustical or seismic through-transmission holograms could be considerably improved using an interferometric technique [23].

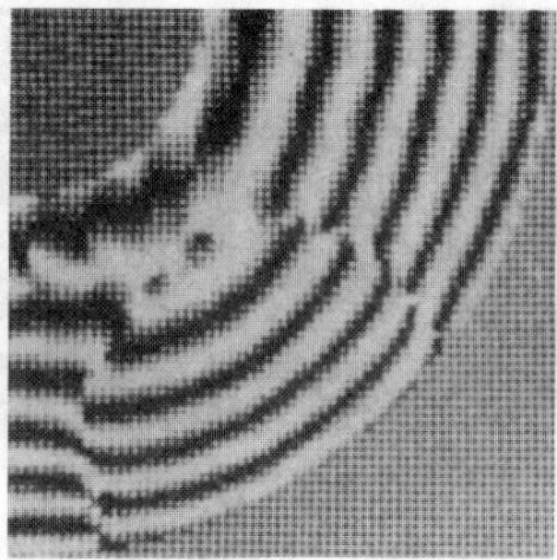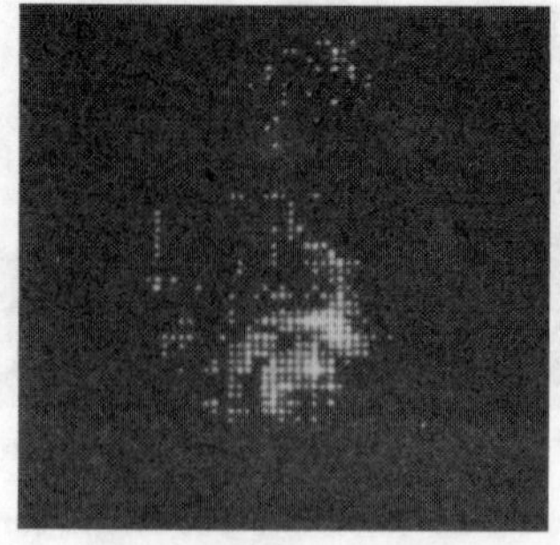

Fig. 9. Computer plot of a scanned 64 × 64 hologram and its computer reconstruction. The subject is a styrofoam sphere at a 4-ft depth in concrete. Left—The hologram. Right—Reconstruction (frequency 125 kHz).

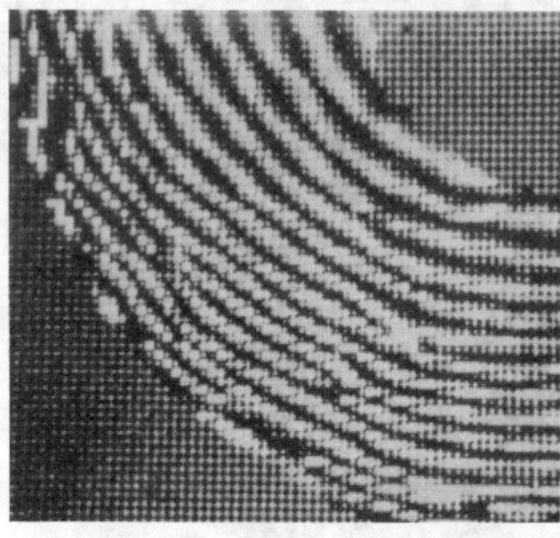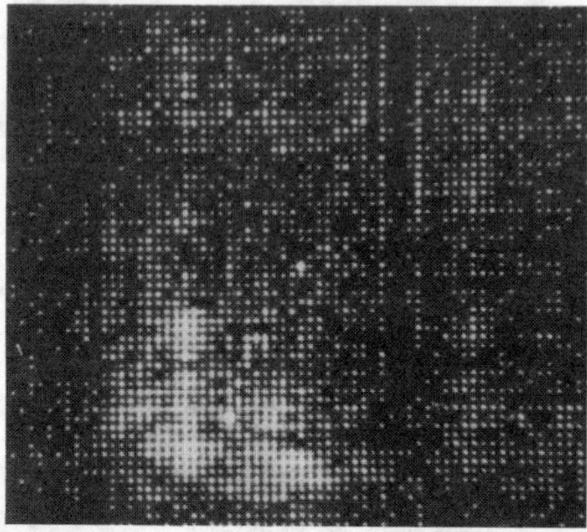

Fig. 10. Hologram and reconstruction of bottom left corner of a buried granite slab at a depth of 4 ft in concrete. Left—The hologram. Right—Reconstruction (frequency 125 kHz).

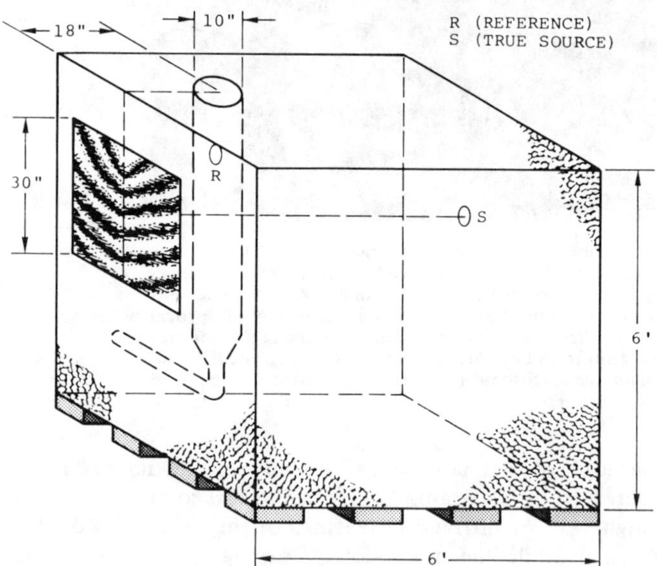

Fig. 11. Experimental setup for making holograms in a large laboratory concrete model unrelated to the experimental setup of Fig. 5. The model contained several objects, one of which was a 10-in diameter cylinder hole that could be filled with various materials. Acoustic pulses at 50 kHz were transmitted from S across the block. A simple timer was used to determine the transit time of the signal (t_0). The appropriate phase angle $\phi = \omega t_0$ was computed using $\omega = 2\pi$ (50 kHz) and a hologram $H = \cos[(2\pi D/\lambda) - \phi]$ was also computed using the reference-source position indicated where D is the distance from R to a point in the hologram array. For details regarding such first-arrival experiments, see [18].

Such techniques are also applicable in principle to deep pulse-echo returns since they too are transmitted through the earth to the surface detectors.

The process in question involves a superposition of two holograms. The first hologram is characteristic of the elastic medium plus a final-state object (after hologram) and the second hologram is characteristic of the elastic medium plus an initial-state object (before hologram). All geometric arrangements, source geometries, and wavelengths are identical in the two cases, except that the reference waves used to make the two holograms are 90° out of phase with respect to each other,[6] and changes are assumed to have taken place in the object or region under study and this region is[7] assumed to be transparent to the seismic or acoustical waves.[7] A reconstruction of this type of composite hologram shows much improved image contrast, especially for objects that introduce small phase shifts. In particular, image contrasts can be made to vary as the first power of small phase shifts rather than as the second power of such quantities as in ordinary holograms.

[6] The reader could be cautioned that this 90° phase shift is different than that employed to remove the unwanted conjugate image. (equations). There the quadrative holograms $\cos(\phi - \phi r)$, $\sin(\phi - \phi r)$ were with respect to the same phase angle ϕ and the two quadrature holograms were treated as the real and imaginary parts of a complex hologram, respectively. In the present case the "quadrature" holograms $\cos(\phi - \phi r)$ and $\sin(\phi' - \phi r)$ are with respect to different phase angles ϕ and ϕ' and both are summed to produce a real hologram $\cos(\phi - \phi r) + \sin(\phi - \phi r)$. If a computer is used to reconstruct such a hologram the conjugate image is removed by computing the complex hologram

$$H = \cos(\phi - \phi r) + \sin(\phi' - \phi r) + i[\sin(\phi - \phi r) + \cos(\phi' - \phi r)].$$

[7] Various things can change the physical properties of an object or region under study such as a change in the p-wave velocity due to an increased stress field which often accompanies the conditions preceeding earthquakes. Artificial changes due to the activities of man such as removal of oil or gas resulting in reduced pressures will also result in changes in p-wave velocities. We will see later that the technique can be applied even if actual changes do not occur.

Consider, for example, the situation where an initial-state hologram made by allowing a scalar seismic or acoustical pressure wave $A_0 \exp(i\phi)$ characteristic of an initial-state object and a synthetic reference wave $A_r \exp(i\phi r)$ are allowed to interfere. Here A_0 and A_r are considered to be real amplitudes and both the object and reference waves are assumed to be monochromatic and spatially coherent.

The intensity recorded on this initial-state hologram is

$$H_1 = A_0^2 + A_r^2 + 2A_0 A_r \cos(\phi - \phi_r). \qquad (5)$$

Now suppose for the sake of argument that natural or man-made changes take place in the phase object (a geophysical phase object is one that introduces phase shifts into incident seismic or acoustical waves by virtue of variations in the pressure-wave velocity, throughout its bulk) so that the final-state amplitude becomes $A_0' \exp(i\phi')$. By allowing this new amplitude to interfere with a reference wave that has been quarterwave shifted from the original, the new intensity recorded on the new hologram is

$$H_2 = A_0'^2 + A_r^2 + 2A_0' A_r \sin(\phi' - \phi_r). \qquad (6)$$

If the two intensities H_1 and H_2 corresponding to the measured initial-state and final-state holograms are superimposed on the same hologram transparency (in the case of laser reconstruction) to form a holographic interferogram $HI = H_1 + H_2$ and if this composite is reconstructed by a light wave represented by an arbitrary complex reference wave U_0, then the transmitted amplitude U through the holographic interferogram will be

$$U = U_0 t_+ \qquad (8)$$

where

$$t_+ = (HI)^{+\Gamma/2} = (H_1 + H_2)^{+\Gamma/2}.$$

The amplitude transmittance t_+ corresponds to a photographic positive, and Γ is the density-log exposure characteristic of the film on which the holograms are stored. For simplicity it is assumed that $\Gamma = 2$ and terms corresponding to simple attenuation of U_0 are dropped from the computation, then the transmitted wave amplitude for the combination is found to be (assuming that $A_0' \sim A_0$ which is a good approximation when pure phase objects are concerned)

$$U = U_0 A_0 A_r \exp(-i\phi)_r \left[(\exp(-i\phi) + i \exp(-i\phi'))\right.$$
$$\left. + (\exp(+i\phi) - i \exp(+i\phi'))\right]. \qquad (9)$$

The first term in this expanded sum corresponds to what we will call the true image amplitude produced by the hologram, and the second-term corresponds to the conjugate image amplitude.

Dropping the slowly varying (with position on the hologram) coefficient $U_0 A_0 A_r$, the intensity in the reconstructed true image is

$$I \sim |(\exp(-i\phi) + i \exp(-i\phi'))|^2 \qquad (10)$$

$$I \sim 2 + i \exp(-i(\phi' - \phi)) - i \exp(+i(\phi' - \phi)). \qquad (11)$$

For small phase differences $(\phi' - \phi) \sim 0$ and

$$I \sim 2 + 2(\phi' - \phi). \qquad (12)$$

Therefore, the reconstructed-image intensity in this holographic interferogram varies as the first power of the difference in phase between the initial and final states. Had there been no quarter-wave shift between the reference waves in the initial

and final cases, the final image intensity would have been given by [23]

$$I' \sim |(\exp(-i\phi) + \exp(-i\phi'))|^2 \sim 4 - (\phi' - \phi)^2. \qquad (13)$$

Hence, it is found that if an ordinary hologram of the object is made, the reconstructed image intensity will vary as the square of a small phase difference $(\phi' - \phi)^2$ rather than linearly with $(\phi' - \phi)$. This means that the image contrast for objects that change have been markedly improved for small phase differences $(\phi' - \phi)$ in the holographic interferogram since the reconstructed image contrast there varies as the first power of $(\phi' - \phi)$. For example, if the reconstructed image contrast is arbitrarily defined (we will see later that a much more advantageous definition may be employed to obtain even better results) as the magnitude of the ratio of the variable part of the reconstructed image intensity to the constant background intensity [23], the image contrast in the reconstructed holographic interferogram would be given by

$$CR(I) = (\phi' - \phi) \qquad (14)$$

and the image contrast in the ordinary hologram [23] would be

$$CR(I') = \frac{(\phi' - \phi)^2}{4}. \qquad (15)$$

If, for example, $(\phi' - \phi)$ corresponds to a one-sixteenth wave shift, then

$$CR(I) = \pi/8 \sim 0.4 \qquad (16)$$

whereas

$$CR(I') = \frac{(\pi/8)^2}{4} = 0.04. \qquad (17)$$

To summarize, we can say that by superimposing two holograms of two different states of an object and reconstructing the composite, it has been shown that the relative image-background contrast for small phase differences can be made to vary as the first power of the phase difference $\Delta\phi = (\phi' - \phi)$ between the initial (ϕ) and the final (ϕ') cases. By comparison, a single final-state hologram would be expected to yield a very poor relative image–background contrast, since for a conventional transmission hologram of a phase object the contrast varies as the square of a small phase angle rather than as the first power of such a quantity. Thus by properly choosing the holograms to be superimposed, one may alter the characteristics of the final reconstructed image in subtle ways. In the next section, another more general interferometric technique is used to obtain a much improved holographic image of an actual unchanging underground fracture zone in oil shale.

C. New Interferometric Techniques

The simplest possible generalization of the amplitude produced by an arbitrary linear combination of transmission holograms, for example, of phase objects is

$$A = \exp(-i\phi) + Z \exp(-i\phi'), \qquad Z = \alpha + i\beta \qquad (18)$$

$$\phi' = \phi + \Delta\phi \qquad (19)$$

where Z is an arbitrary complex number to be determined.

Using A from (18), the image intensity in the image plane of the composite hologram is found to vary as

$$I = 1 + Z \exp(-i(\phi' - \phi)) + Z^* \exp(i(\phi' - \phi)) + Z^*Z \qquad (20)$$

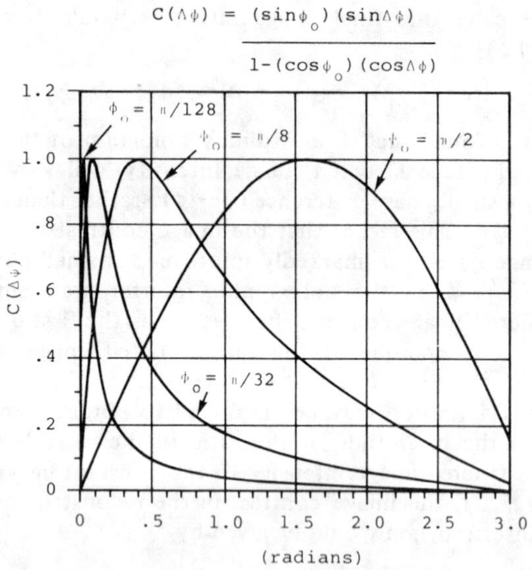

Fig. 12. Relative reconstructed image contrast $C(\Delta\psi)$ for a three-fold hologram for a variety of contours characterized by the phase shift ϕ_0. The width of $C(\Delta\psi)$ at half maximum is roughly $3\phi_0$. Note that $C(\Delta\psi)$ has a maximum value of +1 when $\phi_0 = \Delta\phi$.

or

$$I = (1 + 2\alpha \cos \Delta\phi + \alpha^2 + \beta^2) + 2\beta \sin \Delta\phi. \qquad (21)$$

Now we are free to adjust α and β in any way we like to alter the character of I to improve the reconstructed image. Using this I, we arbitrarily define a new measure of relative image contrast [24] to be the ratio of those terms in I (21) that vary approximately as $(\Delta\phi)$ to the constant background terms plus terms that vary approximately as $(\Delta\phi)^2$. That is

$$CR' = \frac{2\beta \sin \Delta\phi}{(1 + 2\alpha \cos \Delta\phi + \alpha^2 + \beta^2)}. \qquad (22)$$

It is clear that whenever CR' can be arranged to be large, then terms in I that vary $(\Delta\phi)$ will dominate. This ensures that small phase changes between two states will be enhanced, since the functional variation of CR' will be primarily due to terms in $(\Delta\phi)$.

This contrast function (Fig. 12 and equation (22)) is defined for all phase shifts $\Delta\phi$ large or small at every point in the reconstructed image. Therefore, it may be evaluated along any particular phase contour where $\Delta\phi = \phi' - \phi = C$ is some constant. Now, along this contour we desire $CR'(\alpha, \beta)$ to be as large as possible so that terms in $(\Delta\phi)$ will dominate the image along the contour.

Since $CR'(\alpha, \beta)$ may be shown to have its maximum value whenever α, β assume the particular values $\alpha = -\cos \Delta\phi$, $\beta = +\sin \Delta\phi$, namely $CR'(-\cos \Delta\phi, \sin \Delta\phi) = +1$, the contrast for any chosen contour characterized by the phase shift (C) can be made equal to unity by setting $\alpha = -\cos (C)$ and $\beta = +\sin (C)$. Note the very interesting result that CR' is independent of the contour chosen since $CR' = +1$ along any contour and, therefore, $CR' = +1$ for (C) arbitrarily small. This is a very great improvement over the technique discussed earlier.

In the foregoing, we have assumed that a real change occured in the object; i.e., $\Delta\phi = \phi' - \phi \neq 0$. Hence, it has been assumed that new information has been examined in the second of the two hologram "exposures." This assumption makes the underlying ideas easier to grasp. However, this is not an essential requirement. In fact, $\Delta\phi$ can be zero pro-

vided some other change takes place, such as moving the reference source or moving the hologram plane. Such changes can be interpreted as changes in an object, and these changes can still be characterized and enhanced by a proper choice of (C). This flexibility is especially useful, since it allows one to apply the technique to fixed geological objects.

D. Imaging a Crushed Zone in Oil Shale

Fig. 13 illustrates the application of the technique to bring out an image (using the interferometric imaging technique discussed later) of a crushed zone in oil shale (see Fig. 1). The geometry of this experiment is through transmission; however, the enhancement technique may also be applied in principle to the more common pulse-echo geometry. Nor is it required that the so called "interferometric" imaging technique be used as we do here to employ the enhancement technique.

Figs. 13(b) and (e) illustrate ordinary holograms made from this field data. The reference source was placed in the vicinity of the true source so as to produce an interferometric image of the object but owing to the anisotropy the apparent true source position is not its true position. For this reason, fringes appear on these interferometric images that have nothing to do with object information. In fact, without knowledge of the object and the anisotropy of the rock, all of the interferometric images are essentially meaningless (Fig. 13(a) and (d)) with the reference waves moved up the shothole by about 3 ft $(\lambda/16)$. Similarly, these holograms have no meaningful interpretable detail. Now, however, if we use these two states (two positions of the reference source) to produce a threefold composite with a (C) consistent with the source shift $(+\lambda/16)$, the object should be delineated to a certain extent in the interferometric image, and many of the irrelevant fringes should disappear. Figs. 13(c) and (f) bear out this prediction. At the top of the threefold interferometric images is an irregular object that is a crude projected image of the underground fracture zone. This object is now easily delineated.

It should be emphasized once again that these enhancement techniques can be applied in both pulse-echo and through-transmission geometries and in cases where objects do not change. Furthermore, since we are effectively altering the reconstructed amplitudes (18) by altering the recorded holograms, the image enhancement techniques described could also be applied directly to amplitudes reconstructed using various wave equation migration techniques. In the foregoing applications it was assumed that data had already been recorded holographically so that the methods of holographic interferometry were both natural and essential. However, if amplitudes are known (time traces recorded) and these may be migrated to the desired image points, the same kinds of enhancement procedures could be applied in principle to these data by making appropriate choices for the complex number Z. (See (18).)

VII. Computer Reconstruction and Imaging Techniques

Optical reconstructions of acoustic holograms often yield excellent results when the hologram aperture measures many wavelengths, however, when larger wavelengths are used and there are fewer wavelengths in the aperture, optical reconstructions become difficult at best owing to the presence of optical noise and the unavoidable conjugate images. Consequently, an alternate means of reconstructing holograms via the computer is required.

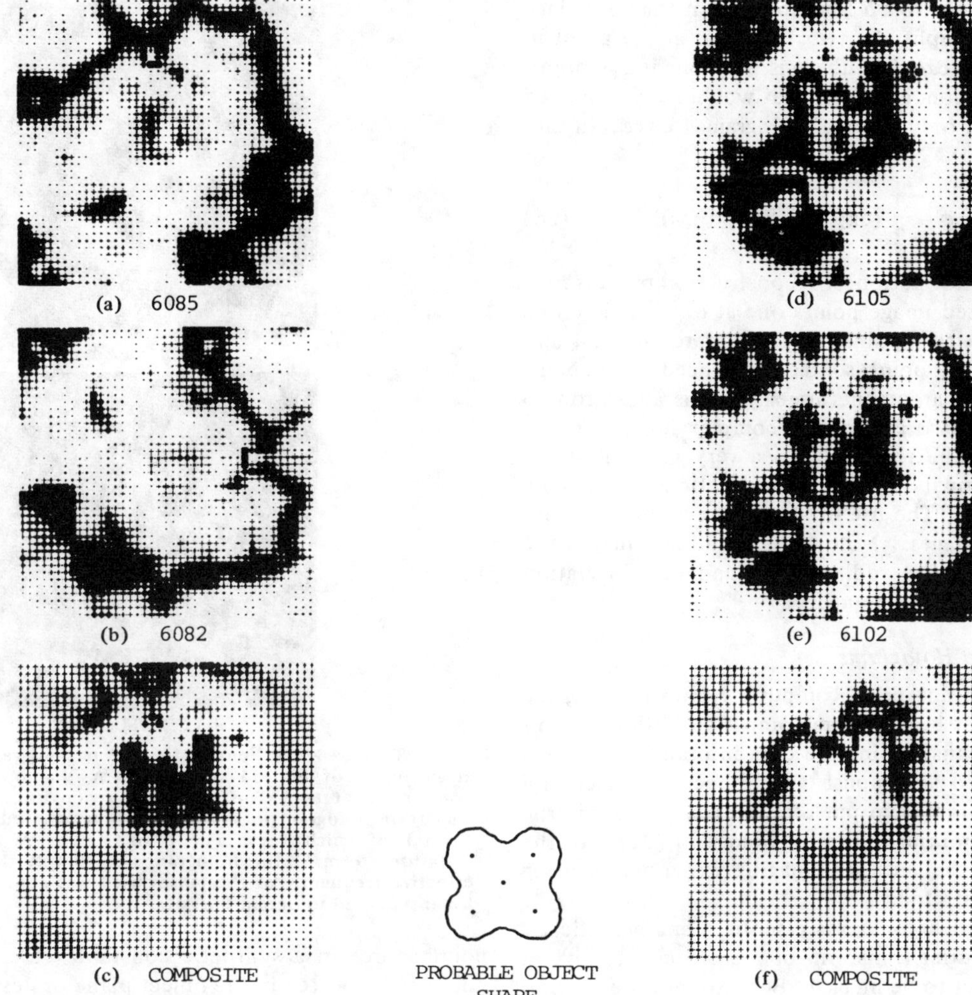

Fig. 13. Holograms made using data from the experiment of Fig. 1 and using synthetic reference sources at different depths as indicated. The true source is at an elevation of 6082 ft. In (b) the true source and reference source are superimposed and in (a) the reference is moved up the shothole by λ/16 or 3 ft. In (c) a composite is constructed and designed to enhance the λ/16 contour. It is clear from this result that only the object appears in the interferometric image. A similar set of holograms is shown in (d) through (f). Here the reference and true source are more widely separated but the two reference sources are close together (6105, 6102). Again only the object appears in the interferometric reconstruction.

There are a number of excellent reasons for using a computer for reconstructing holograms besides the fact that it improves the conventional optically reconstructed images. As we have seen from our earlier discussions on image enhancement techniques, holograms stored in computer memory may be readily added, subtracted, filtered and so on—all such operations being much easier to perform using the computer than their optical counterparts involving physical objects.

A. Removal of Conjugate Images

One of the immediate benefits of computer reconstruction is that the annoying conjugate images can easily be eliminated. This is accomplished by first taking or converting data to the form of a complex hologram the real and imaginary parts of which are in quadrature,

$$H = A \cos \phi + iA \sin \phi = A \exp (i\phi) \qquad (23)$$

where ϕ is the relative phase between the reference wave and the object wave.

The easiest way to see that this removes the conjugate image is to think of a one-dimensional analogy. Call the phase $\phi =$ $\omega_s X$, which is a model for a grating where ω_s is the spatial frequency and X is the distance along the grating and let us suppose that the reconstruction process involves a simple Fourier transformation of this one-dimensional hologram. Since a grating of this sort is very similar to the interference pattern produced by two point sources equidistant from the hologram plant, we expect the reconstruction or Fourier transformation of the grating to give two point sources. Note that all holograms are eventually converted to a form compatible with Fourier transformation in order to utilize computer reconstruction algorithms so that there is no loss of generality in this assumption. Fourier transforming or "reconstructing" H one has

$$A(\omega_s) = \frac{1}{\sqrt{2\pi}} \int H \exp (-i\omega_0 X) \, dx \qquad (24)$$

or

$$A(\omega_s) = \frac{A}{\sqrt{2\pi}} \int \exp [i(\omega_s - \omega_0)X] \, dx = A \, \delta(\omega_s - \omega_0). \qquad (25)$$

Now this is proportional to a δ function so that the only place the "reconstructed" amplitude $A(\omega_s)$ exists is at the point in the image where $\omega_s = \omega_0$, i.e., there is only one image point. Contrary to this situation, consider what would have happened had we reconstructed only the real hologram $A \cos \phi$. In that case

$$H = A \cos \phi = \frac{A}{2} \left(\exp (i\phi) + \exp (-i\phi) \right) \qquad (26)$$

and the Fourier transformation or reconstruction process now gives two reconstructed image points one at $\omega_s = \omega_0$ and one at $\omega_s = -\omega_0$. These two points correspond to the real and conjugate images of a point source referenced by a point source. The foregoing arguments are easily generalized to two dimensions. Hence, by starting with complex holograms the conjugate image may be removed and a very great improvement over conventional optical reconstructions of seismic holograms is achieved. The use of a complex hologram H has other practical advantages. Note that the added quadrature component $A \sin \phi$ carries additional redundant information which tends to improve image quality.

B. Fourier Transform Holograms

In order to take advantage of computer reconstruction, the holographic data must be in a form compatible with the algorithms available for transforming the data into an image. One convenient method to accomplish this, especially for certain geophysical applications, is to put the holographic data in the form of a so-called Fourier-transform hologram [32]. In the following, some of the author's imaging experiments using this approach are illustrated.

A Fourier transform hologram is essentially mathematically equivalent to the Fourier transform of the object intensity in the plane of the object to be imaged. Because they are Fourier transforms they may be readily reconstructed by using an inverse fast Fourier transform routine such as those based on the Cooley–Tukey FFT algorithm.[8]

In order to produce a Fourier-transform hologram from seismic field data, one may begin with a so-called plane wave or on-axis hologram. This type of hologram is simply made with effective local oscillator reference waves in quadrature which are supplied at the time the data is recorded or later from time traces via a computer.

To create a Fourier-transform hologram H' this plane wave complex hologram $H = A \cos \phi + iA \sin \phi$, treated as a vector in the complex plane must be rotated through an angle θ

$$RH = H' \qquad (27)$$

where

$$H = A \begin{pmatrix} \cos \phi \\ \sin \phi \end{pmatrix} \qquad (28)$$

and

$$R = \begin{pmatrix} \cos \theta & -\sin \theta \\ \sin \theta & \cos \theta \end{pmatrix}, \qquad \theta = \frac{2\pi R}{\lambda}. \qquad (29)$$

The phase factor $\theta = 2\pi R/\lambda$ is the phase due to a synthetic

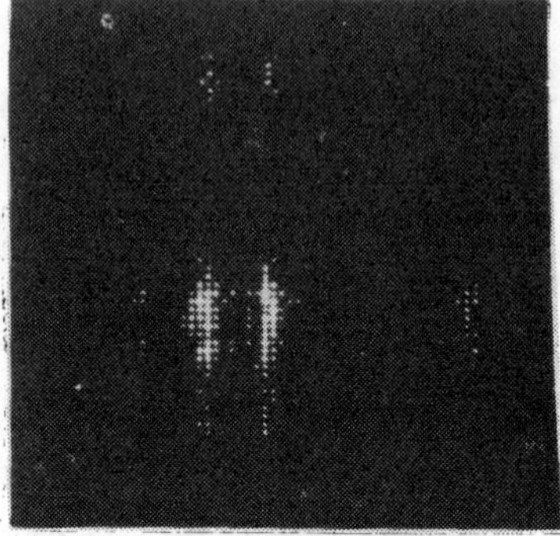

Fig. 14. This 64×64 Fourier transform hologram was made in the arrangement of Fig. 11 for the 10-in. diameter empty cylindrical hole in concrete. The computer reconstruction of the Fourier-transform hologram in this figure shows the edges of the cylinder, the axis of which was at a depth of 18 in below the concrete surface. Data used to make this hologram were simply the first arrivals. The effective frequency of the pulses used was about 50 kHz. A simple timer was used to obtain the data.

point source in a synthetic constant velocity reference medium and is located in the object plane or desired image plane.[9] This "rotated" or "migrated" hologram H' is the Fourier transform hologram and may be readily reconstructed using FFT routines as mentioned earlier. Note that once the data is in the form of a complex hologram, a great variety of phase "corrections" such as θ above can be handled in the same way. Thus corrections due to topographic distortion or velocity variations can be handled using the rotation matrix approach.

The Fourier-transform approach is not only a simple way to prepare data for the computer but it is also very compatible with the kinds of questions one asks of geophysical data. By choosing a point reference at an arbitrary depth Z below the hologram surface (ground surface), one is creating a Fourier transform of the scattered waves from the unknown objects in the vicinity of this depth. Consequently, the reconstructions will consist principally of objects at this depth. By creating a series of such Fourier transform holograms at a series of different depths and lateral locations, from the same initial data, one may reconstruct a series of images at each depth to discover what is actually present. In the not too distant past, before good FFT routines and hard wired systems for carrying them out, one might have successfully argued that the time to reconstruct so many Fourier transform holograms would be prohibitive, but with the advent of this new technology one may seriously consider reconstructing holograms through the interval of interest at fractions of a wavelength increments. These reconstructions can be so fast

---

[8] Examples of algorithms for performing the FFT which is the crucial algorithm in most computer reconstruction processes, are given by N. M. Brenner in "Three Fortran programs that perform the Cooley–Tukey Fourier Transform." Available from M.I.T. Lincoln Laboratory Publications, P.O. Box 73, Lexington, MA 02173.

[9] The reference medium is also assumed initially to have a constant p-wave velocity. Refinement of this approximation can be achieved by introducing various velocity models just as in the wave equation migration schemes.

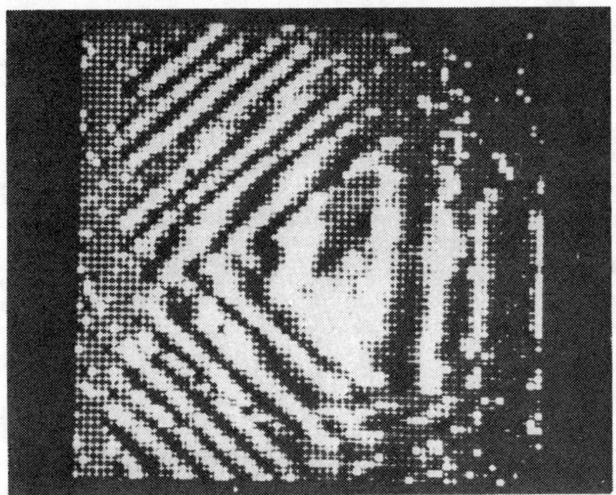

Fig. 15. A 64 × 64 Fourier transform hologram of "Y" hole resolution pattern at 4-in. depth in aluminum. Data was taken as 3.2 MHz in a reflection mode and transmitted to a minicomputer for reconstruction and display. The synthetic point source reference used in making this hologram was located at the center of the "Y" hole pattern. (See Fig. 17 for reconstruction.)

Fig. 16. Example of rectilinear scanner and water tank used to produce holograms. This scanner measures roughly 2 × 2 ft. This scanner was used to produce the hologram of Fig. 15.

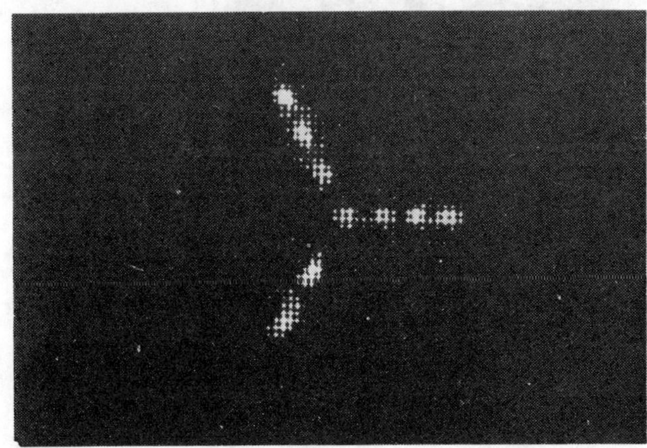

Fig. 17. Computer reconstruction of Fig. 15 showing a "Y" pattern of drillhole tops. Minimum hole spacing, about three wavelengths of ultrasound in aluminum (at 3.2 MHz).

(state-of-the-art hardware and software would allow a 256 × 256 hologram to be reconstructed in a fraction of a second) that it may soon become possible to effectively "focus" at different depths in a near real-time manner using the computer. This would mean that once data had been collected holographically or converted to this form preliminary reconstructions could be done in the field.

C. Examples of Computer Reconstructions

The following are examples of holograms and computer reconstructions of data taken in the laboratory and in the field.

Fig. 11 illustrates an experiment performed in 1974 by the author in a laboratory seismic model. The model consisted of a 6-ft cube of concrete (gravel $\frac{1}{4}$ in or less was used) containing various embedded objects, one of which was a 10-in diameter cylindrical hole. A fixed source transducer located at S generated pulses at about 50 kHz, which propagated to the 30 × 30 in array at H. The source-detector travel time (first arrival time) at each point in the array was measured with a simple timer. The first-arrival data was used in the method described earlier to compute the holograms using a synthetic-point reference provided by a computer program. The synthetic reference source used to produce the hologram was located on the cylinder axis. Fig. 14 shows the hologram and a computer reconstructed image of the bright cylinder edges in the vicinity of the reference source. By moving the synthetic reference source to other positions along the cylinder axis, other parts of the cylinder were also imaged (not shown).

As another example of what can be done using a computer consider Fig. 15. This is a 64 × 64 hologram[10] array (original hologram measured 3 × 3 in) plotted on a CRT screen by a minicomputer. The data was scanned in a rectilinear fashion using a small scanner similar to that shown in Fig. 16. Data from the scanner was converted to a hologram value, digitized and transmitted to a Nova 3/12 minicomputer system. The computer converts the data into new holograms characteristic of different focal depths of interest and then calculates and plots the reconstructed image.

Fig. 17 illustrates the reconstruction of Fig. 15. The target was a "Y" resolution pattern of vertical drill holes at a depth 4 in from the surface in an aluminum block. Data was taken at 3.2 MHz and a synthetic point reference at the center of the "Y" pattern was chosen. The closely spaced holes in the reconstruction are separated by approximately three wavelength of ultrasound. The quality of the reconstructed image is impressive, being somewhat better than the optically reconstructed counterpart (not shown). Holograms made of the same subject but using 256 × 256 scanned arrays are even better owing to the increase in redundant data. One reason for this improvement is the absence of certain aberrations when reconstructing an acoustical hologram with a computer. That is, the reconstructing wavelength is the same in the calculations as in the experiment that produced the data. In optical reconstruction the wavelength of the laser is much shorter than the ultrasound wavelength which leads to aberrations and distortions in the image.

A second reason the computer images shown here are of excellent quality is that the computer generated hologram contains 16 levels of gray rather than the two levels commonly used when a storage oscilloscope is used to store holograms. Typically when a hologram transparency is to be produced, a "print" or "no print" situation is set up to produce high-contrast fringes depending on whether the returned scanned signals are in phase or out of phase with an arbitrary reference

---

[10] Holograms as large as 256 × 256 are also easily-accommodated by the same basic technique but take longer to reconstruct.

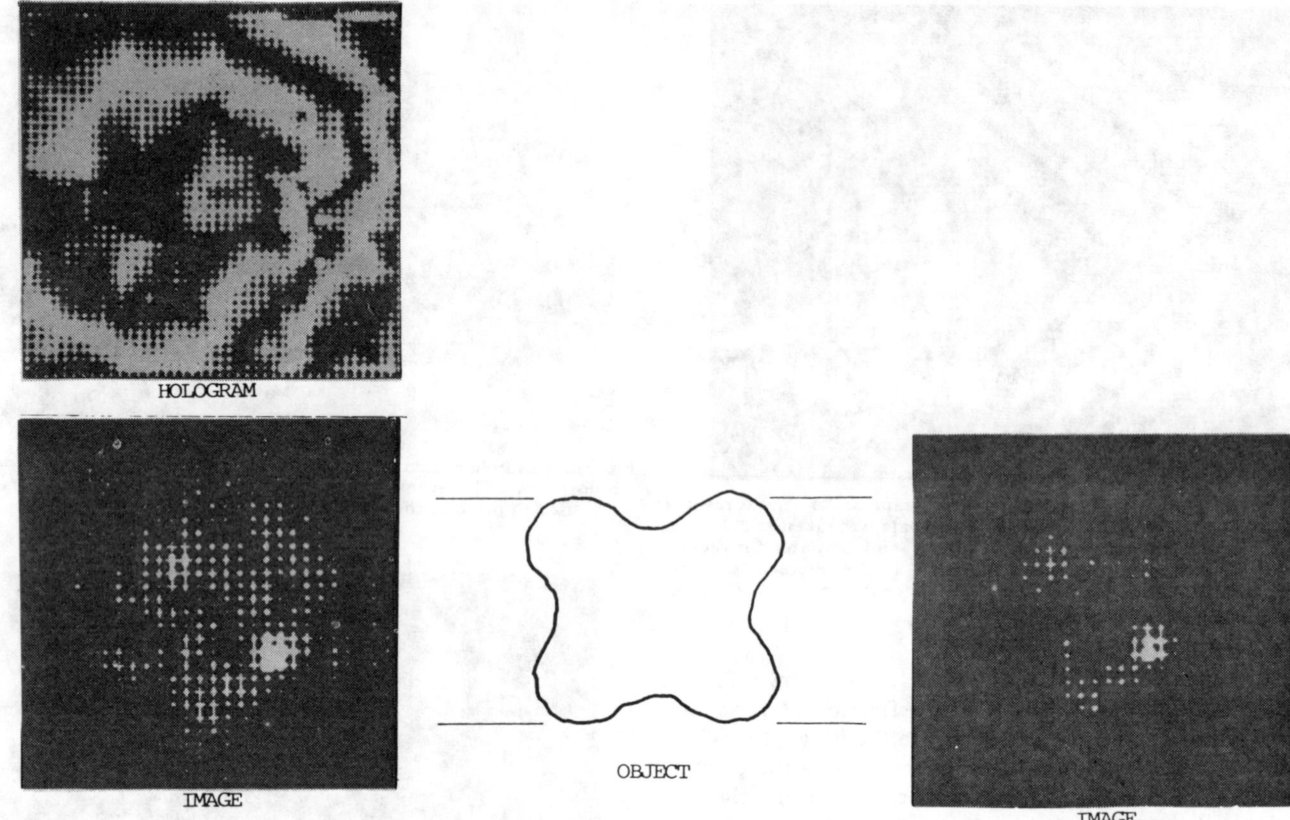

Fig. 18. Illustration of images of computer reconstructed seismic field data at two different contrast levels, showing parts of a four lobed pattern of crushed rock at a depth of 80 ft. The object, shown schematically, was approximately 100 ft in diameter and the hologram measured 226 ft on a side. (See Fig. 1 for further details.)

wave. This results in a loss of gray value information, which results in a loss of image data and explains in part why a computer-generated hologram is far superior to an acoustical hologram stored on film.

All of the foregoing reconstructions and displays were in the horizontal plane or "C" display format. One may also perform reconstructions if desired in the "B" mode where the earth or the specimen is seen in vertical cross section. This is a more natural (traditional) mode of display for seismic data. Note that Farr [11] displayed his field data reconstructions in both the B- and C-scan modes.

Finally we illustrate (Fig. 18) a computer reconstruction of the author's field data discussed earlier (Fig. 1 and Fig. 13). This computer reconstruction is far superior to the laser reconstruction shown in Fig. 2.

D. Backward Wave Propagation or Frequency Domain Migration

The reader will have noticed that in reconstructing the Fourier transform hologram we required a single FFT operation. However, before this could be accomplished certain "rotations" of the plane wave hologram in the complex plane had to be done which introduced what may be called propagation or "migration" phase factors for each point in the hologram array. An alternative way to reconstruct an image is by means of a procedure variously called "backward wave propagation," "backward wave reconstruction imaging" or by some just "migration."

In these techniques which are not holographic in the sense that no reference wave is used to produce an interferogram or hologram, complete time traces are first recorded. From these time traces a given amplitude at a given frequency is obtained by Fourier transformation of the time traces. These amplitudes are then decomposed into their plane-wave components by spatial Fourier transformation. Then appropriate phase factors are introduced to carry each of these plane waves to the desired image plane. Once this "migration" is accomplished the amplitudes are spatially inverse Fourier transformed and an image is calculated by calculating the intensity corresponding to this resultant amplitude. The calculations of phase factors often involve a model of a known or inferred multilayer velocity section.

Even though this technique for reconstructing images takes two spatial FFT operations and a temporal Fourier transformation for each trace it seems to have certain advantages in some cases over the holographic scheme outlined above where only a single spatial FFT is used and no temporal Fourier transformation is required. In particular, after the second spatial transform has been done, one need only supply phase factors to obtain reconstructed amplitudes for focal planes adjacent to the chosen focal plane and no Fourier transformation is required to obtain these amplitudes. In the holographic reconstruction one usually reconstructs a hologram for each focal plane. The interested reader is directed to several excellent papers by Clairbout [26], for details on other wave equation migration techniques which involve similar velocity models and phase factor adjustments. Finally it should be noted that the experiment of Hildebrand and Fandneff [12] in which near surface trenches were being imaged, used a backward wave propagation reconstruction technique or frequency domain migration technique to obtain their images. They used first arrival information to determine their component amplitudes instead of temporally Fourier transforming full time traces. These amplitudes were then spatially Fourier transformed as described above and a two layer velocity model was used to obtain the "migrated" component amplitudes. These amplitudes were then spatially transformed again to obtain an amplitude from which an image intensity could be calculated.

E. Holograms that are Their Own Reconstructions

The reconstruction techniques via computer discussed up to now all involve one or more applications of an algorithm such as the fast Fourier transform for spatially transforming the data array to an image array. There is another approximate way to obtain reconstructions, however, that does not involve such algorithms, and is often useful in obtaining an "image" when holograms are made with effective point source illumination and a depth model of the velocities present is known. The technique usually requires that a transmission arrangement be used but it is also possible to imagine pulse-echo applications[11] using focused array techniques.

By moving the synthetic reference source used in making a through-transmission hologram to the true source position, the number of hologram fringes will be reduced and a more or less realistic projected image should be obtained in the case of a transmission geometry. Note that, qualitatively, an image reconstructed from such a hologram has a functional form given by

$$I \sim \cos(\theta_0' - \theta_0) + \text{(slowly varying terms)} \qquad (30)$$

where θ_0 is a phase angle, $\theta_0 = \theta_0(x, y, z)$ that is characteristic of an unscattered wave, and $\theta_0' = \theta_0'(x, y, z)$ is a phase characteristic of a scattered wave. Now note that a similar function is obtained when a hologram is made by placing the reference source in the same position as the true source. Since the reference source wave describes a reference medium without an object, it is physically similar to the unscattered wave described by θ_0; call it θ_1. The actual source wave transmitted through (or around) the object is physically similar to the scattered wave described by θ_0'; call it θ_1'.

Thus the hologram made with the reference source located at the true source has a functional variation on its surface given approximately by

$$H \sim \cos(\theta_1' - \theta_1) + \text{(slowly varying terms)}. \qquad (31)$$

This is essentially of the same form except for factors of propagation as the image variation described in (30). This means that we can "reconstruct" simple transmission holograms without the laser or FFT routines by merely examining the hologram made with the true source and the reference source superimposed. The hologram is, in a sense, its own reconstruction. Of course, the image plane is now the hologram plane, so that these images are out of focus projected images and depth information will have been lost. However, the quality of these images is often superior to the laser reconstructions in spite of these limitations and it is rapid.

The holograms of Fig. 13 illustrating an image enhancement technique[11] were made in this way and provide an excellent

[11] The image enhancement technique however does not require that this type of interferometric imaging be used. We could also use a computer or a laser to reconstruct the images. The interferometric imaging technique is used here because we have a very simple through transmission geometry and because we wanted to illustrate this approach to imaging.

projected image of the underground fracture zone known to be at the field site.

In the case of a reflection geometry as in large-scale pulse-echo applications, this approach to imaging requires the true point source to be located at the object surface to be imaged. This has been done in ultrasonic imaging where a focused source-receive transducer is used to provide the focusing mechanism. The holograms produced in this way, called surface fringe holograms [27] in many cases provide excellent images of objects. Again it is the hologram itself that is the image and not a reconstruction of this hologram. To apply this technique in the field case would require some type of effective array focusing and this probably rules out large applications for the immediate future. However, it is worth keeping in mind that the transform algorithms for reconstructing holograms are not always a strict necessity in forming images and we should remain open to such possibilities when designing new field experiments.

F. Correlation Holography

It should be noted that the correlation imaging technique described earlier (see (3)) is similar in philosophy to the above interferometric imaging techniques discussed in the previous section in that holograms are compared. In the general technique employed by Farr [12] many different holograms arising from synthetic point scatterers are correlated with the entire measured hologram and this number is taken to be the recorded image intensity of the test point. In the above method the measured hologram is compared with the hypothetical hologram that would have been present had the object not been present.

VIII. CURRENT ANTICIPATED APPLICATIONS

There has been steady progress since the late 1960's in the application of holographic data processing techniques to problems in the earth sciences. In this section, we will begin with a discussion of National Science Foundation (RANN) sponsored work, the eventual purpose of which is to outfit a tunneling machine with an acoustical holography imaging system.

The possibility of using holographic interferometry and related techniques to monitor large underground in-situ oil shale retorts will also be discussed briefly. Finally, the possibility of mapping the focal region of an earthquake zone using the focal region associated sources as they "scan" throughout this region will be discussed.

A. Holographic Imaging Systems for Tunneling Machines

Tunnel boring machines are usually very effective systems for constructing tunnels inexpensively, efficiently, and very quickly in comparison with conventional drill and blast technologies. Unfortunately, the geologic setting in which these systems sometimes operate are unpredictable. Unforeseen hazards to equipment and personnel in the form of bad rock conditions and gas or water-filled cavities are often encountered.

An on-going project at the Holosonics Richland facility to study the applications of holography to these problems is the NSF (RANN) sponsored work mentioned earlier [6], [7]. The purpose of this applied research project is to determine the feasibility of outfitting a tunneling machine with an acoustical holography imaging system. Laboratory experiments involving a large 5-ft diameter scanner in conjunction with a large seismic model are being carried out to test data gathering, data transmission and data processing and display systems.

B. The Experimental System

Fig. 5 illustrates an acoustical scanner designed to test some of the ideas and subsystems that will be needed to outfit tunneling machines with acoustical holography inspection systems. The scanner is 5 ft in diameter and is rail-mounted above a water-covered 10-ft cube of concrete located adjacent to a ten by 10 by 10-ft deep water tank. The concrete cube has numerous permanently embedded objects and various objects may be placed in the water tank and changed at will.

The prototype illustrated in Fig. 5 is not the system that would be used on an actual tunneling machine. No scanner, as such, would be used but rather the rotating head of the machine would be fitted with up to twenty receiving transducers and several sources. Data would be recorded holographically and stored in computer core memory for processing and display calculations.

Several optical reconstructions of holograms taken at a frequency of 125 kHz in the 10-ft-deep water tank are shown in Figs. 6 and 7. These hologram reconstructions were obtained by first photographing an image of the acoustic hologram formed on a storage scope. A transparency of each of these holograms was then illuminated with a laser and the images were formed. These images of objects in water are of excellent quality, but the real test is to determine what can be seen in a rock-like solid such as concrete.

Fig. 8(b) shows a print of a hologram of a line (4-ft long) of six 6-in diameter styrofoam spheres located at a depth of 4 ft in the concrete model. The reconstructed image of the six spheres is also shown in Fig. 8(b). The successful imaging of targets at 4 ft in concrete shown in that figure represents a significant test of the general imaging system in a solid-rock-like material.

In the final tunneling machine application, these laser reconstruction processes would be too time consuming. An entirely different approach to forming images is needed. To fill this need, a computer may be used to reconstruct holograms from digitized holographic data in near real time as the tunneling machine progresses.

C. Computer Reconstruction and Display

The present system for the RANN program study can reconstruct holograms using either the laser method or computer-assisted techniques. The data acquisition scanner (Fig. 5), a data transmission system, a data processing system (Nova 3/12 minicomputer), and a data display system (Tektronix 4013 terminal) have all been linked.

This system makes it possible to transmit acoustical hologram data to a minicomputer where it may be reconstructed using computer software and then displayed for visual analysis. Data organizing and transmission functions are overseen by an MOS Technology KIM-1 microcomputer which is also capable of supplying reference wave phase look-up tables for special reference waves.

Two local oscillator reference waves 90° out of phase are combined with the received signal from the object, and two quadrature hologram values $H_1 \sim \cos \phi$ and $H_2 \sim \sin \phi$ are formed. These hologram values are digitized and transmitted in real time at a rate of 64 kBd (1 Bd = 1 bit/s) to the minicomputer along with the x, y coordinate data specifying the loca-

tion of the scanning transducer. In the present experimental arrangement, the scanner and minicomputer are separated by about one hundred meters, but this distance could be kilometers if necessary.

Next, a minicomputer program is used to "rotate" the complex hologram vector $H_1 + iH_2$ to any new hologram $H_1' + iH_2'$ where the primed hologram is characteristic of a new reference wave that makes possible a reconstruction in the desired image plane. This gives us great flexibility, since it means that only one complex hologram $H_1 + iH_2$ need be scanned and sent to the minicomputer for storage. Other holograms characteristic of other reference waves and other focal depths may be computed from this one set of data. Holograms are reconstructed by simply Fourier-transforming the hologram $H_1' + iH_2'$ where the H' values are calculated using a point reference source at the depth of interest. Input of the depth or distance from the hologram into the computer keyboard produces an image at this depth.

In Fig. 9, a print of a 64 $\times$ 64 hologram array representing a fraction of the circular scan which includes one styrofoam sphere embedded in concrete. This data was plotted by the minicomputer on the display monitor, producing the image seen in Fig. 9. The hologram of the corner of a 4-in-thick granite slab shown in Fig. 10 yields the minicomputer-generated image seen in Fig. 10.

The entire process of scanning, processing, reconstructing and displaying images takes about 10 min with the present system. In a final application, many detectors would be placed on the tunneling machine head, allowing the entire scanning process to take place in several tens of seconds. Since tunneling machines typically have downtimes ranging up to five minutes for each meter of progress, this time is not a limiting factor in the efficiency of the operation.

Reconstruction times can also be reduced drastically by using specialized hardwired systems such as array processors for computing fast Fourier transforms and performing other data manipulations. If all of these systems and subsystems can be effectively ruggedized, the foregoing results make it clear that a practical imaging system for a tunneling machine is a realistic goal.

D. Monitoring Burning Fronts in Oil-Shale Retorts

In a previous section on image enhancement it was shown that if a complex medium changes and if "before" and "after" holograms are made, a considerable amount of subtle information regarding these changes can be extracted. This has led to the idea that such man-made underground features as a modified oil-shale retort could be monitored using holograms during the retorting process.

Knowledge of how the so-called burning front[12] progresses in these retorts is crucial if the efficiency of these systems is ever to be fully understood. Borehole holographic systems and imaging schemes using low-frequency acoustic signals are have been developed by the author and others to study this problem and other problems related to *in situ* oil-shale retorting. The hope is that the retort could be monitored on a day-by-day basis using the special image enhancement techniques and computer reconstruction techniques described earlier.

---

[12] A burning front is not merely a surface temperature change but is accompanied by chemical and physical changes such as changes in Young's modulus and mass density. Thus for example, the p-wave velocity will be altered by retorting.

E. Earthquake Focal Region Mapping

The possibility of imaging very large portions of the earth using holographic principles has always seemed to be an exciting long range goal for those working in applications of seismic holography. Indeed, the term "earth holography" which seems to have been coined by Farr [2] implies this ultimate application. The author considered using natural impulsive sources in making seismic holograms of the earths crust [22] as have several Soviet authors [5].

Recently these and other ideas have materialized into a joint Soviet–U.S. workshop to study these problems currently planned for the late winter of 1978 or Spring of 1979. The purpose of this workshop will be in part to discuss the applications of holography and related techniques to the specific problem of mapping the focal regions of possible earthquake zones.

If applications of this type come to pass they would certainly represent an exciting advancement in the range of problems to which holographic imaging techniques will have been applied.

IX. Conclusions

It is now about 10 years after the first field experiments in seismic holography were performed. Activity and interest in this field extends from the oil and mineral industries to those engaged in mapping earthquake focal regions using natural seismic sources to make holograms. Sufficient practical experience now exists so that even more ambitious and sophisticated experiments are likely to be attempted in the near future.

Like the conventional seismic techniques that have seen continued improvements during the last half century, the newer holographic techniques are also seeing continued qualitative improvements. Because these new techniques open the possibility of new data and image enhancement schemes, there is the promise of eventually extracting even more useful information from seismic data and possibly at less cost. It may very well be that these capabilities could lead to improved techniques for locating scarce energy and mineral resources. Thus the qualitative improvements in data analysis promised by the holographic techniques comes at an opportune time.

Acknowledgment

The author would like to thank Beth Haire for typing earlier versions of this manuscript and Patty Hays for aid in editing the manuscript. The author also thanks Michelle Maes and Vidette Bullock for final preparation of the manuscript after the authors arrival at the University of Houston. He is especially indebted to Robert Steffens (of Holosonics) who, on short notice, designed and built an excellent summation amplifier for use in some of our reciprocity experiments.

References

[1] A. F. Metherell, H. M. A. El-Sum, J. J. Dreher, and L. Larmore, "Introduction to acoustical holography," *J. Acoust. Soc. Am.*, vol. 42, no. 4, pp. 733–742, 1967.

[2] J. B. Farr, "Earth holography: A potential new seismic method," presented at the 38th Annual Meeting of the Society of Exploration Geophysicists (R-17), Denver, CO, Oct. 1968.

[3] D. Silverman, U.S. Patent 34 000 363, 1968.

[4] R. K. Mueller, and N. V. Sheridon, "Sound holograms and optical reconstruction," *Appl. Phys. Lett.*, vol. 9, no. 9, pp. 328–329, Nov. 1966. B. B. Brenden and P. B. Kidmon, U.S. Patent 3 683 679, 1972.

D. Gabor, "A new microscope principle," *Nature*, vol. 161, p. 777, 1948, and "Microscopy by reconstructed wavefronts," *Proc. Roy. Soc.* A, vol. 197, p. 454, 1949. E. N. Leith, and J. Upatnieks, *J. Opt. Soc. Amer.*, vol. 52, pp. 1123–1130, 1962, and vol. 33, p. 1377, 1963.

[5] S. D. Vinogradov, A. V. Nikolaev, P. A. Troitsky, and D. D. Scheimer, "An estimation of possibilities of large seismic arrays in the study of the earth structure by means of seismic holography," Joint USSR-USA rep. on the problem of earthquake forecasting Dushanbe, *Donish*, Book I, vol. 2, 1976 (in Russian).

[6] G. L. Fitzpatrick and T. O. Price, "Acoustical holography goes underground," *Opt. Spec.*, Sept. 1977.

[7] ——, "Scanned acoustical holography for geological prediction in advance of rapid underground excavation," Conf. Proc. sponsored by the National Science Foundation/RANN *Research in Excavation Technology* (770078), Apr. 26–28, p. 53, 1977.

[8] W. E. Leriwell, "Holography at seismic frequency," presented at the European Association of Exploration Geophysicists (EAEG) (Venice, Italy, 1969).

[9] G. L. Fitzpatrick and R. K. Mueller, "Seismic holography," presented at the 82nd Annu. Meeting of the Acoust. Soc. of Amer. (Denver, CO, Oct. 1971). Two experiments were discussed; the author's 1969 field experiment (see [11]) and the Mueller-Steinberg–Farr experiments (see [15]).

[10] G. L. Fitzpatrick, H. R. Nicholls, and R. D. Munson, "An Experiment in seismic holography," *Bureau of Mines Rep. Inv.* 7607, p. 20, 1972.

[11] J. B. Farr, "Earth holography to delineate buried structures," in *Acoustical Holography*, vol. 6, Newell Booth, Ed. New York: Plenum Press, 1975, pp. 435–467.

[12] Private communication, B. P. Hildebrand, and G. A. Fandneff, Batelle Northwest Research Labs, Richland, WA, to be published in *Acoustic Imaging and Holography*, vol. 1, no. 2. New York: Crane Russak, 1978.

[13] R. F. Steinberg, "Seismic holography for underground viewing," *ARPA Rep.* no. 6276, July 1972.

[14] *Handbook of Physics*, E. U. Condon and H. Odishaw, Eds. New York: McGraw-Hill Book Company, 1958, Part 6, p. 79.

[15] B. B. Brenden, "Acoustical Holography," *J. of Physics "E" Sci. Instrum.*, vol. 8, pp. 885–894, 1975.

[16] Willard H. Wells, "Acoustical imaging with linear transducer arrays," *Acoustical Holography*, vol. 2, A. F. Metherell and L. A. Larmore, Eds. New York: Plenum Press, 1970, pp. 87–103.

[17] D. M. Milder, and W. H. Wells, "Acoustic Holography with Crossed Linear Arrays," *IBM J. Res. Dev.*, vol. 14, no. 5, pp. 492–500, Sept. 1970.

[18] G. L. Fitzpatrick, "First-Arrival Seismic Holograms," *Acoustical Holography*, vol. 4, Glen Wade, Ed. New York: Plenum Press, 1972, pp. 381–399.

[19] J. B. Farr, "Acoustical Holography Experiments Using Digital Processing," *Acoustical Holography*, vol. 2, A. F. Metherell and L. A. Larmore, Eds. New York: Plenum Press, 1970, pp. 225–42.

[20] Private Communication, Odd Lovhaugen and Jakob Stamnes, Central Institute for Industrial Research Forkningsv, 1, p. b. 350, Blindern, Oslo 3, Norway; S. Ljunggren, O. Lovhaugen and E. Mehlum, "Seismic Holography in a Norweigian Fjord," presented at the Eighth Int. Symp. Acoust. Imaging (Key Biscayne, FL, May 29–June 2, 1978).

[21] P. N. Keating, R. K. Mueller, and R. R. Gupta, "Conventional and Weak Signal Enhancement Holography in the Presence of Measurement Errors," *Acoustical Holography*, vol. 4, Glen Wade, Ed. New York: Plenum Press, 1972, pp. 251–65.

[22] D. Gabor, G. W. Stroke, R. Restrick, A. Funkhouser, and D. Brum, "Optical Image Synthesis (Complex Amplitude Addition and Subtraction), by Holographic Fourier Transformation," *Phys. Lett.*, vol. 18, no. 2, pp. 116–18, 1965.

[23] G. L. Fitzpatrick, "Phase-Contrast Enhancement Without Spatial Filters for Seismic Holography," *Bureau of Mines Rep. of Inv.* 7721, 1973, p. 17.

[24] G. L. Fitzpatrick and L. P. Yoder, "Threefold seismic or acoustical holographic interferograms for improved reconstructed-image definition and contrast," *Acoustical Imaging and Holography*, vol. 1, no. 1. New York: Crane Russak, Oct. 1978.

[25] G. W. Stroke, *An Introduction to Coherent Optics and Holography*. New York: Academic Press, 1966, p. 270.

[26] J. F. Claerbout, and S. M. Doherty, "Downward Continuation of Moveout-Corrected Seismograms," *Geophysics*, vol. 37, no. 5, Oct. 1972, pp. 741–68. D. C. Riley and J. F. Claerbout, "2-D Multiple Reflections," *Geophysics*, vol. 41, no. 4, Aug. 1976, pp. 592–620.

[27] H. D. Collins, "Acoustical interferometry using electronically simulated variable reference with multiple path techniques," *Acoustical Holography*, vol. 6, Newell Booth, Ed. New York: Plenum Press, 1978, pp. 597–620.

Geomagnetic Depth Sounding by Means of Oceanographic and Aeromagnetic Surveys

GIOVANNI P. GREGORI AND LOUIS J. LANZEROTTI, MEMBER, IEEE

Abstract—The investigation of underground conductivity structures by means of geomagnetic data (i.e., geomagnetic depth sounding (GDS)) has been extensively carried out over land areas using three component recordings. However, the large amount of data collected for many years by airborne and/or shipborne magnetometry all over the world have generally been used to infer only static magnetic anomalies. The time-varying magnetic field has normally been subtracted as an unwanted nuisance. An immediate application of the land-based GDS techniques to airborne and shipborne surveys is not possible because normally these latter surveys measure only the total field intensity. Notwithstanding such a substantial limitation, we discuss three possible techniques for performing GDS analyses by means of aeromagnetic and oceanographic ship surveys. We conclude that GDS analyses can be performed at differing levels of sophistication which can be expected to provide important information on the location (at least) of principal conductivity anomalies associated with, e.g., ocean ridges, volcanic areas, and similar features.

Manuscript received July 20, 1978; revised November 27, 1978.
G. P. Gregori is with Istituto di Fisica dell'Atmosfera (CNR), 00144 Rome, Italy.
L. J. Lanzerotti is with Bell Laboratories, Murray Hill, NJ 07974.

I. INTRODUCTION

GEOMAGNETIC surveys by means of airborne or shipborne magnetometers have long been conducted, covering a large fraction of the earth (see, e.g., [1] and [2]). Most frequently, the quantity measured is the total intensity $|B(t)|$ of the geomagnetic field $B(t)$, but not its direction. Two types of data can be obtained: i) the static geomagnetic field over a site; i.e., the time constant part of the field that is normally associated with the local magnetization properties of the earth's crust and its "geomagnetic anomalies," and ii) the time-varying geomagnetic field; i.e., the field that is normally associated with induction in local conductivity structures and to "conductivity anomalies," where the induced telluric currents are flowing. The time-varying magnetic field data have nearly always been considered unwanted, serving mainly as a nuisance. Its subtraction can raise problems in data analyses, particularly during geomagnetically disturbed periods (see, e.g., [3]).

Reprinted from *Proc. IEEE*, vol. 67, pp. 1029–1034, July 1979.

Geomagnetic depth sounding (GDS) is the name coined [4] for probing the underground conductivity using only the time-varying geomagnetic field. In its usual definition, the technique involves the use of three orthogonal components of the geomagnetic field $B(t)$. We discuss in this paper the possibilities of performing some GDS analyses using only the record of the total field intensity $|B(t)|$ that is most often obtained by aeromagnetic and oceanographic surveys. That is, we emphasize the use of the time-varying portion of the field for this purpose.

II. A Prior Example

We are aware of only one example of an attempt at geomagnetic depth sounding using aeromagnetic surveys that has been reported in the literature [5]. We discuss this important investigation in the following from a point of view rather different than the original. In main, the scope of that investigation was principally concerned with a search for geomagnetic anomalies rather than with conductivity anomalies using GDS techniques.

LeBorgne and Le Mouël [5] used aeromagnetic surveys of northern Morocco and the Alboran Sea and deduced a deep seated "conductivity channel" from the data. The procedure was to use data from a reference station (s; located close to Almeira, Spain, 25 km inland) and to estimate an average magnetic field value $\hat{B}_s$ for the station, employing the average of the total set of measured hourly values between 02 and 03 UT. Le Borgne and Le Mouël [5] assumed that at any given point P (away from the reference station) the measured magnetic field $B_P(t)$ was related to the field at the reference station as

$$|B_P(t)| - B_P = |B_s(t)| - \hat{B}_s. \qquad (1)$$

That is, the instantaneous deviation at any given point P of $|B_P(t)|$ from some average value $\hat{B}_P$, is identical to the instantaneous deviation of $|B_s(t)|$ at the reference station s, from $\hat{B}_s$. From (1) it follows that

$$\hat{B}_P = |B_P(t)| - |B_s(t)| + \hat{B}_s \qquad (2)$$

or $\hat{B}_P$ is equal to the difference between the instantaneous measurements, aside from the constant $\hat{B}_s$. Finally, Le Borgne and Le Mouël [5] used two independent measurements of $\hat{B}_P$, made at times t_1 and t_2, and computed the difference between the two estimates of B_P. They found a systematic difference, depending upon location, and concluded that the results provided evidence for the geographical location of a "deep seated conductivity channel."

Unfortunately, there can be serious errors in employing (1) (and thus (2)) for GDS studies. First, in general, the external origin field can have a scale size substantially smaller than the distance between s and P. Moreover, the scale size can change substantially with time. Second, even if the field scale size is sufficiently large, the underground conductivity structures at the two sites can respond (and likely do) in very different ways to the input signal; such differences can also depend upon frequency. The difference can be expected to be particularly large if either point P or the reference site is located near a conductivity structure itself, such as the coast line near Almeira.

Thus if it is assumed that at different times t_1 and t_2 the external origin field has a different spectral composition, the conductivity structures under s and P will respond differently. The result given by (2) will be substantially different at the times t_1 and t_2. For $t_2 - t_1$ short on the time scale of magneto-spheric and ionospheric processes, the value of (2) at the two times will be quite similar. In addition, for P and s sufficiently close that the conductivities under both sites are similar, the result given by (2) will also be small at a given time. Such effects have been reported [6], [7].

Summarizing, the larger the difference between the two estimates of $\hat{B}_P$ at times t_1 and t_2 (provided that $t_2 - t_1$ is large on the magnetosphere/ionosphere time scale and that s and P are distantly separated), the more singular is the underground conductivity structure at P. This is the solution desired. However, in this case, the initial starting equation (1) is not satisfied! In essence, a "correct" conclusion is reached from incorrect initial assumptions.

In the next section we discuss alternative approaches to the Le Borgne and Le Mouël method in order to overcome limitations inherent either in the initial assumption (1) or in the use of only one reference station.

III. Generalizations

A. Deviations from Linear Relationships

Consider a point P with a field $|B_P(t)|$ and a reference station s with field $|B_s(t)|$. Perform measurements simultaneously at P and s. Plot $|B_P(t)|$ versus $|B_s(t)|$. Whenever the underground conductivity structure is identical at P and s (assuming P and s are sufficiently close so that the external input field can be assumed uniform). then

$$|B_s(t)| = |B_P(t)|. \qquad (3)$$

If several sites $P_1, P_2, P_3, \ldots, P_n$ are considered, then the larger the deviation of $|B_{P_i}(t)|$ is from the simple relation (3), the closer P_i is to some conductivity anomaly. This is equivalent to the Le Borgne and Le Mouël [5] procedure where a linear relationship

$$|B_{P_i}(t)| = |B_s(t)| + \text{const}_i \qquad (4)$$

is assumed. The expression (4) gives parallel lines in a $|B_P(t)|$ versus $|B_s(t)|$ plot, each line characterized by a value of the constant. The conductivity anomaly is located where $|\text{const}_i|$ is a maximum.

Rather than the "additive criteria" assumption (4), a "multiplicative criteria" assumption, e.g.,

$$|B_P(t)| = |B_s(t)| \cdot \text{const}_i \qquad (5)$$

could be used. Such an assumption has been employed by many authors in the framework of other GDS investigations (e.g., [8]–[11]). Equation (5) represents a set of straight lines through the origin, each with a slope depending upon the constant. A conductivity anomaly is expected whenever a slope (a constant) is either a maximum or a minimum with respect to the general trend of the set of computed points.

B. Multiple-Reference Stations

As noted in the second section, the choice of the reference station s can be an important factor in planning an actual analysis. Thus consider several reference stations $s_1, s_2, \cdots, s_m$. Then plot in a $(m + 1)$-dimensional vector space the points with coordinates $(|B_{s_1}(t)|, |B_{s_2}(t)|, \cdots, |B_{s_m}(t)|, |B_P(t)|)$ for different times t. In general $|B_P(t)|$ will be a function of $\{|B_{s_i}(t)|\}$ $(i = 1, 2, \cdots, m)$. The plotted points will thus cluster around a surface of dimension m (at most) in the $(m + 1)$-dimensional space. For example, if $m = 2$, the points should cluster around a surface Γ_P in the 3-dimensional space

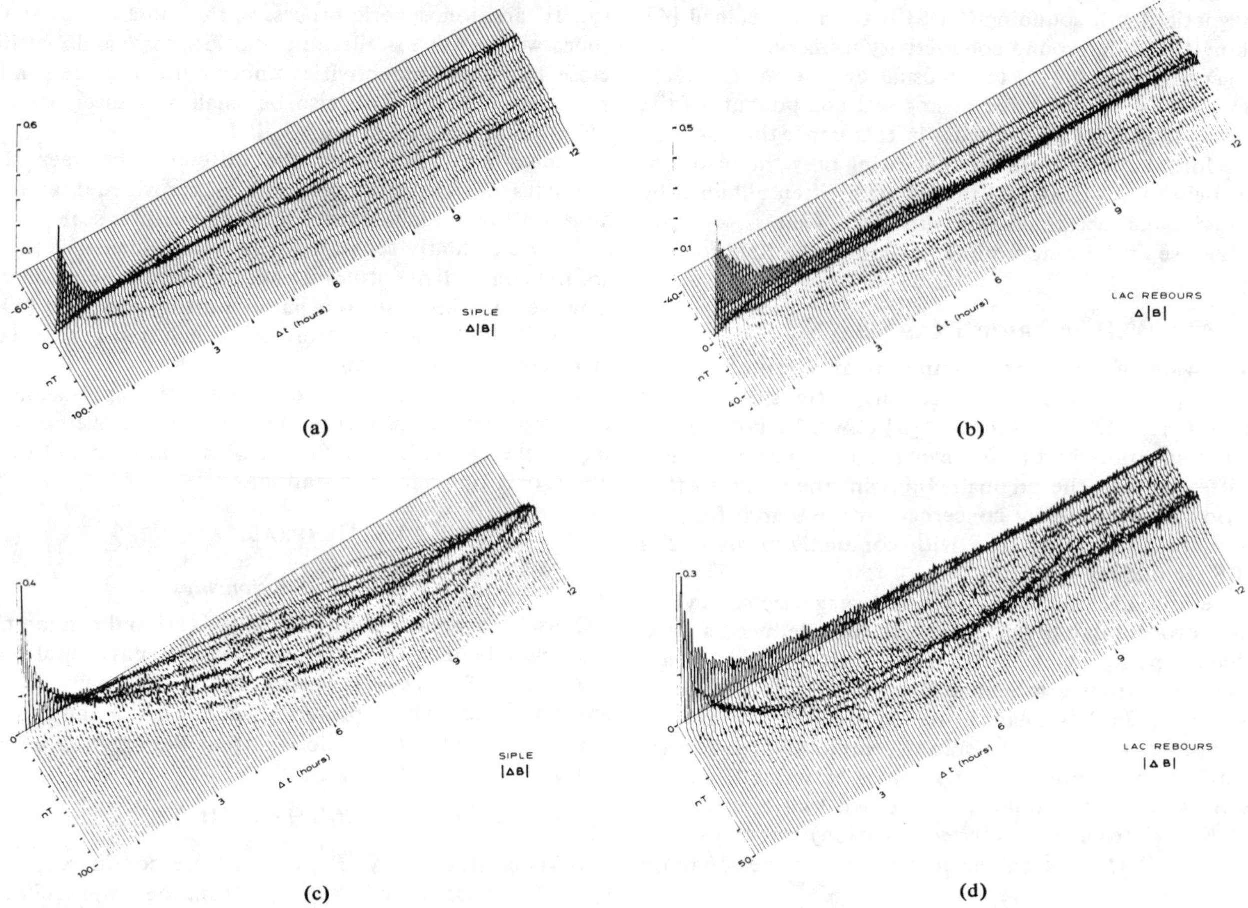

Fig. 1. Plot of $\Delta|B|$ (parts (a) and (b)) and of $|\Delta B|$ (parts (c) and (d)) as defined by (6) and (7), respectively, as a function of Δt. A sequence of data $B(t)$, time spaced at 5 min intervals and covering a total time period of 3 days, 17 h of geomagnetically quiet time were used. For each t we have computed $\Delta|B|$ by (6) (or $|\Delta B|$ by (7)), for each Δt, Δt = 5 min, 10 min, $\cdots$, up to 12 h. At each Δt, the total histogram area is normalized to unit area. Figure parts (a) and (c) are for Siple, while parts (b) and (d) are for Lac Rebours. Comparisons made between parts (a) and (b), and between parts (c) and (d) show considerable differences between the conjugate pair stations.

spanned by $|B_{S_1}(t)|$, $|B_{S_2}(t)|$, and $|B_P(t)|$. The closer P is to a conductivity anomaly, the larger will be the deviation of Γ_P from the general trend observed for the other points P. In this way, the limitations, or biases, introduced by an arbitrariness in the choice of one reference station will be substantially weakened.

C. Parkinson Filtering of the Total Field Magnitude

In essence, the above techniques do not actually contain anything other than a search for a geographical distribution of points which show an anomalous behavior with respect to the general behavior of all the points being considered on a map. The next step is to attempt to split the information provided by different frequency bands, in order to focus on the depth of the conductivity anomalies.

Several filtering procedures have been used in GDS, ranging in sophistication from "visual" techniques (e.g., selecting bay-like events of a given total time duration) to Fourier analysis. In this respect, shipborne or airborne surveys present some difficulty, because the recording "site" changes (generally smoothly) with time. It must be assumed that the data, recorded along a segment of the ship track, have been recorded at a fixed station located at the barycenter of the track segment. In this way, the geographical location of the conductivity anomalies can be inferred by averaging over small areas within some given grid.

A convenient filtering method was employed by Parkinson [12] in studies of coastal effects in geomagnetic data. He considered the differences $B(t + \Delta t) - B(t)$, where Δt is a given preassigned time increment. This filtering procedure is equivalent to applying a high-pass filter, with a reasonably wide window [13], to the data.

Thus we investigate the trend of the quantity

$$\Delta|B| = |B(t + \Delta t)| - |B(t)| \tag{6}$$

and, for comparison, the trend of the quantity

$$|\Delta B| = |B(t + \Delta t) - B(t)|. \tag{7}$$

Obviously, to evaluate (7), the direction of the field as well as the total magnitude is needed.

We have evaluated the feasibility of using (6) and (7) by evaluating data acquired at two land-based, geomagnetically conjugate stations, Lac Rebours, Quebec (47.87°N, 72.45°W, geographic), and Siple, Antarctica (76°S, 84°W, geographic) using multiples of 5 min as Δt. The data were acquired simultaneously at both stations on January 6–9, 1971. These days were very quiet geomagnetically. The equipment has been outlined previously [14]. Figs. 1(a) and (b) show the $\Delta|B|$ trend (number of cases for a given $\Delta|B|$ versus Δt) for Siple and Lac Rebours, respectively. Each histogram, for a given Δt, has been normalized to unit total area. Figs. 1(c) and (d) refer to the analysis for $|\Delta B|$. The results change slightly if

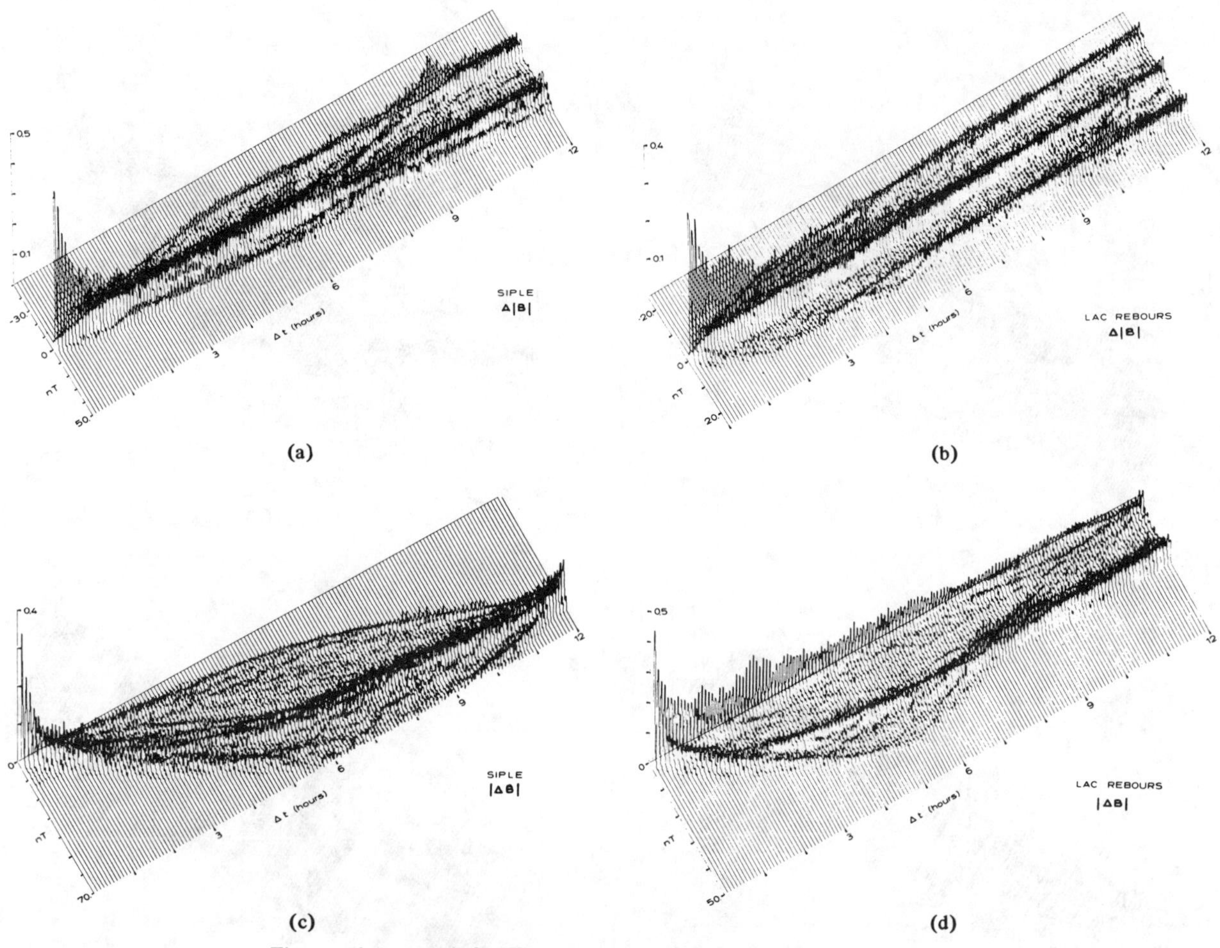

Fig. 2. The same as for Fig. 1, using as the $B(t)$ data base sequence the diurnal average field over the 3 days, 17 h. This prefiltering was done in order to eliminate the noise produced by nonregular time variations. As a consequence of such a prefiltering, the gross features of the histograms are enhanced.

a presmoothing (e.g., the diurnal average over the four days data set) is treated; the results are shown in Fig. 2, corresponding to the Fig. 1 graphs.

In order to attempt an explanation for the observed trends the same procedures have been applied to purely sinusoidal waves of periods 12 h and of 24/26 h ($\simeq 55$ min $+ 23$ s). These results are shown in Figs. 3(a), (b), and Figs. 3(c), (d), respectively. The model wave used has components along the three axes $(\hat{x}, \hat{y}, \hat{z})$ of amplitude $(1, 1, 0)$ and phase $(0, 0, 0)$, respectively. Since only the field intensity is considered, and not its direction, the result is invariant with respect to any rotation of the frame of reference. The "aliasing" effect [13] in Figs. 3(c) and (d) is obvious and is related to the fact that 24/26 h is not an integer multiple of 5 min. Using (6) or (7) explicitly, several symmetries should be found that are indeed observed in Fig. 3.

The interpretation of Figs. 1 and 2 is thus evident: for each given "frequency" a structure having the shape of a "Viking ship" is observed. Each such "ship" for each frequency enters Figs. 1 and 2 with a different statistical weight. The "ship" structure is most clear for the daily variation (smoothed) data set (Fig. 2). A comparison between such diagrams made at different northern hemisphere locations and at Siple is contained in a paper in preparation.

Using data from a shipborne or airborne geomagnetic survey, plots similar to those in Figs. 1(a) and (c) can be drawn from data obtained along each portion of a track. The speed of the ship would have to be adjusted to correspond to the length of the data series acceptable for each given "track." The length of the time step Δt, of course, determines the crustal depth probed. Visual inspections and comparisons of the different shapes will give information on any conductivity anomalies underlying some of the tracks. For example, a simple criterion could be the subtraction of the respective "Viking ships" at any two given geographical points.

Such considerations can be applied also to short Δt. As Hyndman and Cochrane [15] pointed out, shallow sea water effects are pronounced in the frequency range between ~ 20 s and 5 min. Hence, using this frequency range, it is possible to calibrate the method by considering the dependence of the "Viking ship" plots versus sea depth.[1]

---

[1] For the sake of completeness, we should mention that an attempt to estimate water depth by means of simultaneous electric and magnetic field measurements has been made [16]. The most striking result of this nature was reported by Zhigalov [17] using the floating ice station North Pole 6. He reported a remarkable correlation of the geomagnetic field with the depth of the Arctic ocean under the station. He found that the damping of the vertical component was larger when he selected only events with periods shorter than 10 min, consistent with the hypothesis that the water layer is more sensitive to these higher frequencies. Similarly, Heirtzler [18] found, in simultaneously recorded data, that the power spectrum of the geomagnetic field recorded ~ 1000 ft below Fletcher's ice island (T-3) floating in the Artic ocean was ~ 85 percent less than the power spectrum of the field measured on the island.

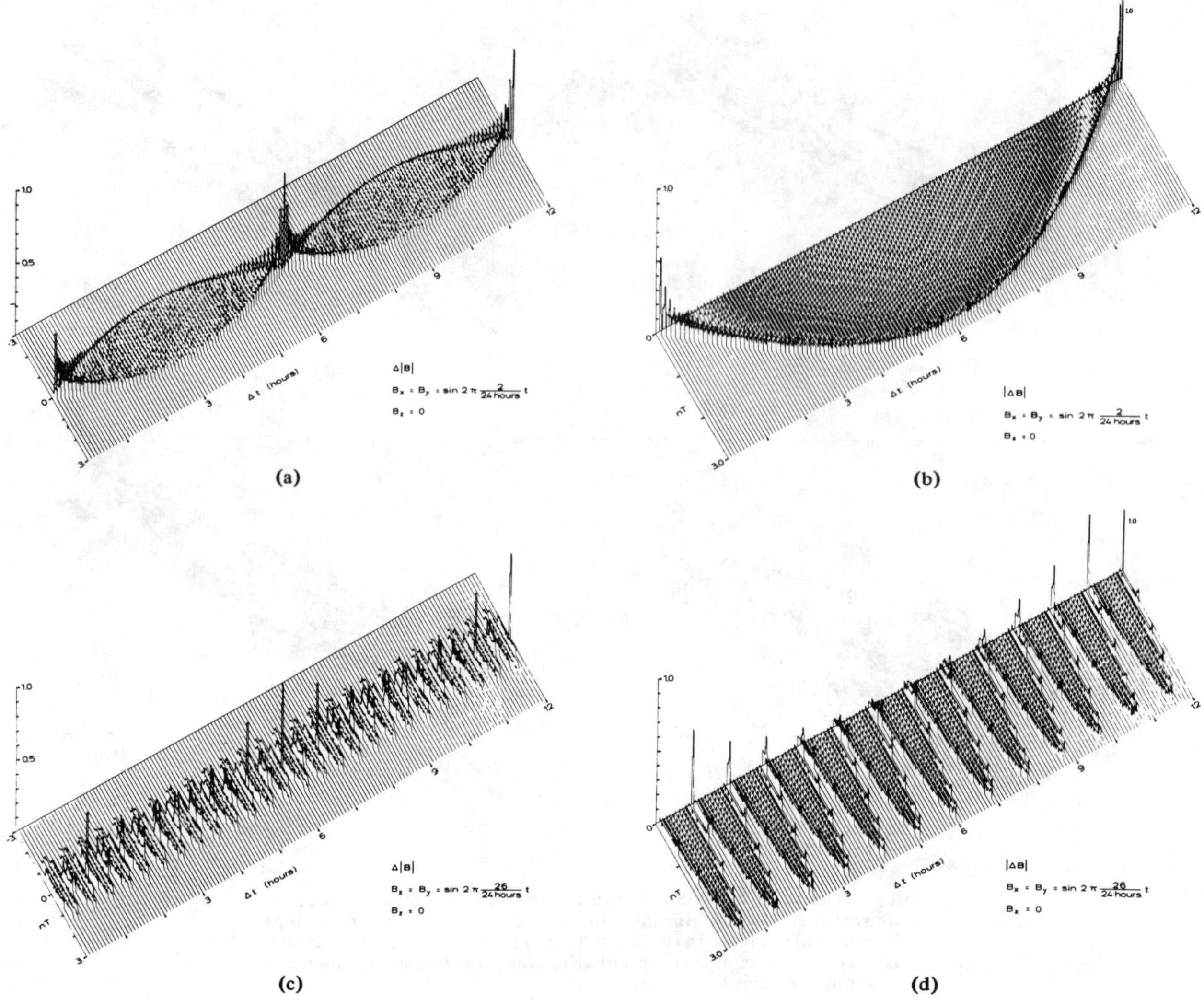

Fig. 3. Plots of histograms of $\Delta|B|$ and of $|\Delta B|$ as in Figs. 1 and 2, but using a set of test data. B_x and B_y are taken equal to a pure sine wave, and $B_z \equiv 0$. Parts (a) and (c) refer to $\Delta|B|$, while parts (b) and (d) refer to $|\Delta B|$. Parts (a) and (b) refer to a pure 12 h period wave; parts (c) and (d) refer to a pure wave of period 24/26 h (55 min, 23 s). In parts (c) and (d) there is an "aliasing effect," related to the fact that the time spacing (5 min) between the different Δt is not an integer submultiple of the period (24/26 h) of the base data set.

IV. Conclusions

In view of the large amount of available aeromagnetic and oceanographic surveys, scanning a large fraction of the earth's surface where essentially no information on the local conductivity anomalies have ever been obtained, we believe that GDS analyses should be carried out using the available data. Such information has great importance for geotectonic investigations on such topics as the nature of oceanic ridges, volcanic islands, island arcs, and geothermal fluxes.

The method of Le Borgne and Le Mouël [5], although based upon an original assumption that is not rigorously consistent with the final product, serves as a good simple procedure for performing GDS studies with total magnetic field data obtained in shipborne and airborne surveys. The first two generalizations discussed in Section III, particularly the use of multiple reference sites, have the potential of providing more substantive results, albeit at the expense of some simplicity.

We believe the third generalization, the use of the Parkinson filter on the total magnitude of the field, has potential for use-fulness in comparisons of observational results at different geographical locations as would be traversed in aeromagnetic and oceanographic surveys. The technique could be calibrated at higher frequencies using shipborne measurements over known ocean depths. A drawback with this procedure is the fact that considerable computer time can be expended in performing the Parkinson filtering. Nevertheless, a systematic exploitation of the technique in connection with other GDS analysis techniques could provide the requisite confidence in its properties and strengths.

References

[1] G. Coulomb, *L'Expansion Des Fonds Océaniques Et Le Dérive Des Continents.* Paris, France: Presse univ. de France. 1969, pp. 1–224

[2] V. Vacquier, *Geomagnetism In Marine Geology.* New York: Elsevier Publishing Company, 1972, pp. 1–185.

[3] M. S. Reford, "Problems of magnetic fluctuations in geophysical exploration," in *Impacts Of Ionospheric/Magnetospheric Processes On Terrestrial Science And Technology,* L. J. Lanzerotti, Ed. Panel on solar system plasma processes of the Study on

Plasma Space Physics, Space Science Board, National Academy of Sciences, Apr. 1978.

[4] J. Bartels, "Erdmagnetische Tiefen-sondierungen," *Geol. Rasch.*, vol. 46, pp. 99–101, 1957.

[5] E. Le Borgne, and J. L. Le Mouël, "A conductivity anomaly in the Western Mediterranean," *Geophys. J. Roy. Astron. Soc.*, vol. 43, pp. 339–355, 1975.

[6] ——, "La variation diurne de l'intensité du champ magnétique terrestre au dessus du Golfe de Gascogne," *Ann. Geophys.*, vol. 27, no. 4, pp. 433–445, 1971.

[7] ——, "Le lévé aeromagnetique du Golfe de Gascogne," *Note de l'Institut de Physique du Globe*, vol. 41, p. 1–55, 1971.

[8] S. M. Mansurov, "Causes of local geomagnetic variations in the Mirny region," *Inf. Bull. Sov. Antark. Ekspeu.*, vol. 2, pp. 37–41, 1958 (English translation in *Soviet Antarctic Expedition, Inform. Bull.*, vol. 1, pp. 82–85, Elsevier, 1964).

[9] R. Shlich, P. Patriat, and M. Ronfard, "Variations diurnes et transitoires de l'intensité du champ magnétique terrestre en Mer Mediterranée," *C. R. Hebd. Séanc. Acad. Sci.*, vol. 260, pp. 623–626, 1965.

[10] B. Caner, W. H. Cannon, and C. E. Livingstone, "Geomagnetic depth-sounding and upper mantle structure in the cordillera region of western North America," *J. Geophys. Res.*, pp. 6335–6351, 1967.

[11] K. A. Poehls, and R. P. Von Herzen, "Electrical resistivity structure beneath the northwest Atlantic ocean," *Geophys. J. Roy. Astron. Soc.*, vol. 47, pp. 331–346, 1976.

[12] W. D. Parkinson, "Direction of rapid geomagnetic fluctuations," *Geophys. J. Roy. Astron. Soc.*, vol. 2, no. 1, pp. 1–14, 1959.

[13] M. Bath, *Spectral Analysis In Geophysics.* New York: Elsevier Scientific Publishing Company, 1974, pp. 1–563.

[14] L. J. Lanzerotti, A. Hasegawa, and N. A. Tartaglia, "Morphology and interpretation of magnetospheric plasma waves at conjugate points during December solstice," *J. Geophys. Res.*, vol. 77, pp. 6731–6745, 1972.

[15] R. D. Hyndman, and N. A. Cochrane, "Electrical conductivity structure by geomagnetic induction at the continental margin of Atlantic Canada," *Geophys. J. Roy. Astron. Soc.*, vol. 25, pp. 425–446, 1971.

[16] W. Swift, and V. P. Hessler, "A comparison of telluric current and magnetic field observation in the Arctic ocean," *J. Geophys. Res.*, vol. 63, no. 3, pp. 1883–1893, 1964.

[17] L. N. Zhigalov, "Some features of the variation of the geomagnetic vertical component in the Arctic ocean," *Izv. Akad. Nauk. SSSR*, vol. 30, no. 4, 1960.

[18] J. R. Heirtzler, "Measurement of the vertical geomagnetic field gradient beneath the surface of the Arctic ocean," *Geophys. Prospect.* vol. 15, no. 2, pp. 194–203, 1967.

Computerized Geophysical Tomography

KRIS A. DINES, MEMBER, IEEE, AND R. JEFFREY LYTLE, MEMBER, IEEE

Abstract—Computerized tomography is used as an aid in geophysical exploration. With this method, detailed pictures of electromagnetic properties in the regions between pairs of boreholes can be reconstructed. The spatial distribution of attenuation or propagation velocity is calculated from line integrals along rays in the plane between boreholes, and displayed as a digital picture. In principle, the transmission of seismic data can also be analyzed by this method as long as it obeys the line integral model. Iterative solution techniques, similar to those used in medical X-ray tomography are applied to solve the large sets of linear equations relating the line integral data and the remote observables. A straight-line ray optics model was used for energy propagation between boreholes. The performance of the reconstruction algorithm is demonstrated using computer-generated data and it is then applied to experimental data collected by continuous-wave electromagnetic transmission probing. Experimental attenuation reconstructions are presented of a proposed underground urban mass-transit site. Both lateral and vertical variations are displayed using these methods.

I. INTRODUCTION

COMPUTERIZED axial tomography has revolutionized medical X-ray imaging because of its ability to display the spatial distribution of X-ray attenuation over cross sections of the body [1]. Tomographic or image-reconstruction methods are applicable to imaging situations where line integrals of a parameter, such as X-ray attenuation, are available as the collected data [2]–[4]. Specifically, when these line integrals can be organized into parallel or fan-beam ray sets called projections, convolutional reconstruction techniques can be used to process data on a projection-by-projection basis in an efficient and accurate manner. These convolution or filtered backprojection methods basically solve a large set of linear equations for the unknown image by taking advantage of the special structure of the coefficient matrix as determined by the choice of scanning geometry [5]–[15].

Early reconstruction efforts made use of iterative algebraic-solution techniques for solving the large sets of sparse equations. Iterative methods are more general than the filtered backprojection methods because they can accommodate arbitrary scanning geometries, although there are some geometries that result in more efficient computational algorithms [16]–[26].

In this paper we apply some of the iterative-solution methods to geophysical line-integral data. These data can be generated by transmission probing through a region using either electromagnetic energy or seismic energy. In so far as signal attenuation rate or propagation velocity characterizes the geology, one can, in principle, image geological structures similar to the way in which medical tomograms are obtained.

Geophysical tomography (geotomography) differs from medical tomography both in physical scale and scanning-geometry characteristics. Geophysical applications require sampling on a larger physical scale than medical applications, therefore, to achieve sufficient received-signal levels over practical distances, lower frequencies must be used in geophysical applications. Spatial resolution in images reconstructed from geophysical signals may be displayed in dimensions of centimeters to meters while medical images are in millimeters. Medical scanners are constructed with a fixed-data collection geometry. Conversely, geophysical problems generally require a new scanning capability for each separate application.

In the problems to be considered here, the scanning paths are boreholes in the ground. Because of the inaccuracies in drilling techniques (i.e., boreholes that wander from a straight-line path) and the fact that preexisting holes must often be used, a fairly general scanning geometry must be considered in the reconstruction algorithm. This factor has led us to consider iterative-solution algorithms that are more versatile than either the convolutional methods or some recently proposed noniteration schemes [27]. In addition, iterative techniques are thought to be more easily adaptable to future applications where refraction effects require ray-bending corrections on large data sets [14], [28], [29].

Our approach is based on an assumed straight line ray-optic model of the propagation mechanism. This approach is known to be approximate, although it is sufficiently accurate if certain criteria, discussed later, are satisfied. The ray-optic approach used is an alternative to the formulations yielding mathematically precise results for earth strata of certain specific form [30], [31].

In Fig. 1, a typical situation, the data-collection system scans the region between boreholes with a signal source located in one hole and a receiver in the other. A multitude of source and receiver locations are used to effectively sample the region between boreholes with a large number of orientations for the transmission paths. The received signals carry time-of-flight information for velocity measurements and amplitude information for attenuation measurements. Note that the region is viewed from only two sides. This is in contrast to medical tomography where the object can be interrogated from all sides of the object. Cross-borehole probing applied in medical tomography would result in spatially truncated projections that are also limited in total view angle [32].

Some possible geotomography applications include: detection of hazardous regions ahead of a mine face, assessing nuclear reactor and waste storage sites, mapping resources at

Manuscript received August 14, 1978; revised December 4, 1978. This work was performed under the auspices of the U.S. Department of Energy, by Lawrence Livermore Laboratory, under Contract W–7405–Eng–48.

K. A. Dines was with the Lawrence Livermore Laboratory, University of California, Livermore, CA. He is now with the Indianapolis Center for Advanced Research, Indianapolis, IN 45202.

R. J. Lytle is with the Lawrence Livermore Laboratory, University of California, Livermore, CA 94550.

Reprinted from *Proc. IEEE*, vol. 67, pp. 1065–1073, July 1979.

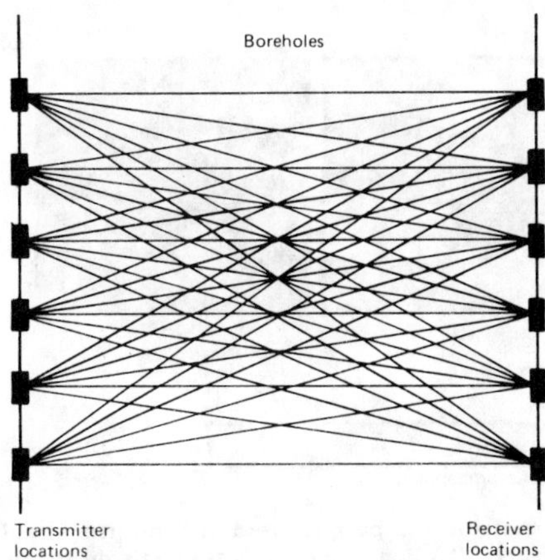

Fig. 1. Cross-borehole sampling using multiple locations for the transmitter and receiver probes.

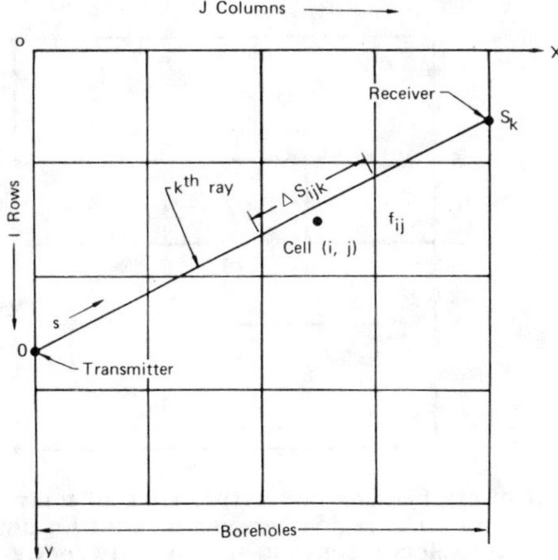

Fig. 2. Discrete model of a region between boreholes showing a typical ray path through the $I \times J$ digital image of attenuation or velocity.

mines to detect deposits that pinch out but are suspected of reappearing elsewhere, and determining the location and volume of oil present in possible secondary oil recovery fields [33]–[37].

In this paper we describe the data interpretation method for straight-ray propagation, test its performance on computer-generated data, and apply it to experimental continuous-wave electromagnetic data from a proposed urban mass transit site.

III. Imaging Model

The model used for cross-borehole probing is shown in Fig. 2, where a typical ray path is indicated for electromagnetic signal propagation. In current geophysical applications the total length of individual rays can range from 1 m to 1.0 km, depending on the characteristics of the host medium and source-receiver capabilities.

The region between boreholes is represented by a two-dimensional area where the distribution of some material parameter, such as velocity $v(x, y)$ or attenuation rate $\alpha(x, y)$, is to be calculated. Attenuation rate is a measure of how rapidly plane-wave energy is dissipated with distance in the medium. If $I(s_0)$ is the power density of the signal at ray-arc length s_0, then a plane wave traveling a short distance Δs, suffers a loss of

$$I(s_0 + \Delta s) = I(s_0) \exp(-2\alpha_0 \Delta s) \tag{1}$$

where $\alpha_0 = \alpha(x_0, y_0)$ is the local attenuation rate in nepers per meter at ray position s_0, corresponding to the coordinates (x_0, y_0) in the plane. We note that attenuation in geological materials is a function of frequency. This is an important factor with pulsed excitations. Signal loss along the entire ray R_k is

$$I(S_k) = I(0) \exp\left[-2 \int_{R_k} \alpha(x, y) \, ds\right] \tag{2}$$

where $I(0)$ is the incident signal intensity at $s = 0$, $I(S_k)$ is the received intensity at the end of the ray $s = S_k$, and the attenuation integral is a line integral taken along the ray. In terms of measured signal intensity data, we have from (2)

$$\gamma_k = -\tfrac{1}{2} \ln \frac{I(S_k)}{I(0)} = \int_{R_k} \alpha(x, y) \, ds \tag{3}$$

where γ_k is the integrated attenuation for the entire signal path.

A similar relationship exists between propagation velocity $v(x, y)$ and the total signal delay Δt_k

$$\Delta t_k = \int_{R_k} \frac{ds}{v(x, y)} \tag{4}$$

where the inverse of velocity appears in the integral. The quantity $1/v(x, y)$ can be imaged and the picture inverted for a direct display of velocity. In terms of the refractive index $n(x, y)$ defined as the ratio of propagation velocity in free space c and velocity $v(x, y)$ in the medium, we have

$$c \Delta t_k = \int_{R_k} n(x, y) \, ds \tag{5}$$

with the optical path length $c \Delta t_k$ being the measured data, and $n(x, y)$ the quantity to be imaged.

Regardless of whether we are dealing with total signal loss (attenuation) or total signal delay (velocity), the same fundamental mathematical relationship exists between the measured data and the quantity to be reconstructed. However, unless the refractive-index function is a constant throughout the region, there will be ray bending with unknown ray paths. This means that one must somehow image the refractive-index function, determine the ray paths, and then use these rays for reconstructing attenuation. If the refractive-index changes are sufficiently small, the rays will be approximately straight. If refraction is significant and straight rays are assumed, there will be distortions in reconstructed pictures.

Three criteria are required for the straight-ray optical model to be a valid approximation of the physical interaction [38]: the separation distance between source and receiver should be much larger than $\lambda/2\pi$, where λ is the wavelength in the medium; the refractive index should vary slowly enough with distance that the field behavior is adequately described by straight-line geometrical optics; and $\lambda \ll \pi\delta$, where δ is the skin depth in the medium. Fortunately, there are many geophysical applications that meet these criteria. An example would be high-frequency electromagnetic cross-borehole probing where the boreholes are separated by five wavelengths, the conduction currents in the probed region are much less than displacement currents (which means $\lambda \ll \pi\delta$), and the local velocity of electromagnetic waves is well approximated as constant throughout the region of interest. For this situation the data on the travel times between source and receiver

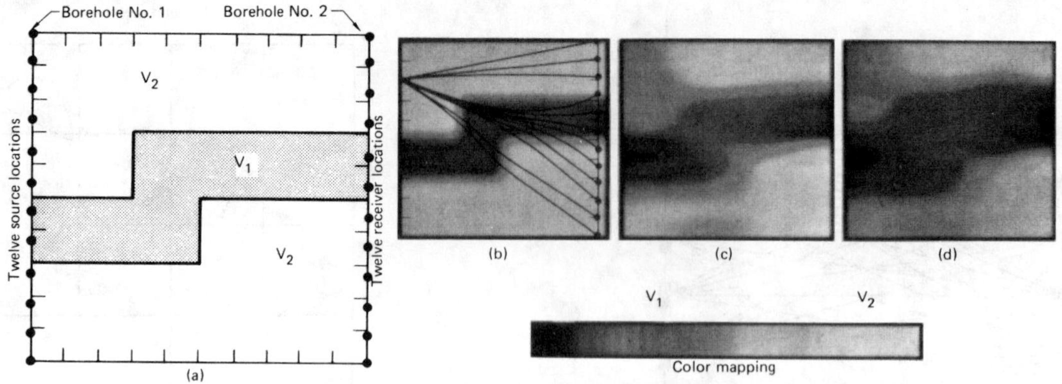

Fig. 3. Effect of ray bending on interpretation of transmission data. (a) The velocity distribution pattern used in computer simulation of the transmission data. The region between boreholes is divided into a 10 × 10 digital picture. (b) Bending of rays transmitted through the simulated 16 percent velocity contrast. The velocity contrast has been smoothed at the edges to give a more gradual change. The color bar shown below Figs. 3(b) through (c) represents the relative velocity scale used. (c) Profile of the 16 percent velocity contrast reconstructed using straight-line interpretation of the bending-ray data. (d) Profile of the 33 percent velocity contrast reconstructed using straight-line interpretation of the bending-ray data.

Note: Fig. 3(b)–(d) appeared in color in the original publication.

would, when interpreted, yield a velocity profile that would be constant regardless of the source–receiver locations. If, however, there were significant attenuation-rate variations throughout the probed region, they would be evident in the amplitude variation results for the different source–receiver combinations. This hypothetical situation is closely representative of an experimental application to be described later. described later.

Corrections for ray bending have been attempted [39]–[41], but were made on relatively small pictures, not the large pictures considered here. Such performance measures and reconstruction examples indicate that significant benefits from ray corrections require a data accuracy in excess of that presently available in our experimental data collection system [41]. We have therefore arbitrarily limited ourselves to those situations where we can ignore ray-bending corrections. Note that some resolution will consequently be sacrificed in the reconstructions if there is ray bending due to a spatially varying velocity profile.

As examples of the effect of ray bending on reconstruction quality, we simulated two hypothetical situations on the computer. Two geophysical profiles (see Fig. 3(a)), with 16 percent and 33 percent velocity contrasts, were modeled. For these profiles, the rays linking source and receiver bend (e.g., see Fig. 3(b)) for the 16 percent contrast. The synthetic transmission data generated using the bending rays can be interpreted using an assumption that the rays traveled in straight lines. Iterative-reconstruction techniques based on this assumption are discussed below. Using these techniques on the synthetic bending-ray data for these profiles, we made reconstructions of the geophysical profile (Figs. 3(c) and (d)). Note that as would be expected, the image resolution is less for the higher velocity contrast. From the limited results given, the authors have tentatively concluded that velocity contrasts of 16 percent or less can be successfully interpreted using a multitude of cross-borehole transmission paths and the straight-line data-interpretation techniques given below. Higher velocity contrasts can also be interpreted using the techniques, but with a degraded resolution.

III. ITERATIVE-RECONSTRUCTION TECHNIQUES

The basic aim of reconstruction is to image a material parameter $f(x, y)$ (attenuation or refractive index) from line-integral

data g_k collected for K signal paths

$$g_k = \int_{R_k} f(x, y) \, ds. \qquad (6)$$

Therefore, given the ray paths R_k, a set of K linear equations can be constructed, and in principle, solved for an estimate of the unknown image $f(x, y)$.

To construct the linear equations that are to be solved on a digital computer, a discrete approximation must be chosen to the function $f(x, y)$. An $I \times J$ grid is superimposed on the picture plane and $f(x, y)$ is approximated by $\hat{f}(x, y)$, whose value is assumed constant over each cell of the grid. The value of $\hat{f}(x, y)$ for the cell centered at the digital picture sample (i, j) may be thought of as the average value of $f(x, y)$ over that cell. The discrete model of the region between holes is an $I \times J$ matrix of cells where $f(x, y)$ is assumed constant within each cell but varies from cell to cell. There are IJ unknown picture values f_{ij}, each corresponding to a cell centered at row i, column j in the matrix of Fig. 2. For each ray, one equation can be written relating these unknowns to the measured data. Doing this for each ray enables one to obtain a system of K equations in IJ unknowns.

$$g_k = \sum_{i=1}^{I} \sum_{j=1}^{J} f_{ij} \Delta s_{ijk}, \qquad k = 1, 2, 3, \cdots, K. \qquad (7)$$

Here, f_{ij} denotes the average value of $f(x, y)$ on the cell (i, j), and Δs_{ijk} is the length of a ray segment that intercepts the cell, as shown in Fig. 2. The summation in (7) is then over all values of i and j, where it is understood that $\Delta s_{ijk} = 0$ for those i and j values for which the associated cell is not intercepted by the ray R_k.

The problem of estimating $f(x, y)$ has now been reduced to solving the set of linear equations in (7). However, several problems remain. First, the data g_k is not known exactly in any practical case as a result of various sources of noise in the system and approximations in the discrete model. Generally this will cause (7) to be inconsistent. Second, the number of independent equations, as determined by the scanning geometry, is usually insufficient to determine f_{ij} uniquely. Finally, in many cases the number of equations are too large for direct matrix-inversion or pseudo-inversion solution techniques. For example, assume the boreholes are separated by 200 m, and we sample a 200 m vertical region. If we desire a resolution corresponding to 1-m × 1-m cells, then there will be 40 000 unknowns and an equation coefficient matrix of perhaps 40 000 × 40 000. Although the equation coefficient matrix is sparse, standard solution methods are impractical.

Efficient iterative-solution methods can be devised to choose an approximate solution to this large system of equations using the insufficient, inconsistent data. Iterative-solution algorithms have recently been used in X-ray probing of the human head and torso. These algorithms have been known for some time, however, not until recently have experimental data been reduced using these methods. The techniques have been extensively applied recently in such varied areas as X-ray tomography, nuclear emission imaging, electron microscopy, ultrasonic imaging, and optical interferometry, among others.

The mathematics governing these reconstruction procedures is well founded [17], [23]. However, a myriad of modifications, both rigorous and heuristic, have been made to the basic approach. Basically, an iterative method such as the algebraic-reconstruction technique (ART) treats one equation at a time [16]. In tomography, this amounts to examining one ray path at a time, a convenient approach because storage of the coefficients Δs_{ijk} in (7) can be avoided. Each equation can be generated from geometry considerations as each ray is encountered in the iterations.

The algorithm for reconstruction begins with an initial guess f_{ij}^0 for every picture sample and calculates an estimate for the data g_k at the end of a chosen ray path,

$$\hat{g}_k = \sum_i^I \sum_j^J f_{ij}^q \Delta s_{ijk} \tag{8}$$

where Δs_{ijk} is as defined in (7). Here f_{ij}^q indicates the estimated picture after the qth iteration. An iteration occurs each time a single ray is examined. Generally, $k \neq q$ because the entire set of rays must be examined several times before a final estimate of f_{ij} is obtained. We wish to determine a set of corrections due to the kth ray, Δf_{ijk}^q, so there will be a zero error for the kth path:

$$g_k = \sum_i^I \sum_j^J (f_{ij}^q + \Delta f_{ijk}^q) \Delta s_{ijk}. \tag{9}$$

Combining (9) with (8) gives

$$\Delta g_k = (g_k - \hat{g}_k) = \sum_{i=1}^I \sum_{j=1}^J \Delta f_{ijk}^q \Delta s_{ijk} \tag{10}$$

where Δg_k is the difference (error in data fit) between the measured value and estimated value for the kth path.

There are an infinite number of possible solutions to (10), because there is only one equation to be satisfied at every iteration, but IJ unknowns Δf_{ijk}^q. We have arbitrarily chosen to minimize the criterion,

$$C = \sum_{i=1}^I \sum_{j=1}^J (\Delta f_{ijk}^q)^{2p}, \qquad p = 1, 2, 3, \cdots$$

subject to the constraint in (10) so that a unique solution is obtained. In (11) p is a positive integer ($p = 1$ for ART algorithms). If $p = 1$, then we speak of minimum energy cor-

rections. A straightforward minimization of (11) subject to (10) leads to the corrections

$$\Delta f_{ijk}^q = \frac{(\Delta s_{ijk})^2 \Delta g_k}{\sum_i^I \sum_j^J (\Delta s_{ijk})(\Delta s_{ijk})^w} \tag{12}$$

for general p, where $w = 1/(2p - 1)$. As mentioned previously, Δs_{ijk} is understood to be zero if the kth ray does not pass through cell (i, j), in which case Δf_{ijk}^q will also be zero. Equation (12) gives the corrections to be applied to each zone to give a zero error for the kth path. The new estimate for the picture is then

$$f_{ij}^{(q+1)} = f_{ij}^q + \Delta f_{ijk}^q, \qquad i = 1, 2, \cdots, I; \\ j = 1, 2, 3, \cdots, J. \tag{13}$$

The process is repeated ray-by-ray until all the rays ($k = 1, \cdots, K$) have been processed several times. Each time a single ray is examined the picture is updated constituting one iteration.

An interesting case arises when p is allowed to approach infinity. When $p \to \infty$ the criterion is (11) is referred to as the L^∞ or minimax norm, or in digital filter design terminology, the Chebyshev norm. In the limit as the integer $p \to \infty$ in (12), we obtain the minimax corrections

$$\Delta f_{ijk}^q = \frac{\mathrm{sgn}\,(\Delta s_{ijk}) \Delta g_k}{\sum_{i=1}^I \sum_{j=1}^J |\Delta s_{ijk}|} \tag{14}$$

where $|\cdot|$ denotes absolute value and

$$\mathrm{sgn}\,(V) = \begin{cases} -1, & V < 0 \\ 0, & V = 0 \\ 1, & V > 0 \end{cases}$$

is the signum function. In tomography, the Δs_{ijk} are distances and therefore nonnegative. For minimax corrections the same value is added to all cells intercepted by the ray in question regardless of the length of the ray segment that intersects the cell. This is simply backprojection which is incidently, one step in the Fourier-reconstruction methods used in tomography. Here we have an iterative backprojection of errors in line-integral data fit. Note that the denominator in (14) is just the total length of the ray between source and receiver.

The ART algorithm with minimum energy corrections ($p = 1$) requires the changes, Δf_{ijk}^q, to be weighted by the ray segment length Δs_{ijk}. In practice though, these ray lengths are often ignored and something similar to minimax corrections are often performed to reduce computation time. The minimax criterion used here leads naturally to a common implementation of ART which, to the authors' knowledge, was previously considered to be an approximation to the $p = 1$ case. Note carefully, that regardless of the value of p chosen for the criterion, the ray-segment lengths must, strictly speaking, be calculated to obtain $\hat{g}_k$ in (8). However, these segment lengths Δs_{ijk} can often be ignored, and the line integral in (8) can be estimated by simply adding the f_{ij}^q for all cells through which the kth ray passes and dividing by the number of contributing cells N_k to obtain the average value of f_{ij}^q per unit length along the ray. With L_k equal to the length of the kth ray, we have

$$\Delta f_{ijk}^q = \text{sgn}\,(\Delta s_{ijk}) \left[\frac{g_k}{L_k} - \frac{1}{N_k} \sum_{i=1}^{I} \sum_{j=1}^{J} f_{ij}^q \,\text{sgn}\,(\Delta s_{ijk}) \right] \quad (15)$$

and the sum in (15) includes the N_k picture cells intercepted by the kth ray. The corrections in (15) are then approximately minimax corrections where calculation of ray-segment lengths is avoided to reduce the computational load. As long as the picture is sampled rapidly enough, compared to its bandwidth, there is little reason why the algorithm with ray lengths included should provide a more accurate estimate of a real continuous picture.

Ray-by-ray techniques that apply corrections to the picture as each ray is processed do not converge in the presence of data inconsistencies. They tend to hunt in a neighborhood of the solution. Convergence behavior can be improved by waiting until all rays have been examined before changing the estimated picture. Methods such as simultaneous iterative-reconstruction techniques (SIRT) that apply changes only after all available rays have been examined and offer some improvement in this area [21], [25].

We have used a simultaneous minimax correction algorithm in the computer simulations and experimental results that follow. The changes implied by all K rays are calculated before changing the picture. An iteration q is now redefined and said to have occurred only after all K rays have been processed. The corrections Δf_{ijk}^q computed in (15) are saved for each ray and combined to obtain the final correction picture for qth pass,

$$\Delta f_{ij}^q = \frac{1}{M_{ij}} \sum_{k=1}^{K} \Delta f_{ijk}^q, \quad \text{for } M_{ij} \neq 0 \quad (16)$$

where $M_{ij} \leqslant K$ is the number of rays passing through the cell at (i, j). The M_{ij} is therefore a ray density map for the scanned region. The changes in (16) are then added to the previous estimate f_{ij}^q to obtain our estimate $f_{ij}^{(q+1)}$ for the next iteration. Iterations proceed until the data residual

$$r = \sum_{k=1}^{K} (\Delta g_k)^2 \quad (17)$$

is on the order of the expected random noise energy in the data or until the residual remains steady.

IV. COMPUTER SIMULATIONS

The reconstruction method previously described was tested on the patterns shown in Fig. 4. Two separate cases were treated. In the first case, values of attenuation were assigned to the various regions resulting in a relatively high-contrast image. The second case simulates low-contrast velocity differences that might be encountered in the field. In both cases, we have assumed straight-ray propagation. Synthetic data corresponding to 100 equally spaced transmitter locations and 100 receiver locations was generated by assuming the image to be piecewise constant on a 100 × 100 cell model. Each picture cell is twice as deep as it is wide, so if Δy is the picture sampling interval in the y direction and Δx is the interval in the x direction, we have $\Delta y / \Delta x = 2$. A ray connects every transmitter to every receiver for a total of 10 000 ray paths. Even though the number of ray paths equals the number of

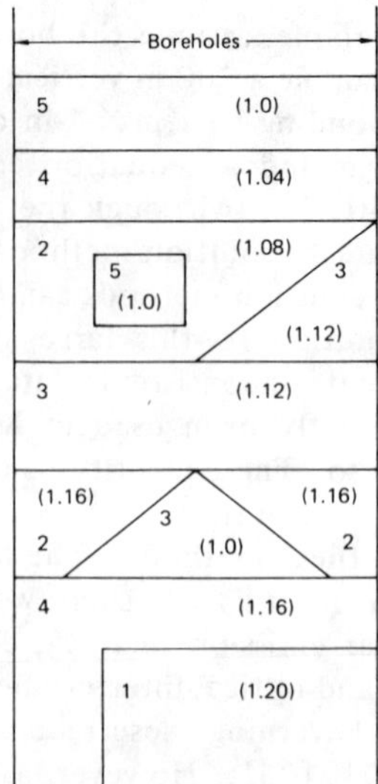

Fig. 4. Relative attenuation and velocity (in parentheses) values in various regions of the simulated test pattern that produce the pictures in Fig. 5(a) and Fig. 5(f).

unknown picture cells, the linear system is underdetermined because the equations are not linearly independent. The ray density is greatest towards the center of the picture and lowest towards the top and bottom. Reconstruction accuracy tends to be better in regions of higher ray density.

When there is no noise in the data, application of the simultaneous correction algorithm in (16) to the high-contrast pattern of Fig. 5(a) for 15 iterations results in the reconstruction of Fig. 5(b). Some artifacts are introduced because of the limited view angles and spatially limited projections. These effects result in the longer ray paths tending to stand out in the picture. Artifacts can be reduced by emphasizing the shorter rays in combining the image corrections due to each ray path. We have found that reconstruction accuracy can be improved in this case by using the weighted corrections below instead of (16).

$$Wf_{ij}^q = \left(\sum_{k=1}^{K} \frac{Wf_{ijk}^q}{N_k^4} \right) \left(\sum_{k=1}^{K} \frac{\text{sgn}}{N_k^4} (Ws_{ijk}) \right). \quad (18)$$

The particular weighting scheme in (18) was arrived at experimentally, but others may be equally appropriate or even better. The general idea of emphasizing the shorter rays is justified on intuitive grounds for three reasons: first, in many practical situations, the geology is dominated by a layered structure so that horizontal rays (shorter rays in this simulation) should be emphasized; second, longer rays affect a larger number of pixels and as a result the total energy in the corrections should be adjusted to be more nearly equal to the shorter rays because there is no reason to assume them to be more important; finally, the longer rays (those at the steeper angles) form incomplete parallel projections (spatially limited) and the truncation effects are diminished by the chosen weighting.

Reconstruction for one iteration and 15 iterations of the weighted algorithm are shown in Fig. 5(c) and Fig. 5(d), respectively. When pseudo-random noise uniformly distributed over ±5 percent of the peak line-integral data value is added to the data, the reconstruction appears as shown in Fig. 5(e). This level of noise is illustrated in Fig. 6(b) where

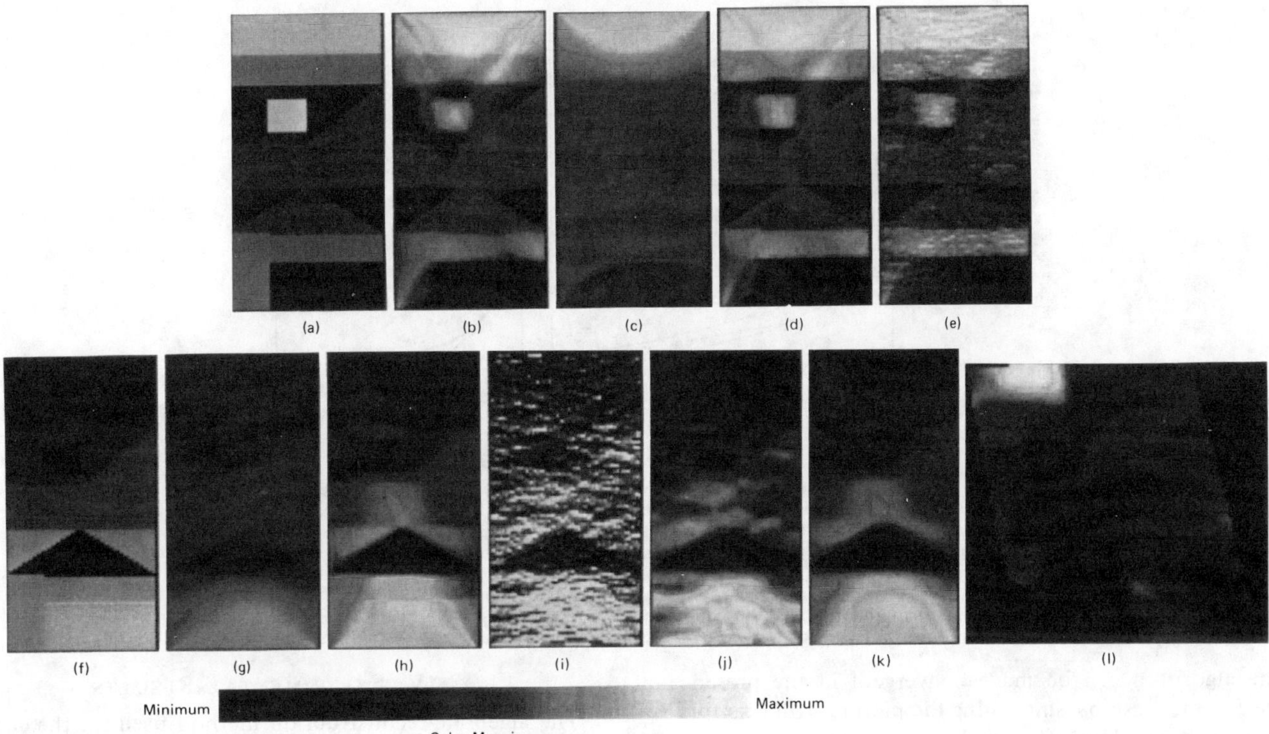

Fig. 5. Reconstruction quantized to 256 gray levels displayed in pseudo-color according to the color mapping shown.
High-contrast simulation: (a) ideal (b) 15 iterations (c) 1 iteration with ray-weighting (d) 15 iterations with ray-weighting (e) 15 iterations with ±5 percent noise.
Low-contrast simulation: (f) ideal (g) 1 iteration (h) 10 iterations (i) 10 iterations with ±5 percent noise (j) 10 iterations with ±5 percent noise and between-iteration smoothing (k) 10 iterations, ideal data with between-iteration smoothing.
Forest Glen experiment: (l) underground attenuation ranging from a minimum of 0.33 Np/m to a maximum of 0.66 Np/m.

Note: This figure appeared in color in the original publication.

the ideal fan-beam projection of Fig. 6(a) is shown plotted along with the noise corrupted projection.

The performance results for the high-contrast pattern are summarized in Fig. 7(a) where the reconstruction error is plotted versus iteration number for the cases discussed. The reconstruction error δ is defined as

$$\delta = e^2/\sigma^2 \tag{19}$$

where

$$e^2 = \frac{1}{IJ} \sum_i^I \sum_j^J (f_{ij} - \hat{f}_{ij})^2 \tag{20}$$

is the average squared error between the $I \times J$ ideal picture f_{ij} and the reconstruction $\hat{f}_{ij}$, and

$$\sigma^2 = \frac{1}{IJ} \sum_i^I \sum_j^J (f_{ij} - \bar{f}_{ij})^2 \tag{21}$$

is the sample variance of the ideal picture, with $\bar{f}_{ij}$ as its sample mean. This error criterion is equal to 1.0 for a mean-value estimate of the picture, and tends to zero as the reconstruction approaches the ideal [25]. It is in effect, a measure of improvement over a mean value (spatial average) estimate for the pattern.

The low-contrast velocity pattern (Fig. 4 and Fig. 5(f)) was chosen to test the algorithm's capability to resolve small changes in velocity (low refraction) using both ideal and noisy data. The results are shown in Fig. 5(g)–(i). Again, noise uniformly distributed over ±5 percent of the projection data peak value was added (Fig. 6(c)). These results show that it is

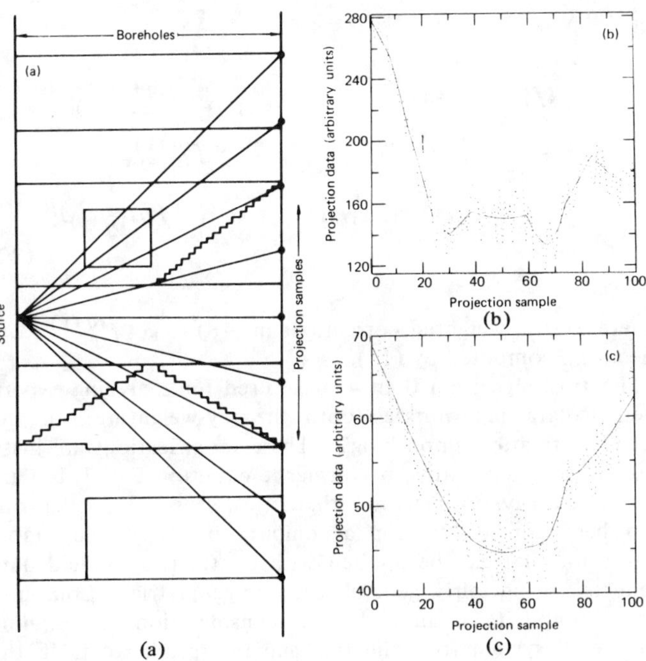

Fig. 6. Typical rays forming a fan-beam projection of the synthetic pattern for computer simulation. (a) chosen projection. (b) ideal (solid line) and noisy (dotted-line) projection for high-contrast pattern of Fig. 4 and Fig. 5(a)–(c) ideal (solid-line) and noisy (dotted-line) projection for low-contrast pattern of Fig. 4 and Fig. 5(f).

more difficult to reconstruct low-contrast patterns in the presence of noise. In addition, the reconstruction error measure chosen in (19) diverges when noise is added (Fig. 7(b)).

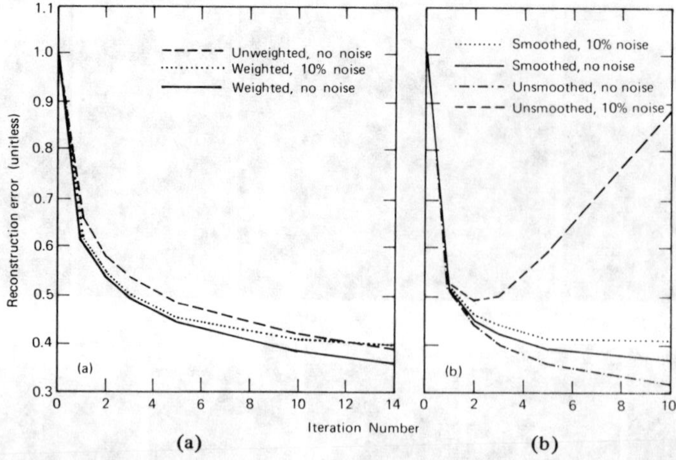

Fig. 7. Performance results for simultaneous iterative reconstruction. (a) Reconstruction error (as computed using Eq. (19)) vs iteration number for the high contrast patterns of Figs. 5(a) through 5(e). Emphasizing the shorter rays (i.e., using ray weighting) improves convergence. (b) Reconstruction error (as computed using Eq. (19)) vs iteration number for the low-contrast patterns of Figs. 5(f) through 5(k). Smoothing the picture after each iteration improves convergence for low-contrast images and noisy data.

The algorithm can be made convergent in the presence of noise for this case by smoothing the picture with a simple 3 × 3 averaging window after each iteration to get the images shown in Fig. 5(j) for noisy data, and Fig. 5(k) for ideal data. Smoothing provides improved stability at the cost of a small sacrifice in resolution which is reflected in an accompanying small loss in accuracy (Fig. 7(b)). In particular, if $f_{ij}^{(q+1)}$ is the reconstructed picture after the qth iteration, we then smooth the picture before proceeding to the next iteration to get $(f_{ij}^{(q+1)})'$,

$$
\begin{aligned}
(f_{ij}^{(q+1)})' = (&f_{(i-1,j-1)}^{(q+1)} + f_{(i-1,j)}^{(q+1)} + f_{(i-1,j+1)}^{(q+1)} \\
&+ f_{(i,j-1)}^{(q+1)} + f_{(i,j)}^{(q+1)} + f_{(i,j+1)}^{(q+1)} \\
&+ f_{(i+1,j-1)}^{(q+1)} + f_{(i+1,j)}^{(q+1)} + f_{(i+1,j+1)})/9
\end{aligned}
$$

$$(22)$$

where we use weighted corrections in (18) to get $f_{ij}^{(q+1)}$ from the Δf_{ijk}^q computed by (15).

The final algorithm that we have used for analyzing experimental data incorporates both the ray-weighting and the between-iteration smoothings. These modifications are justified by the quantitative performance curves in Fig. 7, but are not necessarily optimal in a theoretical sense. However, our aim has been to develop a computationally simple, stable algorithm that can be applied with confidence to field data collected using fairly general scanning geometries. Computational simplicity is an important consideration in designing an overall system for collecting and interpreting data in the field. Presently, the algorithm is implemented on a CDC 7600 computer,[1] although plans are underway to use a small computer system for on-site analysis capability.

[1] Reference to a company or product name does not imply approval or recommendation of the product by the University of California or the U.S. Department of Energy to the exclusion of others that may be suitable.

V. Experimental Results

The algebraic-reconstruction method used for the computer-simulation studies was applied to experimental data collected at a field location called Forest Glen, near Washington, DC. This is the site of a proposed underground mass transit site.

We set up our cross-borehole system on the proposed Georgia Avenue–Forest Glen site of a Washington, DC Metro station to determine whether the technique would be useful in detecting changes in a natural geologic structure. In this study the region had no large contrasts in electrical constitutive parameters (attenuation rate and velocity). Our objective was to determine the detailed structure of the medium.

In regions containing proposed urban transit stations, detailed geologic information from borehole cores and conventional logs is easily obtainable. These data, however, provide only limited information on the geologic structure external to the borehole. If unexpected geologic conditions are encountered between coring boreholes, a different type of excavation equipment may be needed when a station and its feeding tunnel are excavated. The risk of this occurring and the possible difficulties in scheduling the excavation equipment can lead to significant cost overruns.

The data collection and interpretation methods described herein were developed to help alleviate these problems by providing better knowledge of the region between boreholes than has previously been achieved.

We used a continuous-wave frequency appropriate for the data collection, and varied the depths of the transmitting and receiving antennas within their respective boreholes. The transmitter broadcasts an electromagnetic signal, and the magnitude and phase of the received signal is recorded. If there is an electrical anomaly between the two boreholes its presence would be evident in the recorded diagnostic data.

Because the proposed station was to be between 55 and 70 m deep at the borehole slant depth, we sampled a region much larger than necessary, between 46 and 79 m, using available boreholes. We recorded measurements at 0.3- to 0.7-m intervals and performed a total of 1760 measurements using a frequency of 50 MHz.

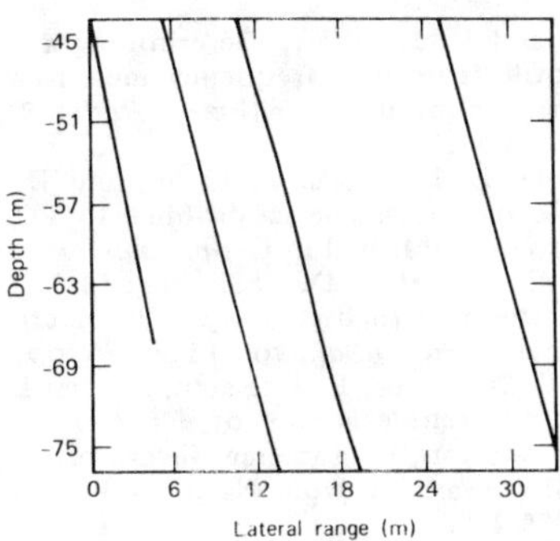

Fig. 8. Borehole trajectories at the Forest Glen site.

Fig. 5(1) displays our interpretation of the Forest Glen attenuation data for the sampled region indicated in Fig. 8. These experimental data were analyzed using the weighted, smoothed iterative-reconstruction technique. The algorithm was terminated after 15 iterations with little change occurring after 5. The image is quantized to 256 levels ranging from 0.33 Np/m to 0.66 Np/m. The color mapping from the minimum attenuation (white) to maximum attenuation (black) is shown in the color bar in Fig. 5.

The presence of the high-attenuation (blue) matches the regions where the individual borehole logs indicated higher than normal weathering or fracture density. The low-attenuation areas (white) correlate with regions of lower fracture density in the rock. Note that both lateral and depth variations in the attenuation profile are easily seen. Using color to represent the attenuation profile portrays the attenuation variations more vividly than a corresponding black and white (or gray level) photograph. Correspondingly, velocity profiles were generated for the regions between boreholes. The velocity profiles were done in strips; i.e., the regions between boreholes 1 and 2, borehoels 2 and 3, and boreholes 3 and 4 were independently determined. There was little variation of velocity [37] within each individual strip (not shown). This makes the straight line ray-optic assumption a valid approximation for this site at the data collection frequency of 50 MHz. Generally, both attenuation and velocity profiles should be determined. For the Forest Glen site, we found that attenuation was a more informative diagnostic than was velocity.

VI. SUMMARY AND CONCLUSIONS

Computerized tomography was adapted and applied to geophysical exploration using data collected by cross-borehole electromagnetic probing. Straight-ray propagation was assumed. A modified iterative-reconstruction technique was developed and used to analyze both synthetic and experimental data. In principle either electromagnetic or seismic data could be reconstructed using the techniques discussed. However, seismic data are likely to require ray-bending corrections to obtain accurate reconstructions. Further work is planned to incorporate ray-bending corrections into the iterative-reconstruction technique.

ACKNOWLEDGMENTS

The authors wish to thank L. L. Cleland of the Lawrence Livermore Laboratory, R. K. MacFarland of the Department of Transportation, and D. A. Linger of the Federal Highway Administration for sponsorship of various phases of this work. Helpful discussions were held with the above individuals and our colleagues at the Lawrence Livermore Laboratory; in particular, A. G. Duba, R. W. Egbert, J. G. Huebel, D. L. Lager, E. F. Laine, E. K. Miller, and J. T. Okada.

REFERENCES

[1] G. N. Hounsfield, "Method and apparatus for measuring X or γ-radiation absorption or transmission at plural angles and analyzing the data," U.S. Patent 3 778 614, Dec. 11, 1973.

[2] R. M. Mersereau and A. V. Oppenheim, "Digital reconstruction of multi-dimensional signals from their projections," *Proc. IEEE*, vol. 62, no. 10, pp. 1319–1338, Oct. 1974.

[3] A. C. Kak, "Algorithms for reconstruction," in *Cardiovascular Imaging and Image Processing* (Proceedings of Conference on Cardiovascular Imaging and Image Processing, Theory and Practice), vol. 72, H. Sandler and H. A. Miller, Eds. Published by Society of Photo-Optical Instrumentation Engineers, 1975, pp. 163–175.

[4] H. J. Scudder, "Introduction to computer aided tomography," *Proc. IEEE*, vol. 66, pp. 628–637, June 1978.

[5] J. Radon, "Ueber die Bestimmung von Functionen durch ihre integralwerte Laengs gewisser Manninfoltigkeiten (On the determination of functions from their integrals along certain manifolds)," *Berichte Saechsische Acadamie der Wissenschaften (Leipzig), Mathematische-Physische Klasse*, vol. 69, pp. 262–277, 1917.

[6] A. M. Cormack, "Representation of a function by its line integrals with some radiological applications—I," *J. Appl. Phys.*, vol. 35, pp. 2722–2727, 1963.

[7] A. M. Cormack, "Representation of a function by its line integrals with some radiological applications—II," *J. Appl. Phys.*, vol. 35, pp. 2908–1913, 1964.

[8] R. N. Bracewell and A. C. Riddle, "Inversion of fan-beam scans in radio astronomy," *Astrophys. J.*, vol. 150, pp. 427–434, 1967.

[9] M. V. Berry and D. F. Gibbs, "The interpretation of optical projection," *Proc. Roy. Soc. London, Ser. A*, vol. 314, pp. 143–152, 1970.

[10] G. N. Ramachandran and A. V. Lakshminarayanan, "Three-dimensional reconstruction from radiographs and electron micrographs: III. Description and application of the convolution method," *Indian J. Pure Appl. Phys.*, vol. 9, pp. 997–1003, 1971.

[11] A. M. Cormack, "Reconstruction of densities from their projections with applications in radiological physics," *Phys. Med. Biol.*, vol. 18, pp. 195–207, 1973.

[12] L. A. Shepp and B. F. Logan, "The Fourier reconstruction of a head section," *IEEE Trans. Nucl. Sci.*, vol. NS-21, pp. 21–43, June 1974.

[13] C. V. Jakowatz, Jr., "Computerized tomographic imaging using X-rays and ultrasound," Ph.D. dissertation, School of Elec. Eng., Purdue Univ., Lafayette, IN, Aug. 1976. (Available from University Microfilms International, Ann Arbor, MI.)

[14] K. A. Dines, "Measurement and reconstruction of ultrasonic parameters for diagnostic imaging," Ph.D. dissertation, School of Elec. Eng., Purdue Univ., Lafayette, IN, Dec. 1976. (Available from University Microfilms International, Ann Arbor, MI.)

[15] K. A. Dines and A. C. Kak, "Ultrasonic attenuation tomography," *Ultrasonic Imaging*, vol. 1, Jan. 1979.

[16] R. Gordon, "A Tutorial on ART (Algebraic Reconstruction Techniques)," *IEEE Trans. Nucl. Sci.*, vol. NS-21, pp. 78–93, June 1974.

[17] S. Kaczmarz, "Angenaberte auflosung von systemen linearer gleichungen," *Bull. Acad. Polon. Sci. Lett., A.*, pp. 355–357, 1937.

[18] K. Tanabe, "Projection method for solving a singular system of linear equations and its applications," *Numer. Math.*, vol. 17, pp. 203–214, 1971.

[19] R. Gordon, R. Bender, and G. T. Herman, "Algebraic reconstruction techniques (ART) for three-dimensional electron microscopy and X-ray photography," *J. Theor. Biol.*, vol. 29, pp. 471–481, 1971.

[20] R. Gordon and G. T. Herman, "Reconstruction of pictures from their projections," *Commun. A.C.M.*, vol. 14, pp. 759–768, 1971.

[21] P. Gilbert, "Iterative methods for the reconstruction of three-dimensional objects from projections," *J. Theor. Biol.*, vol. 36, pp. 105–117, 1972.

[22] G. T. Herman and S. Rowland, "Resolution in ART: an experimental investigation of the resolving power of an algebraic picture reconstruction technique," *J. Theor. Biol.*, vol. 33, pp. 213–223, 1971.

[23] G. T. Herman, A. Lent, and S. Rowland, "ART: Mathematics and applications: a report on the mathematical foundations and on applicability to real data of the algebraic reconstruction techniques," *J. Theor. Biol.*, vol. 43, pp. 1–32, 1973.

[24] J. F. Greenleaf, S. A. Johnson, S. L. Lee, G. T. Herman, and E. H. Wood, "Algebraic reconstruction of spatial distributions of acoustic absorption within tissue from their two-dimensional acoustic projections," in *Acoustical Holography*, vol. 5. New

York: Plenum, 1974, pp. 591–603.

[25] R. A. Crowther and A. Klug, "Three dimensional image reconstruction on an extended field—A fast, stable algorithm," *Nature*, vol. 257, pp. 490–492, 1974.

[26] T. F. Budinger and G. T. Gullberg, "Three-dimensional reconstruction in nuclear medicine emission imaging," *IEEE Trans. Nucl. Sci.*, vol. 21, no. 3, pp. 2–21, 1974.

[27] B. K. P. Horn, "Density reconstruction using arbitrary ray sampling schemes," *Proc. IEEE*, vol. 66, pp. 551–562, 1978.

[28] J. F. Greenleaf, S. A. Johnson, W. F. Samayoa, and F. A. Duck, "Algebraic reconstruction of spatial distributions of acoustic velocities in tissue from their time of flight profiles," *Acoustical Holography*, vol. 6, pp. 71–90, 1975.

[29] D. W. Sweeney and C. M. Vest, "Reconstruction of three-dimensional refractive index fields from multi-direction interferometric data," *Appl. Opt.*, vol. 12, no. 11, pp. 2649–2664, 1973.

[30] J. R. Wait, *Electromagnetic Waves in Stratified Media*. New York: Pergamon, 1970, pp. 8–106.

[31] L. M. Brekhovskikh, *Waves in Layered Media* (translated from the russian by D. Lieberman). New York: Academic Press, 1960, pp. 168–233.

[32] R. N. Bracewell and S. J. Wernecke, "Image reconstruction over a finite field of view," *J. Opt. Soc. Amer.*, vol. 65, pp. 1342–1346, 1975.

[33] R. J. Lytle, D. L. Lager, E. F. Laine, and J. D. Salisbury, "Monitoring fluid flow by using high-frequency electromagnetic probing," Lawrence Livermore Lab. Rep. UCRL-51979 (ERA 1: 17178, available from National Technical Inform. Serv., Springfield, VA), 1976.

[34] D. L. Lager and R. J. Lytle, "Determining a subsurface electromagnetic profile from high-frequency measurements by applying reconstruction technique algorithms," *Radio Sci.*, vol. 12, no. 2, pp. 249–260, 1977.

[35] R. J. Lytle, D. L. Lager, E. F. Laine, and D. T. Davis, "Using cross-borehole electromagnetic probing to locate high-contrast anomalies," to be published in *Geophysics*.

[36] R. J. Lytle, E. F. Laine, D. L. Lager, and J. T. Okada, "Determination of the in situ high frequency electrical properties of permafrost rock," *Radio Sci.*, vol. 11, no. 4, pp. 285–294, 1976.

[37] R. J. Lytle, K. A. Dines, E. F. Laine, and D. L. Lager, "Electromagnetic cross-borehole survey of a site proposed for a future urban transit station," Lawrence Livermore Lab. Rep. UCRL-52484, 1978. (Available from National Technical Inform. Serv., Springfield, VA.)

[38] M. Born and E. Wolf, *Principles of Optics*. New York: Pergamon, 1964.

[39] a) P. Bois, M. LaPorte, M. Lavergne, and G. Thomas, "Essai de determination automatique des vitesses sismiques par mesures entre puits," *Geophysic. Prospect.*, vol. 19, pp. 42–83, 1971.
b) ——, "Well-to-well seismic measurements," *Geophysics*, vol. 37, pp. 471–480, June 1972.

[40] M. LaPorte, J. Lakshmanan, M. Lavergne, and C. Willm, "Mesures sismiques par transmission—Application au genie civil," *Geophysic. Prospect.*, vol. 21, pp. 146–158, 1973.

[41] K. A. Dines and R. J. Lytle, "Iterative reconstruction of underground refractive index distributions from cross-borehole transmission data," Lawrence Livermore Lab., Rep. UCRL-52348 (ERA 3:27006, available from the National Technical Inform. Serv., Springfield, VA), 1977.

Spectral Approach to Geophysical Inversion by Lorentz, Fourier, and Radon Transforms

ENDERS A. ROBINSON

Invited Paper

Abstract—Geophysical inversion seeks to determine the structure of the interior of the earth from data obtained at the surface. In reflection seismology, the problem is to find inverse methods that give structure, composition, and source parameters by processing the received seismograms. The pioneering work of Jack Cohen and Norman Bleistein on general inverse methods has caused a revolution in the direction of research on long-standing unsolved geophysical problems. This paper does not deal with such general methods, but instead gives a survey of some production-type data processing methods in everyday use in geophysical exploration. The unifying theme is the spectral approach which provides methods for the approximate solution of some simplified inverse problems of practical importance.

This paper is divided into two parts, one dealing with one-dimensional (1-D) inversion, the other with two-dimensional (2-D) inversion. The 1-D case treated is that of a horizontally layered earth (Goupillaud model) with seismic raypaths only in the vertical direction. This model exhibits a lattice structure which corresponds to the lattice methods of spectral estimation. It is shown that the lattice structure is mathematically equivalent to the structure of the Lorentz transformation of the special theory of relativity. The solution of this 1-D inverse problem is the discrete counterpart of the Gelfand–Levitan inversion method in physics. A practical computational scheme to carry out the inversion

Manuscript received February 17, 1982; revised May 6, 1982.

The author was with the Departments of Geological Sciences and Theoretical and Applied Mechanics, Cornell University, Ithaca, NY 14853. He is now at 100 Autumn Lane, Lincoln, MA 01773.

process is the method of dynamic deconvolution. It is based on a generalization of the Levinson recursion, and involves the interacting recursions of two polynomials P and Q. This paper treats only much simplified 2-D models. One 2-D method gives the forward and inverse solution for a horizontally layered earth (Goupillaud model) with slanting seismic raypaths. This method involves the Radon transform which is often called "slant stacking" by geophysicists. The other 2-D methods given in this paper are concerned with the process of wavefield reconstruction and imaging known as "migration" in the geophysical industry. A major breakthrough occurred in 1978 when Stolt introduced spectral migration which makes the use of the fast Fourier transform. Another method, the slant-stack migration of Hubral, is based on the Radon transform.

I. Introduction

THE DIRECT problem in geophysics may be thought of as the determination of how seismic waves propagate on the basis of a known makeup of the subsurface of the earth. The inverse problem is to determine the subsurface makeup on the basis of wave motion observed at the surface of the earth. The inverse problem is not unique to geophysics. A large part of our physical contact with our surroundings depends upon an intuitive solution of inverse problems. In many other real-world problems, we must also infer the size, shape, and texture of remote objects from the way they trans-

Reprinted from *Proc. IEEE*, vol. 70, pp. 1039–1054, Sept. 1982.

mit, reflect, and scatter traveling waves. For example, in X-ray computerized tomography [1], it is necessary to combine X-ray scans taken at different angles to form a cross-sectional image which represents the internal details of the scanned structure. In nondestructive testing [2], a reconstruction of three-dimensional (3-D) refractive-index field is made from holographic measurements taken at different angles. In electron microscopy [3], 3-D biological structures are deduced from 2-D electron micrographs taken at different tilt angles. Optimization techniques are being developed for digital image reconstruction from various types of projections [4].

In 1877, Lord Rayleigh [5] treated a physical inverse problem; he was one of the first scientists to do so. Rayleigh considered the problem of finding the density distribution of a string from knowledge of the vibrations. Kac [6] aptly described this inverse problem in the title of his well-known lecture "Can one hear the shape of a drum?" Because seismic waves are sound waves in the earth, we can describe our inverse problem (i.e., seismic exploration) as "Can we hear the shape of an oil field?"

With the introduction of the Schrödinger equation to describe the microphysical world, the scope of inverse problems in physics became enormously enlarged. Over the years, many general inversion procedures were formulated. One of the most elegant approaches was given by Gelfand and Levitan [7] on the solution of a differential equation by its spectral function. This solution leads to an integral equation, the Gelfand–Levitan equation. We will treat the discrete form of the Gelfand–Levitan integral equation in this paper, as well as give a computational scheme, known in geophysics as dynamic deconvolution, for its solution. The word "dynamic" is used to differentiate this deconvolution process from the usual time-invariant deconvolution methods.

The spectral methods used in geophysics are closely connected with the inverse problem [8]. Basically, the spectral approach provides methods for the approximate solution of many simplified inverse problems. We will be concerned in this paper with such specialized solutions and not with the general case. In this sense, this paper deals with the production-type data processing methods in everyday use in geohysical exploration, which serve not perfectly but well.

Since the energy crisis, a greatly increased research effort has been devoted to problems in the geophysical exploration for oil and natural gas. General inverse scattering methods from the mainstream of physics and applied mathematics have been introduced to the geophysical exploration industry. The pioneering work of Jack Cohen and Norman Bleistein has caused a revolution in the direction of research on the long-standing unsolved problems in the seismic exploration for oil. We do not treat these more powerful methods in this paper, but refer the reader to the recent work of Silvia [9], Silvia and Weglein [10], Cohen and Bleistein [11], [12], Mendel and Habibi-Ashrafi [13], Coen [14], Carroll and Santosa [15], Driessel and Symes [16], Stolt [17], Bube and Burridge [18], Zemanian and Subramaniam [19], Gazdag [20], Bamberger, Chavent, and Lailly [21], and Treitel, Gutowski, Hubral, and Wagner [22]. Larner [23] gives a balanced understanding of the entire field of exploration geophysics, from the most difficult physical and mathematical methods to the practical field implementation.

Because we are at a turning point in the methods used in seismic exploration, it is well to summarize where we stand today. Some of the methods presently in use will be replaced by the newer, more powerful methods now being developed, and others may survive, albeit in some modified form.

We divide this paper into two parts, 1-D and 2-D. The 1-D problems are concerned with a laterally homogeneous earth, so the only variation is in the depth dimension z. The basic method which we treat here is the Gelfand–Levitan solution of the inverse problem and the related dynamical-deconvolution scheme. These techniques are closely related to lattice approaches to spectral estimation [24], which use the Levinson recursion [25] and the Burg method [26]. Briefly, dynamic deconvolution is based on the interacting recursions of P and Q polynomials. These polynomials are related to the polynomial A appearing in the Levinson recursion by means of the equation $A_k = P_k - c_0 Q_k$, where $|c_0| = 1$.

We do not give any general solution of the 2-D problem, but instead treat special simplified cases which have proved useful. The 3-D problem is not treated at all because the simplified 2-D methods which we present can readily be extended to the 3-D case. Of course, in such an extension, many facets which depend upon dimension must be respected, but the basic ideas are the same. Today the exploration industry is using 3-D data (lateral dimensions x and y, and depth dimension z pointing downward) more and more, and eventually all exploration will be done with 3-D models. It is here that the general inverse approaches introduced by the pathfinding work of Cohen and Bleistein will reach their greatest effectiveness.

The specialized 2-D methods which we present make use of spectral analysis to solve a much simplified problem, known in the industry as migration. The two spectral techniques used are the 2-D Fourier transform and its related Radon transformation. The Fourier migration method is due to Stolt [27], and the Radon migration method is due to Hubral [28]. The Stolt method, which takes advantage of the efficiency of the fast Fourier transform, was a major breakthrough in seismic migration, and it has led to many other developments.

In brief, the limelight in geophysical exploration is on inverse methods. However, when one looks closer, one sees that underlying these methods are the associated spectral methods. Basically, the spectral approach can be used in conjunction with inversion theory to obtain solutions which give us both physical insight and practical exploration tools. The spectral approach, as exemplified by the 1-D lattice (i.e., layered-earth) methods and the 2-D Fourier and Radon migration methods, has provided practical computational schemes for seismic data processing. These spectral methods work and can be used routinely to solve exploration problems successfully in a large number of cases, even though the complete mathematical inverse solution is yet beyond our reach.

II. One-Dimensional Inversion

A. *The Goupillaud Layered-Earth Model*

The determination of the properties of the earth from waves that have been reflected from the earth is the clasic problem of reflection seismology. As a first step in mathematical analysis, the problem is usually simplified by assuming that the earth's crust is made up of a sequence of sedimentary layers. The well-known *Goupillaud model* [29] (Fig. 1) approximates the heterogeneous earth with a sequence of horizontal layers, each of which is homogeneous, isotropic, and nonabsorptive. This stratified model is subjected to vertically traveling plane compressional waves, and thus it is a normal incidence model. It is assumed that the two-way travel time in each layer is the same and is equal to one time unit. In other words, the one-way

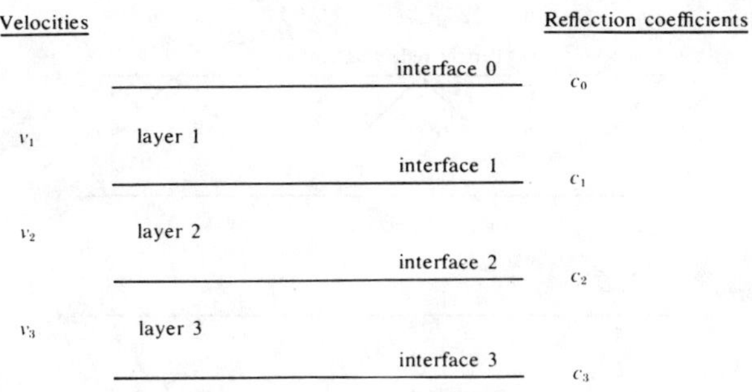

Fig. 1. The Goupillaud model.

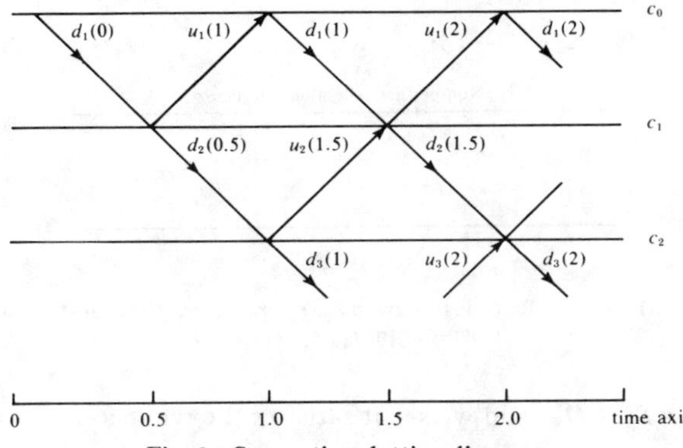

Fig. 2. Space–time lattice diagram.

travel time in each layer is taken to be one-half of the discrete unit of time. The upper half-space (the air) is called half-space 0, the first layer underneath is called layer 1, the next layer underneath is called layer 2, and so on. Interface 0 is the interface at the bottom of half-space 0, interface 1 is the interface at the bottom of layer 1, and so on. Let c_k be the reflection coefficient for downgoing waves striking interface k. The reflection coefficient for upgoing waves striking interface k is thus equal to $-c_k$. We will assume that the amplitudes of our waves are measured in units such that squared amplitude is proportional to energy. Then the transmission coefficient through interface k is equal to $(1 - c_k^2)^{1/2}$ for either upgoing or downgoing waves. All waves are digitized with unit time spacing. Although the waves exist throughout the layers, we will only be concerned with them as measured at the tops of the layers; see Fig. 2. This is done in order to keep the bookkeeping as simple as possible. If the number of the layer is odd, then time is measured at integer values: $n = 0, 1, 2, \cdots$. However, if the layer is even, then time is measured at integer-plus-one-half values: $n + 0.5 = 0.5, 1.5, 2.5, \cdots$. This is because it takes only 0.5 time unit for a wave to traverse a layer. For example, if a downgoing impulse is introduced at time 0 at the top of layer 1, then it arrives at the top of layer 2 at time 0.5, at the top of layer 3 at time 1, at the top of layer 4 at time 1.5, and so on. Because z is used for the depth dimension in geophysics, we will use the Laplace generating function instead of the z-transform. The variable s in the Laplace generating function corresponds to the variable z^{-1} in the z-transform. The downgoing wave at the top of layer k is denoted by $d_k(n)$ if k is odd, and by $d_k(n + 0.5)$ if k is even, where n is an integer. The respective generating functions are

$$D_k(s) = \sum_n d_k(n) s^n \qquad (k \text{ odd})$$

$$D_k(s) = \sum_n d_k(n + 0.5) s^{n+0.5} \qquad (k \text{ even}).$$

The corresponding z transforms are obtained by letting $s = z^{-1}$. Similarly, the upgoing wave $u_k(n)$ for k odd, and $u_k(n + 0.5)$ for k even, is also measured at the top of the layer. Its generating function is $U_k(s)$.

We have thus described the Goupillaud-layered media. Besides its interest in exploration geophysics, the Goupillaud model is of interest in spectral estimation, for it is mathematically the same as a *lattice network*. These networks are useful in building models of many processes which occur in engineering practice, such as the acoustic tube model for digital speech processing, as developed by Gray and Markel [30], and others. As shown by Makhoul [31] and Durrani, Murukutla, and Sharman [32], the lattice model provides methods for adaptive spectral estimation. We now want to discuss some of the properties of this model that have been useful in exploration geophysics.

B. The Lorentz Transformation

When Maxwell derived the electromagnetic wave equation, it soon became known that it is not invariant under the Galilean transformation. However, it is invariant under the Lorentz transformation, and this observation was a key factor in Einstein's development of the special theory of relativity [33]. The *Lorentz transformation* can be written as

$$D_2 = \frac{1}{(1 - c_1^2)^{1/2}} [D_1 - c_1 U_1]$$

$$U_2 = \frac{1}{(1 - c_1^2)^{1/2}} [-cD_1 + U_1]$$

where D_1 and U_1 are, respectively, the time and space coordinates of an event in frame 1, where D_2 and U_2 are, respectively, the time and space coordinates of the event in frame 2, and c_1 (where $|c_1| < 1$) is the velocity (in natural units, such that the velocity of light is unity) between the two frames. The Lorentz transformation is a consequence of the invariance of the interval between events. By direct substitution, it can be shown that the coordinates of two events must satisfy the equation

$$D_2^2 - U_2^2 = D_1^2 - U_1^2$$

on transition from one frame of reference to the other.

We now want to find the relationship between the waves in the Goupillaud model. Instead of the conventional treatment, we will try to put this relationship in a more general setting. We know that the waves in each layer obey their respective wave equation. Let $D_1(s)$ and $U_1(s)$ be, respectively, the generating functions of the downgoing wave and the upgoing wave at the top of layer 1, and let $D_2(s)$ and $U_2(s)$ be the corresponding functions for layer 2. We then say that *wave motion* must be related by the *Lorentz transformation*

$$D_2(s) = \frac{1}{(1 - c_1^2)^{1/2}} [s^{1/2} D_1(s) - c_1 s^{-1/2} U_1(s)]$$

$$U_2(s) = \frac{1}{(1 - c_1^2)^{1/2}} [-c_1 s^{1/2} D_1(s) + s^{-1/2} U_1(s)].$$

The constant c_1 (where $|c_1| < 1$) is the reflection coefficient of the interface between the two layers. This Lorentz transformation is a consequence of the invariance of the net downgoing energy in the layers. By direct substitution, it can be shown that

$$D_2 \overline{D}_2 - U_2 \overline{U}_2 = D_1 \overline{D}_1 - U_1 \overline{U}_1$$

(where the bar indicates that s is to be replaced by s^{-1}; i.e., $\overline{D(s)} = D(s^{-1})$). This equation says that the net downgoing energy in each layer is the same. Because there is no absorption, this energy relation is a physical fact implied by the model.

C. Polynomial Recursions

The Lorentz transformation between two adjacent layers can be written in matrix form as

$$\begin{bmatrix} D_{k+1} \\ U_{k+1} \end{bmatrix} = \frac{s^{-1/2}}{t_k} \begin{bmatrix} s & -c_k \\ -c_k s & 1 \end{bmatrix} \begin{bmatrix} D_k \\ U_k \end{bmatrix}$$

where we have used the symbol t_k to denote the transmission coefficient $(1 - c_k^2)^{1/2}$. Robinson [34] defines the polynomials $P_k(s)$ and $Q_k(s)$, and the reverse polynomials (with superscript R for reverse) given by

$$P_k^R(s) = s^k P_k(s^{-1})$$

$$Q_k^R(s) = s^k Q_k(s^{-1}).$$

These polynomials are defined by the equation

$$\begin{bmatrix} P_k^R & Q_k^R \\ Q_k & P_k \end{bmatrix} = \begin{bmatrix} s & -c_k \\ -c_k s & 1 \end{bmatrix} \begin{bmatrix} s & -c_{k-1} \\ -c_{k-1}s & 1 \end{bmatrix} \cdots \begin{bmatrix} s & -c_1 \\ -c_1 s & 1 \end{bmatrix}.$$

By inspection, we can find the first and last coefficients of these polynomials. We have

$$P_k(s) = 1 + \cdots + c_1 c_k s^{k-1}$$

$$Q_k(s) = -c_1 s + \cdots - c_k s^k$$

$$P_k^R(s) = c_1 c_k s + \cdots + s^k$$

$$Q_k^R(s) = -c_k + \cdots - c_1 s^{k-1}.$$

The polynomials for adjacent layers are related by

$$\begin{bmatrix} P_k^R & Q_k^R \\ Q_k & P_k \end{bmatrix} = \begin{bmatrix} s & -c_k \\ -c_k s & 1 \end{bmatrix} \begin{bmatrix} P_{k-1}^R & Q_{k-1}^R \\ Q_{k-1} & P_{k-1} \end{bmatrix}.$$

This equation gives the *Robinson recursion* [34]

$$P_k = P_{k-1} - c_k s Q_{k-1}^R$$

$$Q_k = Q_{k-1} - c_k s P_{k-1}^R$$

and its inverse recursion

$$P_{k-1} = \frac{1}{1 - c_k^2} (P_k + c_k Q_k^R)$$

$$Q_{k-1} = \frac{1}{1 - c_k^2} (Q_k + c_k P_k^R).$$

Let us now subtract the two recursion equations to obtain

$$(P_k - Q_k) = (P_{k-1} - Q_{k-1}) - c_k s(Q_{k-1}^R - P_{k-1}^R).$$

Let c_0 be the reflection coefficient of interface 0, where $|c_0| = 1$. To be definite, let $c_0 = 1$. If we define the polynomial A_k as $A_k = P_k - c_0 Q_k = P_k - Q_k$, we obtain the *Levinson recursion* [25]

$$A_k = A_{k-1} + c_k s A_{k-1}^R.$$

The *polynomial of the second kind* is defined as $B_k = P_k +$

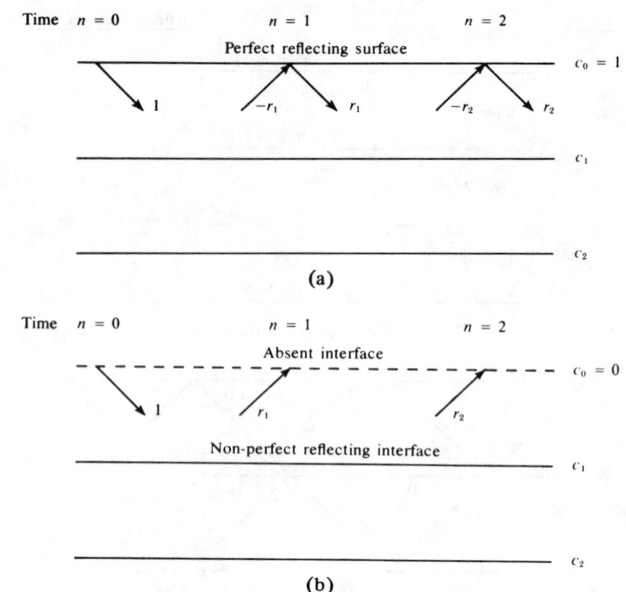

Fig. 3. (a) Free-surface siesmogram $r_1, r_2, r_3, \cdots$. (b) Non-free-surface seismogram $r_1, r_2, r_3, \cdots$.

$c_0 Q_k = P_k + Q_k$, and we see it satisfies the recursion

$$B_k = B_{k-1} - c_k s B_{k-1}^R.$$

The inverse of the Levinson recursion is

$$A_{k-1} = \frac{1}{1 - c_k^2} (A_k - c_k A_k^R).$$

We will now make use of the two recursions given in this section for the analysis of layered-earth (lattice) models; the A recursion for the free-surface case and the P, Q recursion for the non-free-surface case.

D. Free-Surface and Non-Free-Surface Reflection Seismograms

We now want to consider an idealized seismic experiment. The source is a downgoing unit impulse introduced at the top of layer 1 at time instant 0. This pulse proceeds downward where it undergoes multiple reflections and refractions within the layered system. Some of the energy is returned to the top of layer 1, where it is recorded in the form of a seismic trace, which we denote by the sequence $r_1, r_2, r_3, \cdots$, where the subscript indicates the discrete time index; see Fig. 3.

There are two types of boundary conditions commonly imposed on the top interface (interface 0 with reflection coefficient c_0). One is the free-surface condition, which says that interface 0 (the air-earth interface) is a perfect reflector; that is, the free-surface condition is that $|c_0| = 1$. The free-surface condition approximately holds in the case of a marine seismogram taken in a very smooth, calm sea, so the surface of the water (interface 0) is virtually a perfect reflector.

The other condition is the non-free-surface case. For notational convenience, we will choose the non-free surface as interface 1; that is, the air-earth interface is taken as interface 1, which can have an arbitrary (nonperfect) reflection coefficient c_1, where $|c_1| < 1$. Since interface 1 represents the surface of the ground, it follows that interface 0 is not present, that is, $c_0 = 0$. Thus the non-free-surface condition is that $c_0 = 0$ and c_1 is arbitrary.

In summary, an ideal marine seismogram is generated by the

Goupillaud model with the free-surface condition $|c_0| = 1$. To be definite, we will use $c_0 = 1$. Thus the reflection coefficient for upgoing waves is $-c_0$, which is -1, so an upcoming pulse $-r_n$ is reflected into the downgoing pulse r_n. A typical land seismogram is generated by the Goupillaud model with the non-free-surface condition, which for convenience of notation, we take as $c_0 = 0$ and $|c_1| < 1$ (so interface 1 is the surface of the earth). The well-known acoustic tube model [35] for human speech may be described as a Goupillaud-type model with the free-surface condition at the lips.

Kunetz [36] gave the solution for the inversion of a free-surface reflection seismogram. This inversion method yields the reflection coefficient series $c_1, c_2, c_3, \cdots$, from which the impedance function of the earth as a function of depth may be readily computed. Robinson [34] reformulated the Kunetz solution in terms of the Levinson [25] recursion and gave a computer program to do both the forward process (generation of the synthetic seismogram) and the inverse process (inversion of the seismogram to obtain the reflection coefficients). The Kunetz method is covered in the next section.

The celebrated inversion method of Gelfand and Levitan [7] represents the solution of the inversion problem for non-free-surface reflection seismograms. This method has been in the mainstream of physics for many years, and has been further developed and extended by many physicists and mathematicians. The discrete form of the Gelfand–Levitan equation is derived by Aki and Richards [38] for the case of a finite inhomogeneous medium, that is, an inhomogeneous medium bounded by homogeneous media at both ends. In Section II-F, we treat the discrete Gelfand–Levitan equation and give a derivation which holds for an unbounded inhomogeneous medium. We then discuss dynamic deconvolution, which is a means of solving the Gelfand–Levitan equation. Dynamic deconvolution makes use of the interactive recursion of the P and Q polynomials [34]. This recursion for the non-free-surface case represents the counterpart of the Levinson recursion for the free-surface case.

E. The Kunetz Inversion of Free-Surface Reflection Seismograms

Let the source in the Goupillaud model with the free-surface condition $c_0 = 1$ be a unit spike at time 0; see Fig. 3(a). The source gives rise to an upgoing wave in the first layer as a result of reflections and refractions from the interfaces below. We denote this upgoing wave by $-r_1, -r_2, -r_3, \cdots$; that is,

$$u_1(n) = -r_n \quad (\text{for } n = 1, 2, 3, \cdots)$$

represents the wave motion striking the free surface from below. The free surface is a perfect reflector (with upgoing reflection coefficient $-c_0 = -1$). The upgoing wave is reflected back to produce the downgoing wave

$$d_1(n) = r_n \quad (\text{for } n = 1, 2, 3, \cdots).$$

The entire downgoing wave at the top of layer 1 is made up of this reflected portion together with the initial source pulse

$$d_1(0) = 1.$$

We will call $r_1, r_2, r_3, \cdots$, the reflection seismogram. Thus

$$R(s) = r_1 s + r_2 s^2 + r_3 s^3 + \cdots$$

is the generating function of the reflection seismogram. Then

it follows that

$$U_1(s) = -R(s)$$

$$D_1(s) = 1 + R(s).$$

We will now use the invariance property of the Lorentz transformation. The net downgoing energy in layer 1 is

$$D_1 \overline{D}_1 - U_1 \overline{U}_1 = (1 + R)(1 + \overline{R}) - R\overline{R} = 1 + R + \overline{R}.$$

Here we use the convention that a bar over a function indicates that each s is replaced by s^{-1}. If we go very deep, we can assume that we reach a depth where no waves are reflected upward, so we can write

$$U_\infty = 0.$$

Thus at this infinite depth, we have

$$D_\infty \overline{D}_\infty - U_\infty \overline{U}_\infty = D_\infty \overline{D}_\infty.$$

We now come to an important point, which makes the layered earth model (i.e., a lattice network) useful for spectral analysis. Because $\Phi(\omega)$ defined as

$$\Phi(\omega) = D_\infty(e^{-i\omega}) D_\infty(e^{i\omega})$$

is a *bona fide* spectral density function (i.e., nonnegative function of ω), we can use the invariance of the net downgoing energy from layer to layer to establish that

$$\Phi(\omega) = 1 + R(e^{-i\omega}) + R(e^{i\omega})$$

is the same spectral density function. Therefore, the seismogram, completed by the initial pulse and by symmetry

$$\cdots, r_{-3}, r_{-2}, r_{-1}, 1, r_1, r_2, r_3, \cdots$$

is a *bona fide* autocorrelation function. That *the seismogram is the right-half side of an autocorrelation function* is the celebrated result of *Kunetz* [36].

The problem of finding the reflection coefficients $c_1, c_2, c_3, \cdots$ from the free-surface reflection seismograms $r_1, r_2, r_3, \cdots$ represents the inverse problem. The earth's acoustic impedance function is readily computed from the reflection coefficient series.

The Lorentz transformation from layer 0 to layer $k + 1$ may be written as

$$\begin{bmatrix} D_{k+1} \\ U_{k+1} \end{bmatrix} = \frac{s^{-k/2}}{\sigma_k} \begin{bmatrix} P_k^R & Q_k^R \\ Q_k & P_k \end{bmatrix} \begin{bmatrix} 1 + R \\ -R \end{bmatrix}$$

where $\sigma_k = t_1 t_2 \cdots t_k$ is the one-way transmission coefficient through the k interfaces. Using this matrix equation, we solve for D_{k+1}. Then, by replacing s by s^{-1}, we form $\overline{D}_{k+1}$. We also solve for U_{k+1}. We thus find that

$$\overline{D}_{k+1} - U_{k+1} = \frac{s^{-0.5k}}{\sigma_k} A_k(1 + R + \overline{R})$$

where A_n is defined as $A_n = P_n - Q_n$. Since $\Phi = 1 + R + \overline{R}$, we have

$$A_k \Phi = \sigma_k s^{0.5k} (\overline{D}_{k+1} - U_{k+1}).$$

Let us appeal to the physics of the situation; see Fig. 4. The function D_{k+1} is the generating function of the downgoing wave at the top of layer $k + 1$. This downgoing wave is made up of the direct pulse $d_{k+1}(0.5k)$ together with the following pulses: $d_{k+1}(0.5k + 1), d_{k+1}(0.5k + 2), \cdots$. Because the

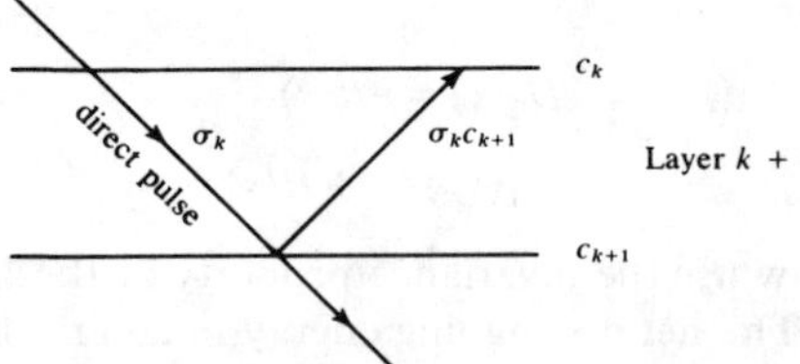

Fig. 4. Reflection of the direct pulse.

direct pulse is the result of only the transmissions through the first k interfaces, we see that the direct pulse is the product of these k transmission coefficients, that is,

$$d_{k+1}(0.5k) = t_1 t_2 \cdots t_k = \sigma_k.$$

Because the time instant of this direct pulse is $0.5k$, we see that

$$D_{k+1}(s) = \sigma_k s^{0.5k} + \text{(terms in higher powers of } s).$$

The function U_{k+1} is the generating function of the upgoing wave at the top of layer $k + 1$. The first pulse in the upgoing wave is the reflection of the direct downgoing pulse at interface $k + 1$. Thus the magnitude of this first upgoing pulse is $\sigma_k c_{k+1}$; that is, the magnitude is equal to the magnitude of the direct downgoing pulse times the reflection coefficient c_{k+1}. Because one time unit elapses for the round trip in layer $k + 1$, the first pulse of the upgoing wave in layer $k + 1$ occurs at one time unit later than the first pulse of the downgoing wave in layer $k + 1$. That is, the first upgoing pulse at the top of layer $k + 1$ occurs at time $0.5k + 1$. Thus

$$U_{k+1}(s) = \sigma_k c_{k+1} s^{0.5k+1} + \text{(terms in higher powers of } s).$$

Using the above expressions, we obtain

$$A_k \Phi = \sigma_k s^{0.5k} \left[\text{(terms in lower powers of } s) + \sigma_k s^{-0.5k} \right.$$
$$\left. - \sigma_k c_{k+1} s^{0.5k+1} + \text{(terms in higher powers of } s) \right]$$

or

$$A_k \Phi = \sigma_k^2 \left[\text{(terms in negative powers)} + 1 - c_{k+1} s^{k+1} \right.$$
$$\left. + \text{(terms in higher powers)} \right]$$

where $\sigma_k^2 = (t_1 t_2 \cdots t_k)^2$ is the two-way transmission coefficient through the k interfaces. Now comes the critical observation. The powers of s from 1 to k are missing on the right-hand side of the above equation. We will exploit this fact. We equate coefficients on each side of this equation for the powers of s from 0 to $k + 1$. We thus obtain the equations (one for each power from 0 to $k + 1$) given by

$$a_{k0} r_0 + a_{k1} r_1 + \cdots + a_{kk} r_k = \sigma_k^2$$

$$a_{k0} r_1 + a_{k1} r_0 + \cdots + a_{kk} r_{k-1} = 0$$

$$\cdots$$

$$a_{k0} r_k + a_{k1} r_{k-1} + \cdots + a_{kk} r_0 = 0$$

$$a_{k0} r_{k+1} + a_{k1} r_k + \cdots + a_{kk} r_1 = \sigma_k^2 c_{k+1}.$$

Here $a_{k0}, a_{k1}, \cdots, a_{kk}$ are the coefficients of the polynomial A_k. We note that $a_{k0} = 1$ and $r_0 = 1$. Now let us look at these equations. As we have seen, the Kunetz result says that r_k is an autocorrelation function. Thus these equations are *normal equations*, and hence the Levinson [25] recursion can be used to solve them. The result is the inversion program [34] that finds the reflection coefficients from the free-surface (marine) reflection seismogram.

F. The Gelfand–Levitan Inversion of Non-Free-Surface Reflection Seismograms

Let us now turn to the non-free-surface reflection seismogram, that is, the seismogram produced by the Goupillaud model with the non-free-surface condition $c_0 = 0$ and c_1 arbitrary; see Fig. 3(b). Let the source be a unit spike. The resulting seismogram is taken to be the upgoing wave in the first layer, that is, by

$$u_1(n) = r_n \qquad \text{(for } n = 1, 2, 3, \cdots).$$

Because interface 0 is absent (i.e., $c_0 = 0$) the upgoing wave is not reflected back into the medium. Thus the downgoing wave at the top of layer 1 is simply the initial source pulse

$$d_1(0) = 1, \quad d_1(n) = 0 \qquad \text{(for } n = 1, 2, 3, \cdots).$$

Let $R(s) = r_1 s + r_2 s^2 + \cdots$ be the generating function of the reflection seismogram. Thus $U_1(s) = R(s)$ and $D_1(s) = 1$. The Lorentz transformation is

$$\begin{bmatrix} D_{k+1} \\ U_{k+1} \end{bmatrix} = \sigma_k^{-1} s^{-0.5k} \begin{bmatrix} P_k^R & Q_k^R \\ Q_k & P_k \end{bmatrix} \begin{bmatrix} 1 \\ R \end{bmatrix}.$$

Thus we obtain

$$D_{k+1} = \sigma_k^{-1} s^{-0.5k} (P_k^R + Q_k^R R)$$

$$U_{k+1} = \sigma_k^{-1} s^{-0.5k} (Q_k + P_k R).$$

We add these two equations to obtain

$$D_{k+1} + U_{k+1} = \sigma_k^{-1} s^{-0.5k} (G_k^R + R G_k)$$

where G_k is defined as

$$G_k(s) = P_k(s) + Q_k^R(s)$$
$$= g_{k0} + g_{k1} s + \cdots + g_{k,k-1} s^{k-1}$$
$$= (1 - c_k) + g_{k1} s + \cdots + (c_1 c_k - c_1) s^{k-1}.$$

Because $g_{k0} = 1 - c_k$, we can find c_k as soon as we can determine g_{k0}. Thus the reflection coefficient series, and hence the impedance function of the earth, can be found directly from the sequence $g_{10}, g_{20}, g_{30}, \cdots$. Let us now show how this sequence is determined.

The direct pulse $d_{k+1}(k/2)$ is the product of the transmission coefficients $\sigma_k = t_1 t_2 \cdots t_k$ and it arrives at time $0.5k$. The first term of U_{k+1} arrives at time $0.5k + 1$. Thus $D_{k+1} + U_{k+1}$ has the form

$$D_{k+1} + U_{k+1} = \sigma_k s^{0.5k} + \text{(terms in higher powers of } s).$$

Thus we have

$$\sigma_k s^{0.5k} + \text{(higher power terms)} = \sigma_k^{-1} s^{-0.5k} (G_k^R + R G_k)$$

which gives

$$G_k^R + R G_k = \sigma_k^2 s^k + \text{(higher power terms)}.$$

This equation shows that the coefficients of $G_k^R + R G_k$ for the powers $1, 2, \cdots, k - 1$ are zero and the coefficient for the power k is equal to σ_k^2; that is,

$$g_{k,k-1} + g_{k0} r_1 = 0$$

$$g_{k,k-2} + g_{k0} r_2 + g_{k1} r_1 = 0$$

$$\cdots$$

$$g_{k1} + g_{k0} r_{k-1} + \cdots + g_{k,k-2} r_1 = 0$$

$$g_{k0} + g_{k0} r_k + \cdots + g_{k,k-2} r_2 + g_{k,k-1} r_1 = \sigma_k^2.$$

This set of equations is the discrete version of the *Gelfand–Levitan equation.*

Given the free-surface reflection seismogram $r_1, r_2, r_3, \cdots$, the Gelfand–Levitan inversion method involves solving the above set of equations for each of $k = 1, 2, \cdots N$. For $k = 1$ the set is

$$g_{10} + g_{10}r_1 = \sigma_1^2.$$

For $k = 2$ the set is

$$g_{21} + g_{20}r_1 = 0$$

$$g_{20} + g_{20}r_2 + g_{21}r_1 = \sigma_2^2.$$

After we solve for $g_{10}, g_{20}, \cdots$, then we can find the reflection coefficients by means of

$$c_1 = 1 - g_{10}$$

$$c_2 = 1 - g_{20}$$

and so on.

If we define $a_{k1} = g_{k, k-1}, a_{k2} = g_{k, k-2}, \cdots, a_{k, k-1} = g_{k1}$, $a_{kk} = g_{k0} - 1$, then the Gelfand–Levitan equations are

$$
\begin{bmatrix} a_{k1} \\ a_{k2} \\ \cdots \\ a_{kk} \end{bmatrix}
+
\begin{bmatrix} 0 & 0 & 0 & r_1 \\ 0 & 0 & r_1 & r_2 \\ & & & \\ r_1 & r_2 & r_{k-1} & r_k \end{bmatrix}
\begin{bmatrix} a_{k1} \\ a_{k2} \\ \cdots \\ a_{kk} \end{bmatrix}
+
\begin{bmatrix} r_1 \\ r_2 \\ \cdots \\ r_k \end{bmatrix}
= 0
$$

which we recognize as this discrete counterpart of the *Gelfand–Levitan integral equation* [7], [9], [38]

$$a(\tau, t) + \int_{-t}^{\tau} a(\tau, \beta)\, r(t + \beta)\, d\beta + r(t + \tau) = 0.$$

G. Seismic Inversion by Dynamic Deconvolution

The Gelfand–Levitan method of inversion, together with its many related methods, has received wide recognition. However, instead of the Gelfand–Levitan approach given in the preceding section, the seismic industry approaches the problem from a different point of view. This alternative inversion computational scheme is the method of *dynamic deconvolution* (dy-decon) [39], [40], [8]. Dy-decon inversion is based upon the physical structure of the reflection seismogram. The key fact is that the reflection seismogram is generated from the reflection coefficient by means of the Einstein addition formula [33]. The recognition of this fact makes the inversion of a reflection seismogram very simple from a computational point of view.

Let us now give the dy-decon computation scheme for the inversion of a non-free-surface reflection seismogram. We use the same conventions as in the preceding section. The field-recorded reflection seismogram $r_1, r_2, r_3, \cdots$ is represented by its generating function $R(s)$, which we now will denote by $R_1(s)$ because the field-recorded seismogram occurs in layer 1. We have

$$R_1(s) = r_1 s + r_2 s^2 + r_3 s^3 + \cdots$$

$$= c_1 s + (\text{terms in higher powers of } s).$$

We know $R_1(s)$ must have this form, because $c_1 s$ represents the first bounce from interface 1. No multiple reflections can appear at the time of the first bounce. Now suppose that layer 2 expands to fill the whole upper half-space, so there is no interface 1. Now the top interface is interface 2. Let the resulting seismogram in this expanded layer 2 be represented

by its generating function

$$R_2(s) = c_2 s + (\text{terms in higher powers of } s).$$

Here $c_2 s$ represents the first bounce. Next, expand layer 3 to fill up the whole upper half-space. The resulting reflection seismogram has generating function

$$R_3(s) = c_3 s + (\text{terms in higher powers of } s)$$

where $c_3 s$ represents the first bounce. Thus conceptually we have a suite of reflection seismograms ($k = 1, 2, 3, \cdots$) with generating functions

$$R_k(s) = c_k s + (\text{terms in higher powers of } s)$$

where $c_k s$ represents the first bounce from interface k. We can, therefore, make the following important conclusion. Given the reflection seismogram for layer k, we can immediately find the reflection coefficient c_k for layer k, because c_k is simply the first coefficient appearing in the seismogram. This conclusion represents the solution of one-half of the inversion problem. The other half of the problem involves determining the suite of reflection seismograms. The given information is the top seismogram $R_1(s)$; this seismogram is the one physically recorded in the field by a seismic crew.

If the current in a river has velocity c_1, and if our motor boat in still water has a velocity R_1, then our motor boat headed upstream will have a velocity R_2 given by

$$R_2 = R_1 - c_1.$$

This equation is the *Newton addition formula.* However, if one attempts to apply Newtonian mechanical laws to ultra-high-speed charged particles, then an insurmountable contradiction is encountered. That is, the simple addition of velocities, as used in the boat example, does not apply in electrodynamics. Instead, one should use the Einstein addition formula for combining velocities. The Einstein formula guaranteed that the resulting velocity will never exceed the velocity of light. Thus the above Newton addition formula should be replaced by the *Einstein addition formula,* which is

$$R_2 = \frac{R_1 - c_1}{1 - R_1 c_1}.$$

Here we assume that all velocities are measured in natural units (i.e., in units such that the velocity of light is unity). Suppose $c_1 = -0.5$ and $R_1 = 0.8$. Then, according to the Newton formula, $R_2 = 1.3$, so R_2 is greater than unity; that is, R_2 is greater than the velocity of light. According to the Einstein formula

$$R_2 = \frac{0.8 + 0.5}{1 + 0.8(0.5)} = 0.929$$

which (necessarily) is less than the velocity of light. The Einstein formula is the correct one to use for ultra-high velocities.

Now let us make the following important observation, which led to the dynamic deconvolution process. A reflection coefficient in magnitude can never exceed unity. A reflection coefficient greater than unity in magnitude is just as impossible from the physics as a velocity greater than the velocity of light. Thus in combining the reflection coefficients of a system of layers, it follows that the Einstein addition formula must be used. As a result, the resulting reflectivity will never exceed unity in magnitude, as required in any physical system.

Now we want to head our boat upstream; that is, we want

to dynamically deconvolve down into the earth. We could use the Newton addition formula and write

$$sR_2 = R_1 - c_1 s.$$

That is, the Newton formula says that we merely subtract the first bounce from R_1 in order to obtain R_2. (The s represents a time shift.) In fact, this formula is approximately true if the reflection coefficients are very small in magnitude, just as the Newton formula for velocities is true if the velocities are very small with respect to the velocity of light. Otherwise, we must use the Einstein addition formula

$$R_2 = \frac{R_1 - c_1 s}{s - R_1 c_1}.$$

Let us now give the inversion algorithm of dynamic deconvolution. We know R_1 (i.e., the field-recorded reflection seismogram). In step 1, we find c_1 as the first bounce of R_1, and then we compute R_2 by the above Einstein addition formula. This computation is easily done by making use of subroutine POLYDV in [34]. So ends step 1. In step 2, we find c_2 as the first bounce of R_2, and then we use the Einstein addition formula to find R_3

$$R_3 = \frac{R_2 - c_2 s}{s - R_2 c_2}.$$

So ends step 2. In step 3, we find c_3 as the first bounce of R_3, and then we find R_4 as

$$R_4 = \frac{R_3 - c_3 s}{s - R_3 c_3}.$$

So ends step 3. Thus given R_1, we can perform the entire deconvolution, and so obtain the sequence of reflection coefficients $c_1, c_2, c_3, \cdots$ and the suite of reflection seismograms $R_2, R_3, R_4, \cdots$. From the sequence of reflection coefficients, we can compute the impedance function of the earth.

Dynamic deconvolution gives the same impedance function as that found by the Gelfand–Levitan discrete inversion method. However, dynamic deconvolution is carried out in terms of physically meaningful quantities (i.e., reflection coefficients and reflection seismograms), so interactive computation can be used to reduce the effects of noise. Also, there are many other features of dynamic deconvolution which make it attractive, such as the option [39] of the determination of the reflection coefficients in the reverse order, i.e., in the order $c_n, c_{n-1}, \cdots, c_3, c_2, c_1$. This reverse order can be useful because in many cases, the most harmful noise appears at the beginning of the reflection seismogram. In such cases, it is better to work backwards in time on the reflection seismogram, leaving its noisy beginning to the end of the computations.

Let us now establish the Einstein addition formula by means of the Lorentz transformation. This proof can be found in most physics textbooks. We have

$$\begin{bmatrix} D_2 \\ U_2 \end{bmatrix} = \frac{s^{-1/2}}{t_1} \begin{bmatrix} s & -c_1 \\ -c_1 s & 1 \end{bmatrix} \begin{bmatrix} 1 \\ R_1 \end{bmatrix}$$

which gives

$$t_1 s^{1/2} D_2 = s - c_1 R_1$$

$$t_1 s^{1/2} U_2 = -c_1 s + R_1.$$

The reflection seismogram R_2 is the result obtained by decon-

volving the upgoing wave U_2 by the downgoing wave D_2; that is,

$$R_2 = \frac{U_2}{D_2} = \frac{R_1 - c_1 s}{s - R_1 c_1}.$$

This equation is the Einstein addition formula.

H. Polynomial Recursion for Dynamic Deconvolution Inversion

Further insight on dynamic deconvolution can be obtained by examining the role played by the polynomials P_k and Q_k. Using the Lorentz transformation for the first k layers, we have

$$\begin{bmatrix} D_{k+1} \\ U_{k+1} \end{bmatrix} = \frac{s^{-k/2}}{\sigma_k} \begin{bmatrix} P_k^R & Q_k^R \\ Q_k & P_k \end{bmatrix} \begin{bmatrix} 1 \\ R_1 \end{bmatrix}.$$

As usual, σ_k is the one-way transmission factor

$$\sigma_k = t_k t_{k-1} \cdots t_1.$$

This equation gives

$$D_{k+1} = \sigma_k^{-1} s^{-k/2} (P_k^R + Q_k^R R_1)$$

$$U_{k+1} = \sigma_k^{-1} s^{-k/2} (Q_k + P_k R_1).$$

The direct downgoing pulse arrives at layer $k+1$ at time $k/2$ and with a transmission loss of $\sigma_k = t_1 t_2 \cdots t_k$. Thus D_{k+1} has the form

$$D_{k+1} = \sigma_k s^{k/2} + (\text{terms in higher powers of } s).$$

This direct downgoing pulse is reflected at interface $k+1$ at time $(k+1)/2$ and produces the initial pulse of the upgoing wave. Because the incident pulse has amplitude σ_k and the reflection coefficient is c_{k+1}, it follows that the initial upgoing pulse has amplitude $\sigma_k c_{k+1}$. This initial upgoing pulse arrives at the top of layer $k+1$ at time $(k/2)+1$. Thus U_{k+1} has the form

$$U_{k+1} = \sigma_k c_{k+1} s^{(k/2)+1} + (\text{terms in higher powers of } s).$$

We now have two equations for U_{k+1}. Equating them, we have

$$\sigma_k c_{k+1} s^{(k/2)+1} + (\text{higher power terms})$$

$$= \sigma_k^{-1} s^{-k/2} (Q_k + P_k R_1).$$

Let us now just pick out the $s^{(k/2)+1}$ term on the right-hand side. The right-hand side is

$$\sigma_k^{-1} s^{-k/2} [(q_{k1} s + \cdots + q_{kk} s^k)$$

$$+ (p_{k0} + \cdots + p_{k,k-1} s^{k-1})(r_1 s + \cdots + r_{k+1} s^{k+1} + \cdots)]$$

so the $s^{(k/2)+1}$ term is displayed as

$$\sigma_k^{-1} s^{-k/2} [(p_{k0} r_{k+1} + \cdots + p_{k,k-1} r_2) s^{k+1}$$

$$+ (\text{higher power terms})].$$

Equating the $s^{(k/2)+1}$ terms on the left and right, we have

$$\sigma_k c_{k+1} s^{(k/2)+1} = \sigma_k^{-1} s^{-k/2} (p_{k0} r_{k+1} + \cdots + p_{k,k-1} r_2) s^{k+1}$$

which gives

$$c_{k+1} = \frac{p_{k0} r_{k+1} + p_{k1} r_k + \cdots + p_{k,k-1} r_2}{\sigma_k^2}.$$

We thus have the following scheme based on the Robinson [34] recursion for P and Q in order to invert the non-free-surface reflection seismogram $r_1, r_2, r_3, \cdots$. As the initial step, we set $c_1 = r_1$, $\sigma_1^2 = 1 - c_1^2$, $P_1(s) = 1$, $Q_1(s) = -c_1 s$. Then we perform the following DO loop from $k = 1$ to the total number of layers that we wish to consider

Compute c_{k+1} by the above formula

Compute $\sigma_{k+1}^2 = (1 - c_{k+1}^2)\sigma_k^2$

Compute $P_{k+1}(s) = P_k(s) - c_{k+1} s\, Q_k^R(s)$

Compute $Q_{k+1}(s) = Q_k(s) - c_{k+1} s\, P_k^R(s)$.

We thus obtain the reflection coefficient series $c_1, c_2, c_3, \cdots$ from which the required impedance function can be calculated.

Finally, let us write down the expression for the reflection seismogram R_{k+1} at layer $k + 1$. It is

$$R_{k+1} = \frac{U_{k+1}}{D_{k+1}} = \frac{Q_k + P_k R_1}{P_k^R + Q_k^R R_1}$$

$$= \frac{\sigma_k c_{k+1} s^{(k/2)+1} + \text{(higher power terms)}}{\sigma_k s^{k/2} + \text{(higher power terms)}}$$

$$= c_{k+1} s + \text{(higher power terms)}.$$

We have thus confirmed the statement made in the preceding section that the first bounce of R_{k+1} is $c_{k+1}\, s$.

In closing our discussion of 1-D inversion, let us mention the *fixed-entropy estimate* [41] of the seismic acoustic log. This scheme is an autocorrecting iterative method, based on a forward model, to compute the acoustic impedance of the earth from the reflection seismogram. This method was offered commercially by Digicon Inc. during 1968–1969 under the trade name S.A.L. (for seismic acoustic log), and it has proved successful as a practical inversion scheme in seismic data processing centers.

III. Two-Dimensional Inversion

A. Plane-Wave Decomposition and Migration

We will now consider two spatial dimensions: lateral coordinate x and depth coordinate z, where the z axis points downward. The other dimension is that of time t. The 2-D methods discussed here involve extremely simple models, so these methods are not truly 2-D in any general sense. We discuss two methods. One treats the forward and inverse problem for a horizontally layered media. This method involves the Radon transform [42], which is often called "slant stacking" by geophysicists. The Radon transform produces a plane-wave decomposition of a wavefield, and thus we can operate on each plane wave separately in order to produce our desired results. The other method we present is a process for wavefield reconstruction and imaging. This process is known as "migration" in geophysics. Although various migration methods have been in constant use by the seismic industry for about forty years, a major breakthrough occurred in 1978, when Stolt [27] disclosed his spectral method of migration. This pioneering work of Stolt is based upon the fast Fourier transform, and it is often called frequency-domain migration or f-k migration (frequency–wavenumber migration). Several universities have seismic research projects which devote large efforts to migration and related problems.

B. The Radon Transform

Let $u(x, t)$ represent the wave motion observed on the surface of the ground ($z = 0$). For fixed horizontal position x, the 1-D function $u(x, t)$ of time t represents a seismic trace.

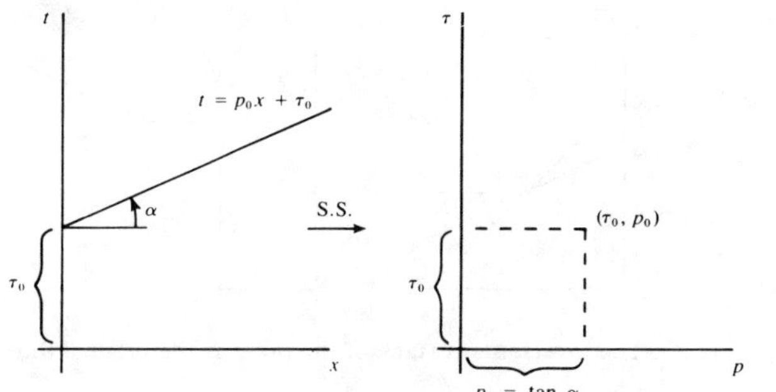

Fig. 5. The slant stack of a line is a point.

The entire suite of seismic traces for all positions x represents the seismic section.

The *Radon transform* [42] of $u(x, t)$ is defined as

$$U_R(p, \tau) = \int_{-\infty}^{\infty} u(x, px + \tau)\, dx.$$

We see that the Radon transform is a function of two variables; τ is called the *intercept* and p is called the *slope*. The reason is that $t = \tau + px$ represents a line in the (x, t) plane (where x is the horizontal axis and t is the vertical axis). This line has slope $p = \tan \alpha$ (i.e., the line makes an angle α with the x axis) and t-intercept τ (i.e., the line cuts the t axis at τ). Geophysicists call the Radon transformation a *slant stack*, as this concept has been in use in exploration seismology since the work of the MIT Geophysical Analysis Group [43] in the 1950's. We may regard the terms *Radon transform* and *slant stack* as meaning the same thing.

The reason for the name "slant stack" is the following. We can perform the Radon transform by sweeping over the wavefield $u(x, t)$ with lines, each given by its slope p and intercept τ. We then add (integrate) all the values on each line and associate the sum (integral) with its slope p and intercept τ. That is, we "stack" all the values of the wavefield on each "slant" line; that is, we "slant stack."

Thus the Radon transform involves summing all the amplitudes $u(x, t)$ along a given line of slope p_0 and intercept τ_0, and plotting that sum at the corresponding point (p_0, τ_0) on the p, τ plane. In brief, the Radon transform has this characteristic; it takes a line of intercept τ_0 and slope p_0 in the x, t space and transforms it into a point (p_0, τ_0) in the new space. That is, the Radon transform converts a line into a point; see Fig. 5. No information is lost because a line is completely described by its intercept and slope.

Now let us look at the *inverse Radon Transform*. This is an inverse slant stack. To be mathematically correct, we must first take the time derivative of the Hilbert transform of $U_R(p, \tau)$. We then slant stack along lines of slope $\tan \beta$ and intercept t; that is, lines $\tau = t + (\tan \beta)p$. Let us find the inverse slant stack of the point (p_0, τ_0). The only slant lines that will contribute are the ones that go through this point. Such a contributing line satisfies

$$\tau_0 = t + (\tan \beta)p_0$$

so its intercept is $t = \tau_0 - p_0 \tan \beta$. For the inverse slant stack, we let x be the negative slope, that is,

$$x = -\tan \beta.$$

Thus the point (p_0, τ_0) for each β gets transformed into the point $(x, t) = (-\tan \beta, \tau_0 - p_0 \tan \beta)$ in the original (x, t) plane.

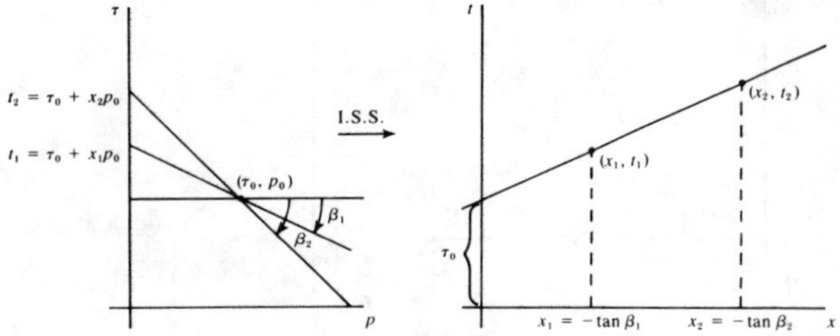

Fig. 6. The inverse slant stack of the point is the original line.

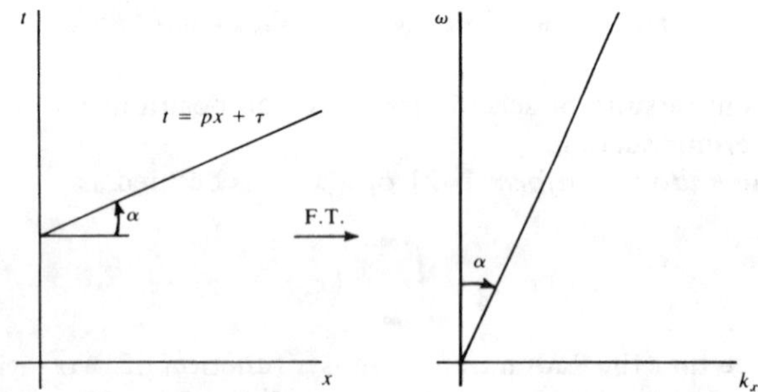

Fig. 7. The Fourier transform of a line is a line through the origin with reciprocal slope. The intercept of the original line is contained in the phase spectrum of the transform line.

As β sweeps out all values, the locus of all these points is the line $t = \tau_0 + p_0 x$, that is, the line of slope p_0 and intercept τ_0 in the (x, t) plane. This is the original line, so we see that the inverse slant stack works; see Fig. 6.

The above heuristic explanation of the inverse Radon transform must be made more precise mathematically. An equation for our heuristic description is

$$u(x, t) = \int_{-\infty}^{\infty} \frac{d}{dt} H U_R(p, t - px)\, dp$$

where H denotes the Hilbert transform.

C. The Fourier Transform

The Radon transform takes a line into a point, and the inverse Radon transform takes the point back into the original line. The 2-D Fourier transform takes a line into another line, and the inverse Fourier transform takes it back into the original line.

Let the function be a delta function $\delta(t - px - \tau)$ along the line $t = px + \tau$ in the (x, t) plane. This line has slope $p = \tan \alpha$ and intercept τ. The *Fourier transform* is

$$\int_{-\infty}^{\infty} \int_{-\infty}^{\infty} \delta(t - px - \tau)e^{-i(\omega t - k_x x)}\, dx\, dt$$

$$= \int_{-\infty}^{\infty} e^{-i[\omega(px+\tau) - k_x x]}\, dx$$

$$= 2\pi e^{-i\omega\tau}\, \delta(p\omega - k_x).$$

Thus the Fourier transform has magnitude given by a delta function along the line $\omega = k_x/p$, and has phase given by $-\omega\tau$. The line makes an angle α with the ω axis and goes through the origin (intercept = 0). The slope of the given line is the reciprocal of the slope of the tranformed line, and the intercept of the given line is locked up in the phase spectrum; see Fig. 7.

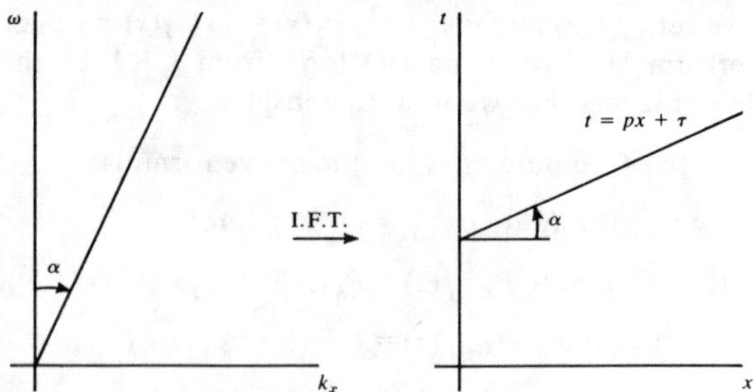

Fig. 8. The inverse Fourier transform gives back the original line.

By taking the *inverse Fourier transform*, we regain the original line; that is,

$$\frac{1}{2\pi} \int_{-\infty}^{\infty} \int_{-\infty}^{\infty} e^{-i\omega\tau}\, \delta(p\omega - k_x)e^{i(\omega t - k_x x)}\, dk_x\, d\omega$$

$$= \delta(t - px - \tau)$$

see Fig. 8.

Because of this interplay between lines, the Radon transform is closely related to the Fourier transform. Let us evaluate the Fourier transform $U(k_x, \omega)$ of the seismic wavefield $u(x, t)$ along the line $\omega = k_x/p$. We have $k_x = p\omega$ so $U(k_x, \omega)$ becomes

$$U(p\omega, \omega) = \int_{-\infty}^{\infty} \int_{-\infty}^{\infty} u(x, t)e^{-i(\omega t - p\omega x)}\, dx\, dt.$$

Because $\tau = t - px$, we have

$$U(p\omega, \omega) = \int_{-\infty}^{\infty} e^{-i\omega\tau} \left[\int_{-\infty}^{\infty} u(x, \tau + px)\, dx\right] d\tau.$$

We recognize the expression within the brackets as the Radon transform $U_R(p, \tau)$. Thus

$$U(p\omega, \omega) = \int_{-\infty}^{\infty} e^{-i\omega\tau}\, U_R(p, \tau)\, d\tau$$

which says that *the Fourier transform of the Radon transform with respect to the intercept variable τ is equal to the 2-D Fourier transform evaluated on the line $k_x = p\omega$.*

D. The Ray Parameter p and the Intercept Parameter τ

Let us now consider a horizontally stratified layered medium in 2-D space (x, z). We assume that the depth axis z points downward, with $z = 0$ indicating the surface. Each interface is represented by a flat (i.e., nontilted) line; line $z = $ positive constant. Let us assume there are N earth layers in total, with interfaces at $z_0 = 0, z_1, z_2, \cdots, z_N$. Layer k lies between interface z_{k-1} (on top) and z_k (on bottom). The thicknesses of the layers are

$$h_1 = z_1 - z_0, h_2 = z_2 - z_1, \cdots, h_N = z_N - z_{N-1}.$$

We let $v_1, v_2, \cdots, v_N$ denote the compressional velocities in the respective layers.

Let an impulsive source be initiated at the surface. Waves will travel down into the earth where they will suffer reflections and refractions at the interfaces. At each surface point $(x, z = 0)$, the resulting wave motion can be recorded in the form of a seismic trace. The seismic trace will include primary reflections (i.e., impulses that have traveled paths directly

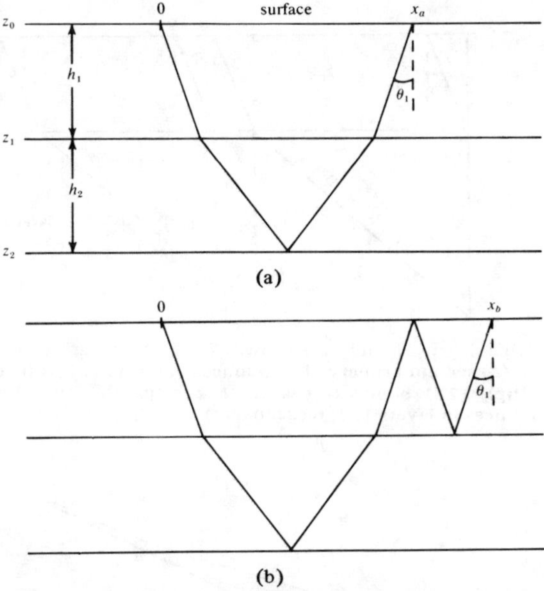

Fig. 9. Primary (a) and peg-leg multiple (b) each with the same value θ_1 of the emergence angle but with different offsets x_a and x_b.

down and back up) and multiple reflections (i.e., impulses that have bounced back and forth within various layers and combinations of layers before returning to the surface). Because the interfaces are flat, there is a symmetry; for each downgoing leg there is a corresponding upgoing leg. Thus we can consider merely the upgoing legs of the ray paths. We thus work with one-way times. The complete times, or two-way times, would then be twice the one-way times that we obtain.

The primary reflection from layer k would have one leg from each layer from interface k up to the surface. A multiple reflection includes extra bounces, so it would have more than one leg in some or all of the layers. For example, a peg-leg multiple has one long leg (corresponding to the primary) and a short leg (corresponding to an extra bounce); see Fig. 9.

Using geometric seismics, we can say that the waves travel along rays. At a given receiver point $(x_1, z = 0)$ on the surface of the earth, the waves will come in from all directions. Let θ_1 represent the angle of emergence of a ray. (All angles are measured from the normal; that is, all angles are measured from the z-axis to the ray.) For example, at a given receiver point $(x_1, 0)$, the primary from interface k would come in at one angle, the primary from another interface would come in at a different angle, and each possible multiple would come in at its own angle. At a different receiver point $(x_2, 0)$, all the angles would be different. To make any sense at all from the received signals, we must do some sorting.

One way to sort is by angle. Let us pick one given angle θ_1, and then move along the horizontal x-axis, and pick out each ray that comes in at that given angle. We throw away all the other rays. We now appeal to Snell's law, which says that p is a constant where

$$p = \frac{\sin \theta_1}{v_1} = \frac{\sin \theta_2}{v_2} = \cdots = \frac{\sin \theta_N}{v_N}.$$

All the ray paths that we have picked out have the same value of the parameter p, which is called the *ray parameter* or *Snell's parameter*. A wave which travels along a path with a fixed value of p is called a *Snell wave*. Thus we have sorted out all the Snell waves for one given value of p, namely, $p = \sin \theta_1/v_1$. What good does this do us?

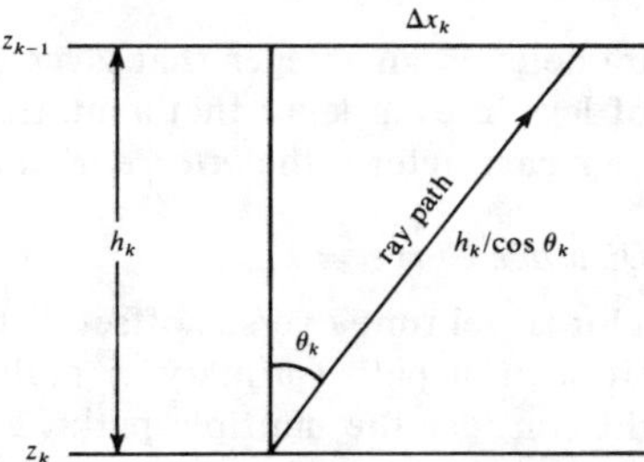

Fig. 10. Upgoing ray path in layer k.

The answer is that we can find an associated parameter τ which has nice properties. Each ray path that we have saved is characterized by the same value of p. We are going to construct our model (i.e., we are going to pick the interface positions $z_1, z_2, \cdots, z_N$) to fit this value of p. In other words, we are going to pick a model (characterized by the value p) to fit our data (all the received signals with a fixed value p).

Let us look at the ray path of one leg in layer k; see Fig. 10. The thickness of the layer is h_k, and the angle that the ray makes with the vertical is θ_k. Thus we have a right triangle with angle θ_k and adjacent, or vertical, side h_k. The travel distance of the wave is the slant distance (i.e., the hypotenuse). The offset distance Δx_k is the projection of the travel distance on the x-axis (i.e., Δx_k is the opposite, or horizontal, side).

The offset distance Δx_k is

$$\Delta x_k = h_k \tan \theta_k.$$

The slant distance is $h_k/\cos \theta_k$, so the travel time is

$$\Delta t_k = \frac{h_k}{v_k \cos \theta_k}.$$

Let us now consider the parameter τ. Its increment $\Delta \tau_k$ for layer k is defined as

$$\Delta \tau_k = \Delta t_k - p \Delta x_k.$$

Let us compute $\Delta \tau_k$. It is

$$\Delta \tau_k = \frac{h_k}{v_k \cos \theta_k} - p h_k \frac{\sin \theta_k}{\cos \theta_k} = \frac{h_k \cos \theta_k}{v_k}.$$

The angle θ_k is fixed because $\sin \theta_k = v_k p$. We will now choose the interfaces of our model so that the thicknesses of the layers are

$$z_k - z_{k-1} = h_k = \frac{v_k}{\cos \theta_k}.$$

In other words, we fit the model to the data; the data consist of all the ray paths with a fixed value of p. Thus for the chosen model, we have

$$\Delta \tau_k = 1$$

for each layer k. The primary from interface k goes through k layers; thus the τ value for this primary is

$$\tau = \sum_{j=1}^{k} \Delta \tau_j = k.$$

Suppose a multiple path goes through layer 1 four times, layer 2 three times, and layer 3 once. Then the τ value for this multiple reflection is

$$\tau = 4 \Delta \tau_1 + 3 \Delta \tau_2 + \Delta \tau_3 = (4 + 3 + 1) = 8.$$

Thus the τ parameter is an integer that gives the sum of the total number of legs in each layer that a multiple path makes. The name of the τ parameter is the *intercept parameter*.

E. The Time–Distance Curve

Let us now plot travel time t versus offset distance x for any given type of reflection path (primary or multiple). For example, we might consider the multiple path $(2, 1)$ which goes through layer 1 two times and layer 2 one time; see Fig. 11. We consider this type of path (a path with 2, 1 bounces in layers 1, 2, respectively) for all values of the ray parameter p; that is, for all possible emergence angles θ_1. For each value of offset x there will be a travel time t. A plot of travel time t versus offset x is called the *time–distance curve* for the multiple path $(2,1)$. Let us designate this curve as $t = f(x; 2, 1)$. This curve is shown in Fig. 12. Also shown are the time–distance curve $t = f(x; 1)$ for the primary from interface 1, the time–distance curve $t = f(x; 1, 1)$ for the primary from interface 2, and the time–distance curve $t = f(x; 1, 2)$ for the multiple with 1, 2 bounces in layers 1, 2, respectively. Except for the case of the first primary $t = f(x; 1)$, there is no explicit formula for such a curve. However, we can find a parametric representation in terms of the ray parameter p. Since $\sin \theta_k = p v_k$, it follows that $\cos \theta_k = (1 - p^2 v_k^2)^{1/2}$ and $\tan \theta_k = p v_k / (1 - p^2 v_k^2)^{1/2}$. Thus the parametric representation of the above time–distance curve $t = f(x; n_1, n_2, \cdots, n_k)$ is

$$x = \sum_k \Delta x_k = \sum_k \frac{h_k p v_k}{(1 - p^2 v_k^2)^{1/2}}$$

$$t = \sum_k \Delta t_k = \sum_k \frac{h_k}{v_k (1 - p^2 v_k^2)^{1/2}}$$

where the index k runs over the value $k = 1$, n_1 times; $k = 2$, n_2 times; and so on, up to $k = k$, n_k times.

Because the ray emerges at angle θ_1 with the vertical, it follows that the wavefront makes an angle θ_1 with the horizontal, as the wavefront is at right angles to the ray. In a small increment of time dt, the wave travels a distance $v_1 dt$ along the ray path. In the same amount of time, the wavefront sweeps out a distance dx along the x-axis, where $dx \sin \theta_1 = v_1 \, dt$, as shown in Fig. 13. Thus the slope of the time–distance curve is

$$\frac{dt}{dx} = \frac{\sin \theta_1}{v_1}.$$

That is, *the slope of the time–distance curve at any point x is equal to the ray parameter p of the ray path that emerges at that point*; i.e.,

$$\frac{dt}{dx} = p.$$

In summary, each type of multiple path has a time–distance curve whose slope at any value of x is equal to the ray parameter characterizing the ray emerging at that point. For example, for the time–distance curve $t = f(x; 2, 1)$, we have

$$p = \frac{dt}{dx} = \frac{df(x; 2, 1)}{dx}$$

where the ray emerging at x has angle $\theta_1 = \sin^{-1}(pv_1)$.

Let us now find out what the parameter τ is. We know that the slope of the curve $f(x; 2, 1)$ is p. That is, the tangent to this curve is a line with slope p. Let τ be the t-intercept of this

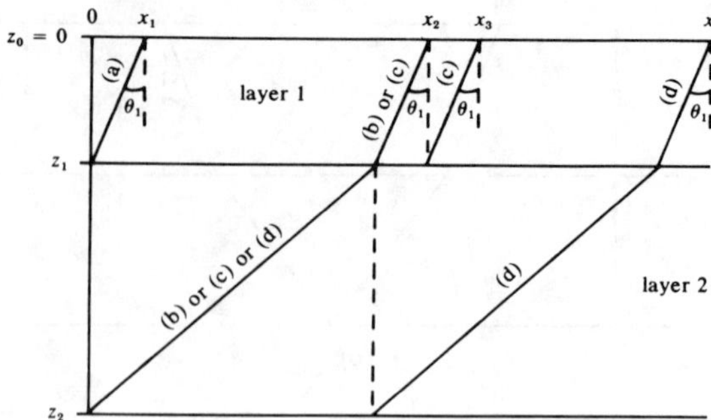

Fig. 11. Upgoing paths only are shown: (a) first primary (1 bounce in layer 1); (b) second primary (1, 1 bounces in layers 1, 2, respectively); (c) multiple (2, 1 bounces in layers 1, 2, respectively); (d) multiple (1, 2 bounces in layers 1, 2, respectively).

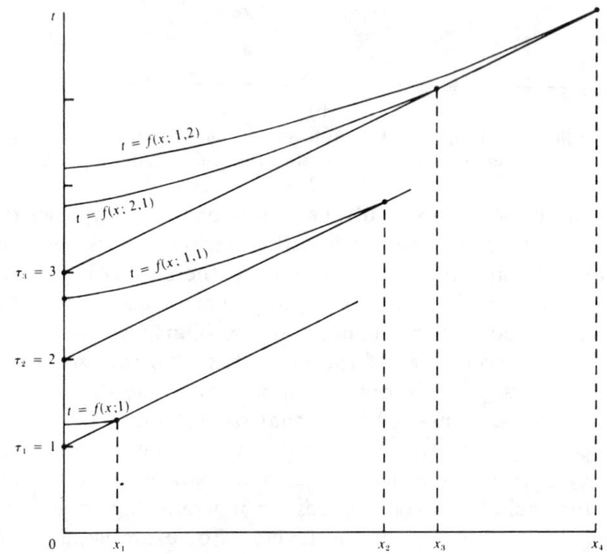

Fig. 12. The hyperbolic-shaped curves are the time–distance curves for the primaries $f(x; 1)$ and $f(x; 2)$ and the multiples $f(x; 2, 1)$ and $f(x; 1, 2)$. The offsets x_1, x_2, x_3, x_4 correspond to the same value of the ray parameter p. When we slant stack at this value of p, the first primary (one leg) gives intercept $\tau_1 = 1$, the second primary (two legs) gives $\tau_2 = 2$, and each of the multiples (each three legs) gives $\tau_3 = 3$.

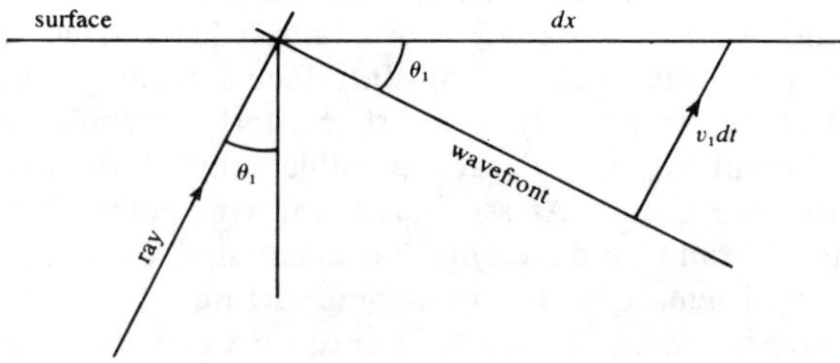

Fig. 13. Geometric demonstration that the slope of the time–distance curve is p.

tangent line, so the equation of the tangent line is

$$t = px + \tau.$$

In the preceding section, we defined $\Delta \tau_k$ as

$$\Delta \tau_k = \Delta t_k - p \Delta x_k$$

so

$$\sum_k \Delta \tau_k = \sum_k \Delta t_k - p \sum_k \Delta x_k$$

which is

$$\tau = t - px.$$

Thus we see that the parameter τ given in the preceding section is the same as the τ given in this section. This explains why we have called τ the *intercept parameter*. The parameter τ is the intercept of the tangent line with the t-axis.

What happens if we slant stack a time–distance curve? A time–distance curve may be thought of as the envelope of its tangent lines. Slant stacking converts each tangent line into a point (p, τ), where p is the slope and τ is the intercept of the line. As an example, let us consider the case of the first primary reflection. The ray-path travel time is t, so the ray-path distance is $v_1 t$, which is the hypotenuse of a right triangle with sides h_1 and x. Thus by the Pythagorean theorem, we have

$$v_1^2 t^2 = x^2 + h_1^2$$

so

$$t = \frac{1}{v_1} (x^2 + h_1^2)^{1/2}.$$

which shows that the first-primary time-distance curve is a hyperbola. This is the one time–distance curve we can write explicitly (instead of implicitly in parametric form). The curve in parametric form is

$$x = \frac{h_1 p v_1}{(1 - p^2 v_1^2)^{1/2}}$$

$$t = \frac{h_1}{v_1 (1 - p^2 v_1^2)^{1/2}}.$$

The intercept parameter τ is

$$\tau = t - px = \frac{h_1 \cos \theta_1}{v_1}$$

where

$$\cos \theta_1 = (1 - p^2 v_1^2)^{1/2}.$$

Thus the above equation for τ together with the Snell equation are

$$\frac{\tau}{h_1} = \frac{\cos \theta_1}{v_1}$$

$$p = \frac{\sin \theta_1}{v_1}$$

which give

$$\frac{\tau^2}{h_1^2} + p^2 = \frac{1}{v_1^2}.$$

Thus the (p, τ) curve is an *ellipse*. This ellipse is the Radon transform (i.e., slant stack) of the time–distance hyperbola

$$t^2 - \frac{x^2}{v_1^2} = \frac{h_1^2}{v_1^2}.$$

F. Dynamic Deconvolution (Inversion) and Dynamic Reconvolution (Construction)

A seismic section $u(x, t)$ gives the amplitude of the received waves as a function of receiver position x and time t. A seismic section represents the received data on the surface of the earth.

Each type of path (primary and multiple) appear as an event on the seismic section. These events lie along the time–distance curves of the respective paths.

Given the seismic data $u(x, t)$, we now want to pick out all the paths that have the same value of the ray parameter p. That is, we want to pick out all the ray paths that emerge at some given angle. As we have said, if we fix the receiver position x, then all the different types of paths come in at different angles. On the other hand, if we fix the angle, then all the different types of ray paths with that emergent angle come in at different receiver positions x.

We recall that we choose the layers in our model for a particular value of p. Consider all the ray paths with the value p. Each ray path will emerge at a different x value. At that x value, the slope of the corresponding time–distance curve will be p. Thus the tangent line at this point will have slope p and intercept τ. The value of τ will depend upon the type of ray path. More specifically, τ is an integer equal to the sum of the number of legs through each layer. For example, for the multiple path with four passes through layer 1, three passes through layer 2, and one pass through layer 3, the value of τ is $4 + 3 + 1 = 8$.

Let us now slant stack the data with slope p. Then the stacked data as a function of τ will be as follows. Every one of the paths has ray parameter with the given value p:

$\tau_1 = 1$: (1) First primary

$\tau_2 = 2$: (1) Second primary, and
          (2) multiple with two passes through layer 1

$\tau_3 = 3$: (1) Third primary,
          (2) multiple with three passes through layer 1,
          (3) multiple with two passes through layer 1 and one pass through layer 2, and
          (4) multiple with one pass through layer 1 and two passes through layer 2.

Thus for fixed p, we obtain a trace as a function of τ. This slant-stack trace satisfies the requirement that the timing of all primaries and multiples are integer valued. Thus this slant-stack trace is the same as a normal incidence trace generated by a Goupillaud model where the reflection coefficients are the ones specified by the ray parameter p. In particular, the multiple arrivals of the slant-stack trace have the same time structure as the 1-D seismic trace generated by the Goupillaud model.

It follows, therefore, we can take this slant stack and invert it by the 1-D methods given in the 1-D part of this paper. In particular, we can use Gelfand–Levitan inversion as implemented by the dynamic deconvolution method.

Conversely, we can construct a forward scheme which generates a seismic section $u(x, t)$ from a given layered model. For each ray parameter p, we find the non-normal-incidence reflection coefficients for each of the layers. We then use the forward Gelfand–Levitan scheme (i.e., dynamic reconvolution) and generate the 1-D seismic trace. This seismic trace will be a function of τ for the given p. Repeating this process for many p values, we obtain $U_R(p, \tau)$. We then apply the inverse Radon transform to obtain the synthetic seismic section $u(x, t)$.

G. Migration

So far we have considered flat layers. Now we want to consider a sloping interface in a constant velocity medium. Sup-

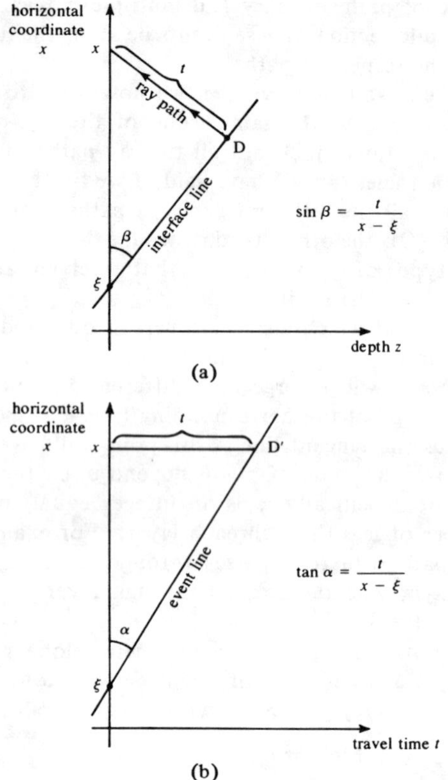

Fig. 14. Wave propagation (a) to (b). Migration (b) to (a). (a) Earth cross section. With velocity $v = 1$, a wave takes time t to travel up from depth point D to receiver x. (b) Seismic section. The depth point appears at D' on the seismic section. The interface with dip $\tan \beta$ and intercept ξ appears as the event with dip $\tan \alpha$ and same intercept. We see that $\sin \beta = \tan \alpha$.

pose the first interface is a line which makes the angle β with the horizontal. We consider a source and receiver at the same surface point x. By Fermat's theorem of least time, the ray path must be a *least time path*. Thus the ray path will be a straight line from the source to the reflecting point on the interface. The same path is used by the reflected wave back to the receiver, and this common ray path will be at right angles to the interface. Thus the ray path will make an angle β with the vertical.

Let the medium have constant velocity v, which for simplicity we take to be $v = 1$. Let us refer to Fig. 14. The interface cuts the surface of the ground at point ξ. We call ξ the intercept. Let x be the coordinate of the receiver. Thus we have a right triangle with hypotenuse $x - \xi$ and angle β. The side opposite β is the ray path $vt = t$. Here t is the one-way travel time along the ray path. Thus

$$\sin \beta = \frac{t}{x - \xi}.$$

On the seismic section, we will plot t versus x. Then the seismic trace at receiver position x will have an event at t. As we vary x, these events will fall on a straight line which intercepts the x axis at ξ; that is, the intercept of the interface line and the intercept of the event line are the same. Let the event line make an angle α with the x-axis. Again we have a right triangle. The side opposite α has length t and the (non-hypotenuse) side adjaccent to α has length $x - \xi$. Thus we have

$$\tan \alpha = \frac{t}{x - \xi}.$$

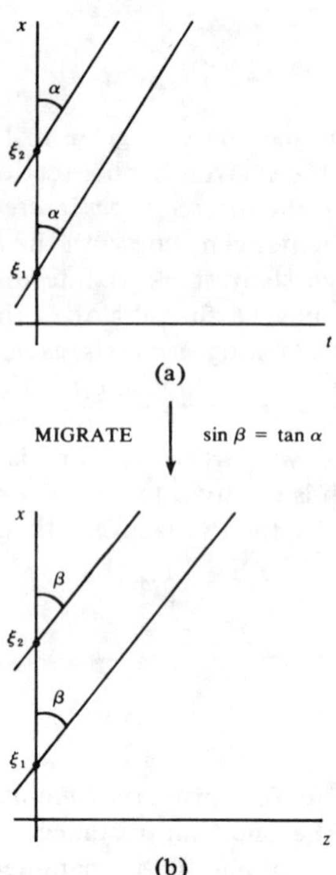

Fig. 15. Mechanical migration: (a) events on a seismic section with dips $\tan \alpha$; (b) each event is rotated about its intercept from $\tan \alpha$ to $\tan \beta$ to produce interfaces of dip $\tan \beta$.

Comparing the above two equations, we have

$$\sin \beta = \tan \alpha.$$

This is the basic equation of migration. *Migration* is the conversion of the event line in the (x, t) plane to the interface line in the (x, z) plane. Each of these lines have the same x-intercept ξ. Thus migration involves rotating the event line around this intercept ξ so as to change the event angle α to the interface angle β, where

$$\beta = \sin^{-1} \tan \alpha.$$

Prior to 1960, migration was performed by mechanical devices; see Fig. 15.

H. Spectral Migration

Each of the events on the seismic section (i.e., the observed data) is represented by a curve in the (x, t) space. Each curve may be considered as the envelope of its tangent lines. Let the equation for a given tangent line be

$$x = \frac{1}{\tan \alpha} t + \xi.$$

Let us now Fourier transform the data; see Fig. 16. The above line will be transformed to line

$$k_x = (\tan \alpha)\omega$$

and with phase spectrum $k_x \xi$. The process of migration transforms the above line into the line

$$k_x = (\tan \beta)k_z$$

and with same phase spectrum. We now inverse Fourier transform. The result gives the corresponding line

$$x = \frac{1}{\tan \beta} z + \xi$$

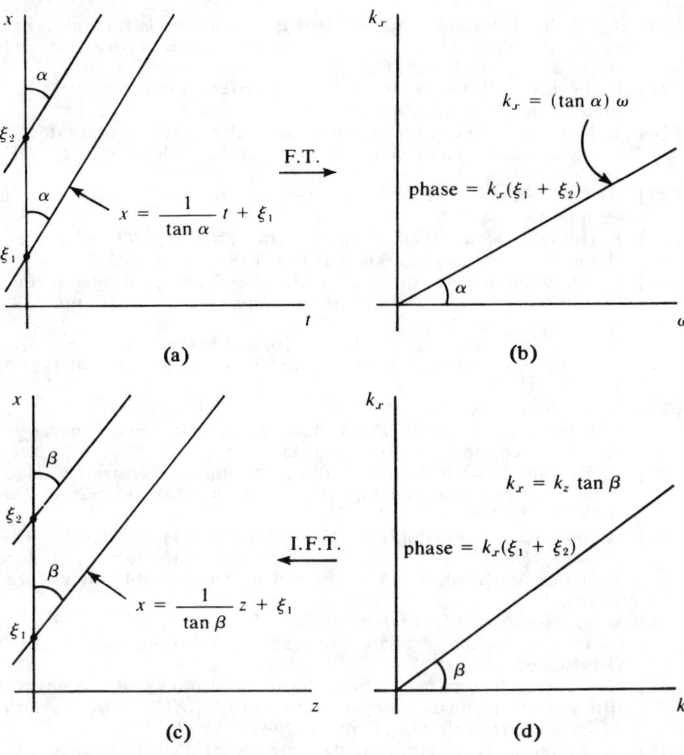

Fig. 16. Spectral migration: (a) events on seismic section with dips tan α; (b) Fourier transform converts all events into same line, with intercepts preserved in the phase; (c) migration changes dip from tan α to tan β; (d) inverse Fourier transform produces interfaces of dip tan β.

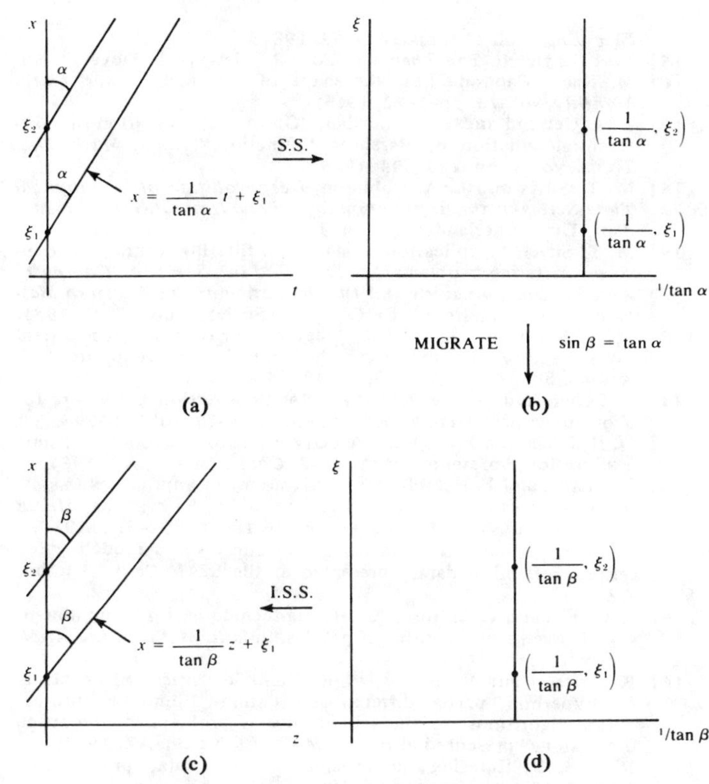

Fig. 17. Slant-stack migration: (a) events on seismic section with dips tan α; (b) slant stacking converts all events into same vertical line; (c) migration moves vertical line to left, from $1/\tan \alpha$ to $1/\tan \beta$; (d) inverse slant stacking produces interfaces of dip tan β.

in the (x, z) space. The interfaces appear as the envelopes of these lines. We have thus described the process of *spectral migration*, or *Stolt migration* [27].

I. Slant-Stack Migration

Each of the events on the seismic section (i.e., the observed data) is represented by a curve in (x, t) space. Each curve may be considered as the envelope of its tangent lines. Let the equation for a given tangent line be

$$\tan \alpha = \frac{t}{x - \xi}$$

which is

$$x = \frac{1}{\tan \alpha} t + \xi.$$

Let us now slant stack the data; see Fig. 17. The above line will be transformed into the point $(1/\tan \alpha, \xi)$. All the tangent lines with slope tan α will fall along the transform line $(1/\tan \alpha) = $ constant in the transform plane. We now move this line left to the position $1/\tan \beta$. We thus shift all such transform lines. This shifting is the process of migration; i.e., the changing of dips. We then inverse slant stack. The result gives the corresponding lines

$$x = \frac{1}{\tan \beta} z + \xi$$

in the (x, z) space. The interfaces appear as the envelopes of these lines. We have thus described the process of *slant-stack migration* (often called *S-two migration*) which is due to Hubral [28].

IV. Conclusion

The problem of the geophysicist is to determine the structure of the interior of the earth from data obtained at the surface of the ground. Ultimately the problem is to find a method that will give structure, composition, and source parameters by processing the whole seismogram. Such a problem is an inverse problem. The forward problem is one which a model of the earth structure and seismic source is used to give properties of seismic motion. When the solution of the forward problem is known, an iteration based on trial and error represents one method of inversion. The parameters of the model are readjusted according to some criterion until some satisfying agreement between the data and the computed wave motion is discovered. This iterative type of approach to the inverse problem has proven to be successful in many applications. Today far more sophisticated inversion methods are being developed for seismic data. In this paper, we have described the present state of the art in which spectral methods in the form of lattice methods, the Fourier transform, and the Radon transform play the key role. An understanding of these spectral methods will provide a firm basis for the appreciation of the exciting new inversion methods which the future holds.

References

[1] H. J. Schudder, "Introduction to computer aided tomography," *Proc. IEEE*, vol. 66, pp. 628–637, 1978.

[2] D. W. Sweeney and C. H. West, "Reconstruction of three-dimensional refractive index fields from multidimensional interferometric data," *Appl. Opt.*, vol. 11, pp. 2649–2664, 1973.

[3] P. F. Gilbert, "The reconstruction of a three-dimensional structure from projections and its applications to electron microscopy," *Proc. R. Soc. London*, ser. B, vol. 182, pp. 89–102, 1972.

[4] T. S. Durrani and C. E. Goutis, "Optimization techniques for digital image reconstruction from their projections," *Proc. Inst.*

Elec. Eng., vol. 127, pp. 161–169, 1980.

[5] Lord Rayleigh, *The Theory of Sound.* New York: Dover, 1950.

[6] M. Kac, "Can one hear the shape of a drum?" *Amer. Math. Monthly*, vol. 73, pp. 1–23, 1966.

[7] I. M. Gelfand and B. M. Levitan, "On the determination of a differential equation by its spectral function," *Amer. Math. Soc. Trans.*, vol. 1, pp. 253–304, 1955.

[8] M. T. Silvia and E. A. Robinson, *Deconvolution of Geophysical Time Series in the Exploration for Oil and Natural Gas.* Amsterdam, The Netherlands: Elsevier, 1979.

[9] M. T. Silvia, "Application of statistical filtering techniques to inverse scattering problems," in *Proc. 2nd Int. Symp. on Computer Aided Seismic Analysis and Discrimination at Southeastern Massachusetts University* (IEEE Computer Society), pp. 20–27, 1981.

[10] M. T. Silvia and A. Weglein, "Method for obtaining a nearfield inverse scattering solution to the acoustic wave equation," *J. Acoust. Soc. Amer.*, vol. 69, pp. 478–489, 1981.

[11] J. Cohen and N. Bleistein, "A velocity inversion procedure for acoustic waves," *Geophysics*, vol. 44, pp. 1077–1087, 1979.

[12] N. Bleistein and J. Cohen, "Velocity inversion. A tool for seismic exploration," presented at the *SIAM Conf.*, Tucson, AZ, 1981.

[13] J. Mendel and F. Habibi-Ashrafi, "A survey of approaches to solving inverse problems for lossless layered media systems," *IEEE Trans. Geosci. Remote Sensing*, vol. GE-18, pp. 320–330, 1980.

[14] S. Coen, "Complete acoustic and elastic layered modeling for seismic reflection data," presented at the SIAM Conf., Tucson, AZ, 1981.

[15] R. Carroll and F. Santosa, "Scattering techniques for a one-dimensional inverse problem in geophysics," *Math. Meth. in the Appl. Sci.*, vol. 3, pp. 145–171, 1981.

[16] K. Driessel and W. Symes, "Coefficient identification problems for hyperbolic partial differential equations. Some fast and accurate algorithms for the seismic inverse problem in one space dimension," presented at the SIAM Conf., Tucson, AZ, 1981.

[17] R. H. Stolt, "Imaging and inversion of seismic data," presented at the SIAM Conf., Tucson, AZ, 1981.

[18] K. P. Bube and R. Burridge, "Solution of the one-dimensional inverse problem of reflection seismology by downward continuation of surface data," presented at the SIAM Conf., Tucson, AZ, 1981.

[19] A. H. Zemanian and P. Subramaniam, "The application of the theory of infinite networks to the geophysical exploration of layered strata," presented at the SIAM Conf., Tucson, AZ, 1981.

[20] J. Gazdag, "Migration of seismic data by phase shift plus interpolation," presented at the SIAM Conf., Tucson, AZ, 1981.

[21] A. Bamberger, G. Chavent, and P. Lailly, "About the stability of the inverse problem in 1-D wave equations. Application to the Interpretation of Seismic Profiles," *Appl. Math. Optim.*, vol. 5, pp. 1–47, 1979.

[22] S. Treitel, P. Gutowski, P. Hubral, and D. Wagner, "Plane wave decomposition of seismograms," presented at the SEG Meet., Los Angeles, CA, 1981.

[23] K. L. Larner, "Computational problems resulting from the discreteness of data sets obtained in seismic exploration," presented at the SIAM Conf., Tuscon, AZ, 1981.

[24] J. Makhoul, "Stable and efficient lattice methods for linear prediction," *IEEE Trans. Acoust., Speech, Signal Processing*, vol. ASSP-25, pp. 423–428, Oct. 1977.

[25] N. Levinson, "The Wiener RMS error criterion in filter design and prediction," *J. Math. Phys.*, 1947.

[26] J. P. Burg, "Maximum entropy spectral analysis," presented at the Soc. Exploration Geophysicists Meet., Oklahoma City, OK, 1967.

[27] R. H. Stolt, "Migration by Fourier transform," *Geophysics*, vol. 43, pp. 23–48, 1978.

[28] P. Hubral, "Slant stack migration," in *Festischrift Theodor Krey*. Hannover, Germany: Prakla-Seismos, 1980, pp. 72–78.

[29] P. Goupillaud, "An approach to inverse filtering of near surface layer effects from seismic records," *Geophysics*, vol. 26, pp. 754–760, 1961.

[30] A. Gray and J. Markel, "Digital lattice and ladder filter synthesis," *IEEE Trans. Audio Electroacoust.*, vol. AU-21, pp. 491–500, 1973.

[31] J. Makhoul, "A class of all-zero lattice digital filters: Properties and applications," *IEEE Trans. Acoust., Speech, Signal Processing*, vol. ASSP-26, pp. 304–314, Aug. 1978.

[32] T. Durrani, N. Murukutla, and K. Sharman, "Constrained algorithms for multi-input adaptive lattices in array processing," in *IEEE ICASSP Proc.*, 1981.

[33] H. Lorentz, A. Einstein, H. Minkowski, and H. Weyl, *The Principles of Relativity: A Collection of Original Memoirs.* London, England: Methuen, 1923 (reprinted by Dover Publ., New York, 1958).

[34] E. A. Robinson, *Multichannel Time Series Analysis with Digital Computer Programs.* San Francisco, CA: Holden-Day, 1967. (Revised edition, 1978.)

[35] H. Wakita, "Direct estimation of the vocal tract shape by inverse filtering of acoustic speech waveforms," *IEEE Trans. Audio Electroacoust.*, vol. AU-21, pp. 417–427, 1973.

[36] G. Kunetz, "Généralisation des opérateurs d'antirésonance à un nombre quelconque de réflecteurs," *Geophys. Prospecting*, vol. 12, pp. 283–289, 1964.

[37] G. Kunetz and I. D'Erceville, "Sur certaines propriétés d'une onde plane de compréssion dans un milieu stratifié," *Ann. Geophysique*, vol. 18, pp. 351–359, 1962.

[38] K. Aki and P. G. Richards, *Quantitative Seismology*, vol. 2. San Francisco, CA: W. H. Freeman, 1980.

[39] E. A. Robinson, "Dynamic predictive deconvolution," *Geophys. Prospecting*, vol. 23, pp. 779–797, 1975.

[40] V. Bardan, "Comments on dynamic predictive deconvolution," *Geophys. Prospecting*, vol. 25, pp. 569–572, 1977.

[41] E. A. Robinson, "Iterative identification of non-invertible autoregressive moving-average systems with seismic applications," *Geoexploration*, vol. 16, pp. 1–19, 1978.

[42] J. Radon, "Uber die Bestimmung von Funktionen durch ihre Integralwerte langs gewisser Manningfaltigkeiten," *Berichte der Sächsischen Akademie der Wissenschaften*, vol. 69, pp. 262–277, 1917.

[43] "The MIT Geophysical Analysis Group Reports," *Geophysics*, vol. 32, 1967.

Acoustic Microscopy—1979

LAWRENCE W. KESSLER, SENIOR MEMBER, IEEE, AND DONALD E. YUHAS, MEMBER, IEEE

Abstract—Acoustic microscopy is emerging as an important analytical technique serving the needs of both biomedical and materials technology. Based upon imaging of specimens with elastic waves at VHF and UHF frequencies, acoustic microscopes reveal structural-mechanical properties with high magnification. A review of the techniques and their applications are presented.

INTRODUCTION

THE acoustic microscope is an analytical tool whose course of development and importance to the scientific community may parallel that of the scanning electron microscope. Though in a relatively early stage of development compared with electron microscopy, the acoustic microscopy field is demonstrating its importance in a broad spectrum of applications, such as biomedical research, materials technology, and quality control. In an earlier article [1], Kessler reviewed the field to about 1973. The purpose of this article is to update the review and provide the reader with an addition to the 1973 comprehensive bibliography. Examples are presented to illustrate the new level of information provided by acoustic micrographs.

By way of contrast to other articles in this volume in which low frequencies (1 to 10 MHz) are employed, acoustic microscopes use frequencies ranging from 100–3000 MHz. In clinical medicine and nondestructive testing, relatively long wavelength (e.g., 0.5 mm) acoustic energy is used to penetrate the depth of the human body or many inches of metal. On the other hand, microscopy, which discriminates structural features down in the micrometer size range, requires appropriately short wavelength ultrasonic energy. Unfortunately, the shorter acoustic wavelengths are often associated with increased absorption losses which decrease penetration depth. The increased absorption is often so severe that in the "microscopy" regime the conventional applications of low-frequency (1–10 MHz) ultrasound are precluded. However, the increased resolution capabilities has lead to variety of new applications.

Modern analytical instrumentation has played an important role in the advancement of technology. Whenever images are formed of an object with a different form of radiation, new information can be gained because of the possible unique interactions which occur between the radiation and the object. An acoustic microscope reveals localized changes in elastic properties of materials by measuring point by point reactions of the specimen to a periodic stress wave. Thus the physical properties of matter which govern sound propagation, namely, the compressibility, the density, and the viscoelasticity are translated into acoustic micrographs. From the pragmatic point of view, the sonically transparent nature of most materials permits internal examination of samples which are opaque to light. Subsurface defects, flaws, inclusions, and disbonded areas are particular areas of materials science and quality control which are amenable to acoustic microscopy. In biomedical research, the capacity to differentiate structure in live tissue without chemical staining makes a new level of experimentation possible. The new structural information that is revealed and the efficiency of visualization without chemical processing of the tissue make the technique of ultimate great value in clinical diagnosis of disease. In materials technology and nondestructive testing, the elastic properties of the sample control its behavior under stress. Acoustic microscopy is used to characterize microelastic structure as well as to find hidden defects and flaws.

II. BACKGROUND

The notion of acoustic microscopy dates back to 1936 when Sokolov [2] proposed a device for producing magnified views of structure with 3-GHz sound waves. However, due to technological limitations at the time, no such instrument could be constructed, and it was not until 1959 that Dunn and Fry [3] performed the first acoustic microscopy experiments, though not at very high frequencies.

The scientific literature shows very little progress toward an acoustic microscope following the Dunn and Fry experiments up until about 1970 when two groups of activity emerged, one headed by C. F. Quate, and the other by A. Korpel and L. W. Kessler. The first efforts to develop an operational acoustic microscope concentrated upon high-frequency adaptations of low-frequency ultrasonic visualization methods. For example, one early system employed Bragg diffraction imaging [4]–[6], which is based upon direct interaction between an acoustic-wave field and a laser light beam. Another example was based on variations of the Pohlman cell [7]. The original device is based upon a suspension of asymmetric particles in a thin fluid layer which, when acted upon by acoustic energy, produce visual reflectivity changes. Cunningham and Quate [8], modified this by suspending tiny latex spheres in a fluid. Acoustic pressure caused population shifts which were visually detectable. Kessler and Sawyer [9] developed a liquid crystal cell that enabled sound to be detected by hydrodynamic orientation of the fluid. In 1973, the Quate group began the development of its present instrument concept [10] which utilizes a confocal pair of acoustic lenses for focusing and detecting the ultrasonic energy. Advancements of this instrument, a scanning acoustic microscope (SAM), have to do with achieving very high resolution, novel modes of imaging, and applications. In 1970, the Korpel and Kessler group began to pursue a scanning laser detection system for acoustic microscopy [11]. In 1974, the activity was shifted to another organization under Kessler, where practical aspects of the instrument were developed. This instrument, the scanning laser acoustic microscope (SLAM), was made commercially available in 1975.

A great variety of methods can be thought of for ultrasonic visualization. Some of these are adaptable for microscopy and there may be many new ones which will be thought of in the

Manuscript received September 20, 1978; revised November 28, 1978. The authors are with the Sonoscan, Inc., Bensenville, IL 60106.

Reprinted from *Proc. IEEE*, vol. 67, pp. 526–536, Apr. 1979.

future when it becomes economical to justify the task. At the present time, in the opinion of these authors, the optimum use of resources seems to be in the area of applications of the technology. Out of these efforts will come the needs and justification for improved techniques. Such improvements may achieve higher resolution, different modes of operation, customized instruments for particular types of samples, etc.

The balance of this article presents theory and applications of the presently employed techniques. Innovations to these techniques have been constantly in process in order to make acoustic microscopy viable as an analytical tool to serve the needs of industrial and scientific communities in biomedicine, materials technology, and quality assurance.

Out of the research efforts of the past five years, essentially two techniques have emerged as viable practical acoustic microscopes: The SLAM and the SAM. The end result of both is the production of high resolution acoustic images; however, the imaging technology, capabilities, and areas of applicability are quite different. In the next section we describe and contrast the operational principles, design philosophy, and capabilities of the two systems.

III. The Scanning Acoustic Microscope

In the (SAM), an incident acoustic wave is launched into a water medium by a piezoelectric transducer bonded onto one end of a cylindrical sapphire rod. The other end of the rod has a concave spherical surface ground into it, causing the acoustic beam to be focused a short distance away. A receiver rod, geometrically the same as the transmitter rod, is colinearly and confocally aligned with the transmitter to achieve maximum signal and resolution. For visualization, a thin sample is placed at the focal zone and it is systematically indexed mechanically. Variations in the sonic transmission are used to brightness modulate a CRT display. The position output signal of the sample drive mechanism is synchronized to the X and Y axes of the display. Horizontal scanning is accomplished by a rod attached to a vibrating loudspeaker cone. The vertical mechanism is a small precision hydraulic piston. A block diagram of the acoustic system is shown in Fig. 1 after Lemons and Quate [10].

Regarding the focusing of waves, in an optical system lens designs are usually quite sophisticated in order to compensate for spherical abberations. Multielement lenses are usually necessary. In the acoustic system, however, the situation is much less involved for 2 reasons. In the first place, the lens in the SAM is always used "on axis" rather than in an imaging mode; here, the sample is moved through the focused beam. In the second place, the spherical abberations which preclude the use of simple lenses in an optical system are minimal in the acoustic system because of the larger refractive index ratio between the lens material and the fluid space in which the rays come to focus [12], [13]. As a comparison, in typical optical systems, a light beam is focused from glass of index 1.5 to air of index 1.0. In the acoustic system the velocity of sound ratio (the reciprocal of the index of refraction ratio) is 7.5 between the sapphire rod and water. Thus the rays from the paraxial region and the far region join focus in a more precise manner than they would if the index of refraction ratio was smaller.

The frequency of operation of the SAM is limited by the ultrasonic attenuation in the fluid (usually water) between the transmitting and receiving rods. The attenuation of signal

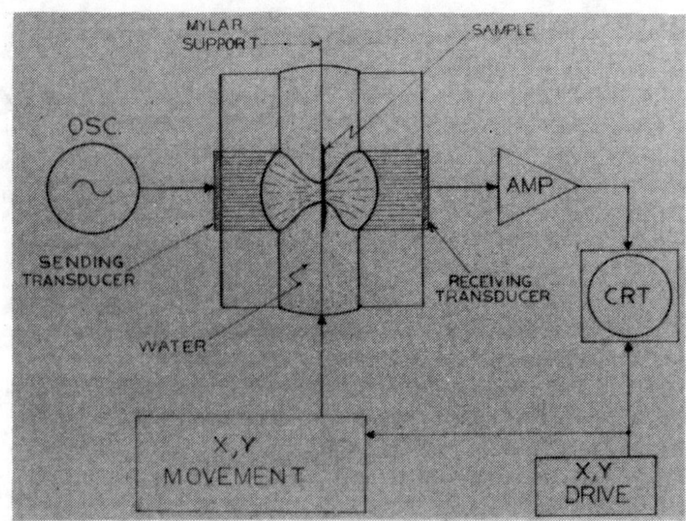

Fig. 1. Schematic diagram of the scanning acoustic microscope (SAM) [10].

depends upon the separation distance between the lens surfaces; this in turn depends upon the lens radius of curvature. The distance can be decreased if the lens radius is made smaller. The first reported experiments in 1973 were at 160 MHz [12] and the lens radius was 1.59 mm. Because of the high velocity of sound ratio, the focal zone is located about 13 percent farther out than the center of curvature of the lens. Therefore, the lens-to-lens separation is about 3.6 mm, and the consequent attenuation loss in the water path, excluding that due to the specimen, is 20 dB at room temperature. In the most recent experiments the reported operating frequency is 3 GHz [14] (Sokolov's proposed frequency) where the wavelength of sound in water (0.5 μm) is comparable to visible light. However, because of the extremely high ultrasonic absorption in water, viz. 8000 dB/cm at 60°, the lens-to-lens distance must be considerably reduced. Thus Jipson and Quate have achieved microscope operation at 3 GHz with a lens whose radius is only 40 μm [14].

The basic advantage of piezoelectric acoustic detection is that it is capable of very high sensitivity [11]. Unfortunately, however, the fluid space between the sample and the lenses must be long enough to achieve acoustic focus, and significant signal is lost in traversing the path. The possibilities of further increases in frequency and, therefore, resolution are based upon finding suitable low-loss fluids as well as fabricating precise lens surfaces with still smaller radii of curvature. A very interesting approach to achieving high resolution in the SAM, suggested by Quate is to operate the instrument with the samples in liquid helium where the wavelength of sound is much shorter than in water, and the absorption losses are orders of magnitude lower [15].

IV. The Scanning Laser Acoustic Microscope

In the SLAM, a specimen is viewed by placing it on a stage where it is insonified with plane acoustic waves (instead of focused waves as in SAM) and illuminated with laser light [16], [17]. The block diagram of this system [18a], [18b] is shown in Fig. 2. Within the sample, the sound is scattered and absorbed according to the internal elastic microstructure. The principle upon which the laser beam is employed as a detector is based upon the minute displacements which occur

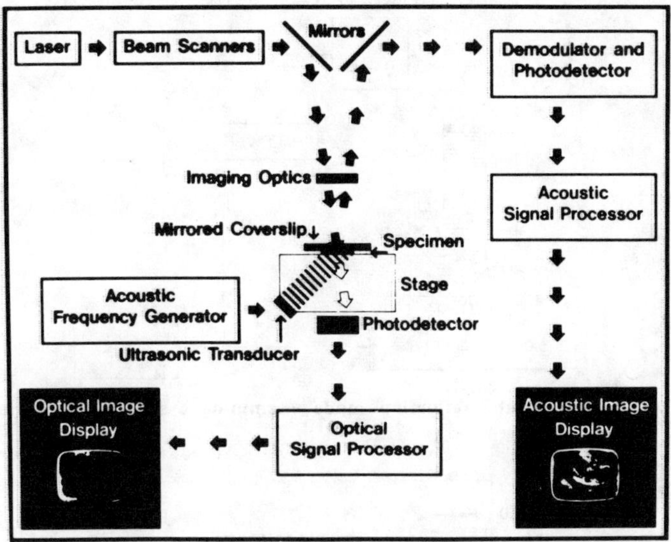

Fig. 2. Schematic diagram of the scanning laser acoustic microscope (SLAM) [18].

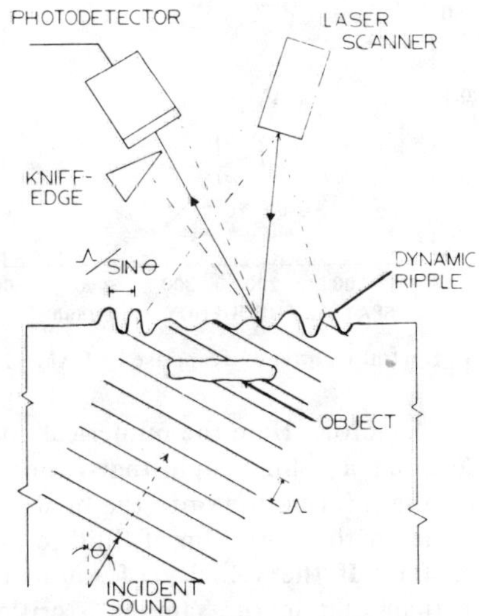

Fig. 3. Laser detection of acoustic energy at an interface [16].

as the sound wave propagates. As shown in Fig. 3, an optically reflective surface placed in the sound field will become distorted in proportion to the localized sound pressure. The distortions are dynamic in that the pressure wave is periodic and the mirror displacements accurately follow the wave amplitude and phase. At every instant of time the mirror surface is an optical phase replica of the sound field. The laser is used to measure the degree of regional distortion. By electronically magnifying the area of laser scan to the size of the CRT monitor and by brightness modulating the display, the acoustic micrograph is made visible. If the sample is made of a solid substance which can be optically polished (as for metallurgical examination), the sample is viewed directly with the laser. However, if the sample is not polished (for example, biological tissue or unprepared solid material), a plastic mirror (coverslip) is placed in contact with the sample to relay the sonic information into the laser beam.

The laser detection process is further explained with reference to Fig. 3. A light beam incident upon the mirror will be re-

flected at an angle equal to the incident angle. When the surface is tilted by an amount proportional to the sound pressure, the reflected light is angularly modulated (spatially). If *all* the reflected light is captured by a photodiode, its electrical output signal will be a dc level only because the light power reaching the detector will not change as a function of angle. However, if part of the light beam is blocked by an obstacle (or knife-edge) then the amount of light reaching the photodiode will depend upon the instantaneous angular position of the beam. Thus the electrical signal output will now consist of a dc component plus a small ac term coherent with the acoustic amplitude.

As a byproduct of the laser scanning technique, a corresponding optical image of the sample is obtained simultaneously as shown in Fig. 2. In the case of optically translucent samples, such as biological material and some solid materials, a "partially silvered" coverslip is employed. Now, a fraction of the probing laser light can penetrate the mirror and sample. This transmitted light is detected and the resulting signal fed to an adjacent CRT monitor, thus constituting an optical image. In the case of a reflective polished specimen such as a metal prepared for metallographic examination, an optical reflection image is produced. The importance of the simultaneous optical image is very great to the user, for it permits newly obtained information, acoustically, to be immediately compared to a familiar optical frame of reference. This is accomplished without repositioning the sample or disturbing its environmental circumstances.

The laser beam scanning technique is based upon the use of an acoustooptical diffraction cell originally developed for a "laser TV" projection scheme [19] in the late 1960's. This was developed because of the difficulties associated with linear mechanical scanning of mirrors for the horizontal deflection at "TV" frequencies, viz. 15.75 kHz. In an acoustooptical cell a traveling ultrasonic wave serves as a diffraction grating for the laser beam. If the interaction distances are sufficiently long, efficient Bragg diffraction occurs and virtually all of the light is diffracted into a single side order whose angular position is a function of the grating spacing. By changing the acoustic frequency to the cell, the output laser beam is made to scan over a range of angles limited by the bandwidth of the transducers. The vertical scanning of the laser beam is accomplished by linearly moving a mirror which is attached to a servo controlled galvanometer. The frame rate of the system is identical to that of standard TV, i.e., 30 frames per second.

The frequency of operation of the SLAM is usually between 100 and 500 MHz, the frequency of choice being dictated by intrinsic attenuation of signal in the sample. Comparing to the SAM, wherein a lossy fluid path is needed to establish focus prior to entering the specimen, the SLAM needs only a thin-fluid film to couple the sound from the stage to the sample. Also thick samples are not as much of a problem with the SLAM except for losses within the samples themselves. Another basic advantage of the SLAM is that the sample remains stationary; the light beam does the scanning and produces acoustic and optical images simultaneously. Like the SAM, the SLAM can be pushed upwards in frequency and down in temperature to liquid helium in order to achieve higher resolution. Unlike the SAM whose resolution limit depends upon the quality of a lens, the limit of resolution in SLAM is governed by the wavelength of the laser light.

V. Resolution

The ultimate resolution of an imaging system of any kind is governed by two factors, the wavelength (λ) of the insonification or illumination and the numerical aperture (NA) of the detection system. The NA is the sine of the half-angle of the response by the detector. For example, an optical system having a lens which is too small to accept (or focus) rays beyond an angle $\pm\theta_m$ from the central ray would have a numerical aperture of $\sin\theta_m$. The classical Rayleigh criterion for resolution states that two distant objects can be resolved when their separation distance d is greater than or equal to $0.66\ \lambda/\text{NA}$. Therefore, with an ideal omni-directional detector, the maximum value of NA = 1, and therefore, d = 0.66 λ.

In the SAM, an acoustic wave is brought to a focus by a lens. The waist dimension of the spot is equal to d (above) in the focus zone. However, the receiver also embodies an acoustic lens, and the combination of lenses in this case actually improves the overall resolution by about a factor of 2. This occurs because the directivity patterns of transmitting and receiving transducers multiply, thereby decreasing the effective spot size. This discussion of resolution in the SAM is valid for focused spots produced in the fluid medium which occupies the space between the two lenses. Soft biological tissues have velocities of sound very close to that of water and, therefore, the resolution critieria are still valid. For solid materials, however, the wavelength of sound is considerably higher than that of a fluid; and, therefore, the resolution *within* the solid is degraded by the longer wavelength of sound as well as by the loss of focus due to aberrations which occur in media with high velocities of sound. If the solid specimens have a thickness limited to the depth of focus of the spot, then the resolution is close to that which would be obtained with biological material. For thick specimens, the resolution is degraded due to loss of focus.

Methods of resolution determination involve the use of test targets and the measurement of spatial frequency response of the system, the so-called modulation transfer function. Weglein and Wilson [20] have measured the modulation transfer function of a SAM operating in the reflection mode shown in Fig. 4. Here, one single lens rod is employed both for transmission and reception of the acoustic energy. This mode is quite useful for inspection of near surface phenomena of a sample since, if penetration depth is limited, the ultimate resolution is governed by the focal spot size in the fluid couplant. Based upon theoretical calculations for spatial frequency response of the SAM, a surprisingly better performance was experimentally observed by Weglein and Wilson. These results, shown in Fig. 5, represent the normalized transfer function for the SAM operating at 375 MHz in the reflection mode. The ultimate limiting resolution appears to be consistent with the calculations; however, there is an enhancement of the low spatial frequency response.

In the SLAM, the effective numerical aperture of the system does not depend upon acoustic lens performance since none are used. Rather, the numerical aperture is limited by the response of the knife-edge detector as a function of insonification angle. The effective numerical apertures for the SLAM is dependent upon the type of samples as will be discussed below. Consider a solid sample that is optically polished on the side being examined by the laser beam. Acoustic energy at any angle but $0°$ (normal incidence) or the critical angle (if it exists), will produce surface tilt and thereby elicit a response by the

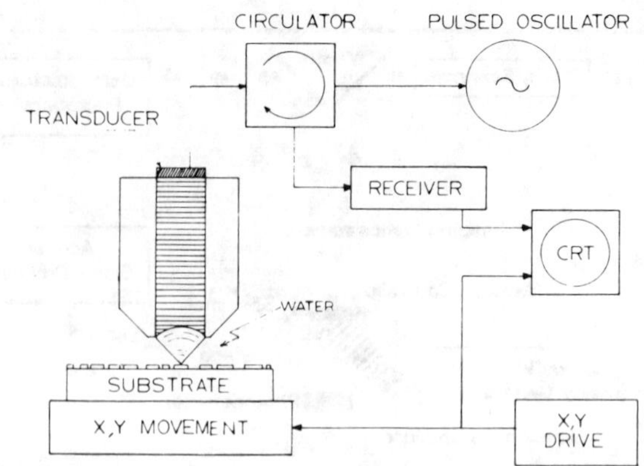

Fig. 4. SAM in the reflection mode examining a substrate material [20].

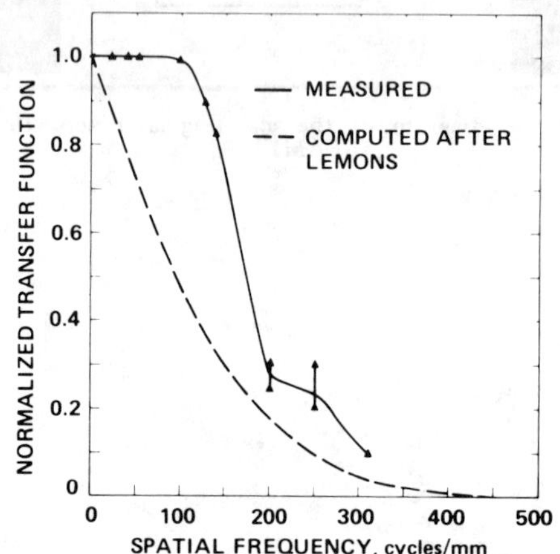

Fig. 5. Spatial frequency response of SAM [20].

knife-edge photodetector. Here the numerical aperture can be close to 1. Consider a solid sample that is not polished. In order to transfer the information onto the light beam, a mirror is placed in contact with a thin film of fluid to promote effective energy transfer. If the velocity of sound in the mirror itself is higher than that in the sample, a critical angle will occur at which the transmitted wave is refracted to 90°. Mirrors can be made from hard materials such as glass as well as from plastic. It is advantageous to use plastics since they characteristically have lower velocities of sound than glass. As long as the velocity of sound in the mirror is lower than in the sample, no critical angle will occur. For soft biological tissue, which has a typical velocity of sound of 1500 m/s, and for a low velocity of sound plastic, typically 2200 m/s, the critical angle will be $42°$ thus restricting the effective numerical aperture to about 0.6.

Aside from pure numerical aperture considerations, there is an opportunity to achieve a factor of about 2 improvement in resolution in the SLAM without a frequency increase. The method is to use transverse acoustic wave illumination instead of compressional mode. It turns out that there is a factor of about 2 smaller wavelengths for the transverse mode for most materials. With plane-wave illumination of a specimen, the choice can be made between the 2 modes. However, in the SAM, since a focused beam is employed, the 2 modes simultaneously exist causing a confusing set of 2 foci to exist within a thick sample.

In the SLAM, optimum resolution is obtained in the near-field zone of the object area imaged. The near-field zone extends inward from the laser viewed surface of the specimen by an amount which depends upon the zone diameter and the sonic wavelength. Outside of the near-field zone, the resolution is degraded, in an analogous manner as with the SAM, when the plane of interest lies outside the focused zone of the acoustic lens.

VI. Imaging Techniques

The usefulness of acoustic microscopy as an analytical tool depends on its adaptability to the problem in need of solution. The basic techniques described above form a good basis; however, numerous modifications and innovations have been necessary to achieve versatility. In this section a variety of imaging modes and acoustic microscopy techniques are described.

Acoustic amplitude transmission images were the first to be demonstrated during the course of the development of both SLAM and SAM. Transmission imaging is still one of the most useful acoustic imaging modes. In this image type, structure within a specimen is revealed by local variations in the transmission of acoustic energy. Attenuation can arise from either absorption of sound by the sample or by reflection and scattering of the sound field by elastic inhomogeneities. Inhomogeneities larger in size than an acoustic wavelength will be individually resolved and will appear as distinct structures on the acoustic micrographs. The size, location, and morphology of these features can be measured and used to characterize the material. When inhomogeneities are smaller than an acoustic wavelength, the attenuation of the beam is the result of scattering. Scattering by smaller structures produces acoustic images with a unique "texture" which can be used to characterize these materials.

In addition to variations in amplitude transmission through a specimen, variations in transit time or phase of the acoustic wave are important. The phase of the transmitted acoustic wave is related to the sonic velocity which is in turn related to the compressibility bulk density. There are a variety of ways that phase information can be incorporated into acoustic images. Two methods—phase contrast imaging and the acoustic interferogram—are described below. Prior to the advent of acoustic microscopy, and, in particular, phase sensitive imaging techniques, measurements of density and compressibility variations at the microscopic level were not possible.

Acoustic phase contrast imaging is directly analogous with optical phase contrast imaging. In phase contrast mode, the brightness level of the monitor is modulated by the relative phase of the transmitted acoustic wave. Thus images are the result of variations in sonic velocity (compared with amplitude transmission images where brightness is controlled by attenuation variations). Aside from the physical properties being revealed, the use of a phase imaging mode may be useful from the pragmatic standpoint of making it easier to "see" low contrast structures. Fig. 6 (Marmor *et al.* 1977) shows an example of a 1-μm section of human retina [21] which is first visualized on an optical microscope (Fig. 6(a)), then mounted on a Mylar support and visualized in acoustic amplitude and acoustic phase. The lack of detail in the optical image is due to the fact that the section is very thin and it has not been histologically stained. (This staining process, though necessary for optical viewing, alters the state of the original tissue and introduces significant artifacts.) Acoustically the

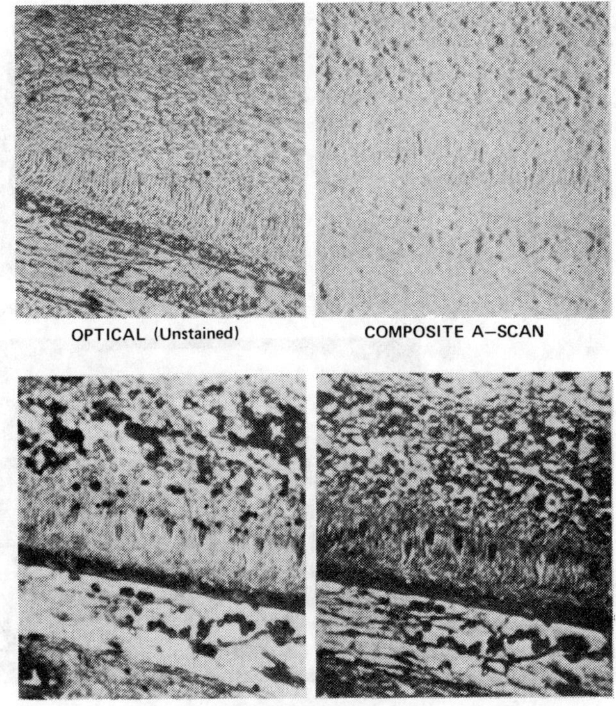

Fig. 6. Optical and SAM acoustic micrographs of a thin (1 μm) unstained section of normal human retina at about 400 X. Both acoustic amplitude (lower left) and phase (lower right) images are shown [21].

structures are differentiated very well without stains (as seen in Fig. 6(b)) and the phase image (Fig. 6(c)) reveals interesting variations of properties within the cell nuclear layers which were not evident in the optical or acoustic amplitude images.

In acoustic interferograms, sonic velocity data is incorporated into the images by superimposing a number of fringes on an acoustic amplitude micrograph. Fig. 7 shows a mouse embryo heart [22] which was maintained alive in the SLAM. This figure is a still frame of a real-time videotape recording of the cardiac contraction. The acoustic frequency is 100 MHz. Optically, the sample is totally opaque due to its thickness. The field of view is 3 mm horizontally and the crossmarks represent 1-mm spacings. In this case the advantage of acoustic microscopy is circumvention of optical opacity in a specimen and differentiation of the tissue structure without introducing stains or fixatives which would interfere with the viability of the live material. The acoustic interferogram (Fig. 7(c)) consists of a series of vertical fringes which arise from the spatial beat note between a $10°$ angular insonification field and an electronically simulated normal incident reference signal introduced into the detector. Whereas a conventional phase image translates phase information to grey levels, the interferogram yields phase information by the lateral shifts of the fringes as the sound propagates through regions with different indices of refraction. In the interferogram shown here, the fringe shifts result from two conditions of the sample: first, the velocity of sound in cardiac tissue is higher than that of the surrounding nutrient fluid bath, thereby causing fringe shifts to the right by an amount dependent on the tissue thickness, and second, it has been found [23] that as muscle contracts, the intrinsic velocity of sound increased a small amount.

Newer additions to the arsenal of acoustic microscopy imaging techniques include reflection and acoustic darkfield imaging. In contrast to transmission imaging schemes where the

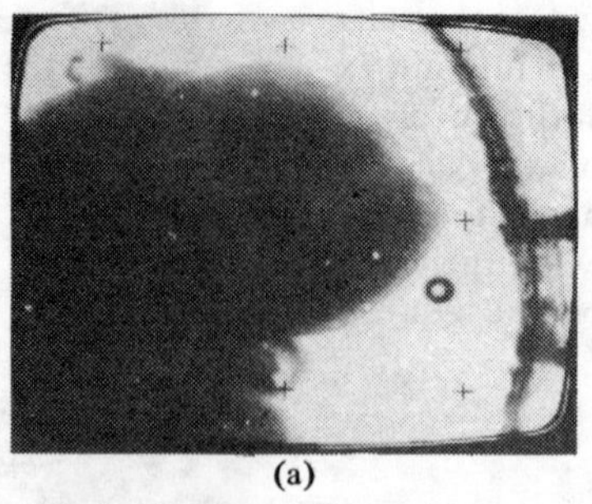

(a)

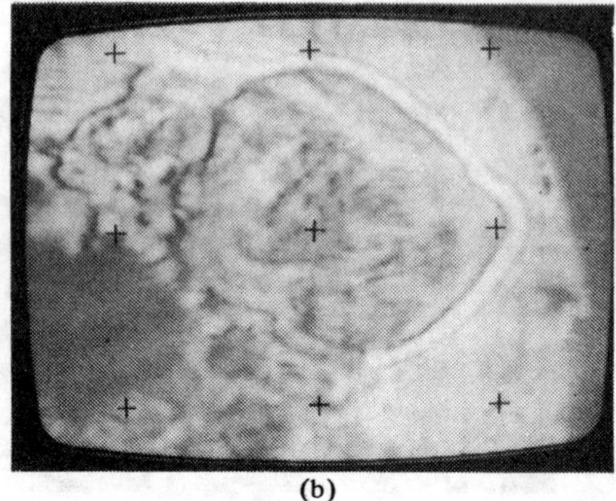

(b)

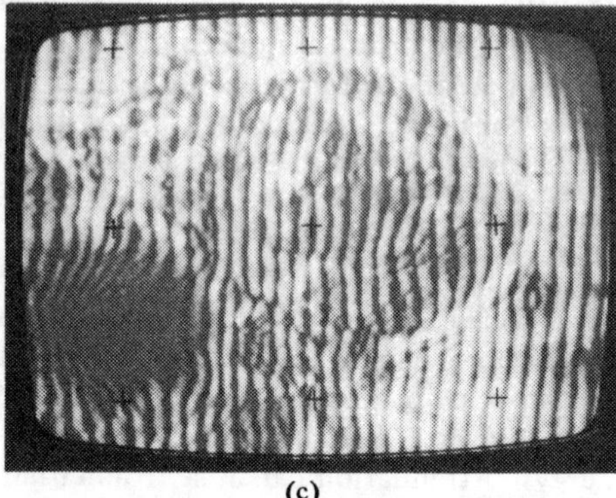

(c)

Fig. 7. Live mouse embryo heart. (a) Optical image. (b) SLAM acoustic micrograph at 100 MHz. Cross-marks are placed 1 mm apart. (c) Acoustic interferogram from which variations in elastic properties of the muscle are determined [22].

structures are revealed when sound is scattered from main beam, these imaging techniques detect the scattered or reflected energy directly.

Acoustic reflection images have been made with the SAM [20], [24] by eliminating one of the transducers and employing the other in a pulse-echo mode. Except for the large difference in frequency, the setup is similar to a conventional pulse-echo system used in nondestructive testing and clinical medicine. (Refer back to Fig. 4.) The technique is very useful for examining near surface phenomena within the reflecting object. An obvious example where this is important is in integrated-circuit technology. A typical sample is shown in Fig. 8 (from [24]) in which the SAM brings out features within the overlapping electrode layers that are not detectable optically.

Acoustic dark-field images in the SLAM can be produced in one of two ways, by insonifying the specimen at an angle corresponding to low knife-edge response, such as normal incidence, or by engaging a sharp band reject filter in the RF output of the photodiode. The latter method is made possible by the fact that when the laser rapidly scans the acoustic field, the perceived electrical frequency is Doppler shifted from that driving the ultrasonic transducer by an amount dependent on the sine of the angle of the incidence [27a], [28]. Thus acoustic energy scattered by an object is incident upon the detector plane with a spectrum of angles of incidence, each angle of which is perceived as a unique electrical frequency. An electrical filter can then be used to spatially filter the content of the acoustic image and produce effects such as dark-field and edge enhancement. Going one step further, the filter can also be so positioned that the image consists only of forward scattered sound or backscattered sound [28]. In this case, forward-scattered and backscattered directions refer to rays with components which are parallel and antiparallel to the direction of the laser scan. This capability is of great value

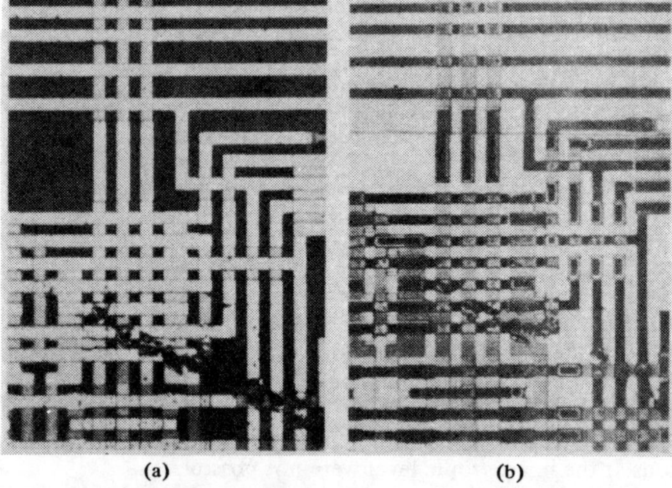

(a)   (b)

Fig. 8. Nomarski optical (a) and SAM acoustic (b) images of an integrated circuit with a silicon-on-sapphire wafer [24].

in analyzing wave patterns existing on surface-acoustic-wave filters, delay lines, and other such devices [29].

Two additional acoustic imaging schemes—nonlinear acoustic imaging and polarization sensitive acoustic imaging—should be mentioned. These methods use the same basic format as normal transmission imaging but differ by the sonic mode used to produce the image. The importance and usefulness of these imaging techniques has only recently been explored.

Nonlinear elastic behavior of materials is a very interesting aspect of the field of mechanics and, with the acoustic microscope, these nonlinear effects can be probed at a very fine level. The basic technique for visualizing nonlinear effects is to excite the specimen at one acoustic frequency while detecting acoustic energy produced at harmonics of the applied frequency. Kompfner and Lemons [30b] produced images with the SAM which displayed the second harmonic images of a biological tissue which was insonified at 400 MHz. Although they found that the resolution was equivalent to that of an 800-MHz image, there were striking features of the image contrast which were not revealed at 400-MHz or 800-MHz regular (nonharmonic) images. Presumably, the detail enhancement was caused by differential nonlinearities of the tissue components; however, the investigators feel that there are still puzzling features of this type image which cannot be explained fully.

For polarization sensitive imaging, samples were insonifed with linearly polarized transverse acoustic waves. Transverse acoustic waves, also known as shear waves, cannot propagate in liquids; therefore, the SAM cannot take full advantage of this shorter wavelength type of insonification. In the SLAM, a transverse wave transducer is bonded onto the quartz stage block and the sample is affixed to the block with a thin film of a viscous gel. Transverse waves transmitted through the sample may be acted upon differently than compressional waves by defects within a sample. For example, particular orientations of flaws may make them difficult to detect with compressional waves. One further aspect of the transverse mode is that similar to electromagnetic waves, there are two polarizations. In the SLAM, only one of these will produce surface ripples. Recall that the SLAM relies upon surface deformation for detection. Therefore, SLAM is polarization sensitive, and if the specimen is insonified by the polarization that produces no surface ripples, the acoustic image will reveal anisotropic elastic properties of the material [26].

VII. Analytical Techniques

Acoustic microscopy, like all microscopic techniques, is primarily a qualitative technique. The information contained in acoustic amplitude or phase micrographs constitute characteristic material signatures. Thus much of the useful information obtained with acoustic microscopy is purely morphological in nature. These data can be used to classify and sort materials, detect and localize flaws and defects in optically opaque samples, and map compressibility and density variations on a microscopic scale.

In addition to the qualitative aspects, techniques have been developed to quantitatively measure elastic properties on the microscopic scale. These techniques include graphic analysis of the acoustic interferograms to obtain velocity data as well as measurement of acoustic transmission levels through samples to obtain quantitative attenuation data. Additional techniques include stereoscopy, acoustic line scan, and acoustic reflectivity profiling. The last two are not true imaging modes or image analysis methods, but instead are new characterization capabilities which have arisen from the microscope technology.

Stereo viewing is an accepted method of depth determination; it also enhances the information gathering process within the eye–brain complex. The technique is commonly used for observing the terrain from aerial photographs as well as for understanding the features of a sample visualized in a scanning electron microscope. The acoustic microscope employs relatively straightforward applications of the standard technique; namely, a set of images is made with the source of insonification at different angles. Thus Bond *et al.* [27b] get the stereo effect on the SAM by rotating the axis of the transmitting transducer-lens with respect to that of the receiving element by an angle θ. The sample is rotated by half the angle θ for reasons of symmetry. For small angles of rotation, say 10°,

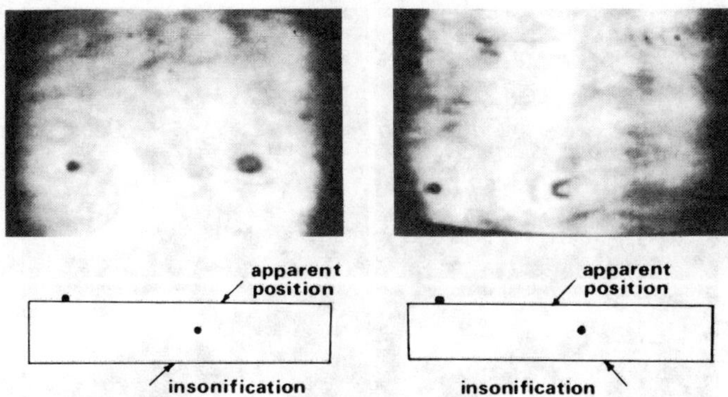

Fig. 9. Defect depth by stereoscopy. SLAM stereo pair of images in which the apparent position of a deep lying defects is shifted by changing the angle of insonification.

the stereo effect appears to be significant in their images of onion skin. For greater angles, however, the images produced in the SAM have accentuated object detail over that which is evident in the perfectly aligned through transmission system. The effect that is occurring has to do with the angular response curve of the system in which energy received at large angles produces a smaller signal than energy at normal incidence. Therefore, when the specimen and transmitter are "off-axis," the low-amplitude scattered energy is detected near the peak in the detector response, thereby producing dark-field enhancement effects.

Depth determination can also be made by simple axial translation of the sample. This method was used by Wang *et al.* [27c] to determine defect locations in joints of various materials.

In the SLAM, the sample is usually insonified on an angle to start with. Therefore, in order to produce a stereo image plane, the sample can simply be rotated on the stage and the set of 2 images recorded directly. An example is shown in Fig. 9 in which a deep lying defect in a homogeneous ceramic material is imaged. In order to record the apparent position shift, a fiducial mark was made on the top surface of the sample. The image shift of the defect with respect to the fiducial can be measured and the depth calculated.

In addition to producing two-dimensional images in the X–Y plane as in the previous examples in this article, the SAM has been used to produce acoustic reflectivity profile. With this technique, graphical spectrum of several materials are produced by axial translation of the object along the axis of the acoustic lens [36]. In this mode the SAM is used in the reflection mode. It is suggested by Weglein and Wilson that in this mode the SAM may have the ability to reveal crystallographic information on a specimen which has otherwise been obtainable by X-ray diffraction alone.

The acoustic line scan mode is an option on the SLAM which permits measurements of sonic velocity variations on a millisecond time scale. This method involves measuring the lateral fringe shifts along a single horizontal line of an acoustic interferogram. This method arose from a need to investigate rapid variations in the elastic properties of viable muscle undergoing contraction [23].

VIII. Applications of Acoustic Microscopy — Examples

The acoustic microscope is an analytical instrument with problem solving capabilities as well as applications to basic and applied research. Illustrations presented below are taken from

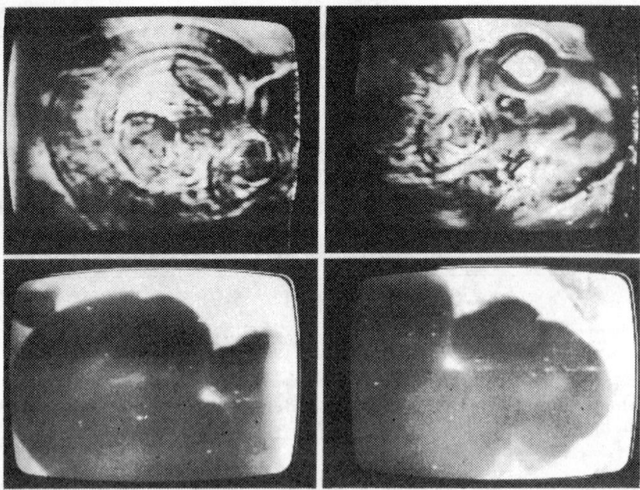

Fig. 10. Mouse embryo at age 10.5 days. Top image set is 100 MHz acoustic transmission and lower images are optical [31].

the biomedical sciences, materials technology, nondestructive testing, and from the electronics components technology.

A. Biomedical

The study of embryos is complicated by the fact that the whole specimen must be optically clarified and selectively stained in order to see internal tissues. These techniques modify the natural state of the tissues and may not be acceptable. A 10.5 day mouse embryo [31] is shown optically in Fig. 10(a). The simultaneously produced acoustic micrograph is shown in Fig. 10(b) and it quite clearly demonstrates a high degree of differentiation for hard and soft tissues. The frequency of ultrasound is 100 MHz and the resolution in tissue is 20 μm. Although this particular specimen was fixed in ethanol, similar studies have been done in the live state, thereby revealing dynamic events such as cardiac activities which were recorded on video tape.

Collagen is an abundant protein in mammals and is responsible for the structural strength of tissues and organs. Acoustic microscopy of fresh collagen [32] carried out at 100 MHz is illustrated in Fig. 11(a) and (b) which are, respectively, a normal acoustic micrograph and an interferogram. Measurements of the fringe shifts in the collagen relative to the surrounding aqueous fluid indicate a velocity of sound which is at least 25 percent higher than soft tissue.

Pathological disease in human liver in shown in Fig. 12 which was obtained at 100 MHz on samples supplied by R. Waag of the University of Rochester Medical School, Rochester, NY. This particular sample shows a metastic adenocarcinoma. Some of these tumor cell nests have necrotic centers which appear darker than the surrounding tumor cells. A transmission acoustic micrograph of a thick section shows collagenous septae as dark bands between glandular nests of tumor cells. The necrotic centers of the tumors appear darker than the peripheral tumor cells. The reduced transmission through the septas and necrotic centers indicates that they attenuate sound more than the surrounding tissue. An acoustic interferogram with fringes bending to the left as they traverse the collagenous septae and necrotic tissue demonstrates that the speed of sound is greater in them than in the adjacent tissue. The distribution of collagen and the architecture of the adenocarcinoma give a markedly different appearence from normal liver.

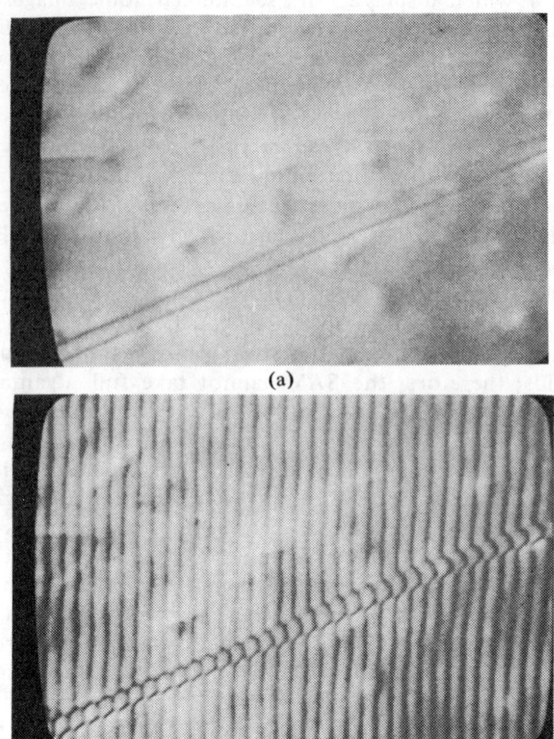

Fig. 11. Acoustic micrograph (a) and interferogram (b) of mammalian tendon at 100 MHz [32].

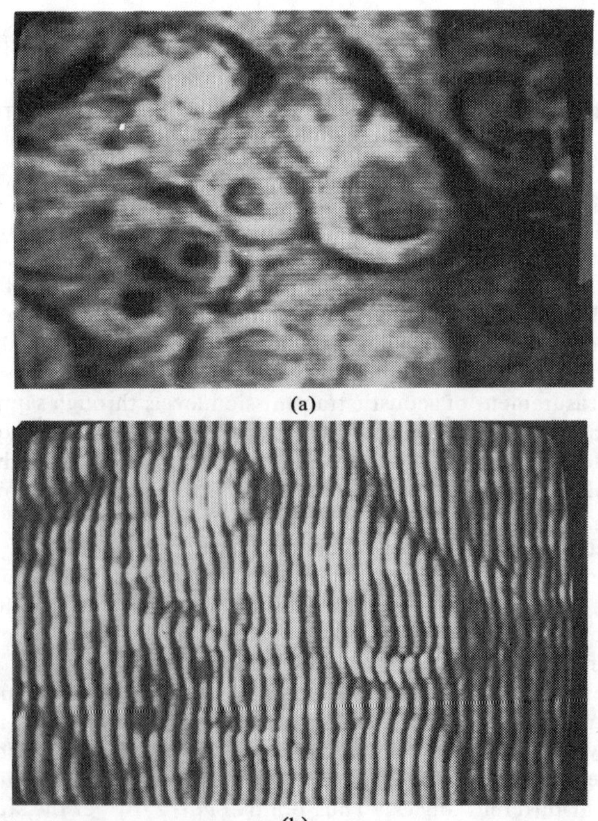

Fig. 12. Human liver with metastatic adenocarcinoma. Acoustic micrograph (a) and interferogram (b) at 100 MHz with SLAM. (Courtesy of R. Waag, University of Rochester Medical School.)

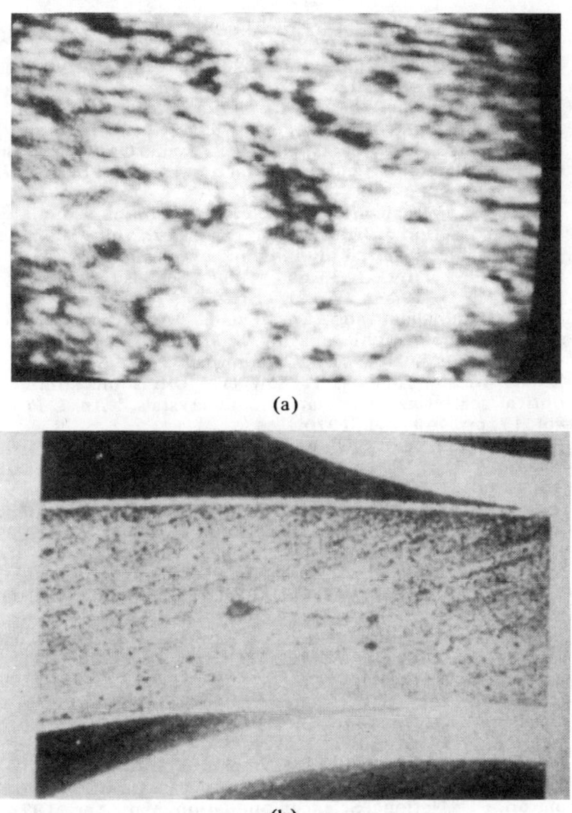

Fig. 13. Ceramic turbine blade showing large defect among a network of porosity (a) acoustic micrograph and (b) sectioned sample revealing laminar flaw [33].

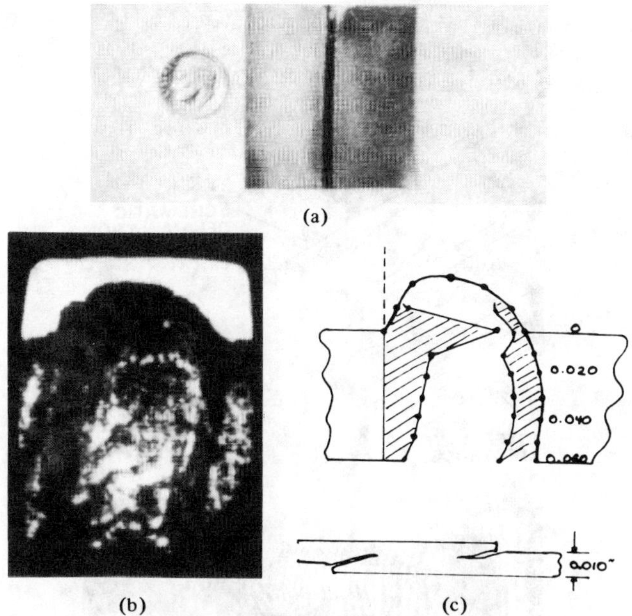

Fig. 14. Seam welded steel can with poor bonding at the lead edge. (a) Optical photograph of sample, (b) 100-MHz SLAM acoustic transmission image with dark zones corresponding to disbonds, and (c) confirming metallographic sectioning of sample revealed approximate disbond areas.

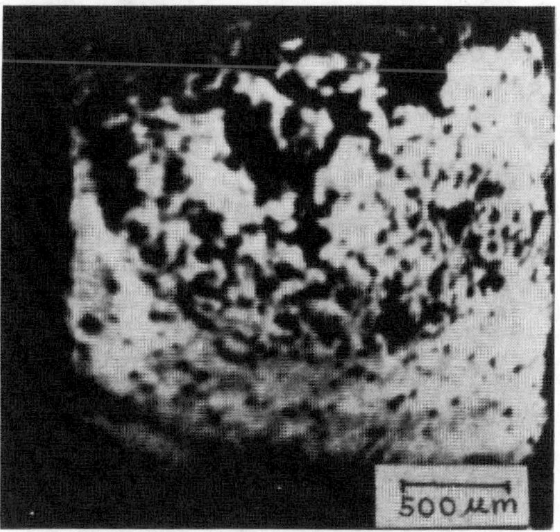

Fig. 15. Acoustic micrograph of a production line silicon–solder–copper bond. Wafer thickness is 100 μm and copper plate is 300 μm. SAM transmission image [34].

B. Materials Technology and Nondestructive Testing

Silicon nitride turbine blades were examined at 100 MHz to define the typical elastic microstructure and to detect the presence of flaws [33a]. Fig. 13(a) shows an acoustic micrograph which shows small pores distributed throughout the sample as well as a much larger laminar defect which could not be detected by radiography even after the flaw was spotted acoustically. Fig. 13(b) shows the flaw optically after the sample was sliced apart to confirm the findings.

The seam welds on steel cans with a thickness of 0.010 in and approximately 0.020 in. thick-weld sections were inspected by SLAM at 100 MHz [33b]. The acoustic micrograph Fig. 14(a) revealed major defects (disbonded zones) along the seam, smaller imperfections within the junction regions and details of the adjacent heat affected metal. Conventional metallographic data obtained by sectioning revealed only the large defects due to the wide separations between the sections as seen in Fig. 14(b). Nine polished and etched sections provided 29 visual data points and required many hours of preparation, whereas the acoustic micrographs containing 40 000 image points each were produced in 0.033 s without destroying the sample.

C. Electronic Components

Acoustic microscopy is a very sensitive method for detecting delaminations of bonded materials. An investigation into solder bonds on a commercially available transistor was carried out at 150 MHz by Tsai *et al.* [34]. Fig. 15 shows a silicon wafer 2.5-mm square bonded to a copper plate by means of Au-Sn solder. The regions of disbond permit no sonic transmission and corresponding dark areas of the micrograph.

Another example is shown in Fig. 16 which is an interferogram (100 MHz) of a ceramic chip capacitor along with a schematic diagram of its construction. The field of view is 4 mm horizontally, and the dark zone in the center correlates with delamination of a layer. In this study, Love and Ewell [35] pointed out that delaminations such as these shorten the lifetime of the component. Each layer is constructed of a high dielectric constant material which has been electroded on both surfaces. Prior to failure, i.e., complete delamination and break of electrical contact, the capacitor behaves normal electrically.

At a frequency of 3 GHz, Jipson and Quate [14] have examined an integrated circuit in the SAM. Fig. 17 shows a reflection mode image of an IC circuit fabricated on silicon. The acoustic reflectivity is a function of the layering structure beneath the aluminum lines connecting to the transistors; thus the dark spots appearing are attributed to subsurface

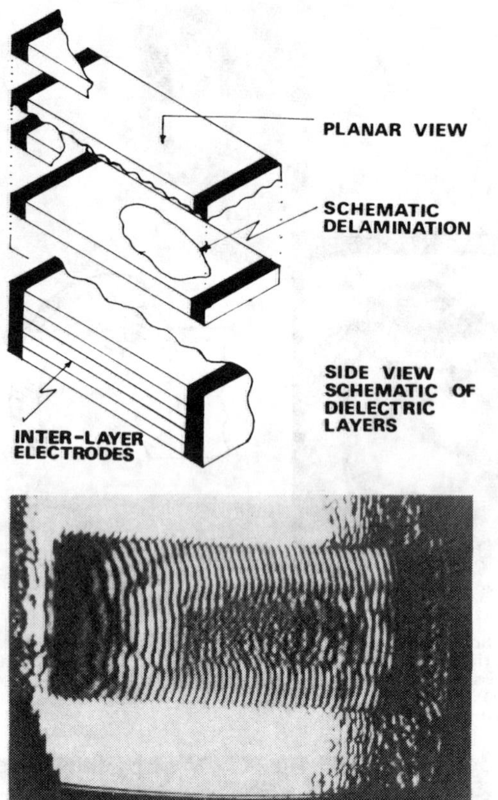

Fig. 16. Ceramic ship capacitor with interlayer delamination. Acoustic interferogram at 100 MHz and SLAM [35].

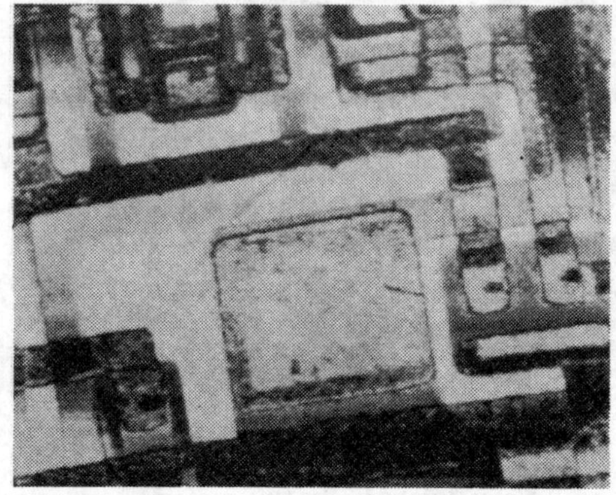

Fig. 17. SAM acoustic image at 3 GHz of an integrated circuit. The line widths are 7 μm [14].

structure such as regions where the oxide has been removed and emitter contacts are formed.

IX. Conclusions

Approximately 35 years after Sokolov first proposed the notion of acoustic microscopy, the technology has now developed to the point where it is practical. Current emphasis is on applications of the technology as well as improvement on the techniques employed. It is anticipated that the SLAM and SAM will soon take their place along the electron microscope as standard analytical instruments.

References

[1] L. W. Kessler, "A review of progress and applications in acoustic microscopy," *J. Acoust. Soc. Amer.*, vol. 55, pp. 909–918, 1974.

[2] S. Sokolov, USSR Patent no. 49 (Aug. 31, 1936), British Patent no. 477 139, 1937, and U.S. Patent no. 21 64 125, 1939.

[3] F. Dunn, and W. J. Fry, "Ultrasonic absorption microscope," *J. Acoust. Soc. Amer.*, vol. 31, no. 5, pp. 632–633, May 1959.

[4] J. Havlice, C. F. Quate, and B. Richardson, "Visualization of sound beams in quartz and sapphire near 1 GHz," paper 1-4 presented to the 1967 IEEE Ultrason. Symp., *IEEE Trans. Sonics Ultrason.*, vol. SU-15, 68, 1968. See also [15] and [17].

[5] H. V. Hance, J. K. Parks, and C. S. Tsai, "Optical imaging of a complex ultrasonic field by diffraction of a laser beam," *J. Appl. Phys.* vol. 38, pp. 1981–1983, 1967.

[6] A. Korpel, "Visualization of the cross section of a sound beam by Bragg diffraction of light," *Appl. Phys. Lett.* vol. 9, p. 425, 1966.

[7] R. Pohlman, "Material illumination by means of acoustic optical imagery," *Z. Phys.*, 1133 697, 1939. See also *Z. Angew. Phys.*, vol. 1, p. 181, 1948.

[8] J. A. Cunningham, and C. F. Quate, "Acoustic interference in solids and holographic imaging," in *Acoustical Holography*, vol. 4, G. Wade, Ed. New York: Plenum, 1972, pp. 667–685.

[9] L. W. Kessler, and S. P. Sawyer, "Ultrasonic stimulation of optical scattering in nematic liquid crystals," *Appl. Phys. Lett.* vol. 17, pp. 440–441, 1970.

[10] R. A. Lemons, and C. F. Quate, "Acoustic microscope—scanning version," *Appl. Phys. Letters*, vol. 24, no. 4, pp. 163–165, Feb. 15, 1974.

[11] A. Korpel, and L. W. Kessler, "Comparison of methods of acoustic microscopy," in *Acoustical Holography*, vol. 3 by A. F. Metherell, Ed. New York: Plenum, 1971, pp. 23–43.

[12] R. A. Lemons, and C. F. Quate, "A scanning acoustic microscope," *Proc. Ultrason. Symp.* 18-21 IEEE Catalog 73CHO 807-8 SU J. de Klerk, Ed., 1973.

[13] —, "Advances in mechanically scanned acoustic microscopy," *Proc. 1974 Ultrason. Symp.*, IEEE Catalog #74CHO 896-ISU, p. 41, J. de Klerk, Ed., 1975.

[14] V. Jipson, and C. F. Quate, "Acoustic microscopy at optical wavelengths," Ginzton Laboratory rep. no. 2790 on Contract AFOSR-77-3455 and NSF APR75-07317; submitted to *Appl. Phys. Letters.* June, 15, 1978 (in press).

[15] "The promise of acoustic microscopy," in *Mosaic*, vol. 9. Washington, DC: National Science Foundation, Mar./Apr., 1978, p. 35.

[16] A. Korpel, L. W. Kessler, and P. R. Palermo, "Acoustic microscope operating at 100 MHz," *Nature*, vol. 232, no. 5306, pp. 110–111, July 9, 1971.

[17] L. W. Kessler, A. Korpel, and P. R. Palermo, "Simultaneous acoustic and optical microscopy of biological specimens," *Nature*, vol. 239, no. 5367, pp. 111–112, Sept. 8, 1972.

[18] a) L. W. Kessler, and D. E. Yuhas, "Structural perspective," *Indust. Rev.*, Jan. 1978, vol. 20, no. 1, 53–56.
b) SONOMICROSCOPE^{TM} 100, manufactured by Sonoscan, Inc., Bensenville, IL 60106.

[19] A. Korpel, R. Adler, P. Desmares, and W. Watson: "A television display using acoustic deflection and modulation of coherent light," *Appl. Opt.*, vol. 5, 1667–1675 1966.

[20] R. D. Weglein and R. G. Wilson, "Image resolution of the scanning acoustic microscope," *Appl. Phys. Lett.*, vol. 31, no. 12, pp. 793–796, 1977.

[21] M. F. Marmor, and H. K. Wickramasinghe, "Acoustic microscopy of the human retina and pigment epithelium," *Invest. Ophth. Vis. Sci.*, vol. 16, no. 7, pp. 660–666, July 1977.

[22] R. C. Eggleton, and F. S. Vinson, "Heart model supported in organ culture and analyzed by acoustic microscopy," in *Acoustical Holography*, vol. 7 L. W. Kessler, Ed. New York: Plenum, 1977, pp. 21–35.

[23] R. C. Eggleton, "Application of acoustic microscopy of the study of muscle mechanics," *SPIE Proc. vol. 104, Multidisciplinary Microscopy*, R. L. Whitmen, Ed. 117–124 Published by Society of Photo-Optical Instrumentation Engineers, P. O. Box 10, Bellingham, WA 98225, 1977.

[24] R. Kompfner, and C. F. Quate, "Acoustic radiation and its use in microscopy," *Phys. Technol.*, pp. 231–237, Nov. 1977.

[25] L. W. Kessler, and D. E. Yuhas, "Listen to structural differences," *Indust. Dev.* vol. 20, no. 4, Apr. 1978, pp. 102–106.

[26] L. W. Kessler, U.S. Patent 4 012 951, Acoustic Examination Method and Apparatus.

[27] a) L. W. Kessler, P. R. Palermo, and A. Korpel, *Practical High Resolution.* New York: Plenum Publishing, 1972, pp. 51–71.
b) W. L. Bond, C. C. Cutler, R. A. Lemons, and C. F. Quate, "Dark-field and stereo viewing with the acoustic microscope," *Appl. Phys. Lett.*, vol. 27, no. 5, pp. 270–272, Sept. 1, 1975.

[27c] S. K. Wang, C. C. Lee, and C. S. Tsai, "Nondestructive visulaization and characterization of material joints using a scanning acoustic microscope," in *Proc. IEEE 1977 Ultrason. Symp.*, IEEE Cat. 77-CH1-264.

[28] D. E. Yuhas, "Characterization of surface flaws by means of acoustic microscopy," in *Program and Abstracts: First International Symposium on Ultrasonic Materials Characterization.* National Bureau of Standards, Gaithersburg, MD, p. 79.

[29] L. W. Kessler, "Real time SAW visualization techniques to aid device design," Paper F-9. 1975 Ultrason. Symp. (IEEE), Sept.

22–24, Los Angeles, CA. Also available as application note SAW-1 from Sonoscan, Inc., 720 Foster Ave., Bensenville, IL 60106.

[30a] H. K. Wickramasinghe, R. Bray, V. Jipson, C. F. Quate, and J. Salcedo, Photoacoustics on a Microscopic Scale. Submitted to *Appl. Phys. Lett.* 1978.

[30b] R. Kompfner, and R. A. Lemons, "Nonlinear acoustic microscopy," *Appl. Phys. Lett.*, vol. 28, no. 6, pp. 295–297, Mar. 15, 1976.

[31] W. D. O'Brien, and L. W. Kessler, "Examination of mouse embryological development with an acoustic microscope," *Amer. Zool.*, vol. 15, p. 807, 1975.

[32] W. D. O'Brien, and S. Goss, In preparation.

[33] a) D. S. Kupperman *et al.*, "Preliminary evaluation of several non-destructive evaluation techniques for silicon nitride gas turbine rotors," *Argonne Nat. Laboratory Tech. rep.*, Materials Science Division, Argonne, IL 60439 (1978). Rep. #ANL-77-89.
b) D. E. Yuhas, and L. W. Kessler, "Acoustic Microscopy," *Principles and Applications*, Paper Summaries, Spring Conf. ASNT, 165–171 (Mar. 1977).

[34] C. S. Tsai, S. K. Wang, and C. D. Lee, "Visualization of solid material joints using a transmission-type scanning acoustic microscope," *Appl. Phys. Lett.*, vol. 31, p. 317, Sept. 1977.

[35] G. R. Love, and G. J. Ewell, "Acoustic microscopy of ceramic capacitors," *Proc. of 28th Electronic Components Conference*, IEEE/EIA, Apr. 24–26 1978 Anaheim, CA.

[36] R. D. Weglein and R. G. Wilson, "Characteristic signatures by acoustic microscopy," *Electron. Lett.*, vol. 14, p. 352, 1978.

Acoustic Microscopy with Mechanical Scanning—A Review

CALVIN F. QUATE, FELLOW, IEEE, ABDULLAH ATALAR, AND H. K. WICKRAMASINGHE

Invited Paper

Abstract—Acoustic waves in liquids are known to have wavelengths comparable to that of visible light if the frequency is in the gigahertz range. The phenomena of Brillouin scattering in liquids is based on such waves. In helium near 2 K acoustic waves with a wavelength of 2000 Å were studied some ten years ago at UCLA. It follows from these observations that an imaging system based on acoustic radiation with a resolving power competitive with the optical microscope is within reach if an ideal lens free from aberrations could be found. Such a lens, which was so elusive at the beginning, is now a simple device and it is the basic component in the acoustic microscope that forms the basis for this review.

In this article we will establish the characteristic properties of this new instrument. We will review some of the simple properties of acoustic waves and show how a single spherical surface formed at a solid liquid interface can serve as this ideal lens free from aberrations and capable of producing diffraction limited beams. When this is incorporated into a mechanical scanning system and excited with acoustic frequencies in the microwave range images can be recorded with acoustic wavelengths equal to the wavelength of visible light. We will present images that show the elastic properties of specimens selected from the fields of material science, integrated circuits, and cell biology. The information content in these images will often exceed that of the optical micrographs. In the reflection mode we illuminate the smooth surface of a crystalline material with a highly convergent acoustic beam. The reflected field is perturbed in a unique way that is determined by the elastic properties of the reflecting surface and it shows up in the phase of the reflected acoustic field. There is a distinct and characteristic response at the output when the spacing between the object and the lens is varied. This behavior in the acoustic reflection microscope provides a rather simple and direct means for monitoring the elastic parameters of a solid surface. It is easy to distinguish between different materials, to determine the layer thickness, and to display variations in the elastic constants on a microscopic scale. These features lead us to believe there is a promising future for the field of acoustic microscopy.

I. Introduction

IMAGING of microscopic objects with optical and electron microscopes has been closely linked to our understanding of physical or biological phenomena. It is hard to conceive of a modern laboratory involved with technology or the advancement of science that is without a microscope of some kind. It has been suggested that the number of instruments in a given country used to extend our "vision" beyond the limits of the unaided eye can be used as an indicator of the progress and advancement of that region.

Electronic microstructures and electronic materials form the basic elements of solid-state electronics—electronics that underlie an ever increasing part of the complex systems that our new technology makes possible. The complexity of these systems comes from an acquired ability to control material uniformity and to fabricate devices on a scale that is determined by the wavelength of light. We not only exploit this wavelength through lithography for the fabrication of devices but we also use this radiation to examine structural details with dimensions of micrometers.

The materials themselves exhibit features with those dimensions either in the form of defects in single crystals or in the alloying of two different materials to produce microscopic regions with inhomogeneous properties. Other noncrystalline materials have a grain structure which can be of this size. The strength of the material itself depends upon these microscopic features.

The entire world of biological structures is largely made up of cellular components that are microscopic in size. The elastic properties of these components are important and they dominate a large number of biomedical problems. The contractile mechanisms involved with cell movement, other contractile processes associated with muscle contraction, the deformability of cells of the blood stream, and the enormous changes in elastic properties that occur when a given cell goes through the mitotic process and divides into two separate cells are examples where the elastic properties are of primary importance.

It may seem that the tools now available for examining microscopic structures form a complete set satisfactory for every task. But there are limitations—by and large the electron microscope in the scanning version is used to examine surface features and it is restricted to objects that can withstand the environment of the vacuum chamber. The optical microscope cannot be used to examine the interior of opaque material. But there is a stronger objection to these instruments which comes from the fact that they cannot be used to examine the mechanical or elastic properties of microstructures. These elastic properties are fundamental—they make a difference as to whether the structures will hold together. The ability to examine these properties on a microscopic scale would increase our knowledge by a wide margin. The alloying spikes of aluminum and silicon, the adhesion properties of the grains that form metal alloys and ceramics, the regions surrounding dislocations and faults in single crystals that are highly stressed, the viscosity and density of intracellular material in biological cells and tissues—all of these form an enormous area in the microscopic world, an area that is worthy of study and an area where we need new tools.

This desire to examine elastic properties on a microscopic scale has motivated our work on the use of acoustic radiation in a microscope. Acoustic waves have always held a potential for microscopic imaging simply because the wavelength of sound at microwave frequencies is small. In crystals of quartz

Manuscript received September 15, 1978; revised February 27, 1979. This research was supported in part by the Air Force Office of Scientific Research and the NBS/ARPA Program on Semiconductor Electronics.

C. F. Quate and A. Atalar are with the Edward L. Ginzton Laboratory, Stanford University, Stanford, CA 94305.

H. K. Wickramasinghe is with the Department of Electronic and Electrical Engineering, University College London, London, England.

Reprinted from *Proc. IEEE*, vol. 67, pp. 1092–1114, Aug. 1979.

at low temperatures acoustic waves with a wavelength of 100 Å have been generated and studied [1]. In liquid helium, wavelengths as short at 2000 Å have been propagated between two parallel surfaces [2]. At room temperature in liquids the acoustic wavelengths have been much longer. Nevertheless progress to date has permitted us to work over short distances in water with wavelengths less than 1 μm.

Much of this article will be devoted to the use of these waves in a focused system wherein the specimen is mechanically scanned to record the image. One primary goal—a goal that has been realized within the past few months [3]—is the construction of an instrument with a resolving power equal to that of the optical instrument. This article will be devoted to a description of that work and a description of some of the micrographs that illustrate the features that can now be studied with acoustic radiation.

We will concentrate almost entirely on the version of the acoustic microscope that uses mechanical scanning and acoustic lens [4]. Before we proceed with the full description we will point out that the essential component in the system is a simple spherical lens formed at the interface between a solid such as sapphire with a high velocity of sound and a liquid such as water with a low sound velocity. There is no spherical aberration in this lens and it can be used to focus the acoustic beam into a waist with a diameter that is less than one wavelength. In water this wavelength is equal to that of visible light (0.5 μm) for a frequency of 3 GHz. The acoustic micrographs at this frequency are beginning to approach the optical micrographs in quality.

The material in this article is confined for the most part to instruments operating above 1 GHz. This region is attractive. There we can compete with the optical microscope in resolving fine detail and we enjoy this competition. Work in the field of acoustic microscopy below 1 GHz is important but it will not be included here since it has been covered in previous review articles [5]–[12]. The early work of Korpel [5] and the current work of Kessler [12] on laser scanning systems has established principles and pointed to areas of investigation [13] where acoustic radiation can play a unique role. The work of Tsai [14] has demonstrated the utility of acoustic waves as a method of probing bonds between opaque materials. Wilson [15] and Weglein [16] have studied integrated circuits with the acoustic microscope and they argue that increased contrast in their acoustic micrographs provides information that is not available in optical micrographs. In France, Bridoux and Torquet [17] in their work have shown that this instrument is useful for opaque objects such as fossils. Attal [18] and Wickramasinghe [19] have taught us that the phase of the output signal contains as much information about the image as does the amplitude of the signal. In Japan, Chubachi [20] has shown that piezoelectric transducers can be fabricated directly on the curved surface of the lens and thereby eliminate the spurious pulses that rattle around inside the crystal that forms the acoustic cell. In England, Bennett, Payne, and Ash [21] have demonstrated that acoustic microscopy is useful for studying the electrolytic deposition of metallic layers. In addition, this field has been discussed in several articles of a more general interest [22]–[26].

II. The Scanning Principle

The "field of view" imaging system where the image appears either on the retina of the observer, on photographic film, or on a fluorescent screen is not a viable alternative for acoustic radiation. Other means must be found. Piezoelectric films are efficient, highly sensitive and they operate over a wide range of frequencies. These could be used to build an array of detectors in the form of an acoustic retina. In such an array careful attention would have to be given to both the phase and amplitude of the signal from each element. The degree of complexity in this system was such that we found that we were continually working on arrays. It was the microscope itself that held our interest. A single piezoelectric detector and a mechanically scanned object is an alternative. An imaging system based on scanning the beam is tightly focused and the image field is constructed point by point as the object is moved in a raster pattern through the focus of the beam.

At first we turned to this system as an expedient, but as we gained experience we found that a scanned system has advantages not found in conventional systems.

The primary drawback for the mechanical scanning system is the speed. It is slow. Several seconds are required to build up a single frame as compared to television rates of 30 frames per second. This will be overcome in time for we have built mechanical systems that operate at 10 frames per second but the work to be reported here will be limited to the systems which use slow scans.

The advantages inherent to scanning systems with focusing were not obvious in the beginning. It is now becoming evident that scanning systems which record a single point at a time exhibit properties different from those that display the entire field of view. In the scanned system there is no problem with coherent radiation. Since the energy at the focus is confined to a diameter that is less than one wavelength in dimension there are no interference fringes of the type that are common with optical microscopes that use coherent laser radiation. These fringes arise from the scattered radiation from two points on the object that are separated by many wavelengths. This point will become clear in a later section when we calculate the response of an abrupt edge for the two systems.

The scanned system is sensitive to transverse phase gradients in the object. In transmission this is an important source of contrast. In the reflection mode the highly focused beam makes it possible to study small variations in the elastic constants across the surface of a solid specimen. This turns out to be an important source of contrast in reflection images. These two points will be discussed at some length later on in this review. And finally, the sequential recording of the image point by point is ideally suited to a system that uses a microprocessor to manipulate, store, and process the image prior to display. The cost of memories is decreasing with time, and microprocessors will be important elements in future microscopes.

III. The Form of the Instrument with Mechanical Scanning

If acoustic imaging systems suffer from the absence of photographic film (sensitive to acoustic radiation) they have an enormous advantage (over optics) in that the wave velocity in solids can be larger than that in liquids by a factor of ten. The sketch of Fig. 1 is useful for explaining this advantage. The large velocity ratio means that there is a large angle of refraction, for a wave is traveling through the solid–liquid interface (Fig. 1(a)). This has two consequences in the microscope: 1) with a spherical interface, rays approaching from the solid will leave in a direction that is nearly radial (Fig. 1(b)), 2) with a plane interface waves approaching from the liquid will find a critical angle for total internal reflection which is much smaller than that encountered in optics (Fig. 1(c)).

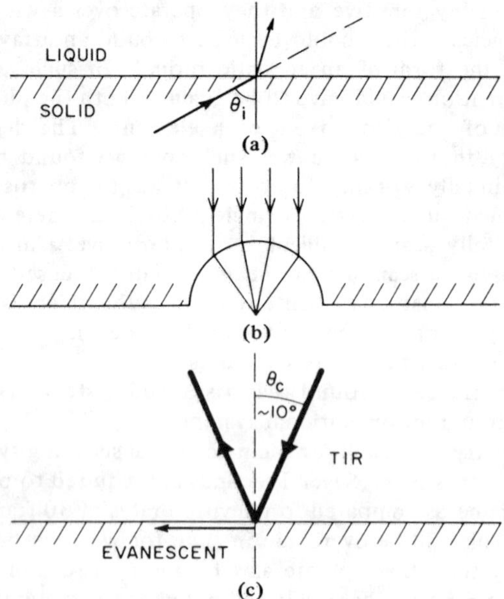

Fig. 1. Illustration of strong refraction of acoustic waves at a liquid–solid interface (TIR—total internal reflection). (a) Snell's law. (b) Lens. (c) Reflector.

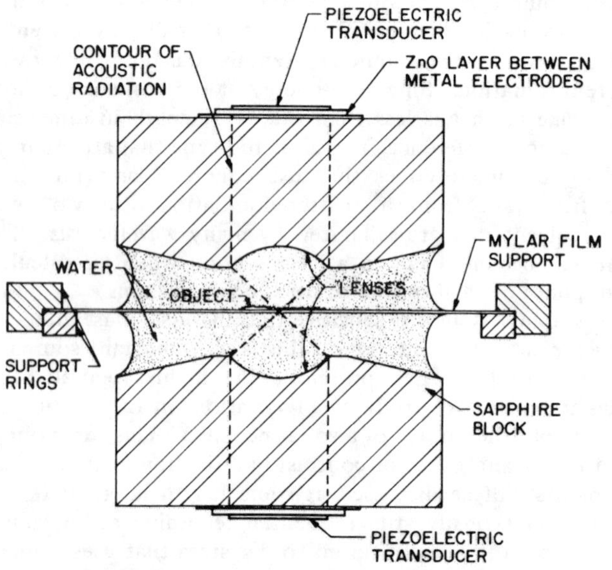

Fig. 2. Sketch of microscope geometry for transmission.

Fig. 3. Scanning acoustic microscope—Mechanical components. (Courtesy of R. C. Addison.)

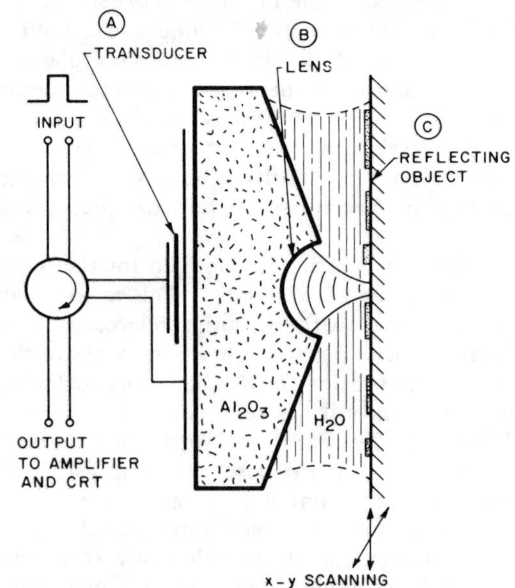

Fig. 4. Sketch of microscope components for reflection.

The first factor permits us to construct a simple, single surface lens that is free from aberrations and focuses the beam to a diffraction limited waist. The second factor permits us to use the reflection mode and sense the elastic properties of the reflecting surface.

The acoustic components of the microscope are shown in Fig. 2 for the transmission mode. A photograph of the mechanical components for this mode is presented in Fig. 3. The essential parts of the reflection mode microscope are shown in Fig. 4.

Referring to Fig. 2, we begin with the electrical input signal to the piezoelectric transducer. It is a sputtered film of zinc oxide sandwiched between the two films of gold. This transducer is extensively used in a variety of microwave acoustic devices [27]. It has proved to be efficient (50-percent conversion effective) and it operates at frequencies that exceed 10 GHz. In our instrument it generates a plane wave that travels through the sapphire crystal to the spherical lens. The ratio of

the radius of the transducer to that of the lens as well as the transducer–lens spacing must be carefully adjusted. The lens is in the Fresnel zone of the radiating transducer and it is surprisingly easy to pick a combination of dimensions that will result in nonuniform illuminations of the lens. At the lens surface the impedance ratio between sapphire and water is nearly 50:1 and this must be overcome with a quarter-wave matching layer. Various combinations have been suggested—gold–quartz [28], glass [29], Arsenic–Tri-Selenide [17]—and they all are effective. Carbon films with an acoustic impedance of 9×10^6 kg/m²-s may be ideal for this purpose but they have not yet been used.

With the sapphire–water combination the beam converges to a focus with a focal length that is 15 percent greater than the radius of curvature. In the transmission mode (Fig. 2) the radiation passes through the object which is supported on a thin Mylar film and it is collected by an output-lens–transducer combination that is similar to the input. In this mode where we use continuous radiation it is possible to monitor either the change in amplitude or the change in phase of the signal as the object is scanned.

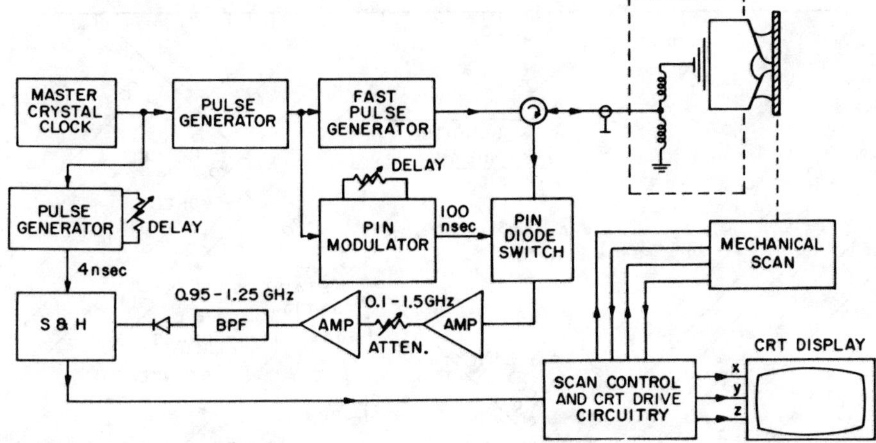

Fig. 5. Block diagram of the acoustic reflection microscope centered at 1100 MHz.

The object itself is mechanically translated through the beam waist by the loudspeaker shown in Fig. 3. This unit moves the object with simple harmonic motion along a straight line at a frequency of 60 Hz over a distance of 0.2 mm. A micrometer drive is used to lift the loudspeaker through this same distance in a time equal to several seconds.

This slow scan speed (5–10 s/frame) makes it necessary to store the image by some method before display. We use two methods: 1) a scan converter, and 2) direct writing on film.

In the reflection mode (Fig. 4) the radiation is pulsed so that the reflection from the object can be distinguished in time from spurious pulses that come from other reflecting points within the system. A block diagram of the reflection mode system is shown in Fig. 5. An avalanche transistor pulser excites the piezoelectric transducer through the circulator. The pulsewidth is selected such that the frequency content of the pulse covers the operating frequency range of the acoustic system.

As an example, a pulse of duration 500 ps can excite the acoustic system centered at 1100 MHz. The return pulse will then be an RF pulse centered at 1100 MHz and of a duration determined by the bandwidth of the acoustic transducer. After being amplified this pulse is detected and its amplitude is used to modulate the intensity (Z-axis) of a television monitor. The images are recorded by photographing the face of this monitor [30].

In addition to a system with increased scan speed, other systems have been explored with features that complement and enhance those discussed here. Two are of primary interest. The nonlinear system where the output transducer is tuned to the second harmonic of the input; in this system the nonlinear properties of the object itself can be monitored [31]. In another system the axis of the output lens is moved from the colinear alignment as shown in Fig. 2 to an off-axis position [32]. It is then possible to detect the energy that is scattered through a wide angle by the object. It is analogous to dark field imaging in some ways since the output transducer does not detect the direct signal from the input when the object is absent.

IV. PROPERTIES OF ACOUSTIC WAVES

It may, at first, seem unnecessary to write down the elementary equations for acoustic waves—no one would take the space to write out the equations for electromagnetic waves—but we feel that it would be useful since acoustic wave properties do

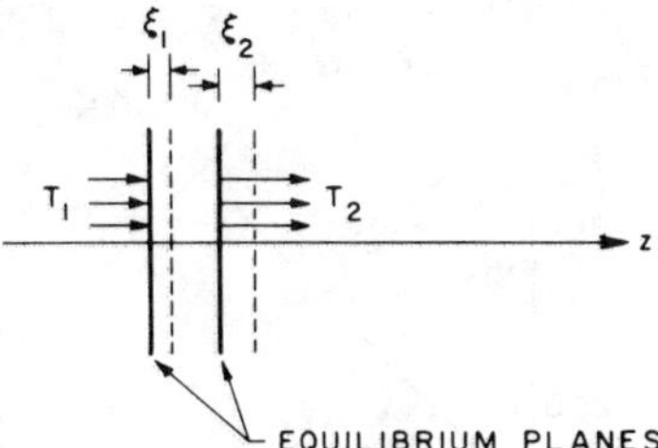

Fig. 6. Sketch of planes and then displacement from equilibrium as used in derivation of wave equation.

not have the familiar ring of dielectric constant or permeability. For that reason we will write out the differential equations. The wave equations that come from these are convenient for defining the terms that we deal with throughout the text.

Acoustic waves come in a variety of forms—shear, longitudinal, and surface—but in liquids the longitudinal wave represents the only mode of propagation. We will, therefore, limit the discussion to longitudinal, or compressional, waves where the direction of the particle motion coincides with the direction of propagation.

In the sketch of Fig. 6 we illustrate two parallel planes spaced by a distance Δz. The medium is liquid with a density ρ_0. The stress on plane 1, denoted by T_1, and on plane 2 by T_2, represents the force per unit of area on these planes. The differential pressure, or net force, on this thin slice is $T_1 - T_2$. The net force acting to compress the slice is $(-\partial T/\partial z)\Delta z$ since T_2 is given by $T_1 + (\partial T/\partial z)\Delta z$. Compressive force will be taken as positive. The mass per unit area of this slice is $\rho_0 \Delta z$. Newton's Force Law gives us the relation

$$-(\partial T/\partial z)\Delta z = \rho_0 \Delta z\, \partial U/\partial t$$

or

$$\partial T/\partial z = -\rho_0\, \partial U/\partial t. \qquad (4\text{-}1)$$

Here U is the velocity of the material in the slab. It is to be distinguished from the wave v_s velocity which will appear later. If plane 1 is displaced from its equilibrium value by an amount ξ the material velocity U is equal to $\partial \xi/\partial t$. If the displacement from equilibrium of plane 1, ξ_1, is equal to ξ_2, the displacement of plane 2, the slab is merely translated along the z-axis. But if ξ_2 is less than ξ_1 the slab is compressed by an amount $\xi_1 - \xi_2 = -(\partial \xi/\partial z)\Delta z$. The strain S is equal to $(\xi_1 - \xi_2)/\Delta z$ or $-\partial \xi/\partial z$. If we differentiate with respect to the time

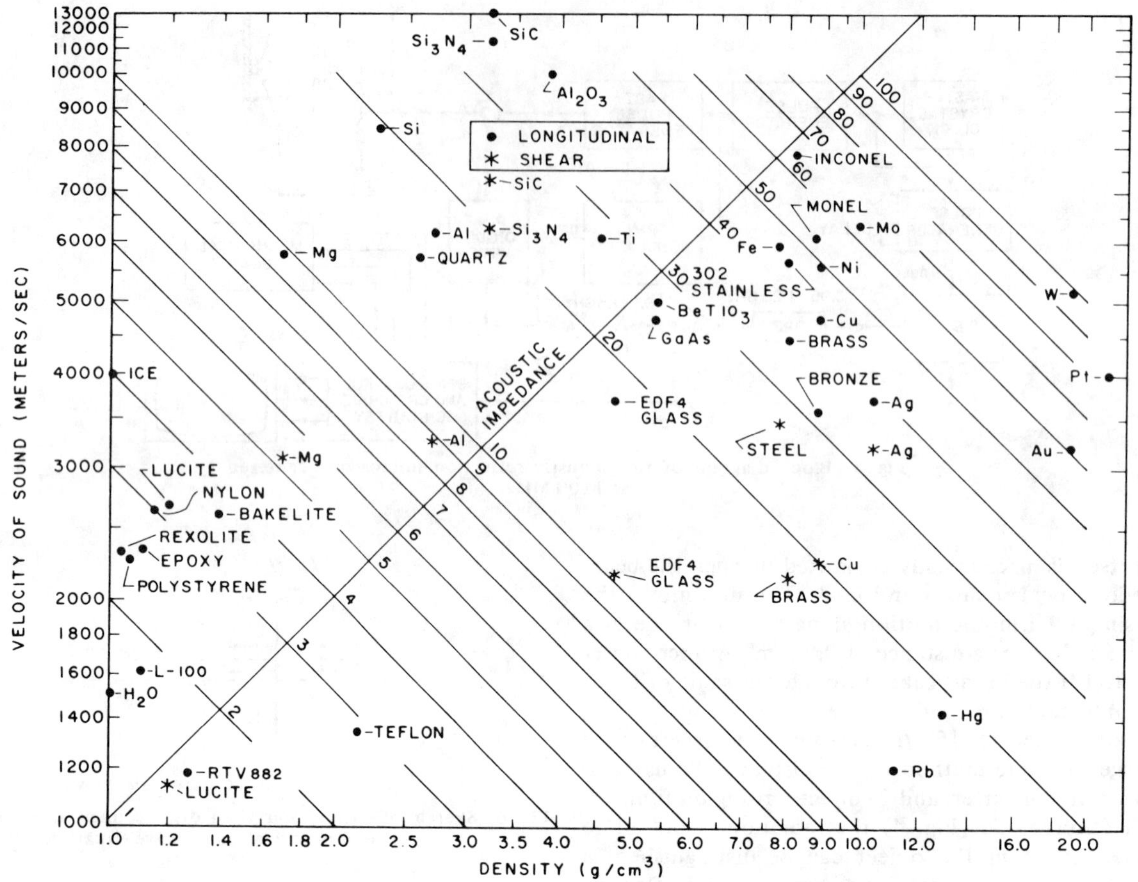

Fig. 7. Chart of material parameters for acoustic waves. (Courtesy of R. C. Eggleton.)

and invert the order of differentiation, we find

$$\frac{\partial}{\partial t}\left(\frac{\partial \xi}{\partial z}\right) = \frac{\partial}{\partial t}(S) = -\frac{\partial U}{\partial z}.$$

We can invoke Hooke's Law, $T = cS$, and write

$$\partial U/\partial z = -\frac{1}{c}\,\partial T/\partial t. \tag{4-2}$$

Here c is the elastic constant for the liquid.

The two equations (4-1) and (4-2) give us the wave equations. We assume lossless one-dimensional propagating waves in the form $\exp(-j(kz - \omega t))$ and the equations take the form

$$kT = \omega \rho_0 U$$

$$kU = (\omega/c)T. \tag{4-3}$$

We find the relation for k to be of the form

$$k = \pm \omega/\sqrt{c/\rho_0} = \pm \omega/v_s \tag{4-4}$$

where

$$v_s \equiv \sqrt{c/\rho_0}.$$

With the forward wave ($k = +\omega/v_s$) we have $T = +\sqrt{\rho_0/c}\,U = Z_0 U$ and with the backward wave ($k = -\omega/v_s$) we have $T = -Z_0 U$.

Here $Z_0 (\equiv \sqrt{c\rho_0})$ is the characteristic impedance of the acoustic wave. It is related to the wave velocity through the relation $Z_0 = \rho_0 v_s$. These three parameters are conveniently plotted in the form as given in Fig. 7. There we see that the wave velocity (m/s) and acoustic impedance (kg/m²-s) for different materials can vary by more than a factor of ten. This large variation underlines the crucial difference between acoustic imaging and optical imaging. The index of refraction, which determines both the wave velocity and wave impedance for optical waves, varies by less than a factor of two from material-to-material. It is for this reason the biological material exhibits a small contrast for optical waves and a large contrast for acoustic waves.

The similarity of (4-1) and (4-2) with the one-dimensional form of electromagnetic waves means that we can take over those solutions directly. The power flow for acoustic waves is given by

$$P = \frac{1}{2}TU^* = \frac{1}{2}\frac{|T|^2}{Z_0}. \tag{4-5}$$

The reflectivity of a wave at an interface by two materials of impedance Z_{01} and Z_{02} is given by

$$\text{Ref} = \frac{Z_{02} - Z_{01}}{Z_{02} + Z_{01}} \tag{4-6a}$$

and the transmission (amplitude) through the interface is given by

$$\text{Trans} = \frac{2Z_{01}}{Z_{01} + Z_{02}}. \tag{4-6b}$$

It also follows that the reflection at an interface can be reduced and the transmission improved with a matching layer one quarter wave in thickness with an impedance equal to $(Z_{01} Z_{02})^{1/2}$. It thus forms an acoustic antireflection coating [29].

The attenuation of these waves is included by rewriting propagation in the form $\exp(+j(kz - \omega t))\exp(-\alpha Z)$ where α is the attenuation coefficient. This parameter has a strong

TABLE I
COMPARISON OF CALCULATED AND EXPERIMENTAL VALUES OF
ATTENUATION AT 1 GHz (FROM WAUK [34])

Material	Acoustic Velocity v	Thermoelastic Attenuation α	Akhieser Attenuation α		Experimental Loss α dB/cm	
			dB/cm		α	α/f^2
Metals	10^5 cm/sec	dB/cm	min.	max.	1 GHz	(GHz)
Al	6.4	20.5				75
Cu	4.4	42				270
Au	3.48	167	--	88		200
Pb	2.07	340				500
Ni	5.31	3.9				
Ag	3.44	250				
Ti	6.33	0.5			10	
W	5.15	2				
Insulators						
Al_2O_3	11.1	0.0015	.20	.80	0.2-0.5	
SiO_2	5.9	0.05	1.64	6.5	2.5	
Fused Quartz					12.1	
YIG	7.20		.35	1.4	2 .34	
YAG	8.56		.16	.64	1.1 0.2-0.32	
Semiconductors						
GaAs	4.73		2.7	10.6	11	
InSb	3.40		14.8	59	16	
					10	
Si	8.43	1.2	2.35	9.4	6.5	
Ge	4.92	1.2	6	24		23 10

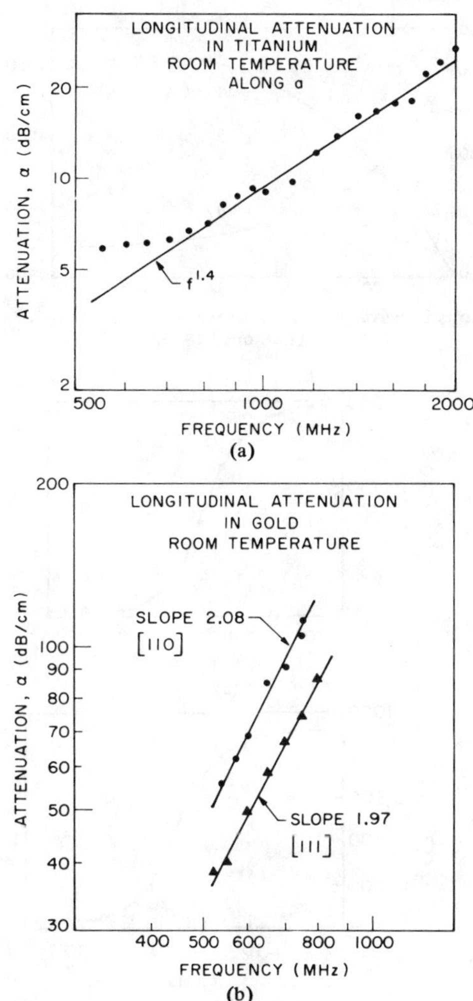

Fig. 8. Attenuation characteristics of (a) titanium and (b) gold (Wauk [34]).

and dominant influence on acoustic imaging at microwave frequencies. Values for typical solids are shown in Table I. In solids the attenuation is moderate and does not affect the microscope in an important way. But in liquids the attenuation is the factor that determines the ultimate resolution of the microscope. It is interesting, and somewhat ironic, to learn that this parameter—utterly different from the physical factors that limit the resolving power of an optical microscope—operates in such a way as to limit the resolving power of the acoustic instrument to a value near the optical limit.

In metals and certain other solids a major source of attenuation is due to thermoelastic heat flow [33]. A longitudinal wave has alternating regions of compression and rarefaction. Compression can produce an increase in temperatures and the flow of heat from this heated region to the cooler region at the rarefaction point represents a source of energy loss. The path length for heat flow of this sort decreases as the frequency increases. This produces a loss per cycle which increases directly as frequency, and hence the overall attenuation increases as the square of the frequency. The values of attenuation as measured by Wauk [34] for two important metals, Au and Ti, are given in Fig. 8.

In insulators an important source of attenuation has been worked out by Akhieser [35]. It can be described in terms of viscous damping of the propagating sound waves due to the "phonon gas," and the phonon–phonon collisions within this gas. Those materials included in Table I show the dramatic decrease from the values for metals. Semiconductors have attenuation coefficients which are intermediate between these values.

The theory that underlies the absorption in liquids is incomplete and we must, therefore, lean heavily on the experimental data [36]. Liquids that appear suitable for the acoustic cell can be placed into three groups—1) water where α/f^2 is independent frequency (it also has a negative temperature coefficient), 2) liquids such as benzene and carbon disulphide which have a strong molecular absorption near 10^8 Hz (and a positive-temperature coefficient), and 3) cryogenic liquids such as argon and helium.

The characteristics of water are shown in Fig. 9 where we see the reduced absorption with elevated temperature [28]. The velocity does increase slightly with heating but it is not an important effect. The high attenuation at low temperatures is attributed to a component in the liquid with an ice-like open structure. It has been found that the absorption coefficient near room temperature can be reduced by as much as a factor of two with the addition of an electrolyte [37]. It means that saline solutions can be used in connection with biological systems.

In the second category we find liquids with a lower velocity than water but a low-frequency absorption that is enormous. This high value of attenuation comes from molecular vibration near 100 MHz. For selected liquids it can be described by a single relaxation time constant τ or more conveniently by a critical frequency $f_c = \frac{1}{2}\pi\tau$ [36]. The absorption is frequency dependent and takes on the following form

$$\alpha/f^2 = B + A/(1 + (f/f_c)^2).$$

In typical cases A is three orders of magnitude larger than B, and it is therefore necessary to work at $f > 100 f_c$ before we

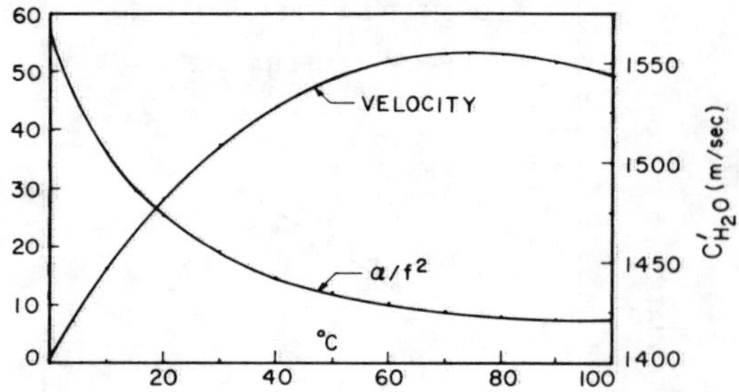

Fig. 9. Acoustic wave properties of water as a function of temperature (Lemons [28]).

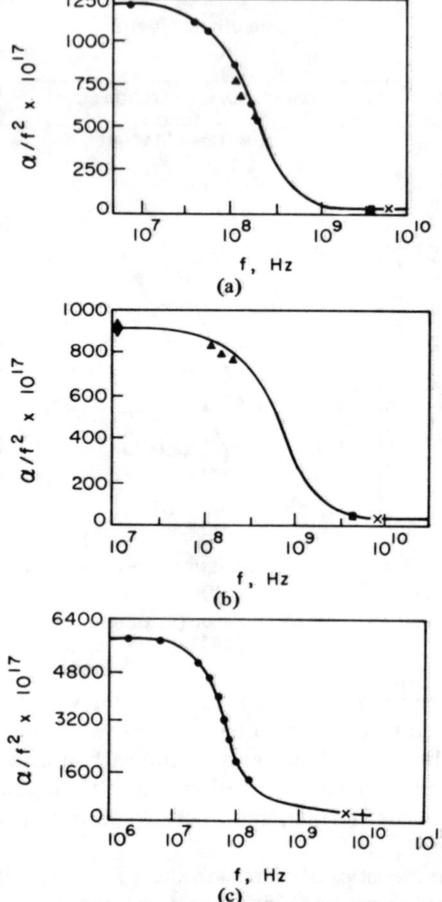

Fig. 10. Absorption characteristics for liquid described with a single relaxation time (Fabelinskii [36]). (a) Methylene chloride. (b) Benzene. (c) Carbon disulfide.

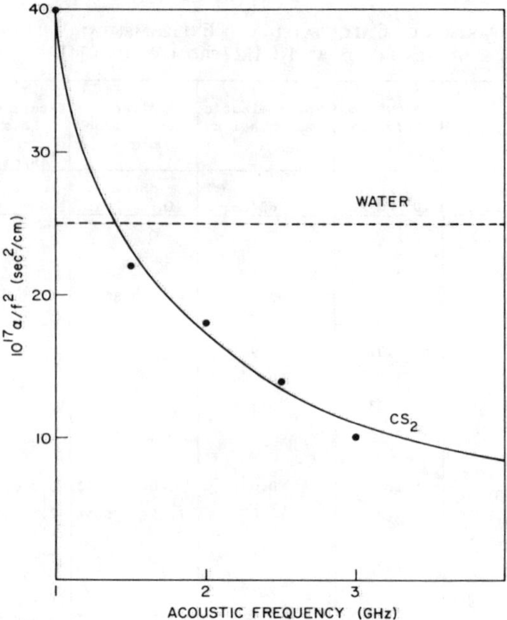

Fig. 11. Detail of absorption characteristic for carbon disulphide as compared to water (Attal [38]).

can neglect the A coefficient in the absorption. The experimental curves taken from the work of Fabelinskii (and reproduced in Fig. 10) [36], are typical of liquids with a single relaxation frequency. The liquid carbon disulphide is interesting at high frequencies since the attenuation and the velocity are both less than water. It is a classic example of high absorption arising from molecular vibrations. In this case it is a bending mode of the CS_2 molecule which peaks near 78 MHz [33]. In Fig. 11 we show on an enlarged scale, the comparative absorption of CS_2 near 3 GHz.

These curves are significant in our work for a most interesting reason. The high-frequency limit is not known for many liquids, and for those liquids where it has been measured, the accuracy is not high. The work in liquids for frequencies greater than 4 GHz has been carried out through Brillouin scattering of laser beams. With this technique liquids with low attenuation coefficients ($\alpha/f^2 < 5 \times 10^{-17}$) are difficult to measure since this corresponds to the limit imposed by the linewidth of the laser itself. If you were optimistic by nature (as we are!), this would suggest that more work needs to be done in this frequency range using the direct method of monitoring of absorption in a variable length acoustic cell.

At cryogenic temperatures liquids have both low attenuation and low velocity [2]. Two hold promise—argon with a velocity of 0.86×10^5 cm/s, and superfluid helium with a velocity of 0.24×10^5 cm/s. But we will not dwell on these possibilities since a discussion of operation at cryogenic temperatures is outside the scope of this review.

The examples included here offer some hope that a liquid might be found with a velocity near 10^5 cm/s and a value of α/f^2 less than 5×10^{-17} s^2/cm. If a liquid with these properties could be found it would permit us to operate the microscope with a wavelength of 0.25 μm.

V. CONVERGING BEAMS

A. Spatial Frequencies

In 1973, Cathey wrote [39]

> The impression of information onto an electromagnetic wave by modulating some parameter, such as amplitude, frequency, or phase, as a function of time is a familiar concept. Spatial information can also be impressed on the wave by amplitude, frequency, or phase modulation. . . .

He goes on in Chapter 5 to introduce the concept of spatial frequencies and he illustrates how these procedures can be used to deal with imaging problems. In earlier work, Goodman [40] and O'Neill [41] made extensive use of the spatial frequency concept to analyze systems for imaging. A large part of this later writing used the work of Ratcliffe [42] as a source. Ratcliffe's article is so clearly written and it sheds so much light on spatial frequency decomposition that it is still today well worth reading. Champeney [43] has discussed the comparative merits of the classical approach using diffraction integrals of this approach based on angular spectrum and spatial frequencies.

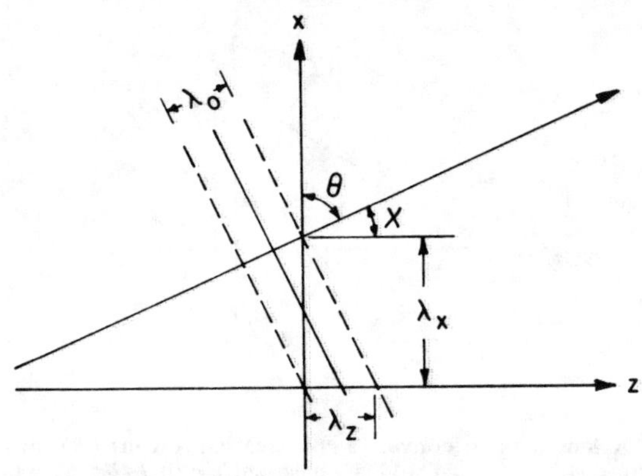

Fig. 12. Sketch for a plane wave in x–z plane showing λ_x and λ_z as components of λ_0. For this wave $k_0 = 2\pi/\lambda_0$, $k_x = 2\pi/\lambda_x = k_0 \cos\theta$, $k_y = 0$, and $k_z = 2\pi/\lambda_z = k_0 \cos\chi$. Wave equation demands that $k_x^2 + k_y^2 + k_z^2 = k_0^2$.

The sketch of Fig. 12 shows the appropriate geometry for a plane wave propagating as

$$\exp\left(-j\omega t + jk_0 \cos\theta x + jk_0 \cos\chi z\right) = \exp\left(-j\omega t + jk_x x + jk_z z\right)$$

where λ_0 is the free-space wavelength and θ, χ, k_x, and k_z are defined in Fig. 12. We will hereafter suppress the exponential time factor and use the following notations:

u amplitude distribution of the actual function of both x and y;

A spectrum of plane waves that are used to constitute the spatial distribution u. It is a function of k_x and k_y.

These two are related via the Fourier transform and this will become clear as we proceed.

We first develop the relation between the spatial distribution and the angular spectrum for a system that is uniform in the y direction. We can, therefore, deal only with the x and z coordinates as indicated in Fig. 12. The amplitude of the plane wave components propagating at the angle θ is denoted by $A(\theta)\,d\theta$, and the component directed along the z-axis is $A(\theta)\sin\theta\,d\theta$. These plane waves can be summed over θ to form the spatial distribution of $u(x)$ at $z = 0$

$$u(x) = \int_{-\pi/2}^{+\pi/2} A(\theta) \sin\theta \exp\left(-jk_x x\right) d\theta. \tag{5-1}$$

We note that k_x will serve as well to denote this component since $k_x = k_0 \cos\theta$. In this treatment where we deal with a single frequency k_0 is constant and we have therefore $dk_x = -\sin\theta\,d\theta\,k_0$. Equation (5-1) takes the form

$$u(x) = -\frac{1}{k_0} \int_{-k_0}^{+k_0} A(k_x) \exp\left(-jk_x x\right) dk_x.$$

For $k_x > k_0$ the waves at $z = 0$ are evanescent and do not propagate. Nevertheless, they can be included without undue difficulty [44] and the limits can be extended to $\pm\infty$. After suitable normalization, this can be written as

$$u(x) = \int_{-\infty}^{+\infty} A(k_x) \exp\left(-jk_x x\right) dk_x. \tag{5-2}$$

In this form we recognize that the spatial distribution at $z = 0$ is the Fourier transform of the angular spectrum distribution $A(k_x)$. It follows directly from this that the angular spectrum

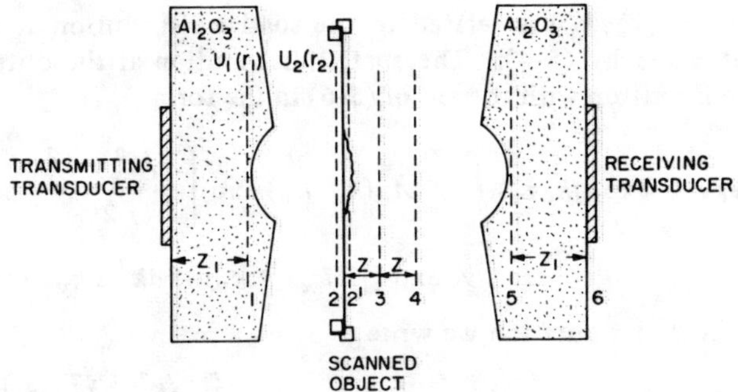

Fig. 13. Sketch of imaging system showing the various planes beginning with the input to plane 1 at the lens to plane 3 at the focal point and finally plane 6 at the output.

$A(k_x)$ is given by the inverse transform of $u(x)$. With a spatial distribution in both x and y, these results can be extended to give

$$u(x, y) = \int_{-\infty}^{+\infty} A(k_x, k_y) \exp\left[-j(k_x x + k_y y)\, dk_x dk_y\right] \tag{5-3}$$

and the inverse

$$A(k_x, k_y) = \frac{1}{(2\pi)^2} \int_{-\infty}^{+\infty} u(x, y) \exp\left[+j(k_x x + k_y y)\right] dx\,dy. \tag{5-4}$$

In more compact notation, equation (5-3) becomes

$$u(x, y) = \mathscr{F}\{A(k_x, k_y)\} \tag{5-3a}$$

and equation (5-4) becomes

$$A(k_x, k_y) = \mathscr{F}^{-1}\{u(x, y)\}. \tag{5-4a}$$

The power of this analytical approach is evident when we consider the problem of determining the spatial distribution $u_1(x, y)$ across a plane 1 a distance z_1 from the input plane. We know the distribution at the input plane to be $u_0(x, y)$. The appropriate geometry for our complete system is sketched in Fig. 13. With the decomposition into plane waves as treated in (5-3), we can easily see the change in each of the plane waves as they move from the input plane to plane 1. It is merely a phase shift given by

$$A_1(k_x, k_y) = A_0(k_x, k_y) \exp\left[+jk_z z_1\right] \tag{5-5}$$

where $k_z = (k_0^2 - k_x^2 - k_y^2)^{1/2}$ as indicated in Fig. 12.

The most illustrative case and one that serves our purpose here is for a beam that is rather narrowly confined around the z-axis. In this case both k_x and k_y are small as compared to k_0 and we have

$$k_z \simeq k_0 \left(1 - \frac{k_x^2 + k_y^2}{2k_0^2}\right).$$

The relation in (5-5) then becomes

$$A_1(k_x, k_y) = A_0(k_x, k_y) \exp\left(jk_0 z_1\right) \exp\left[-j\left(\frac{k_x^2 + k_y^2}{2k_0}\right) z_1\right] \tag{5-6}$$

where $A_0(k_x, k_y)$ is related to the spatial distribution at the input plane by (5-4). The spatial distribution at the output plane is written with the aid of (5-6) in the form

$$u_1(x, y) = \exp(jk_0z_1) \int_{-\infty}^{+\infty} A_0(k_x, k_y) \exp\left[-j\left(\frac{k_x^2 + k_y^2}{2k_0}\right) z_1\right]$$

$$\times \exp[-j(k_x x + k_y y)] \, dk_x \, dk_y \quad (5\text{-}7)$$

or in compact notation we write

$$u_1(x, y) = \exp(jk_0z_1) \, \mathcal{F}^{-1}\left\{A_0(k_x, k_y) \exp\left[-j\left(\frac{k_x^2 + k_y^2}{2k_0}\right) z_1\right]\right\}.$$

$$(5\text{-}7)$$

But we know from the theorems of Fourier transformation that

$$\mathcal{F}^{-1}\{gh\} = \mathcal{F}^{-1}\{g\} * \mathcal{F}^{-1}\{h\} \quad (5\text{-}8)$$

and

$$\mathcal{F}^{-1}\left\{\exp\left(-j\frac{k_x^2 z}{2k_0}\right)\right\} = \left(\frac{k_0}{2\pi z}\right)\exp\left(-j\frac{k_0 x^2}{2z}\right). \quad (5\text{-}9)$$

With these we can write in place of (5-7)

$$u_1(x, y) = \left(\frac{k_0}{2\pi z}\right) \exp(jk_0 z_1) \int_{-\infty}^{+\infty} u_0(x_0, y_0)$$

$$\times \exp\left[\frac{jk_0(x - x_0)^2}{2z_1}\right]$$

$$\times \exp\left[\frac{jk_0(y - y_0)^2}{2z_1}\right] dx_0 \, dy_0. \quad (5\text{-}10)$$

This permits us to move from the input plane to plane 1 just prior to the lens itself (see Fig. 13). In traversing the lens the angular spectrum is modified in phase according to the expression

$$\exp\left[\frac{-jk_0(x^2 + y^2)}{2f}\right] \quad (5\text{-}11)$$

where f is the focal length of the lens (see Fig. 14). At the focal plane itself the distribution is $u_2(x, y)$. It is equal to Fourier transform of the spatial distribution at the lens input $u_1(x, y)$ as modified by the pupil function $P(x_1, y_1)$. That is we can write

$$u_2(x, y) = \left(\frac{1}{j\lambda_0 f}\right) \exp(jk_0 f) \, \mathcal{F}\{u_1(x_0, y_0) P_1(x_0, y_0)\}$$

$$(5\text{-}12)$$

where the transform is now limited by the pupil function to the region

$$k_x = \pm\frac{k_0 x}{f} \quad \text{and} \quad k_y = \pm\frac{k_0 y}{f}.$$

In writing the pupil function in this way we have assumed that the diameter of the beam at the focal plane is much less than the radius of the lens R. In a generalized treatment the pupil function can include numerous interface factors such as the effect of a quarter-wave matching layer. From focal plane we can with (5-10) determine the spatial distribution at a distance z from the focal plane. At that plane we encounter the object

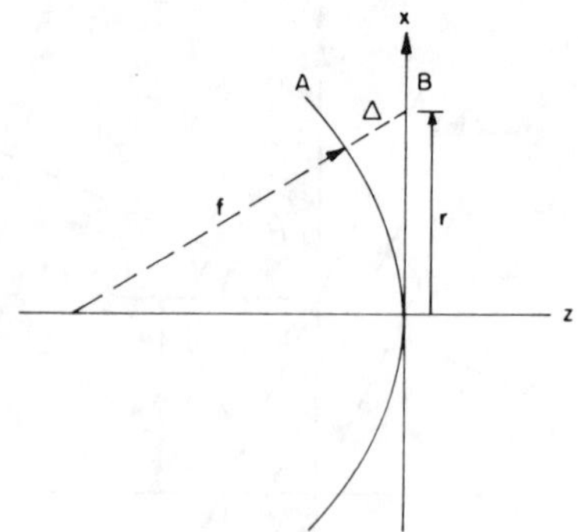

Fig. 14. A lens acts to convert a spherical wavefront (A) into a plane wavefront (b). It must add a phase shift $\exp(-jk_0 \Delta)$ where $f^2 + r^2 = (f + \Delta)^2 \approx f + 2\Delta f$ or $\Delta = r^2/2f = (x^2 + y^2)/2f$.

which either described by a transparency $t(x, y)$ for the transmission mode or a reflectivity $\mathcal{R}(x, y)$ for the transmission mode.

After traversing the object, or being reflected by the object, we can continue this process to again reach the focal plane, transform through the lens, and move from the lens to the transducer to obtain the distribution at plane 6 are denoted by $u_6(x, y)$. This is the output, but it is not that parameter that we measure. Rather we measure the transducer voltage V. This voltage is simply the integral of the distribution $u_6(x, y)$ weighted by the response of the transducer itself at the point x and y, i.e., $s(x, y)$:

$$V = \iint u_6(x, y) \, s(x, y) \, dx \, dy. \quad (5\text{-}13)$$

It is easy to demonstrate that a unit voltage on the transducer will produce a wave distribution in the crystal, plane 0, that is just $s(x, y)$. It has also been shown that the principal of reciprocity can be invoked to demonstrate this feature.

B. Beam Contours and Computed Images

The theory as outlined here can be used to calculate beam contours and spatial frequency content of the converging beam. With these we can compute the images that would be expected for idealized objects. The details of the calculations which do appear in the literature [45] are not appropriate for this review and we will, therefore, proceed directly to the results.

We specify a particular lens at a sapphire–water interface and a frequency of 1 GHz. The lens radius is 75 μm and the focal length is 83 μm. The radius of the transducer is 96 μm and it is spaced 2 mm from the lens. The sensitivity of the transducer $s(x, y)$ is assumed to be uniform over the area of the transducer itself. The spatial frequency transfer function of the system produced by this combination is shown in Fig. 15. In Fig. 15(a) we plot amplitude (dotted) and phase (solid) as a function of the spatial frequencies for an ideal lens which neglects all factors such as absorption in the liquid, mode conversion at the lens surface, and a quarter-wave matching layer on this surface. When all of these factors are included the distributions change to that given in Fig. 15(b). The corresponding beam contours at the focal plane are shown in Fig. 16. The expected resolving power for beam contoured as in Fig. 16(b) is $0.7\lambda_0$, i.e., the instrument is capable of resolving a periodic grating with a full period of $0.7\lambda_0$ which is 1.0 μm for the wavelength in water is 1.5 μm at 1 GHz. These numbers are close to the measured values.

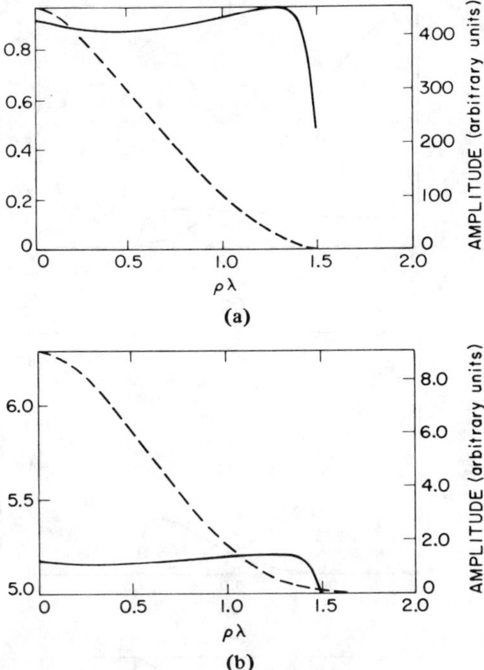

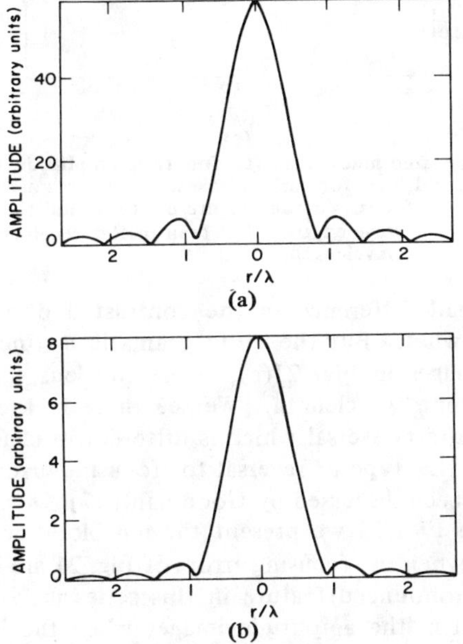

Fig. 15. The amplitude (dashed) and phase (solid) of the spatial frequency transfer function in terms of the spatial frequency ρ and the wavelength λ. Curve (a) is for an ideal system. Curve (b) is for a system with spherical aberration, mode conversion, and absorption in the liquid as described in the text.

Fig. 16. The amplitude distribution at the focal plane for the conditions specified in Fig. 15.

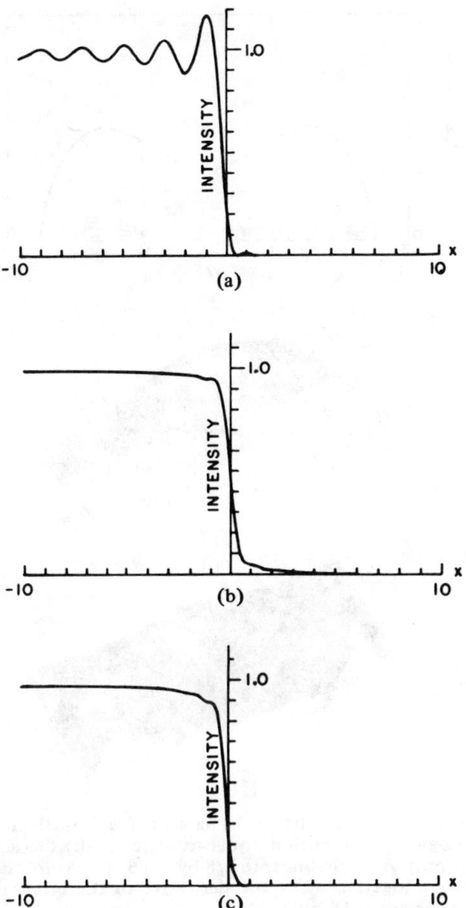

Fig. 17. Calculated one-dimensional images of a step function object. (a) Conventional coherent image. (b) Conventional incoherent image. (c) Image produced by a confocal scanning system using coherent radiation (Lemons [28]).

The theory can also be used to calculate the expected response of an edge and three different systems are compared in Fig. 17 [28]. There we show a conventional incoherent and coherent optical system together with the coherent scanning system. We see that the confocal scanning system (Fig. 17(c)) compares with the incoherent conventional system. The ringing usually associated with coherent radiation (Fig. 17(a)) is missing. The characterizations as shown in Figs. 16 and 17 are often used but it is necessary to consider the image of an individual object with some care. For example, the circular sidelobes on the beam profile of Fig. 16 do not show up in the image of a straightedge as in Fig. 17. They could, however, distort the image of two scattering centers that were closely spaced when their scattering strengths were widely different.

A computed image of the red blood cell is shown in Fig. 18. The object is assumed to be lossless and it only acts to vary the phase of the transmitted beam as shown in Fig. 18(a). The transducer output is plotted in Fig. 18(b) for the phase of the signal and in Fig. 18(c) for the amplitude of the signal. The phase image Fig. 18(b) corresponds quite closely to the object itself. The amplitude image Fig. 18(c) exhibits high contrast even though the amplitude of the scanning beam was assumed to be uniform over the object. The amplitude image of phase objects of this kind does not necessarily conform to the structure of the object. This phenomenon is important for this type of imaging. It can be explained with the aid of the sketch in Fig. 19. We learn from that diagram that a change in object phase over the beam cross section will tilt the transmitted beam. After passing through the output lens the tilted beam will transform into a pseudo-plane propagating off the center of the crystal axis. It will, therefore, be normally incident on the transducer but the transducer response will be diminished as a result of the tilting. The decrease in the magnitude of the output signal is proportional to the gradient of phase in the focal plane. The phase of the transmitted beam is unaffected by this tilt. We do, therefore, expect the phase of the output signal to reproduce the phase of the object with good fidelity. On the other hand, the amplitude of the output signal should

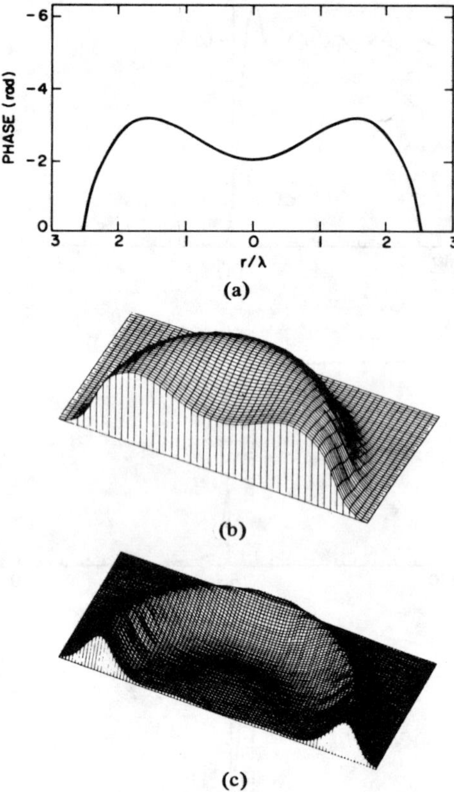

Fig. 18. Ideal red blood cells. (a) Phase profile from Evans and Fung [46] (hemoglobin absorption equal to water). (b) Phase response of transducer output. Grid lines are $\lambda/8$ by $\lambda/16$. (c) Amplitude response of transducer together with the derivative of the phase responses in (b). Grid lines are $\lambda/16$ by $\lambda/32$.

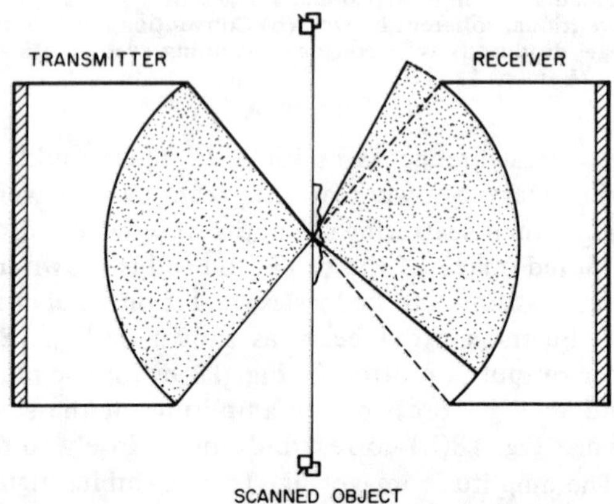

Fig. 19. Illustration of change in illumination of the lens when the beam encounters a transverse phase gradient in the focal plane.

correspond to the phase gradients in the object plane. We see both of these features in Fig. 18(b) and (c).

These ideal properties are changed if the focal conditions are not precise. Defocusing can be of two types—either a) the object is not placed at the focal plane, or b) the spacing between the lens in Fig. 13 does not equal to confocal conditions. These two defocusing conditions are illustrated as follows. In Fig. 20 we show the spatial frequency content of the beam for (a) the in-focus condition, (b) the object defocused from the focal plane by one wavelength, and (c) the lens separation is decreased from the confocal condition by one wavelength. There are changes in both the phase and amplitude of the spatial frequencies, and they alter the images as shown in Fig. 21. The translation of the object from the focal plane

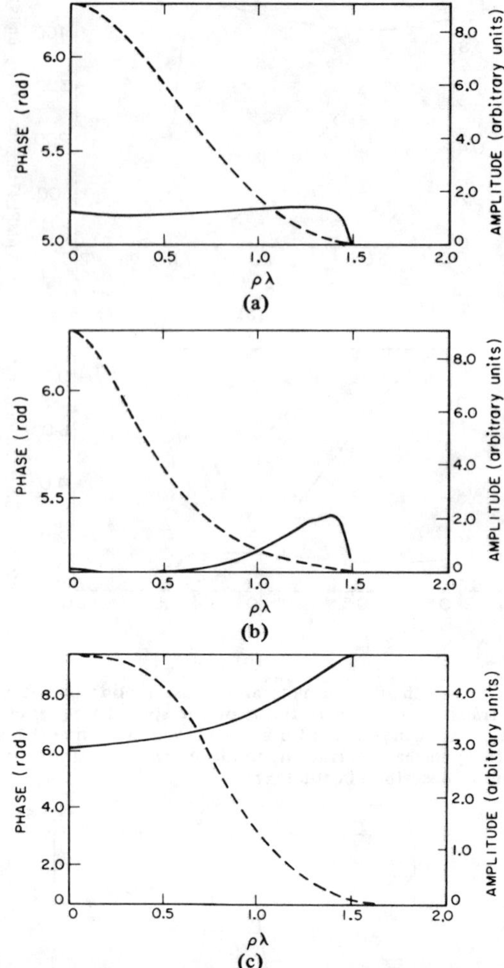

Fig. 20. Spatial frequency transfer function amplitude (dashed line) and phase (solid line) for various cases. (a) Lenses are confocal and the object is at focus. (b) Lenses are confocal and the object is defocused by one wavelength. (c) Transmitter–receiver lens spacing decreased by one wavelength.

makes a small difference in the contrast and broadens the image somewhat. But the more dramatic distinction comes from the images in Fig. 21(c), where the lens spacing is decreased by one wavelength. We see there in the amplitude image a contrast reversal which is different in character from the image. This type of reversal for focusing errors in optical systems has been discussed by Goodman [47].

Finally, in Fig. 22 we present the red blood cell images as they appear when the focusing errors of Fig. 21 are introduced. The most pronounced feature in this series is again the contrast reversal in the amplitude images when the lens spacing decreases (Fig. 22).

C. The V(Z) Curves

For the reflection instrument the output voltage as expressed in (5-14) can be used in a unique way to measure some of the elastic properties of the reflecting surface. The initial distribution at the transducer is $u_0^+(x, y)$, the distribution of the returning field is $u_0^-(x, y)$, and we have

$$V(Z) = \iint_{-\infty}^{+\infty} u_0^+(x', y')\, u_0^-(x', y')\, dx'\, dy'. \quad (5\text{-}14)$$

In writing this form we are anticipating the final result wherein we monitor V as a function of the parameter Z; i.e., the dis-

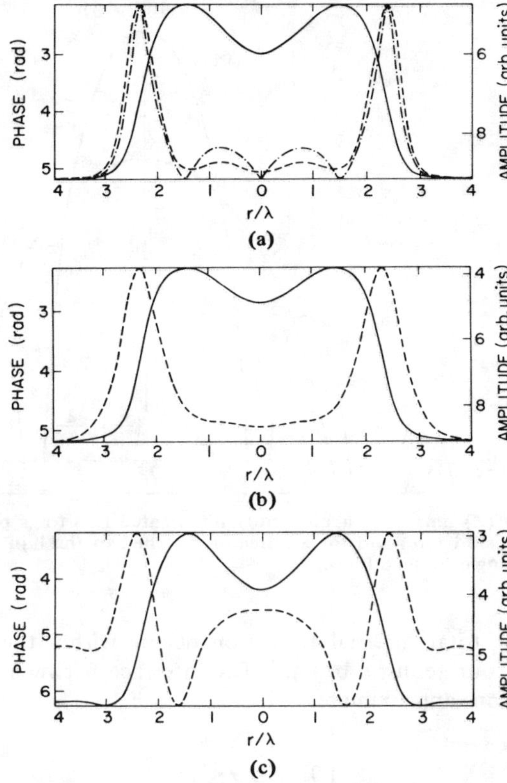

Fig. 21. Computed amplitude (dashed line) and phase (solid line) images of the ideal red blood cell with the conditions specified in Fig. 20.

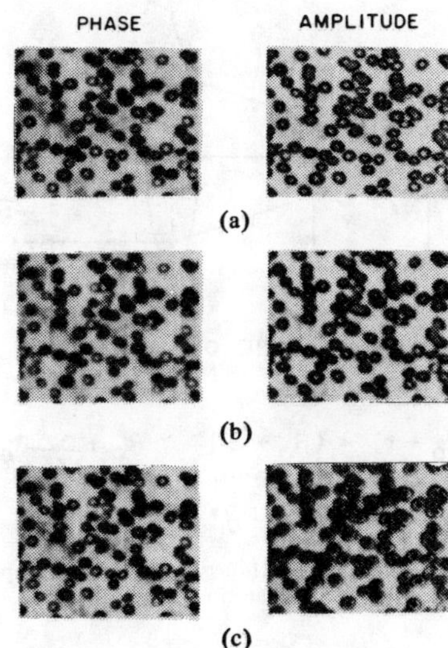

Fig. 22. Experimental images of red blood cells for the three conditions specified in Fig. 20. Note the reversal of contrast in amplitude for (c) the favorable comparison with the theory in Fig. 21(c).

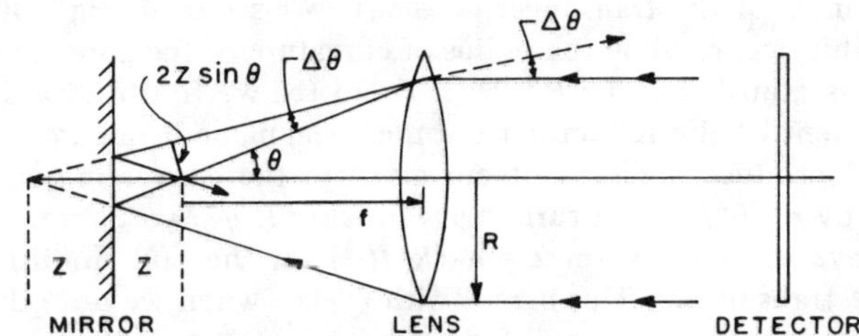

$$\Delta\theta \simeq 2Z \sin\theta / f \qquad \sin\theta \simeq R/f^2$$
$$\Delta\theta \simeq 2ZR/f^2$$
(a)

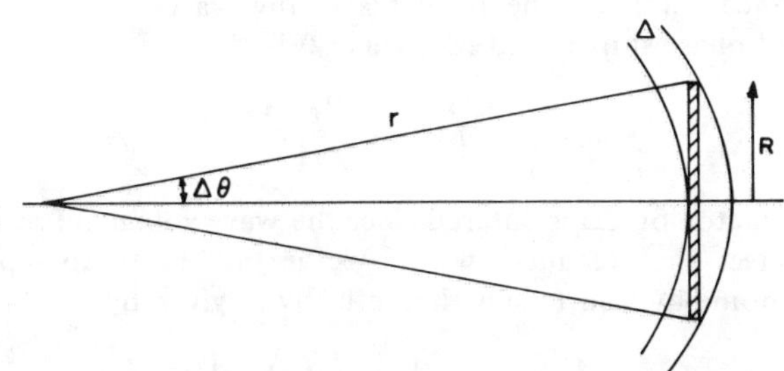

$$r = R/\Delta\theta \simeq f^2/2Z \text{ (From above)}$$
$$r^2 + R^2 = (r+\Delta)^2 \simeq r^2 + 2\Delta r$$
$$\Delta = R^2/2r = (R^2/f^2) Z$$
(b)

Fig. 23. Sketch of rays for a displaced mirror. (a) Reflection from mirror displaced by z from the focal plane. (b) Phase variation across transducer for a spherically diverging wave.

placement of the reflecting object from the focal plane. Equation (5-14) can take on a more suitable form by using the transforms described previously. The details are published elsewhere [48]. The final form for $V(Z)$ is as follows:

$$V(Z) = \iint_{-\infty}^{+\infty} (u_1^+(x,y))^2 (P(x,y))^2$$
$$\times \, \mathfrak{R}\left(\frac{x}{f}, \frac{y}{f}\right) \exp\left(-j\frac{k_0 Z}{f^2}(x^2 + y^2)\right) dx \, dy.$$

Since our problem exhibits circular symmetry about the z axis we can replace $x^2 + y^2$ by r^2 and write [48]

$$V(Z) = \int_0^\infty r(u_1^+(r))^2 (P(r))^2 \, \mathfrak{R}\left(\frac{r}{f}\right) \exp\left(-j\frac{k_0 Z}{f^2}r^2\right) dr.$$

$$(5\text{-}15)$$

An alternative form of this expression and its derivation may be found in the literature [49]. This $V(Z)$ expression has proved to be valuable as a method for studying surfaces. Some results for real cases will be given in a later section. Here we want to gain some understanding of what is to come by analyzing a few simple reflectors.

One straightforward case is that of a lens with a uniform illumination, i.e., $u_1(r) = 1$, and radius R, i.e., $P(r) = \text{circ } (r/R)$ and a perfect reflector $\mathfrak{R}(r/f) = 1$. In this case (5-15) becomes

$$V(Z) = \int_0^R r \exp\left(-j\frac{k_0 Z}{f^2}r^2\right) dr = \frac{R^2}{2} \exp(-jx) \text{ sinc } x$$

$$(5\text{-}16)$$

where

$$x \equiv \pi(R/f)^2 Z/\lambda_0 \qquad \text{and} \qquad \text{sinc } x \equiv \sin x/x.$$

The result in (5-16) is easily understood. When Z is positive the wavefront that impinges on the transducer is spherical with a radius of curvature that depends on Z. As Z is changed we experience an increasing number of cyclic variations of the field across the transducer which gives rise to the sinc curve.

It is instructive to use this concept and calculate the value of Z for the first null in the transducer output. The sketch in Fig. 23 is sufficient for this purpose. We can see from Fig.

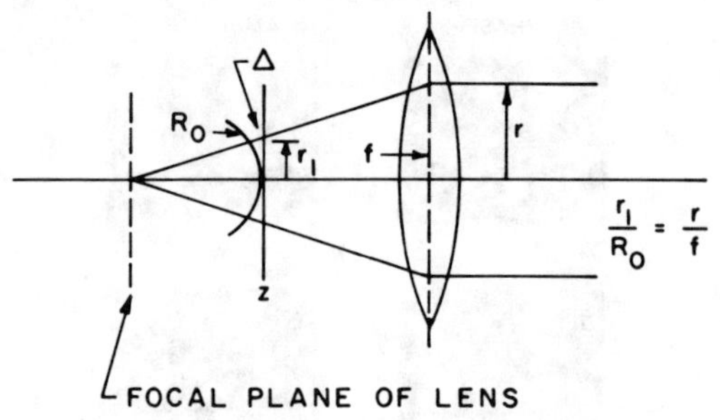

$$R_0 + r_1^2 = (R_0 + \Delta)^2 \simeq R_0^2 + 2\Delta R_0$$

$$2\Delta = r_1^2 / R_0 = R_0 r^2 / f^2$$

Fig. 24. Illustration of phase shifts associated with a spherical dome of radius R_0 centered on focal plane.

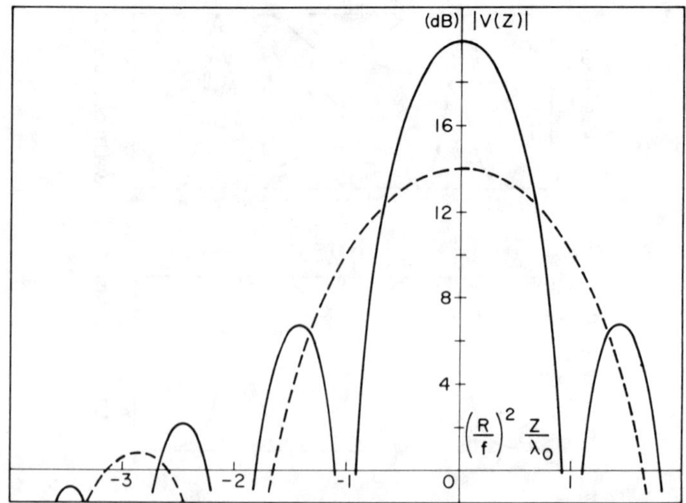

Fig. 25. $V(Z)$ curves of a uniformly illuminated lens for a perfect reflector (solid line) and for a reflector matched to the liquid up to a critical angle (dashed line).

23(b) that the response of the transducer will be reduced to zero when the wave at the outer rim undergoes an additional phase shift of 2π as compared to the portion of the wave at the center of the transducer ($\Delta = \lambda_0$). We see from Fig. 23(a) that this occurs when the radius of curvature of the converging wave is adjusted to be $R^2/2\lambda_0$. From (b) we find that a displacement of the reflector from the focal plane by an amount Z will produce a radius of curvature in the converging wave given by $r = f^2/2Z$. In turn this is equal to $R^2/2\lambda_0$. Therefore, we have the expression $Z = \lambda_0(R^2/f^2)$ for the null condition at the transducer. This agrees with (5-16) when we note that the sinc function has a null for $x = \pi$ (and $Z/\lambda_0 = (R/f)^2$).

In the second example as illustrated in Fig. 24 the reflecting object is a dome with a radius of R_0 and centered on the focal plane. We see from the sketch that on the plane spaced a distance R_0 from the focal plane, the waves suffer an additional phase shift of $k_0(2\Delta)$ where Δ is given by

$$r_1^2/2R_0 = \frac{R_0}{2f^2} r^2 .$$

The factor of 2Δ is entered since the wave going and returning traverses this distance twice. We are at liberty to represent this dome by a surface with a reflectivity given by

$$\mathcal{R} = \exp\left[-jk_0\left(\frac{R_0}{f^2}\right) r^2\right]$$

and in place of (5-16) we have

$$V(Z) = \int_0^R r \exp\left[-jk_0\left(\frac{R_0}{f^2}\right) r^2\right] dr$$

$$= \frac{R^2}{2} \exp(-jx_2)\, \mathrm{sinc}\, x_2 \qquad (5\text{-}17)$$

where

$$x_2 = \pi(R/f)^2 (Z + R_0)/\lambda_0 .$$

This result is similar to (5-16) except that the reflector must be located at $Z = -R_0$ to give the maximum output. This is intuitively correct since at that point the curvature of the dome equals the curvature of the wavefront.

For the third case we consider the special situation where the acoustic impedance of the liquid is equal to that of the solid. However, the velocity ratio is still small and the critical

angle for total internal reflection occurs within the convergence of our acoustic beam. (The interface between mercury and silicon approximates this condition.) The reflectance becomes

$$\mathcal{R} = \begin{cases} 0, & r < R_1 \\ 1, & R_1 < r < R \end{cases} .$$

For this case we can still use (5-17) except that the limits on the integration now extend from R_1 to R. The result is

$$V(Z) = \frac{R^2 - R_1^2}{2}\, \mathrm{sinc}\, \frac{k_0}{2} \frac{R^2 - R_1^2}{f^2} . \qquad (5\text{-}18)$$

It is similar to the first case but the null now occurs at $Z/\lambda_0 = f^2/(R^2 - R_1^2)$ which is larger than that of the perfect reflector. A comparison of (5-18) with (5-16) is shown in Fig. 25 for the case where the area of transducer within R_1 is equal to the area between R_1 at R, i.e., $R = \sqrt{2}\, R_1$.

For the fourth case we choose a reflector that more closely follows the characteristics of the actual liquid–solid interface encountered with real objects. The reflectivity for this case is of the form

$$\mathcal{R} = \begin{cases} 1, & r < R_1 \\ \exp(j\phi), & R < r < R_1 \end{cases} . \qquad (5\text{-}19)$$

With this we can write

$$V(Z) = \int_0^{R_1} r \exp\left[-j\left(\frac{R_0}{f^2}\right) r^2\right] dr$$

$$+ \exp(j\phi) \int_{R_1}^R \exp\left[-j\left(\frac{R_0}{f^2}\right) r^2\right] dr .$$

This when evaluated reads

$$V(Z) = \frac{R_1^2}{2}\, \mathrm{sinc}\, \frac{k_0}{2}\left(\frac{R_1}{f}\right)^2 Z + \frac{R^2 - R_1^2}{2} \exp\left[-j\left(\frac{k_0}{2}\right)\left(\frac{R}{f}\right)^2 Z\right]$$

$$\times \exp(+j\phi)\, \mathrm{sinc}\, \frac{k_0}{2} \frac{(R^2 - R_1^2)}{f^2} Z \qquad (5\text{-}20)$$

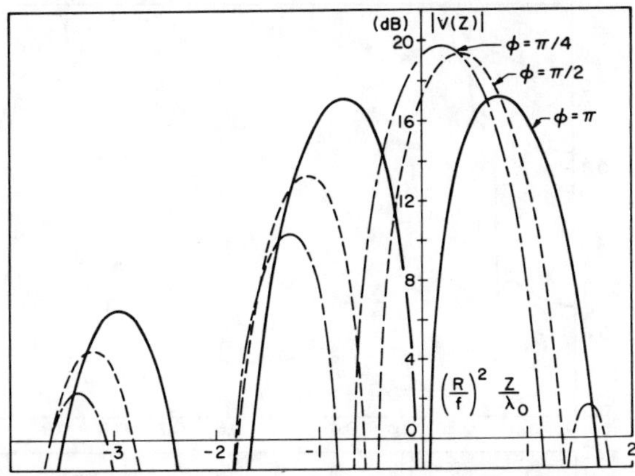

Fig. 26. $V(Z)$ curve of a uniformly illuminated lens for a reflector with a unit amplitude reflectance function. Reflectance function phase is nonzero for angles exceeding a critical value. Different $V(Z)$ curves are for various phase values.

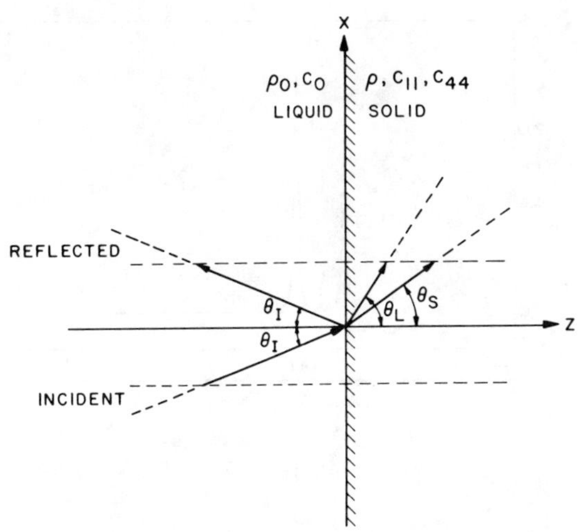

Fig. 27. Acoustic plane wave scattering at a plane boundary between a liquid and an isotropic solid.

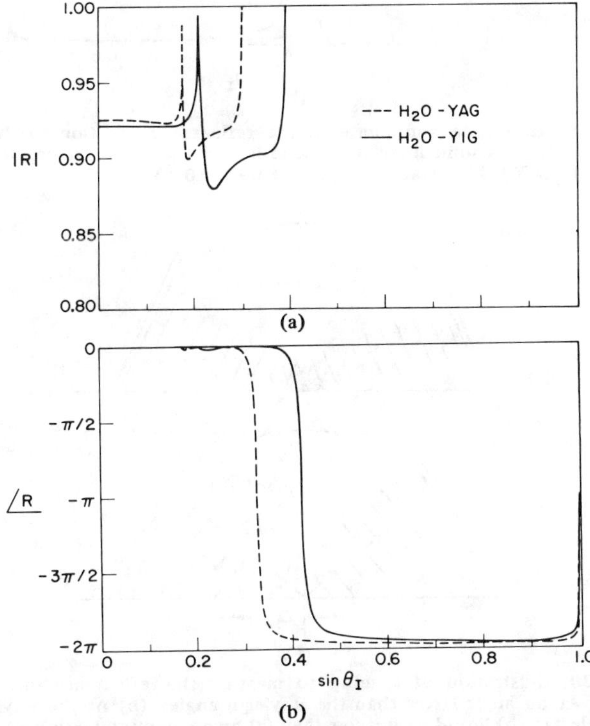

Fig. 28. Amplitude and phase of the reflectance function for H_2O-YIG and H_2O-YAG interfaces.

The curves resulting from different values of ϕ are shown in Fig. 26.

These simple cases tell us a great deal about the character we expect to find in the measured $V(Z)$ curves. A reduction of the reflectivity for incident angles less than the critical angle will tend to broaden the curve and a phase shift for angles greater than the critical angle will tend to displace the curves.

There is one other important feature that comes forth—namely contrast reversal in the images as Z is varied [15], [50]. Assume that we have an image composed of two materials—one with the reflectivity as in the second case, and the other as in the perfect reflector. For $Z = 0$ the perfect reflector would have the larger reflectivity and would appear brighter in the image (Fig. 25). For negative values of Z we see that the contrast is reversed particularly at the null where the ideal reflector goes dark and the reflector with the matched liquid remains fairly bright.

The most important feature that has been left out of these examples is the nonuniform illumination of the lens. This can arise from several factors: diffraction over the length of the crystal, a nonuniform response of the transducer over its cross section, the axis of the transducer displaced from the lens axis through misalignment in the initial fabrication, or the quarter-wave matching layer can exhibit inhomogeneities. For all of these reasons, and more, we find actual distributions to differ from the ideal that has been postulated in the previous examples. The most pronounced effect in the $V(Z)$ curves is the disappearance of the nulls and their replacement with dips of varying degrees of depth.

D. Reflectance Functions

We now attend to the problem of calculating the reflectance of plane waves on a liquid–solid interface as a function of the angle of incidence. The problem is straightforward and it has been treated in the literature [51]. Our needs are somewhat peculiar in that we must cover the entire range of incident angles. The operating frequency is high enough to make the attenuation of the liquid important but for the most part we deal with a linear problem in classical wave theory. The problem is sketched in Fig. 27. We express the reflected wave in terms of the incident wave by the reflection coefficient $\mathcal{R}$. We require both the magnitude and the phase of $\mathcal{R}$ as the incident angle θ (or more properly $\sin \theta$) is varied. In the solid we find that several modes can propagate which involve longitudi-

nal, shear, and Rayleigh waves along the interface. In layered media other modes representing energy propagating within the layer will enter.

For this review it is only required that we present the final form of the reflectance functions since it is this parameter that enters into the expression that we use to calculate the $V(Z)$ curves. A typical result is given in Fig. 28 for two different crystals (YAG and YIG) against water. The magnitude of $\mathcal{R}$ is rather uninteresting since the results would not be altered appreciably if we set $\mathcal{R} = 1$ over the entire range. But the phase $\mathcal{R}$ is crucial. We see that the phase of the reflected wave undergoes a large shift at the critical angle and approaches 2π for large angles. The range near the critical angle is important where the phase relation between the reflected wave and the incident wave undergoes a maximum of change. The boundary conditions that determine this condition require continu-

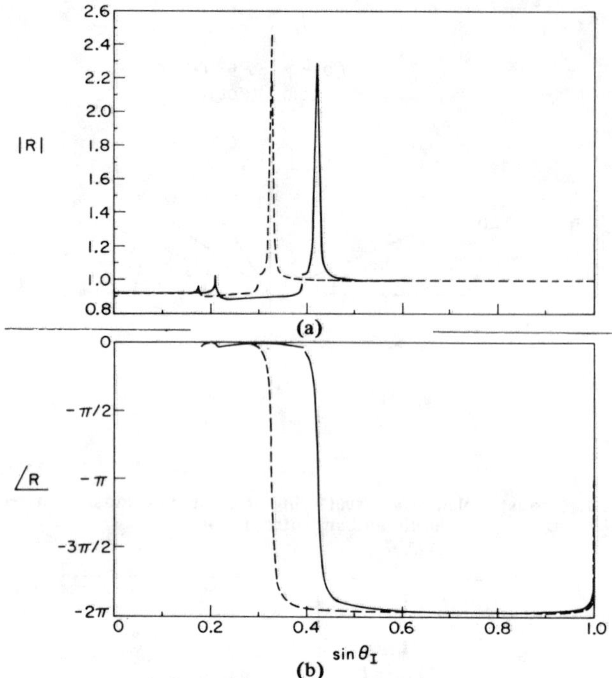

Fig. 29. Amplitude and phase of the reflectance function for lossy–liquid–lossless-solid interface. Solid line H_2O–YIG interface, dashed line H_2O–YAG interface $(\alpha V_0/\omega) = 5.09 \times 10^{-3}$).

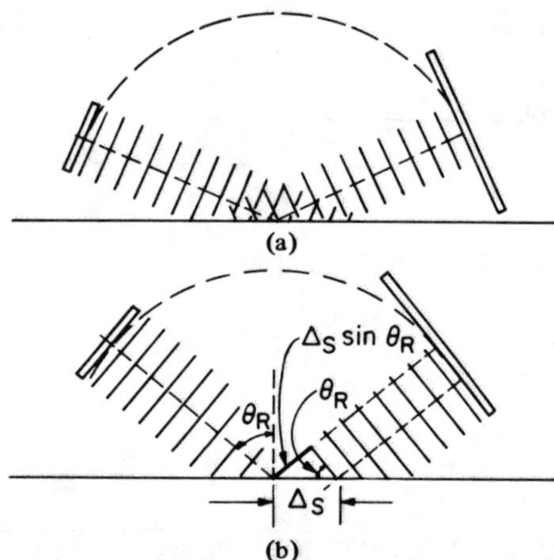

Fig. 30. Illustration of a setup to measure the reflectance function. (a) At an angle larger than the Rayleigh angle. (b) At the Rayleigh angle. In (b) liquid path is less than (a) by an amount $\Delta_S \sin \theta_R$.

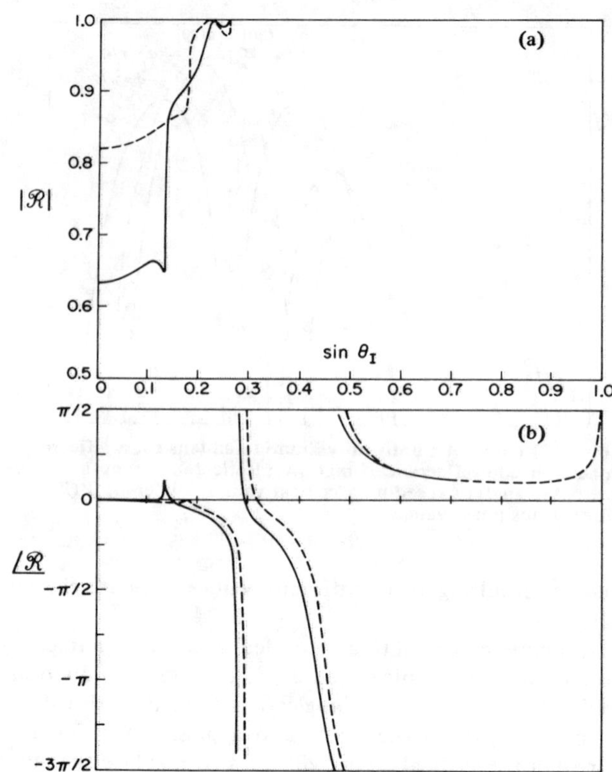

Fig. 31. Reflectance function amplitude (a) and phase (b) for a $\lambda/4$ thick aluminum layer on sapphire (solid line) and silicon (dashed line) substrates.

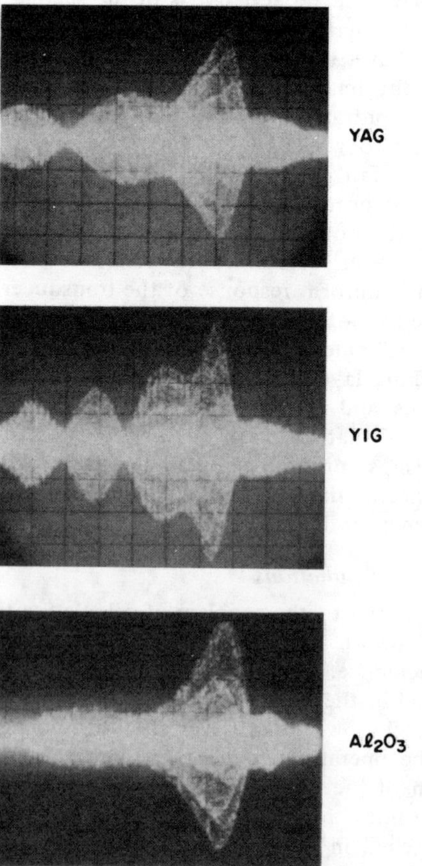

Fig. 32. Long exposure oscilloscope photos of the returning pulses as the distance between the sample and lens is varied. Envelopes show $V(Z)$ curves for different crystals. Horizontal scale 3.75 μm/div (1100 MHz).

ity in both the stress and particle velocity across the interface. If the phase of the reflected wave for normal incidence is equal to the incident wave, it must differ from that value at the critical angle. This follows from the fact that a large component of the Rayleigh interface is excited near the critical angle. When the components of this wave are put into the boundary conditions the phase of the reflected wave must be adjusted to compensate for this addition and the variation of Fig. 28 reflects this adjustment.

As previously mentioned, the acoustic loss of the liquid is important at our frequencies. When this factor is included in the theory, the curves of Fig. 28 are modified and one interesting feature comes in—namely, the magnitude of $\mathcal{R}$ can exceed unity near the critical angle as shown in Fig. 29 [52]. In the literature we find this curve has a dip at this angle for a lossless liquid interfacing with a lossy solid. There the dip is explained by the fact that the Rayleigh wave excited at this

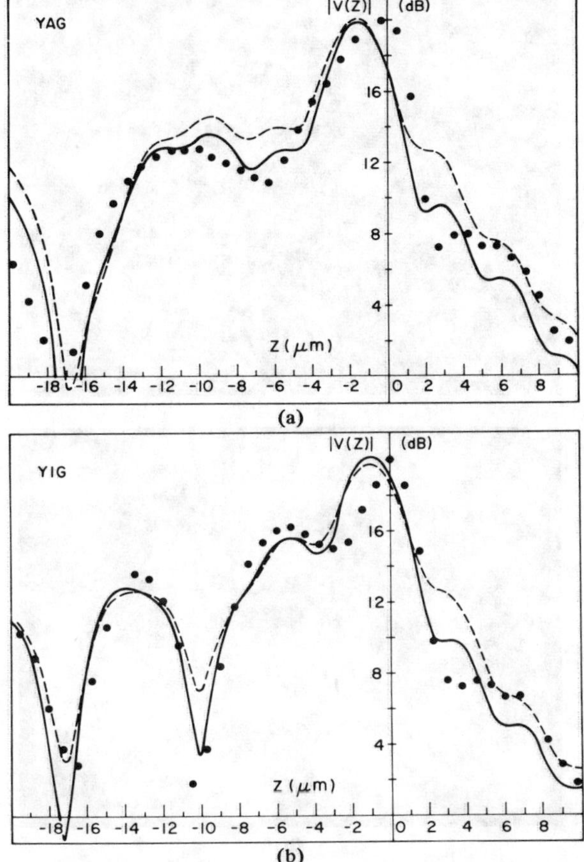

Fig. 33. Experimental (dots) and calculated (dashed lines) $V(Z)$ curves for YAG and YIG crystals at 1100 MHz. Solid lines show the calculated $V(Z)$ curves if an offset of 20 μm is assumed between the axes of the lens and transducer.

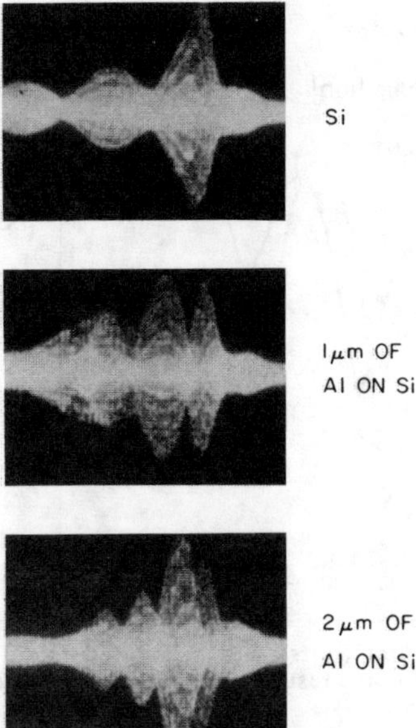

Fig. 34. $V(Z)$ photographs for silicon with different thicknesses of aluminum deposited on it.

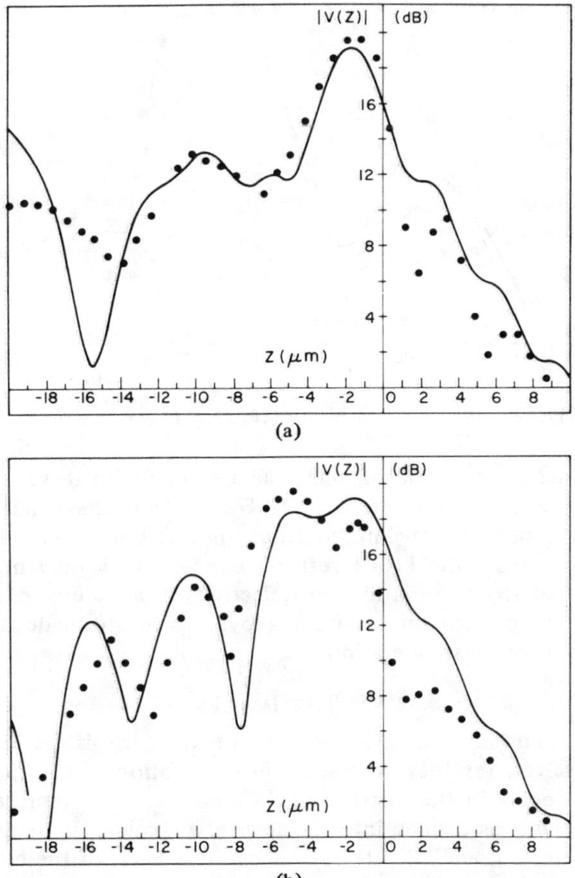

Fig. 35. Experimental (dots) and calculated (solid lines) $V(Z)$ curves for 0.5 μm (a) and 2.0 μm (b) aluminum layer on silicon substrate (1100 MHz).

angle displaces the reflected beam from the position it would have had in a mirror-like reflection—the Schoch displacement [51]. During this lateral displacement the energy is predominately carried by the Rayleigh wave in the solid. The loss associated with propagation in this medium dissipates energy and reduces the energy in the reflected component. For our case with a lossy fluid and a lossless media the situation is reversed. When the reflected beam is displaced along the boundary via excitation of the Rayleigh wave the total path in the lossy liquid is less than it would be for a mirror-like reflection. This point is clarified by the geometry as sketched in Fig. 30. Since the reflection coefficient for the perfect mirror-like reflector is defined as unity, the increased amplitude that appears with the lateral displacement must be accounted for by using a value of $\mathcal{R}$ greater than unity.

Finally we can illustrate the reflectance for a layered medium. In Fig. 31 we show the results for a layer of Aluminum on two substrates—silicon and sapphire. The additional transitions that are found in these curves are due to the various modes such as Love waves and Sezawa waves that are excited in the presence of the layers.

With these curves at hand we can use the theory as developed in the previous section to predict the $V(Z)$ curves. The measured values of $V(Z)$ for single crystals of YAG, YIG, and Al_2O_3 are shown in Fig. 32, and the comparison with the theory is shown in Fig. 33. The effect of layering is shown in Fig. 34, where we have two different thicknesses of Aluminum on Silicon substrates together with some calculations of layering in Fig. 35.

Most crystals exhibit anisotropy in their elastic properties and this has an important bearing on the measured response. In Fig. 36 we show the change in the computed curve when anisotropy is included. The change allows for an improved comparison with the experimental points.

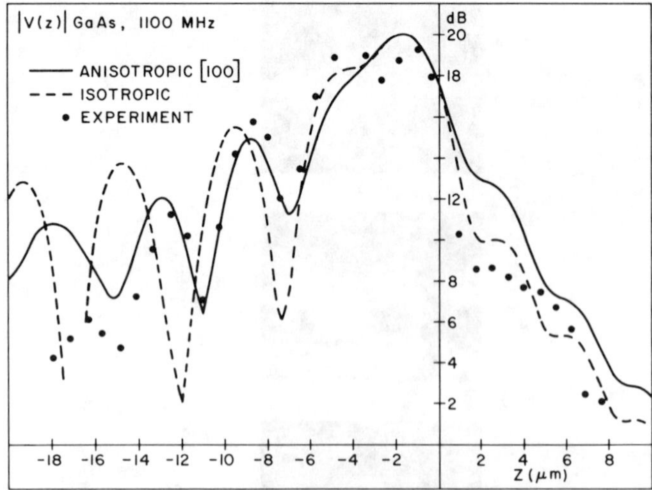

Fig. 36. Experimental (dots) and calculated (solid line) $V(Z)$ curves for GaAs. $V(Z)$ curve resulting from an isotropic calculation (dashed line) is also shown.

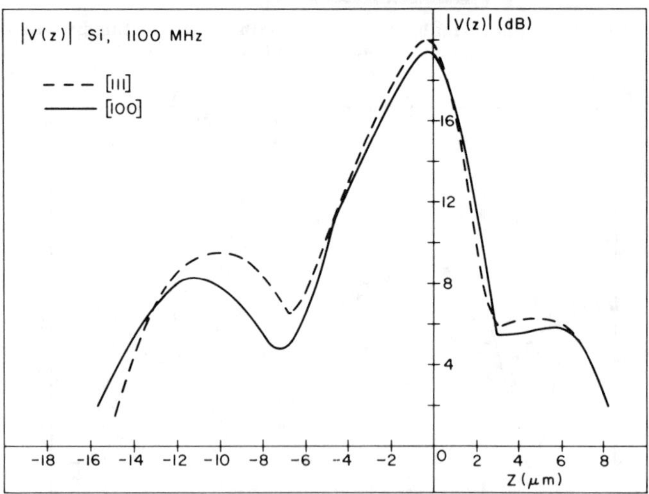

Fig. 37. Measured $V(Z)$ curves for (100) and (111) faces of silicon.

As a final example of what can be done with these curves we show the results of Fig. 37. We see from these that it is possible using this technique to distinguish the [111] reflecting face from the [100] reflecting face. We should not be surprised to see variations in reflectivity as a "source of contrast" in polysilicon or other alloys which are made up of grams of various orientations.

VI. The Images

The end game for a microscope of any form is the images themselves, for they represent the cumulation of all separate components in the instrument. We have selected representative images as divided into the areas of 1) biological specimen, 2) materials, and 3) integrated circuits. Each of these areas will require specially adapted modifications in final versions and the theory for contrast will differ in the three categories. The biological specimen come from cells of the blood and from a tissue section from the human eye. In Fig. 38 we present a comparison of the optical and acoustic micrographs for the human red blood cell. The cells in the optical image are stained and placed under a cover slip. The cells in the acoustic micrograph are unstained but fixed in methanol. We can see that these images in reflection are of good fidelity at this frequency.

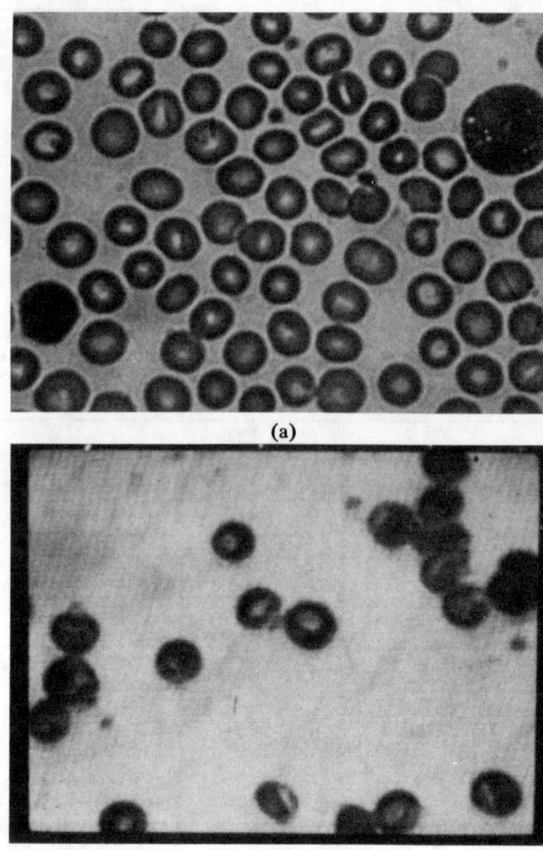

Fig. 38. Normal red blood cells. (a) Optical fixed in methanol with Leishman's stain ($\times$1000 (oil immersion)). (b) Acoustic (1100 MHz) fixed in methanol, unstained, but mounted on silicon wafer with 1.56 μm of SiO_2 ($\times$1000). Cells are from different individuals. (Courtesy of J. Heiserman.)

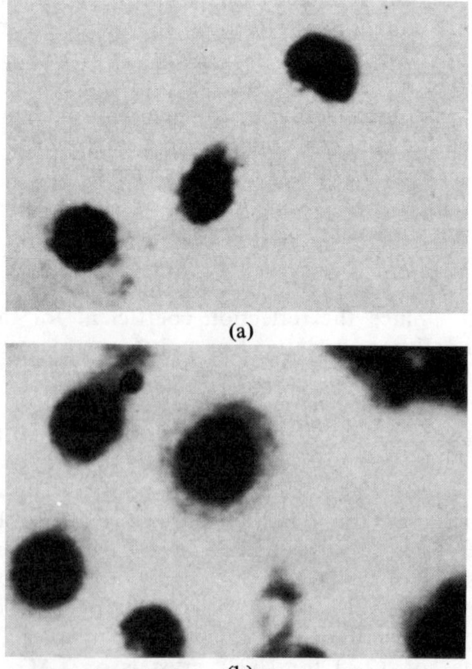

Fig. 39. Acoustic images in reflection (1100 MHz)—Living macrophage cells.

In Fig. 39(a) and (b), we show the appearance of living white cells (macrophage). These are, of course, unstained, and the two different sets of cells display excellent contrast between

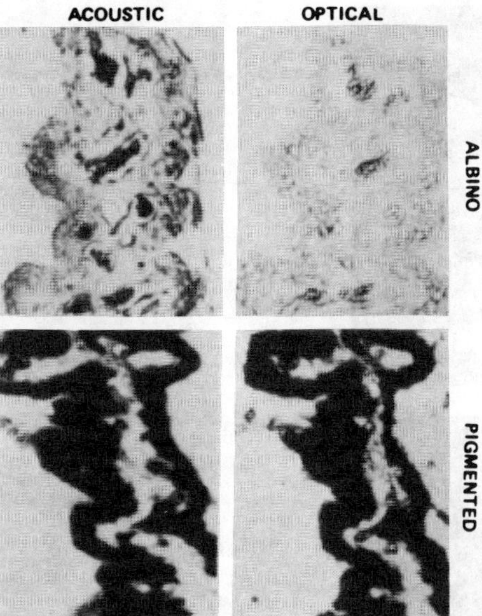

Fig. 40. Sections of iris from an albino and pigmented rabbit (Marmor [53]).

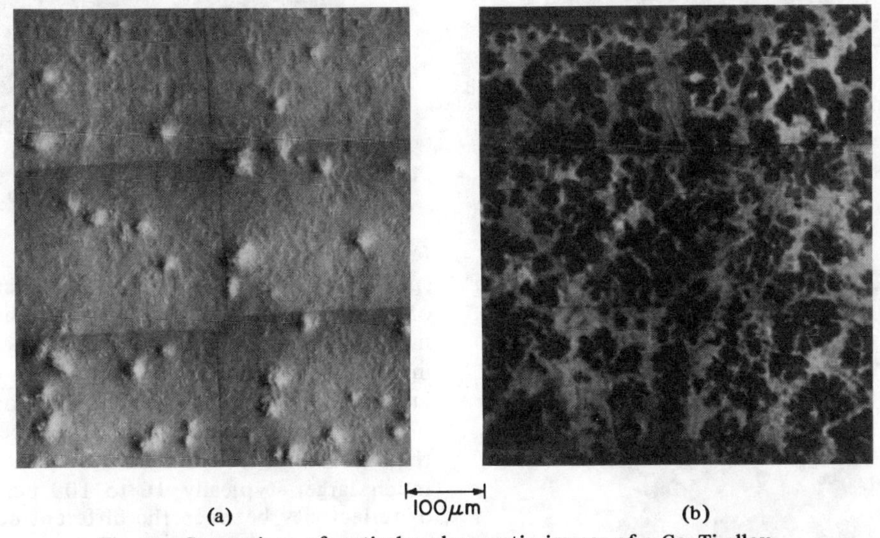

Fig. 41. Comparison of optical and acoustic images of a Co–Ti alloy. (a) Optical D/C. (b) Acoustic. Co–Ti alloy showing 4 phases. Overall composition 59-percent Co, 41-percent Ti.

the nucleus and the surrounding cytoplasm. It suggests that this instrument may be suitable for studying objects of this sort in the living state. And to complete the set we compare the optical and the acoustic images of tissue sections as taken from the retina of a rabbit in Fig. 40 [53]. Again the acoustic image shows the important parts with a contrast that is slightly improved over that of the optical. These images were taken in transmission.

The next sequence of images are included to demonstrate the acoustic response of materials of various kinds. Perhaps the most spectacular is that shown in Fig. 41—a polished surface of a cobalt–titanium alloy. The optical image on the left shows up the hillocks that result from the polishing technique. There is a slight hint of structure in this image but for the most part the optical reflectivity is almost constant over the surface. The acoustic micrograph is quite distinct. There are actually four levels in this image—two in the light grey regions and two in the darkened regions. We have analyzed these particular areas with an X-ray microprobe and find a

one-to-one correspondence between the distribution of phases in this material and the acoustic reflectivity. Stated in a different way, one can determine from the phase diagram for this particular alloy that four different phases—each with a different percentage of titanium—are possible. Each of the four phases has a distinct elastic constant, and it therefore follows from the discussions in Section V that each phase will exhibit a different acoustic reflectivity.

In Fig. 42, we display the optical and acoustic response of another important class of materials. For this sample we coated a silicon wafer with a 1.5-μm layer of photoresist. We then exposed this layer with UV light through a mesh in the form of regularly spaced lines. We followed the conventional procedures for photolithography except for one important difference—we did not develop the photoresist after exposure to the UV light. Because of this omission we do not see the pattern in the optical image of Fig. 42(b) since the optical index change is not sufficient. However, the cross linking in the polymer film that does occur after exposure is sufficient

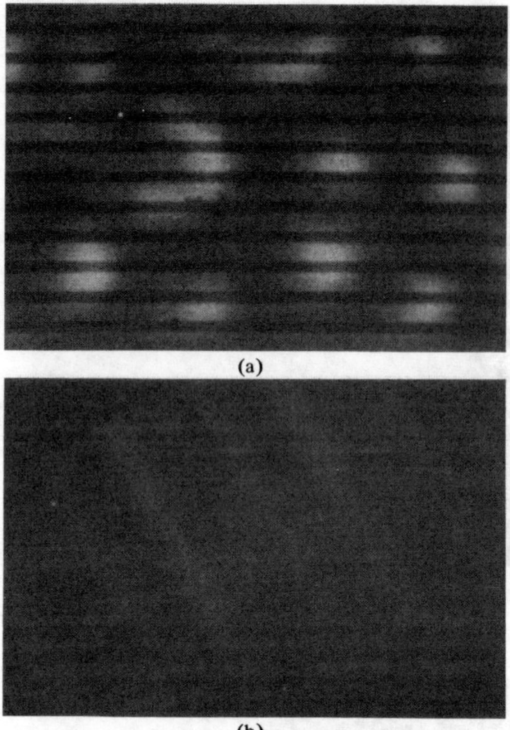

Fig. 42. Comparison of (a) acoustic and (b) optical images of an exposed but undeveloped pattern in photoresist (1.5 μm) on a silicon wafer.

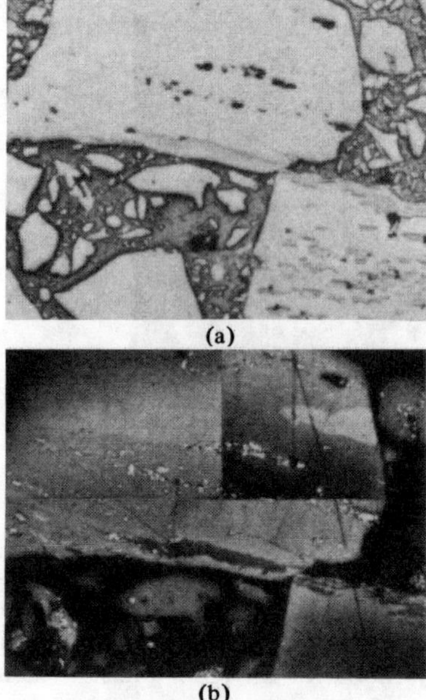

Fig. 43. (a) Optical (×125) and (b) acoustic images in reflection of polished samples of coal. Coal sample from U.S. Steel (medium rank) f = 1100 MHz.

to alter the elastic properties to a degree that permits us to see the bar pattern in the acoustic micrograph. We also see certain light splotches in Fig. 39(a). This may be indicative of unevenness in the thickness of the photoresist but we have not explored this in great detail. We believe that this property will be of technological significance in integrated circuits.

In Fig. 43, we show the comparison for an entirely different class of materials—fossil fuel in the form of coal. The important point here is again the increased contrast in the acoustic micrograph. In a recent article in *Physics Today* reviewing the technology relating to coal it is pointed out that the most ef-

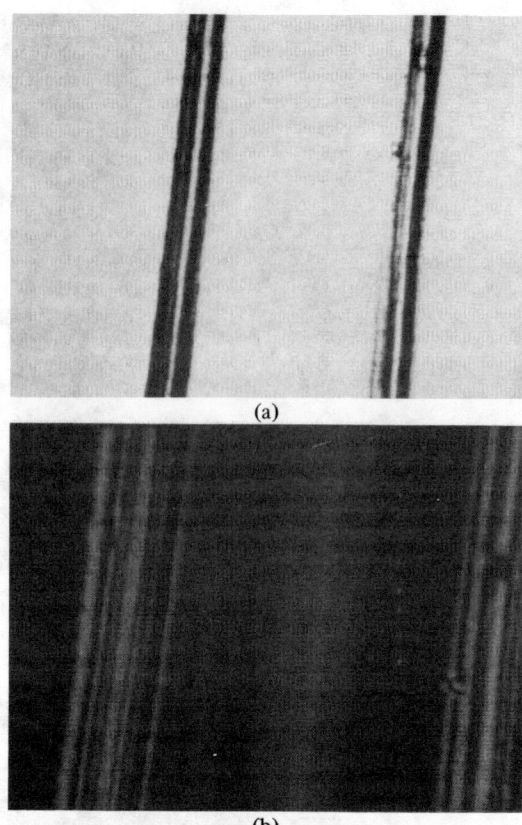

Fig. 44. Acoustic micrographs of polymer (Kevlar) fibers. Transmission at 1400 MHz. (a) ×500. (b) ×800.

fective method for determining the carbon content of coal specimen is the measurement of optical reflectivity. Because of the complexity of this material the optical reflectivity as measured point-by-point across the specimen can be calibrated in such a way as to reveal the carbon content. The point-of-interest here is one of degree. The optical reflectivity varies between 1 and 2 percent and it is between these two limits that the comparison is made. The acoustic reflectivity is much larger—typically 10 to 100 percent—and the variation of reflectivity between the different constituents of the material is greater. This suggests that acoustic microscopy may one day play a role in this field.

Finally, in Fig. 44, we show the acoustic images of polymer textile fibers—Kevlar. This also represents an important class of materials. The various inhomogeneities that show up here are difficult to see in optical images. The changes in elastic parameters appear to be larger than the corresponding changes in the optical index. It could happen that acoustic microscopy will add to the informational content of micrographs in the vast field of fibers.

Now, we turn to a series of integrated circuits—a subject that is probably closer to the professional interest of the readers of *Proceedings*. We begin with a sample of Fig. 45 that is simple—namely, a single layer of oxide 1.56 μm in thickness grown on silicon. There is a pattern in the oxide but it is of secondary interest here. Our primary interest is the large contrast exhibited by this object. This high degree of contrast indicates that we can detect oxide layer thicknesses of a few hundred angstroms.

In Fig. 46 we see an optical image of a MOS transistor fabricated with SOS technology. The cross section of the wafer is shown in the side drawing. In Figs. 47 and 48 we illustrate the

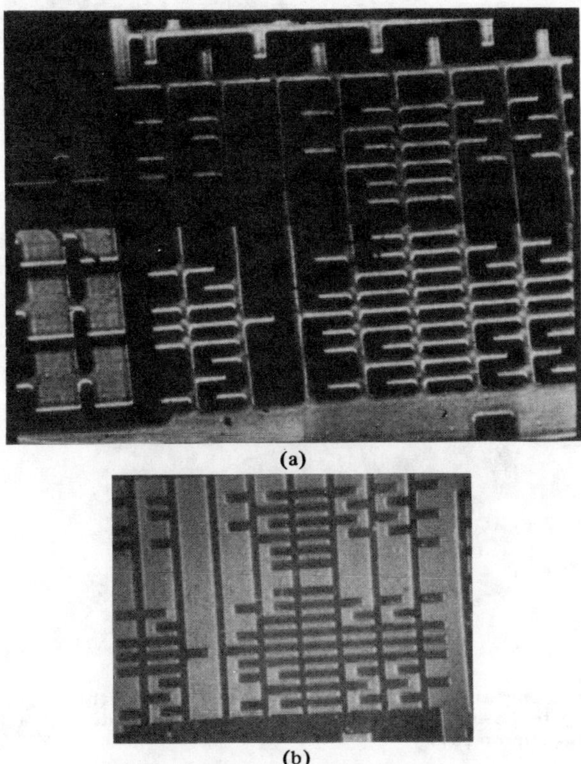

(a)

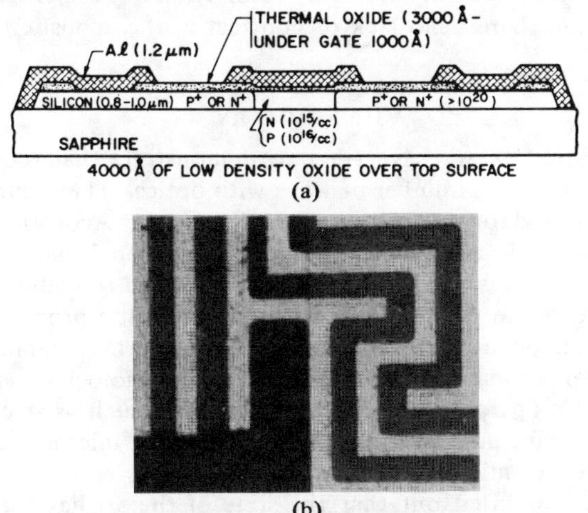

(b)

Fig. 45. Micrographs of silicon wafer coated with oxide. (a) Acoustic ×450. (b) Optical ×350. In (a) dark area has 1.56 μm of oxide—light area has 0.35 μm of nitride.

(a)

(b)

Fig. 46. Cross sectional view and optical image of an SOS–MOS device. Aluminum linewidth is 7.5 μm. (a) Optical brightfield by Koch (×1120). (b) (CMOS transistor profile STDL-4 circuit courtesy of Electronics Research Center, Rockwell International.)

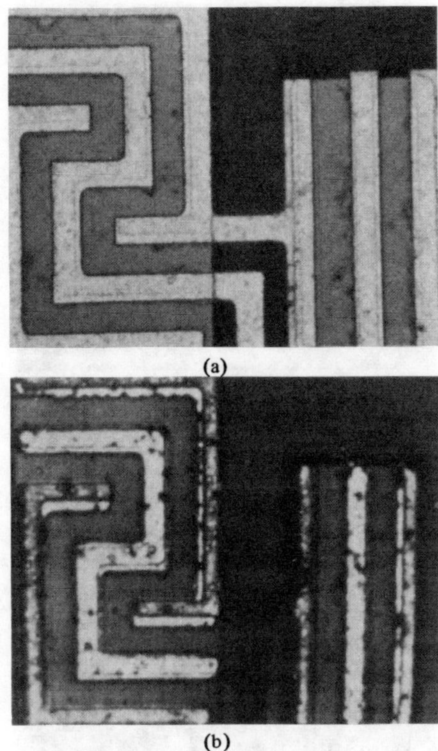

(a)

(b)

Fig. 47. Optical and acoustic comparison of a CMOS device with SOS technology. (a) Optical brightfield by Koch (×1120). (b) Acoustic *f* = 1100 MHz (SOS chip B-STDL-4, Rockwell CMOS).

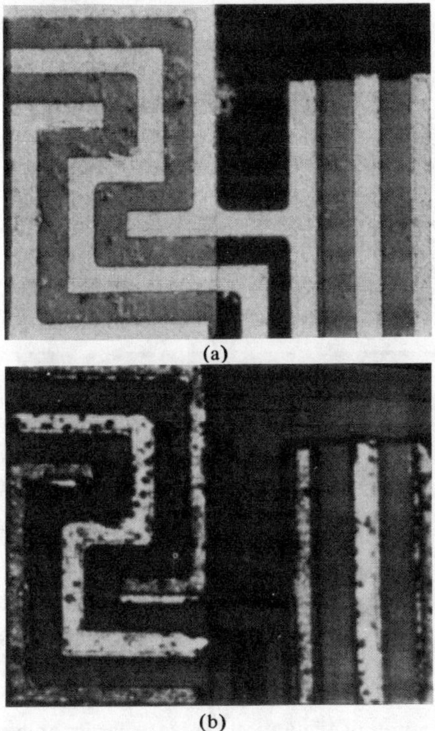

(a)

(b)

Fig. 48. A second CMOS device on the same wafer as that shown in Fig. 47. (a) Optical interference contrast by Koch (×1120). (b) Acoustic *f* = 1100 MHz (SOS chip A-STDL-4, Rockwell CMOS).

appearance of two different devices that were fabricated on the same sapphire wafer. It is instructive to concentrate on the differences between the two devices. It is clearly apparent that the differences in the acoustic micrographs (taken at 1100 MHz) are much larger than they are in the optical comparisons. Here again we suggest that the informational content of the two images is greater than that of the optical alone.

If we move now to a higher frequency (1800 MHz) something new appears—namely, the changes in the oxide thickness beneath an aluminum layer becomes apparent as in Fig. 49 [3]. Again it is the SOS circuit with 3000 Å of oxide between the silicon and the aluminum as shown in Fig. 46. But the oxide thins to 1000 Å at the gate regions and these thinned regions are evident in the acoustic micrograph of Fig. 49(b). In this image and the previous two, the linewidth is 7.5 μm. In Fig. 50 we have the appearance of a circuit as fabricated on silicon [3]. The aluminum linewidth here is 5 μm and we can identify a number of differences between the optical and the

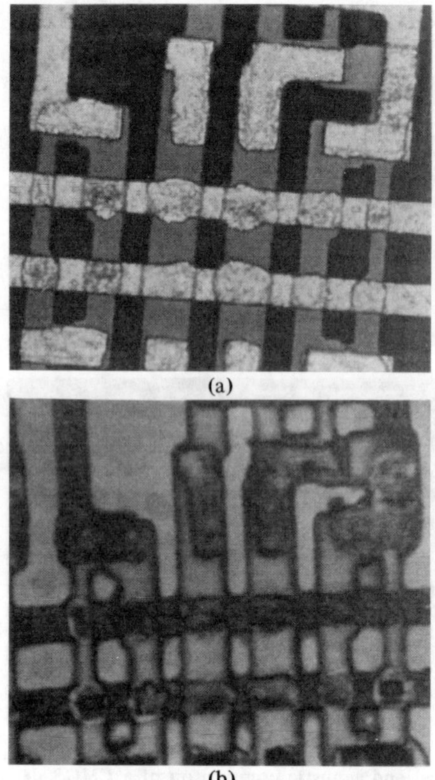

(a)

(b)

Fig. 49. CMOS device showing cross overs (upper aluminum lines) and gates (right and left devices on lower aluminum line). (a) Optical—bright field. (b) Acoustic—1800 MHz. (Courtesy of V. Jipson.)

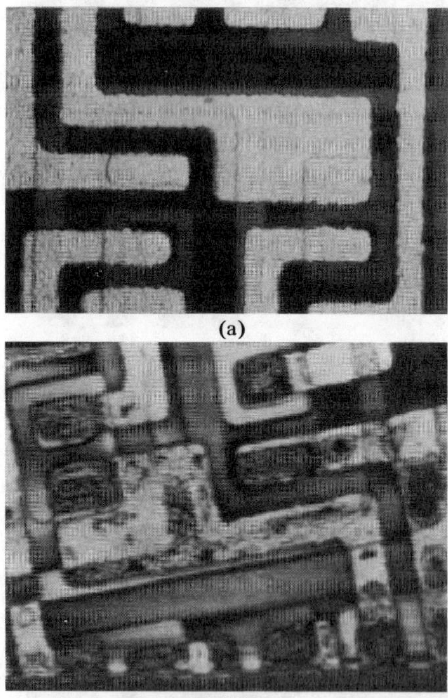

(a)

(b)

Fig. 50. Comparison of the optical (a) and acoustic (b) images of a different region of the same wafer as Fig. 47. Of interest are the dark blotches which appear on the aluminum lines in the acoustic micrograph but are not visible on the optical image (Jipson [3]).

acoustic images. We believe some of the differences are a result of inhomogeneities in the elastic properties of the devices.

The final image of Fig. 51 is placed here to exhibit the micrographs of GaAs devices and to illustrate in a graphic way the

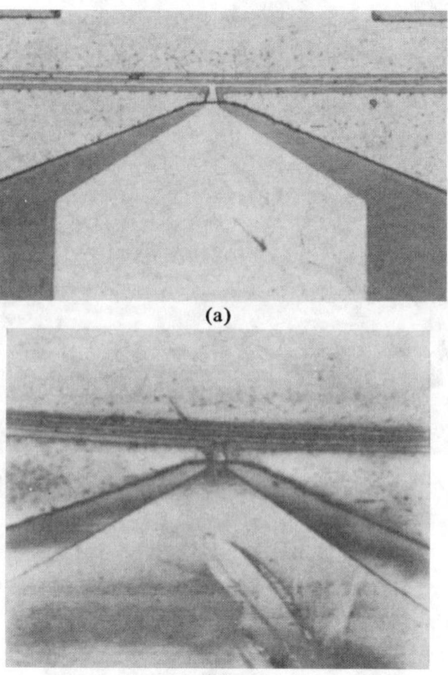

(a)

(b)

Fig. 51. Comparison of the optical (a) and acoustic (b) images of a dual gate GaAs FET. The gate lines are 1 μm wide with a 1 μm spacing (Jipson [3]).

resolution that is now possible with acoustic microscopy. This dual gate FET is made with 1 linewidth spaced by 1 μm. We can see that these lines are easily resolved in both micrographs, and, again, there is no lack of contrast in the acoustic micrographs.

VII. SUMMARY

In this review we have tried to demonstrate that acoustics can compete in a number of ways with optics. They represent a new method for viewing microscopic objects. Acoustic radiation is a viable alternative to more conventional microscopy, and in numerous problem areas it can be used to complement and extend the optical instrument. The elastic properties as monitored on a microscopic scale are important parameters that enter into structures over a range from biological cells, to fossil fuels (particularly coal), to materials such as steel, important in technology through the fabricated microstructures in the field of microelectronics.

We have pointed out that the state of the art has been advanced in the past year. The wavelength used in the best instrument is now equal to that of green light. The theory that is needed to explain the high contrast and the variations in contrast has been worked out. It is now possible to understand a good deal of the information that appears in the images.

We also hold that there is a promising future for a microscope which combines an optical input with an acoustic output—a photoacoustic microscope. In this system the optical input is a laser modulated in amplitude at a microwave frequency. The thermal expansion coefficient of the object produces strains at this modulation frequency. These optically induced strains are to be detected with the acoustic lens and the output transducer. Progress on this suggestion has been intermittent, and for that reason, it is more appropriate to wait for a future review.

We want to leave the reader with the impression that there is still more to come. Shorter wavelengths will be used with a resulting increase in resolving power. Signal processing routines used to enhance the images are evolving, and a dedicated computer to manipulate the electrical signals used to form the image will extend the power of this instrument far beyond what is suggested here. The realm of cryogenic liquids holds great promise, and it should allow us to use wavelengths in the submicrometer region below the optical limit.

We predict the new advances will occur on three fronts—room temperature liquids, cryogenic liquids, and photoacoustics. We end this review with that as our hopeful outlook for the future of acoustic microscopy.

Acknowledgment

A number of people have contributed to the progress in acoustic microscopy as reported here. They have participated both directly and in discussion sessions. Their time was freely given, and we want to express our strong appreciation for their enthusiasm. In the Ginzton Laboratory, M. Chodorow, G. Kino, and the late R. Kompfner have made constructive suggestions since the beginning of the project. At Zenith Research Laboratories, A. Korpel and L. Kessler have shared their ideas on acoustic microscopy with us. R. Wilson and R. Weglein of Hughes Research Laboratories have contributed a number of ideas that will continue to be important. M. Bullis at the National Bureau of Standards and E. Ash at University College London encouraged us to continue in the early stages when the images were lacking in significant detail.

In our own laboratories, the work of R. Lemons has already been referenced and we only need add that he ground the first lens with his own hands. The late W. Bond did much of the early design work and the instrument was constructed by G. Bicker. L. Goddard has shared his expertise with us throughout the program and the performance of the acoustic components is due to his careful work. G. Kotler and J. Vrhel provided the sapphire crystals with precision surfaces and spherical lenses which form the heart of the entire system. V. Jipson set about to improve the resolution and he has shared his high-quality images with us. J. Heiserman has contributed to all aspects of the work with biological specimens. Ms. R. Koch, a member of the Center for Materials Research, has contributed the high quality optical images. Ms. N. Pleibel, of the Cancer Biology Research Laboratory, has provided us with many of the biological cells. We also want to express our appreciation for the samples that we have received from a number of interested friends. These include P. J. Hagon of Rockwell International (the SOS samples), C. Liechti of Hewlett-Packard (the GaAs FET samples), R. Grey of the U.S. Steel Research Laboratory, for suggesting the studies of coal, and P. Tucker of the School of Textiles, North Carolina State University, Raleigh, for suggesting the study of polymer fibers.

References

[1] J. Ilukor and E. H. Jacobsen, "Coherent elastic wave propagation in quartz at ultramicrowave frequencies," in *Physical Acoustics*, W. P. Mason, Ed. New York: Academic Press, 1968, vol. V, ch. 5, pp. 221–231; and C. H. Anderson and E. S. Sabisky, "Spin-phonon spectrometer," in *Physical Acoustics*, W. P. Mason and R. N. Thurston, Eds. New York: Academic Press, 1971, vol. VIII, ch. 1, pp. 2–57.

[2] J. S. Imai and I. Rudnick, "Ultrasonic attenuation in liquid helium at 1 GHz," *Phys. Rev. Lett.*, vol. 22, pp. 694–697, Apr. 7, 1969.

[3] V. Jipson and C. F. Quate, "Acoustic microscopy at optical wavelengths," *Appl. Phys. Lett.*, vol. 32, pp. 789–791, June 15, 1978.

[4] R. A. Lemons and C. F. Quate, "Acoustic microscopy: Biomedical applications," *Science*, vol. 188, pp. 905–911, May 30, 1975, and R. Kompfner and C. F. Quate, "Acoustic radiation and its use in microscopy," *Phys. Technol.*, vol. 8, pp. 231–237, Nov. 1977.

[5] A. Korpel, "Acoustic microscopy," in *Ultrasonic Imaging and Holography*, G. W. Stroke *et al.*, Eds. New York: Plenum Press, 1974.

[6] L. W. Kessler, "A review of progress and applications in acoustic microscopy," *J. Acoust. Soc. Amer.*, vol. 55, pp. 909–918, May 1974.

[7] N. Chubachi, "Acoustic microscopy—A review," *Oyo Butsuri*, vol. 47, p. 75, Apr. 1978 (in Japanese).

[8] C. F. Quate, "Imaging using lenses," in *Acoustic Imaging: Cameras, Microscopes, Phased Arrays and Holographic Systems*, G. Wade, Ed. New York: Plenum Press, 1976, ch. 11, pp. 241–305.

[9] R. A. Lemons and C. F. Quate, "Acoustic microscopy," in *Physical Acoustics*, vol. XIV, R. N. Thurston, Ed. New York: Academic Press, to be published.

[10] L. W. Kessler and D. E. Yuhas, "Acoustic microscopy—1979," *Proc. IEEE*, vol. 67, pp. 526–535, Apr. 1979.

[11] T. G. Rochow and E. G. Rochow, *An Introduction to Microscopy by Means of Light, Electrons, X-Rays, or Ultrasound*. New York: Plenum Press, 1978.

[12] L. W. Kessler, P. R. Palermo, and A. Korpel, "Recent developments with the scanning laser acoustic microscope," in *Acoustical Holography*, P. S. Green, Ed. New York: Plenum Press, 1974, pp. 15–23; and A. Madeyski and L. W. Kessler, "Initial experiments in the application of acoustic microscopy to the characterization of steel and to the study of fracture phenomena," *IEEE Trans. Sonics—Ultrason.*, vol. SU-23, pp. 363–369, Sept. 1976.

[13] L. W. Kessler and D. E. Yuhas, "Structural perspective," *Indus. Res.*, vol. 20, pp. 53–56, Jan. 1978.

[14] C. S. Tsai, S. K. Wang, and C. C. Lee, "Visualization of solid material joints using a transmission-type scanning acoustic microscope," *Appl. Phys. Lett.*, vol. 31, pp. 317–320, Sept. 1, 1977.

[15] R. G. Wilson, R. D. Weglein, and D. M. Bonnel, in *Semiconductor Silicon/1977*, H. R. Huff and E. Sirtl, Eds. Princeton, NJ: Electrochem. Soc., vol. 77, no. 2, pp. 431–440, 1977.

[16] R. D. Weglein and R. G. Wilson, "Characteristic material signatures by acoustic microscopy," *Electron. Lett.*, vol. 14, pp. 352–354, June 8, 1978.

[17] B. Bridoux *et al.*, "Optimization of a transmission acoustic microscope," *J. Appl. Phys.*, vol. 49, pp. 574–579, Feb. 1978.

[18] J. Attal and G. Cambon, "Signal processing in the reflective acoustic microscope," *Electron. Lett.*, vol. 14, pp. 472–473, July 20, 1978.

[19] H. K. Wickramasinghe and M. Hall, "Phase imaging with the scanning acoustic microscope," *Electron. Lett.*, vol. 12, pp. 637–638, Nov. 25, 1976.

[20] N. Chubachi, T. Sannomiya, and T. Iyama, "Scanning acoustic microscope with concave transducers," presented at Joint Meeting, Acoustical Society of America and Acoustical Society of Japan, Honolulu, HI, Nov. 27–Dec. 1, 1978.

[21] S. Bennett, D. Payne, and E. A. Ash, "Reflective geometry for microscopy and NDT," in *1977 Ultrasonics Symp. Proc.*, J. deKlerk and B. R. McAvoy, Eds. (IEEE Cat. No. 77 CH1264-1SU), pp. 161–164.

[22] A. F. Brown, "Seeing with sound," *Endeavour*, vol. 35, pp. 123–128, Sept. 1976.

[23] R. C. Eggleton, "Application of acoustic microscopy to the study of muscle mechanics," in *Multidisciplinary Microscopy*, SPIE Proc. vol. 104, R. L. Whitman, Ed. Bellingham, WA 98225: Soc. Photo-Optical Instrumentation Engineers (P.O. Box 10), pp. 117–124, 1977.

[24] G. Larsen, "Det Akustiske Mikroskop," *Saetrykk av Farmakoterapi*, vol. 33, pp. 49–55, 1977 (in Norwegian).

[25] L. Broomhead, "La microscopie acoustique," *Sci. Avenir*, pp. 71–77, May 1978 (in French).

[26] T. H. Maugh, II, "Acoustic microscopy: A new window to the world of the small," *Science*, vol. 201, pp. 1110–1114, Sept. 22, 1978.

[27] T. M. Reeder and D. K. Winslow, "Characteristics of microwave acoustic transducers for volume wave excitation," *IEEE Trans. Microwave Theory Tech.*, vol. MTT-17, pp. 927–942, Nov. 1969.

[28] R. A. Lemons, "Acoustic microscopy by mechanical scanning," Ph.D. dissertation, Stanford Univ., Stanford, CA, May 1975, unpublished.

[29] R. D. Weglein, "Acoustic properties of sputtered glass at microwave frequencies," *Appl. Phys. Lett.*, vol. 29, pp. 277–279, Sept. 1, 1976.

[30] Further details of the lens design and some of the electronic circuitry can be found in the Annu. Rep. for NSF/RANN, NTIS PB-271443, Apr. 1977.

[31] R. Kompfner and R. A. Lemons, "Nonlinear acoustic microscopy," *Appl. Phys. Lett.*, vol. 28, pp. 295–297, Mar. 15, 1976; and H. K. Wickramasinghe and C. Yeack, "Nonlinear imaging of an edge in the scanning acoustic microscope," *J. Appl. Phys.*, vol. 48, pp. 4951–4954, Dec. 1977.

[32] W. L. Bond *et al.*, "Dark field and stereo viewing with the acoustic microscope," *Appl. Phys. Lett.*, vol. 27, pp. 270–272, Sept. 1, 1975.

[33] K. F. Hertzfeld and T. A. Litovitz, *Absorption and Dispersion of Ultrasonic Waves.* New York: Academic Press, 1959.

[34] M. T. Wauk, II, "Attenuation in microwave transducers and resonators," Ph.D. dissertation, Stanford University, Stanford, CA, July 1969, unpublished.

[35] A. Akhieser, "On the absorption of sound in solids," *J. Phys.* (Akademiia Nauk-Leningrad), vol. 1, pp. 277–287, 1939.

[36] I. L. Fabelinskii, *Molecular Scattering of Light.* New York: Plenum Press, 1968.

[37] T. O. Woodruff and H. Ehrenreich, "Absorption of sound in insulators," *Phys. Rev.*, vol. 123, pp. 1553–1559, Sept. 1, 1961.

[38] J. Attal and C. F. Quate, "Investigation of some low ultrasonic absorption liquids," *J. Acoust. Soc. Amer.*, vol. 59, pp. 69–73, Jan. 1976.

[39] W. T. Cathey, *Optical Information Processing and Holography.* New York: Wiley, 1974.

[40] J. W. Goodman, *Introduction to Fourier Optics.* New York: McGraw-Hill, 1968.

[41] E. O'Neill, *Introduction to Statistical Optics.* Reading, MA: Addison-Wesley, 1963.

[42] J. A. Ratcliffe, *Reports on Progress in Physics*, vol. XIX, A. C. Strickland, Ed. London, England: The Physical Society, 1956.

[43] D. C. Champeney, *Fourier Transforms and Their Physical Appli- cations.* New York: Academic Press, 1973.

[44] ——, *loc. cit.* Section 11.5.

[45] H. K. Wickramasinghe, "Contrast and imaging performance in the scanning acoustic microscope," *J. Appl. Phys.*, vol. 50, pp. 664–672, Feb. 1979.

[46] E. Evans and Y. C. Fung, "Improved measurements of the eryth- rocyte geometry," *Microvas. Res.*, vol. 4, pp. 335–347, 1972.

[47] J. W. Goodman, *loc. cit.* Section 6.4.

[48] A. Atalar, "An angular-spectrum approach to contrast in reflec- tion acoustic microscopy," *J. Appl. Phys.*, vol. 49, pp. 5130– 5139, Oct. 1978.

[49] H. K. Wickramasinghe, "Contrast in reflection acoustic micros- copy," *Electron. Lett.*, vol. 14, pp. 305–306, May 11, 1978.

[50] A. Atalar, C. F. Quate, and H. K. Wickramasinghe, "Phase imaging in reflection with the acoustic microscope," *Appl. Phys. Lett.*, vol. 31, pp. 791–793, Dec. 15, 1977.

[51] L. M. Brekhovskikh, *Waves in Layered Media.* New York: Aca- demic Press, 1960, pp. 100–122.

[52] A. Atalar, "Reflection coefficient for a lossy liquid-lossless iso- tropic solid interface," *J. Acoust. Soc. Amer.*, June 1979.

[53] M. F. Marmor, H. K. Wickramasinghe, and R. A. Lemons, "Acous- tic microscopy of the human retina and pigment epithelium," *Investiga. Ophthalmol. Vis. Sci.*, vol. 16, pp. 660–666, July 1977.

Laser Scanning Microscopy

W. JERRY ALFORD, RICHARD D. VANDERNEUT AND VINCENT J. ZALECKAS, MEMBER, IEEE

Invited Paper

Abstract—In conventional light microscopy, images are formed either by direct imaging of the object at a desired magnification or by imaging the object onto a remote surface and converting the illuminance at that surface to an electrical signal. In laser scanning microscopy, the object or specimen surface is scanned point by point by a focused laser beam. The actual image or other pertinent characteristic of the object is then generated by an electronic system. Use of such scanned laser systems exists today in biomedical research, in the semiconductor microelectronics industry, and in varied other industrial inspection applications. In this paper, we review the basic principles of laser scanning microscopy, discuss advantages as compared to more conventional light microscopy, and illustrate the technique with examples of systems in use today.

I. INTRODUCTION: OVERVIEW OF LASER SCANNING MICROSCOPY

IN CONVENTIONAL light microscopy, images are formed either by direct imaging of the object at a desired magnification or by imaging the object onto a remote surface and converting the illuminance at that surface to an electrical signal. In laser scanning microscopy, the object or specimen surface is scanned point by point by a focused laser beam. The image or other characteristic of the object is then generated by an electronic system. Scanning formats can be such as to lead to real-time video displays or can be configured so as to scan at non-video rates or in a non-raster format, where information about the object is obtained without its real image being generated. The laser is focused to a spot size consistent with the resolution requirements of the application. For many applications, a small spot size together with a large overall field size and limitations in scan speed prevent the formation of "real-time" images. Several examples where this occurs will be cited later in the paper.

High-resolution laser imaging systems have been developed in most cases to overcome inherent disadvantages present in more conventional light microscopy. For example, with increasing magnification and numerical aperture, the depth of focus of a conventional microscope becomes very small. Although it would still be difficult to form real images with scanned laser techniques to any greater resolution and depth of focus as compared to conventional microscopy, through sophisticated techniques such a dynamic focusing it is feasible to conceive of such a system. Also, in applications where a direct image is not required, significant advantages can be obtained by employing scanned laser techniques. For example,

it is possible to detect light diffusely scattered from surface features much smaller in size than the incident scanned beam size. It will be shown how micrometer-sized defects on silicon wafer surfaces can be detected with rastered laser beams focused to 50–100 μm in diameter.

If the application requires a relatively large field to be rapidly covered at high resolution, this can be a tedious and error-prone task when performed on a conventional microscope by a human operator. An example would be the inspection of integrated circuit photomasks. Even when video imaging devices, such as vidicons, CCD's, etc., are coupled to a microscope, limitations in image content and dynamic range are encountered in many applications. Laser scanning techniques have been used to overcome these problems. Also, in laser scanning microscopy various physical characteristics of the object can be monitored. These would include not only reflectance, but others such as surface roughness and topography. Assuming a video scanning format is employed, the result is a video signal that has been preprocessed to exhibit information in a form that is easily handled by image processing hardware or readily recognized via observation of a monitor.

Laser scanning departs from conventional imaging, in which information is acquired by direct imaging of the object at a desired magnification, or by imaging the object onto a remote surface and then converting the illuminance at that surface to an electrical signal. Instead, object scanning is employed to obtain the desired information; there is no direct imaging involved. Fig. 1 illustrates the concept of image and object scanning. In object scanning, detection is accomplished by an arrangement of detectors with wide area coverage. Image scanning, on the other hand, uses a light source with wide area coverage and localizes detection over the image. This certainly has its advantages as a passive technique that can operate with ambient lighting. In most industrial applications, however, and certainly in those requiring image processing, some lighting control is necessary. Object scanning is an active approach in that the illumination (assumed to be a laser) and its movement over the object determine the signal obtained.

The concept of laser scanning to generate an image thus provides a whole series of possible controls and variables to optimize. Basically they can be divided into three major categories—detection, illumination, and scanning. As the object is scanned, detection of the reflected and scattered radiation can be accomplished in a number of ways to maximize information content. The use of multiple detectors is one example. The illumination is controllable via light intensity and spot size, while variations in the scan pattern can be made with the proper deflection apparatus. Each of these three categories will briefly be reviewed in the following.

Manuscript received November 18, 1981; revised December 15, 1981.

W. J. Alford and R. D. VanderNeut are with Ford Aerospace and Communications Corporation, Process Control Products Operation, Charlotte, NC 28208.

V. J. Zaleckas is with Western Electric, Engineering Research Center, Princeton, NJ 08540.

Reprinted from *Proc. IEEE*, vol. 70, pp. 641–651, June 1982.

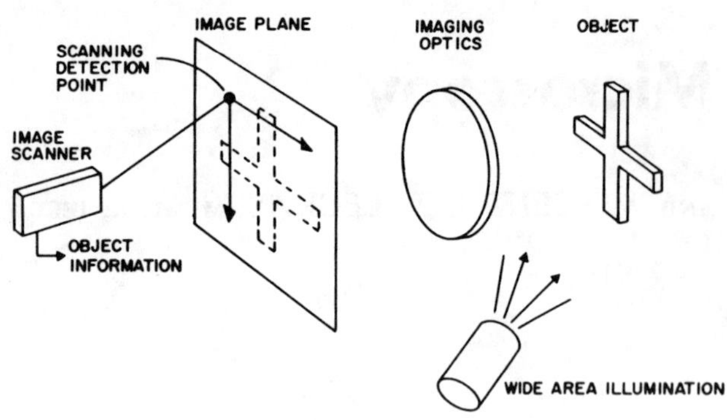

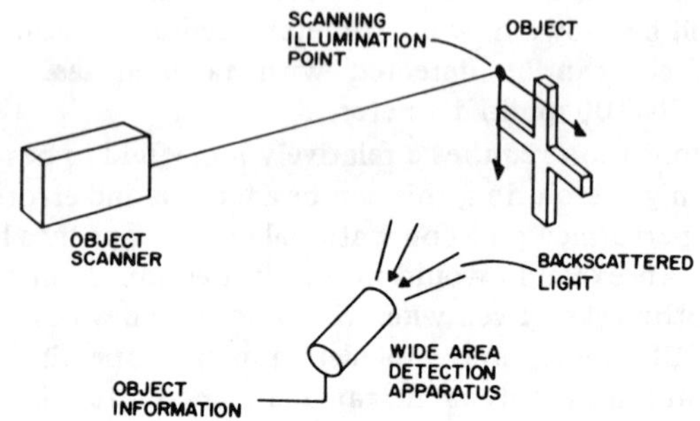

Fig. 1. Illustration of the concept of image and object scanning.

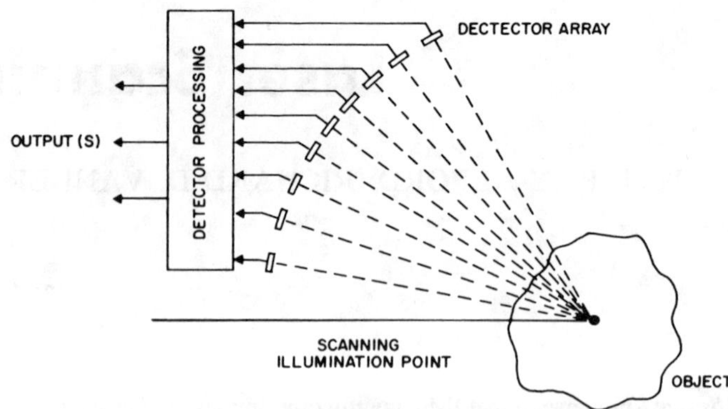

Fig. 2. Illustration of the use of multiple detectors to obtain information on backscattered radiation as a function of reflection angle.

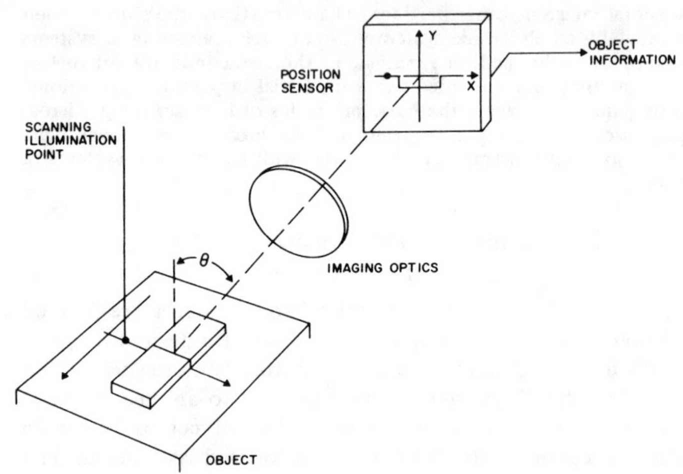

Fig. 3. A possible configuration for monitoring topography using a position detector.

II. LASER SCANNING MICROSCOPE TECHNOLOGY

A. Detection

The most basic detection arrangement is the use of a single detector, where the backscattered radiation from the object is monitored by the detector. The same principles apply for light scattered in the forward direction. The single detector has found utility in past applications involving a scanned laser beam. Applications for optical microscopy [1], [2], semiconductor testing [3], [4], photomask inspection [5], [6], and printed circuit board inspection [7] have been reported. Several of these applications will be explored later in detail. In these areas, scanning with a single detector has been applied to specific objects with a well-defined application.

Although inexpensive photodiodes can be used as the single detector, advantages are obtained using detectors with gain, such as avalanche photodiodes and photomultiplier tubes. Improvement of the signal-to-noise ratio will produce a signal with increased dynamic range, thereby providing more information on object reflectance. Photomultipliers can easily provide a current gain that varies over five decades for a wide range of sensitivities with a linear response [8].

A certain amount of information concerning the object can be obtained with a single detector. Additional information is available by the proper application of multiple detectors with appropriate electronic processing of the detector output. An example is illustrated in Fig. 2, where a series of detectors provides information on the backscattered radiation at various angles. With suitable processing, recognition of object detail is possible by recognition of the scattering profile, since different materials will have different profiles. Thus an object parameter other than reflectance can be used to generate the object signal. Multiple detectors also allow simultaneous observation of variations in reflectance properties. One example is the polarization of the backscattered light [9]. Two detectors with cross-polarizing filters can examine the same object and

obtain information pertaining to the polarization of the reflected beam. This information, when suitably processed, then allows discrimination between various materials in the object regardless of the reflected intensity or image contrast. An example is the observation of gold thin-film patterns on ceramic with a laser scanner [10]. The gold/ceramic ratio was increased from 1.3 to a value near 10 by using two detectors.

Laser scanning with special-purpose detectors can be employed to obtain information in special applications. A quadrant detector has been used for identification of surface defects on the gold contacts of printed wiring boards [11]. In a transmission mode, a similar detector has also been applied to image processing for visualization of phase information from objects [12]. As another example, position detectors such as diode arrays may provide a means of obtaining object contour information. The output from position detectors is proportional to the mean position of the light intensity distribution incident upon them. With laser scanning and an off-axis imaging arrangement, the output from the position detector can be related to object contour. This principle is illustrated in Fig. 3; the off-axis imaging optics provides a perspective of the object such that changes in the contour result in movement of the imaged spot on the detector surface and, therefore, changes in the detector output. Incorporating a laser scanner allows for a rapid, high-speed approach that can access any scan line. Note that other conventional detectors may be deployed to acquire reflectance and/or scattering profile infor-

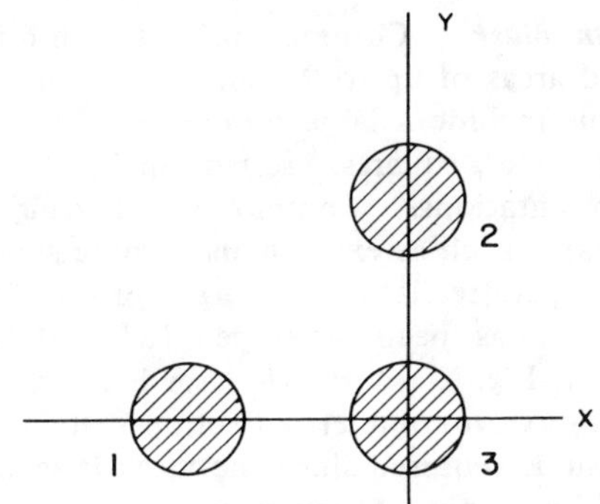

Fig. 4. A two-spot pattern for object differentiation in two dimensions.

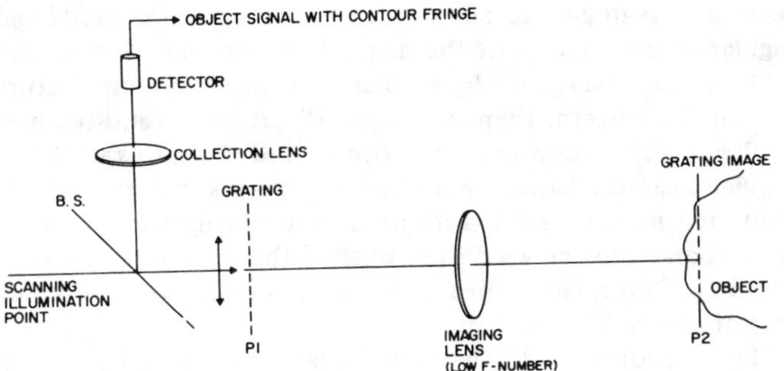

Fig. 5. The optical arrangement for focus contouring.

mation. Thus the contour information can act as yet another input to identify the object detail.

B. Illumination

A second area of importance in laser microscopy is illumination. Variations in the illumination spot during the object scan can be made to maximize the information obtained; these variations can be in spot size, spot shape, and light wavelength, providing a high degree of versatility in illumination. Control of spot shape, as in spot-size control, utilizes information in the vicinity of the scanning spot to optimize the information obtained. This will be illustrated with a discussion of object differentiation and focus contouring.

Object differentiation using multiple spots provides an exact means for obtaining a signal representing the differential of object reflectance. This can be done in two dimensions, thereby providing a capability that simple electronics differentiation cannot provide. Shown in Fig. 4 is an example of a spot configuration that can be used. A multiplexing scheme must be used to separate the signal obtained from each spot. Differentiation in the x direction can be realized by subtraction of 1 from 3, while in the y direction the result is obtained from the difference of 2 and 3 (see Fig. 4).

Focus contouring employs a scanning illumination spot that contains a high spatial-frequency pattern. It is a technique that delineates a single contour on a diffuse object with a bright fringe. Basically, it takes advantage of the short depth of focus obtained with low f/number optics. A similar method is described as a "locus of focus" contour [13]. Fig. 5 serves to better describe the technique. A scanning beam is brought to image plane $P1$. Planes $P1$ and $P2$ are conjugates, so that the image of the scanning beam is at the object plane. The imaging lens is chosen to have a low f/number. By placing a grating with a period much less than the scanning spot size in $P1$, a scanning spot with a high-frequency fringe pattern is incident upon the object. The diffuse radiation collected by that same lens is imaged back to the grating. Due to contour variations on the object, the image will have well-defined grating lines only at those points that are within the depth of focus of the imaging lens. These areas will pass through the grating with maximum intensity. Out-of-focus grating lines, on the other hand, will be reduced by the grating duty cycle. The light passing through the grating on the return is collected and sent to a detector. The resulting signal has a bright fringe delineating those regions within the depth of focus of the imaging lens. The overall image, however, remains in focus due to the relatively small f/number that describes the scanning system.

The potential advantages of wavelength control lie, as expected, in color discrimination. A single scanning spot of multiple wavelength can be detected by any number of detectors, each with a narrow-bandwidth spectral filter. The obvious comparison is to a color camera, which can also discriminate object color. An advantage may be gained with laser scanning in that multiple detectors can provide scattering angle information. Color as a function of scattering angle can be used, therefore, to provide additional object information. In some cases, use of an infrared (IR) or ultraviolet (UV) illumination source may be beneficial. Laser sources with high brightness are available in these regions. Examples of possible applications are transmission studies in silicon (IR) [14] or fluorescence studies [15].

C. Scanning

Three aspects of scanning control are considered. The first is the scan format, or the path of the scanning illumination point in the object plane. The second is scan position information for accurate measurement, if desired, and the third relates to focus variations of the scanning spot.

For most applications, a standard raster scan pattern for the object scan is employed. However, depending on the application, it may be advantageous to employ a different scanning pattern. This would be particularly true for image processing, where a standardized scan format is not necessarily required. As an example, a radial scan for alignment of radially symmetric objects would provide information in a more suitable format for subsequent image processing. In other cases, a spiral scan might be beneficial. Random access capability for the object scan is a possibility as well, depending upon the scanning apparatus employed. Basically, control of the scanning pattern is a means of varying the format of the data as received by the image processor. In doing so, the circuitry for processing the data can be simplified. Obviously, many of the potential advantages for scan control would be based upon the particular characteristics of the object in question.

Scan position information implies precise knowledge of the scanning beam location. Applications for precise measurement and gauging require accurate information relating the signal in time to an object location in space. Using methods of position monitoring for a scanning laser beam [16], accurate beam position information to 1 part in 40 000 has been demonstrated. This is done by splitting a portion of the beam and interrogating the spot in a separate scanning plane with a grating. A time–space relationship is then established by the grating, and drifts of the scanning apparatus or nonlinearities in the scan will not affect measurement accuracy. Fig. 6 illustrates the

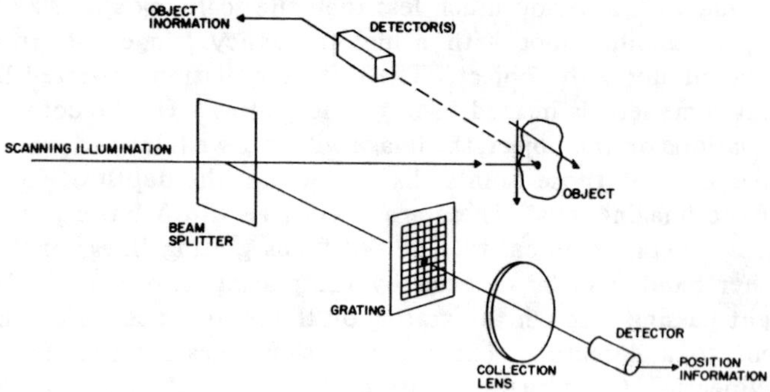

Fig. 6. The use of a two-dimensional grating for accurate monitoring of beam position.

basic configuration. Note that other controls such as multiple detectors can also be employed in the same arrangement to best delineate the measurement points.

Focus control can provide advantages in examining extended objects. Using electrooptic techniques, the possibility exists for variation of the focal point of the scanning illumination spot during the scan. The apparent depth of focus can then be increased by displaying only the information that represents a focused condition. Techniques for autofocus can be applied to recognize the focused positions. Object contour information can also be provided with this approach [17].

III. APPLICATIONS

A. Introduction

In this section we review selected examples of systems designed and developed for specific microscopic inspection or characterization applications. A major part of the industrial and commercial development of such systems has occurred as a result of the inspection needs of the semiconductor industry. Examples of systems for photomask inspection, surface inspection of polished silicon wafers, and patterned silicon wafers will be reviewed. In addition, examples will be used to illustrate the potential of laser microscopy in other areas such as fabric inspection, material characterization, and biomedical research.

B. Photolithographic Mask Inspection

A persistent problem in fabricating thin-film or silicon integrated circuits (SIC's) has been the limitation on the yield of functioning circuits imposed by defective photolithography. Spurious photolithographic defects of micrometer size can lead to short circuits between adjacent conductor paths or other failure-causing effects. Defects in the masks thus reduce the achievable percentage yield of functioning devices.

Laser scanning systems have been developed for the inspection (and ultimately the repair) of both thin-film and SIC masks. For both technologies, the masks themselves are similar in physical characteristics, with the patterns delineated in a thin (opaque) metal film of chrome deposited on a transparent glass substrate. The differences in the two types of masks are found in the patterns themselves. For SIC masks, hundreds or even thousands of patterns are repeated in a regular array ("chip sites"). Hence when the lithographic and other fabrication steps are completed, the same number of devices are fabricated on a common substrate. For thin-film masks, repeated patterns may or many not exist on the same mask. This difference in the masks themselves has led to the development of two unique laser scanning systems for inspection. Each system is reviewed in the following.

1) Thin-Film Masks: Chrome masks for thin-film circuits have patterned areas of up to 9.5 cm $\times$ 11.5 cm in size [18]. Pattern options include a large number of regular geometric shapes (lines, circles, squares, etc.) occurring at an unlimited number of orientations. Commonly occurring defects are irregular in shape, such as extraneous chrome spots, pinholes, etc. A noncomparative laser scanning approach for detection of such defects has been developed [5] and is illustrated schematically in Fig. 7. A He–Ne laser is rastered across the mask by an x–y galvonometer deflection system. No critical mask alignment is required since the mask is scanned using a single focused laser spot. At any point in time, the light transmitted and diffracted from a given point on the mask is collected, immobilized by a descan mirror, and then directed into the optical processing head. The processing head divides the beam into segments to allow a determination of the radial and angular characteristics of the diffraction patterns. If the laser spot size is arranged to be smaller than the minimum feature size on the pattern, then the "regular" nature of valid features results in diffraction patterns with a limited set of radial and angular characteristics. With few exceptions, pattern defects result in anomalous diffraction patterns having radial and angular characteristics which fall outside the set unique to valid features. Defects as small as 5 μm are detectable with a scanned spot diameter of 40 μm.

The position of both the scanned laser spot and the translation table are encoded at all times so that, once a defect is detected, its position can be stored in a minicomputer. Another aspect of this system is the capability to also repair defects once found. This is done using an Nd:YAG machining laser for removal of extraneous chrome. Pinholes are touched up with opaque epoxy [19], [20].

2) AMIS–Automatic Mask Inspection System: A comparative laser scanning approach has been developed [6] for the inspection of SIC masks. It consists of scanning the mask while comparing two adjacent but nominally identical patterns, and registering any deviations on a defect map, which then permits an inspector to view only suspicious locations for defect classification. The system relieves the human inspector from the tedious search for defects, but uses the human's superior pattern recognition power to categorize the defects found and presented by the machine.

The basic system is shown schematically in Fig. 8 and comprises a scanning comparator, a signal processor for its output signals, a display, a scan generator, an operator console, and a data processor. An argon laser is used which produces 5 mW at 488 nm. The beam is scanned by means of a paratellurite acoustooptic deflector [21] involving a beam expander, circular polarizer, and a cylindrical lens to remove astigmatism, none of which are shown. Thereafter, a beamsplitter and movable prisms produce two beams of variable separation to accommodate different pattern spacings on the mask. Since the output from the acoustooptic light deflector varies with deflection angle, a small percentage of one of the beams is directed into a photodetector (PDC), which provides a suitable feedforward compensation signal to the amplifiers in the two signal paths. An adjustable quarter-wave plate follows to permit adjustment of intensity balance of the two channels.

Two imaging lenses produce intermediate scan images at ten times final size. Each of these lenses consists of two elements with adjustable spacing to permit precise matching of the two scan lines. These intermediate images are reduced to final size by means of a 0.1$\times$ photolithographic reduction lens with an 8-mm image field.

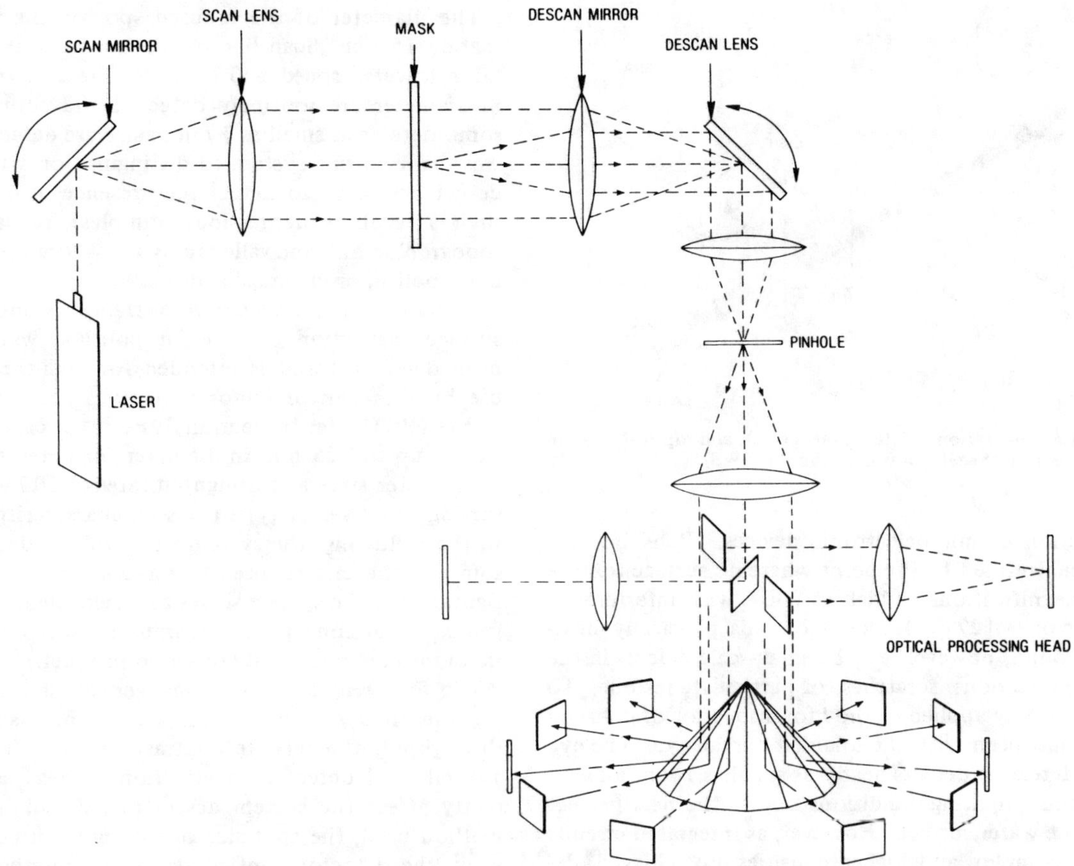

Fig. 7. Schematic illustration of the optical system for thin-film mask inspection.

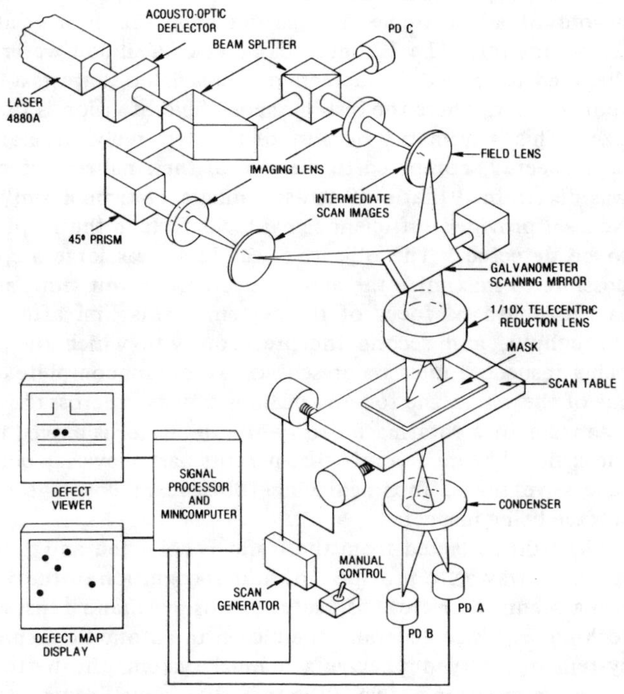

Fig. 8. Schematic illustration of the system for SIC mask inspection.

The reduction lens operates at $f/2.5$ to provide a depth of focus of about 12 μm, adequate to handle bowed masks and to avoid small mismatches between channels due to differences in field lens aberrations. It generates the final size scan lines

on the mask. The light passing through the mask is directed by collector optics common to both channels into the photodetectors PDA and PDB, the output from which constitutes the signals to be processed further.

It is desirable to be able to distinguish surface defects on a mask from intrinsic defects, such as bubbles in the glass substrate, since the former can, in most instances, be removed. Surface defects can be detected by sensing nonspecularly scattered light in coincidence with the normal defect detection signal. Four small fiber-optic bundles are placed in the four quadrants at 45° to the principal axes of the mask under test and 60° to the optical axis of the reduction lens. The four bundles are brought together at an additional photodetector PDD, the output of which is registered if it exceeds a preset threshold. The fiber bundles are oriented at 45° to suppress the scattered light from edges oriented in the x and y directions.

The system is capable of detecting defects with diameters greater than or equal to 3 μm routinely and to 2 μm with high probability [6]. The ultimate detection limit is imposed by the irregularities of image placement on the mask, notably step-and-repeat errors. A system is now available commercially for photomask inspection using the basic comparison scanning approach employed in the AMIS system.[1] This system is capable of detecting mask defects less than 1 μm in size.

C. Semiconductor Wafer Surface Inspection

Highly polished silicon wafers with diameters up to 125 mm and thickness of approximately 0.56 mm are extensively used in the microelectronics industry as starting substrates for the

[1] Manufactured by KLA Instruments Corp., Santa Clara, CA.

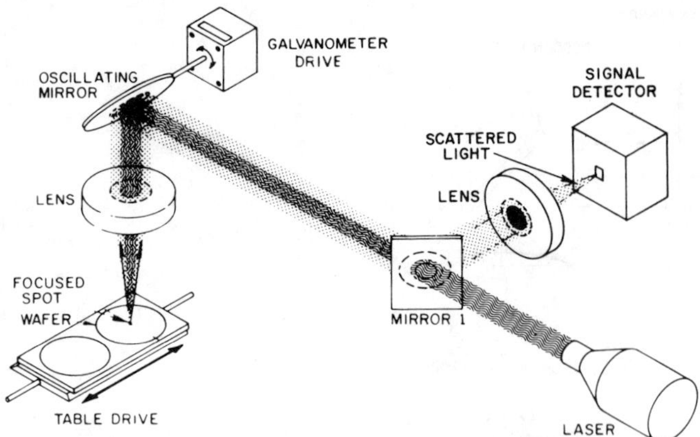

Fig. 9. Schematic illustration of the mechanical and optical system used in the silicon wafer scanner (SWS).

planar fabrication of microelectronic devices. Polishing methods have been refined to the point where no surface texture is visible at magnifications as high as 200X with interference contrast techniques [22]. Imposed on this physically near-perfect background, however, can be small-scale defects in the form of pits, projections, scratches, or particulate residue. To date, the only widely applied method for inspection of polished silicon wafers has been with the unaided human eye. The eye is capable of detecting defects nearly as small as 1 μm in diameter under specific lighting conditions due to the near-perfect condition of the wafer surface. However, as integrated circuits become more complex and higher densities are achieved, defects in the submicrometer range become increasingly important, and are not consistently detectable by a human operator. Additionally, subjectivity of inspection becomes of great concern due to fatigue, boredom, and the like. Variations among inspectors adds to the difficulty in applying specific guidelines for product acceptability. A number of systems have been developed to automate this visual inspection [22]–[25]. The basic principle is the same, namely the surface of interest is scanned by a laser beam and reflected light is monitored to sense the presence of defects. Two systems will be described in more detail in the following.

1) SWS–Silicon Wafer Scanner: One of the earliest instruments developed to automate this visual inspection is called the Silicon Wafer Scanner (SWS) [22]. A simplified schematic is shown in Fig. 9. The beam from a He–Ne laser is expanded and directed onto a galvanometer-driven oscillating mirror, and focused by a lens onto the substrate. Movement of the wafer in a direction perpendicular to the scan results in full coverage of the wafer surface. In the absence of surface defects on the wafer, the light is reflected normally from the surface and follows its incident path in reverse. If, however, the focused spot strikes a defect on the surface, the light is scattered away from this direct return path. This scattered light is detected and serves to indicate the presence of defects. To collect the scattered light, a front-surface mirror with a hole through its center is positioned at a 45° angle in the light path between the source and the oscillating mirror. Scattered light striking the peripheral area around the hole is collected by a lens and focused onto a detector. By coordinating the laser beam scanning and wafer motion with that of the sweep of a storage CRT, a visual indication of the relative location of defects on the surface of the wafer can be obtained. The practical embodiment of the system includes a spot position monitor, used to exclude the outer periphery of the wafer surface.

The diameter of the focused spot on the wafer is approximately 15 μm. Scan line oscillation speed is 85 sweeps/s, and table traverse speed is 0.13 cm/s. Defects greater than 8 μm in diameter are routinely detected and counted and at least some defects as small as 1 μm in size are detected. No attempt was made in this system to distinguish or discriminate among defect types, or to detect the presence of broad area defects such as shallow depressions (dimples), repeating patterns of topographic hills and valleys ("swirls," "orange peel," "waves"), underpolish, or chemical stains.

2) WIS–Wafer Inspection System: A more sophisticated surface inspection system for polished wafers has recently been developed and is intended for high-thruput production use by the semiconductor industry. The system, referred to as the WIS (Wafer Inspection System)[2] is capable of inspecting wafers up to 125 mm in diameter for defects as small as submicrometer sizes at throughput rates of 600 wafers/h. Output sorting as to defect type is also a characteristic of the system. In the following, the system itself will be described as well as some of the criteria used to establish the overall system configuration. The system serves as an excellent example of taking fundamental concepts in scanning microscopy and developing them into an industrially oriented product.

The following considerations were all important in establishing the final system design: area to be inspected, optimum throughput, the relative contrast of the defect with its background, and defect discrimination. These considerations directly affect the system design in determining: the scanning method used, the spot size or instantaneous detection field of view, the detector configuration, and number and placement of detectors.

In the case of polished silicon wafers, where the defects consist primarily of any deviation from a flat polished surface devoid of all scratches and particulates, this is a relatively simple matter. The 125-mm diameter of a silicon wafer with the need to inspect for defects to below 1 μm suggests a flying spot scanner, where the instantaneous field of vision is the spot size. This is primarily because of the extremely large area to be inspected, compared to the size of the smallest defect. It was determined that a 60-μm scanning spot from a 5-mW He–Ne laser provided sufficient signal for defects in the 1-μm range to be detected. The objective was to use as large a spot as possible to maximize the area inspected per unit time, as well as the depth of focus of the system. This first affects the throughput, and second the precision with which the wafer being inspected must be presented. To obtain complete coverage of the wafer, the focused beam is traversed across the wafer by means of a rotating mirror while the wafer is moved under the scanned beam at a rate that permits partial overlap between successive scans, thus achieving 100-percent coverage of the surface being inspected.

The light reflected from the wafer is collected and detected in such a way as to provide optimum recognition of the defects being scanned. Here it is useful to observe manual inspection techniques, since generally the closer an automatic inspection system optically duplicates a manual system, the better will be the correlation between the two. In manual inspection of a silicon wafer, two methods are used. The first utilizes a high-intensity microscope lamp to illuminate the surface, and the operator observes any resultant scattering of light out of its normal reflected path due to pits, particulates, scratches, etc.

---

[2] Manufactured by Ford Aerospace and Communications Corp., Charlotte, NC.

The same results are obtained by using a microscope and observing the wafer surface in the dark-field mode. This same result can be readily achieved in an automated system by placing a detector in a position to only pick up scattered light.

The above dark-field observations give good results for defects that diffusely scatter light because it is not critical that the detector be placed at a specific collection angle. Also, due to the low scatter from a defect-free surface, observable defect size is related to the intensity of the scanning spot rather than the spot size. However, it is also desired to observe the flatness of the polished surface or the presence of polished undulations in the surface such as that resulting from saw marks, spikes, some types of orange peel, etc. This can be readily achieved in an automatic system by causing the reflected light from the surface of the wafer to fall on an aperture placed in front of a detector and sizing the aperture so that any change in slope in the wafer surface causes the reflected beam to move off the aperture.

In manual inspection, observation by the above two methods must be done separately. In the automatic system, the two are combined, providing the ability to instantaneously observe a defect in two different modes, resulting not only in more complete inspection of the wafer than with either method by itself, but the ability to discriminate as to the type of defect.

In both the dark field, where any scattered light is observed, and the light field, where any deviation in the reflected scanned beam is observed, a fiber-optics line-to-spot collector (a bundle that collects linearly distributed optical information and translates it into a circular spot form) is used to configure the results of the scan line into a centrally located detector. In the dark field, the amount of scattered light collected is increased by placing a cylindrical lens in front of the fiber-optics collector. In the light field, the previously described target aperture becomes a narrow slit placed in front of a fiber-optics collector. It might be pointed out here that the same results may be achieved by use of a focusing lens or mirror, however, such elements would require an aperture in excess of 6 in with low f/numbers, and hence would be rather expensive. Although the fiber-optics collectors are somewhat less efficient, their lower cost and greater flexibility makes them a better choice for this application. The detectors used are photomultiplier tubes for the reasons outlined previously. Specifically, they have the sensitivity and frequency response necessary for high-speed scanning, and their large photosensitive area provides a good match for the fiber-optics collectors.

One of several possible system configurations is shown in Fig. 10. Key system components include a He–Ne laser (5 mW), folding optics, focusing lenses, rotating polygon to generate a laser scanning line, automatic wafer-handling system, optical detectors for scattered and specularly reflected light from the wafer, photomultiplier tubes, analog and digital processing circuits, microprocessor, video image of wafer surface with defect location, and hard copy printer.

In operation, the output of the He–Ne laser is focused to a 60-μm spot diameter and scanned across the surface of the wafer. Full surface coverage is provided by moving the wafer orthogonally through the scan line at a speed of 3.5 cm/s. Two fiber-optic collectors detect, respectively, scattered and specularly reflected light from the wafer surface. Photomultiplier tubes convert the collected light into electrical signals which are then processed by analog and digital electronics. These signals are delivered to a microprocessor, which constructs a map of the wafer in its memory along with the location of detected defects. Wafer status is determined and the wafer is

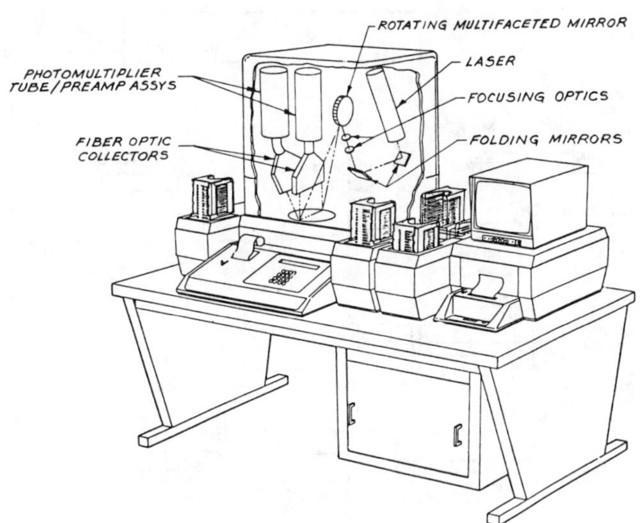

Fig. 10. Overall view of the WIS wafer inspection system.

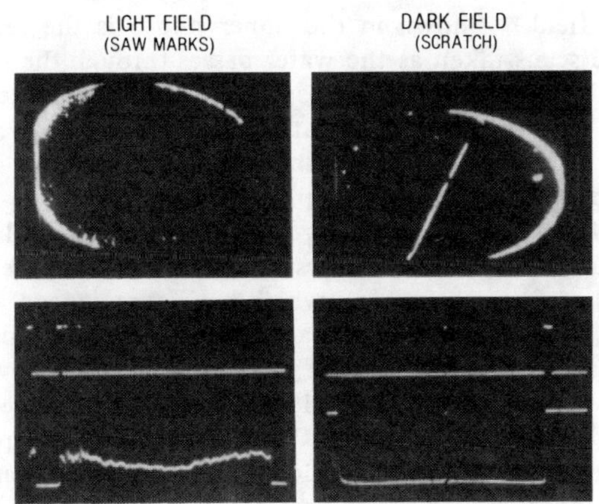

Fig. 11. Illustration of the signal outputs generated by the WIS.

sent to one of four possible stations; i.e., accept, reject, reclean, or repolish, depending on the nature of the defects found.

The processed electronic signals are arrived at by first passing the raw detected signal through appropriate amplifiers of selected frequency response to pass those signals of interest, and then thresholding the resulting signal to detect only those signals that are greater than a predetermined amplitude. Thus by passing the same signals through separate amplifiers of different frequency response and thresholding the unattenuated portion of the processed signal, information is gained as to the frequency of the detected signal. This approach is useful in the light field, where both low- and high-frequency signals are obtained. In the dark field, all signals of interest are high frequency. Here the same processed signal, from which any low-frequency components are removed, is fed to three separate threshold comparators, each at different amplitudes. The amplitude of the signal is determined based on the threshold at which it is detected. Because the scanned spot is generally larger than the defect being scanned, the signal amplitude in the dark field is directly proportional to the defect size. A microprocessor is used for analysis of the above information for defect identification and wafer sorting, as appropriate.

Outputs from the light- and dark-field detectors for a wafer with saw marks and a scratch are illustrated in Fig. 11. (The saw marks show as relatively high-frequency spheres on the left side of the light field trace only, while the scratch shows in

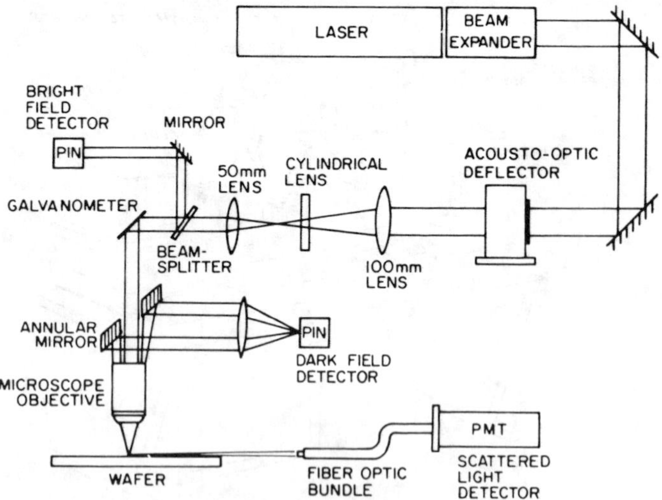

Fig. 12. The laser scanning microscope for patterned wafer surface inspection.

(a)

(b)

Fig. 13. Example of patterned wafer image on the LSM (a) and the result of using the particle detector (b).

the dark field.) Shown in the upper photo is the result of successive scans taken as the wafer passes through the scanner where all bright points on the display are the result of detected defects. The waveforms illustrated in the lower photo are the result of a typical scan across the wafer including the defect, and are the photomultiplier outputs.

3) LSM—Laser Scanning Microscope: Another application to IC wafer inspection involves the detection of defects on patterned wafers, i.e., wafers which have experienced various stages of processing and have patterns etched or deposited on their surfaces. The inspection of patterned wafers for unwanted defects is an extremely difficult task due to the presence of the complex surface pattern. Of interest from an inspection viewpoint is not only the detection of foreign defects (particles, dust, scratches, etc.) but also the pattern itself, i.e., the size of features, their relative location, integrity, etc. Here, the power of the human inspector, with his superior pattern recognition capability, is used for most inspection needs. However, if the problem is simplified somewhat by limiting the inspection to protruding surface particles, for example, a dust particle, laser scanning techniques have been developed to optically discriminate the defect from the pattern and hence a "particulate inspection" of the surface can be performed. One of the predominant defects encountered by a typical semiconductor VLSI manufacturing process is surface particles. Hence there is great interest and need for a system capable of performing this type of inspection. The systems discussed in the previous two examples for polished wafer surface inspection are not directly applicable, since the topography on patterned wafers, i.e., ridges, steps, etc., will scatter incident light in much the same way as defects.

A system called the Laser Scanning Microscope (LSM) has been developed for particle inspection of patterned semiconductor wafers [26]. The LSM illuminates the wafer surface with a scanning laser beam and presents a magnified image of the wafer surface on a television monitor. It has the ability to produce images similar to that of a conventional microscope, but in addition can produce an image of surface particles without imaging the pattern itself. Any or all of these separate images can be combined through electronic addition and/or subtraction to produce other useful images. The optical system of the laser microscope is shown in Fig. 12.

A He–Ne laser beam is expanded and passed through an acoustooptic deflector which scans the beam at the same rate as the horizontal line scan of a television monitor (53.5-μs constant velocity scan followed by a 10-μs flyback period). The scanned laser beam is transferred to a galvanometer scanner by means of a 2:1 telecentric lens system. The galvanometer executes a 60-Hz scan consistent with the television vertical scan rate. The laser beam, now scanned in two orthogonal directions, passes through a flat-field microscope objective and comes to a focus on the surface of the semiconductor wafer executing a raster scan.

Light that is reflected or scattered at low angles form the object is collected by the microscope objective and subsequently collimated. Some of this light passes through the hole in the annular mirror, is reflected by the galvanometer mirror, and is directed to a detector by means of a beamsplitter and an auxilliary mirror. The output of this detector provides a video image very similar to a bright-field microscope image. The remainder of the scattered light collected by the objective is intercepted by the edges of the annular mirror and is directed to a second detector. The video image produced at the output of this second detector contains higher spatial frequency information and corresponds to a dark-field microscope image.

Much of the light scattered from the patterned wafer is not captured by the microscope objective due to its limited aperture. Thus in a conventional microscope, the image information contained in this high-angle scattering is lost. In the laser microscope, this light is also detected to produce an additional video image, namely, that from particles or protrusions on the surface.

The basic goal in the design of the particle imaging system is

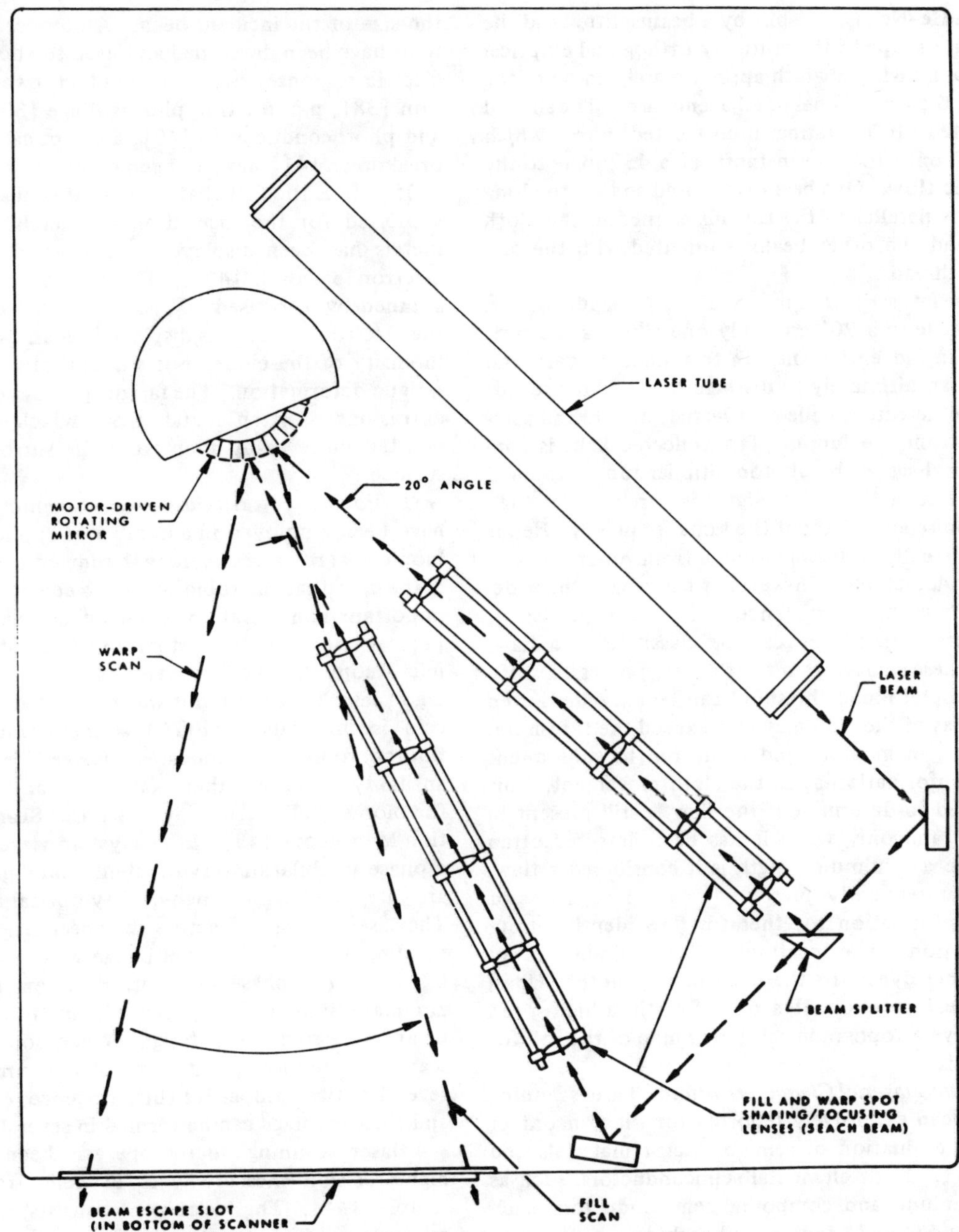

Fig. 14. Woven fabric inspection system.

that of maximizing the signal due to scattering from particles while minimizing the signal due to diffraction from the surface relief pattern. To accomplish this, an array of detectors is placed around the periphery of the wafer and positioned such that only light scattered at angles approaching $90°$ with respect to the surface is detected. Particles scatter a significant amount of light at very high angles due to their inherent shape, whereas the higher diffracted orders scattered from the pattern relief are relatively weak. Further discrimination between the particles and pattern signals is achieved by using a simple comparator circuit following the detector to eliminate any low-level signals from the pattern.

A typical image generated by the system is shown in Fig. 13. A bright-field image of a wafer area containing a 10-μm particle is shown in Fig. 13(a), where the field size is 175×130 μm (16X objective) and the focused spot size is approximately 2 μm. Fig. 13(b) shows the same image field using only the particle detector. As seen, only an image of the particle itself appears, making a visual inspection for particles a relatively simple task.

D. Other Applications

In this section, other applications of laser scanning microscopy are reviewed. A system which was developed for the inspection of woven fabric is discussed. Semiconductor material characterization and biomedical applications are also reviewed.

1) Woven Fabric Inspection: A system developed for the inspection of woven fabrics utilizes a scanning scheme similar to that employed for inspection of polished wafers described earlier (Section III-C2). The system has the capability to detect, identify, and mark the location of single yarn flaws for cloth widths up to 330 cm at throughput rates of 225 m/min [27].

The optical portion of this system is illustrated in Fig. 14.

The beam from a He–Ne laser is split by a beamsplitter and the resulting beams are shaped into mutually orthogonal elliptical shapes, each ellipse having a width approximately equal to the distance between the center lines of adjacent yarns. The shaped beams are reflected off a rotating, multifaceted mirror which directs the beams onto the woven fabric at a 45° angle to the direction of fabric flow. One beam is focused so that the long part of the oval is parallel to the threads aligned in the cloth flow direction, and the other beam is oriented with the perpendicular set of threads.

Since the two beams strike the mirror at a 20° angular offset, and the scan is made in a 20° arc, only one elliptical beam is on the cloth at any given instant. In this manner, warp and fill thread flaws can ultimately be distinguished. Three sets of fiber-optic bundle detectors collect reflected, direct, and scattered laser light from the fabric. The collected light is converted into electrical signals by photomultiplier tubes. In most cases, for a single scan the defect signal is barely larger than the background noise and of about the same frequency. Hence the defects are virtually indistinguishable from other areas of the trace, and undetectable. However, what makes these defects objectionable is their persistence. They must persist for several centimeters before they can be classified as a flaw. Therefore, once these signals from the flaw are processed sufficiently that a predetermined threshold can be exceeded, even though similar areas of the scan may also exceed the threshold, this scan is stored in memory and compared to subsequent scans along with information as to the cloth movement. This information is used to determine if the flaw is still present in subsequent scans, and only when it has been detected often enough to achieve a minimum length is it considered a flaw. The signals are subsequently presented to a microprocessor which links the information together for flaw identification, severity, and location. The location of flaws is indicated by spraying a washable dye onto the edge of the cloth. Upon completion of the inspection of a roll of cloth, a high-speed line printer displays a topographical defect map of the roll for subsequent analysis.

2) Semiconductor Material Characterization: Laser scanning techniques have been extensively reported for the noncontact investigation and evaluation of semiconductor materials and circuits [28]–[35]. Both elemental semiconductors, such as silicon and germanium, and compound semiconductors, such as gallium arsenide and indium phosphide, have been investigated.

The techniques developed can be divided into two broad categories [36]. First, those in which the input and output from the sample under investigation are optical. For example, the IR transmittance, reflectance, and photoluminescence [37] of semiconductor materials can provide information on internal inhomogeneities, impurity precipitations, photoionization effects, and inclusions of foreign material. An instrument called the Scanned Laser Infrared Microscope (SLIM) has been developed for such evaluations [14].

The second category includes those techniques in which an optical input is used to elicit an electrical response. Techniques in this category rely on the fact that incident optical radiation absorbed within a semiconductor will disturb the equilibrium distribution of carriers and hence the electrical properties of the sample. The extent of the modification of the electrical properties depends not only on the illumination but also on the properties of the material itself in the illuminated region. In principle then, techniques could be developed for measuring the electrical properties of a sample with a resolution set by the size of the incident beam. A number of laser scanning systems have been developed and used to elicit a variety of photoelectric responses from semiconductor specimens. Photoemission [38], p-n junction photovoltage [39], bulk photovoltage and photoconductance [40], and optically induced avalanche breakdown [41] have all been studied.

Of note is the fact that somewhat similar mechanisms can be exploited for the inspection of metals. Fatigue damage in metals has been displayed and assessed by means of photoelectron emission [42]. The surface of a fatigue sample is scanned by a focused UV laser, and the spatial distribution of the electron emission is displayed on an oscilloscope. The local intensity of the emission is a quantitative measure of the local fatigue deformation. The fatigue process generates microscopic extrusions of fresh metal, from which electrons are photoemitted more easily than from the surrounding oxide-coated surface.

3) Biomedical Applications: Scanning laser techniques have been employed in a number of applications in the area of biomedical research. Among the advantages of laser microscopy is the fact that microbiological objects need not be stained, an important consideration when living cells are to be observed [1]. A laser scanning system for use in automated fluorescence microscopy has been developed [15]. The system uses an argon laser (488 nm) and was optimized for use with fluorescein isothiocyanate (FITC) stained samples. FITC is the fluorochrome used almost exclusively in clinical fluorescent antibody tests. Another example of an instrument developed for biomedical microscopy is a Laser Scanning Phase Modulation Microscope [43]. In this system a laser flying spot scanner, a phase modulation servo system, and digital image processing are integrated with a high-quality optical research microscope. The laser is rastered across the specimen with galvanometers, yielding a 512×512 pixel image with potential resolution to 0.5 μm. The phase modulation system uses lead lanthanum zirconate titanate (PLZT) ceramic electrooptic light modulators in an innovative servo design. When combined with the laser scanner, it permits point-by-point measurement of any one of several optical properties (birefringence, optical rotation, etc.) and thus an image can be formed in several modes.

A laser scanning microscope has been employed to make high-precision measurements of cells from clinical cervical samples [44]. The instrument consists of a Leitz fluorescent microscope with epi-illumination. Illumination is available from three sources; tungsten and mercury lamps, and a He–Cd 10-mW laser (441 nm). The first two sources are used to locate and identify the cells; actual scanning measurements are made with the laser. The incident and emitted light are separated using a filter and dichroic mirror system to permit illumination below 455 nm and emission above 490 nm. A 0.5-μm spot is produced in the plane of the cells and is rastered across the cell with a vibrating mirror from top to bottom in the field, while the stage (under computer control) moves the slide laterally in 0.5-μm steps following the completion of each laser scan. In this manner, a field 50 μm $\times$ 50 μm is swept out. The specimens are stained with the DNA specific fluorochrome mithramycin, and the fluorescent images analyzed to give information on nuclear size, DNA content, and nuclear shape.

IV. Summary

In this paper we have presented the basic concepts of laser scanning microscopy, and reviewed various applications of the technique, particularly in the semiconductor industry. Laser microscopy was shown to offer several unique advantages over conventional imaging, and it is hoped that the various applications presented demonstrated these concepts.

The recent introduction of several commercial systems employing the principles of laser microscopy serves to illustrate the potential impact that the technique is predicted to have in the future. Improvements in optical system design, the use of shorter wavelengths with the resulting increase in resolution, and the continued use of more powerful electronic signal processing and analysis will extend the applications potential of laser scanning microscopy far beyond what is presented in this review.

REFERENCES

[1] C.J.R. Sheppard, "The scanning optical microscope," presented at the IEEE/OSA CLEA Conf., Washington, DC, June 1977.
[2] C. Cremer and T. Cremer, "Considerations on a laser scanning microscope with high resolution and depth of field," *Microscopica Acta*, vol. 81, no. 1, pp. 31–44, 1978.
[3] D. C. Gupta, B. Sherman *et al.*, "Non destructure semiconductor testing using scanned laser techniques," *Solid-State Technol.*, vol. 14, no. 3, pp. 44–50, Mar. 1971.
[4] D. E. Sawyer and D. W. Berning, "Thermal mapping of transistors with a laser scanner," *Proc. IEEE*, vol. 64, no. 11, pp. 1634–5, Nov. 1976.
[5] D. L. Fehrs, D. R. Munro, and J. D. Cuthbert, "Automatic laser inspection/laser repair system for masks," presented at the IEEE/OSA CLEA Conf., Washington, DC, May 1975.
J. D. Cuthbert, D. F. Munro, and D. L. Fehrs, "A microelectronic mask inspection system based on single spot laser scan techniques," *Japan. J. Appl. Phys.*, vol. 14, Suppl. 14-1, 1975.
[6] J. H. Bruning *et al.*, "An automated mask inspection system—AMIS," *IEEE Trans. Electron Devices*, vol. ED-22, no. 7, pp. 487–495, July 1975.
[7] P. Geise *et al.*, "A laser scanner for PC board inspection," *Electron. Packaging Production*, vol. 20, no. 12, pp. 152–163, Dec. 1980.
[8] R. H. Kingston, "Detection of optical and infrared radiation," in *Springer Series in Optical Sciences*, D. L. McAdam, Ed. New York: Springer, 1978.
[9] J. C. Leader, "Polarization dependence in EM scattering from Rayleigh scatterers embedded in a dielectric slab-theory I," *J. Appl. Phys.*, vol. 46, no. 10, pp. 4371–4385, 1975.
[10] D. P. Jablonowski, unpublished work, 1977.
[11] R. E. Frazee and L. S. Watkins, "Gold contact finger inspection using a scanning laser beam," *IEEE Trans. Ind. Electron. Contr. Instrum.*, vol. IECI-23, pp. 1–7, 1976.
[12] D. Kermisch, "Visualization of large variation phase objects," *Proc. SPIE*, vol. 74, pp. 126–129, 1976.
[13] D. J. Ketcham, "Real time image enhancement techniques," *Proc. SPIE*, vol. 74, pp. 120–125, 1976.
[14] B. Sherman and J. F. Black, "Scanned laser infrared microscope," *Appl. Opt.*, vol. 9, no. 4, pp. 802–809, 1970.
[15] A. F. Slomba *et al.*, "A laser flying spot scanner for use in automated fluorescence antibody instrumentation," *J. Assoc. Advancement of Medical Instrum.*, vol. 6, no. 3, pp. 230–234, May-June 1972.
[16] D. P. Jablonowski, "Interference position monitoring system employing ronchi gratings," *Rev. Sci. Instrum.*, vol. 47, no. 1, pp. 96–100, 1976.
[17] K. A. Stetson, "Holographic surface contouring by limited depth of focus," *Appl. Opt.*, vol. 7, no. 5, pp. 987–989, 1968.
[18] R. W. Berry *et al.*, *Thin Film Technology.* New York: D. Van Nostrand, 1968.
[19] R. A. Kaplan, "A microprocessor-controlled mask inspection and repair system," *Solid-State Technol.*, vol. 17, no. 4, pp. 74–78, Apr. 1976.
[20] D. J. Ehrlich *et al.*, "One-step repair of transparent defects in hard-surface photolithographic masks via laser photodeposition," *IEEE Electron Device Lett.*, vol. EDL-1, no. 6, pp. 101–103, June 1980.
[21] A. W. Warner, D. L. White, and W. A. Bonner, "Acousto-optic light deflectors using optical activity in paratellurite," *J. Appl. Phys.*, vol. 43, no. 11, pp. 4489–4495, 1972.
[22] D. R. Oswald and D. F. Munro, "A laser scan technique for electronic materials surface evaluation," *J. Elect. Mat.*, vol. 3, no. 1, pp. 225–242, Feb. 1974.
[23] A. D. Gara, "Automatic microcircuit and wafer inspection," *Electron. Test*, pp. 60–70, May 1981.
[24] NASA Tech Briefs, "Automatic inspection of silicon wafers," p. 403, Fall 1979.
[25] W. J. Patrick and E. J. Patzner, "The detection of surface defects on silicon wafers by scattered light measurements," in *Semiconductor Silicon*, by H. R. Huff and R. R. Burgess, Eds. pp. 482–490, 1973.
[26] R. L. Schmitt, "The laser scanning microscope," to be published.
[27] L. E. Seidel, "Cloth inspection: A better idea," *Textile Ind.*, Feb. 1978.
[28] E. D. Jungbluth and J. F. Black, "Scanning laser infrared microscopy of doping inhomogeneities in InAs single crystals," *Solid State Commun.*, vol. 13, pp. 1099–1105, 1973.
[29] J. N. Gannaway and T. Wilson, "Examination of grain boundaries in polycrystalline solar cells using a scanning optical microscope," *Electron. Lett.*, vol. 14, no. 16, pp. 507–8, Aug. 1978.
[30] E. D. Jungbluth, "Observations of impurity inhomogeneities in arsenic-doped silicon by scanning laser microscopy," *Appl. Phys. Lett.*, vol. 17, no. 10, pp. 437–440, Nov. 1970.
[31] N. N. Armencha *et al.*, "Leakage current channels in integrated circuits using a laser scanning microscope," *Mikros'laktrinika*, vol. 7, no. 1, pp. 66–69, Jan.–Feb. 1978.
[32] R. E. McMahon, "Laser tests IC's with light touch," *Electronics*, vol. 44, no. 8, pp. 92–95, Apr. 1971.
[33] D. L. Lile and N. M. Davis, "Semiconductor profiling using an optical probe," *Solid-State Electron.*, vol. 18, pp. 699–704, July-Aug. 1975.
[34] P. Shah and L. Crosthwait, "Laser assisted automated surface analysis in process control of large scale integrated circuits," presented at the IEEE/OSA CLEOS Conf., San Diego, CA, 1978.
[35] D. V. Lang and C. H. Henry, "Scanning photocurrent microscopy: A new technique to study inhomogeneously distributed recombination centers in semiconductors," *Solid-State Electron.*, vol. 21, pp. 1519–1524, Nov.–Dec. 1978.
[36] D. L. Lile and N. M. Davis, "Optical techniques for semiconductor material and circuit inspection," *Solid-State Technol.*, vol. 18, no. 6, pp. 29–32, July 1975.
[37] J. F. Black *et al.*, "Scanned-laser microscopy for photoluminescence studies," *Appl. Opt.*, vol. 4, no. 7, pp. 1553–1562, July 1972.
[38] T. H. DiStefano, "Barrier inhomogeneities on a Si–SiO$_2$ interface by scanning internal photoemission," *Appl. Phys. Lett.*, vol. 19, no. 8, pp. 280–292, 1971.
——, "Dielectric breakdown induced by sodium in MOS structures," *J. Appl. Phys.*, vol. 4, no. 1, pp. 527–528, 1973.
[39] J. R. Haberer, "Photoresponse mapping of semiconductors," *Phys. Failure Electron.*, vol. 5, pp. 51–82, 1967.
[40] D. L. Blackburn, H. A. Schafft, and L. J. Swartzendruber, "Nondestructive photovoltaic technique for the measurement of resistivity gradients in circular semiconductor wafers," *J. Electrochem. Soc.: Solid-State Sci. Technol.*, vol. 119, pp. 1773–1778, 1972.
[41] C. N. Potter and D. E. Sawyer, "Optical scanning techniques for semiconductor device screening and identification of surface and junction phenomena," *Phys. Failure Electron.*, vol. 5, pp. 37–50, 1967.
[42] W. J. Baxter, "Laser scanner for exoelectron display and measurement of fatigue damage," *JTEVA*, vol. 5, no. 4, pp. 243–250, July 1977.
[43] E. W. Hansen *et al.*, "Laser scanning phase modulation microscope," presented at the OSA Annual Meet., Orlando, FL, Oct. 1981.
[44] P. J. Mullaney *et al.*, *Models for Low Resolution Slit Scan Measurements Based on High Resolution Laser Scanning Image Analysis: DNA and Nuclear Dimensions, Pattern Recognition*, Elmsford, NY: Pergamon, 1981, vol. 13, pp. 49–55.

Review of Electromagnetic Methods in Nondestructive Testing of Wire Ropes

JAMES R. WAIT, FELLOW, IEEE

Abstract—Wire ropes are used extensively in many life sustaining situations. Elevator and mine-hoist cables are two notable examples, but the support cable for aerial tramways, ski chairlifts and gondolas, helicopter and suspension cables we might also mention. In this review, we will deal mainly with wire ropes used in mine hoists, but the results are also relevant for testing support cables for ski lifts. There is an obvious need to perform tests of the integrity of such ropes without in any way impairing their function. Apart from careful visual examination and measurements of the external diameter, the nondestructive test methods available utilize electromagnetic fields, X-rays, or mechanical waves. Here, we will review progress in the electromagnetic methods.

The early history of the subject will be described briefly, since this provides a remarkably good introduction to the working principles. We will then progress quickly to the current techniques and operating procedures. Next, we will summarize some of the basic papers that deal with the basic concepts and techniques for testing of cylindrical conductors by both electric and magnetic methods. At this juncture, we call our attention to the extensive related work on electromagnetic probing of geophysical targets such as ore bodies and other subsurface conductors. Finally, we turn to the various recent investigations, primarily of theoretical nature, that have been carried out; we include here only the most recent works.

INTRODUCTION

WIRE ROPES are used extensively in many life-sustaining situations. Both elevator and mine-hoist cables are two notable examples, but we might also mention the support cable for aerial tramways, ski chairlifts and gondolas, helicopter, and suspension cables. In this review, we will restrict attention to wire ropes used in mine hoists. There is an obvious need to perform tests of the integrity of such ropes without in any way impairing their function. Apart from careful visual examination and measurements of the external diameter, the nondestructive-test (NDT) methods available utilize electromagnetic fields, X-rays, or mechanical waves. Here we will review progress in the electromagnetic methods.

The early history of the subject will be described briefly since this provides a remarkably good introduction to the working principles. We will then progress quickly to the current techniques and operating procedures. Next we will summarize some of the basic papers that deal with the basic concepts and techniques for testing cylindrical conductors by both electric and magnetic methods. At this juncture, we call attention to the extensive related work on electromagnetic probing of geophysical targets such as ore bodies, and other subsurface conductors. Finally, we turn to the various investigations, primarily of a theoretical nature, that have been carried out; we include here only the most recent works.

Manuscript received May 17, 1978; revised November 16, 1978.
The author is with the Cooperative Institute for Research in Environmental Sciences, University of Colorado/NOAA, Boulder, CO 80309.

SOME EARLY NDT WORK IN ENGLAND

Wall [1] gives an early account of the design and operation of electromagnetic rope testers. The test results were given for specially constructed ropes. Using basically an ac technique, his method makes it possible to detect broken wires within a rope that represent less than 5-percent reduction in the total cross sectional area. As the author indicates, the investigation was motivated by the testing of wire ropes used in collieries in England. The author also indicates that other important applications are to tram cables, airship mooring ropes, and to suspension-bridge ropes.

Wall is an early proponent of the ac method as opposed to the dc magnetic testing favored in more recent times. He lists some of the advantages as follows: a) The rope need not continuously move through the magnetic system, b) The ac signal is easy to detect, and c) Any remnant magnetism due, say to a previous test, is wiped out.

He is interested in testing colliery ropes of the locked-coil type up to 2.25-in diameter. In such locked ropes, the outer and one or more of the inner layers are locked together to form flexible sheaths. This constrains the rope to maintain its circular form as it passes over the winding drum. He then quotes a classical skin-depth formula that gives a guide to the penetration of the ac currents into the core of the rope. He points out cogently, that once the ac energy penetrates through the outer locked-coil sheaths, it will be "practically" uniformly distributed through the remainder of the cross section since the wires are so effectively stranded.

The tests were made by means of a laminated iron yoke that has projecting limbs with machine-tunnelled holes as indicated in Fig. 1(a). The sample length of the rope was fixed concentrically in the holes. A search coil of 20 turns was wound around the center portion of the rope that is midway between the projecting limbs. The relationship between the flux density in the rope and the peak value of the magnetizing excitation at 20 and 50 Hz was measured. Wall was able to ascertain that the flux penetration was almost complete at 20 Hz, but only partially so at 50 Hz.

In the same pioneering paper, Wall studies the effect of mechanical strain on the magnetic permeability with special reference to ac excitation. He also examines the change in the reluctance of the air space due to the eccentricity of the rope in the magnet system.

Wall concludes that "whilst a flaw of about 3 percent of the total cross section is detectable, a flaw of about 5 percent produces a pronounced effect, whilst a flaw of about 18 percent gives a very striking disturbance of the record." Some of his results are summarized in Fig. 1(b).

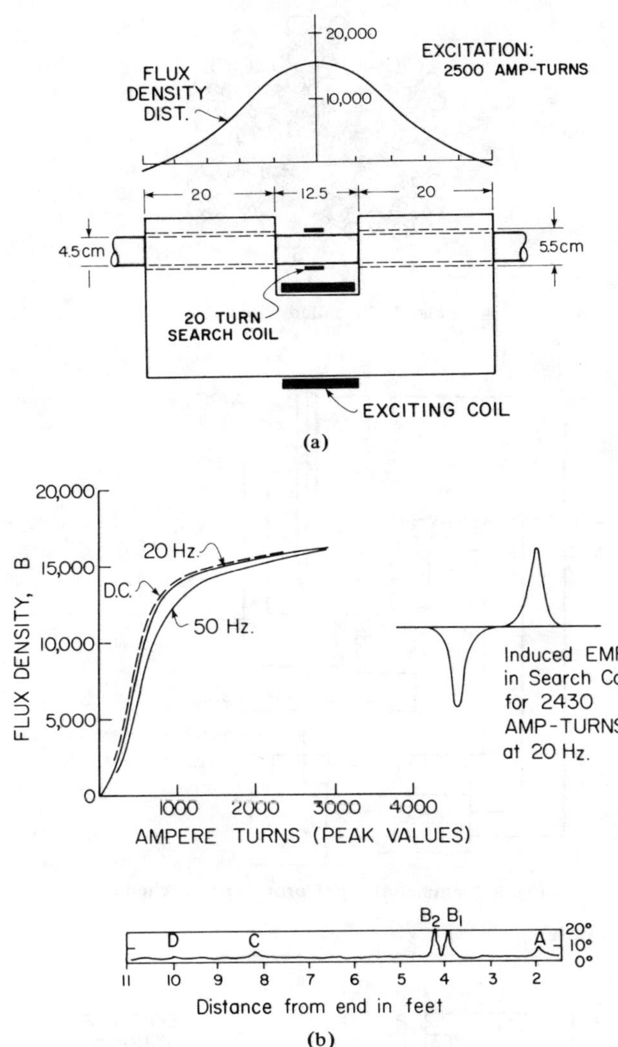

Fig. 1. (a) Sketch of Wall's device [1]. (b) Some data from Wall's test of a locked-coil rope. The B-H curve and the resulting induced EMF in the search coil. (EMF waveform amplitude not given.)

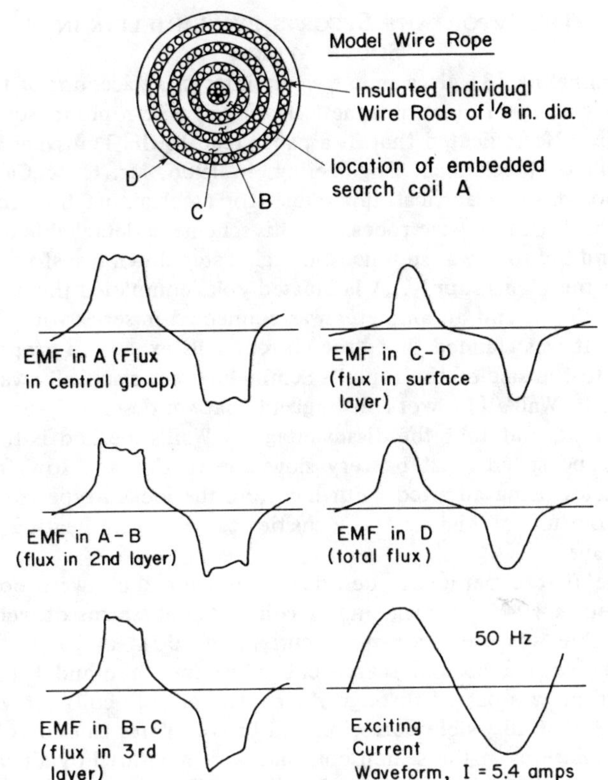

Fig. 2. Special model of a wire rope used by Wall and Hainsworth [2] to study internal fields.

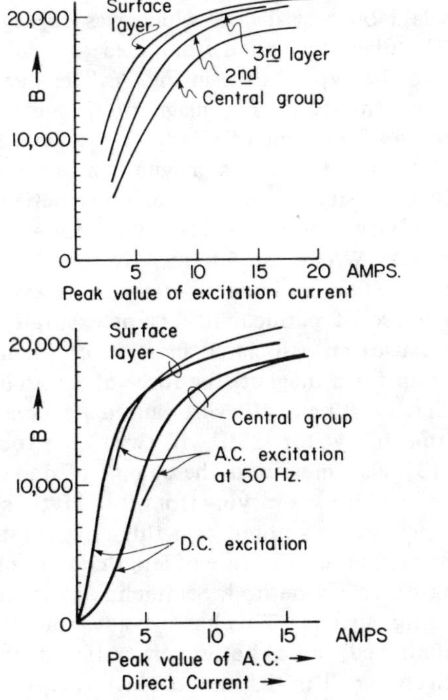

Fig. 3. Some measured data for the special wire rope model. (After Wall and Hainsworth [2].)

In a follow-up study, Wall and Hainsworth [2] investigate the way in which the flux is distributed within the rope. As they point out, this information is relevant to the estimation of the depth of a flaw in a locked coil or similar rope as used in collieries. They feel a mathematical approach to the problem is intractable. Instead, they build up a special sample or physical model with embedded search coils.

The experimental configuration was chosen to be a replica of a locked-coil rope except that the layers of wires were not so close as in actual ropes. Straight mild-steel wire rods of $\frac{1}{8}$ in diameter were employed, each rod was coated with insulating enamel before assembly. A first layer or central group of seven wires was formed and a search coil (A) of two-hundred turns was arranged to embrace this group. A second layer of twenty wires was then added and a search coil (B) embraced this layer. Next came the third layer with a further embracing search coil (C). Finally, a fourth layer of forty-four wires was formed and a search coil (D) embraced it. Each of the four search coils had two-hundred turns. Then by connecting pairs of consecutive search coils in opposition, it was possible to measure the flux magnitude associated with each layer.

The differences between the waveform of the induced EMF's in the various layers are very striking as indicated in Fig. 2.

Also, as indicated in Fig. 3, the B-H response curves are shown for central group and the surface layer. Here the screening effect for the central group is very apparent. For the surface layer, the situation is somewhat different since apparently the ac excitation has the effect of increasing the apparent permeability. To some extent this tends to counteract the eddy current screening.

THE IMPORTANT EFFORTS BY SEMMELINK IN SOUTH AFRICA

Semmelink [3] gives an extremely interesting account of the early history of electromagnetic testing of wire ropes in South Africa. He indicated that in a paper read to the Transvaal Institute of Mechanical Engineering, in 1906, Mr. C. McCann proposed an "electrical apparatus" for ascertaining the cross sectional area of wire ropes. In this scheme, a detachable coil around the rope was supplied through a step-down transformer from the mains supply. A laminated yoke completed the magnetic circuit and an ammeter was connected in series with the coil. It was claimed that "the current falls exactly in proportion to the size of the rope." Semmelink was also well aware of T. F. Wall's [1] work in England that we described above. He points out that the disadvantage of Wall's method is that the rope speed must be very slow due to the very low frequencies being adopted. Furthermore, the locked-type ropes and the use of high-ac flux densities causes severe heating of the rope.

The first experiments described by Semmelink were conducted in 1946. A magnetizing coil of twenty turns of welding cable was used carrying a current of 100 A at 50 Hz together with a coaxial search coil of several thousand turns. The rope was passed through the centers of both coils. It was found that all visible corrosion and broken wires caused voltage variations in the search coil that were measured by a peak reading voltmeter and an oscilloscope. Semmelink [3] then tested about fifty main winding (hoist) ropes. The tensile strength of the wire was either 123/134 tons (2000 lb)/in^2, or 128/140 tons/in^2. The ropes had six strands of approximately thirty wires laid on a sisal core which was impregnated with lubricant. The diameter varied from 1.25 to 2 in. The ropes were similar to the type shown in Fig. 4. The steel was ascertained to have the following magnetic properties: relative permeability = 44 for a magnetizing force less than 1 Oe, maximum permeability = 320 for a magnetizing force of 25 Oe, maximum flux density = 14000 G for a magnetizing force of 200 Oe, retentivity = 9500 G, coercive force = 20 Oe, hysteresis loss = 0.35 W/cm^3 at 50 Hz. He found, what is now generally known, that an increase of tensile stress in the wire causes an increase of permeability. For example, a stress of 65 tons/in^2 causes an associated increase of permeability of 14 percent even for a magnetizing force of less than 1 Oe. He also noted that twisting of the wire caused a decrease of 8 percent of permeability for 180° of twist per foot of wire. Semmelink [3] also measured the change of dc resistance of the wire rope for stresses varying from 0 to 70 tons/in.^{2} Only 1.1 percent increase was noted over this range that was in accord with the percentage increase of length due to elasticity.

In deciding on an ac method, Semmelink chose to employ a low magnetizing current. This has two advantages: a) internal heating is minimized, and b) better penetration of the rope due to the relatively small initial permeability (i.e., he is working on the virgin part of the B-H curve). A schematic of his measuring scheme is indicated in Fig. 5.

In a later paper, Semmelink [4] describes a more sophisticated approach to the eddy-current testing of wire ropes. The schematic diagram of his measurement setup is illustrated in Fig. 6. As indicated, the rope is excited by spaced coaxial coils and the pickup coil is located centrally. The output of the pickup coil is amplified and detected by a phase-sensitive detector.

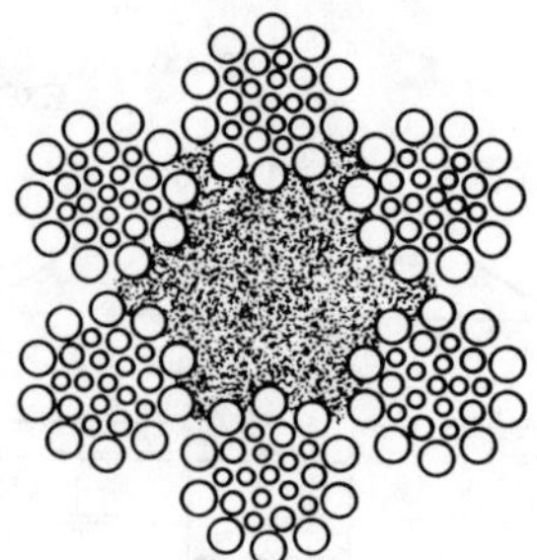

Fig. 4. Stranded wire rope.

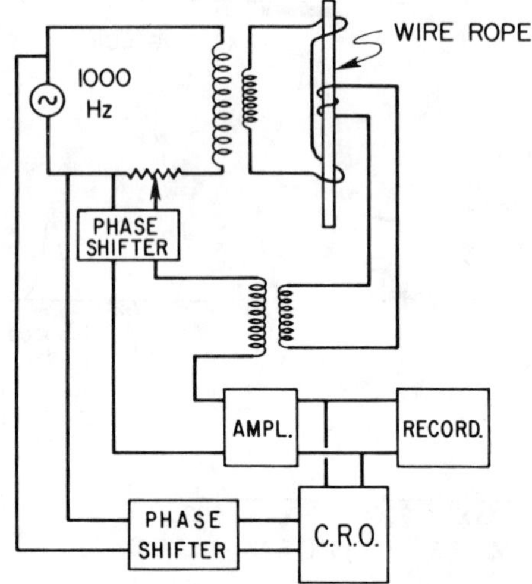

Fig. 5. Semmelink's [3] prototype ac scheme.

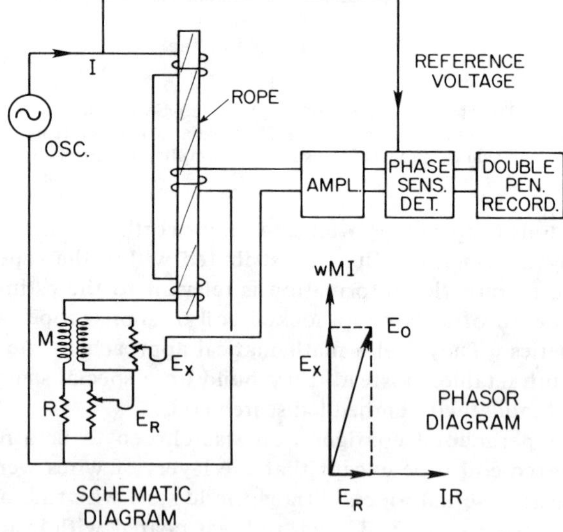

Fig. 6. Improved model use by Semmelink [4].

In the absence of eddy currents, the pickup or search-coil voltage leads the magnetizing current by 90°. However because of the eddy current losses, the phase shift is modified as indicated in Fig. 6. Both the reactive component E_x, and the resistive component E_R, can be balanced out in an appropriate adjustment of the potentiometers. Thus the "output" for a given rope can be indicated on a double pen recorder.

The rope speed during a test depends on the response of the recorder and the detector circuit. Furthermore, due to the choice of a low-operating frequency (e.g., 80 Hz), the response of the detectors cannot be fast and Semmelink chooses a time-constant of 0.1 s. Thus if the shortest variation to be detected along the rope is 10 cm, the rope speed should not exceed 10 cm in 0.1 s (i.e., the rope speed should be less than 200 ft/min).

The coils, wound on a Bakelite former are 6 in long, with 5 in outer diameter, and 3-in inner diameter. The two magnetizing coils have 10 turns each. For a magnetizing current of 1 A, this gives an exciting field at the center of 0.43 Oe. The pickup or search coil also has ten turns. The whole assembly is hinged with spring-loaded contacts to maintain the electrical integrity needed when the two halves are clamped around the rope.

A number of interesting results have been obtained by Semmelink [4]. For example, a decrease of eddy currents causes an increase of flux with a resulting increase on the E_x trace and a corresponding decrease on the E_R trace. This often is associated with decreased contact between the strands. The reverse situation has also been found when there is increased contact between the strands. Such stressful situations occur at the crossover points where ropes pass from one layer to another on winding drums.

Slight corrosion in the rope leads to a deposit of nonconducting material between the wires, and to a reduction of eddy currents. This usually means a decrease of both E_x and E_R traces. Semmelink also indicates that internal corrosion appears to occur usually over relatively short lengths, often at intervals corresponding to the circumference of the drum.

External corrosion manifests itself in a large reduction of the E_x trace but only a small reduction in the E_R trace. Such corrosion can occur over long lengths of the rope (e.g., 1000 ft).

Semmelink [4] found that inadvertent dc magnetization of the rope (e.g., from the earth's magnetic field) could lead to violent transients in the E_x trace when the rope moves at high speed through the coil assembly. In one case, the rope had remained at rest for long periods with one section of the rope extending from the drum to the headgear sheave in a northerly direction.

MORE RECENT APPLICATIONS AND PRACTICES

Hiltbrunner gives a good description of what is known now as the dc magnetic-testing method [5]. This approach has been highly developed in Switzerland for the NDT of tramway wire ropes. Essentially, the method is based on imposing a strong axial magnetic field to the sample by either a solenoid coil and/or permanent magnet. The search coil is oriented in the radial direction and produces a voltage response only when there is some type of lateral nonuniformity.

Lang gives an extensive description of an ac testing device for wire ropes [6]. Although he does not acknowledge the fact, the concept, method, and operational procedure seem to be based on the earlier work of Semmelink [3], [4]. However, Lang uses only one single-turn transmitting coil with a coaxial search coil. Most of his data are shown for a frequency of 30 Hz. Lang found that in all cases of broken wires detected, the "X" trace shows a sharp reduction presumably due to a decrease in the axial magnetic flux. In a number of cases, sections of rope with apparent missing wires were found. This was believed to indicate a wire separation at a faulty spot weld. It is unfortunate that the numerous test results published by

Lang are not accompanied by "ground truth" information on the actual state of the rope. He does show a few interesting comparisons between the measured breaking tensile strength and the "R" and "X" readings at 10 Hz, for locked-coil ropes. Such data however, were not provided for the 30 and 80 Hz tests on the stranded ropes.

Larsen *et al.* describes various devices for both dc and ac rope testing that are currently available [7]. They mention that the Rotesco device, as described by Lang [6], has been successful in 1970 in predicting tensile reductions of about 5 percent, although the extensive comparisons were not "quantitative."

Morgan [8] presents a general review of electromagnetic NDT methods applied to wire ropes. The discussion is entirely qualitative. He makes a number of recommendations for further development in Australia. Morgan and Symes [9] then describe the activities that led to the creation of a government-sponsored project at the University of New South Wales. They give a largely qualitative description of their current research on both methods of testing wire ropes. They also describe some tentative ideas about an ac device that is to operate at a frequency of 1 kHz. Surprisingly, they make no mention of many ac devices that hitherto have been used elsewhere. It is possible that they will find that 1 kHz is rather too high a frequency for effective penetration to the core of most mine-hoist ropes.

Stachurski [10] gives a very useful summary of the physical concepts employed in dc magnetic testing for flaws in wire ropes. A number of interpretative schemes are outlined in a qualitative manner. Also he uses prescribed forms of flaws, breaks, and cracks to calibrate the device. Much useful data on the design and implementation of the defectograph device are also given. It is evident that this Polish group has developed the dc magnetic technique to a high degree.

Egen and Benson [11] describe some interesting tests on a specially prepared rope with prescribed types of imperfections. There were seven types of faults: 1) splice; 2) two to three wires filed halfway through, over a length of about 0.5 in; 3) an added no. 18 AWG wire laid into groove of core; 4) spikes inserted into core and wires were spread apart; 5) three wires of 2 in length were removed from the core; 6) one wire in core was cut; and 7) a 2-in length of core was removed; all of these were done using three dc devices (the Polish MD-8 Defectoscope, the Swiss PMK-75 Kundig device, and the Canadian Rotesco device). None of these devices detected fault no. 6, and the Kundig device did not detect fault no. 2. Otherwise, all other faults were detected by all three instruments. The results indicated, that for the rope tested (i.e., $\frac{7}{8}$ in diameter, 6 × 25, FW, RLL, FC, XIPS), each instrument observed about the same magnetic-field variations. The very similar performance of these three instruments is probably a consequence of the basic similarity of the operating principle of each of these dc devices. It is a pity that the ac Rotesco device was not tested on the same rope.

Bergander [12] describes the Polish dc magnetic device for the NDT of wire ropes known as the Defectograph MD-8 that he developed with Stachurski [12]. The rope being tested moves through the permanent magnet which is magnetized to its saturation point. He claims that a 0.2-percent change of the rope cross section can be detected via a measurement of the external magnetic-leakage field. The EMF induced in the search coil can also be compensated for changes in the rope speed. Using an empirical approach the probe-coil response is related to such parameters as the loss of cross section of the rope, the length over which the loss occurs, and the radial location of the internal flaw.

EARLY THEORETICAL INVESTIGATIONS

Hochschild [13] gives a review of papers by Förster [14]–[18] and presents some useful plots of the current density in conducting cylinders for ac excitation by a solenoidal coil. He points out that no matter how carefully the test-coil system is designed, small defects will go undetected unless, the response time of the instrument is less than the time taken from the defect to pass through the effective region of the coils. For example, a localized defect passing though a 0.03-in-wide differential test coil at 100 ft/min will not be detected unless the response extends upwards to at least 200 Hz. A common limitation on bandwidth is the ink-pen recording devices, whose frequency response seldom exceeds 200 Hz.

McClurg [19] also exhibits some of the results of Förster and colleagues in graphical form. In particular, he shows that the impedance variations of solenoids (i.e., feed-through coils) encircling cylindrical conductors that have surface and subsurface cracks. The empirical data used are from papers by Förster. McClurg discusses the application of these eddy-current techniques to metal-cutting operations where such things as uniformness of the hardness is desirable.

Graneau introduces the interesting concept that induced currents in a conductor, flowing along closed curves, can be represented by a number of filamentary circuits [20]. These currents and the energizing current can then be deduced in principle from a system of circuit equations with both self- and mutual inductances that are postulated from the physics of the problem. Using somewhat heuristic reasoning, Graneau obtains an expression for the current anywhere in the metallic object by infinite series of increasing powers of the energizing frequency. The coefficients are undetermined functions of the filament circuit resistance, and mutual inductances between the filaments. He concludes that there is a clear division between quantities depending on geometry and properties. As a consequence, the induced currents can be expressed as an explicit function of frequency. This is really quite strange since exact solutions of idealized forms such as layered cylinders with external dipole excitation do not exhibit this behavior [21]–[25].

RELATED INVESTIGATIONS IN GEOPHYSICAL PROSPECTING

Electromagnetic methods of NDT of solid conductors are closely akin to techniques that are now used in geophysical prospecting for metallic-ore bodies [21]–[34]. It is unfortunate that these two groups have had little interaction. This writer was involved in the theoretical developments in multifrequency and transient-electromagnetic methods in geophysical exploration. In fact, as long ago as 1950, it was proposed that conductivity and permeability of a spherical-ore body could be ascertained from its electromagnetic response in either the frequency or its time domain. A similar analysis was carried out for a cylindrical-ore body with a specified conductivity and permeability. The basic concept was that geometrical configuration of both the source and receiver coils with respect to the target could be arranged to have a negligible effect of the determination of ore body size, conductivity and permeability. The subject has advanced considerably since

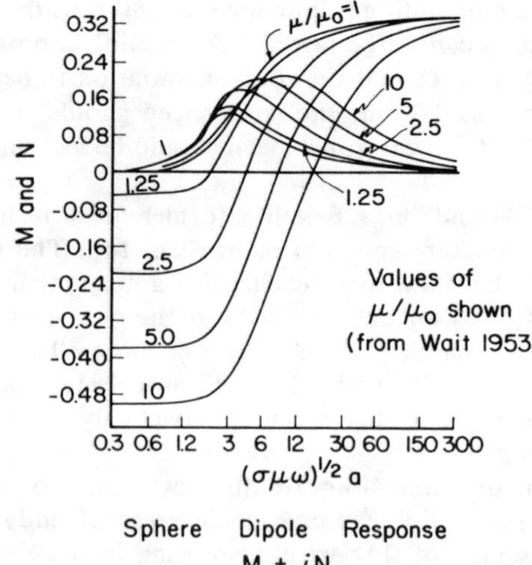

Fig. 7. Induced magnetic dipole for a conducting permeable sphere as a function of its conductivity σ, permeability μ, angular frequency ω, and radius a.

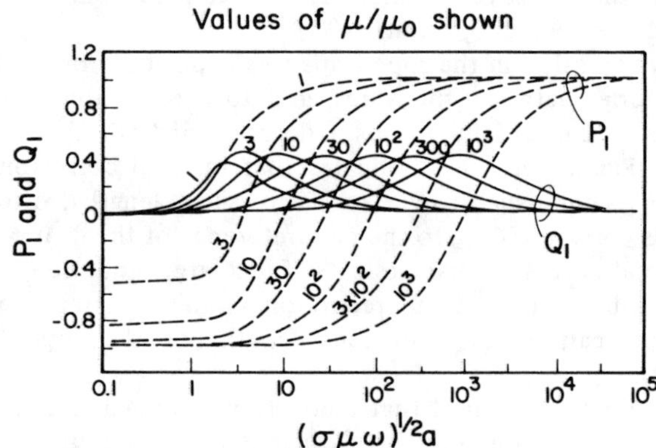

Cylinder   Dipole   Response

$$R_1 = P_1 + iQ_1$$

(from Wait 1952, 1960)

Fig. 8. Induced (line) magnetic dipole for a conducting permeable cylinder.

those "early days" and modern accounts are published regularly in *Geophysics*, the journal of the (U.S.) Society of Exploration Geophysicists, and *Geophysical Prospecting*, the journal of the European Society of Geophysical Exploration.

The work that is relevant to the electromagnetic probing of wire ropes is the analysis of a homogeneous conductive and permeable cylinder of infinite length. In an "early" paper [22], a general solution was given for the total fields produced when a line source or current-carrying cable was located parallel to the cylinder. An exact two-dimensional solution was obtained using a wave impedance approach. The low-frequency version of the general solution was expressed in a quasi-static form and numerical results for the induced dipole term were given. Some examples are shown in Figs. 7 and 8 for the induced magnetic-dipole responses of spheres and cylinders. In each case the ordinates are proportional to the induced-dipole moment. Strictly speaking, the monopole term should also be considered when dealing with cylinders that are effectively infinite in length. This type of analysis was later extended to dipolar excitation of the infinite cylinder when again the monopole or azimuthally independent induced current was not considered in the numerical examples [22].

Further work on this subject was carried out by Hill and Wait [30], where more realistic situations were treated such as the excitation of a conductive cylinder of finite length by an external magnetic dipole where all significant induced monopole, dipole, and multipole contributions were retained in the calculations. The analytical and numerical techniques used in these papers would seem to be applicable in a quantitative analyses of electromagnetic NDT of solid conductors.

MORE RECENT ANALYTICAL STUDIES

Vein [35] points out what is usually accepted—that the mutual impedance between two closed circuits is dependent on conducting solids in the immediate environments. He promotes the concept of transfer impedance but feels ill at ease in relating this to the reciprocity theorem for generally continuous media. With this motivation, he works through the analytical details of a number of classical problems such as the mutual impedance between coaxial-circular loops in the presence of planar, cylindrical, and spherical conductors. He assumes without really providing a justification, that azimuthal symmetry prevails in each case. No real harm is done, however, since no numerical results of any kind are provided. The derivations seem to be unnecessarily complicated, and even then, reliance is made on formulas quoted from exercises in W. R. Smythe's classic text [36].

Burrows, in a significant thesis, exploits the reciprocity theorem in eddy-current testing and the subsequent development of a flaw-detection theory [37]. He is very quick to recognize the limitations of quasi-static theory such as assumed by Vein [35]. But it should be stressed immediately that Burrows actually assumes azimuthal symmetry of his detection coils even though the "flaws" may be asymmetrical. This is a valid procedure but it appears that some fundamental information is lost when both the source and the probe coil fully encircle the cylindrical sample. Burrows represents internal flaws in terms of induced electric and magnetic dipoles, that in turn produce the secondary influence. He also provides some very useful tabulations of the infinite integrals that describe the internal fields within both solid cylindrical and tubular samples of circular cross sections for azimuthally symmetric excitation. These same integrals can be used to predict the response in a corresponding azimuthally symmetric detector coil due to an internal (small) flaw. Actually, this same approach has been followed up very recently by Hill and Wait who did not restrict the results to azimuthal symmetry of the probe coil [38].

Dodd et al. [39] have obtained integral solutions for the vector potential produced by a circular coil for a number of different geometrical configurations. The solutions are limited to axial symmetry. In calculating the exciting fields of a rectangular cross section circular coil, they assume that a straightforward superposition of current over the cross section is valid. This is a quasi-static assumption that probably needs to be investigated, particularly when the coil of finite width and length encircles a highly conducting cylinder.

Dodd et al. quote Burrows' formulation [37] for deducing the secondary-induced voltages due to a defect or flaw in an adjacent conductor. Here they write down a formula for the defect-produced voltage, induced in coil no. 2, by a current in

coil no. 1 in terms of the electric and magnetic scattering matrices for an electrically small defect.

In the same paper, Dodd et al. give explicit solutions in integral form for the rectangular cross sectional coil located over a two-layer planar conductor. Actually, the form of these solutions are very similar to earlier investigations of electromagnetic induction in layered models of the earth's crust. The NDT community is apparently not aware of this extensive literature. An example is the book by Keller and Frischknecht [40] that reviews the current status of such problems at least up to 1965. Of course, Dodd et al. give the explicit form of the fields of a circular coil with rectangular cross section, while the geophysicists restrict their attention to small loops. Dodd et al. also give solutions for various combinations of pickup coils and the corresponding secondary effects due to embedded defects that can be characterized by the polarizability matrices mentioned above.

Cheng et al. [41] have presented a general formulation for the time-harmonic eddy currents, produced by a circular coil of rectangular cross section, for a underlying planar conductor of any number of layers. The integral solutions obtained in a straightforward fashion yield algebraically complicated results. A number of these results could have been obtained by use impedance methods based on analogies with transmission-line theory (see for example [42] and [43]).

Dodd et al. [44] give a formal vector potential solution to a coil coaxial with any number of cylindrical conductors. While they state the derivation is quite general, the solution is only carried through for complete symmetry about the common axis.

Dodd and Deeds [45] give the same solutions for a uniform coil with uniform ac current excitation over a two-layer planar conductor. They then repeat the solution for the coil encircling a two-layer cylindrical conductor of infinite length. A single numerical example is given for the normalized impedance of the coil as over the two-layer planar structure that exhibits the effect of the thickness of the upper layer.

Kahn et al. [46] present an interesting analysis of how eddy currents in a solid conductor are diverted around a surface crack. One of the basic assumptions is that the magnetic field tangent to the surface is a constant even in the presence of the crack. They also present solutions for diffraction by a semi-infinite crack (i.e., a half-plane) in an otherwise infinite medium. Neither of these solutions are "rigorous" as claimed by the authors, but the results do provide considerable insight into how defects, of other than infinitesimal size, will modify to external fields. Kahn and Spal [47] have also presented some results for the calculations of eddy currents in a long cylinder with a radial crack at the surface. Details of the analytical methods are not yet available but presumably the approach is similar to that used in treating the surface crack in the planar conductor. It is appropriate to call attention to the close similarity of such problems to earlier theoretical studies in geophysics, where one is interested in the perturbation of time-varying geomagnetic fields near coastlines [48] and other laterally varying features in the earth's crust [49].

AN ALTERNATIVE FORMULATION FOR SOLENOID EXCITATION

As has been indicated, a common method of NDT of metal rods and tubes is to induce eddy currents by means of an encircling solenoid carrying an alternating current. The impedance of the solenoid is related to the cross sectional area

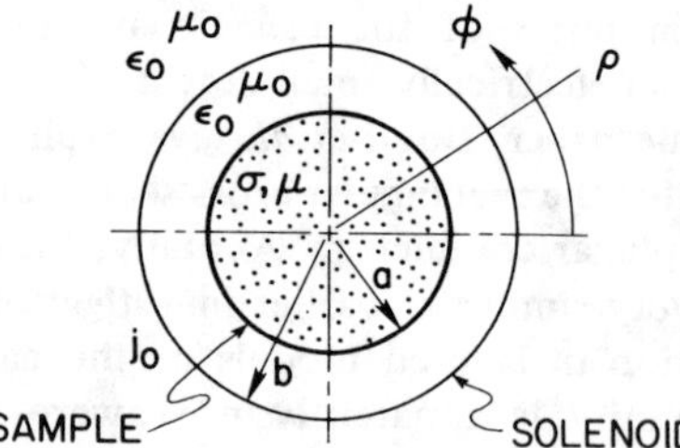

Fig. 9. Cross sectional view of cylindrical sample located centrally.

and the electrical properties of the sample. A formula for this impedance was obtained by Förster and Stambke [16] on the assumption that end effects could be ignored. Also they assumed that the cylindrical sample was centrally located within the solenoid. The same derivation was essentially repeated by Hochschild [13] and Libby [51].

A feature of the Förster–Stambke derivation is that the effect of the air gap is introduced in a somewhat heuristic fashion wherein the field in this concentric region is assumed to be the same as the one for the empty solenoid. We feel it is worthwhile to provide a more general derivation of the impedance formula. We also show it applies to the case of a non-concentric air gap. Finally, we mention the relevance of the current analysis to the dual problem where the cylindrical sample is excited by a toroidal coil.

To simplify the discussion, we consider first the concentric air gap model with a homogeneous cylindrical sample of radius a, with conductivity σ, and magnetic permeability μ. The situation is indicated in Fig. 9 where the solenoid of radius b encloses the sample, both of which are assumed to be infinite in length. Our objective is to find an expression for the impedance of the solenoid per unit length since this is the basis of the NDT eddy-current methods that are commonly used.

In terms of cylindrical coordinates (ρ, ϕ, z), the only component of the magnetic field is H_z, since the exciting current in the solenoid is uniform in both the axial and azimuthal direction. Within the sample, H_z satisfies the Helmholtz equation

$$(\nabla^2 - \gamma^2) H_z = 0 \tag{1}$$

where $\gamma^2 = i\sigma\mu\omega$, and where we have adopted a time factor $\exp(i\omega t)$. Here, ω is the angular frequency that is sufficiently low so displacement currents in the sample can be neglected. If not, we merely replace σ by $\sigma + i\epsilon\omega$, where ϵ is the permittivity. Also, it goes without saying that the field amplitude is sufficiently small that nonlinear effects can be ignored.

For the highly idealized situation described, we can immediately write [52]

$$H_z = A I_0(\gamma\rho) \tag{2}$$

for $\rho < a$, where I_0 is a modified Bessel function of argument $\gamma\rho$, and where A is a constant. From Maxwell's equations the azimuthal component of the electric field is

$$E_\phi = -(1/\sigma)\,\partial H_z/\partial\rho = -A(\gamma/\sigma) I_1(\gamma\rho) \tag{3}$$

also for $\rho < a$. Now we can immediately form an expression for the "impedance" Z_c of the cylinder

$$Z_c = [-E_\phi/H_z]_{\rho=a} = \eta I_1(\gamma a)/I_0(\gamma a) \tag{4}$$

where, $\eta = \gamma/\sigma = (i\mu\omega/\sigma)^{1/2}$ is the intrinsic or wave impedance of the sample material.

Now, for the air gap region $a < \rho < b$, we write corresponding field expressions

$$H_{0z} = B I_0(\gamma_0\rho) + C K_0(\gamma_0\rho) \tag{5}$$

$$E_{0\phi} = -B\eta_0 I_1(\gamma_0\rho) + C\eta_0 K_1(\gamma_0\rho) \tag{6}$$

where B and C are constants $\eta_0 = \gamma_0/(i\epsilon_0\omega) = (\mu_0/\epsilon_0)^{1/2} \cong 120\pi$ in terms of the permittivity ϵ_0, and permeability μ_0, of the air region. Here and above, the Bessel function identities $\partial I_0(x)/\partial x = I_1(x)$ and $\partial K_0(x)/\partial x = -K_1(x)$ have been employed.

Compatible with the requirement that tangential fields must be continuous at $\rho = a$ we can write

$$[E_{0\phi} + Z_c H_{0z}]_{\rho=a} = 0. \tag{7}$$

This immediately tells us that

$$\frac{C}{B} = \frac{\eta_0 I_1(\gamma_0 a) - Z_c I_0(\gamma_0 a)}{\eta_0 K_1(\gamma_0 a) + Z_c K_0(\gamma_0 a)}. \tag{8}$$

In the external region $\rho > b$, the field expressions must clearly have the form:

$$H_{0z} = D K_0(\gamma_0\rho) \tag{9}$$

$$E_{0\phi} = D\eta_0 K_1(\gamma_0\rho) \tag{10}$$

where D is another constant.

Now the solenoid current is idealized as a continuous-current distribution j_0 amperes per meter in the azimuthal direction defined such that

$$\lim_{\Delta\to 0} \begin{cases} H_{0z}(\rho = b + \Delta) - H_{0z}(\rho = b - \Delta) = -j_0 & (11) \\ E_{0\phi}(\rho = b + \Delta) - E_{0\phi}(\rho = b - \Delta) = 0. & (12) \end{cases}$$

Application of these conditions immediately leads to

$$D = C - I_1(\gamma_0 b) B/K_1(\gamma_0 b) \tag{13}$$

and

$$B = j_0 \gamma_0 b K_1(\gamma_0 b). \tag{14}$$

Among other things, this tells us that the magnetic field external to the solenoid (i.e., $\rho > b$) has the form

$$H_{0z} = \{-B[I_1(\gamma_0 b)/K_1(\gamma_0 b)] + C\} K_0(\gamma_0\rho). \tag{15}$$

The quantity of immediate interest is the impedance Z of the solenoid itself. Clearly, within the limits of our basic assumptions,

$$Z = \text{const.} \times E_{0\phi}(\rho = b)/j_0. \tag{16}$$

The corresponding impedance of the empty solenoid is denoted Z_0. Thus it follows that

$$\frac{Z}{Z_0} = 1 - \frac{C}{B} \frac{K_1(\gamma_0 b)}{I_1(\gamma_0 b)} \tag{17}$$

which is explicit since C/B is given by (8).

We now can simplify the impedance ratio formula if we invoke the small argument approximations for Bessel functions of order $\gamma_0 a$ and $\gamma_0 b$. That is, we use $I_0(x) \simeq 1$, $I_1(x) \simeq x/2$, $K_0(x) \simeq -\log x$, and $K_1(x) \simeq 1/x$. This exercise leads to

$$\frac{Z}{Z_0} \cong \left[1 - \frac{a^2}{b^2} + \frac{\mu}{\mu_0} \frac{a^2}{b^2} \frac{2}{\gamma a} \frac{I_1(\gamma a)}{I_0(\gamma a)}\right] = \frac{R + iX}{Z_0} \tag{18}$$

where no restriction has been placed on the magnitude of γa. Here R and X denote the resistance and reactance, respectively.

The formula for Z/Z_0 given by (18) is in agreement with Förster and Stambke [16] (if one remembers they used the old German designations J_0 and J_1 for modified Bessel functions). Förster and Stambke [16], Hochschild [13], and Libby [51] present extensive numerical data for this quasi-static approximation to Z/Z_0 in Argand diagrams in the complex plane for various values of $|\gamma a|$ and μ/μ_0. Two examples, using dimensionless parameters, are shown in Figs. 10 and 11 when the ordinates and abscissas are normalized by X_0 which is the reactance of the empty solenoid. That is, we assume $Z_0 \simeq iX_0$ corresponding to negligible ohmic losses in the solenoid itself. The real parameter α is defined by $\alpha = \gamma a \exp \cdot (-i\pi/4) = (\sigma\mu\omega)^{1/2}a$. In Fig. 10, the sample radius b is assumed to be the same as the sample radius a (i.e., no air gap). Different values of the magnetic permeability are shown. Not surprisingly, when α is small, R vanishes and X/X_0 tends to μ/μ_0. However, in general, the eddy currents have the effect of reducing X/X_0, which is the effective flux, and of introducing a resistive portion R/X_0. In Fig. 11, the relative permeability of the sample $\mu/\mu_0 = 1$ but the filling factor a^2/b^2 assumes different values. The results indicate that the presence of the air gap reduces the sensitivity of the device for probing the conductivity but the effect is predictable.

Actually, if α is sufficiently small (i.e., $|\gamma a| \ll 1$), equation (18) reduces to

$$Z/Z_0 \simeq X/X_0 \simeq 1 + (a^2/b^2)[\mu/\mu_0 - 1] \qquad (19)$$

which is consistent with the curves in Figs. 10 and 11. In this dc limit the results only depend on the magnetic permeability of the sample.

The formal extension of the theory to the case where the exciting solenoid is no longer concentric with the cylindrical sample can also be dealt with. The situation is indicated in Fig. 12. As before, cylindrical coordinates (ρ, ϕ, z) are chosen coaxial with the sample. But now, the shifted coordinates (ρ', ϕ', z) are chosen to be coaxial with the exciting solenoid. The shift is ρ_0 as indicated in Fig. 12 where we do impose the rather obvious physical restriction that $b > \rho_0 + a$. We may show that the field in the nonconcentric air gap has the form [50]

$$H_{0z} = BI_0(\gamma_0\rho') + \sum_{m=-\infty}^{+\infty} C_m \sum_{n=-\infty}^{+\infty} K_{m+n}(\gamma_0\rho') I_n$$
$$\cdot (\gamma_0\rho_0)(-1)^n \exp(-i(n+m)\phi'). \qquad (20)$$

This is valid in the nonconcentric air gap region (i.e., $\rho > a$ and $\rho' < b$). The needed azimuthal component is obtained from

$$E_{0\phi'} = -\eta_0 \partial H_{0z}/\partial(\gamma_0\rho'). \qquad (21)$$

The relevant quantity for the impedance calculation is the "average" field $E_{0\phi'}$ at the solenoid. Then it follows that the impedance Z per unit length of the solenoid with the sample divided by the impedance Z_0 of the empty solenoid is given by

$$\frac{Z}{Z_0} = 1 - \frac{K_1(\gamma_0 b)}{I_1(\gamma_0 b)} \sum_{m=0}^{\infty} \epsilon_m \frac{C_m}{B} (-1)^m I_m(\gamma_0\rho_0) \qquad (22)$$

where $\epsilon_0 = 1$ and $\epsilon_m = 2$ for $m \neq 0$, and where C_m/B is known [50]. Not surprisingly, (22) reduces to (17) for the centrally located sample, i.e., $I_m(\gamma_0\rho_0) = 0$ for $\rho_0 \to 0$ when $m \neq 0$.

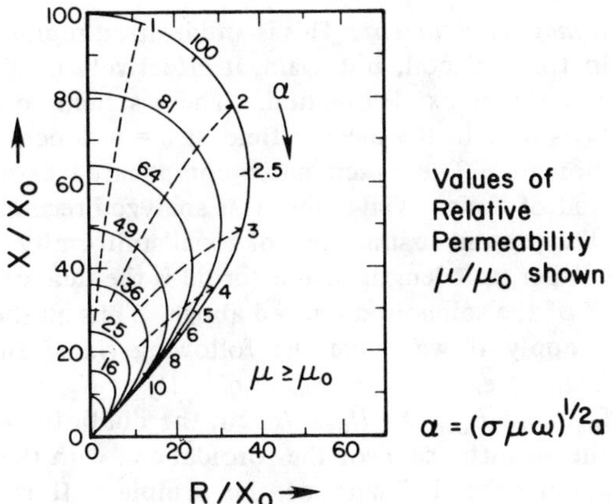

Fig. 10. Argand plot of the impedance $Z = R + iX$ normalized to the reactance X_0 of the empty solenoid, for $a = b$.

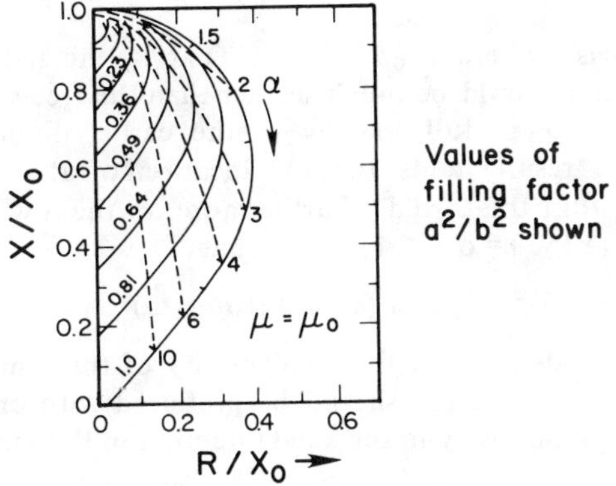

Fig. 11. Argand plot of the impedance $Z = R + iX$ normalized to the reactance X_0 of the empty solenoid, for $\mu = \mu_0$.

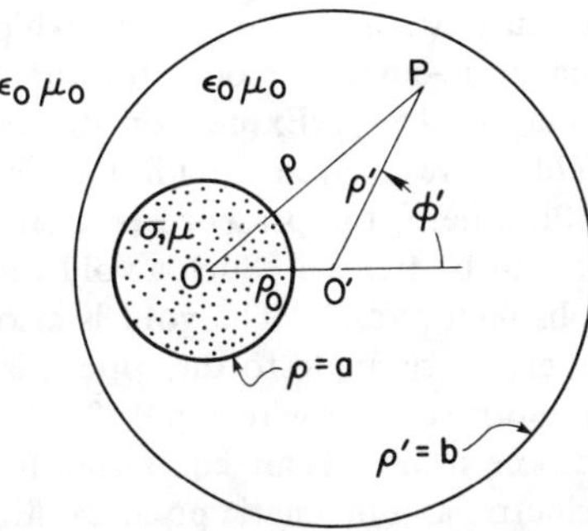

Fig. 12. Cross section view of the nonconcentrically located sample.

We again may invoke the small argument approximations for Bessel functions of order $\gamma_0 a$, $\gamma_0 b$, and $\gamma_0\rho_0$. Lo and behold, these show that Z/Z_0 reduces again to the formula given by (18)! This confirms the conjecture of Förster and Stambke [16] who seemed to be gifted with keen physical insight into such problems. Of course, we do not expect the result to hold in any sense when the dimensions of the solenoid become comparable with the free-space wavelength. In that case, many other complications arise such as the assumed uniformity of the solenoid current.

THE DUAL PROBLEM

There is an extremely interesting dual to the problem we have discussed. That is, rather than exciting the cylindrical sample with an *azimuthal electric current*, we employ an *azimuthal magnetic current*. This is an idealized representation for a thin toroidal coil, but again, it effectively is of infinite length in the z or axial direction. The assumed source discontinuity is now in the electric field at $\rho = b$ which has only a z component. The much more complicated case of the toroidal coil of finite axial extent was analyzed recently [53].

Under the present assumption of axial uniformity, the admittance Y per unit length of the toroid is the dual of the impedance Z of the solenoid discussed above. Thus all the earlier equations apply if we make the following transformations: $i\mu\omega \to \sigma$, $\mu_0 \to \epsilon_0$, $\eta \to \eta^{-1}$, $\eta_0 \to \eta_0^{-1}$, $H_z \to E_z$, $E_\phi \to -H_\phi$, $H_{0z} \to E_{0z}$, and $E_{0\phi} \to -H_{0\phi}$. Then, the dual of (18) is the ratio of the admittance Y of the toroidal coil with the sample to the admittance Y_0 without the sample. It is written explicitly

$$\frac{Y}{Y_0} = \left[1 - \frac{a^2}{b^2} + \frac{\sigma}{i\epsilon_0\omega} \frac{a^2}{b^2} \frac{2}{\gamma a} \frac{I_1(\gamma a)}{I_0(\gamma a)} \right] \qquad (23)$$

for the case where $|\gamma_0 b| \ll 1$. That is, the radius of the toroidal coil should be much smaller than the free-space wavelength. Also, in full analogy to the earlier discussion, the quasi-state result holds for any location of the cylindrical sample within the toroid. Furthermore, in the low-frequency limit where $|\gamma a| = \alpha \ll 1$, we see that

$$Y \simeq Y_0 \left[1 + (a^2/b^2) \left[(\sigma/i\epsilon_0\omega) - 1 \right] \right] \qquad (24)$$

which depends only on the conductivity of the sample. Thus this type of excitation should be preferred with probing the effective conductivity in the axial direction in the sample.

The Prolate Spheroidal Void Model of Hill and Wait

As we have indicated, an appropriate source for excitation of axial-electric currents is a toroidal coil which encircles the rope, and a magnetic-current model for the toroidal source coil has been analyzed [53]. Expressions for both the interior and exterior fields were derived for a homogeneous wire rope. As we shall outline here, the presence of a small slender void within the rope can be treated. Such a void can be considered a model for a broken strand. The void is also allowed to be oriented at any arbitrary angle to the rope axis to account for the winding geometry of the wire rope. The induced electric and magnetic dipole moments are computed from the primary fields and the electric and magnetic polarizabilities of the void. We then obtain expressions for the external fields of electric and magnetic dipoles of arbitrary orientation. Of course, it is these external fields which are the observable quantities in any electromagnetic NDT method. The particular expressions, derived for the external fields of internal electric and magnetic dipoles, should be useful in future analyses of other types of small imperfections in wire ropes. Of course in such cases, the electric and magnetic polarizabilities would be different.

In a previous analysis [53], we analyzed an azimuthal current sheet source which encircled the rope. The current sheet was allowed to have arbitrary width in the z or axial direction and arbitrary azimuthal extent. This source results in fairly complicated expressions for the electric and magnetic fields. Since in this paper we are primarily concerned with the fields scattered by the void, we take the simpler special case for the source shown in Fig. 13. Specifically, a magnetic-current ring of strength K is located at a radius b in the plane $z = 0$. This is

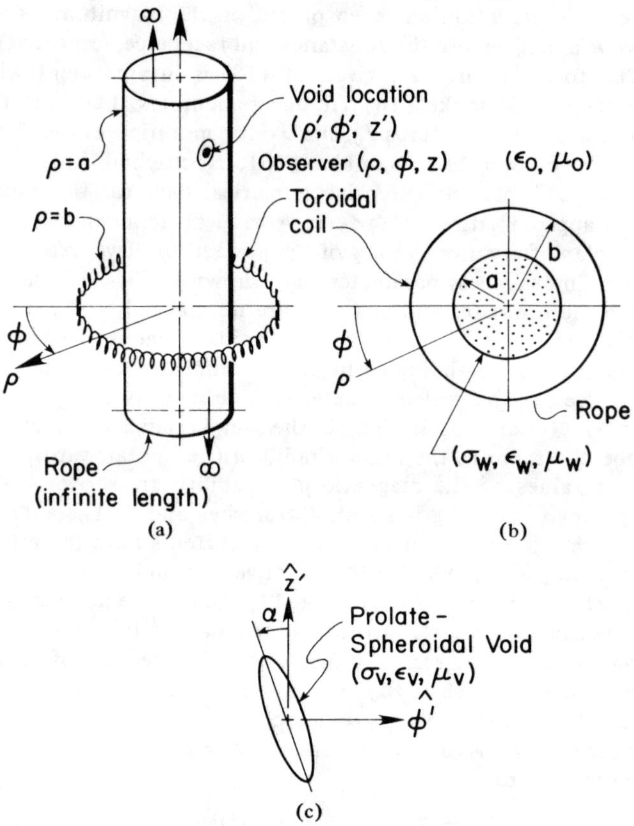

Fig. 13. Thin toroidal coil surrounding a metal rope of infinite length, (a) perspective view, (b) top view, (c) prolate spheroidal void.

a model for a thin toroidal coil which completely encircles the rope. The rope is assumed to be infinitely long and has radius a. It has conductivity σ_w, permittivity ϵ_w, and permeability μ_w. The surrounding free-space has permittivity ϵ_0, and permeability μ_0. For now, we defer discussion of the void properties and consider only the homogeneous rope.

Because of the symmetry of the source and the rope, the fields are transverse magnetic (TM) and independent of ϕ. The magnetic field has only a nonzero azimuthal component H_ϕ^{pr}, and the electric field has only nonzero axial and radial components E_z^{pr} and E_ρ^{pr}. The superscript pr denotes the fields in the absence of the void. These primary fields are derived elsewhere [53], and the explicit forms both inside and outside the rope are given in a recent report [38, Appendix A]. We note that E_ρ^{pr} and H_ϕ^{pr} are zero for $\rho = 0$. On the other hand, E_z^{pr} is nearly independent of ρ inside the rope for sufficiently low frequencies.

We now select a thin prolate spheroid of conductivity σ_v, permittivity ϵ_v, and permeability μ_v, in order to model a broken strand. The prolate-spheroidal shape is a convenient one because its electric and magnetic polarizabilities are known. However, we would not expect a significant difference for a thin circular cylinder of the same length and volume. To account for the winding geometry of the rope, we allow a rotation of the major axis of the spheroid about the ρ' axis by an angle α. Thus the major axis is oriented at an angle α to the unit vector $\hat{z}'$ and an angle $\pi/2 + \alpha$ to the unit vector $\hat{\phi}'$ as indicated in Fig. 1(c).

Since the void has a contrast in both the electric and magnetic properties, both electric and magnetic dipole moments will be induced [36]. The electric polarizabilities for the incident electric field applied along the major axis α^e_{maj}, or along the minor axis α^e_{min}, are given by

$$\alpha^e_{maj} = -V(\sigma_w - \sigma_v) \tag{25}$$

and

$$\alpha^e_{min} = \frac{-2V(\sigma_w - \sigma_v)}{1 + \sigma_v/\sigma_w} \tag{26}$$

where V is the volume of the thin prolate spheroid. Since we anticipate the use of very-low frequencies, we have neglected displacement currents. To include them, σ_w would be replaced by $\sigma_w + i\omega\epsilon_w$, and σ_v would be replaced by $\sigma_v + i\omega\epsilon_v$, in (25) and (26). The magnetic polarizabilities for the incident magnetic field applied along the major axis α^m_{maj}, or along the minor axis α^m_{min}, are similarly given by

$$\alpha^m_{maj} = -Vi\omega(\mu_w - \mu_v) \tag{27}$$

and

$$\alpha^m_{min} = \frac{-2Vi\omega(\mu_w - \mu_v)}{1 + \mu_v/\mu_w}. \tag{28}$$

In order to compute the induced dipole moments, it is first necessary to resolve the incident electric and magnetic fields into components along the major and minor axes. The resultant induced dipole moments can then be resolved into the more convenient ρ, ϕ, and z components. When this is done, the induced electric dipole moments are found to be

$$(Ids)_z = E^{pr}_z(\alpha^e_{maj} \cos^2 \alpha + \alpha^e_{min} \sin^2 \alpha) \tag{29}$$

$$(Ids)_\phi = E^{pr}_z(\alpha^e_{min} - \alpha^e_{maj}) \sin \alpha \cos \alpha \tag{30}$$

$$(Ids)_\rho = E^{pr}_\rho \alpha^e_{min}. \tag{31}$$

In (29)–(31), the primary electric-field components E^{pr}_z and E^{pr}_ρ are evaluated at ρ', ϕ', z'. Similarly, the induced magnetic dipole moments are found to be

$$(Kdl)_z = H^{pr}_\phi(\alpha^m_{min} - \alpha^m_{maj}) \sin \alpha \cos \alpha \tag{32}$$

$$(Kdl)_\phi = H^{pr}_\phi(\alpha^m_{min} \cos^2 \alpha + \alpha^m_{maj} \sin^2 \alpha) \tag{33}$$

$$(Kdl)_\rho = 0. \tag{34}$$

Note that the units of the induced electric dipole moments in (29)–(31) are ampere-meters, and the units of the induced magnetic dipole moments in (32) through (34) are volt-meters. These induced dipole moments are the sources of the scattered field.

The scattered field external to the rope is the observable quantity in any NDT system. Since we anticipate the use of coils for sensors, we have considered the scattered magnetic field components $H^{sc}_\rho(\rho, \phi, z)$, $H^{sc}_\phi(\rho, \phi, z)$, and $H^{sc}_z(\rho, \phi, z)$ [38]. Each of these components can be written as a superposition of the contributions from each of the six induced dipole sources. (Actually there are only five nonzero sources, since $(Kdl)_\rho$ is zero for the specific configuration considered here). Explicit expressions for the three scattered-field components are given elsewhere [38].

The quantities of most interest in NDT are the external ($\rho > a$) magnetic-field components which are observed with the sensing coils. The primary magnetic field has only a ϕ component H^{pr}_ϕ but the scattered magnetic field has all three

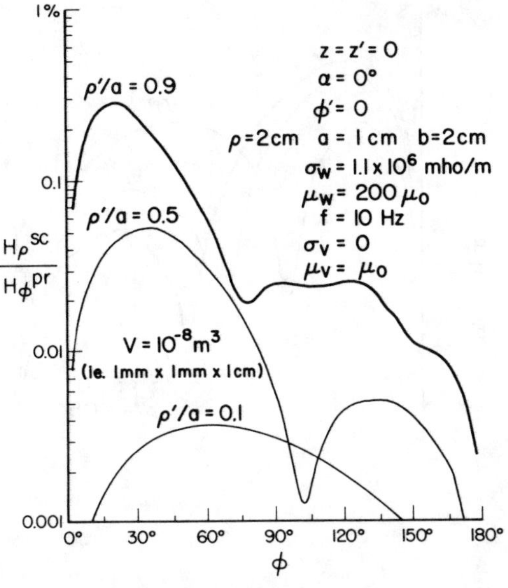

Fig. 14. The normalized magnitude of the scattered radial magnetic field for various void locations ρ'.

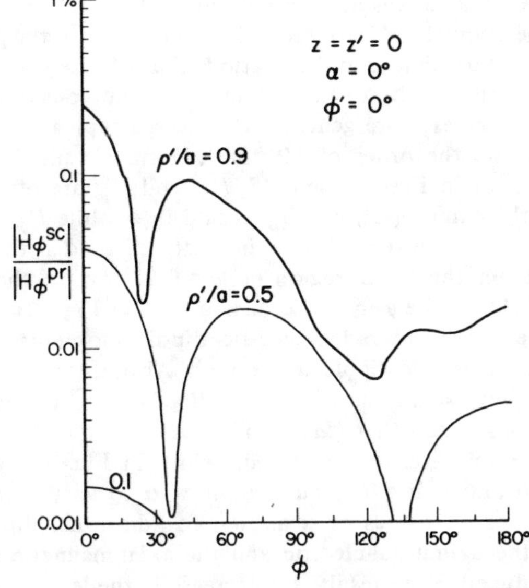

Fig. 15. The normalized magnitude of the scattered azimuthal magnetic field for various void locations ρ'.

components. For the numerical results, the following parametric values remain fixed: $a = 1$ cm, $\sigma_w = 1.1 \times 10^6$ mho/m, $\mu_w = 200 \mu_0$, $b = 2$ cm, frequency = 10 Hz, $\rho = 2$ cm, $\sigma_v = 0$, and $\mu_v = \mu_0$. For this low frequency, the conduction currents dominate, and the permittivities ϵ_w and ϵ_v are unimportant. The above values of σ_w and μ_w are roughly representative of stainless steel, but the permeability of steel is quite variable [54]. For the above parameters, the radius a is approximately one-skin depth. For convenience here, we also choose $z = z' = 0$ and $\sigma' = 0$.

In Figs. 14, 15, and 16, we show the magnitude of the scattered magnetic-field components normalized by VH^{pr}_ϕ as a function of ϕ. The reason for showing the ϕ dependence is that, although the primary field is independent of ϕ, the scattered field varies considerably in ϕ. This variation might dictate the use of multiple-sensing coils spaced in azimuth around

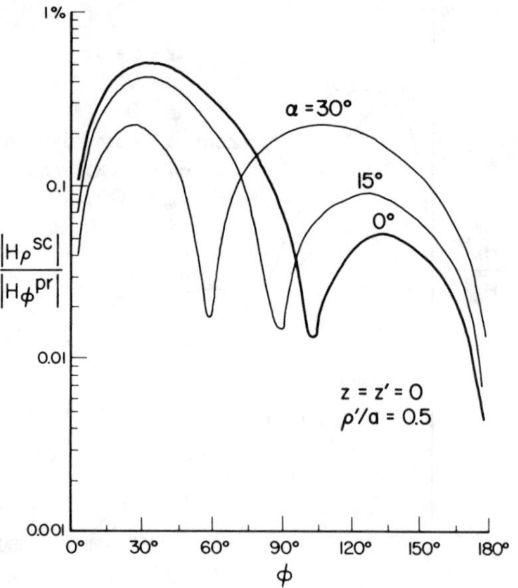

Fig. 16. The normalized magnitude of the scattered radial magnetic field for various void orientations a.

the rope. The curves are normalized by the primary field because the anomalous scattered field is measured in the presence of the primary field and their ratio is thus of interest. We also normalize the results to the volume V of the void in order to make the curves more general. However, a typical value for V might be on the order of $10^{-8} \, m^3$ (=1 cm $\times$ 1 mm $\times$ 1 mm). As indicated in Figs. 14 and 15, H_ρ^{sc} and H_ϕ^{sc} are of approximately the same level, but H_ρ^{sc} is odd in ϕ while H_ϕ^{sc} is even. We also may note the decrease in scattered field as the void is moved from the outer region ($\rho'/a = 0.9$) toward the center ($\rho'/a = 0.1$) of the rope. Because $\alpha = 0°$ in Figs. 14 and 15, only the axial and radial electric dipole moments and the azimuthal magnetic dipole are excited. Also, the radial electric dipole is very small because its exciting field E_ρ^{pr} is small. The calculations reveal that $(Ids)_z$ and $(Kdl)_\phi$ contribute approximately equally to the scattered field. In Fig. 16, we have $z = z' = 0$ and $\rho'/a = 0.5$, but we allow α to vary from $0°$ to $30°$. Nonzero values of α allow two additional dipole moments (the azimuthal-electric and the axial-magnetic dipoles) to be induced. The result is a decrease in the level of H_ϕ^{sc} and H_ρ^{sc} and an increase in the level of H_z^{sc}. These new results are elsewhere [38].

The phase of the scattered field was also computed, but was found to be of less interest. Also, the individual dipole contributions were computed, and they are of individual interest since they will be excited differently for other sources or other void configurations.

Although we have generated numerical results for the specific case of a thin prolate spheroidal void, the formulation given here actually yields the external fields for arbitrary induced electric and magnetic dipole moments. Thus the formulation is useful for any type of rope imperfection that can be characterized by induced electric and magnetic dipole moments. This requires only that the rope imperfection be small in terms of the rope radius and the rope skin depth. Larger imperfections should have a similar qualitative behavior, but could probably be rigorously analyzed only by solving an integral equation for the fields in the imperfection. Also, it would be a simple matter to perform similar calculations for a solenoidal coil of the type used in present NDT systems. The

scattered field calculation remains unchanged, but the primary field would be $TE(E_z^{pr} = 0)$ rather than $TM(H_z^{pr} = 0)$. Some calculations for this case have been carried out by Burrows [37] for the special case, where both exciting and sensing coils are coaxial with the tubular specimen.

CONCLUDING REMARKS

We have attempted to give an overall view of NDT electromagnetic methods. As indicated, the investigations have proceeded along different lines. The very practical and perhaps most useful work to date has been empirical in nature. There has been no attempt made to deduce the magnitude of the secondary fields due to the internal flaw; instead a large number of actual ropes are tested and the results presented. On the other hand, the analytical approaches have considered only highly idealized situations. Nevertheless, some important principles are disclosed that may have an important bearing on operating procedures. For example, the toroidal coil exciter could be utilized in practical schemes in conjunction with localized sensor coils that can characterize the three-dimensional field configuration in an adequate fashion.

A basic theoretical aspect of the NDT problem that we have not really addressed is to account for the anisotropic nature of the effective conductivity and permeability of the wire rope. The spiral construction of stranded wire ropes sometimes described as a "twisted bunch of spaghetti" defies any simple microscopic description. However, from a macroscopic point, we might describe the effective anisotropy by conductivity and permeability tensors. Some preliminary efforts in this direction have begun [55]. It is obvious that much remains to be done.

ACKNOWLEDGMENT

The assistance of Ms. Lana Hope in preparing this report is much appreciated. He also thanks Dr. David A. Hill who provided the results shown in Figs. 14, 15, and 16.

REFERENCES

[1] T. F. Wall, "Electromagnetic testing for mechanical flans in steel wire ropes," *J. Inst. Elec. Eng.*, vol. 67, pp. 899–911, 1929.
[2] T. F. Wall and C. H. Hainsworth, "The penetration of alternating magnetic flux in wire ropes," *J. Inst. Elec. Eng.*, vol. 71, pp. 374–379, 1932.
[3] A. Semmelink, "Electromagnetic testing of winding ropes," *Trans. South African Inst. Elec. Eng.*, vol. 43, no. 5, pp. 113–129, May 1953.
[4] ——, "Electromagnetic testing of winding ropes," *Trans. South African Inst. Elec. Eng.*, vol. 47, no. 8, pp. 206–244, Aug. 1956.
[5] R. H. Hiltbrunner, "Le Controle Magnétique des câbles avec le défectoscope integra," *Économie Tech. Transports*, no. 119, June 1957.
[6] J. G. Lang, "The principle and practice of electromagnetic wire rope testing," *Can. Mining and Metallurgical Bull.*, pp. 415–424, Apr. 1969.
[7] C. H. Larsen, P. A. Egen, R. D. Jones, and H. A. Cross, "Wire rope applications and practices associated with underground coal mining in the U.S.," Final Rep. (from Battelle Laboratories) on U.S. Bureau of Mines Contract No. H0101741, June 22, 1971.
[8] J. P. Morgan, "Investigations on wire ropes in mine hoisting system," *Proc. Australian Inst. Min. Metal*, no. 215, pp. 59–85, 1965.
[9] J. P. Morgan and H. E. J. Symes, "Non-destructive testing of wire ropes," Australian Mineral Industries Research Assoc. Ltd., Bulletin No. 6, (National Library of Australia Card No. ISSN 0313-6973), 1976.
[10] J. Stachurski, "Magnetic testing of steel wire ropes," Rep. from Lab. for Testing Wire Ropes, Univ. of Mining and Metallurgy, Cracow, Poland, 1976.
[11] R. A. Egen and D. K. Benson, "Wire rope retirement criteria and procedures," Progr. Rep. 16 (from Midwest Research Inst., 425 Volker Blvd., Kansas City, MO 64110) on U.S. Bureau of Mines Contract No. J0155187, Nov. 10, 1976.

[12] M. J. Bergander, "Principles of magnetic defectoscopy of steel ropes," presented at the 47th Annu. Convention of the Wire Association, Boston, MA, Nov. 1977.

[13] H. Hochschild, "Electromagnetic methods of testing metals," in *Progress in Non-Destructive Testing*, vol. 1. New York: Macmillan, 1959, pp. 59–109.

[14] F. Förster, "Theoretical and experimental foundation of non-destructive testing using eddy currents I. Test coil methods," *Z. Metallkunde*, vol. 43, no. 5, pp. 163–171, 1952 (in German).

[15] F. Förster and H. Breitfeld, "Non-destructive testing using eddy current methods II. Practical results and industrial applications of methods using test coils," *Z. Metallkunde*, vol. 43, no. 5, pp. 172–180, 1952 (in German).

[16] F. Förster and K. Stambke, "Theoretical and experimental foundation of non-destructive testing using eddy currents III. Quantitative methods of non-destructive testing using test object encircling coils," *Z. Metallkunde*, vol. 45, no. 4, pp. 166–179, 1954 (in German).

[17] F. Förster, "Theoretical and experimental foundation of non-destructive testing using eddy currents IV. Practical apparatus for non-destructive testing using encircling coils for eddy currents," *Z. Metallkunde*, vol. 45, no. 4, pp. 180–187, 1954 (in German).

[18] F. Förster and H. Breitfeld, "Theoretical and experimental foundation of non-destructive testing using eddy currents V. Quantitative testing for cracks in metallic objects using test object encircling coils," *Z. Metallkunde*, vol. 45, no. 4, pp. 188–199, 1954 (in German).

[19] G. O. McClurg, "Non destructive eddy current testing," *IRE Trans.*, vol. IE-11, no. 1, pp. 20–26, 1959.

[20] P. Graneau, "Coupled circuit theory for electromagnetic testing," *Progress in Non-Destructive Testing*, E. G. Stanford and J. H. Fearson, Eds., vol. 2, pp. 163–188, 1961.

[21] J. R. Wait, "A conducting sphere in a time varying magnetic field," *Geophysics*, vol. XVI, pp. 666–672, Oct. 1951.

[22] ——, "The cylindrical ore body in the presence of a cable carrying an oscillating current," *Geophysics*, vol. XVII, pp. 378–386, Apr. 1952. (In eqn. (13), replace μ_2/μ_1 by $n\mu_2/\mu_1$ both in the numerator and denominator, similarly, in (14), replace $(k \pm n)$ by $n(k \pm 1)$. Also, the summations in (66), (67), etc. should include the $n = 0$ terms.)

[23] ——, "A conducting permeable sphere in the presence of a coil carrying an oscillating current," *Can. J. Phys.*, vol. 31, pp. 670–678, May 1953.

[24] ——, "Some solutions for electromagnetic problems involving spheroidal, spherical and cylindrical bodies," *J. Res. Nat. Bur. Stand.*, vol. 64B, pp. 15–32, Jan./Mar. 1960.

[25] S. H. Ward and D. C. Fraser, "A conducting permeable sphere and cylinder in an elliptically polarized alternating magnetic field," *J. Geomagn. Geoelec.*, vol. 18, no. 1, pp. 23–41, 1966.

[26] S. H. Ward, "The electromagnetic method," *Mining Geophysics*, vol. II, pp. 224–372, Oct. 1967. [Ward's quasi-static solution, Sec. 7a, does not include the effect of the induced monopole or azimuthally invariant currents, i.e., the $n = 0$ terms are missed.]

[27] S. K. Singh, "Transient electromagnetic response of a conducting infinite cylinder embedded in a conducting medium," *Geofis. Internacional (Mexico)*, vol. 12, no. 1, pp. 7–21, 1972.

[28] ——, "Transient electromagnetic response of a conducting cylinder in a conducting medium: numerical results," *Geofis. Internacional (Mexico)*, vol. 12, no. 4, pp. 267–280, 1972.

[29] Von J. Meyer, "Über die Richtungsveränderlichkeit des geomagnetischen Induktionspfeiles bei endlicher Leitfähigkeit," *Z. für Geophysik*, vol. 38, pp. 195–221, 1968.

[30] D. A. Hill and J. R. Wait, "Electromagnetic response of a conducting cylinder of finite length," *Geofis. Internacional (Mexico)*, vol. 12, no. 4, pp. 245–266, 1972.

[31] J. R. Wait, "On the electromagnetic induction in elongated ore bodies," *Geophysics*, vol. 38, no. 5, pp. 984–985, 1973. Correction: vol. 39, no. 2, p. 235, 1974.

[32] W. Kertz, "Leitungsfähiger Zylinder im transversalen magnetishen Wechselfeld," *Gerl. Beitr. Geophys.*, vol. 69, pp. 4–28, 1960.

[33] S. H. Ward, "Unique determination of conductivity susceptibility, size and depth in multi-frequency electromagnetic exploration," *Geophysics*, vol. 24, no. 3, pp. 531–546, July 1959.

[34] J. R. Wait, "Electromagnetic coupling between a circular loop and a conducting sphere," *Geophysics*, vol. 18, pp. 970–971, Oct. 1953.

[35] P. R. Vein, "Inductance between two loops in the presence of solid conducting bodies," *J. Electron. Contr.*, vol. 13, no. 5, pp. 471–494, 1962.

[36] W. R. Smythe, *Static and Dynamic Electricity*, 2nd ed. New York: McGraw-Hill, 1950. (3rd revised edition now available.)

[37] M. L. Burrows, "A theory of eddy-current flaw detection," Ph.D. dissertation, Univ. of Michigan, Ann Arbor, 1964 (available from University Microfilms, Ann Arbor, MI, Order No. 64-12,568).

[38] D. A. Hill and J. R. Wait, "Scattering by a slender void in a homogeneous conducting wire rope." *Appl. Phys.*, vol. 16, pp. 391–398, 1978 (and, by same authors, "Electromagnetic field perturbation by an internal void in a conducting cylinder excited by a wire loop," *Appl. Phys.*, vol. 18, pp. 141–147, 1973).

[39] C. V. Dodd, W. E. Deeds, and J. W. Luquire, "Integral solutions to some eddy current problems," *Int. J. of NDT* vol. 1, pp. 29–90, 1969/1970.

[40] G. V. Keller and F. C. Frischknecht, *Electrical Methods in Geophysical Prospecting*. NY: Pergamon, 1966.

[41] C. C. Cheng, C. V. Dodd, and W. E. Deeds, "General analysis of probe coils near stratified conductors," *Int. J. of NDT*, vol. 3, 109–130, 1971/1972.

[42] J. R. Wait, *Electromagnetic Waves in Stratified Media*. New York: Pergamon Press, Chap. 2, 1st ed. 1962 and 2nd ed. 1970.

[43] J. R. Wait, "Fields of a horizontal dipole over a stratified half-space," *IEEE Trans. Antennas Propagat.*, vol. AP-14, no. 6, pp. 790–792, Nov. 1966.

[44] C. V. Dodd, C. C. Cheng, and W. E. Deeds, "Induction coils coaxial with an arbitrary number of cylindrical conductors," *J. Appl. Phys.*, vol. 45, no. 2, pp. 638–647, Feb. 1974.

[45] C. V. Dodd and W. E. Deeds, "Analytical solution to eddy current probe coil problems," *J. Appl. Phys.*, vol. 39, no. 6, pp. 2829–2838, May 1968.

[46] A. H. Kahn, R. Spal, and A. Feldman, "Eddy current losses due to a surface crack in conducting material," *J. Appl. Phys.*, vol. 48, no. 11, pp. 4454–4459, Nov. 1977.

[47] A. H. Kahn and R. D. Spal, "Electromagnetic theory and its relationship to standards," in *Proc. Workshop on Eddy Current Non-Destructive Testing* (National Bureau of Standards, Gaithersburg, MD, Nov. 3–4, 1977) (to be issued as an NBS Special Publication).

[48] J. T. Weaver, "The electromagnetic field within a discontinuous conductor with reference to geomagnetic micropulsations near a coast-line," *Can. J. Phys.*, vol. 41, pp. 484–495, 1963.

[49] J. R. Wait and K. P. Spies, "Magneto-telluric fields for a segmented overburden," *J. Geomagn. and Geoelec.*, vol. 26, pp. 449–458, 1974.

[50] J. R. Wait, "The electromagnetic basis for non-destructive testing of cylindrical conductors," *IEEE Trans. Instrum. Meas.*, vol. IM-27, No. 3, pp. 235–238, Sept. 1978.

[51] H. L. Libby, *Introduction to Electromagnetic Nondestructive Test Methods*. New York: Wiley, 1971, Sec. 5.2, pp. 135–150.

[52] J. R. Wait, *Electromagn. Radiation from Cylindrical Structures*. New York: Pergamon, 1959.

[53] D. A. Hill and J. R. Wait, "Analysis of alternating current excitation of a wire rope by a toroidal coil," *J. Appl. Phys.*, vol. 48, no. 12, pp. 4893–4897, 1977.

[54] A. G. Kandoian, *Reference Data for Radio Engineers*. ITT Corp., New York, 1968, pp. 4–32.

[55] J. R. Wait, "Electromagnetic response of an anisotropic conducting cylinder to an external source," *Radio Sci.*, vol. 13, no. 5, pp. 789–792, Sept./Oct. 1978.

Author Index

<h1 style="text-align:right">Subject Index</h1>

A

Acoustic holography, 83
Acoustic imaging, 1
  classification of papers, vii
  converging beams, 482
  for nondestructive evaluation, 147
  signal processing, 110
  with holography and lenses, 100
  3-D, 110
Acoustic microscopy
  in 1979, 471
  laser, 471
  scanning, 471
  with mechanical scanning, 482
Acoustic-ultrasonic imaging, 1
Adaptive processing, 83
Aeromagnetic surveys
  geomagnetic depth sounding, 440
Aerosol particles
  holography, 13
Ambiguities
  radar, 293, 314
Antennas, 293
  phased arrays, 386
  synthetic, 40
Area detectors, 83
A-scan, 147
Astronomy
  radar, 229, 350

B

Backprojection
  fan-beam reconstruction, 190
  2-D, 258
Backward projection, 66
Bloch equation, 258
Boreholes, 446
Born approximation, 250
B-scan, 125, 147

C

CAT (Computer-aided tomography)
  see Computerized tomography
Character recognition
  by holography, 13
Chirp focused systems, 147
Cinematography
  with holographic screen, 13
  3-D, 13
Classification of papers
  acoustic-ultrasonic imaging, vii
  holography, vii
  microscopy, vii
  microwave imaging, vii
  NMR imaging, vii
  nondestructive evaluation, vii
  optical processing, vii
  seismic imaging, vii
  signal processing, vii
  tomography, vii
Computer reconstruction
  of holograms, 54, 422

Computerized tomography, 1, 220
  comparison with NMR imaging, 258
  geophysical, 29
  mathematics, 163, 179
  nonlinearities, 173
  physics, 163
  with ultrasound, 250
Conductors, cylindrical
  testing, 516
Convolution, 190
Cross correlation
  optical, 40
C-scan, 125, 147

D

Data processing
  optical, 27
Data storage,
  optical, 27
Diffraction tomography, 250
Digital computers
  use in holography, 54

E

Earth rotation effects, 293
Eikonal method, 25
Electromagnetic methods
  use in NDT of wire ropes, 516
Electron microscopy
  application of reconstruction tomography, 229
Entropy optimization, 209
Exploration
  geophysical, 250
  oil, 422, 446

F

Fan-beam geometry
  algorithm, 163, 193
Filtering and filters
  optical, 54
  Parkinson, 440
  spatial, 70
  Wiener, 409
Finite series expansion
  reconstruction methods, 209
Fourier transforms
  geophysical inversion, 455
  holograms, 54, 422
  NMR imaging, 271
  optical, 54, 70
  tomography, 271
Fresnel holograms
  3-D, 54
Fresnel lens, 147

G

Geology
  mapping, 314
Geomagnetic depth sounding
  aeromagnetic surveys, 440
  oceanography, 440
Geometric optics, 229

Editors' Biographies

Hua Lee (S'78–M'80–SM'83) was born in Taipei, Taiwan, Republic of China, on September 30, 1952. He received the B.S. degree in electrical engineering from the National Taiwan University in 1974, and the M.S. and Ph.D. degrees in electrical and computer engineering from the University of California at Santa Barbara in 1978 and 1980 respectively.

In 1980 he joined the faculty of the Department of Electrical and Computer Engineering of the University of California at Santa Barbara as a Visiting Assistant Professor. Since 1983 he has been with the Department of Electrical and Computer Engineering, University of Illinois at Urbana-Champaign where now he is an Assistant Professor. He coedited (with Wade and Schueler) the special issue Digital Acoustical Imaging in the IEEE TRANSACTIONS ON SONICS AND ULTRASONICS (July 1984). His current research interests include optimization of imaging systems, signal analysis and processing.

In 1985, he received the Presidential Young Investigator Award from the National Science Foundation. Dr. Lee is a member of Acoustical Society of America, Eta Kappa Nu, and Tau Beta Pi.

Glen Wade (S'51–A'55–SM'57–F'62) was born in Ogden, UT, on March 19, 1921. He received the B.S. and M.S. degrees in electrical engineering from the University of Utah, Salt Lake City, and the Ph.D. degree from Stanford University, Stanford, CA.

Subsequently, he became an Associate Professor of Electrical Engineering at Stanford and a Consultant for several industrial concerns. In 1960, he joined the Raytheon Company and served as Assistant General Manager of the Research Division. In 1963, he went to Cornell University, Ithaca, NY, as Director of the School of Electrical Engineering and held a distinguished professorship, the J. Preston Levis Chair in Engineering. He joined the Electrical Engineering Department of the University of California, Santa Barbara, in 1966, and has remained there ever since.

Dr. Wade has served the IEEE in various capacities including Editor of the IEEE TRANSACTIONS ON ELECTRON DEVICES, Coeditor of the IEEE JOURNAL OF QUANTUM ELECTRONICS, member of the IEEE Editorial Board, Chairman of the IEEE Educational Activities Board, member of the IEEE Board of Directors and Executive Committee, and Editor of the PROCEEDINGS OF THE IEEE. He received an Eta Kappa Nu Award in the "Outstanding Young Electrical Engineer" competition in 1955. He received a National Electronics Conference Annual Award in 1959. In 1971, he was given a Visiting Professorship Award at Tokyo University from the Japan Society for the Promotion of Science. In 1972, he was awarded a Fulbright–Hays Lectureship in Spain. He was given the Distinguished Teaching Award for 1977 by the UCSB Academic Senate. In 1980, the National Science Council of the Republic of China awarded him a "Special Chair" as a Visiting Professor at the National Taiwan University. He received an IEEE Centennial Award in 1984. He is a member of the American Physical Society, Phi Kappa Phi, Tau Beta Pi, Eta Kappa Nu, and Sigma Xi. He is listed in *Who's Who in America* and in *Who's Who in the World*.